Encyclopedia of
Free Blacks
and
People of Color
in the Americas

Volume I

ENCYCLOPEDIA OF
FREE BLACKS
AND
PEOPLE OF COLOR
IN THE AMERICAS

VOLUME I

Editor:
STEWART R. KING

Associate Editor:
BEVERLY C. TOMEK

Facts On File
An Infobase Learning Company

Encyclopedia of Free Blacks and People of Color in the Americas

Facts On File, Inc.
An imprint of Infobase Learning
132 West 31st Street
New York NY 10001

Library of Congress Cataloging-in-Publication Data
Encyclopedia of free Blacks and people of color in the Americas / edited by Stewart R. King.
    v. cm.
  Includes bibliographical references and index.
  Contents: v. 1. Entries A-J— v. 2. Entries K-Z.
  ISBN 978-0-8160-7212-5 (acid-free paper) 1. Free blacks—America—History—Encyclopedias. 2. Free African Americans—History—Encyclopedias. 3. Blacks—America—History—Encyclopedias. 4. America—Race relations—Encyclopedias. I. King, Stewart R., 1960–
  E29.N3E53 2011 (2012)   305.896'07303—dc23
                      2011017152

Facts On File books are available at special discounts when purchased in bulk quantities for businesses, associations, institutions, or sales promotions. Please call our Special Sales Department in New York at (212) 967-8800 or (800) 322-8755.

You can find Facts On File on the World Wide Web at http://www.infobaselearning.com

Text design by Annie O'Donnell
Composition by Publication Services
Cover printed by Yurchak Printing, Landisville, Pa.
Book printed and bound by Yurchak Printing, Landisville, Pa.
Date printed: December 2011

Printed in the United States of America

10 9 8 7 6 5 4 3 2 1

This book is printed on acid-free paper.

Contents

List of Entries

List of Documents

List of Maps

List of Tables

About the Editors

Stewart R. King holds a Ph.D. in history from Johns Hopkins University. He is the author of *Blue Coat or Powdered Wig: Free People of Color in Pre-Revolutionary Saint-Domingue* (University of Georgia Press, 2001). He is also the author of numerous articles and book chapters, including (with Dominique Rogers) "Housekeepers, Merchants, *Rentières*: Free Women of Color in the Port Cities of Colonial Saint-Domingue, 1750–1790" in Jodi Campbell and Douglas Catterall (eds.), *Women in Port: Gendering Communities, Economies, and Social Networks in Atlantic Port Cities, 1500–1800* (Brill, forthcoming) and "Slavery and the Haitian Revolution" in Robert Paquette and Mark Smith (eds.), *The Oxford Handbook on Slavery in the Americas* (Oxford University Press, 2010). He has a particular research interest in the role of military service in the lives of free people of color in the Atlantic world. He is a professor at the Mount Angel Seminary in Oregon.

Beverly C. Tomek holds a Ph.D. in history from Southwest Texas State University. She is the author of *Pennsylvania Hall* (Oxford University Press, forthcoming) and *Colonization and Its Discontents: Emancipation, Emigration, and Antislavery in Antebellum Pennsylvania* (New York University Press, 2011). She has also written articles for *American Nineteenth Century History* and *Pennsylvania History: A Journal of Mid-Atlantic Studies*. She has served on the editorial boards of *the International Encyclopedia of Revolution and Protest* (Wiley-Blackwell, 2009) and *Encyclopedia of American Social Movements* (M. E. Sharpe, 2004). Her primary field of study is 19th-century U.S. race relations and antislavery. She is an instructor of history at Wharton County Junior College in Wharton, Texas.

Acknowledgments

This encyclopedia would not have been possible without the knowledge, hard work, and dedication of more than 70 authors. I am humbled by their erudition and willingness to contribute their energy to this project in return for little remuneration. I am especially indebted to Beverly C. Tomek, of the University of Houston–Victoria and Wharton County Junior College, whose contributions to the volume were so extensive that she has earned the right to be considered my associate editor. I went into this project with a very good understanding of the role played by free people of color in the societies of 18th- and 19th-century Latin America. I wrote my dissertation and my first book on the society of Saint-Domingue, the modern Haiti, before the Haitian Revolution of 1791–1804. It was that book, and its contention that the divided ruling class of modern Haiti had its genesis in divisions within the group of free people of color before the revolution, that led Facts On File to approach me to prepare this reference work. Tracing the influence of free people of color through the colonial era and into the post-emancipation period is a crucial task for our understanding of black history in the Americas. But to be comprehensive and useful for a general readership, the encyclopedia had to cover the United States as well as South and Central America and the Caribbean islands. I am also grateful to Beverly C. Tomek for her deep understanding of the role of free people of color in the United States and, even more important, for her assistance in finding other contributors and organizing their work.

Andrew Gyory, of Facts On File, deserves as much credit as anybody for the work you hold before you. His careful editing almost always improved articles, and he taught me a great deal about how to be an editor. Andrew's task of an executive editor is a hard one—he has to deal with scholars, with extensive lists of significant publications for scholarly audiences, and teach them how to write for a general audience. He has to teach them how to be editors, how to accept other people's ideas of how to write, and how to help contributors improve their writing. He has to serve as a point of contact between a diverse and individualistic group of academic authors and an organized, professional, and sometimes distant publishing company. All these tasks he performs with great diplomatic skill and unfailing patience. I could never have completed this work without his help and encouragement. His colleague Chief Copy Editor Michael G. Laraque and Copy Editor Susan M. Thornton were impressive in their devotion to making this the best encyclopedia it possibly could be.

The principal editors also owe a great deal to an informal group of assistant editors, some of whom are credited as article authors but all of whom read articles and offered helpful criticism and advice throughout the project. These include Ben Vinson III, of Johns Hopkins University, a specialist in the Spanish Americas; Dominique Rogers, of the Université des Antilles-Guyane, a specialist in free women of color and the French Caribbean; Laurent Dubois, of Duke University, a specialist in the revolutionary period; John Garrigus, of the University of Texas–Arlington, a fellow encyclopedia editor and specialist in the colonial Caribbean; and Michele Reid, of the University of Texas–Austin and a specialist in the Spanish Caribbean. This work is, ultimately, the responsibility of the editors, but if there is merit in it, it is thanks to the assistance of all of these colleagues and many more too numerous to mention.

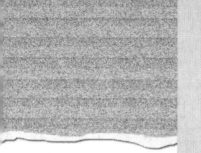

Introduction

Why an encyclopedia of free blacks and people of color? Why should this group of African Americans be considered separately from the mass of their enslaved fellows? There are half a dozen good reference works in English, which are available in most libraries where you will find this book, that discuss the world of African Americans during slavery. However, neither these works nor popular textbooks of African-American history nor general texts of American and Latin American history pay a great deal of attention to the free population of color during the time of slavery. Popular understanding is pretty much ignorant of their very existence, to say nothing of the important role that they played in the history of the countries where they lived. The goal of this reference work is to explore and explain the vital role of the free black community in the Americas, a subject no other encyclopedia has examined.

A few examples will demonstrate the misunderstanding: Frederick Douglass, an American born a slave in Maryland, ran away to the North before the Civil War and worked as a writer, lecturer, and antislavery agitator for many years while slavery continued in the South. Anybody who studies U.S. history has heard of him, but we do not tend to think of him as belonging to a particular group distinct from slaves. François-Dominique-Toussaint Louverture, a Haitian also born a slave before the Haitian Revolution, was liberated by his master and owned his own farm and slaves but led the Haitian people through a terrible war to freedom from slavery. To the extent that Americans are familiar with him, we tend to think of him as a slave. But both of these men were free people of color. It was this status that made it possible for them to make the contributions they did to the welfare of African-American people and the advance of human freedom.

A new generation of scholars has focused attention in historical circles on the free people of color. It was only a decade ago that most English-speaking scholars became aware that Toussaint Louverture, for example, was not a slave when the Haitian Revolution broke out in 1791. New books are published by scholarly presses every year illuminating some new place or sector of society where free people of color made an impact. But the contributions of this new scholarship are only slowly coming to the attention of the general public. Many members of the new generation of scholars have contributed to the work you hold in your hands. We are motivated by a desire to show students and the general public how very important and strong and diverse the free colored people were within slave societies.

There were a lot of them, for one thing, more than most people would guess. Somewhere between 5 and 50 percent of the African-American people in any colony or state where slavery was allowed managed to gain their freedom at some point during their lives. In some places, such as northern Brazil in the 1860s and 1870s, Cuba in the 1600s, or Delaware in the 1850s, where plantation agriculture was weak or slavery itself was dying out, free African Americans became more numerous than slaves, even if the government was not prepared to take the formal step of eliminating slavery altogether. In other places, such as some of the states of the Deep South of the United States, slaves had great difficulty in gaining their freedom because of government regulations and the strength of the plantation economy. However, even in these places, free colored populations grew rapidly thanks to high birthrates. Free colored children also had higher survival rates than either white or slave children everywhere outside the United States. Everywhere, free colored families were large, and children were usually well cared for, so the population increased rapidly by natural means. And everywhere masters had reasons to grant freedom to at least some of their slaves, even if white society as a whole thought that freedom for black people was a dangerous idea.

Free people of color were engaged in a wide variety of activities in the societies in which they lived. They worked at lots of jobs that the white people who were in charge of government and society did not want to do themselves or could not figure out how to do efficiently and yet were unwilling to entrust to slaves. Among the large population of free people of color there were peasants on small remote farms, small businesspeople supplying towns with needed products, skilled workers plying their trades, runaway slaves living in fear of the slave catcher, rebel maroons hiding in mountains, relatives of powerful white people working on their families' plantations, and even well-off farmers and businesspeople who owned their own slaves. In some colonies, free coloreds owned significant proportions of all the land and slaves in the colony and were part of the ruling class, even though they still suffered from racial discrimination. On the other hand, there were many poor free people of color. Even the poorest, though, were careful to preserve their liberty papers, showing that almost all thought that freedom, even in poverty, was preferable to even the most comfortable slavery. Among the poorest of the free coloreds were maroon, or runaway, communities. Living in remote areas, always in danger of attack by colonial militia or police, subsisting by hunting and gathering or working small farms, they led a very difficult life, which was nonetheless preferable to plantation slavery.

Women played an important role in the free colored community. In some places, they exerted more influence over society as a whole than did white women. In general, they had a more respected place in their own community than white women did in white society. The independence that free colored women showed was a threat to established gender roles. Criticism of free people of color by whites was often framed in terms of gender roles: White supremacists argued that free men of color were somehow lacking in manhood because their women were so strong and independent.

White fathers might or might not take as good care of their mixed-race children as their white children, but they were certainly going to provide better education and health care for them than for their unrelated slaves. Even without the assistance of white relatives, though, free colored families generally valued education and sought the best that they could get for their children. And if a slave managed to get some education, often in violation of all sorts of regulations and at the risk of his or her health or life, this could prove a gateway to liberty, as in the case of the activist Frederick Douglass, who said that learning to read "freed his mind" before his body. As a result, those African Americans who managed to acquire an education in slave societies came mostly from or became part of the free colored community.

One consequence of the relatively good economic circumstances, influence, and access to education that free colored communities enjoyed under slavery (relative to the slaves, that is) was that when slavery ended, they were natural leaders of the larger African-American population. Many African-American leaders in the period after emancipation throughout the Atlantic world were people who had been free before slavery was abolished, and to this day many prominent African-American families can trace their ancestry back to preemancipation free people of color.

So these, then, are the themes of this book.

First, Who Were the Free People of Color and Where Did They Live?

The first step in any quest for knowledge is to define your terms. In this encyclopedia, when we talk about a free person of color, we mean someone who had some African ancestors, lived in a colony or independent country in the Americas where slavery existed, but managed to become free for at least part of his or her life while other African Americans continued to suffer under slavery. The period covered here is from the voyage of Columbus forward to the beginning of the 20th century. There were free people of color in Europe before Columbus—in fact, one of them was a sailor in Columbus's first expedition. Portuguese slave traders had been taking people back from Africa to the Iberian Peninsula for two generations by 1492. Since classical times a steady trickle of African slaves had been crossing the Sahara to then be sold to Europeans by North Africans.

But one has to start somewhere. The larger slave trade was the one conducted across the Atlantic to the Americas after 1492, and that is where this book starts. The narrative closes with the aftermath of the end of slavery in the Americas and the role former free people of color played in the new structure of society. In the United States, this was the period of Reconstruction and, following its failure, Redemption and the Jim Crow era. Similar, if not quite so pernicious, situations developed in other countries in the Americas.

We are also limiting ourselves to covering people who became free while other African Americans remained enslaved. One of the most important assumptions of this book is that free people of color were a community. They were different from white people and people of other races because of their African ancestry. Blackness conferred a particularly low status in the Americas, an "indelible stain," as one French commentator put it, because of its association with slavery. Any amount of African ancestry defined one as "other," set one apart from white society in a special way. On the other hand, free African Americans were set apart from their fellows by their freedom. Slavery, it has been argued, was a condition of "social death" under which the slave was so dehumanized that it was as if he or she were dead. The free person had his or her metaphorical life back, even though he or she might not be able to enjoy it on the same basis as someone with no African ancestors because of discriminatory laws and prejudices. Of course, all this being said, there was a good deal of flexibility in all of these terms—black, white, free, slave—that we will explore at much greater length in the articles that follow.

As far as geography is concerned, we are concentrating on the Atlantic world that Columbus made possible. Even more specifically, we are concentrating on the western side of the Atlantic, the Americas, that is, North and South America and the Caribbean islands. There are articles on places and people of Europe, Africa, Asia, and Australia, but only if there was some connection to the Americas. The field of African-American studies in academia is rather sharply divided between researchers who study the United States (and Afro-Canadians) and those who look at the rest of the hemisphere, generally called Latin America. Historians of the United States often do not take many classes or read much of the historical literature about Latin America, and vice versa. It is possible to get through very reputable Ph.D. programs in Latin American history, focusing on black history, without reading more than a dozen books about North American slavery and African Americans. Americanists have the same limitations.

It has been argued that the situation with regard to race and slavery was so different in North America from what was found in the Caribbean, Central America, and South America that one cannot consider the two together. This encyclopedia refutes that assumption. While the United States presented some special challenges to African Americans, both free and enslaved, it existed very much in a spectrum of slave societies along with the other colonies and independent nations of the Americas.

The role of free people of color was especially important in Latin America. Today, most Latinos think of their ancestry as being, in varying proportions, European and Indian. In some places, especially the highland regions of Mexico, Central America, and the Andes, large Indian populations survived contact with the Spanish conquistadores. But European populations were generally very small in these areas during the 16th and 17th centuries, the time when Latino society was being established. In almost all of these countries, imported black slaves outnumbered white immigrants before about 1750. In those lowland regions in the tropical Americas such as Cuba, Brazil, Venezuela, and Hispaniola, where the Indian population almost completely disappeared as a result of tropical diseases carried from Africa, combined with the Eurasian diseases introduced by the whites, the role of free blacks was even more important than in the highland regions. The tropical diseases also kept white populations low in these places. Almost all inhabitants in the late 1700s in the lowland tropical Americas had at least some African ancestry. Because of the economic marginality of these places and the relatively liberal Spanish policy governing manumission, many of these African-American people were free. Free people of color were either the largest population group or second only to slaves in almost all of these countries. In much of Latin America, large numbers of European immigrants arrived in the 19th century as slavery was being abolished. These white

immigrants reinforced the popular self-image of Latinos as descended from Spaniards and/or Indians, as did the ability of light-skinned African Americans to cross color lines in Spanish- and Portuguese-American societies and redefine themselves as mestizo, or mixed Indian-European. In this way, the African heritage of Latin America was lost to public knowledge, only to be recaptured in the late 20th and 21st centuries by new scholarship and cultural revival.

Each colony, state of the United States, or independent country in the Americas that had a significant population of free people of color has an article in this encyclopedia. Additionally, there are articles on cities, states, or regions within countries if they were significant centers of free colored life.

There are also many biographical articles, which give concrete examples of the situations free blacks found in different places and times. Some biographies tell the stories of important individuals such as Toussaint Louverture or Frederick Douglass, people whom anyone interested in the history of a country would know about. Other articles describe the circumstances of little-known people whose lives illustrate some important characteristic of free colored life. We have a biography of a woman merchant in what is now Haiti, a militia officer in Brazil, and a shipbuilder in Philadelphia, for example.

Second, How Did African Americans Get to Be Free and What Did Freedom Mean?

The first question people to unfamiliar with African-American history ask when you tell them you are studying free people of color is "What do you mean? I thought all black people were slaves until Abraham Lincoln (or Vicente Guerrero, or Simón Bolívar, or Toussaint Louverture, or William Wilberforce) set them free?" Free people of color were a standing contradiction of people's racial prejudices in the time of slavery, and they still confound our expectations today. One goal of this encyclopedia is to look at how people gained freedom—as a gift from their master, by ransom or self-purchase, by running away, by rising up in revolution, or simply by being born free. There are also articles about the laws that governed the process of liberation, the treaties between colonies and maroon settlements, and the role played by governments in helping or hindering people seeking their freedom. There are also articles on the special laws that governed African Americans' lives once they gained their freedom—because freedom usually did not mean equality with whites. Finally, there are also articles on the internal divisions along lines of color and class within the free population of color, and how these could change what "freedom" meant to any particular individual.

The issue of racial discrimination and racism is key to an understanding of the situation of free people of color. The law and concept of slavery in the Western world arose from the body of Roman law. For the Romans, any type of person could become a slave, and slaves could become free. As freedmen, they had some duties toward their former masters, often expressed as a condition of "clientage," and the former master had reciprocal duties, called "patronage." But the children of freedmen were Romans, or members of other groups, indistinguishable from other members of those groups. In theory, a freedman might even become a citizen, and some became very influential and wealthy. But in the slave societies of the Americas, the children of former slaves remained black, and blackness, even if diluted by interracial relationships, remained a handicap for all succeeding generations, even up to the present day. The issue of race was commonly confounded with the issue of slavery. Both slaves and abolitionists assumed that if slavery were abolished, an end to racial discrimination would follow, but that turned out not to be the case. Observing how free people of color dealt with this issue of racial discrimination in different historical periods gives us an understanding of how racism evolved.

Third, What Sort of Economic and Social Roles Did They Play in Their Societies?

We answer this question with a series of articles comparing specific fields of activity across the region. There are articles on fields of employment, including farming, crafts, small business, personal services, and urban labor. There were huge differences between countries as to what fields of activity black people were permitted to pursue, and in what fields they were able to achieve success. These articles refer to specific individuals, many of whom are profiled in biographical articles.

In many places, free people of color were key players in the economic life of their communities. As artisans, a trade they were permitted throughout much of the region, they could earn a reasonable living and keep costs of manufactured goods low in what were essentially preindustrial societies separated from their European bases by thousands of miles of treacherous ocean. As labor demands in the economy became more diversified, free black wage-earning workers provided an important economic benefit. Slavery as an economic model is based on a generally unchanging demand for labor—the plantation grows certain products, it requires certain inputs of labor, and these inputs have to arrive at the same time each year and be predictable. As the plantation economy developed a manufacturing (or at least transformative—refining and shipping) sector, this sector demanded a mobile and flexible labor force. Some manufacturers and shippers employed slave labor: Frederick Douglass was hired

out by his master to work on the docks in Baltimore, and this gave him the opportunity to escape. Moving slaves around was risky for the slave owner, however. Slaves might escape, they might be exposed to dangerous ideas, or they might receive opportunities to steal valuable commodities and sell them clandestinely. It was much better from the entrepreneur's point of view to hire free labor and lay off those laborers when they were no longer needed.

There are also articles on how free people of color played special roles in society such as slave owners, landowners, descendants of European nobility, criminals and prisoners, and the like. In many places, there were restrictions that made these roles more difficult for them. There are also articles on the participation of free coloreds in public life in areas such as military service, voting, jury service, or religious life. There are also articles on how color and freed status affected lives in more traditional sociological areas, such as gender and family life.

Religion is a very important theme in this reference. Many free people of color were religious leaders. A basic teaching of Christianity, the dominant though not exclusive religion of the Americas, holds that all human beings are equal in the sight of God. Islam, the religion of many of the African-born slaves, especially in the 16th and 17th centuries, has the same teaching. Many white believers found ways to make their religious beliefs consistent in their own minds with slavery and racism. However, the fundamental teachings of religion both offered solace and strength to slaves and encouraged white believers to take actions that undermined the absolute submission of blacks. African Americans also created their own religions, such as *vodun, santería,* and *candomblé* based on Europeon and African models. Some free African Americans also took on leadership role in Christian groups. Manumission of slaves was often rationalized, by slave masters, as a religious duty. Religious institutions sometimes worked for the amelioration of slavery or even for its outright abolition. Religious life and theological study were highly respected career options for free people of color. A general understanding of the theology and functioning of religious groups is essential to understanding the behavior of believers at this time.

Fourth, What Were Some Special Events or Conditions That Affected Their Lives?

There are a number of articles on topics such as wars, revolutions, natural disasters, development of new crops and industries, scientific advances, legal changes, or cultural and intellectual currents. In some cases, free people of color were players or instigators in these developments. The free black man Benjamin Banneker, for example, was a leading scientist in 18th-century America and helped lay out the city plan for the nation's capital. In 18th-century Haiti, a number of free people of color introduced coffee cultivation and helped make the island the world's leading coffee producer for 50 years. Many of the conditions of free colored life were products of the discriminatory laws people suffered under, and there are a number of articles exploring these laws. Finally, the area of African-American culture has received a lot of attention among scholars. Articles on cultural topics show how free people of color contributed.

Some articles are accompanied by excerpts from documents written at the time. Some of these are from well-known authors, such as Frederick Douglass's speech "What to the Slave Is the Fourth of July?" Others are documents that illustrate some sociological points made in the accompanying article, including certificates of manumission or the accounts of a black-owned business.

How to Use This Book

The articles are arranged in alphabetical order, and you may look up topics as you require. Each article contains suggestions for further reading. Articles are also cross-referenced. In the text, a word or phrase in SMALL CAPITAL letters indicates that there is an article with that title that the reader may elect to consult. At the end of some articles, there are general cross-references that are of broader importance.

If you are interested in the history of a particular place, say, a country or state of the United States, you should first read the article or articles about that place specifically. The main article will contain a list of cross-references to all articles on related cities, regions, or other localities and to all biographical articles about residents of that place. For example, if you are interested in information about South Carolina, go first to the South Carolina article. There, you will find references to an article about the Reconstruction period and about Charleston's free blacks. Also, you will find references to articles about individual South Carolinians, such as Robert Smalls. If you read the biographical articles, you may find references to general articles about that person's trade or profession or about other general conditions that affected his or her life. The article on Smalls for example, would direct you to an article on free people of color working as merchant seamen or in the navy, since Smalls was a harbor pilot and gained his freedom by taking his pilot boat out to the Union navy during the Civil War siege of Charleston, South Carolina.

If you are interested in a particular phase of life or socioeconomic group, start with the general article on that topic. If you were interested in how slaves became free, for example, you would begin with the article on manumission. That article would refer you to articles on running away, marriage between free people and slaves, different specific laws governing manumission in various colonial empires or countries, and so forth. You might also find references to specific country articles or biographical articles that illustrate some related element. Or if you are interested in the role blacks played at sea, go to articles on merchant seamen or naval personnel. They might refer you to biographical articles, regional articles, or articles on other trades and professions, such as merchant or shipbuilding.

We, the authors of this work, hope that it is useful to readers and students.

List of Contributors

K. Wayne Ackerson — Salisbury University
Rose Mary Allen — University of the Netherlands Antilles
Noel Allende-Goitía — Michigan State University
Caitlin Anderson — Harvard University
Cassandra Auble — University of Nebraska–Lincoln
Thomas Bahde — University of Chicago
Ernesto Bassi Arévalo — University of California–Irvine
Madison S. Bell — Goucher College
Angela Bickham — College of William and Mary
Gregory Blake — Independent Scholar
Kenneth Blume — Albany College of Pharmacy
Sylvia Espelt Bombín — Newcastle University
Emily M. Brewer — University of North Carolina
Thomas Brown — Independent Scholar
Barry Cahill — Public Archives of Nova Scotia
Antoine Capet — Université de Rouen
Kim Carey — Kent State University
Caroline Castellanos — University of Texas–San Antonio
Celso T. Castilho — Vanderbilt University
Henry Codjoe — Dalton State College
Laurent Dubois — Duke University
Roy E. Finkenbine — University of Detroit Mercy
Janette Gayle — University of Chicago
Nicole von Germeten — Oregon State University
Laura Gimeno-Pahissa — Universitat Autónoma de Barcelona
Philippe R. Girard — McNeese State University
Alejandro E. Gomez — CERMA
Lynne A. Guitar — El Colegio Americano de Santo Domingo
Elise A. Guyette — University of Vermont
Victoria L. Harrison — Southern Illinois University
Caroline Hasenyager — College of William and Mary
Amy A. Hatmaker — University of Houston–Victoria

Claire Healy — National University of Ireland
Holly Heinsohn — Victoria College
Jesse Hingson — Jacksonville University
Marilyn K. Howard — Columbus State Community College
Matthew J. Hudock — University of Delaware
Curtis Jacobs — University of the West Indies
Martine Jean — Yale University
Aleric Josephs — University of the West Indies
Erin Rahne Kidwell — Georgetown University
Hendrik Kraay — University of Calgary
Summer Leibensperger — University of Houston–Victoria
Carole Levin — University of Nebraska
Yvette Liebesman — St. Louis University
Robert Little — Tarrant County College
Daniel Livesay — College of William and Mary
Janet McClellan — University of Alaska
John McLane — Independent Scholar
Yuko Miki — Washington University–Saint Louis
Dayo Nicole Mitchell — University of Oregon
Aurora Morrison — Independent Scholar
Isabel Morais — University of Saint Joseph
Jennifer Moses — University of Delaware
Arturo Motta — Universidad Nacional Autónoma de México
Ana Janaina Nelson — Independent Scholar
Myron C. Noonkester — William Carey University
Christopher A. Nordmann — Independent Scholar
Genaro Vilanova Miranda de Oliveira — Universidade Federal da Bahia
Forrest D. Pass — Canadian Heraldic Authority
Francisco Quiroz — Independent Scholar
Michele Reid-Vazquez — University of Texas–Austin
Araceli Reynoso Medina — Universidad Nacional Autónoma de México
Daniel Rucker — Independent Scholar

Diana Senior-Angulo	Universidad de Costa Rica	Srividhya Swaminathan	Long Island University
Juan Manuel de la Serna	Universidad Nacional Autónoma de México	Gail Swanson	Independent Scholar
		Inés María Martiatu Terry	Independent Scholar
Thomas H. Sheeler	University of Delaware	Blake Vaughan	Miami University, Ohio
Michael Stone	Hartwick College	María Elisa Velázquez	Instituto Nacional de
Tim Stringer	University of Houston– Clear Lake	Gutiérrez	Antropología (INAH–Conaculata)
Roberto Strongman- Congiu	University of California– Santa Barbara	Pedro L. V. Welch	University of the West Indies

Chronology

1435

▪ *January 13:* Pope Eugene IV issues the instruction *Sicut Dudum* to the king of Spain and the Spanish bishops, forbidding the enslavement of the natives of the Canary Islands and asserting that, even though they were dark-skinned and lived a very "primitive" lifestyle, they were still human and had a basic right to liberty. All Canarian slaves were to be released, and anybody who kept them enslaved was to be excommunicated.

1436

▪ Gil Eanes and Afonso Gonçalves Baldaia guide the first Portuguese ship to visit the Senegal River and return with slaves, beginning the Atlantic slave trade.

1471

▪ *December 21:* A Portuguese ship under the command of João de Santarém reaches the island of São Tomé in the Atlantic off the coast of Central Africa. São Tomé was to become the largest sugar-producing colony in the Atlantic in the early 16th century, owing to the importation of numerous slaves from nearby Congo. The society established there became the model for other sugar-producing colonies in the Americas. Many free São Tomé blacks participated in the colonization of Brazil.

1482

▪ *January 19:* Portuguese establish Elmina Castle in modern Ghana, West Africa, as a center for the slave and gold trade. Local residents are recruited as interpreters and sailors on Portuguese ships; these people and their descendants play an important role as free people of color in the development of Portugal's global trading empire.

1491

▪ *May 3:* King Nzinga a Nkuwu of Congo is baptized as a Catholic, taking the name João and establishing close ties with Portugal. Congo was to be an important source of slaves for the Atlantic slave trade, and Congolese war prisoners were to play an important role in many slave rebellions throughout the Americas.

1492

▪ *October 12:* The first free people of African descent arrive in the Americas; at least three sailors who accompanied Columbus were of wholly or partially African ancestry.

1508

▪ *June 12:* Juan Ponce de León arrives in Puerto Rico with a force of 50 conquistadores, including Juan Garrido, Francisco Meixias and his family, and perhaps other free people of color. These were the first blacks to arrive in Puerto Rico and thus in the future territory of the United States.

1521

▪ *August 13:* The Aztec capital Tenochtitlán falls to a Spanish-Indian army led by Hernán Cortés that includes the Afro-Spanish conquistador Juan Garrido and several dozen other blacks.

1533

▪ Colegio Santa Cruz de Tlatelolco, the first university in the Americas, is founded outside Mexico City. The university admitted nonwhites, including free people of mixed African–Native American ancestry.

1536

▪ *July 1:* The first person known to have crossed the North American continent, the enslaved black Estéban de Dorantes, arrives in Mexico City at the end of his eight-year journey from Florida by way of Texas, Arizona, and Sonora. He was later freed and helped lead another expedition to what is now the southwestern United States.

1537

▪ *June 2:* Pope Paul III issues the bull *Sublimus Dei* in which he condemns the enslavement of Indians and asserts that all people are human and have some basic human rights, especially to family unity and religious services. The Roman Catholic Church position on race and slavery was often contradictory, but this basic requirement remained in force throughout the colonial period.

1538

■ The free black conquistador Juan Garrido files an application to the colonial government in Mexico for a grant of land, citing his service in the conquests of Cuba, Florida, Puerto Rico, and Mexico.

1541

■ *February 12:* Pedro de Valdivia founds Santiago, marking the conclusion of the conquest of Chile. The Afro-Spanish conquistadores Juan Valiente and Juan Beltrán receive land grants in the new city.

1542

■ Sugar cultivation begins in Pernambuco, Brazil, importing technologies and in some cases free and enslaved workers from the Portuguese Atlantic islands and the Algarve district in southern Portugal.

1549

■ Spanish forces destroy the maroon community led by Felipillo in Panama. This may have been the first predominantly African-American maroon community on the mainland of Spanish America.

1555

■ Five African men taken from modern Ghana to England may have been the earliest free Africans to live in England. The men were to be educated and returned to their homeland to help England slave traders as interpreters and cultural intermediaries.

1565

■ *September 8:* Pedro Menéndez de Avilés and an expedition from Cuba including several dozen Afro-Cubans, some free and some enslaved, establish the city of St. Augustine in Florida. This is the oldest European city in North America, and Menéndez's black soldiers were the first free blacks to build their homes in what is now the United States.

1604

■ The Peruvian mixed-race Dominican friar Martin de Porres becomes a full member of the Dominican order. The order generally did not accept nonwhites, but Martin's reputation for sanctity and good works allowed him to overcome discrimination. He was

devoted to serving the poor and was later venerated in the Roman Catholic Church as a saint; he was canonized by Pope John XXIII in 1962.

1605

■ The Spanish Jesuit priest Alfonso de Sandoval begins his ministry among the blacks of Cartagena, Colombia. Sandoval and his successor in the work, Peter Claver, worked tirelessly to protect slaves from the oppression of their masters and to ensure respect of government regulations giving some rights to blacks. Claver was later recognized as a saint by the Catholic Church.

1619

■ *August 15:* A Dutch warship lands 20 captured Africans in Jamestown, Virginia. Blacks were treated as indentured servants, not slaves for life, at this time, so these were probably the first free blacks to arrive in English colonies in mainland North America.

1625

■ *May:* Settlers from St. Kitts arrive at Tortuga island off the coast of Hispaniola and establish the French colony of Saint-Domingue. The first settlers were buccaneers, or hunters, who also fought with the Spanish in neighboring Spanish Santo Domingo. The colony soon was home to many free blacks who sailed with the buccaneers.

1630

■ *March 3:* Dutch capture Recife, Pernambuco, Brazil, beginning a 25-year period of colonial rule during which Dutch planters would learn techniques of sugar cultivation. Brazilian free people of color fought alongside the Portuguese to resist and finally expel the Dutch, thereby staking a claim to better treatment in Brazilian society.

1635

■ *July 8:* The free black militia leader Henrique Dias surrenders the Brazilian fort at Arraial do Bom Jesus to the Dutch, after a long siege. His heroic defense, with only 80 men, helped delay the invaders and rally support for the Portuguese cause. His example led people of color in Bahia to support the Portuguese strongly. Dias was rewarded with a noble title and command of all the free colored soldiers in the province, and he went on to have a military career of 21 years of war against the Dutch and Spanish in which he was never again defeated.

1637

■ Pieter Blower, a refugee from Dutch Brazil, begins sugar cultivation on Barbados. Sugar transformed the island's economy within a decade, and other Caribbean island colonies would imitate Barbados's example. Because free people of color rarely had the resources to cultivate sugar, many small free colored farmers were forced out of business when sugar was introduced.

1640

■ *July:* In Virginia, the runaway black servant John Punch is sentenced to servitude for life, while his four white companions have four years added to their indenture. Punch thus becomes the first legally recognized black slave in the English mainland North American colonies.

1642

■ The Peruvian mixed-race nun Ursula de Jesús begins having mystical visions of an ideal godly society with racial and social justice. Her reputation for sanctity and humility meant that her religious order and society as a whole permitted her to reveal the content of her visions in lectures and in a spiritual autobiography. She became a very influential spiritual figure in 17th-century Peru.

1664

■ Maryland passes a law forbidding free whites to marry slaves or black indentured servants. This is the first miscegenation law in the present-day United States, although it does not affect free people of color directly. A 1691 law in Virginia is the first law in the present-day United States to outlaw marriage between whites and blacks of any status completely.

1670

■ *June 15:* First English and African settlers arrive in Charleston, South Carolina; many early settlers were from Barbados and introduced Caribbean attitudes and laws about race and slavery.

1671

■ *January 18:* The English pirate Henry Morgan, with a crew of 1,400 men operating out of Port Royal, Jamaica, over half of whom were nonwhites, captures Panama. This was the greatest success of the English pirates in the Caribbean and, paradoxically, the act that finally led the English government to withdraw its support from them. Many of Morgan's men were able to retire on their booty in various English colonies and become farmers or artisans.

1685

■ *March 6:* King Louis XIV of France issues the Code Noir, providing some legal rights to blacks, both free and enslaved, but legally defining their subordinate status. This law was the basis for black codes in Louisiana and Florida.

1688

■ *October 3:* An updated slave code in Barbados defines Africans as "heathenish and brutish" and naturally subject to slavery. All Africans were slaves for life, while whites who entered as indentured servants were to serve no more than three years. The Barbados slave code was to provide a model for similar codes in other English colonies both in the Caribbean and on the North American mainland.

1693

■ Brazilian frontiersmen discover gold in the Minas Gerais region. The gold rush allows many slaves to gain their freedom, and Minas Gerais gains a large free colored population in the early 1700s.

1694

■ *February 24:* Brazilian and Portuguese troops make a final assault on the maroon community of Palmares, in Brazil. This was the largest of many maroon communities in the Atlantic world, so large that it became a security threat to the colonial government sufficient to justify sending a large army with artillery to destroy it. The maroon leader Zumbi escapes the field but is captured and beheaded on November 20, 1695.

1697

■ *May 6:* French buccaneers including the free colored Vincent Olivier and many others capture Cartagena, Colombia, and loot an enormous treasure. With their booty, many build plantations in Saint-Domingue, introducing the sugar revolution to that island.

■ *September 20:* Treaty of Ryswick confirms French possession of Saint-Domingue; the French government encourages buccaneers to settle down and become planters. Some free colored buccaneers, like Vincent Olivier, also get lands and slaves.

1712

■ The Afro-Mexican painter Juan Correa is the first to copy the image of the Virgin of Guadalupe, believed to have appeared miraculously on the cloak of St. Juan

Diego. The image has become the national symbol of Mexico.

1713

■ The Puerto Rican mixed-race privateer and merchant Miguel Enriquez is promoted to the rank of captain in the Spanish royal navy and given the exclusive right to provide naval supplies, both to navy ships and to his fellow privateers, on the island. He becomes very wealthy and plays an important role in Spain's growing military power in the Caribbean.

1720

■ Gabriel Mathieu de Thieu, a French naval officer, takes a coffee bush to Martinique and introduces coffee cultivation to the Americas. Coffee proves to be a very good crop for small planters, including free people of color, in the French Caribbean, Spanish colonies, and Brazil.

1721

■ A law in Barbados forbids free blacks to vote and makes the legal testimony of a black less important than that of a white person. Denying the protection of the courts to free blacks becomes a characteristic of British and British-influenced race laws that will spread to the mainland North American colonies, the future United States.

1722

■ Abram Gannibal, a black former slave, freed by Russia's emperor Peter the Great, returns to Russia from his studies in France. In France, the philosopher Voltaire had called him "the dark star of the Enlightenment." In Russia, Peter names him a general and inspector of fortifications. He is probably the first black to hold the rank of general in a European army.

1724

■ *March 9:* King Louis XV of France issues a revised Code Noir for Louisiana. The new code is much harsher on free people of color than its famous predecessor of 1685, which applied to all the other French colonies in the Caribbean, and the Atlantic and Indian Oceans, but still provides more protections than British law in its North American colonies.

1738

■ *January 6:* A treaty between the Accompong Maroons of Jamaica, led by Captain Cudjoe, and the colonial government grants the maroons recognition of their liberty, political autonomy, and land that they will still hold in the 21st century.

1739

■ A law in Barbados requires all persons who want to free one of their slaves to put up a deposit of £40 to ensure that the newly freed person would not become a charge on public charity. The results of this law are a sharp reduction in formal manumissions and an increase in the number of people "living as free." This and other Barbados laws on race become very influential on the other British colonies in the Caribbean and mainland North America.

1744

■ *June 29:* Santa Iglesia (Holy Church) cathedral in Morelia, Michoacán, Mexico, designed by the Afro-Mexican architect Diego Duran, is dedicated.

1751

■ The first volume of the *Encyclopédie* of the French philosopher Denis Diderot is published, introducing a new seemingly scientific racial anthropology.

1758

■ *June:* Joseph Bologne, a mixed-race child of a white planter in Guadeloupe and his African slave mistress, is named a knight of the Gendarmerie du Garde du Roi, one of the royal guard regiments in France. After this time, he is known as the chevalier de Saint-Georges. He was probably the first nonwhite since the Middle Ages to hold a French noble title.

■ *July 20:* The maroon leader and rebel François Mackandal is executed in Cap-Français, Saint-Domingue. Mackandal becomes in death a rallying symbol for Saint-Domingue slaves, and his legend will help motivate slaves to join in the Haitian Revolution in the late 18th century.

■ *September 29:* Philadelphia Yearly Meeting of Quakers forbids all members to own slaves; it is the first formal statement by a governing body of a religious denomination in the present-day United States outlawing slavery.

■ *December:* British forces occupy the French colony on Gorée Island off the coast of Sénégal, Africa. Many of Gorée's free colored businesswomen relocate to the French Caribbean, strengthening transatlantic ties among Senegambia, Saint-Domingue, and the other French colonies. Among the refugees are Anne Rossignol and her family, who become important merchants in Cap-Français, Saint-Domingue.

1760

■ *October 10:* Treaty of Ouca, Surinam, between the colonial government and the Saramaka maroons guarantees freedom and land to the maroons in return for their agreement not to attack plantations and to stop accepting new runaways.

1763

■ *February 23:* Berbice slave rebellion breaks out in Guyana; many free people of color support the colonial government, and when the slave rebels capture most of the countryside, their plantations are destroyed along with those of the whites.

1765

■ *May 10:* The Afro-Caribbean missionary Rebecca Protten and her husband, the Afro-Danish preacher Christian Protten, arrive in the Danish settlement of Christiansborg, in modern Ghana, to establish the Moravian Protestant Church in Africa.

1766

■ Work begins on the Church of St. Francis of Assisi in Ouro Preto, Brazil, designed by the Afro-Brazilian architect Antonio Lisboa "O Aleijadinho." The church is recognized as one of the greatest architectural triumphs of the Portuguese-speaking world.

1767

■ *September 18:* British court declares that Jonathan Strong, a black servant from Barbados, was not a slave but a free man. The case was decided on narrow grounds but provided a precedent for the more famous Somerset case five years later that outlawed slavery in Britain. The British abolitionist Granville Sharp supported Strong in his lawsuit.

1769

■ *June:* White and free colored militiamen in the South Province of Saint-Domingue rebel against increased militia service obligations, presenting the government with the threat of a combination of whites and wealthy free colored planters.

1770

■ Guillaume Raynal's *Histoire des deux Indes* (History of the two Indies) is published. Criticizing both the French monarchy and slavery, Raynal's influential and widely read book was an important intellectual source both for the French abolition movement and for the French Revolution.

1772

■ A five-year struggle begins between the Boni maroons and the colonial government of Surinam that would ultimately lead to a negotiated settlement permitting the maroons to live undisturbed in the far interior of the colony.

■ *June 22:* British courts, in the Somerset case, hold that slavery cannot be enforced under British law, thus making all slaves in Britain free. A similar case in 1778 in Scotland reaffirms that slavery could not exist in Britain.

1773

■ *June 12:* Publication of *Poems on Various Subjects Religious and Moral* by the African-American poet Phillis Wheatley. This was the first book published in the present-day United States by an African American.

1775

■ *June 17:* At the Battle of Bunker Hill in Massachusetts, the free black Peter Salem shoots and kills the British marine commander, Major John Pitcairn.

■ *November 7:* Lord Dunmore issues a proclamation in Virginia offering freedom to any slave belonging to a proindependence master who would join the British army. Ultimately, thousands of blacks would serve in the British army during the War of American Independence, 1775–1783.

1776

■ *September 3:* French regulation called the Police des Noirs permits masters to take slaves to France under certain circumstances, but local courts refuse to implement the regulation in many places, and free people of color preserve their rights.

1777

■ *January 17:* Prince Hall and seven other free blacks petition the Massachusetts legislature to end slavery and grant equal rights to blacks.

1778

■ *April 5:* A decree forbids marriage of whites and people of color in metropolitan France, but many local jurisdictions refuse to enforce it, including Paris, where most of France's free people of color lived at the time.

1779

■ The Saint-Domingue-born free black Jean-Baptiste Pointe du Sable builds a trading post where the Chicago River enters Lake Michigan, becoming the first nonindigenous inhabitant of what is today Chicago, Illinois.

■ *October 9:* Final unsuccessful assault on Savannah, Georgia, by French and American forces during the War of American Independence. The French force contains a unit of black soldiers from Saint-Domingue including many of the future leaders of the Haitian Revolution, while the British force includes the black King's Rangers from Georgia. Some free black soldiers fought among the American rebel forces as well.

1780

- Lemuel Haynes becomes the first African American ordained as a minister of a mainline Protestant denomination when he is licensed as a preacher in the Congregational Church. He serves churches in Vermont, Connecticut, and Massachusetts until his death in 1833.
- *March 1:* Pennsylvania passes the Act for the Gradual Abolition of Slavery, freeing all slaves born after the act was passed at the age of 28; it is first antislavery legislation passed in the United States, though some people remain enslaved in Pennsylvania until final abolition in 1847.
- *September 1:* The New Jersey runaway slave Colonel Tye, fighting for the British during the War of American Independence, is killed in battle. While his rank was a courtesy by the British, he was one of the most prominent free colored soldiers to fight against American independence.

1781

- *June 12:* Quock Walker case first decided by a lower court in Massachusetts, which held that slavery could not exist in the state. Massachusetts is the first American state to outlaw slavery completely.
- *October 14:* An assault on redoubts 9 and 10 of the British position at Yorktown, Virginia, led by French regular troops and the 1st Rhode Island Infantry, a unit composed mostly of free colored soldiers, is successful. The British position is so weakened by this assault that the British general Cornwallis would surrender his army two days later, effectively ending the War of American Independence.

1782

- *August 27:* John Laurens, a prominent white South Carolinian who had encouraged the inclusion of black soldiers in the War of American Independence and called for equality for free blacks, is killed in action at the Battle of the Combahee River, only a few weeks before a ceasefire was to take effect.

1783

- *April 1:* First of almost 3,000 black loyalists from New York and other British-controlled ports in the United States begin to arrive in Nova Scotia, Canada.

- *November 25:* British troops evacuate New York City at the end of the War of American Independence. They take with them several thousand African Americans who had fought on their side and to whom they had promised freedom. American masters, including George Washington, were upset that they could not retrieve their slaves, but there was nothing they could do. Many of these newly freed blacks go on to settle Nova Scotia, Canada, and Sierra Leone.

1784

- *February 26:* Rhode Island passes "An Act authorizing the Manumission of Negroes, Mullattoes, & others, and for the gradual Abolition of Slavery." The state has the densest slave population in the North at the time. The law provides for the gradual elimination of slavery, and the last Rhode Island slaves will not gain their liberty until 1848.
- *March 1:* Connecticut passes a gradual emancipation law that frees all slaves born after the effective date but does not free any born before 1784; the last Connecticut slaves are not freed until 1848.
- *May 24:* Julien Raimond, a mixed-race planter from Saint-Domingue, presents a petition to the French minister of marine, in charge of colonial policy, asking for equal rights for free people of color. This may have been the first formal claim for civil rights in the French colonial world by a person of African descent.

1787

- Ottobah Cugoano, a British free black author, publishes his *Thoughts and Sentiments on the Evil of Slavery and Commerce of the Human Species.* An important abolitionist tract, the book has a powerful influence on British public opinion during the debate over the abolition of the slave trade.
- *April 29:* The Massachusetts free colored Masonic temple founded by Prince Hall receives its official charter from the British Masonic temple, thus becoming the first independent black fraternal order in the United States. Black freemasonry becomes an important tool for organization of free colored communities.
- *May 15:* First ships carrying free blacks from Britain arrive in Sierra Leone, accompanied by the abolitionists John Clarkson and Olaudah Equiano.
- *July 13:* Northwest Ordinance passed in the United States prohibiting slavery in the Northwest Territory, now the states of Ohio, Indiana, Illinois, Michigan, Wisconsin, and Minnesota.
- *September:* New York African Free School opens, the first U.S. school specifically intended for the education of all African Americans. Prominent free colored

leaders from across the country are educated here. The school becomes a part of the regular New York public school system in 1835.

1788

■ Moreau de St-Méry's *Description* of the colony of Saint-Domingue is published. Moreau de St-Méry's racial classification system and ideas about race relations were to become very influential in the early 19th century.

■ *January 18:* The First Fleet of convict transports arrives in Botany Bay, Australia, beginning British settlement of the continent. Among the 1,332 sailors, crewmen, and convicts were several dozen Afro-Britons, Afro-Caribbeans, and African Americans.

1789

■ The first volume of Olaudah Equiano's *Interesting Narrative* is published in Britain. This work, an account of the author's life and journey from Africa to the Americas to Britain and from a peaceful childhood through slavery to freedom, became a best seller and had a great influence on the abolitionist struggle around the world. The book remains a classic to this day.

■ *July 14:* French Revolution begins with the capture of the Bastille in Paris. Parisian free people of color are among the rebels storming the fortress, and the revolution would pave the way for the independence of the first black nation in the Americas, Haiti.

1791

■ *February 22:* The free colored rebels Vincent Ogé and Jean-Baptiste Chavannes are brutally executed in Cap-Français, Saint-Domingue. The cruel execution excited sympathy for the cause of free colored civil rights in France and helped convince the French assembly to grant full equality to free people of color in 1792.

1792

■ *April 4:* French royal decree grants citizenship and the vote to free colored men who owned land.

1793

■ *March 3:* Thomas-Alexandre Dumas, father of *The Three Musketeers* author Alexandre Dumas, appointed a general in the French army and sent to command forces fighting a conservative rebellion in the Vendée region. He was the first nonwhite to hold the rank of general in the French army and the first in any western European army.

■ *August 23:* Léger-Félicité Sonthonax, revolutionary commissioner, abolishes slavery in the North province of Saint-Domingue, first official abolition of slavery in the French Empire.

1794

■ *February 3:* The French National Convention admits three black members, Louis Dufay, Jean-Baptiste Belley, and Jean-Baptiste Mills, as the first blacks to serve in a national legislature in Europe.

■ *February 4:* The French National Convention abolishes slavery throughout the French Empire, making it the first country in the Atlantic world to end slavery. The abolition was later rescinded by Napoléon.

■ *July 29:* Mother Bethel Methodist Church is dedicated in Philadelphia, Pennsylvania. Mother Bethel was the first congregation of what would become the African Methodist Episopal (A.M.E.) Church in 1816. This was the first church entirely led by African Americans in the United States. Bishop Richard Allen, the first pastor, was an enormously important person in the creation of the A.M.E denomination throughout the country.

■ *October 6:* Victor Hugues and an army including many free people of color take control of Guadeloupe, abolishing slavery and extending the French Revolution to the eastern Caribbean. Hugues would rule Guadeloupe until 1798.

1797

■ More than 2,000 Black Carib from St. Vincent arrive in Croatan Island, off the coast of Honduras. This was the largest group of African Americans who were to become the ancestors of the black-Indian populations of the Caribbean coast of Central America.

1798

■ The Connecticut free black Venture Smith publishes his memoir, *A Narrative of the Life and Adventures of Venture, a Native of Africa: But Resident above Sixty Years in the United States of America, Related by Himself,* one of the first slave narratives published in the United States. It will have a great influence on the growth of abolitionism in Connecticut, which had recently passed a gradual abolition bill. Connecticut abolitionists managed to buy the freedom of almost all Connecticut slaves within a few years after the publication of Smith's book.

■ James Forten becomes an independent sailmaker in Philadelphia. He soon becomes one of the wealthiest African-American businesspeople in the United States. He plays an important role in the establishment of black churches and civic institutions and works to protect the rights of blacks in Pennsylvania politics. His children and grandchildren were to be important members of the abolition movement.

1800

- *March:* The garrison of Jacmel, Saint-Domingue, under the command of Alexandre Pétion, surrenders the city to the forces of Jean-Jacques Dessalines, effectively ending the War of the Knives between former free people of color in the South Province, led by André Rigaud, and the predominantly black slave rebels under Toussaint Louverture and Dessalines from the north.
- *October 10:* Gabriel, an enslaved artisan who was living "as free" in Richmond, Virginia, is executed for plotting a slave rebellion; the discovery of the plot led to further restrictions on free people of color in Virginia.

1801

- *October 21:* Magloire Pélage's coup against the governor of Guadeloupe begins six months of free colored rule in the French colony.

1802

- *March 24:* The garrison of La Crête-à-Pierrot, Saint-Domingue, part of the rebel army under command of Toussaint Louverture, evacuates the fort after a monthlong siege in which more than 600 French soldiers die. The evacuation of the fort is caused by artillery fire from a French unit commanded by a free mixed-race officer, Alexandre Pétion. After the fall of La Crête-à-Pierrot, Louverture comes to terms with the French army and surrenders, but before the end of the year, his arrest and French preparations to restore slavery and arrest nonwhite officers drive Pétion and other pro-French Haitian leaders to the rebel side.
- *May 10:* General Antoine Richepanse arrives in Guadeloupe with a large army to reimpose French rule. Guadeloupean free colored forces led by Magloire Pélage do not resist Richepanse, but some free blacks and former slaves led by Pélage's second-in-command, Louis Delgrès, suspect that Richepanse has arrived to reenslave the blacks, and they retreat to the interior of the colony.
- *May 28:* The Martiniquan free colored rebel leader Louis Delgrès and more than 100 companions blow themselves up at Matouba plantation, Guadeloupe, rather than submit to the French army that had arrived to restore slavery to the colony.

1803

- *May 2:* American and French negotiators sign a treaty to sell Louisiana to the United States. The treaty provides that French citizens living in the territory would continue to enjoy their property and rights, and

this was later held to protect land owned by free black Louisianans.
- *November 18:* The Battle of Vertières, fought on the outskirts of Cap-Français, ends the Haitian Revolution. A very important charge that breaks the center of the French position is led by the prerevolutionary free black François Capois ("La Mort"), whose behavior was so conspicuously brave that the notoriously racist French general Rochambeau sends Capois a horse to replace the one that the French shot out from under him.

1804

- *January 1:* Haiti's leaders proclaim national independence. Former slave Jean-Jacques Dessalines is named the first national leader, but many of his chief lieutenants are prewar free men of color.
- *February 13:* Absalom Jones is ordained a priest in the Episcopal Church. He was the first person of African ancestry to be ordained a priest in the Episcopal Church in the United States and may be the first in the entire Anglican Communion around the world.

1805

- *March 2:* Fédon's Rebellion, a free-colored-led nationalist rebellion against British rule, breaks out in Grenada.

1806

- *June 11:* A decree from the king of Spain grants José Manuel Valdes, a Peruvian Afro-Indian surgeon, the right to receive a doctorate from the University of Lima and become the first nonwhite degreed physician in the Spanish colonial world. Surgeons were tradesmen, often also working as barbers, while physicians were degreed professionals with much higher social status.

1807

- *January 25:* New Jersey enacts a law denying the vote to free blacks and women.
- *March 25:* The British Slave Trade Act abolishes the slave trade. British free blacks, including Olaudah Equiano and Quabna Ottobah Cugoano, who were very prominent as advocates for this measure. British blacks had also been important as sailors on slave trading ships.

1808

- *January 1:* U.S. Slave Trade Act abolishes the slave trade in the United States. An 1819 act establishes a naval squadron to intercept slave traders along the African coast and repatriate recaptured slaves to Liberia. Slave prices rise rapidly in the United States, making it much more difficult for people to gain their freedom, and slave states settled after this time generally had harsh restrictions on free people of color and on manumissions.

1809

■ *May 25:* The free mixed-race artisan Francisco Rios leads a riot against colonial authorities in Chuquisaca (modern Sucre), beginning the independence struggle in Bolivia.

1810

■ *May 18:* May Revolution breaks out in Buenos Aires, marking the beginning of Argentina's and Spanish South America's struggle for independence from Spain; Afro-Argentine militia forces play an important role in the fighting and in the subsequent campaigns throughout South America.

■ *June 4:* White and free colored political leaders in Cartagena, Colombia, join together to expel the Spanish governor and declare independence. The free colored faction was very powerful in the politics of the Republic of Cartagena until it was recaptured by Spain in 1815.

■ *September 15:* The Mexican priest Miguel Hidalgo calls for Mexicans to fight for independence from Spain. He also proclaims the end of slavery and of serfdom for Indians, calling on blacks and Indians to join his cause. One of his former students, the Afro-Mexican priest José Maria Morelos, quickly joins the struggle.

1811

■ *July 4:* First Congress of Chile abolishes the slave trade and passes a law of free birth, freeing all persons born after that date.

1813

■ *April 18:* The region of West Florida, including Mobile, Alabama, and the Gulf coast of Mississippi, is captured from Spain and becomes part of the United States. The large free colored population is not protected by treaty but nonetheless remains numerous and relatively well-off in the former Spanish regions of the state.

1814

■ *December 5:* Battle of Urica, Venezuela, where royalist forces under José Tomás Boves, including many free colored cavalrymen from the llanos (plains), defeat proindependence forces and destroy the Second Venezuelan Republic. Boves is killed in the battle, and afterward his successor as leader of the llaneros, José Antonio Páez, throws his support to the independence movement. Free colored cavalrymen from Venezuela become a mainstay of the liberation forces in northern Spanish America from this time forward.

1816

■ St. John's Church, Belize, part of the official Anglican Church, begins a school to educate free colored children. This is the first free school open to nonwhites in the colony and demonstrates the growth of the free colored population as well as the relatively benign racial climate, especially when compared to the English-speaking states of North America, where at the same time it is often unlawful to teach a free colored child to read.

■ *April 10:* Black Methodist congregations, faced with racial discrimination within mainstream Methodism, meet in Philadelphia and organize the African Methodist Episcopal (A.M.E.) Church, the first separate black Protestant denomination. Richard Allen is elected the first presiding bishop.

■ *December 21:* The American Colonization Society is founded in Washington, D.C. The society built on a colonization plan by the free colored leader Paul Cuffe, but most free colored leaders dismissed the plan to resettle them in Liberia.

1818

■ *April 5:* Battle of Maipú, Chile. Forces from Argentina under the command of José de San Martín, including many free people of color from the large black communities of Argentina and Uruguay, defeat royalist forces in Chile and ensure the success of the independence movement there. Black soldiers from Chile and Uruguay played a very important role in the liberation struggles of southern South America.

■ *September 16:* The Connecticut state constitution denies the vote to free blacks.

1820

■ *March 5:* The Missouri Compromise divides the western part of the United States between free and slave territories along the 36°30' parallel of latitude. The compromise will later be modified by the Kansas-Nebraska Act of 1854 and overturned by the *Dred Scott* Supreme Court decision of 1857.

■ *May 30:* Spain ratifies a treaty abolishing the slave trade within its colonial domains, but in fact local officials continue to tolerate an illegal slave trade to Cuba and Puerto Rico until the 1850s. Many Cuban free blacks take advantage of low slave prices from rampant smuggling to establish small plantations in the 1830s and 1840s.

1821

■ *August 24:* In Mexico, the Army of the Three Guarantees, uniting the pro-independence forces under the free mixed-race general Vicente Guerrero and the royalist forces under Agustín Iturbide, enters Mexico City and accepts the surrender of the last Spanish viceroy. This ends the Mexican War of Independence, although fighting between Iturbide's forces and the rebels was to break out again the next year.

- **August 30:** The Constitution of Cúcuta in Gran Colombia (modern Colombia, Ecuador, and Venezuela) declares that all children of slaves born after this date will be free. Slavery will finally be abolished entirely in 1851.
- **October 24:** The Mexican Judicial Council proclaims the law of free birth: All slaves born after this date in Mexico are to be free.
- **December 1:** Representatives of the American Colonization Society buy a 30-mile strip of land near Cape Mesurado in West Africa, leading to the establishment of the colony of Liberia.

1822

- Beverly Hemings, the oldest child of Thomas Jefferson and Sally Hemings, leaves Monticello to move to Washington, D.C., with his white wife. He is accompanied by his younger sister Harriet. Both passed as white, and their further story is lost to history.
- The Haitian prerevolutionary free colored general Jean-Pierre Boyer leads his troops into the Spanish part of the island of Hispaniola, ending a short-lived independence movement there and combining the country with Haiti. He abolishes slavery and establishes racial equality.
- **July 2:** Denmark Vesey, a free black artisan of Charleston, South Carolina, is executed for allegedly planning a slave uprising. Fear of slave rebellion sparked by this discovery led to suppression of many free black institutions and new laws restricting free blacks in the South.

1823

- Delegation of Trinidad free people of color led by Dr. Jean-Baptiste Phillipe appeals to Parliament in Britain for civil rights for free coloreds. Their petition would be granted in 1829.
- **June 1:** Alexander Twilight graduates from Middlebury College in Vermont, the first free black to earn a college degree in the United States.
- **July 24:** Naval battle of Lake Maracaibo, Venezuela: Patriot forces under the command of the Afro-Venezuelan admiral Jose Prudencio Padilla defeat the Spanish navy and ensure the independence of Spanish South America.
- **August 18:** Demerara rebellion breaks out in Guyana; slaves led by Baptist preachers, including whites and free people of color, stop work to try to force

improvements in working conditions. Many leaders are imprisoned or exiled from the colony.

1824

- President Jean-Pierre Boyer of Haiti invites free people of color from the United States to settle in Haiti and what is now the Dominican Republic, then under Haitian control. Many U.S. free blacks are more open to this suggestion than to emigration to Liberia, feeling that it would be better to live under a black government. Several colonies are established between 1824 and 1863.
- **November 22:** Constitution of the Federal Republic of Central America abolishes slavery and establishes equal rights for all racial groups; the central government was weak, and both slavery and racial discrimination persisted in some areas.
- **December 9:** Battle of Ayacucho, Peru, where Peruvian forces under General Antonio José de Sucre defeat royalist forces to seal the independence of Spanish South America. Many of Sucre's men were African Americans from Argentina, Ecuador, Peru, and Colombia.

1825

- **April 18:** Juan Antonio Lavalleja and his tiny band, the "Thirty-three Immortals," including at least two Afro Uruguayans, land near Montevideo and launch a guerrilla struggle against the Brazilian occupying forces. This struggle eventually led to the independence of Uruguay.
- **June 25:** The House of Commons in Britain vindicates the free colored religious leader Ann Gill, from Barbados, who had been prosecuted for leading a black Methodist congregation in her own home after antiblack rioters had burned their church and driven their white pastor out of the colony.

1826

- Madison and Eston Hemings, the two younger sons of Thomas Jefferson and Sally Hemings, are freed by virtue of Jefferson's will. Both live in Virginia for some time, with special permission of the Virginia legislature, since all newly freed people are supposed to leave the state. However, both move to Ohio in the 1830s. They are the ancestors of the many Hemings-Jefferson descendants known in the 21st century.
- **February 8:** The free mixed-race political leader Bernardino Rivadavia becomes president of Argentina; he was the first person to hold that title although the country had been independent from Spain since 1810. He is an example of a successful elite *pardo* since his racial identity was almost unknown even at the time and not an impediment to his political career.

1827

- *March 1:* Pennsylvania passes the first personal liberty law in the North that explicitly protects blacks against kidnapping, forbidding state officials to cooperate with people seeking to reclaim their slave "property" and providing fines for kidnappers. The law was overturned in 1842 by the U.S. Supreme Court in *Prigg v. Pennsylvania.*
- *March 16:* John Russwurm and Samuel Cornish publish the first issue of *Freedom's Journal,* the first African-American-owned newspaper in the United States.
- *December 19:* The Spanish slave ship *Guerrero* runs aground near Key Largo, Florida, touching off an international incident and legal case that foreshadowed the much more famous *Amistad* slave ship case of 1839. Of the 398 slaves on board when the ship ran aground, many are quickly recaptured by a surprise attack from Cuba, but 122 come into the custody of the United States government, and of those 90 survive and are taken to Liberia in 1830.

1828

- *October 2:* Admiral José Prudencio Padilla, a man of mixed race, is executed by the forces of Simón Bolívar. Padilla had tried to work for civil rights for free blacks but met resistance from the government of Gran Colombia (modern Venezuela, Colombia, and Ecuador).

1829

- British government passes laws granting full legal equality to free people of color in its colonies.
- *January 1:* Abdul-Rahman Ibrahim ibn Sori, a slave from what is now the Republic of Guinea, is freed on the request of President John Quincy Adams. Ibn Sori travels the United States seeking funds to purchase the freedom of his family and ultimately moves to Liberia with his wife and two children.
- *August 13:* A mob of more than 200 armed whites, many of them unemployed Irish immigrants, attack the black neighborhood in Cincinnati, Ohio, destroying a number of homes. The police and government officials refuse to intervene, and more than 1,000 Cincinnati blacks leave the city, many moving to Canada.
- *September 15:* President Vicente Guerrero of Mexico, a man of African ancestry, proclaims the complete abolition of slavery.
- *September 28:* David Walker's *Appeal . . . to the Coloured Citizens of the World* is published in Boston; Walker calls for violent resistance against slavery.

1830

- *June 3:* The Spanish slave ship *Fenix,* carrying 82 African slaves, is captured by U.S. Navy vessels in the Florida Straits. A legal case about their status establishes a precedent for the much better-known *Amistad* case in 1839. Thirty-seven of the surviving captives are sent to Liberia in 1835.
- *August 1:* Edward Jordon, Afro-Jamaican journalist, is acquitted of treason; he had been charged by the colonial government because his newspaper had called for the abolition of slavery.
- *September 14:* First Negro Convention is held in the United States, in Philadelphia, Pennsylvania.
- *December 1:* The free colored activists Louis Lescene and John Escoffery return to Jamaica after a seven-year exile imposed to punish their campaign for equal rights. The British parliament in London finally had to intervene to allow them to return home.

1831

- *September 1:* First racially integrated school class in the United States begins at the Canterbury Female Boarding School in Connecticut. Ultimately, almost all white parents removed their children from the school, and free black families from all parts of the country sent their daughters there.
- *December 25:* Jamaican slaves, led by the Afro-Jamaican Baptist preacher Samuel Sharpe, go on strike, beginning the struggle known as the Baptist War. The savage suppression of the strike turned public opinion in Britain against slavery.

1832

- *September 28:* The South Carolina free black Jehu Jones is ordained a minister in the Lutheran Church. He was the first black in the United States to hold that office. He worked in Philadelphia as a missionary to the city's large black population.

1834

- *August 1:* British Slavery Abolition Act of 1833 takes effect, abolishing slavery but establishing a transitional status of "apprenticeship" under which slaves must work for their former masters for wages under government regulation.

1835

- *January 24:* The Malê revolt in Salvador de Bahía, Brazil, breaks out, led by Muslim slaves and free people of color. The outbreak of the revolt was timed to coincide with the beginning of the Muslim month of Ramadan. Harsh repression after the revolt led to attempts, not entirely successful, to end the practice of Islam in Brazil.
- *April 1:* South Carolina passes law making literacy training unlawful for all blacks, free or enslaved. The

free colored teacher Daniel Payne closes his school and moves to Pennsylvania.

■ *August:* The Second Seminole War begins in Florida. The Seminole, including Afro-Indian leaders such as John Horse, refuse to move to reservations and resist attempts to enslave them by white slave raiders. Fighting continues for seven years before most surviving Seminole are rounded up and moved to Oklahoma.

1837

■ James McCune Smith, a New York free man of color, receives a medical degree from the University of Glasgow in Scotland. With his degree, Smith returns to New York and goes into practice as a physician, becoming the first black doctor holding a medical degree in the United States.

■ *September 1:* Cheyney University is founded in Pennsylvania, the first black college in the United States.

■ *November 7:* Sabinada revolt breaks out in Salvador de Bahia, Brazil, among free people of color and slaves seeking independence for northern Brazil and equal rights for blacks. The leader of the revolt is the Afro-Brazilian politician Francisco Sabino Alvares da Rocha Viera. The Salvador free black militiaman Francisco Xavier Bigode is another important leader, who will be killed after the rebels' defeat on March 15, 1838.

1838

■ *January 17:* Pennsylvania state constitutional convention denies the vote to free blacks.

■ *March 1:* The free colored activist Robert Purvis drafts the "Appeal of Forty Thousand Citizens Threatened with Disenfranchisement" protesting Pennsylvania's decision to deny voting rights to free people of color.

■ *November 29:* In anticipation of a papal bull that was issued the next year condemning slavery, the Jesuits of Maryland sell their 272 slaves to Catholic masters in Louisiana.

1839

■ *December 3:* Pope Gregory XVI issues the bull *In Supremo Apostolatus,* in which he unequivocally condemns slavery and the slave trade. He also reiterates and reinforces earlier church teaching that non-Europeans are human beings who have some basic rights.

1840

■ New York passes "An Act more effectually to protect the free citizens of this state from being kidnapped or reduced to slavery," the most strongly worded of the

personal liberty laws in the northern states in that it forbade the practice of kidnapping people even when the former masters had proven that they had property rights in the state the slave left.

1841

■ *March 9:* The U.S. Supreme Court decides in the case of the Spanish slave ship *Amistad* that the slaves who had rebelled against the crew and captured the ship were to be freed, as rebellion on a slave ship was a legitimate act of self-defense. Ultimately, most of the 52 African survivors returned to Africa in 1842.

■ *August 11:* The African-American abolitionist and runaway slave Frederick Douglass makes his first public speech, at the convention of the Massachusetts Anti-Slavery Society in Nantucket.

■ *September 4:* Mass racial violence breaks out in Cincinnati, Ohio, ultimately taking the lives of at least three African Americans and leading to the destruction of an abolitionist newspaper. Police intervention finally suppresses the violence after three days, and the black community feels better protected than in previous race riots in 1829.

1842

■ *March 1:* The U.S. Supreme Court decides, in *Prigg v. Pennsylvania,* that the Personal Liberty Law of Pennsylvania, passed in 1826, is unconstitutional. The Court decides that states could not prohibit the recapture of runaway slaves but that state officials were not required to assist in the capture of slaves. Many states pass laws prohibiting their officials from helping masters recover their slaves, which in turn will spark the Fugitive Slave Act of 1850, which specifically requires states to assist masters seeking their "property."

■ *August 9:* The Webster-Ashburton Treaty between the United States and Canada gives northern Maine to the United States; this area contained several settlements of black Canadians whose ancestors had fled to New Brunswick after the War of American Independence.

1843

■ *March 1:* Peter Ogden, a free colored sailor, organizes the first black Grand United Order of Odd Fellows lodge in New York City. The Odd Fellows would go on to become the largest black fraternal organization, with a much more socially diverse membership than the Prince Hall Masons.

■ *June 1:* The New York free black woman Isabella Baumfree changes her name to Sojourner Truth and begins her career as a speaker for abolition and Christian renewal of the country.

- *August 15:* The National Convention of Colored Citizens meets in Buffalo, New York, first of many "negro conventions" to call for abolition and civil rights in the 19th century in the United States.
- *August 16:* Henry Highland Garnet addresses the National Negro Convention, calling for the use of "any means necessary" to defeat slavery.

1844

- *February 27:* A rebel movement in the Spanish part of Hispaniola drives out Haitian forces, gaining independence for the Dominican Republic. The military chief of this movement is Francisco del Rosario Sanchez, a man of partially African descent. Although, as does Sanchez, most Dominicans have some African ancestry, the troubled history of conquest by Haiti has led most Dominicans to reject blackness and African identity and to prefer a Hispanic identity.
- *June 27:* Oregon's provisional territorial legislature passes the "lash law," banning all free blacks from the territory on penalty of 20–39 lashes. Several early free black pioneers resettle north of the Columbia River in what became the Washington Territory.
- *June 28:* Execution of the mixed-race Cuban poet "Placido" Gabriel de la Concepción Valdéz and 10 companions, accused of complicity in the La Escalera plot, a rebel conspiracy, are executed. Ultimately, hundreds of slaves and free people of color are tried for participation in this conspiracy. Historians are divided on the question of whether any conspiracy took place or whether the accusations were all lies intended to build white solidarity and forestall an independence movement. Placido, in particular, would be seen as a martyr in Cuba and beyond, and his nationalistic poetry became an important cultural expression for Cubans.
- *September:* The Missouri mixed-race pioneer and mountain man George Washington Bush arrives in Oregon with a party of settlers. Oregon has passed discriminatory laws against blacks, so Bush and his white and black companions move north to the Washington Territory to establish the town of Tacoma, Washington. Bush became a successful real estate entrepreneur and was instrumental in attracting the railroad and important port facilities to the town.

1847

- The first volume of Thomas Madiou's *Histoire d'Haiti* is published in Haiti. Madiou's work is an outstanding product of Haitian literature and gives a more balanced view, including the point of view of the poor, black, and enslaved people of Haiti, as opposed to Madiou's contemporary Beaubrun Ardouin, whose story focuses on the point of view of the wealthier mixed-race former free people of color.
- *July 16:* Liberia declares its independence and elects Joseph Roberts as first president.

1848

- The Banda Negra, or Black Edict, in Puerto Rico removes many civil rights from free people of color and creates a very harsh racial environment in the colony. Free people of color were pressured into the cities, where small business and craft employment was still open to them. More than in other Spanish colonies, Puerto Rico's free people of color by the end of the 19th century formed an urban business class.
- *February 2:* Treaty of Guadalupe Hidalgo ends the Mexican-American War; under this treaty, Mexican citizens living in the southwestern United States and California are guaranteed their property rights. Many Afro-Mexicans living in this area are able to escape classification as blacks and suffer less discrimination than blacks from the prewar U.S. territories during the period before the American Civil War. However, the war also creates new territories for the United States, leaving open the possibility that slavery might be expanded there. The political debate about the status of these territories will lead to the American Civil War.
- *April 27:* Second abolition of slavery in the French Empire by the provisional government established after the revolution of 1848.

1849

- *March 23:* The Virginia black slave Henry "Box" Brown climbs inside a large crate, and a friend mails him to an abolitionist leader in Philadelphia. Brown tells the story of his inventive escape in an 1849 book that mocks the institution of slavery and makes Brown a celebrity.
- *July:* Charles Reason, George Vashon, and William G. Allen are appointed professors at New York Central College. They were the first African Americans to hold professorships at a majority-white college in the United States.

1850

- *January 1:* The Maryland enslaved woman Harriet Tubman flees to freedom in Pennsylvania; within months, she will return to Maryland on the first of many trips to rescue other enslaved people. Starting with her own family, Tubman leads hundreds of enslaved people to freedom and helps guide Union soldiers during the American Civil War.
- *July 12:* John Horse and a party of several hundred black Seminoles arrive in Coahuila, Mexico, fleeing

from Oklahoma, where they had been in danger of reenslavement. The Mexican government grants them land and gains their assistance against their own hostile Indians. Horse will remain in Mexico until the outbreak of the American Civil War in 1861, when he returns to Oklahoma to help the Union. Many black Seminoles remain in Mexico, where their descendants still live in the 21st century.

September 4: Brazil passes the Lei Eusébio de Queiroz, abolishing the transatlantic slave trade and declaring free all slaves taken into the country in violation of anti–slave trade regulations that had been previously announced in 1818 and 1844. The mixed-race lawyer Luis Gonzaga de Pinto Gama was foremost among a group of abolitionist lawyers who brought freedom suits under this law. He gained the freedom of more than 500 slaves.

September 18: U.S. Congress passes the Fugitive Slave Act as part of the Compromise of 1850. The law requires public officials in free states to help slave owners hunt down runaway slaves and deprives people who are accused of being runaways of legal protections. Many free people of color flee to Canada to escape reenslavement.

1851

September 11: The Christiana riot takes place in Pennsylvania; free black and white farmers fight Maryland slave catchers to protect runaway slaves, one Marylander is killed, and several are injured. Several of the Pennsylvania rioters are later tried and acquitted.

1852

April 15: The California Fugitive Slave Act is passed, providing that masters can claim slaves that ran away to California with minimal legal process. Several free blacks are threatened with reenslavement under this law.

July 5: Frederick Douglass gives his most famous speech, "What to the Slave Is the Fourth of July?" in Rochester, New York.

1853

The Haitian prerevolutionary free mixed-race journalist, diplomat, and politician Beaubrun Ardouin publishes the first volume of his *Études sur l'histoire d'Haiti* in Paris. Ardouin's work tells the story of the Haitian Revolution and the early years of Haitian independence from the point of view of the mixed-race ruling class, contrasting sharply with the work of his near-contemporary Thomas Madiou, who included an appreciation of the role of poor, enslaved black revolutionaries.

February 8: Washington Territory in the northwestern United States is organized, dividing the former Oregon Territory at the Columbia River. The laws of Washington were more favorable to free blacks, and many black pioneers moved there from Oregon.

July 15: The African-American priest Alexander Crummell arrives in Liberia to begin a 20-year mission to convert Liberians to Protestant Episcopal Christianity and encourage American blacks to move to Africa.

1854

The Brazilian free colored political leader Francisco Gê Acaiaba de Montezuma receives the noble title of viscount of Jequitinhonha. He is probably the first person of African descent to receive a noble title in the Americas.

May 27: The trial of Anthony Burns begins in Boston under the provisions of the Fugitive Slave Act of 1850. Burns was a runaway slave from Virginia who had been recaptured by his master and who was tried in federal court with almost no legal protections. The trial ignored the provisions of Massachusetts's personal liberty law. His case sparked public outrage and led to a riot in which a federal marshal was killed.

May 30: President Franklin Pierce signs the Kansas-Nebraska Act, creating territories in the northern plains states and giving the inhabitants the right to decide whether slavery or free black immigration was to be permitted. This "squatter sovereignty" led to fighting between pro- and antislavery factions in Kansas, with free blacks supporting the abolitionist faction.

June 10: James Augustine Healy is ordained a priest for the Roman Catholic diocese of Boston. He was mixed-race and born a slave in Georgia and is thought to be the first American of African descent ordained a Catholic priest in the United States.

June 25: John Mercer Langston becomes the first black lawyer in Ohio. He would later become a congressman from his native state of Virginia and a leader of a black college there.

October 10: The Jamaican free colored "doctoress" Mary Seacole arrives in Balaclava, near Sevastopol in the Ukraine, to provide medical care for soldiers ill or injured in the Crimean War. She was one of the first professional black nurses and arguably helped the British and French soldiers as much as the much more famous Florence Nightingale.

December 3: The Battle of the Eureka Stockade, Ballarat, Victoria, Australia, an early struggle in the labor organization of mine workers in Australia. The American free colored worker John Joseph was one of the miners' leaders and was the first to be tried, for treason, in Melbourne. His acquittal on all charges was a triumph for the Australian labor movement.

1855

■ The Michigan legislature passes a personal liberty law, designed to make it impossible for people seeking runaway slaves to recapture them in the state, effectively nullifying the Fugitive Slave Act of 1850. Many other northern states follow suit in the next three years. President James Buchanan later called the revised personal liberty laws of the 1850s one of the most important elements in the political crisis that led to the American Civil War.

1856

■ *September 1:* Wilberforce University of Ohio, first historically black college in the United States to be owned by African Americans, begins classes.

1857

■ *March 6: Dred Scott v. Sandford* decided by the U.S. Supreme Court, holding that blacks, whether free or enslaved, could not be citizens of the United States or have access to its courts.

1858

■ *April 27:* The California Supreme Court decides that Archy Lee, a man who had been enslaved in Missouri and was taken to the state by his master and who later claimed his freedom, was not a fugitive slave. This case was an important precedent for California free blacks fighting reenslavement.

■ *June 28:* A party of several hundred black Californians, led by Mifflin Wistar Gibbs, leaves for British Columbia after the government of California barred black children from public schools and passed other antiblack laws.

■ *November 19:* The Afro-Guyanan Sir James Douglas is appointed governor of British Columbia, Canada. He invites blacks from the western United States to move to Canada, and many immigrants arrive from California and the Northwest.

1861

■ *April 12:* The American Civil War begins with the bombardment of Fort Sumter in Charleston, South Carolina; the war would lead to the end of slavery in the United States.

■ *August 1:* The United Brothers of Friendship and Sisters of the Mysterious Ten, the first African-American fraternal organization to admit women and the third-largest African-American fraternal organization, is founded in Louisville, Kentucky.

■ *September 25:* The U. S. War Department confirms the orders of General Benjamin Butler that slaves escaping from Confederate masters were "contraband of war" and could not be returned to their masters.

1862

■ *May 9:* The U.S. Army general David Hunter issues "General Order 11" declaring all the slaves in Georgia, Florida, and South Carolina free and permitting them to enlist in the Union army. The order was partially confirmed in August 1862 by the War Department and then fully ratified by the Emancipation Proclamation.

■ *May 13:* Robert Smalls escapes to freedom in the Confederate navy ship *Planter*, joining the U.S. Navy and ultimately rising to become its first black ship captain.

■ *May 20:* The U.S. Congress passes the Homestead Act, offering government land on very favorable terms to settlers; the lack of racial discrimination in the early administration of this law gave many blacks a chance to settle in the West.

1863

■ *January 1:* President Abraham Lincoln issues the Emancipation Proclamation, abolishing slavery in parts of the United States that were rebelling during the American Civil War and permitting blacks to join the U.S. military.

■ *May 27:* First black troops in battle in the American Civil War: A unit of free blacks from Louisiana fights with distinction at Port Hudson.

■ *June 7:* Black troops at Milliken's Bend, Louisiana, protect an important supply depot from Confederate attackers after white Union troops had fled the field.

■ *July 13:* New York City draft riots break out. The four days of violence would claim at least 120 lives; many of the killed were free people of color attacked by mobs who believed that the American Civil War had been caused by blacks. A black orphanage is burned by the rioters, killing at least some of the children.

■ *July 18:* The African-American 54th Massachusetts Infantry regiment unsuccessfully assaults Confederate positions at Battery Wagner, near Charleston, South Carolina, suffering 272 casualties.

1864

■ The first poems by Brazil's greatest writer, the free colored Joaquim Maria Machado de Assis, entitled *Chrysalids*, are published in the newspaper *Marmota*, by the free colored journalist and entrepreneur Francisco da Paula Brito. The collaboration between the gifted writer and the canny publisher would extend to politics as they both rallied free colored support for the monarchy of Dom Pedro II.

- **October 12:** Brazilian troops invade Uruguay, launching the six-year War of the Triple Alliance among Brazil, Uruguay, Argentina, and Paraguay. Free colored Brazilians played an important role in the nation's military and staked an important claim to full citizenship and equal rights.
- **November 1:** A new state constitution in Maryland abolishes slavery.

1865

- **February 1:** Martin Delaney becomes the first black major in the U.S. Army and the first black to command a regiment, the 104th United States Colored Troops.
- **March 3:** The U.S. Congress establishes the Freedmen's Bureau to help the newly freed slaves. Many pre–Civil War free people of color worked for the bureau as teachers and administrators.
- **April 8:** A new state constitution in Missouri abolishes slavery. Missouri was the last state in the United States to abolish slavery voluntarily. Slaves in the two remaining holdouts, Kentucky and Delaware, as well as some remaining in New Jersey who had not yet received their freedom under the state's gradual abolition law, were freed by the passage of the Thirteenth Amendment to the U.S. Constitution on December 6, 1865.
- **April 9:** Surrender of Confederate forces under Robert E. Lee to the U.S. Army under Ulysses S. Grant at Appomattox Court House, Virginia, effectively ending fighting in the American Civil War. Grant's army includes tens of thousands of free blacks. The surrender terms were very generous and set a precedent that other Confederate soldiers were not going to be prosecuted for waging war against the United States.
- **May 24:** A party of several dozen free blacks from Lençóis, Bahia, Brazil, led by Cândido da Fonseca Galvão, join the Brazilian army to fight in the War of the Triple Alliance. Galvão would later take the name Dom Oba II and, calling himself the "prince" of the African blacks in Brazil, rally support for the monarchy of Dom Pedro II during the political crisis surrounding the abolition of slavery in Brazil.
- **May 29:** The U.S. president Andrew Johnson proclaims an amnesty for most former Confederate officials after the end of the American Civil War. The amnesty allowed the old ruling class of the South to regain power in many places, making the job of incorporating blacks as full citizens much harder.
- **June 19:** Abolition of slavery is proclaimed in Texas, last portion of Confederate-held territory to surrender. June 19 is celebrated in the United States as "Juneteenth," a holiday to mark the abolition of slavery. The last slaves in the United States, in Kentucky and Delaware, were actually freed December 6, 1865, by the Thirteenth Amendment.
- **October 23:** The Afro-Jamaican civil rights leader and Baptist preacher George William Gordon and eight companions are executed after the Morant Bay riots of October 11.
- **December 6:** The Thirteenth Amendment to the U.S. Constitution abolishes slavery. Kentucky and Delaware were the only states in the country to have preserved the institution to that time and thus were the last places in the United States to permit slavery.
- **December 24:** According to tradition, the Ku Klux Klan is founded by Confederate veterans in Tennessee. The organization rapidly spreads to the other former Confederate states. The Klan acts as a terrorist resistance against Union occupation and efforts to include blacks as equal citizens. The Civil Rights Act of 1871 gives the federal government power to suppress the Klan and most groups are wiped out by 1872. Other armed groups continue their campaign of terror against blacks and their white supporters. After the end of Reconstruction in 1877, in most of the South armed repression of blacks is carried out by white-controlled local government.

1866

- **April 6:** The U.S. Congress passes the Civil Rights Act of 1866, guaranteeing blacks equal economic rights. The law is superseded by the Fourteenth Amendment.
- **August:** The first national convention of the National Negro Labor Union is held in New York City. The Prewar free black Alabaman James T. Rapier, a future congressman, attends and is one of the signers of the manifesto of the union.

1868

- The Iowa Supreme Court rules that the Muscatine, Iowa, school district must admit Susan Clark, the daughter of the black activist Alexander Clark, to public schools on a nondiscriminatory basis and that schools in Iowa must integrate. It was to be 86 years before the U.S. Supreme Court followed Iowa's lead in the *Brown v. Board of Education* case from neighboring Kansas and required that all public schools be integrated.
- **July 9:** The Fourteenth Amendment to the United States Constitution proclaims that blacks and all other people born in the United States are citizens and entitled to the equal protection of the law.
- **October 10:** The Ten Years' War breaks out in Cuba, beginning a series of rebellions that would ultimately

lead to the end of slavery and Spanish rule there. Many free blacks fight on the side of the rebels.

1869
- *September 7:* Ebenezer Bassett, an African American from Connecticut, becomes the U.S. minister resident to Haiti. He was the first African American to serve as the chief of a U.S. diplomatic mission abroad.

1870
- *February 3:* Voting rights are guaranteed to black men in the United States by the ratification of the Fifteenth Amendment to the Constitution.

1871
- *April 20:* The U.S. Congress passes the Civil Rights Act of 1871, also known as the Ku Klux Klan Act, making it a federal crime to deprive someone of his or her civil rights. Federal law enforcement protected blacks until after the election of 1876.
- *September 28:* Brazil passes the Rio Branco law, freeing all children of slaves born after that date.

1874
- *June 1:* Patrick Francis Healy, a mixed-race Jesuit priest, becomes the president of Georgetown University, the first African American to head a majority-white university.

1875
- *June 2:* The mixed-race Catholic priest James Augustine Healy is ordained bishop of Portland, Maine, the first American of African ancestry to become a bishop in the Roman Catholic Church.

1877
- *March 2:* The U.S. presidential election of 1876 is resolved by a special commission that votes 8-7 to give the presidency to the Republican candidate, Rutherford B. Hayes. The election had been marred in the South by terrorism and voter intimidation by pro–Democratic Party armed groups. In a compromise, the Republicans concede greater autonomy to southern state governments, controlled by white Democrats, ending the attempt to incorporate blacks as full citizens called Reconstruction.
- *June 18:* The Reverend Simon Roundtree, a free colored minister from Tennessee, becomes the first setter in Nicodemus, Kansas, one of the earliest and best-known settlements of the Exoduster Movement of black westward migration after the American Civil War.

1878
- *June 1:* The African-American composer James Bland publishes "Carry Me Back to Old Virginny," a nostalgic look at plantation slavery that was the Virginia state song from 1940 to 1997.

1880
- *February 13:* Spain adopts a law providing for the progressive abolition of slavery in Cuba. Slaves are to work for their former masters for six years. Slavery finally ends in 1886.

1885
- *September 28:* The Lei Áurea (golden law) in Brazil abolishes slavery. A political crisis over the next several years leads to the abolition of the monarchy in November 1889 and its replacement by a conservative republican government, which, however, does not attempt to reestablish slavery.

1886
- *April 24:* Augustine Tolton is ordained a priest for the diocese of Quincy, Illinois. He is dark-skinned and identified as a black man and is often said to be the first African-American Roman Catholic priest in the United States.

1890
- *October 22:* Edwin McCabe founds Langston, Oklahoma, a black plains farming community that has survived into the 21st century. Oklahoma was a refuge for black pioneers up to the end of the 1800s.

1897
- The free black author Joaquim Maria Machado de Assis becomes the first president of Brazil's Academy of Letters, the foremost literary and scholarly society in the country, comparable to the Modern Language Association in the United States. Machado de Assis is generally recognized as Brazil's greatest novelist.

1898
- Callie House and Isaiah Dickerson, former free people of color from Tennessee, form the National Ex-Slave Mutual Relief, Bounty, and Pension Association, the first group to call explicitly for reparations for slavery. House would ultimately be accused and convicted of fraud for misleading African Americans into believing that America would ever compensate them for their oppression.

Entries A–J

A

ABOLITIONISM AND RESISTANCE TO SLAVERY

It seems natural today to think of free people of color as being opponents of the slave system. After all, as black people they suffered under many of the same restrictions as the slaves, depending on the country where they were living. Many of their relatives were slaves; in many cases, they themselves had been slaves and had experienced firsthand the terrible oppression of the system. We expect that a simple racial solidarity would have been enough to make every free person of color an opponent of the system. Certainly, this was the assumption of much of white society in many places throughout the Atlantic world in the era of slavery. Legal and social restrictions on people of color were often justified by the fear of slave uprising. For example, SOUTH CAROLINA and many other southern states of the United States prohibited free blacks from opening their own churches or preaching the gospel because of fears of a repetition of DENMARK VESEY's rebellion, when a free black preacher was accused of rallying slaves in Charleston, South Carolina, to rebel in 1822. However, free people of color in the Americas were torn between resistance to the slave system and the hope of benefiting from that system.

Many free people of color were SLAVE OWNERS themselves. Many successful merchants, planters, and artisans owned, bought, and sold slaves. ZABEAU BELLANTON, in SAINT-DOMINGUE, the modern Haiti, was actually a slave dealer. WILLIAM "APRIL" ELLISON, of South Carolina, was a very successful manufacturer of cotton gins, but he also made a good deal of money by selling slaves raised in his household into the very profitable internal slave trade in the United States in the 1830s and 1840s. He was a supporter of South Carolina's secession from the United States at the beginning of the AMERICAN CIVIL WAR, 1861–65. These people had benefited from the system. They had profitable businesses, some social respect, and comfortable lives. Disruption of the system held the promise of greater racial equality for them—they still suffered under some restrictions because of their race. Bellanton, for example, was legally prohibited from settling

in France, and when she closed her business and retired to a French port city in 1788, she had to preserve the legal fiction that she was planning to return to the colony. However, disruption of the system also could mean economic collapse and the decline of their businesses. Bellanton sold out and retired just before the outbreak of the HAITIAN REVOLUTION in 1791. Had she remained in the colony, she might well have ended up a penniless exile as did many other prominent free people of color from Saint-Domingue in the 1790s. Ellison died in 1861, the year the American Civil War began, but his city was destroyed by Union troops in 1865, and surely his business would have suffered during the economic turmoil of the war and Reconstruction.

Many free people of color worked for civil rights for their community, even if they were not opposed to slavery itself. Work for civil rights could move a person to an antislavery position. JULIEN RAIMOND, a prominent mixed-race planter from Saint-Domingue, for example, worked in France for the rights of free colored people even before the French Revolution. In 1787, he supported proposals by the royal government to treat free people of one-fourth African ancestry or less who were legitimately born as the equal of white citizens. After the outbreak of the FRENCH REVOLUTION in 1789, Raimond became a member of the French National Assembly, worked with the abolitionist Société des Amis des Noirs, and ultimately supported the abolition of slavery, despite the fact that he and his family owned hundreds of slaves themselves.

Other free people of color worked more consistently for the liberation of all slaves. Denmark Vesey is an example already mentioned, but he was far from the only free black who helped slave rebels and runaways. The prevailing white fear of black solidarity had some basis in fact. The most famous slave rebel, TOUSSAINT LOUVERTURE, leader of the rebel forces in the Haitian Revolution and father of independent Haiti, was a free man of color who owned some slaves and at least one plantation before 1790. Urban slaves in New York who planned an uprising in 1712 had help from free blacks who worked alongside them, who gave them weapons and helped hide them

THE AMERICAN DECLARATION OF INDEPENDENCE ILLUSTRATED.

Published by THAYER & CO. Boston.

An image dating from the early days of the American Civil War in 1861 linking the causes of abolition of slavery and equal rights for people of color. The American eagle in the center lifts a basket with a slave, who is dropping his chains, and a well-dressed man of color intended to represent a free black. Patriotic verses and mottoes connect freedom and equality with the founding documents of America and stress the fundamental equality of all races. *(Library of Congress)*

when the plot was betrayed. Free blacks also cooperated in the 1741 New York conspiracy. Indeed, some historians have treated this incident as labor unrest over poor working and living conditions that affected both free and slave equally. There is no evidence of participation by free people of color in Gabriel's Rebellion in Virginia in 1800, but apparently some radical whites cooperated with Gabriel. Rather than blame those whites, the government of Virginia imposed harsh restrictions on free people of color after the conspiracy failed and blamed them for the uprising. The government suggested that free people of color fleeing the Haitian Revolution had introduced radical notions to Virginia and converted Virginian slaves to the cause of freedom. A free man of color was among the crew members whose lives were spared on the brig *Creole* in 1842, when 145 slaves rebelled, seized the ship, and sailed to the Bahamas. He may have helped the rebels,

or perhaps they spared him out of racial solidarity. Several free men of color accompanied John Brown in his 1859 raid on Harpers Ferry, Virginia, which was intended to be the first blow in a rebellion that would overthrow slavery in the American South. Supporting slave rebellions was dangerous business in the Americas. The most sadistic punishments were reserved for slave rebels. VINCENT OGÉ, a wealthy free man of mixed race who led a rebellion in Saint-Domingue in 1790, was executed by being strapped to a wagon wheel in the town square of CAP-FRANÇAIS/CAP-HAÏTIEN and beaten to death with a sledgehammer—and Ogé had refrained from including slaves in his forces so that he would not be accused of fomenting a slave uprising. He was working simply for civil rights for free people of color. So we can assume that free people of color who worked for slave rebellions were acting out of very strong motives. Most of those accused of rebellion expressed some sort of abolitionist political beliefs, though sometimes the rebellions were more concerned with gaining freedom for a particular group of people than with changing society as a whole. Free people of color were more likely to be educated and in touch with a wider world than slaves, though, and they could introduce a more sophisticated set of ideas to a rebel movement. Toussaint Louverture, for example, lectured his troops about the principles of the French Revolution and persuaded them to agree to switch sides in 1794, from support for the king of Spain to support for the radical French government. He could see that, while the Spanish might grant freedom to individual runaway slaves who fought for them, only a government motivated by the philosophy of the Enlightenment would grant freedom to all slaves.

Another form of resistance to slavery was running away. Many free people of color supported slaves in their decision to flee slavery, either temporarily or permanently. HARRIET JACOBS, author of *Incidents in the Life of a Slave Girl*, lived for seven years in her free colored grandmother's attic in North Carolina before escaping to Philadelphia in 1842. Although Jacobs received help from a free relative, many free people of color in the U.S. South worked as "conductors" on the Undergrond Railroad, an informal network dedicated to helping escaping slaves to travel to the free states and Canada. One of the most famous Underground Railroad workers was HARRIET TUBMAN, who had run away from slavery in Maryland herself and was living as free in Pennsylvania. In Saint-Domingue, the prefect of the Maréchaussée, the rural police and slave-catching force, asked in 1782 for his forces to be given the right to search the home of any free person of color at any time looking for runaway slaves. Hiding runaways was also dangerous, though perhaps not so fatal as helping slave rebels. Still, a free black who helped a runaway slave in many southern states in the United States could be reenslaved as a punishment, and some were. The hero of FREDERICK DOUGLASS's abolitionist novella, *The Heroic Slave*, based on the exploits of one of the leaders of the rebellion on the brig *Creole*, is reenslaved at one point because he tried to help his wife escape slavery.

Free people of color also played a prominent role in the political struggle against slavery. Julien Raimond, JEAN-BAPTISTE BELLEY, and several other French colonial free people of color worked with the Amis des Noirs in the first struggle for abolition in France. Napoléon reestablished slavery in 1804, returning many newly freed people in French colonies to slavery. The later campaign to abolish slavery again in France, which reached a successful conclusion in 1848, was led by a white radical, Victor Schoelcher, from Alsace in France, but he had the support of colonial free people of color. France had a small population of color by that point, but those who did live there worked for abolition. The best-known Afro-Frenchman of the day was the author Alexandre Dumas *père*, the grandson of a Saint-Domingue free colored woman. He was socially prominent, though he suffered some discrimination because of his color, and he lent important support to Schoelcher's campaign during the 1840s.

Britain had a larger population of people of color during the years of the antislavery struggle there. Starting with James Somerset in 1772, people of color fought for their freedom in Britain, aided by evangelical and liberal reformers (see also *SOMERSET V. STEWART*). British people of color were all considered free after the *Somerset* decision, and some British officials considered that it applied throughout the empire. Famously, General Guy Carleton, British overall commander in North America during the WAR OF AMERICAN INDEPENDENCE, 1775–83, used the case to justify his unwillingness to return slaves who had run away from Patriot masters when British forces were evacuating their American bases in 1783. However, the West India planters and slave trade interests were able to protect slavery in the British Empire, and black and white abolitionists in Britain attacked it in a variety of ways. Black abolitionists in Britain, including OLAUDAH EQUIANO and QUOBNA OTTOBAH CUGOANO, gained many supporters for the abolitionist cause by telling the stories of their lives as slaves. Equiano, in particular, worked closely with John Clarkson, GRANVILLE SHARP, William Wilberforce, and Charles James Fox (1739–1806), generating public support for efforts by parliamentary Whigs to end the slave trade. Equiano participated in an effort to collect the signatures of tens of thousands of people on a petition presented to Parliament in 1806 as they were debating the end of the slave trade.

Abolition movements in the northern states in the United States in the years after the American Revolution were led by an uneasy coalition of white activists and politicians and free black agitators. For example, in the *Commonwealth v. Jennison* case in MASSACHUSETTS, which eliminated slavery there in the early 1780s, the free colored man Quock Walker (*see* QUOCK WALKER CASE), who was threatened with RE-ENSLAVEMENT by his former mistress's new husband, had assistance in his suit from white neighbors and a radical lawyer. The PENNSYLVANIA campaign to abolish slavery in the 1790s was led by Quakers, who had lost political power and credibility through their unwillingness to oppose the British during the American War of Independence. They had difficulty working with the large local free colored population, probably because of social class tensions and growing racist ideas. In part because it was poorly coordinated, the Pennsylvania abolition movement was unable to sway rural whites fully and had to settle for gradual emancipation. The last of Pennsylvania's slaves did not gain their freedom until 1847.

The abolition movement in the United States in the 1840s and 1850s included many prominent black figures. The journalist DAVID WALKER, who wrote *An Appeal to the Coloured Citizens of the World* (1829), was an early black abolitionist. Frederick Douglass was famous throughout the world as one of the foremost spokesmen of any color for the abolitionist cause. HENRY HIGHLAND GARNET was another important figure and an opponent of Douglass on a question of tactics: Garnet called for a slave uprising in the South, but Douglass opposed him, arguing that uprisings seldom succeeded and always resulted in death and oppression for slaves. Both men supported the Republican Party and the northern side in the American Civil War, organizing black units for the Union army. Black ministers of religion such as LOUIS WOODSON played critical roles in the United States, given the particularly segregated world of Protestant Christianity in America, in mobilizing black support for the abolitionist cause and helping to give the cause respectability.

In Spanish America, the flexibility of racial definitions meant that some free people of color could overcome racial barriers and rise to high positions in society. Sometimes, this required that they shed a black identity and "pass" for white or mestizo in the eyes of the public, but even so, many retained sympathy for slaves. VICENTE GUERRERO SALDAÑA, the president who decreed the final abolition of slavery in MEXICO in 1829, was himself a free man of color. The *PARDO*, or mixed-race military leaders of the Venezuelan armed forces in the South American Wars of Liberation of the 1810s and 1820s, led many individual people of color to freedom through military service but were unable to bring about the total abolition of slavery. Simón Bolívar, the leader of the northern South American forces and first president of Colombia, attacked

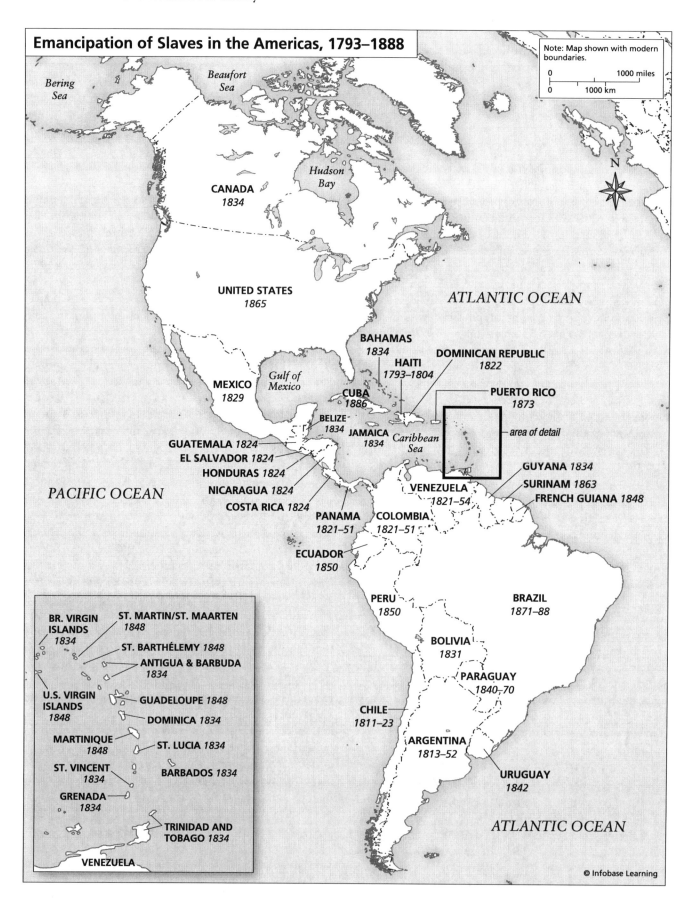

Emancipation of Slaves in the Americas, 1793–1888

Note: Map shown with modern boundaries.

0   1000 miles
0   1000 km

Bering Sea

Beaufort Sea

Hudson Bay

CANADA
1834

UNITED STATES
1865

ATLANTIC OCEAN

N

BAHAMAS
1834

HAITI
1793–1804

DOMINICAN REPUBLIC
1822

Gulf of Mexico

MEXICO
1829

CUBA
1886

PUERTO RICO
1873

BELIZE
1834

JAMAICA
1834

Caribbean Sea

— *area of detail*

GUATEMALA *1824*
EL SALVADOR *1824*
HONDURAS *1824*
NICARAGUA *1824*
COSTA RICA *1824*

GUYANA *1834*
SURINAM *1863*
FRENCH GUIANA *1848*

PACIFIC OCEAN

PANAMA
1821–51

COLOMBIA
1821–51

VENEZUELA
1821–54

ECUADOR
1850

PERU
1850

BRAZIL
1871–88

BOLIVIA
1831

PARAGUAY
1840–70

CHILE
1811–23

ARGENTINA
1813–52

URUGUAY
1842

ATLANTIC OCEAN

BR. VIRGIN ISLANDS
1834

ST. MARTIN/ST. MAARTEN
1848

ST. BARTHÉLEMY *1848*

ANTIGUA & BARBUDA
1834

U.S. VIRGIN ISLANDS
1848

GUADELOUPE *1848*

DOMINICA *1834*

MARTINIQUE
1848

ST. LUCIA *1834*

ST. VINCENT
1834

BARBADOS *1834*

GRENADA
1834

TRINIDAD AND TOBAGO *1834*

VENEZUELA

© Infobase Learning

what he called *pardocracía*—rule by the mixed-race—and preserved slavery until well into the 19th century.

In Brazil, similarly flexible racial lines left the professions open to well-connected and highly talented free people of color. In particular, journalism and education were important avenues to bring the abolitionist message to ordinary Brazilians. The free colored author MARIA FIRMINA DOS REIS wrote a partly autobiographical novel called *Ursula* in 1859 that was enormously popular. The writer Castro Alves, the "poet of the slaves," combined proindependence ideas and racial justice into a potent ideological package in the play *Gonzaga*, often compared with the American *Uncle Tom's Cabin* for the enormous impact it had on the debate over slavery. The law was also an important tool for Brazilian abolitionists, and the mixed-race lawyer José Ferreira de Menezes worked for people suing their masters and published a proabolition newspaper. Menezes's assistant and successor as editor of his paper, JOSÉ CARLOS DO PATROCÍNIO, held elective office in the city government of Rio de Janeiro in the late 19th century and worked to make the city a refuge for runaway slaves in the last days of slavery in Brazil.

Although slaves could never have won their freedom without white allies, blacks both free and enslaved played critical roles in their own liberation struggle. Black people in the Americas sought their freedom through leaders such as have been mentioned here and through many ordinary people who carried out acts of rebellion or flight or who demonstrated in their lives the injustice of the system. Many of these latter were slaves, but free people of color also served, by their very existence, to undermine the racist assumptions on which the slave system depended. Free people of color as coworkers, business partners, employees, coreligionists, and neighbors of white people throughout the Americas demonstrated in their daily lives that black people were human and were capable of the same triumphs and failures as whites. It was much harder for ordinary whites to conceive of a slave as a "chattel," a mere animated piece of property, after living next door to or working alongside a free colored person. The leaders of slave societies were aware of the contradiction that free people of color posed for the basic logic underlying the system, but they could not avoid permitting this class to exist. Slave owners insisted on freeing some of their slaves, and then free people of color refused to disappear, to move away to other places or breed themselves out of existence. Instead, they witnessed to the humanity of black people in their lives and in many cases used their freedom to work actively for the freedom of other blacks through political organization, journalism, and direct subversion of the slave system.

Stewart R. King

FURTHER READING
Alves, Castro. *The Major Abolitionist Poems of Castro Alves.* Translated by James J. Wilhelm. New York: Routledge, 1990.
Andrews, George Reid. "'Our New Citizens, the Blacks': The Politics of Freedom, 1810–1890." In *Afro-Latin America.* New York: Oxford University Press, 2004.
Azevedo, Célia Maria Marinho de. *Abolitionism in the United States and Brazil: A Comparative Perspective.* New York: Garland, 1995.
Douglass, Frederick. *The Heroic Slave.* In *Two Slave Rebellions at Sea: "The Heroic Slave" by Frederick Douglass and "Benito Cereno" by Herman Melville,* edited by George Hendrick and Willene Hendrick. New York: Wiley-Blackwell, 2000.
Equiano, Olaudah. *The Interesting Narrative of the Life of Olaudah Equiano, or Gustavus Vassa the African, Written by Himself.* Edited by Werner Sollors. New York: Norton, 2000.
Jacobs, Harriet. *Incidents in the Life of a Slave Girl, Written by Herself.* Boston: 1860. Available online. URL: http://books.google.com/books?id=1RwEAAAAYAAJ&dq=jacobs+incidents+in+the+life+of+a+slave+girl&source=gbs_navlinks_s. Accessed March 11, 2010.
Quarles, Benjamin. *Black Abolitionists.* New York: Oxford University Press, 1969.
Ripley, C. Peter, and Michael Hembree, eds. *The Black Abolitionist Papers.* 5 vols. Chapel Hill: University of North Carolina Press, 1985–1992.
Walker, David. *David Walker's Appeal.* Baltimore: Black Classic Press, 1997.

ADAMS, JOHN (1735–1826) *second president of the United States (1797–1801)*

John Adams served as the first vice president (1789–97) and second president (1797–1801) of the United States. He was also an impressive scholar, successful lawyer, delegate to the First and Second Continental Congresses, critical advocate of American independence, diplomat, and principal author of the Constitution of the Commonwealth of MASSACHUSETTS. His autobiography, wide-ranging correspondence, and voluminous diary provide many insights into his character and opinions, but he recorded very little about his view of free African Americans and the place they occupied in colonial and postrevolutionary America. Nonetheless, his actions both as president and earlier in his life had a profound impact on the situation of free people of color, especially in his native Massachusetts.

Adams was born on October 30, 1735, in what is now Quincy, Massachusetts. His father was a clergyman and sent him to Harvard College. After graduating in 1755, he studied law, and he became a successful lawyer in Massachusetts before the outbreak of the WAR OF AMERICAN INDEPENDENCE, 1775–83. In one of his most notable cases, he defended the British soldiers accused in 1770 of killing five members of a mob that had been stoning them, one of whom was the free black sailor Crispus Attucks. Adams made his most significant contribution to improving the lot of Massachusetts's people of color when he drafted the first state constitution in 1779. He included language holding that all people were free and equal in rights, and the Massachusetts courts held that this clause made slavery unenforceable in the QUOCK WALKER CASE in 1780.

New England's tiny African-American population, made up of both free and enslaved individuals, meant that Adams had little contact with nonwhites for much of his life. He was a staunch opponent of slavery and deplored its continued existence in the newly created United States, but throughout his long public career, he did little more than attack the institution verbally. Nevertheless, unlike many of his supposedly like-minded antislavery counterparts, Adams maintained his opposition in practice as well as in theory. He and his wife, Abigail, refused to purchase slaves even when it would have substantially eased their frequent economic hardships, and when Abigail and her sisters inherited a family slave, Adams supported their decision to free the woman immediately and employ her for wages. The Adamses periodically engaged free blacks as farmhands and domestics, and Abigail taught a local African-American boy to read and write before enrolling him in the village school and then fought back successfully when the community tried to deny him entrance.

But for all this, Adams appears to have shared most of the racial prejudices of his day. In his diary and correspondence, he often used the word *Negro* as a term of disdain and opposed the enlistment of African Americans in the Continental army. He found miscegenation distasteful, and while he focused his ire on the sexual exploitation of female slaves, it seems doubtful that he approved of interracial sexual activity or marriage for free blacks either. The reaction of Abigail Adams to a performance of *Othello* in the 1790s may be telling: She was appalled at the sight of a black man touching a white woman, even on the stage. While he was living in New York, PHILADELPHIA, and Washington, D.C., Adams's acquaintance with African Americans increased, and his opinion of them probably shifted as well, but it seems clear that they were never the object of much of his attention. Adams died on July 4, 1826.

Caroline Hasenyager

FURTHER READING

"Adams Family Papers: An Electronic Archive." Massachusetts Historical Society. Available online. URL: http://www.masshist.org/digitaladams/aea. Accessed December 15, 2010.

Ferling, John. *John Adams; A Life.* Knoxville: University of Tennessee Press, 1992.

McCullough, David. *John Adams.* New York: Simon & Schuster, 2001.

ADAMS, JOHN QUINCY   (1767–1848)   *U.S. diplomat and sixth president of the United States (1825–1829)*

Born in Braintree, MASSACHUSETTS, on July 11, 1767, John Quincy Adams was the sixth president of the United States, serving from 1825 to 1829. Prior to the presidency, he had served in numerous diplomatic posts and as secretary of state. As a representative from Massachusetts from 1830 to 1848, he was one of the leading antislavery members of Congress, fighting against the "gag law" that blocked antislavery petitions and defending African slaves who had commandeered the *Amistad.*

When the WAR OF AMERICAN INDEPENDENCE, 1775–83, began, Adams was just eight years old. Two years later, he accompanied his father, JOHN ADAMS, on a diplomatic mission to France. He attended school but also helped his father in his diplomatic work and was his father's regular secretary by the end of the elder Adams's stay in Europe in 1788. He was in public service for the rest of his life. He carried out diplomatic missions to France, the Netherlands, Britain, Prussia, Russia, Sweden, Denmark, and Portugal. He was secretary of state under James Monroe and drafted the famous Monroe Doctrine speech, opposing European intervention in the Americas. He was president from 1825 to 1829, and then after being defeated for reelection in 1828, he served in the House of Representatives until dying on February 23, 1848, of a stroke just off the floor of the U.S. Congress, where he had been preparing to make a speech.

As was his father, he was opposed to slavery in principle while remaining open to its existence under certain circumstances. He worked against slavery in the Congress, opposing extension to newly acquired territories in the West. During the debates, he stated that slavery was incompatible with Christianity as he understood it. The Whig Party, which he helped to form, had an ambiguous policy on slavery, opposing its extension but not the right of SLAVE OWNERS to keep their slaves and move them about as they wished within slave states. Toward the end of his life, he voted for the Wilmot Proviso, which would have prohibited slavery in any territories taken in the MEXICAN-AMERICAN WAR, 1846–48. At the age of 73, in the AMISTAD CASE, Adams represented the African slaves who had taken control of a Spanish slave ship and sailed it to the United States. He managed to convince the Supreme Court that since the slave trade was illegal, his clients were like victims of piracy and had the right to capture the slave ship by force. The *Amistad* Africans were freed, and some remained in Massachusetts and Connecticut as free people of color, while most returned to Africa.

Stewart R. King

FURTHER READING
Parsons, Lynn H. *American Profiles: John Quincy Adams.*
    Oxford: Madison House, 1998.

AFRICA

Free people of color from the Americas lived in Africa throughout the era of the slave trade, and their descendants still live there today. There are communities that identify themselves as descendants of people from the Americas living in Senegal, Gambia, Guinea Bissau, Guinea, Sierra Leone, Liberia, Ivory Coast, Ghana, Togo, Benin, Nigeria, Cameroon, Gabon, Republic of the Congo, Angola, and Mozambique (*see* separate articles on Senegambia, Sierra Leone, Liberia, Congo and Angola, and the Slave Coast, Benin, and the Bight of Biafra).

African-American free blacks immigrated to Africa as colonists or merchants. The best-known colonies are Sierra Leone, Liberia, and Gabon. Each of these places was established by European or American colonizers during the period of abolition of the slave trade and, ultimately, of the abolition of slavery itself. There were many motives for colonization efforts. One important motive was suspicion of or hostility toward free people of color. The colonization effort was intended to provide a place where free people of color from the Americas or Europe could resettle away from the white majorities. Many contributors to the American Colonization Society, founded in 1816 and an important early source of funds and recruits for the Liberia colony, were slave owners in the American South who thought, as Thomas Jefferson did, that their society would be better off without any blacks, free or slave. Many southern states required that persons who gained their freedom leave the state, and immigrating to Liberia was an option that was strongly encouraged. Another motive was benevolent paternalism, both by abolitionist whites toward free people of color and of free people of color toward Africans. Granville Sharp, a white British abolitionist and theologian, tried to establish a utopian colony for poor British black people in Sierra Leone. His Sierra Leone Company ultimately became a quite harsh landlord and had to call in government soldiers to break a rent strike in 1799. A famous black Sierra Leonean, the Anglican bishop Ajayi Crowther, established a mission and colony in Yorubaland, in what is now Nigeria, in the 1820s, with the goal of converting the Yoruba to Christianity and teaching them about the advantages of Western civilization.

The African-American colonialists of Liberia also saw their mission as giving the benefits of Christian civilization to what they thought of as the "Dark Continent." A sense of mission permeated their early pronouncements, including the Constitution of 1847 and the charter of Lincoln College of Pennsylvania, which supplied the Liberian colonists with higher education in the early days of the colony.

Free people of color were often employed as merchants on the African coast during the period of the slave trade. In the very early days of European trade with sub-Saharan Africa, from the late 15th century on, Portuguese merchants quickly discovered that they did not understand African cultures well enough to trade successfully. There were Africans who understood Islamic culture, but none who could serve as intermediaries for the Portuguese. To address this problem, Portuguese captains would often leave crewmen on the coast in small "factories" (so called not because they were centers of manufacturing but because they were the offices of commercial agents, called factors). Some of these merchants married African women and established families of mixed race who could carry on their work after the patriarchs had died or moved back to Europe. Because of the harsh disease environment, many died quickly, often before the children, African trading partners, or companions could gain the European cultural knowledge necessary to trade successfully. Portuguese merchant houses responded to this problem by sending in free people of color from Brazil to staff their factories. These Afro-Brazilian merchants had better resistance to tropical diseases because of growing up in a tropical disease environment, albeit one on the other side of the ocean, but the Portuguese attributed their better health to their race. Afro-Brazilian merchants dominated the commercial sector of Luanda, the principal port on the Congo coast, in modern Angola, until the end of the Portuguese colonial era in 1975, and there are still influential merchants of Brazilian ancestry living and working there today. Even in places where Portuguese political rule ended much earlier, as along the Slave Coast of modern Ghana, Togo, Benin, and Nigeria, Afro-Brazilian families remained important intermediaries between the northern European slave traders and their African suppliers. A descendant of a prominent Afro-Brazilian family, Sylvanius Olympio, was the first president of independent Togo in 1964, and his sons are important political figures there today.

Not all free colored merchants on the African coast were involved in the slave trade. Slave trade in the region of Senegambia declined throughout the 1700s. By the end of the 18th century, Senegambia mainly exported "legitimate" cargoes such as peanuts and peanut oil, woven mats, and gum arabic. Much of this transition away from the slave trade was due to the presence of many small Afro-European merchant houses who found it easier to compete with large European firms in these

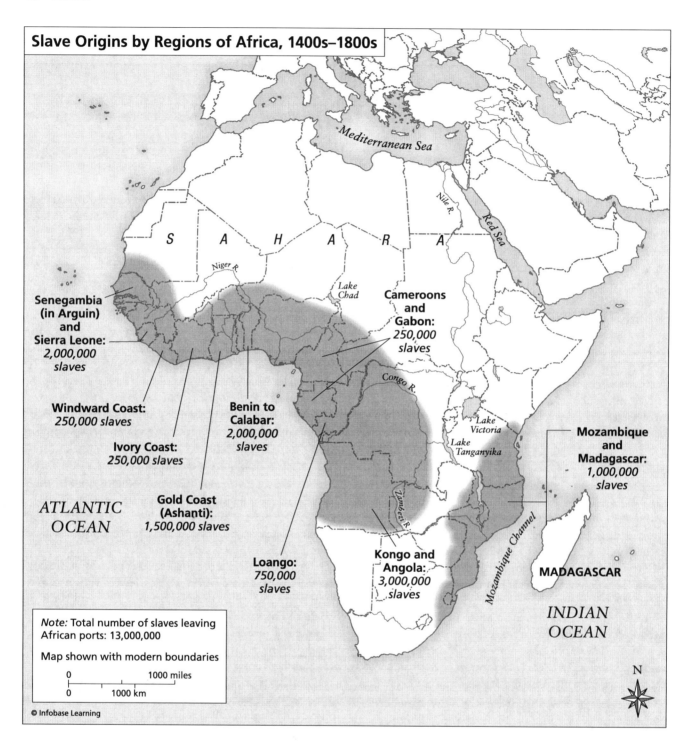

Slave Origins by Regions of Africa, 1400s–1800s

Mediterranean Sea

Nile R.

Red Sea

S A H A R A

Niger R.

Lake Chad

Senegambia (in Arguin) and Sierra Leone: *2,000,000 slaves*

Cameroons and Gabon: *250,000 slaves*

Congo R.

Windward Coast: *250,000 slaves*

Benin to Calabar: *2,000,000 slaves*

Lake Victoria

Lake Tanganyika

Ivory Coast: *250,000 slaves*

Mozambique and Madagascar: *1,000,000 slaves*

ATLANTIC OCEAN

Gold Coast (Ashanti): *1,500,000 slaves*

Zambezi R.

Mozambique Channel

Loango: *750,000 slaves*

Kongo and Angola: *3,000,000 slaves*

MADAGASCAR

INDIAN OCEAN

Note: Total number of slaves leaving African ports: 13,000,000

Map shown with modern boundaries

0   1000 miles
0   1000 km

N

© Infobase Learning

other commodities, which required less capital to make a profit. This trade was mostly organized through the French ports, called the communes, of Senegal. ANNE ROSSIGNOL was a merchant, a free woman of color from one of these communes, Gorée, near modern Dakar. She lived in the French colony of SAINT-DOMINGUE before the HAITIAN REVOLUTION began and had a trading network that extended throughout the Caribbean and across the Atlantic to Africa and Europe.

The descendants of these immigrants from the Americas are still important figures in the independent African countries where they reside. Sierra Leone's Krio people, descended from the black British and North American immigrants, Liberia's Americo-Liberians, Angola's Brazilians, and Ghana, Togo, Benin, and Nigeria's coast traders are all important merchant groups, two centuries after the end of the slave trade.

Stewart R. King

FURTHER READING

Curtin, Philip. *Cross-Cultural Trade in World History.* Cambridge: Cambridge University Press, 1984.

Miller, Joseph C. *Way of Death: Merchant Capitalism and the Angolan Slave Trade, 1730–1830.* Madison: University of Wisconsin Press, 1996.

AFRICAN AND SYNCRETIC RELIGIONS

Many Africans who were taken to the Americas as slaves were already Christians or Muslims, but the majority followed traditional African religions. (*See also* ROMAN CATHOLIC CHURCH and ISLAM.) After arriving in the Americas, sometimes over several generations, most non-Christians formally adopted Christianity. They may have been forced by their masters and the state to profess Christianity, as was common in Catholic countries, or they may have thought it was in their interest to be publicly pious in order to stake a claim to respect from their masters. However authentic or heartfelt these conversions were, though, there were elements of African culture and religious tradition that remained strong in the spiritual practices of African Americans, free and enslaved, throughout the era of slavery and beyond.

The term *syncretism* is often used in a pejorative sense, to suggest that the religious change is somehow false or hypocritical. Christian believers with more traditional practices use it to suggest that the religions so described have adopted Christian terminology and symbols only to hide their continuing devotion to pagan ways. Many anthropologists use the term *acculturation* instead. Syncretism tends to be the more familiar term and describes the mixture of Christian and African religious symbols, names, and even metaphysical concepts in religion as it is actually practiced and believed. Syncretism can begin on either side, that is, fundamentally Christian belief systems can use African concepts or fundamentally non-Christian traditions can make use of Christian symbols or terms. There is no sharp break between the two, but nonetheless we will attempt to provide some broad divisions as part of a discussion of how the tension between African and European spirituality has played out in the Americas.

African Religious Tradition

It is hard to generalize about an entire continent, but there are a few broad elements of African spirituality that had a strong impact on the ways Africans would react spiritually to their new environment in the Americas. First, many African religions are broadly relational, not just about the individual and the divine, but about the family and the relationships among generations, living, dead, and unborn. The dead and the future generations are an important part of any spiritual event, and any person who

is cut off from his or her ancestors—by distance—or from his or her descendants—by sale or premature death without being able to have children—has suffered not just a personal tragedy but a spiritual crisis. African-American religion in the Americas would have to address this need. Next, African religion is often focused on the emotions or feelings of the believer. Believers want to feel a personal connection to the divine through worship. Indeed, believers often feel that the divine is immanent in daily life, and they wish to feel a connection to this divine spirit at all times. Religions that are very intellectual, such less as Islam or Calvinist Protestantism, are less attractive to African converts unless they can develop an emotional element and stress the immanent nature of their God. Third, many, though not all, African traditional religions are animistic: That is, they believe either that God is in everything or that everything in the world has some divine spirit or element. Often, the religious believer performs services in order to gain the favor of or placate the spirits of elements surrounding him or her in nature. As a corollary, religion has a concrete worldly value as well as a spiritual or otherworldly one. That is, by performing religious rituals, the believer intends to induce the spirits of physical objects, people, and animals to help him. Again, Christianity would have to offer some similar promise of help in the real world. And, finally, African religious tradition is oral, and the spoken and sung word is very important in religious contexts. Christianity relies on written scriptures, theological texts, and a body of written laws and regulations. To become attractive to Africans it needed to develop a way for the oral nature of African culture to play itself out, through music, recitation of scripture, lively preaching, and debate and discussion within church communities.

Persistence of African Traditional Religions in the Americas

Most Africans taken to the Americas ultimately converted to Christianity, although in some cases the process took generations, and some preserved their African faith relatively intact. The best-known African religions in the Americas today are *umbanda* and *candomblé* in Brazil. These religions are syncretic, in that they have adopted some elements of Western spirituality, while remaining essentially African in their belief system. *Umbanda* is a relatively recent creation, drawing on African religions and elements of Western spiritism and appealing mainly to urban Afro-Brazilians in the southern part of the country. *Candomblé*, on the other hand, is a relatively pure form of Yoruba traditional religion practiced in northeastern Brazil, mostly among people descended from slaves taken from the Bight of Benin in the 19th century. One concession that *candomblé* makes to its

A group of women prepares offerings for a Jongo festival near Rio de Janeiro, Brazil, in 2008. The Jongo ritual is an African religious dance transplanted to the Americas by slaves, mostly from modern Angola. Similar religious rituals are found throughout the Americas, including *santería* in Cuba and Florida, *vodun* in Haiti, Louisiana, and the Dominican Republic, and *candomblé* in northeastern Brazil. *(Ricardo Moraes/Associated Press)*

Christian surroundings is the use of the images of Christian saints to represent the *orishas*, or gods. But the concept of those gods owes very little to the Christian saints other than choice of a similar figure from Christian tradition so that the images would be symbolically appropriate. The use of Christian images in *candomblé* is frankly described by most practitioners as a means to avoid religious repression rather than being explained, as in other Afro-Caribbean religions, as a way to show the identity of the Catholic and African religious figures. *Candomblé* has also appropriated the gods of other African groups, worshipping them alongside their own in a manner reminiscent of polytheistic practice in the ancient Middle East. The creator gods of *candomblé* are distant figures who do not involve themselves in human affairs or have much interest in the future state of the individual human soul. Instead, the *orishas* and the spirits of nature and the dead are the important divine elements to be worshipped and negotiated with through religious practices.

Other similar survivals of African beliefs were recorded by observers in earlier centuries but have not survived to

our day. Many settlements of runaway slaves, or MAROONS, retained some form of African religious practice for some time. In these cases, though, the mixture of various different African forms introduced by slaves from different parts of Africa often helped undermine the religious identity of the community, opening the way for ultimate conversion to Christianity, especially as Christianity modified itself to become more attractive to Africans.

Afro-Catholic Syncretism
The best known Afro-Caribbean religions are basically Catholic, with syncretic elements from African belief. These include *vodun* of Haiti and the French Caribbean and Spanish American *santería*. Many modern practitioners, such as Dr. Max Beauvoir of Haiti, under the influence of anticolonial thought, have tried to emphasize African traditional elements in these groups. But historically, they owe a great deal to Catholic ideas and deserve to be placed further along the continuum from African to European spirituality than does *candomblé* or the religious practices of the maroon communities in the 18th century.

Vodun existed in the French Caribbean from the late 17th century on. Variants exist today in Louisiana, Martinique, Guadeloupe, French Guiana, and, most famously, in Haiti. *Vodun* has a principal deity, Bondye, or "good God," who is interested in the fate of individual humans and society, unlike *candomblé* and other African traditional religions' creator spirits, who are distant or uninterested. Bondye is depicted as benevolent and powerful, though perhaps not all-powerful. He delegates a good deal of his power to *lwa*, who have individual areas of responsibility and personalities and who can be approached individually. Many *lwa* are derived from various African traditions, principally those of the Ewe of modern Togo and Benin but also Congo and Central Africa. They are often identified with Catholic saints and angels in the sense that believers refer to them interchangeably and appear to believe that they are the same entity. The *lwa* often share the saints' areas of responsibility: For example, Erzulie Dantor, the *lwa* of motherhood, is associated with Our Lady of Czestochowa, a Catholic aspect of Mary the mother of Jesus often invoked by mothers and prospective mothers. Other *lwa* are the spirits of historical figures, such as JEAN-BAPTISTE CHAVANNES or TOUSSAINT LOUVERTURE, while others are the blood ancestors of each worshipper. Serving the *lwa* by sacrifice and various other religious services is a duty of all believers. These duties are often expressed as service to the saints, as is proper and acceptable in Catholicism. Proper service, it is believed, along with forms of initiation, can induce one or more *lwa* to arrive and "ride," or possess, the believer for a time, suppressing or driving out part of his or her own spirit, during which the practitioner will learn important things about the spiritual or physical world or perform acts that he or she might not have been able or willing to perform otherwise.

Vodun changed remarkably after the HAITIAN REVOLUTION and the transfer of Louisiana to American control in the early 19th century, because believers were effectively cut off from the Roman Catholic Church. For as much as half a century in both places, there were almost no priests to teach or serve these communities. In Haiti, the Catholic Church sent no priests because it refused to accept the independence of the country, preferring to wait for France to retake it. In Louisiana, the American Catholic Church had few French-speaking priests and was also reluctant to serve black communities against the objection of white slave-owning Catholics in the South until the time of the AMERICAN CIVIL WAR. *Vodun* became a more independent spiritual tradition during this period without the influence of nonsyncretic Catholic leaders to hold it back.

Santería is a belief system similar to *vodun* that grew up in Cuba in the 18th century and is now practiced throughout the Spanish Caribbean including the mainland and North America. As with *vodun*, modern *santería* believers have tried to reduce the Catholic elements and make the religion more authentically African, and some now refer to the religion as *Lucumí*, after a religious tradition from Nigeria. Historically, though, all believers thought of themselves as Catholics, were baptized, and attended Mass. The Spanish Caribbean had no hiatus of contact with the Roman Catholic Church during the 19th century as Haiti and black Louisiana did, so this growing independence of the tradition from Catholicism has been delayed.

Since one can be both Catholic and *vodun* or *santería*, there were few barriers during the period of slavery for free people of color to participate in these religions. Indeed, the legal restrictions on participation in both groups during the colonial period mostly applied only to slaves. Slaves in Saint-Domingue (the future Haiti) needed passes from their masters to be out after dark and could be whipped if they attended a *vodun* religious service. But no such restrictions applied to free people of color there. In Cuba and Puerto Rico, the Inquisition could question the religious orthodoxy of anybody who attended a *santería* service, but most prosecutions were foiled by the close identification of the spirits with Catholic saints. Indeed, the common name of the religion means "devotion to the saints." Services would be held on saints' days and even led by CATHOLIC CONFRATERNITIES supervised by the priest and authorized by the state. Any unorthodox elements of the service would be kept carefully secret. On the other hand, any known or suspected unorthodoxy in religious practice would be at least a social handicap in any Catholic colony. Public orthodox piety was an important component in the strategy of many free people of color to achieve social acceptance and advancement. Toussaint Louverture, the leader of the rebel forces during the Haitian Revolution, was a devoted Catholic who was never suspected of attending *vodun* services. After his death, though, he was adopted by *vodun* practitioners as a *lwa*.

Protestants and Syncretism
The relatively easy coexistence of Afro-Caribbean syncretic religions and Catholicism was not present at all in Protestant countries. People of color who practiced African traditional religions in Protestant colonies were either ignored or persecuted and did not see their spiritual ideas incorporated in any meaningful way into the dominant faith before the 20th century. If they did wish to create syncretic Afro-Protestant religions, the task was difficult, and acceptance from the dominant culture limited. The Afro-Caribbean tradition of *Obeah* grew up in Jamaica and the other British Caribbean colonies during the period of slavery. *Obeah* has the same roots as the other Afro-Caribbean religions, but there is much less overlap between it and

the Protestant Christianity dominant in Jamaica. *Obeah* appears more a form of folk magic than a coherent religion. Practitioners mostly have conventional Christian beliefs, but with a belief in spirits from Africa or the souls of dead ancestors, and believe that a proper relationship with the spirits can give an individual power to make changes in the natural world. *Obeah* services are held at the request of worshippers who wish to serve a particular spirit, typically with a specific real-world goal in mind.

In the 17th and early 18th centuries, before the beginning of evangelical and Baptist missionary work among slaves in the British colonial world, few slaves were Christians, and most masters did not demonstrate any interest in the religion of their slaves. We have some evidence from this period of slaves actively practicing Islam. Other slaves were no doubt practicing some forms of African traditional religion, though very little documentary evidence has survived. The enslaved woman of color Tituba, who may have been of African or mixed African and Indian ancestry, confessed to witchcraft during the Salem witch trials in Massachusetts (1692). The details of her confession included elements drawn from African spiritual ideas, further confusing the situation and convincing the leaders of Salem that the devil was indeed among them.

When Moravian Baptist missionaries began working among the people of color of Jamaica, one of their expressed goals was to lead the blacks away from what they saw as witchcraft and devil worship. While the Baptist and Pietist movements largely abandoned the requirement for cultural conversion that earlier Protestant faiths had required, they were nonetheless uncomfortable with religious syncretism. In fact, accusations of unorthodox practices in Catholicism that had snuck in through medieval syncretism were among the most common critiques of the Roman Catholic Church during the Reformation. Missionaries from the new sects were hardly likely to be flexible when faced with African spiritual practices.

What they did do, though, was develop Christian responses to the spiritual needs that African-Americans felt. Evangelical and Baptist Christianity are theologically individualistic, stressing the personal commitment to God of each believer. However, in practice, Baptist churches that served African Americans during the 18th and 19th centuries were highly relational, stressing the connection of the believer to a church community and the role of the family in religious life. Providing the worshipper with a substitute for a blood family he or she might no longer have, it helped address a profound spiritual void in the African-American world. Baptist worship was also emotional and participatory, much more so than earlier forms of Protestantism, which tended to appeal to believers intellectually, through study of Scripture or, aesthetically, through music and liturgy that the worshipper

witnessed and appreciated rather than participating in. Evangelical Protestantism was practical in a sense: While not promising magical intervention on specific issues, many Protestant preachers stressed the Old Testament passages where God promised material success to the people of Israel if they followed his law. These texts were taken by African Americans to mean that people who believed in the new faith would gain freedom, respect, and prosperity. And the new faiths were oral in a way that Protestantism was not. Luther stressed the importance of church music and wrote many hymns that remain popular today, but mainline Protestant churches in the 17th and early 18th centuries made liturgy into a spectator activity, performed by the priest and observed by the congregation, who mainly pursued their own individual devotions during the service. Evangelicals and Baptists restored active oral participation in the church service through hymns, common prayer, and especially an emotional and interactive style of preaching.

Another important characteristic of Baptist Protestantism is the independent status of each congregation. Linked to this is the fact that there was no formal process for ordination of ministers, and in fact little study was needed to satisfy most congregations beyond an encyclopedic knowledge of the Bible. This meant that after a relatively short period of teaching and missionary work, many black Baptists could form their own congregations and not be under the tutelage of white church leaders. African cultural ideas could remain strong under such a system, though pressure from other Baptist groups would limit the degree of syncretism. In fact, some black Baptist groups, such as the Spiritual, or "Shouting," Baptists in Trinidad and Grenada, adopted many elements of African spirituality, including Yoruba rituals of fasting and spiritual retreats for purity and the invocation of water spirits. The slave churches in the United States before the Civil War were often similarly syncretic. This was facilitated in their case by the fact that their rituals were either unlawful or at least discouraged by the white power structure, which was, as a result, unable to supervise what was being done and said there. Slave church preachers had even less education in Christian theology than was usual among Baptists as a whole and therefore relied even more heavily on literalist interpretations of selected biblical passages, permitting them more liberty to fit African ideas into their teaching.

Conclusion

African elements were important parts of the spiritual life of people of color in the Americas during the era of slavery. In some cases, African religions continued to claim the loyalty of people of color for long periods without much influence from Christianity. In most places, though, African spirituality infused fundamentally

Christian religious beliefs and practices adopted by people of color. The Roman Catholic Church was more accepting of these African cultural elements, though there were persistent suspicions even there that pagan beliefs were being hidden by a hypocritical or merely superficial adoption of Catholic symbols and terms. In Protestant countries, the attitude of white religious leaders changed over time. In the beginning, African spiritual practices were mostly ignored unless they posed a clear challenge to white authority, through witchcraft, for example. But later, in the 18th and 19th centuries under the influence of evangelicalism, some Protestant church leaders tried to strike a balance between hostility to what were seen as pagan practices and a desire to make their faith accommodating to people of color. This effort, along with the decentralized nature of many Protestant denominations, led to the rise of African-American churches that forged a form of Protestant Christianity that was sensitive to the special spiritual needs of Africans in the Americas.

Free people of color were affected by these developments in religion, though in a manner somewhat different from slaves. Many of the restrictions on attendance at African and syncretic religious services did not apply to free people of color. At the same time, free people of color could hope to rise in the respect of their white neighbors through conventional piety, and thus they might well have rejected too open an adoption of African religious symbols and practices.

Stewart R. King

FURTHER READING

Courlander, Harold. *The Drum and the Hoe: Life and Lore of the Haitian People.* Berkeley: University of California Press, 1986.
Johnson, Paul Christopher. *Secrets, Gossip, and Gods: The Transformation of Brazilian Candomblé.* Oxford: Oxford University Press, 2002.
Metraux, Alfred. *Voodoo in Haiti.* New York: Pantheon, 1989.

AFRICAN METHODIST EPISCOPAL CHURCH
(A.M.E. Church)

The African Methodist Episcopal Church began as a small gathering of free people and former slaves in Pennsylvania and became one of the largest and most powerful churches in the Atlantic world. It would grow from its humble origins in the late 18th century to encompass dozens of countries and almost one million members by the early 20th century.

RICHARD ALLEN always believed that the founding of the African Methodist Episcopal Church was the most important event of his life. Largely through Allen's leadership, the African-American membership grew dramatically

at St. George's, a Methodist church in Philadelphia that had many white parishioners. Upon the completion of a new balcony, the white members evidently assumed that the African Americans would remove themselves to this new, separate worship space. When this did not happen, several whites accosted the African Americans during Sunday services. ABSALOM JONES, a friend and associate of Allen, requested they wait until after the prayer was finished. The whites then sought to remove them physically. With the prayer finished, Jones stood up and led the African Americans from the church. For such an important event, the timing is still contested. Allen claimed the incident occurred in 1787, but other historians have combed St. George's archives and found records of a new balcony in 1792. Other questions remain: Were the African-American parishioners forced out, or did they seek out independence and autonomy?

Did Jones and Allen force the issue, since they were aware of white prejudice and sought either equality or separation? Regardless, Allen and Jones seized the moment.

In March 1793, Allen broke ground on an African church on Fifth Street between Walnut Street and Locust Street in Philadelphia. Despite the early unanimity, some African Americans refused to be associated with Methodism because of their treatment at St. George's. During this period, Methodism was still slowly becoming a distinct denomination separate from the Episcopal Church. Methodism was characterized by a more enthusiastic, less liturgical or scripted form of worship. The sermon was very important in Methodism, as in more extreme dissident Protestant groups, and preaching became the central part of the religious experience for both white and black Methodists. Methodism was also more appealing to working-class, frontier, and immigrant whites, as well as blacks, while the Episcopal Church was the established church in several colonies and had support from elite whites (see also PROTESTANT MAINLINE CHURCHES). Jones was the first African American ordained as a priest in the Episcopal Church. Thus, this first black church became St. Thomas's African Episcopal Church and was led by Jones. Allen still believed in Methodism and led others to a plot he purchased years earlier, in 1791, at Sixth and Lombard Streets. In summer 1794, a pack of mules dragged a converted blacksmith shop to the site. It was dedicated on July 29, 1794. White dignitaries, including Bishop Francis Asbury, founder of American Methodism, who gave the first sermon, attended as well. This church would become known as Mother Bethel, the first African Methodist Episcopal Church. The name *Bethel* was from a prayer offered by the Reverend John Dickins, a well-known white minister who officiated at Allen's first marriage. The prayer was from the book of Genesis. *Bethel* means "temple" in Hebrew and refers to the place where

Jacob carries forth his destiny with the Lord, as a beacon for saving souls. This would prove an auspicious and prophetic name. Bethel was officially incorporated and recognized by the Commonwealth of Pennsylvania in 1796. Starting with only 40 members, within a year Bethel had more than 100 members and by 1810 nearly 400.

The makeup of this early church remains something of a mystery. Of the nine original trustees who signed the charter in 1796, three used only an X, indicating that several important early members were illiterate. There was also clearly a strong presence of African-American women. Both Richard Allen's first and second wives were founding members and would strongly support the church, but women are largely silent in the church's records. Bethel also played an important role in the community by hosting numerous gatherings and meetings, including one in April 1816.

Richard Allen had long struggled with the Methodist Episcopal Church for autonomy and independence. As a condition of the original 1796 Articles of Association, Bethel had a white trustee from the Methodist Church, an ongoing source of tension. In 1805, the new white trustee demanded greater control and the keys and books of the church. Allen refused, instead creating the African Supplement in 1807, revising and repealing the original Articles by the vote of church members. This did not end

The Bethel Methodist Chapel in Philadelphia, founded by Bishop Richard Allen in 1794. This church remains the emotional center of the African Methodist Episcopal Church (A.M.E.) denomination, in honor of the central role played by Bishop Allen and his congregation in organizing the church and spreading its faith throughout the United States and beyond, into the black Atlantic. *(Kean Collection/Getty Images)*

the struggle for control of Bethel. In 1815, the white Methodist elders of the Philadelphia Methodist convention put Bethel up for public auction, thereby hoping to purchase it outright and regain control. Instead, Allen was the high bidder for $9,600. The white elders continued to seek control of the pulpit, but church members stood in the aisle and barred the way. Ultimately, a January 1816 lawsuit reached the Pennsylvania Supreme Court, which ruled in favor of Allen and Mother Bethel. A few months earlier, many members of the Ezion Church in Wilmington, Delaware, had founded a new African Methodist congregation, the first to be unaffiliated with the Methodist Episcopal Church. In Baltimore, Daniel Coker had been corresponding with Allen and, under similar impositions, led his followers to independence as well.

On April 9, 1816, at Bethel Church, 16 men met. They represented roughly one thousand parishioners from four states, Pennsylvania, New Jersey, Delaware, and Maryland. In three days, they created a new organization, the African Methodist Episcopal (A.M.E.) Church, and elected their first bishop, Richard Allen. Though it shared many of the tenets and beliefs of Methodism, this new branch had some differences. They abolished the position of presiding elder, or leader of a regional or national convention, which had proved so troublesome under the old Methodist Church. They also maintained Methodism's strong antislavery position, an issue on which the white church had begun to waver. While the Methodist Episcopal Church stressed personal perfection and expansion, the African Methodist Episcopal Church would also stress social justice and oppose racial prejudice. Alongside several other branches and sects of African Methodism, the A.M.E. would remain the largest group through its activism and outreach.

Portraits of Richard Allen and other African Methodist Episcopal (A.M.E.) bishops, surrounded by scenes including Wilberforce University, Payne Institute, missionaries in Haiti, and the A.M.E. Church book depository in Philadelphia. *(Library of Congress)*

Important agents of this expansion were African-American women, often overlooked or omitted from official A.M.E. records. One example is Jarena Lee. She was adrift personally and spiritually when she heard Allen preach in 1811. Impressed, she felt called to preach herself, but Allen was reluctant. Lee took advantage of a preacher's silence one Sunday and assumed the pulpit. Allen was duly impressed and supported Lee against some opposition, even caring for her son while she traveled the circuit. Allen not only supported her in writing but preached alongside her at meetings and revivals. Lee traveled far and wide, drawing new followers to the fold. Despite this, after Allen's death in 1831, the A.M.E. increasingly sought respectability by marginalizing Lee and other female ministers. Bishop DANIEL A. PAYNE, among others, encouraged them to tend to hearth and home rather than leadership positions in the church. Though Amanda Smith Berry was ordained as the first female minister of the A.M.E. in 1885, her ordination was rescinded two years later.

By 1830, the A.M.E. spread from Philadelphia to the Ohio Valley. Bishop Allen had sent a church elder across the Alleghenies in 1823, and the church had grown to more than 10,000 members by 1826. In 1822, the A.M.E. church in Charleston, South Carolina, was only exceeded by Mother Bethel in Philadelphia. In the aftermath of the DENMARK VESEY slave conspiracy, this Charleston church was targeted by local white authorities and shut down. The Reverend Morris Brown was able to escape from Charleston to Philadelphia, where he was welcomed by Bishop Allen. Brown preached alongside Allen and was eventually sent to Indiana. He would become the second bishop of the A.M.E. Church. Throughout the 1820s, the A.M.E. Church continued to expand, sending missionaries to Haiti and organizing congregations in Canada. Many notable African Americans were members, including DAVID WALKER and HARRIET TUBMAN.

Daniel Payne, who would become the sixth bishop of the A.M.E., was of mixed European, African, and Native American ancestry. He was born in Charleston in 1811 and joined the church in Philadelphia 30 years later. In his time, he would be a minister, a historian, the founder and president of the first A.M.E. college, and, after 1852, bishop. Payne emphasized order and structure in a desire for recognition and respectability. He demanded better education, especially for ministers, and downplayed the emotional worship and nontraditional music that were hallmarks of the early A.M.E. Under his auspices, the A.M.E. Church also began its own newspaper, the *Christian Recorder*. It was based in Philadelphia and launched in 1856. Payne's efforts allowed the tremendous growth of the A.M.E. By the beginning of the AMERICAN CIVIL WAR in 1861, the A.M.E. had more than 50,000 members. Thirty-five years later, thanks to the AME's tremendous efforts to reach the newly freed people, its membership had increased 10-fold.

As it grew in numbers and strength after the Civil War, the A.M.E. turned its attention across the Atlantic, to Africa.

There were numerous missions to West Africa, specifically LIBERIA, during the antebellum years, but these were by white Protestant churches, including many Methodists. The A.M.E. largely avoided Liberia because of a general opposition to the colonization plan and a lack of funds (*see also* EMIGRATION AND COLONIZATION). Beginning in the 1870s, the A.M.E.'s larger numbers and the end of slavery helped change these conditions, and they sent many missionaries to Liberia, as well as other countries in the area. The A.M.E.'s outreach was not limited to West Africa. They also reached into South Africa, establishing the first A.M.E. church there in 1896. By 1910, the A.M.E. had close to 40,000 members in South Africa alone. The A.M.E. remains a thriving national and international church today, as well as a center of African-American culture and community.

Matthew J. Hudock

FURTHER READING

Andrews, Dee. *The Methodists and Revolutionary America 1760–1800: The Shaping of an Evangelical Culture*. Princeton, N.J.: Princeton University Press, 2002.

Campbell, James T. *Songs of Zion: The African Methodist Episcopal Church in the United States and South Africa*. New York: Oxford University Press, 1995.

George, Carol. *Segregated Sabbaths: Richard Allen and the Emergence of Independent Black Churches, 1760–1840*. New York: Oxford University Press, 1973.

Griffith, R. Marie, and Barbara Dianne Savage, eds. *Women and Religion in the African Diaspora: Knowledge, Power, and Performance*. Baltimore: Johns Hopkins University Press, 2006.

Melton, J. Gordon. *A Will to Choose: The Origins of African American Methodism*. Lanham, Md.: Rowman & Littlefield, 2007.

Newman, Richard S. *Freedom's Prophet: Bishop Richard Allen, the AME Church, and the Black Founding Fathers*. New York: New York University Press, 2008.

Park, Eunjin. *"White" Americans in "Black" Africa: Black and White American Methodist Missionaries in Liberia, 1820–1875*. New York: Routledge, 2001.

Payne, Daniel. *History of the African Methodist Episcopal Church*. New York: Arno Press, 1891, 1969.

ALABAMA

Alabama is a state of the United States. It is located in the Southeast, to the west of GEORGIA and of the Appalachian mountain chain. It is mostly flat and well watered, with the exception of the mountainous northern quarter, and the terrain and climate in most parts of the state are suitable for plantation crops, especially cotton. TENNESSEE is to the north, and MISSISSIPPI is to the west. The state has a short coastline around the city of MOBILE, ALABAMA, and to the east of Mobile lies the panhandle region of FLORIDA. The indigenous inhabitants of Alabama were eastern woodland Indians, who lived in villages and some large towns and practiced agriculture. They were organized in multitown chiefdoms when the first European and African travelers appeared in the region in the early 16th century. The first people of African ancestry to enter the territory that is now Alabama were the companions of Hernando de Soto (ca. 1496–1542), who crossed the state in 1541–42. De Soto took several dozen blacks from Cuba, some of whom were free. None of these conquistadores remained in the area, though.

Blacks were living in Alabama as early as 1707, when a Mobile priest baptized Jean-Baptiste, a Negro slave of Jean-Baptiste Le Moyne de Bienville (1680–1767), governor of French LOUISIANA. At that time, Mobile was a part of Louisiana. After the Spanish took control of Louisiana in 1769, the CODE NOIR IN FRENCH LAW, or black code, was adopted in Spanish Louisiana, including parts of Alabama. This legal code offered some protections to people of color, especially those who were free. These legal rights, and the French and Spanish cultural concepts of race and slavery, affected cultural attitudes in the Mobile region long after the area was under the rule of the United States.

Unlike the Mobile region, which had its roots in French and Spanish culture, the rest of Alabama was settled by Anglo Americans from states to the east and north. Except as noted, this entry generally deals with Anglo Alabama and does not include the coastal counties of Mobile and Baldwin with their predominantly Latin heritage.

The table below tracks the evolution of the black population of the territory while under American rule.

This table is based upon federal census figures, which are not always reliable and sometimes undercounted free nonwhites. Nonetheless, it is clear that the vast majority—more than 99 percent—of African-descended Ala-

bamians in the antebellum period were enslaved. In 1850, about 60 percent of the total free colored population resided in five of the state's counties, and two of those were Mobile and Baldwin. In 1860, 70 percent lived in eight counties, with the greatest number of them residing in Mobile, Baldwin, and Madison, in the mountainous north. Free nonwhites typically lived in the cities and towns of the state, such as Mobile, Huntsville, Tuscaloosa, and Montgomery. Mobile contained about 41 percent of the state's total free black population in 1850. Ten years later, nearly half of the state's total of free nonwhites lived in the same area. Mixed-race people constituted 65 percent of the total free colored population in Anglo Alabama in 1860. If Mobile and Baldwin are included, the total jumps to 78 percent of the total number in the state.

Traditional interpretations regarding southern free people of color suggest that manumissions were the result of sexual liaisons involving white male planters and nonwhite slaves. This view, however, is not valid for Alabama. In the late 20th century, the historian Gary B. Mills began an extensive study of free people of color in Alabama, identifying more than 5,700 free blacks by examining traditional genealogical sources such as population, agricultural, slave, and manufacturing schedules of federal census records, and wills, deeds, church records, various civil and criminal court records, estate inventories, city directories, and free papers. Only 11 percent of the free black population of Alabama can be attributed to manumissions. Miscegenation accounted for only 32 percent of the manumissions, and the remaining 68 percent can be attributed to several factors including self-purchase. Manumission took a variety of forms. Caesar Kennedy, a free man of color of Huntsville, manumitted his wife and her seven children in 1821, presumably after having ransomed them from another owner. In his will filed in 1832, William Cureton of Henry County emancipated

AFRICAN-AMERICAN POPULATION OF ALABAMA, 1820–1900

Year	Slaves	Free People of Color	Free People of Color as a Percentage of Total Population	Total Population
1820	34,779	569	0.4%	127,901
1830	117,549	1,572	0.5%	309,527
1840	253,532	2,039	0.3%	590,756
1850	342,844	2,265	0.3%	771,623
1860	435,080	2,098	0.2%	964,201
1870		475,510	47.7%	996,992
1880		600,103	47.5%	1,262,505
1890		678,849	44.9%	1,513,017
1900		827,307	45.2%	1,828,697

his slaves Stephen and Suckey. In Montgomery County, Darby, slave of Ann Goldthwaite, mother of the American painter of the same name, purchased his freedom for $750, probably in the 1850s.

The legislative bodies governing the territory and later the state of Alabama determined the method by which slaves could be freed. In 1805, the Legislative Council and House of Representatives of the Mississippi Territory (which governed present-day Alabama) passed a law on emancipation. It was no longer legal to manumit slaves unless they performed a meritorious act for the owner's benefit or that of the territory. Owners were required to furnish bond and security. The state legislature in 1834 passed an act authorizing the judges of the county courts to manumit slaves. The law required owners to publish in a county newspaper for a minimum of 60 days the name and description of each slave to be emancipated. The legislature stipulated that the newly freed slave was required to leave the state within 12 months after the emancipation and not to return. Failure to comply with this last provision meant the sheriff of the county where the freedman was found could incarcerate the person, who could then be sold into slavery, although this penalty was, in actuality, almost never imposed. Although the Alabama Supreme Court ruled in 1830 that owners could not emancipate slaves by wills, many in the state included such provisions in their wills. Most SLAVE OWNERS did not indicate why they did so, although some masters provided the customary reason that the slaves had performed some type of beneficial service for them.

In the wake of the Nat Turner rebellion in Virginia in 1831, the Alabama legislature, as did some others in the South, enacted restrictive measures regarding nonwhites. Alabama made it unlawful for free people of color to settle within the state after January 1, 1833. Free blacks who did move to the state after this date were given 30 days to leave or suffer 39 lashes. If they remained 20 days after having received this punishment, they could be arrested and sold as slaves for one year. Within 20 days after the end of this year, those free blacks who remained in the state could be sold into slavery.

This law was not enforced as free blacks continued to move to Alabama and even publicly informed officials of their whereabouts. Still, local authorities did nothing. Free blacks such as Peter Brandford of Jefferson County took their free papers verifying their free status outside Alabama for recording to the courthouse after 1833. Before leaving North Carolina in 1834, Lavina Bert obtained a copy of her free paper and presented it to the clerk at the Madison County courthouse the following year. Federal census records also document instances of how the laws were disregarded and demonstrate that free blacks did not avoid public records and public officials who could

have taken steps to have the laws enforced and have them expelled. More than 20 percent of all free nonwhites in Anglo Alabama provided information to the census enumerator in 1850 that showed that they had entered the state illegally. Ten years later two-thirds of these people continued to reside in the state.

Free blacks in the South pursued a variety of economic activities. In Alabama, they were employed in skilled and unskilled positions. Free nonwhites were farmers, carpenters, brick masons, cabinetmakers, bridge builders, tailors, livery stable owners, cooks, butchers, laundry women, stage drivers, cooks, hostlers, and barbers. The state's most prosperous free nonwhites resided in Mobile, Baldwin, Butler, Madison, Montgomery, and Tuscaloosa Counties.

A small number of free blacks in Alabama prospered in the antebellum period. Solomon Perteet of Tuscaloosa County, who was born in Georgia, was a planter. He achieved some economic success as he loaned money, to white men as well as fellow free people of color, and bought and sold land for profit. He made many real estate purchases in Tuscaloosa County, such as the three lots in the city of Tuscaloosa in 1838 and the nearly 120 acres of land that he obtained from the federal government in 1839. He also owned as many as seven slaves. Other elite free blacks in Alabama included John H. Rapier of Lauderdale County and John Robinson of Madison County. Rapier, a prosperous barber in Florence, was born a slave in Albemarle County, VIRGINIA, around 1808 and manumitted in 1829. His successful business allowed him to accumulate about $7,500 worth of property. His son, James T. Rapier (1837–83), served as an Alabama congressman during Reconstruction (see also RECONSTRUCTION IN THE UNITED STATES). Robinson, a livery stable keeper from Virginia, had amassed real estate assessed at $4,000 and a personal estate at twice that amount. He also had a number of descendants who were active as community leaders, including a son who served in the state legislature in the Reconstruction era. Born a slave in SOUTH CAROLINA, Horace King, a slave owner himself, was a successful bridge builder in Alabama and worked on the Alabama state capitol building. During the AMERICAN CIVIL WAR, 1861–65 he repaired bridges for the Confederacy and later served as a member of the Alabama House of Representatives, 1868–72.

Some Alabama free people of color, as did their counterparts in other regions of the South, owned other nonwhites, some of whom were not family members. At his death, Tom Smith of Dallas County, for example, owned his slave wife and their three children as well as 10 other slaves whom his family did not manumit. Solomon Perteet purchased his wife and her child and had them legally freed. He bought and manumitted other slaves as well, but no evidence has been found to suggest that he bought slaves for economic reasons. Throughout the antebellum period, other free blacks owned slaves, such as Silas Pope, a farmer born in Georgia, who owned 10 slaves in 1850.

Some studies of southern free nonwhites maintain that they were more likely than whites to be involved in criminal activities. However, few Anglo Alabama free blacks were engaged in such acts. Only 13 such cases among nearly 3,000 free blacks have been located in extant court records of Anglo Alabama's 48 counties. Charges included gambling, trading with slaves, and the worst possible offense a black man could commit: raping a white woman. Defendants in 10 of these cases were convicted; one conviction was overturned on appeal. The state Supreme Court overturned the death penalty imposed upon John Thurman, who was convicted of rape. In a different case the state Supreme Court overturned a legal judgment against a free nonwhite, who was defended by a local white, accused of inciting a slave revolt. The most common civil action for either race was attempts to collect debts. In many cases, whites sued blacks for unpaid debts, but about a third of the total number of interracial cases in Alabama courts in the antebellum years involved free colored plaintiffs with white defendants. Since the southern counties of the state were governed, for some purposes, under the provisions of the French Code Noir, free blacks in those counties had legal rights, including access to the courts, that were not granted to blacks elsewhere in the American South.

In the antebellum South, religion played an important role in the lives of blacks, both slave and free. Free nonwhites in Alabama were accepted as members by most denominations, including Roman Catholic, Baptist, Methodist, Presbyterian, and Episcopalian, and served as ministers or preachers to others of their race in some cases. For instance, the Alabama Baptist Association purchased Caesar Blackwell, a slave who became an ordained minister (see also BAPTISTS AND PIETISTS). Never legally manumitted, Blackwell lived as a free man, obtained a house and lot in Montgomery, and preached to nonwhites and whites (see also LIVING "AS FREE"). Nathan Ashby, born a slave in Virginia in 1810, purchased his freedom in 1842 and three years later started preaching. He became the leader of the black Baptist church in Montgomery. Mount Hebron Baptist Church in Leeds (Jefferson County) had two free black members in its congregation between 1819 and 1865. Discipline of its white and black members was an important element within the church, as is evidenced when that church excluded slaves, as well as one free man of color, for drunkenness, lying, or swearing. In the Methodist Church, free blacks were licensed to preach or to act as class leaders. Methodist Church members of both races in Montgomery held their services in the same building but at different times during the day. By April 1851, the nonwhite Methodist congregation in Montgomery numbered more than 400 members, most of whom were enslaved. Episcopal churches in Tuscaloosa and Montgomery served free blacks as well (see also PROTESTANT MAINLINE CHURCHES). The Presbyterian Church purchased the freedom of Harrison W. Ellis, who became an ordained Presbyterian minister in 1846, subsequently traveling to LIBERIA, where he led a Presbyterian congregation.

The onset of the American Civil War in 1861 caused great disruption for all Alabamans. The northern part of the state was occupied by federal forces in fall 1862. The U.S. government also controlled Pensacola, Florida, just across the border from Mobile, from spring 1862 on. Alabama blacks fled slavery by the thousands as soon as the northern armies neared their homes. With the EMANCIPATION PROCLAMATION of January 1, 1863, they could be sure that they would find welcome and be given a chance to strike back against their oppressors. A total of 4,969 Alabama men served in the U. S. Colored Troops during the course of the war. An entire division of black soldiers from across the South, about 5,000–6,000 infantrymen and artillerymen, participated in the spring 1865 campaign to liberate Mobile.

After the war, Alabama's small prewar free colored population was able to provide some leadership to the mass of newly freed people. Their role was particularly important in Mobile, where they remained a distinctive community throughout the 19th century.

Christopher A. Nordmann

FURTHER READING
Boucher, Morris Raymond. "The Free Negro in Alabama Prior to 1860." Ph.D. diss., University of Iowa, 1950.
Mills, Gary B. "Free African Americans in Pre–Civil War 'Anglo' Alabama: Slave Manumissions Gleaned from County Court Records." *National Genealogical Society Quarterly* 83 (June 1995): 127–142 and (September 1995): 197–214.
———. "Miscegenation and the Free Negro in Antebellum 'Anglo' Alabama: A Reexamination of Southern Race Relations." *Journal of American History* 68 (June 1981): 16–34.
———. "Shades of Ambiguity: Comparing Antebellum Free People of Color in Anglo Alabama and 'Latin' Louisiana." In *Plain Folk of the South Revisited*, edited by Samuel C. Hyde, Jr., 5. Baton Rouge: Louisiana State University Press, 1997.

ALLEN, RICHARD (1760–1831) *American clergyman*

Richard Allen was born the slave of a Quaker in Pennsylvania in 1760. When the Quakers as a denomination

Richard Allen (1760–1831), American clergyman and founder of the African Methodist Episcopal (A.M.E.) Church. Allen, whose title in the church was bishop, was an important community leader in Philadelphia and, along with his Episcopal colleague Absalom Jones (1746–1818), led the Philadelphia free black community through a period of rapid growth and political turmoil. *(The Granger Collection, New York)*

decided that their members should no longer own slaves, Allen's master sold him and his family but took care to find a master who would treat them decently. Allen's new master, Stokley Sturgis, apparently had a good relationship with Richard. The young man joined the Methodist Church at the age of 17, and he and his brothers were permitted to preach and teach Sturgis's other slaves. Methodism did not explicitly condemn slavery as Quakerism did, but it encouraged masters to treat their slaves with respect, and most Methodists opposed slavery. In the end, Sturgis himself converted to Methodism and decided to give his slaves the opportunity to purchase their freedom. Allen moved to Philadelphia, worked as a bricklayer and as a teamster in the Continental army during the War of American Independence, 1775–83 and by 1783 had earned enough money to buy the freedom of his entire family (*see* LIVING "AS FREE").

Allen was ordained as a minister at the first meeting of the American Methodist Church in 1784, and he began preaching and evangelizing the African-American population of Philadelphia. He drew many black worshippers

to St. George's United Methodist Church despite the fact that the church maintained separate seating and separate services for African Americans. Allen's fellow black minister, ABSALOM JONES, would not accept segregation, especially when church officials ejected him from a service in 1786 for trying to sit in the white portion of the building. Allen and Jones formed a nondenominational black congregation called the Free African Society, but Allen returned to the Methodists shortly thereafter. Jones and Allen worked together to purchase a plot of land and build a black chapel, called Bethel Methodist Chapel, which remained officially connected to the Methodist Church for 20 years. Finally, in 1816, Allen drew black Methodist congregations in the Mid-Atlantic region together to form the African Methodist Episcopal Church. Allen was elected its first bishop on April 10, 1816, a position he held until his death on March 26, 1831. His Bethel Church is today known as the mother parish of the African Methodist Episcopal Church.

Allen also participated in the NEGRO CONVENTION MOVEMENT IN THE UNITED STATES, convening the first such convention in 1830 and serving as its chairman. The convention movement was an important means for political expression and education for blacks in the United States and was the precursor to important civil rights organizations.

Allen was also a conductor on the Underground Railroad, and the Bethel Church continued to help runaway slaves until the end of slavery in the United States in 1865.

Allen initially supported colonization schemes to move free people of color out of the United States to Africa, Haiti, or elsewhere in the Americas. However, faced with strong opposition to these efforts from his fellow blacks in Philadelphia, he joined the opposition to the AMERICAN COLONIZATION SOCIETY's attempt to recruit settlers for LIBERIA.

The African Methodist Episcopal Church was and remains the largest of the "black churches" in the United States. While many African Americans were and are members of white-majority denominations, the predominantly black churches remain a key element in community identity and cohesion. During the period from the Second Great Awakening and the founding of the black churches until the AMERICAN CIVIL WAR, 1861–65, black churches in the North were the center of free black communities. The church provided education, both higher education for a few and primary education for many who were underserved or simply not served at all by the public school system. The church provided social services for the free black poor, legal (and extra legal) services for fugitive slaves, and political expression for the voiceless. After abolition, the black church also provided a rare place where black intellectuals could perform a valued social function and receive a salary during the era of segregation.

Matthew Hudock

FURTHER READING
Newman, Richard. *Freedom's Prophet: Bishop Richard Allen, the AME Church, and the Black Founding Fathers.* New York: New York University Press, 2008.

AMERICAN CIVIL WAR (U.S. Civil War)
(1861–1865)

When the American Civil War began in 1861, whites of the Northern states claimed that it would be a war to preserve the Union rather than a war to end slavery. Black Americans recognized greater potential. Seeing that pressure from their community could influence the goals and outcome of the war, free black intellectuals hoped that they could prove their worth by actively fighting to gain the privileges of American citizenship. Only blacks could make it a successful war for freedom, the abolitionist MARTIN DELANY argued, because "the rights of no oppressed people [had] ever . . . been obtained by a voluntary act of justice on the part of the oppressors." Militant abolitionists such as DAVID WALKER and HENRY HIGHLAND GARNET had chided slaves to stand up and fight in less propitious times, and now that the time was right, black participation would be crucial in securing freedom for the bondsmen and civil rights for all. Abolitionists built upon black service in previous wars to push the government to adopt emancipation as a war goal and extend the right of blacks to participate on the battlefield. Some also offered their skills as laborers, scouts, and spies. Finally, after the war was opened to black participation, they fought for the Union in massive numbers and assisted in efforts to educate the freedmen and prepare them for the future.

Aware that a number of slaves had earned their freedom through service in the WAR OF AMERICAN INDEPENDENCE, 1775–83, and the War of 1812, black leaders saw in the Civil War the chance for a "second revolution," in which they could earn their freedom and demonstrate to the world their equality.

Arriving at similar conclusions, many slaves joined the war effort almost as soon as the fighting began. A group of Virginia slaves seeking asylum behind enemy lines snuck across Chesapeake Bay in May 1861 and presented themselves to General Benjamin Butler, the Union commander at Fort Monroe, Virginia. In so doing, they forced the U.S. government to develop a policy for dealing with black refugees. Instead of returning them to their masters, Butler declared them "contraband," or captured enemy property, and put them to work in camp. Seeing opportunity for freedom, others began to approach Butler's camp, and within two months, he had 900 escaped slaves working as teamsters, blacksmiths, cooks, and laundresses.

Butler's "contraband" set a precedent for black participation in the war. At least 150,000 black laborers assisted in the quartermaster and engineering departments in such capacity by the end of the war, and by 1865, approximately 500,000 slaves joined the effort either as laborers or soldiers. The government was well aware of the value of their assistance. Union soldiers, many of whom entered the war with racist sentiments, began to see the value and skills of the escaped slaves as they came into contact with them. In addition to protecting them from recapture, some even began to argue that black men, slave or free, should be allowed to participate in combat. The Quartermaster General's Report on Negro Labor issued in 1862 concluded that "if black men could wield a shovel they could shoulder a musket." This sentiment strengthened as Northern troops entered the deeper areas of the Confederacy and began to rely more upon contraband assistance. By summer 1862, much of the Northern public even began to see how essential arming former slaves would be to victory, and many, regardless of their views on racial equality or emancipation, began to advocate enlisting black soldiers as an expedient measure.

Union officers began to arm and train blacks for military service before the federal government allowed them to do so. General David Hunter, commander in the South Carolina Sea Islands, sought President Abraham Lincoln's permission to enlist escaped slaves for combat duty in April 1862. When Lincoln failed to respond, Hunter, recruiting on his own authority, finally gained War Department authorization in August. During that same month, Butler, in Louisiana, incorporated several units of free black soldiers in the Union forces under his command. These two groups, Hunter's 1st South Carolina Volunteers and Butler's Louisiana Native Guards, who had previously served in the Louisiana militia and joined the Union army after the fall of New Orleans in May 1862, were the first black Civil War soldiers, the Native Guards the first officially mustered. In the western theater, Senator Jim Lane began recruitment for his 1st Kansas Colored Volunteer regiment at the same time.

The eagerness of both free blacks and escaped slaves to fight converged with the Union's need for as many hands as possible, and blacks won their first major Civil War goal on January 1, 1863, when President Lincoln issued the EMANCIPATION PROCLAMATION. This document not only declared free all slaves in the Confederate states, it also made freedom a war goal and announced

A group of black soldiers in South Carolina poses with their officer and teachers. The man standing on the left may be the abolitionist poet Col. Thomas Wentworth Higginson (1823–1911), and the woman standing next to him may be Susie Baker King Taylor (1848–1912), a free woman of color from Georgia who worked as a teacher for soldiers in the Hilton Head region during the war. *(The Granger Collection, New York)*

the Union's new policy of enlisting African Americans as soldiers and sailors.

In May 1863, the government further sanctioned black participation in battle by creating a Bureau of Colored Troops within the War Department. Black soldiers began to earn acclaim just five days later, in an assault on Port Hudson, Louisiana. Two regiments of free blacks and former slaves from New Orleans participated in this Union assault on the Confederate stronghold on the Mississippi River. Though the Union failed in this effort, the press began to take notice of black heroism. A month later, at Millikens Bend, another battle in Louisiana, both former slaves and free Southern blacks demonstrated bravery that shocked many whites. One Confederate officer was impressed enough to report that the black troops had resisted "with considerable obstinacy," even as white troops "ran like whipped curs."

Black troops displayed bravery in many battles, but none has captured as much attention as the famous assault on South Carolina's Fort Wagner in July 1863. Led by the first black Northern regiment, the 54th Massachusetts Infantry, the attack ended in failure and massive loss of life, but the black soldiers proceeded bravely under unrelenting Confederate fire. William H. Carney earned a Medal of Honor for his bravery in bearing the regimental colors. Though called the "54th Massachusetts," this group of soldiers enlisted from throughout the Union and

was made up mostly of free blacks from Northern cities such as Philadelphia and New York. The Massachusetts governor John A. Andrew put the regiment together in March 1863. Secretary of War Edwin M. Stanton insisted that all black units be led by white officers, so Andrew chose leaders from noted abolitionist families, putting Col. Robert Gould Shaw in charge. Soldiers were then recruited by both white and black abolitionists throughout the North, especially Pennsylvania and New York. Two of the recruits were sons of the nation's most prominent black abolitionist, Frederick Douglass.

Less celebrated but equally important to the Union cause were the naval contributions of African Americans. Well before the Emancipation Proclamation a black sailor gave the Union its first naval victory. On August 7, 1861, a Confederate privateer had captured a schooner, the *S. J. Waring*, off the coast of New York and took black crew members to be sold to slavery in Charleston. William Tillman, the steward, decided that he would not allow himself to be sold, and he convinced a fellow prisoner to help recapture the ship. Though neither Tillman nor his companions had experience in navigation, they managed to take the ship when it was within 50 miles of Charleston, turn it around, and reach New York. Similarly, ROBERT SMALLS, perhaps the most famous slave to contribute to the war, managed to commandeer a Confederate gunboat, the *Planter*, and surrender it to Union forces. He and his crew of fellow slaves waited for the captain to leave the ship on the night of May 13, 1862, picked up their families and friends, and proceeded down the Charleston River, providing the proper signal upon reaching Fort Sumter. Once beyond the range of Sumter's guns, he hoisted a white flag and turned over the vessel to a Union captain. Both black and white newspapers celebrated Small's feat and later reported his promotion as captain of the vessel in 1863.

Seeing that black valor on land and sea forced a number of white soldiers, commanders, and members of the general public to rethink their attitudes, many blacks became confident that despite the failures of past wars, they could help end prejudice by proving themselves on the battlefields. By the war's end, 70 percent of all Northern black males of military age had joined this crusade by enlisting in the Union army. In proportion to the population, black enlistment in the North was three times white enlistment. Black men provided nearly 10 percent of Union fighters, and Northern and Southern blacks participated in 449 engagements, 39 of which were major battles. Approximately 37,300 blacks died while serving, and 21 earned the Medal of Honor. These men had earned citizenship for all African Americans by forcing the government to disregard and even denounce the 1857 *Dred Scott* decision, in which the Supreme Court had declared that blacks were not, and never could be, citizens of the United States.

In addition to acknowledging black citizenship, the U.S. government passed several antidiscrimination measures during the war. In 1862, the Senate repealed an 1825 law barring blacks from carrying the mail, and Congress ruled that blacks could no longer be excluded as witnesses in the courts of the District of Columbia. Following this lead, some states also began to allow blacks to testify in court. Also during the war, Congress admitted blacks to its visitors' galleries for the first time, the Smithsonian began to welcome blacks to public lectures, organizers of the president's public reception on New Year's Day allowed blacks to attend, and black troops were included

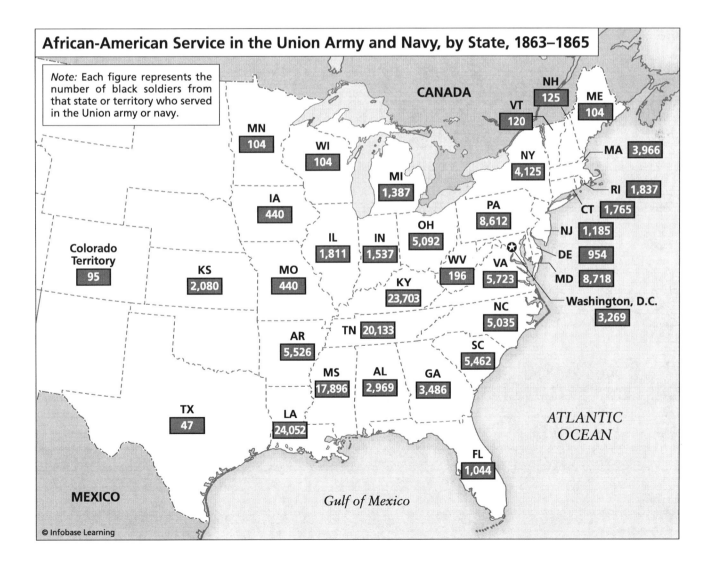

African-American Service in the Union Army and Navy, by State, 1863–1865

Note: Each figure represents the number of black soldiers from that state or territory who served in the Union army or navy.

CANADA

NH 125
VT 120
ME 104
MN 104
WI 104
NY 4,125
MA 3,966
MI 1,387
RI 1,837
IA 440
PA 8,612
CT 1,765
OH 5,092
NJ 1,185
IL 1,811
IN 1,537
WV 196
VA 5,723
DE 954
Colorado Territory 95
KS 2,080
MO 440
KY 23,703
MD 8,718
Washington, D.C. 3,269
AR 5,526
TN 20,133
NC 5,035
SC 5,462
MS 17,896
AL 2,969
GA 3,486
TX 47
LA 24,052
FL 1,044

ATLANTIC OCEAN

MEXICO

Gulf of Mexico

© Infobase Learning

in the Inauguration Day parade on March 4, 1865. Finally, black contributions to the war effort caused many whites to develop more positive attitudes that led to lasting changes in education and public transportation, and legal segregation ended in most parts of the North within three decades of the war's end.

Despite such gains, black soldiers faced enormous discrimination and injustice. To begin with, the sight of a black in the Union uniform offended racists, and in some instances, mobs attacked black soldiers. Also, Confederates treated black prisoners as insurrectionists rather than prisoners of war, brutally murdering them, as in the April 12, 1864, Fort Pillow Massacre, or selling them back into slavery. While Southern maltreatment was expected, black soldiers were often shocked to find discrimination within the Union army as they were denied choice assignments, given inadequate and lower pay than white soldiers, and prevented from rising to the rank of commissioned officers.

However, most blacks chose to stress the good and forgive the bad. For most cases of harassment of black soldiers, optimists could emphasize the dismayed reaction and intervention of white onlookers. Prejudiced actions of officers also were often met with criticism by their superiors or government officials. Also, Confederate threats of murder and enslavement were answered with similar promises of retaliation by the U.S. government and Union officers such as Hunter, who promised he would "at once cause the execution of every rebel officer, and every rebel slaveholder in my possession" if black Union soldiers were executed. President Lincoln took this a step further in July 1863 by pledging retribution against Confederate prisoners if black Union soldiers were to be denied the rights traditionally afforded prisoners of war. Finally, many blacks were encouraged by the support of their commanders, particularly in the struggle for equal pay, which was eventually rectified. The quest for black officers, however, was left largely

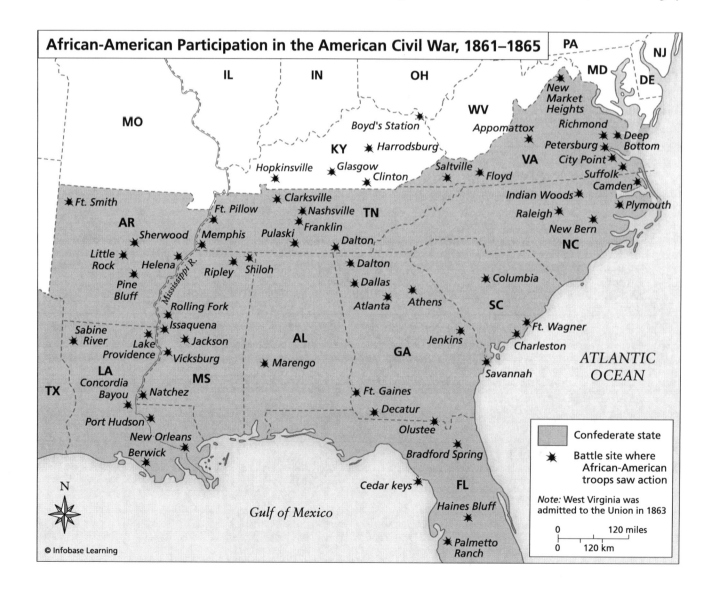

African-American Participation in the American Civil War, 1861–1865

unanswered. At issue was the fact that black soldiers wanted leaders of their own color, but most whites resented the idea of having to salute or take orders from blacks. Though they could not become line officers, blacks could earn commissions as chaplains and surgeons, but such positions did not involve battlefield command. Near the end of the war, Delany was eventually commissioned the first black field officer in the U.S. Army on February 27, 1865, but by that point it was too late for him actively to fulfill the role.

It would have been natural for the Confederacy to use black soldiers, since most American blacks lived in states that joined the Confederacy. Other slave-owning societies had used free blacks as soldiers, and in some cases even slaves, with promises of freedom in return for loyal service. But the Confederacy consistently rejected the idea until the very end of the war. The free-black militia of Louisiana was sent home by the local Confederate commander in 1862, whereupon most of the men in the militia joined the Union army as it gained control of their homes in southern Louisiana. General Patrick Cleburne of the Confederate army, an Irish immigrant, proposed in 1864 enrolling slaves with the permission of their masters and with a promise of freedom, but his suggestion was rejected by higher-ups. As the war was coming to a close in April 1865, General Robert E. Lee, by that time in overall command of Confederate forces, authorized the enrollment of blacks in segregated units similar to the more than 100 regiments in the Union army. Only a couple of hundred recruits were actually enrolled before the fighting ended with a Confederate surrender. An unknown number of blacks, both free and enslaved, served in regular Confederate units, as officers' servants, musicians, teamsters, and other support troops. These men were sometimes carried on the unit's books as soldiers, so that they could draw rations, and their pay may have been given to their masters if they were slaves. The Confederate navy, like that of the Union, enrolled blacks for many jobs. Many Confederate navy ships, like Robert Smalls's *Planter*, were civilian vessels taken into the navy with their civilian crews, which often included blacks. All three groups of men were mostly serving at the orders of their masters or former masters, and no doubt out of personal loyalty and desire for personal advancement rather than ideological conviction. The phenomenon of "black Confederates" has been greatly exaggerated in modern discussions of the subject; it is important to note that the vast majority of black veterans of the Civil War were Union soldiers or sailors.

The battlefield was not the only arena in which free blacks contributed to the war effort. Northern abolitionists such as the former slave HARRIET TUBMAN, as well as more recently liberated slaves, served as scouts, spies, and liberators by heading back south. Tubman, who had led slaves northward along the Underground Railroad for years, earning the nickname "the Moses of Her People," reversed directions and traveled southward to spread the news of emancipation. Sent south at the beginning of the war by the governor of Massachusetts, she not only delivered slaves to freedom and recruited the men as soldiers, she also worked as a spy and a nurse. SUSIE BAKER KING TAYLOR, who had been educated while she was a slave, escaped and joined General Hunter's regiment of former slaves in the Sea Islands as a cook, nurse, and teacher. Garland H. White, once a slave but free before the war began, offered to guide Gen. William T. Sherman's army through Georgia in 1864 and served as a chaplain. Finally, a number of noncommissioned officers, soldiers, and civilians helped educate their fellow soldiers as well as Southern black civilians. The free black abolitionist Satirra Douglas, wife of H. Ford Douglas, traveled to Kansas under the auspices of the Women's Loyal League of Chicago to work in a freedmen's school, and Charlotte Forten, of Philadelphia's noted FORTEN FAMILY, built upon her work in the abolition struggle by also teaching blacks in the Sea Islands. Many of these officers and soldiers were from the North and had encountered Southern blacks for the first time in their army camps.

As the war came to a close, conditions were looking up for the black community. The prewar free people of color, who had been leaders of the crusade for the abolition of slavery a decade before, could concentrate all their energies on civil rights. Their leadership in the army positioned them to become leaders of the postwar black community. Even better, they were leading a movement that appeared to have a promising future. Strides had been made in Northern and Southern education, desegregation had begun in the public facilities in some Northern cities, and blacks were being chosen as jurors and even elected to office. Furthermore, government and military leaders were aware of the important role blacks had played in the war. With military and government leaders praising black efforts for the Union, blacks from both regions shared the optimism that America had awakened. As William Wells Brown explained in *Rising Son*, "One by one, distinguishing lines have been erased, and now the black man is deemed worthy to participate in all the privileges of an American citizen."

Despite such significant advances, there were many obstacles yet to overcome. The Reconstruction period saw both great strides for blacks, led by the prewar free colored community, and great peril from official discrimination and unofficial terrorism from the KU KLUX

KLAN and other violent white supremacist organizations. The leadership role of prewar free people of color lasted less than a generation, as a result of the pervasive post-Reconstruction discrimination that affected all African Americans equally. But during and immediately after the Civil War, the fact that free blacks had served as leaders during the struggle made former black military leaders important players in Reconstruction era politics and important targets for the terrorists.

(*See also* RECONSTRUCTION IN THE UNITED STATES.)

Beverly C. Tomek

FURTHER READING

Cornish, Dudley Taylor. *The Sable Arm: Black Troops in the Union Army, 1861–1865.* Lawrence: University of Kansas Press, 1987.

McPherson, James. *The Negro's Civil War: How American Blacks Felt and Acted during the War for the Union.* New York: Vintage, 2003.

Miller, Edward A. *The Black Civil War Soldiers of Illinois: The Story of the Twenty-Ninth U.S. Colored Infantry.* Columbia: University of South Carolina Press, 1998.

Quarles, Benjamin. *The Negro in the Civil War.* New York: Da Capo Press, 1989.

Redkey, Adam. *A Grand Army of Black Men: Letters from African-American Soldiers in the Union Army, 1861–1865.* Cambridge Studies in American Literature and Culture. Cambridge: Cambridge University Press, 1992.

Wilson, Joseph T. *The Black Phalanx: African American Soldiers in the War of Independence, the War of 1812 and the Civil War.* Hartford, Conn.: 1887.

Wilson, Keith. *Campfires of Freedom: The Camp Life of Black Soldiers during the Civil War.* Kent, Ohio: Kent State University Press, 2002.

AMERICAN COLONIZATION SOCIETY

The American Colonization Society (ACS) was founded in 1816 to relocate free blacks from the United States to an African colony that is now the country of LIBERIA. Important white leaders throughout the United States, including the Reverend Robert Finley of New Jersey; Samuel Mills, a traveling missionary; the American Bible Society founder Elias Boudinot; the New Yorker John E. Caldwell; the Supreme Court clerk Elias Boudinot Caldwell and Justice Bushrod Washington; Francis Scott Key, a well-known Washington, D.C., lawyer; the Speaker of the House of Representatives Henry Clay; the Virginia politicians Charles Fenton Mercer and John Randolph Fairfax; and Representative (later Senator) Daniel Webster were among the founding members. These men shared in common fear of a biracial United States, and that was enough to encourage black resistance

to the organization. To paint a simple picture of immediate resistance by all free blacks to the ACS and Liberian settlement, however, is to oversimplify the story.

Not all free blacks immediately resisted the colonization scheme. As they began planning the ACS, Mills and Finley both contacted PAUL CUFFE, a prosperous sailor of African and Native American ancestry who had already supported a similar British effort at SIERRA LEONE, seeking his support. Cuffe showed interest in the scheme, but he died before the ACS plans took off. While few black leaders of Cuffe's prominence supported the project, the ACS did manage to recruit settlers. These settlers included "recaptives," or Africans rescued from the slave trade; free blacks from throughout the United States; and former American slaves. Most who left for the colony before 1827 were free blacks who applied to the society for passage, but after that point, most settlers were recently manumitted free blacks, many of whom were freed specifically after agreeing to go. Indeed, approximately 6,000 slaves gained their freedom under such conditions between the colony's founding and the AMERICAN CIVIL WAR.

Throughout the 1820s, most emigrants to the colony were free blacks who sought opportunities they were denied in the United States. They saw emigration as the best way to achieve independence and to thrive beyond the confines of American racism. They also assumed that they would be able to participate in governing the colony. What they sought was the chance to earn and enjoy the privileges of genuine citizenship, something they were denied in the United States despite their level of talent or capability. Two free blacks who fit this pattern were Colin Teague and Lott Carey from Richmond. Both elders in the First Baptist Church, they offered to serve as missionaries in Africa, and they promised to send word to other members of Richmond's free black community who were considering making the same move (*see* BAPTISTS AND PIETISTS). Carey died before reporting back, but the fact that many of the colonists who went with him soon returned with negative descriptions of life in Africa discouraged many from following. Soon, few free blacks were interested in volunteering to emigrate. In this climate the bloody Nat Turner slave revolt in Virginia in 1831 led more whites to support colonization, even as fewer free blacks found it appealing.

Black resistance to the ACS began immediately and grew stronger throughout the late 1820s and early 1830s. It began in 1817 when meetings of free blacks in Philadelphia, Richmond, and Washington, D.C., denounced the ACS as a thinly veiled scheme to remove free blacks and thus quiet resistance to human bondage and, as a result, actually strengthen the bonds of slavery. They also feared the prospect of forced deportation, and this fear grew after the Turner revolt.

Resistance to colonization led black leaders to create a vibrant abolition movement that attracted whites who had favored colonization, such as William Lloyd Garrison, and encouraged them to call for immediate abolition instead. (*See* ABOLITIONISM AND RESISTANCE TO SLAVERY.) *Freedom's Journal*, founded in 1827, the first American newspaper operated by blacks, led in this movement, featuring the works of SAMUEL E. CORNISH, JOHN RUSSWURM, and DAVID WALKER. By 1830, white leaders such as Garrison began to listen to the message of these black leaders—that they and their ancestors had played an important role in building the United States and that they had no desire to leave their native land and "return" to a land they had never seen.

As the country's racial climate worsened in the antebellum years, however, some free black leaders found the idea of African settlement more appealing, and some turned to the ACS. Events of the 1850s, such as the FUGITIVE SLAVE ACT OF 1850 and the 1857 *Dred Scott* decision (*see also* SCOTT, DRED) fueled this renewed interest in Liberia or other parts of Africa, and leaders such as HENRY HIGHLAND GARNET, ALEXANDER CRUMMELL, and MARTIN DELANY began to support various emigration schemes. Most abandoned the scheme again when President Abraham Lincoln announced his EMANCIPATION PROCLAMATION in 1863 and the American Civil War became a war for black freedom, but the failure of Reconstruction led many, most notably Delany, to return to the idea again in the 1880s (*see* RECONSTRUCTION IN THE UNITED STATES and EMIGRATION AND COLONIZATION).

Liberia developed a significant population of American-descended people and was able to preserve its independence throughout the late 19th century "scramble for Africa" by European powers. The American Colonization Society gave up administration of the colony in 1847 but continued to support emigrants and some social services in the colony until 1913. The society formally dissolved in 1964 but had been effectively inactive since the 1910s.

Beverly C. Tomek

FURTHER READING

Blackett, R. J. M. *Building an Anti-Slavery Wall: Black Americans in the Atlantic Abolitionist Movement, 1830–1860.* Baton Rouge: Louisiana State University Press, 1983.

Burin, Eric. *Slavery and the Peculiar Solution: A History of the American Colonization Society.* Miami: University Press of Florida, 2005.

McGraw, Marie Tyler. "Richmond Free Blacks and African Colonization, 1816–1832." *Journal of American Studies* 21, no. 2 (August 1987): 207–224.

Mehlinger, Louis R. "The Attitude of the Free Negro toward African Colonization." *Journal of Negro History* 1, no. 3 (June 1916): 276–301.

Miller, Floyd J. *The Search for a Black Nationality: Black Colonization and Emigration, 1787–1863.* Chicago: University of Illinois Press, 1975.

Winch, Julie. *A Gentleman of Color: The Life of James Forten.* New York: Oxford University Press, 2002.

AMERICAN REVOLUTION   *See* WAR OF AMERICAN INDEPENDENCE.

AMISTAD CASE

At a June 1839 Havana slave auction, the Cuban plantation owners José Ruiz and Pedro Montes purchased 53 Africans, mostly from the region north of Liberia, who had been taken from Africa to Cuba in contravention of the ban on the Atlantic slave trade. They were to be transported aboard the schooner *Amistad* to plantations near Puerto Príncipe, CUBA. The ship, with forged papers and $40,000 worth of cargo, sailed from Havana on June 28, 1839.

Four days later, the Africans, led by the charismatic Sengbe Pieh (Joseph Cinqué, 1813–79), broke from their chains, seized the ship, killed the captain and the cook, and ordered Montes to take *Amistad* to Africa. Over the next eight weeks, Montes headed the ship east during the day and west at night, hoping to reach the southern coast of the United States. Instead, *Amistad* reached the eastern tip of Long Island on August 26, 1839. A group of Africans went ashore for assistance.

When the U.S. brig *Washington* arrived to investigate, Lieutenant Thomas Gedney sent a contingent to round up the Africans and then ordered the schooner towed to New London, CONNECTICUT. On August 29, a hearing ruled on complaints of murder and piracy filed by Montes and Ruiz and the status of *Amistad*'s cargo and the Africans as slaves or free men. The court ordered the Africans to stand trial in circuit court for the murder of *Amistad*'s captain and to remain in prison in New Haven, Connecticut, until then.

Abolitionists saw an opportunity to publicize their cause and assist a powerless group of illegally transported Africans. The New York merchant Lewis Tappan (1788–1873) organized a committee to aid the Africans, and Roger Baldwin (1793–1863), a future Connecticut governor and senator, became the lead attorney. After the Africans were transferred to Hartford on September 14, the city took on a carnival atmosphere. Souvenir images of *Amistad* and Cinqué were sold on Hartford's streets, and tourists paid 12 cents for a glimpse of the jailed celebrities.

Death of Capt. Ferrer, the Captain of the Amistad, July, 1839.

Don Jose Ruiz and Don Pedro Montez, of the Island of Cuba, having purchased fifty-three slaves at Havana, recently imported from Africa, put them on board the Amistad, Capt. Ferrer, in order to transport them to Príncipe, another port on the Island of Cuba. After being out from Havana about four days, the African captives on board, in order to obtain their freedom, and return to Africa, armed themselves with cane knives, and rose upon the Captain and crew of the vessel. Capt. Ferrer and the cook of the vessel were killed; two of the crew escaped; Ruiz and Montez were made prisoners.

A newspaper report and illustration of the rebellion on the slave ship *Amistad*, 1839. The *Amistad* case was the most famous of a series of legal cases in U.S. federal courts that confirmed that the slave trade was piracy, that people who were prisoners on slave ships gained their freedom if they made it to the United States, and that the former prisoners were entitled to seek their freedom, even through violence. *(MPI/Getty Images)*

The circuit court confronted five issues: (a) a writ of habeas corpus to release three young girls among *Amistad* captives, (b) criminal law involving the shipboard killings, (c) property law involving assertions that the Africans were legally purchased slaves, (d) admiralty law involving competing salvage claims, and (e) jurisdictional claims about turning the Africans over to President MARTIN VAN BUREN in accordance with the 1795 Treaty of San Lorenzo with Spain. The judge ruled that the court lacked jurisdiction regarding criminal charges, since the incident occurred beyond U.S. waters, but that the court needed to determine the Africans' legal status. Thus, they were held over for the next meeting of the district court.

The trial began on November 19, 1839. Cinqué and various abolitionists testified over the next five days. Abolitionist attorneys argued that the Africans had been illegally kidnapped and therefore were not slaves, property, or salvage. On January 13, 1840, the judge announced his decision. In accordance with salvage rights law, Lieutenant Gedney received one-third of the value of the ship and nonhuman cargo, which would then be restored to the Spanish government. The Africans, having been born free in Africa, were not property and were to be returned to their homeland.

The federal government appealed the decision to the U.S. Supreme Court. Tappan enlisted the Massachusetts representative and former president JOHN QUINCY ADAMS to collaborate with Baldwin. Arguments began on February 22, 1841. Baldwin focused on narrow issues of law, avoiding broad assertions about human rights. Adams

spoke on February 24: "The moment you come to the Declaration of Independence, that every man has a right to life and liberty, an inalienable right, this case is decided," he proclaimed. "I ask nothing more in behalf of these unfortunate men than this Declaration." On March 9, 1841, the Court announced its decision. The Africans had been kidnapped, were not criminals because they had acted in self-defense, and were entitled to their freedom.

To raise funds to transport the Africans back home, Tappan and the abolitionists then organized a show in which the Africans performed and told stories about their homeland. Their life in America was difficult, lonesome, and subject to white harassment, but on December 4, 1841, the 35 surviving Africans boarded the chartered steamship *Gentleman* and reached Freetown, Liberia, 50 days later.

At that point, most of the *Amistad* Africans disappeared from history. One, Margru—Black Snake—adopted the English name Sarah Kinson and returned to the United States in 1846, eventually enrolling at Oberlin College. After graduation, she returned to Africa as a missionary. Cinqué, finding his village destroyed and family gone, disappeared from the records for nearly three decades, later returning, in ill health, to a Christian mission, where he died in 1879.

The *Amistad* case produced mixed results. The Supreme Court decision did not repudiate slavery but ruled on a legal technicality that the Africans had been taken to Cuba *after* the abolition of the slave trade. Supporters of slavery inferred that had the Africans been taken to Cuba prior to abolition in 1820, they could legitimately have been considered slaves and, therefore, property. Nevertheless, the case complicated U.S.-Spanish relations, sparked a missionary movement to Africa, energized the American abolitionist movement, and enflamed the growing conflict over slavery.

See also FÉNIX, GUERRERO.

Kenneth Blume

FURTHER READING

Adams, John Quincy. *Amistad Argument*. New York: S. W. Benedict, 1841. Reprint, Whitefish, Mont.: Kessinger, 2004.

Amistad: Martin Van Buren and John Quincy Adams: Original Manuscripts from the Gilder Lehrman Collection. New York: Gilder Lehrman Institute of American History, 1998.

Barber, John Warner, comp. *A History of the Amistad Captives*. New Haven, Conn.: E. L. & J. W. Barber, 1840. Reprint, New York: Arno Press, 1969.

Gottheimer, Josh. *Ripples of Hope: Great American Civil Rights Speeches*. Cambridge, Mass.: Basic Civitas Books, 2004.

Harrison, Maureen, and Steve Gilbert. *Landmark Decisions of the United States Supreme Court*. Vol. 5. La Jolla, Calif.: Excellent Books, 1995.

Jones, Howard. *Mutiny on the Amistad: The Saga of a Slave Revolt and Its Impact on American Abolition, Law, and Diplomacy*. New York: Oxford University Press, 1987.

Merrill, Marlene. *Sarah Margru Kinson: The Two Worlds of an Amistad Captive*. Oberlin, Ohio: Oberlin Historical and Improvement Organization, 2003.

Trial of the Prisoners of the Amistad on the Writ of Habeas Corpus, before the Circuit Court of the United States. New York: 1839.

United States. Congress. House. Committee on Foreign Affairs. *Schooner Amistad: June 24, 1846*. House Doc. No. 753. Washington, D.C.: Government Printing Office, 1846.

ANGOLA   *See* CONGO AND ANGOLA.

ARDOUIN, BEAUBRUN (1796–1865) *Haitian historian and politician*

Beaubrun Ardouin is recognized today as one of the great figures of Haitian letters. His history of the country is important both for its careful research and for the way it illustrates the point of view of the wealthy class of mixed-race people who had been free before the HAITIAN REVOLUTION. Haitian society and politics are divided along color and social class lines, and the value of Ardouin's work today lies in the way it clearly delineates those lines and shows how they formed in the revolutionary period.

Ardouin was born sometime in 1796, during the Haitian Revolution, one of three sons of a free colored farmer from the South Province. This was a region where free blacks and mixed-race people were better integrated than in the more highly developed parts of the colony. This was the base for the mixed-race leader André Rigaud, and mixed-race political leaders dominated this region until the 20th century. Ardouin's father was a soldier in the revolution and a supporter of JEAN-PIERRE BOYER, a free mixed-race general who later became president of Haiti. Ardouin could not receive a formal education because of the chaotic conditions during the war. Instead, he taught himself literature, philosophy, history, and art out of books his father gave him from the libraries of exiled planters.

Ardouin became a lawyer in 1820, serving in a number of positions in the Haitian governments of Presidents Boyer, Geffrard, and Guerrier, including minister of justice in 1844 and minister without portfolio on two occasions. He was a judge from 1821 until 1831 and a member of the Senate from 1832 until the fall of Boyer in 1844. Both of his brothers were also important writers. His brother Céligny was a political figure as well and was killed by President (later, Emperor) Faustin Soulouque in 1849 because Soulouque found him threatening as a leader of the mixed-race group. Ardouin had to remain in exile in France during Soulouque's reign, only returning in 1857 when he was overthrown. Soulouque represented the black, military, northern faction in Haitian politics, and some of the resentment Ardouin must have felt toward him may have affected his historical writing, much of it done during this period of exile.

Ardouin is best remembered for his 11-volume *Études sur l'histoire d'Haïti*, published in Paris between 1853 and 1860. Ardouin's historical writing attempted to situate the Haitian Revolution that convulsed the island from 1791 to 1804 in the context of other nationalist revolutions in the Americas and denied that it had any special racial or class implications. He argued, primarily but not entirely on racial grounds, that the former free people of color (rather than former slaves) were the natural leaders both of the revolution and of postindependence Haiti. He wanted Haiti to be considered a part of the family of nations in the Americas, and that meant at the time that it could not be a "black" republic. His work was an attempt intellectually to "whiten" the Haitian ruling classes to make Haiti more similar to other countries. He hoped that political developments in his country and growing acceptance of Haiti by foreigners, especially Europeans and North Americans, would lead to the improvement and "civilizing" of the Haitian people. His great intellectual opponent was THOMAS MADIOU, who sought to balance his account and repair the reputation of the great black heroes of the

Haitian Revolution, especially Toussaint Louverture, and to portray the revolution as a successful slave uprising instead of as a national independence movement. Ardouin's interpretation of the events of 1791–1804 has generally not prevailed in modern scholarship. Most 21st-century historians consider the Haitian Revolution as a slave uprising, something unique in history, rather than as a national independence movement like others in the Americas at the time. They see the impact of the revolution around the Americas being linked to its challenge to the racial order existing everywhere else in the region at the time. However, Ardouin's scholarship remains important for the light it casts on the role of free people of color before and during the revolution and in Haiti's early national period. He demonstrates in his own life that former free people of color remained a self-aware group with an influence over society out of proportion to their numbers. And his very careful record of the role played by free people of color in the revolution helps us see the disproportionate role played by free people of color there as well. In this sense, although modern historians reject his racial attitude and larger conclusions about the meaning of the Haitian Revolution, they are indebted to him for ensuring that free people of color are part of the story of blacks in the Americas.

After Ardouin returned to Haiti in 1857, he served as a minister without portfolio, ambassador, and judge. He edited his dead brother's work and wrote legal texts until his death on August 30, 1865.

Stewart R. King

FURTHER READING

Ardouin, Beaubrun. *Études sur l'histoire d'Haiti suivies de la vie du général J.-M. Borgella.* 11 vols. Paris: Dezobry et E. Magdeleine, 1853–1860.

ARGENTINA

Argentina, in the southern part of South America, is often portrayed as a predominantly white European country. Yet throughout the 18th and 19th centuries, the region had a significant population of African descent. These Africans originally arrived as slaves, but as the centuries progressed, an increasing number were emancipated or born free. Africans and Afro-Argentines were central players in many aspects of Argentine history, yet their contribution, even today, is often overlooked.

The Afro-Argentine Population

The majority of forced African migrants arrived in the River Plate (Río de la Plata) region of present-day Argentina during the 18th century. Enslavement in West Africa was often the result of punishment for a crime, indebted-ness, disobedience, indigency, or capture during a war. Records kept by colonial officials often classified the geographic origin of slaves in an arbitrary manner. Ports of embarkation of slaves were regularly considered sufficient indication of the origin of African forced migrants.

The most significant areas of origin of enslaved Africans in the River Plate region were Angola and Congo, encompassing the Kongo and Ndongo kingdoms. Hence, Africans and Afro-Argentines were sometimes referred to as the "caste of Angola." The second largest group originated in Guinea and Western Sudan, encompassing Hausa, Yoruba, Mina, and Mandinga people from the British and French *factorías* on the Gold Coast of Africa. However, from 1750 onward, up to half of all slaves transported to the River Plate were from Brazil.

At certain times during the 17th and 18th centuries, Buenos Aires, the Argentine capital, was supplied solely by slave traders working for the merchants of one country—usually Portugal or England, but France and the Netherlands also held the asiento at different times—and thus the variety of origins of the slaves in Buenos Aires was limited. Relative cultural homogeneity contributed to the African and Afro-Argentine community's ability to form associations and define itself as a group. After 1789, when restrictions on the slave trade were removed, slaves also entered from Mozambique, as well as Brazil, Angola, and Congo.

The journey from the West African coastline to the River Plate took an average of two months. A doctor on a slave ship to the River Plate in the 1750s left an anonymous account of the trip, describing the arduous journey of 70 days and a mortality rate on board of 50 percent

An 18th-century illustration of the skyline of Buenos Aires. After the Viceroyalty of La Plata was established in 1776 with its capital at Buenos Aires, the city became the most important port in Spanish South America and an important entry point for slaves going to Bolivia and Peru. The free Afro-Argentine population grew rapidly, and by the time Argentina gained its independence in 1810, at least 30 percent of the city's people were Afro-Argentines. *(Fernando Brambila, 1794, courtesy Emece Editores)*

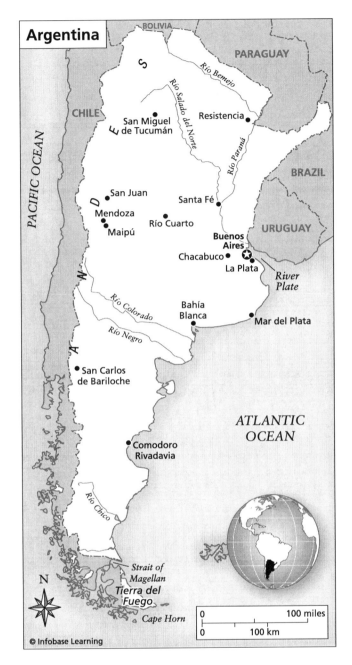

Argentina

BOLIVIA

PARAGUAY

CHILE

Río Bemejo

San Miguel de Tucumán

Resistencia

Río Salado del Norte

Río Paraná

BRAZIL

San Juan

Santa Fé

URUGUAY

Mendoza

Río Cuarto

Maipú

Buenos Aires

Chacabuco

La Plata

River Plate

Río Colorado

Bahía Blanca

Río Negro

Mar del Plata

San Carlos de Bariloche

ATLANTIC OCEAN

PACIFIC OCEAN

Comodoro Rivadavia

Río Chico

Strait of Magellan

Tierra del Fuego

N

Cape Horn

0   100 miles
0   100 km

© Infobase Learning

of African origin in the northern Argentine provinces of Tucumán and Santiago del Estero were 64 percent and 54 percent, respectively. It was possible, in extreme cases, for African ancestry to be simply ignored. This was the case for the sons of an army captain, Gregorio Sanfines, born in 1761 in Buenos Aires of a black father and a mixed-race mother. His sons were listed in records as "*españoles* (Spanish),"indicating that they were considered white. This was only possible for those who were not visibly African and were from the upper echelons of society. Indeed, reclassification had its origins in the early 18th century, when the Spanish monarchy instituted a system whereby a subject could purchase certificates of legal "whiteness" called *cédulas de gracias al sacar.*

Increasing Discrimination

In 1790, the viceroy of the River Plate, Nicolás de Arredondo, declared that all free Africans and Afro-Argentines, together with all indigenous Argentines, had to report to the mayor to prove that they had employment and were not vagrants, on pain of 25 lashes. Throughout the 1790s, the viceregal authorities were suspicious of Africans and people of African origin. There were rumors of a conspiracy involving French aid, with the purpose of freeing all slaves and indigenous people. The flames of these rumors were fanned by news of a successful slave revolt in the future Republic of Haiti, in 1791.

A decade later, the viceregal authorities intensified their curtailment of the activities of African forced migrants, whether enslaved or free. Official fear of Africans' propensity to rebel was manifest in a law prohibiting them from carrying sticks or clubs. From 1804, Viceroy Sobremonte decreed that if Africans and Afro-Argentines did not carry certificates of ownership or employment, they were to be apprehended as vagrants and subjected to two months of public service. Even if this law was never executed in its full harshness, it reinforced the sense that free Afro-Argentines were second-class members of society, whose status was always in doubt.

In Buenos Aires at the turn of the 19th century, Africans resident in Buenos Aires mainly originated from specific small regions in West Africa or were born in Argentina. They were thus less ethnically diverse than plantation slaves in other colonies. This concentration of origin meant that groups of Afro-Argentines acted in a similar way to other immigrant communities, forming clusters from the same region or state. For some Africans in the River Plate, countries of origin therefore remained a significant mark of identity, while others worked hard to join a CREOLE culture, speaking only Spanish and choosing not to pass on details of their origins to their children.

due to lack of exercise and proper nutrition, which caused dropsy and scurvy. The port of Buenos Aires was the entry point for African slaves, who were sent on to work in mines and on estancias (South American ranches) up to the mid-19th century.

In 1770, Alonso Corrió de la Vandera, or "Concolorcorvo," as he was known, the road inspector for the viceroy of Peru, estimated that the total population of the city of Buenos Aires in that year was 22,007, including 4,163 African slaves, mulattoes, and free Afro-Argentines, and 450 free Afro-Argentine soldiers. By the close of the 18th century, almost 50 percent of the population in the Argentine countryside was black. The populations

The urban setting in which Afro-Argentines lived facilitated regular contact with other members of their community and enhanced the possibility of intergenerational cultural exchange. Contact also increased the probability that some Africans and Afro-Argentines would intermarry, both formally and informally. Africans were subject to a loosely defined process of creolization once they moved to America. Distinctions were drawn between new arrivals, or *bozales*, and those who were accustomed to life in Buenos Aires. This led to divisions within the community and generational conflict.

Economic and Social Roles
Many free Africans and Afro-Argentines in the city of Buenos Aires became tradespeople, entered domestic service, pursued careers as artisans, or worked as laundrywomen. Numerous Africans settled in the countryside of Buenos Aires province, some of whom joined the ranks of the gauchos, seminomadic cowboys who did seasonal work on farms and ranches. Other rural Afro-Argentines were employed as agricultural laborers. This was a cause of some trauma to many Africans in Buenos Aires, as working the land was considered demeaning for men in some parts of Congo and West Africa. African men also worked in skilled employment as tailors, blacksmiths, and silversmiths, while women were employed as wet nurses and nannies to children in Spanish-American and European families.

Male and female African street vendors, selling homemade candles, sweets, and brushes, were a common sight in colonial Buenos Aires, though vending had been the preserve of women in the market system in many parts of West Africa. By the beginning of the 19th century, Afro-Argentines dominated many of the workshops in Buenos Aires. Though a large proportion of free Afro-Argentine men joined the army, the principal alternative occupations were those of musicians or skilled craftsmen. In the city, free people of African origin worked as servants, porters, and laborers, as well as being prominent in the militia.

The occupational structure of free Afro-Argentines often replicated that of slaves, and domestic service was considered to imply a degree of unfreedom not far removed from slavery, even for European domestic servants. After being manumitted, many slaves, not possessing the tools, skills, or capital to establish their own businesses, often simply returned to their original employers in return for a low salary.

Africans and Afro-Argentines in the city of Buenos Aires demonstrated a high level of associative activity, founding mutual aid societies and religious lay brotherhoods, or CATHOLIC CONFRATERNITIES, to organize their community. The first Afro-Argentine confraternity was the San Baltasar, founded by clergymen at the Piedad Church in 1772 and authorized by the archbishop of Buenos Aires. Confraternities were organizations that complemented the activities of the Catholic Church, collecting alms, maintaining buildings, paying priests, and arranging celebrations. Significantly, Christian confraternities were a common feature of Central Africa, and people from Congo and Angola were particularly prominent in the confraternities of Buenos Aires. Confraternities were encouraged by the colonial authorities, as they promoted syncretism between African religions and Catholicism. Enslaved and free Africans in Buenos Aires venerated particular saints, such as San Baltasar and San Benito, and various black Virgin Marys.

During the mid-19th century, confraternities were gradually replaced by the less overtly religious and more ethnically defined associations called *nations*. One of the principal functions of the *nation* was that it administrated funds to contribute to the MANUMISSION of members who were slaves. *Nations* were also building societies, burial societies, and cultural associations for Africans and Afro-Argentines. They organized the celebration of feast days and traditional dances such as *tambores*, tangos, and *candombes*. Each *nation* had democratically elected monarchs, who took part in politics. There was a religious element to the *nations*' activities, which was encouraged by the authorities, as it contributed to regulating the societies. The *nations* had a propensity for focusing on utopian visions of the sending country, as was common among European immigrant communities.

From the Catholic Church's and the viceregal administration's point of view, religious brotherhoods were preferable to the *nations* that developed later, which were seen as political forums. *Nations* were perceived as potentially subversive to mainstream society. Because of this and the *nations*' ostentatious celebration of African culture, the colonial viceroy's administration considered them obscene and forbade them. In 1824, eight years after Argentina formally declared its independence from Spain, a government regulation stipulated the procedures for the organization of African societies, which governed manumission, education, morality, productivity, communication with the city police, and the leadership of the organizations.

Most Africans and Afro-Argentines in Buenos Aires, including first-generation forced migrants, spoke Spanish, which they may have learned from traders in West Africa, during the course of the Middle Passage, or, most commonly, of necessity on arrival in Buenos Aires, and in the case of Afro-Argentines, from their parents and those around them. The linguistic influences that did survive the passage and the experience of slavery point to a preponderance of Bantu Africans among the forced migrants. Afro-Argentines eventually developed their own language, *bozal*, and there is a recognizable heritage of the Afro-Argentines in the slang language of Buenos Aires, *lunfardo*.

National Independence

In 1806, a Corps of Indians, Pardos, and Morenos was created by the viceregal government to fight a British invasion, officered almost entirely by African and indigenous people. Despite the newly formed parliament's ostensible gratitude to slaves who fought in defense of the city, only those who were "mutilated and useless for service" were manumitted, along with 70 others who drew lots to achieve their freedom. A festival was organized at the Plaza de la Victoria, present-day Plaza de Mayo, the central square of the city of Buenos Aires, where the redemption of the 70 slaves was paid by the Viceroyalty.

Alexander Gillespie, a British officer, commented during the British invasions of Buenos Aires in 1806 and 1807 that just one-fifth of the urban population of 41,000 in 1806 was white, the rest composed of a "compound breed" of Africans and Europeans. The official statistics for the city at that time—the eve of Argentine independence—show that the population was 29.5 percent of African origin. There were 9,615 Africans, Afro-Argentines, and mulattoes of a total population of 32,558. The disparity between Gillespie's estimate and the census figures reveals much about how racial attitudes differed between British and Spanish cultures. The British officer, influenced by the "ONE-DROP RULE" OF RACIAL IDENTITY, identified every person of any known or admitted African ancestry as a member of the "compound breed," while to a Spaniard, "mulatto" was more than just a bald statement of ancestry, and many people of African descent had officially redefined themselves as white.

During the Argentine wars of independence, both indigenous and African people fought against the Spanish, representing the broader Buenos Aires community and thus joining their ranks. The Buenos Aires revolutionary junta of 1810 granted black soldiers and officers equality with their white counterparts, which effectively meant that Afro-Argentine officers could command white troops.

There were also a number of free Afro-Argentine battalions who fought during the wars of independence. General José de San Martín's Army of the Andes had two exclusively African and Afro-Argentine battalions, the Hunter Battalions Seven and Eight, who fought in the Battles of Chacabuco (1817), Cancha Rayada (1818), and Maipú (1818), as well as in the campaigns of Upper Peru (1820–24). Approximately 2,500 African and

Afro-Argentine soldiers fought in San Martín's army; of these, only 143 returned. While it is probable that many of those who did not return deserted the army in Chile, Peru, or Ecuador, the majority died during the campaign.

In 1813, foreigners were ordered to sell their slaves for a low price so that they could become soldiers, and in January 1815, Carlos de Alvear, leader of the Argentine confederation, required a certain percentage of all slaves, between 15 and 30 percent, to be sold into the army, pending eventual freedom one year after the end of the war. Military service, as well as being a ticket to freedom, was one of the few avenues of social mobility open to Afro-Argentine men, some of whom rose to officer status. The Afro-Argentine officer class was a small minority within the Afro-Argentine soldier population, though black elites never enjoyed the same advantages and opportunities as their white counterparts. Freedom and position for black people were in this context, as in many others, more nominal than practical. The Battle of Sipe-Sipe in 1815 was a turning point; the free black battalions were almost totally wiped out and were replaced by regiments of slaves—earning their manumission—officered by whites.

The Gradual End of Slavery and the Persistence of Racism

Slaves and their children began to gain freedom in 1813 by means of the "Law of the Free Womb," granting freedom to slaves born in the United Provinces of the River Plate, as Argentina was then called, after January 31, 1813. Boys became free men on reaching the age of 20, while girls were granted freedom at the age of 16, or as soon as they were married. In practice, however, many Afro-Argentines born after this date did not escape slavery, possibly because they were not aware of their legal status. Requirements for the acquisition of citizenship for free Africans were more stringent than for immigrants, who had either to reside 10 years in Spanish territory, marry a Spanish person, or contribute financially to the nation. Africans and people of African descent had to provide service to the nation, have legitimate parentage, behave well, and be financially independent.

The most common method of achieving freedom for enslaved men was manumission through service in the Argentine army. Drafted slaves in the armies during the war of independence were granted freedom after five years of service in segregated black regiments and battalions. Their status during their period of service was defined as *liberto*, which granted them an intermediate position between slavery and freedom.

Manumission through military service was not open to women, who commonly bought their freedom by working on their own account while in domestic servitude and saving money, a process known as *coartación* (*see also* COARTACIÓN UNDER SPANISH LAW). The price was commonly set at the sum that the slave owner had originally paid for the enslaved person. In independent Argentina, Africans and Afro-Argentines had the right to purchase their freedom. Slaves who had acquired a skill were at an advantage in that their services were rendered more valuable to an employer. Slaves regularly purchased cheap lottery tickets, some of them lucky enough to win the 300 pesos required at this time to purchase their freedom. This process of gradual emancipation led to the percentage of free Africans and Afro-Argentines among the black population in the city of Buenos Aires nearly tripling between 1810 and 1827 from 22.6 percent to 63.4 percent.

The 1827 municipal census showed, for those for whom a profession was recorded, an overwhelming concentration of Afro-Argentines in skilled, semiskilled, and unskilled manual labor. The percentage for whites in manual labor was 52 percent, as compared with 94 percent for Afro-Argentines. By 1838, 15,000 Africans and Afro-Argentines composed almost one-quarter of the population of the city of Buenos Aires.

The intense racism of the *sociedad de las castas*, the caste society of the Spanish administration, persisted, in society at least, after independence. George T. Love, an English visitor to Buenos Aires in the mid-1820s, juxtaposed what he considered to be polar opposites in the racial hierarchy of the time: "I smiled sometimes to see an elegant *criollo* [Spanish-Argentine] having their cigar lit by a dirty Negro." Afro-Argentines were dramatically disproportionately represented in the prisons; in 1825, of 158 men serving sentences in the provincial presidio, 65 percent were *de color*.

From the independence era and throughout the 19th century, judges and justices of the peace were always white, a custom that continued even during the dictatorship of Juan Manuel de Rosas from 1829 to 1852, despite his reputation for amicable relationships with Afro-Argentines. Popular verses sung by *cancioneros* during the Rosas era indicate that the dictator courted popularity among the Afro-Argentines, particularly through the personages of his wife, Encarnación, and his daughter, Manuelita. In a famous painting of the Rosas family, *Candombe Federal, Época de Rosas* by Martín Boneo, Juan Manuel, Encarnación, and Manuelita Rosas are depicted attending a *candombe* celebration of the Congo Augunga *nation* in front of the *nation's* house. Rosas also employed Afro-Argentines as soldiers and officers in the army. He employed an Afro-Argentine battalion, Restaurador de las Leyes, with an Afro-Argentine commander and major. After the fall of Rosas in 1852, despite the Buenos Aires Constituent Assembly's declaration of abolition that same year, the conditions and visibility of black Argentines deteriorated markedly.

The British abolitionist influence was codified in Argentina in the form of the 1839 Treaty between Great Britain and the Argentine Confederation for the Abolition of the Traffic in Slaves. The treaty was negotiated between the Argentine minister for foreign affairs, Felipe Arana, and the British chargé d'affaires, John Henry Mandeville, and formally abolished the slave trade in the Argentine Confederation. In 1852, the Argentine Constituent Assembly in the province of Santa Fé declared that there were no longer any slaves in the Argentine Confederation and that those who were still on the territory were freed by the constitution. This declaration made Argentina, along with Uruguay, one of the last Spanish-American nations officially to abolish slavery. Shortly thereafter, Buenos Aires split from the Argentine Confederation until 1861, and the provincial constitution of Buenos Aires prohibited the slave trade but stopped short of full abolition.

Aftermath and Conclusion

At midcentury, many mestizos and Afro-Argentines lived in the city of Buenos Aires, clustered in specific districts. After Rosas's fall from power, Afro-Argentine *nations* and events such as *candombes* were stigmatized by their association with the dictatorship. Though both features of the Afro-Argentine community survived, membership of *nations* declined, as many Afro-Argentines chose to integrate fully into Buenos Aires society. Many upper-class Afro-Argentines redefined themselves as *de clase* rather than *de color*, while young Afro-Argentines distanced themselves from the separatism of the *nations*. Afro-Argentine working-class newspapers referred to their readership as the *sociedad de color*.

The historian George Reid Andrews considers this as evidence of attempts to integrate into mainstream Argentine society and to become part of the nascent class system in the city of Buenos Aires. Andrews concludes that this attempt failed and that Afro-Argentines never succeeded in progressing from a caste to a class. In current parlance, the term *de clase* among Afro-Argentines, therefore, simply means a person of color. Growing economic competition among social groups in response to mass immigration and the development of the Buenos Aires economy in the latter quarter of the 19th century led to increasing racial inequality. Furthermore, the availability of cheap immigrant labor removed the city's dependence on Afro-Argentine workers and diluted their influence as a lobbying group.

On a practical level, the acquisition of freedom did not drastically improve the living conditions or social life of Afro-Argentines. Despite formal guarantees of equality in the 1853 constitution, they faced institutional and informal discrimination. Legislation at this time formally outlawed segregation in public schools and in the army. However, as often befell Afro-Americans in the United States during the same period, Afro-Argentines were regularly prohibited from entering certain public places and were even purposefully overcharged for services. Physical punishment was employed in disciplining Afro-Argentine workers. Education was denied them, as were membership in certain religious orders and high government positions. The local authorities excluded Afro-Argentines from education, except in the area of religion. Even in the 1870s, Afro-Argentine students suffered from discrimination in public schools.

Informal racism against Afro-Argentines in Buenos Aires was exacerbated by the fact that their very existence cast doubt upon the literati's assertion that Buenos Aires was a white European city. In 1880, both criollo and Afro-Argentine newspapers carried the story of a scandal that occurred when some theaters and dance halls in Buenos Aires refused to admit Afro-Argentines to their masked balls. Afro-Argentine representatives made an official complaint to the authorities, and the police attempted, unsuccessfully, to force the theaters to admit them to the balls. Despite the fact that the law was on their side when opposing discrimination, Afro-Argentines still had to contend with such racism in a city that theoretically guaranteed them full equality.

One of the few truly famous Afro-Argentines was Antonio Ruiz, who became known by his "war name" of Falucho, and was emblematic of the Afro-Argentine contribution to the war of independence. Falucho was a military sentinel in the River Plate Regiment of the Army of the Andes in 1824. When the regiment capitulated, Falucho refused to honor the Spanish flag and was executed. Bartolomé Mitre, future president of the Argentine Republic, published Falucho's story in 1857, stressing that patriotism could be inspired even in someone he considered a lowly black soldier: "Falucho . . . fell crying *Viva Buenos Aires*! Happy is the country that can inspire such feelings in the heart of a rough Negro soldier!" The entire story, of a submissive but patriotic black soldier, may have simply been an invention of Bartolomé Mitre's in 1857. It fits the mythical paradigm that prevailed in Buenos Aires of Afro-Argentines as submissive and loyal.

By 1895, there were just 305 Africans living in Argentina. The Afro-Argentine population, however, is much more difficult to quantify. A vast problem in studying the Afro-Argentines is the almost ubiquitous perception that they were the victims of history and that their "disappearance" was somehow inevitable. The cessation of migration from Africa from the second quarter of the 19th century meant that there were no newly arrived Africans to replenish the population. There were five principal reasons for the decline: death and injury in wars, intermarriage, low birth rates and high mortality rates, the decline in the slave trade, and reclassification of black people as white or mestizo. No accurate count is possible, because records from this period are spotty at best, and many people deliberately concealed their African heritage.

The African and Afro-Argentine population of Argentina, originally taken to the country as slaves, underwent serious decline during the 19th century, facilitating the invention of the Argentine nation as a country of European immigrants. Today, between 2,000 and 4,000 people claim descent from Africans who arrived in Argentina prior to the 20th century, though some claim that in fact between 500,000 and 2,000,000 Argentines have African roots.

Claire Healy

FURTHER READING
Andrews, George Reid. "The Afro-Argentine Officers of Buenos Aires Province, 1800–1860." *Journal of Negro History* 64, no. 2 (1979): 85–100.
———. *The Afro-Argentines of Buenos Aires, 1800–1900.* Madison: University of Wisconsin Press, 1980.
———. *Afro Latin-America: 1800–2000.* New York: Oxford University Press, 2004.
———. "Race versus Class Association: The Afro-Argentines of Buenos Aires, 1850–1900." *Journal of Latin American Studies* 11, no. 1 (1979): 19–39.
Diggs, Irene. "The Negro in the Viceroyalty of the Rio de la Plata." *Journal of Negro History* 36, no. 3 (1951): 281–301.
Healy, Claire. "Afro-Argentines and Argentine Historiography." *Atlantic Studies* 3, no. 1 (2006): 111–120.
Lewis, Marvin A. *Afro-Argentine Discourse: Another Dimension of the Black Diaspora.* Columbia: University of Missouri Press, 1996.
Mitre, Bartolomé. "Falucho." *Phylon* 5, no. 2 (1944): 136–137.
Naro, Nancy Priscilla, ed. *Blacks, Coloureds and National Identity in Nineteenth-Century Latin America.* London: ILAS, University of London, 2003.
Shumway, Nicholas. *The Invention of Argentina.* Berkeley and Los Angeles: University of California Press, 1991.

ARKANSAS

Arkansas is a state of the United States bordered on the north by MISSOURI; on the east by the Mississippi

River, beyond which lie TENNESSEE and MISSISSIPPI; on the south by LOUISIANA; and on the west by TEXAS and OKLAHOMA. Geography is diverse, ranging from mountains (the Ozarks and Ouachita) to lowland plains. The river valleys of the Mississippi and the Red River are fertile and suitable for plantation crops such as COTTON CULTIVATION and tobacco growing. Spaniards and their Afro-Cuban servants led by Hernando de Soto in 1540 were the first group of Europeans and Africans to visit what is now the U.S. state of Arkansas: They found Native American farming communities and densely populated villages throughout the South. The state's name (like the state of Kansas's name) is derived from the Quapaw Indians. Indian populations declined dramatically in the wake of de Soto's voyage, and when European settlement began in the 17th century, there were few native people remaining in the state.

Colonial History

First explored by the Spanish in the 16th century, the area was part of the land claimed for France in the 17th century by Robert Cavelier, sieur de La Salle. During his voyage down the Mississippi River in 1682, La Salle claimed for France a vast region of land on both sides of the Mississippi River, stretching from the Gulf of Mexico to Canada and including present-day Arkansas. Henri de Tonti founded Arkansas Post in the eastern part of the state in 1686 as a way to connect Illinois and La Salle's planned colony of Louisiana, but the post was abandoned before the Louisiana colony was settled. In 1721, Arkansas Post was reestablished and remained in existence (sometimes a tenuous existence) throughout the colonial period, although the post was sometimes moved in response to attacks by Indians.

Both indentured servants and African-American slaves were taken to Arkansas during this early colonial settlement. Most of the colonists in Arkansas, blacks as well as whites, during this period were hunters or traders who dealt with the Quapaw Indians. The colony supplied NEW ORLEANS, LOUISIANA, with meat from bison and bear along with products made from such animals.

In 1762 and 1763, the French lost their claim to their land in North America in the peace settlements after the SEVEN YEARS' WAR. The Louisiana Territory, including Arkansas, became Spanish in treaties signed on November 3, 1762. Beginning in the 1760s and especially in the 1780s, farming grew in Arkansas.

At the end of the colonial era in 1802, the population of Arkansas Post was fewer than 500, including between 50 and 60 slaves. A few free people of color also lived at Arkansas Post at this time, working primarily as unskilled laborers and in the fur trade.

The Louisiana Purchase and Arkansas Statehood

In 1800, with the Treaty of San Ildefonso, Napoléon Bonaparte regained the Louisiana Territory for France, with plans to develop a colonial empire. But when his forces were unable to secure Saint-Domingue (see also HAITIAN REVOLUTION), Napoléon was certain that any army sent to Louisiana would be easily captured by British forces. Needing cash, he was receptive when the United States offered to purchase New Orleans. The United States bought the entire Louisiana Territory for $15 million in 1803. The area that became the state of Arkansas was initially part of the District of Louisiana and was renamed and redefined several times during the years that followed (becoming the Louisiana Territory in 1805, Arkansas County in 1813, and the Arkansas Territory in 1819). In the 1820s, treaties with the Quapaw, Osage, and Cherokee Indians added to Arkansas lands or helped define its boundaries, and by 1830, most of the Indians in Arkansas had been pushed west as a result of these treaties.

Arkansas was admitted to the Union on June 15, 1836. The population grew dramatically after Arkansas achieved statehood. In 1810, for instance, there were approximately 1,000 whites and slaves in the Arkansas Territory. The population had grown to approximately 30,000 inhabitants in 1830, and that number tripled by 1840. By 1860, there were more than 400,000 inhabitants in Arkansas, including more than 110,000 slaves. Only 144 free blacks were included in this number. The following table shows the evolution of the black population of Arkansas under American rule. The figures are drawn from census records and may not reflect marginalized people such as runaways, Afro-Indians living in a tribal setting, and very poor country people.

As planters moved to Arkansas, they took slaves with them and imported slaves from other states. By the time Arkansas joined the Union, cotton production and slave ownership were beginning to define the delta region of the state, along the eastern and southeastern frontiers, while other areas were still defined by subsistence farming. Between the late 1830s and the early 1860s, the cotton plantation society grew, especially in the south and east of the state, and cotton became Arkansas's most important commercial crop. As the number and wealth of planters grew, the divide between planters and small farmers widened: economically, socially, and politically. This divide lasted through the AMERICAN CIVIL WAR, 1861–65.

By 1860, Arkansas was the frontier for King Cotton in the South: Frontier is the operative word—the state as a whole had prospered in the 1850s as a result of high prices for cotton, but the state's population was still low and primarily rural, and travel in the state was still difficult. Its

AFRICAN-AMERICAN POPULATION OF ARKANSAS, 1820–1900

Year	Slaves	Free People of Color	Free People of Color as a Percentage of Total Population	Total Population
1820	1,600	71	0.5%	14,273
1830	4,570	141	0.5%	30,388
1840	19,935	465	0.5%	97,574
1850	47,100	608	0.3%	209,897
1860	111,115	144	0.0%	435,450
1870		122,169	25.2%	484,471
1880		210,666	25.3%	802,525
1890		309,117	27.4%	1,128,179
1900		366,856	28.0%	1,311,564

largest city was Little Rock, with a population of less than 4,000.

Free People of Color and the Rise of Racial Discrimination

The identity of the first free black or person of color in Arkansas and the way he or she became free are unknown, but it is known that very small numbers of free blacks were in Arkansas Post in the 1720s. Arkansas, as part of the Louisiana Territory, officially was under the same regulations as Louisiana and the larger settlement at New Orleans. By 1724, a set of laws known as the Code Noir was established as a result of concerns about the number of blacks and those of mixed parentage. Based on Louis XIV's Black Code, Louisiana's Code Noir subjected both slaves and free people of color to restrictive legislation, even though the Code Noir declared that people of color, once free (whether born free or manumitted), had the same rights as other free persons (*see also* CODE NOIR IN FRENCH LAW). The code also forbade whites to marry or keep people of color as mistresses, although this restriction was often ignored in the frontier society, where women were scarce.

Indeed, manumission of slaves was easy under French, and later Spanish, law as whites and free persons of color could free slaves in wills, after a period of service, or for other reasons. Slaves also became free in illegal ways—running away and then living as free.

Generally, during French and, to a much greater extent, Spanish rule, the numbers of free people of color grew in Louisiana, and especially in New Orleans, but a large population of free blacks never existed in Arkansas during colonial times. Recall, though, that as late as 1810 the number of residents in Arkansas was 1,000 total. SLAVE OWNERS in Arkansas were usually small farmers, who owned between one and three slaves.

After the United States purchased Louisiana in 1803 and the territory grew and became a state, the number of free blacks in Arkansas remained small, never surpassing the population of 660 in 1858 (at which point the total population was growing toward 400,000). The explanation for such a low number of free blacks is entirely economic. Slaves in the Upper South were being manumitted in the face of agricultural depression, but slaves in the newer areas of the South (e.g., Mississippi, Tennessee, and Arkansas) were in great demand to work the fertile soil.

Free blacks in Arkansas generally resided in rural areas (unusual for the South, where free blacks most often congregated in cities), and they could own land. Marion County perhaps had the largest number of free blacks of any county in Arkansas, and free blacks outnumbered slaves by 1850. Blacks there, such as David and John Hall, could and did own land. David Hall was involved in the fur trade and made whiskey, and he supported his growing family by helping them to gain their own lands and to establish their own cattle herds.

Especially after the bloody Nat Turner slave revolt in Virginia in 1831, free blacks were viewed with suspicion in Arkansas, where some whites, fearing slave insurrections, claimed that the very existence of free blacks acted as a subversive element. Indeed, abolitionism was controversial in Arkansas, as whites vowed to lynch abolitionists of any color. Antiabolitionists worked to establish laws to restrict free blacks' rights and movements. In 1843, for instance, free blacks were prohibited to enter the state, in an effort to stop the growth of that segment of the population. And, in 1859, the legislature passed a law that required free blacks to leave the state by the end of the year: If they did not, they would be jailed and hired out until enough funds had been gained to pay for their transport, or they could choose a master and become slaves again. The law proved effective: In 1858, the number of free blacks was 660; in 1860, the number was reduced to

144. Many of these people moved to KANSAS, a free state, and some returned during the war or in its immediate aftermath.

The American Civil War and Reconstruction

While the secessionist element in Arkansas was strong in the early 1860s, a March 1861 convention decided to remain with the Union. However, after the attack on Fort Sumter and President Lincoln's call for volunteers in April, Arkansans supported secession. On May 6, 1861, Arkansas withdrew from the Union and soon joined the Confederacy. A small group in the north-central part of the state, however, remained staunch Unionists, resisting the authority of the Confederacy and sending troops to fight on the Union side.

Arkansas saw limited formal military action during the Civil War, but Thomas Hindman, sent to Little Rock by the Confederates to command the region, authorized guerrilla warfare against Union forces and their lines of supply. Unionists, both black and white, also organized guerrilla groups to attack the Confederacy. The Union was successful despite the guerrilla warfare, capturing Arkansas Post, Little Rock, Pine Bluff, and other cities by 1863, although fighting continued in parts of Arkansas into 1864. The fighting was sometimes bitter and personal between guerrilla groups, especially when racial conflict joined with class and political divides.

Many slaves seized the opportunity to leave their plantations or farms during this time, and Union officials decided to enlist blacks who were willing to fight. More than 5,000 freedmen in Arkansas would eventually join the Union army in regiments such as the 1st Arkansas Volunteer Infantry Regiment. Confederates who fought these freedmen treated them ruthlessly, killing them even after they surrendered. For example, more than 80 black soldiers were massacred by Confederate forces at Poison Springs, Arkansas, on April 18, 1864. These soldiers belonged to the 1st Kansas Colored Infantry, but many of the Kansas soldiers were actually free Arkansans who had left the state after the 1859 law or who had fled slavery. Some blacks participated in federal land experiments on abandoned plantations at this time, wherein freedmen worked for pay on plantations the federal government had leased. Arkansas blacks were all declared free by the Emancipation Proclamation, January 1, 1863, and their freedom became effective as the state was conquered by the Union army.

Aftermath

After the Civil War ended in 1865, slavery was officially abolished in the United States and Reconstruction began throughout the South. During Reconstruction, Arkansas and other Southern states were placed under military rule (*see* RECONSTRUCTION IN THE UNITED STATES). Arkansas was readmitted to the Union in June 1868 after drafting a new constitution that banned slavery, granted black males the right to vote, and established free public education. Eight blacks were among the 70 delegates who drafted the new constitution.

For a brief time, blacks made progress in the state, holding positions of power in government at the state, county, and local levels, often through the fusion system (wherein blacks and Unionist whites worked together to ensure that both had representation in government). In 1873, for instance, the Arkansas General Assembly included 20 black members. Additionally, blacks in towns gained some degree of prosperity as black commercial districts that housed merchants and craftsmen developed. Many of these individuals were "carpetbaggers," blacks from the North who sought their fortunes in the opportunities of Reconstruction. Black business and fraternal organizations, such as the Mosaic Templars of America, also formed and grew; blacks also formed their own churches. Blacks in rural areas often did not fare as well, as sharecropping developed as a system that largely replaced slavery, and both blacks and poor whites participated.

White Democrats in Arkansas began working toward disenfranchising blacks in the 1880s and 1890s, first using intimidation tactics and then institutionalizing disenfranchisement through literacy tests, residency requirements, and poll taxes. By 1900, white elites were using all-white primaries at both the county and state levels to reduce black participation in government further. Although the most powerful middle-class urban blacks tried to defeat such laws as the segregated passenger coach bill, white supremacists were ultimately successful, and Jim Crow laws that resulted in "separate but equal" transportation, schools, and other public services were passed in Arkansas.

These provisions for segregation and disfranchisement lasted into the 20th century, although leaders of the Mosaic Templars of America and others fought against racial oppression. In 1919, for instance, black sharecroppers attempted to unionize in Elaine, Arkansas. A meeting of the Progressive Farmers and Household Union of America ended in an exchange of gunfire between the blacks guarding the meeting and whites, followed the next day by white mobs' massacring the blacks they believed to be responsible. Twelve black men received the death penalty for their actions but were defended by Scipio Africanus Jones, a prominent black lawyer and politician from a former free colored family, who won their freedom on appeal.

Segregation and discrimination persisted until challenged in the latter half of the 20th century by the Civil

Rights movement. Arkansas was an important center for civil rights activism as the segregationist governor, Orval Faubus, tried to block desegregation of the state's public schools in 1957 and backed down only under the threat of force from federal troops.

Summer Leibensperger

FURTHER READING

Ashmore, Harry S. *Arkansas: A Bicentennial History.* New York: W. W. Norton, 1978.

Bailey, Anne J., and Daniel E. Sutherland, eds. *Civil War Arkansas: Beyond Battles and Leaders.* Fayetteville: University of Arkansas Press, 2000.

Cortner, Richard C. *A Mob Intent on Death: The NAACP and the Arkansas Riot Cases.* Middletown, Conn.: Wesleyan University Press, 1988.

Dougan, Michael B. *Confederate Arkansas: The People and Policies of a Frontier State in Wartime.* Tuscaloosa: University of Alabama Press, 1976.

Finley, Randy. *From Slavery to Uncertain Freedom: The Freedmen's Bureau in Arkansas, 1865–1869.* Fayetteville: University of Arkansas Press, 1996.

Higgins, Billy D. "The Origins and Fate of the Marion County Free Black Community." *Arkansas Historical Quarterly* 54 (Winter 1995): 427–443.

Woods, James M. *Rebellion and Realignment: Arkansas's Road to Secession.* Fayetteville: University of Arkansas Press, 1987.

ARMY   *See* REGULAR ARMY.

ARTISANS

People of color in the Americas often worked as artisans or skilled workers both in rural areas and in the cities. Plantation owners who could afford to spare laborers from the fields would often train slaves to work as carpenters, masons, wheelwrights (makers of carts and carriages), coopers (makers of barrels), millers (skilled workers in mills, especially sugar mills), and blacksmiths and in other skilled trades. This enabled the master to have these expensive tasks performed "in-house," paying only the cost of training the slave. The slaves who received this training could often find ways to earn some income for themselves by working for other employers in their spare time. With money in hand, it would sometimes be possible to buy their freedom, especially if the plantation was suffering financial difficulties—which was often the case with plantations in a volatile commodity market. Many of these skilled slaves thus became free.

Once they were free, the trades were one area of activity that people of color were allowed to practice almost everywhere. The remnants of the medieval European guild system were a slight handicap in Spanish and Portuguese colonies, but in French, Dutch, and English colonies there were almost no restrictions on who could practice a trade. Even in the Iberian colonies, the old rules were increasingly irrelevant. The new rules in the colonies, the ones designed to protect white supremacy and colonial dependence, rarely placed any restrictions on free black tradesmen. Indeed, in some places, it was assumed that all or almost all free black men would go into the trades, and people identified themselves as tradesmen even if they were actually pursuing other occupations. A black man working in a trade was not a very threatening figure to a white political leader, not in the way that a black policeman or militiaman, or a black planter and slave owner, or even a black peasant living in the backcountry might be. Of course, black tradesmen represented competition for white tradesmen, and there were race riots and racially motivated attacks on free blacks in the Northern states of the United States and in Haiti during the early years of the revolution. But working-class whites generally did not have much political power and often—especially outside the United States—were few in number and not well organized. So the skilled trades represented a sector of society where free blacks were welcome, were needed, and could make a respectable living.

The United States: The Northern States

Many free blacks in the North worked at some sort of trade. For example, although he spent most of his time as a writer and lecturer, FREDERICK DOUGLASS worked as a ship's carpenter for part of his time in the North before the AMERICAN CIVIL WAR, 1861–65. James Forten, patriarch of the influential free black FORTEN FAMILY of Philadelphia, first worked as a chimney sweep before being apprenticed to a sailmaker and then becoming a master sailmaker and nautical entrepreneur. The hero of the WAR OF AMERICAN INDEPENDENCE, 1775–83, PETER SALEM worked as a furniture carpenter after the war.

The origins of the Northern free black population, and its historical evolution, almost guaranteed this outcome. Slaves were rarely employed as farmworkers in most places in the North. Most slaves in the North worked in urban areas, either as personal servants or as assistants to businessmen or tradesmen. They had plenty of opportunities learning the trades while slavery existed. Those who could earn good incomes as tradesmen were more likely than personal servants or farmworkers to gain their freedom under slavery. When slavery ended in the North in the late 18th and early 19th centuries, the area entered a long period of economic growth culminating in the American Industrial Revolution of the mid-19th century. Even though immigration from Europe was growing throughout this period, there was a generalized labor shortage, particularly in the Eastern Seaboard cities. Many immigrants entered America with the intention of moving to the frontier and taking up land, and although not all achieved their goal, this desire was shared by many native-born whites who were also free to move west. Free blacks, on the other hand, found it difficult to move to the frontier because of BLACK LAWS IN THE MIDWEST barring African-American settlement in the new states. They were therefore natural targets for recruitment into the trades and industrial employment.

Many blacks who moved to the North from the slave states already had some training in a trade. In some cases, it was this trade that helped them gain their freedom, allowing them to earn money to finance a getaway or ransom themselves. Even those without many skills when they arrived often received training from fellow free blacks and then worked as artisans.

The United States: The Upper South
Many free African Americans in the northern tier of slave states—Delaware, Maryland, Virginia, Kentucky, and Missouri—also worked as artisans. The Upper South had many free blacks. Some of these people had gained their freedom through personal relationships with their master or by self-purchase, as most free colored elsewhere in the Americas did. Others, though, had gained their freedom in a group, as the result of an ideologically motivated manumission by a master convinced that slavery was incompatible with American values. GEORGE WASHINGTON famously called for the liberation of all of his slaves in his will, though some were only actually freed upon the death of his wife, Martha, and many other masters did the same. Slavery was almost abolished by law in Virginia in 1832. At this time, land values were plunging in Virginia, and many plantation owners were in financial trouble, ready to sell freedom to those slaves who could afford it even if they were not ready to set every one of them free—and the slaves who could afford to ransom themselves were often artisans. The large and diverse free colored population in Virginia was limited by law and by competition from the large poor white population from pursuing many occupations or owning large farms. However, many of the skilled trades remained legal and attractive as a way to earn a living.

Farther west, the Upper South states of Kentucky and Missouri had few plantations. Slaves in these states often worked on small farms, where they had to learn a variety of tasks. There was a great deal of informality about job classifications in the West, and many people of color worked at jobs that would be called trades in eastern, urban contexts. As slaves gained their freedom, the rapidly growing frontier economy had plenty of niches in its lower levels for them. Probably a greater proportion were

small farmers there than in Virginia, but the trades were still a popular option.

The United States: The Deep South
There were fewer free blacks in the Deep South, especially outside the old heartlands of slavery in the Carolina/Georgia low country and southern Louisiana. Self-purchase was rare and mass manumissions nearly unknown and generally discouraged by law. Slaves mainly gained their freedom through personal, often familial, relationships with the master. These personal relationships continued after manumission, and so many free blacks in the Deep South lived on or near their native plantations, receiving support from their former masters and working on their behalf. In the United States, it is especially in the Deep South that one encounters the occasional free colored slave owner and planter. People of color who gained their freedom through self-purchase often left the Deep South, either moving to the Upper South near where they were born in order to reunite with separated family members or moving to the North.

The British Caribbean
Jamaican free coloreds, with the exception of members of the large maroon communities, concentrated in the cities. This was because there were harsh laws preventing them from owning large amounts of land or supervising more than a few slaves. Jamaica also had large cities and plenty of work for free colored artisans. In the countryside, large Jamaican plantations occasionally employed a few free black artisans, but the Deficiency Laws that prevented them from hiring free black managers also discouraged employing any but white artisans. In the British Lesser Antilles, the cities were smaller, and slavery had been in existence for longer. This meant that there were fewer opportunities in urban trades and that gifts of land to free coloreds and small purchases had had more time to build up a rural small farmer class. Thus, there were more rural free coloreds and fewer artisans in such places as Barbados, despite a difficult legal climate for black landowners. In those British islands that had been conquered from southern European colonialists, such as Trinidad or St. Lucia, some of the French or Spanish culture, with its larger rural free colored population, survived the British laws.

The French Caribbean
Because French laws permitted land and slave ownership to free people of color on pretty much the same basis as whites, many free coloreds in the French colonies lived in the countryside. This is especially true of people who had family or close patronage relationships with white planters. Those free coloreds without such

relationships, as did the poorer free blacks in North America, gravitated to the cities. The French island colony of Saint-Domingue in particular had a large free black population in its two largest cities, Cap-Français and Port-au-Prince. Many of these people were actually artisans. In addition, many other free coloreds who were engaged in real estate entrepreneurship, moneylending, service industries, or retail commerce would claim membership in a skilled trade because of legal restrictions on their real profession or the higher social status of an artisan. A good example of this phenomenon is the merchant ZABEAU BELLANTON, who owned a shop selling jams and candies but made most of her money from slave trading and real estate speculation. She referred to herself as a *confiseuse*, or baker of sweets, a respectable trade, throughout her career.

Spanish America: Mainland

The medieval guild system was still strong in Spain when the conquistadores entered the Americas in the 16th century. The guild masters sought to establish their power in the Western Hemisphere but were less than completely successful. At the same time, they were losing their power in Spain to a series of reform measures putting power over city government in the hands of the central government. Still, practicing a skilled trade in a Spanish colony required some steps to become certified that were not required elsewhere. Free Africans had been members of guilds in Spain, and there were no explicit racial restrictions on guild membership, but most guild members were white. However, guild membership passed down through families, and so free coloreds who were not the children of guild members had difficulty entering the guilds.

As in other colonies, rural landholders would seek to have African-American slaves or Indian peons trained in skilled trades so that they could avoid having to pay an outsider. In addition, many guild masters and entrepreneurs set up workshops, or *obrajes*, in the cities using Native Americans as workers and African slaves as overseers and technical specialists. Mexico, in particular, saw the importation of many slaves from Africa, especially in the second half of the 16th century, chosen especially for their skills as metal or fabric workers, imported to teach these skills to Indian workers. The colonial government's strong policy of mercantilism kept foreign manufactured goods out of Spanish America and encouraged the skilled trades in the colonies. Slaves working in these skilled positions might often gain their freedom, especially because of the system of *coartación* that made self-purchase easier (*see* COARTACIÓN UNDER SPANISH LAW). Often in the highlands of Mexico and Peru, free black skilled work-

men, surrounded by huge numbers of Native Americans, would achieve racial promotion through social status and marriage to the status of zambo or mulatto, joining the *castas,* or middle racial caste, and over the generations their descendants would lose the African element in their racial identity.

The artisan sector of the economy suffered great decline in the 18th century as the Spanish government, as part of the Bourbon Reforms, loosened its mercantilist policies and let manufactured goods from Britain and China enter its colonial markets. Artisans of all colors suffered, but because of racial discrimination those identified as free coloreds were hit the hardest.

Spanish America: Caribbean

Racial promotion was less likely in areas where African Americans were more numerous, and Indians rare or altogether absent, such as the coasts of Central and South America and the Caribbean island colonies. As can be seen in the specific articles about these colonies, there was a remarkable change in their society when sugar plantations became more common and efficient in the late 18th century. Prior to that time, a large proportion of the people of these colonies were free coloreds. There were few or no Indians, small numbers of whites, and few slaves. All niches in society from the peasantry almost to the very top were filled by people of African ancestry, though lighter skin and European family members still counted for a lot. Nevertheless, in these colonies weak internal markets meant that artisans were few and did not make a good living. An example of a free colored artisan of this time is MIGUEL ENRÍQUEZ of Puerto Rico. One of the most noted pirates of the early 18th century, Enríquez started as a shoemaker in San Juan before going on to become one of the wealthiest men on the island.

Christopher Columbus introduced sugar to what is now the Dominican Republic on his second voyage in the 1490s, but sugar cultivation in Spanish colonies did not take off until after 1750. The new world the sugar revolution created looked a lot more like the Anglo-American social system, where free blacks were restricted to a limited set of economic options, including especially the skilled trades. White immigration grew, but there was still a labor shortage. Many plantations employed free colored skilled workers while the newly vibrant cities also had many economic niches open. This period coincided with the Bourbon Reforms in government, at which time the power of the guilds to restrict who could pursue a trade was pretty much ended. As a result, the skilled trades became an important area for free coloreds in the Spanish Caribbean in the late 1700s, and their descendants remain numerous in small business, construction, and the trades to this day.

Brazil

Portuguese guilds were weaker in the 16th century than those in Spain, and the frontier nature of Brazilian society did not permit them to grow strong there. The 18th-century Bourbon Reforms in Brazil were even more sweeping and modernizing than those in Spanish America, resulting in the suppression of most of the power the guilds had been able to acquire there. As a result, free blacks were able to work more freely in the trades in Brazil than in Spanish America. However, there were also many other areas of activity open to them, similarly to the conditions in the French colonies. Free Afro-Brazilians could own land and slaves, and many did, from small peasant holdings to large plantations. They could move to the frontier, and some of the famous *bandeirantes* (explorers) were of African descent. A mulatto companion of the famous explorer Antônio Rodrigues Arzão, for example, started the fabulous gold rush in Ouro Prêto in 1693.

Conclusion

Artisanal labor was a way that free coloreds could make a living that was both almost universally permitted to them by law and custom and generally well rewarded. As a result, free coloreds were disproportionately found in this sector of the economy in almost every slave society. In some places alternative and more attractive means of making a living were open to free coloreds, and if there were alternative working-class populations (such as poor whites in the United States or mestizos and native peoples in Mexico and Peru) to do the skilled labor, then the free colored dominance of the trades might be lessened.

Stewart R. King

FURTHER READING

Berlin, Ira. *Many Thousands Gone: The First Two Centuries of Slavery in America.* Cambridge, Mass.: Harvard University Press, 1998.

Marable, Manning. *How Capitalism Underdeveloped Black America: Problems in Race, Political Economy, and Society.* New York: South End Press, 2000.

Randall, Laura. "Making a Living: African-Americans in Nineteenth-Century New England." *Humanities* 16, no. 1 (January–February 1995) 38–43.

AUSTRALIA

The institution of chattel slavery did not exist in colonial Australia. This is not surprising in a society founded as a penal settlement in which a consistent supply of coerced indentured labor was a feature from first settlement. This, however, did not exclude the presence in Australia of people of color from the Americas.

Eleven people of African ancestry arrived as convicts aboard the ships of the First Fleet, which established the British foundation settlement in Australia at Port Jackson, to be eventually renamed Sydney, in January 1788. These 11 were all males, most of whom shared a common background of having at one stage in their earlier lives been slaves in the Americas. It is estimated that one-half of these were Loyalist sympathizers from the United States who had run away to join the British during the WAR OF AMERICAN INDEPENDENCE, 1775–83, and the remainder were free people of color from elsewhere in the British Empire. In Britain after the war, these men, for reasons mostly concerned with theft, fell afoul of the law and subsequently were sentenced to be transported to the Australian settlement of New South Wales. Treated in all respects as equals among the general convict population, for what that was worth considering their circumstances, they enjoyed varied degrees of success in their new environment. John Randall, most probably born in New Haven, Connecticut, and 44 years of age when transported, was a former soldier who had served in several significant battles of the SEVEN YEARS' WAR in America, 1755–63, as well as the War of American Independence. He earned his release from the status of criminal forced laborer and a grant of 60 acres of land in 1792, which he sold in 1801. Rejoining the army as a member of the notoriously corrupt New South Wales Corps in 1801, he served in that capacity until 1810. Randall's one official marriage and two common-law wives at different times produced several children, one of whom, Ann, died at the age of 96 in 1911, the last of the original generation of founding African Australians. Among the First Fleet African Americans were John Martin, a seaman; Daniel Gordon, who had either been abandoned or freed by his owner in CHARLESTON, SOUTH CAROLINA, in 1779; and John Caesar, a free black originally from the West Indies (although some sources suggest he had been taken there as a slave from Africa), who was to become BLACK CAESAR, a notorious bushranger operating on the fringes of the colony. George Francisco, whose brief biography includes the fascinating reference to his being a prisoner of war in France during the 1780s, was another First Fleet transportee. John Moseley ran away from his Virginia owner in 1775 and was in Britain in 1783. Found guilty of fraud by impersonation and transported to Australia, he earned his conditional pardon in 1800. Moseley, who died in 1835, prospered and became a dealer in the Rocks area of Sydney, where he maintained a house in which he employed three female servants.

Approximately 1,000 convicts and freeborn settlers of African descent arrived in colonial Australia during the first few decades of the 19th century. The origin of these people was diverse, ranging throughout the British Empire, from the West Indies to Cape Colony, South Africa. North American men of color also featured among the arrivals. William Blue from New York was a freeborn man but was transported to Sydney in 1801 as a convict. Known as "Billy Blue," he was described as a very "black, Black." Blue eventually ran a ferry service on Sydney Harbor. As he progressed in years and eccentricity, Blue dressed in a fanciful naval uniform and a top hat. He became something of a feature of the town, insisting that everyone he met on the streets call him "Commodore." Blue died in 1834, having reached almost 100 years of age. Modern-day Blues Point in Sydney Harbor recalls "Billy Blue."

The next great influx of African Americans into Australia was generated by the gold rushes during the early 1850s. This era saw an unprecedented influx into Australia of people from all corners of the globe. The vast majority of these were seeking gold, and they included many from North America, in particular California. Among these were African Americans. It was not recorded what number of African Americans entered Australia at this time, and it was of no concern for Australian colonial authorities whether an African American was a free man of color or a fugitive slave. Slavery had been abolished in the British Empire by this time, and simply setting foot on British territory made anyone free regardless of his or her prior status. Shipping manifests and the colonial census did not distinguish the race of those marked as American. Estimates are that maybe 2,000 made the journey, but nonetheless "Colored Americans" were a noticeable feature of the frenetic activity that constituted the social and physical landscape of the Australian gold fields. Denied access in much of America to land, the vote, jury service, and many schools and social services, those African Americans inclined to do so would have needed little encouragement to uproot and travel across the Pacific Ocean to seek their fortunes. Unconnected but contemporaneous with the gold rushes was a private venture, publicized in at least one American newspaper, to encourage "Free Negroes" to immigrate to Australia and settle in the continent's tropical north; the harsh climate and unpleasant reputation of the region meant that the scheme attracted no interest.

African Americans left tangible evidence of their presence in Australia during the colony's gold rush era. Place names such as Black Jack Gully, named after an African-American digger who opened it up for mining, and Black-fellow Gully, named after an "American man of color," were features of some diggings. Boston Gully, so called for George Boston, an African American who discovered one

of the richest gold-bearing gullies at the Caledonia diggings, is another example of the lasting mark made on the Australian landscape by African Americans during the 1850s.

In hard times, African Americans, as did other diggers, fell back on the trades they knew. African-American cooks became a feature of what passed for fast-food establishments in Sydney at the time. Other African Americans worked as sailors on coastal ships or in hotels and as domestic servants. Some ran refreshment stands on the diggings, tended market gardens, or managed brothels. In short, they did whatever they needed to do to make ends meet in what were quite often economically very tight circumstances. Even among the hardship some did quite well, such as Henry Johnson, who at one time owned and managed a substantial hotel and, when that business failed diversified into catering for major community events. As with all people, some African Americans got into trouble with the law. One case, which involved a cook who received 10 years hard labor for the "un-English" crime of chasing an intruder out of his kitchen with a knife, reflects more the judge's intolerance of Americans than it does the miscreant's race. When at Ballarat in December 1854 miners took up arms to defend their rights and liberties, among those who did so was JOHN JOSEPH. Joseph was from somewhere on the northeastern coast of the United States, either BOSTON, New York, or Baltimore. It is unclear whether he left America a free man or a fugitive slave. When the military and police attacked the stockade the miners had built, Joseph was prominent in its defense. Captured after resisting during the battle, Joseph and 13 others were accused of treason—a capital crime—and placed on trial. His acquittal set the precedent that led to all the other capital cases' following suit.

A significant aspect of the "Colored American" experience in Australia was the distance, both physical and emotional, it placed between them and the institutionalized racism they had experienced in the United States. "Colored Americans" in Australia celebrated August 1 rather than the traditional July 4 as a special day. This was the date of the British emancipation of slaves in the West Indies, where many of them had lived originally, and no doubt resonated among those with firsthand experience of the inequities they suffered in America. African Australians, including those from the United States, while no doubt subjected to the condescension of whites and the burlesque of public mockery represented by entertainments such as theatrical minstrel shows, otherwise enjoyed a relatively untrammeled existence. This was not because colonial Australian society was a particularly racially enlightened place, but simply that none of the facets of repression designed to maintain the

African either in servitude or at least very much in his place in society had reason to exist in Australia. Unlike for the indigenous or immigrant Chinese population, among whom race was very much the central focus of the relationship with whites, "race" for Africans was not a central fixation in colonial Australia.

The colonial history of Australia, despite its daunting physical distance from North America, offers numerous examples reflecting the African-American experience. Whether or not they were compelled to immigrate to Australia as convicts or did so of their own volition, "free men of color" played a part in the formative years of Australia.

Gregory Blake

FURTHER READING

Potts, E. Daniel, and Annette Potts. *Young America and Australian Gold: Americans and the Gold Rush of the 1850s.* St Lucia, Australia: University of Queensland Press, 1974.

Pybus, Cassandra. *Black Founders: The Unknown Story of Australia's First Black Settlers.* Sydney: University of New South Wales Press, 2006.

———. *Epic Journeys of Freedom: Runaway Slaves of the American Revolution and Their Global Quest for Liberty.* Boston: Beacon Press, 2006.

———. "A Touch of Tar: African Settlers in Colonial Australia and the Implications for Issues of Aboriginality." London Papers in Australian Studies no. 3. London: Menzies Centre for Australian Studies—Kings College London, 2001.

B

BAKER, MOSES (1730?–1823?) *Jamaican religious leader*

Known for his career as a pioneer Baptist preacher in Jamaica, Moses Baker was born around 1730 in New York City to a free black named Elizabeth. His surname was taken from Joseph Baker, a merchant seaman in whose household his mother had been raised. In 1778, Moses Baker married Susannah Ashton, a freeborn black woman who was affiliated with but not a member of the Anglican Church in New York City. Both gained literacy by attending one of the Anglican-sponsored schools for blacks operated by the Society for the Propagation of the Gospel. (*See also* PROTESTANT MAINLINE CHURCHES and EDUCATION AND LITERACY.) As did most free blacks, the Bakers took advantage of the opportunities afforded them by British occupation of New York City during the years of the WAR OF AMERICAN INDEPEDENCE, 1775–83. A British loyalist, Moses worked as a barber and wig-maker, while Susannah catered to a substantial clientele in the city as a dressmaker.

When British occupation of New York neared an end in 1783, the Bakers joined other Loyalists fleeing the city and left for Jamaica. As did the others who constituted the black Loyalist community in postrevolutionary Jamaica, the Bakers faced enormous obstacles. Since they were not Jamaican-born and were suspected by some Jamaican whites of sharing the dangerous republican ideas of the American rebels, they were denied access to formal social and economic networks. Baker rented a small shop after arriving in Kingston and continued his trade as a barber for the next three years. Falling on hard times, he later resorted to working as a farmhand in Leguine, about 15 miles from Kingston. It was there in 1787 that the Bakers reencountered Isaac Lascelles Winn, a Quaker merchant-planter and owner of the merchant ship *Duchess of Gordon,* which plied the ocean between New York and the Caribbean. (*See also* BAPTISTS AND PIETISTS.) Winn remembered Susannah from his dealings in New York and hired her to make dresses for his house servants. This new connection to Winn proved invaluable to the Bakers. Moses had been unable to work for months after an illness left him virtually blind. Pitying the situation in which the skilled and literate family found themselves, Winn agreed to pay for Baker to see a doctor and even offered him a plot of land if he would move to Winn's estate in the western parish of St. James.

Baker's year of blindness had been marked by an intense spiritual struggle. He was not a particularly religious man before moving to Leguine, but conversations with a black man named Cupid Wilkin convinced Baker to submit his life to God. Winn noted Baker's faith and agreed to support his family on the provision that Baker would oversee the religious instruction of Winn's slaves. Baker recovered his eyesight after consulting a physician on a trip to Kingston, where his fellow black American and Baptist preacher George Lisle (1750–1820) baptized him. Baker soon left for Winn's estate, Stretch and Set (later Adelphi), and began preaching among the slaves. As with his contemporary, Lisle, in Kingston, Baker's following grew rapidly. His Baptist congregation met in a chapel known as Crooked Spring, from which Baker expanded his activities in western Jamaica over the next 40 years.

Along with Lisle and a handful of other influential black itinerant preachers, Baker was responsible for the rising number of Christian converts among Jamaica's slave and free black populations during the last decade of the 18th century. Baker had developed an extensive preaching circuit that included a large congregation in Montego Bay and chapels on various estates throughout the island's western parishes. Constant fears among Jamaica's white elite that men like Baker were secretly working to incite slave rebellions resulted in an 1802 law that forbade people to preach without legal sanction. Above age 70 and in failing health, Baker wrote a letter to the Baptist Missionary Society (BMS) in England in which he described the state of affairs in Jamaica and appealed for missionaries to be sent to the island to help him. His letter was published in two parts in the 1803 and 1804 editions of the *Evangelical Magazine,* and in 1814, the first BMS missionary arrived in Montego Bay. Baker's influence on the island continued beyond his death around 1823. His socioreligious networks provided the infrastructure for the later success of BMS missionaries in western Jamaica. By 1840, more then 60 Afro-Christian chapels were dispersed throughout the island. Second-generation Baptist leaders carried on the vision of Baker and his fellow itinerants. Many of them were leaders in the "Baptist War" (1830–32), the largest slave rebellion to occur in the British Caribbean.

J. Blake Vaughan

FURTHER READING
Ballew, Christopher Brent. *The Impact of African-American Antecedents on the Baptist Foreign Missionary Movement, 1782–1825.* New York: Edwin Mellen Press, 2004.

Clark, John, Walter Dendy, James Mursell Phillippo, and David J. East. *The Voice of Jubilee: A Narrative of the Baptist Mission, Jamaica.* London: J. Snow, 1865.

Pulis, John W., ed. *Moving On: Black Loyalists in the Afro-Atlantic World.* New York: Garland, 1999.

Sibley, Inez Knibb. *Baptists of Jamaica.* Kingston: Jamaica Baptist Union, 1965.

Turner, Mary. *Slaves and Missionaries: The Disintegration of Jamaican Slave Society, 1787–1834.* Bridgetown, Barbados: University of the West Indies (UWI Press), 1998.

BAPTISTS AND PIETISTS

Baptist teaching holds that the Baptist religion represents an ancient tradition in Christianity, dating back to the time of the apostles. Baptist churches began to spring up in Europe in the 18th century and almost at once began the project of evangelizing and teaching people of color in the Americas. The majority of blacks in Protestant countries belonged to Baptist and Pietist groups by the time slavery was abolished, and churches with Baptist ideas or affiliation remain an important part of black spiritual life to this day.

The Origins of Baptist and Pietist Churches

Baptists claim as their direct ancestors the earliest Protestant movements, the Hussites in Bohemia and the Lollards in England. These groups differed from the Catholics and from the Lutheran Protestants (*see* ROMAN CATHOLIC CHURCH and PROTESTANT MAINLINE CHURCHES) in that they laid great stress on the egalitarian, participatory, and democratic elements of the Christian message. Some groups called for completely equal sharing of worldly goods, while others accepted a social hierarchy but insisted on democratic organization of society or at least the institution of the church. They also were "believers' churches" in that they accepted as members only those people who could demonstrate to the satisfaction of the membership that they were true believers, often marking their acceptance by baptizing the new convert even if he

or she had been baptized as a baby. Both the Lollards and the Hussites were suppressed by the Catholics, but their ideas persisted. When the Reformation began in northern Europe in the 16th century with the publication of the works of Martin Luther and John Calvin, many dissident groups adopted part of the reformers' ideas while maintaining their own. Luther, Calvin, and the Protestant state churches that were to dominate northern Europe did not accept the ideas of the Anabaptists, or Pietists, as they were called at that time. As state churches, the Lutherans or Calvinists had to accommodate everybody in society; they could not limit membership to the elect. And as departments of national governments, under the authority of kings, the Protestant churches could not accept the democratic form of organization that Pietist groups tended to prefer. Moreover, Pietists during the Reformation were mostly pacifists, like the Moravians of today's Czech Republic or the Mennonites of Germany, and the Protestant countries of northern Europe were engaged in unremitting war against Catholic Europe. Pietist groups were often most successful on the margins of society during the Reformation, among poor country folk living in remote places and among the excluded poor in the cities. The egalitarian nature of their beliefs led them to accept excluded groups. By the mid-17th century, vibrant Pietist groups had sprung up across northern Europe, including the Moravians, Mennonites, Amish, and, most importantly for our purposes, the Quakers of England.

One characteristic that Pietists had in common was an unwillingness to require believers to subscribe to a specific creed or list of beliefs, so one cannot be very precise about their theology. However, most Pietists had fairly conventional Protestant ideas about how people were saved drawn from the writings of John Calvin and some earlier theologians (such as the founder of the English Lollards, John Wycliffe). They tended to believe that people were saved by direct divine intervention and that the human spirit was too weak to overcome the burden of original sin even to start the process of salvation unless God had chosen the person first. However, the harsh Calvinist idea of "double predestination"—that God chose some for salvation but others for damnation—was unacceptable to most Pietists. Many of them tended toward ideas that became known as Arminian, that God chose people on the basis of their faith, which originated in themselves. Essentially, this added to the Calvinist idea that God could choose anybody, the idea that people could choose God, and as a corollary, the idea that believers had an obligation to encourage people everywhere to make the right choice. Preaching equality, love, pacifism, democratic church organization, and limited strictness about specific theological concepts made their ideas very popular among people of color in the Americas.

Pietists in the Americas, Seventeenth–Eighteenth Centuries

The era of exploration led to the founding of Protestant colonies in the Americas after the middle of the 17th century. Pietists were among the first northern European settlers of the Americas. German Mennonites settled in the Delaware Valley of North America in the 17th century, while it was still Swedish and Dutch, even before the English Quaker leader William Penn led his coreligionists to that area, and they spread south from there to the Virginia and Carolina backcountry and the Ohio River valley. Moravian missionaries settled in Jamaica in the mid-18th century. From these bases, these groups sent missionaries far and wide throughout the Protestant colonies, especially after about 1700, when laws forbidding them to preach were mainly relaxed. Everywhere they went, they spoke to Europeans, native people, and African Americans alike. The message was especially attractive to Africans for a number of reasons related to African culture and ideas about spirituality. (*See also* AFRICAN AND SYNCRETIC RELIGIONS.) To summarize and perhaps overgeneralize about a very big and diverse continent, African religions are generally broadly relational, including the whole family, the dead and unborn, as well as the living, into a relationship with God; they are emotional instead of strictly rationalistic; they are practical in that they offer some sort of payoff for the believer in this world; and they are oral and participatory. Pietism stressed the family but also offered a very close-knit church community as almost a substitute family for those Africans who had lost their ancestors and family through being moved across the ocean involuntarily. Pietistic worship was also very emotional, especially when Baptist ideas began to grow after the Great Awakenings of the 18th and early 19th centuries. Intellectualism had a place, especially in Bible study, which was a central element in worship, but often this involved reading or reciting Bible verses in a manner reminiscent, for African Americans, of African storytell-

A service at a Washington, D.C., African-American church, 1870s. The black churches were important as gathering places for the newly freed after abolition in the United States, and their leaders were often people of color who had been free before the American Civil War. Unlike black politicians and lawyers, black preachers were often able to keep their jobs and their leadership roles in the black community even as Reconstruction failed and blacks were forced out of the public sphere. (*North Wind Picture Archives via Associated Press*)

ing. Christianity in general is otherworldly, but Pietists often laid great stress on Bible verses from the Old Testament where God promised freedom and prosperity to the people of Israel if they were faithful to their covenant with him. Pietistic churches were often millenarian, in that they expected the return of Jesus in the relatively short term, and often held that the Kingdom of Christ was going to be a worldly creation, that is, that Jesus would give his followers peace, freedom, and prosperity in this life. This particular idea was very important to syncretic faiths as well, as most famously in Rastafarianism, which grew up after the era of slavery but represents the ideas of older Jamaican syncretic communities. Finally, many Pietists had worship services that were very oral and participatory, unlike the mainline Protestant and Catholic Church services, which were mostly liturgies that were to be observed and appreciated by the faithful. All these aspects made Pietistic faiths very familiar and easy for people of African descent to adopt, and many did. Several prominent early British free blacks were Quakers, including OLAUDAH EQUIANO and QUOBNA OTTABAH CUGOANO, while the Bermudian free black abolitionist writer Mary Prince was a Moravian Baptist.

The Pietists, in particular, were quick to realize that slavery and racial discrimination were wrong. George Fox, the founder of the movement, preached against slavery in the 1640s in England, and by the early 18th century, Quaker meetings began to require their members to get out of the slave trade and ultimately to free their slaves. The Germantown Pennsylvania meeting was the first in North America to do so in 1733, and the influential Philadelphia annual meeting forbade Quakers to own slaves in 1766. Later, many prominent abolitionists were Quakers, including Lucretia Mott, Susan B. Anthony, and Levi Coffin.

The Great Awakenings, Eighteenth and Ninetheenth Centuries

Pietism was very much a minority faith even among Protestants. However, this began to change as a result of two religious movements, one in the mid-18th century and the other in the early 19th century. The First Great Awakening, in the 1730s and 1740s, was the product of British religious leaders in the Church of England, who created the Methodist movement. Methodism bridged the gap between the official, state-supported Protestant denominations and the Pietists by creating a mass religious movement that incorporated many of the Pietist ideas. Salvation was seen to be a process involving the individual's faithful response to God's call. Worship was emotional and participatory, with hymns, enthusiastic preaching, and testimonies from the congregation. The Second Great Awakening in the 1820s and 1830s completed the work by establishing a democratic system of

church government, reinforcing the Arminian theology, and further encouraging missionary activity. The churches that grew out of the Second Great Awakening are what we call today Baptist. They made Pietist beliefs mainstream, particularly in the United States, and had an enormous influence on people of color.

One common feature of Baptist churches was congregationalism. In other words, each Baptist congregation was independent of all others. What this meant was that once a particular local Baptist group was established and operating autonomously, it was under no obligation to adhere to any fixed set of beliefs, worship practices, or externally established rules of any sort. Similarly, there was no formal process for ordination of ministers in the early days. Anybody who could be accepted by a congregation could be a minister. Mostly, this required an encyclopedic knowledge of the Bible but little in the way of theological, philosophical, or general liberal education that a minister in a mainline Protestant or Catholic church would have. Since formal education was next to impossible for blacks to obtain in the English-speaking world, this meant that blacks who felt a call to ministry were most likely to find that call easiest to respond to in Baptist churches.

Another common feature of Baptist churches was scriptural fundamentalism. That is, as did all Protestants, they followed Luther's doctrine of *sola scriptura*, that the Bible contained everything that a Christian needed to know about faith. For the state churches of northern Europe, this meant that church leaders, bishops and priests, had to be able to cite scriptural justification for their decisions, not just "tradition" or the writings of theologians. But for Pietists and especially the newly created Baptist churches, this meant that the Bible was literally inerrant and absolutely true in all respects, without regard to historical context, linguistic issues, or stylistic concerns. This meant that a believer in one of these churches could use a biblical quotation, even a very short one, to provide powerful support for any argument. This also reinforced the importance of the Old Testament. Catholic and mainline Protestant churches had treated the Old Testament as historical background for Jesus's mission, or as prophetic foreshadowing, but for Baptists the Old Testament was a living set of commands and promises from God that applied to them in particular, the "believers' church," as the heirs of Abraham's covenant with God.

Baptist and Pietist Beliefs and Free People of Color

These features of Baptist practice and organization made the faith very attractive to people of color in Protestant countries in the Americas. At the same time, the established or mainline Protestant groups were not especially attractive to people of color for a variety of reasons. As a result, by the middle of the 19th century, enormous numbers of people of color had joined Baptist churches in the Americas.

Baptist and Moravian missionaries in the Caribbean evangelized many slaves and free blacks. The Moravians tried to send a white European missionary to serve each Moravian church in the colonies, but they were unsuccessful in recruiting enough staff, and in any case a challenging disease environment meant that the life expectancy of mission staff was low. Baptist missionary groups generally did not try to maintain resident white pastors after the first few years, and most black Baptist congregations were led by black deacons. Black Baptist groups often had unusual theological teachings, focusing on Old Testament stories of liberation and the coming of the Messiah. Moravian groups also had strong black leaders, such as REBECCA PROTTEN in St. Thomas, Virgin Islands.

In the British Caribbean, most of the white ruling class were mainline Protestants of the Church of England. But in the slave states of North America, many whites, even wealthy ones, belonged to Baptist or Methodist churches after the Second Great Awakening in the early 19th century. This diluted the abolitionist and antisystemic focus of the Baptist movement but also meant that Baptist faith offered a common ground to meet whites similar to what the Roman Catholic Church provided in Catholic countries. The congregational nature of Baptist church organization meant that individual church communities were generally segregated, but this was not always the case. In many cases, the great distances of North America meant that religious services were uncommon, and when a preacher was in town every faithful person, black or white, would attend. As with the Catholic services in Spanish, Portuguese, or French colonies, the whites would receive some privileges—seats in pews, location closer to the altar, and so forth—but everyone would be together in a church that at least theoretically and sometimes aggressively urged the common humanity of all. No white southern Baptist preacher could advocate abolition per se, but it was not uncommon to hear conservative arguments for mitigation of slavery like those offered by many Catholics, drawing from the many biblical passages that regulate slavery and urge slaves and masters to respect each other.

One notable element of black Baptist life throughout the slaveholding world was the phenomenon of "slave churches." Masters preferred to have some control over the religious messages offered to slaves, for obvious reasons. But to the extent that masters also preferred to worship in an all-white environment or, as in the British and Dutch Caribbean, in mainline Protestant churches, people of color were left to their own devices. The congregational nature of Baptist church organization encouraged this.

Ministers in these slave churches were often free people of color, since they had the ability to move about freely and also could learn to read more easily. This was an early and important way in which free people of color could exert leadership in the larger black community. This was particularly true in the slave states of the United States, where other avenues of advancement for free people of color were few. The black church proved to be an enduring institution, surviving RECONSTRUCTION IN THE UNITED STATES, Jim Crow, and the Civil Rights movement of the 20th century as a central focus of black community life. The leaders of the black churches are still community leaders today in many places.

The slave churches were often places where people of color could organize resistance. For example, in 1831, the black Baptist leader Samuel Sharpe, a slave, led a strike or rebellion by up to 60,000 slaves and which was known as the Baptist War. The movement was suppressed with great bloodshed, and the revulsion of the public in Britain contributed to the 1832 decision to begin phasing out slavery in the colonies. The free black DENMARK VESEY of CHARLESTON, SOUTH CAROLINA, who had organized an AFRICAN METHODIST EPISCOPAL CHURCH parish without much official affiliation with the Methodist Church, and the Virginia slave rebel Nat Turner, who preached without having any formal association with a church at all, are additional examples of this phenomenon. Turner drew the inspiration for his rebellion from the Bible. In reaction to Turner's uprising, many Southern states passed laws that made it unlawful to teach slaves to read, but white Baptists, even those who generally supported slavery, routinely violated these laws. Reading scripture was central to the Baptist faith; you might almost say that without Bible Reading one cannot be a Baptist. The religious imperative to teach and convert all people, so central to the Baptist faith, was much stronger than any hypothetical fear that the egalitarian message of Christianity would lead slaves to rebel.

Conclusion

The Baptist and Pietist movements in Protestant Christianity offered a number of elements, both theological and organizational, that made them very welcoming to people of color in the Americas. They were much more democratic, decentralized, egalitarian, emotional, and participatory than the mainline Protestant churches. In the United States, they also offered a common ground for blacks and whites to meet with some recognition of common humanity on both sides.

Both free and enslaved people of color were attracted to these movements. For free people of color, they offered a rare opportunity for leadership within the black community, especially in the American South. Since Baptist groups had a congregational organization and no formal theological creed or doctrinal structure, there was almost no barrier to entering the ministry, unlike the high hurdles black mainline Protestants and Catholics faced entering the priesthood in their churches. The Roman Catholic Church only ordained its first black priest in the United States in 1886. The Episcopal Church in the United States ordained its first black priest, ABSALOM JONES, in 1802, but there was not another one until the 1860s. But black Methodists had been leading congregations since at least the 1780s, and perhaps before. As community leaders and spiritual counselors, these ministers served an important function, as did the faith they taught, by giving organization, hope, and spiritual strength to their communities.

Stewart R. King

FURTHER READING

Raboteau, Albert J. *Slave Religion: The Invisible Institution in the Antebellum South.* Oxford: Oxford University Press, 1978.

Sensbach, Jon. *Rebecca's Revival: Creating Black Christianity in the Atlantic World.* Cambridge, Mass.: Harvard University Press, 2006.

Simpson, George E. *Black Religions in the New World.* New York: Columbia University Press, 1978.

BARBADOS

The island of Barbados is located south of the Greater Antilles, to the east of the Caribbean arc. It is a relatively small island, having a total surface area of about 166.5 square miles. This Caribbean outpost had been settled by Arawak-speaking migrants from the Guianas from as early as the fourth century C.E. However, soon after the arrival of the Portuguese on the island and the later landings by the Spanish, the Amerindian population had largely disappeared. There is some speculation on the reasons for this disappearance, but the evidence for other Caribbean locations would suggest that a combination of factors, probably including epidemic disease caused by vectors introduced by Europeans and a labor regime that disrupted the traditional culture, were responsible. This, of course, does not rule out the possibility that outright genocide might have played its part. In any case, the island's easternmost location, far from Spanish settlements and southward of the main routes followed by Spanish ships, probably explains why there was no permanent Spanish settlement at Barbados.

The English arrived between 1625 and 1627 and began a colonial occupation that lasted for more than 300 years. Within the first few years of the English arrival, some Amerindian labor was imported from the neighboring Caribbean islands and from South America to assist in the cultivation of tobacco and cotton and of tropical staples such as cassava, maize, and ginger. It appears that the Amerindians were also sought for their skill in fishing. Richard Ligon, who lived on the island in the 1650s and wrote the first *History of Barbados*, reported that "the men [Arawak] we use for killing of fish which they are good at; with their own bows and arrows they will go out and [in] a days time, kill as much fish, as will serve a family of a dozen or so persons, two or three days, if you can keep fish so long."

The status of the Amerindians is not clear, but several references to "[Amer]Indians and other slaves" in legislation passed in the island in the late 17th century and Ligon's comments that the English settlers made slaves of the Amerindians who were imported suggest that most, if not all, were in a state of slavery. It would seem, however, that the first group taken out from the South American mainland were considered free, but those who arrived in later importations were enslaved or indentured. It is possible that before the arrival of enslaved Africans, a small mixed population may have emerged, descended from Amerindian women and English settlers. Ligon reports the story of one Amerindian woman, "who chanced to be with child by a Christian servant." The shortage of white

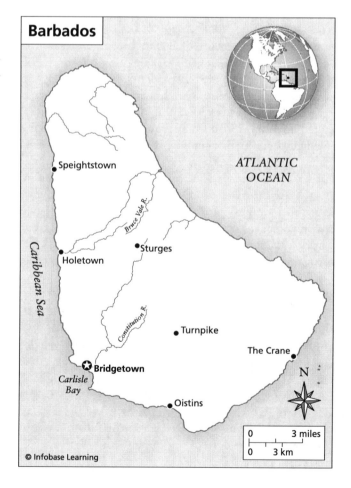

Barbados

Scenes of black life in Barbados in about 1800. The windmill, used for grinding sugarcane, in the background, and the refining house, in the foreground, indicate that this is one of the many successful sugar plantations on the island. Sugar manufacturing was a technically demanding field, and slaves who received training as sugar refiners or millers were valuable and also could earn outside income by renting themselves to other planters when their services were not needed at home. Thus, they could accumulate sufficient resources to ransom themselves, and by 1800, much of the skilled labor on plantations in Barbados was actually done by free colored artisans rather than slaves. *(© Michael Graham-Stewart/The Bridgeman Art Library)*

women in the early years of settlement probably contributed to these unions.

In commenting on the state of affairs, not only in Barbados, but elsewhere, the historian Carl Bridenbaugh wrote, "It would be a long time before family life of the kind that many men and women had known in Old England could be reconstituted in any of the colonies from Maryland southward to Barbados." The historian Richard Dunn's comments on the question of miscegenation in the slave societies of the Caribbean also noted that "there were always fewer white women than white men living in the islands in the seventeenth century." However, he also notes that this might not necessarily be the "key consideration" and points, instead, to the enjoyment of power over the bodies of enslaved women. Indeed, most white men probably felt or presumed that they had rights in law and custom to the bodies of subordinate others.

It was not long, however, before the Amerindians were replaced, first by white indentured servants, and later by African laborers. By the mid-17th century in Barbados,

the sugar revolution was in full sway, and there was a demographic shift to an African majority. Thus, from a situation in the 1630s where there were more than 3,000 white indentured servants and fewer than 1,000 blacks, by 1680, there were just 2,300 white servants and more than 38,000 enslaved Africans. It is at this point that we are able to chart the emergence of a MULATTO group and the appearance of free coloreds in the island. It is important to comment on the use of the term *free coloreds* here. In the local records kept by the various vestries across Barbados, it is not uncommon to find the same individual variously referred to by the vestry authorities as "free mulatto (fm)," "free negro (fn)," and "free colored (fc)." The entries "free man/woman of color," "free colored man/woman," and "free black man/woman" are also common. In order, therefore, to prevent any confusion over the various classifications, this article will use the term *free colored(s)* to cover the wide variety of skin-color gradations that might occur. We might also have used the terms *freedman* and *freedwoman*, but that would tend to obscure the fact that over time there arose in the island a group of people of full or part African origin who were born legally free as distinct from those who might have received manumission. In fact, once an initial manumission had taken place, the descendants of such persons were almost all legally free, rather than "freed/manumitted."

The Sociolegal Context for the Emergence of the Free Colored Population in Barbados

Even before the arrival of the Africans in large numbers, enslavement of Amerindians had been established, and the sexual exploitation of Amerindian women had become an accepted pattern of life among the white settlers. However, it seems that in the very early years of African enslavement, the authorities recognized the dilemma that was posed by the emergence of a nonwhite group and began a process of social engineering that was designed to ensure that slavery was irrevocably linked with racial markers. The first aspects of this process concerned the installation of legal protections for the white indentured laborers.

On September 27, 1661, the House of Assembly, the colonial legislature, passed "An Act for the good governing of servants and ordaining the rights between masters and servants." In this piece of legislation, penalties were invoked to prohibit the importation of persons "to be sold as servants," without the consent of such servants. Clause V of this act also prescribed the penalty of servitude for a period of three years for any free male who impregnated a female servant, "in great prejudice of their respective masters or mistresses whom they serve." No such penalty was ever prescribed for a male impregnating an Amerindian or African woman, probably because, apart from some loss of the mother's labor during the pregnancy, the offspring of such a coupling were the legal property of the enslaver and as such increased the value of his property, thanks to a colonial court decision in 1639 that required African and Indian servants to serve for life and stated that the children of an enslaved woman inherited her condition.

In addition to these distinctions, the act stated that an indentured servant below the age of 18 was to serve "for the space of seven years and no longer" while those older then 18 were to serve "during the space of five years and no longer." At the end of the indenture, each laborer was to receive "four hundred pounds of muscovado sugar for their wages." Thus, the distinction between servants and enslaved people, who were to serve for the entire period of their lives, was enshrined in law.

The distinction between Africans and whites was further codified in the passing of the first slave code in the island in 1661. As Richard Dunn observes, it classified Africans as "an heathenish, brutish, and an uncertaine,

dangerous kinde of people," who were not fit to be governed under English law. On October 3, 1688, the English settlers passed an amended slave code that repeated many of the assertions of the earlier law, declaring that Africans were "of barbarous, wild and savage nature and such as renders them wholly unqualified to be governed by the laws, customs, and practices of our nation." Clause V of this law prescribed severe penalties for any African, enslaved or not, who had the temerity to strike "any Christian." Thus another distinction that would differentiate between Africans and whites was the question of their religious orientation. Even when Africans adopted Christianity, as many eventually did, their earlier identification as a "brutish," "barbarous," or "savage" continued to be applied as a justification for denying them access to fair, equitable systems of justice.

Another legal distinction between Africans and whites was related to the question of redress before the law. "An Act for the Encouragement of White Servants," passed on December 1, 1703, gave servants the right to have a complaint against a master or mistress heard before two justices of the peace. However, enslaved Africans and free coloreds were not guaranteed such rights. Indeed, in 1721, the "Act to keep inviolate and preserve the freedom of elections" held that the testimony of nonwhites was by nature suspect, when it stated that "no person whatsoever shall be admitted as a free holder, or an Evidence in any case whatsoever, whose original extraction shall be proved to have been from a negro, excepting only in the trial of negros and other slaves." The phrase "other slaves" as used in this and similar legislation was probably intended to include Amerindians and mulattoes since in some legal circumstances, the term negro might be understood to mean a person of apparently unmixed African ancestry.

In addition to the distinctions among Africans, Indians, and white servants that appeared in the legal codes, legislation was passed that defined African slaves first as chattel and later as real estate. On April 29, 1668, an act passed in the assembly stated that "all negro-slaves in all Courts of Judicature . . . shall be held, taken, and adjudged to be Estates Real and not chattel." This act was later amended, to ensure that its intent was not misconstrued. The amended act then stated that "by the true meaning of that Act [the 1668 legislation], Negroes may be sued for and recovered by action personal, as they usually were before the making of the said Act: And also, that by the true meaning of the Act aforesaid, Negroes continue chattels for the payment of debts." By seeking further to dehumanize enslaved Africans, the law attempted to classify them in much the same way as a horse or a cart, or some other type of property, real or personal. Later, however, the emergence of a free colored population would challenge this legal prescription.

In 1739, the Barbadian assembly amended the 1688 slave code by requiring "proper maintenance of such negroes, Indians, or mullatoes as hereafter shall be manumitted or set free." This act affirmed that the testimony of any enslaved person would be received "against any free negro, Indian, or mulatto." Additionally, any persons desirous of manumitting an enslaved person were required to deposit £40 (a sum equivalent to about $5,000 in current money) to the church warden of the local vestry. Clearly, the aim was to discourage the manumission of enslaved men and women and, therefore, the growth of a free colored population. This was an important turning point in the life of the free colored community, which had been growing rapidly through MANUMISSION. Though people continued to be freed, the legal restrictions made this more difficult. Many masters allowed favored slaves to work for wages or to go about freely, though the government tried to stop these practices (*see also* LIVING "AS FREE").

Whatever the legal and social prescriptions may have been designed to do, the reality of sexual contact between whites and nonwhites meant that the myth of an "almost human" or "subhuman" African was destroyed. (*See also* INTERRACIAL MARRIAGE and MISCEGENATION.) After all, to admit sexual relations with persons whom the law defined as not quite the same as other humans beings, rather as akin to other kinds of movable chattel, said more about the capacity of the white enslavers for self-denial than about the lack of civilized norms of their slave property. The birth of offspring, some of whom might be as fair-skinned as the male parent, added to the dilemma facing the enslavers. As Richard Dunn observed, "The island colonist who took a Negro Mistress and fathered mulatto children was likely to display some measure of love and responsibility toward his illicit black family. . . . It can be said in the master's behalf that his sexual vices forced him to accept some blacks—his own offspring—as real human beings." Not all enslavers might operate in this way, however, as the records indicate that in some cases, white fathers were as indifferent to their mulatto offspring as to the other enslaved people under their charge. In any case, the emergence and growth of a free colored population in Barbados challenged the notion of an intractable slave society.

The information presented in the following table shows the names of the "Christian Servants" and "Women Negroes" living on Captain William Fontlaroy's plantation in 1654. The white "servants," who were predominantly male, would ultimately receive their freedom if they survived an indenture period, while the "negroes" were by definition, since the 1636 act, slaves for life. The white servants are recorded with their surnames, the "negroes" only by their first name. The gender

LIST OF ENSLAVED PEOPLE AND SERVANTS ON THE PLANTATION OF CAPTAIN WILLIAM FONTLAROY, BARBADOS, 1654

Christian Servants	Women Negroes
William Gould	Abaca
Irish Thomas	Abara
Benjamin Asinoman	Aolu
John jr. Taylor	Bussa
Sarah, a maid servant	Cullabulla
John Hawltey	Cumba
Irish Richard	Hagar
Irish Will	Jappa
David Baylie	Jecina
William Clark	Jocka
Frolise and Eustace	Jug
	Leamo
	Maria
	Mary
	Wombo

balance of Fontlaroy's workforce, with enslaved women of color and indentured white men, reflects a common situation in the Americas, one that would lead to the growth of a mixed-race community.

Manumission of children of color was fairly easy in the early days. Fathers generally respected an obligation at least to see their children freed, and patrons, masters of indentured servants, and charitable citizens often helped men fulfill this obligation if they did not or could not. There were few regulations limiting manumission, and the free population of color grew in the late 17th century as a result.

From the period of settlement up to the 1730s, few official acts or regulations even acknowledged the presence of the free colored population. The 1739 law noted previously shows that their numbers had grown enough to attract the attention of the assembly. One estimate places the numbers at about 107 persons in 1748 and 833 in 1786, a small number in a total population of almost 80,000. The difficulty facing historians is that the various censuses that were conducted over the period often undercounted the numbers of free coloreds. In between the census years, the best sources for estimating the numbers are the various vestry levy books that counted taxpaying islanders. Again, the problem is that many free coloreds may not have paid any taxes since they owned no land and were generally involved in small-scale entrepreneurial activities that would not have been entered into any of the official statistics. Persons living "as free," maroons, and other marginal people of color either would not have been counted at all or would have been considered slaves in any official record. Even with these people added into our estimates of the free colored population, though, their proportion of the population was small by the standards of other Caribbean sugar plantation colonies—no more than 2 or 3 percent of the population before 1800.

After the turn of the 19th century, free coloreds gained as a percentage of the population. By 1833, the year of the abolition of slavery in the British Empire, there were 6,584 free people of color in a total population of 100,242, or more than 6 percent. This rapid growth was common to all the British plantation colonies and was a result of the progressive abrogation of the host of discriminatory laws that had been adopted in the 18th century. Manumission became much simpler. Free people of color could own more kinds of property, including plantation land and slaves. Also, the end of the slave trade in 1807 led to a decline in the profitability of the plantation sector. Though the white planter class remained in power in local politics in Barbados, they lost absolute control over the colony's politics when it became the seat of government of a newly created multi-island Windward Islands Colony in 1833. Barbados's politics came under the direct supervision of a governor who was sent out from Britain. The British government had been trying to rein in the independence of the Caribbean colonial legislatures for some time, and Barbados had had a succession of activist governors from 1794 onward. With large planters losing political and economic power, free people of color had an opportunity to rise in both areas. Voting became an issue for wealthy free coloreds in the 1820s, with Samuel Collymore and the Belgrave family, some of the few colored plantation owners, publicly pressing the assembly for voting rights. They were not granted until 1831, and then only to the propertied elite represented by Collymore and Belgrave. But the rise of a free colored middle class dates to this period, and the economic liberties enjoyed by free coloreds permitted some social mobility.

Free Coloreds in the Urban Environment

For the most part, free coloreds in Barbados, as elsewhere in the English-speaking Caribbean, tended to live in urban areas. There are a number of reasons for this, including the fact that port cities offered far more opportunities for individual income-earning activities than did the rural plantation sector, and that the land in rural areas was largely owned by wealthy planters so that once manumission had been achieved, there was little land

available for free coloreds in such locations. Additionally, it is possible that many free coloreds wished to distance themselves from locations that were closely connected with their previous experience with enslavement. In any case, the available data show that by 1800, 50 percent of the free coloreds lived in Bridgetown, the chief port and capital of Barbados. By 1829, that share had climbed to more than 60 percent. Free coloreds also lived in the three other Barbadian coastal towns at Oistins, Holetown, and Speightstown; the urban free colored population probably exceeded at least 80 percent by the 1830s. By contrast, in prerevolutionary SAINT-DOMINGUE, only about 15 percent of the free colored population lived in towns by 1791.

Another feature of the free colored population was its gender imbalance in favor of females. In part, this related to the greater tendency for the manumission of females (*see also* GENDER ATTITUDES and FAMILY RELATIONSHIPS WITH WHITES). Indeed, it was not uncommon for white males to manumit their mistresses and even to settle property on them. Such was the case of Amaryllis Collymore, who had borne seven children for her white lover, Robert Collymore. This relationship had been continuing for several years before Robert bought Amaryllis and the five children born up to that time (1780) from her enslaver, Rebecca Phillips. Thereafter, Robert used an intermediary, James Scuffield, to whom he sold Amaryllis for the purpose of effecting her manumission. It is unsure why Collymore used this route to achieve his objective. Perhaps, Scuffield was insolvent and might have escaped having to pay the £240 that was required by the law for the manumissions. In his will, Collymore left substantial property, including a plantation called Lightfoots, to Amaryllis and his children.

Another white male, Richard Adamson, made his will in 1776, in which he left property to his mother "in trust" for the "use and behoof" of his slave mistress, Joan, then pregnant with their eighth child. In the will, Adamson specified that his mother was to "permit or suffer my negro woman named Joan to have, hold and enjoy all my said estate to her my said mother given as aforesaid." When his mother died, all of Adamson's property, real and personal, was to be delivered to Joan, by which time the testator expected that "she [would] be a free woman."

The experience of John Perrot Devonish, a mariner who, apparently, had parallel homes in Bristol, England, and Bridgetown, Barbados—a practice that was relatively common among mariners who sailed to the island frequently—further illustrates the trends that were altering the demographics of the free colored population, we might note. Devonish had established a household with a free colored woman named Mercy Katharine Hawes, with whom he had six children. In his will of

1814, he stated: "It is my earnest request . . . that my natural children from a free woman of color named Mercy Katharine Hawes be clothed, fed, [and] maintained out [of] the monies from and out of the sale of my property." It is not clear whether Hawes had descended from a free colored ancestry or whether she had been manumitted, but the tone of the will suggests the latter and that Devonish was the benefactor.

If African women were more favored than men in achieving manumission in Barbados, it must not be assumed that they were passive participants in the process. When the tax for manumission reached £300 for women and £200 for men in the early 19th century, several free colored women formed business and other relationships with whites who acted as agents, procuring the manumission of slave kin and other enslaved persons in Britain, where it cost only 15 shillings, or in other Caribbean locations where the manumission fees were considerably lower than in Barbados. Free colored women such as Susannah Ostrehan and Nancy Clarke were recorded in various legal documents of the period as being involved in several manumissions. The records show that more than 400 enslaved persons were set free by such means from 1795 to 1830.

Although women predominated among the free colored population, men were indeed represented in the urban context. Samuel Collymore, for example, one of Amaryllis's sons, had several ships sailing throughout the region and was a prominent merchant in Bridgetown. Another well-documented Bridgetown resident was William Bourne, who spent £3,000 to purchase his four sons and their mother in 1816. One of these sons, London Bourne, became owner of substantial real estate in the town, including the building known as the Exchange, in which the local mercantile association met. Despite his wealth, London Bourne Junior could not meet socially with his renters. He even employed white clerks to handle his business contacts with whites, but even they were considered his social superiors.

Free Coloreds as Entrepreneurs and Workers
The Bridgetown environment provided vital opportunities for the free colored population. The harbor hosted an average of more than 250 ships per year in peacetime. In some cases, particularly during wartime when convoys were sailing, as many as 200 ships might be found anchored off the harbor in Carlisle Bay in one day. The demand for services created by this maritime traffic was enormous. One area in which free coloreds found an opportunity was in the provision of tavern, hotel, and food services. The Royal Naval Hotel, owned first by Rachel Pringle, later by Nancy Clarke, and located on Madeira Street, and Susannah Ostrehan's hotel, located

on Cumberland Street, were the largest hotels in the island. In general, free coloreds occupied areas in the business sector that were unattractive to whites or that lacked social respectability. Thus, one area that free coloreds tended to monopolize was the prostitution trade. In one account written in 1806 by a medical officer serving in the British navy, George Pinckard, he relates the story of an enslaved woman, Betsy Lemmon, who served as a prostitute in one of the taverns. She took him into her confidence, bemoaning her condition and that of her daughter. There is no confirmation that Pinckard assisted her, but on his return to Barbados in a later trip, Lemmon was a free woman and moreover had acquired her own tavern. Pinckard issued a call to his readers to patronize Lemmon's establishment should they follow him to Bridgetown.

Those free coloreds who sought employment in the port cities also found opportunities as chambermaids, sailmakers, pilots, coopers, ships, carpenters, shipwrights, mariners, and porters, along with several other occupations. Here, too, many found room to maneuver and options that permitted them to improve their lot. On one occasion, Frederick Bayley, a Briton who recorded his experiences on a voyage to Barbados (1826–29), described his encounter with an African pilot who was contracted to guide his ship over the treacherous reefs around the Bridgetown harbor. What surprised Bayley most of all was the ease with which the man took control of the ship and ordered the white mariners to do his bidding. He was a jobbing slave (a slave who paid his master a regular amount of money and was allowed to keep whatever else he earned) and apparently lived a relatively independent life off the proceeds of his trade. Indeed, one route to manumission for such persons was the considerable income that might be derived from their work—income that could be accumulated toward the day when self-purchase was possible. After manumission, many free coloreds continued in those occupations that had gained them freedom in the first place. Additionally, many enslaved saw in the experience of their free colored kin the very routes of their own eventual freedom.

Free people of color in Barbados built some separate community institutions, but in many cases they relied on institutions created for the white community. Free people of any race constituted a tiny minority of Barbados's population, and free people of color were a minority of this small group. There just were not enough free people of color to support black newspapers or many other businesses primarily aimed at the free black community. Predominantly black churches started in the late 18th century, when the Moravian Brethren established three parishes in 1765–66. These churches welcomed slaves and often had free colored preachers (*see also* BAPTISTS AND PIETISTS). However, the majority of free coloreds, especially the wealthy community leaders, were members of the officially established Church of England (*see also* PROTESTANT MAINLINE CHURCHES). This enabled them to connect on a personal level with influential whites but denied them the possibility of taking leadership positions.

Free Coloreds Fighting Discrimination

Despite possessing freedom, livelihoods, and an organized community life, free coloreds faced many legal and social obstacles. When they were defrauded, the law courts often proved hostile. In one case, a free colored woman, Charlotte Belgrave, petitioned Governor Francis Mackenzie, Baron Seaforth (1754–1815, governor 1800–06), in 1804 concerning the case of her husband, Jacob Belgrave, a free colored planter, who had been imprisoned for defending himself against a white male who had struck him first. The white man had apparently cheated Jacob, and when Jacob asked for repayment, the man attacked him. There is no information on the outcome of Charlotte's petition. However, the fact that she had considered petitioning the governor suggests a clear understanding of the power structures. Seaforth had arrived in Barbados with a mandate from the Colonial Office to improve the justice system and to improve the lot of the free coloreds. He outlawed the killing of slaves by masters and implemented many reforms easing the condition of free people of color. It was under his administration that taxes on manumissions were finally reduced.

In 1811, free coloreds petitioned the governor and the Assembly on the question of the right to testimony in court—a right that had been denied them since the passage of the 1721 and 1739 acts. One of the points in the petition was the claim that the free coloreds had "all been baptized and brought up in the Religion of the Established Church of England." Clearly, free coloreds recognized that one of the original premises on which inferiority had been assumed for Africans and their descendants was that they were of a "barbaric" non-Christian background. To claim a Christian connection was, therefore, to claim a certain equality of status and privileges. In 1817, the governor approved a law permitting free blacks who had been baptized in the Church of England to testify in court.

In another step of the struggle, this time in 1824, Samuel Collymore and a number of other free coloreds published an address in the principal local newspaper, the *Globe*, demanding the right to vote and be elected to the House of Assembly. In response, the assembly summoned the leaders to appear before them, and the

Speaker of the House questioned Collymore. "Are you aware," the Speaker asked him, "of any Rights enjoyed by your forefathers which you do not now enjoy?" It was clearly a question that had reference to Collymore's African origins. "Certainly not," Collymore answered. The Speaker probed further, "Do you mean to say that you have a natural and reasonable claim to those Rights and Privileges?" The fight was a long one, and it was not until 1831 that some relief was given in what was termed the Brown Privilege Bill. Under the provisions of this law, free men of color who owned real property worth more than 30 pounds a year in taxes could vote and have full access to the courts. Because of the poverty of most free people of color, only a few could benefit. The bill affected all of 75 people in 1831.

One other aspect of the struggle is worth relating here. In 1794, Governor George Ricketts (governor 1794–1800), who had preceded Seaforth, arrived in Barbados. However, he had with him a free colored mistress who had accompanied him from his previous assignment in Tobago. This mulatto woman was reported to have "enjoyed all the privileges of wife, except the honour of public presiding at his table." The Barbadian historian John Poyer had reported this situation in his *History of Barbados,* which was published in 1808, and he had used this issue to complain that free colored women had succeeded in subverting justice, through their contacts with magistrates and other officials. What made matters worse in Poyer's estimation was that on one occasion, a free colored man, Joseph Denny, had been committed to trial for murdering a white male who had threatened him. However, as Poyer records, the governor's mulatto mistress, Betsy Goodwin, had let it be known that she would intervene on his behalf. Apparently, although a guilty verdict had been recorded, the governor had petitioned the London authorities for a pardon, and this was granted, provided that Denny was transported off Barbados. This incident illustrates that some free coloreds in Barbados understood how to utilize the avenues of power to achieve their objectives. This incident also illustrates the importance of perception in the interpretation of racial politics in slave societies. Poyer, expressing the point of view of the white planter aristocracy, suggests that the governor's judgment was warped by his sexual relationship with a woman of color. On the other hand, the governor may well have seen the pardon as an act of justice, protecting a man of color against unjustified oppression by a member of that planter aristocracy. Ricketts, as had Seaforth and the other governors from the 1790s to the 1830s, immigrated to the colony to try to restrain the excesses and autonomy of the white planter elite and saw the free colored middle class as allies in this struggle.

Free people of color in Barbados were not major players in the struggle for abolition. Several of the most important community leaders were SLAVE OWNERS themselves. In addition, a slave uprising in 1816, though suppressed with great violence by the colonial officials, still frightened all the free inhabitants and made free coloreds unwilling to express themselves too forcefully on the subject of slavery. Most free colored political activism during the period leading up to the 1833 Abolition of Slavery Act was aimed toward gaining equal rights for their own community.

After the abolition of slavery, the economy of Barbados continued to decline. Whites emigrated from the colony, as did many people of color. Barbadian workers could be found around the Caribbean during the 19th and early 20th centuries, working on such projects as the Panama Canal and rail construction in Cuba. The former free colored families remained an important part of the colony's society. Members of the Collymore family are prominent bankers, artists, and politicians in today's Barbados. Members of the Belgrave family play cricket, work as physicians, and teach at the national university. Though small in number, the free colored community was able to perform important services for black Barbadians in the period after the end of slavery because of their education and relative wealth.

Pedro L. V. Welch

FURTHER READING

Bayley, Frederic William Naylor. *Four Years' Residence in the West Indies: During the Years 1826, 7, 8, and 9.* London: William Kidd, 1833. Available online. URL: http://books.google.com/books?id=AiljAAAAMAAJ&source=gbs_navlinks_s. Accessed March 10, 2010.

Beckles, Hilary Mc.D. *A History of Barbados: From Amerindian Settlement to Nation State.* New York: Cambridge University Press, 2007.

Campbell, Mavis. *The Dynamics of Change in Slave Society: A Socio-Political History of the Free Coloureds of Jamaica, 1800–1865.* London: Associated University Presses, 1976.

Cohen, David, and Jack P. Greene, eds. *Neither Slave nor Free: Freedmen of African Descent in the Slave Societies of the New World.* Baltimore: Johns Hopkins University Press, 1972.

Cox, Edward. *Free Coloreds in the Slave Societies of St. Kitts and Grenada.* Knoxville: University of Tennessee Press, 1984.

Dunn, Richard S. *Sugar and Slaves: The Rise of the Planter Class in the English West Indies.* New York: W. W. Norton, 1972.

Handler, Jerome. *The Unappropriated People: Freedmen in the Slave Society of Barbados.* Baltimore: Johns Hopkins University Press, 1974.

Heuman, Gad. *Between Black and White: Race, Politics, and the Free Coloreds of Jamaica, 1792–1865.* Westport, Conn.: Greenwood Press, 1981.

Higman, Barry. *Slave Populations of the British Caribbean, 1807–1834.* Kingston, Jamaica: University of the West Indies Press, 1997.

Newton, Melanie. *The Children of Africa in the Colonies: Free People of Color in Barbados in the Age of Emancipation.* Baton Rouge: Louisiana State University Press, 2008.

Pinckard, George. *Notes on the West Indies: Written during the Expedition under the Command of the Late General Sir Ralph Abercromby: Including Observations on the Island of Barbadoes, and the Settlements Captured by the British Troops, upon the Coast of Guiana.* London: Longman, Hurst, Rees, and Orme, 1806.

Welch, Pedro, with Richard Goodridge. *"Red" and Black over White: Free Coloured Women in Pre-Emancipation Barbados.* Bridgetown, Barbados: Carib Press, 2000.

BARBOUR, CONWAY (ca. 1820–1876) *American steamboat steward, businessman, politician*
While Conway Barbour's early years are a mystery, his adult life demonstrated a striving that typified the self-made man ideal of the 19th century. Born in Virginia around 1820, Barbour, a MULATTO, may have been born a slave but was free by the 1840s. Insured as a slave cabin boy around 1846, Barbour was actually a taxpaying member of Louisville's African-American community and a respected steamboat steward. He and his first wife, Cornelia, a former slave, had two small children in the 1850 census.

In 1854, Barbour represented Kentucky at MARTIN DELANY's Emigration Convention in Cleveland. While Barbour's interest in EMIGRATION AND COLONIZATION was fleeting, his desire for political elevation persisted. He moved Cornelia and their growing family to Cleveland in 1855, possibly hoping to cement his ties to the black political elite. The move also helped to separate his wife, Cornelia, from his mistress, Frances Rankin, with whom he contracted a bigamous marriage in Alton, Illinois, in 1859.

Barbour was a highly visible businessman in Alton during the 1860s. He purchased a lease interest in the Mercantile Restaurant and Hotel around 1863, established the Fifth Avenue Hall in 1865, and became the proprietor of a restaurant and hotel in the city's new train station around 1867. In the midst of the AMERICAN CIVIL WAR, 1861–65, Barbour wrote a letter to the Illinois governor Richard Yates, seeking appointment as a recruiter or Union officer; his offer was ignored. The economic viability of his business ventures, then, is open to question, despite the lavish praise Barbour received in the local newspaper.

Whatever his business prospects, Barbour left Alton, and by June 1870, he corresponded from Lewisville, Arkansas, with the personal secretary of the state's governor, Powell Clayton. In November 1870, Barbour was elected to the Arkansas General Assembly, representing Lafayette and Little River Counties. Particularly interested in penal reform, Barbour spent most of the legislative session (January–March 1871) defending Governor Clayton against impeachment charges brought by Democrats and disaffected Republicans. The impeachment effort failed, and Barbour was rewarded at the session's end with an appointment as tax assessor of Chicot County, Arkansas.

In Chicot County, Barbour developed a rivalry with James W. Mason, also a mulatto and son of Arkansas's largest antebellum slaveholder. In 1872, the two men vied for county sheriff, a contest marked by violence and vitriol. Losing that election, Barbour spent his last years trying to stabilize his fragile financial situation and writing embittered letters to the Little Rock newspaper. He died in Lake Village, the county seat, in August 1876. His brief obituary in the Arkansas *Gazette* referred to him as "formerly a favorite servant of the governor," a hint that Barbour may have been related to James Barbour, Virginia's governor during the War of 1812.

Throughout his career, Barbour attempted to take advantage of possibilities for advancement when and where they arose. As he left no papers, we can only speculate on his motivations. However, his reconstructed public record suggests that Barbour, in his calculating self-reinventions, was a typical 19th-century man on the make.

Victoria L. Harrison

FURTHER READING
Moneyhon, Karl H. *The Impact of the Civil War and Reconstruction in Arkansas: Persistence in the Midst of Ruin.* Little Rock: University of Arkansas Press, 2002.

BECKWOURTH, JAMES (JAMES BECKWITH)
(ca. 1798–1866) *American explorer*
James Beckwourth or Beckwith was born on April 6, by tradition, though whether in 1798, 1800, or 1805 is unclear, in Virginia, the son of a white farmer also named James Beckwith and a mixed-race woman whose name is unknown. His mother's identity may have been hidden to conceal the fact that he was born a slave. He lived with his father and was never treated as a slave. His father moved with him to MISSOURI around 1809 and apprenticed him to a blacksmith. The younger James worked as a blacksmith in St. Louis until 1824. In that year, he joined the fur-trapping expedition organized by William Ashley to explore the Rocky Mountains (*see also* INLAND WEST OF THE UNITED STATES). During the 1820s and 1830s, he became one of the most renowned of the "mountain men." For much of this time, he "passed" as Indian, purporting to be a member of the Crow tribe who had been stolen as a child by the Cheyenne. At one point, he actually went to live among the Crow and was accepted as a member of the tribe, marrying a Crow woman and being initiated into the Dog clan. He fathered a child there, called Black Panther or Little Jim, who may have served in the Crow Scouts, a U.S. Army Indian unit, in the 1860s and 1870s. Beckwourth participated in the Second Seminole War (1835–42) in FLORIDA, ironically fighting men who, like himself, were of partially African ancestry but had Indian identities, the BLACK SEMINOLE. He then opened a trading post in Colorado that became the city of Pueblo, Colorado. He went with the gold rush to CALIFORNIA in 1849, pioneering Beckwourth Pass across the Sierras and operating a toll road, ranch, and inn there for about 10 years. The pass ultimately became the route of the Union Pacific Railroad. One of the guests at his inn was Thomas Bonner, who wrote down Beckwourth's stories and published his memoirs in 1856. These became very successful, but Beckwourth never received any payment for them. Beckwourth returned to Colorado in 1860 and, in 1864, accompanied the Colorado militia leader Colonel John Chivington during his campaign against the Cheyenne, which resulted in the Sand Creek Massacre (November 29, 1864), in which almost 400 Cheyenne and Arapaho Indians were slaughtered. Beckwourth was employed as a scout at Fort Laramie and Fort Kearney in 1866. This was at the beginning of Red Cloud's War (1866–68), in which the Dakota and their Cheyenne allies fought against the United States, supported by their Crow allies. Beckwourth was escorting a shipment of supplies to a Crow village in October 1866, possibly accompanied by his son, Black Panther, when he fell ill, complaining of headaches and nosebleeds. He went to the Crow village, where he died on October 29.

Beckwourth's story illustrates many features of free colored life in the Far West in the mid-19th century. First, as a person of mixed race, he was able to pretend to be an Indian. This may well have gained him better treatment than he would have received if identified as black, especially from white Southerners. The Crow were happy to welcome him as one of their own, as Indians did with many people of African descent throughout North America. Beckwourth worked at a number of jobs and was close to wealth on several occasions, but in each case he left the area before the real money was made. This was a common outcome for pioneers of any race. Even his life story was stolen from him by somebody with better business skills. It is unclear whether his race (either the one he was born to or the one he was perceived as being a member of) made his life more difficult, but it certainly may have been a factor in his many unsuccessful business dealings.

Another interesting feature of Beckwourth's life is that his African-American identity was almost completely overlooked until the 1970s. It took a very diligent researcher, Elinor Watson, in 1972 to resurrect the story. In 1950, Universal Pictures released a film entitled *Tomahawk* about the discovery of the Beckwourth Pass. The part of Beckwourth was played by Jack Okie, a white actor. Beckwourth's memoirs were dismissed as tall tales, while very similar stories from Kit Carson and Jim Bridger were accepted, and these white explorers were lionized.

Stewart R. King

FURTHER READING
Bonner, Thomas D. *The Life and Adventures of James P. Beckwourth*. New York: Harper and Brothers, 1856.

Katz, Loren. *The Black West: A Documentary and Pictorial History of the African American Role in the Westward Expansion of the United States*. New York: Random House, 2005.

Watson, Elinor. *Jim Beckwourth: Black Mountain Man and War Chief of the Crows*. Norman: University of Oklahoma Press, 1972.

BELIZE

The English settlement of British Honduras (today, the independent nation of Belize) was founded on northern Central America's Caribbean coast, bordered to the south and west by GUATEMALA and to the north by MEXICO's Yucatán state. Belize lies within the perimeter of a pre-Columbian Maya culture area stretching from present-day southern Mexico, across the Yucatán Peninsula and Guatemala, into western portions of HONDURAS and EL SALVADOR.

Belize's national territory comprises 8,263 square miles; its most prominent geographic features are the south-central Maya Mountains, the western Mountain Pine Ridge, and the hilly, forested karstic limestone formations of the West and South. The coastal plain consists of mangrove forests that also provided dye woods for European wool manufacturing during the Industrial Revolution. It is characterized by riverine alluvial deposits and generally sandy soil with rather sparse evergreen vegetation. The subtropical rain forests of the interior first attracted English settlement dedicated to extracting mahogany and other tropical timbers. The country's most prominent marine feature is the barrier reef, 135 miles in length, extending from the Mexican border to the Sapodilla Cays—after Australia's, it is the second largest in the world.

Early History

The territory of present-day Belize was inhabited by indigenous Maya-speaking groups long before first contact by Spanish forces in the early 16th century. The Maya civilization flourished throughout Mesoamerica for more than a millennium. Archaeologists estimate that in the territory of present-day Belize alone, the indigenous population numbered between 400,000 and one million in the pre-Columbian and early Spanish colonial periods. There are several hundred Maya archaeological sites in Belize, many originally identified by British Museum expeditions in the early 20th century and later explored more extensively by North American researchers. Maya archaeological sites are situated primarily in limestone areas; among the most important are Altun Ha, Caracol, Cerros, Lamanai, Lubaantun, Nim Li Punit, and Xunantunich.

There is little documentation of early interactions between the Maya and the early English adventurers who arrived to exploit the region's timber. They settled at the mouth of the Belize River and worked the interior. Insects, humidity, tropical storms, and episodic incursions by Spanish forces destroyed many early records of the Baymen (named after their settlement on the Bay of Honduras). Moreover, unlike the Spanish priests, who left extensive chronicles of their activities, the English adventurers-turned-loggers were generally illiterate. Motivated by growing European industrial demand for dyewoods and, somewhat later, mahogany, the loggers left few written documents regarding their activities in the interior and say little about their resulting conflicts with the Maya. Some of the English adventurers probably had African ancestry. The woodcutters were from the same general population as the buccaneers of the Caribbean, many of whom were entirely or partly of African ancestry (*see* PIRACY).

In the early 17th century, Puritan colonists settled Old Providence Island (Isla de la Providencia) and Roatan, off the Central American coast, planting tobacco and gathering silk grass. They employed some African slaves on their farms. In this period, English laws and customs made little distinction between slaves and indentured servants, and in other parts of the English colonial world, blacks imported as slaves gained their freedom after a set period of years. In any case, in frontier societies, the line between free and slave is much more permeable than in more highly developed slave societies. We can assume that there were free people among the Afro-descended population of these early colonies. Some sources suggest that these settlers may also have worked the Cockscomb Coast of Belize (near present-day South Stann Creek, Silk Grass, and Sittee River), taking advantage of the absence of any Spanish settlements along this stretch of the Caribbean littoral. Spanish forces drove the English settlers from Old Providence and Roatan in 1641–42, when the besieged also would have abandoned the Cockscomb.

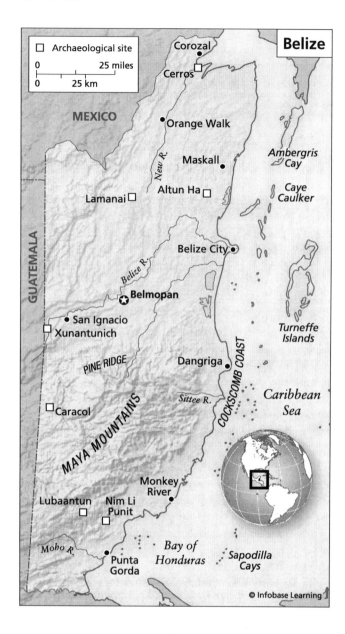

Slavery in Belize

Spain's expulsion of British logwood cutters from Campeche in 1717 sent more settlers south to the Bay of Honduras. A major problem was to secure the necessary labor to expand the timber operations, as British attempts to enslave indigenous Maya groups were unsuccessful. British and Spanish documents alike note an African presence in Belize beginning in the 1720s, referring to blacks imported from Jamaica and Barbados.

Differing from the more common pattern of plantation slavery in most of the Americas, the geography and natural resources of Belize favored a political economy based on extracting local timber resources; this in turn informed a distinctive set of labor relations. The enslaved would spend several months a year working upriver during the dry season, cutting timber and dragging logs to the riverbanks, to be floated downriver during the rainy season. This granted the enslaved a degree of liberty in their work unknown under the more controlled regime of plantation slavery, comparable in the Americas mainly to slaves who worked in alluvial gold mining, as in Brazil's Minas Gerais. As timber workers, male slaves were separated for extended periods from their families, who remained in the British settlement at the mouth of the Belize River, on the Bay of Honduras. This relative freedom permitted enslaved people access to resources, and thus the survivors were more likely to be able to purchase freedom. Also, those willing to exchange a difficult life in the forests for slavery had no difficulty in doing so, and some RUNAWAY SLAVES eventually lived with the Maya.

By the mid-18th century, the enslaved population far outnumbered white settlers in Belize, and by the beginning of the 19th century, slaves constituted about 75 percent of the population. Consequently, whites lived in constant apprehension of slave uprisings, and conditions in the timber camps gave rise to at least four documented slave revolts between 1765 and 1820. Communities of MAROONS existed on the Sibun River and in the Blue Mountains to its north; while these maroons never engaged in prolonged harassment of white settlements, their ultimate fate is unknown (Table 1).

When Spain forced British settlers to evacuate NICARAGUA's Mosquito Coast in 1787, many of the displaced sought refuge in the Belize River area, where mahogany extraction was on the rise. They took their slaves with them, thus more than doubling the local enslaved population. While logwood could be cut by a master and two or three slaves, mahogany required a far more extensive and specialized labor force. Hence, timber entrepreneurs imported growing numbers of enslaved Africans to do the work. After 1770, 80 percent of all male slaves more

Some sources suggest that the English exiles may have sought refuge farther north near the mouth of the Belize River and may have taken the first enslaved Africans, and presumably also the first free people of color, with them to Belize.

After England wrested Jamaica from Spain in 1655, Jamaica-based English buccaneers began attacking Spanish campeche (logwood) ships arriving from the Yucatán, hijacking cargoes to supply dye materials to the expanding English wool industry. After the 1670 Treaty of Madrid, England moved to eradicate piracy, and English buccaneers began cutting their own logwood surreptitiously. They began to establish themselves in the territory south of Yucatán, in the vicinity of the mouth of the Belize River, joining the few survivors of the earlier colonial efforts there.

TABLE 1:
ENSLAVED POPULATION OF BELIZE, 1745–1835

Year	Adult Males	Adult Females	Children	Total Slaves	Belize Total Population	Enslaved Percentage of Total Population
1745	n/a	n/a	n/a	120	170	71%
1787*	n/a	n/a	n/a	1,000	1,300	77%
1787	n/a	n/a	n/a	2,677	3,514	76%
1790	1,091	515	418	2,024	2,656	75%
1803	1,700	675	584	2,959	3,959	75%
1806	1,489	588	450	2,527	3,526	72%
1816	1,645	639	458	2,742	3,824	72%
1820	1,537	600	426	2,563	n/a	n/a
1823	1,440	628	400	2,468	4,107	60%
1826	1,373	577	460	2,410	5,197	46%
1829	1,113	486	428	2,027	3,883	52%
1832	895	435	453	1,783	3,794	47%
1835	768	416	n/a	1,184	2,543	47%

*before arrival of refugees from the Mosquito Coast

than 10 years of age worked in the forests during the dry summer season, in gangs of 10–50 men performing a variety of critical specialized tasks.

From slavery's inception in the 1720s, runaways from logging operations up the Belize River fled to El Petén, Guatemala, and the 18th century was marked by recurrent flights to freedom under Spanish rule in nearby Mexico, Guatemala, and Spanish Honduras. Slaves were adept at turning the situation's inherent contradictions to their advantage: Escape was relatively easy, because men worked in small, largely unsupervised woodcutting groups in the untracked interior, and they were armed with both the knowledge and the tools of the bush.

The stakes were high, however; runaways risked flogging, punitive amputation of body parts, and permanent transportation from the settlement for attempting to escape or aiding others in the effort. Another constraint upon escape was the relatively stable family life that at least some slaves enjoyed, and owners, recognizing the attachment to family occupied in domestic service back in Belize City, exploited this fact as a means of social control.

As formalized by the Spanish Crown in 1752, New Spain's governors were authorized to grant freedom to all Africans who fled British and Dutch slavery in the Western Hemisphere, contingent upon conversion to Catholicism—a policy that persisted into the period of Central American independence after 1821. British colonial reports refer repeatedly to fruitless negotiations with Spanish authorities for the return of runaways.

Ongoing conflict between Great Britain and Spain in the western Caribbean led British authorities to enlist Belizean free men of color in the West India Regiment in the 1790s, to be paid the going rate for regular recruits (see REGULAR ARMY). The Crown further proposed to fill its military ranks by purchasing enslaved males from the English woodcutters, with the proviso that those so enlisted would be liberated upon ratification of peace with Spain. The latter measure proved unnecessary, although some slaves fought alongside the British command in the last major Spanish attack on Belize in 1798. Even so, military recruitment continued into the 19th century, and some slaves sought to pass themselves off as free men when seeking to enlist in the West India Regiment, although punishment included lashing and permanent transportation from the settlement.

Manumission and Abolition
As did their counterparts throughout the English-speaking Americas, SLAVE OWNERS in Belize readily argued—contradicting the evidence at hand—that local slave conditions were superior to those of common wage laborers in Britain, and local newspapers regularly took issue with British abolitionists in a transatlantic debate. While owners couched their supposed temperance in humanitarian terms, as a class they were constrained more by the prevailing atmosphere of slave hostility and

resistance and the small British contingent of the total population.

Evidence is slim regarding the details or extent of MANUMISSION in Belize, although free people of color already were 14 percent of the population by the 1790s. In the early 1800s, manumission upon a master's death was not uncommon, and the enslaved—often along with their children—might be freed in cases of extreme cruelty at the hands of their masters, or when a slave's legal testimony was deemed crucial in a court case. Colonial records report 173 manumissions in the period 1807–16 (from a total slave population of some 2,500).

Free people of color were allowed to set up their own logging operations, provided that they possessed at least four able-bodied male slaves—an indication that an undetermined number of free blacks were able to accumulate sufficient capital to enter the industry. Sustained labor demand enabled slaves to hire themselves out during their free time; although this strategy was for a time officially prohibited, masters with insufficient slave labor plainly abetted the practice, which was legalized by 1810. The system permitted people who were legally enslaved to live just as if they were free (see LIVING "AS FREE"), blurring the lines between free and slave and providing a convenient cover for runaways.

Even with slavery, labor demand led some owners to the legally ambiguous measure of enslaving ZAMBO people (individuals of mixed indigenous and African descent), as had earlier English raiders who took indigenous captives as slaves up and down Central America's Caribbean coast. From the early 19th century, British woodcutters also began to employ men from the free African-Amerindian Garifuna settlements dotting the Caribbean coast from southern Belize to northern Nicaragua.

By that time, the Garifuna (known as the BLACK CARIB during the colonial era) had also established a reputation as mercenaries, and their multilingual talents enabled them to ride the tide of political intrigue and shifting military alliances. The British hired Garifuna to protect Caye Caulker, Belize, while the Spanish hired them to protect the Guatemalan fort at San Felipe (at the mouth of Lake Izabal) from pirates; others served as mercenaries in Spanish Honduras at Omoa and Trujillo. Many Garifuna who supported the losing side in the Honduran civil war fled in 1832 for the Garifuna settlements of Belize; others joined the Miskito Indians to the south on the Río Patuca.

In Belize, free people of color also became higglers (peddlers), among other activities selling rum to the enslaved in defiance of local ordinances. European commentators asserted that people of color and free blacks, many with property, were numerous, and in 1816, St. John's Church in Belize began soliciting contributions to set up a "free school" governed by the colonial superintendent and magistrates, to educate children born of poor free parents.

As elsewhere in the British West Indies, the dominant white population remained relatively small in Belize. In a white population that never exceeded 10 percent of the settlement total after 1790, white men outnumbered white women in Belize by no less than two to one over the ensuing 45 years; during the same period, the proportion of free persons of color more than tripled, from 14 to 45 percent of the total population (Table 2).

The abolition of slavery in the British Empire in 1834 had an impact on the Belize timber entrepreneurs. This impact was somewhat muted by the so-called apprenticeship period (1834–38), a transition that evolved into the advance-and-truck system of free contracted labor that

TABLE 2:
POPULATION OF BELIZE, 1790–1835

Census Date	Slaves	Free People of Color	Whites	Total Population	Percentage Enslaved	Percentage Free People of Color	Percentage White
1790	2,024	371	261	2,656	76%	14%	10%
1803	2,959	775	225	3,959	75%	20%	6%
1816	2,742	933	149	3,824	72%	24%	4%
1823	2,468	1,422	217	4,107	60%	35%	5%
1826	2,410	2,455	332	5,197	46%	47%	6%
1829	2,027	1,591	265	3,883	52%	41%	7%
1832	1,783	1,788	223	3,794	47%	47%	6%
1835	1,184	1,137	222	2,543	47%	45%	9%

Sources: Bolland (1988, 35); John Alder Burdon, ed. *Archives of British Honduras.* Vol. 2. London: 1931–35, 188, 279, 293, 315, 343, 382.

conditioned labor relations in Belize into the 20th century. Under this system, black woodcutters were paid their wages in advance at the beginning of a cutting season. With their wages in hand, they could hire assistants, leave money for their families' subsistence, and purchase tools. Then, they would be contractually obligated to deliver a certain amount of wood (the truck) to the entrepreneur, usually a powerful white sawmill operator. If they failed to fulfill the contract, they could be imprisoned for debt or required to work off the balance of the contract for no wages, effectively a temporary return to slavery. Workers who were not careful or who were unlucky or fell into the hands of unscrupulous entrepreneurs could work years to pay off their debts. This labor system dominated the timber industry in Belize into the 20th century.

As elsewhere in Central America, in Belize an increasingly urbanized African population emerged in the postslavery era. From the administrative center and port of Belize, the CREOLE elite, in concert with absentee foreign capital, directed the country's overall development, shaping its cultural, economic, and political life in a way that reduced most Belizeans, regardless of ethnicity, to the same dependent and impoverished condition. The Crown stopped granting freehold land after emancipation in 1838, effectively preventing former slaves from becoming landowners.

Garifuna and Maya reservations were also established to prevent these groups from owning the land themselves, in hopes of creating a proletarian labor force. Such measures shaped and limited the nature of agricultural development to the benefit of the wealthy Belize merchants and big landowners. Barred from landownership, some free blacks sought to improve their prospects by emigrating. Some settlers and former slaves went to the Bay Islands, the Antilles, or Grand Cayman. Cultural and social ties remained especially strong with the Bay Islands, where white British settlement persisted, augmented by freed English-speaking blacks.

In the decades preceding abolition, 5 percent of the free heads of household controlled some 85 percent of all slave labor, and a similar concentration of landownership. The means of production were controlled by a small number of white settlers, who likewise monopolized import, export, and mercantile activities, giving them an effective chokehold on a highly vertically integrated economy. Property ownership further concentrated with abolition and the consolidation of metropolitan capital that accompanied it.

The writings of colonial officials, diplomats, military officers, newspaper editors, missionaries, and travelers contributed to the racial dichotomy that emerged upon the end of slavery, with considerable attention given to characterizing and demarcating racial and ethnic differences. The small white elite made limited political concessions to a select group of Anglo-identified people of color, the well-positioned offspring of the selfsame white proprietors. The constellation of wealth limited the modes of upward mobility to inheritance or marriage, in which regard colored and black women, together with their offspring, enjoyed a decided advantage, if not always an entirely enviable one.

The growth and differentiation of the free black and colored population necessitated an ideological shift in Belize. Accordingly, there was a selective opening in the years preceding abolition to a chosen few people of color, carefully screened for social and cultural pedigree. But contrary to the persistent underlying social reality of systematic racial discrimination after abolition, propertied whites continued to proclaim to the world that in Belize respectability was attached to merit alone.

Michael Stone

FURTHER READING

Atkins, John. *A Voyage to Guinea, Brasil, and the West Indies.* London: C. Ward & R. Chandler, 1735.

Bolland, O. Nigel. *Colonialism and Resistance in Belize.* Benque Viejo del Carmen, Belize: Cubola Press, 1988.

———. *The Formation of a Colonial Society: Belize from Conquest to Crown Colony.* Baltimore: Johns Hopkins University Press, 1977.

Bolland, O. Nigel, and Assad Shoman. *Land in Belize, 1765–1781.* Kingston, Jamaica: University of the West Indies Press, 1977.

Gonzalez, Nancie L. *Sojourners of the Caribbean: Ethnogenesis and Ethnohistory of the Garifuna.* Urbana: University of Illinois Press, 1988.

Henderson, George, Capt. *An Account of the British Settlement of Honduras; Being a Brief View of Its Commercial and Agricultural Resources, Soil, Climate, Natural History, &c.* London: C. & R. Baldwin, 1809.

Joseph, Gilbert M. "John Coxon and the Role of Buccaneering in the Settlement of the Yucatán Colonial Frontier." *Belizean Studies* 17, no. 3 (1989): 2–21.

———. "The Logwood Trade and Its Settlements." In *Readings in Belizean History,* 2nd ed., edited by Lita Hunter Krohn, 32–47. Belize City: St. John's College, 1987.

BELLANTON, ZABEAU (ELIZABETH)
(ca. 1751–?) *Saint-Domingue merchant*

Zabeau Bellanton was a free woman of mixed race who was born and lived in CAP-FRANÇAIS/CAP-HAÏTIEN, SAINT-DOMINGUE (the future Haiti), until moving to France in 1782. Her life illustrates the circumstances of free women of color in the colony in the decades before the French Revolution. As a merchant, who sold slaves, among other things, she is a very ironic figure, as well as a surprising one. She is a woman who defied limits that society sought to place on her because of her sex and race and who gained great wealth and influence in a society defined by white male supremacy. We know little about her early life and nothing at all about her circumstances after 1782 (*see also* COMMERCE AND TRADE).

Bellanton was born free, probably before 1751, since she was at least 25 years old in her first appearance in official records in 1776. Her mother, Thérèse Bellanton, was black. Zabeau was always described as mulatto, and so therefore her father must have been white, but there is no evidence as to who he was. He certainly did not have any contact with her in her adult years. In the French colonies, fathers were more likely to be involved in the lives of their mixed-race children than in British colonies, but there were still plenty of fatherless mixed-race children. Consequently, women played a more important role in free colored society than in white society, where fathers were more likely to be present and in charge. Zabeau herself had a daughter, Louise Martine Bellanton, described as a *quarteron* (one-fourth African), and again, no white father was in evidence. Zabeau had business dealings with a large number of white men, but there is no sign that any of these had any personal relationship with her. Her daughter was living in France when Zabeau made her will in 1782 and was still a minor. Children of wealthy free colored families were often sent to France for their education.

Bellanton was a wealthy woman. She always described herself as a jam and jelly maker in official documents, but she had much greater resources than a small business would have generated. In 1778, she bought a house for 18,000 livres (about $500,000 in today's terms) from the viscount de la Belinaye, an influential nobleman in France who owned a lot of property in the colony. Stanislas Föache, one of the most important merchants in the colony, was his agent. Interestingly, she paid part of the purchase price in cash, and a larger portion in notes signed by various merchants, including Föache himself. Apparently, Bellanton was selling a lot of valuable items to these merchants on credit. Other notarial acts show that Bellanton was heavily involved in the slave trade, dealing mostly in young African-born slaves who had not been long in the colony. She sold them cheaply, sometimes with the right of repurchase at a predetermined price.

Slaves who arrived in the colonies from Africa often died within a short time. Conventional wisdom says half died in the first five years, though there is a lot of debate about what the real figure was. In any case, a newly arrived slave was worth at most half what he or she would be worth in a couple of years. What Bellanton was doing was selling these newly arrived slaves at a discount to large merchants, who could then resell them to plantations. If they survived, she had the right to repurchase them at a price higher than she received for them, but generally substantially less than they would then be worth. The purchaser had the use of the slave for a couple of years, if he or she survived, at a discount.

Another interesting question is where she obtained the slaves. Under the law, Stanislas Föache and his competitors, the houses of Gobert fils, Bertrand, Faurier frères, Viart, and Bellanton's other debtors, were the legally permitted importers of newly arrived African slaves and would not need to buy them from a mulatto woman. The answer to this question lies in the patterns of French Atlantic trade in the 18th century. The French government wanted to control trade in order to collect taxes and ensure a flow of profits back to the home country. This policy, called mercantilism in English, is known in French as the *exclusif*. The planters in the colonies hated the *exclusif*, not only because they had to pay taxes, but also because the system was unable to deliver the number of slaves they needed at reasonable prices. So, they turned to smugglers. The "interloper" trade in slaves and tropical commodities was one of the most vibrant sectors of the colony's economy. Bellanton appears to have been a broker for smuggled slaves. Another clue to Bellanton's role in this trade was her sale in 1780 of two slaves to a white construction supervisor described as her employee: The slaves (though born in Africa and presumably speaking their own African languages) are said to speak only English. Much of the interloper trade was from the British islands since the British slave traders were much more efficient, transporting more slaves less expensively than their French competitors.

Bellanton moved to France in 1782 and did not reappear in the records of the colony. She freed a number of her personal slaves, took others with her to France (thus effectively freeing them), and made a will giving money to the "honest poor of the parish, both black and white." She charged one of her business associates, Justin Viart, a prominent merchant and lawyer, to see to the upbringing of her daughter. She also left 15,000 livres to her godmother to buy a "little cottage" (which would have been a pretty impressive structure at that price) for her and her mother to live in for the rest of their lives. By her lights, she was a generous, kind mistress to her slaves and a loving daughter and mother.

Stewart R. King

FURTHER READING

King, Stewart. *Blue Coat or Powdered Wig: Free People of Color in Pre-Revolutionary Saint-Domingue.* Athens: University of Georgia Press, 2001.

Rogers, Dominique, and Stewart King. "Housekeepers, Merchants, *Rentières*: Free Women of Color in the Port Cities of Colonial Saint-Domingue, 1750–1790." In *Women in Port: Gendering Communities, Economies, and Social Networks in Atlantic Port Cities, 1500–1800*, edited by Doug Catterall and Jodi Campbell. Leiden, Netherlands: Brill, forthcoming.

BELLEY, JEAN-BAPTISTE (1748 or 1749–1806?)
member of the French Assembly

Jean-Baptiste Belley was one of the most important black politicians of the French revolutionary era. He was a delegate from the colony of SAINT-DOMINGUE to the French National Assembly, one of the first people of color ever to sit in a French parliament. He served alongside the leader of Haiti's liberation struggle, TOUSSAINT LOUVERTURE, in the colonial armed forces and later fought against him during the HAITIAN REVOLUTION.

Belley was born in West Africa in 1748 or 1749 in what is today Sénégal. He claimed to be a native of the island of Gorée, though perhaps this was just where he embarked on his voyage to the Americas. He was taken to Saint-Domingue as a slave in 1750 or 1751. He worked as a servant as soon as he was old enough, received training as a wig maker, and managed to save enough money to buy his freedom before 1776. He was a prominent artisan in CAP-FRANÇAIS/CAP-HAÏTIEN, the wealthiest city in the French empire, in the 1770s and 1780s. Most well-off men and quite a few women wore wigs in the late 18th century, and Belley made some of the best ones in Cap-Français and the North Province. He was also a militiaman and a veteran of the Chasseurs-Volontaires de Saint-Domingue, a regiment of free colored soldiers that was raised in Cap-Français and sent to Savannah, Georgia, and CHARLESTON, SOUTH CAROLINA, during the WAR OF AMERICAN INDEPENDENCE, 1775–83. As a freedman, he had few blood relatives in the city, and it appears that he never married. Instead, he was godfather to dozens of free colored children and witness to many marriages. Through these ties and through his militia service, he accumulated a large circle of friends and clients that made him an important figure in Cap-Français's free colored community.

When the Haitian Revolution began in 1791, Belley's militia company fought to defend Cap-Français's against the rebels. He was wounded in battle and, after free people of color received the vote in 1793, elected as a representative of the colony to the French National Assembly. He traveled to Paris and spoke during the debate when the abolition of slavery was adopted on February 3, 1794. Belley worked for equality between citizens of the colonies and citizens of metropolitan France and published a pamphlet in 1795 supporting this principle and condemning the planters' lobby, the Club Massiac. He lost his seat in 1797 and apparently served in the metropolitan French police. He returned to Saint-Domingue with the expedition of Charles Leclerc in 1802, as a captain of gendarmes. He may have sensed that Leclerc's goal was to reverse all the gains of the Haitian Revolution for people of color; in any case, he was arrested by Leclerc, perhaps at the same time as ANDRÉ RIGAUD and most of the other French officers of color in 1802, and sent back to France. Imprisoned in the fortress of Belle-Isle in Brittany, he was last heard of in 1805, when he managed to get a letter to Isaac Louverture, the son of his old opponent, Toussaint. He

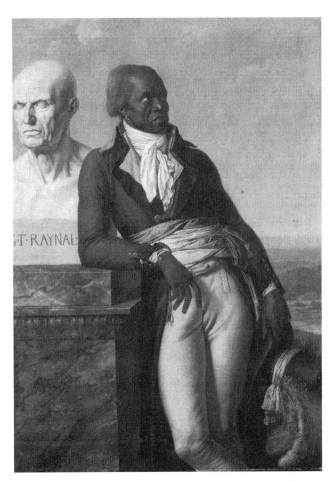

J. B. Belley, Deputy of Saint-Domingue, with a Bust of Guillaume T. F. Raynal, a 1792 portrait, probably made from life, by Anne Girodet de Roussy-Trioson. Belley (1748 or 1749–1806?) was one of the most successful of Cap-Français's free blacks, as an entrepreneur and as a politician. Having gone to Saint-Domingue from Africa as a slave, he became one of the first two people of African descent elected to a national legislative body in Europe. His depiction with the bust of Raynal is intended to refer to Raynal's call for a "black Spartacus" to rise up and free the slaves in the Americas. (Erich Lessing/Art Resource, NY)

died either later in 1805 or early in 1806—several dates are recorded in different sources.

While in the colony in 1802–03, he fathered a son, apparently his only child, to whom he gave the last name Mars. This son went on to become the patriarch of a prominent family in independent Haiti and was the ancestor of the famous Haitian folklorist and intellectual Jean Price-Mars. It is interesting that he used the name Mars: By an edict of 1773, free people of color were to use names "taken from the African idiom" to distinguish them from whites, and many people formally took surnames taken from classical mythology. Most people treated this as a bureaucratic annoyance and rarely if ever used their new "names." Belley was also called Belair and was probably named after the Belair family, French people who lived in Cap-Français, who may have been his former masters. On only two occasions did he use the surname Mars in formal declarations he made before the revolution. He continued using the Belley and Belair names interchangeably throughout his life and was always referred to as Belley during his service in the French legislature. But when the time came to name a son who would live in a free country, he resurrected his "African" name.

Belley also illustrates in his career the many options open to free people of color during the Haitian Revolution. He first fought against the slave rebels and for the revolutionary government of France, apparently wholeheartedly, or at least energetically enough to be wounded. He worked politically for equal rights for free people of color, and then against slavery. He returned to the colony as a supporter of centralized power, against the autonomist or perhaps proindependence policy of Toussaint Louverture. He fought Louverture's forces alongside free colored officers such as ALEXANDRE SABÈS PÉTION and André Rigaud. As did these men, when he saw that the French were planning to restore both slavery and the old racial caste system, he rebelled, was caught, and shipped off to a prison in France as harsh, and as deadly, as the one where his old militia colleague Toussaint Louverture was housed.

In his prerevolutionary life, he demonstrated many of the characteristics of the free black leadership in the North Province. In many colonies, and even in the south and west of Saint-Domingue, free blacks and free people of mixed race were relatively united at least by shared suffering under discrimination. But in the Cap-Français region, because of the great wealth and relative integration of the free mixed-race planter class into white society, prominent free blacks like Belley formed a separate leadership group. They were characterized by their participation in the colonial armed forces and by the way they built networks through acting as godfather and witnessing marriages. Belley and Toussaint Louverture were

of the same class, both lived in the Cap-Français region, and probably knew each other well.

Stewart R. King

FURTHER READING

Fick, Carolyn. "The French Revolution in Saint-Domingue: A Triumph or a Failure?" In *A Turbulent Time: The French Revolution and the Greater Caribbean*, edited by David Barry Gaspar and David Patrick Geggus, 51–77. Bloomington: Indiana University Press, 1997.

King, Stewart. *Blue Coat or Powdered Wig: Free People of Color in Pre-Revolutionary Saint-Domingue*. Athens: University of Georgia Press, 2001.

BIDEAU, JEAN-BAPTISTE   (ca. 1780–1817)
St. Lucian privateer captain

Jean-Baptiste Bideau was a mixed-race man from St. Lucia. He participated in the wars of the FRENCH REVOLUTION and in the SOUTH AMERICAN WARS OF LIBERATION. He first appears in history as the young commander of a privateer—a small private naval vessel operating with the permission of a national navy but working for the profit of its owners—operating out of Guadeloupe (*see also* PIRACY). He was described as a St. Lucian and gave his age as 16. St. Lucia records are very spotty, since the island changed hands several times during this period and the colonial capital of Castries was damaged during the WAR OF AMERICAN INDEPENDENCE, 1775–1783, and burned to the ground during the French Revolution. It is unclear whether Bideau had been free or enslaved in St. Lucia.

In mid-1794, French republican forces commanded by the commissioner VICTOR HUGUES arrived in the island of Guadeloupe, which had fallen into British hands. Hugues was armed with the decrees of the French Revolutionary government that granted citizenship to free people of color and freedom to slaves. These measures assured him of the support of people of color in the islands and allowed him to recruit large land forces. He ultimately succeeded in expelling the British from that island in December of that year. From then on, he also made use of his support among people of color to create a navy of privateers to harass the enemies of France in the Caribbean, in particular Spain and Great Britain. After peace was signed at Basel in 1795 and an alliance was agreed between the French Republic and the Spanish Crown at San Ildefonso in 1796, the authorities of the Spanish Captaincy-General of VENEZUELA allowed those privateers to operate from its coasts and even to dock in its ports, including TRINIDAD AND TOBAGO.

Among the many French vessels operating in Guadeloupe in 1797 was a French brig named *Bouton de Rose* (Rosebud), captained by Jean-Baptiste Bideau. Little is known about his combat record, just that he held a letter of marque (document giving permission to a private ship to operate as a privateer) signed by the French authorities.

After Guadeloupe fell into British hands later that year, Bideau decided to remain in the island under British rule. He ran a ship repair and construction yard. In 1811, attracted by the possibility of serving as a privateer in the Venezuelan republican navy, and maybe acting out of political support for the republican cause, he took his ship to join Venezuela's small fleet. On February 27, 1812, he and the Venezuelan officer Felipe Estevez commanded the naval forces that defeated the royalist navy at the battle of Boca de Macareo (a channel of the Orinoco River). This battle cut the royalist strongholds in the Orinoco delta off from their seaborne lines of communication for several months. In July of that year, immediately after the patriots under FRANCISCO DE MIRANDA had surrendered to the royalist forces commanded by General Monteverde, Bideau was present at the port city of La Guaira (a few miles north of Caracas), where he worked to transport many patriot refugees to Trinidad. In Trinidad, he planned, along with Santiago Mariño (1788–1854), the reconquest of the Venezuelan mainland from a base on the islet of Chacachacare. On January 13, 1813, they took over the coastal town of Güiria in eastern Venezuela in the Orinoco delta, where they established an independent government headed by Bideau. As chief of government, he entered into negotiations with the British governors of Trinidad seeking a trade and navigation treaty. The British had welcomed him as an exile in Trinidad and had been quietly supporting Venezuelan rebels since before 1800.

When the republic Simón Bolívar and his followers had established in Caracas collapsed in late 1814, the royalist army headed eastward. By that time, the town of Güiria was defended by an army composed mostly of free people of color from the French colonies recruited by Bideau. This place was the last republican bastion to fall into royalist hands on February 16, 1815. Before leaving, Bideau made sure to emancipate the slaves from the area, encouraging them to flee into the mountains. After a short stay in Trinidad, he moved to Saint-Bartholomé, Saint-Thomas, and finally the city of Les Cayes, in Haiti. There he met Bolívar, along with many other Venezuelan and Colombian supporters of independence, who had fled South America ahead of a very strong Spanish army that had just arrived (see also CARTAGENA). Bideau took part in the expedition organized by Bolívar in 1816 to the South American mainland, which had material support from the Haitian president, ALEXANDRE SABÈS PÉTION. After taking over the island of Margarita, off the Venezuelan coast, the expeditionary army was defeated at Ocumare de la Costa on September 1816. After this

failure, Bolívar considered committing suicide but was dissuaded by Bideau, who took Bolívar back to Haiti on board the ship *Indio Libre* (Free Indian) There Bideau was appointed commander of the eastern region of Venezuela, including his former stronghold of Güaira and the island of Margarita, by Admiral Brion, Bolívar's British naval commander.

In December 1816, again with the support of Pétion, Bolívar led yet another attack on Venezuelan soil departing from the Haitian port of Jacmel. This time, he succeeded in establishing a new republican government on the shores of the Orinoco River, in the city of Angostura. The rearguard of his army, stationed in the city of Barcelona, was attacked on April 7, 1817, by a 2,000-man royalist army. The proindependence forces took refuge in the Convent of San Francisco, transformed into a stronghold. But ultimately they were slaughtered by the enemy's artillery. Around 1,600 men and women died that day on the republican side, among them the free colored captain from Saint Lucia, Jean-Baptiste Bideau.

Bideau's life illustrates the important role that free people of color played in the nautical realm in the early 19th century. Large percentages of common sailors in the tropical Americas were people of color, and there were few limits on promotion, at least to noncommissioned officer ranks (see MERCHANT SEAMEN and NAVY). It was not uncommon to find black or mixed-race captains, especially of small merchant ships. In European navies, there were very few black commissioned officers before the French Revolution, but the revolution opened up possibilities to everyone. Bideau was obviously a smart and opportunistic young man, who seized on what fortune offered him. After playing an undistinguished role in the struggle for freedom in the French Caribbean, he then rose to considerable importance in the struggle for the freedom of Venezuela before his untimely death.

Alejandro E. Gomez

FURTHER READING
Blanchard, Peter. *Under the Flags of Freedom: Slave Soldiers and the Wars of Independence in Spanish South America.* Pittsburgh: University of Pittsburgh Press, 2008.
Chasteen, John Charles. *Americanos: Latin America's Struggle for Independence.* New York: Oxford University Press, 2008.

BIGODE, FRANCISCO XAVIER   (?–1838)
Brazilian militia officer

Francisco Xavier Pereira (later Bigode) was a free colored militia officer from SALVADOR, BAHÍA, BRAZIL, in the northeastern part of the country. He fought in Brazil's war of independence (1821–23) and again in a very important rebellion of free people of color against conservative rule in 1837.

Left as a foundling in the late 18th century—the year of his birth is unknown—Pereira enlisted in Salvador's black MILITIA in 1797. Known as the 3rd Militia Regiment or the Henrique Dias Regiment, after HENRIQUE DIAS, a 17th-century free colored military leader, this unit enrolled black men and was commanded by black officers. Commissioned second lieutenant in 1805, Pereira was appointed to the paid positions of adjutant in 1809 and major in 1813 under special provisions that allowed black and mulatto militiamen to demonstrate their military qualifications through special examinations. Normally, the posts of adjutant and major were held by regular army officers transferred to the militia, but few regular officers were willing to serve in the segregated militia. In 1820, Bigode reached the rank of lieutenant-colonel and command of the regiment.

His delay in joining the patriot forces in the war for Brazilian independence that was fought mostly in and around Salvador meant that he lost his command in 1822. As a sign of his patriotic identification with the new nation, however, he dropped his Portuguese surname *Pereira* in favor of *Bigode*—moustache—apparently his nickname. In 1828, he returned to command the black militia, now designated the 92nd Militia Battalion. Commanding this battalion, he played a prominent role in the overthrow of the provincial government in 1831.

In late 1831, a new Brazilian government abolished the old segregated militias and established a new integrated national guard, with elected officers. In Salvador, none of the former black militia officers managed to win election in the new units. Bigode and other black and mulatto militia officers repeatedly protested this exclusion and measures that left them receiving lower pensions than their regular army counterparts. They condemned these policies as incompatible with the "impartiality that a free Constitution today affirms," as they said in one of their appeals to the emperor, and called on the Brazilian Empire to recognize that "all black and mulatto men [were] worthy of all military honors and posts."

None of these appeals to equality before the law was accepted, and in 1837, Bigode and many of his fellow militia officers joined the Sabinada Rebellion, a radical liberal and federalist revolt led by FRANCISCO SABINO ÁLVARES DA ROCHA VIEIRA that restored the old segregated militias and abolished the national guard. The Sabinada drew extensive support from Salvador's free black and mulatto population and was seen by many contemporaries as a race war. Bigode resumed his old command; he and his men acquitted themselves well in the fighting. The rebellion was defeated in March 1838, and shortly after surrendering, Bigode was murdered by the vengeful government troops.

Hendrik Kraay

FURTHER READING

Kraay, Hendrik. "The Politics of Race in Independence-Era Bahia: The Black Militia Officers of Salvador, 1790–1840." In *Afro-Brazilian Culture and Politics: Bahia, 1790s–1840s*, 31–56. Armonk, N.Y.: M. E. Sharpe, 1998.

———. *Race, State, and Armed Forces in Independence-Era Brazil: Bahia, 1790s–1840s*. Palo Alto, Calif.: Stanford University Press, 2001.

BISSETTE, CYRILLE-CHARLES   (1795–1858)
French abolitionist and politician

Cyrille-Charles Bissette was born in Martinique in 1795, during the FRENCH REVOLUTION. At that time, France had temporarily abolished slavery, though Martinique was occupied by the British and abolition never took effect there (*see also* FRENCH CARIBBEAN). Bissette's parents were free people of color. His father was half brother to Josephine de Beauharnais (1763–1814), Napoléon's first wife, and was a successful coffee planter.

Bissette became a merchant in Fort-de-France. After the end of the Napoleonic Wars, France regained control of Martinique, and since slavery had been reimposed by Napoléon in 1804, conditions remained much as they had been before the revolution. The first historical reference to Bissette is as a member of the Martinique MILITIA that put down the slave rebellion at Le Carbet in 1822.

In December 1823, an anonymous pamphlet appeared in Martinique denouncing the slave system and exposing the oppression of the slaves. Bissette was revealed to be the author of the pamphlet, and he was arrested by the local authorities for sedition and violation of censorship laws. He was found guilty and sentenced to branding and hard labor in the galleys—a common sentence that in the 19th century no longer meant service as a galley slave but instead some form of hard labor for punishment while imprisoned. After a long legal battle, during which Bissette was branded and publicly exposed in the town square, he was finally banished to France. He continued to work for the abolition of slavery, publishing a newspaper from 1834 to 1848. He was often harassed by the authorities but fought on and became one of the most prominent French abolitionists. He and his colleagues tirelessly called for immediate abolition and finally convinced, among others, Victor Schoelcher (1804–93), an important businessman and abolitionist writer who was to rise to the position of colonial secretary after 1848.

The revolution of 1848 in France gave Schoelcher the opportunity to proclaim the abolition of slavery, and the new constitution granted full civil rights for people of color. As soon as the decree was published, Bissette returned to Martinique, to an ecstatic reception, and declared his candidacy for the Chamber of Deputies. He was elected, but the parliament refused to seat him because of his 1820s conviction for sedition. The superior court in France annulled his conviction, though, and in 1849, he was elected again, defeating Schoelcher by 16,000 votes to less than 4,000. Schoelcher attacked Bissette, accusing him of selling out to the white colonial elite, and the controversy between them was a major political cause célèbre in the Antilles for the rest of the Second Republic. Bissette had the support of the wealthiest whites in the colony, but also of the wealthy free people of color. The two groups had similar economic interests, and Bissette, who shared those interests, appeared to wealthy Martiniquans to be a safer representative than the untried middle-class metropolitan Frenchman Schoelcher. After the coup in 1851 that brought Napoléon III to power, Bissette retired from politics. He lived out his remaining years moving between Paris and Martinique and died on January 22, 1858, in Paris. Schoelcher went into exile, returned triumphantly after the defeat of Napoléon III in 1870, and served as deputy and then senator until his death in 1893, and thus it is that Schoelcher rather than Bissette is remembered as the leading abolitionist of 19th-century France.

Bissette's life is important for many reasons. In addition to his impact on France's decision to eliminate slavery for the second time, he also illustrates the conditions under which wealthy free people of color lived in the early 19th century and the influence they had after 1848. His conviction on charges of sedition would have been impossible had he been an equally prominent white businessman. At worst, he would have been fined for violation of the censorship laws. But a man of color could be branded and sentenced to hard labor for any expression of political dissent. After abolition, he was the consensus choice of newly freed black Martiniquans as their representative to parliament, illustrating the continuing importance of the former free people of color as leaders of the community of color in the French colonies. His close relationship with the white Martiniquan leader Auguste Pécoul and his effort to convince black Martiniquans to forget the oppression of the past and look to a future of shared interests among all the ethnic groups of the colony were also typical of the political role of former free people of color after abolition in many places in the Americas.

Stewart R. King

FURTHER READING
Jennings, Lawrence C. *French Anti-Slavery: The Movement for the Abolition of Slavery in France, 1802–1848.* New York: Cambridge University Press, 2000.

Pame, Stella. *Cyrille Bissette, un Martyre de la Liberté.* Paris: Editions Désormeaux, 1999.

BLACK CAESAR (JOHN CAESAR)   (ca. 1760s–1796) *Australian bandit*

Black Caesar, sometimes known as John Caesar, is regarded as the first bushranger, an outlaw who lived in the unsettled fringes of Australia's early European settlements. Little is known about the early years of his life, though he was probably born sometime in the 1760s. Though a naval lieutenant once described him as a "native of Madagascar," historians point to the West Indies and the United States as his most likely places of birth. *Caesar* was a common name for black chattel slaves in slaveholding societies in the Americas, and his lack of a proper name indicates that he may at one time have been a household slave before arriving in Britain, possibly as a runaway just after the WAR OF AMERICAN INDEPENDENCE, 1775–83. He was said to have a very dark complexion and to stand six feet tall.

On March 17, 1786, Caesar was convicted at the Kent Assizes in London of theft and sentenced to transportation to Australia to work as a laborer for seven years. He left on the convict transport ship for Australia in 1787, arriving at Port Jackson in Sydney in January 1788.

On April 30, 1788, he was charged with theft for allegedly stealing bread from Maitland Shairp, to whom he had been assigned as a convict laborer. The outcome of this trial is unknown. He was charged with theft again on April 29, 1789, and found guilty, and his sentence was changed from seven years to life. A fortnight after this conviction, Caesar left the convict settlement for the bush, carrying with him a musket and an iron cooking pot. He was discovered sometime later and sentenced to death by Judge-Advocate David Collins, who said of him: "This man was always reputed the hardest working convict in the colony." Soon after, Governor Arthur Phillip pardoned him to work in the settlement's vegetable gardens on what is known today as Garden Island in Sydney Harbour.

Caesar ran away yet again in December 1789, taking with him a canoe and some provisions. After stealing a musket, he robbed gardens and frightened away indigenous Australians from their settlements in order to procure food. Defenseless after losing his gun, he was attacked by natives and received multiple spear wounds before being rescued. He was sentenced to hang as soon as he recovered from his injuries but received another pardon from Governor Phillip and was sent to Norfolk Island, a harsh "prison within a prison" for very serious offenders, on March 6, 1790. There he was allocated one acre of land, where he could work three days a week.

At some point, he began living with Ann Poore, and a daughter named Mary-Ann was born in March 1792.

For reasons unknown, Caesar returned to Sydney on March 21, 1793, without his family. He hauled carts in town before escaping to the bush again in July 1794 and was flogged as a punishment after recapture, to which Collins reported Caesar to have declared that "all that would not make him better." Collins stated that Caesar "fled . . . to the woods" again in December 1795 and eventually formed an outlaw gang, earning him the distinction of being the first bushranger in Australian history. The Australian governor John Hunter, who succeeded Phillip, put out a notice on January 29, 1796, that "whoever shall secure this man Black Caesar and bring him in with his arms shall receive a reward five gallons of spirits." A man named John Wimbow, a convicted British highwayman, found Caesar on February 15 at Liberty Plains and shot him. He was said not to have died immediately but been dragged back to the hut of one Thomas Rose, where he succumbed to his wound. Wimbow claimed he shot Caesar in self-defense and had a witness as proof, and both Hunter and Collins repeated this account of the story. In her book *Black Founders*, the historian Cassandra Pybus suggests that Wimbow may have been one of the members of the outlaw gang Caesar had formed.

Caesar's daughter was baptized Mary-Ann Fisher Power in 1806 and moved to Van Dieman's Land, the modern Tasmania, in 1813.

The popularity of Caesar, both at the time and up to the modern day, is testimony to the importance of social banditry in Australia. As the first bushranger, Caesar set a pattern for many rogues and malcontents to follow, and his fame expressed the independence and antiauthoritarian quality of the Australian national character. His status as a person of color perhaps heightened the tension with the established British norms of behavior and ideas about the social order.

Aurora Morrison

FURTHER READING

Gillen, Mollie, and Chris Cunneen. "Caesar, John Black (c. 1763–1796) Biographical Entry." Australian Dictionary of Biography, Online Edition. October 30, 2008. Available online. URL: http://www.adb.online.anu.edu.au/biogs/AS10070b.htm. Accessed December 19, 2010.

Pybus, Cassandra. *Black Founders.* Sydney: University of New South Wales Press, 2006.

BLACK CARIB (Garifuna)

The Black Carib, or Garifuna, are a group of Afro-Indian people who originally came into existence on the islands of the Lesser Antilles in the 17th and early 18th centuries (*see also* BRITISH LESSER ANTILLES). Many of these people were transported to the Caribbean coast of Central America, in BELIZE, GUATEMALA, HONDURAS, and NICARAGUA in the late 18th century. Their lifestyle and history parallel those of other Afro-Indian groups of MAROONS such as the BLACK SEMINOLE.

The indigenous inhabitants of the Lesser Antilles were the Carib, whose ancestors migrated from the interior of northern South America, starting in the 11th or 12th century. The early European visits to the area did not result in the conquest and destruction of the Carib, which was the fate of the Arawak people of the Greater Antilles. Most Carib groups were left pretty much in peace to adjust to the European diseases. Nonetheless, populations fell. In the 17th century, Dutch, French, and English settlers began to appear in the Lesser Antilles. The indigenous inhabitants were not unremittingly hostile but were quite suspicious of the newcomers. The newcomers' slaves, on the other hand, were often welcome in the villages of the Carib. One spectacular shipwreck on St. Vincent in 1675 sent hundreds of Africans into a Carib-dominated area. The Carib and their black neighbors at first lived side by side. But increasingly over the next century, they intermarried, blended cultures and technologies, and advised and helped each other to cope with the hostility of the European colonists. Finally, by the late 18th century, they were one people, speaking an Indian-based Creole heavily influenced by African and French and English roots, farming traditional Indian crops and some imported cash crops, governing themselves with a traditional "big man" oligarchy like those common in West Africa, and fighting fiercely against European colonial expansion. Most Black Carib practiced a syncretic version of Catholicism called Garinagu with many African spiritual concepts (*see also* AFRICAN AND SYNCRETIC RELIGIONS). The Black Carib of St. Vincent were especially well organized and powerful, under the leadership of their paramount chief, Joseph Chatoyer. Chatoyer had made an arrangement with the French colonial officials who ruled St. Vincent before 1763 to leave his people alone on the windward side of the island—a relationship similar to that developed by many maroon communities in the Americas, and like that between the British and the Cockpit Country Maroons in JAMAICA. However, the British were unprepared to honor the agreement on St. Vincent after they took the colony in 1763, and this policy led to a difficult series of wars during the second half of the 18th century.

The Carib had better relations with the French than the British, on the whole, and the history of intermittent warfare between France and Britain during the

18th century gave them a political opening. Especially after the beginning of the FRENCH REVOLUTION in 1789, the Carib proved important allies for the French forces led by VICTOR HUGUES out of Guadeloupe. When the French were finally suppressed in the Caribbean after 1795, the British turned on the Carib and expelled most of them from St. Vincent to the island of Roatan, off the coast of Honduras. From there, the Black Carib moved to the mainland, serving as soldiers for the Spanish and British colonists and settling in the forests alongside the indigenous people. In Central America, they became known as the Garifuna. They preserved their autonomy into the 20th century, resisting the British colonial rulers of Belize and the newly independent states of Spanish Central America. Small groups of Carib remained on many of the islands of the Lesser Antilles and often also preserved a degree of autonomy under British colonial rule.

Stewart R. King

FURTHER READING

Franzone, Dorothy. "A Critical and Cultural Analysis of an African People in the Americas: Africanisms in the Garifuna Culture of Belize." Ann Arbor, Mich: UMI Dissertation Services, 1995.

Gonzalez, Nancie L. *Sojourners of the Caribbean: Ethnogenesis and Ethnohistory of the Garifuna.* Urbana: University of Illinois Press, 1988.

BLACK CODES IN THE UNITED STATES

Black codes were laws that governed the actions of people of African ancestry, both free and enslaved, in the Americas. (*See* CODE NOIR IN FRENCH LAW and LEGAL DISCRIMINATION ON THE BASIS OF RACE for a comparative treatment. This article deals with the British and American legal structure.)

By the end of the 17th century, in both mainland English North America and the Caribbean colonies, a legal system had evolved that distinguished between people on the basis of both race and status. This system was embodied in formal comprehensive black codes passed by most colonies between the 1670s and 1750s, occasionally renewed, and generally strengthened through the 18th and early 19th centuries.

Under these laws, slaves were deemed inherently inferior to free people of any race. They were subject to the jurisdiction of their masters for most legal matters; misdeeds that would normally require the attention of law enforcement, such as assault or robbery, instead were punished by plantation discipline. Personal property or money that slaves were permitted to possess was formally considered the property of their masters, and the mas-

ters could resolve disputes related to property without any reference to the legal system. Whites other than their owners were generally given wide latitude in their dealings with enslaved people, limited only by the fact that in harming a slave they also harmed his or her owner. Slaves had no legal standing whatsoever unless accused of a truly serious crime such as murder and had no recourse against whites who had harmed them. Only their masters could act on their behalf, and then only if the master had suffered some material harm. So, if a white man assaulted a slave who was not his own, his master might at most be able to claim medical expenses or the value of the slave's lost labor. When traveling outside their owners' property, slaves were required to carry a pass and were sharply restricted in their activities. Although many worked for wages with their owners' consent, bought and sold in the market, and otherwise participated in free society, there were sharp legal restrictions on these practices. Owners and slaves often colluded to evade these regulations, but their very existence speaks to the determination of the British legal system to establish a barrier between free and enslaved people. Similar, though much less harsh laws applied to white indentured servants.

Similar, though less harsh regulations also applied to free people of color. The most important of these was the requirement that free people of color be always ready to prove their free status to any white who asked. The assumption of the law was that every black person was naturally a slave, and freedom was an exception to the general rule. Free people of color normally carried their "freedom papers" with them everywhere they went, at least outside their immediate neighborhoods. People who were caught without papers could be taken into custody by almost any white and were at risk of re-enslavement if they could not prove their status quickly. Some colonies restricted the sorts of trades or professional activities free people of color could exercise—the law, medicine, sometimes religious ministry, often innkeeping and gunsmithing, were all activities reserved for whites. Free people of color were also often limited in the amount of land and number of slaves they could own. The intent was to prevent people of color from joining the planter elite, though in a very few cases some individuals were able to exceed this limit. Frequently, wealthy free people of color found themselves obliged to hire white plantation managers or overseers, whom they then had difficulty properly supervising because of the higher racial status of the employee. Disputes between free people of color and whites could be resolved in court, but free coloreds were hampered in their use of the courts both by informal discrimination and sometimes by formal rules that prevented them from testifying against a white. Free people of color were almost never permitted to serve on

A cartoon in *Harper's Weekly* from 1867 by the noted cartoonist Thomas Nast criticizing the Southern states for imposing harsh black codes on their newly freed slaves after the American Civil War. These black codes also applied, in most cases, to prewar free people of color. Sometimes they were based on laws that restricted free people of color before the Civil War, but often they imposed additional restrictions and represented a step backward for free blacks. The Fourteenth Amendment to the U.S. Constitution, ratified in 1868, invalidated the black codes, but restrictions were often resurrected informally during the period of Jim Crow. *(Library of Congress)*

juries, making winning lawsuits difficult. Indeed, they could not hold any other public employment above the most basic service level. Some British colonies—North Carolina and New Jersey in North America, for example—permitted free people of color who met the property qualifications to vote, but because the property qualifications were high, this never amounted to more than a few dozen individuals at any time. This almost total exclusion from public life applied to lower-class whites in the early days of British presence in the Americas, but as political rights extended to a larger and larger spectrum of whites, free blacks were increasingly excluded. This process accelerated after the independence of the United States.

The rapid legal progress that blacks experienced in the British Empire, from the abolition of the slave trade in 1807 to the extension of some legal rights to free people of color in the colonies in the 1820s, through the abolition of slavery itself in 1833, was not matched in the United States. America abolished its own slave trade in 1808,

the earliest date permitted by the U.S. Constitution. This act was welcomed by SLAVE OWNERS in the Chesapeake region, who saw the value of their own slaves shoot up while birthrates remained high. The worst period of legal discrimination against people of African ancestry in the United States was the immediate antebellum period. The newly created southeastern slave states—Mississippi, Alabama, and Florida—enacted black codes that made it almost impossible for free people of color to live there and even increasing the authority of masters over their slaves. Newly freed blacks had to pay large fees or deposits in order to be allowed to remain in the state. Free people of color who left the state could not return in many cases. Some of the "Old South" states of the Atlantic seaboard, with large free populations of color, passed similar laws. Even LOUISIANA, with its looser French ideas about race and status, tightened restrictions after it became a state in 1812. Nonslave states also enacted discriminatory regulations, in some cases banning the entry of free people of color altogether. These restrictions were not seen as unusual: American public opinion saw people of color as not being truly American, as being interlopers only tolerated for their labor. Chief Justice Roger Taney (1777–1864), in the *Dred Scott* decision of 1857, held that blacks were not and could never be citizens of the United States. In so doing, he expressed the attitude of a substantial majority of white Americans, including those who, as did Taney, considered slavery a stain on the national character. (*See* SCOTT, DRED.)

The AMERICAN CIVIL WAR, 1861–65, and the period of RECONSTRUCTION IN THE UNITED STATES made significant changes in the legal status of people of African ancestry (*see also* CIVIL RIGHTS LAWS IN THE UNITED STATES AFTER 1865). As U.S. federal troops captured territory from the Confederate states during the war, state laws controlling the behavior of people of color ceased to have any effect. The public consensus in the North that blacks ought to be excluded from citizenship eroded rapidly as the war took hundreds of thousands of lives and Northerners realized that slavery and racial discrimination were root causes of the destruction. By 1865, Northerners were ready to restructure society fundamentally in the former slave states. The abolition of slavery was carried out in stages, with local federal military commander's extending a form of liberty to runaway slaves as "contraband of war" as early as 1862, President Lincoln's extending freedom to all slaves in Southern-controlled territories with the EMANCIPATION PROCLAMATION of January 1863, some loyal states' changing their constitutions to prohibit slavery between 1863 and 1865, and then the ratification of the Thirteenth Amendment to the U.S. Constitution in December 1865, which ended slavery throughout the United States.

However, what replaced slavery was not equal citizenship. Many whites, both North and South, were not prepared to accept blacks as fully equal members of society. In areas under military occupation, "contraband" former slaves were subject to military regulations. Many were enrolled in the military as soldiers or labor troops. In the loyal states, black codes were enacted or revised to govern both the newly freed and the prewar free people of color. These laws resembled those that had restricted free people of color before the war—limiting access to the courts, restricting occupational choices, and generally defining blacks as second-class citizens. In the former Confederate states, once the war was over, local white elites took the same tack, accepting the end of slavery as an accomplished fact but passing black codes that defined blacks as inferior members of society. These laws often made conditions worse for prewar free people of color, since they were lumped in with the former slaves.

However, Republican leaders in state houses and at the federal level realized that if blacks had the vote, they would be reliable supporters of the party. Blacks saw the Republican-led national government as their protector. Republicans at the national level sealed the alliance by revoking the Southern states' governments and postwar legal structures, black codes and all, after Southerners elected a large number of former Confederate officials to office in the 1866 elections. Discriminatory laws were forbidden by the Fourteenth Amendment, ratified in 1868, and the Civil Rights Acts of 1871 and 1875. Blacks responded by voting in large numbers for Republican candidates, some of whom were blacks and others Southern whites. The Republican governments in the South during the late 1860s and early 1870s established a formal regime of legal equality in most places. Blacks had equal access to the courts, no restrictions on the sort of jobs they could hold or property they could own, schools and other public services were open to them, and they could vote and hold office.

The Reconstruction era spelled the end of formal black codes. Even when the Democrats regained power in the Southern states at the end of Reconstruction, they did not reestablish a generalized system of legal discrimination. Instead, in the era known as Jim Crow, they used unofficial or semiofficial terrorism, discriminatory enforcement of formally nondiscriminatory laws such as literacy requirements for voting, and the careful cultivation of white solidarity to preserve white supremacy.

Stewart R. King

FURTHER READING

Birnbaum, Jonathan, and Clarence Taylor, eds. *Civil Rights since 1787: A Reader on the Black Struggle.* New York: New York University Press, 2000.
Foner, Eric. *Reconstruction: America's Unfinished Revolution 1863–1877.* New York: HarperCollins, 1988.
Waldrep, Christopher. "Substituting Law for the Lash: Emancipation and Legal Formalism in a Mississippi County Court." *Journal of American History* 82, no. 4 (1996): 1,425–1,451.

BLACK LAWS IN THE MIDWEST

All the states in the U.S. Midwest—OHIO, INDIANA, ILLINOIS, MICHIGAN, WISCONSIN, and MINNESOTA—passed laws in the 19th century to protect free blacks and fugitive slaves from being kidnapped or captured into slavery (*see* PERSONAL LIBERTY LAWS), but there were other laws in each of these states that also placed limits on free black citizenship and sometimes even made the migration of free blacks into the states illegal. Collectively, these laws were known as the "black laws." Each state also included specific provisions within their original state constitutions that excluded blacks from basic constitutional protections.

The black laws originated in the slave statutes of Virginia, the Carolinas, Tennessee, and Kentucky, the states from which many white midwesterners migrated, and reflected popular prejudices that blacks were unfit to participate in civil institutions, such as suffrage, public education, the militia, and the legal system. Laws prohibiting black participation in these institutions and establishing punishments for infractions were passed in all the states of the Midwest throughout the antebellum period. In some cases, these laws were not repealed until the end of the AMERICAN CIVIL WAR, 1861–65.

With regard to the black laws, the period between 1800 and 1865 can be divided into two general phases: pre-1850 and post-1850. In the pre-1850 period, the black laws followed a typical model in all of the states of the Midwest. Free blacks were required to post a security bond (usually $500) upon entering the state, which was intended to guarantee that white citizens would not have to support them with public money. Blacks were also required to register with the local courts, usually at the same time they posted bond. At this time, they would receive a certificate of legal residency. This certificate did not grant them citizenship within the state but only established that they were free and legal residents. Blacks were prohibited from marrying whites, joining the state militia, attending public schools, testifying in court against whites, or serving on juries. Illinois, Indiana, and Ohio also passed laws on numerous occasions before 1850 prohibiting any further in-migration of free blacks, which meant that blacks could be charged with a misdemeanor offense for simply entering the state and face either deportation or public auction if they failed to pay the fine. Ohio adopted black laws in 1804 and 1807, then modified them in 1836. Anti-immigration legislation passed in Illinois in 1818, 1829, and 1853. Indiana restricted black immigration in its constitution of 1818 and in laws passed in 1831 and 1852.

In the post-1850 period, some states repealed portions of their black laws, while others strengthened them. These two different responses were largely a result of the FUGITIVE SLAVE ACT OF 1850, as well as the controversial Kansas-Nebraska Act in 1854 and the *Dred Scott* decision of the U.S. Supreme Court in 1857 (*see* SCOTT, DRED). Ohio, Michigan, and Wisconsin repealed portions of their black laws in the 1840s and 1850s, their legislatures condemned the Fugitive Slave Act, and their courts decided against slaveholders who sought to claim fugitives. However, Illinois and Indiana strengthened their own laws and state constitutions, including affirmations of the prohibition on the inmigration of free blacks. Indiana's constitution of 1851 specifically prohibited free blacks from entering the state, and Illinois voters affirmed a series of laws in 1853 that strengthened their black laws already on the books. In 1862, Illinois voters again voted to strengthen the prohibition on free black immigration, and during the Civil War, black migrants were actively prosecuted in the courts.

Thomas Bahde

FURTHER READING

Middleton, Stephen. *The Black Laws in the Old Northwest: A Documentary History*. Westport, Conn.: Greenwood Press, 1993.
———. *The Black Laws: Race and the Legal Process in Early Ohio*. Athens: Ohio University Press, 2005.

BLACK PRESS IN THE UNITED STATES

On March 16, 1827, Samuel Cornish and JOHN RUSSWURM published the first issue of the newspaper *Freedom's Journal* in New York City. A new paper was not a notable event. Thousands of newspapers came and went in early America, some lasting a few weeks and others surviving for several decades. What made *Freedom's Journal* special were its African-American coeditors and authors. They made their opinions known each week in a paper owned and published by them.

Though Cornish and Russwurm created the first black newspaper, they were not the first published African Americans. Beginning in the late 1700s, black authors appeared in print. In the poetry of PHYLLIS WHEATLEY, the protest pamphlets of RICHARD ALLEN and ABSALOM JONES, and antislavery petitions of free blacks, they made themselves heard. However, until 1827, they had no newspaper, of their own.

As the first black newspaper, *Freedom's Journal* established several important precedents and patterns. Though it lasted less than two years, beginning with the first issue it laid out the mission of most future black papers. This would not be a newspaper that strove for objectivity, but neither did most other papers at the time. This paper would advocate for African Americans. As its title suggested, *Freedom's Journal* sought the end of slavery as its primary purpose. The paper would demand equality and fair treatment for African Americans. It would point out white racism and would note when the United States fell short of its democratic promises. *Freedom's Journal* also opposed the removal of African Americans to an African colony by arguing that African Americans were equal citizens and could not abandon their enslaved brethren (*see also* EMIGRATION AND COLONIZATION). This would be a recurring theme in most black papers before the AMERICAN CIVIL WAR, 1861–65, and lead John Russwurm to quit *Freedom's Journal* and the United States to settle in LIBERIA, where he published the local *Liberia Herald*. Cornish began publishing a newspaper under the new name *Rights of All*.

Exact numbers are elusive; however, it is known that there were at least 38 different black papers published before the Civil War. These covered six states and one territory, KANSAS. African-American newspapers were more common in the urban North, mirroring free black populations. New York had well over half with 21, 12 of those in New York City. PENNSYLVANIA was a distant second with six, four in Philadelphia. The only free black newspapers in slave territory were the three published in NEW ORLEANS, LOUISIANA. Black papers were also published as far west as CALIFORNIA. The names illustrate both the variety and the shared mission of these numerous newspapers: *Colored American, Genius of Freedom, Mirror of Liberty, Herald of Freedom, Palladium of Liberty,* and *Emancipator and Free American.* It is important to note that not all of these were published simultaneously as most were short-lived. Still, the journalists and publishers persisted, and when one paper folded, they soon started another.

A persistent problem for newspapers, both black and white, was finances. The black press proved especially transitory since, according to available records, all of them lost money. Black papers depended on white and black readers, but they had far fewer white readers than other papers, and free blacks proved unable to make up the difference. Subscriptions were consistently overdue, and the papers frequently admonished their readers to pay their accounts. Even FREDERICK DOUGLASS, famous escaped slave and orator, lost money on his newspapers.

Douglass, despite his fame and comparative wealth, continued to publish a newspaper until the Civil War. Though the name changed, from *North Star* to *Frederick Douglass' Paper*, its location remained in Rochester, New York. The importance Douglass gave on his newspaper work indicates the importance of the black press to the broader African-American community. It was their voice and their public square. Largely barred from writing in white newspapers and from public gatherings, blacks sought to engage with white critics and advocate for themselves in the public space available to them, their newspapers. They commented on other newspaper articles and political debates as well as broader events. They sought a white audience while always speaking for African Americans. The black newspapers were the ones to attack both slavery and racism consistently, with few exceptions. Before the Civil War, they were the public voice of African America, transitory though it may have been.

With the change from a war to preserve the Union to a war to free the slaves, the free black press took an increasing interest in the American Civil War, especially the enlistment of black troops in the Union army. This seemed both to acknowledge the racial equality the newspapers had long demanded and to secure that equality through shared sacrifice. The two black weekly newspapers still publishing, the *Anglo-African* of New York City and the *Christian Recorder* of Philadelphia, covered the black troops' experience almost exclusively until 1864. The *Christian Recorder* operated from 1852 to 1864 as the official publication of the AFRICAN METHODIST EPISCOPAL CHURCH. In August 1864, the Philadelphia *Press* commissioned Thomas Morris Chester as its sole black correspondent. Chester's dispatches in a white newspaper were an anomaly, but his position allowed him to cover the closing months of the Civil War, including the African-American soldiers who led the Union army into the conquered Confederate capital of Richmond, VIRGINIA.

After the Civil War and the emancipation of the slaves, African Americans continued to use the printed word to confront racism and advance black interests. The mid-19th-century invention of cheap wood-pulp paper and the growing availability of secondhand presses allowed more aspiring black publishers to engage in print production. African-American literacy rates also rose dramatically in these years; immediately after the Civil War, only 5 percent of African Americans could read and write; by 1900, 55.5 percent could. This change dramatically expanded the potential audience for new African-American-oriented publications, including pamphlets, books, and magazines. Newspapers, however, reached the largest audience, because they published every week and were generally more affordable. From 1865 to 1920, the so-called race paper became the most widely produced and consumed form of African-American print culture.

Despite impressive gains in freedom, literacy, political participation, and institution building, the Reconstruction years did not see a great expansion of the African-American newspaper press. Most of the African-American papers that did emerge were financed by the Republican Party and operated primarily as partisan mouthpieces. The party would continue to exert a strong influence on the African-American press—as well as black voters—for the remainder of the 19th century. There were a few exceptions, including the San Francisco *Elevator*, founded in 1865 by the pre–Civil War free black Philip A. Bell (1808–89) after he broke with his publishing partner at the *Pacific Appeal* over Bell's desire to remain politically independent. Nevertheless, several newspaper editors who would become famous from the 1880s to the early 1900s gained experience that would be instrumental to their later successes working on Republican organs during the Reconstruction era.

The end of federal RECONSTRUCTION IN THE UNITED STATES in 1877 (*see also* U.S. ELECTION OF 1876) ushered in a major expansion of the black press. In part, disfranchisement and segregation encouraged the growth

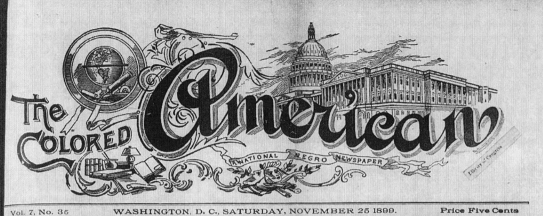

The front page of the November 25, 1899, edition of the *Colored American*. *(Library of Congress)*

because newspaper editing and journalism provided an outlet for a new generation of African Americans largely excluded from party politics and government. Black newspapers existed in virtually every region of the United States, reflecting the slow beginnings of northward migration by former slaves. The newspapers were mostly weekly publications of four to eight pages and generally focused on topics and people seen to be most relevant to African-American readers. News stories and editorials covered topics such as elections and Supreme Court cases about segregation of railways and public accommodations, as well as lynching, riots, and other forms of racially motivated violence.

African-American editors of the late 19th and early 20th centuries were often overwhelmed by the financial hardship and relentless work involved in publishing a newspaper, similarly to the antebellum era. Most titles did not survive even a year in print. Black papers rarely shared in the revenues from selling advertising space, as most businesses that could afford to advertise were white-owned and favored larger, mainstream publications. Many titles originated in rural areas, with subscriptions numbering in the low hundreds; the most prominent urban papers, such as the *New York Age*, the *Pittsburgh Courier*, and the *Washington Bee*, reached subscription rates in the low thousands. The most widely read African-American newspapers could not compete with the largest mainstream dailies, yet they reached much wider audiences than their modest circulation numbers reflect. Subscribers often read the papers aloud to friends and family, and black railroad workers and sailors were known to transport issues across great distances.

Just as mainstream journalism included a small but significant number of white women writers, black newspaper publishing and journalism also offered unique opportunities to African-American women. Ida B. Wells (1862–1931) started editing her first newspaper, the *Memphis Free Speech*, in 1885. Over the next decades her influence would extend across the United States and to Europe, as she became one of the most famous black journalists of her day. Best known for waging a passionate campaign against the late 19th-century rise in occurrences of lynching, Wells bravely reported several such incidences in all of their brutal details. In 1892, three of her friends who owned a grocery store were killed by a white mob. Wells instigated a miniexodus of blacks from Memphis, TENNESSEE, through her editorials in the city's black paper when hundreds of blacks heeded her call to leave the city. This event both demonstrated the power of the black press and aroused white opposition. Damage to the newspaper presses and ongoing threats of violence encouraged Wells to accept an offer to work for the *New York Age*.

The content and tone of the national African-American newspaper press were most influenced by a handful of editors and writers, particularly T. Thomas Fortune (1856–1928) of the *New York Age*, whose editorials were reprinted widely in black newspapers all over the United States. He opined on a variety of issues related to the African-American experience in the United States, especially politics and civil rights. There was no shortage of material to report on, as the end of the Reconstruction gave way to a period in which American imperial national identity was formed along racially and ethnically exclusive lines. Fortune and other major black newspaper editors, including Ida B. Wells; William Calvin Chase (1854–1921), a prewar free black from the District of Columbia; and John Mitchell (1863–1929), generated a running discourse over strategies for combating racism in its various forms across the United States.

In 1895, with his speech at the Atlanta Exposition, the Tuskegee Institute founder, Booker T. Washington (1856–1915), gained prominence as a major African-American leader, in the eyes of many whites and blacks across the United States. Both mainstream newspapers and race papers would for the next two decades pay close attention to Washington's words and activities. His leadership and ideas for black advancement were not uncontested, however. Ambitious to consolidate his power among the African-American elite and to penetrate the sphere of white-controlled politics, Washington saw black newspapers as an important vehicle for accomplishing both goals. Not trained or skilled in either writing or printing, he enlisted the help of two important African-American journalists of this era: T. Thomas Fortune and Victoria Earle Matthews (1861–1907). Washington's accommodationist stances provoked controversy among other black leaders, most famously W. E. B. DuBois (1868–1963) and William Trotter (1872–1934), a descendant of one of the free black CHILDREN OF SALLY HEMINGS and THOMAS JEFFERSON. While Fortune's *New York Age* operated for several years as Washington's mouthpiece, Trotter founded the *Boston Guardian* in 1901 to promote DuBois's ideas.

In 1905, at the height of Washington's influence, DuBois and other opponents formed the Niagara Movement to advocate a more militant approach to securing African-American civil rights and safety. This organization evolved into the National Association for the Advancement of Colored People, which began publication of its own magazine, the *Crisis*, in 1910. As a monthly magazine, the *Crisis* differed from black newspapers per se, but DuBois's desire to edit his own serial publication showed the importance of regular printed news and literary sources in the galvanization of a black civil rights consciousness. Building on the examples of Douglass, Wells, Fortune, DuBois, and many other editors, in 1918,

Marcus Garvey (1887–1940) launched a newspaper called *Negro World* as the official organ of his Universal Negro Improvement Association.

The movement to gain and secure equal rights for African Americans that first found its voice in Cornish and Russwurm's *Freedom's Journal* survived and grew during the 19th century and into the 20th century largely through the pages of black-owned and -oriented newspapers. Despite the hardships of independent newspaper production, African-American editors and journalists persistently protested racism and discrimination, debunked negative stereotypes, and agitated for full civil rights. Most important, this generation of black newspaper editors used their publications to form an alternative arena for public discussions of racial ideologies, political and economic strategies, and social mores that operated outside the mostly racist mainstream media. Although many of the first generation of these editors and journalists had been freed from slavery by the Emancipation Proclamation and the Union victory in the Civil War, a disproportionate role was played by prewar free people of color and their descendants. As in the other learned professions in the post–Civil War era, prewar free blacks had an advantage because they had at least some access to education before the war.

Jennifer Moses and Matthew J. Hudock

FURTHER READING

Bacon, Jacqueline. *Freedom's Journal: The First African-American Newspaper.* Lanham, Md.: Lexington Books, 2007.

Blackett, R. J. M., ed. *Thomas Morris Chester, Black Civil War Correspondent: His Dispatches from the Virginia Front.* Baton Rouge: Louisiana State University Press, 1989.

Detweiler, Frederick. *Negro Press in the United States.* Chicago: University of Chicago Press, 1922.

Giddings, Paula J. *Ida, a Sword among Lions: Ida B. Wells and the Campaign against Lynching.* New York: HarperCollins, 2008.

Kinshasa, Kwando M. *Emigration vs. Assimilation: The Debate in the African American Press, 1827–1861.* Jefferson, N.C.: McFarland, 1988.

Penn, I. Garland. *Afro-American Press and Its Editors.* Springfield, Mass.: Willey and Co., 1891.

Pride, Armistead S., and Clint C. Wilson II. *A History of the Black Press.* Washington, D.C.: Howard University Press, 1997.

Thornbrough, Emma Lou. *T. Thomas Fortune: Militant Journalist.* Chicago: University of Chicago Press, 1972.

Tripp, Bernell. *Origins of the Black Press: New York, 1827–1847.* Northport, Ala.: Vision Press, 1992.

Vogel, Todd, ed. *The Black Press: New Literary and Historical Essays.* New Brunswick, N.J.: Rutgers University Press, 2001.

Washburn, Patrick S. *The African American Newspaper: Voice of Freedom.* Evanston, Ill.: Northwestern University Press, 2006.

Wolseley, Roland E. *The Black Press, U.S.A.* Ames: Iowa State University Press, 1990.

BLACK SEMINOLE

The Seminole tribe of North American Indians came into existence in the 18th century in northern FLORIDA, which was controlled by Spain at the time. The tribe was composed of some Floridian Indians, along with refugee Creek Indians and runaway slaves from the British colonies to the north. The predominantly native and predominantly African-descended Seminole did have somewhat different cultures during the colonial period. African-descended Seminole spoke a language more closely related to Sea Island Gullah, an African Creole, while predominantly indigenous Seminole villages spoke the Seminole language, related to Creek, with loan words from Spanish, English, and African languages. However, the two groups lived closely together, intermarried freely, and thought of themselves as one people by the 1830s.

The indigenous inhabitants of Florida, as in many other places in the tropical Caribbean, suffered enormous mortality rates after the arrival of Spanish settlers in the 16th century. This mortality rate was accelerated by the Spanish practice of gathering Indians into mission villages under the supervision of Spanish religious leaders and military garrisons, where they were more exposed to diseases introduced by the Europeans and their African slaves. By the end of the 17th century, there were very few indigenous Floridians left alive. However, the growing British presence to the north offered another source of immigrants to Florida, starting in the 1720s, as southern woodland Indians fled south to the more accommodating Spanish. After Georgia, established in 1733, began importing significant numbers of slaves in the 1740s, runaway slaves joined this movement. The Spanish encouraged this movement as they had similar developments in other colonies by granting freedom and land to runaway slaves who agreed to obey the precepts of the ROMAN CATHOLIC CHURCH and serve in the MILITIA. Some runaways preferred to live around the Spanish settlements and became fully integrated free people of color, often working as laborers, servants, and artisans for the Spanish. Others, perhaps the majority, preferred to live in the Indian villages, and it is their descendants who evolved into the black Seminole. These people may have preferred the native lifestyle for religious reasons, as they practiced a sort of syncretic Protestant Christianity rather than the officially approved Catholicism. The Spanish authorities in Florida were too weak to enforce religious uniformity, and so Seminole of both ethnic backgrounds developed religious practices that foreshadowed Holiness

A portrait of Abraham, a black man born about 1790 who lived among the Seminole and who served as an interpreter for the U.S. Army during its negotiations with the Seminole in the First Seminole War (1814–19). Most Seminole have at least some African ancestry, and those who had a high proportion of black ancestry were called black Seminole. Some members of this group served the U.S. military during the Indian Wars in the Seminole Scouts, while others emigrated to Mexico and fought in Mexico's Indian wars. *(The Granger Collection, New York)*

or Pentecostal beliefs (*see also* AFRICAN AND SYNCRETIC RELIGIONS).

The word *Seminole* is arrived from the Spanish *Cimarron,* also the source of the English word *maroon,* and the Seminole in many ways resembled other maroon communities throughout the slave societies of the Americas. Because of the relatively large numbers of native people among the ancestors of the Seminole, they preserved a more indigenous way of life than many other maroons. Their crops, their government style, and their collective identity remained native rather than maroon. By 1818, the Seminole had become, as had other quasi-assimilated maroon communities in Spanish colonies throughout the Americas, a recognized part of colonial society with a distinct identity. The period of British rule, from 1763 to 1784, saw a continuation of the previous policy toward those Seminole already living in Florida, although colonists from Georgia objected strongly that their runaway

slaves were still being protected in Florida. The WAR OF AMERICAN INDEPENDENCE, 1775–83, saw rapid growth for the Seminole, as more blacks and Indians fled heavy fighting in Georgia. Some Seminole fought alongside Spanish soldiers at the Siege of Pensacola (March–May 1781), while woodland Indians such as the Creek generally supported the British.

American Rule

Starting in 1810, U.S. pressure on Florida increased, and Indians generally supported the British in their struggle with the Americans. First the Gulf Coast of Mississippi and then the Mobile region of Alabama were incorporated into the United States over the objection of the Spanish and local Indian inhabitants. During and after the War of 1812, American forces under General ANDREW JACKSON launched a series of campaigns against the Seminole and Creek, who had been armed by British agents operating out of Pensacola. Jackson defeated the Indians in Alabama and Mississippi, pursued them into Spanish territory, and destroyed a fort, called the "Negro Fort," at the site of the later Fort Gadsen. American settlers in the interior of Alabama raided the Seminole and Creek settlements, and the Seminole responded by attacking U.S. troops and settlers. The First Seminole War (1814–19) resulted in the American occupation of Florida, and Florida officially became part of the United States after the Senate ratified the Adams-Onís Treaty in 1821.

The Seminole were promised a reservation in central Florida, but their rights were progressively violated, both by the government and by white settlers, who were not restrained by the U.S. government. Among other outrages, slave catchers were indiscriminately rounding up dark-skinned Seminole, claiming them as runaway slaves, and selling them into the vibrant U.S. internal slave trade. The Seminole responded by claiming many African-descended members as slaves of other members, but this was a pretense intended to protect those African Americans from white slave catchers. In fact, the African-descended Seminole lived as equals to the predominantly Indian groups around them. There were no plantations in Seminole areas as were found among the southeastern woodland Indians such as the Cherokee. At least 1,000 Seminole were described as slaves in the 1820s. Under the Indian Removal Act of 1830, the Seminole were to be transferred to OKLAHOMA, and they were permitted to take their "slaves" with them. The Seminole wholeheartedly resisted removal, and the Second Seminole War, 1835–42, marked the high point of African-Seminole cooperation. The black Seminole leaders John Caesar and John Horse (1812–82) supported the militant Seminole leader Osceola in resistance to the U.S. troops, and they drew hundreds of slaves from Florida plantations into their ranks. The black warriors fought hard, but ultimately the U.S. Army was able to break their resistance. The U.S. general Thomas Jessup offered emancipation to some of the black Seminole, and about 500 of them took him up on his offer and accompanied the defeated Seminole to Oklahoma. Other black leaders retreated to the Everglades of South Florida and maintained their resistance. After the Third Seminole War (1855–56), some of these survivors took a ship and sailed to Andros Island in the Bahamas, where there they formed a cohesive community that still exists today.

John Horse and his supporters went to Oklahoma, where they established a settlement along with other Seminole at Wewoka, but in the 1840s, they found themselves under increasing pressure from neighboring Indian tribes and white slave raiders. Even some predominantly indigenous Seminole cooperated in this discrimination, pursuing claims to ownership of their African-descended "slaves" and attempting to set up large cash-crop farms in emulation of their Cherokee and Creek neighbors. Finally, in 1848, the U.S. government decided to disarm the black Seminole and imprisoned Horse and his chief supporters at the Indian prison. In 1849, Horse escaped and, accompanied by several hundred of his followers, crossed Texas to free soil in Mexico. Horse's flight to freedom bears comparison to the more celebrated, and less successful, flight of Chief Joseph of the Nez Perce (1840–1904) in 1877. Horse's people were offered sanctuary by the Mexican government. They supported the government of Benito Juárez (1806–72), himself a Zapotec Indian, during the Wars of the Reforma, 1857–61, and the French invasion, 1863–68, and were rewarded with lands at Nacimiento and Laguna de Parras in Coahuila state in northern Mexico. Their descendants remain there, a distinctive group called the Mascogos. Some of these people returned to the United States in 1870 at the invitation of the U.S. Army, forming a unit called the Negro Seminole Scouts. They worked closely with the black 9th and 10th Cavalry Regiments, the Buffalo Soldiers, in the wars against the western Indians. Four Seminole scouts won the Medal of Honor for actions against Apache and Comanche Indians. The unit was disbanded in 1914, and many of the descendants of these soldiers live around Brakettville, Texas, where their unit was stationed.

The black Seminole who remained in Oklahoma experienced increasing isolation from fellow Seminole during the remainder of the 19th and 20th centuries. The pervasive climate of racism in the United States during that period and the slightly better treatment of Indians than blacks meant that the predominantly indigenous Seminole found it to their advantage to distinguish themselves from their black cousins. The progressive growth of this barrier meant that many black Seminole were ultimately denied membership in the Seminole tribe when it was formally organized under U.S. government patronage. Today, they are referred to as Seminole freedmen and have fought in the courts to gain recognition as members of the Seminole Nation. The descendants of the few black and indigenous Seminole who remained in Florida have organized themselves separately as the Miccosukee Seminole Nation.

Stewart R. King

FURTHER READING

Brown, Canter. "Race Relations in Territorial Florida, 1821–1845." *Florida Historical Quarterly* 73, no. 3 (January 1995): 287–307.

Goggin, John M. "The Seminole Negroes of Andros Island, Bahamas." *Florida Historical Quarterly* 24 (July 1946): 201–206.

Landers, Jane. *Black Society in Spanish Florida*. Urbana: University of Illinois Press, 1999.

Littlefield, Daniel F., Jr. *Africans and Seminoles*. Westport, Conn.: Greenwood Press, 1977.

Mulroy, Kevin. *Freedom on the Border: The Seminole Maroons in Florida, the Indian Territory, Coahuila, and Texas*. Lubbock: Texas Tech University Press, 1993.

Porter, Kenneth Wiggins. *The Black Seminoles: History of a Freedom-Seeking People*. Edited by Thomas Senter and Alcione Amos. Gainesville: University of Florida Press, 1996.

BLAND, JAMES A.   (1854–1911) *American musician*

From the 1870s through 1890s, minstrel shows reached the height of popularity in the United States. Perhaps the most prolific black composer of popular music for these traveling revues was James A. Bland, credited with writing more then 700 songs. Most famously, Bland wrote "Oh Dem Golden Slippers" (theme song of the Philadelphia Mummer's Parade for more than 50 years) and "Carry Me Back to Old Virginny" (Virginia's state song from 1940 to 1997).

Bland was born on October 22, 1854, in Flushing, Long Island, New York, to Allen M. and Lydia Ann Bland. The family later moved to PHILADELPHIA, PENNSYLVANIA, where Bland taught himself to play banjo by listening to street performers. After the family moved to Washington, D.C., Bland graduated from high school, worked as a House of Representatives page, and occasionally performed as a musician at select clubs and homes. Accepted by Howard University, he studied law, until his overwhelming love of traditional spiritual songs led him to return to a career in entertainment. He graduated from Howard at age 19 with a liberal arts degree, and by 1875, he had joined his first minstrel troupe, in a lead role of the Original Black Diamonds of Boston. The following year he joined the Bohee Minstrels.

Composers such as Bland would often sell all rights to a given song for 10 or 15 dollars. He only registered 40 of his songs in the Library of Congress. Performing in minstrel shows provided the only way for black professional entertainers of the time to gain fame and work in concert venues, and indeed this path allowed Bland to be billed as the "World's Greatest Minstrel Man" and made his songs popular across the country.

Bland earned great acclaim when he traveled to London in 1881 with Haverty's Genuine Colored Minstrels, gaining the sobriquet "Idol of the Music Halls." He continued to tour Europe, in part because he could perform there without blackface makeup, which was still the accepted norm in the United States for white and black minstrel performers alike. Singing his songs, dancing, and playing banjo, Bland reached the peak of his fame.

He returned to the United States in 1901 but found the public's interest in minstrel shows waning. After working with a number of minstrel troupes, Bland wrote a musical comedy, *The Sporting Girl*, which was a critical and popular failure. Over the next few years, he faded into obscurity, poverty, and sickness, as he contracted tuberculosis. He died on May 5, 1911, and was interred at an unmarked grave in Bala Cynwyd, Pennsylvania. Eventually, in 1939, a monument was built on the gravesite.

The musician and writer Elijah Wald noted in his book *Escaping the Delta* that though music by African Americans rarely received its due critical acclaim until the Harlem Renaissance of the 1920s, the "plaintive, melancholy" performance style of "Old Virginny" (first published in 1879) found praise from many listeners. As a performer, Bland possessed skills both "tear-jerking" and comedic.

In 1997, "Old Virginny" was removed from its place as state song, after frequent complaints that the lyrics condoned slavery. Since 1948, The Lions Clubs of Virginia have awarded a music scholarship to young musicians in Bland's name.

Daniel Rucker

FURTHER READING

Randel, John M., ed. *Harvard Biographical Dictionary of Music.* "Bland, James A(llen)." Cambridge, Mass.: Harvard University Press, 1996.

Southern, Eileen. *The Music of Black Americans: A History.* 3rd ed. New York: W. W. Norton, 1997.

Wald, Elijah. *Escaping the Delta: Robert Johnson and the Invention of the Blues.* New York: HarperCollins, 2004.

BLANKE, JOHN (unknown) *African trumpeter in England during the 16th century*

Africans began to be a part of European life in the 15th century, as the Portuguese Atlantic trade began to supplement the small flow of slaves across the Mediterranean. By the early 16th century, the first Africans were penetrating the farther corners of Europe, including England. African personal servants, both enslaved and free wage earners, were a sign of wealth, and Africans working in highly visible positions, such as musicians, were very much in demand. John Blanke is an example of such a servant. Many details of his personal life have been lost to history, but what we do know illustrates the role free blacks played in England at the beginning of its colonial expansion.

African trumpeters began to be visible at the Spanish and Italian courts in the 15th century, and by the next century, the practice of employing them was spreading. In the reigns of Henry VII (1485–1509) and Henry VIII (1509–47), there was a black trumpeter at the English court. Royal disbursement accounts maintained by John Heron, treasurer of the chamber, record regular compensation paid to a black trumpeter who was referred to as John Blanke. This name, possibly given to him by someone at the English court, was probably ironic—Blanke for "white." He may have arrived in England in 1501 as part of the royal retinue of Catherine of Aragon when she married Arthur, King Henry VII's eldest son. (After Arthur's death, she married her husband's brother, Henry VIII.) She had several black people among her entourage who were to become part of her household staff upon her marriage to Arthur.

How Blanke became a court entertainer is unclear; however, records exist of several payments made to him for eight pennies a day. He also appears in the Great Tournament Roll of Westminster, a pictorial narrative commissioned by Henry VIII in 1511 to commemorate the birth of his first son with Catherine. He is the only black trumpeter among other musicians. He stands out not only because of his skin color. While other trumpeters are bareheaded with shoulder-length hair, Blanke's hair is hidden out of sight under a turban. Otherwise, he was dressed as the other trumpeters were. That he was allowed to wear this different headwear, obviously important to his cultural identity, suggests his skill and value as a musician, as it was a rare occurrence for an African musician not to be wearing the standard court costume.

The fact that Blanke was chosen to perform in royal events and appears consistently in the royal treasury accounts spanning more than a decade indicates that he was highly regarded by the royal court. The degree of esteem in which he was held is further evidenced by the fact that Blanke was allowed to marry. The 1512 Exchequer Accounts of Henry VIII record that the king sent him a gift of clothes to mark the occasion. Unfortunately, we do not know the final fate of John Blanke, as he disappears from the historical record.

Carole Levin and Cassandra Auble

FURTHER READING

Earle, T. F., and K. J. P. Lowe, eds. *Black Africans in Renaissance Europe.* Cambridge: Cambridge University Press, 2005.

Fryer, Peter. *Staying Power: The History of Black People in Britain.* London: Pluto Press, 1984.

Habib, Imtiaz. *Black Lives in the English Archives, 1500–1677: Imprints of the Invisible.* Burlington, Vt.: Ashgate, 2008.

BOLIVIA

Bolivia is one of the most geographically and ethnically diverse countries in South America. It is surrounded by BRAZIL, PERU, CHILE, PARAGUAY, and ARGENTINA. The western part of the country includes the Andes mountain range; the altiplano (highlands), where its current capital, La Paz, is located; and a series of steep river valleys, known as the Yungas. The eastern half encompasses several tropical lowland areas. Bolivia has been troubled by deep-seated internal problems and instability. Historically, it has had two rival centers of political power. When it established independence from Spain in 1825, Bolivia established its first capital in Sucre (formerly called Chuquisaca), located in the valleys closer to the geographical center of the country. However, in 1898, Sucre and La Paz, the largest city in the country's mountainous western half, fought in a brief civil war in which the forces in La Paz won. As a result, Bolivians reached an agreement to place the country's judiciary in Sucre while locating the legislative and executive branches of government in La Paz.

Of approximately 9 million Bolivians today, most (more then 60 percent) are indigenous, but there are various subgroups. The largest of these include Aymara, Quechua, and Guaraní-speaking peoples, among others. Those who are counted as mestizos (half European and half Amerindian) constitute between 30 and 40 percent, and European-descended peoples are approximately 5–15 percent, many of whom are fairly recent arrivals. Only a fraction of Bolivia's total population is made up of people of African descent, who are mixed with other ethnic groups. Throughout Bolivia's history, the minority of European-descended peoples have controlled the political and economic power of the country.

Bolivia has relied primarily on natural resources to drive its economy, but it is one of the poorest countries in the Americas. Much of the wealth generated from

the extraction of natural resources has either left the country or been concentrated among a small number of wealthy Spanish families. When Spain conquered the region by the mid-1500s, it established a lucrative silver mining operation at Cerro Rico, located near the town of Potosí, which, by 1670, became the largest city in the Americas. Spaniards used indigenous laborers to work the mines in order to extract silver to be exported to Europe. By the late 18th century, however, silver production had declined dramatically. During the late 19th and early 20th centuries, Bolivia exported tin and oil, lucrative commodities during the Industrial Revolution, but demand for tin, in particular, had all but collapsed during the 1930s as a result of the worldwide Great Depression. In addition, when Bolivia was defeated by Chile during the War of the Pacific (1879–83), it lost both its access to the Pacific Ocean and its nitrate fields along its southwestern boundary. More recently, Bolivia has relied on natural gas exports, but it has struggled to develop this resource without private foreign investments. In general, much of the wealth generated from these boom-and-bust cycles has not been distributed well throughout Bolivia's population. Some governments during the 20th century nationalized key industries, including oil extraction in 1937 and tin mining in 1952, but these efforts largely failed to solve the problem

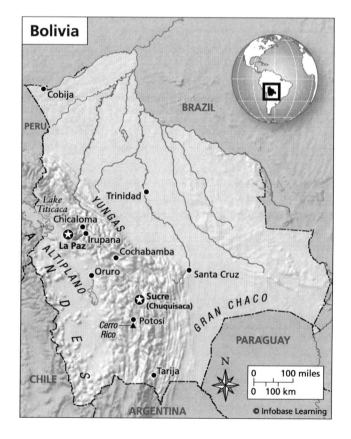

of the maldistribution of wealth that pervades the country's history. Many indigenous Bolivians farm coca, which may be turned into coca for tea or cocaine paste. Various programs to control coca production have failed altogether.

The Era of Colonial Slavery

In the mid-16th century, the Spanish Empire took control of the region, known as Upper Peru, and began a large-scale operation to extract silver near Potosí. They relied primarily on indigenous laborers who were already working in the area, but many Amerindians began to die off, largely as a result of epidemic diseases, such as smallpox. In response, Spanish authorities in Upper Peru authorized the importation of a modest number of African slaves from the South American port cities of Lima and Buenos Aires. The total number of African slaves imported into the region is not known, but by 1549, slave populations tended to be concentrated in Potosí and worked primarily in the Casa de Moneda (Royal Mint), where coins were minted during the colonial period. Although these slaves largely avoided working in the mines, they still worked in extremely harsh conditions. Potosí's cold climate negatively affected those without adequate shelter, and slaves worked with dangerous materials, such as mercury, in order to separate the silver. As did many other urban slaves in Buenos Aires, Santiago, or Lima, some slaves in Potosí worked as domestic servants. However, many black and mulato slaves worked in sugar plantations and vineyards in more temperate climate zones in Upper Peru, such as the Yungas, or river valleys, located in Bolivia's central regions. Regardless of where they worked, many of these slaves had low life-expectancy rates. Over time, many of these slaves also mixed with other people. After 1767, some African slaves were sold into slavery into Bolivia from Chile when the Spanish Crown forced the Jesuit order to leave its colonies in the Americas.

With the decline of silver mining by the late 18th century, colonial Spanish authorities authorized the transfer of slaves to work in other parts of Upper Peru, including the large landed estates in Yungas and coca leaf plantations in the mountainous regions of the North. In 1793, approximately 90 percent of coca production occurred in the central river valleys. By the early 19th century, parish and colonial government records show the creation of small but vibrant communities of people of color in Yungas. Songs and dances preserved by many Afro-Bolivians in the region today also demonstrate the presence of vibrant mixed-race slave populations. Scholars estimate that approximately 25,000 blacks, slave and free; mulattos; and other African-descended peoples settled in Yungas to work on large plantations.

Independence and Integration

In 1825, as a result of the efforts of South America's heroes of independence, Simón Bolívar and Antonio José de Sucre, Bolivia declared its independence from Spain. Slaves and free people of color fought on both sides during the wars of independence in South America. However, this was especially the case in Bolivia. Blacks played key roles in the earliest phases of the wars of independence. On May 25, 1809, Francisco Ríos, a free mulatto also known as "El Quitacapas," led a riot against colonial authorities in Chuquisaca (Sucre). Black soldiers also fought against Spanish forces in the Battles of Irupana (October 25) and Chicaloma (November 11), located in the Yungas, the same area where many black and mulatto PEASANTS had settled. The wars of independence were a long struggle for Bolivia, and in 1825, Sucre had negotiated a peace settlement with Spanish soldiers in Upper Peru to end the war. When Bolivia, in response to a direct appeal by Simón Bolívar, adopted its formal constitution in 1826, it ended the slave trade. Free womb laws, which granted freedom to all persons born after a certain date while those older remained enslaved, gradually ended slavery, but powerful landed interests kept delaying the effects of these decrees. Over the course of the 19th century, many Afro-Bolivians were not technically slaves, but many were still tied to large landed estates as debt peons. Debt peonage in Bolivia remained a strong institution until after the 1952 national revolution, so many of the descendants of Bolivia's slaves did not gain true freedom until the second half of the 20th century.

By the late 19th century, other Afro-Bolivians had migrated to larger cities, such as La Paz or Santa Cruz, a city in the more tropical East. According to Bolivia's 1900 national census, Bolivia had a free black population of 3,939, most of whom were concentrated in these cities. Still, the decline in Bolivia's population of free people of color was due in large measure to racial mixing with other groups, although intermarriage occurred at different rates depending on the community. In Chicaloma, for example, free people of color have intermarried more readily with Aymara peoples, and they have adopted Aymara cultural traits. In communities in northern Yungas, on the other hand, free people of color are culturally separate from the Aymara and seek to preserve their African heritage. The decline in the numbers of free people of color in this area is more due to the fact that younger generations are migrating to the cities. When they arrive, they are more likely to choose mates from other races and socioeconomic groups. Their descendants often adopt other ethnic identities rather than calling them Afro-Bolivian, a process known as "whitening" that is common throughout the Iberian Americas (see "WHITENING" AND RACIAL PROMOTION). This process of urban migration was accelerated after the 1952 revolution freed the rural poor. In the following year, Bolivia passed a reform program, which broke up large landed estates and passed ownership to peasant workers, established universal suffrage, nationalized tin mines, and abolished harsh treatment of workers and forced labor. This meant that people of color could have the opportunity either to own their own land or to migrate out of rural areas.

Contemporary Realities

Today, Afro-Bolivians live in diverse settings in both rural and urban contexts. Rural dwellers live mainly in the semitropical areas of Yungas, Irupana, Inquisiri, and Alto-Beni. Today, in Yungas, in particular, the remaining people who are identified as Afro-Bolivians live in scattered houses on mountainsides and depend mainly on subsistence farming, but they also grow coca, citrus, and coffee to sell in local markets. Afro-Bolivians also live in many cities, such as Santa Cruz, Cochabamba, and La Paz, and they have blended indigenous, European, and African cultural traditions. Linguists and anthropologists have found a persistence of African cultural patterns that have survived in various forms since the colonial era. The Morenada and Caporal are two dances that incorporate African rhythms. The Caporal dance, in particular, is danced to Saya music, which is derived from African rhythms and beats but played with traditional Andean musical instruments.

Afro-Bolivians have also been active in Bolivian politics. Several members of the community have been elected as leaders of various municipalities. However, activism appears to be channeled through organizations outside political institutions. In 1998, Monica Rey and Juan Angola Maconde, a historian and activist, founded the Movimiento Cultural Saya Afroboliviano (Afro-Bolivian Saya Cultural Movement), an advocacy group for Afro-Bolivian history. Angola Maconde also founded the Fundación de Afro Descendientes Pedro Andaverez Peralta (FUNDAFRO), named after the Afro-Bolivian hero of the Chaco War, 1932–35, between Bolivia and Paraguay, which serves as a liaison between scholars around the world and communities of free people of color. These leaders argue that the history of people of color in Bolivia has largely been overlooked. More recently, with the election of Evo Morales, Bolivia's first indigenous president, in 2005, political and social activists for people of color are hopeful that their concerns will be heard.

Jesse Hingson

FURTHER READING

Angola Maconde, Juan. "Los afrodescendientes bolivianos." *Journal of Latin American and Caribbean Anthropology* 12, no. 1 (April 2007): 246–253.

Bridikhina, Eugenia. *La mujer negra en Bolivia.* La Paz, Bolivia: Librería Editorial Juventud, 1995.

Busdiecker, Sara. "Where Blackness Resides: Afro-Bolivians and the Spatializing and Racializing of the African Diaspora." *Radical History Review* 103 (Winter 2009): 105–116.

Crespo, Alberto. *Esclavos negros en Bolivia.* La Paz, Bolivia: Librería Editorial Juventud, 1977.

Gutiérrez Brockington, Lolita. *Blacks, Indians, and Spaniards in the Eastern Andes: Reclaiming the Forgotten in Colonial Mizque, 1550–1782.* Lincoln: University of Nebraska Press, 2006.

Klein, Herbert S. *Bolivia: The Evolution of a Multi-Ethnic Society.* 2nd ed. New York: Oxford University Press, 1992.

Lipski, John M. "Afro-Bolivian Language Today: The Oldest Surviving Afro-Hispanic Speech Community." *Afro-Hispanic Review* 25, no. 1 (Spring 2006): 179–200.

THE BONDWOMAN'S NARRATIVE   See Crafts, Hannah.

BOSTON

Though the black population of Massachusetts in general was small during the colonial and revolutionary period, the city of Boston had a vibrant black community by the 1750s. By 1752, the city had more than 1,500 black residents, and this meant that roughly 10 percent of the city's residents were of African descent. Most of these people were slaves. Indeed, by the 1760s, the population contained only about 18 free blacks. Even so, their presence established the base of what would be a strong free black community by the mid-19th century.

Slaves in Boston faced a different situation than slaves in most parts of British North America. Instead of the arduous fieldwork expected of slaves in the Southern and some of the middle colonies, Boston slaves generally worked as coachmen, doormen, footmen, cooks, maids, or butlers in the households of wealthy whites. Most lived and worked in close contact with their masters, and this led to a paternalistic relationship that sometimes worked to their advantage. For one thing, this meant a greater respect for slave marriages and slave families. It also meant that masters were more likely to allow slaves to hire themselves out during their free time, and many were able to earn enough money eventually to buy their own freedom. Slaves in Boston also enjoyed legal rights that many of their counterparts in other places did not. Perhaps most importantly, they were allowed to use the courts to file lawsuits. Indeed, it was this right that ultimately led to the end of slavery in Massachusetts in the early 1780s after a slave named Quock Walker sued for his freedom (*see* Quock Walker case).

Even though Boston slaves had these advantages, they still faced the threat of being sold, and they had to deal with a level of isolation that slaves in the Southern and middle colonies did not have to face. Because they lived and worked so close to their masters, they often had few black acquaintances. Because the master/slave relationship was one based on domination, and because they were deprived of the chance to meet other blacks and form real friendships, most lived fairly lonely lives. This made special occasions when blacks could get together, such as election day, all the more important. In Boston, blacks were not allowed to participate in official elections, but they were allowed to hold their own celebrations on the Common and have their own election day festivities. They gathered to enjoy food and drink, play music and dance, hold parades, and compete in sporting contests. They also elected their own "governors" or community leaders who could be called upon to settle disputes within their community.

Three notable black Bostonians of the colonial and revolutionary era were PHILLIS WHEATLEY, Crispus Attucks, and PRINCE HALL. Wheatley gained celebrity as a black poet after being taught to read and write by the family who owned her. Though freed after gaining fame, she never profited economically from her poetry and died in poverty. Attucks, also known as Michael Johnson, was of African and Native American ancestry and was a sailor, as were many black men in Boston. One of the victims of the Boston Massacre in 1770, he is best known as a martyr to the American revolutionary cause. Gaining his freedom just after the Boston Massacre, Hall, a leather dresser and caterer, is remembered primarily as the Grand Master of the African Masonic Lodge in Boston, America's first black Masonic lodge (see FREEMASONRY). This group, as did the similar African Society of that city, promoted social, economic, and political improvement of free blacks by fighting for the abolition of slavery, the end of the slave trade, and free education for black children. Thanks to a petition Hall and his associates presented to the court in February 1788, the Massachusetts General Court passed an act to end the slave trade and to assist the families of people who were kidnapped into slavery.

Free blacks faced a number of challenges in Boston. Though legally free and enjoying legal equality, they had few civil rights. They paid taxes, but most were not allowed to vote. Whether by custom or law, their children were not allowed to attend public schools, and they faced much job discrimination. In many cases, their situation was so desperate that they were forced to indenture their children until their 21st birthday. Even so, they fought to change their situation by building community associations and mutual aid societies such as those mentioned.

The free black community saw a number of gains in the first decades of the 19th century. By 1808, the community had an important meeting place, the African Meeting House, which also housed a black school, and in 1815, the wealthy white businessman Abiel Smith left money in his will to fund a new school for the city's black residents. Two years later, a Sabbath School was organized, and it was renamed the Abiel Smith School. In the 1820s, JOHN RUSSWURM was hired as an instructor at the Smith School. New black-led reform organizations also began to emerge in the 1820s as well. One such group was the Massachusetts General Colored Association, which was formed in 1826 when black Bostonians met in DAVID WALKER's used clothing store to discuss ways to fight racism in the North and slavery in the South. Despite such progress, Walker grew increasingly disenchanted and three years later issued a famous "Appeal to the Colored Citizens of the World," calling for slaves to rise against their masters.

Despite white racism and the tensions it created, black Bostonians had formed a vibrant community by the 1830s, the decade that saw the epicenter of American abolition move to their city. The free black population of Boston reached its postindependence height as a percentage of the total population in 1830, when blacks made up 3.1 percent of the total population. Most blacks lived on the lower slopes of Beacon Hill, though the city was never completely segregated. From 1830 to 1860, the native black population was increasingly augmented by blacks from other parts of the North, as well as former slaves from the South, some of whom had escaped from their owners. This meant that, despite racial similarity, the black community had a number of different dialects and cultural backgrounds. Most were relegated to low-skilled domestic service occupations with low pay. Those who had skilled or entrepreneurial positions were usually hairdressers, barbers, blacksmiths, or used clothing dealers (see ARTISANS). The very top tier of this free black society consisted of a small professional class of doctors, ministers, teachers, and lawyers.

Though economically poor, the black community was culturally rich. In addition to a strong oral tradition, Boston blacks enjoyed a high rate of literacy. Even if the schools were segregated, the black community clearly shared the concern for education that was a hallmark of New England culture, and by 1860, only 8 percent of Boston's blacks were illiterate (see EDUCATION AND LITERACY). This combination of oral culture and literacy helped to produce one of the nation's first black historians, William C. Nell, who wrote about black contributions to the WAR OF AMERICAN INDEPENDENCE, 1775–83, and the War of 1812. Family bonds were reinforced through residential patterns, which often included the practice of

Titled *The 54th Massachusetts regiment, under the leadership of Colonel Shaw in the attack on Fort Wagner, Morris Island, South Carolina, in 1863,* this mural appears in the Recorder of Deeds building in Washington, D.C. The 54th Massachusetts was one of the first black regiments raised for the Union army during the American Civil War. It was organized in Boston, Massachusetts, and although members of the unit were from many different states, Boston's free black community contributed a large share. The unit's commander was a white Boston abolitionist, Col. Robert G. Shaw. The doomed assault on the Confederate defenses at Fort Wagner was an early demonstration of the aggressiveness and determination of black soldiers. *(Library of Congress)*

boarding extended family or other members of the black community. This fostered close-knit communities centered around well-organized family units.

Black Bostonians formed a number of formal and informal associations to improve their community. The African Society that was founded in 1796 lived on through the antebellum years, serving as a mutual aid and charity organization that provided financial relief to its members during hard times and served as a job placement agency. Meeting at the African Meeting House on Beacon Hill, it also supported widows, orphans, and the infirm while providing for burials and administering wills. It also served as a guardian of the community's morals by spreading values of self-help and temperance. The Masonic Lodge founded by Prince Hall also continued to play a large role in the community by providing free firewood, sponsoring food drives, providing a form of unemployment insurance, and offering loans to its members and their families. Of course, these organizations were only available for those who could manage to pay the dues, but they were not elite institutions because there were no exclusions based on skill or socioeconomic status, per se.

In addition to these broad associations, there were a number of specific clubs and organizations that had more specific purposes. One example was the Adelphic Union Library Association, formed in 1838 to sponsor lectures and foster intellectual debates. The Histrionic Club was a drama group formed in the late 1840s, and there were also debating societies such as the Boston Philomanthean Society and the Young Men's Literary Debating Society.

All but the latter were open to women as well as men. In addition to these, there were a number of women's groups such as the Afric-American Female Intelligence Society, a literary and mutual aid organization formed in 1832; the Daughters of Zion, founded in 1845; and the Female Benevolent Firm, founded in 1850. Youth organizations included the Juvenile Garrison Independent Society, founded in the early 1830s to provide education as well as community service, as well as youth choirs such as the Garrison Juvenile Choir and the primary School Number Six Choir.

The church was the center of the community in many ways. Boston's black community gained its own church in 1805, when the African Baptist Church was officially organized under the leadership of the Reverend Thomas Paul (*see* BAPTISTS AND PIETISTS). The meetinghouse was built a year later using only black labor, and by 1819, it was an established community institution with more than 100 members. Nathaniel Paul followed his father's lead and also preached in the church, which was closely affiliated with the American Baptist Home Mission Society. The community gained other churches, including the AFRICAN METHODIST EPISCOPAL CHURCH in 1818, the African Methodist Episcopal Zion Church in 1838, and the Twelfth Baptist Church in 1840. These churches, especially the African Baptist Church, played important roles in the antislavery and social protest movements. Boston's black church leaders who also served as black abolitionist leaders included Peter Randolph, John T. Raymond, Samuel Snowden, John Sella Martin, Leonard Grimes, and Jehiel C. Beman.

Perhaps because of its position at the epicenter of the immediate abolition movement (as opposed to those advocating progressive abolition, who were active throughout the North), Boston produced a number of the nation's top black activists. Lewis Hayden, an escaped slave from Kentucky, made his way to Boston, where he established a clothing store and a home that served as a gathering place for community activists, as well as a station on the Underground Railroad. A member of the Boston Vigilance Committee, he helped to aid fugitives along their way to freedom, and he organized laborers, seamen, and other members of the lower end of black Boston society to help with such antislavery efforts as the attempted rescue of the fugitive slave Anthony Burns in 1854. He was known especially for drawing the working class into the movement and for helping them by providing financial aid and emotional support. He also funded a number of community initiatives, including a Harvard scholarship for poor black medical students. Robert Morris was one of Boston's few black attorneys, and instead of participating in the type of direct action Hayden was known for, he was known for donating his legal services. He also helped rescuers such as Hayden obtain access to the courtrooms where fugitives were being held. He also worked with the Vigilance Committee by serving on the finance council. Other noted leaders included the historian William C. Nell, John S. Rock, and Charles Lenox Remond. Collectively, they fought against discrimination, and their work spread beyond the antislavery movement and into the realm of civil rights.

One of the main focuses of the antebellum civil rights movement in Boston was the integration of public schools. Black schools were given inadequate facilities and materials, and they were located in inconvenient places for many families, causing many young black students to walk miles out of their way or, in one noted case, to take an expensive ferry to school every day. Nell, John T. Hilton, and Jonas Clark joined in 1844 to organize a drive to end this situation, and in 1846, the Primary School Committee was presented petitions to integrate all Boston public schools. The petitions were denied, but the struggle continued in 1849, when the Negro School Abolition Society formed to apply more pressure. After a successful boycott of the black Smith School and a noted case in which Benjamin Roberts sued the city on behalf of his daughter Sarah, Boston schools were finally integrated in 1855.

Black Bostonians handled discrimination in employment in a different way. Unable to force white employers to change their practices, black leaders responded by creating businesses of their own and hiring black workers. The master blacksmith Hosea Easton formed an iron manufacturing company to employ and train black work-

ers, and Benjamin Roberts established a printing office to do the same. Jehiel Beman ran an employment agency for blacks. Finally, some of the city's white abolitionists, especially William Lloyd Garrison, hired blacks and helped others find employment with friendly whites.

Overall, Boston was known for having a fairly liberal racial climate, compared to many cities. By the 1850s, the public schools were desegregated, many public theaters and other entertainment venues were open to blacks, and travel accommodations for blacks were better there than in many places. Also, the Boston Lyceum accepted black patrons, and black Bostonians were only excluded from the vote in many cases by tax restrictions. This was significant because by this time many northern states had adopted constitutions that prohibited blacks from voting. In theory at least, then, black Bostonians could vote and hold office. Finally, Boston's black community benefited in many way from close ties to the white abolitionists in their city. Though leaders such as Garrison have been justifiably criticized for their patronizing attitude toward black leaders, the lengths to which they went to help their black neighbors and to fight against slavery were appreciated by their black neighbors, even as they began to question Garrison's mild tactics more and more after 1850.

By the 1850s, Boston's black leaders, like most throughout the free states, were becoming more and more militant. The FUGITIVE SLAVE ACT OF 1850 left all free blacks in danger of being kidnapped into slavery, and it led to an increase in the capture and trials of fugitive slaves. Notable fugitive slaves with ties to the city included William and Ellen Craft, Fred Wilkins (also known as Shadrach), Thomas Sims, Washington McQuerry, and Anthony Burns. Shadrach and Burns were both the subjects of dramatic rescues in the city, and Sims's and McQuerry's supporters fought hard to win their freedom as well, to no avail. These dramatic cases made more and more white Bostonians aware of, and sympathetic to, the plight of both slaves and free blacks and perhaps made them more willing to elect an abolitionist governor, John A. Andrew, in 1860.

The election of Governor Andrew paved the way for a milestone in the history of black Boston. After the AMERICAN CIVIL WAR erupted in 1861, blacks from throughout the North tried to enlist in the Union army. Nowhere were they immediately accepted, but Andrew worked to convince the federal government to allow him to raise black troops. After meeting many times with President Abraham Lincoln, he was given permission to proceed. The result was the 54th Massachusetts Infantry, the first black regiment. White abolitionists raised funds, secured the participation of white officers, and enlisted black leaders including FREDERICK DOUGLASS, Charles Lenox Remond, and MARTIN DELANY to lead in recruiting efforts. Andrew wanted to be able to promote qualified blacks to officer ranks, but he was denied this request, so all commissioned officers were white. By May 1863, enough black recruits had volunteered that a second unit, the 55th Infantry, was created. At least 40 percent of Boston's eligible black men volunteered to serve in these regiments, a very high percentage and much higher than the proportion of white Northerners who served in the Union army.

After the war, black Bostonians continued their civil rights struggle. John S. Rock, irritated at the slow pace of desegregation of public accommodations and the growing pace of ghetto formation, complained about worsening job prospects and the popularity of black-face minstrel shows in the city. Even so, a number of black leaders gained a degree of prominence in Boston politics. Lewis Hayden was elected the nation's first black state representative in 1865, and John J. Smith, a barber, abolitionist, and recruiter of black troops, became the first black to serve on the Boston Common Council and the third African American to serve in the state House of Representatives. Thanks to his efforts, the city had its first black member of the police force.

Beverly C. Tomek

FURTHER READING

Deming, Brian. "Slaves and Free Blacks in Colonial Boston." Suite 101.com. Available online. URL: www.suite101.com/content/slaves-and-free-blacks-in-colonial-boston-al74078. Accessed October 4, 2010.

Greene, Lorenzo Johnston. *The Negro in Colonial New England.* Boston: Atheneum Press, 1968.

Horton, James Oliver, and Lois E. Horton. *Black Bostonians: Family Life and Community Struggle in the Antebellum North.* New York: Holmes & Meier, 1979.

Kendrick, Stephen, and Paul Kendrick. *Sarah's Long Walk: The Free Blacks of Boston and How Their Struggle for Equality Changed America.* Boston: Beacon Press, 2004.

BOWSER, MARY ELIZABETH (1839–?)
American Civil War spy for the United States

Mary Bowser was an important Civil War intelligence operative for the U.S. eastern armies during the 1864 campaign in Virginia. She worked inside the household of the president of the Confederate States and was able to pass important operational and political intelligence.

Bowser was born a slave in 1839. She belonged to Henry Van Lew, a hardware merchant in Richmond, VIRGINIA. After her master's death, his widow, Elizabeth Van Lew (1818–1900), a staunch Quaker, freed all their slaves in 1851. American Quakers had been opposed to slavery since the 1750s, and a substantial Quaker population in southside Virginia and northeastern NORTH CAROLINA clung to their abolitionist ideas (*see also* BAPTISTS AND PIETISTS). Bowser continued to live with her former mistress, working as an employee in the hardware shop. Virginia had enacted a number of harsh laws against free people of color starting in the 1830s, and in principle all freed people were supposed to leave the state. This law was widely flouted by masters who wanted to keep their former slaves around them, and nobody appears to have troubled Van Lew and Bowser. Bowser did leave the state for several years between 1850 and 1860 to be educated at the Quaker School for Negroes in PHILADELPHIA, PENNSYLVANIA, one of the first institutions in the United States to offer advanced education to black women. By 1860, she was once again living with Van Lew in Richmond.

In May 1861, Virginia seceded from the United States and joined the Confederate States of America. The Confederate capital was moved from Montgomery, ALABAMA, to Richmond. Mary married Wilson Bowser on April 16, 1861, just days after the Civil War began, and moved in with him while maintaining close ties to the Van Lew family. Elizabeth Van Lew made no secret of her distaste for the Confederacy but adopted a somewhat crazed public persona and was tolerated as "Crazy Bet," a harmless eccentric. Behind this facade, Van Lew was managing a team of up to a dozen highly placed spies: secret Union sympathizers who worked for the Confederate government. Her information was priceless to the U.S. military forces trying to capture Richmond. The chief of intelligence on the Union general Ulysses Grant's staff in 1864 called her the best intelligence source he had in the Southern capital.

Van Lew recruited Bowser for her network sometime in 1863. At that time, Bowser adopted a cover identity as "Ellen Bond," a dull-witted but reliable free black house servant. Van Lew persuaded a friend to introduce "Bond" to Varina Davis, the First Lady of the Confederacy. Bowser worked as a part-time employee at several functions at the Confederate White House, but the real payoff occurred in 1864, when several of Davis's slaves were sent back to Mississippi in fear that the rapidly advancing U.S. forces would capture the city. Bowser was hired full-time as a housecleaner at the Confederate White House. Nobody suspected at first that this seemingly dull drudge was actually an educated woman with a photographic memory, able to read and memorize documents she found on the president's desk or in his files and correctly interpret conversations she overheard. Since servants were treated as almost part of the furniture, she was able to avoid suspicion for some time, although it quickly became apparent to Confederate counterespionage that there was a leak somewhere in the president's staff. Finally, in January 1865, suspicion fell on Bowser. She was able to flee, after attempting to set fire to the house. Her trail becomes hazy at this point, though Van Lew's biographer believes that she escaped and spent the remainder of her life in Philadelphia. In 1995, the U.S. Army inducted her into the Military Intelligence Hall of Fame at Fort Huachuca, New Mexico.

Stewart R. King

FURTHER READING

Downing, David C. *A South Divided: Portraits of Dissent in the Confederacy.* Nashville: Cumberland House, 2007.

Forbes, Ella. *African American Women during the Civil War.* New York: Routledge, 1998.

Pendelton, Anthony, Capt. USAF. "From Slave to Spy: Mary Elizabeth Bowser." *Air Intelligence Spokesman Magazine,* November 2004.

Varon, Elizabeth. *"Southern Lady, Yankee Spy": The True Story of Elizabeth Van Lew, a Union Agent in the Heart of the Confederacy.* New York: Oxford University Press, 2003.

BOYER, JEAN-PIERRE (1776–1850) *Haitian revolutionary leader and president*

Jean-Pierre Boyer was born of mixed parentage in PORT-AU-PRINCE, in the French colony of SAINT-DOMINGUE (modern Haiti) in February 1776. He always claimed February 15th as his date of birth, but no records of it were kept. Sent to France for education, he returned to his home, where he first worked as a tailor. In 1792, Boyer joined the French army.

Haiti in the 1790s was a tense area of competing interests. French colonists of various political sympathies who were upset at their government before and during the FRENCH REVOLUTION were planning a revolt, as were mulattos of various political sympathies who were upset at their limited political and social status. In the middle of this environment a slave revolt broke out and developed into a full-blown civil war. Boyer fought alongside TOUSSAINT LOUVERTURE, was promoted to captain, and became a protégé of the southern mulatto leader ANDRÉ RIGAUD. When Rigaud and Toussaint fell out, Boyer supported the former and had to flee the island for France when Rigaud's forces were crushed.

The chaos continued as French, British, and even Spanish troops intervened in Saint-Domingue. Boyer returned to the calony in 1802 as part of an invading French army but soon abandoned his new allies to join with his fellow mulatto general ALEXANDRE SABÈS PÉTION. After Toussaint's capture by the French, Jean-Jacques Dessalines (1758–1806) took control and later declared himself emperor after Haiti's independence was achieved. Dessalines proved to be a cruel ruler and was murdered in 1806 as part of a larger plot.

Henry Christophe, who had also served with Toussaint and Dessalines, was proclaimed provisional head of the new government, while Pétion was appointed chairman of a committee charged with drafting a constitution. Christophe rejected this convention and tried to remove it militarily by marching on Port-au-Prince. He failed, and Pétion was elected president by the national assembly in 1807. Unable to contact the South and West, Christophe abandoned these departments to establish his own rule in the North. He set up a presidency and eventually declared himself king of Haiti and his territory a kingdom in March 1811. To Pétion and his supporters, Christophe was a dangerous usurper and a troublemaker. Boyer, meanwhile, was appointed commander in chief of Pétion's army and had fought off the attempted takeover of Port-au-Prince by the forces of Christophe, recaptured the South after a rebellion led by his old patron Rigaud, and notched several other crucial victories against Christophe.

Christophe had the advantage of being well connected with important figures in Britain, such as the abolitionist Thomas Clarkson, who provided him with considerable advice and guidance in his relationship

Jean-Pierre Boyer (1776–1850), Haitian military and political leader. Boyer reunited Haiti after the end of the Haitian Revolution and ruled the country relatively peacefully for 25 years. A military leader of mixed race, he generally commanded respect from other military leaders and from the mixed-race business class. *(© Gianni Dagli Orti/CORBIS)*

with France and also on domestic issues. As were later leaders, however, Christophe was faced with his territory's limited economic potential, especially given the collapse of the rich sugar plantation sector during the revolution.

In 1818, Pétion died, and Boyer was chosen president of the southern Haitian Republic. Boyer got along no better with his northern rival, and there was constant bickering between the two leaders. Eventually, there were several uprisings against Christophe, who committed suicide in 1820. Boyer then incorporated Christophe's territory into his own. Finally, Boyer also put the eastern part of the island, the modern DOMINICAN REPUBLIC, under his rule, creating a unified Haiti. Several years later, Boyer managed an agreement with the French wherein, in exchange for a sizable payment, the French would relinquish all claims to their former possession. This payment proved to be such a burden to the Haitian government that it had nothing to spare for developing the country.

As president, Boyer faced many of the same problems as later Haitian leaders. Although he worked diligently to improve the administration and increase educational opportunities, Haiti's agricultural sphere had been severely damaged by years of infighting. Attempted agricultural reforms under the framework of Boyer's Code Rurale failed to alleviate the growing poverty of the populace and to assure the few remaining intellectuals that Boyer had any viable solutions. He attempted to thread a path among the competing interests of the mulatto business elite, the military leadership, and the rural poor and was successful for many years. However, after an earthquake that further damaged the economic situation, Boyer was overthrown by Charles Rivière-Hérard in January 1843. The former president fled to Jamaica and later to France, where he died on July 9, 1850.

K. Wayne Ackerson

FURTHER READING
Ackerson, Wayne. *The African Institution (1807–1827) and the Antislavery Movement in Great Britain.* Lewiston, N.Y.: Mellen Press, 2005.

Cole, Hubert. *Christophe: King of Haiti.* New York: Viking Press, 1967.

Newcombe, Covelle. *Black Fire: A Story of Henri Christophe.* New York: Longman's, 1940.

BRAGANÇA, ISABEL OF.   *See* ISABEL OF BRAGANÇA.

BRAGANÇA, PEDRO I OF.   *See* PEDRO I.

BRAGANÇA, PEDRO II OF.   *See* PEDRO II.

BRAZIL
Geography
Colonized by Portugal in 1500, Brazil is a huge country, taking up almost half of South America. It is very diverse geographically, culturally, and in every other way. The country stretches from the northern Tropics to the southern temperate zone and from the foothills of the Andes across thousands of miles to the Atlantic Ocean. Geographically and culturally, the country has five main regions. The first is the northeastern coastal zone. This was the first area settled by Europeans and their African slaves and was the most productive sugar region. It consists of a fertile and well-watered coastal plain, then dry scrubland. The coast has many fine harbors, including especially Salvador de Bahia and São Luís in Maranhão. Many small rivers descend from the Brazilian Highlands to the south and west, carrying water that can be used for waterpower or irrigation. This was an area especially well suited for plantation agriculture. Inland from the northeastern coast is a drier region, well suited to ranching. To the south lies the southeastern coastal region, and the cities of Rio de Janeiro and São Paulo. Today the most heavily urbanized section of the country, here development lagged in colonial days, in part because the mountains are close to the coast and there is little flat land for sugar development. Also, the climate is not quite as suitable as in the Northeast for sugar cultivation. However, the mountains are ideal country for coffee growing, and in addition the region offers easy access to the interior. Inland from Rio and São Paulo are the mining regions of Minas Gerais and Goiás. Goiás surrounds the modern capital of Brasilia, which was not developed until the 20th century. Both of these provinces are rich in minerals, especially gold. The discovery of gold in Minas Gerais in the late 17th century sparked rapid urban development both there and in the coastal cities. Both provinces are mountainous and heavily forested, and the gold is found in widely scattered placer deposits. This condition encouraged a "wild west" frontier society in these areas, permitting rapid social advancement—and equally rapid falls—for prospectors, bandits, and speculators of all races. The far south of Brazil, which includes a good deal of what is now URUGUAY, ARGENTINA, and PARAGUAY, was a frontier region for much of the colonial period. There was some mining, but the principal activities were ranching and exploitation of the local native population. The Brazilian settlement at Colonía do Sacramento on the Plate River in Uruguay was an important slave trading and smuggling port, providing goods and services to the Spanish colonies on the Plate and in BOLIVIA and

Brazil

VENEZUELA
COLOMBIA
GUYANA
SURINAM
French Guiana
(FRANCE)
ATLANTIC
OCEAN

Río Negro
Amazon R.
Manaus
Amazon R.
Madeira R.
Marajó Is.
Belém
São Luís
Fortaleza
Arraial do
Bom Jesus
Pernambuco

Rio
Branco

PERU
Río Xingu
Río Araguaia
Río Tocantins
Río São Francisco

PALMARES
Recife

BOLIVIA
Brasília
Goiás
Minas Gerais
Belo
Horizonte

Salvador
de Bahia

PACIFIC
OCEAN
Río Grande

N
Río Paraná
São Paulo
Santos
Rio de Janeiro

PARAGUAY
CHILE
ARGENTINA

☐ Historic place
Goiás Province name and border

0   400 miles
0   400 km

Pôrto Alegre

© Infobase Learning
URUGUAY

PERU. The final region, the far northern and northwestern interior, was little developed in colonial times. Expeditions of slave raiders and merchants from São Paulo, the famous *bandeirantes* penetrated this area during the 17th and 18th centuries. After independence in 1821, rubber, lumber, and gold industries grew up here. To the north is the Amazon River basin. Much of the region is heavily forested, although there is more open country in the highlands along the border with Bolivia and Peru. Until the 20th century, the regions were not linked effectively by land. Coastal shipping was the rule, and during the

colonial period, some provinces had more reliable links with PORTUGAL or African ports than with other Brazilian regions.

Early Colonial Period (1530–1700)

The indigenous population of Brazil was as diverse as its geography. However, no dense settled populations of native people survived contact with Europeans so as to be conquered and ruled as the Spanish had done in the Andes. Recent research indicates that the Amazon basin did indeed house a dense agricultural population at the beginning of the 16th century, but that population was decimated by disease before Europeans settled the area. The mountains and coastal plains of northeastern Brazil were inhabited by the Tupí, who were agriculturalists and had a civilization similar to that of the eastern woodland Indians of North America. As did the North American Indians, they alternately fought European expansion and sought accommodation. They took in RUNAWAY SLAVES and developed Afro-Indian communities of MAROONS. Unlike in North America, however, the disease environment of tropical Brazil was more hostile to native people, with tropical diseases that entered from Africa finding a more congenial home. Thus, the Tupí contribution to the Brazilian maroon culture was less than the native contribution to, for example, the BLACK SEMINOLE or the Afro-Cherokee culture in North America (see also BRAZILIAN MAROONS). The Portuguese colonists put captured Tupí Indians to work as slaves on their plantations, a system that reduced their population and destroyed their culture. Ultimately, the Tupí culture was almost completely exterminated, surviving only in the remote mountainous parts of this region. The states of Minas Gerais and Goiás hosted relatively dense Indian populations related to the Guaraní of Paraguay. These Indians had time to adjust to the new disease environment before they had to confront more than scattered slave raids. By the 18th century, they were prepared to resist strenuously. The gold miners clashed repeatedly with the Indians in this region, and finally suppressing them had to wait until after national independence. Some of these Indians lived alongside runaway slaves and formed cross-racial alliances, while other local Indians joined the *caçadores do mato*, or rural slave-catching police.

The first European presence along the coast of what is now Brazil was French, as traders stopped to buy brazilwood for dyes, timber for naval supplies, and food. The Portuguese decided to prevent the French from installing themselves in what Portugal saw as its territory, based on the 1494 Treaty of Tordesillas with Spain, and allocated lands along the coast to nobles as hereditary captaincies. The captains were supposed to pay the cost of settlement themselves, but ultimately the Portuguese Crown had to subsidize these settlements, and most became bankrupt in the end anyway. The captains wanted to trade with the Indians for goods they could sell to passing ships, but the few settlers they could recruit wanted to farm, mostly using enslaved native labor. Duarte Coelho, the captain of Pernambuco, managed to satisfy all the various stakeholders by developing sugar production starting in 1542. He started out using enslaved native labor, much of it purchased from the only other successful captaincy, that of São Vicente, who specialized in slave raiding, but ultimately he and other Brazilian planters turned to Afri-

can slaves. Portugal had already been using Africans on plantations in southern Portugal and the Atlantic islands of Madeira and São Tomé, so this was a natural decision. Brazil rapidly became the world's largest sugar producer and imported about half of all slaves taken to the Americas by the Atlantic slave trade.

Among the early Portuguese settlers were free people of African descent. Portugal had been importing slaves from Africa for more than a century by the time the captains established themselves on the coast of Brazil. In addition, Portugal had had forts on the coast of Morocco since the early 15th century, through which they traded with Moroccan slave traders, who took slaves up from the Niger River valley across the Sahara. Portugal's slave laws, like Spain's LAS SIETE PARTIDAS, were based on Roman legal principles that saw freedom as human's normal condition and slavery an unfortunate, although sometimes necessary, exception. This is not to say that slaves in Portugal were always well treated, but the legal system and cultural concepts favored at least some people who sought their freedom, if they were prepared to accommodate society's expectations in terms of religious behavior and culture. Racialist ideas had not yet really developed in the European mind in the 16th century, meaning that people of color who acted Portuguese could be largely accepted as full members of the society. Contrary to the almost-universal practice elsewhere in the Americas, or to the norms in Brazilian society after the middle of the 17th century, in early colonial times the children of white men and Indian or African women were thought of as free whites. In later centuries, many a prominent old Brazilian family had to conceal the racial status of some female forebears. Even after formal, legal adoption of the general norm that the status (free or slave) of the child follows that of the mother, and that people of mixed-racial origin were mulattos, of a lower status than pure whites, there were still individuals who looked somewhat African and had some known African ancestors who were nonetheless treated as whites because of their social standing and long ancestry in the colony. Portugal never developed strong prejudices or laws against MISCEGENATION, or even INTERRACIAL MARRIAGE, although there were governmental positions that only someone officially recognized as white could hold. Sometimes marriage of a white man and a black or Indian woman meant that the man would be ineligible for government posts. Certainly there was plenty of prejudice against people of mixed race, though perhaps less than against pure blacks. Marriage, interracial or intraracial, was actually quite rare in early colonial Brazil by the standards of the Christian world. Most people lived in informal relationships. MANUMISSION remained common throughout the era of slavery: Masters had almost complete latitude to decide to free their slaves and the government intervened to liberate slaves, to reward good service or to punish masters for mistreatment.

For all these reasons, we have almost no sense of how many free Brazilians in the early colonial period had African ancestry, or even of the somewhat smaller number who would have been considered mixed-race or black. We can only guess that the proportion was at least as high as that found in Spanish America at the same time—which in some places was as high as 50 percent. More than half of all free non-Indian Brazilians in the 17th century had at least some African ancestry.

The colony faced many difficulties in its first century and a half of existence. Defeating the Indians was difficult, and as the conquest proceeded, there was a labor crisis, as African slaves were deemed vital to replace the declining supply of Indians. Runaway slaves formed maroon communities; the most important of these *quilombos*, as they were called, was Palmares, located in the mountains between Recife and Salvador. Palmares resisted Portuguese and Dutch attack for almost a century, at the end under their king ZUMBI, later a hero of Afro-Brazilian struggle. They were only finally subdued when regular forces were called from all over the colony for a major attack in 1694. Foreign countries intervened on several occasions. Most notable among these, the Dutch invaded in 1630, holding some of the most profitable sugar areas until 1654. Resistance to the Dutch offered opportunities to people of color to serve in the armed forces, to escape slavery, and to profit in business. One important commander of the Portuguese forces was the free black HENRIQUE DIAS, who led Brazilian forces at the Siege of Arraial do Bom Jesus in 1635. The invasion also helped create a sense of shared suffering and collective purpose between elite free people of color such as Dias and Portuguese whites that helped free coloreds gain acceptance, especially in the Northeast. In the Southeast, expeditions out of São Paulo began to explore the interior starting in the mid-17th century. Some early explorers of the Brazilian interior were JESUITS sent as missionaries, who established a chain of mission villages along the Paraná River. The mission villages had conflicts with São Paulo merchants and slave raiders, and ultimately the Jesuits were driven out of Brazil and their villages destroyed. The Paulista *bandeirantes* included many people of color. In his expedition of 1674, the famous Paulista Fernão Dias Pais had about 20 people described as Afro-Brazilians among his almost 600 men, including the mixed-race captain Belchior da Cunha. It was during this expedition that gold was first discovered in Minas Gerais. Dias Pais's mixed-race son was said to have been the first to find a nugget of gold; it is unclear whether the son's mother was an African or Indian slave.

Late Colonial Period (1700–1821)

The southeastern region became the economic and political heart of the colony after the discovery of gold in Minas Gerais in the 1670s, and then in Goiás after 1720. At the same time, the sugar plantations in the Northeast were experiencing hard times as competitors in the Caribbean were entering to the market with lower production costs and shorter journeys to the European market. Rio de Janeiro and São Paulo offered an easy route to the mining areas and profited enormously. At the same time, the interior experienced a huge and sustained economic boom. Boom times generated slave imports. In the coastal cities, slaves worked as urban laborers, craftsmen, and servants and on farms. In the interior, slaves worked primarily as miners. Mining in particular offered many opportunities for a slave to improve his condition. Since the gold was found in widely scattered placer deposits in streambeds, miners could not be supervised directly. Instead, slaves would be equipped by their masters, who would then send them off into the wilderness with instructions to return in a certain period. Since the masters had no way of controlling what the slave did with his time or the gold he found, masters would demand a certain fixed payment each trip. Slaves who hit a rich strike could earn enough to purchase their freedom in one trip. Slaves who failed to find anything might be harshly punished if they returned, might be tempted to try to remain in the mountains as maroons until they found enough to satisfy the master, or might even try to seek freedom. These conditions led to the rapid growth of a population of free Afro-Brazilians in and around the gold fields. The port cities and the internal mining towns such as Ouro Preto developed significant free Afro-Brazilian populations in the 18th century. One famous mixed-race citizen of Minas Gerais was ANTONIO LISBOA "O Aleijadinho," an architect and sculptor who designed and decorated many of the churches of Minas Gerais in the late 1700s. Other, less well-known free people of color worked as ARTISANS and craftsmen, especially in the building trades, as Lisboa did. The beautiful buildings of Ouro Preto have been designated a world heritage site by UNESCO.

The free colored population grew in the other cities of Brazil during this period. With relatively easy manumission and a limited flow of working-class white immigrants, the working class and small business community of the coastal cities was predominantly free colored by the end of the 18th century. One example of this community is ROSA MARIA DA CONCEIÇÃO, a seamstress and small businesswoman from Bahia in the Northeast, who died at an advanced age in 1843. She was a freed slave, born in Africa. Illiterate, she had the notary's assistance to draw up her will, but she was wise enough in the ways of the world to protect her possessions through legal processes when she thought they were being misappropriated by a white man. She was a member of a CATHOLIC CONFRATERNITY that provided some social services for her, and she appears to have been a pious member of the ROMAN CATHOLIC CHURCH. In a time when FREEMASONRY and the ideas of the Enlightenment were undermining religious piety among educated elite whites, free people of color were among the most active parishioners in many parts of the Catholic Americas. Another example, a more prosperous woman, was CHICA DA SILVA, widow of a diamond broker in Minas Gerais. She educated her daughters in the best convent, moved in the highest circles of society, and seemed to suffer no handicap from her background of slavery and illegitimacy. Poorer free people of color worked alongside slaves who were permitted to hire themselves out. In Bahia around the turn of the 19th century, workers formed *cantos*, often organized among people who had the same African origin or ancestry; free coloreds were often chosen as leaders because of their greater mobility. By the turn of the 19th century, free people of color were a majority of the African-descended population and were more than one-third of the total population of the colony. Brazil was really an outlier in this regard, having a much higher proportion of its population recognized as free people of color than any other place in the Americas.

Ironically, free people of color played an important role in one of the bleakest chapters in Brazil's history, the persistence of the African slave trade into the late 19th century. The slave trade between Brazil and the Portuguese African colonies was permitted for some time after other countries such as Britain abolished the slave trade, as it was considered in some sense an internal trade. Brazilian merchant families dominated the trade, even on the African end on supposedly Portuguese soil. These Brazilian merchants formed close relationships with Angolan and Mozambiquan merchants. Often these relationships, as was common on the African coast, included marriages, which produced a population of Luso-Africans who carried on the trade after their fathers' retirement or death. However, some of the Brazilian merchants were free people of color from Brazil, descended from people who had made the Middle Passage across the Atlantic in previous generations.

Another important role that free people of color filled in late colonial society was that of defender of the colony against its internal and external enemies. The colonial armed forces were full of free people of color. The black regiments of the Brazilian MILITIA in Salvador were named after Henrique Dias. FRANCISCO XAVIER BIGODE, a fighter in the independence movement, served in this regiment from in 1797 and rose to the rank of lieutenant colonel under the old regime, as a result of his performance, patronage by whites, and special exceptions to the general rule that the top command positions would be held by whites.

Also in the late colonial period, free people of color began to be admitted to the professions: law, medicine, the priesthood, journalism, and the professional civil service. As in the case of Bigode's promotion to field grade rank in the army, admission of free people of color to high positions was exceptional, open to only a few people with very high skills and important white patrons. Sometimes these exceptions were as a shock to the uninitiated. The British traveler Henry Koster remarked on this phenomenon in 1820. He asked his servant about a particular local official, the Capitão-môr, or militia commander. "Was he not a mulatto man?" Yes, said the servant, he was a mulatto but is so no longer. Koster wondered how this could be, and the servant replied, "Can a capitão-môr be a mulatto man?" The man had not been formally promoted to whiteness by some official process, but assuming the office normally restricted to whites meant that he was socially redefined as white.

This process of redefinition, or *whitening*, was working throughout Brazilian society in the 19th century (*see* "WHITENING" AND RACIAL PROMOTION). People of mixed race whose appearance and social standing permitted it were slowly integrated into the white population. Brazilian culture had a high tolerance for African physical appearance among people defined as white, so it was uncommon for anybody to move in the opposite direction, that is, for someone defined as white to have a child who was defined as free colored. A similar process at work in Spanish America led to the near-disappearance of people of African descent in such places as MEXICO and Argentina. In Brazil, this was not possible, especially given the fact that Brazil continued slave imports at a vigorous pace throughout the 19th century, landing a total of about 1.9 million persons between 1811 and 1870. Still, the fact that many Brazilians socially defined as white have African ancestors means that we must increase our estimate of the effect of Africans and Afro-Brazilians on the national culture.

Independence and the Nineteenth Century (1821–1889)

Brazil became an independent empire in 1821, as the result of a revolution that was much bloodier in Portugal than it was in Brazil and can almost be seen as the independence of Portugal from Brazil. There was some fighting in Brazil, especially in the Northeast, and free colored militiamen such as Bigode played an important role. Skilled urban free coloreds like Bigode generally supported the House of Bragança during the first few disturbed decades of Brazilian independence. The late 1820s and 1830s were marked by almost-continuous rebellions and conflict between liberal and conservative forces. The first emperor, Dom PEDRO I, abdicated in 1831, going to Portugal to fight to establish his daughter on the throne. Dom Pedro had liberal principles and sought liberal reforms in Brazil and Portugal, though he wanted to keep political power centralized in his own hands. His successor, Dom PEDRO II, was only five years old when he ascended the throne; his father may have hoped to keep control over Brazil through a long regency, but in fact local elites seized control of the regency council and implemented many conservative ideas. Among these was dissolution of the free colored militias, integrating them into multiracial regular units with white officers. This centralized control of the armed forces in the national government and reduced the importance of free colored and regional elites. The national government also persisted in protecting the slave trade, despite signing agreements with the British and others to end it. Dom Pedro's constitution guaranteed equal rights for all free Brazilians of any color, but a series of government measures protected state governments and individuals who wanted to discriminate on the basis of race during this period. These measures sparked local revolts, including the revolt in 1837 that cost Bigode his life, which was led by FRANCISCO SABINO ÁLVARES DA ROCHA VIEIRA. It was also during this period (1825–28) that Uruguay rebelled and gained its independence, led by a group of liberal notables that included at least two men of partially African ancestry. Brazilian rebels generally proclaimed their loyalty to the young Dom Pedro II, who was known to share his father's liberal ideas. In 1840, at the age of 14, Dom Pedro II overthrew his regency council and seized power, pardoning a variety of defeated liberal rebels from the preceding decades, including Sabino.

A period of prosperity and internal peace under the long rule of Dom Pedro II (1840–89) proved a golden age for Brazilian free people of color. Many of the most famous Afro-Brazilians were active during this period. Among these were Brazil's greatest novelist, JOAQUIM MARIA MACHADO DE ASSIS; the poet and publisher FRANCISCO DE PAULA BRITO; the engineer and positivist philosopher ANDRÉ REBOUÇAS; and the poet and teacher ANTÔNIO GONÇALVES TEIXEIRA E SOUSA. Intellectual life, publishing, and letters were important avenues of advancement for free people of color. Increased literacy, including public education, which was established in the cities in the 1860s, opened up a market for works of literature, and liberal principles of freedom of speech allowed these men generally to publish whatever they wanted. Literacy rates increased during the period, though the mass of poor country people were still generally untouched by education.

Brazilian slaves also took advantage of a more prosperous and liberal society to gain their freedom. Purchasing letters of manumission became even easier during the mid-19th century. In addition, poorer states that did not have many slaves often welcomed runaways from the coffee centers of São Paulo and Rio, who could settle as freed persons and help build up the local economy. And blacks moved from the countryside to the cities, sometimes with manumission papers in hand and sometimes simply LIVING "AS FREE" and hoping that nobody noticed in the bustling urban environment. In the last years of the empire, the trickle of migrants became a flood.

The War of the Triple Alliance (1865–70) was an important step in the lives of free people of color, as many volunteered from across the country to fight for Brazil. The forces of tiny Paraguay inflicted many defeats on the Brazilian-Uruguayan-Argentine alliance in the early going, and national unity and the liberal government were in peril. The patriotic rallying of young men from across the county proved the salvation of Brazil. Black soldiers hoped that their service would make the broader society think of them as citizens, and to some extent this happened. Brazil's victory in the war gave a major boost to the abolitionist movement.

Paradoxically, the abolition of the slave trade in 1850 resulted in a step backward for free people of color in Brazil. With the increasing price of slaves after the cutoff of new imports and the increase in coffee production in the hinterland of Rio de Janeiro, manumissions declined. At the same time, free people of color found it more expensive to buy their own slaves and advance themselves economically.

Abolition and the First Republic (1889–1930)

Free people of color were an important constituency for abolitionists (see also BRAZIL, ABOLITIONIST MOVEMENT IN). Free people of color who met the strict property and education limitations could vote in imperial Brazil, and they made up as much as 10 percent of the electorate. Of course, this was much smaller than the percentage of blacks in the total population, or even the free population, reflecting the relative poverty and poorer education of free people of color. They were reliable supporters of liberal causes, and the liberal politicians knew that it was wise to protect their interests. The emperor, as a supporter of most liberal reforms, benefited from their support. Teixeira e Sousa was an exception, as he was a dissident for most of his public career, calling attention to abuses of people of color by local officials and accusing the national government of doing little to protect them. But monarchist free blacks ranged from the educated elite such as Rebouças or the lawyer and politician Francisco Gê Acaiaba de Montezuma, viscount of Jequitinhonha, to the free black veteran and "prince" Cândido da Fonseca Galvão (Dom Obá II). Dom Obá traveled with a band of forest rangers from the backcountry of Bahia to fight for Brazil in the War of the Triple Alliance. It is unclear what his actual service was, but he had a reputation for bravery after the war. He moved to Rio de Janeiro and was recognized as the leader of the city's African-born population. He regularly attended Dom Pedro's imperial receptions, where he was granted considerable honors. He rallied poor black support to the monarchy throughout the troubled decade of the 1880s. He and his followers cheered the decision by the regent Princess Imperial Isabel of Bragança to end slavery in 1888. The monarchy did not long survive abolition of slavery, as landed elites took their revenge in 1889. Dom Obá was forcibly retired after participating in promonarchy demonstrations in 1890 and died shortly thereafter.

The abolition movement benefited from the rapid degeneration of Brazil's slave system during the years after the war with Paraguay. Hundreds of thousands of slaves fled, sometimes being offered protection by states on the frontier or in underdeveloped regions that wanted to increase their populations. An abolitionist consensus spread throughout Brazilian society, though the planter class in the coffee regions insisted that some provision be made to ensure them a steady labor supply.

The first outcome of the revolution was that the new leadership decided not to offer compensation to slave owners who had lost their "property" at the time of final emancipation, even though the lack of compensation had been one of the major grievances of local elites from the coffee districts of São Paulo and Rio. However, the new power structure gave great power to regional elites through a federalist constitution. Local elites tended to be conservative, but not universally. One result was that conditions for black Brazilians varied widely from state to state and even within states, as local governments either protected blacks or tried to exclude them from political power and economic independence. The national government supported white immigration, which had been strong throughout the 19th century, giving land grants in the North and Southwest to new arrivals. Rapid white immigration, combined with whitening of people of mixed race, meant that Afro-Brazilians declined as a share of the national population from an estimated 67 percent in 1800 to 47 percent in 1900. The migration of blacks from rural areas to Brazil's cities dates back at least to the 18th century, but the process accelerated sharply

in the late 19th century as industrialization really took hold. The favelas of Rio and São Paulo had their origins in this period, as factory workers settled where they could. An urban population, even a very poor one, has access to education and social mobility that they would not have in the countryside. Blacks became important members of Brazil's labor movement. One of the most important outbreaks of labor unrest during this period was the "Revolt of the Whips" in 1910. The sailors on four Brazilian navy battleships in the harbor of Rio de Janeiro mutinied against the use of physical punishment, ranging up to 250 lashes, against the mostly black sailors. One important leader of the sailors was João Cândido Felisberto (1880–1969), who was born free in Rio Grande do Sul, son of a black ranchhand. He and the other leaders were punished and dismissed from the service, but the navy reformed its judicial system and began promoting black sailors to higher ranks.

Patronage and hierarchy were important parts of the conservative republican idea of "order"—crucial to Brazil's self-identity as the national motto was (and is) "Order and Progress." Blacks who subscribed to the system of hierarchy by gaining the patronage of local elites could receive protection, social advancement, and other benefits. One example, from the historian Kim Butler's *Freedoms Given, Freedoms Won* (1998), is the case of Josepha da Silva Santos, a woman of color, in 1895. The father of Josepha's daughter had taken the girl and had given her as a servant to a Portuguese family. The immigrant family mistreated the girl. Josepha's older son, a policeman, intervened and in turn was mistreated by the Portuguese family. Josepha called on the chief of police, who under the rules of patronage and hierarchy was responsible for looking out for the family of "his" policeman, a client. Instead of a modern, liberal idea of equal justice for all, under which the mother would be able to appeal the mistreatment of her child to the courts, a similar outcome may have been achieved (the final outcome of the case is not recorded) by a sort of transitional feudalism that preserved traditional hierarchies of class and race.

The other half of the republican ideology was "progress," and specifically racial progress. The dominant philosophy of race during the period of the First Republic was the idea that Brazil was a "racial democracy" evolving a robust, hybrid people through miscegenation and immigration and that any racial troubles were on their way to extinction along with an identifiable Afro-Brazilian population. This philosophy is similar to the assimilationist attitude toward immigrants found in the United States at the time, sometimes called the "melting pot" model. Brazilians, or perhaps the Portuguese in general, were seen as having a unique ability to assimilate and uplift tropical peoples through race mixing and the universalist effects of Catholic Iberian civilization. This idea was perhaps best expressed by a historian of the succeeding generation, GILBERTO FREYRE (1900–87), in his masterpiece *Casa-Grande & Senzala* (in English, *The Masters and the Slaves*). Many prominent Afro-Brazilians supported this philosophy, both through their private decisions to "whiten" themselves or their children or through publicly affirming a collective Brazilian identity for themselves and other dark-skinned people. Even the rebel black sailor Cândido joined a movement in the 1930s called "integralism," which was a kind of fascism modified for South American conditions and included some of these same racial ideas.

Conclusion

Brazil has the largest population of African descent in the Americas, with almost 93 million of the nation's 170 million people self-identifying as black or *pardo*. In addition, millions more Brazilians who self-identify as white or Indian also have unacknowledged African ancestry, thanks to assimilation and "whitening." African culture has had profound effects on Brazilian culture, from Afro-Caribbean religions (*see also* AFRICAN AND SYNCRETIC RELIGION) to the samba in music and dance, from a martial arts style called capoeira imported by Congo slaves to broadly held assumptions about family, society, and government. Much of this African influence, of course, was transmitted by slaves. Free people of color, especially the well-educated, mixed-race elite, often tried as best they could to escape their African roots and consciously displayed European cultural markers whenever possible. However, because their position gave them freedom to move around and gave them access to at least some wealth and social position, free people held communities of color together. There was occasional division between black and mixed-race people and between those from long-established free families and the newly freed in Brazil, but very little compared to that seen in French and British colonies. Very light-skinned people of color might whiten and disappear from the community altogether. But there was a generally strong sense of common identity and purpose. By deleting elite Afro-descended people from the socially defined Afro-Brazilian population, the phenomenon of "whitening" actually reduced the importance of former free colored elites after general abolition. In any case, the general collapse of the slave system in the 1880s, with hundreds of thousands of people fleeing into freedom, meant that the distinction between old free coloreds and those freed by general abolition was largely academic. Today, Afro-Brazilians are again beginning to speak of themselves as a people,

aided by government programs created during the post-1984 democratic era designed to root out and destroy the vestiges of racial prejudice that still hamper the social mobility and full acceptance of those with more obvious African ancestry. However, internal divisions based on former status are of little importance today.

Stewart R. King

FURTHER READING
Andrews, George Reid. *Afro-Latin America, 1800–2000*. New York: Oxford University Press, 2004.
Barman, Roderick. *Brazil: The Forging of a Nation, 1798–1852*. Palo Alto, Calif.: Stanford University Press, 1988.
Bethell, Leslie ed. *Colonial Brazil*. Cambridge: Cambridge University Press, 1987.
Burns, E. Bradford. "The Intellectuals as Agents of Change and the Independence of Brazil." In *From Colony to Nation: Essays on the Independence of Brazil,* edited by Russell-Wood, 211–246. Baltimore: Johns Hopkins University Press, 1975.
Butler, Kim. *Freedoms Given, Freedoms Won: Afro-Brazilians in Post-Abolition Sao Paulo and Salvador*. New Brunswick, N.J.: Rutgers University Press, 1998.
Degler, Carl. *Neither Black nor White: Slavery and Race Relations in Brazil and the United States*. Madison: University of Wisconsin Press, 1986.
Frank, Zephyr. *Dutra's World: Wealth and Family in Nineteenth-Century Rio de Janeiro*. Albuquerque: University of New Mexico Press, 1982.
Freyre, Gilberto. *The Masters and the Slaves: A Study in the Development of Brazilian Civilization*. Translated by Samuel Putnam. New York: Alfred A. Knopf, 1946.
Graden, Dale. "The Origins, Evolution, and Demise of the 'Myth of Racial Democracy' in Brazil, 1848–1998." In *La reconstrucción del mundo en América Latina*, edited by Enrique Pérez Arias. Lund, Sweden: Cuadernos Heteroqénesis, 1998, 181–197.
Graham, Richard. "Free African Brazilians and the State in Slavery Times." In *Racial Politics in Contemporary Brazil*, edited by Michael Hanchard. Austin: University of Texas Press, 1999.
Klein, Herbert. "Nineteenth-Century Brazil." In *Neither Slave nor Free: The Freedmen of African Descent in the Slave Societies of the New World,* edited by David W. Cohen and Jack Greene, 84–133. Baltimore: Johns Hopkins University Press, 1972.
Miller, Joseph. *Way of Death: Merchant Capitalism and the Angolan Slave Trade, 1730–1830*. Madison: University of Wisconsin Press, 1996.
Reis, João José. *Slave Rebellion in Brazil: The Muslim Uprising of 1835 in Bahia*. Baltimore: Johns Hopkins University Press, 1995.
Russell-Wood, A. J. R. *The Black Man in Slavery and Freedom in Colonial Brazil*. New York: Palgrave Macmillan, 1982.

Schwartz, Stuart. "The Manumission of Slaves in Colonial Bra-
zil: Bahia 1648–1745." *Hispanic American Historical Review*
54, no. 4 (1974): 603–665.
———. "Tapanhuns, Negros da Terra, and Curibocas: Common
Cause and Confrontation between Blacks and Natives in
Colonial Brazil." In *Beyond Black and Red: African-Native
Relations in Colonial Latin America*, edited by Matthew
Restall, 81–114. Albuquerque: University of New Mexico
Press, 2005.

BRAZIL, ABOLITIONIST MOVEMENT IN

Africans and Afro-Brazilians formed an integral part of
the abolitionist movement that pressured the Brazilian
government to end slavery on May 13, 1888, making it the
last country in the Americas to end slavery. The area that
received nearly 40 percent of the African slave trade, Brazil still counted approximately 1.3 million enslaved men
and women in 1880, the year the abolitionist movement
emerged. Like the U.S. and British antislavery campaigns,
the Brazilian movement was characterized by its popular, urban, and decentralized nature. Scores of abolitionist societies formed in the 1880s, consisting of members
of a wide range of social groups, such as students, merchants, port workers, and theatrical companies. Within
these antislavery clubs, free people of color were a driving
force, participating directly not only in the liberation of
slaves, but also in the process of wide-scale mobilization
that was redefining the relationship between society and
politics. That is, the importance of Brazilian abolitionism
transcends the dynamics of slave emancipation; it is also
at the center of an important shift in the country's political culture.

The abolitionist movement of the 1880s represented the
emergence of Brazilian popular politics, and it was the
influence of public pressure, combined with the slaves'
own initiatives for freedom, that forced an abolition law
that was "immediate" and without "compensation" for
SLAVE OWNERS in 1888. The abolition law could have been
further delayed and might have happened under different
terms were it not for the critical contributions of Africans and Afro-Brazilians to the abolitionist movement.
As politicians, lawyers, journalists, and teachers, a generation of free coloreds played a crucial role in a transformative moment in Brazilian history in creating and
mobilizing an abolitionist consciousness in Brazil.

The literary and theatrical arts were an essential medium to foment an abolitionist sentiment, for
without a generalized antislavery consciousness, a
full-fledged movement could not have evolved. The
writings of the Afro-Brazilians MARIA FIRMINA DOS
REIS and Antônio de Castro Alves (1847–71) were part
of the early cultural and intellectual attacks on slavery.

Maria Firmina dos Reis, a mulatta schoolteacher from
the northern province of Maranhão, wrote Brazil's first
antislavery novel, *Ursula*, in 1859. Alves, a mulatto from
the northeastern province of Bahia, wrote poetry and
theater works that caused great ferment among literary
and legal student circles in Bahia, Rio de Janeiro, Recife, and São Paulo in the late 1860s. Alves's words were
still a source of inspiration at abolitionist events in the
1880s, even a decade after his death. The "poet of the
slaves," as Alves was called, published his first antislavery poem in 1863 and in 1868 recited his famous "The
Slave Ship." In addition, Alves wrote a theatrical piece,
Gonzaga, which integrated an abolitionist theme into
the story of the independence-minded Minas Gerais
Conspiracy of 1789. *Gonzaga*, along with *Uncle Tom's
Cabin*, was among the abolitionist plays most staged in
1880s Brazil.

A marked feature of the struggle for abolition, the
advocacy of slaves' freedom through the courts gained
prominence in the 1860s and 1870s. Luiz Gama (1830–82),
an Afro-Brazilian lawyer who himself had been illegally
enslaved as a child, worked tirelessly in São Paulo to free
Africans who had been "illegally" imported to Brazil
after the 1831 ban on the African slave trade. Gama also
regularly wrote newspaper articles on antislavery, and he
was the mentor to a group of abolitionists who operated
an "underground railroad" between the coffee fields of
São Paulo and the province's port city of Santos.

Once established in the early 1880s, the abolitionist movement expanded and grew more influential as
a result of its campaign through the press. Newspapers in every major urban area of Brazil carried news
about abolitionism, usually promoting the cause, but
sometimes also arguing that movement espoused a too
"immediate" and therefore "reckless" transition to free
labor. Through the abolitionist press, Afro-Brazilians
remained a visible and active part of the public debate
over slave emancipation. In Rio de Janeiro, then the
national capital, the *Gazeta da Tarde* was arguably
the most comprehensive and nationally recognizable
paper. The founding editor, José Ferreira de Menezes (?–1881), a mulatto lawyer, and his apprentice, the
mulatto JOSÉ CARLOS DO PATROCÍNIO, were powerful
forces within Brazilian journalism. Upon Ferreira's
death in 1881, Patrocínio assumed control of the *Gazeta*,
and his reprinting of parliamentary debates on slavery
and constant news about the provincial antislavery
campaigns turned the paper into the foremost source
on Brazilian abolitionism. Patrocínio parlayed his visibility into a position as an alderman on the municipal
council of Rio de Janeiro in 1886, an election that was
especially important because it occurred amid an anti-
abolitionist backlash in Brazil. In addition to Patrocínio,

the writings of another mulatto, ANDRÉ REBOUÇAS, an engineer and professor at the Polytechnical Institute in Rio de Janeiro, changed the way Brazilians understood abolitionism. Most important, Rebouças advocated an abolition plan that also included an agrarian reform and land distribution for the former slaves as a way to reinvigorate the agricultural economy. Rebouças's 1883 work on the modernization of agriculture was of great importance to Joaquim Nabuco, a lawyer and politician, the man who was regarded as the leader of the Brazilian abolitionist movement.

At the "everyday" level of promoting abolition, Afro-Brazilians were also of invaluable importance; unfortunately, much less biographical information exists on those from more humble origins. People such as "Pio," a freedman who lived in rural São Paulo in the 1880s, and others such as Sebastião Grande de Arruda, a man of African ancestry who had served in the navy during the Paraguayan War (1864–70), figure among the lesser-known participants of Brazilian abolitionism. Both were engaged in regional "underground railroads": Pio worked as a transporter of slaves from the coffee fields in the Southeast to the safe haven of Santos (São Paulo), and Arruda helped escort slaves from the sugar fields of the Northeast to the "free" lands of Ceará, the Brazilian province that abolished slavery in 1884, four years prior to the national abolition law. The free coloreds in Brazil, oftentimes but not necessarily people who had been slaves, were also essential in protecting and sustaining the communities of runaway slaves that formed across Brazil, most famously those in Campos (Rio de Janeiro) and Santos (São Paulo), places that entered the nation's consciousness because of attention from the abolitionist press.

Free coloreds, in short, shaped the trajectory of the abolitionist movement. Their contributions to the rise of Brazilian abolitionism still need to be better studied, however. In particular, scholars have to look more closely at the practices of abolitionism in order to capture the role that "everyday" people and, in particular, women played in advancing the cause of abolition.

Celso T. Castilho

FURTHER READING
Azevedo, Célia Maria Marinho de. *Abolitionism in the United States and Brazil: A Comparative Perspective.* New York: Garland, 1995.
Conrad, Robert. *The Destruction of Brazilian Slavery.* Berkeley: University of California Press, 1972.
Donald, Cleveland, Jr. "Slave Resistance and Abolitionism in Brazil: The Campista Case, 1879–1888." *Luso-Brazilian Review* 13, no. 2 (Winter 1976): 182–193.
Drescher, Seymour. "Brazilian Abolition in Comparative Perspective." *Hispanic American Historical Review* 68, no. 3 (August 1988): 429–460.
Graden, Dale. *From Slavery to Freedom in Brazil: Bahia, 1835–1900.* Albuquerque: University of New Mexico Press, 2006.
Nabuco, Joaquim. *Abolitionism: The Brazilian Antislavery Struggle.* Translated and edited by Robert Conrad. Urbana: University of Illinois Press, 1977.
Toplin, Robert. *The Abolition of Slavery in Brazil.* New York: Atheneum, 1972.

BRAZIL, LAWS ON RACE AND SLAVERY
Historical Background before the Independence of Brazil in 1822
The history of the slave trade in Brazil started at the beginning of the colonial era in 1532 and extended up until after independence from Portugal in 1822. From the first half of the 16th century, the transatlantic slave trade supplied human cargo from Africa. Slaves were taken mainly from the west coast of Africa, but also in smaller numbers from the Cape Verde Islands, the Cape of Good Hope, the east coast of Mozambique, and sometimes areas in the interior. Slaves were transported in the so-called black ships and entered through the ports of Rio de Janeiro, Salvador, Recife, and São Luis. They were first sold to work in Bahia and Pernambuco in the Northeast of Brazil, on sugarcane plantations and other agricultural establishments and in domestic service. Later slaves were transported to work on coffee cultivation in the central South (the provinces of São Paulo and Rio de Janeiro, and some parts of Minas Gerais), in the gold and diamond mines of Minas Gerais, and in all sorts of jobs in towns and cities. Between the 16th and 19th centuries, according to historical records and estimates, a total of around 3,600,000 African slaves arrived in Brazil.

Although Portugal abolished slavery on February 12, 1761, it did not extend the abolition to its colony of Brazil. During the 18th century, there were a number of local independence movements against the Portuguese Crown, including, for example, the Conjuração Baiana, which occurred in Bahia in 1798, and also sought the abolition of slavery.

From the Independence of Brazil to the Abolition of Slavery, 1822–1888
After the independence of Brazil from Portugal on September 7, 1822, Brazil became a constitutional monarchy with a representative congress, the Brazilian Empire, under the emperor Dom PEDRO II, until the establishment of the republican government on November 15, 1889. Slavery continued to play a dominant economic and political role in the 19th century until its abolition in 1888.

After Brazil's independence, calls for the abolition of slavery became louder, with the country feeling international and internal pressures. The expansion of British industrial capitalism, in particular Britain's sugar production and interests in its colonies in the West Indies, compelled Brazil to pass laws to improve the country's image. Between 1817 and 1871, Britain signed bilateral treaties with several countries that entitled foreign (mostly British) warships to conduct searches and capture vessels on the high seas suspected of being involved in the slave trade and allowing British admiralty courts to decide the disposition of the ships and return the crews of such ships to their own countries for trial.

For example, in 1826, Brazil and Great Britain signed an anti–slave trade treaty aimed at abolishing the slave trade within the next three years. In addition, the Constitution of 1824 and the Penal Code of 1831 sought to curb violence against slaves and improve their working conditions. Brazil also passed and enforced the Slave Trade Law of 1831. This law stipulated that slaves found on vessels from Africa were to be returned to their ports of origin or to other foreign ports, while those slaves who disembarked in Brazil would automatically be released. Nevertheless, Brazil's agreement with Great Britain and its own legislation were never effectively enforced, and the transatlantic slave trade between Africa and Brazil continued. In August 1845, the British Parliament passed 'the Aberdeen Act, which authorized British naval intervention in the transatlantic slave trade by boarding and seizing suspected vessels in any part of the world, even in Brazil's own territorial waters. Slaves then were to be transferred and released in their port of origin, and offenders were to be prosecuted in joint Brazilian-British admiralty courts on charges of PIRACY.

In 1850, facing Great Britain's naval power and the threat of destruction of Brazilian ships, as well as active resistance such as mass slave escapes and rebellions, along with epidemics eventually related to the recently imported African slaves, Brazil gradually introduced more antislavery legislation. International trade in slaves was forbidden by the so-called Eusébio Queirós Law (named after the minister of justice of the empire) and the Law Number 581 of September 4, 1850. The passage of this legislation outlawed the international slave trade to Brazil. It sanctioned shipowners, sea captains, and pilots of transported slaves, as well as those who collaborated in the slave's disembarkation on Brazilian shores. They could be tried by the imperial government instead or by local judges. These measures were finally effective in sharply reducing the international slave trade to Brazil, although there was still some illegal importation of slaves up to the abolition of slavery in 1888.

Despite the end of the international slave trade and the gradual abolition of slavery throughout most of the Americas in the 19th century—particularly in the United States in 1865—as well as the increase in campaigns for the abolition of slavery, there was still a strong internal demand for slaves in Brazil. Between 1850 and 1888, in particular during Brazil's 1877–78 period of severe drought, the northeastern landowners resorted to a system of interprovincial slave trade in order to manage the reduced supply of slave labor and its increasingly high costs. Itinerant slave traders took and sold slaves from the sugarcane and cotton plantations located in the northeastern coastal areas, which were in decline, and took them to the flourishing central and southern coffee plantations in the provinces of São Paulo, Rio de Janeiro, and Minas Gerais (see COTTON CULTIVATION and SUGAR CULTIVATION). In 1854, the Law Nabuco de Araújo (named after the minister of justice and father of the famous abolitionist poet) threatened punishment of local authorities who persisted in covering up the illegal slave trade.

Between 1850 and 1870, facing restrictions on the arrival of new slave shipments and consequent labor shortages and reduced profits, Brazilian coffee plantation owners also progressively replaced slavery with European immigration. A national movement had also emerged in the 1860s, when a group of Brazilian intellectuals, including some journalists, writers, and politicians, and supported by several organizations and newspapers in Rio de Janeiro and São Paulo, began an active campaign promoting the abolition of slavery. After the end of the War of the Triple Alliance against Paraguay (1866–70) many former slaves who had enlisted in the army in exchange for their freedom in response to a law of 1866 refused to work for their former masters. In 1871, the Conservative Party passed the Rio Branco Law (free-birth legislation), also known as the Lei do Ventre Livre (Law of the free womb), of September 28, 1871, which emancipated all children born to slave parents from 1871 on. The SLAVE OWNERS would raise the children until they were eight years old. Upon reaching that age, the so-called freeborn children were to serve their mothers' masters without pay until they reached the age of 21 or they were released to the state, and their masters were entitled to an indemnity.

In 1884, Ceará became the first province to abolish slavery in its territory in Brazil, after a successful abolitionist movement led by the traditional harbor boatmen (jangadeiros), who refused to transport slaves from aboard the ships anchored in the harbor to land, starting on January 30, 1881. In 1884, the so-called Dantas Bill decreed the movement of slaves from state to state to be illegal, increased the redemption funds to persuade more landlords to free slaves, and granted freedom to 60-year-old slaves. In 1885, the imperial government promulgated a similar law, the Saraiva-Cotegipe Law, which became

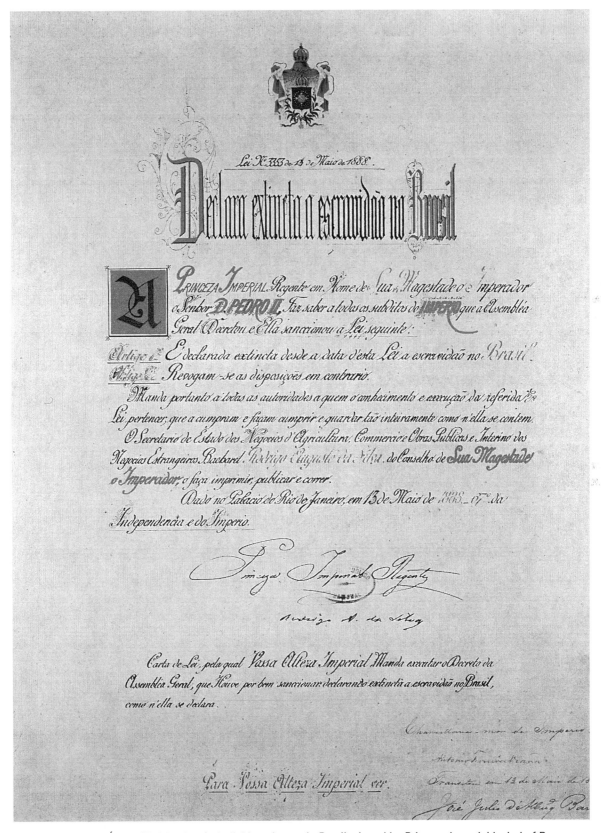

The text of the Lei Áurea (Golden Law) abolishing slavery in Brazil, signed by Princess Imperial Isabel of Bragança. Elite resistance to the law ultimately led to the fall of the Brazilian monarchy, but the conservative republican government that took power in 1889 did not revive slavery. Brazil was the last country in the Americas to abolish slavery. *(© Museu Historico National Rio de Janeiro Brazil/Gianni Dagli Orti/The Art Archive)*

known as the Law of the Sexagenarians (Lei dos Sexagenários). Slaves who were 60 years old were released, and those under 65 years old were required to work for a period of three years. After turning 65, they were freed upon providing indemnities to their owners.

Between 1885 and 1888, many slaves escaped from the coffee plantations in São Paulo Province with support and encouragement from abolitionists, who sometimes also purchased their letters of manumission (cartas de alforría), while the military refused to chase the fugitives. On May 13, 1888, during the absence of the emperor Dom Pedro II in Europe, his daughter, Princess Imperial ISABEL OF BRAGANÇA, (1846–1921), acting as regent, acquiescing to the international rejection of slavery and pressures from the abolitionists, promulgated the so-called Golden Law (Lei Áurea), which abolished slavery in the empire. Thus, Brazil become the latest country in the Western world to ban slavery, a fact that had several consequences and was the origin of an economic crisis that contributed to the fall of the monarchy and the proclamation of a republic in 1889.

The First Decade after the Abolition of Slavery, 1888–1898

The enactment of the Lei Áurea granted freedom to the black slaves without any indemnity and generated radical changes in their social, economic, and working conditions. Although the abolition of slavery created freedom of movement and freedom of choice, freedmen were impoverished, illiterate, and oppressed as they remained in a position of dependency. Unlike previous antislavery legislation, which had been preceded by long public discussions, the Lei Áurea had been immediately and unexpectedly approved. Wealthy and powerful slaveholders were not willing to, nor prepared to, release their slaves from servitude and accept the new legal status of their former slaves. They refused to accept that slavery had been unconditionally outlawed. Slavery ended earlier in the Northeast region than in the central and southern regions. Many slaves moved from the Northeast to the Southeast region because the state subsidized train transportation. On the coffee plantations, which continued to demand an increasing number of workers, the landlords continued, through necessity, to domesticate the new arrivals and subject them to harsh treatment. Yet, many former slaves chose to remain in the areas where several generations of their forebears had lived and worked, relying on a network of family and relatives and thus satisfying the needs for labor of landlords who employed all members of the family working together on the plantations. Some masters forced their former slaves who refused to work without pay to remain on their plantations, held them in private

confinement, and subjected them to corporal punishment. Some former slaves rebelled, asked for police protection, and managed to have their stories published in the newspapers.

On the other hand, landlords complained about former slaves whom they accused of becoming vagrants and thieves, blaming them for trespassing on their properties, arson, and the theft of animals and food supplies. Former slaves who were released were often forced by economic necessity to submit to the demand of landowners who continued to exploit them by paying the minimal salaries, for example, in the rubber industry in the Amazonian forest. Many of the newly freed could not find jobs, for instance, in the state of Paraíba, where the coffee plantations were in decline and were being progressively replaced by cattle production, which required less manpower. Other former slaves migrated to big cities like Rio de Janeiro, where employment was scarce and the lack of accommodation compelled them to live in slums. In the 1890s, one of the consequences of the Lei Áurea was an economic crisis. The sugarcane plantation owners who were not willing or prepared to replace the slave workers with free workers organized the Society for the Promotion of Immigration (Sociedade Promotora de Imigração) to recruit a workforce from Europe and Asia. Despite all the constraints, plantation work remained a vital source of revenue for the former slaves and their families, despite little change in their working conditions and living standards.

Stewart R. King

FURTHER READING

Camargo, Oswaldo de. "The Long Struggle for Liberation: Reflections on the Abolition of Slavery in Brazil." UNESCO Courier. Available online. URL: http://findarticles.com/p/articles/mi_m1310/is_1988_June/ai_6553006. Accessed November 27, 2008.

Góes, José R. *A paz nas senzalas. Famílias escravas e tráfico atlântico, Rio de Janeiro, c. 1790–c. 1850.* Rio de Janeiro: Civilização Brasileira, 1997.

Kowarick, Lúcio. *Trabalho e vadiagem: A origem do trabalho livre no Brasil.* São Paulo: Brasiliense, 1987.

Schwartz, S. B. *Slaves, Peasants, and Rebels: Reconsidering Brazilian Slavery.* Blacks in the New World series. Champaign: University of Illinois Press, 1992.

BRAZILIAN MAROONS (QUILOMBOLAS)
Origins and General Characteristics

Brazilian maroons, or *quilombolas,* were escaped slaves who, when grouped together, founded settlements known as *mocambos* or *quilombos.* (*See also* MAROONS.) Flight was a common strategy of slave resistance throughout the duration of Brazilian slavery, which lasted more than three centuries until its abolition in 1888. The earliest record of these groups dates back to the 16th century, during the period of Portuguese colonization. They varied widely in size and composition, ranging from a few individuals to several thousand members in exceptional cases, and included men, women, and children. *Quilombos* could last from a few weeks to many years, some of them becoming permanent settlements that outlasted abolition. They were found throughout Brazil wherever there was slavery, from urban centers to rural plantation zones and the Amazon frontier.

During the early colonial period these settlements were generally known as *mocambos*; the term *quilombo* gained currency from the late 17th century onward. Both terms derive from the West Central African Kimbundu language of the CONGO AND ANGOLA region and signify a hideout and a male military society, respectively. Although many slaves in Brazil originated in this region, *quilombos* encompassed slaves of various ethnicities and origins.

While *quilombos*, like maroon communities elsewhere, were previously believed to be isolated communities of slaves recreating an African society in the Americas, it is now accepted that they were characterized by creative cultural adaptation and the diversity of their inhabitants. African- and native-born slaves predominated, but the communities also included freed people, Indians, military deserters, and fugitives, some of them white. The reasons for fleeing slavery were manifold. A substantial number fled in order to leave their enslavement permanently behind, but for some it was a bargaining tactic. By absenting themselves from work, some *quilombolas* were able to negotiate better conditions for their captivity with their masters. Still others fled for only short periods to gain temporary respite or to visit friends and kin. Whatever the individual intentions of each runaway slave, flight destabilized the rigid structures of slave society.

For their sustenance, *quilombos* practiced economic activities such as mining, timber harvest, and subsistence agriculture, thus maintaining social and commercial relations with enslaved and free people. Slave hiding was an illegal but common practice. *Quilombolas* often relied on slave hiders, who sheltered them out of compassion, fear of retaliation, or the need for *quilombola* labor. Many *quilombos* also relied on raids of nearby plantations and towns in order to obtain food and livestock, tools, and sometimes people. For this reason, they were frequently located on the outskirts of population centers, and their proximity was perceived as a constant threat by residents at the same time that they provided a refuge for many slaves.

Because of the menace they posed to slave society, *quilombos* were frequent targets of expeditions by law enforcement and bush captains, known as *capitães-do-mato*, who received a reward in exchange for capturing escaped slaves. Many bush captains were former slaves and colored freed people, but Indians were also employed. Nonetheless, it is important to remember that the relationship between *quilombos* and the rest of society was not exclusively antagonistic.

The *Quilombo* of Palmares (1604?–1694)

Numbering up to 20,000 residents and lasting nearly a century, the *quilombo* of Palmares, in reality a federation of nine settlements, was the largest and longest lasting of its kind in Brazilian history. Located in the mountains spanning the present-day states of Alagoas and Pernambuco and surrounded by protective palisades *(palmares)*, Palmares endured numerous raids by the Dutch, who invaded northeastern Brazil in the early 17th century, and by the Portuguese, who regained control in 1654. Between 1672 and 1680, there was a military expedition against it almost every year.

Palmares was an organized state governed by a leader who exercised control over subordinate chiefs in the outlying settlements and commanded great reverence from them. The names of two of its leaders, Ganga Zumba and ZUMBI, his nephew, point to a strong Angolan influence in the settlement's political and religious organization and suggest a royal lineage. Palmares was in fact referred to as *angola janga* (little Angola) by its residents, but as time progressed, there were an increasing number of native-born and mixed-race inhabitants as well as Indians and a few whites. The religion practiced was a mixture of Christian and African elements. Those who were captured in raids were enslaved, while those who joined voluntarily were considered free.

As in other *quilombos* and *mocambos*, Palmares's relations with local inhabitants were not always adversarial. Agriculture was practiced on the *quilombo*, but the residents relied on commerce with surrounding populations in order to obtain weapons and other necessities.

Even so, the threat to social order posed by Palmares remained undiminished. After a sustained attack by the Portuguese, Ganga Zumba, tired of war, signed a peace treaty with the governor of Pernambuco in 1678, in which he agreed to return any new fugitives and pledged loyalty to the Portuguese Crown in exchange for recognition of the *quilombo*'s freedom. This act was perceived as accommodationist by some of Palmares's own residents, and, in 1680, Ganga Zumba was assassinated by his nephew and military commander, Zumbi.

Zumbi's rule over Palmares was marked by numerous attacks, the last led by the veteran Indian hunter Domingos

Jorge Velho. The final battle, in February 1694, ended with the death of hundreds of slaves through murder and suicide. Zumbi himself was betrayed, captured, and decapitated by the colonial authorities on November 20, 1695, in order to send a message to any slaves attempting to follow the path of those in Palmares.

Today Zumbi dos Palmares has become the symbol of the Movimento Negro (black movement), and the date of his death, November 20, is designated as Black Consciousness Day in Brazil.

Maroons and the Abolition of Slavery

Slaves continued to escape their captivity after Brazil achieved its independence in 1822. Authorities were constantly fearful that the maroons would incite slave insurrections, which continued to abound in Brazil throughout the 19th century. Slave restiveness intensified in the 1870s with the promulgation of gradual emancipation laws, and large-scale flights became common in the 1880s as the institution of slavery showed clear signs of unraveling. By this time, the majority of the maroons were native-born as a result of the cessation of the transatlantic slave trade in 1850. While many slaves deserted their masters of their own accord, they were frequently aided by abolitionists, who guided them to freedom through "underground railroads" to provinces that had already abolished slavery, such as Ceará. Many maroons also fled to abolitionist *quilombos*, notably that of Jabaquara near the port city of Santos, São Paulo. These places became safe havens for maroons, who received the abolitionists' protection against masters who continued to oppose refuse their emancipation.

After abolition, many of the *quilombolas* remained on or near their settlements and became rural peasants and urban laborers with uncertain claims on citizenship during the First Republic (1889–1930).

Quilombos and Contemporary Politics

In recent years, *quilombos* have become the topic of heated debates triggered by the promulgation of Article 68 in the 1988 Brazilian federal constitution, which authorized the granting of titles to lands held by black communities that were recognized as "*quilombos* remnants" *(remanescentes de quilombos)*. Many of the communities who claim or have been guaranteed title to their lands in fact do not have their origins in runaway slave communities in the strictly historical sense, as some were founded during slavery by freed people or traced their origins back to the post-emancipation period. This has inspired a reconceptualization and amplification of the idea of "*quilombos* remnants" to include rural black communities established without land titles, based upon a common origin linked to slavery. The criteria remain far from settled, however. For example, the rural focus of these remnant communities has been challenged by "urban *quilombos*," who also claim their place in the past and the present.

Yuko Miki

FURTHER READING

Castro, Hebe Maria Mattos de. "'Terras De Quilombo': Land Rights, Memory of Slavery, and Ethnic Identification in Contemporary Brazil." In *Africa, Brazil, and the Construction of Trans-Atlantic Black Identities*, edited by Boubacar Barry, Elisee Akpo Soumonni, and Livio Sansone, x, 293–318. Trenton: N.J.: Africa World Press, 2008.

Gomes, Flavio dos Santos, and H. Sabrina Gledhill. "A 'Safe Haven': Runaway Slaves, Mocambos, and Borders in Colonial Amazonia, Brazil." *Hispanic American Historical Review* 82, no. 3 (2002): 469–498.

Machado, Maria Helena Pereira Toledo. "From Slave Rebels to Strikebreakers: The Quilombo of Jabaquara and the Problem of Citizenship in Late-Nineteenth-Century Brazil." *Hispanic American Historical Review* 86, no. 2 (2006): 247–274.

Price, Richard. *Maroon Societies: Rebel Slave Communities in the Americas*. 3rd ed. Baltimore: Johns Hopkins University Press, 1996.

Reis, Joao José. *Slave Rebellion in Brazil: The Muslim Uprising of 1835 in Bahia*. Johns Hopkins Studies in Atlantic History and Culture. Baltimore: Johns Hopkins University Press, 1993.

Schwartz, Stuart B. *Slaves, Peasants, and Rebels: Reconsidering Brazilian Slavery*. Urbana: University of Illinois Press, 1992.

BRITAIN

Britain was the base of the largest slave-trading and slave-employing empire of the Atlantic world. British slave traders carried millions of people across the Atlantic, taking them to British colonies and to colonies of other European nations. British attitudes toward people of color strongly affected the treatment of African Americans, both free and enslaved, in mainland North America, the Caribbean, and even South and Central America. British laws on race and slavery formed the basis for laws in the United States. Thus, it is important to understand British laws and the way Britain treated its own people of color to understand this influence on the situation in the Americas. Moreover, Britain was home to a relatively large free population of color in the 18th century, and these people played an important role in economic, cultural, and political events in Britain, in the empire, and throughout the Atlantic world. They were prominent as abolitionists, cultural figures, and workers.

English Attitudes toward Others in the Sixteenth and Seventeenth Centuries

In 16th and 17th centuries, the English people had a very strong sense that their country and they themselves were the best. One foreign ambassador scornfully remarked that the English described leaving England with such regret it was as if they were going out of the world—that is, they viewed England as if it were the entire world. The English monarchs had long wished to control all of Britain and, after the conquest of Wales in the 13th century, made many attempts on Scotland and Ireland. Particularly in the late 16th and the 17th centuries, there was great hostility, especially with the Irish, as the English conquered Ireland with savage violence that was justified by dehumanizing them as both the "other" and "different." This became even easier after the Protestant Reformation swept England in the 16th century while most of the Irish remained Catholic.

In 1573, Queen Elizabeth I instructed Walter Devereaux, earl of Essex (1541–76), to devote himself to destroying Scottish settlements in Ulster in northern Ireland. But Essex soon became so frustrated by the Gaelic chiefs, even those who professed loyalty to the English, that he massacred hundreds of Irish people. Elizabeth praised Essex for advancing such a "barbarous" race to "civility." At the same time, Sir Humphrey Gilbert (1539–83), British military commander in Ireland during the Geraldine Rebellion (1569–73), virtually declared war on every Irish man, woman, or child in the southern province of Munster. Essex and Gilbert clearly believed they were exempt from any ethical constraints when they dealt with the native population in Ireland. Conditions became even more horrific in the mid-17th century under Oliver Cromwell (1599–1658), British military dictator during the English Civil War (1641–58), when he massacred the inhabitants of Drogheda, calling them "barbarous wretches."

This same attitude of dehumanization was in evidence when England began to attempt to establish colonies in the Americas in the late 16th and 17th centuries. Indeed, after his time in Ireland, Gilbert had wished to establish a colony in North America. However, he died at sea, so the first Englishman actually to do so was Gilbert's younger half brother, Sir Walter Raleigh (1552–1618). The colonies established in the 16th and 17th centuries adopted the policy of driving out or exterminating native inhabitants. In northern colonies, such as Massachusetts, English settlers established small farms. In the southern colonies of North America and ultimately in the Caribbean, where the white population faced greater challenges due to tropical diseases, larger landholdings were the rule, worked at first by indentured immigrants from Europe, including Ireland, and finally by slaves from Africa. In both cases, the English were very unwilling to consider the subordinated peoples as members of the national community.

The English essentially transferred their negative attitudes toward the Irish to Native Americans and Africans. The English found justification of their exploitations of Africans in the long-held beliefs that black was a demonic color and those whose skin was black were wicked and lecherous. There was a widespread belief that black Africans were descended from Noah's son Ham, and that God had damned Ham's posterity for his wickedness and disobedience. This attitude was also promoted by the bizarre descriptions of Africans found in many travel narratives. Such books were filled with descriptions of the various peoples of Africa as monstrous in both body and behavior. But the English not only read about Africans in the 16th century; they actually experienced them. The first African community was established in Edinburgh around 1500. A Portuguese ship captured a Scottish ship, so King James IV ordered his navy to capture a Portuguese one. Since it was a slave ship, the Africans were taken to Edinburgh and established a community there. Some of them became entertainers at the king's court, including one who was a drummer. One woman, possibly named Elen or Helenor, was given a beautiful dress for the tournament of the black knight and the black lady, with James playing the black knight and a kiss from the black lady the prize of the tournament.

As the slave trade grew in the 16th century, more Africans arrived in Europe, including in England. In the early 1500s, there was a black trumpeter at the court of Henry VII and Henry VIII (see JOHN BLANKE). In 1554–55, John Lok took five Africans to England so they could learn to be translators and "friends" of the English (see FIVE AFRICANS BROUGHT TO ENGLAND IN 1555). But the English interaction with Africans became more pernicious as the century progressed. Myths and negative perceptions about Africans allowed the English easy consciences about participation in the slave trade. Africans began being transported into England in small numbers in the 1570s. Most of them were household servants, but some were prostitutes for wealthy English and Dutch who were in England. Sir Walter Raleigh and his wife, Elizabeth, had a black servant or slave, as did the earl of Dorset. A late 16th-century census of foreigners in the London parish of All Hallows listed several Africans.

There were also black entertainers, both dancers and musicians, at the courts of Elizabeth I, who ruled from 1558 to 1603, and her successor, James VI of Scotland and I of England, who ruled from 1603 to 1625. The ways Africans were used in entertainments could be demeaning. At the baptism of James's son Henry in 1594, the organizers had originally intended the royal carriage to be pulled by a lion, but they feared the lion might be too difficult to control. They substituted a black man who was given rich and exotic apparel and chains of pure gold. In the 1617 Lord Mayor's Show in London, there were black men mounted on horses disguised to look like griffins and camels.

But while Queen Elizabeth had several black dancers and musicians at her court, as the economy took a downturn in the last decade of her reign, the Africans became an all too easy target. In 1601, Elizabeth issued a proclamation expressing her discontent at what she claimed was the great number of black people living in her kingdom. She appointed a certain Caspar van Zenden, a merchant of Lubeck, to transport them out of the court. Even though the proclamation declared that most of the blacks living in England were infidels who had no understanding of Christ or his gospel, there were no exceptions for the Africans who had converted to Christianity. But while the end of the 1590s was a time of poor harvests, inflation, and great destitution for many English people, expelling the few black people in England would hardly have solved these serious problems. Despite this decree, many of the black people in England stayed. And their numbers only increased throughout the 17th century.

Legal Background

The Acts of Union of 1707 with Scotland and 1800 with Ireland created the United Kingdom. The Westminster Parliament claimed the right to legislate for the entirety of British territory around the world. However, for most matters each colony had its own legislature and its own set of laws. Moreover, Britain had no written constitution against which proposed laws could be measured. Each jurisdiction had its own constitution, composed of laws and royal acts and judicial decisions, and each was different from the other. This confusing diversity in British laws makes it difficult to make definitive statements about the legal treatment of race and slavery throughout the British colonies.

Nonetheless, there are some common features to the way the British legal system dealt with these matters. The idea of the "one drop" rule of racial identity—that any black ancestry defined one as black—evolved during the time of slavery and really only had its full effect in the United States in the 19th century. Still, legal discrimination against people of African ancestry was harsh and did not distinguish between people considered black or brown. In almost all British colonies, people of African ancestry were not granted equal access to the courts, meaning that their property rights were not fully enforced. In some places, they were forbidden to sue or testify against whites, while in others they had formal access to the courts but the fact that jury membership was limited to whites meant that they had difficulty prevailing. Often, they were prohibited from owning certain types of property, especially slaves, or restricted to small numbers of slaves or small amounts of agricultural land. Laws in JAMAICA, called Deficiency Laws, counted free people of color as half a white person for purposes of determining the appropriate ratio of slaves to free people on a plantation, for example; as a result, free colored SLAVE OWNERS had to hire white managers or pay discriminatory taxes. In most places in the American South, laws passed in the early 19th century prohibited blacks from buying slaves, though those who already owned slaves could keep them, and a substantial class of free black planters still existed in LOUISIANA and formerly Spanish FLORIDA up until the AMERICAN CIVIL WAR.

Free People of Color in the British Isles

In Britain itself, slavery had disappeared in the early Middle Ages. Even formal serfdom was nearly extinct by the 16th century, so that there was no legal framework for slavery at all. British common law, reinforced by a 16th-century court decision related to a serf from Russia, held that the air of England made one free, but the application of this principle to African-American slaves was not tested in court until 1772. In that year, the British courts declared James Somerset a free man, despite the fact that Charles Stewart had bought him legally in Barbados and taken him to Britain as a domestic servant (see SOMERSET V. STEWART). The Somerset case did not totally close the door to slavery in Britain but ruled that the British courts and government officials could not keep a person enslaved against his or her will. Masters still took slaves to Britain but could not make them keep working or return to the colonies. A similar case in Scotland in 1776 found that slavery could not exist under Scottish common law. These two legal decisions emancipated about 15,000 people, the estimated number of slaves who either were living in Britain at the time or entered later and took advantage of the decisions. These newly freed persons were joined by free people of color from all over the British Empire who immigrated between 1772 and the 1820s. Britain had no consistent set of laws like the Police des Noirs in France that tried to keep people of color out of the mother country. Instead, people of color became an important part of the working class population of the English and Scottish port cities and had a niche as personal servants. The black coachman, valet, or page boy was almost an obligatory accessory for people of fashion in late 18th-century Britain. The military, both ground forces and Royal Navy, employed many blacks in the 18th century (see also REGULAR ARMY and NAVY). At the end of each of the many wars of that century, a new influx of demobilized black soldiers and sailors arrived in London and the other port cities of the British Isles. In particular, after the end of the WAR OF AMERICAN INDEPENDENCE, 1775–83, many black loyalists migrated to Britain rather than face the wrath of the victorious Americans. Some of these immigrants went on to Sierra Leone in the 1790s, but many more remained or returned after short stays in Africa, including sailor and abolitionist writer OLAUDAH EQUIANO.

As immigrants, blacks were not covered by the Poor Law, which required indigent people to be cared for by the Church of England parish of their birth. Some poor blacks were cared for by their baptismal parishes, typically in the port cities, but others became beggars. The black poor—and Asian immigrant poor—were a social concern in the late 18th and early 19th centuries, and the strong minority racial component of urban poverty was one reason Parliament created harsher new poverty laws in the 19th century.

Unlike free colored populations in the Americas, the free colored population of the British Isles was not balanced by gender. The high number of military and naval veterans and the preference of employers for men as valets, butlers, and coachmen meant that few women of color were taken to Britain. There was some intermarriage between men of color and Englishwomen, but this was rare because of prevailing cultural prejudice, though there were no laws against intermarriage as there were in many places in the Americas. Most personal servants were forbidden to marry as a condition of employment. As a result, the free colored population of the British Isles did not grow naturally, sustaining its numbers by immigration. Immigration slowed after the end of the slave trade (1807), and especially after the abolition of slavery in the British Empire (1833), though there were a number of immigrants from the United States in the 1850s, including the abolitionists FREDERICK DOUGLASS and HENRY "BOX" BROWN. Douglass returned to the United States after a few years. There were still thousands of people of color living in Britain (many of whom may have been wholly or partly of Asian ancestry) in the 20th century when immigration from the West Indies began to build again, but the number was down from its high point in the 1810s. Historians estimate that perhaps 50,000–100,000 black people lived in Britain in 1808, between 0.5 and 0.9 percent of the population.

Free people of color in Britain were active in the movements against the slave trade and slavery itself in the 18th and early 19th centuries. Olaudah Equiano and QUOBNA OTTOBAH CUGOANO were important participants in the abolition movement, publishing books and pamphlets and speaking to a wide variety of audiences. When JOHN CLARKSON began researching the slave trade, it was black seamen on slave ships who were his early informants. The actor and playwright Ignatius Sancho published pamphlets supporting the British war effort in America during the War of American Independence and calling for the use of black soldiers in that conflict.

Carole Levin

FURTHER READING

Dabydeen, David, John Gilmore, and Cecily Jones, eds. *The Oxford Companion to Black British History.* Oxford: Oxford University Press, 2000.

Fryer, Peter. *Staying Power: The History of Black People in Britain.* London: Pluto Press, 1984.

Levin, Carole. "Shakespeare and the Marginalized 'Others.'" In *A Concise Companion to English Renaissance Literature,* edited by Donna B. Hamilton. Oxford: Blackwell, 2006.

Morgan, Phillip D. "The Black Experience in the British Empire, 1680–1810." In *Black Experience and Empire,* edited by Phillip D. Morgan and Sean Hawkins. Oxford: Oxford University Press, 2004.

BRITAIN, ABOLITIONIST MOVEMENTS IN
Early Antislavery Ideas

Though evidence of antislavery protest in Britain can be found dating back to the first English slaving voyage in 1555, no organized social movement coalesced until the end of the 18th century. Early antislavery protest typically arose from clergy, who objected to the use of biblical arguments to justify the enslavement of human beings. These sermons rarely proposed any concrete solutions and served more as commentary on an unpalatable practice. However, Britain's engagement with African slavery grew over the course of the 18th century until the nation became the largest transporter of slaves in the world. The granting of the Spanish asiento—essentially an exclusive contract to supply Spanish colonies with slaves—and the demand from Britain's own profitable sugar colonies made slave trading a very lucrative component of British commerce. However, the increase in trade and the number of Britons involved in the institution began to evoke sympathetic reactions as awareness of the atrocities of slavery spread.

British slaveholders returned to the mother country with their slaves and created situations in which slavery could be confronted more directly. Arguably the first antislavery crusader, GRANVILLE SHARP, used the atrocities committed by slaveholders to challenge openly the legality of slavery in England. The case of James Somerset (1772) (*see* SOMERSET V. STEWART) is noteworthy for two reasons—first, because Sharp and his colleagues successfully argued that slavery had not been established by positive law in England, and, second, because Somerset became the first person of color freed by a British court. His case reverberated through the legal system and seemed to threaten the legality of slavery even in the colonies. James Somerset became a symbol of the beneficence of British civil law and provided the first spark for the movement to abolish the slave trade.

Abolition of the Slave Trade

The Quaker community was the first to campaign actively against African slavery and the slave trade, beginning as early as the 1760s (*see* BAPTISTS AND PIETISTS). The push to eradicate slaveholding and slave trading within their own community began in the American colonies—Pennsylvania in particular—but soon moved to Great Britain. American Quakers, such as Anthony Benezet (1713–84), swiftly realized that total abolition of slavery would not be feasible, and so they proposed a more incremental method of dismantling the institution. Quaker writings against slavery focused more specifically on the transatlantic slave trade—the abolition of which would limit the number of slaves in the colonies and presumably lead to gradual emancipation. American Quakers worked with their London counterparts to push for abolition through Parliament, presenting the first petition to abolish the slave trade in 1783. Though the petition was unsuccessful, a small group of six London Quakers began to organize and use print as a medium of disseminating their ideas. They also reached out to fellow activists, such as Granville Sharp and JOHN CLARKSON, and in 1787 formed the London Abolitionist Society. In 1788, they gained a powerful ally in William Wilberforce, a member of Parliament, who instituted the first official parliamentary inquiry into the atrocities of the Middle Passage.

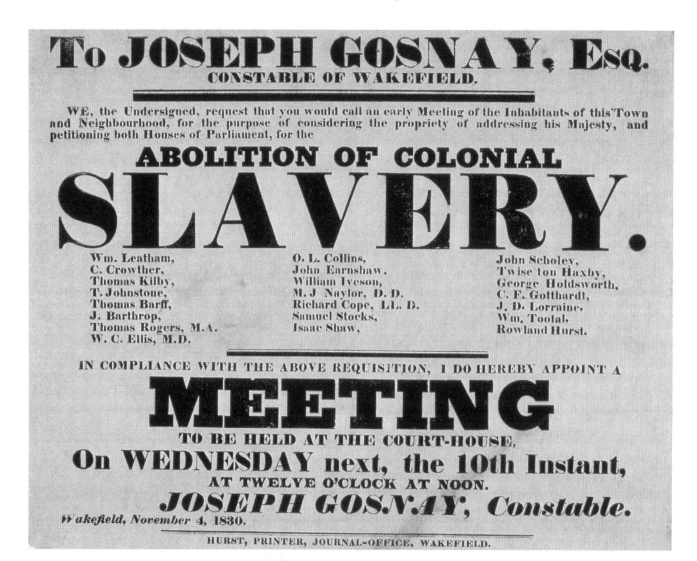

Announcement of a public meeting in Britain calling for the abolition of slavery, 1830. Working-class and middle-calss Britons generally supported the end of slavery. Many thousands of white Britons attended meetings and signed petitions calling on Parliament to abolish the slave trade and slavery between the 1780s and 1830s. In 1833, Parliament passed a law for gradual abolition, and slavery was finally abolished in the British Empire in 1838. *(English School/Getty Images)*

The movement to abolish the slave trade benefited greatly from the work of free people of color in Great Britain and its colonies. The most persistent line of argument used by proslavery writers emphasized the inability of Africans to think and act in the same civilized manner as Europeans. Though race theory had far from solidified in the 18th century, authors such as Edward Long felt comfortable asserting "facts" about African inferiority. However, even Long could not deny the genius of writers like Francis Williams (ca. 1697–1762), the son of free blacks from Jamaica who was educated at Cambridge and published poetry in Latin. In 1772, James Ukawsaw Gronniosaw published the first slave narrative in English and claimed for himself an African-British identity. The African-American poet Phillis Wheatley, who met Granville Sharp on her visit to England, published an elegant book of poetry in London in 1773 with testimonials from several Britons regarding the authenticity of her verse. The success of her writing led her owner to free her shortly after her return to America, and her book of poetry was often cited as evidence of African capabilities.

As anti–slave trade sentiment gained ground in the 1780s, two significant publications by Afro-Britons contributed to the dialogue about the inequities of slavery. In 1782, friends of IGNATIUS SANCHO, a greengrocer and freedman in London, published his letters posthumously. This collection of letters revealed how Sancho positioned himself with relation to London society and on the topic of slavery. He detailed several schemes for the improvement of society that illustrated his belief in his own voice as a citizen of Great Britain. He also had an impressive list of correspondents, including the novelist Laurence Sterne, who credited his own antislavery views to Sancho. Though not as stridently opposed to slavery as the writers who followed, Sancho often used typical descriptors, like "Black-a-moor," in a tongue-in-cheek manner that subtly questioned the limitations of such labels. Additionally, his letters revealed a keen mind and sharp wit that were the match of any "white" Englishman.

In 1787, QUOBNA OTTOBAH CUGOANO published a scathing attack on the slave trade that directly challenged the Christianity and civility of the traders. He drew upon his own experiences as a former slave who had suffered the cruelties of the Middle Passage to point out the hypocrisy of Britain's engagement with the slave trade. How could a country that so valued liberty sanction this gross injustice? Though Cugoano was not the first to pose this question, he was the first to question it from the position of African superiority. He passed judgment upon the supposed civility of Britons in a harsh manner and questioned the behavior of "apostate Christians," a label he applied to all those involved in slave trading and slaveholding. More importantly, Cugoano presented his

indictment without any European intermediaries—no editors or amanuenses. Thus, he provided the abolitionist movement with a strong and confident voice of native authenticity whose attack on slave trading could not be easily dismissed by slavery advocates.

The most significant contribution by a free person of color in the fight to abolish the slave trade was made by OLAUDAH EQUIANO, a former slave known alternatively as Gustavus Vasa. He made critical contacts with abolitionists including Granville Sharp and was briefly involved with the Sierra Leone resettlement project to transport poor blacks from London to West Africa. Though his association with the leaders of the project soured, he did point out several abuses of authority that negatively affected the project. Equiano's greatest contribution was the publication of his *Interesting Narrative* in 1789. He became a celebrity figure in the abolitionist movement because of both the success of his narrative and his charismatic personality. He went on speaking tours throughout the British Isles, and his book became a best seller. His description of an idyllic childhood in Africa contradicted proslavery claims about the barbarity of the continent, and his poor treatment at the hands of unscrupulous traders reinforced the evils of slavery. Equiano became an important spokesperson for African potential and stated that the only actual benefit to slavery was the introduction to Christianity, which did not require enslavement. He advocated that the British go on missions of conversion rather than preying upon the greed of Africans who engaged in the slave trade and the misery of those trapped by it.

From 1788 to 1792, Parliament heard arguments and testimony for and against the African slave trade. The public sentiment built against slavery, and small towns across the country produced petitions, participated in boycotts of West India sugar, and mobilized in an unprecedented manner. Severe political upheavals in France and Haiti evoked fears of similar revolution in Great Britain and the West Indies. The movement to abolish the slave trade stalled in the House of Commons until the turn of the century. On March 25, 1807, both houses of Parliament officially abolished the transatlantic slave trade in a decision that was hailed as a victory for both liberty and the British nation.

Abolition of Slavery

Abolishing the slave trade seemed to be the first step in abolishing slavery altogether; however, that did not prove to be the case. When the abolitionists organized in London, they believed that cutting off the supply of slaves to the colonies would force plantation owners through necessity to treat their existing slaves in a more humane fashion. In time, many owners might be persuaded to emancipate their slaves and to reintegrate this freed workforce into Caribbean society. However, the trade in new slaves from Africa did not prohibit the trade of existing slaves between colonies in the Caribbean. Also in some areas, such as the southern United States, slave populations had been reproducing and could be traded between colonies in the Americas. In less than a decade, the failure of early abolitionist hopes became apparent. From 1816 to 1823, the British Caribbean witnessed a series of slave revolts that resulted in increased fear among slaveholders and worsening conditions for slaves. While no revolt matched Toussaint Louverture's dramatic liberation of Haiti beginning in 1791, the British revolts did serve to revive the abolitionist movement in Great Britain.

The new abolitionist movement, beginning in the 1820s, mobilized an even greater segment of the British population and incorporated many new voices. Women took a strong role in forming their own abolitionist societies, running boycotts, and collecting signatures in petitioning campaigns. This new movement was hampered, however, with questions about the manner in which abolition should take place. Veteran campaigners, such as John Clarkson, believed that immediate abolition would create turmoil, so he advocated that slavery be abolished gradually. In contrast, activists such as the Quaker Elizabeth Heyrick published pamphlets advocating immediate abolition. By 1830, the campaigns to abolish slavery merged and advocated immediate emancipation for all slaves in British territories.

The most influential book published in this second abolitionist campaign detailed the atrocities of slavery as perpetrated on a woman. *The History of Mary Prince* (1831) chronicled for the first time the cruelties of West Indian plantation slavery. Mary Prince was born into slavery in Bermuda and endured countless acts of brutality. She had several capricious masters who flogged her for simple offenses and separated her from her husband when she dared to wed without permission. In 1828, she traveled to London with her current master, who threw her out onto the streets. She took refuge in a Moravian church and found a position with Thomas Pringle, an antislavery activist. A friend of Pringle's named Susanna Strickland wrote down Prince's story, and they published the sad tale in London. As with Equiano's autobiography a generation earlier, Prince's narrative became the best seller of the antislavery movement in the 1830s. Her simple language and the horrors she endured resonated particularly well with British women, who proved to be excellent organizers of this second campaign.

The renewed mobilization of abolitionists in 1831 had an unlikely consequence in the West Indies. In 1831–32, massive slave revolts ripped through Jamaica, and the British military barely managed to quell the uprisings. The decision to abolish slavery seemed very prudent in light of the unrest; however, Parliament was unwilling to legislate immediate abolition. Also, the West India planters complained about the overturning of their livelihoods and demanded compensation as abolition became more of a reality. In 1833, Thomas Fowell Buxton introduced a bill for abolition, but Parliament agreed to abolish slavery gradually by having slaves step into temporary "apprenticeships" that did not differ substantially from enslavement. This "apprenticeship" period, originally designed to last six years, immediately sparked renewed protest in Great Britain so Parliament shortened it to four years. On August 1, 1838, slavery was officially abolished in British territories.

Srividhya Swaminathan

FURTHER READING

Bacon, Jacqueline. *The Humblest May Stand Forth: Rhetoric, Empowerment, and Abolition.* Columbia: University of South Carolina Press, 2002.

Carretta, Vincent. *Equiano the African: Biography of a Self-Made Man.* Athens: University of Georgia Press, 2005.

Carretta, Vincent, and Philip Gould, eds. *Genius in Bondage: Literature of the Early Black Atlantic.* Lexington: University Press of Kentucky, 2001.

Myers, Norma. *Reconstructing the Black Past: Blacks in Britain, 1780–1830.* London: Frank Cass, 1996.

BRITISH ANTI-SLAVERY ACTS

In the early 19th century, Great Britain sought to abolish the slave trade and the institution of slavery itself through several parliamentary enactments. The most significant of these were the 1807 act prohibiting the involvement of British subjects in the African slave trade and the 1833 act abolishing slavery within the British colonies. The fulfillment of the promise inherent in these acts would, however, require further enactments over the course of the next hundred years, as well as multiple attempts to create effective enforcement mechanisms. Britain's continuing acquisition of new colonies, many of which had their own institutions of slavery, further limited the efficacy of these landmark enactments. The British abolition movement, which had begun in earnest in 1783 with the submission of an antislavery petition to Parliament by the Quaker Society Committee on the Slave Trade, would not succeed in totally abolishing slavery throughout the British Empire until 1928, when Parliament outlawed slavery in Sierra Leone (ironically the first British colony specifically founded for freed slaves). Nonetheless, the 1807 and 1833 acts laid firm foundations for freedom and inspired abolition movements elsewhere.

The Quaker Society's 1783 petition to Parliament would be followed by many others in following years (*see also* BAPTISTS AND PIETISTS). Many such petitions were signed by freed Africans, especially those from the growing community of freed slaves in London, and were further supported by the publication of two works by former slaves—*Thoughts and Sentiments on the Evil and Wicked Traffic of the Slavery and Commerce of the Human Species* by QUOBNA OTTOBAH CUGOANO in 1787 and the autobiographical *Interesting Narrative of the Life of Olaudah Equiano or Gustavus Vassa, the African,* in 1789 (*see* EQUIANO, OLAUDAH). In 1792, Parliament received 500 antislavery petitions. The momentum of the British abolition movement was interrupted in the 1790s, however, by fears of sedition and insurrections fueled by perceptions of the potential influence of the FRENCH REVOLUTION, which had abolished slavery in French colonies in 1794. When Napoléon restored slavery throughout the French Empire in 1802, the British were given an additional patriotic motive to support the cause of abolition. Antislavery efforts began to be received favorably again in both Houses of Parliament. Support for plantation owners by the Crown and the royal family's own oft-stated support of slavery delayed passage of legislation until 1806, when abolitionists succeeded in persuading the House of Lords to pass the Foreign Slave Trade Bill prohibiting British traders to sell slaves in foreign territories. Seizing on this opportunity, abolitionists amended this bill to end the British slave trade completely. In this final form, the bill passed both Houses of Parliament in March 1807 by overwhelming margins, 100-36 in the House of Lords and 283-16 in the House of Commons, and received the Royal Assent to become law as An Act for the Abolition of the Slave Trade.

The British were not, however, the first to outlaw the slave trade. Denmark had passed a law in 1792 that made it illegal to import slaves into the Danish colonies in the Caribbean after 1803. The French revolutionary government had abolished both the slave trade and slavery in 1794, but both were reinstated by Napoléon in 1802. The Netherlands also abolished the slave trade in 1803. Britain's 1807 act would be followed by legislation in the United States later that year, and then in Sweden, France, Spain, and Portugal from 1813 to 1815. The year 1815 would also see Austria, Britain, France, Portugal, Prussia, Russia, Spain, and Sweden issuing a joint anti–slave trade declaration at the Congress of Vienna.

The British act of 1807 made it illegal as of May 1, 1807, for any British subject or foreign resident in the United Kingdom or any British colony, dominion, or territory to engage in any aspect of the slave trade. The penalty for doing so was set at £100 "for each slave so purchased, sold, bartered, or transferred, or contracted or agreed

William Wilberforce *(Library of Congress)*

for." The act further made it illegal "to fit out, man, or navigate . . . any Ship or vessel for the purpose of assisting in, or being employed in the carrying on of the African Slave Trade," or to procure or otherwise be concerned in such an enterprise. Any such ships could be lawfully seized by "Officers of Customs, or Excise, or Navy" and would be forfeited. A grace period was included for any slave-trading vessels that departed Britain before May 1, 1807, and landed in the West Indies before March 1, 1808. It was also made illegal to insure such vessels, with a penalty of £100 and treble the policy's premium. Any Africans on board seized slave-trading vessels would be forfeited to the Crown and given the option to enter into a period of British military service or a 14-year apprenticeship without any possibility of pensions or future support afterward.

The common challenge facing the 1807 act and subsequent laws and treaties would be the highly profitable nature of the slave trade itself. Each new loophole found and exploited by slave traders necessitated yet more legislation, royal proclamations, and treaties to counter it. The dominance of Britain's naval power on the high seas meant that the greater part of enforcement efforts fell to the British. The British Admiralty would finally form a dedicated Anti–Slave Trade Squadron in 1818 to patrol the West African coast, with a squadron being formed for the Indian Ocean in the early 1830s. By 1860, the West African squadron alone had seized almost 1,600 ships, freeing an estimated 150,000 slaves. At the height of enforcement, however, the vessels seized and forfeited amounted to nearly 50 percent of the slave-trade vessels. Clearly outlawing the slave trade alone was insufficient.

In the face of continued opposition, an increasing public awareness of the horrors of the slave trade and the growing involvement of London's community of free persons of color in the British abolition movement gave new impetus to legislative attempts to abolish slavery itself. In August 1833, Parliament passed An Act for the Abolition of Slavery throughout the British Colonies; for promoting the Industry of the manumitted Slaves; and for compensating the Persons hitherto entitled to the Services of such Slaves. As the title indicates, the act did not simply abolish slavery and unconditionally free slaves throughout the British Empire. As with the 1807 Slave Trade Act, the 1833 act allowed for a one-year grace period before taking effect on August 1, 1834. Rather than immediately freeing slaves throughout Britain's overseas colonies and territories, the act converted their status as slaves into that of indentured servitude as "apprenticed Labourers" in order to ameliorate any economic impact on the prior slaveholders. The act also specifically excluded "the Territories in the Possession of the East India Company, or to the Island of Ceylon, or to the Island of Saint Helena," effectively limiting its geographical coverage.

An even more significant sign that the act was perhaps more concerned with the interests of slaveholders then the slaves themselves was the provision mandating a £20 million fund (equal to more than £1 billion today) be set up to compensate slaveholders for their lost property interests. Almost half of the act is concerned with establishing and administering this compensation fund. The new apprentices' interests were, however, considered to the extent of limiting the number of hours the "Employer" could force them to work each week to 45 with a further provision limiting overtime hours to 15. Nor could the "Employer" split up families in the event the services of "apprenticed Labourers" were legally transferred to another. The "Employer" was also required to continue providing housing, food, and clothing and prohibited to administer any form of corporal punishment on his or her own authority. The mandated period of indentured servitude could not be renewed or otherwise prolonged by the "Employer." The act limited the length of these new apprenticeships to August 1, 1840, for praedial (agricultural) apprentices "attached to the Soil," and August 1, 1838, for all others. Voluntary discharge by the "Employer" before those dates was allowed, as was the purchase of such early discharge by the apprentice. No compensation whatsoever was provided to the newly freed persons of color for their trials and suffering as slaves.

A further significant provision of the 1833 act gave statutory authority to and expanded the rule of SOMER-

SET V. STEWART case (1772) that any slave taken into Britain could not be compelled to accompany the slaveholder when he left the country, effectively freeing such slaves as long as they remained in Britain. Section 3 of the act provided "that all Slaves who may at any Time previous to the passing of this Act have been brought with the Consent of their Possessors, and all apprenticed Labourers who may hereafter . . . be brought, into any part of the United Kingdom of Great Britain and Ireland, shall from and after the passing of this Act be absolutely free to all Intents and Purposes whatsoever." Neither the 1807 act nor the 1833 act totally ended slavery or the slave trade on its own. Nearly 40 more acts and some 20 international treaties over the next century, as well as significant enforcement measures, would be required. Even then, an increasing indifference would set in by the late 19th century, ensuring that the issue of slavery and its evils would in some form last into the present day.

Erin Rahne Kidwell

FURTHER READING
Blackburn, Robin. *The Overthrow of Colonial Slavery, 1776–1848.* New York: Verso, 1988.
Drescher, Seymour. *From Slavery to Freedom: Comparative Studies in the Rise and Fall of Atlantic Slavery.* New York: New York University Press, 1999.
Eltis, David, et al., eds. *The Abolition of the Atlantic Slave Trade: Origins and Effects in Europe, Africa, and the Americas.* Madison: University of Wisconsin Press, 1981.
Gerzina, Gretchen. *Black England: Life before Emancipation.* London: Allison and Busby, 1995.
Jennings, Judith, ed. *The Business of Abolishing the British Slave Trade, 1783–1807.* Portland, Ore.: Frank Cass, 1997.
Kielstra, Paul Michael. *The Politics of Slave Trade Suppression in Britain and France, 1814–48: Diplomacy, Morality and Economics.* New York: St. Martin's Press, 2000.
Martin, S. I. *Britain's Slave Trade.* New York: Macmillan, 1999.
Sherwood, Marika. *After Abolition: Britain and the Slave Trade since 1807.* New York: Palgrave MacMillan, 2007.

BRITISH LESSER ANTILLES

The Antilles are a chain of islands that run from near the coast of CUBA in the northwest to Trinidad and Tobago off the coast of South America in the southeast. The term is also applied in this case to other groups of small islands located in the western Caribbean or just outside the Caribbean in the Atlantic Ocean that were under British rule for all or part of the period 1600–1900. The island groups profiled here include the Cayman Islands, Montserrat, the Turks and Caicos, the Bahamas, the British Virgin Islands, Anguilla, St. Kitts and Nevis, Antigua and Barbuda, St. Lucia, St. Vincent and the Grenadines, and Barbuda. Similar cultural and environmental conditions existed in Dominica, Barbados, and Trinidad and Tobago.

There are two basic geographical types of Caribbean islands. The first, typified by the Bahamas and Turks and Caicos, is low-lying and composed of sandy soil. Rainfall is limited, and subsurface water difficult to find. Soils are relatively infertile, and these islands are not well suited for plantation agriculture. The other type of island, typified by Grenada, is mountainous and volcanic. The mountains catch rainfall, and the windward sides of these islands can be very well watered. They do not tend to have much flat land, however, and so prospects for cultivation of sugar, the most profitable plantation crop in the Caribbean, were somewhat limited on most of these islands. However, they were good locations for coffee production, and where sugar plantations were feasible, the climate

was nearly ideal. The mountain forests also provided refuge for runaway slaves and indigenous groups resisting European rule. The more southerly islands, south of Martinique, are also off the track usually followed by Atlantic hurricanes, and thus the chance of a disastrous storm's damaging production is much lower than in the Greater Antilles islands to the north and west.

Indigenous people from South America, called the Kalinagos, conquered the islands of the Lesser Antilles occupied by the earlier Taino inhabitants starting in the 11th or 12th century. The islands of the western Caribbean were still inhabited by the Taino when Europeans arrived in 1492. Columbus first made landfall in the Americas somewhere in the Bahamas and visited or at least sighted most of the islands of the Caribbean during his four voyages in the region. Spain claimed all the islands of the Caribbean by virtue of the Treaty of Tordesillas (1494)

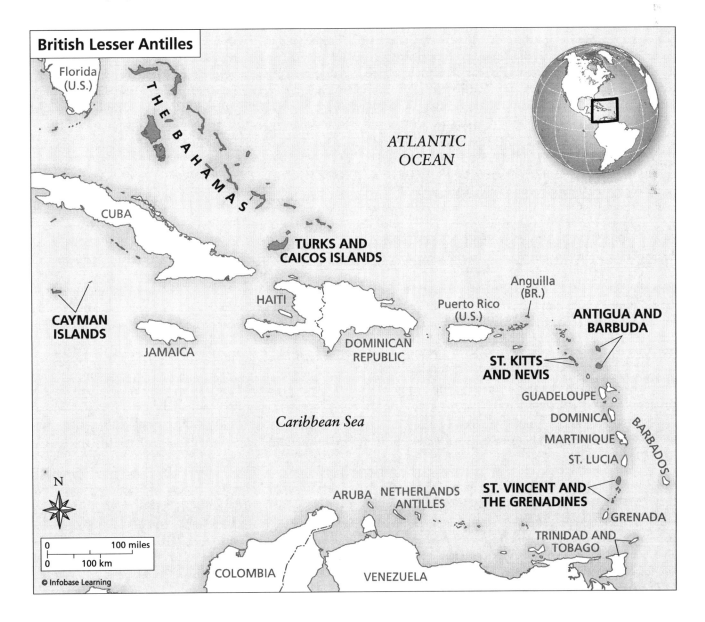

with Portugal but did not settle the smaller islands. The islands of the western Caribbean were subject to Spanish slave raids up through the middle of the 16th century, resulting in almost complete depopulation. In the eastern Caribbean, the inhabitants were pretty much left alone and were able to develop resistance to European diseases and a healthy suspicion of the motives of European visitors and welcome runaway slaves and even some wandering Europeans to their numbers. After Spain ceased to be a serious threat to their existence, they often found themselves in a multicornered struggle with the English, French, and Dutch, who were eager to divide the islands among themselves. In so doing, they held up the advance of European colonialism for two centuries after 1492. The decisive moment occurred in 1763, when the British managed to gain the ascendancy in the region after the SEVEN YEARS' WAR, 1756–63.

The Afro-indigenous cultures created between 1492 and 1763, including the BLACK CARIB of St. Vincent and the Garifuna, later transplanted to the coast of Central America, were especially resistant to European rule. The smaller islands of the Caribbean were first settled by Europeans and their African slaves after 1600. These islands changed hands many times, with some being occupied at different times by France, Denmark, the Netherlands, and Spain, but by the end of this period, all the island groups indicated were under British rule, where they remained for the most part until the 20th century.

Plantation agriculture, cultivating sugar, coffee, indigo, and other crops, came into being on all the islands where geography permitted by the middle of the 18th century. Many of these islands were extremely productive sources of plantation crops during the 18th century. None rivaled the Greater Antilles islands of Cuba, JAMAICA, and Hispaniola (Haiti/SAINT-DOMINGUE) as producers of plantation commodities, but they were important secondary producers, especially in the protected British Empire market. They were also important, though secondary, destinations for slaves imported from Africa. About 1.3 million slaves were delivered to these islands during the period of the Atlantic slave trade, or about three times the number imported into North America.

Free People of Color in the British Caribbean

The appearance, growth, and development of free people of color as a distinct social group in the Americas may be perceived as an unintended consequence of the development of a social order that was constructed upon the trade in and enslavement of African people. This colored group arose, in the main, from the sexual unions of European males and enslaved African females and were, to a large measure, a consequence of a general scarcity of European women, particularly during the "frontier" period, that is to say, the period when slave society was in its embryonic phase, the period from 1600 to the early 1700s in these islands.

In addition, as a result of the Europeans' borrowing of their medieval social traditions, the planter class had acquired by custom "seigniorial rights" to every unattached female under its direct ownership and control. Although LAS SIETE PARTIDAS and the CODE NOIR had specific statutes on paper against the sexual unions between Europeans and Africans, the practice continued even in the Spanish and French colonies. For the British colonies, however, no such laws existed. (*See also* MISCEGENATION.)

The Spanish and Portuguese developed a hierarchical order of the gradations of "white" blood that these people of color were supposed to have in their veins. This system was then adopted by the non-Iberian nations that established colonies and slave societies. This order also included those who had indigenous ancestry. The people who were regarded as having the greatest amount of "white blood" were afforded the highest social status. Some of these terms used in the British Caribbean included the mulatto, who was a person whose parents were African and European. Other gradations included the sambo, mustee, *cabre*, octoroon, and quadroon. These terms were meant to create divisions among the people of color, though generally most mixed-race thought of themselves as one racial group in the British Caribbean.

The free colored group became a third class in a society that was originally constructed for two. Since the slave laws in every British colony by the 18th century held that every person assumed the free or slave status of his or her mother, almost every free colored person—or his or her ancestors—was born enslaved. Usually the favorites of their parents, these mixed-race children were often manumitted when they reached the age of maturity and were often given land or finance with which they were expected to lead an independent adult existence. This is one striking difference between the British Caribbean and the North American colonies, where many mixed-race people were kept as slaves. Many were also sent abroad to be educated and often returned to the land of their birth, endowed with professional qualifications that were the basis of their livelihood.

The exotic look of these people of mixed ancestry was not unnoticed by the Europeans. Almost every European male who visited the Caribbean and recorded his observations spoke of the beauty and grace of the free colored people, particularly the women. One of their most important observers was the Italian artist Agostino Brunias. As a member of the entourage of Sir William Young after he was appointed commissioner for the sale of lands in the Ceded Islands in 1764, Brunias traveled through much of the eastern Caribbean with his patron. His paintings showed his fascination with them and their lifestyle. He captured them on canvas as they went about some of their most menial daily tasks and their recreational activities. His paintings showed them to be fond of self-adornment, particularly in the area of dress, as well as music and dancing. Though commentators have argued that Brunias's work may not have been always grounded in reality and ignored the fragile social order of slave society during this crucial period of the 18th century, his aquatint of the *Cudgelling Match between English and French Negroes in the Island of Dominica* of 1779 may have telegraphed the Anglo-French conflict that arose in the Lesser Antilles during the period of the French Revolution. Brunias's works nevertheless remain a unique record of life for the free people of color during this period.

As in other slave societies of the Americas, blacks as well as people of mixed race were able to gain their freedom. Free blacks were somewhat differentiated from people of mixed race, often suffering under increased social discrimination while generally being treated the same under the law. In some colonies, there were separate social services or duties for free blacks, such as separate MILITIA companies or separate accommodations in the established church.

Most of what is known today of the free coloreds has been confined to the relative few who managed to acquire significant personal wealth, social position, and influence. Some were significant landowners and SLAVE OWNERS, but the majority of free people of color tended to gravitate toward the urban centers. In an age when one's physical characteristics determined one's legal status, it was prudent for the free coloreds to live in the towns, where the lines between slavery and freedom had become blurred. It was there that they found life to be the least free of restrictions, though discrimination remained very strong. In Barbados, for example, London Bourne (1793–1869) was wealthy enough to own buildings that could be rented by the white business class for the meetings of the association of businessmen, but Bourne himself was not allowed to be a member of the body.

The presence of free colored people in significant numbers in the urban areas also facilitated slaves' running away and LIVING "AS FREE" in the towns. (*See also* RUNAWAY SLAVES.) With the lines becoming so blurred, enslaved people who took unauthorized leave of their masters' estates easily blended with the free people of color in the towns—to whom many of them were related—who often gave them shelter. With their help, many of these urban maroons remained hidden for many years without detection. For the literate among them, it was also easy to forge or a fabricate certificates of freedom that enabled them to move about freely. The towns

also served as a gateway for those maroons who found sanctuary on the ships that plied the maritime highways of the Americas.

For the majority of the free coloreds, however, everyday life appeared to be much nearer to the experience of the enslaved than the whites. In the towns, they had daily contact with those enslaved who lived and worked in these urban centers. The evidence suggests that they acquired many of their folkways from the enslaved, and the movement from a life of enslavement to that of personal freedom may not have involved as much change as might be expected, particularly for those who lived in the towns. The enslaved were the only people to whom the free coloreds could claim a real social connection within slave society. This is especially true in the British Caribbean because of the generally harsh legal restrictions on free people of color (*see also* BRITAIN).

The most precious commodity in slave society was personal freedom. The slave laws also permitted the enslaved to purchase their own freedom, and as soon as the free colored group attained a critical demographic mass in any given colony, the established order began to pass laws to restrict both the growth in their population and their personal freedom. Jamaica, captured from Spain in 1655, was the only one where the English legislature took the cue of the Spanish colonies and passed laws giving the rights and status of white persons to those free coloreds who were three generations removed from African ancestry. For the most part, free blacks and free people of mixed race were lumped together and suffered under a variety of legal handicaps limiting their right to practice certain professions and to own land, slaves, or personal property of certain types (especially weapons and high-status clothing).

The free colored people, nevertheless, continued to thrive as a social group. Freed from the rigorous daily work regime of plantation labor, they showed themselves to be the social group best able to increase their population by natural means. In Grenada, for example, by 1783, they composed 53 percent of the free population of that colony. With such a decisive demographic superiority over the white population, they felt the full brunt of the institutionalized discrimination meted out to them by the local members of the British colonial establishment. With their significant wealth, these free coloreds resented the restrictions placed upon them.

As a social group recently emerged from slavery, they tried to identify with their colonial rulers, who thought that they made an excellent buffer between them and the enslaved masses. However, the people of color were never promised social equality in return. Their socially acceptable means of protest—the petition and the memorial to the authorities in Britain, for example—failed to achieve relief from the state-sponsored persecution to which they were often subjected. However, as social equality was not forthcoming, they tended to identify with the country of their birth. Neither African nor European, they regarded the land of their birth as their home. The Europeans were regarded as interlopers.

The beginning of the FRENCH REVOLUTION in the 1790s brought to a head many of the social conflicts that had been in train for decades, particularly after the French became the first major European nation to abolish slavery in 1794. The French Revolutionary message of "Liberty, Equality, and Fraternity" was a heady and explosive message to the colored masses in the Lesser Antilles. In most of the Lesser Antilles, social unrest was the order of the day. While some writers have observed that the incidence of slave resistance experienced a lull during the late 18th century, this seems mostly true for the colonies in the Lesser Antilles that were acquired before 1763.

For the colonies acquired after 1763, Dominica, Grenada, St. Vincent and the Grenadines, and Tobago, however, the British in particular experienced special problems of governance with people who were of European but not necessarily of British origin. The free coloreds were at the center of most of the open revolts and rebellions that arose between 1789 and 1803. In Grenada, for example, most of the white French, a few white British, and the majority of the free coloreds, led by the free colored Julien Fédon, headed the French against British rule and chattel slavery. In Dominica, the resistance to British rule during this period was led by such free coloreds as Jean-Louis Polinaire and his colleague, a man named Petit, who survived the destruction of the rebel forces and ultimately joined the French invading forces. French forces, led by VICTOR HUGUES, operating out of Guadeloupe, attacked British forces throughout the area and offered support to rebels in British colonies. In St. Vincent, the revolutionary movements were led by Chatoyer, the chief of the so-called Black Carib, a community composed of MAROONS, or runaway slaves, and Carib Indians, and a number of free coloreds who joined the French revolutionary forces. In St. Lucia, which had been French until the outbreak of the Revolution, the free coloreds were in the forefront in the struggle against British conquest and domination, their fortunes joined with those of revolutionary France. The French defeat at the start of the 19th century also meant the end of French social power. As the revolutionary movements were put down one by one, their leaders and followers found themselves convicted of high treason, their properties confiscated. The French cultural influence remained, but the French no longer possessed much social power and influence.

In the older established colonies of Britain, the free people of color became part of the emerging "Creole" society. By the end of the 18th century, particularly in Barbados, the enslaved Africans and free coloreds began to lose their sense of common ethnic identity. The free coloreds were busy distinguishing themselves in the lower echelons of the business class, where they engaged in the wide range of intermediate occupations between those that were traditionally allocated for the white ruling class and those of the enslaved Africans.

In such newly acquired British territories as Trinidad, the experience of dealing with subject peoples of European but non-British origin in such colonies as Grenada informed their decision. They decided not to grant a colonial legislature to that colony, opting instead for a new system of colonial rule: Crown Colony government. The British rulers thought that this expedient was necessary in order to prevent the legislature from being controlled by people whom they regarded as "foreigners." Trinidad, a Spanish colony, had been colonized during the late 18th century mainly by white and free colored French Roman Catholic settlers from the eastern Caribbean.

The colony, though neutral for much of the French Revolution, was a place to which many "republicans" had fled for refuge and was a source of supplies for the revolutionary movements to the north. It possessed a large free colored population when the British conquered the colony in 1797. The grant of representative institutions in the style of those in Barbados and Jamaica would have placed local government in the hands of a non-British majority in Trinidad. It was the beginning of a long political struggle between the colony's British rulers and their subject peoples that would last for almost a century.

With France fading to a colonial power of the second rank behind Britain during the 19th century, the free coloreds began the slow process of accommodation in the colonial society. They mainly identified with the colonial power and sought to work within the socially acceptable boundaries in order to defend and advance their rights.

Abolition and Beyond

Free people of color, such as OLAUDAH EQUIANO, were important members of the abolitionist coalition in Britain in the late 18th century. The struggle against slavery in Jamaica featured the contributions of black Baptist leaders, most of whom were enslaved (see BAPTISTS AND PIETISTS). But in the British Lesser Antilles, the revolutionary impulse was more associated with the French Revolution Wars and Napoléon. Disruptions in the Lesser Antilles and the desire to cripple the competing French colonies of Guadeloupe and Martinique were part of the calculations that led Parliament to abolish the slave trade in 1807. However, there was not much antislavery agitation among free people of color in the smaller islands from 1807 up to the time of the end of slavery in the 1830s.

The predominantly accommodationist free colored community continued, nonetheless, to provide the leaders for black society during and after this period. Preabolition free people of color and their descendants remained particularly dominant in the areas of urban real estate and artisan production well into the 19th century. As in Jamaica, though, the racial distinction would overshadow the former status distinction, with the "browns," or mixed-race, mostly but not all former free people of color, occupying a higher social niche than the "blacks," or wholly Afro-descended, most but not all of whom had been slaves until 1833.

Curtis Jacobs

FURTHER READING

Brizan, George. *Grenada: Island of Conflict*. London: Macmillan Education, 1998.

Cox, Edward. *Free Coloreds in the Slave Societies of St. Kitts and Grenada, 1763–1833*. Knoxville: University of Tennessee Press, 1984.

Dyde, Brian. *A History of Antigua: The Unsuspected Isle*. London: Macmillan Caribbean, 2000.

Hall, Neville. *Slave Society in the Danish West Indies*. Edited by B. W. Higman. Mona, Jamaica; Cave Hill, Barbados; St. Augustine, Trinidad: University of the West Indies Press, 1992.

Honychurch, Lennox. *The Dominica Story: A History of the Island*. London: Macmillan Caribbean, 1984.

Steele, Beverley. *Grenada: A History of Its People*. London: Oxford: Macmillan Education, 2003.

Welch, Pedro. *Slave Society in the City: Bridgetown, Barbados, 1680–1834*. Oxford: Ian Randle Publishers and James Currey Publishers, 2003.

Welch, Pedro, and Richard Goodridge. *"Red" and Black over White: Free Colored Women in Pre-Emancipation Barbados*. Bridgetown, Barbados: Carib Research, 2000.

BROWN, HENRY "BOX" (ca. 1815–?) *escaped slave, abolitionist*

Henry "Box" Brown was born on a plantation in Louisa County, Virginia, and as it is the case with most slaves, no one knows the real date of his birth, although it is usually given as sometime in 1815. He became a leading orator against slavery, but above all, he became a celebrity thanks to his unusual escape from bondage. Brown escaped from the plantation hidden in a wooden box, an experience he would later explain in his *Narrative of the Life of Henry Box Brown, Written by Himself.*

According to his own autobiographical account, Brown enjoyed a pretty happy life as a slave child. With his master's death in 1830, Brown was sold to another family; that gave him the opportunity to work at his new master's

tobacco factory, and therefore, he was able to save some money for the first time in his life. He hoped this money would help him buy his own freedom in the near future.

The same year, Brown married Nancy, a slave owned by his first master's family. They had several children; the exact number is unknown. Although their masters agreed on never separating the couple, some months afterward, Nancy's owner sold her to an extremely cruel family, who then sold her to a man named Samuel Cottrell. Nancy's new owner promised Brown he would never sell Nancy if he would pay him half of Nancy's price. Soon Cotrell blackmailed Brown by obliging him to pay $50 every year if he did not want him to sell Nancy and their children. Since Brown could not raise the money Cotrell demanded from him, Nancy's owner eventually sold her and their children to a North Carolina slave trader in 1848.

This incident encouraged Brown to seek his freedom. With the help of a white accomplice named Samuel A. Smith, a storekeeper, to whom he paid $86 from his savings, he devised a plan to have himself shipped to Philadelphia inside a box. Brown contacted an African-American carpenter named John Mattaner and obtained a crate that measured about 25 cubic feet. He himself was five feet eight inches tall and weighed about 200 pounds. Before dawn on March 23, 1849, he was hidden in the wooden box and nailed into it by his accomplices. Brown carried a bladder of water and a gimlet he could use to bore holes in the box in case he needed more air. Smith shipped the box, marked as dry goods, via the Adams Express Co, an express delivery service, to James McKim, a prominent abolitionist living in PENNSYLVANIA. Brown's box traveled by many means of transport: train, ferry, steamboat, and wagon. Sometimes the box was not handled with care, but Brown was never discovered. Three hundred and fifty miles later, and after 27 hours of travel, the box arrived safely in PHILADELPHIA, PENNYSLVANIA, where it was delivered to McKim. In 1850, Brown's "unboxing" was immortalized in a lithograph by Samuel Rowse: *The Resurrection of Henry "Box" Brown at Philadelphia*. Samuel A. Smith, Brown's accomplice, was imprisoned from October 1849 until June 1856 for trying to box two other potential fugitive slaves. He would later be received as a hero among African Americans in Philadelphia. It is unclear whether Smith and McKim had been in contact before Brown's escape, but apparently Smith was an active antislavery campaigner.

Almost immediately, Henry Brown adopted his middle name, "Box," and joined the American Anti-Slavery Society. He became a prominent abolitionist who campaigned against slavery. Being illiterate, he told his story to Charles Stearns, a white man who became Brown's amanuensis and wrote his life story: *Narrative of the Life*

The Resurrection of Henry Box Brown at Philadelphia, a lithograph by Samuel Rowse published in 1850. Brown (ca. 1815–?) escaped from slavery by having himself mailed in a small crate to a Philadelphia abolitionist. He went on to be a public speaker, describing his escape and his experiences in slavery. Some antlslavery activists criticized him for revealing his escape method, arguing that others could have used it had he kept it a secret. *(Library of Congress)*

of Henry Box Brown who Escaped from Slavery Enclosed in a Box 3 Feet Long and 2 Wide Written from a Statement of Facts Made by Himself. With Remarks upon the Remedy for Slavery. By Charles Stearns (1849). As did many other slave narratives, Brown's became a huge success.

Brown constructed a panorama called *Mirror of Slavery*, an invention that consisted of a moving scroll with scenes that included the origins of the African slave trade, views of the South, slaves' punishments, and images of Brown's life in slavery and his adventurous escape. With the panorama, Brown wanted to denounce the participation of all Americans as accomplices in African-American enslavement. As the historian Richard Newman explains, Brown asked for a $150 loan from Gerrit Smith, an abolitionist, and encouraged Josiah Wolcott (1814–85), a minor New England painter, to paint the panorama. Brown also contacted the African-American printer Benjamin F. Roberts, who wrote the lecture, "The Condition of the Colored People in America," that would be recited while the panorama was being exhibited. The panorama was inaugurated on April 1850 in Boston and then moved to other northeastern cities. Brown would take his *Mirror of Slavery* to BRITAIN as well in 1850–51.

As a runaway slave, Brown remained at risk of recapture, and after the FUGITIVE SLAVE ACT OF 1850, he emigrated to Britain. In Europe, Brown also became popular and traveled around the continent explaining the miseries of slavery. He was very popular, above all because of his unusual escape from bondage. Later on, Brown participated in lighter shows where he appeared together with singers and ventriloquists. He would usually emerge from a box on stage at some point in the show. He became a controversial figure in the abolitionist movement both because he revealed the means of his escape and because he turned his experiences into profitable but somewhat crude entertainment. The abolitionist and fellow free black FREDERICK DOUGLASS criticized him for his disclosure of the method he used to escape from slavery. According to Douglass, that would prevent other slaves from using that method that had proven useful to Brown for fear of being caught.

In 1851, a new edition of Brown's narrative with some significant stylistic changes was published in Manchester, England. The original title was changed to *Narrative of the Life of Henry Box Brown, Written by Himself* and was soon followed by a second edition published in Boston in 1852. In his narrative, Brown follows the pattern of other antebellum slave narratives and denounces violence against slaves, the systematic sexual abuse of black women, and the enslavers' religious hypocrisy.

Brown remained in Europe for the rest of his life, marrying a white British woman some time in the 1860s. He worked as an entertainer, doing hypnotism and stage magic. He made a tour in the United States in 1875, working with his second wife, but appears to have then returned to Britain and retired. He never appears to have sought out his first spouse or family, even after the AMERICAN CIVIL WAR freed all slaves in the United States in 1865. Henry "Box" Brown's place and date of death remain unknown.

Laura Gimeno-Pahissa

FURTHER READING

Brown, Henry Box. *Narrative of the Life of Henry Box Brown.* Edited by Richard Newman. New York: Oxford University Press, 2002.

Ernest, John. "Outside the Box: Henry Box Brown and the Politics of Antislavery Agency." *Arizona Quarterly: A Journal of American Literature, Culture, and Theory,* 63, no. 4 (Winter 2007): 1–24.

BUCHANAN, JAMES (1791–1868) *fifteenth president of the United States (1857–1861) and diplomat*

President of the United States from 1857 to 1861, James Buchanan was the last president to govern before the outbreak of the AMERICAN CIVIL WAR (1861–65). His presidency was marked by increasing political crisis. His efforts to avert the crisis were ineffective. He also is believed to have had great influence over the Supreme Court's decision in the case of *Dred Scott v. Sandford* (1857), which had serious negative implications for free people of color and made the war almost inevitable. He is generally thought to be among the worst American presidents.

Buchanan was born on April 23, 1791, near Harrisburg, PENNSYLVANIA. He had a humble social background; his father was an Irish immigrant who managed a hotel. Living in small-town Pennsylvania, he would have encountered a few people of color, both free and enslaved, during his early life but probably would not have significant contact with them. His father was a Federalist and a supporter of the policies of Alexander Hamilton. James Buchanan studied law and was elected to Congress in 1814 as a Federalist and opponent of the War of 1812. He served in Congress until 1831. He was by then a member of the Democratic Party, as were many northern immigrants and their families, and a supporter of President ANDREW JACKSON (1829–37), who appointed

him ambassador to Russia from 1832 to 1833. This was the first of several diplomatic assignments he was to hold, culminating in his appointment as secretary of state under President FRANKLIN PIERCE (1845–49). While serving as ambassador to Britain, Buchanan had a hand in drafting the Ostend Manifesto (1854), which threatened Spain with war if it did not sell Cuba to the United States. Expansion of U.S. territory into the Caribbean and Central America had been a dream of Southerners for many years, with the hope that these would constitute new and profitable territories for slavery. Buchanan, however, can claim credit for modifying the harsh tone of early drafts of the manifesto, allowing Spain a way out of the negotiations without war.

For many years, Buchanan had a very close friendship and lived with the Alabama senator William Rufus King (1784–1853), who served as vice president in the Pierce administration. Buchanan's close relationship with King may have made him more sympathetic to the Southern point of view on national affairs than other Northern Democrats.

Buchanan's presidency was marked by the fallout from the Supreme Court decision in the *Dred Scott* case, decided only two days after his inauguration in 1857 (*see* SCOTT, DRED). Buchanan and Chief Justice Roger Taney (1777–1864) were fellow alumni of Dickinson College and political allies, and Buchanan is widely assumed to have had a hand in forming Taney's sweeping opinion in the case. Taney went beyond the specific issues in the case to invalidate the Missouri Compromise and all federal laws forbidding slavery in the territories, even the Democratic Party's cherished "squatter sovereignty" idea of giving the (white) inhabitants of each territory the right to decide whether slavery should be allowed. Taney also ruled that blacks, whether enslaved or free, could never be citizens of the United States and had "no rights a white man was obliged to respect." Buchanan expected that the Court's decision would end all discussion of the issue of slavery in the territories, but in fact the broad range and underlying logic of Taney's decision made Northern whites feel threatened. There was no reason why Taney's argument against the validity of laws forbidding slavery in the territories could not also apply to laws forbidding slavery in Northern states, and some Southern "fire-eater" proslavery agitators were prepared to launch test cases to see whether Southern slaves could be taken to Northern states and put to work on farms and in factories. Northerners who had treated slavery as an issue that only affected people in faraway places now realized that it affected them too, and the United States became, as the future president ABRAHAM LINCOLN said in a speech on June 16, 1858, reacting to the *Dred Scott* case, a "house divided against itself."

President Buchanan further aligned himself with the Southern interest when he pushed hard to have Kansas admitted to the Union as a slave state. A proslavery convention, supported by armed militia from MISSOURI, had passed a draft constitution opposed by the majority of white Kansans, who were mainly antislavery people from Northern states. Buchanan's support of this armed coup d'état tied him inextricably to the proslavery cause. Buchanan's fellow Democrat, the Illinois senator Stephen Douglas, rallied Northern Democrats to oppose this measure, in defense of the "squatter sovereignty" principle he had put into the Kansas-Nebraska Act of 1854. Buchanan's defeat by Douglas in the succeeding intraparty feud isolated and weakened him. When the final crisis of secession occurred, Buchanan had no political allies on whom to rely.

The election of 1860 saw the Democrats splitting into three factions: Southerners led by Vice-President John Breckinridge, who favored full implementation of the *Dred Scott* decision and the expansion of slavery; a Northern faction, led by Douglas; and a Constitutional Unionist faction, still seeking compromise. With the Democrats badly split, the Republican candidate Abraham Lincoln won the election without a single popular vote from a dozen states in the South. In the winter of 1860–61, many of those states began to take steps to secede from the United States. In February 1861, they formed the Confederate States of America. Buchanan was still president but exercised little power and did little to stop them. His vice president, Breckinridge, and secretary of war, John Floyd, were destined to become Confederate army generals in 1861. Many of his allies in Congress were packing their bags to move to the new Confederate capital of Montgomery, ALABAMA. Buchanan himself did not support secession and looked for ways to compromise. He invited the former president JOHN TYLER (1841–45), of Virginia, still neutral between the two sides at the time, to put forward peace proposals. After Floyd moved U.S. Army weapons to Southern arsenals where they could be taken over by the Confederates, Buchanan fired Floyd but was unable to prevent many of the weapons from falling into enemy hands.

After leaving the presidency on March 4, 1861, Buchanan quit all involvement in politics. The Civil War began a month later. In 1866, he published a memoir defending his actions in the final crisis, which was the first presidential autobiography. He died on June 1, 1868, in Pennsylvania.

Buchanan left office with the country divided between warring factions that were to kill and wound almost 1,000,000 Americans during the next four years. In this, he cemented his reputation as one of America's worst presidents. As far as his actions specifically affected free people of color, his legacy was quite harmful. His support for the *Dred Scott* decision, often considered the worst Supreme Court ruling in American history, effectively barred all blacks from citizenship. Avenues of legal defense for people of color threatened with reenslavement were closed, and people of African descent lost access to the federal courts. James Buchanan's public life provided no benefits for free people of color and may be considered a disaster for them.

Stewart R. King

FURTHER READING

Baker, Jean. *James Buchanan.* New York: Times Books, 2004.

Birkner, Michael J., ed. *James Buchanan and the Political Crisis of the 1850s.* Cranbury, N.J.: Susquehanna University Press, 1996.

Buchanan, James. *Mr. Buchanan's Administration on the Eve of the Rebellion.* New York: Appleton, 1866. Available online. URL: http://deila.dickinson.edu/theirownwords/title/0010.htm. Accessed March 30, 2010.

BUSH, GEORGE WASHINGTON (ca. 1779–1863) *Anglo-American businessman and pioneer*
George Washington Bush was born about 1779 in PENNSYLVANIA, the son of an Afro-British sailor and an Irish indentured servant woman. He lived as a young man with a white merchant in Philadelphia who gave him a good education and encouraged him to go into commerce. Bush worked as a merchant and trapper in the West, for the Hudson's Bay Company and the Northwest Company in CANADA, and for smaller concerns in the LOUISIANA Territory (*see* INLAND WEST OF THE UNITED STATES). He fought for the United States in the War of 1812 and was a veteran of the victorious Battle of New Orleans in January 1815. When the merchant he had lived with as a young man died in the 1820s, he left Bush a substantial inheritance, which Bush used to buy land and try to farm in Missouri. He married Isabella James, a German-American woman, in 1831 and started a large family, but racial discrimination, which was especially violent because of his marriage to a white woman, forced him from the state in 1844.

Bush led a party composed of his family, his neighbor, a white man originally from KENTUCKY named Michael Simmons, and several of Simmons's relatives along the Oregon Trail to the OREGON Territory. His long experience in the western wilderness was invaluable to the party. Upon arrival, though, they discovered that the Oregon legislature had passed antiblack laws, and so they moved across the river into WASHINGTON, which was then administered by Britain. The group formed a settlement at Bush Prairie, now called Tumwater, on Puget

Sound. Bush and wife and his six surviving sons and the Simmonses and their relatives all obtained land in 1845 under the British regulations, which did not discriminate on the basis of race. In fact, when the Bushes arrived in the area, the governor of the British colony of Victoria, in theory responsible for the Puget Sound region, was JAMES DOUGLAS, a man of mixed race.

Bush was a welcoming figure for other pioneers moving north from Oregon. He helped newcomers with food and tools, helped them file land claims, and served as a central figure in the rapidly growing settlement. Ironically, though, the growing presence of settlers from the United States in the region that is now the state of Washington, including the Bushes, led the British to agree to draw the border of British Columbia at the 49th parallel, and the Bushes once again became residents of the United States. Oregon's discriminatory laws applied to them, and the Bushes and their neighbors had to go to the U.S. Congress in the 1850s for a declaration that their land claims were valid. Bush was an important participant in peace negotiations with the Nisqually Indians that settled a long-running conflict in 1854.

Bush died on April 5, 1863. He is an outstanding example of the often unappreciated role black pioneers played in the settlement of the American West. Many trappers and fur traders were people of mixed race, with either black or Native American ancestry. Their skills were essential for the migrants to cross the wilderness successfully. Many of them tried to transition to a more settled life as farmers, only to encounter racial discrimination, sometimes from the very people they had helped to arrive in the territory. Bush and his family were lucky that their neighbors stood by them, and George Washington Bush is recognized today as one of the founders of the state of Washington.

Stewart R. King

FURTHER READING:

City of Tumwater, Washington. "Articles on George Washington Bush." Available online. URL: http://www.ci.tumwater.wa.us/research%20bushTOC.htm. Accessed January 19, 2011.

Katz, William. *The Black West: A Documentary and Pictorial History of the African American Role in the Westward Expansion of the United States.* New York: Harlem Moon, 2005.

Oldham, Kit. "George W. Bush Settles with His Family at Bush Prairie Near Tumwater in November 1845." Available online. URL: http://www.historylink.org/index.cfm?DisplayPage=output.cfm&File_Id=5646. Accessed December 27, 2010.

C

CAESAR, JOHN. *See* BLACK CAESAR.

CALIFORNIA

California is a state of the United States. It is located along the Pacific Ocean and stretches from the border with MEXICO in the south to OREGON in the north, with Nevada and Arizona forming the border to the east. California is the second-largest state by area in the continental United States. There are a narrow coastal plain and a large interior valley that are both well watered and fertile. The coastal plain is broader in the South, but water is scarce there—southern California was lightly inhabited rangeland until the 20th century. The Sierra Nevada, a large range of mountains with rich mineral deposits, runs along most of the eastern boundary of the state. The indigenous inhabitants of California had not acquired horses or developed agriculture before European settlers arrived and lived in small bands by fishing, hunting, and gathering.

Early European Presence

European explorers first visited California in the 16th century, but permanent settlement did not take place until the late 18th century, when the Franciscan missionary Junipero Serra (1713–84) founded a chain of mission settlements between 1764 and 1784. Some Mexican settlers and government officials followed the missionaries, and the colonial government of New Spain gave large land grants to soldiers and government officials. These officials and their descendants transformed their land grants into large ranches. The indigenous population suffered extensively from disease, and so the ranches were mostly staffed by laborers imported from Mexico, some of whom were free people of African descent. Ranchers also imported a few slaves, though the institution was never strong and there was no plantation agriculture. A small population of free people of color grew up alongside the larger mestizo group and declining Indian population, to some extent merging into the larger population thanks to the permeable color line in Spanish-American culture. Mexico abolished slavery definitively in 1829, and though the law was not universally enforced, there do not appear to have been significant numbers of slaves in California at the time of the MEXICAN-AMERICAN WAR, 1846–48. California had a population of more than 92,000 in the census of 1850, after it became an American state, of which somewhat more than a thousand—just above 1 percent—were identified as free blacks or mulattos.

Gold Rush and Statehood

In 1849, gold was discovered in the foothills of the Sierras, and over the following decade, hundreds of thousands of people from all over the world descended on California to seek their fortunes. The California gold rush drew people of African descent as well as American whites, Asians, and immigrants from Latin America and Europe. By 1852, the black population of the state had more than doubled, to more than 2,000, with significant communities in San Francisco, in Sacramento, and at the gold fields. The newly established state government of California struggled to deal with this very diverse population. Some California officials had attempted to enshrine slavery in the state constitution, but a majority of Northern immigrants, supported by representatives of mine workers, rejected this initiative, and California entered the Union as a free state. There were also attempts, likewise thwarted by antislavery forces, to forbid all black immigration. Some Southern white immigrants had taken their slaves with them and wanted to be allowed to continue the practice. There were several cases in the 1850s in which the abolition of slavery was tested in California courts. An early case was *in re Frank Galloway*, in 1851. A Missouri man named Galloway had taken his 18-year-old slave Frank with him to work in his mining operation. Having heard that California was a free state, Frank decided to claim his freedom in 1851. His owner, Galloway, had him seized by law enforcement officials in San Francisco, citing the federal FUGITIVE SLAVE ACT OF 1850, which required governments in free states to assist in the recovery of fugitives. Frank's defenders successfully argued that since his master had taken him to the state voluntarily, thus Frank had not crossed state lines in his flight and so was not a fugitive slave under the mean-

A 1999 U.S. postage stamp commemorating the 150th anniversary of the California gold rush depicts a racially mixed group of miners. Many immigrants to California from the American South took slaves with them who ultimately became free under California law and court decisions, and many free blacks also traveled west to seek their fortunes in the gold fields. Like other western states, California enacted laws that made it difficult for free blacks to settle, and many California free blacks immigrated to British Columbia in the 1850s when gold was found there. *(U.S. Postal Service/Associated Press)*

ing of the act. In response to this case, proslavery lawmakers passed the California Fugitive Slave Act in 1852, which remained in force until 1855, which allowed masters who had taken slaves with them from slave states to take them back again, even against their will. Several free people of color were reenslaved under the provisions of this act. The state legislature also made it unlawful for blacks to testify in court cases. The most celebrated case of this series was the Archy Lee affair of 1858–60. Lee was taken across the plains from MISSISSIPPI by his master, Charles Stovall, who taught school in Sacramento. Stovall allowed Lee to work for wages and took either all or some proportion of his pay. The precise arrangement between them was a matter for debate during the case, since Lee's supporters asserted that Stovall recognized that Lee was free and took some portion of his wages as a form of rent. In 1858, Stovall decided to send Lee back to Stovall's father in Mississippi, but Lee refused to go and took refuge among the free black population of Sacramento. Stovall had Lee arrested, and Lee's friends sued. The case was decided in state courts and then appealed to federal courts under the federal Fugitive Slave

Act. California law held that masters who were temporarily in the state could keep their personal slaves during their stay, but the California Court of Appeals and a U.S. commissioner for the Fugitive Slave Act found that Stovall had established a residence and that Lee was thus free. The federal commissioner had considered the issue and finally decided that Lee was not an interstate fugitive. The case garnered national attention, as the AMERICAN CIVIL WAR, 1861–65, was nearing, and tension over slavery was at a heightened state throughout the country.

California blacks responded to pervasive discrimination by speaking out through the NEGRO CONVENTION MOVEMENT IN THE UNITED STATES, at conventions held in 1855, 1856, and 1857. A guiding spirit in this movement was William H. Newby, originally from Virginia. Newby was a businessman in San Francisco who was also a correspondent of FREDERICK DOUGLASS's various newspapers and published at least one short-lived black newspaper himself. Under Newby's leadership, the conventions protested antiblack legislation, built community solidarity, and provided a mechanism to rally support for

AFRICAN-AMERICAN POPULATION OF CALIFORNIA, 1850–1900

Year	Free People of Color	Free People of Color as a Percentage of Total Population	Total Population
1850	962	1.0%	92,567
1860	4,086	1.1%	379,904
1870	4,272	0.8%	560,247
1880	6,018	0.7%	864,694
1890	11,322	0.9%	1,208,130
1900	11,045	0.7%	1,485,053

individuals threatened with reenslavement. Newby himself left the state in 1857 to move to Haiti, where he was to serve as secretary in the French diplomatic mission.

Despite the legal oppression they experienced, a growing number of free blacks occupied important places in California society in the mid-1850s. A miner called Black Dick supposedly hit a big strike in Tolumne in 1849, taking almost $100,000 worth of gold to San Francisco, where he gambled most of it away. A black mining community called Negro Hill grew up on the American River, with considerable amounts of gold produced in the early 1850s. There are at least 30 places in California with *Negro* or a similar word in their names, suggesting the important role played in early settlement by black pioneers and prospectors. A produce farmer named Stephen S. Hill in Tolumne had a farm worth $4,000 in the 1850s, a significant sum at the time. Hill was threatened with reenslavement under the California Fugitive Slave Act of 1852, and his neighbors intervened, first to get him legal representation, and then to spirit him away from his supposed master and help him escape to CANADA. As pressure grew on the free black population of California, Canada soon seemed to offer better opportunities. A free person of African descent originally from GUYANA, SIR JAMES DOUGLAS, was governor of what is now British Columbia between 1858 and 1864, and a new gold rush was beginning along the Fraser River. In April 1858, several ships carrying around 700 free blacks set out from San Francisco for Victoria, British Columbia. This exodus significantly reduced the black population of California. Still, the 1860 census recorded a free colored population of 4,086, which was a little more than 1 percent of the total population of the state.

After the American Civil War ended in 1865, California's black population stagnated, reaching only 11,000 in 1900 of a total population of almost 2,000,000. White leaders were working hard during this period to exclude Asian immigrants—the U.S. government passed the Chinese Exclusion Act in 1882—but the hostility to nonwhites also spilled over to the black community. As American

citizens, blacks could not be forced out of the state, but pervasive discrimination made California an uncomfortable place for blacks to settle in the postwar years. Nonetheless, the small black population remained vibrant, creating schools, churches, and other cultural institutions. Blacks attended universities, practiced professions, and went into business. The black population of the state began to grow again in the 1920s as part of the "great migration" of African Americans from the South, and especially during and after the World War II as a result of the industrialization of California.

Stewart R. King

FURTHER READING

California State University Sacramento Library. "The California Underground Railroad." Available online. URL: http://digital.lib.csus.edu/curr/. Accessed December 19, 2010.

Katz, William. *The Black West: A Documentary and Pictorial History of the African American Role in the Westward Expansion of the United States.* New York: Harlem Moon, 2005.

Lapp, Rudolph. *Blacks in Gold Rush California.* New Haven, Conn.: Yale University Press, 1977.

CANADA

Free people of color in Canada (British North America, 1783–1867) fell into three broad categories: the freeborn or manumitted or emancipated slaves, fugitive slave refugees from the United States, and emigrants from the West Indies before and after the official end of slavery in the British Empire in the 1830s. Free people of color were concentrated in the Maritime Provinces of New Brunswick and Nova Scotia and in southwestern Ontario. Canada provided refuge to fugitive slaves from the United States even while slavery existed on its own soil. For a century or more, free people of color coexisted with slave persons of color. The 100 or so blacks recorded in the 1767 census of greater Nova Scotia (then including both New Brunswick and Cape Breton Island) were free. They prob-

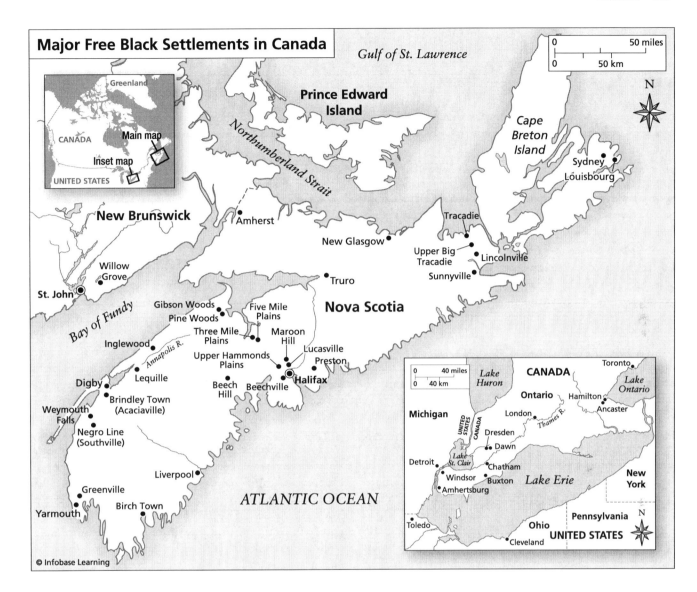

Major Free Black Settlements in Canada

ably formed part of the New England Planter migration, 1759–64, which included free black persons. Barbara Cuffy, for example, was a manumitted slave who became a proprietor in Liverpool Township on Nova Scotia's South Shore. Black slaves were to be found in every one of the old colonies before and after the final conquest of French Canada by the British in 1763 and in due course themselves became part of the population of free people of color.

The Maritimes

Pride of place belongs to Nova Scotia, where the first major influx of free people of color took place at the end of the WAR OF AMERICAN INDEPENDENCE, 1775–83. During the war, British martial-law measures aimed at disrupting the Patriot home front declared slaves of rebels free in return for fleeing their owners, and many thousands went. In 1782–83, some 3,000 fugitive slaves who had reached and remained behind the British lines were given free passage to Nova Scotia; the alternative was repossession by their American owners in line with Article VII of the Treaty of Paris, which ended the war. These freed blacks established several settlements in mainland Nova Scotia: Birch Town (at least three communities, all named in honor of the British military commandant of New York City who had signed the former slaves' passports), Preston (Halifax County), Negro Line (Annapolis County), Brindley Town/Conway (Digby County), and Upper Big Tracadie/Little Tracadie (Guysborough County). The Birch Town west of Shelburne on Nova Scotia's South Shore was for a few years the largest freed black community in North America. New Brunswick (set off from Nova Scotia in 1784) saw most of its freed blacks settle in or around the new city of Saint John and northward along the Kingston Peninsula. A few blacks who were Loyalists also settled in Nova Scotia; noteworthy among them were Catherine Abernathy, the schoolmistress and lay preacher, and

Stephen Blucke (fl. 1776–96), paramount black leader in Nova Scotia during the first postwar decade.

The arrival of thousands of American Loyalist slaveholders with their human property decisively reinforced slavery in the old American colonial society that was pre-Loyalist Nova Scotia. As far as government and people were concerned, freed blacks were for all practical purposes indistinguishable from slaves salvaged from the United States by their Loyalist owners. The inspection roll ("Book of Negroes") included indiscriminately both freed blacks and Loyalists who were black. The freed blacks themselves, especially the handful who had seen military service with the British, took a very different view of their status and entitlements. Their claims were not respected, however, and they did not prosper. If they received land at all, it was small in size, of poor quality, remotely or inconveniently situated, and begrudgingly or belatedly given or promised and not given. The threat and sometimes the reality of reenslavement by dispossessed white Loyalists hung over the freed blacks, and they were not shown anything like the same consideration as Loyalists such as Blucke, who were freeborn or manumitted blacks, and as a result fared a good deal better.

The freed blacks were understandably receptive to the prospectus of the SIERRA LEONE Company, created in 1791 by the English Committee for the Abolition of the Slave Trade, which offered to relocate former slaves in West Africa. The rationale was that if neither the slave trade nor slavery could be abolished in the short term, then the lives of freed blacks might be made easier and more secure in a faraway territory where slavery was prohibited. The powers that were in Nova Scotia enthusiastically promoted and cooperated with the scheme because they believed it was in the public interest to do so. The presence of so many recent fugitive or claimed slaves living cheek by jowl with so many held slaves potentially threatened the social order. The antislavery activists among the governmental elite also feared that the continued presence of so many former fugitive slaves, whose status remained until 1794 an international controversy between Great Britain and the United States, would undermine their efforts to destroy slavery by legal if not constitutional means.

Not all the freed blacks supported the West African resettlement scheme. Among those who opposed it was Stephen Blucke, who was not persuaded that the freed blacks would be any better off in Sierra Leone than they were in Nova Scotia. Another prominent Loyalist, Joseph Leonard, disagreed with Blucke, however, and took most of Digby's freed blacks with him to Sierra Leone. The West African emigration scheme effectively divided both Loyalist blacks and freed blacks. Yet their interests and prospects were not identical; a significant number of the freed blacks hoped that in Sierra Leone they would be truly free, as they were not in Nova Scotia and could not be while slavery was in the ascendant.

In January 1792, some 1,200 freed blacks—less than half the 1783 immigrant population—accompanied JOHN CLARKSON, the Sierra Leone Company's agent, to West Africa. This exodus temporarily obliterated some of Nova Scotia's freed black communities, including Preston, and depopulated others. Such a mass migration was a tragedy for African Nova Scotians in that it deprived them not only of significant numbers but also of high-quality leadership when they needed it most. The leaders of the freed blacks were either Loyalists such as Richard Corankapone (New Brunswick) and Blucke or former military servicemen such as Thomas Peters (Nova Scotia), a noncommissioned officer in the Black Pioneers, the only black military unit in the British army establishment during the war. The places of consummate leaders like Corankapone, Peters, David George, Boston King, Joseph Leonard, and Moses Wilkinson, all of whom departed, could not easily be filled and were not. The departure of the freed blacks arrested the development of African Nova Scotians for many years and probably delayed the extinction of slavery.

There was no further significant black immigration to the Maritime Provinces until 1796, when the MAROONS of JAMAICA—proudly independent guerrillas fighting slavery—arrived. Their superior social status among local blacks was confirmed by the province's lieutenant-governor's taking one of their women as his mistress; their progeny survive to this day. The maroons were settled among the freed black remnant at Preston but found the climate—not to mention the state of dependence and subservience in which the freed blacks lived—oppressive; in 1800, they, too, removed to Sierra Leone. A few stayed behind, their settlement surviving as Maroon Hill, just beyond metropolitan Halifax. No further immigration took place until after the War of 1812, when absconding slaves from the Carolinas and Virginia who reached the British lines were given protection by the Royal Navy and in due course new homes in Nova Scotia and New Brunswick.

These "Black Refugees," as they were known, founded communities such as African Grant/Willow Grove (northwest of Saint John, New Brunswick) and Refugee Hill/Beech Hill/Beechville, Five Mile Plains, Lucasville, and Upper Hammonds Plains (Halifax County, Nova Scotia). Africville, a now-lost community on the northernmost fringe of peninsular Halifax, was founded later by out-migrants from Upper Hammonds Plains. The Black Refugees also gave a new lease on life to barely surviving freed black settlements such as Preston, which with its satellites quickly became and remains the largest black community in Nova Scotia. Unlike the black refugees of the American War of Independence, who were dispersed throughout the province, those of the War of 1812 were settled almost entirely in Halifax County. Segregating the newcomers from the indigenous former slave population, which was distributed largely outside Halifax County, was conducted with a view to relocating the Black Refugees. But the gradual abolition of slavery had changed the calculus. In 1821, an attempt was made to resettle the Black Refugees in Trinidad. Fear of reenslavement, however, was a key factor in the refusal of the vast majority to leave a colony where slavery was moribund for another where it was still very much alive.

The gradual abolition of slavery in Nova Scotia also had demographic consequences, giving rise to distinct communities of former slaves such as Gibson Woods, The Pines/Pine Woods (Kings County), Greenville (Yarmouth County), Inglewood and Lequille (Annapolis County), Lincolnville and Sunnyville (Guysborough County), Three Mile Plains (Hants County), Black Town (Shelburne County), and Weymouth Falls (Digby County). Former slaves were not welcome in the white communities where they had lived and worked while enslaved.

Though more than a generation separated the Black Refugees of 1815 from the freed blacks of 1783, as African Americans they shared both the fugitive slave experience and, in the case of Southern blacks, the same or similar places of origin or domicile in the United States. In both cases, moreover, the treaty ending the war in which they asserted their freedom by running away provided for repossession by their former owners. In both cases the British dishonored this treaty obligation in order to preserve and protect the fugitive slaves' newfound liberty. The British further secured the freedom of the Black Refugees of 1815 by paying compensation to their former owners; they had not done that for the freed blacks of 1783.

The presence of the Black Refugees, allied to the increase in the population of free people of color wrought by emancipation of all the slaves, caused Halifax merchants to fear the economic consequences of the abolition of slavery in the West Indies. Nova Scotia's economy was utterly dependent on West Indies trade, which slave labor supported. By 1824, when the campaign to abolish slavery in the West Indies was in its final phase, Halifax merchants were petitioning the British government to "go slow" on slavery abolition. Ten years later, when emancipation became a reality, the Nova Scotia legislature passed an act prohibiting the immigration of liberated slaves. It was disallowed by the home government: "This Act prohibits the access to the Province of a class of Your Majesty's Subjects, who have, by a recent Act of Parliament, been relieved from the disabilities formerly affecting them, and to whom it is not fitting that new

disabilities, from which the other classes of Your Majesty's Subjects are exempt, should be extended" (Order in Council, March 4, 1835). The earl of Aberdeen, foreign and colonial secretary, took the view that the ill treatment that the Black Refugees had received in the nearly 20 years since their arrival in Nova Scotia would be "the best possible security" against newly emancipated slaves' immigrating to the colony.

Lord Aberdeen's prognosis proved incorrect. Nova Scotia became and remained for a century a preferred destination for West Indian emigrants. Most settled in Halifax City, home to Nova Scotia's oldest black quarter, which still survives and where in the later 1820s William Scarth Moorsom, a resident Englishman, would observe, "The large proportion of people of colour daily seen about the streets of Halifax strikes a European stranger sensibly." By 1851, fully one-third of Nova Scotia's 5,000-strong black population lived in Halifax County. Black people of diverse origins and backgrounds gradually coalesced, building strong ethnic community institutions centered especially around the black churches, both Methodist and Baptist.

Halifax's African Methodist Episcopal (A.M.E.) Zion Church, established as a foreign mission from Baltimore in 1846, ministered principally to recent West Indian immigrants. In 1857, the British North America Mission Annual Conference was established, comprising the Maritime Provinces and Bermuda. The principal strength of black Methodism, however, was among fugitive slaves in Ontario who took their religious affiliation with them and were soon followed by their ministers, who had been strenuously involved in both the Underground Railroad and antislavery activism. In Nova Scotia, the African Baptists, who established themselves by the early 1820s, were numerically stronger and more widely dispersed than the African Methodists, whose historic congregations all eventually disappeared. The African Baptist Association, founded in 1854 by the Reverend Richard Preston (d. 1861), a slave-born Baptist minister whose mother had entered Nova Scotia as a Black Refugee, was a centripetal force and remains an important organization.

After 1834, people of color founded abolitionist societies, fraternal organizations, and friendly societies and celebrated Emancipation Day (August 1). By the late 19th century, the coal mines and iron and steel works of industrial Cape Breton and Pictou Counties were attracting immigrants from the West Indies as well as rural out-migrant blacks to towns where they had never lived except as slaves and where their presence was deeply resented. In 1990, African Nova Scotia comprised nearly 50 communities. Fully half were historic rural black settlements founded either by slaves emancipated locally or by African-American refugees from slavery.

The same could not be said of Prince Edward Island, a colony separated from greater Nova Scotia in 1769 and the only one in British North America to legislate a germinal slave code. There was no freed black immigration such as populated Nova Scotia and New Brunswick in 1783 and again in 1815, and so the relatively small number of free people of color were exclusively former slaves and their descendants. Concentrated in Charlottetown, the island's capital, most of the black population by 1911 had been assimilated, had died out, or had out-migrated. In New Brunswick, on the other hand, where fewer freed blacks and Black Refugees settled than in Nova Scotia, people of color rapidly urbanized, becoming and remaining a significant presence in Saint John and, to a lesser extent, Fredericton, the province's capital.

Ontario
If the focus of the first and second waves of fugitive slave migration was the Maritime Provinces, then that of the third and last was Ontario (Upper Canada/Canada West, 1791–1867), the northern extension and terminus of the Underground Railroad. The history of free people of color in central Canada begins with the gradual abolition of slavery in the first quarter of the 19th century and ends with the Thirteenth Amendment to the U.S. Constitution in 1865, which abolished slavery. Upper Canada was the only British North American colony to legislate against slavery, in 1793, and antislavery sentiment there was always strong. Yet Ontario, like New Brunswick, was a Loyalist creation and, until the outbreak of the War of 1812, was more a refuge for slaveholders than for fugitive slaves. This was indirectly due to the Northwest Ordinance of 1787, which banned slavery from those U.S. territories bordering Ontario and drove the slaveholders farther north into Canada— a migration further encouraged by a 1790 act of Parliament favoring "late Loyalists." Moreover, neither Upper nor Lower Canada (Quebec) had any experience of fugitive slaves as war refugees.

American fugitive slave interest in Ontario came about as a result of the decline and disappearance of slavery there. Black people had a firm friend in Sir Peregrine Maitland, lieutenant-governor, 1818–28 (and of Nova Scotia, 1828–32). As early as July 1818, the new lieutenant-governor was advised by Chief Justice William Dummer Powell that American fugitive slaves who reached Upper Canada were legally free, a view not shared by American authorities including Secretary of State (and future president) JOHN QUINCY ADAMS. A few months before the end of his administration in 1829 some 200 free people of color meeting in Ancaster (southwest of Hamilton) petitioned Lieutenant-Governor Maitland for the establishment of a black township. In 1829, black people from Cincin-

nati, dispossessed by the revival of Ohio's dormant slave code, resettled in Ontario. Free blacks, no less than fugitive slaves, were at high risk not only from slave catchers and bounty hunters but also from contract kidnappers. The operation of the U.S. Fugitive Slave Act, moreover, first enacted in 1793, raised the issue of extraterritorial recognition of rights and whether American private law could be enforced outside the jurisdiction where slavery was outlawed. Fugitive slaves also faced the threat of criminal extradition, alleging that they had committed crimes during their escapes. This was illegal in their case under Canadian law, but American masters nevertheless attempted this strategy and occasionally succeeded.

Between the end of British colonial slavery in the 1830s and the outbreak of the AMERICAN CIVIL WAR in 1861, freed blacks, assisted by white antislavery activists and philanthropists, founded at least four distinct communities in Upper Canada. The first of these, Wilberforce, established late in the lifetime of the famous British abolitionist William Wilberforce (1759–1833) for whom it was named, was perhaps, according to the early 20th-century historian Fred Landon, the least successful as "an experiment in the colonization of freed Negroes." More successful was Buxton, founded in 1848 by a Presbyterian minister, the Reverend William King (1812–95), and named in honor of the late Sir Thomas Foxwell Buxton, who years before had succeeded Wilberforce as leader of the antislavery group in the British House of Commons. Another settlement was the quasi-commune of Dawn, near Dresden, founded by Josiah Henson (1789–1883), a fugitive slave; Elgin—the fourth and last—was also founded by King. The end of slavery in the United States removed the raison d'être of these communities, and they went into terminal decline, their population absorbed by white cities and towns. Amherstburg, Chatham, Dresden, Hamilton, London, St Catharines, Toronto, and Windsor all developed a significant black presence. Until after World War II, when Afro-Caribbeans began to immigrate in numbers directly to the large metropolitan or industrial centers, the black population of Ontario consisted mostly of fugitive or emancipated slave descendants.

Another part of Canada to receive an influx of free people of color between passage of the last U.S. Fugitive Slave Act in 1850 and the end of the American Civil War in 1865 was the Pacific coast (lower mainland) of British Columbia. Blacks who settled there, however, were fleeing racism not slavery, and what they found was similar to what they had left behind in the Pacific Northwest and California.

Free People of Color: The Canadian Experience
Free people of color in Canada faced numerous hardships and obstacles. They had to cope with the persistence

of slavery; with the memory of enslavement and the ever-present danger of its chief consequence, racism; and with racism's legacy: prejudice, segregation, and unequal access to social and legal justice. Though black people could no longer be owned, they could still be discriminated against and oppressed with impunity. What rights they enjoyed were partial and selective. Though enfranchised in Nova Scotia as early as 1837, as late as the 1960s African Canadians in Ontario and Nova Scotia had to endure separate schools. Just as free people of color formed organizations to promote the abolition of slavery in the United States, so their descendants formed organizations to resist and combat racial discrimination at home. The experience of free people of color in Canada has been that of African Americans writ small. It began as resistance to slavery and continues as resistance to racism. So desperate was the situation that by 1865 three-quarters of the black population of Ontario had reemigrated back to the United States. Though slavery disappeared from Canada earlier than the West Indies or the United States, its insidious impact lasted longer because its existence has never been properly acknowledged by either the Canadian government or the Canadian people. This in itself is witness to persistent, if not perpetual, racism and explains the failure of black Canada in all its rich contradiction to integrate into the mainstream of African diaspora or British Empire history.

Barry Cahill

FURTHER READING
British Columbia Black History Awareness Society. "A Resource Guide on Black Pioneers in British Columbia." Available online. URL: http://digital.lib.csus.edu/cdm4/item_viewer. php?cisoroot=/curr&cisoptr=264&cisoBox=1&rec=2. Accessed December 27, 2010.
Fergusson, Charles Bruce. *A Documentary Study of the Establishment of the Negroes in Nova Scotia between the War of 1812 and the Winning of Responsible Government.* Halifax: Public Archives of Nova Scotia, 1948.
Ogg, Frederic Austin. "Slave Property as an Issue in Anglo-American Diplomacy, 1782–1828." Unpublished Ph.D. thesis, Harvard University, 1908.
Pybus, Cassandra. *Epic Journeys of Freedom: Runaway Slaves of the American Revolution and Their Global Quest for Liberty.* Boston: Beacon Press, 2006.
Ripley, C. Peter, et al., eds. *The Black Abolitionist Papers.* Vol. 2: *Canada, 1830–1865.* Chapel Hill: University of North Carolina Press, 1987.
Silverman, Jason H. *Unwelcome Guests: Canada West's Response to American Fugitive Slaves, 1800–1865.* Port Washington, N.Y.: Associated Faculty University Press, 1985.
Simpson, Donald George. *Under the North Star: Black Communities in Upper Canada before Confederation.* Trenton, N.J.: Africa World Press, 2005.
Walker, James W. St. G. *The Black Loyalists: The Search for a Promised Land in Nova Scotia and Sierra Leone, 1783–1870.* 1976. Reprint, Toronto: University of Toronto Press, 1992.
Whitfield, Harvey Amani. *Black Refugees in British North America, 1815–1860.* Burlington: University of Vermont Press, 1976.

CAP-FRANÇAIS/CAP-HAÏTIEN *(Le Cap, Cap-François)*
Colonial Period: Growth and Development
Throughout the colonial period, Cap-Français was the largest city and commercial center of the French colony of SAINT-DOMINGUE, the modern Haiti. Although the city was gravely damaged during the HAITIAN REVOLUTION, burned first in 1794 and again in 1801, it remained the second-largest city, after the capital, PORT-AU-PRINCE, in the new nation of Haiti under its new name, Cap-Haïtien. The city is located on the north coast of the island of Hispaniola, around a large protected harbor. Sailing ships from France found it easiest and quickest to call first at Cap-Français, and so the city became the colony's commercial capital and principal port. It was also the principal market town and port for the many plantations of its hinterland. More than a hundred ships arrived here each year by the late 18th century, delivering slaves from Africa and from other Caribbean ports, manufactured goods from Europe and Asia, and food from North America and taking the products of the plantations to European and North American markets. The largest part of the colony's legal slave imports passed through Cap-Français, numbering as many as 25,000 a year in the 1780s, and the city had an enormous slave market.

To the south and east of the city lies the Plaine du Nord, or northern plain, which was the most fertile sugar-growing region in the colony. The plain was the first area of the colony to be developed for sugar cultivation, and by 1791, sugar fields covered almost every available acre of the plains. The surrounding hillsides were thickly forested in the 17th century, but by 1791, they, too, were intensively cultivated, producing coffee, food for sale to the plantations, indigo, and other plantation crops.

Cap-Français was the capital of the North Province of the colony and the seat of one of its two supreme courts (Conseils Supérieurs). Before the revolution, the city was called the "Paris of the Antilles" because of its wealth and sophistication. In addition to government facilities, the city boasted a theater, a "Société des Philosophes" with a library, several hospitals, a beautiful church, and many fine stone houses that would not have been out of place in wealthy districts of Paris. According to the census of 1788, Cap-Français had a population of about 7,500, making it

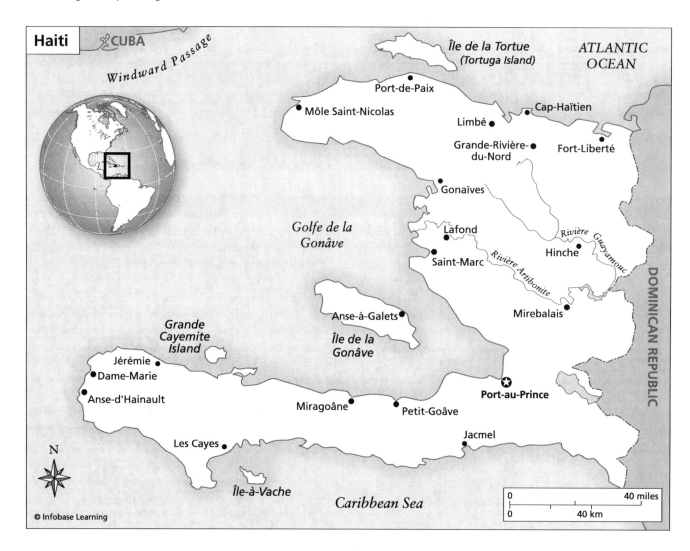

one of the largest cities in the Caribbean. Of these, about 1,400, or 19 percent, were free people of color, meaning that the city also had the largest concentration of free people of color in the colony.

The urban and rural populations of free coloreds were different in Saint-Domingue, as in many parts of the Americas. Discriminatory laws against free people of color, passed during the 1760s and 1770s, were most strictly enforced in the cities. In reaction to these laws, and thanks to a vibrant rural economy, most wealthy and well-connected free coloreds made their homes outside the city, though most were obliged to go to town occasionally to do business. The poorest free people of color in the colony did not have the resources to set themselves up in business or be trained in a trade, and thus they remained peasants in the countryside. As a result, the free colored people of Cap-Français were middle-class, owning small businesses, practicing a trade, or offering services. Many had small farms near the city and clearly hoped to prosper enough to be able to join the planter class in the countryside.

The urban environment was unhealthy everywhere in the 18th century, and this was true of Cap-Français, as well. Parents knew this and often sent children and vulnerable elders outside the city to live with relatives. As a result, the free population of the city, both whites and blacks, tended to be young and childless. Wealthy free people of color were often married. Members of the middle and lower classes, though, often did not marry, because marriage was expensive, requiring legal documents, payments to priests, and customary presents and feasts that could cost as much, put together, as an ordinary workingman could earn in a couple of months. In addition, it was difficult to overcome racial prejudice and the stigma of their own illegitimacy and attract a marriage partner. Whites and free coloreds had intermarried freely before the 1760s, but growing prejudice made this uncommon by the late 18th century. Slaves were married by the JESUIT missionaries of the ROMAN CATHOLIC CHURCH before 1763, but when the Jesuits were expelled from the colony, nobody took over their missions to the slaves. So even though they were frequently parents and often involved in informal sexual relationships, the majority of the city's free coloreds in 1791 were single.

A young, mostly single, childless, middle-class population in a very prosperous city could be expected to have a lively social life, and this indeed was true of the free coloreds of Cap-Français. The stereotype of free coloreds in the colony, popularized by white travelers' accounts and the anti–free colored propaganda of the revolutionary period, portrayed all free colored women as prostitutes or concubines of white men (see PROSTITUTES AND COURTESANS). This was not true of the vast majority of free colored women in the colony, but Cap-Français was home to several hundred young single women of color, many of them mixed-race, who were frequently courted by white men, from whom they expected lavish presents but not marriage.

But most of Cap-Français's free people of color, male and female, worked as businesspeople and participated in the enormous commercial vitality of the town. The mixed-race businessman VINCENT OGÉ, leader of the rebel forces in the early days of the revolution, owned warehouses, town houses for rental, and ships engaged in the interisland trade and lived in a stately house, with his widowed mother. A mixed-race businesswoman, ZABEAU BELLANTON, was an important buyer and seller of slaves, as well as having a number of other small businesses, and may have played an important role in the enormous illegal trade of the island. She retired before the revolution and apparently lived out her days in comfort in France. Alongside these remarkably wealthy individuals were many smaller businesspeople, from retail shopkeepers to skilled tradesmen to real estate developers.

While the great sugar plantations were mostly owned by whites, free people of color owned many of the smaller plantations in the hinterland of Cap-Français. These small planters often had business interests in the city. Indeed, many of them had started as urban businesspeople and had then reinvested their profits in a farm. Owning a plantation gave social status in the society of the colony, even to a person of color. So the declaration by Pierre Augustin in a notarized bill of sale in 1782 that, having purchased a plantation in the neighboring parish of Limbé, he was no longer to be referred to as a wig-maker resident in Cap-Français but instead as a planter is understandable in social terms. It does not mean that Augustin, or any of his fellow planters, abandoned his urban interests. TOUSSAINT LOUVERTURE, future leader of the Haitian revolutionary forces, who had a plantation in Haut du Cap a few miles from the town, also had urban real estate interests through his wife and visited the town regularly. While Toussaint was born and raised in the countryside, many cases such as that of Augustin suggest that retirement to the countryside with age and perhaps with the maturation of children who could take one's place in the urban environment was a common practice.

Many public institutions in the town were not open to them—they could not join the Sociète des Philosophes or belong to the library. When institutions were open to them, it was often on a discriminatory basis: People of color had to sit in the lesser seats at the theater and could not have the padded kneelers in church. There were some social institutions that were specific to people of color, as, for example, the Maison de Charité, the poorhouse and hospital, of the free coloreds. One institution that was important to them was the colonial armed forces. Many free men of color, especially free blacks and those mixed-race individuals with no known family ties to whites, were very active in the MILITIA and seem to have used it as a way to connect to each other and to build patronage relationships with their white officers. The Catholic Church had a role in their lives probably greater than it did for whites; free people of color in Saint-Domingue were about twice as likely to include specific religious language in their wills as whites.

Thus, the free population of color in Cap-Français during the colonial period was like that of other port cities of the Caribbean in many ways. The wealth of the urban environment gave them many opportunities to make a living and, for some, to become wealthy. They tended to be young and single, and they had an uninhibited social life. On the other hand, like people of color throughout the Americas, they were apparently more devout than their white neighbors. In other ways, they were unlike populations of color found in other colonies. The connection with the rural free population of color was much stronger than that found in British colonies, for example, where people of color were sharply limited in ownership of land and slaves. The important role military service played in their lives was in striking contrast to the situation found in British colonies, although similar to the situation in Spanish colonies where there were many people of African ancestry.

Cap-Français/Cap-Haïtien during the Revolution

All discussions of Saint-Domingue/Haiti must include a investigation of the effects of the Haitian Revolution, one of the most decisive political events in the Americas. For Cap-Français, this event was truly decisive as it resulted in the devastation of the "Paris of the Antilles" and the demotion of the city, under its new name, to the sleepy secondary port city that it is today.

The first shots of the Haitian Revolution were fired only a few miles from Cap-Français, in the rural district of Grande Rivière, where Vincent Ogé and JEAN-BAPTISTE CHAVANNES rallied the free men of color of the province to strike for equal rights in 1790. Their movement was a failure, as regular troops from the city's garrison quickly overwhelmed their small force of militiamen and rural constables, chasing them into the Spanish part of the island, from whence they were extradited back to Cap-Français for public torture and execution.

Ogé and Chavannes did not welcome slaves into their movement; indeed, they both owned slaves themselves, and their political goal was full inclusion of wealthy free people of color in a slave-owning society. But when the slaves rebelled, in 1791, Cap-Français's free people of color played an important role. The first leaders of the slave uprising were slaves themselves, but the man who kept the movement together and led it to its final victory, Toussaint Louverture, was a free man of color, a resident of a suburb of Cap-Français before the revolution. Many of the wealthy free people of color fought for the French, in defense of their slave-worked plantations, while poorer free coloreds, such as Toussaint, often supported the slave rebels. In their first uprising, the slaves tried and failed to capture the city, and then they besieged it off and on for two years. When the French government finally abolished slavery in 1794, Toussaint Louverture and the rebel slaves became loyal French soldiers, and Cap-Français was his headquarters. During one of the internecine struggles of the revolution, the city was set aflame and many structures burned.

During the revolutionary period, the distinction between former free people of color and former slaves eroded, especially among the soldiers of Toussaint's army. Former free coloreds had the education, military background, and resources to serve at higher ranks, though, and many of Toussaint's officers were from this class.

After his final victory over the forces of the South Province, led by the free colored general ANDRÉ RIGAUD, Toussaint moved his headquarters to Port-au-Prince and left his general Henry Christophe, who had been a slave at the outbreak of the revolution, in command in Cap-Français. Christophe rebuilt the city and established something of an independent power base in the North. When Napoléon sent an expedition to crush the autonomy of Toussaint's government and reestablish slavery, the fleet arrived first at Cap-Français. General Leclerc, the French commander, ordered Christophe to evacuate the city, but Christophe replied that Toussaint must give any such orders and that if the French tried to land without permission, he would burn the city to the ground and fight to the death in the ruins. He performed the first half of his vow, though after sharp fighting he and his surviving troops surrendered to Leclerc. The French finally captured Toussaint and sent him off to prison in France, and the revolution seemed over.

However, political miscalculations byLeclerc—allowing the blacks to realize that his mission was to reestablish the slave system—combined with the ever-increasing toll of disease among the French forces encouraged the colony's people to resist. Christophe and the other officers of Toussaint's army slipped away one by one to take up arms in the countryside. The main army was in the West, around Port-au-Prince, but Christophe waged a determined insurgency against the French forces in the North so that they could not go to the aid of their comrades in the West. The French responded with brutal violence, hanging or drowning most of the former free coloreds who had fled for protection to Cap-Français. Finally, the French were defeated, with the climactic battle taking place at Vertières, just outside the walls of Cap-Français, in November 1803. The French survivors surrendered to the British navy and were evacuated to JAMAICA, and the Haitian army marched in on January 1, 1804. The overall commander, Jean-Jacques Dessalines, the first ruler of independent Haiti, marked the occasion by changing the city's name to Cap-Haïtien and slaughtering most of the few white inhabitants who had remained behind.

The city never recovered from the devastation of the wartime years. Cap-Français's role had always been as a commercial center, and the mainstay of that commerce was sugar and coffee cultivation. The plantation system never recovered, despite the best efforts of Toussaint and Christophe. They had redistributed the plantation land to military officers, many former free people of color, and required all former slaves to work on their former plantations for a set wage, on pain of imprisonment at forced labor. Former slaves were not interested in working on plantations, though, even for wages, and in the unsettled condition of the times no amount of force could make them. They mainly moved to the mountains and began subsistence farming, while the enormous sugar fields lay fallow. To this day, there are large uninhabited tracts in the Plaine du Nord, while peasants intensively cultivate the hillsides.

The former free people of color gravitated to the town in the postindependence years. What small commerce still continued provided a living for a greatly diminished population.

Stewart R. King

FURTHER READING

Geggus, David. "The Major Port Towns of Saint-Domingue in the Later Eighteenth Century." In *Atlantic Port Cities: Economy, Culture, and Society in the Atlantic World, 1650–1850*, edited by Franklin Knight, and Peggy Liss, 87–116. Knoxville: University of Tennessee Press, 1991.

King, Stewart. *Blue Coat or Powdered Wig: Free People of Color in Pre-Revolutionary Saint-Domingue.* Athens: University of Georgia Press, 2001.

Moreau de St.-Méry, Médéric Louis Élie. *Description Topographique, Physique Civile, Politique et Historique de La Partie Française de l'Isle de Saint-Domingue.* Paris: printed privately, 1788 [1797]. Reprint of second edition, edited by Blanche Maurel and Etienne Taillemite. Paris: Société de l'Histoire des Colonies Françaises, 1958.

CAP-HAÏTIEN.   *See* CAP-FRANÇAIS/CAP-HAÏTIEN.

CAPTAIN CUDJOE   (dates of birth and death uncertain, active 1690–1739)   *Jamaican maroon leader*

The history of Africans in the Americas throughout the slavery era was often one of revolution and resistance. Nowhere was this demonstrated more than in the Caribbean colonies, where, by 1700, slaves greatly outnumbered their European masters. On the islands, notably in JAMAICA, slaves organized large-scale uprisings and rebellions—repeatedly and often violently. Planters lived in constant fear of a slave revolt. Perhaps the most famous of all the rebels in the Caribbean were the runaway MAROONS of Jamaica. Known for their daring, love for liberty, self-sufficiency, and political independence from British rule, they established one of the most enduring communities of freed blacks and a remarkable record of successful resistance to plantation society.

The greatest and best-known of the Jamaican maroons was "Captain Cudjoe," who was selected by his community to lead a group of slaves from Clarendon parish who rebelled in 1690 against their masters and sought refuge in the interior parts of the island. The mountains where they fled, called the Cockpit Country, were unsuitable for sugar cultivation, and coffee had not yet been introduced into Jamaica. Thus, the maroons had a stronghold that was also not especially attractive to European settlers. Cudjoe's date and place of birth are not exactly known, but his name *Cudjoe* suggests he was from the Gold Coast, now modern-day Ghana. Active from 1690 to 1739, he was portrayed by a contemporary observer, a British officer named R. C. Dallas, as a "fearless soldier," "illiterate," an "unshapely Coromantee," and "a bold, skillful, and enterprising man." *Coromantee* was the anglicized spelling of the Gold Coast port of Koromantine, where slaves who either were Akan or had been enslaved by Akan were sold into the Atlantic slave trade. Cudjoe is a common name among Akan and other peoples of the region. Dallas, who met him for the first time during peace negotiations in 1739, described him as a

> rather a short man, uncommonly stout, with very strong African features and a peculiar wildness in his manners. He had a very large lump of flesh upon his back. Around his head was tied a scanty piece of white cloth so very dirty that its original color might have been doubted. He wore no shirt and his clothes . . . were covered with the red dirt resembling ochre. He had on a pair of loose drawers that did not reach to his knees and a small round hat with the rims pared so close to the crown that it might have been taken for a calabash. Such was the

chief, and his men were as ragged and as dirty as himself: all were armed with guns and cutlasses.

Cudjoe and fellow maroons, who were possibly his brothers and sister or else pseudokin, Nanny, Accompong, Johnny, and Quao, caused severe problems for the British. Surviving in the mountains of northern Jamaica and forming a loose confederation of runaway slaves and small gangs, they continuously harassed the planters by raiding plantations for weapons and food, burning crops, destroying cattle, trading with slaves and enticing them to run away, sometimes even carrying off slaves by force. By 1730, these former slaves, under Cudjoe, had terrorized the whites to such an extent that Britain sent two additional regiments to protect the planters. The planters lived in constant fear and had complained to the British legislators, who made Cudjoe's capture and execution the primary objective of the colonial army. But Cudjoe and his band of fugitive slaves stood their ground. Armed and battle-ready, they fought frequent battles with the European militias for nearly 30 years. As Thomas Thistlewood, a plantation overseer in Jamaica's Westmoreland parish, noted in his diary, "Col Cudgoe's Negroes behaved with great bravery." Cudjoe had grown so strong that some of the old British settlers thought it was best to abandon their plantations and return home. It was commonly said, "General Williamson the British Commander rules Jamaica by day and Captain Cudjoe by night."

Cudjoe's successful exploits were too much for the British to bear. In 1734, the government decided to make a redoubled effort to capture him. The British built forts and outposts near the maroon settlements and employed hundreds of Central American Afro-Indians to hunt them down. Cudjoe and his maroons prevailed, but in due time, despite their victories, the superior arms of the slaveholders began to wear them down. One of the maroon camps on a high mountain was attacked, and nearly everyone was killed. But Cudjoe devised a clever scheme, escaped to another part of the island, and staged yet another major raid. Cudjoe's men fought on for another four years. In desperation, the government planned another expedition against him. But it was unsuccessful, and in the end, the colonial authorities reversed course and sought a peace treaty with Cudjoe and the maroon forces. In 1739, after some 50 years of warfare, the British agreed to a treaty that granted Cudjoe and his people full independence and a large tract of land, more than 1,500 acres in the Clarendon area, for farming. They also agreed to exempt the maroons from all taxation in perpetuity and grant them permission to hunt anywhere on the island, except within three miles of a white settlement. In return, the Jamaican maroons promised to return all runaway slaves whom they found or who entered their settlements.

The Jamaican maroons became a settled community of free people of color after this peace treaty. They still had run-ins with the local authorities, and a large group of them were exiled from the colony in the 1780s, first to Nova Scotia in CANADA and then to SIERRA LEONE, where they combined with the American black Loyal-ists and recaptured slaves to be the ancestors of the Krio people. But Cudjoe's descendants in the Trelawney area remained neutral in that conflict and still live in Jamaica today. The Cockpit Country maroons remained separate from the other Jamaican populations of color—the plan-tation slaves and the urban free colored community—and even after abolition retained a separate identity.

Henry Codjoe

A 19th-century engraving of the meeting between Captain Cudjoe and the British colonel John Guthrie in 1739, in which the Jamaican colonial government agreed to recognize the independence of Cudjoe's maroon colony, give them title to the land they occupied, and agree not to harass them as long as they refrained from attacking plantations and allowing slaves to run away and join their group. The descendants of Cudjoe's band of maroons still inhabit Trelawney Town in the Jamaican mountains. *(The Granger Collection, New York)*

FURTHER READING

Blackburn, Robin. *The Making of New World Slavery: From the Baroque to the Modern, 1492–1800.* London: Verso, 1997.

Campbell, Mavis C. *The Maroons of Jamaica, 1655–1796.* Trenton, N.J.: Africa World Press, 1990.

Craton, Michael. *Testing the Chains: Resistance to Slavery in the British West Indies.* Ithaca, N.Y.: Cornell University Press, 1982.

Hall, Douglas. *In Miserable Slavery: Thomas Thistlewood in Jamaica, 1750–86.* Kingston, Jamaica: University of West Indies Press, 1989.

Harris, Joseph E. *Africans and Their History.* New York: Meridian Press, 1998.

CARTAGENA

Colonial Period (1521–1808)

From the beginning of the colonial period in the 16th century, Cartagena in present-day Colombia became one of the most important strongholds and commercial cities in Spanish America. The reasons for this lie, on the one hand, in the natural protection the bay offered against the attack of pirates and privateers and, on the other hand, in its location adjacent to the mouth of the Magdalena River, the main route for entering into the interior of the Vice-Royalty of New Granada (today's Colombia). For more than three hundred years, Cartagena received the fleets regularly dispatched from Spain loaded with European goods, the same ones that would return to Europe loaded with the treasures in gold, silver, and other products from the Americas. In addition, because of its position facing the Caribbean, it also established commercial connections with island possessions of other colonial powers, most commonly through contraband. By the late 18th century, this activity had become the most important part of the city's economy, despite the efforts imperial authorities undertook to suppress it. It was for these reasons that it became the center of a large continental trade network that stretched from its immediate hinterland, through New Granada, and down to Quito and Peru.

As was generally the case in Spanish America, the city and its immediate hinterland, including the Magdalena Valley, were tied together under the same municipal government, and so this article will deal not only with the immediate urban area but also with the surrounding province.

One of the activities Cartagena was renowned for was its participation in the African slave trade. It has been estimated that from the 16th to the 19th century more than 200,000 slaves were introduced to the South American mainland through Cartagena's port alone. Many of them remained within the boundaries of the Province

of Cartagena, but most were sent farther away to work in haciendas, mines, and textile factories *(obrajes)* and to perform other kinds of manual labor in Peru, Quito, and other parts of New Grenada. As happened in other parts of Hispanic America, the absence of white women favored MISCEGENATION between the conquerors and black and Indian females. Along the northern coast of South America, including New Granada and the Captaincy-General of Venezuela, and other parts of the Hispanic Caribbean, such as CUBA and SANTO DOMINGO, where the Indian population had been decimated, most of the interracial unions took place between Spaniards and their female slaves. In consequence, the Caste (CASTA) sector there was formed mostly of mixed-blood individuals of Euro-African heritage, known together as PARDO. As the Spanish legislation on slave MANUMISSION allowed Spanish men to emancipate the children they had with their women slaves, many *pardos* attained freedom. This was the most important reason behind the spectacular growth of that racial sector, which became the most numerous in Cartagenian society, outnumbering whites, slaves, Indians, and free blacks.

By the end of the 18th century, that tendency continued still, as *pardo* single women were very numerous, almost twice as many as their male counterparts. This phenomenon encouraged informal unions with white males, increasing through their offspring the mixed-race population of the city. According to an estimate based on census records from 1777, the city had 13,690 inhabitants, of whom 4,034 were whites, 2,584 slaves, 88 Indians, and as many as 6,745 "Free People of all Colors" *(Libre de todos los colores),* nearly half the population. It is important to underline that the latter was a residual category that included all those persons who were not either white, Indian, or slave, such as ZAMBOS (persons of mixed African and native ancestry), mestizos (persons of mixed Native and European ancestry), free blacks, and, most commonly, mixed-blood individuals of European and African ancestry. The many mixtures resulting from the unions of blacks, *pardos*, and Europeans astonished the Spaniards as at times they may seem to violate a certain chromatic logic: A Sevillian priest who lived in Cartagena in the late 17th century, Alonso de Sandoval, described how dark-skinned parents could have lighter-skinned children, and how sisters of Afro-European ancestry could be different from each other in both color and phenotype.

To establish order on the confusion generated by so many mixtures, the Spaniards made use of categories already existing in the Iberian Peninsula and even created several more, as represented in New Spain's Casta Paintings (Pinturas de Castas). The categories existing in Cartagena were described by the Spanish travelers Jorge Juan and Antonio de Ulloa in the report they made for the

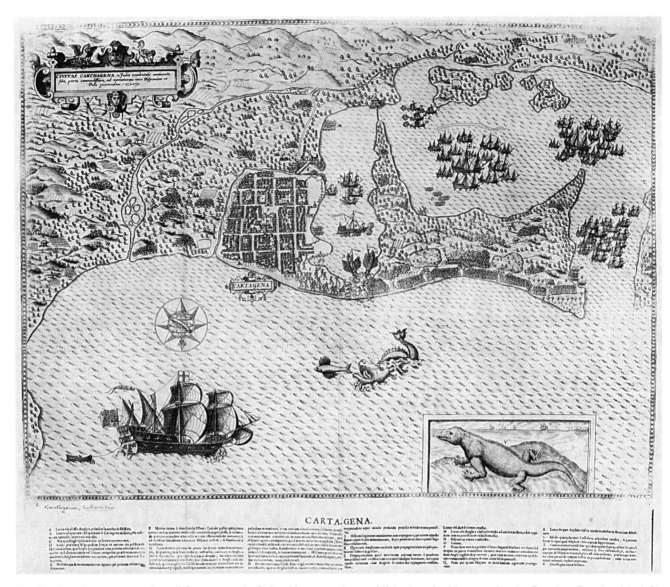

Hand-colored map engraving of Cartagena de Colombia, recently established and without walls, by Baptista Boazio, titled *Sir Francis Drake in Cartagena, 1585.* Cartagena was one of the most important slave-trading ports in the Spanish Empire in the 17th century. The Jesuit mission in Cartagena, responsible for evangelizing the newly arrived slaves, protected some of them against their masters and helped others obtain their freedom. The city eventually gained a large free black and mixed-race population, which played a role in the proindependence coalition during the Colombian War of Independence (1808–21). *(The Granger Collection, New York)*

Spanish government, *Secret News on America (Noticias secretas de América)*, after a scientific expedition they made to Peru, Quito, and New Granada in 1735. In this text, Juan and Ullúa describe from a scientific perspective—much earlier than Alexander von Humboldt and Médéric-Louis-Élie Moreau de St-Méry—the origins of the many racially mixed categories they observed there, including zambo (offspring of black or *pardo* plus Indian), mulatto (of white and black), *tercerón* (of white and mulatto), quadroon (of white and *tercerón*), and quinteron (of white plus quadroon).

According to this and other testimonies, when a person belonged to the highest levels of Euro-African misce-genation (quadroons, *quinterones*), he or she could hardly be visually differentiated from whites. This was a crucial issue in the Hispanic world, where one's "quality" *(calidad)* conditioned one's status in society, establishing limitations or granting privileges to each person. The logic behind this valorization originated in the Iberian idea of the "purity of blood" of Old Christians, an outgrowth of the fears southern Spaniards felt from the 16th century onward of Muslim and Jewish converts to Catholicism (New Christians) and their descendants living among them. In the Americas, particularly in places where free people of color were numerous, African ancestry also made one unqualified to be considered white or Spaniard.

Other factors taken into account to establish the "quality" of the person was the class or status background of his or her family. Thus a qualification would be positive if one had aristocratic ancestry, or very negative if in the family tree could be found a stain of illegitimacy. This latter aspect affected in particular mixed-blood individuals such as *pardo*s, whose ancestors had often been conceived outside marriage.

Free coloreds experienced many limitations in Spanish America from having an inferior condition, including social segregation, such as being prohibited to walk the streets alongside whites, or formal measures of discrimination, such as prohibition from employment in the public sector, restrictions on the right to bear arms, or be promoted beyond the grade of captain in the militia. Nevertheless, by the end of the 18th century, many of the wealthiest and most "whitened" Cartagenian *pardo*s had successfully crossed the line of color and gained some of the privileges reserved to whites, such as being addressed as *don* or *doña* in legal document, or becoming priests and nuns. One free person of color was appointed professor in the local Catholic seminary, and some had even managed to marry their daughters to renowned whites. Normally, *pardo* elite attempts to improve their socioracial status would be opposed by the white Creoles in a violent manner, either individually (through attacks and insults) or collectively (from the local town hall or *cabildo*).

The color hierarchies also affected the way individuals made a living. Thus, in Cartagena, manual labor was performed mostly by free blacks and zambos, never by whites and seldom by *pardo*s; higher-skilled professions, such as different sorts of craftsmen (carpenters, blacksmiths, barbers) mostly by *pardo*s, but also by whites; and other more specialized activities, such as shopkeepers and bakers, mostly by whites but also by *pardo*s. That hierarchical notion also shaped the spatial distribution in Hispanic-American cities. In Cartagena, whites and free coloreds often lived by one another in the same borough, block, or even building. Nevertheless, there were two urban areas where this hardly happened: The area surrounding the cathedral was inhabited by whites belonging to the elite, as living there was a symbol of social status, while the *barrio* of Saint Mary de Getsemaní, outside the city walls, where 30 percent of the population of the city lived, was inhabited mostly by free coloreds. In general, they overwhelmingly dominated the human landscape of Cartagena, as was reported by the travelers Juan and Ullúa, who asserted that "you do not see other people in all the city streets; in the farms, and the towns; and it is only by chance that you come across white people." By the end of the 18th century, the population of the Cartagena had grown to 17,600, and most of it was still "of all colors."

The 18th century was a period of reform in Spanish America. These reforms were instituted by the new ruling House of Bourbon, which rose to power in Spain as a result of the War of the Spanish Succession (1700–14), and so they are called the Bourbon Reforms after their architects. The reforming spirit was first felt as early as 1720, but the reforms had their greatest effect after mid-century, when Spain and its American colonies entered a period of economic growth and more effective government. Among the costs of the reforms, though, were budgetary restrictions on local government, which reduced investment in the city's defense forces. Many free coloreds relied on MILITIA service for at least a part of their income. This and other factors fostered an economic crisis that would affect the most populous sectors of the city, causing distress among them. This factor is essential to understand what happened when Cartagena established an autonomous government that caused disorder in the metropolis in 1810, a process in which free coloreds played an important role.

Struggle for Independence (1808–1821)

When news from Spain began to arrive of the setting up of assemblies, or juntas, after Napoléon's occupation of Spain in 1808, local white CREOLES reacted in an attempt to create autonomous governments. By 1810, the city was in a deep economic crisis, due to the irregular arrival of funds from the viceroyalty's central government in Bogotá, and to growing commercial competition with the cities of Mompox and Santa Marta. This situation had been aggravated because of the growing vigilance against contraband (the main income source of the city) carried out by Spanish coast guards, and the austerity policies introduced as part of the Bourbon Reforms from the late 18th century, which had increased from the arrival of Governor Don Francisco Montes in October 1809. Among these policies stood out the suspension of public works on the city's defenses and the transfer of two battalions from the Fijo garrison (composed of peninsular Spaniards) to Bogotá, the capital, to cut down expenses. These decisions left many colored individuals without work, since their employment depended very much on tasks and occupations associated with the defense of the city.

This situation facilitated the work of white creoles to gain their support for the cause of forming an autonomous government in Cartagena. For this purpose one of them, José María García de Toledo, contacted colored leaders (some of them members of the local *pardo* militia garrisons) of the districts of the Cathedral, Saint Toribio, and, most specially, Saint Mary de Getsemaní. His objective was to establish an alliance with them, so the *pardo* militias would intervene to control any reaction by the remaining troops of the Fijo regiment, when the time came to overthrow Montes. Perhaps the most important of those leaders was Pedro Romero, a *pardo* blacksmith born in the region of Matanzas, Cuba, who lived in the district of Getsemaní around 1756. Romero must have been very prosperous as he had his own workshop located at the entrance of Getsemaní, with his two sons and his brother. The high socioeconomic level he had among the Cartagena free colored community is apparent from the fact he had married some of his daughters to white men and that six months earlier he had made a request to the king to waive racial restrictions for his son, so he could be accepted in the university to study philosophy.

Although initially Romero did not much like the plan proposed by García de Toledo (probably fearing loses of his socioeconomic status), shortly afterward, according to testimony in a court of inquiry into the rebellion, he became convinced that the project was possible and would result in a good outcome for the free people of color, and he agreed to cooperate. The alliance between white creoles and free coloreds became evident on June 14, 1810, when members of the town hall *(cabildo)* of Cartagena finally decided to oust the governor. On that day, their actions were supported by an important faction of the town's free blacks, mulattoes, and zambos coming from different parts of the city, headed by their own leaders. Together they forced the Spanish governor (whom they also accused of being pro-French and anti-creole) to quit his position. He was replaced by Colonel Don Blas de Soria. Then, the *cabildo* took over the local colonial government, creating for its defense two battalions of volunteers: one of whites and another of free coloreds. This latter was named Patriotic Lanceros of Getsemaní, in honor of the courageous behavior shown by the inhabitants of the district of the same name, and was placed under the command of Pedro Romero, who was promoted to colonel.

Two months later, on August 14, following the model of those that had been previously formed in Spain, an autonomous government was established: the Supreme Government Assembly of Cartagena (Junta Suprema de Gobierno de Cartagena). This crucial step intended to set up a government not only at the same political level as the one established in the Spanish city of Cádiz but also equal to the one created in Bogotá nearly four weeks earlier. As soon as it received word of the events in Cartagena, the Supreme Regency Council in Spain—the political entity that replaced the junta of Cádiz as head of the imperial government—condemned the action of the Cartagena assembly and appointed a new governor: Jose Dávila. On his arrival at the city gates, the city government forbade him to enter. As a result, he had to stay in a fortress nearby. This decision divided local whites as it meant disobeying the regency, while the *lanceros* of Getsemaní

supported it enthusiastically. During the days Dávila remained near the city, this colored garrison guarded the assembly while many people of color gathered around the palace of government where it had its meetings. Some of them also began to insult whites (both creole and Spaniards) who were royalists, an action that was immediately condemned by García de Toledo, who had been elected president of the assembly. In a decree dated November 9, he threatened to punish those who continued "insulting, murmuring and interpreting in the worst way the most innocent actions of many honest Spaniards." This situation fostered a wave of migration of local whites (including the temporary governor, Blas de Soria) mainly toward Santa Marta, a city that was starting to become a royalist bastion.

Notwithstanding its refusal to allow the entrance of the governor appointed by the regency, Cartagena's assembly had not yet officially broken with Spain. In fact, on December 31, 1810, a public ceremony was organized to recognize the imperial court assembled in the region of Leon, in northwestern Spain, formed by delegates summoned from throughout the empire, including America. That same month, the Cartagena assembly approved an electoral regulation renewing the mandate of the assembly, in which citizens from all towns of the province were invited to take part. This initiative could be interpreted as an expression of the white assembly leaders' willingness to grant further political rights to free coloreds, as it allowed all male householders regardless of the color of their skin (excluding individuals employed by others, those with a criminal background, and the enslaved) the right to vote. Nonetheless, the elections could not take place as the cities of Simití and Mompox decided to form their own autonomous governments. Moreover, the latter town had decided to become a province of its own and not to send delegates to Cartagena's assembly, but to the one in Bogotá. These decisions would put it on a collision course with the assembly of the province.

Mompox was located within the borders of the Province of Cartagena, generating a good part of its fiscal revenues. When in September 1810 the Supreme Assembly of Cartagena realized that the people of Mompox sought to separate themselves from the rest of the province, a confrontation between the cities broke out. This town had followed a very similar political course to that already seen in Cartagena: On August 6, 1810, many white creoles had overthrown the colonial government, with the support of the local free colored population. Those whites were of a more radical political tendency than their counterparts in Cartagena, as is shown by the fact that many of them emancipated their slaves immediately after the coup had succeeded. Among them was Vicente Caledonio Gutiérrez de Piñeres, a prosperous businessman, who would later become president of Mompox's assembly. Here, the town hall had also formed battalions of white and *pardo* volunteers, who were defeated by Cartagena's forces when they ran out of ammunition. The conflict would end on January 23, 1811, with the occupation of Mompox by Cartagenian forces.

The campaign against Mompox was commanded by the Spanish officer Antonio Jose de Ayos. This encouraged royalist whites in Cartagena to carry out an attempt to overthrow the autonomous government and impose the authority of the regency council in Spain. The coup took place on February 14, 1811, and although it was quickly controlled by the military high command, whose members remained loyal to the Supreme Assembly, it did not prevent an angry reaction by the free colored population. Testimonies describe hundreds of armed mulattoes, free blacks, and zambos running in the streets, chasing and arresting the whites implicated in the conspiracy, some of whom were imprisoned in the barracks of the *pardo* battalion commanded by Pedro Romero. This situation made whites feel threatened by free coloreds, thus triggering a new exodus toward Santa Marta and producing a fracture in the alliance that until then had supported proautonomist white creoles and free colored leaders.

At this time, news arrived from Spain that the Cortes of Cádiz, the national assembly of Spain, had denied equal representation to American Spaniards and refused equality of rights to all free persons of African descent. These developments pushed free colored leaders closer to the position of the more radical whites. These were in favor of absolute independence from Spain and equality of rights for all citizens, including free coloreds. Their leader was paradoxically a man from Mompox, who had been appointed delegate before the province's first assembly of 1810. His name was Gabriel Gutiérrez de Piñeres, brother of the former president of that city's autonomous assembly. Among the leaders were yet another of his brothers, Germán, and a lawyer from Corozal, Ignacio Muñoz, who also was son-in-law of Pedro Romero. They were opposed to white conservatives, whom they accused of adopting aristocratic attitudes and of having ferociously crushed the self-government initiative of Mompox. They had been exerting pressure for a declaration of independence from Spain from at least mid-1811, through articles published in their newspaper, *El Argos Americano*, and petitions they raised before the Supreme Assembly.

By November 11, 1811, tired of waiting for a decision, they decided to act. Members of the colored battalion took positions on the city walls, aiming the batteries of cannons at the barracks of the Fijo and white regiments, while Romero and Gutiérrez de Piñeres gathered the people in a church in the district of Getsemaní. Then they assaulted the armory and forced the opening of the main city gate. Once in front of the government palace, they sent a delegation into the room where the assembly met, demanding that its members immediately declare independence from Spain. They also made other demands, including equality of rights for all free coloreds and the appointment of colored officers for the *pardo* and artillery battalions. Under such pressure, members of the assembly had no alternative but to declare that same day the independence of the Province of Cartagena. They also agreed on summoning elections to form a constituent assembly that would grant a constitution to the newborn state of Cartagena, ruled by the electoral law approved on December 1810. The inclusive character of this law in relation to nonwhites led to three *pardos'* being elected as constituents, among whom was Pedro Romero. The constitution sanctioned on June 5, 1812, not only granted suffrage to free coloreds, but also suppressed the slave trade and opened the doors for the establishment of a manumission fund.

The hegemony of the radical faction headed by Gabriel Gutiérrez de Piñeres in Cartagena political life extended until the end of 1814. During that time, as a result of the downfall of the Venezuelan Second Republic in 1814 and the offering of "Letters of Marque" by the independent government to privateers to finance the war against Spain, the streets began to show the presence of many outsiders, mostly French Antilleans and Venezuelans. After a controversial election to choose a new constituent assembly and an intense political struggle between conservatives and radicals, the government was handed over to the Venezuelan Pedro Gual. Fearing a popular insurrection and the eventual formation of a government led by colored people headed by the mulatto Pedro Medrano, the new governor made an alliance with white conservatives, other Venezuelans, and the French Antilleans. Then the colored military units were withdrawn from key positions, their members disarmed, and the brothers Gutiérrez de Piñeres expelled to the United States—although on their way there they stopped in Haiti.

In August 1815, the army dispatched from Spain under the command of General Pablo Morillo to reconquer the mainland of northern South America surrounded the city of Cartagena by land and sea. After two months of siege, the defenders made a desperate attempt to escape to the Caribbean. Many were caught, tried, and executed, while others managed to reach Haiti. Among the latter was Pedro Romero, but he died shortly after his arrival of starvation. The brothers Gutiérrez de Piñeres, who were already in Haiti, did not have better luck: Germán died at Les Cayes, whereas Gabriel and Vicente Caledonio (who in 1816 had joined Simón Bolívar in a campaign against the coast of Venezuela) were executed, along with some relatives and many other patriots, at the fortress of

Barcelona. The royalist occupation of Cartagena would last until October 10, 1821, when after a long siege the Spanish governor decided to surrender the city after receiving the news that proindependence vessels commanded by Admiral José Prudencio Padilla (a *pardo*) had crushed the Spanish fleet at Animas Bay.

National Period (1821–1900)

The 1821 recapture of Cartagena by proindependence forces from royalist hands marked the final victory of the patriotic forces in the region. As a result of the violence of the independence war and successive migrations, its population had been reduced to 11,929, a third less than it had been in 1809. The city had been greatly affected by the conflict, in particular the barrio of Getsemaní, where most lower-class residents including many free people of color lived, half of which had been destroyed. Although the city had declined from the level of wealth it had attained in colonial times, it still was the most important city on the Caribbean coast of Colombia because of its position near the mouth of the Magdalena River. In 1821 in Cucuta, a new constitution was adopted for Gran Colombia, a short-lived republic formed by the present-day countries of Ecuador, Venezuela, and Colombia. The constitution included a manumission fund for gradually abolishing slavery and ensured the political equality of all free citizens without distinctions of color. It also established an indirect system of representation, very similar to the one designed in Cartagena in December 1810, in which free colored men were allowed to vote.

Notwithstanding the inclusive nature of that constitution, free coloreds were still regarded with suspicion by many white creoles. From 1822 to 1824, whites from the towns of Algarrobo and Majagual several times accused the Alcalde Mayor of the latter city, Valentín Arcia, who was a free mixed-race man, of promoting race war against them. For this reason he was arrested and tried in Cartagena, where he remained imprisoned for three years until the central government ordered him released. According to the testimony presented during the trial, he had warned the whites that if they continued to treat the people of color badly, they would turn against them. The unrest among poorer colored people was more intense in the city of Mompox, where disturbances broke out in 1823 when authorities attempted to recruit more men for the republican armed forces. The troops of Gran Colombia were still fighting royalist forces in Peru and Bolivia, and free nonwhites made up a large percentage of both sides' armies. The former regional commander, the *pardo* Colonel Remigio Marquéz, was accused of encouraging "insolent" behavior and of having fostered a racial conflict.

The mistrust many white creoles manifested toward free coloreds was shared by many members of the political elite, in particular by the president of the republic, the Venezuelan "Liberator," Simón Bolívar. Bolívar had often expressed his concerns about the free coloreds' taking over the government and establishing *pardo* rule or *Pardocracia*, as he called it. Previously, at Angostura in 1817, he had accused the *pardo* general Manuel Piar, who had challenged his leadership, of promoting race war, for which he was executed by a firing squad after having been found guilty by a military court. In 1828, colored lower classes revolted once again, this time in Cartagena, against Bolívar's plan to reform the constitution of 1821. A very prestigious colored officer, the *pardo* admiral José Padilla, headed the movement, which led to his arrest by Bolívar's followers on charges of sedition. When Padilla attempted to reconcile himself with the president of the republic, he was tried and executed for sedition. After the collapse of Gran Colombia, a new constitution was established for the Colombian Republic alone in 1830. It again ensured the people formerly called "Free of All Colors" *(Libres de todos los colores)* the right to citizenship, in the same terms as did the constitution promulgated in Cucuta almost a decade earlier.

The free Afro-Colombian population of Cartagena and its surrounding region continued to be the largest and strongest such community in the country throughout the 19th century. With legal rights assured, they worked for social equality. One common means of attaining social equality throughout Spanish America was assimilation into the larger community. A process of "whitening" and racial promotion through intermarriage and adoption of Hispanic cultural elements had been occuring since colonial times; this accelerated after independence when the legal restrictions on Afro-Colombians were removed. Nonetheless, with such a large population of African descent, the Cartagena region retains a distinctively Afro-Caribbean culture, and its people have a "coastal" identity that celebrates their African character. The region's best-known musical style, *cumbia*, uses the *guacharaca*, a percussion instrument with African roots. In the late 20th century, a revival of African identity and culture encouraged more Afro-Colombians to seek or acknowledge their African identity, making today's Cartagena the most distinctively Afro-Caribbean city of Spanish South America.

Alejandro E. Gomez

FURTHER READING

Bethell, Leslie. "The Independence of Spanish South America." In *The Independence of Spanish America,* edited by Leslie Bethell. New York: Cambridge University Press, 1991.

Grahn, Lance. "Cartagena and Its Hinterland in the Late Eigh-teenth Century." In *Atlantic Port Cities: Economy, Culture, and Society in the Atlantic World, 1650–1850*, edited by Franklin Knight and Peggy Liss, 168–195. Knoxville: University of Tennessee Press, 1991.

Helg, Aline. "Simón Bolívar and the Spectre of Pardocracia: José Padilla in Post-Independence Cartagena." *Journal of Latin American Studies* 35, no. 3 (August 2003): 447–471.

Lynch, John. *Simón Bolívar: A Life*. New Haven, Conn.: Yale University Press, 2006.

McFarlane, Anthony. *Columbia before Independence: Economy, Society and Politics under Bourbon Rule*. New York: Cambridge University Press, 1993.

CASTA

Casta is a general term used in Spanish America for any person of mixed race and was not considered derogatory in the past. This included those people referred to as *pardos*, mulattos, mestizos, and a wide variety of other racial definitions. There is a famous series of paintings from Mexico, the Casta Paintings (Pinturas de Castas), created by variety of artists in the 18th century, which illustrate the various subdivisions of the *casta* group and, by the way these groups are depicted, tell us what characteristics of mind, character, education, and social standing were associated in the public mind with each group.

Stewart R. King

FURTHER READING

Katzew, Ilona. *Casta Paintings: Images of Race in Colonial Mexico*. New Haven, Conn.: Yale University Press, 2004.

CATHOLIC CONFRATERNITIES

Confraternities are lay social organizations formed by free men and women of color in colonial Latin America. They helped enslaved Africans and their descendants, both free and enslaved, forge an enduring link to the ROMAN CATHOLIC CHURCH. Both men and women joined and led these Catholic organizations. In Spanish, confraternities were called *cofradías, hermandades, congregaciones,* or *cabildos*. In Portuguese, the term was *irmandade*. Afro-Catholic confraternities existed in many cities throughout colonial Latin America, many of them poor and marginalized. Unfortunately, many records have been lost over the centuries, and for that reason, most of the evidence is restricted to brotherhoods in Cuba, Brazil, and Mexico. Although brotherhoods in all of these regions shared many characteristics, variations in the diffusion of the African diaspora led brotherhoods in each area to develop noticeable differences.

While clergymen encouraged and helped found confraternities, lay people maintained them. Africans and their descendants who lived in Iberia from the mid-15th century had their own Catholic brotherhoods. The Portuguese introduced their confraternities to all of their colonial outposts, including those in Africa. In the Americas, these organizations continued to thrive well into the 19th century and exist in Brazil even today. In Spanish America, Africans and their descendants organized and led brotherhoods based in parish churches. Convent churches and cathedrals often had several confraternities, which were established in chapels and side altars throughout the edifice. Confraternities revolved around maintaining a chapel and celebrating festivals connected to the Holy Sacrament, Jesus, the Virgin Mary, or Benedict of Palermo, a Franciscan friar who was the son of African slaves. The Virgin of the Immaculate Conception and Our Lady of the Rosary were two of the most popular recipients of confraternal devotion. Other confraternities dedicated themselves to honoring an aspect of Catholic doctrine connected to Jesus Christ. Throughout the African diaspora in Latin America, brotherhoods existed wherever Africans were eager to maintain their social ties, religious beliefs, and heritage.

Other confraternities focused their activities on Holy Week processions, in which they presented various aspects of the Passion of Christ. In colonial Mexico, people of color founded at least 60 brotherhoods, and among those, at least eight practiced public flagellation as part of a penitential procession during Holy Week. Members viewed these practices as a way to recreate and experience Christ's suffering and crucifixion and as a display of their Christian piety. Men, women, and children walked in the penitential processions, although only men participated in the flagellation. Women carried candles and images of saints. Penitential brotherhoods had names such as the Exaltation of the Holy True Cross and the Tears of Saint Peter or the Humility of Christ.

As organizations that drew people together socially, confraternities celebrated yearly fiestas, which included music, dances, food, drinking, and firework displays, all financed by the brotherhood. Confraternities also had important charitable functions, including care for sick members. In addition, confraternities provided shrouds and burials for their members, as well as annual masses for the souls in purgatory, since many feared that their souls would languish in purgatory because they lacked sufficient family and friends to pray for them after death. Members believed that prayers were more effective and more likely to receive saintly intercession when said by a group. For this reason, if an individual could afford to pay the dues, he or she might join numerous confraternities. Slaves also feared that their bodies would be neglected when they died and treated as debris to be thrown away. Confraternity members who failed to attend a fellow member's funeral lost the privilege of having a large funeral entourage themselves.

The brotherhoods elected or appointed their officials, including secretaries, treasurers, and majordomos, the most important office, which ultimately controlled the funds and organized the fiestas. Majordomos, almost always men, often had to make up losses with their own money, which was a vehicle for them to demonstrate community spirit, wealth, and status. Many confraternities allowed membership for both men and women and were open to all races and classes. Often, membership fees were minimal or nonexistent. Some confraternities specified that members had to be from particular African nations, American-born creoles, mulattoes, or mestizos (of European and indigenous ancestry). Most Afro-Latin American brotherhoods admitted slaves, although they often limited leadership positions to free people of color. Confraternities raised money by charging membership dues, investing in properties and businesses, or begging for contributions on a scheduled day of the week. Some African confraternities cooperated in order to buy the freedom of a particular member. Women of African descent played leadership roles in all of these activities.

Confraternities in Cuba and Brazil had a much more direct and long-lasting tie to African organizations than was the case of those in colonial Mexico. From the 16th century forward, Afro-Cubans belonged to Catholic confraternities derived from Spanish traditions, but new slave arrivals formed organizations more directly connected to African traditions. Afro-Brazilian brotherhoods flourished in ways unmatched in Spanish America. In Minas Gerais, Salvador de Bahia, and elsewhere, Afro-Brazilian *hermandades* grew to the point of independently controlling their own church buildings. Many African brotherhoods divided along the lines of ethnolinguistic groups, such as Angolan, Jeje, or Nagô. Despite maintaining strong African beliefs, these confraternities were actually located in churches and dedicated to Catholic saints.

From the time of their early foundations in Bahia in the 1600s, the most popular advocation for Afro-Brazilian brotherhoods was the Virgin of the Rosary. Although Africans appreciated the charity and social activities of the brotherhoods, churchmen focused on their spiritual benefits. From the perspective of the Catholic Church, this was the prime reason for their existence; enjoying an afterlife in heaven, to them, superseded earthly manumission. Slaves from the Mina coast as well as Central Africa enthusiastically organized dozens of Rosary brotherhoods in towns throughout the region of Minas Gerais, which generally lacked a strong presence of the official Catholic Church. By the end of the 18th century, many of these organizations had their own lavish official churches. Their processions were lengthy and opulent, and members dressed in white silk, carrying statues encrusted with gold and diamonds.

Nicole von Germeten

FURTHER READING

Howard, Philip A. *Changing History: Afro-Cuban Cabildos and Societies of Color in the Nineteenth Century.* Baton Rouge: Louisiana State University Press, 1998.

Kiddy, Elizabeth W. *Blacks of the Rosary: Memory and History in Minas Gerais, Brazil.* University Park: Pennsylvania State University Press, 2005.

von Germeten, Nicole. *Black Blood Brothers: Confraternities and Social Mobility for Afro-Mexicans.* Tallahassee: University Press of Florida, 2006.

CÉDULAS DE GRACIAS AL SACAR

A Spanish royal decree issued on February 10, 1795, established standard fees for some 71 exemptions to regulations of social and monetary statutes ranging from powers of attorney to the official age of majority. Called *cédulas de gracias al sacar*, these exemptions also granted nonwhites the right to escape various legal restrictions placed on them because of their color. Functioning as de facto certificates of whiteness, they entitled free people of color to bypass restrictions regarding dress, marriage, education, and employment in late colonial Spanish America. Most of the buyers of these certificates procured them for the purposes of obtaining a university title, joining the church hierarchy, securing a public office, or attaining the honorific title of *Don*.

The intriguing name of *gracias al sacar* (the grace of purchase) has engendered much confusion in the historical literature, where several critics mistake them as certificates that allowed the holder to be "thankfully extracted" from the ranks of the color. Similar to a *perdón*, a *gracia* is a prerogative outlined in the legal code of LAS SIETE PARTIDAS (the traditional legal code of Castile, enacted 1252–84) that allows the monarch to extend a benefit to one of his subjects as an act of royal kindness. In this sense, here *gracias* is more akin to the meaning of "mercy" or "grace" than an expression of gratitude. When these *gracias* were acquired through payment to the Crown, they received the name of *al sacar*, which here implies "purchase" rather than "removal." Thus, *gracias al sacar*, in the Spanish legal tradition, implies the dispensation of a royal exemption purchased by the bearer.

The 1795 *cédulas* allowed an exemption of the qualities of *pardo* and *quinterón*—two racial categories used in

Spanish America—for 500 reales and 800 reales, respectively. In order to raise additional revenues, the Crown increased the fees in the Real Cédula de 3 de Agosto de 1801 de "Gracias al Sacar," which repeated almost verbatim the text of the 1795 decree. The fee for racial waivers increased from 500 to 700 *reales* in the case of *pardos* and from 800 to 1,100 *reales* for *quinterones*.

The separate fees for these two racial categories raise a number of questions that historical research has not yet fully explained. It is not entirely clear why exemptions existed only for the categories of *pardo* and *quinterón* and not for the many other color and lineage gradations recognized by the colonial practice of *castas.* (See CASTA.) It would appear that the complex ethnosocial nomenclature of the Spanish *casta* system was simplified in late colonial legal discourse. In the *cédulas,* the category of *pardo* seems to have applied to mixed-race individuals of visible African or Amerindian background. Since the *casta* system allowed for the children of a *quinterón* and a Spaniard to be considered biologically white, the category of *quinterón* was likely to be ascribed to mixed-raced individuals so light that they could pass for white. Therefore, the *gracias al sacar* appear to cover the entirety of the mixed-race spectrum of the Spanish colonial world by reducing it to only two categories that distinguish individuals of visible and imperceptible non-European lineage. But this raises another important question: Why should the whiter *quinterón* have to pay a greater fee than the darker *pardo* for a certificate of whiteness? The difference in fee probably functioned as a fine for passing. It is also likely that the Crown assumed that the *quinterón* occupied a more privileged socioeconomic position than the *pardo* and would therefore be better prepared to pay more for a full measure of entitlement.

The *gracias al sacar* were dictated by the financial and imperial considerations of the Spanish Bourbon monarchs. The revenue from the *gracias* was used to finance the Spanish military activities against France and Britain. The *gracias* also responded to the desire to counterbalance an increasingly politically suspect criollo, or native-born, elite in the American colonies. It sought to neutralize this restless elite by adding to its ranks wealthy colored subjects who would be loyal to the Crown. Also, by drawing out potential leaders from the ranks of the colored masses, it sought to prevent popular insurrections. As they sought to avert criollo independence movements or slave uprisings like those in contemporary Saint-Domingue (see HAITIAN REVOLUTION), the *gracias* became ingenious ways to harness demographic shifts of power to ensure the continuation of Spanish colonial rule. However, it remains unknown how the *gracias al sacar* galvanized the resentment of the criollo elite and thereby fueled the revolutionary wars that led to the independence of Spanish America (*see also* SOUTH AMERICAN WARS OF LIBERATION).

One of the most notable *gracias* cases concerns José Ponciano de Ayarza, who in 1797 requested a dispensation of color from the Crown. Citing his distinguished military service in the Spanish colonial city of Portobello, Panamá, the king granted him and his children waivers of the quality of *pardo.* After a series of bureaucratic entanglements with university officials and colonial administrators in the New Granadan capital city of Bogotá, Ponciano de Ayarza used this *gracia* to enable his son to graduate from the University of Santa Fe, which until then had been closed to people of color. But the *gracia* had its limits: In spite of the dispensation of color, the Crown refused Ponciano de Ayarza's request for the honorific noble title of *Don.* Indeed, the *cédulas de gracias al sacar* did not in truth enable the bearer to gain full entry into the ranks of the elite. After his voyage to Venezuela during the first decade of the 19th century, one French traveler observed that the only benefit one *pardo* family acquired through the purchase of a racial dispensation certificate was the right for the women to carry rugs to the church so as not to dirty their dresses as they knelt to pray during the Mass, a privilege then granted only to elite white families.

The *cédulas de gracias al sacar* reveal the social constructedness of race. Undermining biological theories of race, the *gracias al sacar* expose how powerful groups assemble racial categories for strategic affiliations at convenient historical moments. The implication that color might be removable through payment reveals the religious and criminal metaphors underlying the construction of subordinate ethnicities in Latin America. Unlike Anglo-Saxon North America, where race was legally defined as an intrinsic and heritable stigma, Latin American racial formations represented color as a religious or criminal condition that, like sin or an infraction, could be atoned for through the purchase of an indulgence or the payment of a fine. As such, the *gracias al sacar* shed historical light on the Spanish phrase *"el dinero* blanquea," literally, "money whitens."

Roberto Strongman-Congiu

FURTHER READING
Mörner, Magnus. *Race Mixture in the History of Latin America.* Boston: Little, Brown, 1967.

Santos, Rodulfo Cortes. *El regimen de "las gracias al sacar" en Venezuela durante el período hispánico.* Caracas: Academia Nacional de la Historia, 1978.

Twinam, Ann. *Public Lives, Private Secrets: Gender, Honor, Sexuality and Illegitimacy in Colonial Latin America.* Palo Alto, Calif.: Stanford University Press, 1999.

Wright, Winthrop R. *Café con Leche: Race, Class and National Image in Venezuela.* Austin: University of Texas Press, 1990.

CHARLESTON, SOUTH CAROLINA

The English colonial city of Charles Towne, South Carolina (today known as Charleston), was founded in 1670. Many of the original white inhabitants immigrated to this new city on the mainland from the Caribbean island of BARBADOS. It can be said that Carolina was a colony of a colony, in that many of the inhabitants left one English colony to found another. Charleston is located near the coast beside a fine harbor. The surrounding countryside is low-lying with many navigable creeks and rivers, permitting easy access by water. The climate and landscape are very suitable for plantation agriculture.

Attracted by the lure of vast tracts of inexpensive land, white planters from Barbados arrived in Carolina accompanied by their slaves. As a result, from its inception, the region around Charleston quickly developed into a society based on slavery. Despite its initial attraction, there was a sinister side to life in the country. Much of the low-lying area surrounding Charleston was marshland. Before the lands were cleared and settled, many who arrived in the region quickly died of a variety of diseases, most characterized by high fevers. The cause of death was frequently malaria, a disease spread by infected mosquitoes.

Colonial Period

Whites who survived were ready to recreate their prosperous plantation lifestyle in mainland North America. One of their first tasks was clearing the land. Slave labor was instrumental in accomplishing this arduous task. Once the land was cleared, the new residents set their sights on the implementation of animal husbandry. Residents of the new colony started raising cattle in the typical English manner. A common pastureland was placed in the center of the community. Animals would be fed and tended throughout the mild weather months. Later, during the harvest season, most would be butchered, leaving a few prime animals to replenish the herd in the spring. The residents soon discovered that the winters in Carolina were mild, and no special care was needed to ensure survival of the herds. As a result, the herd size grew quickly with little effort of the landowners. Settlers were easily able to provide adequate food for themselves and for new settlers to the region who soon followed.

Assured that adequate food was available, planters turned their attention to their prime concern: which crops would enable them to attain and maintain a semifeudal plantation lifestyle in their newly founded colony. Because the climate in Charleston varied from that of Barbados, planters sought crops that would be successful in their new location. The abundant land was exceptionally fertile in and around Charleston. The soil quality and the mild climate made this an attractive agricultural region. In addition, the natural port at the junction of two rivers, the Ashley and the Cooper, provided settlers the ability to export crops easily from the vicinity of Charleston to Europe and the Caribbean. By 1740, the city became one of the largest British cities in North America, with a population of more than 6,000 people.

At the end of the 17th century, rice cultivation was introduced into the region. Historians believe that white planters were originally unsuccessful in their attempts to grow the lucrative crop. Eventually, slaves imported from Africa conveyed the necessary knowledge and skills for farming the labor-intensive crop (*see* SIERRA LEONE). As rice farming became firmly established in the marshlands of the region, the demand for slave labor rapidly increased. Assigning the care of crops to the hands of slaves and overseers, planters would leave the swampy areas and move to the seaside at Charleston, where the environment was healthier during the hot summer and autumn. By the end of December, the fever season had ended, and life in the countryside could return to normal until the following summer.

Despite their success in growing rice, planters in Carolina were wise enough not to concentrate on just one crop. Indigo, a plant used in the creation of blue dye, emerged as another important crop in and around Charleston.

The WAR OF AMERICAN INDEPENDENCE, 1775–83, had a profound effect on Charleston. The city was captured by the British in 1780 and remained under British occupation until 1783. During this time, the British colonial government freely recruited people of color into its locally raised military. These black loyalist soldiers and their families numbered more than 25,000, or about one-fourth of the black population of the state. Many were people who had been enslaved on plantations owned by rebels and thus gained their freedom during the war, but many were prewar free people of color who thought that the British government was more likely to improve their lot than an independent government dominated by the white Carolina planter class. When Britain made peace and left the region, many of these black Carolinians followed them, decimating the free black population of Charleston.

Early National Period (1783–1860)

In the years following the war, at the dawn of the 19th century, Charleston's population quickly grew to more than 20,000 people with blacks outnumbering whites. This was a trend that would continue through the 1850s. The black population in the region was larger than the white because the majority of residents were slaves. Although there were a growing number of free blacks in the region, their population remained relatively small, numbering 586 in the 1790 census and growing to just above 3,000 by the eve of the AMERICAN CIVIL WAR, 1861–65, in 1860. Nonetheless, this was one of the largest concentrations of free people of color in the United States, surpassed only by New York City; PHILADELPHIA, PENNSYLVANIA; and NEW ORLEANS, LOUISIANA.

During the 1790s, black slaves on the Caribbean island of Saint-Domingue overthrew the white planter society on the island (*see* HAITIAN REVOLUTION). This event led to the creation of the establishment of the black-run nation of Haiti. During the years of rebellion and chaos on Saint-Domingue, hundreds of free colored refugees escaped their island homeland and found safe haven on the North American mainland in cities with large black populations such as Charleston. Free, light-skinned African Americans occupied a social position midway between those of whites and slaves. They were not embraced by whites, nor did they align themselves with the slaves. Instead, they created a unique place in society where they served as a buffer between the races.

These free mulatto refugees posed serious concerns for Charleston's whites. Although the free mulatto émigrés simply wanted to live life unmolested in their adopted homeland, whites living in Charleston feared the newcomers would try to impart ideas of freedom and revolution to slaves living in the region. Fears of instability clouded the lives of whites as the mulatto population became firmly entrenched in Charleston's society.

Although Charleston's whites were firmly committed to the institution of slavery, they lived in constant fear of the possibility of slave insurrections. Their fears escalated after the successful slave revolt on the island of Saint-Domingue. White fears of insurrection were certainly justified as brutalized slaves sought the means to escape and practiced acts of resistance toward owners and overseers. White fears were confirmed in 1822, when the former slave DENMARK VESEY was implicated in a conspiracy to lead a slave revolt. As part of the hysteria that emerged, Vesey and others were publicly hanged as a warning to others who might consider such actions.

A small percentage of slaves living in and around Charleston were able to gain MANUMISSION despite living heavily restricted lives. Some slave children were born to slave mothers and white fathers. Some of these unions were consensual, but more often the children were a result of white men's forcing slave women to engage in nonconsensual sexual relations (*see also* FAMILY RELATIONSHIPS WITH WHITES). Occasionally, these slaves, both mothers and their children, were given their freedom. In addition, some offspring were granted special privileges such as an education or the privilege of specialized training. Slaves who were capable of earning a living and able to support themselves financially were more likely to be manumitted than those who were

destined to become wards of the community. In some cases, faithful slaves were rewarded with manumission in the wills of benevolent masters. Others were able to earn and save money selling commodities or their labor in the marketplace. Skilled craftsmen, or ARTISANS, were sometimes allowed to hire out their time with the permission of their owners. In these cases, the slave would guarantee the master an amount of money agreed upon for his daily labors. Any money earned beyond that amount would belong to the slave (*see* LIVING "AS FREE"). In this way some talented and dedicated individuals could earn enough money over time to purchase their freedom and that of family members.

Clearly life was difficult for slaves in antebellum South Carolina, but it was difficult for free blacks as well. Conscious of the possibility of cooperation between slaves and free people of color, white legislators created complex legal codes to maintain control and to define class separations between free blacks and their slave counterparts. Such laws and restrictions imposed by whites created an environment that left many free blacks with lives almost as restricted as the lives of the slaves. Most free people of color lived in constant fear of being re-enslaved and tried to live as inconspicuously as possible (*see* RE-ENSLAVEMENT). Any encounter with powerful whites or any hint of impropriety could result in the loss of freedom. If an individual was charged with a crime or his identity was mistaken for that of another individual, he could be sold into slavery. A free black with connections to powerful whites who could serve as benefactors or liaisons was in less peril than others who lacked those relationships. As a result, it was in the best interests of free blacks to maintain strong, respectful relationships with members of the white community whenever possible.

In cities like Charleston, free people of color built communities and lived their lives in societies parallel to their white counterparts. Most free blacks were poor and worked as common laborers on farms, in town, or on the docks. Some free blacks were merchants, artisans, or tradesmen. These individuals and their families lived a middle-class life and associated primarily with other blacks of their class. Those blacks at the top of the social pyramid were wealthy, often cultured, and comparatively well educated. Some had studied in private schools in the North or in Europe. They lived a lifestyle that mirrored, yet remained separate from, that of the white planter class. These wealthy blacks owned businesses or plantations and sometimes owned slaves just as their white counterparts did. When necessary, black and white men had business relationships, but they never mingled socially. Interracial social relationships were considered unacceptable by the white community.

One such successful black businessman was William Ellison, who emerged from slavery by becoming a free person of color in 1816, when he was just 26 years old. As a slave he was a skilled tradesman and learned to build cotton gins. After he purchased his freedom, he continued at that trade and was successful at his craft. He was so skilled that his cotton gins were in great demand, and he became known throughout the region. His talent and reputation as a cotton gin maker enabled three generations of Ellisons to live as prosperous members of the free black population for decades. Ellison used his cotton gin manufacturing business as a cornerstone with which to create a financial empire that included both land and slaves. These assets placed Ellison in an economic stratum at the pinnacle of black society in South Carolina. While few could duplicate this level of economic achievement, Ellison did serve as an example of what could be accomplished by African Americans who were free, dedicated to hard work, and conscious of the steps they needed to take to remain in the good graces of the white population they served. No free African Americans could garner any level of success unless they catered to and understood their place with regard to influential members of white society.

After securing his freedom and establishing a business, William Ellison chose to marry. He married a free woman of color, Mary Thomson Mishaw, whose father, John Mishaw, belonged to the exclusive Brown Fellowship Society, an African-American social organization in Charleston. Ellison's brothers, Henry and Reuben, married sisters, Mary Elizabeth and Harriett Ann Bonneau. Their father, the schoolteacher Thomas Bonneau, also belonged to the Brown Fellowship Society. These marriages firmly established the Ellison men as an integral part of Charleston's free black community.

Just as in the white community, social relationships were the foundation of black society. The important aristocratic social organization Charleston's Brown Fellowship Society was organized in 1790. Membership in the society was limited to 50 of the most prominent free black men in Charleston's society and was determined by skin color, social standing, and wealth. Dark-skinned African Americans were not included (darker-skinned men created their own organizations, which served similar purposes). One common criterion for determining who was or was not acceptable was the brown paper bag test. To qualify for membership, an applicant had to have skin that was the color of a brown paper bag or lighter. This sort of test was not confined to this one organizations, nor was this kind of test exclusive to the city of Charleston. It was a technique that was employed wherever exclusive African-American organizations existed.

This method of limiting social interaction served the purpose of securing elite status for those who qualified.

The Brown Fellowship Society served a number of purposes within Charleston's free black society. Inductees paid a fee to join and contributed monthly dues. The money collected was used to fund a credit union system that allowed members to borrow money from the organization to expand a business or remodel a home. It was also used to fund a benevolent society for members and provided financial aid in time of illness, injury, or death. Although the financial functions were important to the members of the society, the organization also served as a social club for members and their families. It provided activities where people could gather to foster beneficial social connections with like-minded people in a world that excluded African Americans from the dominant society. Family membership in the society enabled those of marriageable age to locate suitable spouses who would help them maintain their presence at the pinnacle of Charleston's black society, thereby concentrating their wealth, power, and status within a very limited population.

Social organizations were not the only groups to emerge within the free black community of Charleston. In 1816, a new church, called the AFRICAN METHODIST EPISCOPAL CHURCH (A.M.E.) was organized by Bishop Richard Allen in Philadelphia, Pennsylvania. This was the first church in America to be organized and run entirely by and for African Americans. In 1818, discouraged by the restrictions imposed on members of their race, the majority of African-American Methodists living in Charleston decided to separate from the Methodist Church. At that time they organized their own Methodist church and aligned it with the A.M.E. Church of Philadelphia. In this religious environment, free blacks developed leadership and organizational skills. This first attempt at creating a self-sustaining black church in Charleston was short-lived. After Denmark Vesey's slave conspiracy against the white planter aristocracy surfaced in 1822, Southern whites feared the possibility of future slave uprisings that might emerge from any group of African Americans regardless of whether that group was religious or secular. In an attempt to ward off any possibility of black insurrection, civic authorities closed the black-run church just weeks after Vesey's hanging and prevented any further attempts at reorganization. Black Methodists had no choice but to return to established white congregations, where they were excluded from all leadership positions and segregated from white congregants.

In addition to starting religious institutions, prosperous free people of color in Charleston began to establish private schools for their children. During the first decade of the 19th century, the Brown Fellowship Society spon-

CLASS No. 1.

Comprises those prisoners who were found guilty and executed.

Prisoners Names.	Owners' Names.	Time of Commit.	How Disposed of.
Peter	James Poyas	June 18	Hanged on Tuesday the 2d July, 1822, on Blake's lands, near Charleston.
Ned	Gov. T. Bennett,	do.	
Rolla	do.	do	
Batteau	do.	do.	
Denmark Vesey	A free black man	22	
Jessy	Thos. Blackwood	23	
John	Elias Horry	July 5	Do. on the Lines near Ch.; Friday July 12.
Gullah Jack	Paul Pritchard	do.	
Mingo	Wm. Harth	June 21	Hanged on the Lines near Charleston, on Friday, 26th July.
Lot	Forrester	27	
Joe	P. L. Jore	July 6	
Julius	Thos. Forrest	8	
Tom	Mrs. Russell	10	
Smart	Robt. Anderson	do.	
John	John Robertson	11	
Robert	do.	do.	
Adam	do.	do.	
Polydore	Mrs. Faber	do.	
Bacchus	Benj. Hammet	do.	
Dick	Wm. Sims	13	
Pharaoh	— Thompson	do.	
Jemmy	Mrs. Clement	18	
Mauidore	Mordecai Cohen	19	
Dean	— Mitchell	do.	
Jack	Mrs. Purcell	12	
Bellisle	Est. of Jos. Yates	18	
Naphur	do.	do.	
Adam	do.	do.	
Jacob	John S. Glen	16	
Charles	John Billings	18	
Jack	N. McNeill	22	
Cæsar	Miss Smith	do.	
Jacob Stagg	Jacob Lankester	23	Do. Tues. July 30.
Tom	Wm. M. Scott	24	
William	Mrs. Garner	Aug. 2	Do. Friday, Aug. 9.

A list of the names of the accused conspirators executed by the government of South Carolina in the Denmark Vesey case in 1822. Vesey was the only free person of color to be executed. *(The Granger Collection, New York)* sored a school employing one teacher, Thomas Bonneau, to educate the children of its members. Soon, because there were so many requests by members to enroll their children in the school, additional teachers had to be hired to meet the growing demand. DANIEL A. PAYNE, who was educated in the school sponsored by the society, went on to open his own school in Charleston. Payne's school became the most popular school among free people of color because it offered the most advanced curriculum available for blacks in the city.

In the aftermath of Nat Turner's slave revolt in Virginia in 1831, whites across the South began to fear the influence that educated blacks could assert. They feared that educated blacks would challenge white authority and perhaps even encourage slaves to revolt. In 1834, South Carolina enacted legislation that outlawed education for free blacks. Despite the restrictive legislation, some schools continued to educate wealthy free blacks in secret, away from the watchful eyes of white authorities. Fear regarding the influence of abolitionists and the very real possibilities of slave insurrection continued to increase throughout the 1840s and 1850s as abolitionist influence spread and as sectional differences in the United States grew in intensity. In reaction to those fears, legislators in South Carolina passed more stringent laws in an attempt to maintain firm control of the black population and the way of life that governed the South. The lives of the slaves changed little under the tightening restrictions; however, the privileges of free blacks were constantly threatened under the changing legal environment.

During the 1850s, the United States steadily moved toward civil war. Since the formation of the nation, South Carolina was at the forefront of the debate regarding the institution of slavery in America. South Carolina was the state most determined to protect the institution of slavery from any interference by the federal government. As the ongoing controversy edged toward war, it became clear that if war occurred, it would probably commence there. Free blacks in Charleston had everything to lose and little to gain if the nation went to war. Financially they were aligned with white society. They shared business and financial concerns with their white counterparts. They stood to lose their money, their businesses, and their homes if war occurred. Conversely, the slaves understood that if war began, it would be a war about slavery. If South Carolina and its supporters won such a conflict, it would ensure that slavery would survive in the South for a long time to come. If the North prevailed, slavery, the foundation for all of Southern society, might be dismantled. Although the fate of black SLAVE OWNERS was intimately entwined with that of their white counterparts, free blacks had only limited access to the decision-making process. Free black slave owners had virtually no voice in the political affairs of their nation. They could only wait and see what would ensue.

The American Civil War and Its Aftermath (1860–1900)

In 1860, four political parties fielded candidates for the presidency of the United States. When the votes were tallied, the Republican, Abraham Lincoln, was elected. Lincoln and the Republican Party opposed the extension of slavery in the West, and South Carolinians, fearing the new administration would be hostile to their interests, quickly entertained thoughts of secession. On November 10, 1860, just four days after the presidential election, South Carolina began the process of withdrawing from the Union by calling for a state convention, which proclaimed a formal act of secession on December 20. That action virtually guaranteed there would be war among the states. In early 1861, other Southern states followed the example set by South Carolina and seceded from the Union, and together those states formed the Confederate States of America. The fighting actually began in Charleston, when South Carolina armed forces bombarded and captured the federal-controlled Fort Sumter at the mouth of the harbor on April 12–13, 1861. No one was killed in the battle. Paradoxically, a war that would take almost a million lives, devastate the South, and end slavery began with a bloodless battle in a predominantly black city.

Slaves were instrumental in the Confederate war effort. One significant individual was ROBERT SMALLS. In the years before secession, Smalls was hired out by his owner to work on the wharves and ships in Charleston harbor. Over time, he convinced his owner, Henry McKee, to allow him to hire out his own time. When his owner accepted Smalls's terms, Smalls became his own agent, paying McKee 15 dollars a month for his labor. Anything Smalls was able to earn above that amount was his to keep.

Robert Smalls was intelligent and ambitious. Serving as an assistant to ship captains on the vessel *Planter*, Smalls mastered sailing the complex channels of Charleston harbor. When war broke out, the Confederacy commandeered the use of *Planter*, and because Smalls was a slave, he was ordered to remain with the ship. On May 13, 1862, Smalls was working as a ship pilot. In the early hours of the morning, he commandeered the ship while the white crew was ashore for an evening of entertainment. He successfully sailed the ship through the harbor, past Southern ships and sentries, and delivered it safely to the Union forces. Smalls stole himself, as well as selected members of the black crew and their families, from slavery. Smalls and his band of followers became free people of color as they crossed into the safety of Northern-controlled waters.

The confiscation of *Planter* is remembered as an important event in the Civil War. Not only did Smalls deliver a ship of considerable value to the Union, but he also gave his considerable expertise and knowledge of Charleston's waters to the Union navy. After his escape with *Planter*, Smalls continued his career of public service to the United States. In fall 1862, Smalls traveled to New York to lobby for funds in support of the Port Royal Experiment. At Port Royal, South Carolina, slaves abandoned by plantation owners fleeing the devastation of war were given the opportunity to manage and run the plantation where they had previously been enslaved. To a degree, this experiment proved successful, and it continued into Reconstruction.

Robert Smalls was also active in lobbying for funds to be used in educating former slaves on the Sea Islands off the coast of South Carolina. Using his own funds, he purchased a building, which he converted to a schoolhouse. After acquiring the facility, Smalls returned to the North, where he raised funds to purchase books and supplies for the school. His wife, Hannah, served as treasurer for the funds Smalls raised.

Smalls's service to his country did not end with the financial lobbying in which he engaged. He soon became active in Republican Party politics, eventually running for the U.S. Congress from the district at Beaufort, South Carolina. Once elected, Smalls served in the U.S. House of Representatives from 1875 to 1886. He provides an example of the role played by former free people of color in the postwar period, known as Reconstruction (*see* RECONSTRUCTION IN THE UNITED STATES).

Another outstanding example is the career of MARTIN DELANY, a free black physician from Pennsylvania, who went to South Carolina as an officer in the Union army—one of the few blacks to gain a commission during the war. He worked in the military occupation of South Carolina, then with the FREEDMEN'S BUREAU. After leaving the military, he stayed in Charleston and went into politics. Blacks constituted the majority of South Carolina's population and remained influential in its politics much longer than in other Southern states. Delaney was twice elected as a state judge and worked with the former Confederate general and governor Wade Hampton (1818–1902) to try to achieve racial reconciliation in the state. Ultimately, though, South Carolina succumbed to the same forces that had led to growing racial injustice in the rest of the South, and the era called Jim Crow began. Blacks were forced from public office, sharply restricted in employment and education, restricted to living in certain areas of the city, and denied public services or offered them on a segregated basis.

In the years following the end of Reconstruction, the social status of the former free blacks in and around Charleston slowly diminished. Once all blacks were free, skin color, not social standing, became the defining social characteristic in the nation. The formerly free persons of color struggled to maintain their elevated status against the rising tide of discrimination under Jim Crow. At the same time, they struggled to maintain their economic status while facing the same trials experienced by formerly wealthy whites in the devastated South. Increasingly, the free African Americans who once served as liaisons between the races (because of their wealth, education, and social position) found themselves lumped together with blacks who had formerly been slaves and with whom they had nothing in common except skin color. After the Civil War, slavery as an institution was destroyed; however, another century would pass before the aftereffects of slavery would be adequately addressed in the United States.

Kim Carey

FURTHER READING

Fraser, Walter J., Jr. *Charleston! Charleston! The History of a Southern City.* Columbia: University of South Carolina Press, 1989.

Johnson, Michael P., and James L. Roark. *Black Masters: A Free Black Family in the Old South.* New York: W. W. Norton, 1984.

Powers, Bernard E., Jr. *Black Charlestonians: A Social History, 1882–1885.* Fayetteville: University of Arkansas Press, 1994.

Uya, Okon Edet. *From Slavery to Public Service: Robert Smalls 1839–1915.* New York: Oxford University Press, 1971.

Wood, Peter H. *Black Majority: Negroes in Colonial South Carolina from 1670 through the Stono Rebellion.* New York: W. W. Norton, 1974.

CHAVANNES, JEAN-BAPTISTE
(1748–1791) *Haitian revolutionary*

Jean-Baptiste Chavannes was a free man of mixed race who lived in SAINT-DOMINGUE, the French colony that became Haiti. Along with VINCENT OGÉ, he led the rebel forces during the first outbreak of violence in the HAITIAN REVOLUTION. He was a military veteran who had served in the colonial MILITIA and in the French forces that fought in North America during the WAR OF AMERICAN INDEPENDENCE, 1755–83. He was also a planter and SLAVE OWNER.

Chavannes's name is sometimes spelled Chavanne in contemporary documents. This may have been an intentional misspelling in response to a law that prohibited free people of color from using the names of whites, even their own relatives. Often people changed the spelling of the family name slightly, as did Ogé, whose father was named Joseph Augé, and JULIEN RAIMOND, whose father spelled his name Raymond.

Chavannes was born in 1748 in Grande-Rivière du Nord, a rural parish near the border with the Spanish side of the island of Hispaniola. His parents were also free people of mixed race. His father was also named Jean-Baptiste Chavannes, and his mother was Marie Marthe Castaing Chavannes. Her family was from the outskirts of CAP-FRANÇAIS/CAP-HAÏTIEN), where her brother was a close friend of Ogé. It was a large family, as was common with free people of color in Saint-Domingue; Jean-Baptiste had at least three brothers and one sister who survived to adulthood. As the oldest son, after his father's death sometime between 1777 and 1783, he managed the family plantation. It was big enough to provide small but respectable farms for each of the younger children upon their marriages and have enough left over to rent for 15,000 livres a year in 1786, the equivalent of $375,000 in today's terms. Chavannes does not appear to have been a very successful planter; the rental in 1786 was apparently forced on him by his creditors.

Unlike many free colored planters, Chavannes had good relations with poorer free blacks. He often was a godfather for newly freed people or the children of poor blacks in his neighborhood. He was also a militia sergeant and built relationships both with the largely black militia noncommissioned officer corps and with the white militia officers, one of whom rescued him when he had financial difficulty in 1786. His militia comrades supported him in his rebellion, and many of them went on to support the larger rebellion led by TOUSSAINT LOUVERTURE. There is no evidence that he knew Toussaint, but they were from the same part of the country and knew many of the same people. Toussaint's commander in the early stages of the revolution, Georges Biassou, cited Chavannes's experience when negotiating with the colonial government.

Chavannes volunteered for the French army in 1779, persuaded by the charismatic French admiral Count d'Estaing, who was organizing an expedition to Georgia. d'Estaing recruited more than a thousand free colored men from the North Province. Many of them were relatively poor free blacks, some with unclear titles of liberty. Few of the wealthy planter class signed up for the expedition; Jean-Baptiste was an exception. He fought in the Savannah campaign of 1779, distinguishing himself during the free colored regiment's only major battle, covering the French retreat from the British fortifications. After the expedition, Haitian tradition holds that he continued to serve in the United States for the remainder of the war. Most of the regiment was sent to various islands in the Caribbean. He returned to the colony in 1783. He and his comrades were very disappointed by the lack of response by white society to their service. They and d'Estaing had hoped that military service would help overcome prejudice against free coloreds. Neither the government nor white public opinion responded. Free people of color had experienced increasing racial prejudice since the 1760s, and this would only worsen as the revolution approached.

The Revolution Begins

Chavannes was not involved in Vincent Ogé's failed approach to the French National Assembly at the beginning of the FRENCH REVOLUTION. But when Ogé returned to the colony in October 1790, he met with Chavannes. The two signed a letter to the colony's governor on October 21, 1790, calling for equal voting rights for free coloreds in local elections. The National Assembly had passed a law calling for elections, but the law did not mention voting rights for free blacks. Ogé and Chavannes suggested that since the law contained no restriction on the basis of race, all races should be included. The colony's governor and white public opinion felt, on the other hand, that without specific instructions from Paris to include free coloreds, they could be excluded, and so the appeal was rejected.

At the same time, they began to gather armed free colored men around them on a camp established in a plantation in Grande-Rivière. The police, who were free people of color, would not do anything to stop them, and indeed one of their closest supporters was a constable of the rural police.

On October 27, 1790, an attempt was made by regular troops from the Cap-Français garrison to arrest Ogé and Chavannes. The soldiers, who numbered only a few dozen, retreated without a confrontation. The next day, the pair and their supporters went to all the neighboring plantations and collected their weapons. On October 30, a force of about 800 soldiers, militiamen, and constables from Cap-Français, probably at least half free coloreds, confronted 400 free coloreds in a battle that lasted most of the morning. The government troops were forced to withdraw to the town.

The free colored rebels celebrated, but their leaders knew that the next attack would be even more powerful. Ogé sent messengers to prominent free coloreds across the island but received no response. The rebels built field fortifications at their camp. Chavannes and other free colored rebels encouraged Ogé to enroll slaves in the army, promising them their liberty in return for their services. It is said that Chavannes even had 30 male slaves of his own, though given that his largest plantation was rented to the militia commander of the region, it is doubtful he actually owned many slaves at the time. Ogé refused to enroll slaves, though, even with the permission of their masters. He did not want the movement for free colored civil rights to lead to a hugely disruptive slave rebellion, though he had accepted the idea of gradual, compensated emancipation of slaves in discussions with the Amis des Noirs and the Club Massiac in Paris the year before.

When the colonial governor arrived in person the next day with 3,000 men and artillery, the small force of free colored rebels could not resist them. They fled into the hills, with many returning to their homes. Ogé,

Chavannes, and 23 of their closest supporters, including Ogé's four brothers, Chavannes's two brothers, and two free black militia sergeants, fled across the border to the Spanish side of the island.

The End

In the past, the Spanish had sheltered runaway slaves, and in later years, they would provide refuge for Toussaint Louverture's slave rebel army, but in 1790, they were trying to remain on good terms with the French, and so they extradited the pair and their men to Cap-Français. Chavannes and Ogé were sentenced to death on February 21, 1791. The execution was barbaric. Both men were forced to their knees before the door of the church to repent of their crimes publicly. Chavannes refused and instead called for freedom for all blacks. Then, they were beaten with hammers until all their major bones were broken, then tied to a wagon wheel and left to die in the main square. Chavannes's head was put up on a spike alongside the road where he had fought his last battle.

Aftermath

The barbarity of the execution and Chavannes's steadfast courage gained the admiration of colonial witnesses, including many blacks. Indeed, the propaganda value the government had clearly hoped to gain from this public auto-da-fé clearly backfired, as blacks were enraged and many whites overcome with pity and remorse. The French Parliament responded by passing a law on April 4, 1792, that gave equal citizenship to free people of color. The revolutionary commissioner, Léger-Félicité Sonthonax, was sent to the island to enforce this decree, and it was he who ultimately declared the abolition of slavery and recruited Toussaint Louverture to lead the colony's armies.

In later years, Chavannes seemed a lesser figure than Ogé. But his legacy is less mixed, since he supported including slaves in the rebellion—though, significantly, not calling for general abolition but instead freeing individual slaves who were willing to fight. Nevertheless, his name has returned to today's news, borne by another rural rebel, Chavannes Jean-Baptiste, who has organized peasants in Haiti and fought courageously for the rights of poor country people against a variety of governments in Port-au-Prince from 1973 to the present.

Stewart R. King

FURTHER READING

Dubois, Laurent. *Avengers of the New World*. Cambridge: Belknap, 2005.

King, Stewart. *Blue Coat or Powdered Wig: Free People of Color in Pre-Revolutionary Saint-Domingue*. Athens: University of Georgia Press, 2001.

CHAVIS, JOHN (ca. 1763–1838) *American educator and religious leader*

John Chavis was one of the earliest black educators in the mid-Atlantic South and was among the most highly educated men of color in the country during his lifetime. Before Chavis's three years of service during the WAR OF AMERICAN INDEPENDENCE, 1775–83, little is known about his early life and education. Even his date of birth is unclear. He was probably born free around 1763, but where is not known.

By 1789, Chavis was tutoring the orphans of a wealthy white man in Virginia. In 1792, Chavis studied for the Presbyterian ministry as a private student of John Witherspoon, president of the College of NEW JERSEY (now Princeton University). Chavis also attended Liberty Hall Academy (now Washington and Lee University) in Virginia. Starting in 1800, Chavis worked as a Presbyterian circuit rider, preaching to both slave and free congregations in the mid-Atlantic states. (*See also* PROTESTANT MAINLINE CHURCHES.)

In 1807, Chavis moved to Raleigh, NORTH CAROLINA, with a license to preach, but no parish. Nonetheless, Chavis continued to address both black and white audiences. Chavis's preaching career ended in 1832, after North Carolina clamped down on the liberties of free people of color in the wake of the Nat Turner rebellion.

After the pulpit had been denied him by law, Chavis sermonized in print, in "Letter upon the Doctrine of the Extent of the Atonement of Christ" (1837). He attacked prejudice and intolerance and indirectly criticized the institution of slavery as a product of man, and not God's will.

In 1808, Chavis founded a school in Raleigh. At first, he taught black and white students integrated in the same classes. After complaints from parents, Chavis segregated his school, teaching whites in the morning and blacks in the evening. Chavis developed a reputation for academic rigor. Prominent white families sent their college-bound sons to prepare with Chavis. His alumni included numerous politicians and jurists.

Chavis corresponded with one of his former students, senator Willie Mangum of North Carolina, from 1823 to 1836. In these letters, Chavis described himself as a Federalist and felt free to criticize ANDREW JACKSON and states' rights ideology.

Yet Chavis also opposed a constitutional amendment abolishing slavery. As a free black man who associated with prominent whites, Chavis walked a fine line. Presbyterians of the early republic believed that slavery was inconsistent with the revolutionary principles of liberty. However, they did not support immediate emancipation and instead advocated first converting and educating blacks in order to prepare them for freedom. Having attended Presbyterian colleges and worked as a Presbyterian minister, he upheld the church's stance on slavery until the end of his life—oppositional, yet conservative and accommodationist.

Chavis's biography has been misused in a number of ways since his death. Chavis's story became popular among Southern whites during the 1880s to support their contention that the slave era was characterized by benevolent interracial tolerance. More recently, the *African American Registry* described Chavis as a "dedicated opponent of slavery" and "an influential abolitionist leader in the South"—despite the fact that Chavis opposed immediate emancipation. He died in June 1838 in Orange County, North Carolina.

Thomas Brown

FURTHER READING

Des Champs, Margaret B. "John Chavis as a Preacher to Whites." *North Carolina Historical Review* 32 (April 1955): 165–172.

Hudson, Gossie H. "John Chavis, 1763–1838: A Social-Psychological Study." *Journal of Negro History* 64 (Spring 1979): 142–154.

Knight, Edgar W. "Notes on John Chavis." *North Carolina Historical Review* 7 (July 1930): 326–345.

Othow, Helen C. *John Chavis: African American Patriot, Preacher, Teacher, and Mentor (1783-1838)*. New York: McFarland, 2001.

Savage, W. Sherman. "The Influence of John Chavis and Lunsford Lane on the History of North Carolina." *Journal of Negro History* 25 (January 1940): 14–24.

CHICAGO, ILLINOIS

The Haitian-born explorer and entrepreneur Jean-Baptiste Pointe du Sable is widely credited with being the first free black settler in the Chicago region in the late 18th century. However, free blacks did not begin to settle in the area in any number until the 1830s, and even then the community was quite small. As in other parts of the state of Illinois, free blacks in Chicago were subject to the restrictive and prejudicial black laws (*see* BLACK LAWS IN THE MIDWEST and ILLINOIS), which limited their access to the courts, prevented them from voting, and made them subject to threats of kidnapping and transportation to the slave states. The black laws, as well as Chicago's location in the far northeastern part of the state, kept the free black population of the city small until the 1850s.

According to the Chicago city census of 1837, the year the city was incorporated, there were just 77 free blacks of a total population of 4,066, or only about 2 percent of the overall population. Most of the free blacks in the 1830s were migrants from Kentucky, Missouri, and the states of the Old Northwest, although a few were from as far away as Pennsylvania, Virginia, and North Carolina. When the federal census of 1840 was taken, it listed only 53 free blacks in the city. By 1840, however, there were a number of children and young adults in the community, indicating a growing population. In the Illinois state census of 1845, the free black population had grown to 140. This growth was part of a population boom that was also taking place in the city at large. Although the black population was larger than it had ever been, it remained less than 2 percent of the city's overall population of nearly 12,000. When the federal census of 1850 was taken, Chicago showed continued rapid growth. The entire population of the city now stood at nearly 30,000, with free blacks numbering 323—now only a little more than 1 percent. The city continued to grow over the next decade, and by 1860, on the eve of the AMERICAN CIVIL WAR, 1861–65, the 955 black residents made up less than 1 percent of the city's 109,260 people. Many of these free blacks were refugees (or fugitives) from the slave states who had escaped through the networks of Illinois's Underground Railroad. From Chicago, many blacks who fled slavery also later emigrated into CANADA or to Haiti.

Although the lives of Chicago's free blacks were constrained by the black laws and the fear of kidnapping, many of them also started businesses, bought property, established churches, and raised families. Many blacks chose to live near each other in the First and Second Wards, but others lived in racially integrated neighborhoods across the city, and there was no official policy of residential segregation. In 1845, a black grocer named Hanson was already in business, and in 1847, the first black church was organized and the first black-owned saloon established. Blacks also owned and operated barber shops, blacksmith shops, stage lines, and tailoring establishments. By 1854, blacks owned a total of 15 homes and stores within the city, as well as two churches. Those who were unable to operate establishments of their own worked in shops owned by both blacks and whites and as draymen, porters, hostlers, janitors, laborers, and servants. Black women were typically not employed outside the home, unless as servants or washerwomen, but they played an important role in forming social networks within the community, organizing the black churches, and participating in the activities of the Underground Railroad.

Because of Chicago's large size and ties to eastern cities, the abolition movement was stronger there than in other parts of the state of Illinois. (*See* ABOLITIONISM AND RESISTANCE TO SLAVERY.) Fugitive slaves frequently sought refuge in Chicago, sometimes on their way farther north, but they also often settled within the community. Although many of the black laws were not strictly enforced within the city, blacks were still unable to vote or access many aspects of the justice system. Many abolitionists turned their efforts toward the repeal of the black laws, as well as the abolition of slavery.

The black Chicagoan most active in the fight against the black laws was John Jones, who was born free in North Carolina to a free mulatto mother and a white father. When he was a young boy, Jones's mother apprenticed him to a tailor in order to prevent him from possibly being sold into slavery. Jones traveled with his guardian to Tennessee, where he met his future wife, Mary Richardson, the daughter of a free blacksmith. When the Richardsons moved to Illinois, Jones remained in Memphis to finish his apprenticeship and save enough money to join Mary in Illinois. The couple were married in Alton, Illinois, in 1844 and shortly thereafter moved to Chicago. On their journey, the couple was briefly detained on suspicion of being fugitive slaves, a danger faced by all free black travelers in the state.

When the Joneses arrived in Chicago, they rented a small apartment, and John established a successful tailoring shop. The couple developed relationships with Chicago's abolitionists, including the physician Charles Dyer and the lawyer Lemanuel Covell Paine Freer. It is unclear when Jones first developed his anti–black laws stance, but as a businessman and friend to local abolitionists, Jones would have been exposed not only to abolitionist rhetoric but also to the discrimination of the laws themselves. During the state Constitutional Convention of 1847, Jones made public his opposition to the black laws in the columns of the *Western Citizen*, where he defended the rights of blacks against those who wanted even more severe restrictions written into the new constitution. In 1848, John Jones and the Reverend Abraham Hall were elected by black Chicagoans to be delegates at the Colored National Convention in Cleveland, Ohio. FREDERICK DOUGLASS was chosen president of the convention, and Jones was chosen vice president. In 1850, Jones was part of a rally at the African Methodist Church (*see also* AFRICAN METHODIST EPISCOPAL CHURCH) to resist the passage of the FUGITIVE SLAVE ACT OF 1850. The Chicago Common Council agreed with the city's black activists and called on the city to resist enforcement of the law. During the 1850s, Jones worked to assist possibly hundreds of escaped slaves make their way into Canada, and the Jones home became a significant point along the Underground Railroad. In 1853 and 1856, Jones attended statewide conventions of blacks, speaking on the necessity of repealing the black laws and resisting the Fugitive Slave Act. During the American Civil War, Jones published an influential pamphlet condemning the black laws, which helped lead to their repeal in 1865.

Thom Bahde

FURTHER READING

Gliozzo, Charles A. "John Jones: A Study of a Black Chicagoan." *Illinois Historical Journal* 80 (Autumn 1987): 177–188.

Reed, Christopher R. "African American Life in Antebellum Chicago, 1833–1860." *Journal of the Illinois State Historical Society* 94 (Winter 2001–2002): 356–382.

———. *Black Chicago's First Century.* Vol. 1, *1833–1900.* Columbia: University of Missouri Press, 2005.

CHILE

Chile is a country situated along the southwestern coast of South America. From north to south, it stretches a distance of 2,700 miles, but its territory from west to east is narrow, covering only 110 miles on average. Chile shares its northern border with PERU and BOLIVIA, a region rich in natural resources, such as copper and nitrates. This has led to numerous disputes between Chile and its northern neighbors, most notably the War of the Pacific (1879–83), in which both Peru and Bolivia lost territory. Chile also shares its long eastern border with ARGENTINA, where the rugged Andes Mountains prevent easy travel. The rough terrain in this part of the country is also difficult to survey; as a result, Chile has had various border disputes with its eastern neighbor. Chile's western coastline is the Pacific Ocean, which has allowed it to take advantage of a thriving oceanic trade. Chile's fertile central valley between the Andes and a chain of coastal mountains represents the heart of its agricultural economy, and this is also where its capital, Santiago, is located.

Chile was a Spanish colony from 1536 to 1818, but the Spaniards could not conquer the entire region all at once for several reasons. The Andes Mountains prevented Spanish colonization from Argentina in the East. The first Spanish conquistadores arrived from Peru in the north after their conquest of the Inca Empire in the 1530s. Lima, one of the most important capitals of the Spanish colonial empire, also dominated Chilean politics, and colonial administrators there hesitated to develop the region for fear that it might become a rival colony. Fierce resistance among the region's indigenous populations, including the Araucanian and Mapuche, also proved difficult to overcome. Thus, Chile's colonial economy was largely based on war.

Chile has traditionally promoted itself as a European country. Its first historians rarely included people of color in their writings. More recently, the military government of Augusto Pinochet (r. 1973–90) had a record of prohibiting African immigration into the country. Although traces of Chile's African heritage are rarely seen, more than 90 percent of the population may be considered mestizo, a mixture of European and indigenous ancestry.

Conquest and Colonization

Free people of color and their descendants have contributed significantly to Chile's historical development,

particularly during its colonial history from the 16th to the 19th century. When Diego de Almagro (1475–1538), a Spanish conquistador, led the first expedition from Peru into Chile in 1536, he had several African personal servants with him. Largely because of indigenous resistance, this attempt to conquer the region failed. However, by 1541, Pedro de Valdivia (1500–53) returned, accompanied by African slaves, who helped him penetrate into Chile's central valley and establish Santiago as the capital. Most notably, Juan Valiente (1505–53), a free black veteran from Mexico, and Juan Beltrán are two of the best-known soldiers of color from this era. By 1550, they and a small group of other African and Afro-Spanish conquistadores settled in and near Santiago, where the enslaved among them were rewarded with freedom and they received grants of land and the right to receive the tribute and service of Indians, known as *encomiendas*, for their services.

Colonial Spanish authorities established a war footing in response to the region's hostile indigenous population. They imported African slaves to supplement labor demands not met by local indigenous populations and to help them fight in the wars against resistant Araucanian and Mapuche people. Slaves filled a variety of roles as domestic servants, agricultural workers, craftsmen, carpenter, cobblers, jug makers, masons, miners, ARTISANS, overseers, and soldiers. Labor demands grew in 1552 after gold was discovered. Still, Spanish colonial administrators believed that African slave labor could be better utilized in other parts of the empire in the Americas, and Chile remained a relatively minor destination for the slave trade. Moreover, Santiago's distance from major slave markets in South America, such as Lima, Buenos Aires, and Potosí, Bolivia, made importing large numbers of slaves too expensive. Still, slave traders established a monopoly in Bolivia, Paraguay, and western Argentina, and most used the overland passage from Argentina to transport slaves into Santiago.

While insufficient documentation makes it difficult to pinpoint the exact numbers of slaves imported, scholars estimate that more than 3,000 African slaves were introduced into Santiago and as many as 20,000 into Chile as a whole by the early 17th century. By 1810, on the eve of Chile's independence from Spain, Santiago had the highest concentration of enslaved and freed persons of color within Chile, constituting approximately 10 percent of the city's total population of about 30,000.

The population of freed persons of color grew slightly by the end of the 18th century. Because of the costs associated with African slavery, it was not a solution to the shortage of labor in Chile's colonial agrarian economy. Chilean latifundias were in a better position to employ a large number of poor Spaniards and freed persons of color. One reason was that the majority of enslaved persons of color became urban domestic servants, particularly in Santiago. Often those considered loyal by their owners were manumitted, but slaves were also more likely to be able to buy their freedom or were freed after their masters died. As a result, communities of freed persons of color, working as domestic servants, often took root beyond the household (*see also* HOUSE-KEEPERS). Hundreds also joined the ranks of the Spanish colonial MILITIA; however, they were organized into separate units with their own officers. Manumission was granted so often that by the end of the 18th century, the total population of freed persons of color outnumbered that of slaves.

Freed and enslaved persons of color also frequently interacted with ecclesiastical institutions. On the one hand, many priests and nuns saw persons of color as social delinquents, especially mixed-race groups, such as mulattoes and ZAMBOS, who were labeled as being sexually promiscuous or born out of wedlock (*see also* ROMAN CATHOLIC CHURCH). However, Catholic authorities were among the first to champion the rights of African slaves to marry and not to be forcefully separated from their families. In 1627, Alonso de Ovalle, a Catholic priest, arrived in Santiago and proselytized freed persons of color. He helped them organize their congregation into a *cofradía* (religious brotherhood), Nuestra Señora de la Candelaria de los Mulatos, which promoted traditional Catholic teachings while also allowing them to incorporate their own dances and songs into church rituals (*see also* CATHOLIC CONFRATERNITIES). Indeed, many persons of color identified with the figure of Jesus Christ as a person who was like them: He had suffered. On matters pertaining to the *cofradía*, members had the right to vote, unusual in the Americas at the time.

Wars of Independence and Abolition

By the early 19th century, African slavery ceased altogether because cheaper labor from indigenous and European immigrant sources became more readily available. As a result, a few prominent politicians, including Manuel de Salas (1754–1841) and José Miguel Carrera (1785–1821), called for its abolition. In 1811, a revolutionary regime in Chile formally ended the slave trade and established a free womb law, which granted freedom to all people of color at birth.

In the early 19th century, when Chile began its movement for independence, a growing number of free colored soldiers fought against Spanish rule. Many already had experience in Chile's colonial militia. These soldiers appealed to their superiors that their services justified exemption from the payment of tributes, but their requests were often denied. More could be recruited because revolutionaries promised all slaves their freedom if they enlisted in patriotic armies under Bernardo O'Higgins (1778–1842). As a result, many served in the armies of O'Higgins and José de San Martín (1778–1850), one of Argentina's military leaders, as they completed Chile's liberation from Spain in 1817. Indeed, many members of San Martín's army were themselves Afro-Argentinian free persons of color. In 1823, Chile was one of the first republics in the Americas to abolish slavery completely.

Population Decline

The numbers of free persons of color declined dramatically during the colonial period, mainly as a result of MISCEGENATION, a process that began at the very moment the first Africans arrived in Chile. If they were allowed to choose mates, slaves tended to do so outside their racial group. Indeed, the acceleration of race mixing in Chile directly affected the social rank of native and African women because their status often depended upon the social rank of their husbands, friends, and lovers. By 1620, the combined number of African slaves and free people of color (approximately 22,500) significantly outnumbered the white population (approximately 15,000), but the free people of color mixed very quickly with the indigenous and European populations and stopped being identified as Afro-Chileans.

This process accelerated because the slave trade declined dramatically, thereby decreasing the number of newly imported slaves to replenish African populations in Chile. Although the slave trade flourished in other parts of Spanish America as commercial relations with other regions increased, it declined in Chile because cheaper labor became available in the market, and it was no longer profitable. The percentage of persons categorized by authorities as *negro* (pure African) declined so dramatically during the colonial period that they had almost completely disappeared by the middle of the 19th century. Indeed, by 1813, there were only approximately 33,000 blacks and mulattoes compared to more than 280,000 Spaniards. Even in Santiago, where the largest concentration of persons of color lived, pure blacks had virtually disappeared from the city. Most scholars agree that social and biological mixture with a rapidly growing number of Italian and Spanish immigrants meant that people identified as persons of color would nearly disappear by the early 20th century.

In addition to miscegenation as the main cause for the depopulation of persons of color in Chile, historians are now beginning to take a serious look at the role of forced migration. In this interpretation, Chile was merely a launching point from which African slaves were sent to all parts of the Spanish Empire. For example, JESUITS had established numerous estancias in colonial Chile and elsewhere in the Americas during the colonial period. African slaves worked in the sale of *aguardiente*, and their numbers actually grew between 1732 and 1767 via internal growth rather than by importation. However, when the Spanish Crown ordered the expulsion of all Jesuits from the Americas in 1767, all Jesuit property, including their African slaves, was sold at auction to those outside the region. In fact, many of these slaves were sent to Bolivia's mines, leading to the dramatic depopulation of persons of color, who otherwise might have been free people of color had they remained in Chile.

By the 20th century, as in Argentina and Uruguay, social and biological mixture coupled with a rapidly growing number of European immigrants meant that free people of color and their descendants would disappear. Although hundreds of years of race mixture have guaranteed that the percentage of African blood is minuscule, recent blood samples taken from various residents in Santiago, for example, confirm the historical and biological presence of Africans in Chile's gene pool. In addition, studies of names among the Aymara tribes in Chile and Bolivia reveal the influence of African-derived naming systems for their children. This presents very strong evidence that frequent cultural contact occurred between African and indigenous peoples.

People of color still live in various parts of the country as a result of relatively recent migrations. In Arica, Chile's northernmost town (once a Peruvian city before it lost control to Chile as a result of the War of the Pacific in 1884), for example, a resurgence of cultural pride in the country's African past has occurred in recognition of the migration of people of color from Peru to the area in the late 19th and early 20th centuries. Public festivals, such as the Pascua de los Negros, demonstrate the fact that Afro-Latin American and African cultural traits have mixed with modern Catholic rituals. The founding of a group calling itself Oro Negro (Black Gold) has raised awareness of Chile's rich African heritage and has rejected the deep-seated national idea of *la raza chilena*, the notion promoted by the first historians of Chile and modern leaders that the country's heritage may be understood by studying only its Spanish and indigenous roots.

Jesse Hingson

FURTHER READING

Carmagnani, Marcello. "Colonial Latin American Demography: Growth of Chilean Population." *Journal of Social History* 1 (1967): 179–191.

Fagerstrom, René Peri. *La raza negra en Chile: una presencia negada.* Santiago, Chile: Editora Hilda López Aguilar, 1999.

Flusche, Della M., and Eugene H. Korth. *Forgotten Females: Women of African and Indian Descent in Colonial Chile, 1535–1800.* Detroit: Blain Ethridge Books, 1983.

Mellafe R., Rolando. *La introducción de la esclavitud negra en Chile, tráfico y rutas.* 2nd ed. Santiago, Chile: Editorial Universitaria, 1984.

Sater, William F. "The Black Experience in Chile." In *Slavery and Race Relations in Latin America*, edited by Robert Brent Toplin, 13–50. Westport, Conn.: Greenwood Press, 1974.

CHRISTIANA RIOT

As sectional tensions in the United States mounted in the 1850s, Southern states sought federal protection for their right to own human property, and they found such protection in the Compromise of 1850 and the associated FUGITIVE SLAVE ACT OF 1850. This act allowed SLAVE OWNERS a great deal of power in recapturing runaway slaves and required private citizens to assist the slave owners or face severe fines. The law met with much resistance from the antislavery and free black communities. One of the best-known cases occurred in Christiana, Pennsylvania, on September 11, 1851.

The Christiana "Riot" began when a Maryland farmer, Edward Gorsuch, pursued four escaped slaves across the state border to the home of William Parker, a fugitive slave living in Christiana who had allowed them refuge. Parker, who was free by Pennsylvania law, had already participated in a number of Fugitive Slave Act resistance efforts, as had many of his neighbors. Indeed, when Gorsuch arrived to claim the fugitives, he found himself in conflict with a secret society that had been formed in southern Pennsylvania specifically to prevent fugitive captures. Thanks to the efforts of Samuel Williams, an agent from Philadelphia, the resistance group knew of Gorsuch's impending approach and had prepared.

Gorsuch was seeking the return of Noah Buley, Nelson Ford, and George and Joshua Hammond, four slaves who had escaped from him in 1849. He learned in September 1851 that the men were living near Christiana, a town known as a major point on the Underground Railroad, and he assembled an armed posse that included his son Dickinson, his nephews Joshua Gorsuch and Thomas Pearce, two other Marylanders, two Philadelphia constables, and the Philadelphia-based U.S. deputy marshal Henry H. Kline.

This force, however, proved no match for Parker and his well-organized interracial resistance network, which included his wife, Eliza, and a number of armed black men who were at his home when the slave catchers arrived. Gorsuch's forces surrounded the house, and Eliza Parker sounded a horn to alert neighbors of the attack. Men and women descended upon the Parker property from every direction with guns, clubs, corn cutters, and other tools for defense. When the fighting was over, several dozen blacks and two known white sympathizers, the Quaker shopkeeper Elijah Lewis and the miller Castner Hanway, had assembled to defend the fugitives. Two of the raiding party were wounded, but Edward Gorsuch was the only one to die in the standoff, which lasted almost an hour and would symbolize the deadly turn that the struggle against slavery had taken. The runaway slaves and Eliza Parker fled to CANADA, where they became free.

After the attack, 37 local black men and one white man were charged with treason under the Fugitive Slave Act. Only one was even tried—the white Castner Hanway—who, ironically, had offered shelter to some of the wounded Marylanders after the battle. He was acquitted by a Pennsylvania jury on November 15, 1851. The acquittal gave further evidence of public opposition to the Fugitive Slave Act in the North and gave Southerners further cause to fear Northern public opinion as a threat to the slave system.

Beverly C. Tomek

FURTHER READING

Bordewich, Fergus M. *Bound for Canaan: The Underground Railroad and the War for the Soul of America.* New York: HarperCollins, 2005.

Forbes, Ella. *But We Have No Country: The 1851 Christiana, Pennsylvania Resistance.* Cherry Hill, N.J.: Africana Homestead Legacy, 1998.

Nash, Roderick W. "William Parker and the Christiana Riot." *Journal of Negro History* 46, no. 1 (January 1961): 24–31.

Slaughter, Thomas P. *Bloody Dawn: The Christiana Riot and Racial Violence in the Antebellum North.* New York: Oxford University Press, 1991.

CIVIL RIGHTS LAWS IN THE UNITED STATES AFTER 1865

The first legacy of the end of the AMERICAN CIVIL WAR in 1865 for African Americans was the end of slavery. This was accomplished in several steps—slaves emancipated themselves by escaping, and the EMANCIPATION PROCLAMATION of January 1, 1863, ended slavery in territories controlled by the Confederacy, although those territories would have to be conquered by Union forces before freedom would actually be established there. The African-American holiday of Juneteenth, celebrated June 19, marks the effective date of the Confederate surrender in TEXAS in June 1865, the last military district of the Confederacy to recognize the Union victory. The slave states that remained loyal to the United States during the war were not affected by the proclamation, and they mainly ended slavery through their own constitutional acts between 1862 and 1865. The last holdouts, DELAWARE and KENTUCKY, saw slavery end with the adoption of the Thirteenth Amendment to the U.S. Constitution, on December 6, 1865.

The end of slavery left open the question of the future status of African Americans in the reunited country. Most states, in the North as well as in the South, had laws that restricted free blacks in some ways, ranging from complete prohibitions on migration to requirements for bonds or residential segregation. White leaders in Southern states, with large African-American populations and devastated economies, thought they needed harsh restrictions to prevent racial revolution and ensure continued white supremacy. They quickly passed state laws, called black codes, that extended the regime of discrimination and segregation that had applied to free people of color to all blacks. These developments represented net progress for former slaves. They remained free people—all Southern states were obliged to ratify the Thirteenth Amendment and outlaw slavery in their constitutions—and especially given the disrupted nature of Southern society in the immediate aftermath of the war, many of the legal restrictions were hard to enforce. But for free people of color in the South, and especially in the Upper South, the new laws were actually more restrictive than what had preceded them.

Northern public opinion had evolved during the course of the war, though. More than a quarter of a million African-American men fought in the ranks of the U.S. Army. Tens of thousands had given their lives in the struggle. As the army demobilized at the end of the war, the white state regiments mostly went home, leaving the remaining force with a very high percentage of black soldiers. America's security against outside aggression and renewed rebellion depended on black soldiers in the late 1860s. The war, which had begun as a struggle for union, evolved into a struggle for racial justice, a goal Lincoln proclaimed in his famous Gettysburg Address in 1863. So the North reacted harshly to the black codes enacted by the South. Congress barred Southern representatives and established military governments for the Southern states.

Congress also took action to ensure equal rights for blacks throughout the country. The Civil Rights Act of 1866, the first major piece of legislation of what would come to be called congressional Reconstruction, prohibited discrimination in legal proceedings, housing, and employment based on race or ethnicity. There was no federal enforcement of the law, however, and victims of discrimination were required to take their cases to the federal courts at their own expense. During the Reconstruction period (1865–77), federal courts in the South were ready to help plaintiffs, and the law was widely used. In addition, the FREEDMEN'S BUREAU, a relief organization set up by the army to aid displaced people in the South, helped black workers who had been discriminated against in employment file suits under this law. It was a very effective tool for blacks to advance themselves economically in the late 1860s.

CELEBRATION AT BALTIMORE ON MAY 19th 1870.

THE FIFTEENTH AMENDMENT AND ITS RESULTS.

Respectfully dedicated to the colored Citizens of the U.S of America A.D.1870. by Schneider & Fuchs. 184 N.Eutaw St.
Baltimore Md.

An 1870 poster entitled *The Fifteenth Amendment and Its Results* depicting a parade in Baltimore, Maryland, celebrating the ratification of the Fifteenth Amendment to the U.S. Constitution. The amendment was intended to guarantee black men the right to vote in the United States. On the bottom left and right are portraits of the prominent prewar free black leaders Frederick Douglass and Hiram Revels. The decision to grant the vote to African-American men was extremely controversial, especially in the former slave states. By the 1880s, most Southern blacks had lost the right to vote as part of the informal system of discrimination called Jim Crow, though some Southern blacks continued to be active in Republican Party politics and hold appointed offices under Republican administrations up until the 1940s. The situation was less harsh in border states such as Maryland and Missouri, where urban blacks were able to preserve some political influence through the Jim Crow era. *(Library of Congress)*

The Republicans in Congress feared that the laws they were passing could be overturned by shifts in the political winds, and they wanted to lock progress on racial equality into the Constitution. They passed the Fourteenth Amendment to the U.S. Constitution in 1866, and it was ratified in 1868, thanks in good measure to the requirement that Southern states ratify it before being allowed to send representatives to Congress. The amendment is probably the single most far-reaching change to the Constitution. It provides that every person born in the United States is a citizen with equal rights, overturning the 1856 Supreme Court decision in *Dred Scott v. Sandford* that blacks could not be citizens. It extends to the citizens

directly those rights that the Bill of Rights merely forbade the federal government to violate. That is, after 1868, every citizen had rights to free speech, freedom of religion, jury trial, and so forth, that state and local government entities could not violate. It threatened to deprive states of their representation in Congress if they disenfranchised blacks or other groups of people. It gave great power to the federal government to enforce racial justice.

In response to the progress blacks were making, whites in many Southern communities organized branches of the Ku Klux Klan and similar terrorist groups. Terrorism became a real security problem both for black communities and for the federal government as a whole by

1870. In response, Congress passed the Force Act of 1870 and the Civil Rights Act of 1871. Both laws permitted federal troops and law enforcement to attack terrorist groups directly. Many white terrorists were tried by military tribunals and imprisoned, while others were killed during military operations or summarily executed. The centrally organized Ku Klux Klan shut down operations almost immediately, while other groups limited operations or went underground. The Civil Rights Act of 1871 went further, giving people who had been attacked or discriminated against by state or local government officials acting in their official capacity to bring suit in federal courts. This provision was far-reaching, though it was many decades before it truly benefited black communities. In the 1960s and after, it became a central piece of the legal strategy of civil rights organizations addressing pervasive discrimination in the country. In the 1870s, however, the gradual political failure of RECONSTRUCTION IN THE UNITED STATES meant that local police and government officials could take over the role of the terrorist organizations and keep blacks "in their place" without fear of repercussions from the federal government. The federal Posse Comitatus Act of 1878 prevented the federal armed forces from acting as law enforcement officials, effectively placing the enforcement of civil rights laws in the hands of local officials, since the federal law enforcement agencies were generally active only in the western territories. This act removed the last vestiges of protection from Southern blacks.

The right to vote was an important goal, and many black activists and their white allies in Congress thought it would be the key element of protection for civil rights for blacks. Before the Civil War, each American state was responsible for determining the eligibility of voters in its own territory, subject to very broad guidelines in federal law. The Fourteenth Amendment to the U.S. Constitution had threatened to reduce the representation of states that systematically denied the right to vote to citizens on the basis of their race, but this provision was not used, and Southern states still placed roadblocks in the way of black voting participation. Thus, Congress proposed the Fifteenth Amendment in 1869, and it was ratified by the required three-fourths of the states in 1870. The amendment was supposed to ensure nondiscrimination in voting against black men. For the first decade or so after its passage, it worked as designed. Blacks were in the minority in almost all states, with the exception of South Carolina and Mississippi, but across the South, they were able to form alliances with white Republicans and control state governments. Even after the withdrawal of federal troops in the late 1870s, these coalitions continued to wield political power. Often, the elected officials and other black political leaders were prewar free people

of color. ROBERT SMALLS served five terms in the U.S. Congress from South Carolina between 1875 and 1887, after the withdrawal of federal troops from the state. HIRAM REVELS served as a U.S. senator from Mississippi in 1870–71 and continued to be active in the Republican Party until his death in 1901. Blanche Bruce (1841–98) was also a U.S. senator from Mississippi, from 1875 to 1881, after the withdrawal of federal troops there, and was the first African American to win convention votes for a major party's nomination to national office, gaining eight votes for vice president at the 1880 Republican National Convention. Complete exclusion of black voters from the election process in the South took more than a quarter-century after the end of Reconstruction, with the process only reaching its culmination after the turn of the century. Southern states used a combination of hurdles to reduce black participation to a tiny fraction of the electorate after 1900. States imposed burdensome registration procedures; enacted strict eligibility standards for voters, such as literacy tests that were theoretically nondiscriminatory but were actually administered so as to exclude blacks and admit whites; charged high poll taxes that excluded all poor people; and, as a last resort, turned to terrorist violence against blacks who managed to overcome the other hurdles. Even in the first decades of the 20th century, Southern black Republicans were an important constituency within the party structure for Northern white Republican leaders. President Theodore Roosevelt (1858–1919, served 1901–09) faced criticism from white Southerners for his intraparty alliance with blacks.

The last major piece of civil rights legislation during Reconstruction was the Civil Rights Act of 1875. This law prevented discrimination in "public accommodations," which included transportation, housing, food and lodging services, and other businesses serving the public. This progressive law would have enforced racial equality throughout the country. It was not enforced after the removal of federal troops from the South and was found unconstitutional by the Supreme Court in 1883. More than eight decades later, the provisions of this law were reenacted in the Civil Rights Act of 1964, this time accepted as constitutional by the courts, and form the basis of civil rights protections that people of color enjoy in the United States today.

Ultimately, the failure of Reconstruction was a failure of political will of the Northern people and the Republican Party and not a failure of legislation. Congress provided the tools to enable the army and the federal government to enforce equality throughout the country. Ultimately, though, Northern whites accepted national reconciliation with Southern whites, a reconciliation that excluded blacks. Discrimination became pervasive throughout the country, especially in the South. Southern blacks who tried to stand up for their rights under the law found the court system closed to them, administered by the same white elites who oppressed them in other ways. Juries were stocked with whites who would seldom vote for a black plaintiff. Congress would not use the enforcement mechanisms that might have punished Southern states for discrimination. It was not until the middle of the 20th century that blacks were able to relaunch their campaign for racial justice; then, with the political support of many whites, these laws became important tools to force the reluctant minority of resistant whites to live up to their legal obligations.

Stewart R. King

FURTHER READING

Berlin, Ira, Barbara J. Fields, and Steven F. Miller, eds. *Free at Last: A Documentary History of Slavery, Freedom, and the Civil War.* New York: New Press, 1995.

DuBois, W. E. B. *Black Reconstruction in America, 1860–1880.* New York: Free Press, 1998.

Fitzgerald, Michael W. *Splendid Failure: Postwar Reconstruction in the American South.* Chicago: Ivan Dee, 2008.

Foner, Eric. *Nothing but Freedom: Emancipation and Its Legacy.* Baton Rouge: Louisiana State University Press, 2007.

———. *Reconstruction: America's Unfinished Revolution, 1863–1877.* New York: HarperPerennial, 2002.

CLARK, ALEXANDER (1826–1891) *American civil rights activist, health care worker, soldier, and diplomat*

Alexander Clark's life illustrates many aspects of black life on the northern plains in the mid-19th century. He was able to take advantage of the opportunities that freedom offered to gain an education, get involved in politics, and rise in society. Although little known, he fought for civil rights, was a sergeant major during the AMERICAN CIVIL WAR, 1861–65, and served as U.S. ambassador to Liberia.

Clark was born free in PENNSYLVANIA sometime in 1826. His parents sent him to Cincinnati, OHIO, in 1839 to learn barbering. Barbers were also surgeons and provided general medical care to the poor and people who lived far from other medical resources. Clark moved to the frontier in IOWA in 1842, opening a barbershop in Muscatine, at the time one of the largest communities of people of color in the territory. Sixty-two free blacks were counted in Muscatine in the 1850 census. Clark was a leader in this small community, helping to organize the AFRICAN METHODIST EPISCOPAL CHURCH, an important community institution. He married and started a family and accumulated real estate through land grants and wise investments.

Clark was a delegate to the 1853 National Negro Convention in Rochester, New York, convened by the abolitionist FREDERICK DOUGLASS (*see also* NEGRO CONVENTION MOVEMENT IN THE UNITED STATES). Many midwesterners attended this convention, as the convention movement had its start among free blacks in the lower Midwest. Iowa had a Negro Convention of its own in 1857, which met in Clark's Muscatine A.M.E. church and to which Clark was also a delegate. The Negro Conventions were an important way that blacks could participate in political debates, since they were generally not permitted to vote even in the Northern states. Conventions passed resolutions and organized support for black civil rights. Many midwestern states had even passed laws forbidding blacks to enter or settle there or imposing special taxes on them; Iowa's legislature passed several anti-immigration measures in the 1840s and 1850s. The Iowa convention was particularly concerned about voting rights for blacks, which Iowa had denied in its new state constitution. But the convention also addressed an important issue for Clark, the right of blacks to equal educational opportunity.

Most midwestern states had set up public educational systems, on the model of the New England states where some early settlers had originally lived. The system of free public education, supported by local property tax receipts, was a major engine for economic growth and social promotion for white settlers in the Midwest and Far West. It was fast on its way to becoming the standard model for education throughout the United States. However, almost universally, blacks were not allowed to participate.

With the beginning of the American Civil War, the situation of blacks in the Midwest began to change. At first, white Iowans, as did other Northern whites, wanted to keep the war a "white man's struggle." Iowa generally opposed the ABRAHAM LINCOLN administration's moves toward black emancipation. Alexander Clark was at first refused when he offered to recruit black soldiers to serve in Iowa regiments. But the increasing manpower demands of the U.S. Army, the increasing reluctance of whites to volunteer for service, and the increasing polarization of the country as the war ground on led Iowa's governor to accept Clark's assistance in 1863. He ultimately recruited 1,157 men into the 1st Iowa Volunteers of African Descent (later the 60th Infantry, United States Colored Troops). Many of these men were runaway slaves from Southern states, but the army permitted Northern states to count Southern blacks toward their manpower quotas if state officials recruited and equipped them. However, more than 20 percent of the fewer than 2,000 Iowa blacks served in the war. Blacks were rarely granted commissions as officers in the U.S. Army during the Civil

War, so Clark had to settle for being the regiment's sergeant major, the highest noncommissioned rank. The regiment served in Arkansas from 1863 until the end of the war, fighting in the battle of Big Creek, July 25, 1864.

After the war, Clark returned to Muscatine. In 1868, he coordinated a campaign with the Iowa Republican Party to strike the word *white* from the Iowa Constitution and law code. The measure was adopted by referendum, and Iowa's laws became, at a stroke, the most egalitarian in the Midwest. The previous year, Clark had sued the school district of Muscatine to force them to permit his daughter to attend public school. In part on the basis of the new law, the state Supreme Court found in his favor, requiring that all children in Iowa be educated together. After the end of RECONSTRUCTION IN THE UNITED STATES, racial prejudice against blacks began to grow, and gains in civil rights were rolled back during what became known as the Jim Crow era. Clark bought a regional black newspaper, the *Chicago Conservator*, in 1880 and wrote editorials calling for civil rights and cultural acceptance of blacks. Before the war, he, as had many other black leaders, had opposed colonization schemes under which blacks would be resettled in LIBERIA or elsewhere outside the United States (*see also* EMIGRATION AND COLONIZATION). But when President Benjamin Harrison appointed Clark to the post of ambassador to Liberia in 1890, Clark accepted the honor. He died in Liberia the following year on May 31, 1891.

Clark's story exemplifies some of the features of black life on the frontier in the mid-19th century. He suffered discrimination: Even though his neighbors were firmly opposed to slavery, they did not want free blacks living around them. Clark and other blacks in the Midwest were always outsiders trying to gain acceptance into the society around them. The events of the Civil War gave them a respite, but racial prejudice did not disappear and regained strength in the following decades. The leadership of people such as Clark, who had been prominent free blacks before the war, was important to help the black community remain strong during the period of discrimination to come.

Stewart R. King

FURTHER READING

Frese, Stephen J. "From Emancipation to Equality: Alexander Clark's Stand for Civil Rights in Iowa." *History Teacher*, 40, no. 1 (November 2006). Available online. URL: http://www.historycooperative.org/journals/ht/40.1/frese.html. Acccesd December 20, 2010.

Jackson, Marilyn. "Alexander Clark: A Rediscovered Black Leader." *Iowan* 23 (Spring 1975): 45.

Schwalm, Leslie A. *Emancipation's Diaspora: Race and Reconstruction in the Upper Midwest.* Chapel Hill: University of North Carolina Press, 2009.

CLARKSON, JOHN (1764–1828) *British abolitionist and naval officer*

The younger brother of the dedicated abolitionist Thomas Clarkson, John Clarkson also joined William Wilberforce's campaign and is best known for founding the West African colony of SIERRA LEONE for former American slaves and black Loyalists whom the British government had located to Nova Scotia after the WAR OF AMERICAN INDEPENDENCE, 1775–83.

Born on April 4, 1764, in Wisbech—an inland port 90 miles from London—Clarkson was raised by his mother after his clergyman father died in 1766. In 1777, at age 12, he entered the Royal Navy, assisting Britain in its war against the American colonies and their European allies. Promoted to midshipman at age 14, he embarked on a warship, not to return home for four and a half years. He attained lieutenancy at age 18, serving only briefly in this capacity before the war officially ended in 1783. His years in the service strongly influenced Clarkson, who often witnessed the brutalities of naval discipline and observed enslaved workers in his 18 months protecting British interests in the West Indies.

As did most officers in peacetime, Clarkson found himself unemployed; he lent his support to the abolitionist cause, to which his more famous brother had dedicated his life. Together, the Clarkson brothers bent their efforts toward the plan to establish a utopian self-governing settlement in Sierra Leone for former British slaves. GRANVILLE SHARP and other organizers imagined that the so-called Province of Freedom would serve as both a trading post for African products and a base for the spread of Christianity. When the initial 1787 settlement, called Granville Town, destabilized within two years as a result of poverty, disease, and hostile nearby slave traders, the settlement was abandoned. The London-based friends of the settlement, initially crestfallen, were reenergized by the 1790 arrival in London of Thomas Peters, a black emissary from Nova Scotia. Peters, who represented 200 former slaves, communicated his cohorts' desire to move to the new province. In 1791, after once again failing to outlaw the slave trade, Parliament passed a bill to form the government-run Sierra Leone Company. Clarkson volunteered to follow Peters to Nova Scotia to organize the new colonists for a migration financed by the British government, leaving behind his fiancée, Susan Lee. Now 27, the lieutenant faced the staggeringly difficult task of signing up emigrants, facing the ire of white slavers, and coordinating the 15-ship fleet for what was a rough passage to Africa. They landed in March 1792.

Clarkson's "Mission to America," his journal of the historic migration from Halifax to Sierra Leone, offers a frank account of his accomplishments and blunders and records his personal investment in the black settlers and their futures. He oversaw the surveying and distribution of land, mediated disputes, advocated settlers' needs before the British government, and, in the four months before his December 1792 departure, served as governor. The settlement weathered several crises under his watch, from unrealized expectations to challenges to his authority, to funding shortfalls. Upon his return, Clarkson received no public praise because of his outspoken critiques of the company's failings. He married Lee in 1793, and though he never returned to Sierra Leone, he corresponded with its black leaders for the rest of his life.

Retiring from public life and from the navy, Clarkson settled into the lime trade in the hamlet of Purfleet in Essex. The Clarksons had 10 children, of whom six died young. He died at age 63 on April 2, 1828.

Emily M. Brewer

FURTHER READING

Clarkson, John. "Mission to America" (Birchtown, Nova Scotia, Canada: Black Loyalist Heritage Society Online Digital Project). Available online. URL: http://www. blackloyalist. com/canadiandigitalcollection/documents/diaries/mision. htm. Accessed February 28, 2010.

Clifford, Mary Louise. *From Slavery to Freetown: Black Loyalists after the American Revolution.* London: McFarland, 1999.

White, Ellen Gibson. *John Clarkson and the African Adventure.* London: Macmillan Press Ltd, 1980.

COARTACIÓN UNDER SPANISH LAW

Coartación was a legal procedure in Spanish law under which a slave could demand that his or her master set a price for MANUMISSION, and upon the receipt of that price, the slave would be freed. Although the term was used throughout Spanish America, the legal procedure was only fully legally enforceable and formalized in CUBA and PUERTO RICO in the 19th century, after Spain's mainland colonies gained their independence. Even there, the system was always under attack by SLAVE OWNERS, and the colonial governments were suspicious of a procedure that seemed to undermine the authority of the master and the color line.

The origin of *coartación* lies in the LAS SIETE PARTIDAS of King Alfonso X of Spain (1252–84). This law code established slavery as a legal institution in Spain but guaranteed certain rights to the slaves that were not found in other European countries' slave laws. Most importantly, Las Siete Partidas held that freedom was the natural condition of all individuals and that slavery was a vile exception. Thus, any steps toward to freedom that were consistent with public order were to be encouraged. Of course, local lawmakers, fearing disruption of the slave

system by slaves who thought they had a right to freedom, diluted this liberal impulse as much as they could. However, since the *coartado* had to pay for his or her freedom, masters had a direct financial interest in *coartación*. The basic legal principle remained in place and was an important touchstone for those who wished to seek their freedom through the courts.

In Spanish America before the rebellions of the 19th century, this continuous tension of the humane general principle, the generally restrictive application of the principle, and the self-interest of at least some masters in wishing to profit from their slaves' desire for freedom led to the development of a wide variety of customs that were sometimes referred to as *coartación*. In VENEZUELA and COLOMBIA, slaves who purchased their freedom were called *coartados*, although they apparently had no legal right to appeal to the courts to set their price against their masters' wishes. However, masters and slaves who wanted to arrange self-purchase often appealed to local dignitaries or the courts to help them set a fair price even when there was no legal requirement. The advantage to including a third party was that the agreement was then more solid and might survive the death or departure for Spain of the original master. In Spanish LOUISIANA and FLORIDA, the formalized procedure established in Cuba was also a part of the legal code but appears to have been rarely used. Louisiana's plantations operated under French cultural assumptions about MANUMISSION, which considered self-purchase illegitimate, while Florida had few slaves during the period of Spanish rule. Portuguese BRAZIL and other places in the Spanish Americas also had self-purchase, though the term *coartación* was rarely used in those places.

In the Spanish Caribbean, once a slave was *coartado*, that is, when a price had been fixed, the slave gained certain legal rights, often including the right to ask to be sold to a particular person or the right to refuse to be sold to a prospective master. At a minimum, if a *coartado* slave was sold, the agreement for self-purchase remained in force as between the slave and the new master. *Coartados* were still slaves: That is, they were obliged to work for their master, had no right to wages, were subject to some forms of punishment from their masters, their children would still be slaves, and so forth. But they had made a significant step along the road to freedom. Masters were often very much opposed to *coartación*, and records of many legal cases in both Cuba and Puerto Rico still attest to the ferocity of the struggle around slaves' rights to self-purchase. For example, in 1855, Maria, a slave of Carlota Dascar of Santiago de Cuba, sought her freedom through the courts. The *síndico*, or protector of slaves of the city, took Maria into his house to protect her from abuse by the mistress. The mistress then sued the *síndico*. The principal point of disagreement appears to have been the price that Maria should pay for her freedom, as her mistress demanded an extraordinarily high 600 pesos, which the courts finally reduced to 450 pesos. In order to pressure Maria to agree, her mistress sought to sell her to another master, but Maria insisted on, and got, a formal discharge from the court entitling her to seek a purchaser of her own liking. Finally, Maria received a favorable decision from the court of appeals and was able to purchase herself.

Coartación granted the slave the right to purchase himself or herself, but not necessarily the resources. With an ordinary workingman's wages averaging less than a peso a day, slaves would have to work for years to accumulate enough money to purchase their freedom. Presumably, many people would work together to gather the money, and *coartados* were often people with valuable skills. As with other forms of manumission, women were the most common beneficiaries—one study shows that almost two-thirds of the people who gained their freedom through *coartación* in Puerto Rico were women. For a family, gaining formal manumission of female members had a multiplier effect since all children born after manumission would themselves be free. Additionally, women may have had better access to money through participation in the marketplace; often small commerce in the plantation Americas was dominated by women of color, both free and enslaved.

Not all *coartación* agreements were consummated by the formal manumission of the slave. In fact, probably as many people lived out their lives as *coartados* as actually achieved formal manumission. Since masters could and often did permit *coartados* to move about freely seeking work on their own account, perhaps in return for a small payment, this status was often a way for slaves to enjoy many of the benefits of freedom while their masters gained a small cash income (*see also* LIVING "AS FREE"). This appears to have been especially true of men who had craft skills. Since male slaves did not pass on their status to their children with free women, it made more economic sense for a man to remain a slave, if he was allowed to work for wages on his own account, and devote his resources to achieving the freedom of his partner and children. If the master tried to interrupt this arrangement, the slave could always have recourse to the courts and the formal process.

Coartación often made economic sense for masters, as well. The price for freedom was set at the beginning of the process, when the slave was young and at his or her most productive. Often, if the slave had to work for many years to gain the resources to fulfill the contract, the actual market value of the slave would have fallen. In the mean-

time, the master would be receiving regular payments, since *coartados* often paid in installments rather than a lump sum. Finally, the master would have the price of a young healthy slave in return for surrendering rights over an elderly and no longer productive one.

Coartación was blamed for disrupting the "natural" subordination of slaves. It was suspended in Cuba after the revolt led by José Antonio Aponte in 1812. Aponte, a free black, had gained his freedom through self-purchase (though not, apparently, with the assistance of the courts), and the government felt that the prospect of self-purchase made slaves "arrogant." The practice was swiftly reestablished, both because the government of Spain insisted and because masters missed the potential income. However, some masters continued to object, as Carlota Dascar of Santiago de Cuba did, arguing that court-ordered self-purchase unlawfully deprived her of her property rights.

In sum, *coartación* was a legal institution that held potential benefits for both slave and master. However, it diluted the authority of masters over their slaves and created an ambiguous class of people who were neither entirely free nor fully enslaved. On the other hand, governments liked the fact that it demonstrated liberality and helped give slaves a sense of having a place in the social system and hope for the future.

Stewart R. King

FURTHER READING

Bergad, Laird W. *The Comparative Histories of Slavery in Brazil, Cuba, and the United States*. Cambridge: Cambridge University Press, 2007.

Figueroa, Luis A. *Sugar and Slavery in Nineteenth-Century Puerto Rico*. Chapel Hill: University of North Carolina Press, 2005.

de la Fuente, Alejandro. "Slaves and the Creation of Legal Rights in Cuba: *Coartacíon* and *Papel*." *Hispanic American Historical Review* 87, no. 4 (2007): 659–692.

CODE NOIR IN FRENCH LAW

Like the rigorously structured French château of Versailles where it was conceived, the 55 articles of the Code Noir—or Black Code—sought to impose order and rationality on French colonial slave society when first passed in 1685. It offered guidelines for the policing of slavery and articulated the rights of freed slaves up until the FRENCH REVOLUTION a century later. The code applied in the overseas colonies, where Africans labored in the Caribbean sugar islands (Saint-Domingue, Guadeloupe, Martinique, and St-Christophe), and Native Americans and Africans toiled in French possessions in mainland North America, from Louisiana to Illinois to Canada. Both Versailles and the Code Noir owe their existence to

Homo sum; humani nihil a me alienum pu... Ter...

Je suis Homme; et rien de ce qui intéresse l'Homme ne m'est étranger.

The Code Noir, an illustration engraved by Louis-Joseph Masquelier, from *Voyage à L'Isle de France* by Bernardin de Saint-Pierre. This 1773 allegory demonstrates that the Code Noir, the French Black Code, was seen, in at least some ways, as protecting blacks against their masters. The freedman, carrying his broken chain, holds up a copy of the Code Noir and tells his former master, "I am a man, and nothing that interests a man is foreign to me." *(The Bridgeman Art Library)*

Jean-Baptiste Colbert, King Louis XIV's most influential minister for domestic affairs from the early 1660s until his death in 1683. Although the Code Noir was adopted two years after Colbert's death, it is the culmination of legal reforms he set in motion during his tenure.

The preamble to the code touts as its twin goals "to maintain the discipline of the Catholic Church and to order things concerning the position and status of slaves." Beyond the first article's dictate for the exile of all Jews from the colonies, numerous articles require adherence to orthodox Roman Catholicism. Slaves were to be baptized into the church and raised in the faith (Art. II); colonists were not to practice any other faith openly (Art. III); those vested with authority over slaves were to be Roman Catholic (Art. IV); all subjects and slaves were to observe the Sabbath and refrain from working on Sundays and on Catholic holidays (Art. VI); and non-Catholic subjects could not be legally married, and their children were to be considered bastards (Art. VIII). This emphasis on Catholicism complemented the Edict of Fontainebleau, also passed in 1685, which outlawed Protestantism in France and extended orthodox Roman Catholicism universally across France and its overseas territories.

The Code Noir legally defined slaves as chattel that could be bought and sold, and it set forth guidelines for the treatment and punishment of slaves. Regarding marriage and children: Masters could not force slaves to marry, but neither could slaves marry without their masters' permission (Art. XI); the child of two slaves became the property of the mother's master (Art. XII); the child of a freeman and a female slave was to be born a slave, and the child of a freewoman and a male slave was to be born free (Art. XIII). Regarding slaves' behavior: Slaves could not carry weapons, except when sent hunting (Art. XV); slaves of different masters could not gather under any pretext, else risk the possibility of corporal punishment or death (Art. XVI); they could not sell sugarcane or other commodities (Arts. XVIII and XIX); a slave who struck his master or a member of the master's family would be punished by death (Art. XXXIII); a slave who ran away for a month would be branded with a fleur de lys on one shoulder the first time, a second fleur de lys brand and a cut hamstring the second time, and death the third time (Art. XXXVIII); and a member of a slave nuclear family could not be taken or sold separately (Art. XLVII). Regarding masters' rights and duties: Beyond the dictates for slaves' religious instruction, masters were to nourish and care for slaves who were sick or infirm with age, regardless of whether the sickness was curable, and abandoned slaves were to be treated by a hospital and their care billed to their masters (Art. XXVII).

While the Code Noir nominally protected slaves from capricious and cruel treatment by their masters, there was little enforcement, and compliance varied widely. Violations of the code—and even the murder of slaves—was unpunished. Perhaps inspired by the marquis de Lafayette's experiment in Guiana of paying a salary to slaves and refraining from corporal punishment, King Louis XVI issued a series of royal decrees from 1784 to 1786 to improve slave conditions. These decrees included provisions for slaves' food and private plots of land and regulated the punishment masters could employ. Although planters in the colonies thwarted the application of these decrees, the new regulations spurred rumors that the king had freed the slaves, and these rumors helped spark many of the slave revolts in the early 1790s.

According to the original Code Noir, freed slaves (*affranchis*) were to enjoy the same rights, privileges, and immunities enjoyed by freeborn people (Art. LIX). Therefore, people of African descent who were emancipated were to be the legal and political equals of French whites. However, as the number of free blacks in the colonies multiplied; became educated, entrepreneurial, and wealthy; and sought equality with the white colonists, the Code Noir was modified in the 18th century in order to stymie their ambitions and to reinforce white supremacy. The majority of the repressive legislative changes were made in the final decades of the colonial regime.

The Code Noir de la Louisiane (black code of LOUISI-ANA) was passed in 1724 "for the regulation and administration of justice, police, discipline and trade of black slaves in the Province and colony of Louisiana." The two codes both address the exile of Jews and the universality of the ROMAN CATHOLIC CHURCH, but the Louisiana version prescribes stricter regulations, including a dictate against MISCEGENATION and white-black cohabitation and marriage (Art. VI); a requirement that masters bury baptized slaves in consecrated cemeteries (Art. XI); a prohibition against masters' substituting rations of brandy instead of food and clothing for their slaves (Art. XVIII); and guidelines for prosecuting masters who inflict inhumane and barbarous treatment on their slaves (Art. XX).

The Code Noir stands apart in the body of European legislation as among the most far-reaching official codifications of race, slavery, and liberty. The provisions regarding free people of color in the 1685 code provided for the most egalitarian treatment of this group of any colonial law code in the Americas. Unfortunately, as they were watered down or ignored in actual fact, free people of color in French colonies actually suffered significant discrimination. However, the legal provisions remained an important tool for free colored activists seeking civil rights for their community, and for individual free people of color defending their rights through the legal system.

Emily M. Brewer

FURTHER READING

Dubois, Laurent. *A Colony of Citizens: Revolution and Slave Emancipation in the French Caribbean, 1787–1804.* Chapel Hill: University of North Carolina Press, 2004.

Eckberg, Carl J. *Code Noir: The Colonial Slave Laws of French Mid-America.* Naperville, Ill.: Center for French Colonial Studies, 2005.

Stearns, Peter N. "The Free People of Color in Louisiana and St. Domingue: A Comparative Portrait of Two Three-Caste Slave Societies." *Journal of Social History* 3, no. 4 (1970): 406–430.

Stovall, Tyler. "Race and the Making of the Nation: Blacks in Modern France." In *Diasporic Africa: A Reader,* edited by Michael A. Gomez, 200–218. New York: New York University Press, 2006.

COFFEE CULTIVATION

In its role in the lives of free people of color, coffee was probably the most important crop in the plantation complex in the Americas. It was an important secondary crop in terms of its economic role, contributing less to the overall Atlantic economy than SUGAR CULTIVATION, the giant, and also somewhat less than the late-coming but important COTTON CULTIVATION. Unlike sugar, though, coffee can be produced efficiently on a quite small farm and does not require much specialized equipment in order to prepare it for market, making it an ideal starter crop for people with little capital, such as free people of color.

Coffee grows on bushes as a small red cherrylike fruit. The bushes take four or five years to mature and begin bearing fruit and then are productive for another 15–20 years. The berries are picked when fully ripe and dried, typically in the sun. Once dry, the fruit is stripped off, leaving the seed. Seeds must be roasted before use, but this can be done by the consumer or at an intermediate point; the dried and unroasted seeds keep well. Processing thus requires very little in the way of gear or specialized labor. The bushes can be intercropped with food crops and actually benefit from being planted alongside nitrogen-fixing crops such as beans and squash. The bushes can also be intercropped with trees, and some varieties grow better in shade than in full sun. The intercropped trees can be fruit producers or be harvested for firewood. All these features make coffee a useful crop for small farmers.

Another characteristic of coffee cultivation is that the planter must wait several years before his or her investment bears fruit. Poor whites who immigrated to the colonies to make their fortune were often trying to build their plantations with borrowed money. It was easier for a white man with decent connections to borrow money than for a free person of color. However, servicing their debt for the years of waiting for the bushes to mature was an insuperable handicap for most poor whites. Free colored planters, on the other hand, did not have the same chance to borrow money as whites. Their financing was either from their white relatives or from their savings. They also had no social position to maintain and could live as peasants on the food produced on their farms while waiting for the coffee bushes to mature.

Coffee was first domesticated in Ethiopia sometime during the first millennium A.D. From East Africa, the habit of coffee drinking spread to the Islamic world, and from there to Europe, thanks to the Crusades and other, more peaceful cultural contacts between the Middle East and Europe in the Middle Ages. The mountains of East Africa and the Arabian Peninsula were ideal country for coffee bushes: high altitudes, relatively warm temperatures, moderate but not excessive rain. Europeans and Middle Easterners imported their coffee from East Africa until the 17th century, when coffee bushes were first grown in the mountains of Indonesia and South Asia, introduced by Indian and Dutch merchants. The French acquired coffee plants from the Dutch and introduced coffee to the Caribbean island of Martinique. From Martinique, the drink spread throughout the French colonial world, then to the Spanish and Portuguese Americas in the 18th and 19th centuries.

Everywhere it was introduced in the Americas, coffee instantly appealed to sugar planters as a way to make profitable use of their more distant and mountainous lands. In the 18th century, coffee became a leading crop throughout the Caribbean, wherever high mountains and sufficient rainfall permitted it. The largest coffee-producing colonies in the late 1700s were SAINT-DOMINGUE, Cuba, Colombia, and Martinique. In the 19th century, Brazil became a large coffee producer, surpassing the Caribbean islands and producing most of the coffee consumed in the world until after 1950, when smaller producers in Asia, South America, the Caribbean, and Africa began to tap a growing market for higher-quality coffee. Most sugar colonies, especially the islands of the Caribbean, contained remote mountainous interior areas that were outside the effective control of the colonial government. Governments often awarded land grants in these areas, to encourage development, but without a crop that could be grown there profitably, the planters had no incentive to work these lands. Sugar required flat, well-watered fields, and in any case sugar is a bulky crop, which was best grown near water for greatest efficiency in transportation. The interior wastelands were worse than useless to the slave society, because they were a standing invitation to slaves who wanted to run

A COFFEE PLANTATION, LAS NUBES

WEEDING AND PROTECTING THE YOUNG PLANT FROM THE SUN

TRANSPLANTING THE YOUNG COFFEE TREE, ANTIGUA

A FULL-GROWN COFFEE-TREE, LAS NUBES

An 1877 illustration of coffee cultivation in Guatemala. Coffee proved to be a very profitable crop for free colored farmers in the Tropics. It required only a small labor force and little in the way of technologically sophisticated equipment, and a farmer could make a good crop with only the labor of his or her family or at most a few slaves. The plants grew on steep hillsides, often the kind of marginal land that free colored farmers could afford to buy. The demand for coffee in Europe grew rapidly between 1750 and 1850, providing plenty of room in the market for small producers and little incentive for large white landowners to try to force their smaller black neighbors out of business. *(Library of Congress)*

away and form settlements of MAROONS. But with coffee, this dilemma was resolved.

As the coffee revolution spread across the Americas, it coincided in many colonies with the final offensive against the maroons. Colonial governments that had been content to fence the runaways off in seemingly useless interior areas, even making treaties with them to prevent them from receiving new runaways, suddenly found that there was a profit to be made in depriving the maroons of their lands. The maroon settlements that survived this period did so by having the good fortune of living in an area where coffee cultivation was not possible, as in SURINAM or North America, or by integrating as villages of freed people, as in Jamaica or the fugitive Haitian maroons in the DOMINICAN REPUBLIC.

As the maroons moved out, though, other free people of color moved into these areas. Planters commonly

gave their remote plots of land to favored free people of color, their children, or others. These plots were also easy assets for planters to sell to free coloreds for quick cash when economic times were tough. At first, free people of color ranched or grew food on these lands (*see* PROVISION GROUND FARMING), but once coffee was available, free colored farmers turned to it with enthusiasm. In 1780, one of the wealthiest men of any color in Saint-Domingue was JULIEN RAIMOND, a free man of color who was a coffee planter and owned plantations worth at least half a million livres, about $15 million in today's terms. Another less successful Dominguan coffee planter of color was JEAN-BAPTISTE CHAVANNES, one of the earliest leaders of rebel forces in the HAITIAN REVOLUTION. His was only one of dozens of similar families in Saint-Domingue. The Brazilian coffee boom of the 19th century also saw many free people of color grow rich, and then saw many of them lose everything as prices collapsed.

Coffee was a profitable crop under most circumstances, but as with all agricultural commodities, its price could vary sharply. Once again, this was an advantage for free people of color, as they were commonly less exposed to fluctuations because of their typically lower burden of debt. Most of the countries that had the geography and climate required for coffee bushes to grow well—high altitude, relatively dry climate, no frost—were also places where, for the most part, free people of color could own land and slaves. There were a few exceptions, including Jamaica, where it was very difficult for a person of color to be a planter (*see also* PLANTERS AND PLANTER AGENTS), but for the most part, the physical geography and political/social conditions lined up well. For all these reasons, coffee was a very important crop for free farmers of color and a doorway to the exalted status of planter for a lucky few.

Stewart R. King

FURTHER READING

Trouillot, Michel-Rolph. "Motion in the System: Coffee, Color, and Slavery in Eighteenth-Century Saint-Domingue." *Review*, v 3 (Winter 1982): 331–338.

Wild, Anthony. *Coffee, a Dark History*. New York: Norton, 2007.

COLOMBIA

Introduction: Defining Free People of Color in the Colombian Context

Phrases such as "free people of color," "free coloreds," and "free men of all colors" are generally used to refer to people of African descent who were not slaves. This use fits neatly in U.S., Caribbean, and Brazilian plantation societies where contact with Europeans led to a stark decline (bordering extinction) in native populations and massive imports of African slaves. Through MANUMISSION (never very common before the late 18th

Simón Bolívar (1783–1830) is shown liberating the slaves of Colombia in 1819. In fact, slavery persisted in Colombia until 1851, and Bolívar's major achievement in race relations was establishing the principle of equality among whites, Indians, and free people of color. *(Museo 20 de Julio de 1810 Bogotá/Gianni Dagli Orti/The Art Archive)*

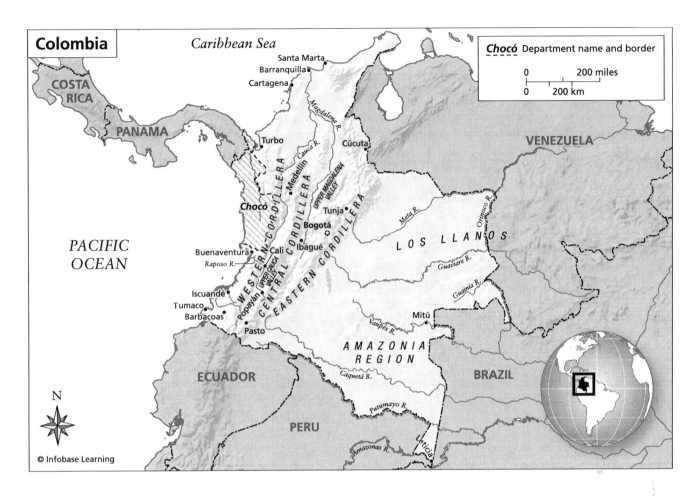

century) and sexual unions between whites and African slaves, these societies witnessed the appearance and slow growth of a free population of African descent. The near-extinction of native peoples resulted in biracial societies in which free people of color, necessarily, were of African descent. In societies with larger native populations at the time of contact with Europeans, Indians—though greatly decimated—were able to survive initial contact and recover to become one of the most notable sectors of the population. The availability of indigenous labor in places such as the former Aztec and Inca Empires (approximately present-day MEXICO and PERU, respectively) reduced the need for massive import of African slaves. Interracial sexual unions, therefore, did not necessarily result in offspring of African descent. Thus, though African slaves were imported in every corner of the Americas, in societies with a significant indigenous component, free people of color seldom were of African descent. Or, more accurately, free people of African descent constituted a small portion of the free colored population.

During the colonial period and throughout the 19th century, the area that constitutes present-day Colombia stood somewhere between these two demographic configurations. While many free people of color in Colombia (or New Granada, as it was called during the colonial period)

were indeed descendants of African-born people transported to the Americas as slaves, the term also included all kinds of people who did not neatly fit within the established categories of *blancos* (whites), *indios* (Indians), and slaves. In other words, the term *libres de todos los colores* (free people of all colors) was a residual category that included people who were variously referred to as mulattoes, *pardos*, mestizos, zambos, and by many other terms. More than a racial category, it should be understood as a status category that encompassed all men and women who were neither slaves, nor tribute-paying Indians, nor whites, nor rich or well connected enough to be able to obtain CÉDULAS DE GRACIAS AL SACAR that made them legally white. As an analytical category, thus, free people of color is far from being a self-explanatory concept that broadens our understanding of colonial and 19th-century Colombian society. In fact, the term is full of ambiguity. On the one hand, the use of the term (and the number of people who fall under it) strengthens the depiction of Colombia as a country characterized by racial mixture (i.e., the idea of Colombia as a mestizo nation). On the other hand, it leads to the false idea that free coloreds constituted a political community united by a defined set of experiences and goals. The historian Alfonso Múnera has provided a useful definition of the term that helps offset its ambiguity. In his words, "The expression *libre de todos los colores* makes reference to a person that given his [or her] social condition could prove that he [or she] was not subject to any kind of servitude or special contribution."

In places such as Colombia's Caribbean and Pacific coasts—sparsely populated before the Spanish arrival and more affected by native population decline as a result from contact—free people of color tended to be of African descent; in central areas—densely populated by Native Americans even after the decimation that resulted from first contact with Spaniards—the African component was less well-recognized among the free colored population. In both areas, however, after the initial phases of Spanish colonization, free people of color (of African descent or not) constituted the majority of the population. Despite their numbers, their image remains blurry, and a scholarly interpretation of who were the free people of color in Colombia is still lacking. As the historian Margarita Garrido recently wrote, "We still know very little about the *libres de todos los colores'* view of themselves, of others and of the society they lived in."

Geographical Context

Colombia is located at the northwestern tip of South America. It occupies an area of approximately 400,000 square miles (roughly the area occupied by California, Arizona, and New Mexico combined). It is the only South American country with coasts on the Caribbean Sea and the Pacific Ocean. It is crossed from south to north by three long cordilleras that—even today—make the journey from east to west a long, painful one. In between these cordilleras run Colombia's two main rivers—the Magdalena River and its biggest tributary, the Cauca River—which merge north of the Central Cordillera and then continue until the Magdalena's encounter with the Caribbean Sea in northern Colombia. The three cordilleras (Eastern, Central, and Western) and the Magdalena and Cauca Rivers divide Colombia into nine clearly defined geographic regions: (1) the Caribbean region, historically dominated by CARTAGENA—Colombia's main port through the colonial and early national periods; (2) the Eastern Cordillera region, dominated by Bogotá; (3) the Upper Magdalena Valley, agricultural region largely responsible for supplying Bogotá; (4) the Central Cordillera region, area of internal colonization developed during the 19th century; (5) the Upper Cauca Valley, agricultural region developed since the colonial period around the towns of Popayán and Cali; (6) the Southern Highlands, densely populated by indigenous groups in the vicinity of Pasto; (7) the Pacific Lowlands, largely populated by people of African descent; (8) the Eastern Plains, frontier region historically isolated from the center of the country;

and (9) the Amazonia, Colombia's most isolated region. Throughout most of Colombia's history (and certainly during the colonial and early national periods), topography limited interregional communication. This relative regional isolation has led major historians of Colombia to refer to it as "a nation in spite of itself" (David Bushnell) and as a country of "fragmented land, [and] divided society" (Frank Safford and Marco Palacios).

Free People of Color during the Conquest, 1500s–1560s

The conquest of the territory that was later called New Granada began during the first years of the 16th century, when South America's Caribbean coasts were first explored by Spaniards. During the first four decades of the 16th century, especially between 1526 and 1539, Spanish conquistadores founded what were to become the major colonial towns, some of which are still among Colombia's most important cities. Santa Marta (1526) and Cartagena (1533), on the Caribbean coast; Cali (1536) and Popayán (1537), in southwestern Colombia; and Santa Fe (1538), in central Colombia, were all founded during this period.

During the first half of the 16th century, Indians—despite the drastic population decline produced by contact with Europeans—constituted the majority of the population. A small number of Spaniards and African slaves complemented the population of New Granada. This triracial division of society, in theory, allowed no space for the emergence of free people of color. In practice, however, there was plenty of space for the appearance of such a group. Since during this initial period of conquest the vast majority of Spaniards entering to Colombia were men, sexual relations between Spaniards and Indian women rapidly led to the emergence of a small population of mestizos. Though not usually referred to as free people of color, mestizos were neither Indian nor white, and since they were not slaves, they can be regarded as free people of mixed ancestry. While there are no precise records for the number of African slaves who took part in the conquest of New Granada, on the basis of other more documented conquests (i.e., those of Mexico and Peru), it seems safe to assume that some of these slaves were rewarded with their freedom.

Thus, by the middle of the 16th century, the population of New Granada consisted of a large, though declining, indigenous population, several thousand Spaniards, and a small minority comprising blacks (slaves and free) and mestizos. According to the 16th-century chronicler Juan López de Velasco, in 1560 of a total of 1,275,000 people living in New Granada, 8,000 were whites—most of them born in Spain, but at least some of them criollos (sons and daughters of Spanish parents born in the Americas); 1,260,000 were Indians; and 7,000 were blacks, mulattoes;

and mestizos (probably mestizos constituted the vast majority of this last group).

The Place of Free People of Color in the Established Colony, 1570s–1770s

After the initial turmoil of the conquest period, New Granada developed into a possession of secondary importance within the Spanish-American territories. While great amounts of silver made Peru and Mexico the centers of Spanish colonization, New Granada's gold was not sufficient to turn this territory into one of the main Spanish overseas possessions. Its almost peripheral status played an important role in the relaxation of authority, which, in turn, coupled with native depopulation as the result of conquest and substantial imports of African slaves, led to a massive increase in the free colored population. From a small, virtually nonexistent minority in the middle of the 16th century, free people of color rose to become nearly half of New Granada's population by the last decades of the 18th century.

This dramatic increase in the numbers of free people of color is explained by two interconnected trends: First, as a result of *mestizaje* (racial mixing) more people were born into the ranks of free people of color. Second, throughout the colonial period, it became increasingly common for slaves to secure freedom. *Mestizaje*, initially between Spanish men and indigenous women, continued to increase the number of free people of color. The offspring of these unions continued to bear free children. Furthermore, the importation of nearly 123,000 slaves—including many women—between the 1550s and the 1770s eventually led to a surge in the number of free people of African descent. Through manumission, a common practice in Spanish America, and purchase of freedom, many of these slaves became *libertos* (freed). Conjugal unions between *libertos* and mestizos further contributed to the increase in free people of color. Through *mestizaje*, manumissions, and purchases of freedom, free people of color's numbers increased to the point that, by the middle of the 18th century, they constituted the vast majority of the population of New Granada. Of this large number, a significant minority were people who had some African ancestry.

By the second half of the 18th century, as a result of native population recovery after the depopulation caused by the conquest and the cumulative imports of African slaves, certain demographic characteristics that were to characterize 19th- and 20th-century Colombia became apparent. The central and southern highlands, given the pace of native population recovery, developed a free colored population that was more Indian than African. Because most of the African slaves were imported to work in the mines of western New Granada and the plantations of southwestern and Caribbean New Granada, these regions developed populations of free people of color who were also free people of African descent. Benefiting from legal options to obtain freedom (manumission or purchase), a significant number of slaves and their descendants moved into the ranks of free people of color. When these opportunities were not readily available, many slaves opted to gain freedom through less legal means. Thus, *cimarronaje* (i.e., the practice of running away and settling into *palenques* or communities of MAROONS) became a common phenomenon in these regions.

Maroons: Slaves or Free Blacks?

Throughout the Americas, slaves commonly responded to maltreatment by escaping individually or collectively to found, or become accepted into, settlements called *palenques*. Though still officially property of a master, cimarrons (runaway slaves) often managed to secure freedom on a permanent basis. Either by remaining fugitives until their death or by reaching agreements with the Spanish authorities, successful runaway slaves became de facto free.

In colonial New Granada, *palenques* provoked complaints reiterated by authorities throughout the colonial period. Famous and long-standing *palenques* were founded sometime during the 17th century in the provinces of Popayán, in southwestern New Granada, and Cartagena, on the Caribbean coast. During the 18th century, colonial authorities launched intense campaigns of pacification geared toward the incorporation of runaway slaves and groups of unconquered Indians. The *palenque* of Castillo, in Popayán, and the *palenque* of San Basilio, in Cartagena, were among the most famous targets of these campaigns. After several unsuccessful attempts to subjugate their inhabitants, both settlements were offered peace treaties that would provide their residents freedom and the right to remain unmolested by colonial authorities. In exchange, cimarrons had to promise to reject new runaway slaves. The cimarrons of Castillo and San Basilio followed different paths. While the former chose to reject the treaty, the latter complied with its conditions. As a result, the Spanish authorities launched another expedition against Castillo, which led to the cimarrons' final defeat in 1745. On the contrary, the acceptance of the treaty by the cimarrons of San Basilio secured them permanent freedom and led to its establishment as an officially recognized community of free blacks.

Cimarronaje, thus, was both an attractive and a dangerous strategy. As shown by the examples of Castillo and San Basilio, running away to found a *palenque* could lead to two opposite outcomes: obtaining legal freedom provided runaways complied with some conditions or being defeated and either killed or returned to slavery.

POPULATION OF NEW GRANADA, 1778–1780

Provinces	Whites		Indians		Free People of All Colors		Slaves		Total	
Tunja	101,658	45.00%	32,107	13.58%	97,897	41.41%	4,767	2.02%	236,429	29.83%
Cartagena	13,850	11.70%	19,416	16.40%	75,490	63.77%	9,626	8.13%	118,382	14.93%
Santa Fe	28,057	28.88%	32,054	33.00%	35,573	36.62%	1,463	1.51%	97,147	12.26%
Popayán	9,768	15.15%	11,363	17.63%	29,949	46.46%	13,380	20.76%	64,460	8.13%
Antioquia	7,866	16.97%	2,034	4.39%	27,535	59.39%	8,931	19.26%	46,366	5.85%
Mariquita	12,336	26.15%	4,436	9.40%	26,313	55.79%	4,083	8.66%	47,168	5.95%
Santa Marta	4,566	11.43%	8,504	21.29%	22,882	57.29%	3,988	9.98%	39,940	5.04%
Pamplona	3,399	12.44%	4,475	16.38%	17,980	65.80%	1,471	5.38%	27,325	3.45%
Neiva	5,908	22.33%	3,850	14.55%	15,810	59.76%	888	3.36%	26,456	3.34%
Girón	1,470	21.02%	126	1.80%	4,596	65.68%	804	11.50%	6,993	0.88%
Los Llanos	1,558	7.45%	15,189	72.63%	4,046	19.35%	119	0.57%	20,912	2.64%
Chocó	332	2.26%	5,414	36.93%	3,160	21.55%	5,756	39.26%	14,662	1.85%
Riohacha	351	8.89%	633	16.03%	2,513	63.62%	453	11.47%	3,950	0.50%
Barbacoas	521	7.87%	512	7.74%	1,678	25.36%	3,907	59.04%	6,618	0.83%
Pasto	10,075	37.63%	15,592	58.24%	922	3.44%	184	0.69%	26,773	3.38%
Iscuandé	612	22.25%	363	13.20%	855	31.08%	921	33.48%	2,751	0.35%
Raposo	99	3.10%	290	9.07%	549	17.17%	2,259	70.66%	3,197	0.40%
Tumaco	512	16.31%	156	4.97%	490	15.61%	1,981	63.11%	3,139	0.40%
TOTAL	206,094	26.00%	158,534	20.00%	364,627	46.00%	63,413	8.00%	792,668	100.00%

Source: Anthony McFarlane, Colombia before Independence: Economy, Society, and Politics under Bourbon Rule, Cambridge: Cambridge University Press, 1993.

The Census of 1778–1780

The first official and detailed count of the population of New Granada that shows that free people of color constituted the majority of the population is the countrywide census that was taken between 1778 and 1780. Ordered by Archbishop Viceroy Caballero y Góngora, this census constituted an integral part of the Bourbon Reform project. As such, it was developed as an instrument to facilitate the collection of taxes. Therefore, census takers were mainly concerned with classifying people according to fiscal categories. As a result of this interest, the census classified people as whites, Indians, slaves, and free people of color. Free people of color, thus, constituted not so much a socioracial category but a residual fiscal category that encompassed nonwhites who were neither slaves nor subject to Indian tribute. Furthermore, the census data should be read cautiously because the population numbers they present only refer to the population incorporated into the Spanish administrative sphere. That is, hundreds of thousands of unconquered Indians and free blacks and mestizos living in rochelas (small illegal settlements established at the margins of colonial domination) were not counted in the census. As has been suggested by Aline Helg, up until the 1770s, only considering Caribbean Colombia,

"those who escaped the control of the government, the church, and the law amounted to some 100,000 persons, or probably one of every two inhabitants in Caribbean New Granada." While neither authorities nor other contemporaries referred to these unconquered peoples as libres de color, there is no doubt that most of them were both free (some not legally so) and of mixed race. Despite these caveats, the 1778–80 census remains the most detailed count of New Granada's population at the end of the colonial period. While its numbers should be read critically, the quantitative information it provides about free people of color is invaluable. Qualitative information about this population group is more difficult to obtain.

A brief presentation of some of the census data regarding free people of color suffices to establish the quantitative importance of freemen of all colors (see above table). Free people of color constituted 46 percent of the total population of New Granada. Their numbers surpassed those of any other group in 10 of 18 provinces. They constituted the absolute majority (more than 50 percent) in eight of 18 provinces. Tunja, New Granada's most populated province, was also the province with the highest number of free people of color. Even in Popayán, the province with the highest number of slaves, free people of color constituted the majority of the population. In Cartagena, free people of color accounted for more than 60 percent of the province's population. They were only outnumbered by whites in Tunja, Tumaco, and Pasto; by Indians in Chocó, Pasto, and Los Llanos; and by slaves in Chocó, Tumaco, Raposo, Iscuandé, and Barbacoas (the provinces of the Pacific Lowlands).

Qualitative information to indicate who were the free people of color is more difficult to get. In fact, a detailed study that allows us to move beyond characterizing free people of color as a faceless crowd remains to be written. With the available information, it is safe to say that free people of color lived in both cities and countryside. In rural areas they were mostly engaged in agricultural labor, both for a master and for their own benefit. They were also occupied as *bogas* (boatmen who were largely responsible for the transportation of people and merchandise up the Magdalena River). In urban settings, they formed the majority of the labor force. In the important cities of Santa Fe and Cartagena, free people of color worked as tailors, carpenters, small vendors, cobblers, goldsmiths, masons, grocers, and barbers. In Cartagena, they were also predominant among the workers of the shipyards and increasingly important in the MILITIA. While generally they lived a meager existence, a handful of *libres de color* succeeded in obtaining important positions that allowed them to climb up the economic and social ladder and avoid the invisibility to which most free coloreds were doomed. The wars of independence provided a unique opportunity for some free people of color to inscribe their names (and to some extent their faces) in the historical record.

Free People of Color and the Wars of Independence

After 1808, when French forces invaded the Iberian Peninsula and took the Spanish king captive to France, people of all classes and races in the Spanish-American territories were faced with the question of what to do in the absence of the king. While initially most people, including free people of color, chose to postpone any decision, very quickly Spanish Americans were forced to choose among three main options: support the republicans, support the royalists, or remain at the margins of the conflict. As shown by the 19th-century Colombian politician and historian José Manuel Restrepo, many rural dwellers, most certainly free people of color, chose the latter option. In Restrepo's words, most free people of color throughout New Granada decided to "seek refuge in the woods instead of fighting against Spanish troops." Others, however, became actively involved in the struggle, following closely events in both Spain and New Granada.

Linking events in Spain with occurrences in New Granada, historians have argued that free people of color became supporters of independence after the Spanish legislature passed a decree in 1811 known as the Cortes de Cádiz that denied citizenship to free people of African descent. This certainly holds true for provinces, such as Cartagena and Popayán, where the vast majority of free people of color were also of African descent. In fact, as has been shown by Alfonso Múnera and Marixa Lasso, the 1811 Cádiz decree, coupled with commercial restrictions that limited the availability of cheap, foreign flour in Cartagena, was crucial to the radicalization of independence leaders such as Pedro Romero, the mulatto artisan from Cartagena, and JOSÉ PRUDENCIO PADILLA, the *pardo* sailor who became admiral of the republican navy during the wars of independence. Their active republicanism was countered by the open royalism of free people of color in provinces with a less marked African component, such as Pasto and Santa Marta, whose predominantly Indian-descended free colored population, after suffering the devastation produced by republican troops, decided to side with the Spanish forces.

The wars of independence also affected the legal status of slaves and Indians. For most slaves this struggle provided an opportunity to become free. New Granadan slaves participated in the independence struggle not so much as convinced republicans or royalists but as individuals seeking to take advantage of the promises of freedom made by their republican or royalist masters. As a result, all over New Granada slaves were to be found fighting for both rival armies. For Indians, the wars of independence, if won by republicans who wished to turn Indians into citizens with no corporate rights (i.e., into free people of color), represented a threat to their communal landholdings. This threat explains why Indian groups in the provinces of Pasto and Santa Marta remained even after the wars were over the most ardent defenders of the king. For both slaves and Indians, the wars of independence represented an opportunity to become, or the threat of being transformed into, free people of color. Their desire or unwillingness to become *libres de color* played an important role in their decisions to support the republican or royalist parties.

The Abolition of Slavery

After Colombia achieved independence from Spain in 1819, the new republican government only differentiated between citizens (all free persons), slaves, and *uncivilized*, independent indigenous groups. Of course, this inclusive definition of citizenship was only theoretical, and day-to-day discrimination continued to limit the opportunities of nonwhites. As for slaves and *uncivilized* Indians, their long struggle to secure freedom and self-determination continued. Slaves continued to achieve freedom on an individual basis until 1851, when slavery was finally abolished. From there on, former slaves became free but, just as "Indian" citizens, discriminated against nevertheless.

From 1851 until 1991, when a new constitution officially recognized ethnic diversity, all Colombians became theoretically equals, and the idea of a mestizo nation, where there were not whites, blacks, or Indians, but a single mixed-race population, reigned. In practice, as has been shown by Peter Wade, this apparent legal equality was used to conceal crucial differences that, through the 19th and 20th centuries, worked to perpetuate discrimination against nonwhites while maintaining the appearance of a successful racial democracy.

Ernesto Bassi Arévalo

FURTHER READING

Bushnell, David. *The Making of Modern Colombia: A Nation in Spite of Itself.* Berkeley: University of California Press, 1993.

Garrido, Margarita. "'Free Men of All Colors' in New Granada: Identity and Obedience before Independence." In *Political Cultures in the Andes, 1750–1950,* edited by Nils Jacobsen and Cristóbal Aljovín de Losada, 165–182. Durham, N.C.: Duke University Press, 2005.

Helg, Aline. *Liberty and Equality in Caribbean Colombia, 1770–1835.* Chapel Hill: University of North Carolina Press, 2004.

Lasso, Marixa. *Myths of Harmony: Race and Republicanism during the Age of Revolution, Colombia, 1795–1831.* Pittsburgh: University of Pittsburgh Press, 2007.

McFarlane, Anthony. *Colombia before Independence: Economy, Society, and Politics under Bourbon Rule.* Cambridge: Cambridge University Press, 1993.

Múnera, Alfonso. "En busca del mestizaje." In *Fronteras imaginadas. La construcción de las razas y de la geografía en el siglo XIX colombiano,* 129–152. Bogota: Planeta, 2005.

Safford, Frank, and Marco Palacios. *Colombia: Fragmented Land, Divided Society.* New York: Oxford University Press, 2002.

Sanders, James E. *Contentious Republicans: Popular Politics, Race, and Class in Nineteenth-Century Colombia.* Durham, N.C.: Duke University Press, 2004.

Wade, Peter. *Blackness and Race Mixture: The Dynamics of Racial Identity in Colombia.* Baltimore: Johns Hopkins University Press, 1993.

COLONIZATION. *See* AMERICAN COLONIZATION SOCIETY; EMIGRATION AND COLONIZATION.

COMMERCE AND TRADE

In the Americas during the 17th to 19th centuries, people of color often dominated the small retail market even in places where they were relatively few in numbers. They often faced discrimination and legal handicaps in growing their businesses and moving into international trade.

Nevertheless, some extraordinary individuals managed to have great success in business, even while experiencing harsh discrimination. Of course, the many differences among the various colonizers in the area of law and cultural attitudes toward people of African ancestry, and even among different colonies under the same colonial master for geographical and socioeconomic reasons, made conditions very different from place to place.

During the FRENCH REVOLUTION of the late 18th century, the free colored political leader JULIEN RAIMOND said his people were the "natural bourgeoisie" of the Caribbean islands. He was alluding to the middle status of free coloreds, between a white ruling class and enslaved workers, and laying claim to a French association of bourgeois with higher moral standards than the (supposedly) debauched aristocracy of the revolutionary period. If *bourgeois* is taken in its literal meaning, as city dweller, Raimond was wrong. The majority of free colored people in the French Caribbean colonies lived in rural areas and were peasants or small farmers, while the members of Raimond's own class were great PLANTERS with huge lands, large slave workforces, and small urban interests. But taking *bourgeois* as meaning what it means in modern class analysis, an entrepreneurial middle class changing the old society by applying ideas of individualism, profit, rational utility, equal rights, and pragmatism, then he was probably closer to the truth than he realized.

Small Retail Businesses

One important component of being bourgeois is seeking profit through business. It was here that free people of color in Raimond's home of Saint-Domingue and throughout the Americas made a great contribution to the societies where they lived. In many cases, people of color began their association with business even before they gained their freedom. Masters often gave slaves free time during the workweek to tend their own small plots of land, especially in Latin America. This was supposed to provide food for the slaves, allowing the master to avoid having to pay for rations, but slaves sometimes grew extra or planted cash crops. Slave women, in particular, were very active in small retail commerce, selling the proceeds of the family plot—or sometimes things they might have stolen or gleaned from the master's fields. Of course, success in commerce meant that the slave received some money, and with money she could buy her freedom, especially if the master was experiencing financial distress, a not-unusual condition for plantation owners in a volatile commodities market. Then, she might well continue in business as a free woman. The colonial travelers Alexander von Humboldt (who mainly visited Spanish America between 1799 and 1804) and Girod de Chant-

A photograph taken in 1908 or 1909 of the market in Bridgetown, Barbados. This was long after the end of slavery there (in 1834), but the importance of women of color in commerce in the Caribbean is apparent. Women of color made up the majority of sellers in almost every commercial community along the Atlantic coast of the tropical Americas, even in those places where there were relatively large Indian and white populations. *(© Royal Geographical Society, London, UK/The Bridgeman Art Library)*

rans (a military officer stationed in the French Caribbean during the AMERICAN WAR OF INDEPENDENCE, 1775–83), both noted the prevalence of free coloreds in the marketplaces of the Americas.

The authorities were often concerned about this phenomenon. First, they were worried because of the avenue it provided for slaves to sell property stolen from their masters. Next, there was a more generalized concern that people of color were breaking a color line, taking control of an important sector of society and appropriating resources that should flow to whites. There were occasional legal crackdowns, either on slaves selling in the marketplace or on colored retail merchants in general. The government could not dispense with the black retail sector, though, as frequently there was no other way to distribute food and daily necessities. In places where there was a substantial population of poor whites who could take over the retail sector, as in the northern United States, free coloreds were even more limited in their ability to rise in business and were often limited to serving the black community.

Wholesale and International Trade

There were often legal and customary restrictions on the ability of people of color to succeed in business, especially at the higher levels. The first problem was legal: People of color in many places either could not sue whites at all or were very unlikely to be able to have a court find in their favor. The fact that most free colored retail merchants were women just added sex discrimination to racial discrimination to make the problem even worse. Without the ability to go to law to enforce a contract, a businessperson was taking a terrible risk buying or selling on any terms other than cash. One common result of the widespread European policy of mercantilism and the near-universal reliance on gold and silver for currency was a persistent cash shortage in the American colonies. Almost all transactions beyond the most basic were on the basis of credit, and private commercial paper circulated through the economy almost as it were paper money. Collectively, these conditions proved a very effective barrier to free colored businesspeople in moving beyond the basic retail level where deals could be made with small amounts of cash or barter.

A second problem was the shortage of credit available to free blacks. While they could be sued by white creditors and often were, white merchants resisted granting credit to free blacks of all professions and levels of society. When one compares business or plantation records from white-owned and colored-owned enterprises, it is striking how much less debt the free colored proprietors accumulated. While some of this difference may have been natural conservatism or better business sense among the free coloreds, it probably reflects the difficulty they faced in finding anybody willing to lend to them.

One way to escape this trap was through having white patrons, often family members. In places where white fathers could acknowledge their mixed-race children, those children could benefit from the protection of their fathers (and half brothers, uncles, and other relatives) and do business on the same level. One example is VINCENT OGÉ, leader of the first stage of the Haitian Revolution in 1790 and 1791. Ogé was the mixed-race son of a prominent white planter. He went into business with capital given him by his father and then took over much of his uncle's business. Ogé owned ships that traded among Haiti, France, and the United States and had extensive real estate interests on the island. He did experience racial discrimination, most notably when he became involved in revolutionary politics, and was broken on the rack in punishment. The PHILADELPHIA, PENNYSLVANIA, businessman James Forten (see FORTEN FAMILY)also benefited from a white patron, this time not a family member but a former employer, Robert Bridges, who provided him training, capital, and business contacts to help launch his business career in the 1780s. Forten overcame racial prejudice to become one of the wealthiest African Americans in the United States before the Civil War.

Specialty or Service Businesses

Another way to evade these restrictions was to create a business that principally served other people of color. Of course, most people of color were slaves and had very little to spend, and even most free blacks were poor. This made for a limited market, but some free black businesspeople made a profit serving it. Personal grooming products, along with clothing, offered an important market as urban free coloreds often spent heavily on such products,

and whites in slave societies were accustomed to obtaining clothing and beauty products and services from people of color. Thus, they might have been willing to shop at a store owned by a person of color for such products while they would not buy groceries or other products from someone of another race.

The whole area of personal services was one that people of color were associated with from slavery. Slaves who worked as domestic servants had many opportunities to acquire money or otherwise advance themselves. First, it was traditional in many slave societies for a guest to tip the servants, even if they were slaves. Masters themselves might reward their servants, in extraordinary cases even with liberty. Slaves could use domestic occupations to make money on the side, by taking in other people's laundry or mending other people's clothes in their spare time. Working in close proximity to the master meant being close to small pieces of valuable property that might be appropriated, or received as gifts, and then sold through the vibrant colored retail sector. Money in the hands of a slave could be profoundly liberating: Either she could buy her freedom if the master was having financial troubles or she could make her escape more easily. Once free, it would be natural for someone with these skills to continue using them to make a living, at least until some better opportunity came along. An example is the African-born Pierre Augustin of CAP-FRANÇAIS/CAP-HAÏTIEN, Haiti. He was a barber and wig maker as a slave, and after he bought his freedom in 1776, he continued to work in the same profession for some years. Wealthy people in the French world—whites and free coloreds—wore elaborate and expensive wigs in the 18th century, and Augustin was one of the principal suppliers in this exceptionally wealthy city. Augustin did so well out of his business that he was able to reinvest his profits in agricultural land and slaves and become a small plantation owner in his own right. Augustin is an example of one extreme of the successful businessman of color, who rose from below the hatches of a slave ship to slave ownership during a time of great prosperity. Economics, cultural conditions, and geography all affected the African-American business experience in different places.

The United States: The North

Commerce and trade among free blacks in the Atlantic world varied greatly from region to region. In the northern United States, free blacks faced huge obstacles in business both because the legal climate was especially hard for them and because the culture and society offered few niches for them. In most free states, blacks could not testify against a white person in a lawsuit, and even when they were permitted, their testimony received less weight.

Blacks in many places were forbidden to engage in some businesses that were thought to be especially likely to produce disruption in the racial order, such as saloon keeper or stable owner. In some places, the law required them to have a white partner or to pretend to be the employee and not an owner in order to be permitted to do business within city limits. Even in those places, such as Massachusetts, where they had legal equality, the prejudice of the white public meant that they would have problems receiving equal treatment from courts or government.

This was the situation for blacks everywhere in the United States, but in the North, there was the additional problem that a large group of poor whites were living in the cities and also trying to succeed in business. The great tide of immigration from Europe to America in the middle of the 19th century mostly washed ashore in northern ports. In Boston, New York City, and Philadelphia, the competitive climate was difficult. However, free blacks were in the North before most of the European immigrants began to arrive. The first blacks in PENNSYLVANIA arrived in 1681 with William Penn. Free black communities grew for a century and a half without intense competition from poor free whites. Most poor whites who immigrated to the colony during the 18th century moved to the country, either at once if they had the resources or after a period working in the cities as indentured servants. Either way, they were not direct competitors for the free black businesspeople. The big rush of European immigration dates from the Irish potato famine in 1845. Some free blacks, such as Forten in Philadelphia, had already made successful businesses. There was ongoing tension between white immigrants and blacks in northern cities, marked by several bloody race riots, including the NEW YORK DRAFT RIOTS, 1863.

As a result, most black businesses in northern states were small and/or served a predominantly black clientele, with a few striking exceptions such as the Forten Family. Ambitious northern blacks mainly chose other paths, such as journalism, religion, or other professions.

United States: The South
In slave states in the American South in the 19th century, far fewer poor whites lived in the cities than in the North. Fewer immigrants entered the South, and native-born poor whites tended to be farmers. Blacks, both free and enslaved, made up a much higher proportion of the population of the cities. Moreover, Southern whites were more accustomed to receiving personal services from blacks. These factors created a market niche for free black businesses. In the Deep South, there were fewer free African Americans than in the Upper South. Those people who did gain their freedom in the Deep South and who did not move out of the region entirely generally stayed

closer to their native places in the countryside. Cities and towns in the Deep South, though, often had small black retail sectors similar to those found in the Caribbean colonies. This institution existed in the cotton country of the Deep South for the same reason as in the sugar- and coffee-growing regions of Latin America, that masters sometimes permitted slaves to cultivate food crops for themselves on small plots of land rather than buying rations for them. Slaves or free blacks who lived in the countryside might go to town for a day to sell their surplus in a marketplace. This practice was much less common in the Upper South, where plantations were often cultivating food crops anyway and had plenty to spare to feed the slaves. There were few large-scale black businesspeople in the South; one exception was WILLIAM "APRIL" ELLISON of South Carolina, who owned as many as 70 slaves by 1860 and was the largest manufacturer of cotton gins in the state.

The British Caribbean
In most British Caribbean colonies, discriminatory laws prohibited free people of color to own more than a small amount of land or supervise slaves directly. As a result, free blacks concentrated in the cities or moved to the outskirts of the settled areas to live as peasants or MAROONS. Moreover, the British Caribbean colonies had the most highly developed SUGAR CULTIVATION regions. Masters here commonly permitted slaves to cultivate their own crops, though general British colonial policy opposed this practice. A 1738 law in Montserrat, for example, forbade planters to allow slaves to cultivate their own food, but this law was widely ignored, especially after slaves protested the law during a strike—which planters called a rebellion—in 1768. Since Britain controlled the sea-lanes during the 18th century, it would have been possible for planters to import food for their slaves and use all available land for more cash crops. Some did, and the market for foodstuffs permitted plantations on the periphery of the plantation zone, as in the Upper South of the United States, to shift to food cultivation. But this was a risky decision, because even a temporary interruption in the flow of supply ships could lead to starvation among the slaves, which would cause economic hardship for the planter. Masters in the British Caribbean gave private plots of land to slaves almost as commonly as those in the French or Dutch Caribbean. The result, as in the neighboring colonies, was a strong black retail sector. Whites dominated wholesale and international commerce in the British world, though, being less handicapped by traditional old regime expectations of noble behavior, which forbade those aspiring to noble status, as most large planters did, to soil their hands with "trade." Therefore, there were few opportunities for free coloreds

to break in. In Jamaica, there were large towns with big commercial sectors where black-owned businesses could grow, but in the smaller colonies of the British eastern Caribbean there was less opportunity.

The French Caribbean

Vincent Ogé, discussed earlier, is but one example of a free colored participant in large-scale international commerce. Another is ANNE ROSSIGNOL, who arrived, apparently voluntarily, as a free immigrant, from the French colony in Senegal but who made her home in Saint-Domingue in the 1770s and 1780s. Rossignol had business contacts around the Atlantic, from France to Africa to mainland North America to the British and French Caribbean colonies. She bought and sold slaves and tropical products, owned real estate, and loaned money to planters. Benefiting from the relatively favorable legal climate for free coloreds in the French Empire, and from the support of white business partners and patrons, she and Ogé were able to do business without much apparent handicap.

People of color dominated the small retail sector in Saint-Domingue, although in the 1760s and 1770s a wave of white immigration to the colony created competition. Poor whites complained at the time of the FRENCH REVOLUTION that they had been discriminated against by the powerful whites, who preferred free colored businesses to theirs. In the code of behavior of the French old regime, noblemen and those who aspired to nobility could not engage in trade. Since almost all large planters and government officials in the colonies hoped that the great wealth of their plantations would enable them to become nobles, they were happy to leave business activities they could not engage in to their free colored relatives and clients. Of course, the white partners could count on good deals and preferential treatment, and perhaps a share of the profits in these businesses. The French government wanted to encourage racial solidarity among whites and put various restrictions on the economic activity of free coloreds from the 1770s, but these were often ignored or circumvented by local white elites and the colonial governments they controlled in favor of their free colored clients and business partners.

Spanish America: The Mainland

In the heartland of Spanish America—the highlands of Mexico and South America—free people of color did not commonly own commercial businesses. There were some free Afro-Mexicans and Afro-Peruvians who owned businesses, but these were mostly skilled tradesmen selling their services or products they had manufactured. This is because most slaves who were taken to these areas were taken there to work in manufacturing rather than agriculture. If they gained their freedom, they often continued to work in a skilled trade rather than beginning a more entrepreneurial business. Once established in a trade, guild restrictions meant that one was more or less guaranteed a good living and the right to pass on one's business to one's heirs. Going on to bigger business or getting involved in other lines of work, like an entrepreneur of a later century, was not encouraged by society or the laws. Spanish society valued craft work higher than mere commerce. As the legal restrictions were gradually lifted during the period of the Bourbon Reforms in the 18th century, the free colored business community declined. Manufacturing became less profitable as foreign goods were allowed into the marketplace, and free colored ARTISANS tended to move away or take up other lines of work. At the same time, the free population of color was becoming absorbed in the larger category of CASTAS, or mixed-race people of all descriptions, and losing its independent African identity.

Spanish America: The Caribbean

African identity was not in any danger of disappearing in the Spanish Caribbean. Indeed, the 18th century saw renewed large-scale importation of slaves into the islands, especially Cuba and the coastal areas of South America and Mexico where sugar could be grown. Before about 1750, the population of these areas was almost entirely free, and people of color were in the majority, and almost all roles in society except the very highest were filled by them. There were few slaves, and also fewer whites than free coloreds. The economy was very weak, though, and towns were small. Thus, while there was not much of a commercial sector, what did exist was open to free coloreds. After sugar revolutionized the Spanish Caribbean, the society there began to resemble the Anglo-American model more closely. Most basic labor was done by slaves, but many higher-status positions in society were closed to people of African ancestry. Racial discrimination began to impede the rise of free colored entrepreneurs. Nevertheless, there were small businesspeople of color among the leaders of the Cuban independence movement of the 19th century: José Antonio Aponte, executed after a plot in 1812; "Placido" GABRIEL DE LA CONCEPCIÓN VALDÉS, executed after the La Escalera Conspiracy; and ANTONIO MACEO Y GRAJALES, the "Bronze Titan" of the TEN YEARS' WAR, are all examples.

Brazil

In the northeastern sugar-growing regions of the Portuguese colony of Brazil, people of color were very numerous and filled many roles in society, as in the Spanish Caribbean. However, this area had a slightly different history than did Cuba and Puerto Rico, and these differences made life harder for free colored businesspeople there. The enormous influx of new slaves in the late 18th century that Brazil also experienced did not enter an area almost devoid of slaves, as in Cuba. Instead, northeastern Brazil had been able to continue functioning as a slave society, albeit on a reduced scale, since the late 16th century, when it was the biggest sugar producer in the world. Brazil had few white immigrants in the 17th and 18th centuries, but the greater wealth and connection of this area to the global economy made for a more harshly stratified society. White elites limited access by free coloreds to the higher levels of business.

In the southwestern mining region of Minas Gerais, settled in the 18th century, free Afro-Brazilians played a very important role in business. The 18th-century mulatto architect and builder ANTONIO LISBOA "O Aleijadinho," for example, became wealthy and created significant works of art that bear comparison with European examples of the high baroque. However, he was only one of many free black or mixed-race businessmen in Minas Gerais. The wealth of the mines and the open frontier society produced a situation where talent was much more likely to result in financial success. The distance from Portugal and the hardships of the voyage meant that white immigration was slow, and many niches in the economy were left for free Afro-Brazilians.

The metropolitan areas on the southeastern coast, Rio de Janeiro and Saõ Paolo, had large free colored populations but had sterner laws and social customs against free colored businesses.

Throughout the Americas, commerce and trade offered an opportunity for free people of color to earn a living and for some lucky individuals to amass great wealth. Restrictions on free colored business activity under law or by (white) prejudice were common, varied widely, and hindered but did not stop people of color from doing business. This was an area where women could play an important independent economic role, though sex discrimination often hindered their advancement. Nonetheless, the wealth of the Atlantic economy, fueled by slave labor on the plantations, was great enough that there was business for everyone.

Stewart R. King

FURTHER READING
Horton, James O., and Lois E. Horton. *Black Bostonians: Family Life and Community Struggle in the Antebellum North.* New York: Holmes and Meier, 1999.
Johnson, Michael, and James Roark. *Black Masters: A Free Family of Color in the Old South.* New York: Norton, 1986.
Miller, Joseph. *Way of Death: Merchant Capitalism and the Angolan Slave Trade, 1730–1830.* Madison: University of Wisconsin Press, 1988.
Socolow, Susan. "Economic Roles of the Free Women of Color of Cap Français." In *More than Chattel: Black Women and Slavery in the Americas,* edited by David B. Gaspar and Darlene Hine, 279–297. Bloomington: Indiana University Press, 1996.

INCORPORATION PAPERS OF THE GRASSERIE MARIE JOSEPHE, FORT-DAUPHIN, SAINT-DOMINGUE, 1785

The following incorporation papers dated July 12, 1785, were for the establishment of a small retail business in Fort-Dauphin, a medium-sized city in a sugar-growing region of the French colony of Saint-Domingue (present-day Haiti), near Cap-Français.

One of the two partners in this establishment is a free black woman, Marie Josephe. She does not appear to have had a surname, or any white ancestors or relatives. Her color and lack of family connections would place her in the lowest class of free people in the colony. The other partner, Sieur Guillemet, was a white man. By law and custom, whites were preferred to free blacks in most things in the colony. The very use of the title sieur, or lord, in this legal paper indicates that he was to be considered a superior person. In similar documents in France, only members of the upper classes, nobles or very distinguished bourgeois, would get a sieur in front of their name, but in the French Caribbean colonies, any white person rated one. Marie Josephe is referred to by her name alone. At least she avoided the somewhat insulting la nommée ("the so-called") that would often be put before the names of free colored people in official documents. In France, this term would only be used for criminals, beggars, and other "undesirables."

Not only was Marie Josephe a person of color, she was also a woman. Women in old regime France were generally assumed to be incapable of taking care of their own affairs. Most women would have been legally prevented from executing any sort of contract without the formal permission of some man, either a father, a brother, a husband, or a son. Women of color sometimes escaped this situation, through illegitimate birth, remaining unmarried, or taking legal steps to preserve their independence. The economic independence and power of free colored women was one of the distinguishing characteristics of the class in the French colonies. White men found this feature disquieting, and gender stereotypes often appear in the comments of white colonists on the free colored class.

Racial and gender prejudice aside, though, Marie Josephe appears to have been the dominant partner in the business. From internal evidence and other papers with the same two principal actors, it appears that the relationship between the two of them was only business. Marie Josephe provided the cash to get the store started, while Guillemet provided his managerial talents. Marie Josephe did not trust his management too far, though; notice in the last paragraph that he was forbidden to give credit to anyone. Presumably this means he could not do it without her permission. In fact, given the shortage of actual cash in the colony thanks to the French policy of mercantilism, almost every transaction was for some form of credit. People usually had accounts at businesses they dealt with regularly, settling up periodically, like after the sale of their crop. Otherwise, buyers could write a personal check or IOU to pay for the transaction, and then those IOU's would circulate throughout the local economy like cash, ultimately being presented for payment at harvest time.

Another feature of interest is the wide variety of products to be sold at the store. The name Grasserie suggests that the principal product for sale is oil and grease, but there is also wine, cheese, pepper, vinegar, rum, various food items, and even paper. French and Creole cooking uses a lot of oils, and apparently this was also true in the 18th century. It is possible that the business also sold prepared food.

The creation of an indoor retail facility, instead of a marketplace stall, puts this business at the cutting edge of a commercial revolution going on at the time. As the boutique replaced the market, then the large store replaced the boutique, consumers could satisfy their needs more easily and comfortably.

A note on money and symbols: The standard money of account in France before the Revolution was the livre, or pound. A mark of silver (eight ounces) was worth 51 livres tournois, which was the standard money of metropolitan France. Just to make things more confusing, the metropolitan French money was worth about 20 percent more than the colonial money because of government currency manipulation. One livre was a poor day's pay for a workingman in the colony. Two to three livres would rent a room for a week in Fort Dauphin. The livre was divided into 20 sols, or shillings, each of which was further subdivided into 12 deniers, or pennies. The symbols used for these currencies were: # = livre, s = sol, d = denier.

To further confuse scholars from a later era, most coins actually in circulation in the colony were not denominated in livres but were instead gold and silver coins from various places, which would be weighed to assess their value. The most common large coin used in the colony was the gourde, worth 20 livres, which gave its name to the modern Haitian currency.

Appeared before me, Leprestre, and my colleague, notaries in the town . . . of Fort Dauphin . . . this 12th day of July, 1785, *Sieur* Guillemet and Marie Josephe, *negresse libre*, of this town. The two parties engage themselves in a society for a duration of one year . . . renewable on agreement without further formalities . . . [on the following terms]:

The following is the starting stock of the store:

Marie Josephe's contribution:
a barrel of wine containing 10½ demi-johns,[1] 66#
3 full demi-johns [of wine], 24#15s
25 pounds of *"morne"* @ 61#17s6d the quintal,[2] 15#8s3d[3]
25 pounds of cheese @ 20s/pound, 25#
a pound of pepper, 3#
12 large plates @ 25s, 15#
4 large oval plates @ 25s, 5#
2 goblets, 15#
1 *"entomier"*, 4#2s6d[4]
12 pots of cooking oil @ 20s, 12#
5 pounds of candle wax @ 25s, 7#10s
one *"duedane"* of grease, 3#[5]
50 empty bottles @ 7s6d, 18#15s
17 empty demi-johns @ 12#, 204#[6]
7 *"echelles"* (shelf units) @ 6#5s, 57#15s
4 boards 9 feet long @ 15s the French foot, 25#15s[7]
52 feet of planks @ 7s6d, 19#10s
10 others of *"halle"* for *"garniture,"* @ 1#10s, 15#[8]
two tables, one missing its legs, with two empty barrels, 18#
a pint measure, 1#10s
3 pots of olive oil, 4#10s
pair of iron scales, 8#5s
11 pounds of weights for scales, 8#5s
1 cabbage, 3#[9]
1 large jar, 49#10s
1 *terrine de France*, 4#2s[10]
2 chairs, 8#5s
1 wicker cover for jar, 1#10s
1 large scale in wood with two platforms, 6#
2 demi-johns of vinegar, 30#
Total contribution of Marie Josephe 838#

Contribution of *Sieur* Guillemet
84 feet of wood at 7s6d, 41#
1 table and two barrels, 8#
1 pair of scales and 14 pounds of weights, 44#15s
4 chairs @4#2s6d, 16#10s
50 empty bottles @ 7s6d, 18#15s
11 demi-johns, some empty, some full, 15#, 165#
1 small *"entommier,"* 1 *gaudet*, 1 *pinte*, 6#[11]
1 jar, 27#
1 small *jarre de Provence*, for butter, 12#[12]
1 coffee mill, 16#
1 block of sugar, 42 pounds @ 20s, 42#
7 (illegible, maybe glasses or plates) @ 3#, 21#
9 oval plates @ 25s, 10#
3 small plates @ 20s, 3#
8 plates @ 10s, 4#[13]
55 pots of grease @ 25s, 67#10s
7 pots of fine oil @ 1#10s, 10#10s

18 pots of (illegible, some other sort of oil), 9#
17 bottles of fine oil @ 33# the doz., 45#
4 *"sirzaim de Casthe"* @ 3#10s, 14#[14]
½ a ream of paper,[15] 6#
1 (illegible) 85#
4½ spools of thread @ 16#10s, 74#5s[16]
8 demijohns of Taffia, 66#
1 barrel of Taffia, 92#[17]
1 small table, 12#
4 shelves @ 8#5s, 33#
2 pieces of *"macoute"* @ 5#5s, 10#10s[18]
1 sack of lentils, 8#5s
3 panniers of *"pomponilles"* 4#10s[19]
some rice, 12#
Total contribution of Sr. Guillemet, 1062#10s

Marie Josephe also put in 232# in cash to make immediate purchases. She also loaned the society 230# more in cash, to be returned to her at the first accounting.[20]

Rules of the business: Guillemet will manage the firm. The store will do business in a building already leased by Marie Josephe, paying a rent of 5 *gourdes* (= 100#) per month. There is a kitchen, a small back room, and a street front gallery, which the two associates will share.[21] Starting now, the society will pay the rent instead of Marie Josephe. Merchandise will be bought in Cap, and any bill must be signed by both partners before it can be paid. Guillemet is forbidden to give credit to anyone. There will be monthly accountings.[22] The society will rent a slave.[23]

---

[1] A modern demijohn contains anything from 20 to 60 liters; the measurement in this case probably closer to the lower figure.

[2] A quintal is 100 pounds or about 45 kilograms.

[3] It is unclear what *"morne"* is.

[4] A serving dish.

[5] A large barrel full of recycled cooking grease.

[6] Glass was expensive and difficult to obtain and stores often insisted that people bring their own containers. This is a practice in markets today in developing countries.

[7] Probably shelving.

[8] *"Halle"* was cheap wood, probably not well cured. The high cost of lumber reflects the growing size of the city and increasing difficulty people had in finding wood as forests were cleared for farming. The area around Cap Français (now Cap Haitien) today is heavily deforested, but this was already becoming a problem more than 200 years ago.

[9] This was an entry that was very difficult to understand. The word used is *"choux"* which is the plural of cabbage, but the document says there was one of them. Given the price, presumably one barrel is intended. The mountains of Hispaniola are cold and damp enough to grow European vegetables and presumably there was a market for them among white immigrants who wanted to eat the food of their home.

[10] A large pot, used to keep water (and anything placed in it) cool. A sort of refrigerator.

[11] The latter two items are bottles or barrels of various sizes for measurement.

[12] For preserving and keeping butter cool.

[13] With all the plates and glasses and kitchenware, it is possible they were also preparing and serving food.

[14] It is unclear what this was.

[15] Paper was very expensive—a ream of paper cost almost two weeks' wages for a poor working man, the equivalent of more than $1000 in modern terms.

[16] Big spools, from the price.

[17] Taffia is low-quality rum, not well aged, consumed by the working class in Haiti today and often a part of rations given to slaves in the eighteenth century.

[18] The word *"macoute"* in modern Haitian Creole means "backpack" and is best known for its association with the Duvalier regime's militia the *tontons macoutes*. But in colonial times it referred to a type of wood preferred for construction of high-quality furniture.

[19] A type of fruit.

[20] They expect to make a profit of 230 *livres* in a year beyond what they need for living expenses. On a capital of a little over 2,000 *livres* this is a nice rate of return. The document says the loan will be repaid at the first accounting but we can assume that that meant an annual accounting as the incorporation papers said the business was to be established for a period of one year, renewable by mutual agreement.

[21] Presumably, Guillemet lived in the building. The kitchen may have been for his use and it may also have been used to prepare food to serve to customers.

[22] None of the accountings were notarized, unfortunately. The monthly accountings were presumably not formal processes but simply a way for Marie Josephe to check up on Guillemet's work. This passage suggests that she was not present all the time and may have been a "silent partner" in the business.

[23] Renting slaves was very common. You could rent a slave for a year for about one-fifth of what he or she would cost to buy outright. Average monthly rentals for an adult slave range around 20 to 40 *livres*.

Source: Archives Nationales de France, Centre des Archives d'Outremer, Notarial archives of Saint-Domingue, volume 1298, July 12, 1785.

COMMONWEALTH V. JENNISON   See QUOCK WALKER CASE.

CONCEIÇÃO, ROSA MARIA DA   (?–1843)
Brazilian woman

A freedwoman originally from the coast of Africa, Rosa Maria da Conceição was a former slave of Clemente Luiz, a man of mixed race of African and European descent. She lived in Bahia in northeastern BRAZIL. We know very little about her life, but what we do know, from her will and some public documents, illustrate how free black life changed during the early 19th century in Brazil.

Conceição wrote her will on February 1, 1836. When she died on March 24, 1843, the will was read and inserted in the official records, and an inventory of her property was also taken to be used in formal distribution of assets according to Brazilian inheritance law. Childless, Conceição left all of her possessions to her executor and the heirs of her former master, who had perhaps given her a house. According to the historians Richard Boyer and Geoffrey Spurling, Conceição's complaint, in her will, of frauds perpetrated on her is evidence of the importance of material possessions for freed slaves. Illiterate, she was led to believe that those who helped write her first will not only were doing so in good faith but would also keep her valuables for her for safekeeping. Her faith in them was misplaced, however, and her possessions were in danger of being misappropriated, or at least she felt they were, when she made a second will.

The importance of the ROMAN CATHOLIC CHURCH for the freed community in Brazil is also apparent in her will. She expressed the wish to be buried in Saint Francis Monastery. Conceição was a member of Our Lady of the Rosary of Shoemaker's Hollow, a CATHOLIC CONFRATERNITY, which allowed freed slaves some social status in Brazilian society.

The fact that she had been freed by a man of color is also significant. Aside from the provision that his heirs can have her small house if they wish it, the will does not reveal anything about her relationship with him: Many times, family members, friends, patrons, companions, godparents, or other benefactors would buy slaves with the intention of liberating them. But in other cases, free people of color owned slaves for the same reasons that whites did, to make use of their labor, and freed them for the same reasons as whites did, in return for payment or as a reward for good service (*see also* MANUMISSION).

Ana Janaina Nelson

FURTHER READING

Boyer, Richard, and Geoffrey Spurling, eds. *Colonial Lives: Documents on Latin American History, 1550–1850*. New York: Oxford University Press, 2000, 279–293.

CONCEPCIÓN VALDÉS, GABRIEL DE LA (PLÁCIDO) (1809–1844) *poet*

Gabriel de la Concepción Valdés, popularly known as Plácido, was one of the most important poets of Cuban romanticism. He was a MULATTO living in a society where slavery was permitted. Out-of-wedlock relationships were common between white men and black or mulatto women, although such conduct caused the white man to lose status. Plácido's birth, on March 8, 1809, was even more severely condemned by society because his mother was a white woman. His mother was Concepción Vázquez, a Spanish dancer, and his father, Diego Ferrer Matoso, was a prominent hairstylist and a mulatto. His mother was born in Castile in Spain, and she loved poetry. Plácido's father was an extremely polite man, also an admirer of poetry. He was a member of a mulatto family renowned for their excellence in hair grooming. They went as far as possible in their economic position. They owned a carriage, which at that time was considered a sign of privilege usually denied to people of color. After giving birth, his mother decided to place him at the orphanage known as Casa de Beneficencia y Maternidad. She left a card expressing her desire to name him Gabriel de la Concepción. Valdes was the last name given to children left there if they were not to be registered under their parents' names.

Plácido's background was a cause of prejudice, disdain, and even envy among his contemporaries and later generations. At the time, he was subject to prejudice both as a person of mixed race and as an orphan, but he managed to overcome this prejudice and gain an education. Formal elementary education was open to free people of color, and while the university admitted only whites, Plácido managed to get a better education on his own than he would have had at the university.

Plácido's elementary schoolteachers were two prominent intellectuals, Pedro del Sol and Francisco Bandaran. His art teacher was Vicente Escobar, the most famous portrait painter in Cuba of his day. Among other artistic crafts, he was a silversmith and made ornamental combs for the elaborate hairstyles worn by women of the time. Working as ARTISANS was common for free people of color in Cuba, and silversmiths were among the best paid of the artisans.

Plácido also worked at the well-known editor José Severino Boloña's typographic studio. There he met famous intellectuals such as Bachiller y Morales and the Gonzalez del Valle brothers. They realized that Plácido was a child prodigy with a great talent for poetry. Plácido read and translated French, including the works of Racine, Corneille, and Molière. At the time, the University of Havana was a very mediocre education center with scant resources. The university he was not allowed to attend was weaker than the cultural atmosphere he was exposed to through his work.

Through Plácido's position as poet and mulatto, he was surrounded by people of all social strata. He was acquainted with prominent white intellectuals such as Domingo del Monte, but probably because of scorn or personal or intellectual contempt, del Monte took an ambivalent attitude toward Plácido. Plácido enjoyed a respected position as a poet, but at the same time, he was very proud and defiant, sympathizing with the poor and racial minorities in recognition of his racial and social origins. It was said his dress habits were sober and clean, but he did not disdain to wear the footwear of the poor, showing the leather's inner side, or using open collar shirts without a necktie. He dressed both with dignity and in ways that transgressed social rules. His teacher, Jose Severino Bolona, publisher of one of his books, suggested that he wear a dress jacket, a necktie, and a tall hat for a portrait, but Plácido insisted on wearing an unbuttoned shirt with no necktie.

Plácido cultivated the sonnet and other lyrical forms such as the popular stanza. He gained fame in social gatherings with his extraordinary gift of improvisation, creating delicate and ingenious verses from even the most difficult "cue." He astonished his public and was acclaimed everywhere. He often challenged other poets, including his friend, Francisco Poveda, considered one of Cuba's greatest popular poets, to poetry competitions. One of Plácido's most renowned poems was inspired by a sculpture named the *Fountain of the Indian*, also known as *The Noble Havana*, located in one of Havana's parks.

Mirad, La Habana, allí color de nieve
gentil indiana de estructura fina
dominando una fuente cristalina
sentada en trono de alabastro breve
. . . sin alma, sin calor, sin sentimiento
hecha a golpes con el hierro duro
jamás murmura de su suerte aleve

See, Havana, there colored like snow
finely built comely Indian lady
a crystalline fountain dominating
on a brief alabaster throne she sits
. . . , soulless, without warmth or feeling
Hammered out of hard iron
of her treacherous fate never a murmur said

Plácido's Era

In Cuba, there were three political tendencies during the 19th century: reform, independence from Spain, and support for annexation to United States. Racial, classist, and national conflicts played a role in these conflicts. Abolitionism emerged with different overtones as a result of British influence. It was linked to practical and economic "progress" rather than to humanitarian goals. Fear of blacks due to the HAITIAN REVOLUTION was rooted in Cuban society. The Cuban ruling class decided to use black people for economic development and start a racial-ist project to "whiten" the island by encouraging white immigration and ethnic mixture. This was their way of eliminating blacks, a goal thought to be achievable in the span of 50 years. In the nations of the Spanish-American mainland, this "WHITENING" AND RACIAL PROMOTION process made considerable progress during the 19th century. Light-skinned mixed-race people such as Plácido were assimilated into the ranks of the mestizo or even white populations. Darker-skinned people were encouraged to intermarry or were socially and culturally marginalized. The result was precipitous decline in the reported Afro-descended population; Cuba hoped to emulate this "achievement."

After the Haitian Revolution ended in the early 19th century, Cuban oligarchs developed SUGAR CULTIVATION on plantations to take the place Haiti had once occupied at the summit of the plantation economy. Cuban sugar plantations were huge and required enormous financing, which was only available from mainland North America. U.S. investment entailed American ideas about race, harshening the climate of racial exclusion and exploitation of free people of color as well as of slaves. Ironically, these absolutist North American ideas about race also sidetracked the "whitening" project, as people such as Plácido were increasingly reminded of their status and not permitted to assimilate.

The existence of a small bourgeoisie of educated blacks and mulattoes, some of them wealthy business owners or free professionals with military training, aroused concern among whites, who thought that free people of color could be natural leaders of a slave revolution as they had been in Haiti. As the conservative politician Francisco de Arango y Parreno (1765–1837) remarked, "They [free people of color] are dangerous [like slaves]. They are all black . . . they all have the same complaints and the same motives to dislike us."

The La Escalera Plot

In 1843, massive organized insurrections took place in Havana and Matanzas provinces. By the end of March, an uprising of 250 slaves took place at a sugar mill named Alcancia, followed by slave uprisings at La Luisa, La Trinidad, and La Aurora sugar mills. Simultaneously, slaves working at a railroad construction site between Cardenas and Bemba rose too. Rumors spread in Havana about possible revenge on the white population. In November 1843, a great uprising at a sugar mill named Triunvirato expanded to other nearby sugar mills. A prominent figure was a black slave, a woman named Fermina Lucumi, who was apprehended and executed. In January 1844, the colonial government started a process that led to the worst repression in Cuban colonial history. Plácido was caught up in the repression of the Conspiracy of the Escalera, or LA ESCALERA PLOT, so called because those tortured were tied to a ladder and whipped, often to death.

Praise of Plácido the poet along with rumors that he could be king or president of Cuba endangered his life. His importance as a cultural figure made it essentially impossible for him to remain neutral. It is improbable that Plácido was head of the conspiracy, but his wife, Maria Gila Morales, and her mother and other relatives were accused of involvement in the plot, and, therefore, the authorities assumed he was also involved.

Free black and mulatto creoles promoted liberal and abolitionist ideas. They claimed to be working for both Cuban independence and the end of slavery. They hoped to unite into a multiracial Cuban nation with white Cubans of similar ideals. The Spanish Crown was afraid to lose their Cuban colony, and the dominant class was afraid to lose their privileges as SLAVE OWNERS. The Spanish authorities and the slave-owning class considered it a dangerous conspiracy and a threat to their interests.

The Escalera torture served the purpose of terrorizing slaves, eliminating a free black and mulatto middle class, and intimidating liberal and abolitionist white intellectuals. No whipping or death sentences were imposed on whites, but slaves were taken out of sugar mills, tortured, and murdered. More than 300 blacks and mulattoes were executed, and more than 700 sent into exile. Others were deprived of their authorization to engage in trades and professions they were qualified for and made destitute. Amid the repression of the Escalera, Plácido was arrested and condemned to death.

On June 28, 1844, Plácido was executed. The death of Plácido and the other accused conspirators suppressed any possible rebellion. Historians are still divided as to whether any true conspiracy existed, or whether the whole affair was just an overreaction by the colonial government to isolated slave rebellions and a calculated measure to rid the colony of its powerful free colored middle class. The harsh repression provided the pro-independence faction with a host of martyrs, however, and Plácido was the most notable among them. During the TEN YEARS' WAR, 1868–78, the rebels had a Plácido Brigade. The Afro-Cuban leader Juan Gualberto Gómez (1854–1933), the deputy commander of the Cuban forces during the War of Independence (1894–98), eulogized Plácido and called him a model for all Cuban patriots. Plácido's poetry has become a national treasure and has influenced many Spanish-American poets. The 20th-century Cuban poet José Lezama Lima (1910–76), originator of the neobaroque school, named Plácido as an important literary influence.

Inés María Martiatu Terry

FURTHER READING

Castellanos, Jorge. *Plácido, Poeta Social y Politico.* Miami, Fla.: Ediciones Universal, 1984.

Paquette, Robert. *Sugar Is Made with Blood: The Conspiracy of La Escalera and the Conflict between Empires over Slavery in Cuba.* Middletown, Conn.: Wesleyan University Press, 1990.

CONGO AND ANGOLA

The Kingdom of Kongo was formed in Africa in the late 14th century near the border of the modern nations of Congo and Angola. The kingdom was ruled by the *mwene*, or king, who had direct authority over the central provinces near the capital of São Salvador and received tribute and confirmed local rulers in more distant provinces. This was a rather conventional political organization for many African medieval states, but Kongo added two innovations that made it a major power in the late 15th and 16th centuries. The first was a powerful standing army of heavy infantry, which numbered at least 20,000 in the 16th century. The second was a flourishing trade, cultural connection, and military alliance with Portugal, starting in 1491, when the Portuguese explorer Diogo Cão brought missionaries and Mwene Nzinga a Nkuwu converted to Catholicism, taking the name of João I. After João died in 1506, his son Alfonso was involved in a succession struggle, and in 1509, he won a decisive battle that he attributed to the miraculous intervention on the battlefield of the Virgin Mary and Saint James. Alfonso made Catholicism the state religion of Kongo, and the Kikongo people remain overwhelmingly Catholic to this day.

The Portuguese established their main trading post at Luanda in modern Angola, just outside the area of effective Kongo sovereignty. They sent trade goods, including firearms, to the *mwene* in return for slaves captured during Kongo's wars of expansion, and received private merchants from Kongo and its tributary states. The *mwene* did not approve of the Portuguese trading with others and often protested, especially when in 1526 some of the slaves who were sold through Luanda proved to be captives from the Kongo Royal Army. But in general, relations between Kongo and Portugal were good and mutually beneficial, so long as Kongo remained strong. The Kongo army of professional infantrymen, now armed with muskets, either imported from Europe or manufactured locally, was able to defeat any possible challenger, including the Portuguese. At the beginning of the 17th century, however, Kongo entered a period of political instability. Seeing an opportunity in the decline of their trading partner, the Portuguese jumped into Kongolese internal politics, invading the kingdom on several occasions. Their first major invasion was defeated in 1622, and Kongo planned to throw the Portuguese out altogether with the assistance of the Dutch. Dutch ships cooperated with Kongo troops in a successful attack on the Portuguese in 1647, capturing Luanda. The Portuguese returned, however, and launched an all-out offensive. In 1665, the *mwene* was killed, along with the mixed-race Capuchin priest Francisco de São Salvador, who had tried to prevent the war. The kingdom fell apart in a terrible civil war, which lasted until 1716. By the end of the war, the Portuguese were dominant over the whole region, though Kongo preserved nominal independence until the 19th century.

The ports of Angola, Luanda and Benguela, were the largest slave-trading ports in Africa. As many as one-half of all the people who crossed the Atlantic on the Middle Passage embarked at Central African ports. Northeastern

Brazil was the principal destination for the Portuguese trade from Angola, and this area preserves Angolan cultural traditions to this day. However, slaves from Angola went all over the Atlantic. Portuguese merchants did not control all of this trade: Thanks to commercial agreements between Portugal and England in the 17th century, English ships carried more than one million people from Angola to the Americas. Many countries' ships traded in these ports, including Americans', and as many as half of all slaves imported directly from Africa to what became the United States were from Angola. The French entered this trade as well, especially after 1750, as the demand from their growing colony in Saint-Domingue overwhelmed the supply from their own bases in Senegambia.

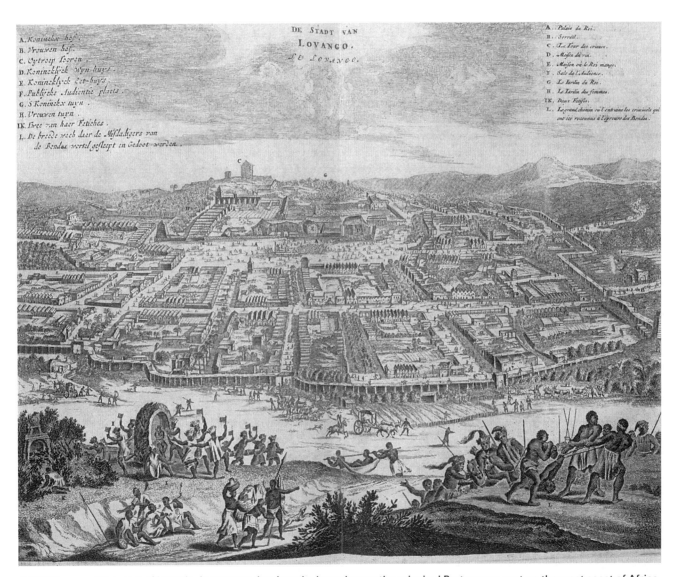

A 1686 image of the port of Luanda, in present-day Angola. Luanda was the principal Portuguese port on the west coast of Africa, through which hundreds of thousands of slaves traveled on their way to the Americas. Many of the merchants of Luanda were free people of color, often mixed-race descendants of Congolese and Portuguese merchant families. Others were free people of color from Brazil who traveled across the Atlantic to work with Portuguese merchants. Luanda was a large city, even in the 17th century, and grew even larger in the 18th and 19th centuries as the slave trade grew. *(Schomburg Center/Art Resource, NY)*

A renewal of internal strife in Kongo in the 1770s led to an expanding supply of slaves for sale in Angola. Many thousands of Angolans ended up in SAINT-DOMINGUE just before the outbreak of the HAITIAN REVOLUTION in the 1790s, and Kongolese military veterans formed an important cadre in the rebel armies of that war.

The "Portuguese" who traded and fought in Angola were mainly free people of African descent. Portugal, like Spain, was very open to social promotion by non-Europeans, especially if they had other components of high social status, such as highly placed white parents, obvious Catholic piety, and wealth. The governors and bishops of Angola were generally white peninsular Portuguese nobles, but intermediate leaders ranging from military commanders to important priests and missionaries to wealthy merchants were people of color. Some of these were the descendants of white Portuguese and Africans, while others were free people of color from the Americas. Angola was intimately linked to Brazil and indeed was subordinate to the Viceroyalty of Brazil for part of the 18th century. Even after Brazilian independence, while Angola remained part of the Portuguese empire, commercial links remained strong. The merchant houses of Angola employed many Brazilians, including free people of color, and in the 19th century, most of the capital invested in Angola, especially after the end of the slave trade, was from Brazil.

Stewart R. King

FURTHER READING

Miller, Joseph C. *Way of Death: Merchant Capitalism and the Angolan Slave Trade, 1730–1830.* Madison: University of Wisconsin Press, 1996.

Thornton, John. "'I Am the Subject of the King of Congo': African Ideology in the Haitian Revolution." *Journal of World History* 4 (1993): 181–214.

———. *Warfare in Atlantic Africa, 1500–1800.* London: UCL Press, 1999, esp. chap. 5.

CONNECTICUT

Connecticut is a small state in New England, in the United States. It borders NEW YORK STATE, RHODE ISLAND, and MASSACHUSETTS and has a long coastline along Long Island Sound. It is predominantly rural, with small cities along the coast and rivers that lead north. The farmland is not very fertile, and the climate makes it unsuitable for plantation agriculture. During the colonial and antebellum eras, the economy focused on small farming; resource extraction, especially logging; and manufacturing.

From its colonial beginnings in the 17th century, Connecticut participated in the slave system. Slaves in the colony worked in a number of endeavors, including farming and household labor. They also worked in business and on ships. In general, most slaves in this colony worked very closely with their masters because most slaveholders owned one or two slaves or, in some cases, one family of slaves. By the time of the WAR OF AMERICAN INDEPENDENCE, 1775–83, there were approximately 5,100 slaves in Connecticut, about 3 percent of the overall population, alongside about 400 free people of color. As in the other future states, slaves in Connecticut began immediately to forge their own identities and communities.

Connecticut was founded in the 1630s by colonists from neighboring Massachusetts and included slaves from the beginning. The first slaves were Pequot Indians taken captive by the settlers during the Pequot Wars (1635–37), but Africans were also imported by the late 1670s. In Fairfield County, the chief producer of grain in New England, these slaves worked the fields and tended animals such as dairy stock and horses. In other parts of the colony, slaves worked in the timber industry and made barrels, as well as being employed in the shipyards and iron mines. In the agricultural areas, slaves made up as much as 10 percent of the population by the time of the War of American Independence. One famous man who began life as a slave in Connecticut was VENTURE SMITH, a farmer who purchased his freedom in the 1760s and served in the Continental army.

Slaves began forging their own families and cultural identity immediately. They retained a number of African cultural practices such as bodily markings and hair braiding. They also developed a rich oral culture that allowed them to preserve their cultural memories and traditions. It was difficult to retain much of their African heritage, however, because slaveholdings were small, and slaves and owners often worked, ate, and sometimes slept in close proximity. Since Connecticut, as were the other New England colonies, was founded as part of a religious mission, slaves in this state were quite familiar with Christianity, in this case, Congregational Protestantism (*see also* PROTESTANT MAINLINE CHURCHES). They were allowed to become church members, and some were even encouraged to marry in the church and have their children baptized.

Some slaves, such as Venture Smith, managed to gain their freedom through a number of means. In Smith's case, freedom was through self-purchase. The relatively small size of slaveholding units, the cultural similarity between masters and slaves, and the generally urban occupations and relatively high-skill levels of slaves were all factors that tended to lead to high levels of MANUMISSION. Indeed, there were respectable numbers of free blacks in Connecticut before the War of American Independence, but most blacks became free through the process of gradual emancipation. The General Assembly of Connecticut took its first action against slavery in 1774 by putting an end to slave importation into the colony. A few years later, town boards were empowered to evaluate freedom requests on an individual basis, and in many cases, they only allowed for freedom under the provision that former masters continue supporting the slaves they sought to free. As in many places in the Atlantic world, governments were afraid that masters would use liberal manumission laws to "free" slaves who were unable to work, thus throwing them on the government or church for their support. Blacks participated in the emancipation process by petitioning the legislature for their freedom, and many fought in the American Revolution under the promise of emancipation. Gradual emancipation became law in Connecticut in 1784, when the state legislature passed a bill providing for the freedom of children born to enslaved women after March 1, 1784, upon their 25th birthday. (This age was later lowered to 21.) In 1794, the Connecticut Society for the Promotion of Freedom, a group founded by white emancipationists, almost succeeded in a quest to pass a bill that called for complete abolition of slavery in the state. Despite the failure of their bill, this group, as did others of its time, fought to protect

blacks from kidnapping and to fight slavery on a case-by-case basis. By 1800, the state still had a population of 1,000 slaves, but it also was home to more than 5,000 free blacks, almost completely reversing the ratio found only a quarter-century before.

Once freed, blacks faced the jealousy and fear of their white neighbors. Smith managed to amass a nice estate, which included houses, more than 100 acres of property, and ships, but his story was atypical. Most free blacks were kept in more lowly circumstances by a system of discrimination, supported by whites, both native and immigrant, who feared job competition. Before 1814, black property owners could vote, but that year the legislature took this right away by arguing that only white men should exercise this privilege, and this ruling made its way into a revised state constitution in 1818 despite an organized opposition campaign led by the black community leaders William Lanson and Bias Stanley. Even many white antislavery leaders advocated African colonization, fearing that true integration remained an elusive goal (*see also* EMIGRATION AND COLONIZATION and AMERICAN COLONIZATION SOCIETY).

Homes in Bridgeport, Connecticut, built by a black family named Freeman in 1848. The neighborhood was called Little Liberia in the 19th century because of the number of free blacks who lived there. *(Douglas Healey/Associated Press)*

AFRICAN-AMERICAN POPULATION OF CONNECTICUT, 1790–1900

Year	Slaves	Free People of Color	Free People of Color as a Percentage of Total Population	Total Population
1790	2,764	2,808	1.2%	237,946
1800	951	5,330	2.1%	251,002
1810	310	6,453	2.5%	261,942
1820	97	7,380	2.7%	275,248
1830	25	8,047	2.7%	297,650
1840	54	8,105	2.6%	310,015
1850		7,643	2.1%	370,799
1860		8,027	1.7%	460,147
1870		9,668	1.8%	537,454
1880		11,547	1.8%	622,700
1890		12,302	1.6%	746,258
1900		15,226	1.7%	908,420

Even so, by the time of the 1830 census, Connecticut had approximately 8,000 free blacks, concentrated primarily in the urban areas of Hartford, New Haven, New London, and Middletown. Many of the newcomers were in Connecticut because they had fled enslavement in the South. They were employed in a number of jobs in the maritime and cloth industries, and many were domestic servants. Some, such as the stonemason and stable owner William Lanson (1776–1851), were successful entrepreneurs. Lanson's fortune amounted to more than $10,000 in the 1820s, though he subsequently lost everything and died in the poorhouse.

The free black community created its own social and spiritual institutions, which allowed them collectively to endure the hardships they faced and enjoy their freedom. Lanson became in many ways a leader of this emerging free black community. He, along with Bias Stanley and Scipio Augustus, founded New Haven's first black Congregational church, the African United Ecclesiastical Society, in 1825. A year later, they formed the African Improvement Society and a black temperance society. Other Hartford blacks founded the African Religious Society. The Reverend Jehiel Beman, a leader of the Middletown black community, led in the founding of an AFRICAN METHODIST EPISCOPAL CHURCH in 1828.

White resentment and resistance grew as the black community began to achieve autonomy and success. For one thing, the American Colonization Society gained in popularity throughout the 1820s, supported by important ministers such as Leonard Bacon in New Haven. Also, black entrepreneurs such as Lanson faced assaults upon their possessions as whites seized his properties by hav-

ing them condemned as centers of prostitution, drunkenness, and other vices.

Whites also made it increasingly difficult for blacks to obtain education in Connecticut. Black children were not allowed to attend white schools, and though blacks responded by creating their own schools, these institutions often were forced to make do with inadequate resources and resistance from the community. In one incident, free blacks from PHILADELPHIA, PENNSYLVANIA, and their white abolitionist allies resolved to build a manual labor school in New Haven, Connecticut. The mayor called a town meeting to consider the plans, and he, the aldermen, the common council, and a number of citizens of New Haven ultimately resolved to resist the school. In a second incident, in 1833, Prudence Crandall, a white abolitionist who operated a boarding school for girls in Canterbury, agreed to admit a black student, Sarah Harris. Local residents became outraged, but their anger only prompted Crandall to close her existing school and open a school exclusively for black girls. Opposition intensified, and the locals had Crandall arrested under a law that forbade teaching blacks who did not reside in the community. Her first trial ended in a hung jury, but she was later convicted. She was eventually exonerated on a technicality, but her school was closed in 1834. Even so, white resistance to such efforts to benefit blacks continued.

Connecticut blacks joined in the abolition movement from the 1830s until the outbreak of the AMERICAN CIVIL WAR, 1861–65. In one well-known case, the slave ship *Amistad*, which had been captured by its human cargo, was first sailed into the port of New London (*see* AMISTAD CASE). The Connecticut free black population and white abolitionists rallied to defend the slave rebels and ultimately brought the case to the U.S. Supreme Court, where the slaves' actions were found justified. In 1838, the Connecticut legislature passed a personal liberty law, one of the first such in the nation, which ensured a jury trial for all people sought as fugitive slaves before they could be sent back into slavery. State officials were directed not to cooperate with slave catchers who did not have a Connecticut court order. The relative security this law offered fugitive slaves encouraged the growth of Connecticut's black population, which reached 8,627 by 1860.

Upon the outbreak of the American Civil War in 1861, Connecticut blacks joined their fellows throughout the North in volunteering to serve the U.S. armed forces. The army rejected black recruits until 1863, after President Lincoln issued the EMANCIPATION PROCLAMATION. However, many Connecticut blacks served in the navy, given the state's maritime heritage and the concentration of blacks in the port cities. New London, in particular, was an important naval shipbuilding center during the war and had a large black population. The U.S. Navy had never had any restrictions on blacks' serving at the enlisted level. About 100 Connecticut men joined the two famous black Massachusetts Infantry Regiments, the 54th and 55th Massachusetts.

In the aftermath of the war, Connecticut remained a relatively welcoming environment for blacks. In general, racial discrimination was less harsh in New England than elsewhere in the northern states. A system of de facto residential segregation kept black and white communities largely separate, and schools and other public services in white areas were better funded. Nonetheless, black community life was possible; there were educational and economic opportunities and a small middle class. One outstanding example of this group was Alfred DuBois (1833–95), the father of the black intellectual and civil rights leader W. E. B. DuBois (1868–1963). The elder DuBois was born in Haiti but grew up in New Haven, the son of a merchant and a child of relative privilege. Lacking a large urban area, though, the state did not experience the rapid growth in black populations that neighboring New York and Massachusetts did. By 1900, while the state's population had almost tripled, the black population stood at 15,296, nearly twice what it had been in 1860.

Beverly C. Tomek

FURTHER READING

Gilder Lehrman Center for the Study of Slavery, Resistance & Abolition. *Citizens ALL: African-Americans in Connecticut, 1700–1850.* New Haven, Conn.: Yale University. Available online. URL: http://cmi2.yale.edu/citizens_all/index.html. Accessed December 20, 2010.
Hinks, Peter. "Digging Deeper." *Citizens ALL: African-Americans in Connecticut, 1700–1850*, a Web site produced by Gilder Lehrman Center for the Study of Slavery, Resistance & Abolition. New Haven, Conn.: Yale University, 2007.
McManus, Edgar. *Black Bondage in the North.* Syracuse, N.Y.: Syracuse University Press, 2002.
———. *Law and Liberty in Early New England: Criminal Justice and Due Process, 1620–1692.* Amherst: University of Massachusetts Press, 1993.
Stone, Frank Andrews. *African American Connecticut: The Black Scene in a New England State, Eighteenth to Twenty-First Century.* Bloomington, Ind.: Trafford, 2008.

CORNISH, SAMUEL E. (ca. 1795–1858)
American minister and newspaperman

Samuel E. Cornish was one of the first African Americans to work as a journalist (*see* BLACK PRESS IN THE UNITED STATES). He was an important voice in the African-American abolition movement and a minister in the Presbyterian Church.

Cornish was born free in DELAWARE in about 1795. As for many people during this period, his childhood and early years are undocumented. In 1815, at around the age of 20, he moved to PHILADELPHIA, PENNSYLVANIA. There he began teaching at a school run by John Gloucester, the minister of the First African Presbyterian Church. Cornish began training to become a Presbyterian minister in 1817 and was officially licensed to preach two years later. Both of his brothers also became ministers in the AFRICAN METHODIST EPISCOPAL CHURCH, but Cornish chose to join and remain a part of a predominantly white church community (*see also* PROTESTANT MAINLINE CHURCHES).

In 1820, Cornish became a missionary to slaves on the eastern shore of MARYLAND. His repugnance for Christian slaveholders led him to leave the area and move to New York City. There he continued his ministry with the New York Evangelical Missionary Society of Young Men. About a year after his arrival, he helped found the first African American Presbyterian Church in New York City, the First Colored Presbyterian Church. In 1822, Cornish switched his allegiance from the Philadelphia presbytery of the Presbyterian Church to New York City's, formalizing his new residence in the eyes of his church. Despite being recruited to replace the deceased John Gloucester in 1823, Cornish stayed in New York and became pastor of the First Colored Presbyterian Church in 1824. Cornish was also active in many groups and societies, including the Haytian Emigration Society, though he became disenchanted with this project and remained a lifelong opponent of African colonization (*see also* EMIGRATION AND COLONIZATION). Cornish was still a minister when he teamed with JOHN

Russwurm in March 1827 to publish the first African-American newspaper, *Freedom's Journal.* As the older man, Cornish was labeled senior editor, but he resigned after only six months. The parting was evidently amicable, until Russwurm switched the paper's position on African colonization and left for Liberia in 1829. With the demise of *Freedom's Journal* and departure of Russwurm, Cornish began another paper, the *Rights of All.* It only lasted six monthly issues. Both papers sought to provide a public service to the black community by facilitating communication and to serve as a voice calling for the end of slavery and improved treatment for free blacks in the North.

After this, Cornish continued to work for the abolition of slavery and the improvement of African Americans. At the First Annual Convention of the People of Colour in 1830, he was elected to collect funds for a proposed manual labor college. He was also active in the Phoenix Society, focused on literacy and education, and the New York Committee of Vigilance, which worked to prevent the kidnapping of free blacks into slavery. Cornish served on both the Board of Managers and Executive Committee of the American Anti-Slavery Society and continued to publish articles in abolitionist newspapers such as the *Emancipator* and the *Liberator.* In 1837, he resumed his editing in what was, for a time, the most important black newspaper in the country, the *Colored American.* A year later, the prominent black abolitionist and physician James McCune Smith (1813–65) became his assistant at the newspaper. The financial difficulties from the loss of a libel suit brought by David Ruggles, a free black involved in a freedom suit, caused them both to leave the *Colored American* in 1839. With eight other African-American clergymen, Cornish was among the founders of the American and Foreign Anti-Slavery Society in 1840. The society became one of the most important voices in the abolition movement in the United States. He also cowrote *The Colonization Scheme Considered* with Theodore Wright, arguing that the African colonization movement was racist and proslavery. In his later years, Cornish continued to complain in print about the condescension and racism of white abolitionists while applauding their efforts. Cornish also continued his clerical and missionary work throughout his life. Samuel Cornish died on November 6, 1858, in New York City.

Matthew J. Hudock

FURTHER READING

Alexander, Leslie M. *African or American? Black Identity and Political Activism in New York City, 1784–1861.* Urbana: University of Illinois Press, 2008.

Bacon, Jacqueline. *Freedom's Journal: The First African-American Newspaper.* Lanham, Md.: Lexington Books, 2007.

Harris, Leslie M. *In the Shadow of Slavery: African Americans in New York City, 1626–1863.* Chicago: University of Chicago Press, 2003.

Swift, David E. *Black Prophets of Justice: Activist Clergy before the Civil War.* Baton Rouge: Louisiana State University Press, 1987.

Tripp, Bernell. *Origins of the Black Press: New York, 1827–1847.* Northport, Ala.: Vision Press, 1992.

CORNWALLIS, COUBA (17??–1848) *Jamaican innkeeper and medical caregiver*

Couba Cornwallis was a lodging-house keeper who lived in Port Royal, Jamaica, during the 18th and 19th centuries. The date of her birth is not yet ascertained, but by 1780 she was already operating a lodging house and was a noted traditional healer, or "doctress," in Jamaican parlance. She died in 1848.

Port Royal was once a parish in Jamaica but is now a part of the parish of Kingston. It has historical and cultural significance for the island, as it was the chief city in the 17th century, the seat of the island assembly and the base of the buccaneers who helped England gain recognition for its colonies from Spain. This rich city was destroyed by a major earthquake in 1692 and fire in 1704 but became an important naval station in the 18th century.

It is in what was left of this former parish that Cornwallis, a former slave woman, established her lodging house. She was described as light-colored, suggesting that she was sambo, or Mulatto. In 18th-century Jamaica, her lighter skin color would have put her one step up on the social ladder, and Manumission would have added to her social elevation. She, as like quite a few colored women of her day, had a white male patron who purchased her freedom and secured her economic well-being, providing her with a lodging house. This favor would have opened the door to economic independence for her. Marriage to her patron was impossible because of the racial difference. Her patron was a young naval officer stationed in Port Royal, Captain William Cornwallis (1744–1819), who like all British naval officers at the time, was white. Thus she became the mistress of this officer (and took his surname). He later became an admiral and commanded Britain's largest fleet during the Napoleonic Wars.

As a lodging-house keeper, Couba Cornwallis was part of a tradition in Jamaica whereby free black and colored women operated lodging houses, which often operated as convalescent homes for transient whites. With the Port Royal location, she would probably have done a thriving business, as the town was the home of Fort Charles, an important part of the naval defense for the British in the Caribbean.

The strategic placement of her lodging house accounts for her survival in the historical records as more than a faceless lodging-house keeper. She was popular among the soldiery, whom she often nursed. She served two of Britain's sons of noble birth while they served their motherland in the Caribbean; she is remembered as the person who nursed young Horatio Nelson (1758–1805) back to health in 1780 and who cared for the future King William IV (1765–1837).

Horatio Nelson, later Lord Nelson, returned from an British expedition against the Spaniards in Nicaragua suffering from malignant fever, dysentery, and poisoning by manchineel. Being very weak, he had to be carried ashore to Cornwallis's lodging house. It was not surprising that this sailor would have been sent to her lodging house. She, as an expert healer, had knowledge of traditional cures for a number of diseases. Couba Cornwallis, as did many other Afro-Caribbean lodging-house keepers, had a heritage in CREOLE healing art. (See also MIDWIVES AND TRADITIONAL HEALERS.) Her knowledge of herbal cures was the common heritage of the African diaspora during and after slavery, but there were specialists among healers, and Cornwallis was one such specialist. Not only were Cornwallis and other lodging-house keepers known for their love of nursing and their skills in herbal healing, they had a reputation of being compassionate to the sick and suffering among the white travelers to the Caribbean. They catered to the board and lodging needs of those travelers. Given the inadequacy of medical care and inadequate knowledge of tropical diseases in the Caribbean at the time, the work of women like Cornwallis was vital to the well-being of those men (and women) who were far from home. Their care and service were comparable to those of gentlewomen in Europe who used their homes for convalescent care of the sick.

Cornwallis not only nursed Lord Nelson back to health before he could be sent to the Port Royal hills for convalescent care but also nursed the future king William IV, who fell ill while he was a young midshipman on a visit to Jamaica. In recognition of her service, Cornwallis received royal recognition from the future Queen Adelaide, who sent her a gown. It is said that Cornwallis kept this dress for her burial.

Aleric Josephs

FURTHER READING

Josephs, Aleric. "Mary Seacole: Jamaican Nurse and 'Doctress.'" *Jamaica Historical Review* 17 (1991): 48–65.
Kerr, Paulette A. "Victims or Strategists? Female Lodging-House Keepers Jamaica." In *Engendering History—Caribbean Women in Historical Perspective;* edited by Verene Shepherd, 197–212. Kingston, Jamaica: Ian Randle, 1995.
Wilkins, Nadine. "Doctors and Ex-Slaves in Jamaica, 1834-1850." *Jamaica Historical Review* 17 (1991): 19–30.

CORREA, JUAN   (1646–1716)   *Mexican master painter*

Juan Correa was one of the most distinctive artists of Mexico's baroque period. Among the many images that he painted were angels, cherubs, and the unique (based on the best evidence we have) representations of children of *color quebrado* (broken color) that strongly imply his own Afro-descendant origins. He was also the first painter to copy the image of the Virgin of Guadalupe, which was said to have appeared miraculously on the *tilpa* (cloak) of the man to whom the Virgin appeared. The painting has subsequently become an important symbol of Mexican identity. He achieved the level of veedor (supervisor) of his artisan guild and was a recognized and respected artist of his time.

As an inheritor of an important social and artistic process at the mid-17th century in New Spain, this Afro-Mexican painter was, on one side, a representative of the mestizo, an emergent social group in Mexico, and, on the other, of developing international baroque culture. Using images and religious symbols of his epoch, Correa and the apprentices at his workshop reproduced baroque style, colors, movements, and gestures included in chapels, sacristies, altarpieces, convents, and churches throughout New Spain, popularizing the new artistic aesthetic and adding a Mexican element to it.

As a result of the research initiated more than 20 years ago by a group of art historians headed by Elisa Vargas Lugo, Juan Correa's work is perhaps the best known of the viceroyalty period painters of New Spain. It was known that the mestizo descendants of Indians, Spaniards, and Africans were employed as apprentices and officers in the guild's workshops, yet for modern scholars of the viceregal period, it is still surprising that a mestizo, especially one with African ancestry, achieved the rank of guild master and, even more surprisingly, became a recognized artistic authority. In that lies the importance of a detailed analysis of Correa's life and his prolific production, not only for the sake of accurate art history in Mexico, but also for the ethnic and social dynamic that contemporary Mexico inherits.

Born sometime in 1646, Juan Correa was the son of a famous barber surgeon, also named Juan Correa, employed by the Mexican Inquisition, and Pascuala de Santoyo, a *morena libre* (free mixed-race) daughter of Bartolomé and María de Santoyo, described in her will as "black parents" *(negros mis padres).* Internal evidence in the will suggests that one of his mother's parents was a *bozal,* or person born in Africa. Pascuala had also given birth to two sons during a previous unmarried relationship. She personally owned 500 hundred pesos of her own assets, a fairly considerable sum for a black woman at that time. Furthermore, the viceroyalty's treasurer, Alonso Santoyo, an important patron who may have been a former master, bequeathed to her rental property. With her husband she gave birth to two other children: José, a Maestro Dorador (master gilder), and Juan Correa. Correa's father was born in Mexico City, son of a Spaniard and a woman born in Cádiz, who is reputed to have been a MULATTO or Moorish woman, though there is no proof of her racial status. The father of Juan Correa was an eminent surgeon of the Holy Office and later anatomy professor of the Royal and Pontific University of Mexico; he was the first surgeon to perform an anatomic dissection in 1646.

Information in the will of Correa's mother shows the complex and heterogeneous *afromestizo* world of 17th-century New Spain. In this period, there were a variety of social and ethnic categories. For example, Correa's parents had the ability to *labrar casas* (build houses, that is, within the official town limits, which gave them rights as citizens of the town). Some of these houses were willed to their sons, who firmly established their economic position in Calle del Aguila, a very well-situated location in downtown Mexico City. According to documents, the real estate was valued at the considerable sum of 3,679 pesos. The Correas' wealth allowed them to lend 300 pesos to their son José, who bought his wife, Tomasa Gutierrez's, freedom from slavery, and an additional 50 pesos for their grandson's liberty as well. Underlining the complex ethnic diversity in 17th-century New Spain, Juan Correa, the artist, owned and enjoyed the services of a 50-year-old black slave, whom he sold for 235 pesos to a *bachiller* (lawyer or amanuensis). Other archival records show that one of Correa's half brothers was a Franciscan friar, a finding that challenges the commonly accepted idea that only Spaniards and criollos (children born in America of Peninsular Spaniards) were accepted at New Spain's convents.

During his life, Juan Correa married twice; the dates of the ceremonies are unknown, as are the ethnic origins of his wives. He had no children from his first marriage because of the premature death of his wife María de Paéz. The marriage to Ursula de Montoya, his second wife, had in four children: Miguel, Francisco, Diego, and Felipa. Two of them became artists. Their first son became an officer in the colonial government, and Diego became a master artisan but died at an early age.

There is no accurate information on Correa's early years, but he surely was apprenticed to the painter's guild and later reached master status. Even so, on the basis of the similarities in his brushstrokes, drawings, and expressions with the well-known painter Antonio Rodriguez, some art historians maintain that Correa was trained in his workshop.

The exact date of Correa's acceptance into the guild is unknown, but there is evidence that points to his being a contemporary of other well-known painters. In 1687, new regulations placed stricter requirements on guild members to prove their skills. At the time Correa was examined for mastery, he was 41 years old. His examiners were such outstanding artists as Cristobal de Villalpando, Juan Sánchez Salmerón, and Joseph de Rojas. But because of the dating of his earlier paintings, we know he had started working independently at least 20 years earlier.

Correa was elected *veedor* (examiner) of his guild in 1706; *veedor* was an important position in the institutional hierarchy. To gain this responsibility a master needed to have a good reputation and experience in the office. *Veedors* were the persons responsible for implementation of the orders and laws of the city that related to the practices of the guild. They were also members of the juries that examined the master and officer candidates.

Further, Correa acted as evaluator of goods and executor of wills for fellow artisans. For example, for several months he acted as executor of the will of a free *pardo* (Afro-Mexican) by the name of Mateo de Aguilar, a gold and silver merchant and native of the town of Real y Minas de Taxco and owner of an considerable fortune. Aguilar was one of a significant and growing number of wealthy people of mixed race in Mexico at this time.

In his life as a master painter, Correa accepted several mulatto apprentices in his workshop and helped educate José Ibarra (1688–1756), who later became an important artist. He provided economic support to other *afromestizos* and was godfather to a sizable number of children of diverse ethnic origins. Correa died in 1716.

During the late 17th and early 18th centuries, Correa was well known and appreciated in New Spain's society. Correa and the members of his workshop created many important paintings commissioned by civil and ecclesiastical authorities. His paintings covered all types of iconography of the time: archangels, devotions to the Blessed Virgin Mary, allegories, saints, and souls in purgatory, including a screen decorated with humanistic themes. Their work was distributed across the main regions in New Spain's territory, including Guatemala, which at that time were part of the viceroyalty. Some of them even traveled to Spain. Many of these pieces—of which some 400 were signed, and some 40 others were attributed to his brush—remain part of the religious buildings that commissioned them to this day. Among them are the sacristy in the metropolitan cathedral in Mexico City, the church of the Convent of San Francisco in Guadalajara, the sacristy of the Church of San Diego in Aguscalientes, the Asunción parochial Church in Pachuca de Hidalgo, the sacristy of Durango's cathedral, and the Toluca Cathedral. Some others belong to Mexico's city museums, such as the National Viceroyalty, the National Museum of Interventions, el Museum del Carmen, the Franz Mayer, the National Museum of Art, the National Art Gallery, St. Charles Museum, and many other museums and regional cultural institutions. Correa's pieces are also located in foreign museums, particularly in Spain, and in some private national and foreign collections.

María Elisa Velázquez Gutiérrez

FURTHER READING

Maquivar, Consuelo, coordinator. *Memoria del Coloquio El arte en tiempos de Juan Correa*. Mexico City: Museo Nacional del Verreinato, Instituto Nacional de Antropologia e Historia, 1994.

Vargas Lugo, Elisa, and Gustavo Curiel. *Juan Correa, su vida y su obra. Cuerpo de documentos*. Mexico City: Universidad Nacional Autonoma de Mexico, 1991.

Velázquez, Maria Elisa. *Juan Correa, mulato libre, maestro de pintor*. Mexico City: Consejo Nacional para la Cultura y las Artes, 1998.

COSTA RICA

Costa Rica is a small nation in Central America bordered on the north by NICARAGUA, on the southeast by PANAMA, to the east by the Caribbean Sea, and to the west and southwest by the Pacific Ocean. Coconut Island, in the Pacific Ocean, also belongs to Costa Rica. The Caribbean coastal regions are low-lying and heavily forested, while a chain of mountains parallels the Pacific coast. As in other parts of Central America, the central highlands, and particularly an important central valley with easy access to both coasts, are the most heavily inhabited section of the country.

Colonial Period (1502–1823)

Christopher Columbus arrived on his fourth and last voyage to the Americas at the island of Cariari on the Caribbean coast in September 1502. His caravels anchored near that island, close to what today is the city of Limón. Impressed by the exuberant vegetation and by the jewelry and gold decorations worn by the indigenous population, Columbus baptized this land with the name *Costa Rica*, or rich coast.

Castilla de Oro, or Panama, was the first place on the mainland of the Americas where African slaves were carried, and although it is unclear exactly when they arrived, documentary evidence shows that they were present by 1513. The fusion of races and nationalities progressed among the different ethnic groups from the earliest days of colonization. On September 25, 1513, Vasco Núñez de Balboa became the first Spaniard to reach the Pacific Ocean in what is now Panama. He was accompanied by a black man called Nuflo de Olano, whose free or enslaved status was not recorded.

In 1522 and 1523, Gil Gonzalez Davila explored the Pacific coast of Costa Rica and Nicaragua. Later in the 1520s, Fernández de Córdoba began colonization in Nicaragua. Among the members of both these Spanish expeditions were an unknown number of African slaves and probably also some black or mixed-race free people from Seville or the Caribbean colonies.

The conquest of Costa Rica was a consequence of the first establishments of Spaniards in Panama and Nicaragua. Already by 1526, Panama had entered into a more stable phase of exploitation, which would speed the importation of African slaves, in order to replace indigenous populations that had been devastated by diseases introduced by Spanish and African immigrants and by the labor demands of the Spanish conquistadores.

Costa Rica remained almost unexplored until 1561, when Juan de Cavallón, the *alcalde* (mayor) of Nicaragua, initiated explorations in the territory. The central valley of Costa Rica, with natural exits toward both the Caribbean and the Pacific, became the principal axis of colonization, with the most important port and early settlements on the Pacific coast. Ultimately, with population growth and economic development, the colony spread out of the central valley to populate the highlands, by this time almost denuded of native inhabitants.

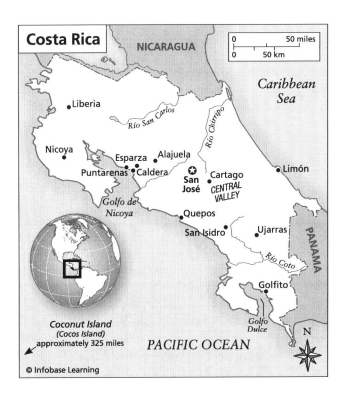

POPULATION OF COSTA RICA, 1522–1801

Year	Spaniards	Indians	Mulattoes	Blacks	Mestizos	Total
1522		27,200				
1569	113	17,166	170	30		17,479
1611	330	14,908	250	25	25	15,538
1700	2,146	15,489	2,291	154	213	19,293
1720	3,059	13,269	2,193	168	748	19,437
1741	4,687	12,716	3,065	200	3,458	24,126
1751	7,807	10,109	2,987	62	3,057	24,022
1778	6,046	8,104	6,053	94	13,915	24,212
1801	4,942	8,281	8,925	30	30,413	52,591

Source: Thiel, "Monografía para la población de Costa Rica," in *Revista de Costa Rica*, San José, 1921

A Spanish royal decree of March 30, 1563, attached the provinces of Nicaragua and HONDURAS, as well as Costa Rica, to the Panama Audiencia. The effective autonomy of local government under this system contributed to the independence of Central America from MEXICO and PERU during the colonial period. In addition, Costa Rica, in particular, was a frontier zone throughout the colonial period. A small mining industry and some farms and ranches provided enough to support a colony but not enough wealth to attract large imports of any commodity. African slaves were expensive anywhere in Spanish America, and few of them were taken to Costa Rica.

The total numbers were very small, when compared to those of Mexico or Panama: 2,915 slaves taken legally to Costa Rica between 1600 and 1825. There was a significant illegal trade in slaves, especially in the early 18th century, before the British were granted official permission, the *asiento*, to import slaves. Governmental estimates of the illegal trade were in the range of several hundred a year for the early 18th century. Overall, however, we can estimate that no more than 5,000 slaves were taken to the colony during its entire history. Nonetheless, African slavery became an important part of the socioeconomic system of colonial Costa Rica in the late 16th and 17th centuries. Many of the African slaves were imported into the country to work at Golfo Dulce, located on the Pacific coast of Costa Rica near the border with Panama, which was an important early center of settlement. As elsewhere in Central America, the frontier conditions and relatively ill-defined racial lines in Spanish society meant that some slaves were able to gain their freedom and move into the ranks of free people of color.

Free people of color formed an important intermediate stratum between slaves and the very small Spanish population. The colonial militias of the 17th century were organized to face native resistance as well as English, French, or Dutch presence on the coast. The first black

and mulatto MILITIA companies were organized by Governor Juan Fernandez de Salinas y de la Cerda in 1650. He designated a free mixed-race man named Diego de Zuñiga as the captain and commissioner of the black and mulatto militia of Cartago city, which was then the capital, and later in the 1600s, the mulatto Lucas de Contreras served as captain of infantry of the free mulattoes of Esparza city.

Free Afro–Costa Ricans contributed to the development of new social structures in rural areas, especially in the central valley and in the Guanacaste and Caribbean regions. Slave imports were low as the early prosperity of the area dissipated and the Spanish colonial economy as a whole entered a long period of decline. In a pattern familiar throughout Spanish America, African-descended people often intermarried with indigenous and white people, and their descendants sometimes were able to redefine themselves racially. In this way, they disappeared into other population categories, causing declines in the reported African percentage among the general population.

There are no sources that give a complete total for the free Afro-descended population in the province of Costa Rica in the 18th century, only three partial registers of 1776, 1782, and 1783, corresponding to the cities of Cartago, Ujarras, and San José. In Cartago, there were 95 PARDOS, a term that referred to all African-descended people. In the village of Ujarras, near Cartago, in 1782, there were 125 *pardos*. The city of San José, the largest city and capital after 1824, had 706 mulattoes in 1783, in addition to an unknown number of free blacks. In each case, the register recorded a much larger number of free black women than men: 87 to eight in Cartago, 71 to 54 in Ujarras, and 530 to 176 in San José. There are a variety of possible explanations for this phenomenon, but the most likely is that free black men were more marginalized socially than women and thus more likely to be undercounted. Considering the probable undercount and the phenomena of "WHITENING" AND RACIAL PROMOTION, it is likely that as much as 40 percent of the population had at least some African ancestry in the 1780s. The table on page 196 is based on government statistics and estimates by a historical demographer and makes no distinction between free and enslaved people of African ancestry, but it offers a sense of the evolution of the black population of Costa Rica during the colonial period.

African slaves were first imported into Costa Rica in the 16th century in order to work in placer gold mines. Mining, as was common throughout the Americas, was a dangerous industry for newly imported Africans, but it was also one that offered the possibility for quick freedom, either by running away from a remote mine site or by finding enough minerals to buy one's freedom. The mines were quickly exhausted, though, and by the late 16th century, the few African slaves who remained in the country were carried to Nicoya and Esparza on the Pacific coast to work in INDIGO CULTIVATION. With the subsequent decline of dye plantations, many blacks went to the capital of Cartago, either as free urban ARTISANS, as personal servants, or as enslaved employees in workshops. Again, servants and artisanal workers each had access to money and a much better chance than agricultural workers to obtain their freedom. Later, blacks did move into general agriculture and COFFEE CULTIVATION, either as free peasants or as enslaved laborers.

By 1801, blacks had disappeared almost completely through mixed marriages; as a result, their children would become members of another racial category. However, in the late 19th century, the introduction of black Caribbean workers would give a new ethnic composition to the country. Without this black migration from the islands, an identifiable community of African descent would not exist in Costa Rica today.

Early National Period (1823–1870)
Costa Rica gained its independence, along with Nicaragua, Honduras, EL SALVADOR, and GUATEMALA, from Mexico in 1823 as part of the Federal Republic of Central America. The WAR OF MEXICAN INDEPENDENCE, 1810–21, against Spain had not touched Costa Rica at all, aside from disruptions in trade. After independence there was almost immediate liberation of the remaining slaves, decreed by the National Constituent Assembly of the Federal Republic in April 1824. The republic's leaders were liberals and believed strongly in racial equality. They were opposed in each of the member countries by conservative factions, including powerful landholders and the ROMAN CATHOLIC CHURCH. The conservative faction in Costa Rica was weak, however. As the liberal governments in the other countries of the Federal

Republic were overthrown one by one in the 1830s, Costa Rica remained loyal to the concept of Central American union under Juan Mora Fernandez. Fernandez's policy of free trade and lowering of barriers to consolidation of landholdings allowed the growth of the coffee industry. Coffee plantations employed local labor but also began to encourage immigration from the Caribbean, welcoming the first of a new wave of free blacks to the country. Finally, in 1838, Costa Rica accepted the dissolution of the Central American union and declared itself separately independent.

In 1856–57, an American "filibusterer," William Walker, invaded Central America in an attempt to create a conservative Central American empire where plantation slavery could flourish. American Southern whites had dreamed of acquiring territory in Spanish America that could counterbalance the growth of the Northern industrial section of that country and maintain the political balance between free and slave states. Walker's expedition was one of many such attempts in the 1850s. With the help of local conservatives, he briefly became the president of Nicaragua. In 1857, he invaded Costa Rica. The liberal president, Rafael Mora Porres, rallied town militias to face the invader. One of these militiamen, a man of African ancestry named Juan Santamaria from the town of Alajuela, nicknamed *el erizo* (the Porcupine) because of his spiked hair, lost his life while setting a filibusterer strongpoint ablaze. In the late 19th century, liberal intellectual and political leaders identified Santamaria as a symbol of Costa Rican nationalism, and the day of his death became a national holiday.

By the 1850s, Afro–Costa Ricans were highly assimilated and had almost completely vanished in public statistics and the public concept of Costa Rican identity. The national legend of Juan Santamaria, as it was created after 1891, played down the importance of his mother, Manuela Santamaria, because she was identifiably Afro-mestiza. Santamaria was a symbol not of the contributions of Afro-Costa Ricans but of a national identity, undivided and primarily Hispanic, that could be contrasted with the newly arrived African-descended immigrants of the 1890s.

Afro-Caribbean Immigration and Racial Discrimination (1870s–1940s)
Coffee and cocoa cultivation became important to the national economy in the 1830s, but rapid growth in these sectors only began in 1871 with the initiation of railroad construction. It was at this time that Costa Rica became an important destination for MIGRATION by Afro-Caribbean people. In addition, in the 1870s, fruit production became an important economic sector. As a result of these developments, Costa Rica received a diverse group

of new, mostly black immigrant workers from places such as Cuba, Haiti, Saint Lucia, Saint Kitts, Great Cayman, Trinidad and Tobago, Jamaica, the Dominican Republic, Providence Island, Aruba, Barbados, Guyana, San Andres, and Curaçao; other immigrants joined them from: Belize, Honduras, Nicaragua, and Colombia, among others.

Notable among these places of origin was Jamaica, at that time a British colony, which was an important source of migrant labor throughout the Caribbean region. Many Jamaicans arrived in Limón on the Caribbean coast. The Afro-Caribbean community settled in that region adopted Jamaican as their primary cultural identity, so the majority spoke English and were affiliated with Protestant churches. At the turn of the 20th century and with some help from natural demographic growth as well as immigration, the Limón jurisdiction became a province. By this time, Afro-Caribbean people made up about 3 percent of the national population.

That condition enabled American transnational corporations, especially the United Fruit Company, to hire Afro-Caribbean workers at a very low cost in the early 1900s. In most cases, the Afro-Caribbeans who worked in banana plantations paid the cost of their transportation to the place where United Fruit needed them.

A new agricultural sector came into being, narrowly tied to the railroad and to the Afro-Caribbean immigrants and their descendants. From Guacimo in the Old Line to Port Limón, extending toward the south to Cahuita and Old Harbour, these zones were at the beginning more linked to local roads. Before railroad construction began, one of the main economic activities was cocoa cultivation, usually in small plots and often by farmers of mixed race. Although cocoa continued to be an important export, many of these small producers were forced out of the market by large producers and by the economic and political power of the United Fruit Company, and they became landless agricultural laborers alongside the more recent Afro-Caribbean immigrants.

In 1873, a year after the American financier Henry Meiggs Keith initiated railroad construction, the Costa Rican government began to create the infrastructure required by the project, including buildings, roads, and a water system. At the same time, the Costa Rican government established specific legal measures for the Caribbean region, designed to control the Afro-Caribbean population, based on the concept of "public hygiene." These ideas to a certain extent grew out of the prevailing racial ideology of the United Fruit Company but were also based upon a national myth of a "white and egalitarian" Costa Rica. This national myth dominated public identity in Costa Rica in spite of the heterogeneous origins of its population, evident since the very early colo-

nial epoch. The defenders of these ideas were the liberal elites, who proposed to safeguard the social order and national morality by means of the exclusion and selective repression of immigrant blacks, based on criteria associated with race, culture, morality, and hygiene. Such strategies cemented liberal political dominance and national identity of the Costa Rican population, above all because the elites saw imminent danger of degeneration of the national white population caused by the black immigrants, considered as members of an inferior race.

Thus, during the first years of railroad construction and the banana plantation boom, the attitude of the government concerning the Afro-Caribbean population changed, although not in a final or decisive way. A colonization law of 1862 specifically prohibited Chinese and African immigration. Almost a decade later, given the new labor situation, in 1874, the government decided to grant residency to the existing Afro-Caribbean workers.

On the other hand, the collapse of the banana boom in the 1920s coincided with the worst economic crisis seen by the Costa Rican central valley. This took place alongside an increase in "scientific racism" on a worldwide basis. The impact of this period in Costa Rica's racial politics was recognizable. It also explains to a great extent the antiblack legislation and the public racist protest that characterized the years of 1924 and 1925, when racialist rhetoric joined with nationalist language to identify Afro-Caribbean immigrants as the "other" and a threat to Costa Rican identity.

Thus, the first of a series of petitions was presented to Congress in 1925 by various white workers in the banana industry, requesting that blacks not be permitted to occupy positions in company offices, as salespeople, and in other similar specialized occupations. And it is here that the second moment of hostility experienced by the Afro-Caribbean population occurs: In the middle of the decade of the 1930s, with the backdrop of the Great Depression and during the general strike of 1934. One of the outcomes of the strike that year was the prohibition of the employment of people of color in the Pacific zone of the country, where the new operations of the United Fruit Company would take place. The objective was to control the Afro-Caribbean laborer contingent, considered at the time harmful to the country. It was intended that Afro-Caribbeans leave Costa Rica, since the major source of jobs in Limón was about to disappear with the transfer of United Fruit operations to the Pacific region. Later, in 1942, with the purpose of dismantling the migratory networks around the Afro-Caribbean population, a legal prohibition on immigration was enacted, restricting the entry of other nonwhites as well.

It was not until 1949, after a bloody civil war ousted the political faction most identified with the racist policies of the earlier decades, that the new constitution would recognize the descendants of the Afro-Caribbean immigrants as Costa Rican citizens. Today, however, the Limón province remains the poorest part of the country, and many Afro-Costa Ricans remain landless and exploited agricultural workers on large fruit and coffee plantations.

Diana Senior-Angulo

FURTHER READING

Acuña, María de los Ángeles y Chavarría, Doriam. *"El mestizaje: La sociedad multirracial en la ciudad de Cartago (1738–1821)."* Tesis de Licenciatura en Historia, Universidad de Costa Rica, 1991.

Aguilar Bulgarelli, Oscar. *La esclavitud negra en Costa Rica. Origen de la oligarquía económica y política nacional.* San José: Editorial Progreso, 1997.

Cáceres, Rina. *Negros, mulatos, esclavos y libertos en la Costa Rica del siglo XVII.* México-D.F.: Instituto Panamericano de Geografía e Historia, 2000.

Meléndez, Carlos y Duncan, Quince. *El negro en Costa Rica.* San José: Editorial Costa Rica, 1989.

Senior-Angulo, Diana. "La incorporación social en Costa Rica de la población Afrocostarricense durante el siglo XX, 1927–1963." Tesis de Maestría en Historia, Universidad de Costa Rica, 2007.

COTTON CULTIVATION

Cotton became the principal plantation crop in the interior of the Southern states of North America in the 19th century after the invention of the cotton gin permitted the profitable cultivation of the short-staple (short-fibered) cotton that grows best there. Prior to that, long-staple cotton, more easily cleaned by hand, had been a secondary crop on the Atlantic coast of North America, in the Caribbean, and in tropical South America. Both types of cotton can be cultivated on small farms, making use of the labor of family members or a limited number of slaves or hired laborers. Even large cotton plantations in the American South in the years before the AMERICAN CIVIL WAR, 1861–65, typically employed only a few dozen field slaves, as compared with the hundreds of slaves and tens of thousands of dollars of equipment needed for profitable SUGAR CULTIVATION. Cotton did not require a lot of sophisticated equipment; even the cotton gin was fairly easy to manufacture in a small blacksmith's shop and thus within the means of a small farmer. Short-staple cotton is native to South Asia and when introduced to the Americas enjoyed a long holiday from its various diseases and insect pests, so yields were very high. As a result, cotton was a potentially valuable crop for free people of color in those places where they were allowed to own or rent land.

Cotton is relatively bulky, typically being packaged for sale in bales 18 cubic feet (0.5 m³) in volume and weighing 500 pounds (225 kg). A good farmer in the early 19th century could expect a yield of about one bale of short-staple cotton per acre, so a moderate farm would produce 20 or 30 of these heavy packages each harvest. This is a difficult load to transport, so cotton farming developed near transportation routes: rivers, seaports, roads, canals, and rail lines. Land in these areas was more expensive than land in remote places, constituting a constraint on poor farmers. However, land in frontier regions in the American Southeast was fairly inexpensive, and in addition, the custom of sharecropping was introduced.

Originally developed in the poor areas in Great Britain where the ancestors of many of the white settlers of the backcountry South came from, sharecropping permitted a land-rich but capital-poor landlord to put his land into the hands of a poor, but free, tenant without any money's changing hands. The landlord and tenant would divide the crops at the harvest, with the share of each governed by contracts based on ancient customary law. The landlord would often be responsible for marketing the combined product of all of his tenants—to the extent that any of it went to market—with the cash divided also according to contract and ancient custom. The contracts were typically for a year, though they could be for longer periods, but in Britain, tenants expected to remain on the same piece of land for many generations. The landlord obviously had the advantage in any such arrangement, especially if there was no shortage of potential tenants. Unlike the master-serf relationship that existed in the wealthier parts of Britain, most tenant farmers in the north of England, lowland Scotland, and Northern Ireland were free people who were tied to their landlords by kinship in clans, and this fact moderated the exploitative nature of the sharecropping system. These "Scotch-Irish" landlords transplanted the system to their new homes, and at first the sharecropping tenants were kinsmen or at least countrymen. But with the introduction of free blacks into the system, this tie of kinship was lost, and sharecropping became a very abusive system. Still, there were few alternatives, and the system permitted a huge amount of cotton to be grown by small farmers, many of them blacks, along with the even larger quantities grown by white farmers with enough capital to own some dozens of slaves.

Cotton became the engine of enormous economic growth in the American South in the two generations before the Civil War. This was a period when restrictions on free people of color were growing ever harsher. But tenant farming remained an option for free people of color in many states, and landownership was possible for those free black families who had acquired

A woman cultivating cotton by hand in Mississippi in the 1930s. Cotton was an important crop for free people of color in the American South and in the Caribbean because it could be grown on small plots by hand labor. (© *Dorothea Lange/ Bettmann/CORBIS*)

areas it had difficulty competing with sugar cultivation for prime real estate. On the sugar islands, land close to seaports and roads was used for sugar, and mountainous land was used for COFFEE CULTIVATION. Cotton might be a secondary crop that could keep a small farm going in the mountains until the coffee bushes matured. This was the case with the farm of ANTONIO MACEO Y GRAJALES, the "Bronze Titan," the hero of Cuba's struggle against slavery and Spanish rule in the late 19th century. His father grew cotton for a while in the mountains behind Santiago de Cuba, then switched to coffee and made most of his money as a muleteer, transporting other people's crops to market.

Like sugar and the other crops of the plantation complex, cotton was both a very important cause of the exploitation and enslavement of blacks and a means for those who gained their freedom to advance economically. The relative ease and low expense involved in entering cotton cultivation, and the sharecropping system that grew up around it, allowed free people of color to grow this crop probably more easily than some of the others of the plantation Americas.

Stewart R. King

FURTHER READING

DuBois W. E. B. *The Souls of Black Folk: Essays and Sketches.* Chicago: McLurg & Co, 1903, esp. chaps. 6 and 7.
West, Jean M. *King Cotton: The Fiber of Slavery.* "Slavery in America: History." Available online. URL: http://www.slaveryinamerica.org/history/hs_es_cotton.htm. Accessed December 21, 2010.

CRAFTS, HANNAH (dates unknown) *American novelist*

Hannah Crafts is believed to be the author of an original manuscript titled *The Bondwoman's Narrative*, possibly the first novel written by a black woman who had been a slave. After purchasing the handwritten manuscript at auction, Henry Louis Gates, Jr., humanities professor at Harvard University and literary critic, verified the authenticity of the manuscript and worked toward its publication. On the basis of the dating of the manuscript's paper and ink and scholars' careful consideration of textual clues, Gates argues that the work was written between 1853 and 1861. The manuscript was published by Warner Books in 2002 and became a bestselling novel.

The Bondwoman's Narrative is the story (possibly autobiographical) of a young black woman's journey toward freedom. The narrator, Hannah, describes her life as a mulatto slave on a haunted plantation in Virginia and tells of her two escapes from slavery. After the second

their land before restrictive laws were passed. Black PEASANT farmers might well grow a few acres of cotton for market, and individuals who gained freedom during this period with the consent of their masters might well move into sharecropping on an undeveloped bit of land owned by their former masters or another white. In this way, free blacks shared, albeit in a restricted way, in the bounty of King Cotton. When the Civil War ended in 1865, there was a small class of black capitalist farmers who were able to weather the storm and be the central figures in communities of color that sprang up after the war. The scholar W. E. B. DuBois noted in his *Souls of Black Folk* (1903) that several of the well-off farm families whose children he taught while teaching in a blacks-only school in Tennessee had ancestors who had been free before the war.

Cotton also grew in the rest of the Americas, outside the United States. Indeed, long-staple cotton was first domesticated by Native American farmers in PERU some 7,000 years ago, long before agriculture spread to western Europe. Cotton was grown in the Caribbean and the mainland of South America, though in the plantation escape, Hannah finds a home in an all-black fugitive community in NEW JERSEY, where she becomes a schoolteacher, marries a Methodist preacher, and reunites with her mother and with slaves she knew who had also found their way to freedom.

Research is still ongoing about the author and the work. Not even the author's name is certain: Hannah Crafts may be an assumed name or pseudonym. She may have been black and/or a former slave, or she may have been neither. Drawing on other scholars' research as well as his own, Gates speculates that either Jane Johnson (a slave whose escape was well documented) or Hannah Vincent (a free black Sunday school teacher who lived in New Jersey) was Hannah Crafts.

Some consider *The Bondwoman's Narrative* to be an autobiographical slave narrative, but the tale may be a fictionalized autobiography or may be entirely fictional. Autobiographical slave narratives, of which hundreds were published between the late 1700s and early 1900s, were often meant to contribute to the abolitionist movement by revealing the cruelties of slavery, but they also reveal a literary culture that soundly defies the contemporary cultural stereotypes of slaves as ignorant and unteachable.

Indeed, if the work is an autobiographical slave narrative, Hannah Crafts's account reveals a slave who was probably self-educated and portrays prejudices toward field slaves as compared to house slaves. It is also an *unedited* manuscript, which means that no white editor censored the work or worked to make it appeal to a white audience, as was common with published slave narratives (although the extent to which they were edited or censored is also a matter of debate).

Whether the work is an autobiographical slave narrative or an entirely fictional novel, Crafts was influenced by works published in the mid-1800s, and the work shares characteristics with gothic, romantic, sentimental, and slave narrative genres.

Summer Leibensperger

FURTHER READING

Andrews, William L. *To Tell a Free Story: The First Century of Afro-American Autobiography, 1760–1865.* Urbana: University of Illinois Press, 1986.

Crafts, Hannah. *The Bondwoman's Narrative.* Introduction by Henry Louis Gates, Jr. New York: Warner Books, 2002.

Gates, Henry Louis, Jr., and Hollis Robbins, eds. *In Search of Hannah Crafts: Critical Essays on* The Bondwoman's Narrative. New York: Basic Civitas Books, 2004.

Williams, Adebayo. "Of Human Bondage and Literary Triumphs: Hannah Crafts and the Morphology of the Slave Narrative." *Research in African Literatures* 34, no. 1 (spring 2003): 137–150.

CREOLE

The term *creole* has many meanings in the slave societies of the Americas. In general, it means someone born in the Americas, as opposed to Europe or Africa, but within that broad category it can have many meanings.

In Spanish America, the term *criollo* generally referred to whites born in the colonies. Blacks born in the colony might occasionally be referred to as *criollos negros*, but this usage was unusual, and instead the African-born were referred to as *bozales*, while those born in the colony received no special description. White creoles were considered somewhat degraded in the Spanish racial hierarchy, both because race mixing was feared and because the Spanish government preferred European-born whites for high government and church positions. Creole blacks, on the other hand, were thought of as being more civilized and trustworthy.

In the French colonies, the term was used broadly for all persons born in the colony, both whites and blacks. Free people of color were assumed to be creoles, although on rare occasions someone would be referred to as a creole of some place if he or she was from a different colony. Black creole slaves were generally more valuable than African-born slaves and more likely to gain their freedom.

In the British Caribbean, the term was used in much the same way as in the French Caribbean, though whites were rarely referred to as creoles. In British North America, this practice was almost unknown, and the term *creole* became synonymous with *black*. As African-born slaves became more and more scarce after the 1770s, the term fell out of use in most of the United States. Instead, the rare African-born blacks would be referred to as African. In Louisiana, the creoles (the term is usually capitalized) were people of mixed race who descended from French colonists who lived there before the colony became a Spanish possession in 1763. They benefited from somewhat better treatment under Louisiana law as compared with other free people of color because of the terms of the treaty that transferred Louisiana to the United States in 1803. The treaty preserved the generally favorable laws that applied to free people of color under the French and Spanish rulers. The treaty was increasingly ignored or superseded by state laws but continued to reflect white society's view that the creoles were more civilized than black immigrants from the eastern colonies and their descendants. The Louisiana Creoles preserve a distinct identity to this day.

Stewart R. King

CROWTHER, SAMUEL AJAYI   (ca. 1809–1891)
British Anglican clergyman

Samuel Crowther was born around 1809 in Osogun, Yorubaland, in today's Nigeria. He was kidnapped and sold to Portuguese slave traders in 1821. His ship was captured by the British navy, and he was freed and taken to Freetown, SIERRA LEONE. He lived in Freetown under the protection of the Anglican Church Mission Society, and he was baptized as an Anglican in 1825. In 1826, he went to Britain and attended school but suffered in the cold climate. He returned to Sierra Leone in 1827 and was one of the first students at Fourah Bay College, now one of the foremost universities in West Africa. He was interested in languages and in the Christian evangelization of Africa. After graduation from college, he became a teacher for the Church Mission Society. In 1841, he accompanied a white missionary priest on an expedition to the falls of the Niger, in Hausaland, several hundred miles into the interior of Africa in modern Nigeria. After the failure of the mission, he was sent to Britain, where he studied for the priesthood and was ordained in 1843. He returned to Nigeria, this time to Yorubaland, where he had greater success in implanting the Anglican Church. He translated the scriptures and the Anglican Book of Common Prayer into several African languages, including Yoruba, Igbo, and Nupe. He was elected bishop in 1864 and was the first black to hold that position in the Church of England.

The liberal leadership of the Anglican Church and missionary society that permitted Crowther to rise so far in the hierarchy gradually died out, and imperialistic and racist attitudes toward Africans and African Americans in the British Empire hardened as the 19th century wore on. Crowther was attacked, and several of his African subordinates were fired. He himself kept his position, but white subordinates were sent out from Britain with power to overrule him on financial matters. He struggled for the autonomy of the African church for the rest of his life, but with little success. After he died in 1891, the next black bishop of the Anglican Communion was not ordained until 1952.

Bishop Crowther's life illustrates several important trends in the experience of free people of color in the British Empire. First was the role of the British decision to abolish the slave trade and to work actively for its end in other countries. Crowther was destined for a life as a sugarcane or coffee worker in Brazil, assuming he survived the Middle Passage, had he not had the good fortune to encounter the British navy on his way. His ship was taken as a pirate, and he became a free person of color without even having to set foot in the Americas. Approximately two million people crossed the Atlantic from Africa after Britain's decision to end the slave trade in 1807. However, the European merchants responsible for transporting and selling them found the job increasingly difficult, faced with the consistent opposition of the British armed forces and intermittent interference from

other countries' navies, including those of the United States and France.

Crowther's relationship with the Anglican Church, in both its positive and negative aspects, illustrates the confused relationship between Christianity and people of color in the Atlantic world. The Anglican Church was primarily a national church at the time. (*See also* PROTESTANT MAINLINE CHURCHES.) That is, membership in the Church of England was equivalent to being British—non-Anglican Protestants, Roman Catholics, and Jews living in Britain were in many senses second-class citizens. In the colonies, Anglicanism was the religion of the upper classes, with the lower ranks of society filled by those non-Anglican Britons who found life at home uncongenial. Joining the Anglican Church for a nonwhite was a daring decision, staking a claim to citizenship and social status that was totally in opposition to the low status imposed by race. On the other hand, Anglicans had led the push for abolition of the slave trade, especially William Wilberforce and William Pitt the Younger. The evangelical movement in the Anglican Communion called for the propagation of the gospel to all people and recognized the spiritual equality of all Christians. The great flourishing of the evangelical movement in the mid-19th century receded as the century drew to a close, though it never died out. The old Tory tradition of Anglicanism as the "British upper classes at prayer" became dominant again for a while, and nonwhites were no longer so welcome. Eventually, it took decolonization and the parallel independence of non-British Anglican Churches before Africans could once again lead Anglican dioceses. Today, the biggest Anglican Church in the world is the Church of Nigeria, founded by Crowther.

The suppression of Crowther's movement for autonomy of African Christianity parallels the suppression of Sierra Leone's drive for internal democracy at the same time. The freed former slaves and rescued transportees of Sierra Leone thought of themselves as free citizens and argued that they should have the right to self-government. The Sierra Leone Company disagreed and sent governors with plenipotentiary powers. The colonists were forced into submission by the British armed forces, supported by relocated Jamaican MAROONS, and Sierra Leone did not gain significant self-government until 1953, when the chief minister of the colonial government became responsible to the local parliament instead of to the colonial ministry of London.

Stewart R. King

FURTHER READING

Ade-Ajayi, J. F. *A Patriot to the Core: Bishop Ajayi Crowther.* Santa Rosa, Calif.: Spectrum Books, 2001.

Curtin, Philip D. *Africa Remembered: Narratives by Africans of the Era of the Slave Trade.* Madison: University of Wisconsin Press, 1967, chap. 9.

CRUMMELL, ALEXANDER (1819–1898)
American missionary and journalist

Alexander Crummell was an important supporter of black emigration from the United States to LIBERIA in West Africa. He worked for the integration of the American Episcopal Church and introduced that form of Protestant Christianity to Liberia, where it remains an important part of the religious mix of the country (*see also* PROTESTANT MAINLINE CHURCHES). He remains famous because of an obituary written by the black intellectual W. E. B. DuBois (1868–1963), republished in his epochal 1903 work, *The Souls of Black Folk*. DuBois portrays Crummell as an example of the contradictions implicit in the lives of black intellectuals and comments on Crummell's decision to leave the country and try to live in Africa.

Alexander Crummell was born in New York on March 3, 1819. He grew up in a family dedicated to abolition and education. Crummell's father, Boston Crummell, emancipated himself shortly before the WAR OF AMERICAN INDEPENDENCE, 1775–83, by simply telling his owner that he would no longer be a slave and then leaving his master's house. Boston worked for abolition and believed that education was the first step in making a difference. Thus, Crummell attended the city's First African Free School. Later, Crummell attended the Noyes Academy in Canaan, New Hampshire, which was established by white abolitionists for black education. Members of the town, however, did not accept the school and demolished the building with a team of oxen. Crummell persevered and continued his education at the Oneida Institute in Whitesboro, New York, another school created by white evangelicals that was open to black students. Ironically, the president of the Oneida Institute at the time, Beriah Green, was opposed to proposals to settle free blacks in Africa and preached several controversial sermons against the AMERICAN COLONIZATION SOCIETY.

Raised in the Episcopal Church, Crummell wished to become a priest. He moved to Boston in 1844 and was ordained a priest in the diocese of Massachusetts at the age of 25. The Episcopal Church in most parts of the United States was a church of the social elite, almost entirely white, and not strongly influenced by the evangelical movement that had made so many Protestants in the North abolitionists. Crummell was never able to have an assignment as a priest in the United States. One bishop, in Pennsylvania, would have accepted him but only if he agreed not to sit in the annual assembly of priests that made policy decisions for the diocese, and he was not willing to do that. Aided by abolitionist friends, Crummell left for Britain in 1847 to pursue further education at Cambridge. Without a sense of belonging either to the church or to American society, Crummel was drawn to the idea of moving to Liberia or SIERRA LEONE. British abolitionists had established Freetown in Sierra Leone as a homeland for people of color who wished to repatriate to Africa. Many early settlers were from the United States at the time of the War of American Independence, while others were rescued from slave ships by the British navy. The American Colonization Society founded Liberia as a home for free people of color from the United States. Crummell moved to Africa in 1853 and worked in Freetown and Monrovia, Liberia, for 20 years. He mainly engaged in missionary work with both Africans and immigrants from the Americas, striving for a republic of black Christians. He also served as a professor at the College of Liberia. There he wrote and published his first book, *The Future of Africa*, in 1862.

Poor health, dwindling emigration to Liberia, and continued conflict between immigrants and Africans in Sierra Leone led Crummell to return to the United States in 1872. He settled in Washington, D.C., and focused on establishing a black church centered on not only worship but also social service. In 1873, the Episcopal bishop of Washington, a white Marylander, appointed him missionary-at-large to the city's African-American population. He led black parishioners from a segregated church in northwestern Washington to found Saint Luke's Church in 1880. St. Luke's today is one of the most prominent Episcopal churches in the city, with a racially mixed congregation. Crummell worked within his church community to combat racism. First, he organized the black Episcopal clergy to fight racism in the church, as well as establish support programs for local blacks. When white bishops sought to form a separate diocese within the church to oversee black parishes in the United States, Crummell organized the Union of Black Episcopalians to resist the separation and insist on equal participation of black and white Episcopalians in the life of the church. His efforts were successful: Today, the Episcopal Church has many black members, especially in the Mid-Atlantic region, where Crummell worked, and two of the 14 bishops who have served the District of Columbia since its creation as a separate diocese have been African American.

Next, he turned to education as a means to overcome poverty and racism for all Americans. He aided in the establishment of the American Negro Academy, an organization of educated African Americans who focused on black education. Crummell went on to write *Greatness of Christ* and *Africa and America*. He also maintained an active interest in missionary work in Africa. However, recent critics note that Crummell never appreciated

African religion and culture. Along with many missionaries at the time, he opposed any "enculturation" of Christian worship into African forms and insisted on conversion to Western forms of worship as well as adoption by converts of a more Western lifestyle. Alexander Crummell died in Red Bank, New Jersey, on September 10, 1898, leaving an impressive legacy, in the battle against racism, the struggle for united education for blacks, and the pastoral care of black Christians.

Caroline Castellanos

FURTHER READING
DuBois, W. E. B. "Of Alexander Crummell." In *The Souls of Black Folk*. New York: Oxford University Press, 2007, 145–152.
Haskins, James. *African American Religious Leaders*. Hoboken, N.J.: Wiley, 1941.
Moses, Wilson Jeremiah. *Alexander Crummell: A Study of Civilization and Discontent*. New York: Oxford University Press, 1989.

CUBA

Cuba is the largest island in the Caribbean, extending almost 750 miles northwest to southeast, and about 90 miles wide at its widest spot. Its northernmost point is only about 125 miles south of Florida, while at its easternmost point, it is about 50 miles from Hispaniola. At its eastern point, it is about 125 miles from the Yucatán Peninsula in Mexico. The island has extensive flat, well-watered areas in the West, well-suited to plantation agriculture. In the East, it is mountainous, with narrow coastal plains, much like the topography of neighboring Hispaniola or Jamaica. The island was inhabited by the Taino and Ciboney peoples in the 15th century when Spanish explorers, led by Christopher Columbus, arrived. Estimates of their number before 1492 vary between 100,000 and 500,000. They cultivated a number of products, including tobacco, that the invaders enthusiastically adopted. They also mined the small amounts of gold in the island's rivers. The Spanish first settled in Hispaniola and raided the neighboring islands for slaves, devastating the coastal areas of Cuba and weakening the population before the ultimate conquest.

Origin of the Free Colored Population

In 1511, Spain initiated its conquest of Cuba; it began establishing settlements in the colony a year later. Between 1550 and 1650, the indigenous population was further decimated through Spanish enslavement and diseases, which rapidly decreased their numbers from approximately 112,000 in 1511 to just 2,000 by 1650. To replace the labor force, Spain began importing enslaved

Africans to the island. By 1650, African slaves totaled 5,000. The large numbers of Spanish men in Cuba, combined with the scarcity of European and Indian women, led to frequent liaisons with African women. Although few of these unions resulted in legal marriage, some men freed their racially mixed offspring, typically called mulattoes or PARDOS because of their brown or fair complexions. They were soon joined by Africans, who were often categorized as blacks, or *morenos*, because of their darker skin, who also acquired freedom. The combination of these two groups expanded to form a new sector of society: free people of color.

Early Population Growth: From Slaves to Free People of Color

As the colony developed over the 16th through the 18th centuries, slaves and free people of color remained a key feature of Cuba's population. During this period, slaves and the emerging free sector of color were located primarily in the burgeoning cities. The Spanish settlers' distaste for manual labor, the sheer lack of Spanish immigrants, and racial prohibitions on professional occupations relegated a variety of economic activities to enslaved Africans and their free descendants. Consequently, bondsmen and bondswomen became active, and moderately autonomous, participants in the local economy, often monopolizing positions as skilled tradesmen, market vendors, tavern owners, and innkeepers, as well as day laborers and domestics. These occupations enabled some slaves to earn enough money to purchase their freedom and construct new lives within the slave system.

MANUMISSION, in which slaves were freed by their owners or through self-purchase, had been a common Iberian practice, as well as a feature of Castilian law. In the colonial Cuban context, it was not uncommon for owners to free their slaves upon the master's death. The complex process of self-manumission depended heavily on social relationships, usually among the slave, the owner, and third parties who witnessed monetary exchanges, particularly because slaves typically paid in installments. The practice of *coartación*, established in Cuba as early as 1590, permitted slaves to enter into an agreement with their owner to purchase themselves for a fixed price. In theory, the price could not be altered. The bondsmen or bondswomen would then make a down payment on freedom, which would shift their status from slave to *coartado*, until they had paid the agreed price and became legally free. In practice, *coartación* rarely worked without difficulties. Individuals unable to complete the payment process remained in a state between slave and free, unless they could find assistance from families or organizations in the free community of color. (*See also* COARTACIÓN UNDER SPANISH LAW.)

In spite of the difficulties in self-manumission, slaves continued to utilize their economic skills, earnings, social networks, and legal options to gain their freedom. In doing so, they forged a free community of color with the same kinds of abilities and understandings of colonial society. Because of the restrictions of *limpieza de sangre* (purity of blood), colonial officials excluded free men of color from all professions and civil positions, such as government bureaucrats, lawyers, doctors, priests, nuns, and pharmacists. These prohibitions forced free people of color to find places for themselves in the economy as domestic and manual laborers and skilled ARTISANS. A large proportion of young women obtained their freedom through manumission during the colonial era, often as a result of their involvement in coerced sexual relationships with their owners. They also gained access to funds for self-purchase by working as domestic servants, street vendors, and tavern operators in urban areas. The substantial numbers of freed women fueled the growth of this free community, as all children born to nonslave women were also free. At the same time, free people of mixed race were able to benefit from official or unofficial "WHITENING" AND RACIAL PROMOTION and leave the ranks of those recognized as being of mixed race. By 1774, there were approximately 30,000 recognized free people of color in Cuba, who composed 10 percent of the total population.

The free community of color expanded exponentially during the late 18th and early 19th centuries. Between the 1774 and 1841 censuses, Cuba's free sector of color increased by almost 80 percent. A similar development took place among whites (76 percent), as the Spanish Crown promoted immigration to its Caribbean territories, and among slaves (83 percent), who were imported in larger numbers to serve the labor needs of SUGAR CULTIVATION, which was also increasing exponentially during the period, and other areas of agriculture. Natural reproduction remained the primary impetus for increasing the number of free blacks and mulattoes in the colony.

Immigration also augmented the number of free blacks and mulattoes in Cuba during this period. Families of free blacks and mulattoes resettled in Cuba when Britain claimed Spanish Florida at the end of the French and Indian War (1756–63). Free people of color were also among the thousands of refugees fleeing the HAITIAN REVOLUTION and who arrived in Cuba between 1791 and 1808. Politics curtailed their stay, and most were expelled after the French emperor, Napoléon Bonaparte, usurped the Spanish throne in 1808. Most departed for U.S. ports, including NEW ORLEANS, LOUISIANA, Savannah; GEORGIA; PHILADELPHIA, PENNSYLVANIA; and BOSTON, MASSACHUSETTS. Those who stayed lent their expertise to Cuba's coffee industry. British efforts to police transatlantic slave trading during the 1820s and 1830s, under the auspices of the British and Spanish Mixed Commission for the Suppression of the Slave Trade, created yet another category of free people in Cuba, the *emancipados*.

Classified between slave and free, *emancipados* were Africans liberated from captured slave ships. Britain transferred thousands to Cuban authorities, whereupon they worked essentially as slaves for the government. Overall, the years from the start of the 19th century to 1843 witnessed a flourishing and heterogeneous free sector of color.

Occupations, Social Organizations, and Military Service

As Cuba entered the 19th century, the presence and influence of free blacks and mulattoes in the colony strengthened tremendously. By the late 1830s, most free people of color in the cities occupied the lower economic levels of society as laundresses, cooks, stevedores, porters, coachmen, and day laborers. Those in the rural areas were employed in cattle raising, fishing, mining, and agriculture. Hundreds traversed the cities and rural areas as regional peddlers. Free people of color also flourished in the skilled crafts, especially as carpenters, tailors, shoemakers, tobacco processors, and masons. Some financially successful skilled artisans, such as Charles Blackely, accumulated modest wealth in the form of property and slaves. After emigrating from the U.S. South, Blackely became a prominent dentist in Cuba, whose real estate, slaves, and dental equipment were evaluated at almost 8,000 pesos at the time of his death in 1850. From the perspective of colonial authorities, however, men and women like him constituted a dangerous example for slaves in a slave society.

The areas of health care and education represented some of the highest occupational levels open to free blacks and mulattoes. Tourist guides in the 1830s, which listed the most reputable professionals and artisans in Cuba, included numerous free people of color. The dentist Andrés Dodge, the midwife María Vicenta Carmona, and the bloodletter José de la Encarnación Muñoz were named consistently. The teachers Juana Pastor and Gabriel Doroteo Barba established and advertised their schools for adults and children of color. In 1836, there were 31 schools for free *pardo* and *moreno* children. By 1861, the number of students registered had increased rapidly, and literacy rates among free people of color reached 10 percent.

During this era, free men of color dominated the arts, particularly music and literature. In 1827, they composed 53 percent of the musicians. The 1839 tourist guide spotlighted the popular orchestra director Claudio Brindis de Salas. Two of the most prominent literary figures to emerge in the first half of the 19th century were GABRIEL DE LA CONCEPCIÓN VALDÉS, called "Plácido," and Juan Francisco Manzano. In the 1830s and early 1840s, Plácido, born to free parents, won numerous awards, had his work featured in local newspapers, and obtained the patronage of colonial aristocrats. During his lifetime, he published two volumes of verse and wrote more than 440 poems. Juan Francisco Manzano published his first poetry in 1821 as a slave. With the aid of Domingo Del Monte, a wealthy CREOLE (Cuban-born) intellectual, Manzano obtained his freedom and wrote his autobiography. Antonio Medina y Céspedes, also a poet, established *El Faro*, the first newspaper for people of color, in 1842. This wide range of occupational activities highlighted the free sector of color's heterogeneity and talent.

In addition to their contribution to Cuba's economic vitality, free *pardo* and *moreno* men took on active roles in the colonial military starting in the 16th century. Free men of color were among the earliest settlers of Cuba. They included JUAN GARRIDO, later among the first Spaniards to enter Mexico City. Spanish authorities established the first MILITIA company of color in the early 17th century. After Britain occupied Havana in 1762–63, Spain rapidly expanded the participation of free blacks and mulattoes in the military. By 1770, the original company had increased to three full battalions and 16 companies. Roughly one in five free men of color participated in the armed services, far beyond their proportion in the overall population. Although segregated racially, military service enabled free men of color to become officers and, eventually, to command *moreno* and *pardo* troops. Incentives, such as a *preeminencias*, which provided license and fee exemptions, and the *fuero militar*, which gave soldiers the right to receive formal training, carry weapons, access military courts, and receive pensions for themselves and their families, attracted numerous skilled artisans of color into Cuba's armed forces.

To sustain and improve their communities, free people of color and slaves formed *cabildos de nación*, which were socioreligious and cultural mutual aid associations organized around African ethnicities. For instance, *cabildos de nación* Lucumí, Carabalí Arará, Congo, Gangá, Mandinga, and Mina represented a substantial proportion of the African groups that arrived in Cuba during the colonial period (*see* CATHOLIC CONFRATERNITIES). They used these organizations, first founded in Cuba in the 16th century, to establish and maintain ethnic identities and cultural traditions. In 1755, the ROMAN CATHOLIC CHURCH officially recognized *cabildos* in order to stimulate religious conversion and instruction of slaves. However, rather than completely abandoning indigenous religious doctrine, many Africans and their descendants integrated elements of Christianity into their own belief systems, ultimately leading to the emergence of *santería*, which revolved around Yoruba deities and Catholic saints, and *palo monte*, which derived from Congelese spiritualism (*see also* AFRICAN AND SYNCRETIC RELIGIONS). The arrival of thousands of enslaved Africans in the early 19th century stimulated the growth of *cabildos de nación* throughout Cuba.

These associations played an important role for the free population of color by addressing social needs, expanding the number of free blacks and mulattoes, and fostering an autonomous space for them within colonial society. An elected *capataz* (king) led each *cabildo*, and many also elected a *matrona* (queen). In many instances, women were a majority of the association members, and they often guided the organization's leadership and internal affairs. Freeing family members became a driving force behind economic goals. Havana manumission records of 1810 and 1811 revealed that 79 percent of the 954 slaves who gained their freedom through self-purchase received support from a *cabildo*. Many organizations also purchased land or homes for organizational use and rented out these properties to help generate funds for manumission, as well as festival celebrations and skilled trades workshops. More secretive all-male associations, called Abakuá societies, emerged in the 1830s. Their members, called *ñáñingos*, adhered to closed initiation rites, sacred written symbols, and strict organizational discipline. As the 19th century progressed, colonial authorities grew suspicious of *cabildos* and other societies of color and implicated the leaders, who were often militiamen and artisans, in rebellions and conspiracies.

Race, Rebellion, and Emancipation

An escalation of regional uprisings and warfare in the 19th century fused politics, race, and nation throughout the Americas. Major slave revolts in the Caribbean, the United States, and South America spread ideologies of freedom, equality, and revolution in the region. Similar rebellions occurred in Cuba, which had now become a full-fledged slave society. For instance, inspired by the Haitian Revolution, José Antonio Aponte, a free *moreno* carpenter, retired military officer, and leader of a *cabildo de nación*, united urban and rural slaves and free people of color with the goal of ending slavery and Spanish rule in Cuba in 1812. In 1835, two free men of color, Juan Nepomuceno Prieto, the *capataz* of a Lucumí *cabildo* and a retired militia officer, and Hermengildo Jáurequi led the Lucumí Conspiracy. As did Aponte, they wanted to abolish slavery and overthrow the colonial government. Similarly, several *pardo* and *moreno* militia officers organized a revolt in 1839. Pilar Borrego, a survivor of the Aponte Rebellion, and Captain León Monzón, Sub-lieutenant José del Monte del Pino, and Sergeant José Dabares organized an unsuccessful rebellion in eastern Cuba. In spite of these and numerous other smaller uprisings, Cuba continued to import increasing numbers of enslaved Africans for agricultural production as it became the world's largest sugar producer.

In 1843, a series of large slave revolts broke out in March, May, and November, which became known as the LA ESCALERA PLOT (the Ladder Conspiracy). Suspicious of these increasingly organized insurgencies, Cuban officials connected the rebellions to a conspiratorial plot among slaves, free people of color, and British abolitionists designed to destroy slavery and give Cuba its independence. In the ensuing repression, authorities arrested and sentenced thousands in connection with the conspiracy and executed the accused leaders, who included the poet Plácido (Gabriel de la Concepción Valdés), the dentist Andrés Dodge, the tailor Francisco Uribe, and numerous other influential free people of color. In addition, officials curtailed occupational avenues, dismantled militia of color, and restricted unauthorized *cabildo* meetings. Thereafter, free people of color and slaves suffered harsh prohibitions on their employment, activities, and gatherings.

The Escalera rebellions and the 1845 treaty between Spain and Britain to end the slave trade intensified the tensions associated with poor race relations and slavery in Cuba. In response, authorities encouraged white immigration from Spain to offset the predominance of free people of color in the skilled trades. They also reasoned that European immigration would establish a greater equilibrium between the colony's white and black populations, which had reached a black majority of 58 percent (15 percent free people of color and 43 percent slaves) in 1841. To contend with reduced legal slave imports, planters imported immigrant laborers from China and Indians from the Yucatán to augment the agricultural workforce. Meanwhile, they increasingly turned to the United States to supply slaves illegally and to provide investment capital to the plantation sector. As this economic relationship deepened, some Cuban elites and intellectuals and American officials called for annexation to the United States in order to protect Cuban slavery, enhance commercial profitability, and foster modern progress. Annexation sentiments waned, however, as the United States became embroiled in civil war and then abolished slavery in 1865.

In 1857, the Cuban government granted a general amnesty for all political prisoners, which enabled hundreds of free people of color who had been imprisoned, banished, or exiled overseas to return. It also reinstated the militia of color. Unfortunately, this decision coincided with a sharp economic downturn in the colony. Hundreds of commercial businesses, factories, and plantations failed, and creole landowners, including some free people of color, forfeited their property to Spanish creditors. Although the colony imported almost 90,000 slaves between 1856 and 1860, the plantation system's labor supply had become strained. As the white population expanded to a 57 percent majority, they displaced free people of color from their previous positions. For instance, in Havana, white workers supplanted free mulattoes and blacks as cigar makers, carpenters, shoemakers, blacksmiths, butchers, and barbers, all areas in which they had previous predominated or formed a large proportion. In addition, when authorities authorized mutual aid associations for the general public to assist those devastated from financial ruin, it stipulated that they be racially segregated. Moreover, in 1864, officials prohibited free people of color born in Cuba to form or join *cabildos*; only African natives were authorized to do so. The restrictions on associations curtailed the African-descended population's ability to provide support for their community in the face of financial hardship.

By the mid-1860s, island reformists increasingly voiced concerns that modern industrial advances in production were incompatible with slavery. Planters, however, who were shocked by the civil turmoil abolition caused in the United States, preferred a controlled and gradual emancipation that would preserve property and the established racial hierarchy. Meanwhile, some Cubans in the United States radicalized their calls for separation and began advocating immediate abolition. Using the newspaper *La Voz de América* (The voice of America), their ideas promoting the inclusion of all races and classes in the independence movement circulated in the United States and parts of Cuba. Similarly, the Spanish Abolitionist Society, formed in Madrid in 1865, asserted that free blacks worked just as productively as whites and that it was the brutality of slavery that hindered an individual's work ethic. Nevertheless, Spanish Peninsular and Caribbean elites viewed the rightful citizens of the Spanish nation as white and not of African descent.

These and other conflicts erupted into warfare in 1868. On one side of the Atlantic, a series of coups d'état in Spain empowered those who opposed colonial reforms for slavery, labor reforms, and white immigration to the colonies. Instead, Spanish leaders imposed new taxes and tariffs on foreign goods, exiled opponents, censored publications, and increased their military presence in Cuba. Furthermore, profits from the sugar boom in prior decades eluded slaveholders in eastern Cuba, exacerbating existing resentment over the economic monopoly of Spanish and western plantation elites. In October 1868, the eastern sugar planter and slave owner Carlos Manuel de Céspedes initiated Cuba's first war for independence, the TEN YEARS' WAR, 1868–78, by declaring Cuban independence, freeing his slaves, and inviting them to join him in spreading liberty and ending colonial rule. During the decade of war, thousands of slaves, free people of color, whites, and Chinese joined the rebellion. The multiracial insurgent army forced the separatist leadership to uphold its principles and abolish slavery in the eastern part of the island. Perhaps the best known black leader to

emerge from the war was ANTONIO MACEO Y GRAJALES, a free mulatto and former mule driver, who rose to the rank of general. Mariana Grajales, Maceo's mother, has been heralded for her unwavering bravery attending to fallen soldiers on the battlefield during the Ten Years' War and for her commitment to the abolition of slavery and Cuban independence throughout the final decades of the 19th century. Similarly, María Cabrales, Maceo's wife, worked as a nurse during the insurgency. Quintín Bandera, the son of free black parents and a former bricklayer, also gained prominence as a general. Guillermo Moncada, a free black carpenter, became a military captain. The rebel republic also installed free men of color as local-level public officers. As slaves and free people of color became involved in the Ten Years' War, they embraced ideals that would free them from slavery and colonialism and that embraced them as Cuban citizens.

In the midst of the war, in 1870, Spain established the Moret Law, which freed all children born to slaves since 1868 and all slaves aged 60 and older, Thus, this law, which stopped short of full abolition, became a bargaining tool for Spain in the war against the insurgents. In February 1878, insurgent and Spanish leaders negotiated the Pact of Zanjón to end the prolonged conflict. Its terms granted freedom to slaves and dissolved Chinese laborers' contracts for those who had participated in the war, but it did not abolish slavery or colonial control. Unwilling to accept these terms, General Maceo, along with an array of black officers such as Rafael Fromet and Moncada, numerous white soldiers, and hundreds of other free people of color and slaves, reignited the insurgency in what became known as the Little War (1879–80). Ironically, Cuba's separatist leadership, particularly former elite white supporters, rejected the rebellion as unpatriotic. Because of the predominantly black military leadership and armed forces of the new revolt, Spanish officials insisted that this was a race war in which the rebels aimed to create not simply a sovereign nation but an independent black republic. Spanish officials forced the white rebels who surrendered to sign statements attesting to these racial aspirations. They continued to make these claims even after black officers finally surrendered in June 1880.

Events in the 1870s and 1880s accelerated the growth of the free population of color. War and the Moret Law increased the proportion of free blacks to 19.2 percent of the colony's population and decreased slaves to 13.6 percent. In January 1878, the Spanish government abolished slavery and replaced it with an eight-year apprenticeship system called the *patronato*. However, little had changed from the previous system. The former slaves, now called *patrocinados*, continued working for their former owners for a nominal wage. Free people of color, individually or through *cabildos*, often assisted slaves in acquiring full freedom from these apprenticeships. In 1886, Spanish and Cuban officials ended the *patronato*, making all persons of African descent in Cuba legally free.

Post-Emancipation Society

The transition from slavery to post-emancipation society proved challenging for Afro-Cubans. Colonial hierarchies and old patterns of discrimination continued to obstruct opportunities in employment, landownership, and education. Possibilities to correct these inequalities emerged with another separatist movement, the final War for Independence from Spain (1895–98), in which Afro-Cubans again actively participated in order to obtain their rightful share in the new Cuban nation. Despite their important participation in the Ten Years' War and the Little War and the efforts to achieve abolition of slavery—which finally occurred in 1886—colonial hierarchies and old patterns of discrimination persisted. Racial divisions continued to obstruct Afro-Cubans' opportunities in employment, landownership, and education. As the independence movement gained new momentum in the 1890s, Afro-Cubans began a new set of struggles pressing for full citizenship and equality.

The post-abolition Afro-Cuban community remained a heterogeneous mixture in the late 1880s and 1890s. Stratification reflected socioeconomic distinctions between long-standing free and semiprofessional families and the recently emancipated. For instance, after the government repression of the La Escalera Plot in 1844, most free black and mulatto artisans reestablished their economic standing and expanded their participation in journalism, music, literature, and religion in ways that corresponded to Spanish cultural forms. In doing so, some adopted the dominant society's racial prejudices, which forged a wedge between them and Africans and former slaves. In addition, cultural friction intensified between native Africans and Afro-Cubans whose families had resided in the colony for generations or centuries. Cuban authorities had restricted membership in *cabildos de nación*, socioreligious and cultural mutual aid associations, to Africans and their immediate descendents in the 1860s. By the late 1880s, the divisions sharpened among Afro-Cubans and the approximately 13,000 African natives, primarily the Yoruba from the Slave Coast, Benin, and the Bight of Biafra, and the Congo from northern Congo and Angola. Native-born Cubans of African descent established more Europeanized *sociedades de color* (societies of color), which were generally designed to remove the vestiges of slavery and, frequently, African traditions. In spite of these internal differences, virtually all Cubans of African descent shared the overarching difficulties shaped by colonialism, slavery, and racism.

In the broader society, a variety of discriminatory practices prevailed. Although legalized employment segregation did not exist, as a result of educational biases, there were few Afro-Cuban doctors and lawyers. Spaniards predominated in the business arena, and white Cubans typically held positions as sales personnel and clerks. In addition, some skilled trades and unions in the tobacco and railroad industries refused to admit Afro-Cubans. Thus, blacks and mulattoes largely continued to occupy pre-abolition positions in agriculture, such as harvesting sugarcane, and as servants, laundresses, tailors, seamstresses, masons, and shoemakers.

Landownership also proved problematic because it was one of the qualifications for voting, and by 1889, regional distinctions in landownership produced distinct patterns. In the western sugar territories, only 2 percent of Afro-Cubans in the rural areas rented or owned land. In eastern Cuba, however, roughly 30 percent of both Afro-Cubans and whites gained access to agricultural land production. These disparities, particularly in the western provinces, led to black and mulatto disenfranchisement because suffrage rights were granted on the basis of landownership, rather than specifically on race.

Furthermore, educational and institutional discrimination fostered inequality. By the late 1880s, literacy rates for Afro-Cubans were at 11 percent, a rate two-thirds lower than for whites. Children of color continued to have limited access to public elementary schools, and Afro-Cuban individuals, particularly women, continued to establish separate schools for their community. In addition, the majority of high schools and colleges were private and denied black students admission. Authorities also segregated hospitals and prisons, creating precarious health conditions and reinforcing criminal stereotypes.

Afro-Cubans also found themselves barred from full participation in public organizations and spaces. For instance, in the early 1880s, authorities gave Cubans of color access to public squares and parks, but whites quickly established segregated areas. Newly formed mutual aid associations for Spanish immigrants, who assisted members in gaining access to education, health care, and entertainment, excluded Afro-Cubans. Numerous hotels denied blacks and mulattoes accommodations, theaters excluded them from the best seats, and restaurants, bars, and cafés often either refused them service or overcharged them. Thus, for most Cubans of African descent, persistent racism and discrimination forced them to live partly in an integrated and unequal public space and partly in a private, segregated world in which they were full participants.

To counter these effects, Cubans of African descent established more societies of color, which often had a more mainstream Catholic and Spanish appearance, to attend to their members' spiritual and social needs. African-influenced secret associations also became more prevalent in the 1880s. Abakuá societies, the all-male secretive organizations that had existed since the time of slavery, flourished in the cities. These groups became symbols of fear for cultivating African cultural and religious traditions that police claimed centered on witchcraft and criminality. In order to challenge cultural and social discrimination and to claim as citizens, Afro-Cubans developed new ideologies and organizations.

Individuals primarily from the mulatto and black middle class fostered beliefs that countered white supremacy. In particular, they asserted social and racial equality based on blacks' positive attributes. In 1887, they established the Directorio Central de las Sociedades de la Raza de Color (Central Directory of the Societies of the Race of Color), which united the black organizations against colonial society. Under the leadership of the journalist Juan Gualberto Gómez, the Directorio advocated the enforcement of current civil rights and pushed for future gains. Their demands included equal protection under the law and free public education for children of African descent. The organization also published *La Igualdad* (Equality), which become the most prominent Afro-Cuban newspaper of the 1890s. Gómez and *La Igualdad* helped spread a new sense of pride among Afro-Cubans by insisting that a shared African ancestry connected all blacks and mulattoes. In addition, Gómez stressed their worth to Cuba through their crucial economic roles and fundamental participation in the Ten Years' War and in the abolition process. The Directorio also urged Afro-Cubans to organize black political organizations to aid their push for civil rights. Cubans in the United State also supported Gómez's stance. Rafael Serra y Montalvo, an Afro-Cuban tobacco producer, with the support of José Martí, the white leader of the Cuban Revolutionary Party, established La Liga (League), an organization that united working-class Afro-Cubans and Afro–Puerto Ricans in New York City and Cubans in Tampa, Florida.

Some Afro-Cuban intellectuals, however, disagreed with Gómez's message. In particular, the journalist Martín Morúa Delgado insisted on a racial division between mulattoes and blacks. He also attacked Gómez's proposal for a black political party as a ploy to take over Cuba and insisted on integration, self-improvement, and patience, rather than civil agitation, as the best method for Cubans of color to gain full rights. Similarly to Gómez, Morúa used his newspaper, *La Nueva Era* (The new era), to disseminate his ideas. General Antonio Maceo promoted some of Morúa's ideas. He especially supported multiracial organizations as the means to achieve racial equality and independence. Both men asserted that Cubans of color must win their rights, not as blacks and mulattoes, but as Cubans. Both groups would put their differences aside for a time, to support a new insurgency that promised to create a nation based on racial democracy.

War and Independence
In 1895, the War for Independence (1895–98) erupted in Cuba. José Martí, who had established the Cuban Revolutionary Party in 1892 while in exile in the United States, chose Gómez to organize separatist activities on the island. In February 1895, Cuban rebels staged simultaneous revolts throughout the colony. Under the military leadership of the Afro-Cuban generals Antonio Maceo and Quintín Bandera, the entire country joined the rebellion for sovereignty from Spain.

Male and female Afro-Cubans participated in the war effort. Agricultural laborers, such as Ricardo Batrell Oviedo, a 15-year-old sugar worker who could not read or write, were typical recruits. After the war, however, Batrell became the only black soldier to write a memoir of his experiences. Women also took part in the insurgency as nurses near the battlefield, as soldiers, and as organizers raising funds for the insurgency. María Hidalgo fought in the liberation army for two years. María Cabrales, Antonio Maceo's wife, organized the José Martí's Women's Club in New York City and the Cuban Women's Club in Costa Rica to raise money for the war. Other organizations run by Cubans in Florida also contributed to war activities.

The new rebellion demonstrated both the possibilities and the limits of post-emancipation society. On the one hand, the Liberation Army was a multiracial military force that promoted Afro-Cuban commanders. Black and white Cubans and foreign observers admired General Maceo's long-standing leadership in Cuba's quest for independence and Afro-Cuban equality. After his death during an ambush by Spanish forces in December 1896, he was heralded as a war hero. On the other hand, white rebel generals often challenged General Maceo's leadership by ignoring his orders and accusing him of aspiring to political power. Similarly, Batrell's war memoir described numerous episodes of mistreatment by white officers, such as reduced distribution of ammunition to troops that were predominantly black and mulatto. Afro-Cubans used these examples to fuel their fight for racial equality in the army and as citizens.

As the war came to a close, Calixto García, the white general of the Liberation Army and a veteran of the armed independence movement, began shifting assignments and appointing new commanders. García authorized these changes to remove Afro-Cuban officers from their command on the grounds that men of color were less prepared to lead academically and culturally, in comparison to whites. For example, the army officer Martín Duen, who had been a cook prior to the war, was removed from his position as a regiment leader. Batrell contested these kinds of actions, arguing that white men were now garnering all the credit for the victories and sacrifices Afro-Cuban officers and soldiers had made during the insurgency.

U.S. intervention in the war in 1898—in what Americans would call the Spanish-American War—denied Cuban independence and Afro-Cuban equality. U.S. leaders viewed Cuba's ability to govern through a lens that defined civilization as whiteness, rather than accepting the fact that Cubans had abolished slavery and aspired to eliminate racism. Consequently, after achieving victory over Spain, U.S. authorities made the island an American protectorate in 1898. The United State granted Cuba its independence in 1902, but the Platt Amendment enabled the American government to intervene in Cuban affairs indiscriminately. This arrangement transformed Cuba into an American neocolony and escalated Afro-Cubans' inequalities. Segregationist policies and discriminatory practices resumed and became more widespread. Afro-Cuban cultural practices were suppressed. Immigration legislation favoring European workers displaced Cubans of color, except in the rural areas. For agricultural production, sugar companies imported migrant laborers from Jamaica and Haiti, who were, in turn, stigmatized as socially and culturally unbeneficial to Cuban society.

To overturn racist laws and to fight for greater equality, Afro-Cubans became an important factor in the electoral process. Cubans of color represented 32 percent of the voting population, and politicians realized that they could not ignore these votes if they wished to gain public office. In 1908, at least 14 Afro-Cubans, including Silverio Sánchez, Ramiro Cuesta, Rafael Serra, General Agustin, and Alberto Castellanos, were elected to Congress in Cuba. To assist Afro-Cubans in obtaining fuller participation in the government, Evaristo Estenoz established the Partido Independiente de Color (PIC) (Independent Party of Color), a black political party, and began publishing the newspaper *Previsión* (Foresight) to disseminate their ideas and issues. Opponents accused the group of being racially exclusive and using race to supersede national identity. The PIC's main goals, however, were to foster Afro-Cuban involvement in the government and to integrate Afro-Cubans into broader society. Members were harassed, arrested, and charged with conspiring to overthrow the government and establish a black republic. Although no evidence of these plans ever surfaced and the accused were found not guilty, authorities dissolved the organization in 1910 by declaring political organizations based on race illegal. Barred from participating in elections, the PIC organized an armed demonstration in 1912. Government forces killed thousands of Afro-Cubans, including Estenoz, sending the message that authorities would violently repress any challenges to the social order.

Post-abolition events, particularly the War for Independence and the 1912 massacre, set the stage for Afro-Cubans' continuing struggles for full citizenship and equality in the remainder of the 20th century. Tremendous gains in these areas emerged during and after the 1959 Cuban Revolution, as Afro-Cubans persisted in their efforts to transform the legacies of slavery, colonialism, and neocolonialism into full social, cultural, political, and economic equality.

Michele Reid-Vazquez

FURTHER READING
Primary Documents
Batrell Oviedo, Ricardo. *The Narrative of Ricardo Batrell, a Black Mambí in Cuba.* Translated by Mark A. Sanders. Minneapolis: University of Minnesota Press, 2009.
Manzano, Juan Francisco. *Autobiography of a Slave.* Translated by Evelyn Picon Garfield. Detroit: Wayne State Press, 1996.

Films
Rolando, Gloria, director. *Roots of My Heart.* Cuba: Images of the Caribbean, 2001.
Solas, Humberto, director. *Cecilia.* New York: Latin American Video Archives, 1998.

Secondary Sources
Casanovas, Joan. *Bread, or Bullets! Urban Labor and Spanish Colonialism in Cuba, 1850–1898.* Pittsburgh: University of Pittsburgh Press, 1998.
Childs, Matt D. *The 1812 Aponte Rebellion in Cuba and the Struggle against Atlantic Slavery.* Chapel Hill: University of North Carolina Press, 2006.
Chomsky, Aviva, Barry Carr, and Pamela Maria Smorkaloff, eds. *The Cuba Reader: History, Culture, Politics.* Durham, N.C.: Duke University Press, 2003.
de la Fuente, Alejandro. *Havana and the Atlantic in the Sixteenth Century.* Chapel Hill: University of North Carolina Press, 2008.
———. *A Nation for All: Race, Inequality, and Politics in Twentieth-Century Cuba.* Chapel Hill: University of North Carolina Press, 2001.
———. "Slaves and the Creation of Legal Rights in Cuba: Coartación and Papel." *Hispanic American Historical Review* 87 (2007): 659–692.
Díaz, María Elena. *The Virgin, the King, and the Royal Slaves of El Cobre: Negotiating Freedom in Colonial Cuba, 1670–1780.* Palo Alto, Calif.: Stanford University Press, 2000.

Ferrer, Ada. *Insurgent Cuba: Race, Nation, and Revolution, 1868–1898*. Chapel Hill: University of North Carolina Press, 1999.

Helg, Aline. *Our Rightful Share: The Afro-Cuban Struggle for Equality, 1886–1912*. Chapel Hill: University of North Carolina Press, 1995.

Howard, Philip A. *Changing History: Afro-Cuban Cabildos and Societies of Color in the Nineteenth Century*. Baton Rouge: Louisiana State University Press, 1998.

McLeod, Marc C. "Undesirable Aliens: Race, Ethnicity, and Nationalism in the Comparison of Haitian and British West Indian Immigrant Workers in Cuba, 1912–1939." *Journal of Social History* 31, no. 3 (Spring 1998): 599–623.

Pérez, Louis A., Jr. *Cuba: Between Reform and Revolution*. 3rd ed. New York: Oxford University Press, 2006.

Prados-Torreira, Teresa. *Mambisas: Rebel Women in Nineteenth-Century Cuba*. Gainesville: University Press of Florida, 2005.

Reid, Michelle. "Protesting Service: Free Black Response to Cuba's Reestablished Militia of Color." *Journal of Colonialism and Colonial History* 5, no. 2 (Fall 2004).

Sartorious, David. "My Vassals: Free-Colored Militias in Cuba and the Ends of Spanish Empire." *Journal of Colonialism and Colonial History* 5, no. 2 (Fall 2004).

Scott, Rebecca J. *Slave Emancipation in Cuba: The Transition to Free Labor, 1860–1899*. Princeton, N.J.: Princeton University Press, 1985.

CUDJOE   *See* CAPTAIN CUDJOE.

CUFFE, PAUL (1759–1817) *Connecticut merchant*
One of the first socially and financially successful Americans of color, Paul Cuffe was born in Connecticut on January 17, 1759, to a former slave father and a Native American mother. Paul and his siblings received little formal education, and he left home as a teenager to make his own way, working on whaling ships. Cuffe was captured by the British during the WAR OF AMERICAN INDEPENDENCE, 1775–83, spending three months in a British jail in New York. In 1783, he married Alice Pequit, a local Indian woman. The couple had seven children.

After the war, New England was growing and developing and seemed to promise opportunities for black men. Cuffe purchased a shoemaker's shop, traded, whaled, and eventually owned several ships, personally sailing to many varied locations. While the arrival of a black sea captain was often shocking enough, Cuffe's crews were predominantly composed of black and Indian seamen. By 1800, Cuffe was quite well off and owned about 200 acres and a windmill in addition to the shoemaker's shop.

Cuffe was increasingly respected and connected with his local community of Westport, Connecticut. Cuffe set up a racially integrated school on his land, one of the first such schools in the United States, and socialized with and joined the Quakers. Partly because he still perceived a color divide between him and his white Quaker peers, however, Cuffe began to focus on more external opportunities.

The early 19th century was a stressful and perilous period for the United States. Naval and diplomatic problems between Americans and the British led first to several incidents on the high seas and then to President Thomas Jefferson's Embargo Act, which essentially prevented any foreign trade. This law, strongly condemned in New England, hampered the maritime activity of the region.

On his voyages, Cuffe began to speak with local abolitionists, who saw in him a prime example of how slavery was keeping down an entire population. Cuffe was successful, ambitious, hardworking, and a self-made man, and this combination was a powerful argument in favor of what most abolitionists sought. British antislavery activists also learned of Cuffe and began to see him as a use-

A silhouette of Paul Cuffe (1759–1817) and one of his ships. Cuffe was a ship captain and merchant based in Connecticut. He traveled widely in the Atlantic basin and knew many early abolitionists. He became a supporter of immigration to West Africa and personally led one expedition to Sierra Leone shortly before his death. *(Library of Congress)*

ful figure. As a Quaker, Cuffe also presumably exhibited the attributes desirable for all Christians and admired by humanitarians. One group especially interested in Cuffe was a new antislavery organization in Britain, the African Institution, founded in 1807.

News of West African affairs was relatively easy to come by in the ports of New England, and Cuffe began regular transatlantic trading, whaling off the African coast, and trading with the West Indies. Cuffe also became increasingly familiar with the British colony of SIERRA LEONE, established in 1787 partly as a refuge for London blacks. The Embargo Act effectively ended many promising trade efforts, however.

Later, Cuffe revealed that he had been considering a journey to Sierra Leone and mentioned the possibility that his family might relocate to the West African colony. These thoughts were relayed to the African Institution, who encouraged Cuffe's efforts through letters. Finally, in December 1810, Cuffe left for Sierra Leone, where he arrived in March 1811. Cuffe met with the governor and others and then left for Britain, where he visited several cities and met with members of the African Institution, who were eager and willing to facilitate as best they could any of Cuffe's efforts to develop Sierra Leone. A delegation from the group even met with the British government to request a land grant for Cuffe.

The embargoes between Britain and the United States made it difficult for a citizen of one nation to travel to the territory of the other, however, much less to conduct business between them. Cuffe ran the risk of having his ships and cargoes seized. The War of 1812 also posed other practical problems. Cuffe did eventually take 34 immigrants to Sierra Leone, but by 1817, his health was quickly declining. On September 7, 1817, Paul Cuffe died in the presence of his family and friends in Connecticut. His estate was valued at around $20,000, a quite remarkable sum for a black person, or indeed for anyone, at the time.

K. Wayne Ackerson

FURTHER READING

Ackerson, Wayne. *The African Institution of London (1807–1827) and the Antislavery Movement in Great Britain.* New York: Mellen Press, 2005.

Harris, Sheldon. *Paul Cuffe: Black America and the African Return.* New York: Simon & Schuster, 1972.

Thomas, Lamont. *Paul Cuffe: Black Entrepreneur and Pan-Africanist.* Champaign-Urbana: University of Illinois Press, 1988.

CUGOANO, QUOBNA OTTOBAH

(ca. 1757–ca. 1803) *British antislavery writer*

Quobna Ottobah Cugoano was one of the most influential antislavery writers in late 18th-century Britain. His antislavery works, especially his 1787 book, *Thoughts and Sentiments on the Evil and Wicked Traffic of the Slavery and Commerce of the Human Species*, framed the debate over the slave trade in terms of the humanity and human rights of the enslaved. He had a lasting influence on the antislavery movement, and his book was influential throughout the abolition struggle of the 19th century and even into the Civil Rights movement of the 20th century.

Quobna Ottobah Cugoano was born around 1757 in a village in Ghana, possibly near Ajumako. He belonged to the Fante people and was raised in the house of a chief, who was the ruler of Ajumako and Assinie. Cugoano did not belong to the royalty himself, however. Around 1770, when he was about 13 years old, Cugoano was kidnapped by fellow Africans, who sold him into slavery. As he later wrote in his 1787 book, his experience of the Middle Passage was so traumatic that he defined it as a "situation [that] may be easier conceived than described." He was transported from Cape Coast Castle to Grenada in the West Indies, where he remained enslaved until a Briton took him to Britain in 1772. There he learned to read and write and was baptized John Stuart, a name he used for the next 15 years. He became free thanks to the British courts' decision, in SOMERSET V. STEWART, that masters had no enforceable rights over their slaves on British soil. By the 1780s, Cugoano worked as a house servant in Britain, including employment in the house of Richard Cosway (1742–1821), court painter to the prince of Wales. Cugoano appears in Richard Cosway's 1784 etching *Mr and Mrs Cosway* and served as the model for *Pompey* in another painting by Cosway. Through Cosway, he met many important figures in British public life, including the prince of Wales, later King George IV (1762–1830).

Inspired by the growing abolitionist movement in Britain in the late 18th century, Cugoano published *Thoughts and Sentiments on the Evil and Wicked Traffic of the Slavery and Commerce of the Human Species*, which attacked the traditional biblical and theological views that served to justify slavery and appeared in numerous 18th-century treatises on the institution. In his work, Cugoano used an objective prose to present his arguments for immediate abolition of slavery. One of his main attacks was on the supposed "Christianity" of many slave traders and masters. He described overseers as "hard-hearted [bosses who] have neither regard to the laws of God, nor the life of their fellow-men." Cugoano's book is considered to be the first abolitionist text written by an African in England, and it presented several arguments in favor of the liberty of enslaved African men and women. He became a well-known public figure between 1786 and 1791. In a celebrated case in 1786, he worked with OLAUDAH EQUIANO and the white abolitionist GRANVILLE SHARP to rescue a free black man named Henry Demane, who was in danger of being kidnapped back into slavery in the West Indies. In 1791, he released a shorter edition of his book, in which he argued that slaves had a duty to humanity to escape from slavery. He also expressed support for the emigration of British blacks to Sierra Leone (see also EMIGRATION AND COLONIZATION). After the publication of this book, Cugoano disappears from history. Equiano wrote in a letter in 1803 that he had heard that Cugoano had died but gave no further details.

In *The Origins of Modern African Thought* (1967), Robert July characterized Cugoano as one of the most influential personalities on 19th- and 20th-century African thought. Cugoano became a prominent figure among the free blacks who inhabited London in the 18th century. He often corresponded with abolitionist personalities such as Sharp and JOHN CLARKSON.

Laura Gimeno-Pahissa

FURTHER READING

Cugoano, Q. O. *Thoughts and Sentiments on the Evil of Slavery.* Edited by Vincent Caretta. London: Penguin, 1999.

Gates, H. L. *The Signifying Monkey.* Oxford and New York: Oxford University Press, 1988.

Gates, H. L., and C. T. Davis. *The Slave's Narrative.* Oxford and New York: Oxford University Press, 1985.

July, Robert W. *The Origins of Modern African Thought: Its Development in West Africa during the Nineteenth and Twentieth Centuries.* 1967. Reprint, Trenton, N.J.: Africa World Press, 2004.

D

DANISH VIRGIN ISLANDS

The Virgin Islands are a group of islands in the Caribbean lying to the east of PUERTO RICO and are the northwesternmost of the Leeward Islands chain. The eastern part of the island group, including Tortola and Virgin Gorda, was originally settled by the Dutch in the 17th century and then captured by England in the Third Anglo-Dutch War in 1672. The western part of the island group, including St. Croix, St. John, and St. Thomas, was settled by a variety of European colonizers but unified under Danish rule in 1733. The United States purchased the islands from Denmark in 1917, and they are now known as the U.S. Virgin Islands.

The islands are small, volcanic, and rocky. There is little land suitable for plantation agriculture. Nonetheless, in the 18th century, a plantation economy developed, especially on St. Thomas. The islands also benefited from the presence of fine harbors at Charlotte Amelie, St. Thomas, and Christiansted, St. Croix. Interisland trade, often smuggling, became an important part of the islands' economy in the 18th century, with goods imported cheaply by British shippers and then reexported to neighboring Puerto Rico, the French island colonies, and even the Spanish mainland colonies on the other side of the Caribbean. One important part of this trade was slaves, imported in many cases from Denmark's own colony on the West African coast in today's Ghana. Many sailors and dockworkers, and even some shipowners and officers, in the interisland trade were free people of color (see also MERCHANT SEAMEN).

Most people of color on the islands worked as agricultural laborers, however. As with enslaved people everywhere in the plantation zone, their working conditions were terrible, and harsh repression was the rule. A violent rebellion in 1733 by members of one Ghanaian ethnic group overthrew Danish rule on St. John for almost a year. The Danish governor escaped and was able to restore himself to power with the help of French troops from Martinique and island blacks who were not members of the rebel ethnic group. Repression of all blacks, free and enslaved, increased after the uprising, though. One factor that helped ameliorate the conditions in the colony was the work of Moravian Brethren missionaries

(see also BAPTISTS AND PIETISTS). The Moravians were opposed to slavery, as were many other Pietistic groups such as the Quakers and Baptists. Moravian missionaries established churches and trained Afro-Caribbean people to serve as preachers and evangelists. When the Danish authorities and white colonists began persecuting the German missionaries, driving some of them out of the colony, their Afro-Caribbean assistants were able to carry on their work. Many of these lay preachers were free people of color. One of the most famous was REBECCA PROTTEN, who was probably the first woman ordained a minister in any Christian denomination in modern times when she was made a deacon of the church in 1739.

The free colored population of the islands grew during the 18th century, exceeding 1,000 in 1792, along with 22,000 slaves and about 2,000 whites. Denmark ended its participation in the Atlantic slave trade in 1803, becoming the first European country to outlaw the slave trade. After that time, the slave population began to decline slowly, while free blacks grew in number. The plantation economy declined, and many whites abandoned the colony. While the civil servants and soldiers who governed the colony were Danish, most of the civilian white inhabitants were natives of other European countries and had little reason to stay if their plantations were no longer valuable. A few planters stayed on and in fact prospered and grew their businesses, picking up the land and slaves of their departing neighbors at a discount. However, most landowners in the colony were people of color by the 1830s. In 1848, as revolutionaries marched on Copenhagen demanding a liberal constitution, people of color in Frederiksted besieged the colonial governor's palace demanding an end to slavery. Both free people of color and slaves were part of this demonstration, which threatened to turn into a violent rebellion. Governor Peter von Scholten (1784–1854) had been pushing for reform of the slave laws anyway, and faced with serious labor unrest, he declared the end of slavery in the colony on July 3, 1848.

After emancipation, the colony experienced an economic boom as the interisland shipping business became the mainstay of the local economy. Until the 1870s, the

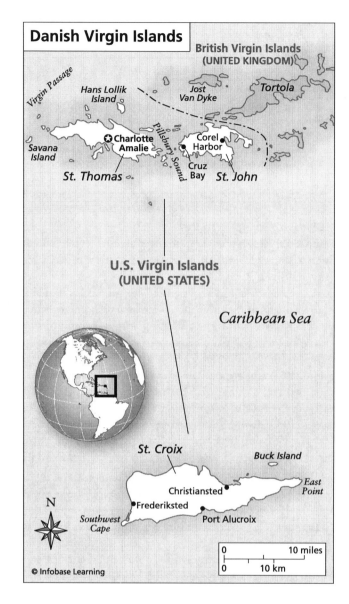

Danish Virgin Islands

British Virgin Islands
(UNITED KINGDOM)

Virgin Passage

Hans Lollik
Island

Jost
Van Dyke

Tortola

Pillsbury Sound

Charlotte
Amalie

Corel
Harbor

Savana
Island

St. Thomas

Cruz
Bay   St. John

U.S. Virgin Islands
(UNITED STATES)

Caribbean Sea

St. Croix

Buck Island

N

Christiansted

East
Point

Frederiksted

Southwest
Cape

Port Alucroix

0   10 miles
0   10 km

© Infobase Learning

British Royal Mail packet ships made their first Caribbean stop in Charlotte Amelie, where interisland shippers could transship cargoes to other colonies nearby. While large white-owned merchant houses controlled much of this trade, the small, often Afro-Caribbean-owned shippers who had been in the business since the 18th century often profited handsomely. Technological and political changes in the 1880s meant a decline in this trade. Finally, the colony became such a burden on the Danish treasury that the government agreed to sell it to the United States during World War I.

Stewart R. King

FURTHER READING

Danish National Archives. "A Brief History of the Danish West Indies, 1666–1917." Available online. URL: http://virgin-islands-history.dk/eng/vi_hist.asp. Accessed April 13, 2010.

Hall, Neville A. T. "Apollo Miller, Freedman: His Life and Times." *Journal of Caribbean History* 23 (1989): 196–213.
Lawaetz, Eva. *Free Coloured in St. Croix, 1744–1816.* St. Croix, privately published, 1979.
Olwig, Karen Fog. *Cultural Adaptation and Resistance on St. John: Three Centuries of Afro-Caribbean Life.* Gainesville: University Press of Florida, 1985.

DÉDÉ, EDMOND   (1827? 1829? –1903) *American musician, conductor, and composer*

Edmond Dédé, an accomplished Creole (*see* CREOLE) violinist, clarinetist, conductor, and composer, was born in New Orleans, Louisiana, in 1827 or 1829 to free black parents who had migrated from the French West Indies. Like other black musicians and artists of the time, Dédé became an expatriate, fleeing the United States's restrictive laws and prejudice.

Dédé studied the violin first in New Orleans, then briefly in MEXICO, and finally in Paris. In New Orleans, he studied clarinet under Constantin Debarque (variously spelled Debergue or Deburque) and violin under Ludovico Gabici but worked as a cigar maker by trade, saving money for a trip to Paris. His move to Mexico in 1848 may have been prompted by a post-Mexican-American War environment that changed race relations in New Orleans. In 1857, Dédé moved to FRANCE, where he completed his musical education in Paris at the Paris Conservatoire; he studied under Jacques-François Fromental Halévy and Jean-Delphin Alard.

Dédé's career lasted more than four decades, earning acclaim in Europe especially. He was a composer of classical (or concert) music and composed orchestral works, operas, and operettas, including *Le serment de l'Arabe, vaillant belle rose quadrille, Le palmier overture*, and *La sensitive*. Dédé became the director of the orchestra of L'Alcazar in Bordeaux, France, and was a member of the French Society of Authors, Composers, and Editors of Music and the Society of Dramatic Authors and Composers in Paris.

In May 1865, Dédé's *Quasimodo Symphony* was performed in New Orleans at the Orleans Theater. The symphony was conducted by Samuel Snaer, Jr., and performed by an orchestra composed of black musicians.

Notably, he returned to New Orleans in 1893 (after surviving the October 1893 wreck of the steamship *Marseilles*), playing the violin in several successful concerts, but he returned to France the following year.

Dédé married Sylvie Leflat, a Frenchwoman, in 1864. They had a son, Eugène Arcade. Dédé died in France sometime in 1903, leaving the opera *Le sultan d'Ispahan* unfinished.

Summer Leibensperger

FURTHER READING

Cuny-Hare, Maud. *Negro Musicians and Their Music.* Washington, D.C.: Associated Publishers, 1936.

Dédé, Edmond. *Edmond Dédé* (audio CD). Hot Springs Music Festival, Richard Rosenberg, conductor. Naxos 8.559038, 2000.

Kein, Sybil, ed. *Creole: The History and Legacy of Louisiana's Free People of Color.* Baton Rouge: Louisiana State University Press, 2000.

Koster, Rick. *Louisiana Music: A Journey from R&B to Zydeco, Jazz to Country, Blues to Gospel, Cajun Music to Swamp Pop to Carnival Music and Beyond.* Cambridge: Da Capo Press, 2002.

Logan, Rayford W., and Michael R. Winston, eds. *Dictionary of American Negro Biography.* New York: W. W. Norton, 1982.

Southern, Eileen. *Biographical Dictionary of Afro-American and African Musicians.* Westport, Conn.: Greenwood Press, 1982.

Trotter, James M. *Music and Some Highly Musical People.* Boston: Lee and Shepard, Publishers, 1881.

DELANY, MARTIN (1812–1885) *American abolitionist and military officer*

Best known for an African emigration scheme he developed in the 1850s, Martin Robeson Delany has been called "the father of black nationalism." He was born on May 6, 1812, in Charles Town, Virginia (now West Virginia), to a free black woman named Pati Peace. His father, Samuel Delany, was a skilled slave who was allowed to work for wages in his free time and, with his wife's help, bought his freedom. Both parents claimed royal African ancestry, and his grandfather and father were known for refusing to allow whites to punish them. His mother taught her children to read and write despite Virginia laws against black literacy and was forced to flee to Chambersburg, PENNSYLVANIA, after her sons allowed their ability to be discovered. Samuel Delany joined them after securing his freedom.

Thus, by age 11, Martin Delany was able to enjoy the security of a stable two-parent family. Though always aware of the slave catchers ubiquitous in southern Pennsylvania, the Delanys also enjoyed the stabilizing influence of the broader community of 35–40 black families in the Chambersburg neighborhood known as Kerrstown. These families worked together and set up their own Methodist Episcopal congregation, which included a Sabbath school as well as a regular school for the children, funded by a self-imposed "occupation tax" paid in addition to state taxes, which were given to the white schools (*see also* AFRICAN METHODIST EPISCOPAL CHURCH and EDUCATION AND LITERACY). This financial sacrifice allowed Martin to attend school at an age when many children already worked.

After he turned 19, Delany moved to PITTSBURGH, PENNSYLVANIA, to further his education. A new abolitionist crusade, based on the call for immediate, uncompensated emancipation, was beginning, and Delany arrived just after local black leaders met formally to pledge resistance to the AMERICAN COLONIZATION SOCIETY, a group formed to create a settlement of American blacks in Africa and promote transporting American blacks to the colony of LIBERIA. Delany became friends with the chair of this meeting, the War of 1812 veteran and successful barber John B. Vashon (*see also* VASHON FAMILY). Through the efforts of Vashon and another local black leader, the Reverend LEWIS WOODSON, Delany would be groomed to play his own role in the antebellum freedom struggle. He began by founding the Theban Literary Society in 1832 and the Young Men's Moral Reform Society of Pittsburgh in 1834. He also served as an officer in the Philanthropic Society, a group that helped fugitive slaves find safety in Pittsburgh. His work with this group earned him the position of diplomat between the black and white communities.

Throughout his antislavery career, Delany supported a concept of self-elevation that had three main components—moral uplift, educational attainment, and economic self-sufficiency. He believed that self-elevation could lead to racial uplift, which would force whites to accept racial equality. This, in turn, would lead to the abolition of slavery by defeating proslavery arguments that bondage alone ensured good behavior among blacks.

Though he maintained his belief in this agenda throughout most of his life, a number of factors led Delany to consider emigration to escape the bounds of American racial prejudice. He began considering this idea when black Pennsylvanians lost the vote in 1839, when a new constitutional convention amended the state charter by adding the word white to the section describing voter qualifications. That winter, Delany traveled to the South to investigate the suitability of the independent TEXAS republic as a safe haven for free blacks. During this trip, he began to formulate his novel *Blake.* Abandoning Texas emigration, however, he returned to Pittsburgh and was elected to the board of managers of the Pittsburgh Anti-Slavery Society. Soon after his return, Delany served on a committee to organize a state convention to discuss strategies for regaining the vote. After that he founded a newspaper, the *Mystery,* which lasted four years, until he and FREDERICK DOUGLASS joined forces in the *North Star* in 1847.

Delany's affiliation with the *North Star* gained him recognition in the national antislavery ranks. Though he

Martin Delany (1812–85) is known as the "father of black nationalism" for advocating black-led immigration to Central America, Africa, and the Caribbean before the American Civil War. For a brief period, he studied medicine at Harvard, until the university dismissed him because of his race. He organized blacks to fight in the Union army during the Civil War and was commissioned a major, the first black field officer in the U.S. Army. After the war, he worked for racial reconciliation in South Carolina; finally, frustrated with the failure of Reconstruction, he returned to the idea of immigration in his final years. *(National Portrait Gallery, Smithsonian Institution/Art Resource, NY)*

stepped down as editor in 1849, he continued to send correspondence until summer 1850, when he and Douglass entered a heated exchange in the paper's columns after Douglass condemned Samuel R. Ward for speaking at a biracial meeting in which blacks were relegated to the balcony of their own church in Philadelphia. Douglass criticized Ward for acceding to racism for the benefit of reaching a larger audience, and Delany condemned Douglass for contributing to dissent and hostility in the black abolitionist ranks.

His disagreement with Douglass was not the only reason Delany left the *North Star.* After years of studying medicine with doctors in Pittsburgh, he was accepted by Harvard Medical School, and he eagerly left to pursue this opportunity. In December 1850, however, he was dismissed from the program after a group of white students petitioned the dean, Oliver Wendell Holmes (1809–94),

arguing that the presence of blacks devalued their diplomas. A year later, he suffered a further assault on his dignity when he was denied a patent for an invention that would have facilitated the uphill transportation of goods by train on the ground that patents could only be granted to citizens of the United States. As the Supreme Court stated in its *Dred Scott* decision in 1857, blacks were not considered citizens of the United States.

Indeed, 1850 was a low point for the antislavery and civil rights campaign, as it also saw the passage of the new FUGITIVE SLAVE ACT OF 1850, which brought about one of the most militant periods in the struggle for freedom and equality. Many black and white abolitionists alike began to encourage civil disobedience and outright resistance to the law, and Delany warned that fugitive slaves were not the only ones who should fear for their freedom. He pointed out that the law was especially dangerous for Northern free blacks because, unlike Southern free blacks, they usually did not possess documentation of their status.

The Fugitive Slave Law prompted an immediate mass exodus of free blacks to a number of locations beyond the borders of the United States, and it led Delany to write his influential emigrationist treatise, *The Condition, Elevation, Emigration and Destiny of the Colored People of the United States* (1852). Despite his embrace of emigration at this time, he continued to resist white-led efforts at colonization to Liberia. Instead he concluded that the safest places to go were the provinces of Central and South America and the Caribbean, places where people of color already made up the majority of the population. In 1853, he issued a call for a convention in Cleveland in which emigrationists could meet and discuss such details. During the meeting, Delany presented a Declaration of Sentiments as well as his "Report on the Political Destiny of the Race on this Continent," which collectively argued that blacks would never gain equality until given a true political voice. He then issued a report favorable to Canadian settlement and visited Chatham, Ontario, CANADA, in 1856.

In 1857, the Supreme Court's declaration in the *Dred Scott* case that no blacks could enjoy the privileges and protections of American citizenship caused a renewed interest in emigration, and Delany began to reconsider Africa. Yet he continued to resist the American Colonization Society's efforts for emigration to Liberia. Through William Nesbit, who had visited Liberia, Delany had learned of the unsafe conditions and unhealthy climate of the country. He also learned of the prevalence of slavery in the country and the "injurious effect" of white missionaries upon the indigenous population. He continued to resist the American Colonization Society, then, even as he developed his own African plan.

Delany's plan is best described as a "city upon a hill," which would showcase black ability and force Americans, and the rest of the world, to recognize racial equality. His plan was to take a carefully screened group of talented blacks and lead them in creating a self-sufficient African colony, with primary emphasis on economic progress. Ultimately, he decided that growing cotton to compete with American slave-grown produce in the British market would be the best way to achieve his goal. He explored Africa as part of the Niger Valley Exploring Party in 1859 and negotiated a treaty with the Egba of Abeokuta, in today's Ogun State, Nigeria.

A number of factors ended Delany's consideration of emigration. First, he lacked the funds to establish his colony. Also importantly, his colony, like Liberia, was planned upon the faulty assumption that Western culture was superior and should to be spread throughout the world. Thus, he, as did his white counterparts who helped found Liberia and Sierra Leone, failed to appreciate African culture on its own merits. Finally, the AMERICAN CIVIL WAR, 1861–65, put the final damper on his plans by offering him renewed hope that blacks could be accepted in the United States.

Soon after the war broke out, Delany, like most black leaders, enthusiastically offered his support to the federal government. Although at first turned away, finally in 1865, he met with President Abraham Lincoln and Secretary of War Edwin Stanton and was commissioned the first black field officer in the U.S. Army. After the war, he served with the FREEDMEN'S BUREAU in SOUTH CAROLINA. He held several positions in the South Carolina government during RECONSTRUCTION IN THE UNITED STATES, finally joining forces with the former Confederate army general and governor Wade Hampton (1818–1902) in an attempt to achieve racial reconciliation in the state. His hope for racial justice in America only ended with the death of Reconstruction, at which point he again embraced the American Colonization Society and their program for at Liberia. He died on January 24, 1885, feeling that he had lost his struggle for racial equality.

See also GARNET, HENRY HIGHLAND.

Beverly C. Tomek

FURTHER READING

Adeleke, Tunde. *UnAfrican Americans: Nineteenth-Century Black Nationalists and the Civilizing Mission.* Lexington: University of Kentucky Press, 1998.

———. *Without Regard to Race: The Other Martin Robinson Delany.* Jackson: University Press of Mississippi, 2003.

Blackett, R. J. M. *Building an Anti-Slavery Wall: Black Americans in the Atlantic Abolitionist Movement, 1830–1860.* Ithaca, N.Y.: Cornell University Press, 1983.

Levine, Robert. *Martin Delany, Frederick Douglass and the Politics of Representative Identity.* Chapel Hill: University of North Carolina Press, 1997.

Miller, Floyd. *The Search for a Black Nationality: Black Colonization and Emigration, 1787–1863.* Chicago: University of Illinois Press, 1975.

Ullman, Victor. *Martin R. Delany: The Beginnings of Black Nationalism.* Boston: Beacon Press, 1971.

DELAWARE

Delaware is a state of the United States. It is located along the Atlantic coast on the southern bank of the Delaware River. Most of the state is surrounded by MARYLAND, but there is a short border with PENNSYLVANIA to the north and NEW JERSEY to the northeast. The largest population center is Wilmington, and surrounding New Castle County, in the North. The state is flat and well watered, and climate and landforms are appropriate for the cultivation of tobacco, wheat, and corn. Transportation links with the interior are more difficult than for Maryland; the Delaware River runs north to PHILADELPHIA, PENNSYLVANIA, one of the country's largest cities in the colonial era, but there is no transport by water routes beyond there to other northern cities or to the West. Delaware was not geographically tied to the rest of the slave-owning Southern colonies but instead to the Northeast. The indigenous inhabitants of Delaware were the Lenape, or Delaware, whose lifestyle was similar to that of other eastern woodland peoples such as the Powhatan Indians in Virginia. They had relatively good relations with the early European settlers, trading furs with the Swedes and Dutch who settled the area beginning in the 1630s. But in the 1660s, the area fell under the control of England, first as a part of New York and then as Pennsylvania. The southern portion of the colony was claimed by Maryland until the Mason-Dixon surveying expedition of 1763–67. Indian populations were driven out or marginalized by the British, who established tobacco cultivation on the model of Maryland and Virginia. Slaves were imported directly from Africa and from the British West Indies, and Delaware became a remote outpost of the Atlantic plantation world.

Free African Americans lived in a tenuous situation in Delaware. From the WAR OF AMERICAN INDEPENDENCE, 1775–83, to the AMERICAN CIVIL WAR, 1861–65, Delaware amassed the largest percentage of free blacks of any slave state in the United States. Still, Delaware did not legally abolish slavery until national ratification of the Thirteenth Amendment—which Delaware's legislature rejected—in 1865. This duality of freedom and lingering slavery marked free blacks as second-class citizens during

Delaware's history despite their best efforts to create communities, institutions, and stability.

Slavery existed early on in Delaware. From 1639 through the 1660s, Swedish and Dutch colonists took slaves to the region, but the institution expanded after the English took control of the area in 1664. By the War of American Independence, slaves accounted for 20–25 percent of the colony's population, a larger proportion than all colonies to the north and lower than those to the south. Few Africans attained freedom during Delaware's colonial history. Slaveholders sometimes freed old or infirm slaves, but laws passed in 1731, 1740, and 1767 required masters to pay indemnity bonds to county governments to provide for aged freed people. Slaveholders often found these requirements cumbersome and refused to manumit their slaves. Moreover, many slaveholders refrained from MANUMISSION out of fear that former slaves would attack former masters and because they wanted to leave slave property to their heirs.

By the American Revolution, the role of slavery in the colony had changed, and more slaveholders began to free their slaves. Delaware's legislature did not abolish slavery outright, but in 1776, a new state constitution did outlaw slave imports. Several antislavery societies pushed for general emancipation during and after the Revolution, but lack of popular and financial support hindered antislavery efforts. Economic concerns, however, may have done more to increase manumission. A shift from tobacco production to less labor-intensive crops like corn and wheat made slaves an economic drag for many slaveholders. Delaware's slaves also generated less money than nearby Virginian slaves in the slave trade.

Despite the lack of legislative emancipation, the free black population grew rapidly during the 19th century. In 1790, Delaware's 3,899 free blacks accounted for 30.5 percent of the black population and 7 percent of the total population. By 1820, the number of free blacks had risen to 12,958, amounting to 74 percent of African Americans and 13 percent of the total population. Forty years later, on the eve of the American Civil War, free blacks numbered 19,839 (92 percent of all blacks and 18 percent of the total population). The proportion of Delaware's free black population was larger than that of any other slave state in the United States. Most free blacks lived in the country: 84 percent living in rural areas in 1800, and 75 percent in 1860. The black population was concentrated in Kent County, in the middle of the state, until the 1830s, when blacks began moving to New Castle County and Wilmington in the North.

Serious challenges faced free blacks. Perhaps the most serious was economic. Manumission worked by imposing a period of "quasi-freedom" on blacks intended to control their labor. All freed people undertook a period of temporary indentured labor that predated their actual manumission. In addition, the state legislature passed vagrancy codes in 1807, 1811, and 1849 that limited the amount of time free blacks could spend out of state. (Leaving the state widened job opportunities for black men.) These laws also authorized local authorities to hire out black children and the unemployed. As a result, most free black men worked as unskilled laborers until midcentury. In the 1850s, black labor patterns shifted. Increasing numbers of black men found semiskilled or skilled work as farmers, tenant farmers, blacksmiths, masons, barbers, watermen, carpenters, and bricklayers. Gender mattered when finding a job. Whereas men saw increasing opportunities, women often worked in the same small range of jobs: domestic servants, seamstresses, cooks, and washerwomen. Location also mattered. In Dover, in central Delaware, only 3 percent of working black males were skilled in 1860. Farther south, in Milton, 22 percent held skilled jobs. The majority of skilled and semiskilled workers lived in Wilmington, where 26 percent of black males held skilled positions in 1860. In Wilmington, however, increasing competition with immigrant labor pushed many blacks into personal service jobs while the newcomers moved into manufacturing and professional services (e.g., as doctors and lawyers) in the 1850s.

White Delawareans circumscribed free black life in other ways. Laws limited African Americans' access to gun ownership and limited the size and times of black public meetings. Free blacks also faced violence. Further, despite white fear of free black violence, the opposite tended to be true. In the 1830s, 100 percent of white-on-black crimes involved assault, compared to 18 percent of black-on-white crimes. Free blacks also lived with the threat of kidnapping. In colonial Delaware, kidnappers sold free blacks to slave traders. After a 1787 law barred blacks from testifying against whites, the risk increased, and it remained constant until the Civil War. These dangers complicated African-American efforts at building stable communities. In some areas, such as family structure, blacks were successful. In others, including education, blacks failed to achieve lasting results.

Black families demonstrated remarkable stability. Whereas slavery subjected families to separation through sale, free blacks used their freedom to ensure their families' survival. Between 1800 and 1860, the number of African Americans living in all-black households rose from 72 percent to 84 percent. In addition, most children grew up in two-parent households, especially in the country: Approximately 84 percent of households in the country and 70 percent in Wilmington had two parents in the mid-19th century. A disproportionate demand for female domestic workers in Wilmington skewed the city's population toward women, therefore reducing their ability to find husbands.

African-American attempts to build autonomous institutions had mixed success. Some success occured in religion. In the 1790s, a free black man named Peter Spencer (1782–1843) tried to separate from Asbury Methodist Episcopal Church over issues of segregation and leadership. He struggled against Asbury's leaders for years before establishing "Old Union" (African Union Methodist Church) in 1813—three years before RICHARD ALLEN founded the celebrated Mother Bethel Church of the AFRICAN METHODIST EPISCOPAL CHURCH in Philadelphia. Free blacks belonged to five major congregations before the Civil War, which grew to eight churches after the war. Churches served as sites for black protest as well as worship. In the 1830s, blacks in Old Union issued petitions opposing the AMERICAN COLONIZATION SOCIETY, founded to relocate free blacks beyond U.S. borders. Beyond churches, other organizations were less successful. Benevolent organizations, such as the African Benevolent Association, founded in Wilmington in 1820, and the Sons of Benevolence, established in 1830, suffered from lack of funds and government support. State legislators rejected many attempts to incorporate black societies, resulting in their inability to draw financial assistance from state and local government.

Education presented the greatest difficulties. Delaware passed no statutes preventing African Americans from receiving education, but in the 1820s, a law denied state aid for black students. Moreover, white public opinion opposed integrated public schools. A Quaker abolitionist established a school in Wilmington as early as 1801, but funding problems forced it into frequent closings, and it averaged only 30 students per year. In the 1810s, abolitionists formed the African School Society to collect funds. It managed to expand average attendance to 40 students of both sexes, but its petitions for state assistance yielded only mixed results. Churches also ran schools, but most children received little education. No schools existed in Sussex County in southern Delaware, and in 1860, 65 percent of blacks 20 years and older in Wilmington and 95 percent in Sussex County were illiterate.

On the eve of the American Civil War, modest social stratification marked African-American life. The starkest stratification emerged in rural areas. Farmers accrued most of the wealth held by rural residents though they accounted for only 15 and 9 percent of free blacks in 1850 and 1860, respectively, Wilmington's black population was similarly divided. A small minority, 4.5 percent, held real estate in 1850 and 1860. Real estate holders generally were in the ranks of the service trades, waiters, and washerwomen. Interestingly, race and nativity played a role in property ownership. Mulattoes and blacks who migrated to Delaware were more likely to own property than native-born blacks. Finally, despite some evidence of upward mobility, the majority of black workers did not move up the socioeconomic ladder.

The Civil War precented opportunities and disappointments blacks. Hoping to prove their patriotism to hostile whites, 954 black men—both free and enslaved—served in the Union army, composing 8 percent of Delaware's

AFRICAN-AMERICAN POPULATION OF DELAWARE, 1790–1900

Year	Slaves	Free People of Color	Free People of Color as a Percentage of Total Population	Total Population
1790	8,887	3,899	6.6%	59,094
1800	6,153	8,268	12.9%	64,273
1810	4,177	13,136	18.1%	72,674
1820	4,530	10,146	13.9%	72,749
1830	3,292	15,855	20.7%	76,748
1840	2,605	16,919	21.7%	78,085
1850	2,290	18,073	19.7%	91,539
1860	1,798	19,826	17.7%	112,210
1870		22,794	18.2%	125,015
1880		26,442	18.0%	146,608
1890		28,386	16.8%	168,493
1900		30,697	16.7%	184,735

Union soldiers. Their service rang hollow, however, in the state legislature. Controlled by Democrats sympathetic to the South, it rejected calls for emancipation and considered arming slaves only late in the war. Democrats also resisted efforts to extend voting rights—formally denied since 1776—to black men. In perhaps the strangest occurrence in Delaware history, the state legislature refused to ratify the Fifteenth Amendment, which prohibited disfranchisement on the basis of race, until 1901. (Nevertheless, enough states ratified the amendment to make it law in 1870.)

In the years following the war, blacks faced continued hardship, particularly in the areas of civil rights, education, and employment. Though the Fifteenth Amendment prohibited racial discrimination at the polls, Democrats used other tactics to disfranchise black voters. One strategy involved removing blacks from tax lists since taxpayer status made one eligible to vote. Whites eventually replaced tax fraud with literacy requirements most blacks could not meet. The effectiveness of literacy requirements points to continuing problems with black education. In 1875, the state legislature allowed black schools to be funded through black property taxes, but with so few owning property, the law was ineffective. The success of black schools was uneven. In 1910, 72 percent of black children aged six to nine attended school, compared to 75 percent of native-born whites and 69 percent of foreign-born whites. Little correlation existed, however, between literacy and upward mobility, and in 1890, only 50 percent of blacks were literate. Employment posed continuing challenges to black workers. Increasing competition with European immigrants destabilized black labor. Despite the emergence of organized labor, most unions barred blacks, and black workers lacked entry into apprenticeship programs. By contrast, immigrants gained access to both unions and apprenticeship opportunities.

By the dawn of the 20th century, Delaware's black population had endured much hardship. They had faced stubborn discrimination in all aspects of their social, political, and economic lives. They resisted attempts to keep them marginal characters in Delaware's history. Though they sometimes failed in those efforts, they succeeded in establishing and maintaining fundamental aspects of their lives, including their families, churches, and social networks.

See also EDUCATION AND LITERACY; FAMILY; RACISM AND RACIAL PREJUDICE.

Thomas H. Sheeler

FURTHER READING

Essah, Patience. *A House Divided: Slavery and Emancipation in Delaware, 1638–1865.* Charlottesville: University Press of Virginia, 1996.

Heinegg, Paul. *Free African Americans of Maryland and Delaware: From the Colonial Period to 1810.* Baltimore: Clearfield, 2000.

Marks, Carole, ed. *A History of African Americans of Delaware and Maryland's Eastern Shore.* 2nd ed. Wilmington: Delaware Heritage Commission, 1998.

Williams, William Henry. *Slavery and Freedom in Delaware, 1639–1865.* Wilmington, Del.: SR Books, 1996.

DELGRÈS, LOUIS (1766–1802) *Guadeloupean military officer and rebel leader*

Louis Delgrès was a Martinican *homme de couleur*, or free man of color, who became famous, even legendary, for his resistance against French troops in Guadeloupe in 1802, and for his choice to commit suicide along with his troops on the heights of Matouba rather than surrender (*see also* FRENCH CARIBBEAN and FRENCH REVOLUTION). He was born free in Martinique, probably on August 2, 1766. He is thought to have been the son of a French official, also named Louis Delgrès, who worked in the colonial government in the 1760s, and a free woman of color. He was a sergeant in the MILITIA starting in 1781. He signed the manifesto of the exiled Martinican revolutionaries in DOMINICA in 1792. In this document, he said he was a property owner and was born free and listed 1766 as his birth date.

Starting in 1789, a series of often violent conflicts broke out on the island of Martinique, pitting partisans of revolutionary ideology against defenders of the royal order. Delgrès, along with many other men of color, participated in these conflicts on the pro-revolutionary side. In 1792, the royalists gained the upper hand in Martinique, and a group of republicans gathered in exile on the nearby British island of Dominica. Claiming to be the proper representatives of Martinique, they elected representatives to send to metropolitan France. Delgrès participated in this election, the first in French history that was racially integrated in terms of both those who participated and those who were elected, one of whom a man of color.

In 1794, when the British invaded Martinique with the assistance of local royalists, Delgrès was taken prisoner and shipped across the Atlantic. He was eventually released to metropolitan France and became part of a unit called the Bataillon des Antilles. Delgrès became a lieutenant in the unit, promoted at the same time as MAGLOIRE PÉLAGE, who would fight alongside him for the next several years until the two ended up on opposite sides in 1802. Although they were unable to regain control of Martinique until the British ceded it back to them in 1802, the French did recapture Guadeloupe from the British in 1794, after slavery had been abolished in the French Empire by the National Convention in Paris.

Delgrès was sent to Guadeloupe in 1795, and from there he was dispatched as part of an invasion of the British island of St. Lucia. Delgrès was promoted to captain in St. Lucia and then sent to fight the British in Vincent, where the French allied with the BLACK CARIB who lived there. With an infusion of reinforcements sent across the Atlantic, the British ultimately defeated the French in both St. Vincent and St. Lucia, and Delgrès was once again imprisoned. He was again released to metropolitan France, where after a brief mobilization in a new Compagnie des hommes de couleur he spent time in Paris.

In 1800, he was assigned to a military unit that accompanied new commissioners being sent to govern the island of Guadeloupe. Widely respected by the soldiers under his command, many of them formerly enslaved, he became a leader among those who were suspicious of French intentions during these years. In September 1801, after the white governor of the island, Jean Baptiste Raymond Lacrosse (1765–1829), passed over the man of color Magloire Pélage for promotion, small insurrections broke out in the military. Lacrosse arrested many popular officers, and on October 21, he tried to have Pélage arrested. Soldiers and local laborers rose up, and Lacrosse was expelled from the island. Pélage took control, creating a new autonomous government in Guadeloupe, and Delgrès was placed in command of Fort-St-Charles in the administrative capital of the island, Basse-Terre.

Delgrès, however, was at odds with Pélage's regime, which sought to appease metropolitan leaders and demonstrate their loyalty to France in part by using military force to keep the former slaves working on plantations. Delgrès refused to follow orders to round up plantation laborers who had taken refuge in Basse-Terre. Such laborers seem to have trusted Delgrès, for when French troops arrived on the island in May 1802, they presented themselves to him in large numbers, asking for weapons to fight.

The French mission to the island was led by the General Antoine Richepanse and had been sent from France a few months after a similar mission was sent under the command of General Charles Leclerc to SAINT-DOMINGUE. Both missions had as their secret goal to destroy the autonomous regimes that had emerged in the Caribbean, to prepare for the reversal of emancipation. Much of the population of Guadeloupe was suspicious of French intentions, and many openly feared a return to slavery. So when French troops, welcomed by Pélage at Pointe-à-Pitre, began disarming all the soldiers of African descent they could, many grabbed their weapons and prepared to resist. Delgrès became the leader of the resistance movement, rallying his troops in Basse-Terre and allying with many plantation laborers who wanted to fight the French as well.

On May 10, 1802, Delgrès issued a famous proclamation in Basse-Terre, explaining why he was fighting the French. Addressed "TO THE ENTIRE UNIVERSE," as a "CRY OF INNOCENCE AND DESPAIR," it claimed Richepanse was committed to reestablishing slavery on the island and taking away the power of men of African descent. "Let us dare say it. The maxims of even the most atrocious tyranny have been surpassed today. Our old tyrants permitted a master to emancipate his slave. But it seems that, in this century of philosophy, there exist men, grown powerful thanks to the distance that separates them from those who appointed them, who only want to see men who are black or take their origins from this color in the chains of slavery." Delgrès promised white citizens that they would not be harmed. But, he insisted, "Resistance to oppression is a natural right." The proclamation inspired the rebels of Basse-Terre, who swore to defeat Richepanse or "bury themselves in the ashes of the colony." Their rallying cry became "Vivre libre ou mourir"—To live free or die.

Delgrès's troops had initial success resisting the disembarkation of French troops into Basse-Terre in May 1802. But when Pélage requested that the French allow him and his troops, who had been imprisoned, to fight against Delgrès, the tide began to turn. Delgrès decided to split his troops, sending the officer Joseph Ignace up the island to attack Pointe-à-Pitre, while he orchestrated a nighttime retreat from Fort-St-Charles in order to fight the French in the hills above Basse-Terre. As they continued to fight, Delgrès's troops flew a French tricolor with the white ripped out of it—the same flag that would become the standard of resistance in Saint-Domingue a year later. Surrounded on a plantation at Matouba, on the heights of the Soufrière volcano that dominates the island, Delgrès decided to commit suicide with his followers rather than surrender. On May 28, 1802, he mined the plantation with kegs of powder and as the French approached set them alight, ending the rebellion with a massive explosion.

Delgrès has, in the past decades, become a hero in Guadeloupe, remembered for his courageous defense of emancipation and racial equality. In 1948, a plaque was placed at Matouba commemorating his struggle there. The fort where he made his last stand has gone through several name changes since 1802. After the reestablishment of slavery in the island, it was renamed after General Richepanse, who died of fever shortly after Delgrès's death and is buried in the fort. In 1962, however, local administrators removed the name of the French general who had reestablished slavery on the island from the fort in their town, giving it back the original name of Fort-St-Charles. And in 1989, a group of local administrators, including the writer Daniel Maximin, lobbied successfully to have the name of the fort changed to Fort-Louis-Delgrès, and plaques and chronologies commemorating his struggles within it. In 1998, Louis Delgrès's name was placed, along with that of Haitian Revolutionary TOUSSAINT LOUVERTURE, in a hall in the French Panthéon, the temple of heroes, in Paris. And in 2002 a large statue of Delgrès was placed along a major avenue in the town of Pointe-à-Pitre. Historians, activists, musicians, poets (notably Aimé Césaire), and even comic book artists have all recounted the story of Delgrès during the past decades, and today he is widely known and respected in Guadeloupe.

Laurent Dubois

FURTHER READING

Dubois, Laurent. *A Colony of Citizens: Revolution and Slave Emancipation in the French Caribbean, 1787–1804.* Chapel Hill: University of North Carolina Press, 2004.

DIALLO, AYUBA SULEIMAN (JOB BEN SOLOMON)   (ca. 1701–ca. 1773) *African merchant*

Ayuba Suleiman Diallo was born around 1701 in Bondu, in the modern nation of Sénégal, near the headwaters of the Gambia River (*see also* SENEGAMBIA). He was from a family of Muslim religious leaders in what was then the Kingdom of Futa, which included much of central Sénégal along with the Futa Djallon highlands region of today's Republic of Guinea. This was a prominent kingdom that was created in the late 17th century by a Fulbe jihad. The kingdom endured into the late 19th century, when it was conquered by the French. In the early 18th century, the Fulbe were exporting many slaves, prisoners captured in their wars of expansion, mostly through the British Royal African Company slave-trading port James Island, at the mouth of the Gambia River. Diallo was involved in the trade with the British, and in 1730, he traveled to the Gambia region to sell slaves and buy imported British goods. He was captured by personal enemies and sold to a slave ship captain. He tried to arrange a prisoner exchange or ransom, but negotiations fell through and the ship left port, carrying him eventually to Annapolis, MARYLAND.

In Maryland, he became an agricultural laborer in Kent County on the eastern shore. He had the habit of going into the woods to perform the Islamic prayers, but when he was mocked by a child, he decided to run away. He was recaptured, and while he was in prison waiting for his master to get him, a lawyer named Thomas Bluett met him. Bluett discovered that Diallo was a Muslim and was literate in Arabic. He was also impressed by Diallo's

aristocratic manner and was convinced that he was "no common slave." Bluett then found another slave who was from Senegambia and spoke Wolof, a language of a neighboring group that Diallo also spoke. With translation, the men discovered that Diallo was of high social status. Bluett convinced Diallo's master to permit Diallo to write a letter to the Royal African Company.

The letter made its way to Britain, where the director of the company, James Oglethorpe (1696–1785), confirmed Diallo's identity from company records and offered to buy his freedom for £45. Diallo was freed in 1733, and he and Bluett traveled to Britain. The pair wrote a biography of Diallo, which is one of the first authentic slave narratives in English. Diallo then returned to the Futa in 1734 and resumed his former life. He lived there for almost 40 more years, dying around 1773.

Diallo's story is important for several reasons. For one thing, he is a well-documented example of a Muslim cleric who immigrated to the Americas and practiced his religion (*see also* ISLAM). The degree to which Islam was successfully transplanted to the Americas before the 20th century is hotly debated, but here is an example of

A book illustration taken from a drawing probably made from life of Ayuba Suleiman Diallo, an African merchant who was temporarily held as a slave in Maryland from 1731 to 1733. Diallo received permission from his master to write to his friends in the British Royal African Company, and they ransomed him and sent him back to his homeland. Diallo thus became one of the few Africans to return from the Americas. As a Muslim clergyman, he practiced his religion in Maryland and was literate in Arabic. *(Schomburg Center/Art Resource NY)*

a Muslim resident in America. The reaction of whites to his religion is also enlightening—both his master and Bluett felt that being a Muslim made him more "civilized" and more worthy of regaining his freedom. Next, he is one of the few examples of an African who made a round trip across the Atlantic in the time of the slave trade. His intelligence and social standing permitted him to escape from a peril few found any way out of other than death. Finally, he illustrates the close relationships that existed between African and European merchants in the era of the slave trade. Once the British slave-trading company offices in London received his letter, they were able to verify his identity from their records. They knew who their African counterparts were, and they valued them—enough, in this case, for Oglethorpe, an extremely important individual in British society, to buy him and spend a considerable sum for his travel to Britain and back to Africa.

Stewart R. King

FURTHER READING

Bluett, Thomas. *Some Memories of the Life of Job, the Son of Solomon, the High Priest of Boonda in Africa; Who Was a Slave About Two Years in Maryland; and Afterwards Being Brought to England, Was Set Free, and Sent to His Native Land in the Year 1734.* London: Richard Ford, 1734. Available online. URL: http://docsouth.unc.edu/neh/bluett/bluett.html. Accessed December 22, 2010.

Curtin, Philip. *Africa Remembered: Narratives by West Africans from the Era of the Slave Trade.* 1967. Reprint, Long Grove, Ill.: Waveland Press, 1997.

DIAS, HENRIQUE (?–ca. 1662) *Brazilian soldier*
Henrique Dias was an important leader of Brazilian forces during the struggle against the Dutch invasion in the 17th century. He remains an iconic figure for Afro-Brazilians in the military, and several units and military installations at different times have been named after him.

Nothing is known of Dias's status at birth nor of his early life; he first attracted notice in the early 1630s, during the wars between the Dutch West India Company and Luso-Brazilian settlers. The Dutch sought to gain control of the sugar plantation districts of Pernambuco from 1630 to 1654, when they were finally expelled (*see also* BRAZIL). In the course of these conflicts, Dias emerged as the leader of the black troops—both slave and free—mobilized by the Luso-Brazilians. In 1636, he received the title of governor of the blacks charged with attacking the Dutch. During the truce between the Dutch and the Portuguese (1638–45), Dias and his troops were ordered to Angola, but they apparently did not leave Brazil before the resumption of hostilities. He led the black troops in the final campaign against the Dutch (1645–54) and, after the war, received membership in the Order of Christ and other rewards from the king of Portugal. In 1656, he traveled to Lisbon to seek greater rewards and lobby for the freedom of the slaves who had fought with him (he judged the rewards that he had received to be less than those received by white commanders, and masters were seeking to reclaim slaves who had fought against the Dutch). He also requested that the government maintain his troops as a MILITIA regiment. Dias was successful in winning the rank of minor nobility for his sons-in-law and royal orders that the slaves who had fought under him be freed, either voluntarily by wealthy masters or via modest compensation from the treasury for poor masters. He never profited much from his fame, and he slipped back into obscurity after the end of the struggle against the Netherlands. Most biographers agree that he died in 1662, though the circumstances and even the year are uncertain.

His militia regiment eventually gave rise to the black militia units that proliferated in 18th-century Brazil. Dias entered the pantheon of heroes of the so-called restoration of Pernambuco and, through the 19th century, served as a symbol of black patriotism and incorporation into the nation, albeit in a subordinate way.

Hendrik Kraay

FURTHER READING

Mattos, Hebe. "'Black Troops' and the Hierarchies of Color in the Portuguese Atlantic World: The Case of Henrique Dias and His Black Regiment." *Luso-Brazilian Review* 45, no. 1 (2008): 6–29.

Mello, José Antônio Gonçalves de. *Henrique Dias: Governador dos crioulos, negros e mulatos do Brasil.* Recife: Massangana, 1988.

DOMINICA

Dominica (pronounced do-min-NEE-ka), sitting between Martinique and Guadeloupe in the eastern Caribbean, is just less than 300 square miles. It is a volcanic island, with forested peaks of 5,000 feet drawing rain clouds, and geothermal activity continues with sulfur springs and a boiling lake. Today it is remarkable for the Carib Territory (the last substantial population of indigenous Caribbean people), providing location shots for the *Pirates of the Caribbean* movie franchise and ecotourism, especially hiking and bird-watching.

Early History

Mountainous Dominica offered little flat land for European plantations, and the indigenous Carib were largely able to maintain their hold on Dominica, despite sporadic slave raids from the Spanish during the 1500s. They traded with European ships reprovisioning at Dominica and helped their fellow Carib raid European settlements in nearby islands. In 1686, the French and English agreed that Dominica would be considered neutral territory and left to the indigenous people. Despite the treaty, French settlers moved into the island to cut wood and produce food to meet the needs of nearby plantation islands. Some of these immigrants were free people of color, and some owned slaves. This is the first recorded presence of people of African descent in the island, though some of the Carib Indians may have been runaway slaves like their better-known fellow tribesmen on St. Vincent (*see also* BLACK CARIB). From 1727, the French establishment at Martinique backed the settlers with force, pushing the Carib into the northeast corner of the island.

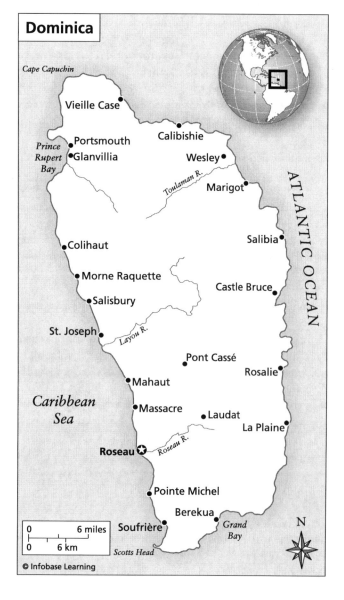

Dominica remained a de facto French island until the 1760s. The British captured Dominica in 1761, and the treaty that ended the Seven Years' War in 1763 confirmed British possession. Dominica was occupied by the French from 1778 but returned to the British in the 1783 treaty that ended the WAR OF AMERICAN INDEPENDENCE, 1775–83, and stayed British until full independence in 1978. French and Catholic influence remained strong throughout—family names and place-names were still French-dominated, and even today, Dominicans speak a French creole as well as the official language of English. Both French and British colonists took slaves to the island and tried to develop a plantation sector. Plantations here remained small, and the island was of limited economic importance. This relative poverty meant that racial discrimination remained less onerous here than in other French and British islands in the Caribbean. The fact that whites and blacks worked side by side on small farms meant that master-slave relationships tended to be more feudal and personal. This could be bad or good from the point of view of the slave, depending on the personalities involved. But it meant that slaves had an easier chance to develop patron-client or other personal relationships with whites that might lead to freedom.

Dominica was strategically important despite its small size and mountainous terrain. The good harbor of Prince Rupert Bay at Portsmouth provided the British a naval base in the heart of French territory. The capital, however, was placed at Roseau as Portsmouth was swampy and therefore unhealthy. Making Dominica a free port in 1766 allowed the British to profit from trade with the French but also allowed the inhabitants to maintain their French connections. Despite its role in trade, Dominica was generally a poor colony and afflicted with frequent hurricanes.

The Nineteenth Century

Although there were free people of African ancestry on the island—runaway slaves, the children of Indians and blacks, and free blacks and mixed-race people who had been manumitted—from the earliest days of European settlement, the 19th century in Dominica was the century of free people of color. Population estimates tell the story of the increasing free population of color and of white flight: A few hundred Carib remained isolated in the forests, and several hundred MAROONS also populated the interior, raiding the plantations until they were finally subdued in 1815.

The population of free people of color grew noticeably during the FRENCH REVOLUTION and Napoleonic Wars, 1789–1815. Dominica's French heritage and location between Martinique and Guadeloupe meant that the French Revolution had a strong impact on the island

POPULATION OF DOMINICA, 1791–1831

Year	Whites	Free People of Color	Slaves
1791	2,000	500	15,000
1815	1,100	2,600	19,000
1831	750	3,900	14,000

(see also FRENCH CARIBBEAN). Many French free coloreds and free blacks immigrated to Dominica, some with slaves and capital to set up as planters. Several French revolutionary papers were published and circulated in the island, including a pamphlet exhorting free people of color to rise up and demand their rights. As in many French colonies, much of the colony's defense forces consisted of free men of color. In 1795, the free colored MILITIA in the Colihaut region petitioned for equal rights, citing the racial equality established by law in the neighboring French colonies. In 1802, the governor disbanded the free colored militia, concerned they would betray the colony. British colonial governments provided arms and ammunition to French royalists to fight VICTOR HUGUES and his policies of racial equality in Guadeloupe between 1794 and 1798.

The paintings of Agostino Brunias, who traveled the West Indies and lived in Dominica from 1764 to 1796, have left us a visual record of free people of color in the late 18th century. Dominica stood out among the British islands in having a significant class of free colored planters, generally concentrated in coffee and cocoa rather than sugar. Not all free people of color were planters, however. An 1820 tax roll identified only 400 individuals or partnerships who owned slaves, a fraction of the 2,800 free people of color. The term "free people of color" also included clerks, fishermen, seamstresses, small farmers, day laborers, sailors, and ship captains and incorporated those who were of either mixed or unmixed African descent. The weakness of the plantation economy in Dominica meant that extra land was available for enslaved people to grow provisions, enabling a higher rate of MANUMISSION and self-purchase. Furthermore, taxes on manumission also produced a class of people who were effectively free but lacking formal papers (see also LIVING "AS FREE").

In Dominica, free people of color were not allowed to vote, serve in the assembly, serve on parish boards, or sit on juries. Their ability to give evidence in court was limited; they faced different fines or jail terms for various offenses. While there were no limits on their acquisition of property, they were barred from certain occupations such as tavern-keeper. Manumission was taxed, and free people of color entering the island were required to prove their freedom and pay a tax. In 1821, free men of color in

Dominica launched a collective movement for equality, holding public meetings, electing a representative committee, and circulating petitions. They argued that the crops they produced and the taxes they paid entitled them to equal standing with whites but also spoke of the right of all men to justice and the rights of a British subject. The push for civil rights was spearheaded by the propertied elite, but petitions were signed by a range of men.

British Dominica was governed by a locally elected assembly in conjunction with an imperial governor. The petitions to the local assembly went nowhere in the 1820s, but after systematic investigation, by 1829 the British imperial government had made it a matter of West Indian policy to end discrimination against free people of color. After a brief attempt to limit free people of color from voting or running for the assembly, in 1831 the Dominica assembly passed a law to eliminate all disabilities. The imperial government also ended disabilities against Catholics in 1832. That year, free men of color voted for the first time and peacefully elected three men of color to the assembly.

As the British government sought to end slavery and reorganize the Dominican government into a federation ruled from Antigua, free men of color allied with the imperial government to oppose the white plantocracy of Dominica. In particular, Joseph Fadelle, a lawyer and free man of color, established himself as a noisy advocate for better treatment of free people of color and apprentices, and the newspaper the Dominican was founded as the mouthpiece of liberals and free men of color. Dominica became known for bitter factionalism, at one point shutting down the government entirely. Rattled by an attempt by the white majority in the assembly to increase the property qualification for voting, free men of color sought to take over the assembly at the December 1837 election. Terrified by crowds and riotous behavior at the polls, whites aborted the electoral process, leaving four of 19 seats empty. The assembly ceased to function for some six months, just as it was most needed to pass laws to facilitate emancipation in August 1838. Under imperial reprimand, a new government was reestablished in May 1838, but white planters abstained from involvement, abdicating all power to the men of color.

Prior to emancipation, the free colored elite had generally associated themselves with the whole of free people of color, poor and rich, and consciously sought to include free blacks in their claims to rights. The colored majority in the assembly had also softened the post-emancipation police state established in other British colonies. However, class and color stratification played a larger role after emancipation. Some free men of color, particularly those associated with the Methodists and antislavery activists in Britain, continued to advocate for the freedmen. But in general these elite free people of color were not trusted by the former slaves or poor free blacks. In 1844, the colored-dominated assembly sought to take a census. The rumor that the census was preparation for restoring slavery, in combination with ongoing disputes over land and squatters, sparked a full-scale revolt known as "la guerre négre," in which some 1,200–1,500 freedmen gathered with arms to resist the census. The revolt was suppressed, with most prisoners pardoned, and elite free coloreds continued to dominate the assembly in what was called a "Mulatto Ascendancy" until self-government was abolished for crown colony rule in 1898.

Dayo Nicole Mitchell

FURTHER READING

Chace, Russel. "Protest in Post-Emancipation Dominica: The 'Guerre Négre' of 1844." Paper presented at the Conference [Association] of Caribbean Historians, UWI Mona, Jamaica, April 15–20, 1983.

Government of Dominica, ed. *Aspects of Dominican History.* Dominica: Government Printing Division, 1972.

Honychurch, Lenox. *The Dominica Story: A History of the Island.* 1975. Reprint, London: Macmillan Education, 1995.

Trouillot, Michel-Rolph. "The Inconvenience of Freedom: Free People of Color and the Political Aftermath of Slavery in Dominica and Saint-Domingue/Haiti." In *The Meaning of Freedom: Economics, Politics, and Culture after Slavery,* edited by Frank McGlynn and Seymour Drescher, 147–182. Pittsburgh: University of Pittsburgh Press, 1992.

DOMINICAN REPUBLIC

Hispaniola, the Caribbean island today shared by the Dominican Republic and Republic of Haiti, was the site of the first permanent European settlement in the Americas, the hub of Spain's rich new empire. In the course of building that empire, thousands of African slaves were taken to Hispaniola, where they were "seasoned" to plantation life. Less known and studied is the fact that today's Dominican Republic is where the first free people of color in the Americas carved out their fortunes as well. The colony was named after St. Dominic (1170–1221), founder of the Dominicans, by the Spaniards, and was called Santo Domingo in Spanish and Saint-Domingue in French.

The principal city in the Spanish part of the colony was also named Santo Domingo. Today, the city has regained its colonial name, while the former Spanish colony is called the Dominican Republic.

It is no coincidence that Christopher Columbus finally received support for his great enterprise of the indies in 1492, the same year as the last act in the long Reconquest of Spain when Christians overpowered Muslims in the nation. King Ferdinand and Queen Isabella had exhausted their treasury in battling to expel the Moors who had dominated Spain since the eighth century, thus they were now open to Columbus's idea of a trade route to the riches of the Indies, as Asia was then called by Europeans. Throughout those almost 800 years of Moorish occupation, thousands of people of color, both enslaved and free, intermingled their genes and customs with those of the already diverse peoples of the Iberian Peninsula. Thus, it should be no surprise that many of the "Spaniards" who conquered and settled Hispaniola were *ladinos*, although most early documents do not distinguish them from other Spaniards.

Ladinos were people of African descent who had been "hispanicized." That is, they had lived or been born in Spain, were baptized Catholics, had Spanish names, spoke Castilian, and were acculturated to Spanish life. The *criados* (loyal men or retainers) of the colonial Spanish officials on Hispaniola were frequently free or enslaved *ladinos*, who fulfilled important household roles and acted as the officials' legal and business representatives, military attaches, and overseers of their mines, ranches, and plantations. Through faithful service, *ladino* slaves could earn freedom. Many of the island's early colonial ARTISANS, tradesmen, and merchants were also free *ladinos*, and some free *ladinos* were conquistadores, landowners, and *encomenderos* in their own right (an *encomendero* was a Spaniard with a royal grant of Indians to work for him in exchange for providing them with the fundamentals of Christianity). Among those who are known to have lived on Hispaniola in the 15th century are Antón Mexía, Francisco Piñon, and JUAN GARRIDO, who was a *criado* to both Juan Ponce de León (1474–1521) and Hernán Cortés (1485–1547). *Criada*, the feminine version of the word, was a colonial era euphemism for both indigenous and African concubines, many of whom were granted freedom for themselves and their mixed-blood children by the Spaniards who loved them.

Other slaves brought directly from Africa—known as *bozales*—worked alluvial gold deposits found throughout the island. Many Africans had developed mining, refining, smelting, and goldsmithing skills in their native lands, as well as techniques for forging iron and steel. Documents indicate that at least 120 African slaves were sent to Hispaniola's royal mines in 1504 and 1505, but many obviously arrived earlier, for in 1503, Governor Nicolás de Ovando had written to the king, complaining that he did not want any more African slaves—neither *ladinos* nor *bozales*—sent to Hispaniola because they ran away and convinced local Taíno Indians to run away with them.

We will never know how many people of color entered Hispaniola in those early years. Records are scarce, for the island was a frontier, far from the European mainland, and it was tropical, a climate where parchment does not long survive. Additionally, most of the *bozales* were imported illegally, sold to Spaniards by the Portuguese, who monopolized trade with western Africa. It did not take *bozales* long to realize that slavery under the Spaniards was far more onerous than slavery in Africa, so they ran away, as did many *ladino* slaves. Having no relatives on the island to help them and not knowing the land, where to find water, or what was edible, it made sense to join with the Taíno. Together, these Indians and Africans who ran away to freedom were called *cimarrones*, or MAROONS in English.

The *cimarrones* kept to the isolated, mountainous or peripheral, often less fertile and more arid regions of the island, preferring difficult lives as freedmen to life under Spanish dominance. They grew and gathered their own food, eating what Taíno had relied on for centuries, but adding pork, beef, and chicken to the mostly marine proteins that had been available before the arrival of the Spaniards, for many pigs, cows, and chickens had also become *cimarrones* and, encountering no natural enemies, propagated rapidly.

By 1519, a large percentage of the Taíno of Hispaniola had run off or died (the first smallpox epidemic in the Americas hit in 1518–19), and the easily mined gold had run out. The island's economic salvation was sugarcane, and West Africans had already learned to grow and process it in the Atlantic islands and in plantations on the Iberian Peninsula. The Spanish Crown attempted to fulfill the constant requests of the colonists to send more African slaves by issuing a license to the governor of Bresa to import 4,000 *bozales*. The more African slaves there were on the island, however, the more runaways and rebellions there were.

The first mass rebellion on Hispaniola took place on the plantation belonging to Governor Diego Colón (Columbus's eldest son and heir) on Christmas Day 1521. Twenty-plus slaves initiated it, mostly Wolof from Cape Verde in today's SENEGAMBIA. They convinced another 20 or more slaves to run away with them and headed west toward the town of Azua, stealing provisions from a cattle ranch and killing several Spaniards along the way. They were probably planning to join Enriquillo, the era's most powerful Taíno cacique, and his men. Enriquillo had counseled cooperation with the Spaniards but finally rebelled against them in 1519, motivating hundreds of other Taíno and Africans to join him in the southern-central mountains of Bahoruco, near the modern border with Haiti.

Most of those first Africans who rebelled en masse were free for only a week, for Colón led patrols that supposedly shot six of them and hanged the rest. Their heads were stuck on pikes along the road to Azua, a warning to others not to follow in their footsteps. But slave ordinances promulgated on January 6, 1522—the first in the Western Hemisphere—indicate that not all were killed or captured, and the desire to be free could not be so easily quenched.

The first African *cimarrón* whom we know by name is SEBASTIÁN LEMBA, who joined Enriquillo in the late 1520s or early 1530s and captained up to 400 men. Lemba was killed in 1547, after almost 20 years of freedom, by another African slave, who gained his own freedom by doing so. Other African *cimarrones* whose names were recorded in documents of the era include Diego de Ocampo, at large for more than 10 years, and Diego de Guzmán. As was Lemba, both were captains under Enriquillo. In the 1540s, documents name Dieguillo de Ocampo, another slave from the same area as Diego de Ocampo, an African-born *cimarrón* captain who led raids in La Vega and Santiago, and in the 1550s, an African *cimarrón* captain named Juan Vaquero, who had led raids against the Spaniards for years, was captured and put to death. Spaniards feared that all of the approximately 12,000 African slaves on the island would rise up in rebellion.

In early 1548, Spanish authorities on Hispaniola discovered a large community of fugitive slaves in the easternmost mountains of Higüey. The leader's name was Juan Criollo. Although he and his people did not raid Spanish plantations or attack Spaniards along the roads and hold them for ransom as other *cimarrónes* did, it was feared they might do so. A Spanish patrol captured Criollo and destroyed the community. There were many other African *cimarrón* communities, however, which came to be called *manieles*.

In the mid-16th century, the main Spanish treasure fleet that provided the principal commercial connection between Spain and the colonies in the Americas was rerouted through Havana instead of Santo Domingo. That, along with the discovery of gold and silver in quantity on the mainland and security worries caused by the runaway slaves, put an end to Hispaniola's nascent sugarcane industry. While it would thrive in Saint-Domingue, the western part of the island later named Haiti, in the 1700s, it would not recover in Santo Domingo until the late 1800s. Most of the island's white population fled to the mainland, and Hispaniola sank into poverty. In 1604–06, the Crown ordered the island's governor, Domingo de Osorio, forcibly to remove all the population in the north and west, the modern Haiti, to new sites nearer the city of Santo Domingo because these mostly mixed-blood peoples were illegally trading with Spain's enemies, the French, English, and Flemish.

Enslaved Africans took advantage of the chaos—while their owners resisted the "devastations" of the forced move—to escape and form their own *manieles*. One of these was Tomasillo, who founded a free community in the mountains south of Puerto Plata from which he and his people continued to sell contraband. "Whites! Whites!" they yelled when a Spanish troop led by the Delgado brothers attacked them in 1608. Next, the Delgados went after Pablo Mandingo and other fugitive slaves, including a couple named Luis Angola and Lucrecia Biáfara, from a *maniel* just outside Santo Domingo (note how their origin in Africa is indicated by their names: Luis from Angola in Central Africa and Lucrecia from Biafra in what is today southeastern Nigeria). In 1609, Captain Estéban Peguero discovered another *maniel* just seven leagues from the capital, and there was another in Hozama with hundreds of slaves, one near Higüey, one in Seibo and in Cotuí, and several in the mountains of Bahoruco, one of which had already enjoyed 80 years of freedom. In 1649, a *maniel* headed by Juan Angola was discovered just north of Baní with a population of more than 200 Africans. On the offshore island of Tortuga and along Hispaniola's north coast, fugitive slaves and foreign privateers began butchering wild cattle and selling the meat (dried on green-stick racks that the Taíno called *bucanes*) to passing ships—they were called buccaneers.

As the colony experienced economic decline in the 17th century, slavery also declined. While it was never abolished, by the beginning of the 18th century, almost all people of color in the colony were free. And with the departure of the white settlers for greener pastures on the mainland and the extermination of the remaining Taíno, almost all the free inhabitants of the island were of at least partially African descent. In a sense, the history of the free people of color of Santo Domingo from this point forward is the history of the colony. However, the older established and lighter-skinned free colored families began self-identifying as white, preserving divisions on the basis of skin color.

By 1677, the French, encountering little Spanish opposition, had already established a dozen sugarcane plantations on the western third of Hispaniola, and runaway slaves from these plantations were already seeking refuge among the Spaniards. Thus was born San Lorenzo de Los Minas in the 1720s, a community of a former slaves (mostly Minas from Angola) just outside Santo Domingo. The runaways were granted freedom in exchange for agreeing to help fight the French. Thirty years later, Los Minas was so large that it supported three black MILITIA companies—comprising more than 1,000 men.

There were other *manieles* all over the island, even in Samaná, the northeasternmost peninsula, that were populated by fugitive slaves from the French plantations. The largest *maniel* of all, located in the Sierra de Ocoa, was called Maniel and was home to more than 600 fugitive families. To survive, the *manieles* were in isolated regions, but their residents traded gold, hides, and tobacco in the Spanish towns for goods that they could not produce themselves. In the process, they gathered information about the cry for freedom, liberty, and brotherhood that was getting louder on the French side of the island during the HAITIAN REVOLUTION that began in 1791.

At the end of October 1796, more than 200 black slaves on the Boca de Nigua plantation just west of Santo Domingo rebelled—the largest revolt ever on the Spanish side of the island—declaring liberty for all and forming a revolutionary government. The rebellion was quickly put down, and the leaders, Francisco Sopo, Antonio Carretero, Petit Juan, Pedro Viejo, and Tomás Congo, were hanged and quartered. Just five years later, however, TOUSSAINT LOUVERTURE marched into Santo Domingo unopposed to take over "Spanish Haiti," for the majority of the island's populace was in favor of unification under the new Haitian Republic. On January 26, 1801, Toussaint declared freedom for all former slaves and proclaimed racial equality.

The next two decades in Hispaniola were chaotic. In February 1802, the French retook Spanish Haiti and reinstated slavery. Battles between the French and Haitians were constant, with Spaniards caught in the middle. The populations of entire towns were slaughtered. The French occupation force often did not distinguish between Haitian rebels and Spanish inhabitants, especially since the Spanish shared the Haitians' African ancestry to some degree. Desperate, in 1809, residents asked to become a Spanish colony again. The Iberian Spaniards were astonished to find out how "colored" the "Spaniards" of Spanish Haiti were and told them that if they lived in CUBA, they would be slaves. Nonetheless, Spain was becoming more liberal. In 1812, its new Cádiz Constitution granted the same political rights to all criollos (Spaniards born in the Americas) as peninsular Spaniards had and opened all the universities and seminaries to free descendants of Africans. They did not, however, abolish slavery.

Wanting a return to Haitian rule, to freedom, a number of slaves and free people of color, led by José Leocadio, Pedro de Seda, Pedro Henríquez, and Marcos, rebelled against the Spaniards. Despite their executions and José Núñez de Cáceres's (1772–1846) brief attempt in 1821 to create the Independent State of Spanish Haiti, most of the populace favored Haitian rule. In February 1822, JEAN-PIERRE BOYER, president of Haiti, marched unopposed to take over Spanish Haiti, once again declaring slavery to be abolished across the island. In 1844, Spanish patriots declared and successfully fought for their independence from Haiti and signed into law a resolution that the new Dominican Republic would never permit slavery to be reestablished within its territory.

During the remainder of the 19th century, the Dominican Republic evolved a society where Spanish identity was in a difficult balance with African ancestry. Conservative Dominicans continued to hope for annexation by Spain, and colonial rule was reestablished for a brief period in the 1860s. One of their hopes was that Spanish rule would facilitate white immigration, leading to a whitening of the Dominican population. This process was under way in Spanish-owned Cuba and PUERTO RICO, though immigration there was slowed by incidents of civil disorder. The Dominican Republic, on the other hand, attracted relatively few white immigrants in the 19th century, and the African-born segment of the population continued to grow as immigrants arrived from Haiti. The Dominican Republic, thus, was one of the few countries in Spanish America where the black and mulatto population grew in the late 19th century. The population of Haiti was (and remains) at least twice that of the republic, and the history of repeated occupations from the western part of the island made ruling elites very fearful. These racial fears led to heightened discrimination against people of obvious African ancestry, and to increasingly desperate attempts by Afro-Dominicans to change their racial identity by calling themselves mestizos or Indians or

anything but black or mulatto. The racial discrimination and the desire to reaffirm a Hispanic identity led to a terrible act of genocide, the slaughter of tens of thousands of black Dominicans and Haitian immigrants in 1937 by the troops and secret police of the dictator Rafael Leonidas Trujillo (1891–1961). Trujillo always justified his actions by saying that he was defending the country's Hispanic identity against Haitian immigrants and said the soldiers distinguished between Spanish-speaking Dominicans and Creole-speaking Haitians. In fact, many dark-skinned Dominicans whose families had been living in *manieles* for generations predominantly spoke the Creole of the western part of the island and so were also caught up in the massacre.

Lynne Guitar

FURTHER READING

Cruz, Shamil. "African Americans in the Caribbean and Latin America." Available online. URL: http://www.poaa.com/blacks_latin_america_etc.htm. Accessed December 22, 2010.

Deive, Carlos Estéban. *La esclavitud del negro en Santo Domingo (1492–1844).* Santo Domingo: Museo del Hombre Dominicano, 1980.

———. *Los guerrilleros negros: Esclavos fugitivos y cimarrones en Santo Domingo.* Santo Domingo: Fundación Cultural Dominicana, 1989.

Gage, Thomas. "Maroons and Free Blacks in Spanish America in the 1600s: Three Documents." Available online. URL: http://nationalhumanitiescenter.org/pds/amerbegin/power/text9/GageSpanishMaroons.pdf. Accessed December 22, 2010.

Moya Pons, Frank. *The Dominican Republic, National History.* New Rochelle, N.Y.: Hispaniola Books, 1995.

Price, Richard, ed. *Maroon Societies: Rebel Slave Communities in the Americas.* 3rd ed. Baltimore: Johns Hopkins University Press, 1996.

DOMINICANS, THE *(Order of Preachers, Roman Catholic religious order)*

The Dominican order was founded by St. Dominic (1170–1221), a Spanish Catholic gentleman whose uncle was an archbishop. He was greatly affected by the plight of poor people suffering in a famine in Spain in 1191 and dedicated his life to poverty. When visiting southern France, he encountered the Cathar movement, which the ROMAN CATHOLIC CHURCH saw as heretical. The church's response to the Cathars seemed to Dominic to be too reliant on pomp and wealth and harsh pronouncement of anathemas—formal religious condemnations of unorthodox beliefs—and directed exclusively at the upper classes. Dominic soon created a monastic community that shared

The Dominican friar Bartolomé de Las Casas (ca. 1484–1566). Las Casas was a stalwart defender of the Indians and helped formulate the Catholic Church's position, expressed in Pope Paul III's letter *Sublimus Dei* (1537), that all people of all races were human beings with souls and should have basic human rights. *(The Bridgeman Art Library)*

the life of ordinary people in order to preach orthodox Catholic doctrine to them. The Dominicans thus became one of the "mendicant" orders of friars, who lived in voluntary poverty and worked with excluded people to teach the Catholic faith. The Dominicans were not so severely devoted to poverty as the Franciscans, in part because they needed resources to operate schools, which became an important part of their mission. Dominican theologians and academics, including St. Thomas Aquinas (1225–74), have been very important to the development of Catholic thought. The Dominicans also supported the Inquisition with theologians and ordinary investigators, working against the Cathars in the Middle Ages and against Protestants, Jews, and Muslims in the early modern period.

As Spain and Portugal began colonizing the Western Hemisphere in the late 15th and 16th centuries, they called upon the Dominicans, as well as the other orders of friars, to evangelize the Americas. Dominican friars were among the earliest Catholic religious leaders to live in Hispaniola, MEXICO, and PERU. A young planter in Spanish SANTO DOMINGO, Bartolomé de Las Casas (ca. 1484–1566), heard a Dominican preacher condemn the mistreatment of Indian slaves and was so moved that he joined the Dominicans himself and worked throughout the remainder of his life to protect the Indians in Spanish America. Las Casas was instrumental in the Spanish government's adoption of the New Laws of the Indies (1542), which laid out the legal framework for the treatment of both Indians and blacks in the Americas. Las Casas was only one of many members of religious orders who confronted the abusive treatment of nonwhites by Spanish colonial officials. Other examples include his fellow Dominican St. Louis Bertrand (1526–81) in PANAMA; Archbishop Juan de Zumarraga (1468–1548), a Franciscan, in MEXICO; and St. Peter Claver (1580–1654), a Jesuit, in CARTAGENA, COLOMBIA.

Dominicans were important members of the Inquisition in Spanish America, as they had been in Spain and France. The Inquisition was particularly concerned with the orthodoxy of religious practice among free people of color. Indians, for the most part, were not subject to the Inquisition, as they were assumed to be insufficiently trained in proper Catholic beliefs to be held responsible for complete orthodoxy. Instead, their religious training was overseen by their parish priests, many of them in the religious orders. But all free people of African descent were subject to the Inquisition, and many of them were accused of religious unorthodoxy or blasphemy because of syncretic religious practices (see also AFRICAN AND SYNCRETIC RELIGIONS). Historians have found the records of the Inquisition an invaluable source for understanding the persistence of African culture in the Americas. Contrary to its public image, the Inquisition in the Americas

rarely "relaxed" offenders to the civil authorities for punishment, which could include death by burning or other forms of torture. Instead, their preference was to force people found guilty of syncretic practices to renounce their beliefs publicly and then impose some form of public humiliation as penance (the auto-a da-fé). Public recantation and formal humiliation of syncretic practitioners had a powerful effect on fellow believers, while a messy execution could often strengthen the faith of the unorthodox. Lesser punishments could be imposed and often were for blasphemy or other religious offenses. Fines and public humiliations for these offenses were quite common irritants in the lives of urban free people of color, as well as mestizos and poorer whites.

All the religious orders, including the Dominicans, occasionally enrolled nonwhites. Most nonwhite Dominicans, like St. MARTIN DE PORRES, were restricted to lower levels in the order's hierarchy. Martin spent most of his career as a lay brother and was only promoted to full membership in the order after his saintly reputation became widely known. He was never ordained a priest. The Dominicans were unusual in that their internal organization was democratic, with all full members of the order having a vote. Therefore, they were more reluctant than the other mendicant orders to give full membership to people of low social class—even St. Martin was the illegitimate son of the royal governor of Panama.

Stewart R. King

FURTHER READING
Cavallini, Giuliana. *Martin de Porres: Apostle of Charity.* Charlotte, N.C.: TAN Books, 1979.
Silverblatt, Irene. *Modern Inquisitions: Peru and the Colonial Origins of the Civilized World.* Durham, N.C.: Duke University Press, 2004.
Zagano, Phyllis. *The Dominican Tradition (Spirituality in History).* Collegeville, Minn.: Liturgical Press, 2006.

DORANTES, ESTÉBAN DE   (ca. 1500–1539)
Afro-Spanish explorer

Born around 1500, Estéban de Dorantes was a sub-Saharan African, possibly from the modern nations of Senegal or Mauretania, who was taken as a slave, probably while still a child, across the Sahara to the Portuguese enclave of Azemmour, Morocco (see also SENEGAMBIA). The Spanish records referred to him as *negro alárabe*, or Arabized black, perhaps suggesting that he was born in Morocco of African ancestors. In any case, during a famine in Morocco, he was sold to a Portuguese slave trader, who ultimately delivered him to Andrés Dorantes de Carranza, a Spaniard living in Seville. Estéban and his master lived for some years in Spain, and then Andrés

Dorantes joined Pánfilo de Narváez's expedition to conquer FLORIDA and took his servant with him.

Narváez took some 400 people, mostly Spaniards but with a number of Africans and Indians, to establish Spanish rule in Florida. Arriving on the coast in April 1528, they established a base near the modern Tampa, Florida. Narváez and a group of about 300, including Estéban and his master, proceeded inland to conquer the local Indians. The Indian defenders adopted guerrilla tactics and harassed the expedition. After four fruitless months, the survivors regrouped along the Gulf Coast of western Florida. The group they had left behind on the coast had tired of waiting for them and returned to Cuba. Narváez was quite ill, and the new leader, Álvar Núñez Cabeza de Vaca, suggested that they build boats and try to reach MEXICO by sea. They set sail in September, but a hurricane destroyed their ships and drove the survivors ashore near Galveston, Texas. Most of the survivors quickly died of disease or were killed by Indians, but Estéban, Andrés Dorantes, Cabeza de Vaca, and another Spaniard named Alonso del Castillo found a way to survive for six and a half years.

Estéban was the key to the survival of this little group. He dressed in any sort of flashy clothes that they could muster and went to Indian villages. His remarkable appearance and natural acting talent (and perhaps some real medical skills) convinced the Indians that he was a shaman and a healer. The Indians would care for Estéban, and he shared his food with his white companions. The Indians would also introduce the group to their neighbors, and in this way, passing from one Indian tribe to the next, they travelled from south Texas across the continent to Arizona, then to Sonora, Mexico, where they finally encountered a group of Spanish slave raiders in March 1536.

Estéban and his companions arrived in July 1536 in Mexico City, where they made a report to the viceroy and to the archbishop of Mexico City, Juan de Zumárraga. There was a great power struggle going on between the archbishop, and by extension, the ROMAN CATHOLIC CHURCH, and the Spanish civil administration over the treatment of the Indians. Zumárraga took advantage of the story of Estéban and his companions to show that a policy of kindness and cultural sensitivity would produce more results in terms of converts and expansion of Spanish rule than the current policy of violent conquest. He had to report the story of the survivors with care, because much of what they did had little to do with Catholic proselytism. However, it was true that Estéban and the others had succeeded in voyaging without any violence for more than six years in the interior of northern Mexico and the American Southwest, in areas that Spanish parties travelling up from Mexico found almost impassable because of the hostility of the local Indians.

Cabeza de Vaca returned to Spain and published a highly colored version of his adventures, in which Estéban appears, though in a minor role. All sorts of wild stories about the wealth of the area can be found in Cabeza de Vaca's book, which was wildly popular. These stories provoked more expeditions of conquistadores, who sought out the advice of those who had gone before. It is unclear when or whether Estéban ever formally gained his freedom. Older sources said he was a free black, and colonial records show that the government purchased him from Andrés Dorantes in 1538. Estéban's most recent biographer believes that instead of freeing Estéban, the viceroy, Antonio de Mendoza, kept him as his own slave. In any case, Estéban was employed as the chief scout of an expedition to the rumored "Seven Cities of Gold," thought to be in what is now the American Southwest. The expedition was headed by Marcos de Niza, a Franciscan missionary, who hoped to take advantage of Estéban's skills to induce Indian villages to accept the Catholic faith peacefully. Estéban was in charge of a party of Mexican Indian scouts. He left the expedition after Easter 1539, in northwest Mexico, on an extended scouting trip to find Indian villages that might be willing to listen to Niza. He was apparently killed at the Zuñi pueblos in what is now Arizona sometime that spring.

The story of Estéban is remarkable. He was the effective leader of the first recorded group of people to travel across the North American continent from the Atlantic to the Pacific coast. He explored a good deal of northern Mexico and what is now the southwestern United States. He was one of what we have come now to realize were dozens or hundreds of black conquistadores who made invaluable contributions to Spanish expansionism in the Americas. His methods were not at all those of his Spanish contemporaries, though. He foreshadowed in some ways the missionary and exploratory work of French JESUITS in northeastern North America, but his example, for all the urging of Archbishop Zumárraga and the Franciscans, had little impact on Spanish religious practice. He was a man of many identities who lived in at least three very different worlds in his lifetime: the Mediterranean, Spanish America, and Native America.

Stewart R. King

FURTHER READING

Cabeza de Vaca, Álvar Núñez. *Chronicle of the Narváez Expedition.* Translated by Fanny Bandelier; revised and annotated by Harold Augenbraum; introduction by Ilan Stavans. New York: Penguin, 2002.

Goodwin, Robert. *Crossing the Continent, 1527–1540: The Story of the First African-American Explorer of the American South.* New York: HarperCollins, 2008.

Oviedo y Valdés, Gonzalo Fernández de. *General and Natural History of the Indies.* Book 35. Translated by Basil Hendrick. Published as *The Journey of the Vaca Party: The Account of the Narváez Expedition, 1528–1536.* Carbondale: Southern Illinois University Press, 1974.

DOS REIS, MARIA FIRMINA   *See* REIS, MARIA FIRMINA DOS.

DOUGLAS, SIR JAMES   (1803–1877) *Canadian business leader and statesman*

Sir James Douglas was a significant figure in the British North American fur trade but is best known as the first governor of the Colony of British Columbia, today a province of CANADA.

Born on August 15, 1803, in New Amsterdam, in the Dutch colony of Berbice (present-day Guyana), Douglas was the illegitimate second child of Martha Ann Ritchie, a free colored woman originally from BARBADOS, and John Douglas, a merchant planter from Glasgow, Scotland, who had prospered from his investments in West Indian sugar and cotton plantations. Douglas was raised by his mother and grandmother until the age of nine, when John Douglas took James and his brother Alexander to Scotland, where they attended the respected Lanark Grammar School.

In 1819, young James returned to the Americas, this time to Canada, where he entered the service of the North West Company (NWC) as an apprentice clerk. Founded in 1776 and headquartered in Montréal, the NWC was one of the largest enterprises competing for control of the lucrative North American fur trade. East of the Rocky Mountains, it aggressively challenged the monopoly of the London-based Hudson's Bay Company (HBC). By the first decade of the 19th century, the NWC had extended its operations to the largely unknown territories beyond the Rocky Mountains, and it was there that Douglas made his name.

In 1820, the year after Douglas arrived in North America, the NWC merged with the HBC. The HBC acquired the NWC's trading posts west of the Rocky Mountains, and in 1825, Douglas, who had been working at various posts in the Saskatchewan and Peace River districts, was reassigned to Fort St. James in what is now northern British Columbia. There, in 1828, he married Amelia Connolly, the daughter of a Scottish fur trader and a native Cree woman. "Country marriages" between Indian or mixed-race women and non-Indian men were common during the fur trade era because there were few non-Indian women in the fur trade country and because these intimate relationships helped to solidify business relationships between the company and its Indian sup-

pliers. Two years after their marriage, James and Amelia moved to Fort Vancouver (present-day Vancouver, Washington), where James had been transferred to fill an accountant's position at this important HBC depot. There he won the admiration of the chief factor, Dr. John McLaughlin, and served as second in command of the company's Columbia Department.

By the terms of an 1818 convention, British subjects and American citizens had equal rights to trade and settle in the "Oregon Country," which extended from the Rocky Mountains to the Pacific Ocean and from California to Alaska. By the 1840s, however, the influx of American settlers made continued joint occupancy by the two countries untenable. In 1843, Douglas sailed to Vancouver Island seeking a new site for an HBC headquarters. At the southern tip of the island, he founded a new trading post and named it Fort Victoria after Queen Victoria. His action was prescient, for in 1846, the Oregon Boundary Treaty set the 49th parallel as the boundary between British and American possessions, and the HBC was forced to abandon Fort Vancouver. In 1849, the British government granted the company exclusive trading rights on Vancouver Island and organized the island as a colony. Richard Blanshard was appointed the first governor, but relations between Blanshard and Douglas, now the senior HBC official west of the Rockies, were frosty, and Blanshard resigned after less than a year. Douglas was appointed to replace him, and during his term in office, he presided over settlement promotion efforts and the organization of a colonial administration. However, the colony failed to attract many settlers, and as late as 1858, Vancouver Island was home to only a few hundred non-Indian residents.

This changed with the discovery of gold on the banks of the Fraser River on the mainland, as yet an unorganized fur trade preserve. Within a matter of months, as many as 30,000 miners, predominantly Americans from CALIFORNIA, streamed into the region. Fearing that the American settlers would demand annexation to the United States, as had happened in California and OREGON, Douglas proposed to the British government that the mainland territory be organized into a separate crown colony. London assented, and on November 19, 1858, the Colony of British Columbia was officially proclaimed, with Douglas as its governor. He also retained the governorship of Vancouver Island, although the two colonies remained constitutionally separate.

Douglas's leadership style was autocratic and authoritarian. Believing, with good reason, that the American miners remained loyal to the United States and that they would use democratic institutions to promote annexation, he hesitated to establish an elected assembly in British Columbia, and he was vilified by the local press.

However, he also undertook an ambitious program of road construction, and perhaps because of his own ancestry, he pursued a policy of racial accommodation that was remarkably progressive for its day. The treaties he negotiated with native groups around Fort Victoria, still called "the Douglas Treaties," were the only formal treaties signed in British Columbia before the 1990s. Most intriguingly, he encouraged blacks fleeing persecution in California to settle on Vancouver Island, and his decision to enfranchise black settlers provoked criticism from his political rivals, who feared that black voters would help to elect legislators sympathetic to the governor. He also encouraged the formation of a black MILITIA unit, the Victoria Pioneer Rifle Company, known informally as the "African Rifles."

In 1863, Douglas was knighted for his service to the British Crown, and the following year he resigned his governorships. In retirement, he opposed the unification of Vancouver Island and British Columbia in 1866 and was not enthusiastic about the federation of British Columbia with Canada in 1871. He died on August 2, 1877, in Victoria, British Columbia. Historians have treated him kindly, and even his critics acknowledge that without his firm resolve the British Pacific possessions would probably have been annexed to the United States. This creole from Guyana is now justly regarded as "the father of British Columbia."

Forrest D. Pass

FURTHER READING

Adams, John. *Old Square-Toes and His Lady: The Life of James and Amelia Douglas.* Victoria, Canada: Horsdal & Schubert, 2001.

Kilian, Crawford. *Go Do Some Great Thing: The Black Pioneers of British Columbia.* Vancouver, Canada: Douglas & McIntyre, 1978.

DOUGLASS, FREDERICK (1818–1895) *American orator, journalist, reformer, and statesman*

The most prominent African American of the 19th century was born into slavery as Frederick Augustus Washington Bailey, in Tuckahoe, MARYLAND, the exact date uncertain although Douglass later concluded it was February 14, 1818. Douglass saw his mother, Harriet Bailey, only four or five times because she was sold to another slave owner 12 miles away and died when Douglass was eight or nine. He believed that his father was the white plantation owner Captain Aaron Anthony.

Douglass lived initially with his maternal grandmother but in 1824 was moved to the plantation of Colonel Edward Lloyd and in 1825 was sent to Baltimore to live with the Hugh Auld family. He served the household for seven years, all the while discovering the world of ideas and politics and learning how to read, largely by using old newspapers and a rhetoric textbook.

Douglass returned to a plantation near St. Michael's, Maryland, in 1832 and in 1833 organized a secret school for slaves. The school was eventually broken up by a white mob, and he was hired out to a "slave breaker." He continued to rebel by organizing another secret school in 1836 after he had been transferred to yet another farmer. When in that year Douglass tried to escape but was discovered, Auld returned him to Baltimore, where, for the next two years, he worked as a caulker in various shipyards. He also met his future wife, Anna Murray, a free woman of color, and took advantage of his situation to talk to and learn from free blacks about the issues of the day—particularly the growing controversy of slavery.

In September 1838, Douglass escaped his bondage by impersonating a sailor and traveling north. He and Murray married in New York City and then settled in New Bedford, MASSACHUSETTS, where he worked as a caulker and engaged in other manual labor. To protect himself against slave catchers, he selected a new name: Frederick Douglass.

Over the next decade, his family expanded and his reputation spread. He began reading William Lloyd Garrison's militant the *Liberator*, and his political and social thinking grew and evolved. In August 1841, attending the convention of the Massachusetts Antislavery Society in Nantucket, he was asked to speak. Thus began his career as an abolitionist and orator. The officers of the Antislavery Society, seeing his skill and charisma, enlisted him as an agent, and over the next four years he became one of their star speakers. Anyone who heard him was impressed by his tall stature, his flowing hair, his baritone voice, and the moral clarity of his words.

From 1841 to 1843, he gave hundreds of speeches throughout NEW YORK STATE and New England. He made his first visit to Rochester, New York, in 1842 to attend a convention of blacks, and in 1843 he participated in the One Hundred Conventions tour throughout Upstate New York, OHIO, INDIANA, and western PENNSYLVANIA. At the 1843, National Convention of Colored Americans in Buffalo, the Reverend HENRY HIGHLAND GARNET delivered an impassioned address calling for a slave uprising—a call that Douglass convinced the convention not to endorse, thereby initiating a Garnet-Douglass rivalry that continued for 40 years.

Ironically, Douglass was such a stirring and articulate speaker on the lecture circuit that rumors spread that he had not actually been a slave, despite the experiences he recounted at the lectern. Partially in response to those doubts, in 1845 he published the first of three versions of his autobiography: *Narrative of the Life of Frederick Douglass, an American Slave.* The volume became a best seller in the United States and Britain; was soon was translated into French, German, and Dutch; and transformed Douglass into the best-known black man in the world.

But the volume endangered his personal freedom by revealing his location and his previous identity. In August 1845, therefore, he sailed to Europe, where for 20 months he toured England, Scotland, and Ireland, giving antislavery lectures and being feted by prominent reformers. His new supporters also provided funds to begin an antislavery newspaper, and English Quakers helped him to raise funds to purchase his freedom from Hugh Auld. In 1846, consequently, he was able to purchase his freedom for £150, and in August 1847, he returned to the United States a legally free man of color.

Douglass also returned to the United States with the confidence to disagree with the Garrison-dominated abolition movement. He ignored Garrison's advice by moving to Rochester in November 1847 and launching the *North Star*, a weekly newspaper, which in later years became *Frederick Douglass' Paper* and finally *Douglass' Monthly*. Rochester was a center of social, religious, and political reform movements, but initially, residents were not happy about having *North Star* associated with their city. The New York *Herald* urged them to dump the printing press into Lake Ontario.

Nevertheless, the newspaper, with a largely black readership, enabled Douglass to declare his independence from the white Garrisonian abolitionist establishment. Residing in Rochester also put him in contact with other reform movements—particularly the women's rights movement—and facilitated his involvement with the Underground Railroad.

He also resumed a grueling lecture schedule, sometimes spending six months of the year on the road. He needed the lecture fees to support his newspaper, which he had mortgaged his home to subsidize. In addition, he strengthened his connections with women's rights leaders, particularly Elizabeth Cady Stanton, and attended the 1848 Seneca Falls Convention, where he spoke in favor of women's right to vote. In the same year, at the Free Soil Convention in Buffalo, he endorsed that party's call for prohibiting slavery extension and was elected president of the Negro Convention Movement in the United States, meeting in Cleveland.

Traveling in England in 1848, Douglass met Julia Griffiths, who returned to Rochester with him, took up residence in the Douglass house, and tutored the Douglass children and his wife, Anna. Over the next three years (1848–51), Griffiths served as Douglass's "office manger" and was seen with him constantly, a cause of some scandal in Rochester, whose residents were unac-

A lithograph portrait of Frederick Douglass (1818–95), from a photograph, as he looked in the years after the American Civil War. Douglass was an escaped slave from Maryland, who became an author, lecturer, journalist, and one of America's foremost activists for abolition and civil rights. Douglass pointed out the fundamental contradiction between slavery and American ideals in his famous speech "What to the Slave Is the Fourth of July?" *(Library of Congress)*

customed to seeing a black man and a white woman together. Under Griffiths's guidance *North Star* ceased to be a money-losing operation by 1851.

During the turbulent 1840s and 1850s, as conflict over slavery intensified, Douglass moved steadily away from the "moral suasion" of William Lloyd Garrison and toward more militant political tactics. Although in 1843 he had opposed Garnet's call for a slave uprising, in 1849 he publicly expressed his wish for a bloody uprising in the South. In 1850, *North Star* denounced the harsh Fugitive Slave Act of 1850 enacted by Congress, and he began to call widely for resistance to the act.

His increasingly radical stance seemed to peak in 1852, when he published a novella, *The Heroic Slave*, in which the title character leads a violent slave uprising. The story was based on an 1841 rebellion aboard the slave ship *Creole*. In addition, on July 5, 1852, Douglass delivered his greatest address, one of the finest speeches in American history: "What to the Slave Is the Fourth of July?" In it, Douglass denounced America for its betrayal of the ideals of the Declaration of Independence and Constitution but, at the same time, expressed optimism that America's future was destined to be better and more just.

In June 1856, the new Republican Party nominated John C. Frémont for the presidency. Douglass endorsed Frémont and the party's platform calling for prohibition of slavery in the territories. Later that summer, the German journalist Ottilie Assing (1819–84) arrived in Rochester to interview Douglass. Assing was destined to spend the next 22 summers with Douglass, assisting with his writing and tutoring his children. Although the intimacy of the relationship is unclear, she apparently believed that Douglass would eventually marry her, because when he married a different white woman in 1884, two years after the death of Anna, Assing committed suicide, even as her will made Douglass her sole beneficiary.

In 1858, John Brown visited the Douglass home to work on plans for the Harpers Ferry raid that he hoped would spark a slave rebellion. Douglass's acquiescence to the visit signaled his growing radicalization on the slavery issue, even though he declined to assist in raising funds or actually participate in the raid. When Brown was arrested, Douglass, knowing that some of Brown's papers would include his name, fled to the safety of Canada and then sailed to Britain. He returned to the United States in May 1860 when he learned that his youngest child had died. By then, he had begun to consider alternative solutions to America's race dilemma—including resettlement of blacks in Haiti (*see also* EMIGRATION AND COLONIZATION).

But in the 1860 election, the Republicans, led by ABRAHAM LINCOLN, took the presidency in a sectional vote boding ill for the nation's future. When the nation split apart and the AMERICAN CIVIL WAR began in 1861, Douglass encouraged President Lincoln to make emancipation a goal and called for the use of black troops in the Union army. After the EMANCIPATION PROCLAMATION took effect in 1863, Douglass recruited for the 54th Massachusetts, a black infantry regiment, and worked for equality of black and white soldiers. When Lincoln was assassinated on April 14, 1865, Douglass spoke at a memorial service organized by African Americans in New York City.

In the postwar decades, Douglass turned to the new challenges of racial justice, urging former abolitionists to direct their energies to the work of equal rights. But African Americans were not the only citizens lacking full rights. In 1866, Douglass attended the convention of the Equal Rights Association, which addressed, in part, the proposition that black men should not be granted the right to vote unless all women also received it. The divergence between proponents of women's rights and African-American rights was highlighted when Douglass signaled his disagreement with the proposed "all or nothing" strategy and indicated that voting rights for black

Americans needed to be first. He devoted his energy on behalf of the Fifteenth Amendment to the Constitution and criticized President ANDREW JOHNSON's failure to endorse black voting rights.

Despite that criticism, President Johnson offered Douglass—the most prominent African American in the nation and a staunch Republican—the post of commissioner of the FREEDMEN'S BUREAU in 1867. Douglass might have wanted a federal appointment, but he supported General Oliver O. Howard in the position and therefore declined the offer. He continued to lecture around the country and work for African-American rights.

In 1870, he purchased the weekly *New National Era*, headquartered in Washington D.C. He edited the paper until 1871, when President ULYSSES S. GRANT appointed him assistant secretary to the commission of inquiry exploring U.S. annexation of Santo Domingo. The three commissioners traveled to Hispaniola to investigate conditions there, but Douglass, as secretary, remained in the United States. But he supported annexation and urged members of his race to support the plan.

In 1872, after Douglass's home in Rochester was destroyed by fire, he moved his family to Washington, closer to the locus of political activity and power. Douglass actively supported President Grant's reelection, expecting to be rewarded with a federal appointment. When Grant won the election but failed to offer Douglass a position, he returned to the lecture circuit. But two years later, because of his prestige, he was elected president of the Freedmen's Savings and Trust Company, the troubled institution that had been created to assist former slaves in adjusting to life as free citizens by learning the habits of personal financial management and thrift. By 1874, the bank was suffering from overexpansion, mismanagement, and the effects of the panic of 1873. Douglass took with him his prestige, connections with congressional leaders, and considerable personal funds, but by that point conditions at the bank had passed anything that even a Douglass could do. The bank failed in June 1874, and thousands of African Americans lost their life savings. Douglass, in turn, lost $10,000 that he had invested in the bank.

The year 1877 brought the inauguration of President Rutherford B. Hayes and the end of RECONSTRUCTION IN THE UNITED STATES and federal commitment to racial justice. Douglass remained a staunch supporter of the party of Lincoln and an advocate of moderation and individualism, positions for which the newer generation of African-American leaders criticized him. He remained, nevertheless, the preeminent leader of his race. Hayes appointed him U.S. marshal for the District of Columbia (1877–81), a minor position but recognition of his contributions to the work of the party and reform.

In 1878, he purchased a nine-acre estate in the Anacostia area of Washington. In 1881, President James Garfield appointed him recorder of deeds for the District of Columbia (1881–86), and in the same year, he published the third version of his autobiography, *Life and Times of Frederick Douglass.*

In 1882, his wife of more than 40 years, Anna Murray Douglass, died. Two years later, Douglass resigned as recorder of deeds and married his secretary, Helen Pitts, a white woman from Honeoye, New York, 20 years his junior. The interracial marriage was controversial within both the Pitts and Douglass families and American society generally, but Douglass brushed off the criticism. He and his new wife toured Britain, France, Italy, Egypt, and Greece (1886–87) and then returned to the United States in time for Douglass to campaign for another Republican presidential candidate, Benjamin Harrison.

Harrison was elected, and in 1889, he appointed Douglass minister-resident and consul general to Haiti and chargé d'affaires to Santo Domingo (1889–91). Since the United States was becoming increasingly interested in establishing a naval base at Môle Saint-Nicholas in Haiti, Douglass had a potentially important role to play in representing U.S. foreign policy in the Caribbean. Haitians knew about his career and his stature, so he was well received and began his responsibilities with considerable political credibility. But his activities in Haiti were less than successful, and he tended to be used by Secretary of State James G. Blaine to further American expansionist interests. Although he supported the naval base plan, he became the scapegoat when Haiti rejected the offer, and he resigned, partially in response to criticism of his role.

In the last few years of his life, Douglass continued to work for racial justice, even at a time when racial conflicts and lynchings were increasing. He served as the only African-American official at the World's Columbian Exposition in Chicago, leading the Haitian legation to that exposition (1892–93). His long-standing belief in the importance of economic empowerment for his race moved him to the ill-advised decision to let unsavory promoters use his name in creating a fraudulent manufacturing company in Virginia that, purportedly, would employ hundreds of blacks but that, in actuality, was a scam.

Douglass died at his home in Washington, D.C., on February 20, 1895. The best-known and most influential African American of his era, and one of the greatest orators of American history, he devoted his life to reform and to racial justice. Throughout a long career marked by frequent triumphs and occasional setbacks, he never lost his faith in America's possibilities. The Civil Rights movement of mid- to late-20th-century America can justifiably be seen as the legacy of Frederick Douglass.

Kenneth Blume

FURTHER READING

Blassingame, John, ed. *The Frederick Douglass Papers, Series One: Speeches, Debates, and Interviews.* 5 vols. New Haven, Conn.: Yale University Press, 1979–1992.

Blight, David W. *Frederick Douglass' Civil War: Keeping Faith in Jubilee.* Baton Rouge: Louisiana State University Press, 1989.

Brown, William Wells. *The Black Man, His Antecedents, His Genius, and His Achievements.* New York: Thomas Hamilton, 1863.

Diedrich, Maria. *Love across Color Lines: Ottilie Assing and Frederick Douglass.* New York: Hill & Wang, 1999.

Douglass, Frederick. *Frederick Douglass, Autobiographies.* Edited by Henry Louis Gates, Jr. New York: Library of America, 1994.

Foner, Philip S., ed. *Frederick Douglass. Selected Speeches and Writings.* Abridged and adapted by Yuval Taylor. Chicago: Lawrence Hill Books, 1999.

Huggins, Nathan Irvin. *Slave and Citizen: The Life of Frederick Douglass.* Boston: Little, Brown, 1980.

Lampe, Gregory P. *Frederick Douglass: Freedom's Voice.* East Lansing: Michigan State University Press, 1998.

Lawson, Bill E., and Frank M. Kirkland, eds. *Frederick Douglass: A Critical Reader.* Oxford, U.K.: Blackwell, 1999.

McFeely, William S. *Frederick Douglass.* New York: Norton, 1991.

Oakes, James. *The Radical and the Republican: Frederick Douglass, Abraham Lincoln, and the Triumph of Antislavery Politics.* New York: Norton, 2007.

Quarles, Benjamin. *Frederick Douglass.* Washington D.C.: Associated Publishers, 1948.

"WHAT TO THE SLAVE IS THE FOURTH OF JULY?" SPEECH BY FREDERICK DOUGLASS, JULY 5, 1852

One of the greatest American orators of the 19th century, Frederick Douglass (1818–95) delivered more than 2,000 speeches and built an oratorical reputation with his sonorous voice and dramatic delivery. Initially an advocate of the "moral suasion" approach to abolition, by 1852 Douglass—who had escaped from slavery in 1838—had begun to advocate more militant strategies.

Douglass's address occurred as the controversy over American slavery was intensifying. The Fugitive Slave Act of 1850 required federal marshals to return runaway slaves, made assisting runaway slaves a crime, and denied suspected runaways the right to a trial. In 1852, Harriet Beecher Stowe published Uncle Tom's Cabin—*an immediate best seller that attacked the institution of slavery. Meanwhile, many Northern blacks fled to Canada, fearful of being sent south as "fugitive slaves."*

Douglass spoke at the Rochester Ladies' Anti-Slavery Society, Corinthian Hall, Rochester, New York. Invited to speak on

July 4, he chose instead July 5—a traditional preference for African-American speakers.

This address is often considered Douglass's greatest speech, and the preeminent antislavery speech. A "rhetorical masterwork of irony," according to the historian Robert E. Terrell, it follows the structure of the African-American jeremiad: (a) a reminder of the promises of freedom inherent in America's founding documents, (b) an outline of America's failures to deliver on the promise, and (c) a prophecy of future success and happiness. If Uncle Tom's Cabin is "the fictional masterpiece of American abolitionism," the historian David W. Blight has written, then Douglass's address is "abolition's rhetorical masterpiece."

Douglass's audience of 600 white abolitionists must have cringed at the ferocity of his indictment of America's hypocrisies. But the address ends with a soaring articulation of 19th-century optimism about a better future. When Douglass concluded, the audience burst into thunderous applause.

Mr. President, Friends and Fellow Citizens . . . This, for the purpose of this celebration, is the 4th of July. It is the birthday of your National Independence, and of your political freedom. This, to you, is what the Passover was to the emancipated people of God. It carries your minds back to the day, and to the act of your great deliverance; and to the signs, and to the wonders, associated with that act, and that day. This celebration also marks the beginning of another year of your national life; and reminds you that the Republic of America is now 76 years old. . . .

[Douglas goes on tell the story of America's independence.]

I leave, therefore, the great deeds of your fathers to other gentlemen whose claim to have been regularly descended will be less likely to be disputed than mine!

My business, if I have any here today, is with the present. The accepted time with God and his cause is the everliving now.

Trust no future, however pleasant,
Let the dead past bury its dead;
Act, act in the living present,
Heart within, and God overhead.[1] . . .

We have to do with the past only as we can make it useful to the present and to the future. To all inspiring motives, to noble deeds which can be gained from the past, we are welcome. But now is the time, the important time. Your fathers have lived, died, and have done their work, and have done much of it well. You live and must die, and you must do your work. You have no right to enjoy a child's share in the labor of your fathers, unless your children are to be blest by your labors. You have no right to wear out and waste the hard-earned fame of your fathers to cover your indolence. Sydney Smith tells us that men sel-

dom eulogize the wisdom and virtues of their fathers, but to excuse some folly or wickedness of their own. This truth is not a doubtful one.

There are illustrations of it near and remote, ancient and modern. It was fashionable, hundreds of years ago, for the children of Jacob to boast, we have "Abraham to our father," when they had long lost Abraham's faith and spirit.[2] That people contented themselves under the shadow of Abraham's great name, while they repudiated the deeds which made his name great. Need I remind you that a similar thing is being done all over this country to-day? Need I tell you that the Jews are not the only people who built the tombs of the prophets, and garnished the sepulchres of the righteous? Washington could not die fill he had broken the chains of his slaves. Yet his monument is built up by the price of human blood, and the traders in the bodies and souls of men, shout—"We have Washington to our father." Alas! that it should be so; yet so it is.

The evil that men do, lives after them,
The good is oft' interred with their bones.[3]

"What have I, or those I represent, to do with your national independence?"

Fellow-citizens, pardon me, allow me to ask, why am I called upon to speak here to-day? What have I, or those I represent, to do with your national independence? Are the great principles of political freedom and of natural justice, embodied in that Declaration of Independence, extended to us? and am I, therefore, called upon to bring our humble offering to the national altar, and to confess the benefits and express devout gratitude for the blessings resulting from your independence to us?

Would to God, both for your sakes and ours, that an affirmative answer could be truthfully returned to these questions! Then would my task be light, and my burden easy and delightful. For who is there so cold, that a nation's sympathy could not warm him? Who so obdurate and dead to the claims of gratitude, that would not thankfully acknowledge such priceless benefits? Who so stolid and selfish, that would not give his voice to swell the hallelujahs of a nation's jubilee, when the chains of servitude had been tom from his limbs? I am not that man. In a case like that, the dumb might eloquently speak, and the "lame man leap as an hart."[4]

But, such is not the state of the case. I say it with a sad sense of the disparity between us. I am not included within the pale of this glorious anniversary! Your high independence only reveals the immeasurable distance between us. The blessings in which you, this day, rejoice, are not enjoyed in common. The rich inheritance of justice, liberty, prosperity and independence, bequeathed by your fathers, is shared by you, not by me. The sunlight that brought life and healing to you, has brought stripes and death to me. This Fourth [of] July is yours, not mine.

You may rejoice, I must mourn. To drag a man in fetters into the grand illuminated temple of liberty, and call upon him to join you in joyous anthems, were inhuman mockery and sacrilegious irony. Do you mean, citizens, to mock me, by asking me to speak to-day? If so, there is a parallel to your conduct. And let me warn you that it is dangerous to copy the example of a nation whose crimes, lowering up to heaven, were thrown down by the breath of the Almighty, burying that nation in irrecoverable ruin! I can to-day take up the plaintive lament of a peeled and woe-smitten people!

By the rivers of Babylon, there we sat down. Yea! we wept when we remembered Zion. We hanged our harps upon the willows in the midst thereof. For there, they that carried us away captive, required of us a song; and they who wasted us required of us mirth, saying, Sing us one of the songs of Zion. How can we sing the Lord's song in a strange land? If I forget thee, O Jerusalem, let my right hand forget her cunning. If I do not remember thee, let my tongue cleave to the roof of my mouth.[5]

Fellow-citizens; above your national, tumultous joy, I hear the mournful wail of millions! whose chains, heavy and grievous yesterday, are, to-day, rendered more intolerable by the jubilee shouts that reach them. If I do forget, if I do not faithfully remember those bleeding children of sorrow this day, "may my right hand forget her cunning, and may my tongue cleave to the roof of my mouth!"[6] To forget them, to pass lightly over their wrongs, and to chime in with the popular theme, would be treason most scandalous and shocking, and would make me a reproach before God and the world.

My subject, then fellow-citizens, is AMERICAN SLAVERY. I shall see, this day, and its popular characteristics, from the slave's point of view. Standing, there, identified with the American bondman, making his wrongs mine, I do not hesitate to declare, with all my soul, that the character and conduct of this nation never looked blacker to me than on this 4th of July!

Whether we turn to the declarations of the past, or to the professions of the present, the conduct of the nation seems equally hideous and revolting. America is false to the past, false to the present, and solemnly binds herself to be false to the future. Standing with God and the crushed and bleeding slave on this occasion, I will, in the name of humanity which is outraged, in the name of liberty which is fettered, in the name of the constitution and the Bible, which are disregarded and trampled upon, dare to call in question and to denounce, with all the emphasis I can command, everything that serves to perpetuate slavery—the great sin and shame of America!

"I will not equivocate; I will not excuse"[7]; I will use the severest language I can command; and yet not one word shall escape me that any man, whose judgement is not blinded by prejudice, or who is not at heart a slaveholder, shall not confess to be fight and just.

But I fancy I hear some one of my audience say, it is just in this circumstance that you and your brother abolitionists fail to make a favorable impression on the public mind. Would you argue more, and denounce less, would you persuade more, and rebuke less, your cause would be much more likely to succeed.

But, I submit, where all is plain there is nothing to be argued. What point in the anti-slavery creed would you have me argue? On what branch of the subject do the people of this country need light? Must I undertake to prove that the slave is a man? That point is conceded already. Nobody doubts it.

The slaveholders themselves acknowledge it in the enactment of laws for their government. They acknowledge it when they punish disobedience on the part of the slave. There are seventy-two crimes in the State of Virginia, which, if committed by a black man, (no matter how ignorant he be), subject him to the punishment of death; while only two of the same crimes will subject a white man to the like punishment.

What is this but the acknowledgement that the slave is a moral, intellectual and responsible being? The manhood of the slave is conceded. It is admitted in the fact that Southern statute books are covered with enactments forbidding, under severe fines and penalties, the teaching of the slave to read or to write.

When you can point to any such laws, in reference to the beasts of the field, then I may consent to argue the manhood of the slave. When the dogs in your streets, when the fowls of the air, when the cattle on your hills, when the fish of the sea, and the reptiles that crawl, shall be unable to distinguish the slave from a brute, then will I argue with you that the slave is a man!

For the present, it is enough to affirm the equal manhood of the negro race. Is it not astonishing that, while we are ploughing, planting and reaping, using all kinds of mechanical tools, erecting houses, constructing bridges, building ships, working in metals of brass, iron, copper, silver and gold; that, while we are reading, writing and cyphering, acting as clerks, merchants and secretaries, having among us lawyers, doctors, ministers, poets, authors, editors, orators and teachers; that, while we are engaged in all manner of enterprises common to other men, digging gold in California, capturing the whale in the Pacific, feeding sheep and cattle on the hill-side, living, moving, acting, thinking, planning, living in families as husbands, wives and children, and, above all, confessing and worshipping the Christian's God, and looking hopefully for life and immortality beyond the grave, we are called upon to prove that we are men!

Would you have me argue that man is entitled to liberty? that he is the rightful owner of his own body? You have already declared it. Must I argue the wrongfulness of slavery? Is that a question for Republicans? Is it to be settled by the rules of logic and argumentation, as a matter beset with great difficulty, involving a doubtful application of the principle of justice, hard to be understood? How should I look to-day, in the presence of Americans, dividing, and subdividing a discourse, to show that men have a natural right to freedom? speaking of it relatively, and positively, negatively, and affirmatively. To do so, would be to make myself ridiculous, and lo offer an insult to your understanding. There is not a man beneath the canopy of heaven, that does not know that slavery is wrong for him.

What, am I to argue that it is wrong to make men brutes, to rob them of their liberty, to work them without wages, to keep them ignorant of their relations to their fellow men, to beat them with sticks, to flay their flesh with the lash, to load their limbs with irons, to hunt them with dogs, to sell them at auction, to sunder their families, to knock out their teeth, to bum their flesh, to starve them into obedience and submission to their masters? Must I argue that a system thus marked with blood, and stained with pollution, is wrong? No! I will not. I have better employments for my time and strength, than such arguments would imply.

What, then, remains to be argued? Is it that slavery is not divine; that God did not establish it; that our doctors of divinity are mistaken? There is blasphemy in the thought. That which is inhuman, cannot be divine! Who can reason on such a proposition? They that can, may; I cannot. The time for such argument is past.

At a time like this, scorching irony, not convincing argument, is needed. O! had I the ability, and could I reach the nation's ear, I would, to-day, pour out a fiery stream of biting ridicule, blasting reproach, withering sarcasm, and stern rebuke. For it is not light that is needed, but fire; it is not the gentle shower, but thunder. We need the storm, the whirlwind, and the earthquake. The feeling of the nation must be quickened; the conscience of the nation must be roused; the propriety of the nation must be startled; the hypocrisy of the nation must be exposed; and its crimes against God and man must be proclaimed and denounced.

What, to the American slave, is your 4th of July? I answer: a day that reveals to him, more than all other days in the year, the gross injustice and cruelly to which he is the constant victim. To him, your celebration is a sham; your boasted liberty, an unholy license; your national greatness, swelling vanity; your sounds of rejoicing are empty and heartless; your denunciations of tyrants, brass fronted impudence; your shouts of liberty and equality, hollow mockery; your prayers and hymns, your sermons and thanksgivings, with all your religious parade, and solemnity, are, to him, mere bombast, fraud, deception, impiety, and hypocrisy—a thin veil to cover up crimes which would disgrace a nation of savages.

There is not a nation on the earth guilty of practices, more shocking and bloody, than are the people of these United States, at this very hour.

Go where you may, search where you will, roam through all the monarchies and despotisms of the old world, travel through South America, search out every abuse, and when you have found the last, lay your facts by the side of the every-day practices of this nation, and you will say with me, that, for revolting barbarity and shameless hypocrisy, America reigns without a rival . . .

[Douglass goes on to detail the horrendous abuses of the slave system.]

You boast of your love of liberty, your superior civilization, and your pure Christianity, while the whole political power of the nation (as embodied in the two great political parties), is solemnly pledged to support and perpetuate the enslavement of three millions of your countrymen. You hurl your anathemas at the crowned headed tyrants of Russia and Austria, and pride yourselves on your Democratic institutions, while you yourselves consent to be the mere tools and bodyguards of the tyrants of Virginia and Carolina.

You invite to your shores fugitives of oppression from abroad, honor them with banquets, greet them with ovations, cheer them, toast them, salute them, protect them, and pour out your money to them like water; but the fugitives from your own land you advertise, hunt, arrest, shoot and kill. You glory in your refinement and your universal education; yet you maintain a system as barbarous and dreadful as ever stained the character of a nation—a system begun in avarice, supported in pride, and perpetuated in cruelty.

You shed tears over fallen Hungary, and make the sad story of her wrongs the theme of your poets, statesmen and orators, till your gallant sons are ready to fly to arms to vindicate her cause against her oppressors; but, in regard to the ten thousand wrongs of the American slave, you would enforce the strictest silence, and would hail him as an enemy of the nation who dares to make those wrongs the subject of public discourse!

You are all on fire at the mention of liberty for France or for Ireland; but are as cold as an iceberg at the thought of liberty for the enslaved of America. You discourse eloquently on the dignity of labor; yet, you sustain a system which, in its very essence, casts a stigma upon labor. You can bare your bosom to the storm of British artillery to throw off a threepenny tax on tea; and yet wring the last hard-earned farthing from the grasp of the black laborers of your country.

You profess to believe "that, of one blood, God made all nations of men to dwell on the face of all the earth," and hath commanded all men, everywhere to love one another; yet you notoriously hate, (and glory in your hatred), all men whose skins are not colored like your own.

You declare, before the world, and are understood by the world to declare, that you "hotel these truths to be self evident, that all men are created equal; and are endowed by their Creator with certain inalienable rights; and that, among these are, life, liberty, and the pursuit of happiness;" and yet, you hold securely, in a bondage which, according to your own Thomas Jefferson, "is worse than ages of that which your fathers rose in rebellion to oppose," a seventh part of the inhabitants of your country.

Fellow-citizens! I will not enlarge further on your national inconsistencies. The existence of slavery in this country brands your republicanism as a sham, your humanity as a base pretence, and your Christianity as a lie. It destroys your moral power abroad; it corrupts your politicians at home. It saps the foundation of religion; it makes your name a hissing, and a by word to a mocking earth. It is the antagonistic force in your government, the only thing that seriously disturbs and endangers your Union.

It fetters your progress; it is the enemy of improvement, the deadly foe of education; it fosters pride; it breeds insolence; it promotes vice; it shelters crime; it is a curse to the earth that supports it; and yet, you cling to it, as if it were the sheet anchor of all your hopes. Oh! be warned! be warned! a horrible reptile is coiled up in your nation's bosom; the venomous creature is nursing at the tender breast of your youthful republic; for the love of God, tear away, and fling from you the hideous monster, and let the weight of twenty millions crush and destroy it forever! . . .

Allow me to say, in conclusion, notwithstanding the dark picture I have this day presented of the state of the nation, I do not despair of this country. There are forces in operation, which must inevitably work The downfall of slavery. "The arm of the Lord is not shortened,"[8] and the doom of slavery is certain. I, therefore, leave off where I began, with hope. While drawing encouragement from the Declaration of Independence, the great principles it contains, and the genius of American Institutions, my spirit is also cheered by the obvious tendencies of the age.

Nations do not now stand in the same relation to each other that they did ages ago. No nation can now shut itself up from the surrounding world, and trot round in the same old path of its fathers without interference. The time was when such could be done. Long established customs of hurtful character could formerly fence themselves in, and do their evil work with social impunity. Knowledge was then confined and enjoyed by the privileged few, and the multitude walked on in mental darkness. But a change has now come over the affairs of mankind. Walled cities and empires have become unfashionable.

The arm of commerce has borne away the gates of the strong city. Intelligence is penetrating the darkest corners of the globe. It makes its pathway over and under the sea, as well as on the earth. Wind, steam, and lightning are its chartered agents. Oceans no longer divide, but link nations together. From Boston to London is now a holiday excursion. Space is comparatively annihilated. Thoughts expressed on one side of the Atlantic are, distinctly heard on the other. The far off and almost fabulous Pacific rolls in grandeur at our feet. The Celestial Empire, the mystery of ages, is being solved. The fiat of the Almighty, "Let there be Light,"[9] has not yet spent its force. No abuse, no outrage whether in taste, sport or avarice, can now hide itself from the all-pervading light.

The iron shoe, and crippled foot of China must be seen, in contrast with nature. Africa must rise and put on her yet unwoven garment. "Ethiopia shall stretch out her hand unto God."[10] In the fervent aspirations of William Lloyd Garrison, I say, and let every heart join in saying it:

God speed the year of jubilee
The wide world o'er!
When from their galling chains set free,
Th' oppress'd shall vilely bend the knee,
And wear the yoke of tyranny
Like brutes no more. . . .[11]

---

1 Wadsworth Longfellow, "Present"
2 Matthew 3: 8–9
3 William Shakespeare, *Julius Caesar*, Act III, Scene 2.
4 Isaiah 35:6
5 Psalm 137: 1–4
6 Psalm 137: 5
7 William Lloyd Garrison, *Liberator,* January 1, 1831
8 Isaiah 59:1
9 Genesis 1:3
10 Psalm 68:31
11 William Lloyd Garrison, "Triumph of Freedom"

SOURCE: The full text of the address has been widely reproduced. *Frederick Douglass Selected Speeches and Writings,* edited by Philip S. Foner, abridged and adapted by Yuval Taylor, "Introduction" by Yuval Taylor, 188–206. Chicago: Lawrence Hill Books, 1999.

DUMAS, THOMAS-ALEXANDRE (THOMAS-ALEXANDRE DAVY DE LA PAILLETERIE)
(1762–1806) *French general*

Thomas-Alexandre Davy de la Pailleterie was born on March 25, 1762, in Jérémie, SAINT-DOMINGUE. His father was a French nobleman, the marquis de la Pailleterie. His mother was a free black woman, Marie-Césette Dumas, who may have been married to the marquis. It is unclear whether they were married because a nobleman would have been required to surrender his title if he married a woman of color under French law. In any case, Thomas-Alexandre and his three siblings were born free. He took his father's name and was known as de la Pailleterie until 1786. At that time, his father remarried, and in order to avoid criticism for his former relationship with a woman of color, he asked young Thomas-Alexandre to start using his mother's name.

After Dumas's mother died in 1774, he and his father moved to France. Even if Dumas had been born to

Thomas-Alexandre Dumas (1762–1806), French military officer. Fantastically strong and brave, Dumas led Napoléon's cavalry during his invasion of Egypt in 1798. His son, Alexandre Dumas, wrote *The Three Musketeers* and other adventure stories. *(Giraudon/The Bridgeman Art Library International)*

can ideals by ordering his officers to give up their gold and silver badges of rank. In 1794, he was deputy commander of the army sent to put down the rebellion in the Vendée, a particularly brutal guerrilla war fought between peasant rebels and the revolutionary government. The royalist rebels called him "the black devil." In 1796–97, he served under Napoléon in Italy, participating with distinction in the siege of Mantua. In one battle, he held a bridge alone against attacking Austrian cavalry until his own troops arrived to relieve him.

Dumas commanded the cavalry in the expedition to Egypt in 1798. He served with distinction in the early phase of the campaign but criticized Napoléon's plan to invade Syria. Napoléon dismissed him, and he set sail for France. His ship was wrecked, and he was taken prisoner by the Austrians. After two years in prison, he returned to France broken in health. He died on February 26, 1806. His only child, Alexandre Dumas *père* (1802–70), was the author of *The Three Musketeers, Man in the Iron Mask*, and many other adventure stories. One grandson, also named Alexandre (1824–91) and called *fils* (son), was also a popular author and playwright best known as the author of the story that became Verdi's opera *La Traviata*.

Stewart R. King

FURTHER READING

Maurois, Andre. *The Titans: A Three-Generation Biography of the Dumas*. Translated by Gerard Hopkins. New York: Harper, 1957.

DUNMORE, JOHN MURRAY, EARL OF
(1732–1809) *earl of Dunmore, last British royal governor of Virginia*

Known as Lord Dunmore, John Murray is most famous for waging a series of campaigns against Native Americans that became known as Dunmore's War and for issuing a proclamation in 1775 promising freedom to slaves who agreed to fight for the British in the WAR OF AMERICAN INDEPENDENCE, 1775–83. Dunmore's proclamation was the first large-scale emancipation of slaves in American history. Many of the former slaves whom Dunmore recruited later settled in CANADA and SIERRA LEONE.

Dunmore was born in Scotland in 1732, the son of William Murray, the third earl of Dunmore, and his wife, Catherine. He served in Parliament, succeeded his father as earl in 1756, and was appointed as the governor of NEW YORK, in 1770. When Virginia's governor died, Dunmore replaced him as the royal governor of the Colony of Virginia, a post he held from 1771 until 1776, when he returned to Britain.

married parents, his African ancestry made him ineligible for many of the benefits otherwise open to the children of nobles. His father arranged for him to join the French army as an enlisted man in 1786, serving in the Queen's Regiment of Dragoons. He was a good soldier and rose to the rank of corporal. In 1789, his regiment was stationed in Picardy, where he met and married Marie Elisabeth Louise Labouret, an innkeeper's daughter.

During the early stages of the wars of the FRENCH REVOLUTION, Dumas distinguished himself for his strength, bravery, and fighting spirit. The revolution opened up the military, and all other fields, to careers open to talent, which in the military meant to the toughest fighters. It is no accident that the high ranks of Napoléon's armies were full of prerevolutionary noncommissioned officers such as Dumas, who, like him, were very aggressive fighters. Stories are told about Dumas's strength: that he could pick up his own horse, or that in attacking one Austrian position, when his soldiers could not get over the wall, he picked them up one by one and threw them over. He was given a commission as an officer after he singlehandedly captured 12 Austrian skirmishers.

He rose rapidly through the ranks and in 1793–94 commanded a small army in the Alps with the rank of general of division. He cleared the passes of Piedmontese troops and distinguished himself for his republi-

Initially popular, Dunmore lost support as the colonial revolutionary movement gained momentum and he clashed with colonial leaders. He dissolved the Virginia House of Burgesses in 1773 and again in 1774 for its of procolonial actions, and he angered many by removing gunpowder from the magazine in Williamsburg in April 1775, after fighting had began in Lexington and Concord, MASSACHUSETTS. In June 1775, faced with a violent uprising, he took refuge aboard the warship HMS *Fowey* at Yorktown and thereafter began conducting raids for supplies and inviting slaves to join his forces.

In November 1775, Dunmore issued a proclamation that declared martial law; called all men to fight for royal forces, declaring those who would not to be traitors; and promised freedom to "all indented Servants, Negroes, or others" who would leave their proindependence masters to join royal forces.

His goals in recruiting slaves were practical rather than humanitarian: He hoped to gain new troops for his own forces, who were at that time cut off from British forces in BOSTON; deprive proindependence forces of labor; disrupt the economy; and create panic among the colonists who feared slave insurrections. As for the latter, Dunmore wanted Virginian planters to be consumed with protecting their assets from a domestic threat rather than investing their efforts and resources in war against Britain.

The publication of the proclamation outraged colonists, who responded by strengthening restrictions on meetings among slaves and warning slaves that they should not be tempted by Dunmore's offer. They also spread rumors that Dunmore, a slave owner himself, intended to sell slaves who escaped to his forces in the West Indies. In December 1775, Virginians issued the Virginia Declaration, which stated that slaves who had run away to join Dunmore's forces would be pardoned if they returned within 10 days but punished if they did not. The penalty for insurrection was death.

Ultimately, the Dunmore proclamation helped galvanize white colonists against British rule, as many saw the action as one more attempt to threaten private property. Further, the active recruitment of slaves by the British later led General GEORGE WASHINGTON to reverse his earlier opposition to enlisting free blacks and slaves to fight for the patriot cause and to accept their recruitment.

Approximately 800 black men were eventually inducted into what became known as Lord Dunmore's Ethiopian Regiment; they were issued uniforms with "Liberty to Slaves" inscribed upon them. The regiment was initially successful in battle, defeating the Virginia militia at the Battle of Kemp's Landing on November 15, 1775. However, Dunmore's forces were stopped by proindependence troops at Great Bridge on December 9. The Ethiopian Regiment suffered several hundred casu-

alties, and Dunmore had to retreat to his ships. By June 1776, illness in the form of smallpox and battle casualties had decimated Dunmore's forces, including the Ethiopian Regiment. In August, Dunmore left Virginia and sailed north to New England, taking his regular forces and about 150 blacks, including men, women, and children, with him. Among them, apparently, was the New Jersey runaway black COLONEL TYE, who went on to lead a very successful loyalist raiding force in New Jersey. General Washington's slave HARRY WASHINGTON may also have accompanied Dunmore on his withdrawal, or he may have left with another group of British raiders who attacked the Potomac estuary in 1776.

Dunmore's proclamation and the promises of other British leaders, especially the top commander, General Sir Henry Clinton (1730–95), led perhaps 100,000 blacks to join British forces. They served primarily as laborers, servants, or cooks, although some, such as those in Dunmore's Ethiopian Regiment, were soldiers. Many succumbed to disease or harsh conditions, some died in battle, and others remained the property of their loyalist owners or were recaptured by rebel owners. In the end, approximately 5,000 of the blacks who fought or served with the British were freed by their service. Many were transported to Nova Scotia, Canada, where some of the skilled workers found employment. Many of the former fieldhands ended up working as sharecroppers on land owned by white men. In 1792, prompted by an offer from a London abolition group, more than 1,000 Canadian blacks, most of them veterans of the American war, led by Harry Washington, traveled to and settled in Sierra Leone, establishing the city of Freetown.

From 1787 to 1796, Dunmore served as colonial governor of the Bahamas. During this time, many white SLAVE OWNERS from the American South who had fought against independence resettled in the Bahamas, and Dunmore's experience as governor of Virginia may have led them to feel that he would understand their culture better. A number of the blacks taken to the Bahamas and elsewhere in the British Caribbean at this time claimed that they had been freed as a result of war service. Dunmore's government and the governments of the other colonies did little about this problem, and ultimately some of these people were able to bring their freedom suits to courts in Britain, and some regained their freedom. Dunmore retired in 1796, returned to Scotland, and died on February 25, 1809.

Summer Leibensperger

FURTHER READING
Frey, Sylvia R. *Water from the Rock: Black Resistance in a Revolutionary Age.* Princeton, N.J.: Princeton University Press, 1991.

Holton, Woody. *Forced Founders: Indians, Debtors, Slaves, and the Making of the American Revolution in Virginia.* Chapel Hill: University of North Carolina Press, 1999.

Lanning, Michael Lee. *African Americans in the Revolutionary War.* New York: Citadel, 2000.

Nash, Gary B. *Race and Revolution.* Madison, Wisc.: Madison House, 1990.

Schama, Simon. *Rough Crossings: Britain, the Slaves, and the American Revolution.* New York: Ecco, 2006.

DURÁN, DIEGO (1721–1795) *prominent free black architect in colonial Mexico*

Diego Durán achieved fame and success as an architect in the colonial city of Valladolid (now called Morelia), MEXICO. Durán is most known for his work on the town's aqueduct and contributions to the local cathedral. He also worked on the San Juan de Dios hospital. Spanish authorities, in adherence to the race-based hierarchies of their American colonies, labeled Durán a mulatto; however, he preferred the title of *maestro*, in reference to his career as a master architect.

Durán had both Amerindian and African ancestors. His father was probably descended from African slaves who worked on sugar-growing plantations in the 1600s. Durán's mother was of Native American ancestry. Both her father and brother worked as master builders in early-18th-century Valladolid, and Durán inherited both their surname and their careers. Durán's birth date is unknown. He was baptized in Valladolid in 1721, four years after his parents' marriage. The priest described the entire family as free mulattoes, so Durán's mother assumed the racial label given to her husband and her son. This kind of racial label was fluid at the time and depended often on the whim of the government or ecclesiastical official who was describing the person during an encounter with colonial bureaucracy. In the 18th century, many free men of African descent achieved similar success as craftsmen and tradesmen in colonial Mexico.

Durán had a large family, another sign of his success and prosperity. Three times a widower, he married in 1742, 1749, 1764, and 1765. At his church wedding ceremonies, the priest described his first two wives as mulattoes, the third Spanish and the fourth mestizo (of indigenous and European descent). After the death of his third wife, Durán was left with only one daughter, but his fourth wife bore six living children. She also took significant wealth into the marriage, including three large urban houses, and managed to outlive her husband. Because women often died in childbirth, it was common for affluent men of African descent to marry several times: Duran's longevity and wealth made him desirable many times over as a husband and demonstrated his desire to

pass on his wealth to his offspring, just as he benefited from the trade knowledge of his ancestors. The continuation of his legacy may have been an important factor motivating Durán.

Through the family profession, marriage, connections, and his own ambitions, Durán became a wealthy man. Later in life, he lived in a house worth more than 4,000 pesos, a huge sum at the time. One sign of his good reputation and high social status was the fact that Durán was often involved in many property transactions and loans after the mid-18th century. In his role as an architect, Durán frequently assessed properties donated to the ROMAN CATHOLIC CHURCH or purchased by his peers. From the 1740s until his death some time in 1795, Durán led a Catholic brotherhood with a free black membership based in a Valladolid church. (*See also* CATHOLIC CONFRATERNITIES.) Durán worked hard to raise the status of this free black fraternal organization, demonstrating both his devotion to religion and his desire to ensure his good reputation as well as that of his peers, despite the racial prejudices built into the Spanish colonial system.

Nicole von Germeten

DU SABLE, JEAN-BAPTISTE POINTE (ca. 1745–1814 or 1818) *first free black settler of Chicago*

Jean-Baptiste Pointe Du Sable is generally acknowledged as the first free black settler of present-day CHICAGO, ILLINOIS. Although the details of much of his life remain somewhat uncertain, scholars have been able to piece together much useful information. Du Sable was probably born around 1745, either in SAINT-DOMINGUE to a mother of West African ancestry and a French father, or to a free black woman and an unknown French father near Montréal, Canada. He was raised as a Catholic and probably spent some time as a young man in FRANCE, where he acquired an education. Sometime in the mid-1760s, he apparently arrived in LOUISIANA to seek his fortune. Du Sable lived in New Orleans for a short time, working for a group of French priests. In the late 1760s or early 1770s, he traveled up the Mississippi River into present-day MISSOURI, where he trapped and traded to earn a living. He may also have lived in CANADA for a brief period before arriving in Chicago in the mid-1770s. At the time, the site that would become the city of Chicago was already a Potawatomi trading center, which probably included a good deal of French colonial business as well. Du Sable established himself as a fur trader and businessman. Over the next 25 years, Du Sable achieved a degree of financial success and started a family with a Potawatomi woman named Kittiwaha (or Catherine). While in Chicago, the couple had two children, named Jean-Baptiste and Suzanne.

In the 1790s, Du Sable may have held a subchieftaincy or some other position within the Potawatomi, but when the Potawatomi signed a treaty with the U.S. government in 1795, yielding control of a small plot of land that would become American-controlled Chicago, Du Sable's monopoly on the region's trade began to suffer. American speculators and entrepreneurs entered Chicago by 1800, when the region was governed by the United States as part of the Indiana Territory. This may have led to Du Sable's decision to move southward to present-day Peoria, ILLINOIS. By 1804, however, Du Sable sold his property there and moved to an area governed alternately by the Spanish and French on the western side of the Mississippi River. Du Sable's decision to leave the Indiana Territory may have been prompted by the territory's growing hostility to free blacks and people of color. In 1803, laws were passed that prevented blacks from testifying against whites in court, and legal opinion tended to favor the view that all blacks in the territory were subject to laws that governed slaves and servants. This would have made conducting business with his American neighbors potentially dangerous for Du Sable. In 1804, Du Sable apparently arrived in St. Charles, in present-day Missouri, where he again entered the business of land speculation and entrepreneurship. Du Sable was nearly 70 years old in 1813 when he signed over control of his properties and holdings to his granddaughter, Eulalia (daughter of Suzanne and Jean-Baptiste Peltier), with the understanding that she would care for him in his old age and bury him in the Catholic cemetery at St. Charles. Du Sable died at St. Charles either in 1814 or in 1818.

Thomas Bahde

FURTHER READING

Grivno, Max L. "'Black Frenchmen' and 'White Settlers': Race, Slavery, and the Creation of African-American Identities along the Northwest Frontier, 1790–1840." *Slavery and Abolition* 21 (December 2000): 75–93.

Kaplan, Sidney. *The Black Presence in the Era of the American Revolution, 1770–1800.* Greenwich, Conn.: New York Graphic Society, 1973.

Meehan, Thomas A. "Jean Baptiste Point du Sable, the First Chicagoan." *Journal of the Illinois State Historical Society* 56 (1963): 439–453.

Reed, Christopher Robert. *Black Chicago's First Century.* Vol. 1, 1833–1900. Columbia: University of Missouri Press, 2005.

Reef, Catherine. *Black Explorers.* New York: Facts On File, 1996.

DUTCH CARIBBEAN ISLANDS

Free people of color lived throughout the Dutch Caribbean, which consisted of SURINAM on the South American mainland, the island of Aruba just to the north of VENEZUELA, and the five islands of the Netherlands Antilles. The Netherlands Antilles consists of Bonaire and Curaçao, situated near Aruba in the southern Caribbean (together they are called the Dutch Leeward islands or the ABC Islands), as well as Saba, Sint Eustatius, and (Dutch) Sint Maarten, the southern part of an island that is shared with French Saint Martin, near Saint Kitts and Nevis in the northeastern Caribbean (known as the Dutch Windward Islands). This entry deals only with the six Dutch Caribbean islands and excludes Surinam.

Enslavement

During the early phases of the transatlantic slave trade in the 16th and 17th centuries, both Curaçao and Sint Eustatius were major transit ports for enslaved Africans taken on Dutch ships to the surrounding islands. During the high tide of this trade in enslaved people, from 1658 to 1675, Dutch slavers carried more than 50 percent of their cargoes to the Dutch Antilles. One hundred years later, this percentage dropped to 13 percent. Curaçao was an attractive transit harbor for the trade between the Dutch Republic and nearby regions on the Spanish mainland after the Dutch had concluded a peace treaty with Spain in 1648.

Plantations on the islands of the Dutch Caribbean were characterized by the fact that most did not produce just one major crop for export. Generally, plantations were small in size in comparison with those in the rest of the Caribbean. Nowhere on these islands did large concentrations of enslaved people exist as on the sugar plantations of, for example, JAMAICA and Surinam. More than 80 percent of the SLAVE OWNERS on the Dutch Antilles owned fewer than 10 enslaved people.

Sint Maarten, Sint Eustatius, and Saba also did not have a "typical" plantation economy. Saba did have one sugarcane plantation, but most of the small number of enslaved worked in the household. In Sint Maarten and Sint Eustatius, cash crop production included tobacco and later SUGAR CULTIVATION, COTTON CULTIVATION, and INDIGO CULTIVATION. Both Sint Maarten and Bonaire used slaves in the salt industry as well. The island of Bonaire as a whole was a plantation of the Dutch West India Company. The small numbers of slaves worked in the salt industry and in dyewood. When the company dissolved in 1791, the Dutch government confiscated its properties and continued its operations in Bonaire. The enslaved people were owned directly by the Kingdom of the Netherlands and were known as government slaves. Slaves on average constituted only one-third of the population of the Dutch

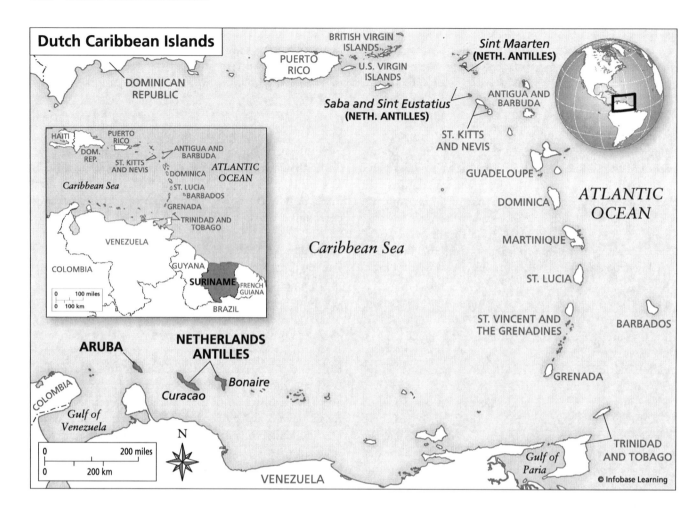

Antilles. Even though the Dutch Caribbean islands were not monoculture plantation societies, they shared certain features common to all slave societies.

As in other Caribbean slave societies, slavery determined the social fabric and shaped the lives of whites, freed nonwhites, and enslaved Africans on the Dutch Caribbean islands. In the social hierarchy during slavery times, people of African descent were at the bottom, either as enslaved or freed persons. The Dutch and other Europeans were the leading class, while in Curaçao next in line were the Sephardic Jews, who, after having arrived in the 17th century, dedicated themselves mostly to commerce. A classic study of the island in Dutch by Harmannus Hoetink (1931–2005) introduced the theory of a segmented society to describe the society of that moment. A segmented society is composed of several groups of different race, ethnicity, language, religion, and social class that coexist but hardly mingle. There is a lack of consensus of values among the several ethnic groups, which manifests itself in differences in institutions such as marriage and family, in education and economics, and in religion, language, and folklore. Consequently, these ethnic groups are engaged in con-

tinuous conflict, while one cultural minority tends to uphold the social order politically. The society of the Dutch Caribbean islands followed this pattern in the eighteenth century.

In all six Dutch Caribbean island societies, those of mixed color could transcend their social position within the social hierarchy. In the course of time, the growing numbers of freed persons led to increased organizational complexity of the societies. Scholars have long recognized that in order to understand slavery as an institution and the status of the free person of color within slave societies, one must have a better understanding of the potential for, as well as the rate of incidence of, MANUMISSION in these societies.

With the increase of free colored people, one's skin color/tone and other physical features became deciding factors for social mobility. Hair texture and the degree of one's skin pigmentation became important markers of identity and status. The enslaved of mixed race were also categorized as colored: the term "colored people," in Papiamentu, the creole language of the Dutch Leeward Islands, *hende di kolo*, meant that one had a lighter, therefore more "appropriate," skin color, and consequently slightly better chances for upward mobility. This term is even used to this day by elderly or more conservative people in the islands. In Sint Eustatius, the process of MISCEGENATION was called "building up the race." On all these islands, Afro-Dutch women especially could reach certain positions on account of their lighter complexion. As slaves, for example, they were more likely to be chosen to work within the household.

One of the distinguishing features of slavery on the Dutch Caribbean islands was that the number of manumitted people, both black and of mixed race, grew considerably through frequent manumissions. These islands stood out among other Caribbean societies for their comparatively large free black population. The figures for the end of slavery in 1863 can be seen in the table below.

In the 19th century, the free population of color consisted of manumitted people and their descendants. Some of the manumitted were formerly enslaved people whose families, or who themselves, had been able to buy their freedom. Slaves who were skilled ARTISANS, in particular, had better opportunities to buy their own freedom. In addition, some masters freed their enslaved in an act of humanitarian concern and sometimes sought to provide for them by giving them a piece of land or another present. Some of these manumitted persons had blood or sexual ties with their former masters. Others were old and disabled people whose owners simply disposed of them as economic liabilities: They gained their freedom when their owners could or would no longer continue sustaining them. When times were bad for the inflexible and inefficient plantations, many slave owners were forced to let go of their enslaved because they lacked the means to feed and house them. Many of these manumitted stole food to prevent starvation. In order to counter this phenomenon, the government levied a tax on manumissions in 1761. The publication of this particular rule had to be repeated several times, suggesting that owners did not abide by it. As a consequence of these various factors, the Dutch Antilles had

proportionally more manumitted than did neighboring plantation colonies. However, the group of manumitted did not enjoy a smooth transition from enslavement to freedom and was left to fend for itself. By entering freedom under the worst social conditions, these disadvantaged formerly enslaved people continued to be socially marginalized.

The history of Curaçao and the rest of the Netherlands Antilles is different from that of Surinam. In comparison to Surinam, the white population was proportionally larger and settled in the countryside rather than in a single large city. There was also more intermixing between the races in the islands, and the proportion of free colored people to slaves was also larger than in Surinam. The commonness of miscegenation led to a significant number of people of mixed race in the society. The relationship between the masters and their colored mistresses and offspring was marked by social ties that seemed less racially polarized and to a certain extent even harmonious. In this multiracial society, the group of mixed origins enjoyed a privileged status relative to the black population. Within the total freed population, the proportion of people of mixed race was relatively high, as most of the time the illicit colored offspring of the white slave masters were granted manumission by their white fathers.

The sexual relationships between black slave women and white owners resulting in children of color have been considered by some scholars to be the ultimate expression of the slave master's power over the life of his enslaved. In these societies, female slaves gained social advantage from the practice of cohabiting with a European male. Several studies, however, have shown that the colored people were not exempt from stereotyped ideas about race and slave background. There was some degree of antipathy against them among the white elite. Planters would still regard and treat them with contempt. They were often considered arrogant and pretentious and were therefore disliked.

POPULATION OF PEOPLE OF COLOR OF THE DUTCH CARIBBEAN ISLANDS, BY STATUS, ON THE EVE OF EMANCIPATION (1863)

	Aruba	Bonaire	Curaçao	Saba	Sint Eustatius	Sint Maarten
Freed	2,398	1,828	14,328	1,105	864	1,337
Percentage	83%	69%	67%	62%	45%	43%
Enslaved	502	819	6,985	666	1,085	1,741
Percentage	17%	31%	33%	38%	55%	57%
Total	2,900	2,647	21,313	1,771	1,931	3,078

Source: Luc Alofs, et al. . . . p. 60.

The social position of free people varied. Some colored people became prosperous. However, a large part of the free population confronted basic problems in terms of participating economically and socially in the society. As the number of free black people increased, the society could actually become more racially rigid.

In adapting to their new situation of freedom, freed persons faced several options. The first option was agriculture. However, in Curaçao this was hindered by the unfavorable climate of the island. Qualified artisans could gain a livelihood by working as carpenters, masons, shoemakers, or tailors. Other possibilities were connected with commerce and the shipping industry, which were principal economic activities on the islands. Men of color worked on ships as sailors or helped to build or repair interisland schooners and others vessels. This was especially important because of the role Curaçao and Sint Eustatius served as ports for (often unlawful) trade with other countries' colonies in the region.

People also continued to leave for different places in the region where there were better job opportunities. These migrants did not move at random but chose their destinations whenever they had the opportunity. Most of the time it was the men who migrated, and consequently there were more women than men among the freed population on the island. The women had to take control of their lives in order to survive the extremely poor conditions in which they remained behind.

In the 19th century, there was an increased attempt to convert the Afro-Antillean population to Christianity. The ROMAN CATHOLIC CHURCH became central to this effort on the Dutch Leeward Islands of Aruba, Bonaire, and Curaçao. In that century, this church increasingly convinced the Protestant (Dutch Reformed) colonial government of the importance of educating the enslaved. The Catholic Church would play a very important part in the dynamics within which the cultural encounter between enslaved, freed, and free people took place. It became an important machinery of cultural control during the 19th century.

Post-Emancipation Period
On August 8, 1862, the Netherlands passed the Emancipation Law, which abolished slavery in the Dutch colonies the following year on July 1, 1863. On that day, 11,654 enslaved were freed on the six Dutch Caribbean Islands, about 35 percent of the total population. In Surinam, 33,621 enslaved became free: 55 percent of the total Surinamese population of approximately 60,000. In Surinam, the owners were given 300 guilders per slave by way of "compensation." On the islands, the sum was 200 guilders, with the exception of Sint Maarten, where the owners received 100 guilders because the colonial government had considered the enslaved on that island as free people since 1848, when the neighboring French colony had freed all its slaves.

Freedom brought no substantial change as no economic base or social recognition was achieved. Furthermore, the formerly enslaved had no voice in the shaping of government policy until the 20th century. The coercive forces and the mechanisms by which those in power exercised control over the lives of the poor continued to exist.

In Curaçao, for example, the planters retained strong control through the *paga tera* system (literally, paying for the land you live on). Under this system, some former slaves would remain living on the plantation, occupying the provision grounds as well as the house to which they had access during slavery. In return, they were obligated to work for free for the landowners during certain periods of the year.

Leaving the islands to find work abroad became a much-practiced custom in all the Dutch Caribbean societies. (*See also* MIGRATION.) The black working class in these societies made use of their newly acquired mobility to look for social and economic opportunities outside their own society on a large scale. Migration was an option and a coping strategy for members of the poorer classes to seek temporary or permanent alleviation from poverty.

After 1863, former slaves left Sint Eustatius to work in St. Croix, St. Thomas, Trinidad, Bermuda, and Antigua. In 1864, 400 men left the island to work in Venezuela but returned home with fever. From Sint Maarten, some former slaves left for the DOMINICAN REPUBLIC directly after 1863; there they settled in the province of San Franscisco de Macoris. Other Dutch Antillean migrants made their way to PANAMA to work on the Panama Canal, to the coast of Central America, and to PUERTO RICO and CUBA.

The Dutch Caribbean was anomalous in the Caribbean world as the number of slaves imported was very high, but there was not a very strongly developed plantation society. Instead, many people of color, both free and enslaved, worked in urban occupations and on smaller farms and fisheries, all occupations that allowed a greater chance for freedom than large plantations. That the Dutch culture was Protestant and northern European, according to the TANNENBAUM HYPOTHESIS, predisposed these colonies to have harsher treatment of slaves and stricter color lines than the Spanish or Portuguese colonies. However, the lack of a strong plantation sector and close contact with Spanish America meant that the Dutch islands had large free colored populations who received relatively fair treatment. There was a great contrast in this regard between the islands and the mainland colonies of Surinam and the Dutch enclaves in what is now GUYANA, where slaves were harshly treated and racial lines sharply drawn.

Rose Mary Allen

FURTHER READING

Allen, Rose Mary. *Di Ki Manera. A Social History of Afro-Curaçaoans, 1863–1917.* Amsterdam, Netherlands: SWP, 2007.

Alofs, Luc, et al., eds. *Geschiedenis van de Antillen: Aruba, Bonaire, Curaçao, Saba, Sint Eustatius, Sint Maarten.* Zutphen, Netherlands: Walburg Pers, 1997.

Antoin, F. D. *Lantamentu di katibu na Boneiru.* Bonaire, Netherlands Antilles: National Printing Bonaire, 1997.

Emmer, Pieter Cornelis. "Jesus Christ Was Good, but Trade Was Better: An Overview of the Transit Trade of the Dutch Antilles, 1634–1795." In *The Lesser Antilles in the Age of European Expansion,* edited by Robert L. Paquette and Stanley L. Engerman, 206–222. Gainesville: University Press of Florida, 1996.

Gibbes, F. E., N. C. Römer-Kenepa and M. A. Scriwanek. *De bewoners van Curaçao, vijf eeuwen lief en leed, 1499–1999.* Willemstad, Curaçao, Netherlands Antilles: Nationaal Archief, 2002.

Lampe, A. "Yo te nombro libertad. Iglesia y Estado en la sociedad esclavista de Curazao (1816-1863)." Ph.D thesis, Free University of Amsterdam, 1988.

Oostindie, Gerrit Jan. *Het paradijs overzee. De "Nederlandse" Caraïben en Nederland.* Amsterdam, Netherlands: Bert Bakker, 1997.

Rupert, Linda M. "Inter Imperial Trade and Local Identity: Curaçao in the Colonial Atlantic World." Ph.D. thesis, Duke University, 2006.

ECUADOR

Ecuador is located on the northwest coast of South America and shares its northern border with COLOMBIA and its southern border with PERU. To the east in the 19th century lay BRAZIL; later Peru and Colombia took most of Ecuador's Amazonian territories. Ecuador has a diverse heritage reflected in its population and geography. Today, most of Ecuador's population is indigenous and mestizo with approximately 5 percent considering themselves of African descent. The country is divided into three main geographical zones: a coastal zone, which encompasses more than 400 miles of coastline along the Pacific Ocean; the sierras (Andes), which run through the middle of the country; and the eastern lowland jungle region. Ecuador's political boundary also extends to the Galapagos Islands, situated several hundred miles off the coast of South America. The country's topography has been difficult to overcome. The construction of modern roads and railroads connecting Quito, the inland capital, and Guayaquil, its largest city, began only in the late 19th and early 20th centuries, This helps to explain the intense regionalism that still exists within the country. Ecuador also has a rich indigenous past. For the past 10,000 years, numerous tribal groups and polities have settled the area. Quito, its present capital, and Cuenca, in southern Ecuador, were prized cities of the Inca Empire.

When Spaniards conquered the region in the early 16th century, they turned Quito into a key seat of government with an *audiencia*, or a special court of appeal. It remained under the control of the Viceroyalty of Peru (Lima) until it was transferred to the jurisdiction of the Viceroyalty of New Granada (Bogotá) in present-day Colombia in 1739. This administrative change allowed Spanish officials to collect taxes more efficiently and better govern its empire. In 1765, in Quito, riots targeting the imposition of new taxes challenged Spanish authority. Napoléon's invasion of Spain, beginning in 1808, cast Spanish authority over its colonies in doubt. In Ecuador, local responses remained subdued until 1822, when Simón Bolívar, known as "the Liberator," secured the independence of the Republic of Gran Colombia, which included the territories of present day Colombia, Venezuela, PANAMA, and Ecuador. Later that year, he liberated Quito. Bolívar sought to keep the various regions of Gran Colombia together, but his efforts failed shortly after the wars of independence ended. Venezuela left in 1829, and Ecuador and Colombia followed suit in 1830. Ecuador's postindependence governments were polarized between liberals and conservatives. Liberals established their political base in the port city of Guayaquil and sought to emulate European methods of economic development while conservatives were based out of Quito and sought to preserve colonial institutions. Throughout the 19th century, these groups fought in violent civil wars over control of the government. Political instability continued into the 20th century, even though the military became intricately involved in Ecuadorian politics.

Colonial and Early National Histories of Ecuador's Free People of Color

The history of Ecuador's free people of color reflects the country's intense regionalism and diversity. The majority of Ecuadoreans consider their country, once encompassing the northern half of the Inca Empire, as purely indigenous, and many largely ignore its African heritage. This belief is widespread despite the fact that, according to the 2001 national census, "Blacks and *mulatos*" numbered more than 632,000 of a total population of 12.6 million people. Most of these Afro-Ecuadorians are located in diverse geographical zones, such as Esmeraldas on the Pacific Coast, Imbabura, and Carchi. The largest concentrations of people of African descent currently live in cities, such as Guayaquil, Esmeraldas, and Quito, although scattered populations may be found in rural settings, such as the sierras in Mira, Juncal, and the Chota River valley.

As was the case within most Spanish colonies, African slaves were imported to work in the agricultural and mining sectors of the imperial economy. Spanish authorities in Quito regulated the importation of African slaves into the region. Slaves mined gold primarily in what is today Northwest Ecuador, which included Playa de Oro and San José de Cachavi y Guembi.

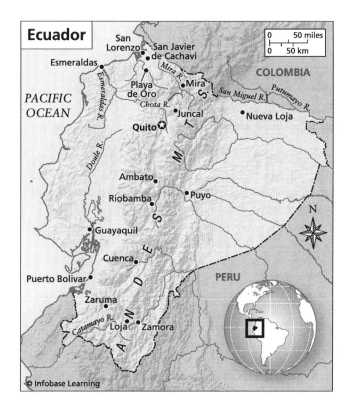

A thriving slave trade also developed in the sierras. Between 1580 and 1700, the JESUITS bought slaves to labor in their SUGAR CULTIVATION and wine operations in the Chota and Mira River valleys. Scholars estimate that by the early 18th century, the order was cultivating as much as 10 percent of Ecuador's land. The presence of Jesuit sugar plantations represented a fundamental shift from the Amerindian cultivation of coca and other traditional Andean crops. By the early 1700s, African slaves had supplanted indigenous laborers as the main source of labor on large landed estates. Indeed, the Chota Valley in Imbabura province became the second-largest slaveholding area in Ecuador.

Escaped slaves formed their own settlements, known as *palenques*, throughout Ecuador. (*See also* MAROONS.) In 1553, the first such community was established when 23 slaves from West Africa found themselves shipwrecked off the coast of what today is called Esmeraldas, located on Ecuador's northern Pacific coast. Scholars credit an African named Antón for saving the small colony by making alliances with the Pidi tribe. Several years later, another black leader, Alonso Sebastián de Illescas, learned local indigenous languages and cultures in order to keep the small colony of former slaves alive. He and his descendants intermarried within the area's indigenous populations. During the colonial period, Esmeraldas evolved into an important multicultural settlement and attracted hundreds of escaped slaves from both Ecuador and Colombia. Other *palenques* were formed among both

blacks and indigenous peoples, particularly the Chachi Indians, which established the so-called Republic of the Zambo, along the Cayapas River in northwestern Ecuador. Other distinct communities in Loja, Zaruma, and Zamora, located in southern Ecuador, were founded by black slaves, who escaped from working in the region's gold mining operations. Spanish imperial armies more often crushed these types of settlements, but many survived because they lived in areas too remote for imperial forces to reach. Like the maroons, African slaves often challenged Spanish colonial authority. In the late 1780s, in Ibarra, just north of Quito, slaves on one large estate refused to work until an abusive owner was removed. Many slaves gained liberty through MANUMISSION, a relatively simple process in Spanish America. Slaves could purchase their own freedom using funds they earned by extra work when their masters did not need them, or by gift or will of their masters. Once free, the population of Afro-Ecuadorians grew rapidly by natural growth. Afro-Ecuadorians suffered under some forms of discrimination, enough to push them together as a community. They were not permitted to hold certain offices, such as commissioned officers in the military, the priesthood, or other prestigious jobs, but they could own land and businesses, and many did. By 1800, free people of color outnumbered slaves in the colony by 28,000 to 5,000.

During the wars of independence against the Spanish Crown in the 1810s and 1820s, many free black communities allied themselves with both patriot and royalist forces (*see also* SOUTH AMERICAN WARS OF LIBERATION). However, the free people of color in Esmeraldas decided that they stood a greater chance at autonomy if they sided with anti-Spanish forces. In 1820, they led a key insurrection against the Spanish army at Rio Verde. As he fought his way south from Colombia, Simón Bolívar wanted to attract support from local communities. Thus, in the following year, Gran Colombia's central government decreed that all slaves born after July would be free. Despite opposition from local SLAVE OWNERS, Bolívar also liberated slaves on his military campaigns toward Peru. However, the breakup of the confederation into three independent republics in 1830 delayed manumission for some communities. Authorities often used the political chaos as justification to postpone enforcing antislavery decrees.

Still, the numbers of slaves declined gradually as Ecuador secured its independence, first from Spain and then from Gran Colombia. In 1825, Ecuador counted 8,000 slaves, but by the 1850s, this number had dropped to 2,000. In 1821, Ecuador ended the slave trade. As in most parts of Spanish America, free womb laws—stating that all persons born after a certain date were free—starting in 1821, ensured that many would remain enslaved for at least another generation. However, owners of large landed estates made certain that stronger antislavery laws would not be enforced until the late 19th century. Other systems of forced labor, including debt peonage, kept black and indigenous populations tied to large landed estates. In 1851, Ecuador's government abolished slavery once and for all.

Conservatives and liberals, at odds with each other for much of the 19th century, sought to curry favor with free and slave communities. The liberal president José Urbina (1808–91) formed an elite Afro-Ecuadorian presidential guard, called the Tauras. This group was a mainstay of his regime until conservatives took power in 1860. Under the leadership of Eloy Alfaro (1842–1912), liberals returned to power in 1895. In order to consolidate his power, Alfaro recruited soldiers from Esmeraldas. They were instrumental in helping liberals secure a victory over conservative forces, particularly in Quito. After Alfaro's death in 1912, black troops loyal to him retreated to Esmeraldas and continued armed resistance against the government until 1916.

Today, Afro-Ecuadorians have made tremendous achievements in politics, sports, entertainment, and literature, among other areas of life. In 1995, Mónica Chalá (1966–) became the first Afro-Ecuadorian to win the Miss Ecuador competition. One of the most prominent political figures in the late 20th century was Jaime Hurtado González (1937–99). Known as the "Champion of the Poor," he began his political career in the late 1970s and helped found the Movimiento Popular Democrático, closely tied to Ecuador's Communist Party. In 1988, he ran for president. Although he failed to be elected, Hurtado fundamentally altered Ecuadorian politics by attracting more people to leftist causes. He became an important figure in Ecuador's national parliament. During the 20th century, several black writers, including Adalberto Ortiz (1914–2003), Nelson Estupinan Bass (1912–2002), and his wife, Luz Argentina Chriboga (1940–), drew inspiration from their experiences within their home province of Esmeraldas. Their work has gained national and international recognition.

Jesse Hingson

FURTHER READING

Antón Sánchez, John. *Sistema de indicadores sociales del pueblo Afroecuatoriano.* Santiago de Chile: CEPAL, 2005.

Rahier, Jean Muteba. "Blackness, the Racial/Spatial Order, Migrations, and Miss Ecuador, 1995–1996." *American Anthropologist* 100, no. 2 (June 1998): 421–430.

Whitten, Norman E., Jr. *Class, Kinship, and Power in an Ecuadorian Town: The Negroes of San Lorenzo.* Palo Alto, Calif.: Stanford University Press, 1965.

———, ed. *Cultural Transformations and Ethnicity in Modern Ecuador.* Urbana: University of Illinois Press, 1981.

———, ed. *Millennial Ecuador: Critical Essays on Cultural Transformations and Social Dynamics.* Iowa City: University of Iowa Press, 2003.

Whitten, Norman E., Jr., and Diego Quiroga. "Ecuador." In *No Longer Invisible: Afro-Latin Americans Today,* 287–317. London: Minority Rights, 1995.

EDUCATION AND LITERACY

As with many poor and excluded people in the early modern world, people of color in the Americas saw education as a way out of their situation and sought it enthusiastically at all levels. As with many other means of social promotion, a racially stratified system made it more difficult for people of color to gain education in many places. Features of black culture and society also contributed to the desire to seek education, especially literacy training.

The first step in any kind of education in the modern world is literacy training. This does not, however, diminish the importance of oral culture and memorization in both the African cultures where American blacks' ancestors originated and African-American culture itself. Memorization of scripture was especially important. Omar Ibn Said, an Islamic cleric from the Futa Djallon in modern Guinea, was a slave in North Carolina from the early 1800s until his death in 1864. He was literate and wrote several Arabic manuscripts during his life but attracted the attention of blacks and whites in the region because of his ability to recite the entire Koran from memory. Rebecca Protten, a free mixed-race Protestant religious leader in the Caribbean and Africa in the 18th century, first gained the attention of white Moravian missionaries with her ability to recite long passages from the Bible from memory in two languages.

Literacy is the key to modern learning, however, and becoming literate was an important first step for people of color. Many important skills required book learning. Modern political consciousness could also result from books: Frederick Douglass, born in 1818, famously attributed his unquenchable desire for freedom to his having learned to read at an early age, while still a slave in Maryland. In addition, for followers of Protestant Christianity, reading the scriptures was the key to understanding God's will, and no person could consider himself or herself a Christian without a deep understanding of the Bible. (*See* Protestant mainline churches and Baptists and Pietists.)

Masters realized that literacy was dangerous, but they also valued it, creating a classic "prisoner's dilemma" whereby the slave owners' common good (preventing people of color from becoming literate and thus disrupting the social order) clashed with their individual good (having employees who could read and keep records). Abdul Rahman Ibrahim ibn Sori, another literate Muslim from West Africa, became a slave on a small Mississippi plantation in the early 1800s and was the only literate person there, including the master. When he reestablished contact with former business contacts and sought his freedom, it took the direct intervention of President JOHN QUINCY ADAMS to convince his master to let him go. The master was reluctant because he was too valuable. Only he could read the plantation's records (which were written in Arabic). Whites in the United States also often shared blacks' devotion to reformed Protestant beliefs that placed a high value on the ability to read the Bible. White believers often sought to train slaves and free blacks in literacy as part of a missionary effort.

American Southern states generally adopted laws in the early 1800s that hindered or outright prohibited literacy training for people of color. These laws were often seen as a response to a number of rebellions and plots, such as Nat Turner's Revolt in 1831, in which literate blacks had played a role. These laws were widely violated and evaded by masters, slaves, and free people of color. In some cases, they did not apply to free people of color, as in LOUISIANA, where the wealthy free colored "Creole" community actually supported a school during the period of slavery there. In the North, the laws were often less harsh. Prudence Crandall (1803–90), a white Quaker schoolmistress from CONNECTICUT, admitted a black student to her school in 1831. The state government responded with a law forbidding schools to admit out-of-state blacks—though the student in question, Sarah Harris, was a Connecticut native. The school closed, but Connecticut rescinded its law in 1838. Other Northern states had schools where African-American students could be educated separately from whites, and while these sometimes provoked white public opposition, they were legal and very popular.

Other countries in the Americas generally did not restrict literacy training for blacks by law, as the United States did. There were occasional regulations about black education in the Protestant colonies of the Caribbean, but these mostly restricted the content of educational messages that could be delivered to blacks. For example, the Moravian missionaries in the DANISH VIRGIN ISLANDS, the group that Rebecca Protten belonged to, were criticized, assaulted by mobs, warned by governors and judges, and ultimately almost driven from the colony by whites upset at the egalitarian nature of their teachings, but there does not appear to have been any criticism of literacy training per se. Cuban colonial authorities closed black schools in the wake of the LA ESCALERA PLOT (1844) because of concerns about the content of education being offered there, but the ROMAN CATHOLIC CHURCH schools continued to accept black students and most private schools eventually reopened.

The prospect of formal education was very attractive to people of color. Slaves were rarely educated in this manner, though some people, such as Frederick Douglass, managed to get some part of a formal education at second hand by listening to white children at their lessons. Some people who were LIVING "AS FREE" received formal education, including the children of the

The townspeople of Canterbury, Connecticut, setting fire to Prudence Crandall's School for Young Ladies of Color in 1834. This is an example of the hostility of white communities to education for people of color. *(The Granger Collection, New York)*

HEALY FAMILY of Georgia, two of whom became the first priests of African ancestry from North America, who had a tutor provided by their white father while they were still legally slaves in GEORGIA in the 1840s. Formal education was an option that was enthusiastically pursued by free people of color in many places. Free public education was a North American innovation. Separation of blacks and whites in the public sphere was also strongest in the United States, so it is not surprising that the first black schools were formed in the Northern states of the United States. The Philadelphia Abolition Society founded a colored school in 1774. The Pittsburgh African Educational Society, founded in 1829 by John B. Vashon of the VASHAN FAMILY was among the first black schools to be led by blacks. In OHIO, the Harveysburg Free Black School, founded in 1831, was among the first schools to accept black students without any payment, though it was not a public school but instead founded by Quakers. Quakers and other Pietistic groups, such as the Moravians in the Danish Virgin Islands, were among the first to offer formal education to blacks. However, Catholic religious orders such as the JESUITS were not far behind. The Healy brothers were students at the College of the Holy Cross in Worcester, MASSACHUSETTS (today a university, but at that time also a secondary school), in 1844.

Formal education for blacks outside the United States was limited by the fact that most of these places made no attempt to educate more than a tiny minority of their populations of any color. Roman Catholic parishes began to sponsor parish schools in the late 18th century, which were supposedly open to any child in the parish. These schools, however, were rare in the Americas outside urban areas and often offered little more than rote memorization of the catechism and perhaps very rudimentary literacy. Good primary and secondary schools in Latin America were normally open only to well-off city dwellers and the landowning class. However, if people of color were members of the ruling class, as was sometimes the case, they could have access to good education. The Haitian liberation leader and first president ALEXANDRE SABÈS PÉTION, a free man of mixed race, was formally educated in Haiti at a Catholic school run by the Christian Brothers in the 1760s and then attended the French national military academy. Sometimes, especially intelligent and hardworking poor boys could have access to a high-quality education, often with the expectation that they would go on to become priests. One of the heroes of the Mexican liberation struggle, JOSÉ MARIA MORELOS, was a poor boy who advanced in society through education, first attending a school kept by a relative and then being trained for the priesthood.

Stewart R. King

FURTHER READING

Woodson, Carter G. *The Education of the Negro Prior to 1861.* Originally published 1917. Available online: URL: www.gutenberg.org.ebooks/11089. Accessed December 23, 2010.

ELLISON, WILLIAM "APRIL" (1790–1861)
American plantation owner

William "April" Ellison was born enslaved on a SOUTH CAROLINA plantation in April 1790. He received the name April because it was common for slaves in the period to name children after the month or day of the week when they were born. Between 1800 and 1802, Ellison was purchased by William Ellison, a white slave owner whose surname he ultimately took. By the time Ellison was 10, he was assigned work as a cotton gin apprentice and was taught a variety of skills including carpentry, blacksmithing, machining, reading, writing, and bookkeeping for the next six years at William McCreight's gin building shop in Winnsboro, South Carolina. Ellison stayed on at the gin shop for another eight years, during which he married at about age 21.

On June 8, 1816, William Ellison appeared before a magistrate to gain permission to free April. Ellison was given his freedom at age 26. Using skills he had been taught, Ellison soon became a successful businessman and mechanic, working as a master gin builder and repairman. In 1820, he purchased two slaves to work in his shop. Also in 1820, Ellison had his name officially changed to William, the name of his former owner, who was possibly also his father. The Ellison family joined the predominately white Episcopal Church, and Ellison was allowed to seat his family on the ground floor, typically an area reserved for wealthy white families who had to "buy" their pew with contributions to the church. (*See also* PROTESTANT MAINLINE CHURCHES.) It was common practice at the time to require blacks and poor whites to sit in the balcony. From 1822 through the 1840s, Ellison's gin business grew. He acquired additional slaves on the way to becoming one of South Carolina's primary cotton gin manufacturers and repairers. Machines built by Ellison were sold and sent as far as MISSISSIPPI. In fact, it is believed that Ellison's business had become so dominant in the state that several white-owned competitors went out of business, an exception to the general principle that whites only did business with other whites.

Ellison purchased 54.5 acres of farmland and moved into a large home in 1838. Within 10 years, he owned 350 acres, and in 1860, he owned 900 acres. His slave ownership also doubled during these years, growing from 30 in 1840 to more than 60 by 1860. (*See also* PLANTERS AND PLANTER AGENTS.) The land on his farm was used mostly for COTTON CULTIVATION, except for a small part set aside to raise food for his family and slaves. Ellison had a reputation as a harsh slave master, and his slaves were said to be the worst fed and clothed in the district. Despite his business success, most of Ellison's plantation income appears to have come from slave "breeding," a business that was looked upon with disdain throughout the South. Most Southern states had laws that made it illegal to sell slaves younger than age 12 or to sell inherited slaves altogether. Except for a few females Ellison kept as "breeders," he sold most of the women and children for about $400 each. Ellison was a supporter of the Confederate cause and died on December 5, 1861.

Holly Heinsohn

FURTHER READING

Johnson, Michael P., and James L. Roak. *Black Masters: A Free Family of Color in the Old South.* New York: W. W. Norton, 1984.

Lemelson Center. *Fixing a Gin: Math and History at Your Desk.* Available online. URL: http://invention.smithsonian.org/centerpieces/whole_cloth/u2ei/u2ma. Accessed December 11, 2008.

EL SALVADOR

El Salvador is the smallest country in Central America, located along the Pacific Coast between GUATEMALA and NICARAGUA. To the north, it borders HONDURAS. The country is mountainous, with many volcanoes. The coastal strip is narrow, but the highlands have good soil and supported a large population in precolonial times. The soil and climate favor some plantation crops, including INDIGO CULTIVATION, cacao growing, and COFFEE CULTIVATION.

Unlike all of the other Central American countries, El Salvador lacks a Caribbean coast and thus is home to no Afro-Caribbean-Indian population similar to the Garifuna, Miskito, and BLACK CARIB. This does not mean that there are no Afro-descended people in El Salvador, however. The first free people of color entered El Salvador with the conquistador Pedro de Alvarado (1485–1541) in 1526. He established the colonial capital of San Salvador in that year, and among his companions was a young free colored servant named Juan Valiente (1505?–53), who went on to become one of the most important conquistadores in CHILE. Juan Bardales (?– 1551) was also a companion of Alvarado, who went on to take up land in Honduras and become a leading citizen of Tegucigalpa.

In 1548, the New Laws of the Indies went into force in Central America. These Spanish laws freed most surviving Indian slaves and encouraged the importation of Africans to replace them in Spanish plantations and mines. By this time, the native population of El Salvador had fallen to below 10,000, and the native culture had been almost destroyed. Most surviving native people were living on large farms owned by the conquistadores and were rapidly acculturating. El Salvador had a brief boom in the mining sector in the mid-16th century, and more than 10,000 African slaves were imported to work in the mines. Throughout the 16th century, no more than 1,000 whites lived in the colony. Thus, the majority of 16th-century ancestors of modern Salvadorans were Africans.

Mining, especially placer mining for gold, which was the largest product in El Salvador, had a high mortality rate but also offered an avenue for slaves to gain their freedom. Placer miners worked independently, with panning dish and shovel alongside remote streams. If they were enslaved, they were usually required to turn over a fixed amount of product to their masters on each trip. Striking it rich, a slave could earn enough to buy his freedom within one or two trips. Failing to find anything, he had a strong motive to run away to avoid punishment and little supervision to stop him. El Salvador rapidly developed a free African and Afro-mestizo population as well as communities of MAROONS. Starting in the 1670s, as the placer gold fields declined, indigo became an important product. More slaves were imported to work in this field, which remained an important sector of the economy into the 19th century.

Most slaves imported to the colony were men, who established relationships with Indian women. Since the women were free, their mixed-race ZAMBO children were also legally free. Thus, El Salvador gained a large free mixed-race population. By 1779, 31 percent of the colony's inhabitants were mixed-race, for a total of more than 25,000 people. Some of these were Euro-Indian mixes, or mestizos, but most were zambos, that is, Afro-Indians. Raised by Indian mothers, however, these zambo children mainly inherited an Indian culture that had been strongly affected by the European conquerors. Although slave imports continued on a lower level into the 18th century, by the beginning of the 18th century, most Salvadorans were primarily aware of their Indian ancestry and looked to European cultural models.

New Spain, which included MEXICO and what is now the Central American nations, gained its independence from Spain in 1821 after a bloody 10-year struggle. Some of the most important leaders of the independence struggle, including the rebel top commanders José María Morelos and Vicente Guerrero Saldaña were free Afro-mestizos. The war had little impact in El Salvador, however, other than disrupting trade routes. The Central American nations declared independence from Mexico in 1823, forming the United States of Central America, and El Salvador became an independent nation in 1839. Their constitution of the Central American Federation of 1824 outlawed slavery. Conservative local elites in the various countries managed to prevent this provision of the constitution from taking full effect, but most slaves in El Salvador were free by 1856 when the liberal president Gerardo Barrios (1813–65) proclaimed the emancipation of the few still held in captivity.

People with some African ancestry make up a substantial percentage of El Salvador's population today—by some estimates as much as 50 percent. However, this fact is little known or acknowledged. Almost no Salvadorans today self-identify as Afro-Latinos. A series of conservative Salvadoran governments, starting in the 1870s, both forbade black immigration to the country and did their best to convince Salvadorans that their identity was solely Hispanic and Indian. Thanks to the flexibility of racial lines in Latin American culture, this effort was largely successful. Nonetheless, Afro-Caribbean rhythms dominate in Salvadoran popular music. The national musical instrument, the marimba, is directly descended from African instruments. As has much of Spanish America, El Salvador has lost sight of its African roots and is only now beginning to rediscover them.

Stewart R. King

FURTHER READING

Andrews, George. *Afro Latin America, 1800–2000.* New York: Oxford University Press, 2004.

Dzidzienyo, Anani, and Susan Oboloer. *Neither Enemies nor Friends: Latinos, Blacks, Afro-Latinos.* New York: Palgrave Macmillan, 2005.

EMANCIPATION PROCLAMATION

President ABRAHAM LINCOLN often spoke of the abolition of slavery as a good end but repeatedly denied dur-ing the 1860 campaign and afterward that he sought to abolish slavery as a matter of policy. Lincoln actually was a frequent target of more ardent abolitionists who thought his commitment to the cause to be tepid at best. He was nominated as the Republican candidate in 1860 only because the abolitionist faction of the party was unable to muster enough votes for the NEW YORK STATE senator William Seward, their foremost spokesman, or the alternative antislavery candidate, Edward Bates of MISSOURI. Most abolitionists would also have accepted the former OHIO senator Salmon Chase ahead of Lincoln. Lincoln's position on slavery was that it should not be extended into the western territories, and that free states should not be required to change their policies and accept or support the institution, but that slavery could not constitutionally be interfered with in the states where it existed.

The AMERICAN CIVIL WAR began in April 1861, one month after Lincoln's inauguration. As the war entered its second year, it became increasingly obvious that slaves were an important military asset for the Confederacy. Slaves built military fortifications, transported supplies, worked as servants for officers, and tended the sick and wounded of the Confederate army. They also did much of the agricultural work in the South, at least on the very productive plantations, supporting the Southern economy and freeing white men for military service. Northerners soon realized that, if freed, Southern blacks could be an important military asset for the United States forces. Abolitionists, such as FREDERICK DOUGLASS, had been urging Lincoln to enlist Northern free blacks as soldiers since the beginning of the war. The much larger numbers of blacks in the South could provide an important reservoir of manpower for the United States in what was increasingly obvious was going to be a protracted war of attrition. Congressman Thaddeus Stevens had put forward a bill to confiscate the slaves of supporters of the Confederacy, which became law in July 1862. As a matter of course, slaves who ran away from their masters in Confederate territory and made it to U.S. Army camps were not sent back by 1862 but were instead treated as "contraband of war" and put to work in support of the U.S. military.

Lincoln soon believed that emancipation would be central to Union victory since it would deprive the Confederacy of its labor supply. He initially had opposed freeing slaves by executive order, fearing that state governments could nullify such action. Early Confederate military victories, however, convinced him that emergency executive action was necessary to turn the tide of the war. Lincoln also knew that European perceptions of the United States were important, and he feared that BRITAIN and FRANCE might

A U.S. Army officer reads the Emancipation Proclamation to Louisiana blacks and black Union soldiers in 1863. Almost all slaves in Union-controlled parts of Louisiana had already been freed as "contraband of war," that is, property owned by rebels that might have been used to support the Confederate war effort, but the Emancipation Proclamation promised them that they would never be returned to slavery and that all other slaves in the rebel states would be free as soon as the Union army could take control of the area where they lived. *(North Wind Picture Archives via Associated Press)*

recognize the Confederacy. So long as the war was merely a struggle between two sections of the country over the power of the central government, it was conceivable that Britain and France, the great powers of the age, could intervene to force peace and the acceptance of an independent Confederacy. But if Lincoln could redefine the war as a struggle of freedom versus slavery, no western European government would have been politically able to tell its people that it was going to war on the side of slavery. Thus, in summer 1862, Lincoln began considering the possibility of declaring the abolition of slavery in those areas under the con-

trol of the Confederacy. He wrote a draft, probably in July, and showed it to his vice president and cabinet. Secretary of State William Seward advised him to wait for a major battlefield victory before issuing the proclamation publicly, arguing that such a declaration at a time of military weakness could look like desperation. Lincoln accepted the advice, and after the Union victory at Antietam on September 17, 1862, he issued the Preliminary Emancipation Proclamation, dated September 22, 1862. This proclamation declared that slaves in states still in rebellion on January 1, 1863, would be "forever free."

In this 1865 illustration, Thomas Nast celebrates the emancipation of Southern slaves with the end of the American Civil War. *(Library of Congress)*

The Preliminary Emancipation Proclamation did not free slaves in areas under the control of the U.S. forces, which at the time included the slave states of TENNESSEE, MARYLAND, KENTUCKY, DELAWARE, and MISSOURI, the part of Virginia that was shortly to become the state of West Virginia, and the Gulf Coast of LOUISIANA, including NEW ORLEANS, LOUISIANA. Slaves in those areas were freed by the actions of their own state legislatures or by the Thirteenth Amendment to the U.S. Constitution, ratified in December 1865. The Emancipation Proclamation issued on January 1, 1863, was perhaps Abraham Lincoln's most important written document and his greatest accomplishment as president. The proclamation declared free all slaves held in areas then rebelling against the federal government.

The Emancipation Proclamation divided contemporaries. Since it did not free slaves in areas under direct federal control, some critics, including Frederick Douglass, charged that it lacked the authority to free any slaves. Others, however, thought that it went too far. In the early months of 1863, thousands of Union troops deserted, angry that abolition of slavery and not the preservation of the Union now appeared to be the primary goal of the federal war effort. The Emancipation Proclama-

tion set the nation on the course of abolition that once begun could not be stopped. In January 1865, Congress passed the Thirteenth Amendment abolishing slavery, and the states ratified it in December. The Emancipation Proclamation changed the course of the American Civil War and ensured Abraham Lincoln's status as one of the nation's greatest presidents

The Emancipation Proclamation has remained one of the foundational documents of America. The date of the proclamation, or a date in June recognizing the reception of the news in the South called Juneteenth, is a holiday among African Americans.

Stewart R. King

FURTHER READING

Holzer, Harold, Edna Greene Medford, and Frank J. Williams. *The Emancipation Proclamation: Three Views (Conflicting Worlds: New Dimensions of the American Civil War)*. Baton Rouge: Louisiana State University Press, 2006.

"Preliminary Emancipation Proclamation: A Virtual Visit." New York Public Library. Available online. URL: http://www.nysl.nysed.gov/library/features/ep/. Accessed December 23, 2010.

EMANCIPATION PROCLAMATIONS, 1862, 1863

The following is the full text of the two proclamations, the first issued by President Abraham Lincoln on September 22, 1862, after word of the Union victory at Antietam reached Washington, D.C. President Lincoln issued the second one on New Year's Day 1863, ratifying and enforcing the first.

Preliminary Proclamation

By the President of the United States of America

A PROCLAMATION

I, Abraham Lincoln, President of the United States of America, and Commander-in-Chief of the Army and Navy thereof, do hereby proclaim and declare that hereafter, as heretofore, the war will be prosecuted for the object of practically restoring the constitutional relation between the United States, and each of the states, and the people thereof, in which states that relation is, or may be suspended or disturbed.

That it is my purpose, upon the next meeting of Congress to again recommend the adoption of a practical measure tendering pecuniary aid to the free acceptance or rejection of all slave-states, so called, the people whereof may not then be in rebellion against the United States, and which states and may then have voluntarily adopted, or thereafter may voluntarily adopt, immediate, or gradual abolishment of slavery within their respective limits; and that the effort to colonize persons of African descent upon this continent, or elsewhere, with the previously obtained consent of the governments existing there, will be continued.

That on the first day of January in the year of our Lord, one thousand eight hundred and sixty-three, all persons held as slaves within any state, or designated part of a state, the people whereof shall than be in rebellion against the United States; shall be then, thenceforward, and forever free; and the executive government of the United States including the military and naval authority thereof will, recognize and maintain the freedom of such persons, and will do no act or acts to repress such persons, or any of them, in any efforts they may make for their actual freedom.

That the executive will, on the first day of January aforesaid, by proclamation, designate the States, and parts of states, if any, in which the people thereof respectively, shall then be in rebellion against the United States; and the fact that any state, or the people thereof shall, on that day be, in good faith represented in the Congress of the United States, by members chosen thereto, at elections wherein a majority of the qualified voters of such state shall have participated, shall, in the absence of strong countervailing testimony, be deemed conclusive evidence that such state, and the people thereof, are not then in rebellion against the United States.

That attention is hereby called to an Act of Congress entitled "An Act to make an additional Article of War" Approved March 13, 1862, and which act is in the words and figure following:

Be it enacted by the Senate and House of Representatives of the United States of America in Congress assembled. That hereafter the following shall be promulgated as an additional article of war for the government of the Army of the United States, and shall be obeyed and observed as such:

Article—. All officers or persons in the military or naval services of the United States are prohibited from employing any of the forces under their respective commands for the purpose of returning fugitives from service or labor, who may have escaped from any persons to whom such service or labor is claimed to be due and any officer who shall be found guilty by a court martial of violating this article shall be dismissed from the service.

SEC. 2. And be it further enacted, that this act shall take effect from and after its passage.

Also to the ninth and tenth sections of an act entitled "An Act to suppress Insurrection, to punish Treason and Rebellion, to seize and confiscate property of rebels, and for other purposes," approved July 17, 1862, and which sections are:

SEC. 9. And be it further enacted, that all slaves of persons who shall hereafter be engaged in rebellion against the government of the United States, or who shall in any way give aid or comfort thereto, escaping from such persons and taking refuge within the lines of the army; and all slaves captured from such persons or deserted by them and coming under the control of the government of the United States; and all slaves of such persons found or being within any place occupied by rebel forces and afterwards occupied by the forces of the United States, shall be deemed captives of war, and shall be forever free of their servitude, and not again held as slaves.

SEC. 10. And be it further enacted, That no slave escaping into any State, Territory, or the District of Columbia, from any other State, shall be delivered up, or in any way impeded or hindered of his liberty, except for crime, or some offence against the laws, unless the person claiming said fugitive shall first make oath that the person to whom the labor or service of such fugitive is alleged to be due is his lawful owner, and has not borne arms against the United States in the present rebellion, nor in any way given aid and comfort thereto; and no person engaged in the military or naval service of the United States shall, under any pretence whatever, assume to decide on the validity of the claim of any person to the service or labor of any other person, or surrender up any such person to the claimant, on pain of being dismissed from the service.

And I do hereby enjoin upon and order all persons engaged in the military and naval service of the United States to observe, obey, and enforce, within their respective spheres of service, the act and sections above recited.

And the executive will in due time recommend that all citizens of the United States who shall have remained loyal thereto throughout the rebellion, shall (upon the restoration of the constitutional relation between the United States, and their respective states, and people, if that relation shall have been suspended or disturbed) be compensated for all losses by acts of the United States, including the loss of slaves.

In witness whereof, I have hereunto set my hand and caused the seal of the United States to be affixed.

Done at the City of Washington, this twenty second day of September, in the year of our Lord, one thousand eight hundred and sixty two, and of the Independence of the United States the eighty seventh.

Abraham Lincoln
By the President:
William H. Seward
Secretary of State

Final Proclamation

By the President of the United States of America

A PROCLAMATION.

Whereas, on the twenty-second day of September, in the year of our Lord one thousand eight hundred and sixty-two, a proclamation was issued by the President of the United States, containing, among other things, the following, to wit:

That on the first day of January, in the year of our Lord one thousand eight hundred and sixty-three, all persons held as slaves within any State or designated part of a State, the people whereof shall then be in rebellion against the United States, shall be then, thenceforward, and forever free; and the Executive Government of the United States, including the military and naval authority thereof . . . will do no act or acts to repress such persons . . . in any efforts they may make for their actual freedom.

That the Executive will, on the first day of January aforesaid, by proclamation, designate the States and parts of States, if any, in which the people thereof . . . shall then be in rebellion against the United States; and the fact that any State, or the people thereof, shall on that day be, in good faith,

represented in the Congress of the United States by members chosen thereto at elections wherein a majority of the qualified voters of such State shall have participated, shall, in the absence of strong countervailing testimony, be deemed conclusive evidence that such State, and the people thereof, are not then in rebellion against the United States.

Now, therefore I, Abraham Lincoln, President of the United States, by virtue of the power in me vested as Commander-in-Chief, of the Army and Navy of the United States in time of actual armed rebellion against the authority and government of the United States, and as a fit and necessary war measure for suppressing said rebellion, do, on this first day of January, in the year of our Lord one thousand eight hundred and sixty-three, . . . designate as the States and parts of States wherein the people thereof respectively, are this day in rebellion against the United States, the following, to wit:

Arkansas, Texas, Louisiana, (except the Parishes of St. Bernard, Plaquemines, Jefferson, St. John, St. Charles, St. James Ascension, Assumption, Terrebonne, Lafourche, St. Mary, St. Martin, and Orleans, including the City of New Orleans), Mississippi, Alabama, Florida, Georgia, South Carolina, North Carolina, and Virginia, (except the forty-eight counties designated as West Virginia, and also the counties of Berkley, Accomac, Northampton, Elizabeth City, York, Princess Ann, and Norfolk, including the cities of Norfolk and Portsmouth[)], and which excepted parts, are for the present, left precisely as if this proclamation were not issued.

And by the virtue of the power, and for the purpose aforesaid, I do order and declare that all persons held as slaves within said designated States, and parts of States, are, and henceforward shall be free; and that the Executive government of the United States, including the military and naval authorities thereof, will recognize and maintain the freedom of said persons.

And I hereby enjoin upon the people so declared to be free to abstain from all violence, unless in necessary [self-defense]; and I recommend to them that, in all cases when allowed, they labor faithfully for reasonable wages.

And I further declare and make known, that such persons of suitable condition, will be received into the armed service of the Unites States to garrison forts, positions, stations, and other places, and to man vessels of all sorts in said service.

And upon this act, sincerely believed to be an act of justice, warranted by the Constitution, upon military necessity, I invoke the considerate judgment of mankind, and the gracious favor of Almighty God.

Sources: "Preliminary Emancipation Proclamation." Available online. URL: http://www.nysl.nysed.gov/library/features/ep/. Accessed May 4, 2011. Also available at http://www.ashbrook. org/library/19/lincoln/emancipationproclamation.html. Accessed May 4, 2011.

EMIGRATION AND COLONIZATION

From the point of view of white elites, free people of color were incompatible elements in a racially based slave system. This was true everywhere in the Americas, and especially in the United States, where a republican ideal of the equality of all free people coexisted poorly with laws and customs decreeing white supremacy over nonwhites. Many white elites wanted to remove all or almost all free people of African ancestry from their societies in order to resolve the contradiction. Indigenous peoples in the United States and in Spanish America were often moved to reservations or Indian villages. Naturally, the idea of special reservations for free blacks suggested itself. In many places, governments or private members of the white ruling class launched schemes to move free people of color to colonies or settlements outside the area settled by whites and slaves. In some cases, individual leaders within the free colored community cooperated in these efforts, though in general free people of color preferred to remain in place. These efforts did succeed in creating some lasting settlements but were unsuccessful in their intended goal of removing all free people of color from any of the places where these policies were attempted.

Migration of free people of color took place in many different ways. Sometimes, people were obliged to move out of a territory upon being freed, while in other situations the desire to move originated with the freed persons themselves. (Voluntary, private migration that was not part of a publicly endorsed scheme is the subject of another article; *see* MIGRATION.) In some instances, groups of free people of color went to special settlements

Emigrants awaiting transportation to Liberia (1880). After the failure of Reconstruction in the United States, some African Americans immigrated to countries where they would be more welcome. Liberia, founded in 1821 as a refuge for free people of color from the United States, was a popular destination after the Civil War. *(American School/Private Collection/The Bridgeman Art Library International)*

or regions, generally in areas where slavery was not permitted. Sometimes movements were international, and sometimes they remained within the borders of a particular colony or to other regions within the same colonial empire or large country. These movements were generally supported by the white population, but sometimes this support manifested itself in government or private charitable funding and in other cases merely as more or less friendly encouragement. Free people of color often resisted colonization schemes, arguing that they were rightful citizens of the countries where they lived when they gained their freedom and had the right to stay. Sometimes, white elites also opposed colonization schemes and forced emigration, especially if they had family members or clients of color.

Obliging or encouraging slaves to leave a territory upon gaining their freedom was a characteristic of laws in the United States. Once the Northern states abolished slavery in the early years after independence, and it became obvious that the United States was going to be divided into free and slave territory, white leaders in the slave states almost universally decided that free blacks belonged somewhere else, not living near their slaves. Some states, especially those in the Upper South, such as VIRGINIA AND WEST VIRGINIA and KENTUCKY, made MANUMISSION more difficult after the 1820s, including imposing significant taxes or bonds on newly freed people, which they could avoid by moving permanently to other states. They also, as did many Northern states, forbade immigration by free people of color from other states. But they did not entirely outlaw manumitted people's remaining in the state, and many did choose to stay. In the Deep South states, on the other hand, there were strict laws requiring people who gained their freedom to leave the state within a short period after the manumission was granted, and enforcement made it difficult for people to remain. Some did, but they were rare. And, of course, the most common form of manumission was for the master to simply take his slaves to a Northern state, avoiding all the paperwork but making it impossible for the newly freed person to return without risk of legal trouble, even RE-ENSLAVEMENT, if the original master had died or become bankrupt and the heirs were opposed to the grant of freedom.

These individual or family migrations from the South to the North were encouraged or obliged by the states' laws, but they might well have been the freed persons' wishes as well. Plenty of slaves made the dangerous journey from south to north against their masters' will, seeking freedom at the risk of their lives or severe punishment. A dominant ideology of white supremacy was growing fast in the 1830s, and increasingly harsh laws controlled free blacks' activities in many onerous ways. Despite these factors, many free blacks chose to stay: The South was their home, many

had enslaved family members they did not want to leave, and others were protected by white patrons (who may have been family members). After the end of slavery, many who had left returned to their native states—a prominent example is JOHN MERCER LANGSTON, a mixed-race Virginian, who was moved to OHIO by his family, apparently without any formalities of manumission (his mother may have been free before his birth); there he attended college and had a career in law and public service. After completing a tour as U.S. minister to Haiti in 1885, he moved back to Virginia, where he was president of the state teacher's college for blacks and served a term in the U.S. House of Representatives.

Arriving in the Northern states, or, later, in CANADA, the free people of color often formed distinctive communities. Racial prejudice was present throughout the Northern United States and even in Canada, and the black immigrant population generally chose to live together. In some cases, this desire to settle together was encouraged or even made obligatory by laws and social customs in the host territories. In the Midwest and West after the end of slavery, many cities and towns adopted "sundown" ordinances that required blacks to be outside the city limits during the nighttime hours. These laws replaced or supported pervasive social customs that required people of color to live in specially designated black districts. These districts were often in unincorporated areas outside city limits and thus did not receive city services: law enforcement, fire protection, city schools, and so forth. These settlements took on some of the characteristics of colonies, in that they had a distinctive culture and ethnic population. They ultimately assimilated into the larger population with the arrival of more Southern blacks in the Great Migrations of the late 19th and early 20th centuries and the end of segregation during the Civil Rights movement of the mid-20th century.

The largest era of internal colonization in the United States was after the Civil War, when the newly freed, led in many cases by prewar free blacks, established settlements in the West. The EXODUSTER MOVEMENT, or KANSAS Exodus of 1879, led by the prewar MICHIGAN free black Benjamin Singleton, led as many as 40,000 Southern blacks to Kansas and Colorado after the outcome of the U.S. ELECTION OF 1876 showed that the federal government was not going to protect blacks' rights in the South. The attitude of Southern governments and white public opinion toward blacks was bizarrely contradictory: On the one hand, Southern whites knew they needed black labor to keep agriculture productive, but on the other hand, they imposed such a harsh system of racial discrimination that they were clearly encouraging blacks to leave. The Exodusters established a number of predominantly black towns in Kansas, of which Nicodemus is the best known and almost the only one still largely inhabited by the descendants of the immigrants. OKLAHOMA was later proposed as a potential refuge for Southern blacks fleeing oppression after the failure of RECONSTRUCTION IN THE UNITED STATES. EDWIN P. MCCABE, a free black lawyer from ILLINOIS, helped establish some 80 black communities in Oklahoma and worked unsuccessfully to be named territorial governor. These communities were self-contained and preserved the distinctive culture of their inhabitants better than the black neighborhoods and towns in the North, because they were not surrounded by large numbers of white settlers. However, the increasingly harsh racial climate around the turn of the 20th century and the "dust bowl" drought of the 1920s drove many of these people to the cities of the North and Midwest, and the colonies generally only exist today as ghost towns or historical monuments. As in the earlier migration of freed blacks before the Civil War, this migration did little to reduce the population of blacks in the South, drawing off something around 1 percent of the total population.

International migration was an option for free people of color that did create more clearly defined colonies. Many philanthropic American whites in the early 19th century wanted to move free people of color to Africa. THOMAS JEFFERSON encouraged migration in his *Notes on the State of Virginia* (1785). PAUL CUFFE, a free black merchant from MASSACHUSETTS, worked with Northern evangelists and Southern white leaders to establish a regular shipping connection between BOSTON and SIERRA LEONE, which would carry black emigrants to Africa and return valuable cargoes to the United States. Cuffe's business never prospered, but his idea led to the establishment in 1816 of the AMERICAN COLONIZATION SOCIETY (ACS). The ACS had as its founding leaders important politicians including Henry Clay of Kentucky (1777–1852), Daniel Webster of Massachusetts (1782–1852), and John Randolph (1777–1833) of Virginia. The ACS raised significant funds from private benefactors and state governments in the South and a small sum from the federal government. The funds were sufficient to establish a number of colonies along the West African coast that ultimately became the independent nation of LIBERIA, along with a colony established separately by the state of Maryland. Other American colonization schemes included a plan to send blacks to Haiti after the American Civil War, supported by then U.S. minister FREDERICK DOUGLASS, and a plan to move American blacks to BRAZIL in the 1880s that was derailed by the fall of the imperial government and its replacement by a republic that was much less friendly to people of color. After 1888, Brazil had a policy of favoring white immigration, and the American black group's plans were stalled, though

a number of individual blacks emigrated from America to Brazil.

International migration of free people of color was a strategy adopted by other countries. The British especially put important resources into establishing a colony in Sierra Leone as a home for people of color from Britain and the American colonies. The first group of settlers in Sierra Leone, in 1787, consisted of free blacks from Britain. The British local governments found caring for the large population of indigent free blacks, many of whom were servants or navy personnel who had grown too old to work, very expensive. Unfortunately, the coast of West Africa was not a healthy place for a population of mostly elderly or handicapped Britons. Most of the first group died within a few years of their arrival. The second group, entering in 1791 under the auspices of the Sierra Leone Company and its director GRANVILLE SHARP, were black veterans of the loyalist forces during the WAR OF AMERICAN INDEPENDENCE, 1775–83. They also had very high mortality rates, but they were family groups of young people whose men often had recent combat experience. Their settlements in Freetown, the capital, and other parts of the colony survived and ultimately thrived. A group of Jamaican MAROONS joined them in 1799, arriving just in time to put down a rebellion by the earlier colonists that threatened white domination over the colony. The British based their Atlantic anti–slave trade patrols out of Freetown's marvelous harbor, and thousands of recaptured Africans joined the American exiles. The Sierra Leone and Liberia colonies ultimately developed into distinctive minority populations in their respective countries that dominated the politics of both places until the late 20th century. The "Americos" of Liberia provided most of the senior civil servants and all the political leaders of the country until a military coup in 1980, and the Krio-speaking minority of Sierra Leone dominated the civil service and the professions until the civil war there in the 1990s.

Many of the Sierra Leone settlers were from CANADA, especially Nova Scotia, and the black settlements established there after the American Revolution were intended to be separate colonies. However, discrimination both by the colonial government and by the local white population undermined the integrity of these communities, and they generally either moved on to other destinations within the British Empire or became a permanent semi-assimilated subordinate caste within Nova Scotia society.

Internal colonization was also tried in the British Empire when the BLACK CARIB of the Lesser Antilles, a group who included many free blacks, were moved to the coast of Central America, particularly BELIZE. This was not an attempt to remove all free blacks from the territory, though, but instead to remove a particular group of free coloreds that was especially challenging to the social order because of their indigenous lifestyle and repeated wars with the settled population of the colonies. The government of Jamaica had similar goals when removing some of the maroons from the mountains in the northern part of the island. These people went ultimately to Sierra Leone, after first being settled in Nova Scotia, Canada.

The Spanish colonies generally integrated people of African descent better than British ones, but there were some special colonial projects there as well. In Cuba, the famous settlement of El Cobre, in the eastern province of the island, was a distinctive community of free people of color, protected by the Spanish king, who were specialists in mining the mineral deposits. They preserved their culture throughout the colonial period and the various wars of late 19th-century Cuba, and their descendants today still think of themselves as a distinct community. Mexico hosted a community of American black Indians, the Black Seminole, who fled the Indian settlements in Oklahoma when faced with racial discrimination by whites and Indians.

The French colonies in Senegambia were more like the British and American models, in that free people of color from France were sometimes encouraged to move there as a result of official discomfort with the presence of large numbers of people of African descent in France. However, there was never a large organized colonization society or concerted governmental effort, and instead the citizens of the French towns on the coast of Senegambia, the famous women merchants called *signares*, were mostly the descendants of white French men and their African partners. The culture of these people was thus more purely African, and these populations assimilated more completely into the African population than did the Sierra Leonean or Liberian immigrant groups.

Brazil received some American black immigrants but was unwilling to permit the immigration of large groups of blacks to establish separate colonies. Brazilian people of color were an important component in the settlement of the ports of the Congo and Angola coast, and to a lesser degree in slave-trading ports elsewhere on the African coast, in the 18th and 19th centuries. These were not designed as colonies for blacks in the same sense as Liberia and Sierra Leone, however. Instead, the Portuguese and Brazilian merchants who wished to trade on the Central African coast tended to choose black or brown Brazilian employees because of the mistaken belief that they were more resistant to tropical diseases. The Afro-Brazilian population of Angola assimilated smoothly into the larger African population in the 20th century, in a similar manner to the French-African mixed-race people of Senegambia, and unlike the immigrant populations of Liberia or Sierra Leone.

Stewart R. King

FURTHER READING

Anderson, Eric. "Black Émigrés: The Emergence of Nineteenth-Century United States Black Nationalism in Response to Haitian Emigration, 1816–1840." *49th Parallel: An Interdisciplinary Journal of North American Studies* 1 (Winter 1999). Available online. URL: www.49thparallel.bham.ac.uk/back/issue1/emigres.htm. Accessed December 23, 2010.

Angrand, Jean-Luc. *Céleste ou le temps des signares.* Paris: Éditions Anne Pépin, 2006.

Diaz, Maria Elena. *The Virgin, the King, and the Royal Slaves of El Cobre: Negotiating Freedom in Colonial Cuba, 1670–1780.* Palo Alto, Calif.: Stanford University Press, 2000.

Dixon, Chris. *African America and Haiti: Emigration and Black Nationalism in the Nineteenth Century.* Westport, Conn.: Greenwood Press, 2000.

Dorsey, Bruce Allen. "A Gendered History of African Colonization in the Antebellum United States." *Journal of Social History* 34, no. 1 (2000): 77–103.

Garrison, William Lloyd. *Thoughts on African Colonization.* Boston, 1832. Reprint, New York: Arno Press, 1968.

Harris, Joseph, ed. *Global Dimensions of the African Diaspora.* Washington, D.C.: Howard University Press, 1982.

Miller, Joseph C. *Way of Death: Merchant Capitalism and the Angolan Slave Trade, 1730–1830.* Madison: University of Wisconsin Press, 1988.

Nash, Gary B. *Forging Freedom: The Formation of Philadelphia's Black Community, 1720–1840.* Cambridge, Mass.: Harvard University Press, 1988.

Shick, Tom. *Behold the Promised Land: A History of Afro-American Settler Society in Nineteenth-Century Liberia.* Baltimore: Johns Hopkins University Press, 1980.

ENCYCLOPÉDIE

Published in 27 volumes over a period of more than 20 years, 1750–1772, the *Encyclopédie ou Dictionnaire raisonné des sciences, des arts et des métiers* (Encyclopedia or carefully thought-out dictionary of the sciences, arts, and activities) was an attempt to include all knowledge on any subject in one set of books. This ambitious attempt was doomed by the rapid increase in human knowledge during the very period it was being compiled. Nonetheless, it allows us to gauge attitudes and ideas held by the most educated and respected people in Europe in the 18th century. The articles on race, and especially on Africans and African Americans, were to have enormous impact on educated people's ideas about these subjects, not only in France, but throughout Europe, for a century and more.

Even though it is generally known after the name of its two famous editors, Denis Diderot (1713–84) and Jean le Rond d'Alembert (1717–83), a large number of the entries in the *Encyclopédie* (17,000 of 68,000) were written by Louis de Jaucourt (1704–79)—including those on foreign countries, and especially that on the "*traite des nègres*" (trade in Negroes, or slave trade), which he vehemently condemned. Despite this condemnation, de Jaucourt reflected many of the racial views and stereotypes of the time. His use of the term *nègres*—a close cognate to the English "nigger" with similarly negative connotations—was the standard word in France for all black people until recently. De Jaucourt—and the *Encyclopédie* as a whole—is patronizing and condescending toward non-European peoples, an attitude inconsistent with their belief in a conception of humankind that insisted on common human rights whatever the place or circumstances of one's birth.

The philosophers of 18th-century France tended to distinguish between the way they perceived non-European countries in the present and the glory that those countries had enjoyed in ancient times. It may be argued that the first level of their stereotyped view of the world was based on cultural values, as the entry on "Barbarians" makes clear: "The name that the Greeks gave out of contempt to all the nations who did not speak their language—at least as well as they. . . . It is like we French, who regard as boorish anything that is not similar to our customs. The Greeks and Romans were eager to dominate even more by the mind than by the force of arms, as we try to do with our fashions."

Thus, the nearer to the French yardstick, the more acceptable what we now call a civilization was in their eyes. But at the same time, they were aware that 18th-century French values have no universality—they are the result of fashion, essentially a transient criterion. And it is precisely this aspiration to a universal culture or civilization that was the object of all their efforts—one only has to remember how Voltaire derided the established religions of his time because they were parochial, with the Muslims worshipping God on Friday, the Jews on Saturday, and the Christians on Sunday. An enlightened man could only conceive of one "universal" day. Nonetheless, it was difficult even for the philosophers of the Enlightenment to escape their own parochial value set. Therefore, the inhabitants of the non-European world met with increasing respect in the *Encyclopédie* as they approached French or European intellectual and cultural standards.

"Turks apply themselves a lot to medicine, geometry, geography, etc, and morals," says the *Encyclopédie* approvingly. On the other hand, the judgment is more ambiguous for the peoples of Asia. The encyclopedists recognize that this continent has produced great civilizations in the past. For instance, the East Indies used to have great philosophers: "The peoples of this country had such a reputation for their wisdom among the Greeks that their philosophers never thought it below their dignity to visit them. . . . As far as their moral philosophy was con-

cerned, everything in it was noble and elevated. For them, there was only one good, namely wisdom." But then, the *Encyclopédie* continues, they went through a phase of decline: "What a difference between this philosophy and the one which is currently proffered in the Indies!"

In the case of the Japanese, the reasoning is slightly different—they were above the Europeans at one time: "Japan, with a population as numerous proportionately as that of China, and no less industrious, while the nation is prouder and braver, possesses almost everything that we have, and almost everything that we have not. The peoples of the Orient once were superior to our Western peoples, in all the arts of the mind and of the hand." Again, however, there is a caveat: "But how we have caught up with lost time! . . . The oriental peoples are only barbarians, or children, in the fine arts, in spite of their antiquity and all that Nature has done for them." In other words, the peoples of Asia were not intrinsically inferior to those of 18th-century Europe—one only had to look at their past achievements in the things of the mind—but the question was whether they would be able to keep pace with the Westerners, who were making such rapid progress.

The "Indians" of the Americas could not have been more different: "A large part of North America is peopled with savages, most of them still ferocious, and who feed on human flesh." The archetype were the Iroquois: "All are savage warriors, comparatively united, now attached to the English, now to the French, according to where they believe their interests lie. . . . Their largest trade is in beavers, which they barter against brandy, which they passionately love. . . . Their religion is only a medley of childish superstitions, in keeping with their barbarous mores."

It is, however, the Africans who receive the most negative descriptions in the *Encyclopédie*, especially those of Senegal, France's largest colony in Africa at the time (*see also* SENEGAMBIA): "They steal each other and strive to sell one another to the Europeans who trade in slaves along their coasts." The people of Southern Africa suffer even more at the hands de Jaucourt: "The Hottentots are not Negroes. . . . They would only be tanned if they did not blacken their skin with grease and tallow, which they mix to smear themselves with. . . . Their hair, glued together by their horrible dirtiness, looks like the fleece of a black sheep full of excrement. . . . Their language is strange: they chuckle like guinea-fowls. . . . The women are much smaller than the men, and most of them have a sort of excrescence, or skin, which grows over their pubic bone and drops to the middle of their thighs, like a kind of apron. . . . For their part, the men. . . are all semi-eunuchs—not that they are born like this, but because one of their testicles is removed from them at the age of eight, or sometimes later."

The entry in the *Encyclopédie* on "Character of negroes in general" is full of contradictions. It begins with an entirely negative judgment: "If by chance one meets with honest Negroes from Guinea (the vast majority are always vicious), most of them are prone to lechery, vengefulness, theft and lying. Their stubbornness is such that they never confess their faults, whatever punishment is imposed upon them; even the fear of death does not move them. In spite of this kind of firmness, their natural bravery does not shelter them from the fear of sorcerers and spirits, which they call *zambys*."

The assessment is slightly more positive for the descendants of those transported across the Atlantic: "As for the Creole negroes, the workings of education make them a little better; they always retain something of their origins, however; they are vain, contemptuous, conceited, with a love for finery, gambling and above all else women; the latter are in no way different, following the ardor of their temperament without restraint; besides, they are prone to quick passions, tenderness and attachment." This can be seen as a reflection of the attitude common among SLAVE OWNERS in the Americas, in French as in other colonies, about CREOLE blacks. Yet, this is followed by what can only appear as a complete refutation of the damning comments with which the entry opens: "The negroes' faults are not so universally widespread that one does not come across very good subjects; many planters own whole families made of perfectly honest people, much attached to their masters, whose conduct would shame many whites. All are usually brave, courageous, sympathetic, charitable, submissive to their parents, and especially to their godfathers and godmothers, and full of respect for old people."

So, it seems clear that de Jaucourt had no real respect for African people—but again, these members of the "black race" were members of a higher entity called the "human race," and as such they should be treated on an equal footing with their white brothers. It is to be noted, however, that the *Encyclopédie* does not have a lengthy formal treatment of "race," with the very short entry only mentioning the genealogical sense, "extraction, line, lineage," and referring the reader to "birth, nobility." What strikes the modern reader is that despite these negative views, especially of black people, the entry on "Negroes" unambiguously insists on their common stock with the whites: "Are so many different men issuing from the same mother? It is impossible for us to doubt it." One physiological proof given is that "the entrails of negroes and the skins found there are the same color as in white men." This position is in contrast to a common idea about race in the 19th century, called polygenesis, which held that different races had different origins. De Jau-

court's position is closer to the position consistently held by the ROMAN CATHOLIC CHURCH in the 18th and 19th centuries, and thus the orthodox belief in France, that all human beings were descended literally from one mother, Eve.

More than that, the *Encyclopédie* argues that it is behavior, not skin color, that determines barbarity, as the "Slavery" entry indicates: "The right of property over things and over men are very different rights. . . . . The peoples who have treated slaves as goods of which they could dispose at will have only been barbarians. . . . Slavery is a state which is not only humiliating for the person who is submitted to it, but for humanity itself, which is degraded." Many commentators have pointed out the contradictions often found in the *Encyclopédie*. Still, despite the negative image given of Africans, the *Encyclopédie* forcefully denounces the "trade in negroes. . . in order to reduce them to slavery, a commerce which violates religion, morals, natural laws, and all the rights of human nature."

The *Encyclopédie* had a special impact on the lives of free people of color in the Americas because, of all people of African descent, they were the most likely to have contact with educated Europeans and to seek education themselves. The attitudes expressed in the work were the attitudes that they were likely to encounter when they did mix in intellectual circles or seek higher education. A few notable free people of color were important participants in the intellectual world of the Enlightenment: ABRAM PETROVICH GANNIBAL studied in France and met Voltaire in the 1720s. Voltaire called him the "dark star of the Enlightenment." He corresponded with Diderot and d'Alembert. JOSEPH BOLOGNE, CHEVALIER DE SAINT-GEORGES, was a prominent musician in Paris at the time the *Encyclopédie* was being written. As counterexamples to stereotypes, they may have had an influence on the growth of those stereotypes, or at least on the editors' willingness to admit of exceptions to the general rules they were proposing.

Antoine Capet

FURTHER READING

Bernasconi, Robert, and Tommy Lee Lott, eds. *The Idea of Race*. New York: Hackett, 2000.

Diderot, Denis, and Jean le Rond d'Alembert. *Encyclopédie ou Dictionnaire raisonné des sciences, des arts et des métiers*. (Originally published Paris, 1750–1772). Available online. URL: http://encyclopedie.uchicago.edu. Accessed December 23, 2010.

Eze, Emmanuel, ed. *Race and the Enlightenment: A Reader*. New York: Wiley-Blackwell, 1997.

Frederickson, George. *Racism: A Short History*. Princeton, N.J.: Princeton University Press, 2003.

ENRÍQUEZ, MIGUEL   (1672–1743)   *Puerto Rican merchant and privateer*

Enríquez was an Afro–Puerto Rican born sometime in 1672 of a slave mother, a woman of mixed race named Graciana Enríquez, and an unknown white Spanish father. His grandmother was a black woman taken as a slave from Angola. He was the youngest of four siblings, all of whom were born free. In the Spanish colonies in the 17th century, especially in peripheral areas like Puerto Rico, children followed the condition of their father rather than, as was much more common in the slave societies of the Americas, of the mother. We do not know today who Enríquez's father was, but he must have been known at the time since he passed his free condition to his children at birth. Enríquez was, for a while, the wealthiest man of any color on the island and played an important role in Spain's long struggle to preserve its colonial empire in the Americas in the 18th century. His life illustrates the ambivous situation of free blacks and free people of color, the agency they displayed in the face of open and hostile discrimination and prejudice, and the kind of social negotiation and racial struggle that shaped the history of Puerto Rico.

We do not know much about Enríquez's early life. When he was involved in a series of legal cases in later life, he was described as a shoemaker by trade. However, he clearly was a master seafarer by 1700 and so must have been one of the MERCHANT SEAMEN or in the NAVY. There were many free people of color in both fields in the late 17th century. During the War of the Spanish Succession from 1701 through 1714, he became a private armed corsair licensed by the Spanish Crown to intercept British and other enemy ships. The war pitted a varying cast of European powers against Britain and Austria, but for most of the struggle, Spain was allied with FRANCE against BRITAIN. The British had not yet attained the total naval superiority they were to enjoy after the turn of the 19th century, and Spanish privateers could cause great harm and make great profits from attacking British merchant ships. Enríquez was phenomenally successful in his new position. In 1713, after more than a decade of war, he was named Capitán de Mar y Guerra y Armador de los Corsos de Puerto Rico (captain of sea and war and provider [of supplies] for the corsairs of Puerto Rico) and was eventually made a Caballero de la Real Efigie (knight of the royal image). (*See also* PIRACY.) These official military positions were very influential and profitable posts, and it would have been quite unusual during the course of Spain's colonial rule in the Americas for a person of color to hold office at this level.

Enríquez became a rich person in San Juan. From initially owning one armed ship, he ended up with 25, he operated stores where he sold what he captured in his raids, and he owned a sugar mill with 60 slaves. By 1735, he owned more than 250 slaves, more than anyone else on the island. He was active in the local slave trade. Between 1716 and 1733, acting as a licensed corsair, he captured 20 ships, with slaves as part of their cargo, and sold 176 slaves.

His active participation in the slave trade prompted him to try to influence foreign policy. In an effort to damage the British and Danish economies and impair their sovereignty in the Caribbean, in the early 17th century, the Spanish Crown instituted a policy granting freedom to any slave who escaped from the colonies of Protestant countries on the condition that he or she agree to be baptized as a Catholic Christian. (*See also* ROMAN CATHOLIC CHURCH.) The policy remained in effect until 1724, and even after that time, Spanish colonial governors were generally welcoming to runaway slaves who might make good citizens. This policy was especially important in relatively underpopulated colonies like Puerto Rico since it attracted new free citizens. A good proportion of the free blacks and free people of color in Puerto Rico were runaway slaves from Danish St. Thomas and British islands. When the governor of St. Thomas, retaliating for the Spanish policy, made a similar offer of freedom to Puerto Rican slaves who would run away to the colony, 23 of Enríquez's slaves fled there on a single night. Enríquez's commitment to the slave trade was such that on one occasion he captured a boat full of runaway slaves from the Virgin Islands heading for their promised freedom in Puerto Rico and tried to sell them in San Juan as slaves, but the sales were stopped and the runaways welcomed as free blacks by government officials. After this, Enríquez put his economic power and political influence into overturning the Spanish policy granting freedom to runaways from other islands, which he and other SLAVE OWNERS on the island saw as a threat to the slave system as a whole. Enríquez hoped that if Puerto Rico ceased to be a haven for runaway Virgin Islanders, the British and the Danish governments would also cease to welcome runaway Puerto Ricans.

Enríquez had an informal relationship with a free woman of color named Ana Muriel, starting sometime before 1714 and lasting the rest of his life. His wealth and influence allowed him to include Ana Muriel in public acts, including public masses that he sponsored. This was unusual because normally an informal sexual relationship with a woman of color would never be publicly celebrated, even if it was widely known. Among his friends were Governor Francisco Danío Granados (served 1720–24), Governor José Antonio de Mendizabal y Azcue (served 1724–30), and Bishop Fray Fernando de Valdivia (served 1718–25).

The alliance between Governor Danío and Enríquez was an example of state power working together with private businesspeople that used legal means to do illegal trade. During this time, smuggling and illegal trade were common in Puerto Rico. This was in part due to Spanish laws that dictated that the only legal port of entry was San Juan. San Juan was far from many of the other population centers of the island, and with little internal infrastructure, it was nearly impossible to trade through only one port. Other mercantilist regulations made imported goods more expensive and handicapped development of plantations. With the tacit support of the governor, who was also a local planter and consumer of imported goods, merchants such as Enríquez smuggled from the neighboring British and Dutch colonies and kept the economy functioning. However, it was this alliance of convenience that caused Enríquez's demise. Governor Matías de Abadía (served 1731–43) allied with aristocratic white leaders of the San Juan social and political elite who resented Enríquez's wealth and power. He was hated both because of his race and because he was involved in trade, an "ungentlemanly" occupation. Enríquez's enemies started by denying him the use of his military titles, thus also lifting from him the immunity to civil law traditionally granted to military officers. Then, they went after his finances.

Enríquez's economic activities positioned him as an important moneylender, which made him more vulnerable to his enemies. For example, he loaned the government enough to pay the salary for the entire San Juan military garrison in 1725. However, the white male–dominated Puerto Rican society of his time could not tolerate for long time a PARDO with such financial and social success, especially when some of his wealth was gained at their expense. By 1735, Enríquez's former legitimate activities, which helped him to achieve a noblelike status, became his ruin. His debtors, prominent government and church officials, became the people that could not tolerate him. In his dire hour of need, in spite of his wealth and service to the royal Crown, he was treated as any other low-class pardo. He was accused by the white ruling class of being a man of inferior category, a poor mulatto shoemaker, who had risen above the rightful position of a "member of a despicable race," as the criminal complaint put it.

In 1735, Miguel Enríquez fled prosecution and sought refuge in the Monastery of Saint Thomas to avoid arrest. His enemies celebrated parties and fandangos, dancing and singing songs with lyrics referring to the defeated enemy. Miguel Enríquez, once the richest and most powerful person in the island, died sometime in 1743 as a poor refugee confined to a monastery. Subsequently, race relations in the island became more stringent, creating the basis for a more repressive and segregated situation for both slave and free Afro–Puerto Ricans.

Miguel Enríquez was born and lived in an island where color distinctions among pardo (socially prominent brown), moreno (ordinary mixed-race), and negro (black) were consequential for social mobility. He grew up in a society that constantly reminded unfree and free blacks and pardos that there was no lower status than to be a black. A pardo, such as Enríquez, was slightly ahead of the black, but color still marked him as inferior. This view of colored people in the island was part of the contradictions of 17th- and 18th-century colonial life. Despite the disadvantages free colored people labored under, however, they enjoyed degrees of freedom: They could travel, own stores, acquire land, inherit property, and acquire an education, among other things. During his life, Miguel Enríquez was witness to both the possibilities and the struggle of unfree and free blacks and pardos.

Noel Allende-Goitía

FURTHER READING

Kinsbruner, Jay. *Not of Pure Blood: The Free People of Color and Racial Prejudice in Nineteenth-Century Puerto Rico.* Durham, N.C.: Duke University Press, 1996.

Lopez Cantos, Ángel. *Miguel Enríquez.* Sevilla: Consejo Superior de Investigaciones Científicas, Escuela de Estudios Hispano-Americanos, 1998.

Sued Badillo, Jalil, and Angel Lopez Cantos. *Puerto Rico negro.* Rio Piedras: Editorial Culture, 1986.

EQUIANO, OLAUDAH *(Gustavus Vassa)*
(1745?–1797) *British seaman and abolitionist writer*

An African-born (Igbo) slave employed as a sailor, Olaudah Equiano eventually purchased his freedom, then became a prominent abolitionist author in Britain.

According to his 1791 autobiography, *The Interesting Narrative of the Life of Olaudah Equiano*, Equiano was born in or around 1745 in the Igbo region of present-day Nigeria. Captured at the age of eight, he was sold multiple times until he reached the Gulf of Guinea, where he was sold to European traders and shipped to the West Indies (*see also* SLAVE COAST, BENIN, AND THE BIGHT OF BIAFRA). His account of the Middle Passage describes the many horrors of the slave trade. In what is no doubt the most affecting passage in the book, Equiano, at about the age of 11, is separated from his sister, with whom he has lived in captivity for several months, and is sent off to another owner, who ultimately sells him to a European buyer to be sent to the Americas. In 2005, however, the historian Vincent Caretta, argued that Equiano was probably born in SOUTH CAROLINA in 1747 and invented his African birth to emphasize better the horrors of the Middle Passage. The prominent historian of the Atlantic slave trade Paul Lovejoy, on the other hand, concludes from the records of the slave trade and the internal evidence in the *Interesting Narrative* that he was actually born in Nigeria. The rest of his life, however, is not in dispute.

Landing in BARBADOS in May 1754, the young Equiano failed to attract a buyer and was transshipped to Virginia, where he was purchased by a Mr. Campbell. Various masters renamed Equiano Michael, then Jacob, and finally Gustavus Vassa, after the 16th-century Swedish king who freed his country from Danish rule. It was under this name that he was known for the rest of his life, until he used his birth name in his autobiography. He was used for field and household duties until he was sold to the naval lieutenant Michael Henry Pascal.

Equiano traveled extensively as the servant of Pascal and other officers to whom he was loaned and served in the SEVEN YEARS' WAR, 1756–63, on the British warships *Roebuck, Preston, Savage, Royal George, Namur,* and *Aetna* (*see also* NAVY). He participated in the attack on Louisburg in CANADA, the naval battle of Lagos Bay, and the attack on Belle Isle en Mer. As the servant of an officer, Equiano was treated fairly well and befriended Pascal's white servant Richard Baker. While in London to recover from chilblains (an inflammation of the skin), he stayed with the Guerin family (Pascal's bankers), learned to read, and was baptized in 1759.

Equiano expected to be freed at war's end because of his record of good service and relative independence in the British navy. But there was no legal obligation to free slaves on British soil until the *SOMERSET V. STEWART* case (1772), and Pascal decided instead to sell Equiano to Captain James Doran. Equiano landed in Montserrat in 1763. Sold again to Robert King, a Quaker and a relatively humane owner, he was employed as a clerk and sailor (*see also* MERCHANT SEAMEN). Given on loan to Captain. Thomas Farmer, he traveled extensively between the West Indies and North America, carrying tropical goods and slaves. He used such opportunities to trade on his own account and earn cash. In 1766, he bought his own freedom from his owner.

Now a free man, Equiano continued his career as a sailor on the Caribbean–North American route. When the *Nancy* was wrecked in the Bahamas in 1767, his courageous actions helped save the crew. He found it difficult to live the life of a free colored sailor, however, because unscrupulous whites repeatedly attempted to re-enslave him and he no longer had any white patron. His former employer, Captain Farmer, was uninterested in standing up for Equiano in one such incident in Savannah because he was now free. The threat of RE-ENSLAVEMENT eventually convinced Equiano temporarily to leave the Western Hemisphere.

Equiano then traveled to the Mediterranean, where he witnessed more slave trafficking, this time in the Ottoman Empire. After another voyage to JAMAICA, he joined Constantine John Phipps's 1773 expedition to the Arctic Circle. Aimed at finding the Northwest Passage, the expedition included the young Horatio Nelson (1758–1805). While he was in London in 1774, a spiritual crisis led Equiano to join a church, and he eventually embraced evangelical Methodism because it posited that everyone, including blacks, could achieve salvation.

After another wreck off Spain in 1775, Equiano participated in an attempt to create a slave plantation on the Miskito Coast of Central America (*see also* NICARAGUA). The colony was a failure, and Equiano had to leave after quarreling with fellow settlers. Several attempts by whites to re-enslave him on the return voyage convinced Equiano to settle permanently as a servant in London in 1777 (he only crossed the Atlantic one more time, to PHILADELPHIA, PENNSYLVANIA, in 1785).

It was in Britian that Equiano, who had never seemed opposed to slavery as a concept in his earlier life, became an abolitionist. He helped organize the 1787 expedition to create a settlement for freed slaves in SIERRA LEONE but was prevented from leaving with the expedition when he denounced corruption and mismanagement in the project. By 1788, he was also a prominent writer in abolitionist newspapers in Britain.

Equiano's renown stems from his autobiography, which he financed and published himself (rather than abandoning the copyright to a printer, as was then customary). Equiano promoted and sold the book during countless tours in the British Isles. It went through nine editions during his lifetime and probably netted him the sizable sum of 1,000 pounds. The book was only the second account of the slave trade published by a former slave, thus providing a rare occasion to understand its impact through the eyes of one of its victims. At a time when blacks were widely viewed as uncouth and illiterate, Equiano also insisted that he had written the book himself to strengthen further the effect of its vivid, moving style.

Equiano has been interpreted in various ways, as befits an Atlantic man whose intellectual roots lay in Africa, the Caribbean, mainland North America, and Britian. He prided himself on his African heritage: His autobiography identified him as "Equiano, the African" and dedicated many positive pages to his alleged youth in present-day Nigeria. He was also a typical American free person of color, who did his best to distance himself from his humble origins as a slave and initially did little to combat the enslavement of others after he obtained his own emancipation. His spiritual life and political activism in his later years also bore witness to the impact late-18th-century British society had on his intellectual development.

Equiano married Susanna Cullen, a white British woman, in 1792 and had two daughters, Ann and Joanna.

He died on March 31, 1797, by which point he had become the richest and most famous man of color in Britain.

Philippe R. Girard

FURTHER READING

Caretta, Vincent. *Equiano the African: Biography of a Self-Made Man.* Athens: University of Georgia Press, 2005.

Equiano, Olaudah. *The Interesting Narrative of the Life of Olaudah Equiano.* Edited by Robert Allison. 1791. Reprint, Boston: Bedford Books of St. Martin's Press, 1995.

Lovejoy, Paul. "Autobiography and Memory: Gustavus Vassa, Alias Olaudah Equiano, the African." *Slavery and Abolition* 3 (December 2006): 317–347.

THE INTERESTING NARRATIVE OF THE LIFE OF OLAUDAH EQUIANO, OR GUSTAVUS VASA, THE AFRICAN, WRITTEN BY HIMSELF (1789)

According to his autobiography, Olaudah Equiano was born in 1745 in what is now southeastern Nigeria, enslaved at age 11, sold to British slave traders, endured the Middle Passage to the West Indies, and subsequently was taken to Virginia and purchased by a planter. A month later, he was purchased by Michael Henry Pascal, a Royal Navy officer, who renamed him Gustavus Vassa (or Vasa), took him to London, and carried him along in a man-of-war for action in the Seven Years' War. At war's end, Pascal rescinded his promise to free Equiano (Vassa) and instead sold him to the West Indies, the cruelties of which Equiano vividly describes. In the West Indies, Equiano show-cased his keen business savvy and amassed enough money to buy his own freedom in 1766. During his tenure in the Indies, he acquired and supervised plantation slaves. Eventually, he set forth for adventurous and commercial voyages, traveling to North America, the Mediterranean, the West Indies, and the North Pole. A near-death experience in the Arctic fright-ened him about the possibility of eternal damnation, and, after returning to London, he converted to Methodism in 1774. Having previously served as a slave and as a sailor on a slave ship, he then joined a small but vocal group of abolitionists in Britain; to support the cause he wrote letters to newspapers and, in 1789, published his Interesting Narrative. *He married a British woman in 1792 and had two daughters, one of whom survived to adulthood. When he died on March 31, 1797, he left a consider-able estate from the profits of his publications.*

In the early 21st century, biographical discoveries have thrown into question many of the details Equiano reports in his autobiography. Somewhat controversially, the University of Maryland professor Vincent Carretta has uncovered baptismal and naval records that suggest that Equiano was born around 1747 in South Carolina and first arrived in Britain long before his narrative states. The prominent historian of the Atlantic slave trade Paul Lovejoy, on the other hand, concludes from the records of the slave trade and the internal evidence in the Interesting Narrative *that he was actually born in Nigeria and that the docu-ments asserting that he was born in the Americas represented an attempt to claim a higher status (and thus value) for him as a creole slave. Opponents of the abolition movement claimed at the time that the* Interesting Narrative *was fiction in order to dis-credit it. If Equiano fabricated stories about an African upbringing and the often-quoted account of the Middle Passage in a slave ship, he deserves even greater credit for his literary accomplish-ment. His story, contrivance or truthful account, spoke vividly to a British readership primed to abolish the slave trade, a goal accomplished 10 years after his death. His autobiography went through a stunning nine editions, and today his work is consid-ered a classic in the genre of the slave narrative.*

In the following excerpts, Equiano describes his hopes for his own liberty, his observations of cruelty in the West Indies to slaves and to free blacks, his purchased freedom, the treatment of free blacks in Savannah, and his perspective on a voyage to Sierra Leone.

Chapter Four: Equiano's Hopes for Liberty

I thought now of nothing but being freed, and working for myself, and thereby getting money to enable me to get a good education; for I always had a great desire to be able at least to read and write; and while I was on ship-board I had endeav-oured to improve myself in both. While I was in the Ætna par-ticularly, the captain's clerk taught me to write, and gave me a smattering of arithmetic as far as the rule of three. There was also one Daniel Queen, about forty years of age, a man very well educated, who messed with me on board this ship, and he likewise dressed and attended the captain. Fortunately this man soon became very much attached to me, and took very great pains to instruct me in many things. He taught me to shave and dress hair a little, and also to read in the Bible, explaining many passages to me, which I did not comprehend. I was wonderfully surprised to see the laws and rules of my country written almost exactly here; a circumstance, which I believe tended to impress our manners and customs more deeply on my memory. I used to tell him of this resemblance; and many a time we have sat up the whole night together at this employment. In short, he was like a father to me; and some even used to call me after his name; they also styled me the black Christian. Indeed I almost loved him with the affec-tion of a son. Many things I have denied myself that he might have them; and when I used to play at marbles or any other game, and won a few halfpence, or got any little money, which I sometimes did, for shaving any one, I used to buy him a little sugar or tobacco, as far as my stock of money would go. He used to say, that he and I never should part; and that when our ship was paid off, as I was as free as himself or any other man on board, he would instruct me in his business, by which I might gain a good livelihood. This gave me new life and spirits; and my heart burned within me, while I thought the time long till I obtained my freedom. For though my master had not promised it to me, yet, besides the assurances I had received that he had no right to detain me, he always treated me with the greatest kindness, and reposed in me an unbounded confidence; he even paid attention to my morals; and would never suffer me to deceive him, or tell lies, of which he used to tell me the consequences; and that if I did so God would not love me; so that, from all this tenderness, I had never once supposed, in all my dreams of freedom, that he would think of detaining me any longer than I wished.

In pursuance of our orders we sailed from Portsmouth for the Thames, and arrived at Deptford the 10th of December, where we cast anchor just as it was high water. The ship was up about half an hour, when my master ordered the barge to be manned; and all in an instant, without having before given me the least reason to suspect any thing of the matter, he forced me into the barge; saying, I was going to leave him, but he would take care I should not. I was so struck with the unexpectedness of this proceeding, that for some time I did not make a reply, only I made an offer to go for my books and chest of clothes, but he swore I should not move out of his sight; and if I did he would cut my throat, at the same time taking his hanger. I began, however, to collect myself; and, plucking up courage, I told him I was free, and he could not by law serve me so. But this only enraged him the more; and he continued to swear, and said he would soon let me know whether he would or not, and at that instant sprung himself into the barge from the ship, to the astonishment and sorrow of all on board. The tide, rather unluckily for me, had just turned downward, so that we quickly fell down the river along with it, till we came among some out-ward-bound West Indiamen; for he was resolved to put me on board the first vessel he could get to receive me. The boat's crew, who pulled against their will, became quite faint different times, and would have gone ashore; but he would not let them. Some of them strove then to cheer me, and told me he could not sell me, and that they would stand by me, which revived me a little; and I still entertained hopes; for as they pulled along he asked some vessels to receive me, but they could not. But, just as we had got a little below Gravesend, we came alongside of a ship which was going away the next tide for the West Indies; her name was the Charming Sally, Captain James Doran; and my master went on board and agreed with him for me; and in a little time I was sent for into the cabin. When I came there Captain Doran asked me if I knew him; I answered that I did not; ''Then,'' said he ''you are now my slave.'' I told him my master could not sell me to him, nor to any one else. ''Why,'' said he, ''did not your master buy you?'' I confessed he did. ''But I have served him,'' said I, ''many years, and he has taken all my wages and prize-money, for I only got one sixpence during the war; besides this I have been baptized; and by the laws of the land no man has a right to sell me:'' And I added, that I had heard a lawyer and others at different times tell my master so. They both then said that those people who told me so were not my friends; but I replied—it was very extraordinary that other people did not know the law as well as they. Upon this Captain Doran said I talked too much English; and if I did not behave myself well, and be quiet, he had a method on board to make me. I was too well convinced of his power over me to doubt what he said; and my former sufferings in the slave-ship presenting themselves to my mind, the recollection of them made me shudder. However, before I retired I told them that as I could not get any right among men here I hoped I should hereafter in Heaven; and I immediately left the cabin, filled with resentment and sorrow.

Chapter Six: Injustices to Free Blacks in the West Indies

While I was in this place, St. Kitt's, a very curious imposition on human nature took place:—A white man wanted to marry in the church a free black woman that had land and slaves in Montserrat: but the clergyman told him it was against the law of the place to marry a white and a black in the church. The man then asked to be married on the water, to which the parson consented, and the two lovers went in one boat, and the parson and clerk in another, and thus the ceremony was performed. After this the loving pair came on board our vessel, and my captain treated them extremely well, and brought them safe to Montserrat.

The reader cannot but judge the irksomeness of this situation to a mind like mine, in being daily exposed to new hardships and impositions, after having seen many better days, and been, as it were, in a state of freedom and plenty; added to which, every part of the world in which I had hitherto been seemed to me a paradise in comparison of the West-Indies.

While we lay in this place [Montserrat] a very cruel thing happened on board of our sloop which filled me with horror; though I found afterwards such practices were frequent. There was a very clever and decent free young mulatto-man who sailed a long time with us: he had a free woman for his wife, by whom he had a child; and she was then living on shore, and all very happy. Our captain and mate, and other people on board, and several elsewhere, even the natives of Bermudas, all knew this young man from a child that he was always free, and no one had ever claimed him as their property: however, as might too often overcomes right in these parts, it happened that a Bermudas captain, whose vessel lay there for a few days in the road, came on board of us, and seeing the mulattoman, whose name was Joseph Clipson, he told him he was not free, and that he had orders from his master to bring him to Bermudas. The poor man could not believe the captain to be in earnest; but he was very soon undeceived, his men laying violent hands on him: and although he shewed a certificate of his being born free in St. Kitt's, and most people on board knew that he served his time to boat-building, and always passed for a free man, yet he was taken forcibly out of our vessel. He then asked to be carried ashore before the secretary or magistrates, and these infernal invaders of human rights promised him he should; but, instead of that, they carried him on board of the other vessel: and the next day, without giving the poor man any hearing on shore, or suffering him even to see his wife or child, he was carried away, and probably doomed never more in this world to see them again. Nor was this the only instance of this kind of barbarity I was a witness to. I have since often seen in Jamaica and other islands free men, whom I have known in America, thus villainously trepanned and held in bondage. I have heard of two similar practices even in Philadelphia: and were it not for the benevolence of the Quakers in that city many of the sable race, who now breathe the air of liberty, would, I believe, be groaning indeed under some planter's chains. These things opened my mind to a new scene of horror to which I had been before a stranger. Hitherto I had thought only slavery dreadful; but the state of a free negro appeared to me now equally so at least, and in some respects even worse, for they live in constant alarm for their liberty; and even this is but nominal, for they are universally insulted and plundered without the possibility of redress; for such is the equity of the West Indian laws, that no free negro's evidence will be admitted in their courts of justice.

Chapter Seven: Equiano Gains His Freedom

We set sail once more for Montserrat, and arrived there safe; . . . . When we had unladen the vessel, and I had sold my venture, finding myself master of about forty-seven pounds, I consulted my true friend, the Captain, how I should proceed in offering my master the money for my freedom. He told me to come on a certain morning, when he and my master would be at breakfast together. Accordingly, on that morning I went, and met the Captain there, as he had appointed. When I went in I made my obeisance to my master, and with my money in my hand, and many fears in my heart, I prayed him to be as good as his offer to me, when he was pleased to promise me my freedom as soon as I could purchase it. This speech seemed to confound him; he began to recoil: and my heart that instant sunk within me. "What," said he, "give you your freedom? Why, where did you get the money? Have you got forty pounds sterling?" "Yes, sir," I answered. "How did you get it?" replied he. I told him, very honestly. The Captain then said he knew I got the money very honestly and with much industry, and that I was particularly careful. On which my master replied, I got money

much faster than he did; and said he would not have made me the promise he did if he had thought I should have got money so soon. "Come, come," said my worthy Captain, clapping my master on the back, "Come, Robert, (which was his name) I think you must let him have his freedom; you have laid your money out very well; you have received good interest for it all this time, and here is now the principal at last. I know Gustavus has earned you more than an hundred a-year, and he will still save you money, as he will not leave you:—Come, Robert, take the money." My master then said, he would not be worse than his promise; and, taking the money, told me to go to the Secretary at the Register Office, and get my manumission drawn up. These words of my master were like a voice from heaven to me: in an instant all my trepidation was turned into unutterable bliss; and I most reverently bowed myself with gratitude, unable to express my feelings, but by the overflowing of my eyes, while my true and worthy friend, the Captain, congratulated us both with a peculiar degree of heart-felt pleasure. As soon as the first transports of my joy were over, and that I had expressed my thanks to these my worthy friends in the best manner I was able, I rose with a heart full of affection and reverence, and left the room, in order to obey my master's joyful mandate of going to the Register Office. As I was leaving the house I called to mind the words of the Psalmist, in the 126th Psalm, and like him, "I glorified God in my heart, in whom I trusted." These words had been impressed on my mind from the very day I was forced from Deptford to the present hour, and I now saw them, as I thought, fulfilled and verified. My imagination was all rapture as I flew to the Register Office. . . . All within my breast was tumult, wildness, and delirium! My feet scarcely touched the ground, for they were winged with joy, and, like Elijah, as he rose to Heaven; they "were with lightning sped as I "went on." Every one I met I told of my happiness, and blazed about the virtue of my amiable master and captain.

When I got to the office and acquainted the Register with my errand he congratulated me on the occasion, and told me he would draw up my manumission for half price, which was a guinea. I thanked him for his kindness; and, having received it and paid him, I hastened to my master to get him to sign it, that I might be fully released. Accordingly he signed the manumission that day, so that, before night, I who had been a slave in the morning, trembling at the will of another, was become my own master, and completely free. I thought this was the happiest day I had ever experienced; and my joy was still heightened by the blessings and prayers of the fable race, particularly the aged, to whom my heart had ever been attached with reverence.

As the form of my manumission has something peculiar in it, and expresses the absolute power and dominion one man claims over his fellow, I shall beg leave to present it before my readers at full length:

Montserrat.—To all men unto whom these presents shall come: I Robert King, of the parish of St. Anthony in the said island, merchant, send greeting: Know ye, that I the aforesaid Robert King, for and in consideration of the sum of seventy pounds current money of the said island, to me in hand paid, and to the intent that a negro man-slave, named Gustavus Vassa, shall and may become free, have manumitted, emancipated, enfranchised, and set free, and by these presents do manumit, emancipate, enfranchise, and set free, the aforesaid negro man-slave, named Gustavus Vassa, for ever, hereby giving, granting, and releasing unto him, the said Gustavus Vassa, all right, title, dominion, sovereignty, and property, which, as lord and master over the aforesaid Gustavus Vassa, I had, or now I have, or by any means whatsever I may or can hereafter possibly have over him the aforesaid negro, for ever. In witness whereof I the above-said Robert King have unto these presents set my hand and seal, this tenth day of July, in the year of our Lord one thousand seven hundred and sixty-six.

ROBERT KING.

Chapter Eight: Treatment of Free Blacks in Savannah

After our arrival we went up to the town of Savannah; and the same evening I went to a friend's house to lodge, whose name was Mosa, a black man. We were very happy at meeting each other; and after supper we had a light till it was between nine and ten o'clock at night. About that time the watch or patrol came by; and, discerning a light in the house, they knocked at the door: we opened it; and they came in and sat down, and drank some punch with us: they also begged some limes of me, as they understood I had some, which I readily gave them. A little after this they told me I must go to the watch-house with them: this surprised me a good deal, after our kindness to them; and I asked them, Why so? They said that all negroes who had light in their houses after nine o'clock were to be taken into custody, and either pay some dollars or be slogged. Some of those people knew that I was a free man; but, as the man of the house was not free, and had his master to protect him, they did not take the same liberty with him they did with me. I told them that I was a free man, and just arrived from Providence; that we were not making any noise, and that I was not a stranger in that place, but was very well known there: "Besides," said I, "what will you do with me?"—"That you shall see," replied they, "but you must go to the watch-house with us." Now whether they meant to get money from me or not I was at a loss to know; but I thought immediately of the oranges and limes at Santa Cruz: and seeing that nothing would pacify them I went with them to the watch-house, where I remained during the night. Early

the next morning these imposing ruffians slogged a negro-man and woman that they had in the watch-house, and then they told me that I must be slogged too. I asked why? and if there was no law for free men? And told them if there was I would have it put in force against them. But this only exasperated them the more; and instantly they swore they would serve me as Doctor Perkins had done; and they were going to lay violent hands on me; when one of them, more humane than the rest, said that as I was a free man they could not justify stripping me by law. I then immediately sent for Doctor Brady, who was known to be an honest and worthy man; and on his coming to my assistance they let me go.

This was not the only disagreeable incident I met with while I was in this place; for, one day, while I was a little way out of the town of Savannah, I was beset by two white men, who meant to play their usual tricks with me in the way of kidnapping. As soon as these men accosted me, one of them said to the other, "This is the very fellow we are looking for that you lost;" and the other swore immediately that I was the identical person. On this they made up to me, and were about to handle me; but I told them to be still and keep off; for I had seen those kind of tricks played upon other free blacks, and they must not think to serve me so. At this they paused a little, and one said to the other—it will not do; and the other answered that I talked too good English. I replied, I believed I did; and I had also with me a revengeful stick equal to the occasion; and my mind was likewise good. Happily however it was not used; and, after we had talked together a little in this manner, the rogues left me.

Chapter 12: Equiano Leads an Expedition of Free Blacks to Sierra Leone

On my return to London in August [1786] I was very agreeably surprised to find that the benevolence of government had adopted the plan of some philanthropic individuals to send the Africans from hence to their native quarter; and that some vessels were then engaged to carry them to Sierra Leone; an act which redounded to the honour of all concerned in its promotion, and filled me with prayers and much rejoicing. There was then in the city a select committee of gentlemen for the black poor, to some of whom I had the honour of being known; and, as soon as they heard of my arrival they sent for me to the committee. When I came there they informed me of the intention of government; and as they seemed to think me qualified to superintend part of the undertaking, they asked me to go with the black poor to Africa. I pointed out to them many objections to my going; and particularly I expressed some difficulties on the account of the slave dealers, as I would certainly oppose their traffic in the human species by every means in my power. However these objections were over-ruled by the gentlemen of the committee, who prevailed on me to go, and recommended me to the honourable Commissioners of his Majesty's

Navy as a proper person to act as commissary for government in the intended expedition; and they accordingly appointed me in November 1786 to that office and gave me sufficient power to act for the government in the capacity of commissary. . . .

I proceeded immediately to the execution of my duty on board the vessels destined for the voyage, where I continued till the March following.

During my continuance in the employment of government, I was struck with the flagrant abuses committed by the agent, and endeavoured to remedy them, but without effect. One instance, among many which I could produce, may serve as a specimen. Government had ordered to be provided all necessaries (slops, as they are called, included) for 750 persons; however, not being able to muster more than 426, I was ordered to send the superfluous slops, &c. to the king's stores at Portsmouth; but, when I demanded them for that purpose from the agent, it appeared they had never been bought, though paid for by government. But that was not all, government were not the only objects of peculation; these poor people suffered infinitely more; their accommodations were most wretched; many of them wanted beds, and many more cloathing and other necessaries. For the truth of this, and much more, I do not seek credit from my own assertion. I appeal to the testimony of Capt. Thompson, of the Nautilus, who convoyed us, to whom I applied in February 1787 for a remedy, when I had remonstrated to the agent in vain, and even brought him to be a witness of the injustice and oppression I complained of, I appeal also to a letter written by these wretched people, so early as the beginning of the preceding January, and published in the Morning Herald of the 4th of that month, signed by twenty of their chiefs.

I could not silently suffer government to be thus cheated, and my countrymen plundered and oppressed, and even left destitute of the necessaries for almost their existence. I therefore informed the Commissioners of the Navy of the agent's proceeding; but my dismission was soon after procured, by means of a gentleman in the city, whom the agent, conscious of his peculation, had deceived by letter, and whom, moreover, empowered the same agent to receive on board, at the government expense, a number of persons as passengers, contrary to the orders I received. By this I suffered a considerable loss in my property: however, the commissioners were satisfied with my conduct, and wrote to Capt. Thompson, expressing their approbation of it.

Thus provided, they proceeded on their voyage; and at last, worn out by treatment, perhaps not the most mild, and wasted by sickness, brought on by want of medicine, cloaths, bedding, &c. they reached Sierra Leone just at the commencement of the rains. At that season of the year it is impossible to cultivate the lands; their provisions therefore were exhausted before they could derive any benefit from agriculture; and it is not surprising that many, especially the lascars, whose constitutions are very tender, and who had been cooped up in ships from October to June, and accommodated in the manner I have mentioned, should be so wasted by their confinement as not long to survive it.

Thus ended my part of the long-talked-of expedition to Sierra Leone; an expedition which, however unfortunate in the event, was humane and politic in its design, nor was its failure owing to government: every thing was done on their part, but there was evidently sufficient mismanagement attending the conduct and execution of it to defeat its success.

Source: Documenting the American South database. Available online. URL: http://docsouth.unc.edu./neh/equiano1/menu.html. Accessed December 23, 2010.

ESCALERA PLOT   *See* LA ESCALERA PLOT.

EXODUSTER MOVEMENT

Also known as the Exodus of 1879, the Exoduster Movement led about 40,000 African Americans from the South into KANSAS and Colorado. It was the best-organized and best-known part of a larger movement of people from former slave states to the West in the years after the AMERICAN CIVIL WAR, 1861–65.

There were free people of color living throughout the American West in the years before the American Civil War. In many cases, blacks were among the first explorers of these territories as mountain men and trail guides (*see also* INLAND WEST OF THE UNITED STATES). Because the West was a frontier area, the harsh racial discrimination that existed elsewhere in the Unites States, both North and South, was weather there. Blacks could be independent economic actors and enjoy dignity in the West. As the frontier closed in the late 19th century, however, this looser racial climate was giving way to more pronounced racism, in a pattern common across the Americas. But the earlier experience had led blacks to think of the West as whites did, as a land of opportunity where the differences between people were less important and hard work and sacrifice would be rewarded.

As the hope of racial justice in their Southern homes faded with the end of RECONSTRUCTION IN THE UNITED STATES, many Southerners began to consider leaving their homes to seek a better situation. Northern whites were not very welcoming. Although the Black Codes restricting the rights of African Americans were overturned by the Fourteenth Amendment to the U.S. Constitution and the postwar Civil Rights Acts (*see also* CIVIL RIGHTS LAWS IN THE UNITED STATES AFTER 1865 and BLACK CODES IN THE UNITED STATES), informal discrimination in the North was still strong. Many blacks looked to the West. Foremost among them was Benjamin Singleton (1809–92). He had been born in slavery in TENNESSEE and had run away to MICHIGAN in 1846. At the time, Michigan had been a state for less than 10 years and was still the frontier. Singleton lived a frontier lifestyle for many years, helping other blacks escape to CANADA and living by his wits. Singleton returned to Tennessee when Union soldiers liberated the state, and he became a community leader in Nashville. Together with a black minister and other local leaders, he founded a real estate office in 1874 to help black Tennesseans acquire land there. But landowners were reluctant to sell to blacks, and the courts were unwilling to protect black landowners against neighbors and conmen. In 1875 and 1876, Singleton and his partners traveled to Kansas to look for suitable places for black settlements. In 1877 and 1878, Singleton led parties from the Nashville area, totaling about 2,300 people, to establish towns, the most famous of which was Dunlap, Kansas. A group of settlers from KENTUCKY independently established the most famous Exoduster settlement, Nicodemus, Kansas, in 1877. The idea spread rapidly through Southern black communities, and in 1879, as many as 50,000 people migrated to Kansas, MISSOURI, OKLAHOMA, Colorado, IOWA, and ILLINOIS. Although Kansas whites were generally abolitionist in their political beliefs before the war, many were horrified to see so many blacks settling in the state, many almost penniless after the long trip. Few of these migrants were directly associated with Singleton's group, and his colonies were generally well financed. He went before the U.S.

Congress and the Kansas legislature in 1880 to defend the black settlers and call for assistance to those too poor to establish themselves successfully. He ultimately lost control of his settlement at Dunlap to the Presbyterian Church.

Ultimately, antiblack prejudice became more virulent in Kansas and Colorado, as it did in the rest of the country after the end of Reconstruction. The black settlements on the plains seemed less like refuges as discrimination harshened. Ironically, the legal case that finally overturned segregation in the United States, the 1954 *Brown v. Board of Education* decision, originated in a lawsuit against school segregation in Topeka, Kansas. In addition, poor weather and a financial crisis put a lot of pressure on all plains farmers in the 1890s. Many of the black settlements were wholly or partially abandoned by the turn of the century. Nicodemus, Kansas, is still inhabited by descendants of the Exodusters. Dunlap had no black inhabitants in 2000.

Stewart R. King

FURTHER READING

Athearn, Robert G. *In Search of Canaan: Black Migration to Kansas, 1879–80.* Lawrence: Regents Press of Kansas, 1978.

Hamilton, Kenneth Marvin. *Black Towns and Profit: Promotion and Development in the Trans-Appalachian West, 1877–1915.* Urbana: University of Illinois Press, 1991.

Painter, Nell Irvin. *Exodusters: Black Migration to Kansas after Reconstruction.* Lawrence: University Press of Kansas, 1986.

FAMILY

The family is the basic institution of society. Family life for people of color in the Americas was especially important because their color meant they were excluded from many other social institutions. The black family was very strong during slavery. At the same time, family life was especially difficult for people of color for a variety of reasons. Families might be divided by the status of slavery, by race, or by distance. Male and female roles within the family might well be different from those found in white society. Parent-child relationships might also be different, and the role of elders was also affected by these conditions. Some people were unable to maintain normal family relations thanks to the harsh conditions found in slave societies and formed alternative pseudokin networks to provide some of the benefits that normal family life would offer.

The common view of black family life during slavery was, until recently, that families were weak and divided. The black family was seen as an institution that had been troubled for hundreds of years, indeed, since Africans arrived in the Americas. Stereotyped views of black life that sprang from this false preconception led to unsuccessful public policy initiatives in the 20th century, such as welfare regulations and cuts, and much political posturing. Proponents of this point of view commonly argued that the system of slavery offered no formal recognition of slave marriages, and that was true in many places, though not in Spanish and Portuguese America. They also pointed out that parents could be sold separately. They referred to the well-known risk of sexual victimization of female slaves by their masters. They logically connected these points together to paint a picture of a gravely imperiled institution among slaves. Among free people of color, they argued, most people gained their freedom as individuals, not in family groups. The newly freed, more commonly women than men, entered into their new status as atomized individuals, and thus free black society during slavery was equally bereft of strong families, at least for most individuals. The predominance of women among the newly freed meant that traditional patriarchal assumptions were overturned. This analysis, however, is inadequate as a description of the family life of blacks, both slave and free, in most places in the Americas. Particularly in the case of free people of color, the first priority for many seemed to be reestablishing broken family linkages and advancing the interests of the family even before those of the individual.

In truth, though, all the factors cited previously did pose challenges to the slave family. In some ways they paralleled challenges faced by poor white families in Europe. The lack of legal status for slave relationships was a feature of black life in the Atlantic world, one of the many components of the "social death" experienced by slaves. But marriages between free people and even between free and slave in many places did have legal status, and free people of color were very likely to marry. In fact, in most plantation colonies in the Americas outside the United States, free people of color were more likely to marry than whites, mostly because of the unbalanced sex ratio among whites in many places. As did blacks in the Americas, poor whites in Europe had difficulty formalizing their marriages, because marriages cost money and because they were often unable to prove that earlier relationships had been properly ended. Just as blacks who became free formalized their marriages, it was not uncommon for a poor couple in Europe who achieved economic success to marry. Sexual victimization of servants by employers was a common feature of the lives of poor European women, though they may have had better access to the courts and social elites to complain than did black slave women. Rates of illegitimacy were highest among the poor in all the western European countries that owned slave colonies in the Americas. But this victimization did not stop the European women from establishing families. Separation of slaves by sale parallels separation of European families by distance, through the migration of the husband to cities or colonies in search of work, for example. And yet European families often reestablished themselves when the husband returned from the city, or the wars, or the NAVY, and similarly slave families often reestablished themselves after one partner gained freedom.

A marriage celebration in the United States in the 1870s. Family celebrations such as marriages, baptisms, and funerals were important in all black societies in the Americas, especially since they faced discrimination or outright bans in other public venues for entertainment and sociability such as theaters, churches, and schools. *(North Wind Picture Archives via Associated Press)*

Many black families consisted of some members who were enslaved and others who were free. A common strategy for a slave family would be to seek MANUMISSION for one female member. Women were more frequently chosen because the children of a free mother were free. It was not unknown for free people to marry slaves. Under the CODE NOIR IN FRENCH LAW, such a marriage required the permission of the master of the enslaved party but resulted in the tax-free manumission of the slave and, if a woman, all her children with the free groom. In Spanish and Portuguese America, marriage to a slave did not automatically free the slave but gave the free spouse the right to purchase the partner's freedom. In British America and the United States, such marriages did not convey many benefits and thus were rare but not unknown, although masters had to give permission. Even though society might pay some respect to the marriage bond, the status division was a hardship for the family in many ways. The family could not dispose of the labor power of one of its spouses. There was always the danger of sale, limited but not entirely eliminated by any legal recognition granted to the relationship. And even if one of the partners were free, the

children might still be slaves, thus imposing additional costs and hardships on the family.

INTERRACIAL MARRIAGE was also possible and not uncommon in some places. Marriage between free people of mixed race and whites was an unremarkable occurrence in Spanish America, leading ultimately to the point that they disappeared into the white population, one of the many manifestations of "WHITENING" AND RACIAL PROMOTION. Public acceptance of these relationships varied from place to place and from time to time. As a general rule, the more profitable the plantation complex was, and the more slaves there were as a proportion of the population, the less common interracial marriage. So, for example, in SAINT-DOMINGUE in the 1720s and 1730s, in a sample from South Province, 17 percent of religious marriages were interracial—and this underestimates the actual number of such pairings because many light-skinned free people of color had already crossed over the racial line and were considered to be white by the keepers of the statistics. By the 1780s, however, in a sample from the North and West Provinces of Saint-Domingue, only 4 percent of marriage contracts were for interracial relationships. In the meantime, the marriage laws and religion of the colony had remained the same, but the slave population had increased by a factor of 10, and slaves made up 80 percent of the colony's population by 1788. The rate of interracial marriage varied as a function of the religion and historical background of the colonizing power. As a general rule, interracial marriage was stronger where the colonial power was Catholic and Mediterranean. Marriage was one of the key variables of racial attitudes explored by the historian Frank Tannenbaum in his seminal 1947 work *Slave and Citizen*. A racial difference within the family was always a hardship, however, even in the most accepting places. Racial attitudes hardened in most places during the 18th century, and people who were in interracial marriages lost racial status. For example, white men in French colonies who were married to women of color could no longer aspire to noble status after 1755 and could not hold officer's commissions in the MILITIA (an important component of status in colonial society) after 1776. Interracial marriage was generally prohibited in the British colonies from the middle of the 18th century on. Where interracial marriage was too burdensome or actually unlawful, interracial families still existed, just without the benefit of formal marriage.

Just as poor white families might be torn apart by distance, through the operation of naval or military conscription, or by long voyages by husbands to cities or colonies in search of work, so, too, could black families in the Americas be divided by distance. This was especially true of marriages that involved a slave, because all the colonies maintained significant internal slave trades, even after the elimination of the international slave trade. Slaves in the Chesapeake Bay region of Virginia, MARYLAND, and DELAWARE in the 19th century might well be "sold south" to plantations in the rapidly growing COTTON CULTIVATION states. Slaves in the Lesser Antilles in the early 18th century risked being sold to the larger islands or to the mainland. Slaves from the Northeast of BRAZIL after 1820 or so might be sold to the COFFEE CULTIVATION growing regions of southern Brazil. Slaves from Uruguay before 1810 might find themselves on their way to Potosí in Bolivia. Free partners might find themselves obliged to uproot themselves or alternatively might be forced to abandon their partners. Some black churches, in their marriage services, inserted the words "or distance" into the conventional promise "until death do us part." But given the importance of the family for people of color in slave societies, as they so often lacked alternative social institutions to which they could belong, many people followed their spouses as best as they could. Even free families of color might be divided by the same sort of social forces that divided poor white families in the metropolis: economic

dislocation, debt, military or merchant sea service. The FREEDMEN'S BUREAU of the U.S. Army after the AMERICAN CIVIL WAR, 1861–65, did an impressive public service by helping to reunite black families that had been sundered by sale.

The unique pressures on the black family did affect gender roles. (*See also* GENDER ATTITUDES.) A common family pattern among free people of mixed race outside the United States was a relationship between a white father and a black mother with their mixed-race children where the couple was not married. Interracial relationships were frowned upon, but were, of course, present everywhere. Without the benefits of marriage, though, these relationships assigned great responsibility and great authority to the mother. Even if the father was prepared to support the family financially and lend his social position and network to further their ambitions, everything they owned was at least formally the property of the mother and her children. Women were responsible for managing the assets of the family, buying and selling land and slaves, running the family business, doing all sorts of things that in the conventional gender order of that day were supposed to be taken care of by men. The greater autonomy of mothers translated into a greater autonomy for women in all areas of free colored life. Mothers trained their daughters to fulfill the same roles as they did. Mothers trained their sons to think it normal that their female partner would play a role in the family business. Since these women were often among the wealthiest and most visible free women of color in any colony, their lifestyles set a pattern for many others below them in the social hierarchy. It is important to note, however, that women in West African society had a traditional role in marketing and small business that might well have played into the greater autonomy and economic activity of women of color.

The status divisions of slavery also affected the role of elders. Very often in free families of color, older members might still be enslaved. Even if the family were living under the protection of some white patron who was helping them gain their freedom, as in the case of the children of Sally Hemings and Thomas Jefferson (see HEMINGS, SALLY, CHILDREN OF), putting resources into gaining the freedom of an older person past childbearing and working years was hard to justify. Sally Hemings remained de jure a slave throughout her life, though the white daughter of Jefferson who inherited her after his death gave her "her time," allowing her to live as she wished (see also LIVING "AS FREE"). This would tend to decrease their natural authority within the family. Hemings's children generally moved away to the Midwest to avoid discriminatory laws against people of color. This was another problem that society in the Americas posed for the relationship with elders—they might well be living many miles away as both white and black populations were very mobile. The absence or relative powerlessness of elders in the black family helped weaken the extended family, giving priority to the immediate family of parents and children. It also helped the black family respond more readily to changes in society, since elders with presumably more conservative values were not able to slow adoption of new ideas. This may be one explanation for the rapid adoption of the 19th century's new religious movements—evangelicalism and Baptist reforms—and of the century's new moral code.

The harsh conditions affecting the black family during slavery left many individuals without blood kin to rely on. For these people, black society created a wealth of pseudokin networks, that is, social groupings that provided some of the benefits of family networks to unrelated people. Families provide affection and emotional support, conservation and secure transmission of assets to the next generation, a safety net in case of emergencies, and a network of trusted associates for business and sociability. Various social institutions in the Americas provided some of these benefits for people of color. CATHOLIC CONFRATERNITIES in the Spanish and Portuguese world provided safety nets through health and burial insurance, as well as social networking and friendship. The FREEMASONRY and secular fraternal organizations in North America and the Caribbean did so for some free people of color, though these institutions date back only to the last decades of the era of slavery. Across the Americas outside the United States, the free colored MILITIA was a very important social institution that fulfilled many of these functions. Especially in places where the military threat was strong and white men few, free coloreds served as militiamen. The militia company could be a network to provide social support to its members in the case of an emergency. The company put the soldier in contact with officers who were generally upper-class whites, potential patrons and protectors. Even fellow servicemen could prove important members of the network. Studies in SAINT-DOMINGUE and Veracruz, MEXICO, show free colored militiamen preferring their fellow soldiers as godfathers to their children, business partners, and husbands or fathers-in-law for their daughters.

In conclusion, although the black family suffered under intense hardships during the time of slavery, it was a resilient institution and very important in black life.

Stewart R. King

FURTHER READING

Gutman, Herbert G. *The Black Family in Slavery and Freedom: 1750–1925.* New York: Pantheon Books, 1976.

MacAdoo, Harriet Pipes, ed. *Black Families.* London: Sage Publications, 2007.

Tannenbaum, Frank. *Slave and Citizen.* Boston: Beacon, 1992.

FAMILY RELATIONSHIPS WITH SLAVES

Free people of color often had family members who were enslaved. Some were married to slaves, though in many cases a marriage between a free person and a slave would result in the automatic or greatly simplified MANUMISSION of the slave (*see also* MARRIAGE BETWEEN FREE AND SLAVE). But free people of color might also have parents, children, or other close family members who were enslaved. Gaining the freedom of enslaved family members was a crucial goal for many free people of color. Different social and legal systems in different colonies and states made this process more or less difficult, depending on a wide range of circumstances.

It was very common throughout the Atlantic world for an enslaved family to seek the freedom of women of childbearing age first. This is because it was almost universally true that the children of a free woman were free themselves, regardless of the status of the father or older siblings. Thus, freeing a woman also freed all of her subsequent children. It is this, much more than any sexual complaisance, that fevered racist propaganda imagined, that accounted for the high percentage of women who received manumission in most places in the Americas. Less commonly, older people were often freed voluntarily by masters, both as a reward for long service and because their labor was relatively valueless. Governments were suspicious of manumissions of elderly slaves, though, concerned that they were simply attempts to dump unprofitable workers on communal charity. White fathers of enslaved children also sought the freedom of their children, though governments also frowned upon this as a reward for "immorality." Manumissions were difficult to achieve, though, as they required the permission of the master, often only given after a substantial payment was made, and also the permission of governments, again often requiring a substantial tax. Many manumissions were informal, that is, people would remain officially enslaved but would be given "their time" or "bush freedom" (sometimes in exchange for a payment). These manumissions are hard to document and further complicate an understanding of the relationship between free and enslaved persons of color. Some people sought freedom by running away (*see also* MAROONS and RUNAWAY SLAVES). Men were more likely to run away than women, because women would probably be responsible for child and elder care. However, a runaway who was able to get to a place where his freedom was relatively secure, a free territory or a maroon village, would seek to liberate additional family members beginning with women of childbearing years.

Because of the difficulty of obtaining government permission for manumission, it was not uncommon for a free person to be the legal owner of the enslaved kin. It might cost the equivalent of a few hundred dollars in today's money to buy a young child or elderly person from a master, but the tax demanded by the government for registration of the manumission would be in the thousands of dollars. This situation would be acceptable in the short term, but if the "master" died, or was bankrupt, or some other crisis erupted within the family, the ransomed family members would be in danger of RE-ENSLAVEMENT. This was much more common than a simple kidnapping or judicial punishment, feared by all free people of color, as a means of re-enslavement.

The most common family relationship between a free person of color and a slave was that between a free mother and her enslaved children and partner or husband. The prevalence of manumissions of women meant that populations of free people of color were demographically skewed toward women, though not so much as might be expected given the high birthrate and substantial proportion of most free colored populations that was born free. These women had to work not only to support themselves but also to accumulate substantial amounts of capital to obtain the freedom of their relatives. The prevalence of women working outside the home, especially in commerce and hospitality, led to unfortunate gender stereotypes of free people of color (*see also* COMMERCE AND TRADE, GENDER ATTITUDES, and PROSTITUTES AND COURTESANS).

Another common relationship between free and enslaved family members was that between a free adult daughter and her parents. It was usually not a good investment to seek the freedom of enslaved parents since they were unlikely to outlive the free family member, so in many cases one finds a parent the legal property of his or her daughter. Though one presumes that traditional patriarchal family structures were not totally upended by such a situation, this might have tended to reinforce the power of women in the society and to undermine the power of older generations. And occasionally cases were recorded of free children who became gravely ill or injured and made wills in which they tried to provide for the formal manumission of their parents. One such case was of a mixed-race soldier in the French army during the WAR OF AMERICAN INDEPENDENCE, 1775–83, Jean-Charles Floissac, who made his will before departing for GEORGIA in 1779 and called on his executor, a wealthy white man who may have been a relative though probably too young to be his father, to pay for the freedom of his mother out of his earnings.

Laws and social customs in many places recognized and protected family relationships between free and slave. The most common protections were for marriages. In Spanish, Portuguese, and French colonies, married couples had some protection by the ROMAN CATHOLIC CHURCH from separation by sale and other disruptions of family life. In general, Catholic canon law codes dating from the Middle Ages put family ties above other social bonds, including slavery. To the extent that a country accepted the guidance of the Catholic Church on family legal matters, these protections extended not only to marriages but also to other family ties. French customary law also recognized a mother's right to oversee her children up to the age of 10, in theory preventing an enslaved child from being sold away from his or her mother. Free women claimed this right in two recorded cases in the French Caribbean, though in both cases they were given the option to purchase their child by the court, and it is unclear whether they had the resources to actually do so. In many other cases, though, slave children younger than 10 were sold without their mothers, suggesting that the legal provision was ignored or circumvented. Catholic priests were much more active in the Spanish colonial world than in BRAZIL or the French colonies in defense of their black parishioners. Free black mothers often appealed to church law in MEXICO and elsewhere on the mainland to prevent sales of their enslaved children. A 1786 law that was officially in effect in South America, LOUISIANA, FLORIDA, and CUBA but not Mexico or Central America enshrined these protections in the statute books and made priests responsible to the state to protect family life. In Dutch colonies, blacks who were acculturated and members of the Reformed Church could also sometimes gain assistance from their church officials. In the British colonies, the only protection was from the poor law administrators in each parish, who did not want motherless children or solitary elderly put onto the charity rolls. If the child was enslaved and the parent free, as was generally the case, they usually did not intervene. In the United States, even this protection was not present, since most states disestablished their churches and had no official poverty programs whatsoever. In any case, British law and the laws of states of the United States after independence in the 1770s placed the property rights of SLAVE OWNERS above the family ties of slaves in almost all circumstances.

Stewart R. King

FURTHER READING

Dunaway, Wilma. *The African-American Family in Slavery and Emancipation.* Cambridge: Cambridge University Press, 2003.

Gutman, Herbert G. *The Black Family in Slavery and Freedom, 1750–1925.* New York: Vintage, 1977.

FAMILY RELATIONSHIPS WITH WHITES

The traditional view of free people of color is that they were the children of white men and their enslaved black women. In fact, the majority of free people of color in many colonies throughout the Americas were black rather than mixed-race. Mixed-race free people of color often had no relationships with their white relatives. Nonetheless, a significant group of people of color considered themselves members of white families and were accepted by the whites, at least in private. Public acceptance and cultural attitudes toward these relationships were conditioned by many factors, including the status of the white relatives, the attitudes of religious and secular authorities, and evolving attitudes toward race. As a general rule, across the plantation world family relationships between whites and people of color were more difficult to acknowledge and more harmful to both parties if they became known as racial attitudes hardened.

The relationship between white fathers and their children of color was the best known and prototypical family tie between white and black. There were many such relationships. MISCEGENATION was extremely common, and many sexual relationships between white men and women of color lasted for decades and produced numerous children. In Spanish, Portuguese, and French colonies, there was at least some pressure from the ROMAN CATHOLIC CHURCH on these couples to marry. Under French law, if a free man married a slave woman, she and all the children they had had together were freed without payment of a MANUMISSION tax. Even if the couple did not or could not marry (for instance, if the white man had a wife in Europe already), there were legal provisions and cultural mores requiring some sort of support for the children. Under French common law, fathers of illegitimate children were required to provide a living allowance for their children, though they could meet this requirement by giving them job training or some capital assets such as land and slaves. Often, telltale language in wills, apprenticeship agreements, and formal donations of goods made by white men to mixed-race children in French colonies announced that a particular grant or apprenticeship was provided "in lieu of a living allowance." Courts occasionally enforced payment of living allowances to mixed-race illegitimate children against the legitimate heirs of a white father who died without a will, especially if the mixed-race children had powerful patrons in the colony. Legitimate children of mixed race were the natural heirs of their white fathers and frequently inherited large estates over the objections of more distant white relatives in the French, Spanish, and Portuguese worlds. In the Spanish colonies, the Catholic Church oversaw family law and was quite ready to enforce the rights of illegitimate children against fathers or their

heirs. Spanish men who married slaves also obtained easier manumission for them and their children. Mixed-race children whose parents were married in the Spanish world could be formally granted some of the privileges of whiteness, through the process of *CÉDULAS DE GRACIAS AL SACAR* (official certificates of dispensation from the laws applying to free people of color). Informally, white society could accept light-skinned free people of color who were of legitimate birth and simply allow them to blend into the larger society. Even illegitimate children could benefit if their fathers were influential and took an interest in their success. For example, St. MARTIN DE PORRES, a mixed-race Peruvian man who joined the order of DOMINICANS as a low-ranking lay brother in the late 16th century, was allowed to become a full member of the order, a rank usually reserved for whites at the time, when his father, the Spanish governor of PANAMA, intervened on his behalf.

If the children were enslaved, cultural mores insisted that they be freed. A French traveler in SAINT-DOMINGUE reported that young men newly arrived in the colony were sometimes lured into relationships with female slaves, and then when the slaves became pregnant the masters would sell the children to their fathers at exorbitant prices. This is probably exaggerated, but it shows the strength of the social expectation that white fathers must at least free their mixed-race children. Mixed-race people were much more likely to gain their freedom in French, Spanish, and Portuguese colonies than were blacks.

In British and Dutch colonies, and in the United States, there was no formal requirement that fathers care for or free their mixed-race children. British poor laws placed the established Protestant Church in charge of looking out for the destitute. Illegitimate children who had to be taken care of by the parish had to name their fathers, and the fathers could then be fined to pay the costs of their children's upkeep (if the relationship could be proved). The social cost of being sued by the parish for child support was usually enough to ensure that at least some provision was made for free colored children. Similar provisions did not exist in the Dutch colonies, though the Dutch Reformed Church would often attack a white man cohabiting with his slave for immorality and oblige him to free and support his children as a punishment. Marriages between white men and women of color were extremely unusual in the Protestant world, even forbidden in some colonies, especially in North America. Formal manumission was more difficult in the British colonies too, and there was little social pressure to free one's children. Nonetheless, people sought to free their children, and some succeeded in obtaining a place for them in their families. Famously, John Custis (1678–1749), a leading politician in Virginia and the father of Daniel Parke Custis (1711–57)—first husband of Martha Dandridge Custis Washington (1731–1802), who later married GEORGE WASHINGTON—became the father of a mixed-race boy, also named John but called Jack, in 1739. As a member of the Governor's Council, John Custis had no difficulty obtaining governmental permission for young Jack's manumission in 1744. John's will divided his property between his two sons, with Jack committed to the care of his elder half brother until he reached adulthood. Neither the father nor the elder brother appears to have found this arrangement unusual, though it did create some scandal in Virginia society. Jack Custis died at the age of 12, apparently of meningitis. Martha Dandridge Custis Washington, on the other hand, kept her half sister Ann Dandridge in slavery throughout her life. Ann only gained her freedom after Martha's death in 1802, as a gift from Martha's grandchildren, who were her heirs. However, the conditions of Ann's enslavement were relatively mild—many observers at the time and later thought that she was a free colored woman, and a biographer of Washington only found the record of her manumission in the 1990s.

Mainland North America differed from the Caribbean and South American slave societies by having large populations of poor whites. It was not uncommon for white women, often poor indentured servants, to have relationships with enslaved black men. Unlike the reverse situation, which could be winked at under patriarchal norms, this was a severe violation of the evolving racial code and could result in very harsh punishment for all concerned. The black father was in danger of losing his life if identified, and the white mother might well find her indenture lengthened or a large fine imposed. However, the child was free from birth. Family relationships between white mothers and free mixed-race children were not uncommon in the Southern colonies. Many old free colored families in the South trace their ancestry to such unions. As white people who had an acknowledged family tie, the white matriarchs would provide important protection to their children and grandchildren in these very oppressive societies.

Other degrees of kinship with whites than parenthood were also important for free people of color. As noted, young Jack Custis was cared for by his half brother. Half siblings could be very important in the lives of people of mixed race, if both sides were aware of the relationship, but they were not an unmixed blessing. For the white children, the parallel black family was living evidence of their father's lack of monogamy, at least theoretically demanded by the common Christian culture. On the other hand, the cultures of the whites of almost all plantation areas were very patriarchal, and family ties were enormously important. This led to compromises, such as white families' supporting mixed-race kin without publicly acknowledging their relationship, and conflict, such as white families' suing their mixed-race half siblings for the return of assets given or willed to them. The hypocrisy inherent in these tangled relationships is evident in the diary of Mary Chesnut, a SOUTH CAROLINA white woman, who observed in the 1860s: "Like the patriarchs of old our men live all in one house with their wives and their concubines and the mulattoes one sees in every family exactly resemble the white children and every lady tells you who is the father of all the mulatto children in every body's household, but those in her own she seems to think drop from the clouds, or pretends so to think." The pretending was necessary, as the women were caught between the competing values of marital fidelity and family ties. Sometimes, the outcome was bad for the mixed-race children and their mothers, who might well suffer unusually harsh treatment from stepmothers and white half siblings. Mixed-race slaves were still more likely to be freed in North America than were blacks, but the margin was not nearly so great as in Catholic countries, and the social protections for the children of informal unions were much weaker. Often the concealment of these informal unions was so successful that subsequent generations, at least on the white side, would be entirely unaware of the connection. The CHILDREN OF SALLY HEMINGS are a well-known example of this phenomenon: It is clear from DNA evidence and the accounts of observers at the time that Sally Hemings maintained a long-term relationship with her master, THOMAS JEFFERSON, after his wife, her half sister, died in 1782. Jefferson freed her children, and most of them moved to the Midwest and established a large family there. The Hemings descendants were always aware of their famous ancestor, but the white descendants of Thomas Jefferson through his surviving legitimate child have persistently refused to acknowledge the relationship, even in the 21st century as the evidence has become overwhelming.

Family relationships of people of color with whites were full of contradictions for both sides. White relatives could be lucrative patrons, perhaps powerful enemies. White relatives could be a source of pride for mixed-race families, and a source of shame as a reflection of the subordination of slavery. As with many other features of free colored life, having a white relative was an opportunity, but one that had to be treated with caution to prevent falling back into the abyss of poverty and subordination.

Stewart R. King

FURTHER READING

Degler, Carl. *Neither Black nor White: Slavery and Race Relations in Brazil and the United States.* Madison: University of Wisconsin Press, 1986.

Gordon-Reed, Annette. *The Hemingses of Monticello: An American Family.* New York: W. W. Norton, 2008.

Gutman, Herbert G. *The Black Family in Slavery and Freedom, 1750–1925.* New York: Vintage, 1977.

FÉDON'S REBELLION (1795–1796)

Fédon's Rebellion occurred in the British Caribbean colony of Grenada between 1795 and 1796. It took its name from Julien Fédon, a free colored planter who was the leader of this spectacular antislavery and anticolonial movement. It was, simultaneously, an unsuccessful revolution, a slave rebellion, an episode of the FRENCH REVOLUTION, and The Brigands' War, 1794–98, and an abortive, protonationalist war of independence (*see also* BRITISH LESSER ANTILLES).

The underlying causes of the rebellion are located in the preceding century and a half of resistance to slavery under French rule immediately prior to the establishment of British rule in 1763. After Britain's capture of Grenada in 1762—during the SEVEN YEARS' WAR, 1756–63—was confirmed by the treaty of 1763 between Britain and FRANCE, conflicts between the more numerous Roman Catholic French and the Protestant British settlers over the French participation in the colony's civic affairs dominated Grenada's internal politics until 1779, when, during the WAR OF AMERICAN INDEPENDENCE, 1775–83, France captured the colony in 1779 but ceded it back to Britain in 1783. (*See also* ROMAN CATHOLIC CHURCH and PROTESTANT MAINLINE CHURCHES.)

The restoration of British rule led to the intensification of the state-sponsored persecution of the French Roman Catholics. Their church buildings were forcibly seized by acts of the Grenada legislature; the glebe (or cultivated) lands owned by the Roman Catholic Church for more than a century were also seized by the Protestants; all Roman Catholic marriages, burials, and baptisms were declared null and void unless they were solemnized before Protestant clergymen. They then lost the institutionalized minority they held in the Grenada legislature. On January 28, 1793, their social and political condition reached new depths when Ninian Home (1732–95) arrived at Grenada with the appointment as lieutenant governor.

Home was an implacable enemy of the French Roman Catholics in Grenada from the start. The second Speaker of the Grenada Assembly and owner of two plantations, he was a prominent member of the "Ultra-Protestants," who resisted all attempts by the British to honor its commitments in the treaties of 1763 and 1783 to provide a measure of civic and religious rights to the French Roman Catholics of Grenada.

Home's arrival at Grenada on January 28, 1793, was at a crucial moment in Caribbean and world history.

Exactly a week before, in France, King Louis XVI was executed by guillotine. On February 1, Britain joined the First Coalition against France in the French Revolutionary War. In August 1793 in SAINT-DOMINGUE, Léger-Félicité Sonthonax (1763–1813) declared general abolition in Saint-Domingue.

The evidence suggests that Home's appointment was the event that finally alienated the French and mixed-race French-descended Roman Catholics from allegiance to Britain and drove them toward armed revolution against British rule and chattel slavery. With the migration of many white French Roman Catholic families to nearby Spanish Trinidad to avail themselves of the opportunities afforded by the Cedula de Población of 1783—a measure taken by the Spanish colonial government to increase the population of Trinidad by inviting French and other refugees from nearby wars to immigrate and set up plantations (*see also* TRINIDAD AND TOBAGO)—the leadership of the French community passed to the free people of color, who were the largest single group of free people in Grenada. By September 1793, the revolutionaries had already chosen their headquarters—Belvidere—Fédon's estate in the center of Grenada and, apparently, the leader of the revolution, Fédon himself.

The planning was greatly aided by the deployment of the British garrison to assist in the capture of the French eastern Caribbean empire in 1793; France's abolition of slavery in February 1794 by (the Decret du 16 Pluviôse) and the arrival off Guadeloupe of a French expedition led by VICTOR HUGUES in June 1794 to recapture France's empire and implement the decree. In July 1794, however, the French Revolution entered a new phase with Robespierre's fall, but Hugues and his followers continued to take the French Revolution to the British. Hugues gave military, ideological, diplomatic, and financial assistance to the Grenada revolutionaries.

The abortive revolution began with simultaneous attacks on the towns of Gouyave and Grenville, and the capture of Speaker Home and other senior officials on the night of March 2–3, 1795. Fédon then sent a Declaration and Summons to surrender the colony to him and the French Revolutionary forces. The British refused, and Grenada was subjected to nearly two years of bloody civil war, with unprecedented savagery on both sides, during which the issues of war and treason were inextricably bound.

On August 10, 1795, the surviving members of the Grenada legislature passed the Act of Attainder, which declared several hundred revolutionaries by name guilty of high treason unless they surrendered to justice by September 1, 1795. Another law confiscated their estates. The British also created several armed battalions of enslaved Africans in order to help them to defeat the revolutionaries. For long periods, only these armed slaves stood between the British and complete social revolution in Grenada.

By October 1795, the French military and civil authorities established an official presence on Grenadian soil. France never sent a large force, but two demibrigades of the revolutionary army—between 1,000 and 2,000 soldiers—and a few hundred officials served in the island during the struggle. They established their capital at Gouyave, renamed Port Libre, and there appear to have been established the rudiments of a government. The Grenadan revolutionary forces included the several hundred hard-core rebels who had been identified by name in the Act of Attainder, with their families and dependents. They could put two to three thousand men in the field with weapons for at least short periods, though most of the men were farmers or farmworkers who continued to work in the fields. With the British confined at St. George's, the remainder of Grenada's territory was mostly controlled by the revolutionaries.

This was the situation in early 1796, during which the historian Michael Craton said that Grenada deserved to be called a "black republic under arms." In their moment of greatest strength, however, the revolutionary movement was split in two. Differences between the Grenadians led by Fédon and the French resulted in the division of the revolutionaries into two separate commands. By the time a British Expeditionary Force consisting of nearly 10,000 soldiers supported by the heavy guns of a dozen warships arrived in June 1796, the revolutionaries were divided, outnumbered, and outgunned. The French military and civilian personnel surrendered to the British on June 10, 1796, and the revolutionary stronghold was captured by the British on June 19, 1796.

Most of the leading revolutionaries were captured, brought to trial, identified by name in the Act of Attainder, hanged, and beheaded—that is, except Julien Fédon himself. He was never captured and made to suffer an ignominious death at the hands of the British. He was thought at first to have drowned on his way to Trinidad in 1796 but in 1814 was believed to have escaped to CUBA, where, oral tradition holds, he died during the 19th century.

Fédon's rebellion represents the high-water mark of the French Revolution in the Lesser Antilles. After the British forces regained control of Grenada, they went on to restore British fortunes elsewhere in the islands, ultimately wresting control of the region from the French. Later Antillean nationalists looked back to Fédon as a progenitor, and the revolutionaries are honored today as the fathers of independent Grenada.

Curtis Jacobs

FURTHER READING

Brizan, George. *Grenada: Island of Conflict*. London and Basingstoke: Macmillan Education, 1998.

Cox, Edward. *Free Coloreds in the Slave Societies of St. Kitts and Grenada, 1763–1833*. Knoxville: University of Tennessee Press, 1984.

Craton, Michael. *Testing the Chains: Resistance to Slavery in the British West Indies*. Ithaca, N.Y: Cornell University Press, 1982.

Steele, Beverley. *Grenada: A History of Its People*. London: Macmillan Education, 2003.

FENIX slave ship

The *Fenix* was a Spanish ship engaged in the Atlantic slave trade that was captured by the U.S. Navy in 1830. The slave trade was then unlawful under international law, although SPAIN and BRAZIL continued to import slaves from Africa into the 1850s. The controversy over what was to be done with the liberated slaves on board the *Fenix* was a decisive moment in the development of American attitudes toward slavery and toward free people of color. This case foreshadowed the more famous AMISTAD CASE of 1839–41.

On June 3, 1830, the *Kremlin*, an American merchant ship of Boston commanded by Christopher J. Hall, when sailing off Santo Domingo was pursued by the *Fenix*, a Spanish ship commanded by Francisco Pablo de la Torre. An American warship, USS *Grampus*, commanded by Isaac Mayo, encountered the ships and learned from the *Kremlin* of the attempted PIRACY. After cannon fire from the *Grampus*, the *Fenix* surrendered. Aboard were a crew of 19, all Spaniards, and 82 male and female captive Africans, 24 days from the coast of Calabar, on the Bight of Biafra in West Africa (*see also* SLAVE COAST, BENIN, AND THE BIGHT OF BIAFRA). American sailors under the command of Lt. James P. Wilson took charge of the ship and confined the Spaniards as prisoners, not for slave trading, but for piracy.

The small *Fenix*, formerly the New York pilot boat *Trimmer*, was taken to NEW ORLEANS, LOUISIANA, by way of Key West and Pensacola, FLORIDA. From Key West, where the *Fenix* arrived on June 18, escorted by the *Grampus*, the ship was escorted to Pensacola by the US Revenue Cutter *R. C. Pulaski*, sailing on June 24. Two of the Africans had died before the arrival at Key West.

Upon arrival at Pensacola, only 77 Africans were aboard, indicating that there had been more deaths. Commodore Jesse D. Elliott, commanding U.S. naval forces in the West Indies, later wrote that he furnished the Africans with fresh provisions in quantity and that their condition improved quickly, but some still succumbed to the rigors of the journey.

The *Fenix* arrived in New Orleans on July 19, after being escorted partway by USS *Natchez*, a vessel that had been in Pensacola, and the *Grampus*, which rejoined it after investigating the *Fenix* in Havana, where it had been bound. Upon arrival in the city, only 74 Africans were living.

There, a series of hearings were held in the U.S. District Court before Judge Samuel H. Harper. The court determined, much to the dismay of Lieutenant Wilson, that there was not enough evidence for the charge of piracy. The Africans, represented by an attorney, demanded their freedom. Judge Harper declared that they were indeed free, as they had been illegally transported in the slave trade, but that to release them unconditionally would be unwise, for LOUISIANA had passed a law the previous year that free persons of color who entered the state after 1828 should be compelled to leave it.

The administration of President ANDREW JACKSON ordered that the Africans remain in the custody of the court in New Orleans while their case was being resolved, and that in order to cover the cost of housing them, they could be hired out as slaves. The government also argued before the court that the Africans were not covered by existing anti–slave trade law, since they were not intended to be imported into the United States.

On September 21, 1830, Deputy Marshal O. H. Burlingame noted there were only 61 Africans still living. U.S. Attorney John Slidell, in forwarding this report, told the court that from the necessity of confining the Africans and from other causes their health had suffered. In fact, the mortality rate in this case was not unusual for slaves taken to Louisiana from Africa during the era of the slave trade, and there is no suspicion that their treatment was unusually harsh.

In 1831, President Jackson sent a message to Congress asking for suitable legislation for the maintenance of the Africans. They were, however, hired out to William McQueen and to Judge Joshua Lewis in Louisiana. Four years later, after many more deaths, Secretary of the Navy Mahlon Dickerson made arrangements with the AMERICAN COLONIZATION SOCIETY for their transportation to LIBERIA. Only 37 Africans of the 82 found on board the *Fenix* ever again saw the shore of their native continent. They sailed from New Orleans in late May 1835, on the brig *Louisiana*. After a stop at Norfolk, Virginia, they arrived at Liberia on August 11, still known by their African names, which were recorded in New Orleans. They were settled with other Africans released from the *Antelope* and the *GUERRERO* slave ships at New Georgia.

The story of the *Fenix* shows the hardships that people recaptured from slave traders endured. Even though the slave trade had been illegal under U.S. law since 1808, the *Fenix*'s unwilling passengers were kept as slaves in the United States for four years, and then the survivors—for only about half survived, a death rate quite consistent with mortality rates among newly arrived slaves throughout the Atlantic world—were sent back, not to their homes, but to a land that was only marginally more familiar to them than Louisiana. The *Fenix* case also prefigured the much more famous *Amistad* case, in which the free status of people who were imprisoned in the illegal slave trade was confirmed by the U.S. Supreme Court.

Gail Swanson

FURTHER READING

Lee, Byron A. *Naval Warrior: The Life of Commodore Isaac Mayo*. Linthicum, Md.: Anne Arundel County Historical Society, 2002.

Report of Mr. Kennedy, of Maryland, from the Committee on Commerce of the House of Representatives of the United States on the African Slave Trade. Washington, D.C.: Gales and Seaton. 1843. Reprint, Manchester, N.H.: Ayer Company Publishers, 1971.

FILLMORE, MILLARD (1800–1874) *thirteenth president of the United States (1850–1853)*

Millard Fillmore was the first Northerner since the brief tenure of WILLIAM HENRY HARRISON to hold the presidency. He took office on July 10, 1850 (after the sudden death of President Zachary Taylor), in the midst of a crisis over the status of the territories acquired by the United States in the MEXICAN-AMERICAN WAR, 1846–48. Fillmore, though a Northerner, was more open to compromise than Taylor had been. He ultimately accepted the Compromise of 1850, including the FUGITIVE SLAVE ACT OF 1850, which had a very negative impact on the lives of free people of color.

Fillmore was one of the few American presidents actually born in a log cabin, in Moravia, NEW YORK, on January 7, 1800. His parents were poor farmers, and he was apprenticed to a weaver as a boy. He received only six months of formal education but was able to qualify as a lawyer after being tutored by an older lawyer. He lived in rural New York for most of his life, having little contact with people of color. Fillmore rose through the ranks of the Whig Party in New York, serving as state legislator and congressman and running unsuccessfully for governor in 1844. In 1848, he was nominated for vice president alongside Zachary Taylor, as a representative of mainstream Whig and Northern opinion with the popular but politically untested Taylor. Taylor died after only 14 months in office, and Fillmore served the remainder of Taylor's term, until March 4, 1853.

Two fugitive slaves, Anthony Burns and Thomas Sims, are returned to their masters by U.S. Federal Marshals and troops under the provisions of the Fugitive Slave Act of 1850. This painting depicts the two men together, but actually the events occurred three years apart. Both caused great unrest in Massachusetts and contributed to the political decline of the Whig Party, to which President Fillmore belonged. *(© North Wind Picture Archives/Alamy)*

Fillmore's presidency was marked by the political crisis over the status of the newly acquired territories in the present-day Southwest. Southerners insisted that the new territories be open for slavery, at least south of the Missouri Compromise line, which was the southern border of Missouri, extended westward. Northerners, including many Whigs, argued that the principles of the Northwest Ordinance (1787) should apply to all newly acquired territories and thus that slavery should be banned, perhaps with the exception of TEXAS, which had been admitted directly as a state.

As a congressman in 1844, Fillmore had voted against the admission of Texas as a slave state. However, as president, he actively supported the Compromise of 1850. This measure had originally been proposed by the Whig leader Henry Clay but was put into its final form by the Democrat Stephen Douglas. Under the compromise, CALIFORNIA was to be admitted as a free state, even though part of its territory extended south of the Missouri Compromise line. The territories south of the line were to be left open for slavery if their people wished it, and ultimately the principle of "squatter sovereignty" meant that the white male inhabitants of each of the territories could choose to allow slavery or not. And, most importantly for free people of color, the new Fugitive Slave Act of 1850 would make it much harder for Northern states to protect their black citizens against RE-ENSLAVEMENT by southerners who claimed to own them. The Compromise of 1850 put off the AMERICAN CIVIL WAR, 1861–65, by 10 years, perhaps allowing the North to make more progress in regional unity and industrialization that helped ensure ultimate victory. At the time, though, it was seen by the Northern public as weakness, and it destroyed the Whig Party. Fillmore was the last president to hold office as a Whig, and in the 1852 election, a variety of third parties tried to lay claim to its role as the principal opposition party to the predominant Democrats in American politics. The remnant of the Whigs nominated the Mexican War general Winfield Scott in 1852, denying Fillmore renomination. In 1856, Fillmore ran for president as the candidate of the anti-immigrant, anti-Catholic American Party, popularly called the Know-Nothings. By this time, most Northern Whigs had, like ABRAHAM LINCOLN, joined the new Republican Party. Fillmore continued to oppose the Republicans throughout the Civil War and supported President ANDREW JOHNSON during the

Reconstruction period (*see* RECONSTRUCTION IN THE UNITED STATES).

Fillmore's legacy for free people of color is troubling. While an opponent of slavery and the first president not to have owned slaves since JOHN QUINCY ADAMS, he approved the draconian Fugitive Slave Act of 1850. The concept of "squatter sovereignty," accepted in the decision to admit New Mexico as a slave territory and further codified in the Kansas-Nebraska Act under his successor, Franklin Pierce, in 1854, also spelled acceptance of harsh restrictions on free people of color in the western territories (*see also* OREGON, and INLAND WEST OF THE UNITED STATES). This willingness to compromise with the South over the expansion of slavery into the territories ultimately led to armed struggle in KANSAS. Fillmore died on March 8, 1874.

Stewart R. King

FURTHER READING

Smith, Elbert B. *The Presidencies of Zachary Taylor and Millard Fillmore*. Lawrence: University Press of Kansas, 1988.

FIVE AFRICANS BROUGHT TO ENGLAND IN 1555

In 1555, the English trader John Lok took a group of Africans to England. The English were interested in breaking the Portuguese monopoly on trade with western Africa and believed the best way to accomplish this was to gain support from the local inhabitants. The plan was to return with the slaves to England, where they would be taught English and later returned to Africa as interpreters and "friends" of England. Lok sailed to West Africa along the coast of Guinea, an area controlled by PORTUGAL and associated mainly with slavery. He took five men from Shama, a town on the coast of present-day Ghana, and returned to England. A published account of Lok's travels described the men as tall and strong, and it was said they enjoyed English meat and drink but hated the cold, moist weather. Three of these black men were known among the English as Binne, Anthonie, and George; however, no names are recorded for the other two men.

In the 1550s, the London merchant William Towerson led three trading voyages to Guinea. In the second one, in 1556, he took with him three of the black men, one of whom was George. These men acted as interpreters and "friends" of the English. They were able to convince other Africans that it was safe for them to board English ships for trading purposes and facilitated public relations between African locals and English merchants. When the returning travelers got back to the area where they were known, they were enthusiastically welcomed. Some wept with joy to see them, while others asked where Anthonie and Binnie were

and were relieved to hear they would be returned on the next voyage. When they arrived at Shama itself, the men's relatives rushed out to meet them, including one of their aunts. Their friends greeted them as jubilantly as if they, too, were family. There was so much joy in the reunion that the English observers expressed themselves surprised that "savages" could have such deep feelings.

The story of these men is an early example of the important role that free Africans and African Americans would play in the Atlantic slave trade. The European slave traders could not function efficiently as pirates, kidnapping people along the coast of Africa. African governments were too well organized to permit this sort of behavior over the long term. One ship captain could get away with a piratical raid, but the next ships to arrive on that coast would find an armed and suspicious population able to resist capture or at least make acquiring slaves by force too expensive in lives and time. Slavers needed local people to work with them. Taking people from coastal villages, either by force or with the consent of local officials, became the rule, along with the allied practice of leaving European crewmen on the coast with friendly locals to establish a base for subsequent voyages. These European sailors, if they survived, would often establish families who would carry on their business for generations. Between these two expedients, the slave traders created a Euro-African class of "coast traders" who survive to this day as a distinctive group, especially in what used to be called the "slave coast," the original home of these five men (*see* SLAVE COAST, BENIN, AND THE BIGHT OF BIAFRA).

Carole Levin and Cassandra Auble

FURTHER READING

Fryer, Peter. *Staying Power: The History of Black People in Britain*. London: Pluto Press, 1984.

Hakluyt, Richard. *Voyages and Discoveries: The Principal Navigations, Voyages, Traffiques and Discoveries of the English Nation*. Edited by Jack Beeching. Harmondsworth, England, and Baltimore: Penguin Books, 1972.

Law, Robin. *The Slave Coast of West Africa 1550–1750: The Impact of the Atlantic Slave Trade on an African Society*. Oxford: Clarendon Press, 1991.

Levin, Carole. "Backgrounds and Echoes of Othello: From Leo Africanus to Ignatius Sancho." *Lamar Journal of the Humanities* 22, no. 2 (Fall 1996): 45–68.

Scobie, Edward. *Black Britannia: A History of Blacks in Britain*. Chicago: Johnson Publishing Company Inc., 1972.

FLEETWOOD, CHRISTIAN ABRAHAM

(1840–1914) *American soldier and civil servant*
Christian Fleetwood was a Civil War soldier and one of the few black American soldiers to win America's highest

A photograph of Christian Fleetwood (1840–1914), taken shortly after the end of the American Civil War. Fleetwood, born free in Baltimore, Maryland, served as a senior noncommissioned officer in the Union army during the Civil War. He was one of the few blacks to win America's highest military medal, the Medal of Honor, before the 1970s. He went on to a successful career in the civil service and was a senior officer in the District of Columbia National Guard in the 1890s. *(Library of Congress)*

military honor, the Medal of Honor, before the 1970s. He went on to have a successful career in the civil service.

Fleetwood was born to free black parents in Baltimore, MARYLAND, in 1840. He received a good education, thanks to the generosity of a wealthy white sugar merchant, John Brunes. He graduated from Ashmun Institute (later Lincoln University, the oldest historically black college in the United States) in Oxford, PENNSYLVANIA, in 1860. He worked for the AMERICAN COLONIZATION SOCIETY before the AMERICAN CIVIL WAR, 1861–65, and made a brief trip to SIERRA LEONE and LIBERIA. He also briefly published a newspaper in Baltimore, the *Lyceum Observer*.

When the American Civil War began in 1861, Maryland free men of color were eager to serve in the United States armed forces. The army, however, was composed of state regiments mustered by the state governments and then turned over to the national army for service. The states set the requirements for enlistment, and Maryland was unwilling to permit blacks to serve even after President ABRAHAM LINCOLN made it clear that blacks were acceptable in the final EMANCIPATION PROCLAMATION, issued on January 1, 1863. Some Baltimore blacks enlisted in the NAVY, which had no racial limitations on enlistment. Some blacks from southern Maryland went to the District of Columbia or the U.S.-controlled post at Fort Monroe, Virginia, to enlist in regiments organized there. But it was not until July 1863 that the army established a camp outside Baltimore, named after its commander, Colonel William Birney of the 2nd Infantry, United States Colored Troops (USCT), and began enrolling Maryland blacks directly without going through the intermediary of the state government. Ultimately, he raised enough manpower in the Baltimore area to staff seven regiments of the USCT, including Fleetwood's 4th Infantry. Birney accepted anyone who volunteered, free or slave. He was unwilling to return recruits to Marylanders who purported to be their masters and indeed was accused of raiding slave pens for manpower. However, educated free blacks were preferred for leadership positions, and Fleetwood was rapidly promoted to sergeant major of the regiment, the highest noncommissioned rank. Almost all commissioned officers of the USCT were whites.

The 4th USCT was sent to Fort Monroe in August 1863. It participated in a number of actions in the Virginia theater. Many of its assignments were lacking in glory—white officers had little faith in the black troops' fighting qualities, and they were often assigned to building fortifications and roads, guarding prisoners, hauling supplies, and the like. But the 4th USCT, with Fleetwood, swept the creeks and inlets of the James estuary for small Confederate gunboats; attacked rebel posts near Richmond, the Confederate capital; and impressed the army's leadership with its ability to march and fight. The regiment was assigned to General Benjamin Butler's (1818–93) Army of the James in April 1864 and participated in the Bermuda Hundred landing. Butler's army was attempting to cut the rail line connecting Richmond and Petersburg but was defeated at the Battle of Dewry's Bluff (May 12–16, 1864). Fleetwood and his men worked on fortifications until September 1864, when they were sent into battle at Chaffin's Farm (September 28–29, 1864). The Union army was once again attempting to break through the defenses of Richmond by attacking along both sides of the James River. The Northern defenses were anchored by a Confederate fort on a bluff overlooking the river called Fort Harrison. The 4th USCT and seven other regiments of black soldiers stormed the fort and the adjoining lines of trenches.

The fort itself was carried, but Fleetwood's portion of the attack became bogged down in front of well-manned Confederate trenches. The flag bearer for the regiment was shot, and Fleetwood and another soldier seized the flag. When the regiment began to fall back, Fleetwood used the flag to rally some of the soldiers and form a line to protect the flank of the other regiments pressing the attack. For his heroic deeds at Chaffin's Farm, Fleetwood was awarded the Medal of Honor, America's highest military decoration.

After Chaffin's Farm, the much-depleted 4th USCT, along with much of Butler's army, was sent off to the coast of NORTH CAROLINA. Fleetwood participated in the capture of Fort Fisher, guarding the mouth of Wilmington harbor, in January 1865. The regiment campaigned in North Carolina for the remainder of the war, participating in the capture of Wilmington, Raleigh, and Goldsboro. Despite the unanimous recommendation of his officers, the War Department would not grant Fleetwood a commission as an officer. His service ended when the regiment was disbanded, May 4, 1866.

After the war, Fleetwood lived for a while in OHIO, then moved to Washington, D.C., in 1867, and went to work for the War Department's FREEDMEN'S BUREAU. Many bureau employees were prewar free blacks. Fleetwood worked for the War Department until he retired in 1891 with a disability pension based on deafness caused by combat in the Civil War, although he must have been able to hear a little as he worked as the choir director at a D.C. black church. Fleetwood helped to organize a black battalion of the D.C. National Guard, though he was passed over for command. He also organized a Cadet Corps in the black high school in the district. Some graduates of this corps went on to become officers in World War I, among the first blacks to be commissioned officers in the U.S. Army.

In 1869, Fleetwood married Sara Iredell (1811–1908), another prewar free black from D.C. who was one of the first registered professional nurses in the United States. She was supervisor of nurses at the Freedmen's Bureau Hospital in the district and an important figure, along with Clara Barton (1821–1912), in the professionalization of nursing in the United States.

Fleetwood and Iredell were typical of the so-called first generation of freedom: black professionals who took advantage of prewar educational opportunities and the brief opening during the war and the period of RECONSTRUCTION IN THE UNITED STATES to have successful careers. As a highly decorated black soldier, Fleetwood was a standing contradiction to racist ideas about blacks' fighting abilities in the U.S. military in the bleak years of Jim Crow in the armed services. Iredell was a founding mother of the profession of nursing. Their contributions

were all but forgotten by the larger society, but they were trailblazers along the route that black professionals of later decades were to follow.

Fleetwood died just after the outbreak of World War I, on September 28, 1914.

Stewart R. King

FURTHER READING

Longacre, Edward. *A Regiment of Slaves: The 4th United States Colored Infantry, 1863–1866.* Mechanicsburg, Pa.: Stackpole Books, 2003.
McPherson, James. *The Negro's Civil War: How American Blacks Felt and Acted during the War for the Union.* New York: Vintage, 2003.

FLORIDA

Florida is a peninsula extending from the southern part of North America into the Caribbean Sea. The modern state also extends 250 miles along the coast of the Gulf of Mexico, as far as Pensacola Bay. The Spanish/British colony that existed until 1821 included the Gulf Coast territories of what are now the states of MISSISSIPPI and ALABAMA. The southern part of the state is low-lying and swampy and was not heavily inhabited until the late 19th and early 20th centuries. The densest settlement before the AMERICAN CIVIL WAR, 1861–65, was along the northern border of the state and especially around the important ports of St. Augustine, Pensacola, and Mobile. Bordering the state to the north are GEORGIA and Alabama.

Florida's colonial period was marked by various transfers of the swampy Florida terrain among the Spanish, the British, and the Americans. After a period of exploration between 1513 and 1565, Florida belonged to the Spanish from 1565 to 1763, with the majority if not all of settlement in the northern portion of the state. The British eventually captured Florida and held it from 1763 to 1783. The Spanish took Florida back at the end of the WAR OF AMERICAN INDEPENDENCE, 1775–83, in which Spain supported the Americans, and held it from 1784 to 1821 before the Americans finally secured the land area in 1821. While the Spanish held Florida, slavery laws allowed for the freedom of slaves of African descent more readily than British and American law. The predominant Catholic faith allowed the Spanish to see the enslaved people as people who could actually rise from their enslavement once they fully accepted and practiced the Catholic religion (*see also* ROMAN CATHOLIC CHURCH). The Spanish even invited enslaved people to make their way from Britain's Carolinas to Florida under the promise of freedom for service. To this end, in 1738, a group of 38 newly freed men were allowed to establish Garcia Real de Santa Teresa de Mose, also known as Fort Mose (*see also* MAROONS and RUNAWAY SLAVES).

Fort Mose is considered the first legal free black town in what is now the United States of America. Located two miles north of St. Augustine, this town was used as a city for the founding men and their wives as well as a fortress against the British. The almost 100 residents maintained themselves through farming and harvesting shellfish. Much like the neighboring town, it also was served by Franciscan priests. The first settlement of Fort Mose only lasted two years before the British general James Oglethorpe, governor of Georgia, took and occupied it. During this time, the residents moved back to St. Augustine until the Spanish retook Fort Mose in 1742. At that time, Florida's new governor tried to make the original residents move back to Fort Mose, but the town's former residents were reluctant. Historians believe that this reluctance was due to new family connections in St. Augustine and the dangers of attacks by Native Americans. Soon, however, 67 residents of the new Fort Mose resettled the town. The town, however, was rebuilt to be larger and more heavily defended. The free people of color who established the new Fort Mose were from various places in Africa, including Arara, Carabeli, Congo, Gamaba, Ganga, Guinea, Lucumi, Mina, and Samba. Some of the residents were also Native American. The leader of this group was Mandiga. The priests were concerned for this group because the group members were heard praying in their native languages. As new runaway slaves left CHARLESTON, SOUTH CAROLINA, and Savannah, Georgia, in the mid-18th century, they added to the population of Fort Mose and made it more CREOLE and less African in its culture. At the end of the SEVEN YEARS' WAR in 1763, however, Florida became a British colony under the Treaty of Paris, and Fort Mose was completely dismantled. Many of the residents moved to CUBA instead of becoming part of the British colony.

Fugitive slaves and free people of color also found refuge within Florida's Indian population. Some fugitive slaves and free people of color, however, found themselves enslaved by Florida's Indian population. Each person of African descent, free or enslaved, who was affiliated with the Native Americans, especially the Seminole, had his or her own stories regarding how they or their ancestors went to live with Florida's Native American peoples. Native Americans did not always readily accept persons of African descent into their tribes, and some research shows that even the Seminole, who later became closely linked with a number of people of African descent, apparently had no black people living with them in 1774. By the 1780s, however, Native Americans along with white residents in Florida enslaved numerous people of African descent. For example, even though the Creek tribe signed the Treaty of

New York in 1790 and the Treaty of Colerain in 1796 stating that they would return fugitive slaves living in their territory that included Florida, reportedly some Creek tribe members utilized slaves as farm laborers. In the case of the Seminole, reportedly the people of African descent, both slave and free, began to take on the customs and language of the tribe. The term BLACK SEMINOLE came to characterize the infusion of the people of African descent into the Seminole way of life even as the people of color were not fully considered Native American. As a result of this infusion, when the Seminole were expelled from Florida and moved to the American West between 1838 and 1843, approximately 500 people of African descent went with them. Many of these people, seeking to return to Spanish-owned territory, where they would experience less discrimination, moved on to northern and central MEXICO and were at the core of an important Afro-Mexican community.

During the colonial period, Spain imported enslaved Africans in order to work mainly in the East Coast city of St. Augustine. Because the Spanish could not find ways to maintain self-sustaining crops in the swamplands (as they did in the Spanish West Indies), there was little need for a large agricultural slave population. During the American Revolution and British rule, however, the British took about 8,000 slaves to Florida in order to escape the Americans. As a result, INDIGO CULTIVATION provided the staple crop. After the American Revolution and the subsequent period of Spanish rule, the United States gained control of Florida and found that the middle of the state was fertile enough for some COTTON CULTIVATION. Thus, more slaves were taken to the state in hopes of establishing strong cotton plantations. Jackson, Gadsden, Leo, Jefferson, and Madison Counties began to see some cotton production, but not as much as in other parts of the southern United States. South Florida boasted some SUGAR CULTIVATION plantations in the 1820s, but again not as much as the West Indies. The Seminole Wars of the 1830s completely destroyed these plantations, and it was not until after the 1840s that new sugar plantations began to sprout up in South Florida. These plantations, however, yielded little significant production. The 1850s census records show thousands of cotton plantations but only 200 large enough for 30 or more slaves, and only a few were recorded as having more than 200 slaves. About 60,000 blacks lived in Florida in 1860, of whom around 1,000 were free.

In the 1840s, when free white Floridians began to publicly fear abolitionist activities in their state, there were a few significant legal acts that sought to contain the state's free people of color. In 1845, a revenue act assessed higher county taxes on free people of color than on free white citizens. In 1847, cities were to require free people of color

AFRICAN-AMERICAN POPULATION OF FLORIDA, 1830–1900

Year	Slaves	Free People of Color	Free People of Color as a Percentage of Total Population	Total Population
1830	15,501	844	2.4%	34,790
1840	25,717	817	1.5%	54,477
1850	39,310	932	1.1%	87,447
1860	61,745	932	0.7%	140,424
1870		91,689	48.8%	187,748
1880		126,690	47.0%	269,493
1890		166,180	42.5%	391,422
1900		231,209	43.7%	528,542

to obtain legal guardians who were white city residents of high reputation. These guardians were supposed to vouch for the good character of the free people of color as well as be held responsible for their overall public actions. It has been noted that this requirement was not widely adhered to, especially in the cities like Pensacola and St. Augustine, where free people of color contributed to a significant portion of the local economy. It also has been noted that although the guardianship act did not make a great difference, many free people of color did carry documents that affirmed their status as free instead of enslaved.

After 1850, many free white Floridians sought to limit the movements and activities of Florida's free people of color. These free people of color, as in other Southern states, were generally seen as threats to the slavery establishment in as much as they may have given hope to the enslaved and were seen as taking away free white Floridian money and jobs. An 1855 act sought to prohibit free people of color from moving to Florida. An 1856 act prohibited free people of color to possess firearms. This act also stated that if an enslaved person purchased his or her freedom in Florida, then he or she had 30 days to leave the state or be sold back into slavery by the sheriff. An 1857 act stated that if a free person of color were found guilty of teaching a slave to read, that person was to be fined, imprisoned, and/or whipped up to 39 lashes. An 1858 law allowed free people of color to select their own masters and become slaves or, if their habits were publicly deemed idle or dissolute, free people of color could be arrested and eventually sold into slavery by public auction. And in 1861, as the American Civil War approached, state law required each free person of color older than 12 years old to register with the county probate judge. This registration included documenting name, age, color, sex, and occupation and paying a one-dollar fee. An extra dollar was assessed if they moved to a different county. The penalty for not registering included becoming the slave of

whoever caught them. Again, cities such as Pensacola and Key West were less stringent in enforcement of this law. South Florida and the Keys, indeed, were frontier areas where racial prejudices common in more settled areas were diluted. Racial attitudes were more like those found in nonplantation areas of the British Caribbean, such as the Bahamas or Cayman Islands, than anywhere in the United States.

Close to 1,000 free people of color are estimated to have lived throughout Florida in the 1850s and 1860s, with the majority living in the towns of Pensacola, Jacksonville, Tallahassee, and St. Augustine. While more and more legal restrictions were being placed upon Florida's free people of color, their presence in the 1850 and 1860 census records shows that the people who decided for one reason or another to stay in Florida continued to survive and in some cases thrive. The census records show that free people of color were employed in jobs such as barbers, bricklayers, brick masons, butchers, cabinetmakers, carpenters, cigar makers, farmers, grocers, laborers, mariners, masons, sailors, ship cooks, shoemakers, tailors, and tiners. Real estate and personal wealth were also recorded in the Florida 1850 and 1860 census records, with free people of color listed as having wealth between $200 and $5,000. Birthplaces were also recorded in the census records. Not only were free people of color listed as being born in the state of Florida, but many were born in states such as Alabama, Georgia, LOUISIANA, MARYLAND, MISSISSIPPI, NEW YORK, NORTH CAROLINA, PENNSYLVANIA, SOUTH CAROLINA, and Virginia, as well as in the District of Columbia. Still others were listed as being born in Africa, Bahamas, Havana, Martinique, and San Domingo.

Florida was lightly affected by the American Civil War, most of the state remained under the control of the Confederate authorities throughout the war. The United States held Fort Pickens, at the mouth of Pensacola Bay, throughout the war and established a base at

Jacksonville in 1862. Many black Floridians fled to the protection of the U.S. forces, and about 1,000 enlisted in the U.S. military. They served primarily in United States Colored Troops regiments raised in South Carolina. These units participated in the one serious attempt by U.S. forces to recapture the state that culminated in the Confederate victory at Olustee in February 1864. After this battle, Union forces held their coastal bases for the remainder of the war. Slavery in Florida was initially abolished by the EMANCIPATION PROCLAMATION in January 1863, but it did not take actual effect in most of the state until the end of the war and the ratification of the Thirteenth Amendment in 1865.

After the Confederate surrender in May 1865, the former free colored population of the state did not preserve much collective identity. The small number of prewar free people of color, combined with the pervasive discrimination against all people of color in the postwar society, meant that all blacks struggled equally. The population of far southern Florida and the Keys was something of an exception, as people in the region only slowly adopted Southern culture and racial attitudes as they became more fully incorporated into the state's economy, and blacks whose ancestors had lived in those areas before the Civil War retained a sense of being part of the "Conch Republic" in a way that blacks from farther north could not share.

Angela Bickham

FURTHER READING

Berlin, Ira. *Slaves without Masters: The Free Negro in the Antebellum South*. New York: New Press, 1992.
Deagan, Kathleen, and Darcie MacMahon. *Fort Mose: Colonial America's Black Fortress of Freedom*. Gainesville: University Press of Florida, 1995.
Landers, Jane. *Black Society in Spanish Florida*. Urbana: University of Illinois Press, 2001.
Reiss, Oscar. *Blacks in Colonial America*. Jefferson, N.C.: McFarland, 2006.
Singleton, Theresa A., ed. *"I, Too, Am America": Archaeological Studies of African American Life*. Charlottesville: University Press of Virginia, 1999.
Smith, Julia Floyd. *Slavery and Plantation Growth in Antebellum Florida, 1821–1860*. Gainesville: University Press of Florida, 1973.

FONSECA GALVÃO, CÂNDIDO DA (DOM OBÁ II)
(ca. 1845–1890) *Brazilian army officer and Afro-Brazilian "prince"*

Cândido da Fonseca Galvão was one of the most colorful characters in the political turmoil of the late imperial period in Brazil. He gained fame as a noted supporter of the Brazilian Empire and as a spokesman for the value of African identity. The combination of dedication to monarchy and a very modern connection with his African roots seems strange to modern observers but made sense to urban free people of color at the time, giving him a large following. He remains an important figure in Brazilian folklore.

The son of a freed Yoruba man, Galvão was born around 1845 in Lençóis, in the interior of the province of Bahia, Brazil. Nothing is known of his early life, but in 1865, at the start of the War of the Triple Alliance (1864–70), Galvão led 30 volunteers from his hometown to the provincial capital of Salvador. For this service, he was commissioned *alferes* (second lieutenant) in one of the all-black companies of Zuavos (light infantry) then being raised by the Bahian government. Galvão probably did not see action, for he was invalided out in August 1866, just before his Zuavo company went into action at the Battles of Curuzu and Curupaiti the following month.

After the war, Galvão received an honorary second lieutenant commission and spent time in the old soldiers hostel in Rio de Janeiro. He eventually returned to Bahia but could not find stable employment. Around 1880, he joined the migration of Afro-Brazilians from the economically depressed Northeast (including Bahia) to Rio de Janeiro, the national capital.

In Rio de Janeiro, Galvão took the name Dom Obá II and presented himself as the ruler of the city's Afro-Brazilian people. His claims to descent from African royalty were widely accepted by lower-class Afro-Brazilians, though mocked by the mainstream press. Dom Obá II frequented Emperor Pedro II's public audiences and used his connections to assist his people in their dealings with the state.

Dom Obá II regularly published articles in an opposition newspaper, *O Carbonário*, on topics ranging from the political questions of the day to larger social issues. These texts offer a unique window into popular understandings of Brazilian society at the time of the abolition of slavery, which occurred in 1888. Dom Obá II drew on an eclectic set of sources, including the Bible, Yoruba proverbs, and his reading of the mainstream press, to condemn racial discrimination and the rough treatment that men and women of color received from the authorities.

As a well-known popular monarchist, Dom Obá II did not long survive the republic that was proclaimed in November 1889. After he participated in a monarchist demonstration in December 1889, the government stripped him of his honorary military rank. His death in mid-1890 was, however, widely reported in the press, and he remained an important figure in Rio de Janeiro's folklore.

Hendrik Kraay

FURTHER READING

Kraay, Hendrik. "Patriotic Mobilization in Brazil: The Zuavos and Other Black Companies." In *I Die with My Country: Perspectives on the Paraguayan War, 1864–1870*, edited by Hendrik Kraay and Thomas L. Whigham, 61–80. Lincoln: University of Nebraska Press, 2004.

Silva, Eduardo. *Prince of the People: The Life and Times of a Brazilian Free Man of Colour*. Translated by Moyra Ashford. London: Verso, 1993.

FORD, WEST (early 1780s–1863) *American farmer*

West Ford was the mixed-race son of a mulatto slave named Venus who was the property of John Augustine Washington (1736–87), the brother of GEORGE WASHINGTON. He was born on John A. Washington's plantation in Westmoreland County, Virginia, in the early 1780s; the exact date is a subject of debate. Venus was said to have claimed that George Washington was the boy's father, though some of the president's biographers have disputed the claim on the basic of the possible timing of Ford's birth and Washington's known visits to his brother's plantation. Additionally, Washington had no other children and may have been sterile as a result of a childhood illness. Other possible fathers include John Augustine and his two sons, Bushrod and Corbin. Bushrod Washington (1762–1829), who was to serve as a justice of the Supreme Court, left West Ford a substantial legacy of 160 acres of good farmland and some money and tools when he died, leading many to assume that he was his father. Ford's recent biographer, Linda Bryant, however, accepts the paternity of George Washington, so the question must, as with many similar cases of mixed-race children, remain open.

George Washington took an interest in the boy from an early age, however. Washington visited his brother's plantation regularly between 1785 and 1791, while he was resident at Mount Vernon, to see his relatives, and he always took young Ford riding or hunting and to the local Episcopal church. It was at this time that Ford met Washington's longtime personal servant WILLIAM LEE, who was beginning to suffer from the alcoholism that was ultimately to kill him.

John Washington died in 1787, and Bushrod and Corbin gave West Ford to their mother. She freed him in her will when she died in 1802, and he was actually free by 1806. In 1812, Ford married a free black woman who lived near Mount Vernon, some distance from his home in Westmoreland County. He may have met her through his friends in Washington's service. Ford lived in Mount Vernon for some time, helping to care for William Lee during his final illness. Ford used bleeding to treat Lee's alcoholic comas, and this treatment may have contributed to his death.

In 1829, Ford inherited a farm in Fairfax County, Virginia, near Washington, D.C., from Bushrod Washington, and his family moved there by 1831. In 1857, he divided his farm, by that time more than 200 acres, among his children and returned to Mount Vernon to live full-time. By the 1850s, there were no longer any heirs of Washington living at Mount Vernon, and Ford cared for the property. The Mount Vernon Ladies' Association, who acquired the property in 1853, allowed Ford to live on there and provided him a pension. He gave tours of the facilities and spoke about his life with the Washingtons (though never publicly claiming any family relationship). He died in 1863, in the midst of the AMERICAN CIVIL WAR, 1861–65 as plantations and smaller farms throughout Virginia were devastated by passing armies.

Ford's property in Fairfax County (now in the city of Alexandria, Virginia) went on to become the black farming community of Gum Springs. The area was under Union military control from a very early point in the conflict. Ford's children welcomed many RUNAWAY SLAVES and newly freed people and helped reconnect people to Virginia families they had been sold away from, sometimes many years before. Many black farmers settled in the area, and the Ford descendants became the core of an important black community during the period of RECONSTRUCTION IN THE UNITED STATES and afterward. The Ford Descendants Association still exists.

Ford and his family are an example of a common phenomenon among free people of color in the American South. As a free person of color, Ford had limited options during the period of slavery. He remained under the protection of his influential family, as a resident or neighbor of Mount Vernon and the Washingtons. But in the chaotic conditions during the Civil War and afterward, their connections, skills and education, and the new freedoms accorded black people in general helped to make the Fords important community leaders. In this way, at least in the United States, the free black community was able to make some of its most important contributions after the formal difference between them and other blacks had been wiped away by abolition.

Stewart R. King

FURTHER READING

Bryant, Linda. *I Cannot Tell a Lie: The True Story of George Washington's African American Descendants*. Bloomington, Ind.: iUniverse Star, 2004.

"The Legacy of West Ford." The West Ford Descendants' Organization Web site. Available online. URL: http://www.westfordlegacy.com/home.html. Accessed December 23, 2010.

Wiencek, Henry. *An Imperfect God: George Washington, His Slaves, and the Creation of America.* New York: Farrar, Strauss & Giroux, 2004.

FORTEN FAMILY   *American businesspeople, activists, authors*

The Forten family was one of the most prominent free black families in the antebellum United States. Based in PHILADELPHIA, PENNSYLVANIA, the Fortens were leaders in their community and in the fight to end slavery and achieve racial justice. James Forten, the family patriarch, was born on September 2, 1766, in Philadelphia. He was the first person in his family with that surname. His forbears had been known as Fortune, but he would make the name Forten famous. He would achieve success in business and use his personality and pen to work for a better America, a legacy he would pass on to his children and grandchildren.

James Forten's great-grandfather was a slave in PENNSYLVANIA in the time of William Penn, the colony's 17th-century founder. His grandfather gained his freedom and married a free woman. His father, Thomas, worked as a sailmaker in the loft of Robert Bridges. Thomas was literate and Anglican, two characteristics that made him unusual in the African-American community (*see* PROTESTANT MAINLINE CHURCHES). James's mother, Margaret, gave birth to Abigail in 1763 at the age of 41 and James three years later. His father's sister, Ann Elizabeth Fortune, was an exceptional woman. She owned enough property to write a will. She bequeathed all of her property to Ann, except her slave woman, Jane, who gained her freedom.

James probably worked alongside his father in the sail loft during his childhood. Thomas Fortune died in late 1773 or early 1774. Though James was able to attend the Friends' African School, he left sometime in 1775 to work for a local storekeeper (*see also* BAPTISTS AND PIETISTS for more on the Quakers and blacks). In the tumult of the WAR OF AMERICAN INDEPENDENCE, 1775–83, 14-year-old James Forten joined an American privateer, or privately owned warship. The ship set sail in July 1781, and the first voyage was remarkably successful, capturing several ships. Forten signed up for another voyage just after his 15th birthday; one day after leaving port, they encountered a British warship and were captured. Forten was ordered to keep an eye on the British captain's youngest son. As they neared New York City and its prisoner ships, the British captain offered to send Forten to England as his son's companion. Forten could have enjoyed friendship, the protection of a wealthy patron, and legal equality. Instead he politely refused, saying he would never be a traitor to his country. Though Forten later had the

opportunity to escape from the prison ship by hiding in an officer's sea chest, he gave up his spot to a white Philadelphian, Daniel Brewton. Brewton never forgot this act of kindness, and they became lifelong friends. After nearly seven months, Forten and some of his companions were freed in a prisoner exchange.

James Forten worked for Robert Bridges for 13 years, moving from apprentice to foreman to junior partner. After the Revolution, in 1798, Bridges prepared to retire. Though Bridges had several children, he sought a better future for them than labor as ARTISANS and sold his loft to James Forten. When the firm changed hands, all of the apprentices, most of them white, voted to stay and continue their education under Forten. Throughout his long ownership, Forten employed both blacks and whites, and he tried to convince others that this interracial success was a model for the country. Many of his African-American employees were family and friends, including his nephews, his sons, and James Cornish, the younger brother of the New York minister SAMUEL E. CORNISH.

By this time, James Forten also owned several pieces of property in Philadelphia. He leased these properties to citizens of all classes and colors. Throughout this period, Forten became more involved in the African-American community. There is no record of community leadership before 1796, when he became a church vestryman in the first election at St. Thomas's African Episcopal Church, whose pastor was the first African-American priest in the Episcopal Church, ABSALOM JONES. Forten served as a vestryman numerous times, was an officer of the African Lodge of Masons, and helped raise funds for black schools and colleges (*see also* FREEMASONRY). James Forten also signed several antislavery petitions and wrote to sympathetic politicians. He also lent money at interest, including to his friend and minister Absalom Jones.

Over the ensuing years, Forten looked out for his niece and three nephews after the death of their father in 1805. His namesake, James Forten Dunbar, worked as a sailor for many years and was still in the navy when the Civil War began in 1861. On December 10, 1805, Absalom Jones presided at James Forten's wedding to 20-year-old Charlotte Vandine. She was of mixed background and light complexion and would eventually bear nine children. Almost exactly nine months after their wedding, Margaretta, named in honor of Forten's recently deceased mother, was born. Other children followed in the coming years: Charlotte in 1808, Harriet in 1810, James, Jr., in 1811, Robert Bridges in 1813, Sarah Louisa in 1814, Mary Isabella in 1815, Thomas Willing Francis in 1817, and William in 1823. Their names recognized family, friends, and supporters.

When the Pennsylvania legislature considered an oppressive and racist law in early 1813, Forten replied in a public series, "Letters from a Man of Colour." Though unsigned, his authorship was probably an open secret since he had frequently used that phrase to identify himself before. He drew on the rhetoric of American liberty to argue for African-American equality. The next year, Forten helped organize more than 2,000 African Americans to build defenses around Philadelphia against a potential British invasion during the War of 1812.

The restoration of peace in 1815 encouraged James Forten and his New England friend PAUL CUFFE in their African emigration plan. Despite Forten's interest, the creation of the AMERICAN COLONIZATION SOCIETY in late 1816 and the corresponding rejection of African colonization by the African-American community in Philadelphia forced Forten to rethink his position (*see also* EMIGRATION AND COLONIZATION). Instead, Forten became one of the leading opponents of African colonization, and late in life, he would either forget or omit mentioning his early support. Despite his ongoing opposition to African colonization, Forten supported a plan for emigration to Haiti, and two of his apprentices as well as his brother-in-law settled there. In many of these community endeavors, Forten worked alongside his friend Absalom Jones and his associate RICHARD ALLEN.

After Jones's death in 1818, Forten took an active role in finding his successor. He had earlier sought to install an assistant minister of his choosing but been rebuffed by other vestrymen. The effort to find a permanent minister proved equally contentious, and after nearly a decade, a white minister was appointed. Eventually, William Douglass, an African-American minister from Baltimore, would take the pulpit of St. Thomas in 1835. Forten at last had the well-educated African-American minister he had long sought.

Beginning in the 1830s, Forten became friends with the white abolitionist William Lloyd Garrison. Though many years younger and from a very different background, Garrison shared Forten's hatred of slavery and colonization. Forten supported Garrison by finding subscribers to his newspaper, the *Liberator*, and loaning Garrison money when he needed it. James Forten's letters and writings appeared many times in Garrison's newspaper. Forten's son-in-law ROBERT PURVIS also supported Garrison's efforts.

The brothers Robert and Joseph Purvis were close friends of the Forten family. Born in Charleston to a Briton and a free black woman, in 1810 and 1812, respectively, Robert claimed an early antislavery education, either ignoring or forgetting the fact that both his parents bought and sold slaves. The brothers moved to Philadelphia in 1820 and knew the Forten family through both church and school. Robert Purvis married Harriet Forten on September 3, 1831. Though Purvis was often mistaken

for white and some of his father's friends advised him to seize the opportunity, Purvis declined. Robert and Harriet lived in the Forten home for the first months of their marriage but soon purchased a new home nearby. Robert Purvis was a founding member of the American Anti-Slavery Society in 1833. For the rest of his life, James Forten would often serve as an officer in the organization, frequently alongside his sons and son-in-law. Not to be left out, within days of the creation of the American Anti-Slavery Society, Charlotte Forten, three of their daughters, and a future daughter-in-law helped create the interracial Philadelphia Female Anti-Slavery Society.

Sarah Louisa Forten achieved renown as an antislavery writer and poet before marrying at a relatively late age, in her mid-20s. Her first published poem was at age 16 in the *Liberator*, though she used a pseudonym. Sarah published numerous poems during her life, most advocating abolition and equality. On January 8, 1838, Sarah married her brother-in-law, Joseph Purvis. They were married in a small civil ceremony in Vermont, avoiding the large formal wedding at the Forten home their siblings had had. They settled west of Philadelphia, and Sarah withdrew from the Philadelphia Female Anti-Slavery Society and stopped writing as she gave birth to eight children in 12 years and helped to run the family farm. After numerous financial setbacks, Sarah died at the family home in 1884.

Margaretta, the eldest child, also published occasional poems and was an active worker in the abolition movement. She never married, and after her father's death in 1842, she became a teacher. She would remain a strong influence and source of comfort for her extended family until her death in 1875.

James Forten, Jr., traveled and spoke in support of abolition. He married Sarah Vogelsang, from a wealthy New York City family, on January 13, 1839. Less than a year later, James Vogelsang Forten was born. Robert Forten was also an effective antislavery speaker and accomplished individual. He constructed a nine-foot-long telescope, which was exhibited at the Franklin Institute in Philadelphia, and wrote poetry about ancient Rome. Robert married one of his sisters' friends, Mary Virginia Wood, on October 18, 1836. Their first child, Charlotte, was born the following August. Their youngest son, William, attended the Oneida Institute in Upstate New York. His classmates included HENRY HIGHLAND GARNET and ALEXANDER CRUMMELL. Though he left after two years, he would become an antislavery crusader as well.

Throughout the 1830s, the Forten family was beset on all sides. Pennsylvania officially stripped all blacks of the right to vote. One of James Forten's sons was attacked by a white mob. In fact, white mobs regularly rampaged through the streets of Philadelphia, attacking abolitionists and free blacks and, in 1838, burned down Pennsylvania Hall. In 1835, James Forten was elected president of the convention movement (*see also* NEGRO CONVENTION MOVEMENT IN THE UNITED STATES). The next year, Forten, his sons, and his son-in-law, Robert Purvis, renamed and refocused the organization. Now known as the American Moral Reform Society, they sought to better America society and remove any marker or denotation of color. This proved rather divisive, as former friends accused them of being ashamed of their color. They were not, they were seeking to live in an America where color was irrelevant.

After a lingering illness, James Forten died on March 4, 1842. Thousands of people of all complexions turned out to pay their respects. Tributes were spoken and published throughout the spring. The proceeds from the sale of Robert Purvis's tribute to his father-in-law benefited the abolition movement.

Unfortunately, James Forten had numerous loans at the time of his death. The owners of the sail loft, James, Jr., and Robert, had a difficult time collecting on these debts. Their troubles dragged on for a decade, with their brother-in-law Robert Purvis suing them in court more than once. They sold the sail loft in the mid-1840s to two former employees. James, Jr., moved to New York City, where his wife became a teacher. Though Sarah Vogelsang Forten died in 1852, her husband and son both fought in the NAVY during the Civil War. After the war, James Vogelsang Forten, James Forten's grandson, settled in NEW JERSEY and started a family. Denied a military pension, he slowly sank into poverty and died in 1907.

Robert Forten had stayed in Philadelphia and weathered the bankruptcy as best he could. He cared for his daughter Charlotte and remained close to Robert and Harriet Purvis. While living in England, Robert learned that blacks could serve in the Union army, and he returned to enlist in 1864 at the age of 50. Eventually promoted to sergeant major, he helped recruit new soldiers until becoming ill after drilling his men in the rain. Robert Bridges Forten died on April 25, 1864. His widow took almost three years to secure his pension.

Charlotte, Robert's daughter from his first marriage, was more fortunate. She was sent to school in New England in 1853 and began keeping a journal. It was a habit for most of her life and detailed her meetings and friendships with abolitionists, poets, and authors. She became a teacher and secured a post teaching freed people during the Civil War on the Sea Islands of South Carolina. Her correspondence was published in the *Atlantic Monthly*. After the war, she eventually settled in Washington, D.C., where she worked for the Treasury Department and married Francis J. Grimké in 1878 at age 41. Grimké

was the nephew of the white reformers Sarah and Angelina Grimké, who recognized him despite his mixed parentage. Theirs was a happy marriage, and Charlotte Forten Grimké died on July 22, 1914.

Harriet and Robert Purvis purchased a mansion outside Philadelphia in 1843, after Robert had been forced to guard their home during another Philadelphia riot. At this new home, they entertained guests of all shades and legal statuses; a hidden room was added for RUNAWAY SLAVES. Their marriage was a true partnership, as both worked fervently for abolition and equality. During the Civil War, she raised funds while he worked to recruit black troops. After the war, they both continued their work for African-American and women's suffrage. Harriet died in 1875. After Robert died in 1898, Elizabeth Cady Stanton paid tribute to him for his work for women's suffrage.

William, the youngest child of James and Charlotte Forten, continued their antislavery work. He was an active member of the Vigilance Committee before the Civil War and strong supporter of the Equal Rights League after it. He became involved in politics and was a staunch supporter of the Republican Party. As the family finances and his political influence dwindled, he moved into a home for the aged and infirm. He died in 1909 at the age of 86.

Charlotte Forten, widow of James Forten, proved a shrewd businesswoman and recouped some of the family's losses. She buried two of her sons, all five of her daughters, and nine grandchildren. She died in 1884, days short of her 100th birthday.

The Forten family is an example of African-American accomplishment. They were well known, frequently visited, and often cited by white abolitionists. Though this life occasionally became burdensome and they bemoaned the lack of privacy, they usually welcomed the opportunity to assist in the effort for abolition and equality. Through their proud history they strove to be successful, work for abolition, and achieve equality.

Matthew J. Hudock

FURTHER READING

Gernes, Todd. "Poetic Justice: Sarah Forten, Eliza Earle, and the Paradox of Intellectual Property." *New England Quarterly* 71 (June 1998): 229–265.

Nash, Gary. *Forging Freedom: The Formation of Philadelphia's Free Black Community, 1720–1840*. Cambridge, Mass.: Harvard University Press, 2003.

Winch, Julie. *A Gentleman of Color: The Life of James Forten*. Oxford: Oxford University Press, 2002.

———. *Philadelphia's Black Elite: Activism, Accommodation, and the Struggle for Autonomy, 1787–1848*. Philadelphia: Temple University Press, 1988.

FRANCE
French Colonialism and Racial Attitudes: Background

Unlike England and the Netherlands, France had some limited contact with people of color during the Middle Ages and had some legal precedent for slavery. Starting in the 10th century, important markets in the Champagne region of northern France drew together merchants from North Africa and Asia, eastern Europe, and Italy with northern European merchants. Europeans wished to purchase spices and manufactured goods from the more developed civilizations of the Middle East and East Asia and sell their own agricultural produce, particularly woolen cloth and wine. Some of these foreign merchants maintained agents in France. There were also slaves from North Africa and eastern Europe living in medieval France. The Crusades, starting in the 11th century, strengthened ties between France and the Middle East. Naval warfare and raiding across the Mediterranean took slaves and prisoners of war to France, and sent French people to live as slaves in Africa and the Middle East. Some of these people were ransomed and returned, with a sense of a larger world. People of color were unusual, but not unknown, in French medieval society. Slavery was also a legally defined state in at least some areas of medieval France, with customary rules governing the relationship between master and slave in force in many of the provinces. Until the 18th century, France did not have a unified legal code, but instead each province had its own Parlement, or supreme court, which would register edicts from the king and make its own laws. The southern and western French jurisdictions that had laws related to slavery in the Middle Ages were also those that contributed the most settlers to France's early colonial expansion and thus set the pattern for France's race relations in the Americas. Paris, on the other hand, did not recognize slavery after the 11th century and by the 17th century was asserting that slavery could not exist on the territory of France.

Race in the way we think of it today was an unknown concept in medieval France. Frenchmen sometimes spoke of the "French race" in the 15th and 16th centuries, though even this nationalistic idea of race was not so firmly established as in England at the same time. Mostly, people in France divided the world on the basis of religion—Christians and non-Christians, Catholics and Protestants. Nonwhite Christians from Ethiopia or the Middle East were fully acceptable, and even non-Christians who lived up to the ideals of chivalry could be accepted as members of the human family and honored for their virtues. Medieval chansons de gestes, romantic tales of chivalry, often featured noble African heroes or antagonists, and the Egyptian sultan Saladin (1137–93),

who defeated and drove the crusaders out of Palestine, was seen as one of the greatest knightly heroes.

Racial Attitudes in the Age of Discovery and Colonization

When France began to establish colonies in the Americas in the 16th century, it was in the midst of its own civil war. Three political factions fought a series of increasingly bloody conflicts, with the winner, the House of Bourbon, drawing much of its support from France's minority Protestant community. Most French were Catholics, but the Protestants were numerous in the port cities and among the merchant class. The Bourbons began to colonize the Americas as a strategic move, to attack the Spanish and Portuguese who were allied to their enemies, the House of Guise. Henry of Navarre, the Protestant head of the House of Bourbon, took power as Henri IV in 1589, but only after converting to Catholicism. "Paris is worth a Mass," he famously said, but his successors on the throne took their religion much more seriously.

By the beginning of the 18th century, the French Crown was just as serious as the Spanish in insisting that colonial expansion could only be justified by a national mission to expand the ROMAN CATHOLIC CHURCH. This meant that society must be an ordered community, with a place for everyone, even slaves, and mutual responsibilities of service and protection uniting everyone. The famous CODE NOIR IN FRENCH LAW, or Black Code, promulgated in 1685, began with an affirmation of the Catholic identity of France and its colonies and insisted on the rights of slaves to decent treatment and of free people of color to a place in society. However, the Frenchmen who settled France's colonies in the tropical Americas were more pragmatic. Many of them were from the south, or from the western port cities, areas that had been hotbeds of Protestant, or Huguenot, support during the civil wars. Through their regional culture and historical background, they were already accustomed to the idea of strangers living among them, and through their religion they were more individualistic and prepared to see some people excluded from the community. (See also PROTESTANT MAINLINE CHURCHES and BAPTISTS AND PIETISTS.) This is not to say that Protestants were more likely to engage in racial discrimination than Catholics. It is the nature of the discrimination that was different. In the Catholic world, people were prepared to believe that there were "natural" differences between the races, as this concept began to grow out of the ideas of the Enlightenment, which justified a lower status for people of color, but regardless of status, considered everyone part of the community with at least a defined place and rights. Protestants, especially Calvinists, either accepted people as members of the "elect," or those who had been chosen to be saved, and treated them as equals or rejected them as among the damned and thus could justify almost any sort of treatment. This difference accounts, in part, for the paradox that the Protestant nations generally treated their slaves and free people of color more harshly, and yet the great moral movement of abolitionism first appeared in the Protestant churches. Most French colonists were not Protestants, though its first overseas colonies, in CANADA (1534), BRAZIL (1555), FLORIDA (1562), and Petit Gôave, in SAINT-DOMINGUE (1580), were majority Huguenot. In some cases, the French colonists of the 17th and 18th centuries or their ancestors were nominally Catholics but had converted from Protestantism at the same time as the Bourbons, or during the mid-17th-century persecution of Huguenots under Louis XIV. But Protestant attitudes toward the other were part of the cultural makeup of those areas that sent the most colonists to the Americas, especially in the early days, when the culture and common law of the colonies were being developed.

The early French colonists had few or no slaves. Their colonies were trading posts, seeking to trade with the Indians for products such as furs or dyewoods. The settlers farmed for themselves and for sale to the trading companies. In the Caribbean, the early French settlers were *boucaniers*, or buccaneers—originally hunters who sold meat dried on a *boucan*, or barbecue, to passing ships—and then pirates. The famous pirate haven at Tortuga, the largest in the Caribbean in the 17th century, was primarily inhabited by Frenchmen and ultimately part of the French colony of Saint-Domingue. Other ports open to French pirates existed at St. Kitts, Guadeloupe, French Guiana, and Martinique. Pirate society was famously racially mixed and egalitarian. (*See also* PIRACY.) But the pirate society ultimately declined as European governments became better organized and decided they could dispense with private armed forces. In the 17th century, the pirates of Tortuga were an important part of France's ability to project power in the Caribbean. Their most famous exploit was the capture of CARTAGENA de Colombia in 1697. After the Treaty of Ryswick in that year formally acknowledged France's claim to Saint-Domingue, France encouraged the pirates to settle down. Those who refused were ultimately hunted down by regular naval forces. Of the compliant, those who could be socially defined as whites often became planters, and the darker-skinned ones became MERCHANT SEAMEN or free black farmers.

The Eighteenth Century

French colonies in the Caribbean and Canada became enormously wealthy during the course of the 18th century. Canada spread largely through the efforts of traders and missionaries, deploying a small population of Europeans and Indian/white mixed-race subalterns across a huge territory in the interior of North America. There were some Afro-Canadians in French colonial days, but very few. The Caribbean colonies, on the other hand, became the most highly developed slave societies in the Americas. France concentrated development in a few colonies, using monopoly corporations to control the flow of resources. Saint-Domingue, and to a lesser extent Martinique, developed dominant SUGAR CULTIVATION sectors and important COFFEE CULTIVATION industries. Hundreds of thousands of slaves were imported from Africa. Especially after France lost Canada to the British at the end of the SEVEN YEARS' WAR, French colonial interest was overwhelmingly focused on Saint-Domingue. By 1790, it was the wealthiest colony in the world, with housing prices higher than those in Paris or London and white elites living a lifestyle that people in Europe could only imagine.

The racial egalitarianism of pirate days disappeared during the early 18th century, to be replaced by an increasingly strong color line. The colonies developed a caste society. Blacks were increasingly excluded from social institutions, ultimately including the white family. Whites and blacks had sexual relations and sometimes long-lasting relationships that clearly took the place of stable marriages in the lives of both partners, but these relations could not be publicly acknowledged. This led to the growth of a numerous and wealthy group of free people of color, who were isolated from their white kin by the color bar and from other blacks by slavery. Colonial governments and the imperial government at home passed increasingly harsh laws to enforce the separation of the races: Blacks were excluded from the professions, from roles in the church, from some trades; were required to use names "drawn from the African idiom" instead of the names of their white relatives; could not hold officer's commissions in the MILITIA, wear certain types of clothing, or ride in coaches; and faced a whole host of other restrictions. In France itself, there was a concerted effort, the Police des Noirs, to exclude people of color from the country, though it was ultimately unsuccessful. All these measures were intended, many scholars now suggest, as a "divide and conquer" strategy to prevent the growth of a CREOLE nationalism among elite whites and free people of color. Instead, whites were taught to have racial solidarity that transcended the class-based solidarity among the planter class. With whites so enormously outnumbered in all the Caribbean colonies, especially in Saint-Domingue, this meant that they were dependant on the national government and could not think about independence.

Revolution, Reconstruction, and Abolition

Revolutionary ideas took hold of France in the late 18th century and had profound repercussions in France's empire and in the treatment of people of color in France. The basic principles of the FRENCH REVOLUTION, which began in 1789, were individual freedom and responsibility, the elimination of all inborn distinctions between people and equal treatment under law for everybody, and a strengthening of national community through cultural solidarity and governmental centralization. It was an open question whether or how these principles were meant to apply outside France. In Europe, France sought to export its revolution from the earliest stages, but generally not through expansion of French national territory but instead by encouraging other nations to have their own revolutions. In the early 19th century, Napoléon did ultimately annex significant portions of Europe to France, but for the most part, he preferred to establish quasi-independent republics under French oversight. Revolutionary governments thought of France's colonies, at different times, as integral parts of the national territory and full participants in the revolution, as dependent territories to be ruled much as they had been under the old regime, or as quasi-independent nations in their own right, under the leadership of France but autonomous in domestic matters. A strong abolition movement grew up in France at this time, organized around the Société des Amis des Noirs and Abbé HENRI GRÉGOIRE. A free man of color from Saint-Domingue, JULIEN RAIMOND, had been working for civil rights for free people of color even before the French Revolution. He became a deputy to the National Assembly and a legislative commissioner to Saint-Domingue after free people of color were granted equal rights.

The colonial peoples had their own sense of their roles in the great revolutionary struggle. Poor whites in the colonies thought of themselves as *sans-culottes*, or working-class rebels. They saw the PLANTERS AND PLANTER AGENTS as their aristocratic foes. The planters tended to be royalists and dreamed of an imagined stable organic community in which everybody knew his or her place and worked hard and white elites took care of everybody. The free people of color heard talk of equality and the end of inherited differences among people and thought it should apply to them. And the slaves knew that what they wanted were liberty and equality. These colliding visions of what the revolution meant resulted in violent multisided civil wars in all the French colonies in the Americas. The most striking was the HAITIAN REVOLUTION, which cost France tens of thousands of military casualties and ultimately led to the independence of Haiti. After some early hesitation, France reacted to the situation in its colonies by trying to apply revolutionary ideas, granting equal civil rights to free people of color in 1792, and freeing the slaves in 1794.

But the situation was out of hand, and Haitian leaders were pushing for autonomy, if not actual independence. Faced with the collapse of the plantation economy in its colonies and the near-universal refusal of slaves to continue working as they had, France under Napoléon launched military expeditions to reconquer its colonies. Napoléon decided, and his successors agreed, that the colonies could no longer be considered integral parts of the republic but instead were separate territories to be governed under different rules—generally, those of the old regime with its legal distinctions of race and slavery. France regained its Caribbean colonies, aside from Saint-Domingue, though Guadeloupe also put up a fight under LOUIS DELGRÈS. Slavery was reestablished and the plantations rebuilt. The British obliged France to end its slave trade, however, and slave populations became stagnant. Europeans had eschewed the habit of consuming cane sugar during the long years of blockade and embargo during the Revolutionary and Napoleonic Wars (1791–1815), substituting beet sugar, which could be grown in Europe. Cane sugar from Guadeloupe and Martinique found a market, but it was not the dominant commodity that it had been before 1789. Slavery continued in the French Caribbean colonies until 1848, when the republican government that rose to power in the revolution of that year abolished it once again, this time permanently. Guadeloupe, Martinique, and French Guiana remain part of France to this day, with a population that is largely black and mixed-race. Since 1946, they have been integral parts of France, no different from any other part of the national territory, and their citizens have the same rights as any other French people.

Free People of Color in France

People of color have lived in France at least since Roman times. In the late Middle Ages, there were hundreds or perhaps thousands of people from North Africa and the Middle East living in or visiting France at any given time, and some of them were of sub-Saharan African ancestry. The sainted French king Louis IX (1214–70) is said to have taken home a black African servant from the seventh Crusade who had taken care of him while he was a prisoner of the Egyptians. The Spanish expelled as many as a million of their Moorish subjects in the 16th century. Many of these refugees made their way farther into Europe, with large numbers settling in France. Since Morocco had conquered the bend of the Niger in what is now Mali and Guinea in the 15th century, many Moroccans had some African ancestry, though for Europeans at the time their religious identity was their most notable characteristic. These long-established populations of color began to be joined by people of African descent from the Americas in the 17th century.

At first, small numbers of African-American servants accompanied their masters to Europe. As in BRITAIN, by the middle of the 18th century, a black manservant, page boy, or coachman was an essential accessory for a person of fashion in Paris. In addition, the French army and navy recruited men of color, and many of these servicemen remained in France when they mustered out. Vincent Olivier from Saint-Domingue was one such. He entered France as a released war prisoner after the Treaty of Ryswick (1697); he had been a prisoner of the British, who captured him on his way back from the sack of CARTAGENA de Colombia. He was presented at court, and Louis XIV was sufficiently impressed by his height, strength, and good looks to enroll him in the royal guards. Olivier served in the French military for about 30 years, rising to the rank of captain, and then retired to a farm in Saint-Domingue. Many of his comrades remained in France. The free colored population of France was fairly well gender balanced, mainly because the newly arriving immigrants, predominantly men, were able to find wives. Restrictions on intermarriage with whites were weak or nonexistent in France, and there were already small populations of color when the new immigration started. As a result, numbers of free people of color in France grew throughout the 18th century.

One problem was that the legal status of people of color in France was ambiguous. Legal reform in the 18th century eroded the autonomy of the regional Parlements and subjected the provinces to the legal regime of Paris, which did not recognize slavery. Ultimately, though there was consensus that slavery could not exist in the country, the government did not want to interfere with the property rights of masters who wanted to import their slaves. At the same time, elites began to see the growing population of people of color as a threat to the social order. In the colonies, the new discourse was of white solidarity. At home, liberal thinkers wanted to preclude the possibility that slavery would be reestablished in the country and called for the exclusion of people of color in general. Their logic seems to have been similar to that of the proponents of exclusionary laws in Northern states in the period before the AMERICAN CIVIL WAR, 1861–65: to avoid white workers' being displaced by slaves and to avoid disruption of the social order, ban not only the practice of slavery but blacks themselves. The government responded with a series of edicts, in 1716, 1738, and 1774, that placed increasing restrictions on the immigration of people of color, either enslaved or free. The edicts were never fully implemented, though they did make free black migration to France more difficult. Some ports were closed to black visitors, depending on the attitude of their provincial court. The Parlement of Paris, where the largest group of free people of color lived, refused to register the first two edicts, though, and the third, while registered, never entered into force because of the political crisis over the status of the Parlements in the 1780s.

In the meantime, colonial free people of color continued to move to France. ZABEAU BELLANTON, for example, a Saint-Domingue mixed-race merchant, moved to France in 1782 regardless of the law. THOMAS JEFFERSON took two personal servants, Sally Hemings and her brother, James, to France during his service as ambassador in the 1780s. Both were given wages while they were there, and Jefferson at least was aware that they were free under French law. But they returned with him to Virginia in 1789 and again became slaves. The free colored population of France never reached the levels found in Britain, in part because of the governmental effort to keep them out and in part because of assimilation. After a few generations, the descendants of free people of color who married white French people would be considered whites, for example, the Dumas family. The two authors, Alexandre Dumas *père*, author of *The Three Musketeers*, and his son Alexandre Dumas *fils*, a playwright, were considered white, although Dumas *père* had a black grandmother (*see* THOMAS-ALEXANDRE DUMAS). In the same way, a few centuries before, the descendants of Moorish refugees or Middle Eastern immigrants had assimilated into Frenchness. Many people of color lived in the country without notifying the authorities, or indeed, as in the case of the Hemings, without being fully aware of their status as free or enslaved. There are no reliable figures on the number of people of color who lived in the country, but scholarly estimates range from 5,000 to 15,000 in the 1780s, at the high point. By the turn of the 20th century, when substantial immigration began again from the French colonies in Africa and the Caribbean and from the United States, there were no more than a few thousand people socially defined as "black" living in France. Black people were so rare as to be a novelty and valuable as entertainers, domestic servants, and sports stars. American blacks in particular appreciated the more relaxed French attitude about race, and many refugees from Jim Crow lived in Paris in the 1920s and 1930s.

Stewart R. King

FURTHER READING
Blankaert, Claude. "Of Monstrous Métis? Hybridity, Fear of Miscegenation, and Patriotism from Buffon to Paul Broca." In *The Color of Liberty: Histories of Race in France*, edited by Sue Peabody and Tyler Stovall, 42–72. Durham, N.C.: Duke University Press, 2003.
Peabody, Sue. *"There Are No Slaves in France": The Political Culture of Race and Slavery in the Ancien Regime.* Oxford: Oxford University Press, 2002.

FREEDMEN'S BUREAU

The Freedmen's Bureau, formally known as the Bureau of Refugees, Freedmen, and Abandoned Lands, was a temporary relief agency established by the U.S. Congress on March 3, 1865. Its charge was to provide aid and protection both to white refugees and to the four million Southern blacks newly freed by the AMERICAN CIVIL WAR, 1861–65.

Part of the U.S. Department of War, the bureau provided relief assistance in the form of food, clothing, and health care; managed abandoned and confiscated properties in the South; supervised labor relations between freedmen and planters; settled disputes between freedmen and whites and among freedmen; and supported education. The bureau existed from 1865 to 1872; most of its work was conducted between June 1865 and December 1868.

"What Shall Be Done with Slaves . . . Contraband . . . Freedmen?"

As the fighting in the Civil War began in 1861, fugitive slaves made their way toward Union lines expecting freedom, but in the early stages of fighting, Union army commanders struggled with what should be done with them. All slaves would not be declared free until the adoption of the Thirteenth Amendment on December 18, 1865. Lacking any formal policy, some of the commanders returned escaped slaves to their owners, but soon Gen. Benjamin F. Butler's (1818–93) policy of treating slaves as "contraband of war" became widespread. Under this system, slaves were treated as any other kind of enemy property or resource—something to be confiscated to weaken the enemy. Many of the "contraband" slaves were put to work, most often as laborers for the Union army.

As the Union gained more and more territory, the number of slaves under the Union's charge grew; many of these slaves were freed by President ABRAHAM LINCOLN's EMANCIPATION PROCLAMATION on January 1, 1863, but the question of what should be done with the new freedmen remained.

To Union generals in the South, the question was not an abstract one—there were freedmen to be fed and housed. Some of the freedmen became soldiers or sailors; others lived under poor conditions in freedmen's camps near army posts; many were put back to work on leased plantations saving crops of cotton, sugar, and corn standing in the fields. The government leased abandoned plantations to speculators, and freedmen signed labor contracts under which they were promised wages, food, housing, and medical care in return for their work. The system, however, was rife with corruption.

As the Civil War drew to a close, the question "What shall be done with slaves?" was still unanswered. As the historian W. E. B. DuBois (1868–1963) put it in his 1901 article "The Freedman's Bureau," "Peremptory military commands, this way and that, could not answer the query; the Emancipation Proclamation seemed but to broaden and intensify the difficulties; and so at last there arose in the south a government of men called the Freedmen's Bureau."

The Beginnings of the Freedmen's Bureau

On December 14, 1863, Representative Thomas D. Eliot (1808–70) introduced a bill in Congress to create a Bureau of Emancipation (his was the second such bill; the first was proposed in January 1863 just after Lincoln issued the Emancipation Proclamation). It was a controversial bill, and its constitutionality was fiercely challenged. A version of the bill passed the U.S. House of Representatives on March 1, 1864 (largely through efforts by Radical Republicans), and after extensive arguments about whether the bureau should be housed within the War Department or the Treasury Department, Congress finally passed the Freedmen's Bureau Act on March 3, 1865. President Lincoln signed the bill that day.

The bill created the Bureau of Refugees, Freedmen, and Abandoned Lands (renamed from the Bureau of Emancipation to suggest the bill and its bureau were inclusive) within the War Department. Intended to last for one year after the war, the bureau was charged with "the supervision and management of all abandoned lands, and the control of all subjects relating to refugees and freedmen from rebel states."

Various constituents promoted the bill, including freedmen's aid societies, cotton-mill owners, and Radical Republicans. Cotton-mill owners saw the bill as a way to control the freedmen's labor, thereby increasing profits. Radical Republicans saw the bill as one more way to control the process of Reconstruction in the Southern states, thereby increasing power by solidifying political strength in the North and East (see also RECONSTRUCTION IN THE UNITED STATES). Ultimately, Radicals did not want Southern Democrats to return to power and did not want wartime legislation to be repealed. They were willing to give the vote to freedmen, a very controversial idea at that time, to help ensure Republican control of the South. The bureau, they thought, would be in an ideal position to help influence the vote of freedmen.

It was in this environment that President ANDREW JOHNSON appointed the Union army General Oliver O. Howard (1830–1909) as the first commissioner of the Freedmen's Bureau in May 1865. The bureau had four divisions: financial affairs, government-controlled lands, medical affairs, and records (which included education programs). The act provided for assistant commissioners, one for each of 10 districts, and Secretary of War Edwin M. Stanton (1814–69), a Radical Republican, directed Howard in the appointment of the assistant commissioners. The law did not, however, provide any funding for the bureau, so bureau agents were usually taken from the military, at least initially, and funding was from the military budget. Some of those agents assigned to the bureau were African-American officers, but when many Southern whites were angered by the move, these officers were moved into less controversial posts (often in education) or discharged.

Howard immediately went to work learning about the conditions of the freedmen within the states and about the activities of the freedmen's aid societies. He began fighting for equal rights for freedmen and attempted to enlist freedmen's aid societies to collaborate on education efforts, but he faced early difficulties due to Stanton's Radical Republican commissioners and poor funding. The next few years saw both successes and failures for the Freedmen's Bureau.

Successes, Failures, and Corruption

Broadly stated, the bureau's goal was to help freedmen in the transition from slavery to self-sufficient citizenship. More specifically, the bureau sought to accomplish that goal by assisting freedmen and other refugees with their immediate needs during and after the war by managing abandoned and confiscated property (initially intended to be rented to freedmen), by helping freedmen establish fair labor contracts, by obtaining justice for freedmen in state courts, and by supporting education for freedmen.

Relief and Medical Care

The law that established the bureau provided that freedmen and other refugees and their families could be issued "provisions, clothing, and fuel." The bureau quickly went to work helping the millions of freedmen and whites who

A Freedmen's Bureau panel hears legal cases in Tennessee in 1866. For blacks seeking justice, the Freedmen's Bureau courts often functioned as alternatives that were less discriminatory than the state and local courts. The courts frequently sat informally, as this picture shows, and heard the stories of poor black petitioners, many of whom were illiterate and unaccompanied by lawyers. (North Wind Picture Archive via Associated Press)

had been displaced by the war and who were living in poverty.

Perhaps the bureau's most important task immediately after the war was the distribution of food and clothing. Without funding, the bureau drew on supplies from the army to feed and clothe freedmen and refugees. In August 1865, the bureau was handing out nearly 150,000 rations per day. A ration consisted of enough food (meat, flour, cornmeal, etc.) to last a week. The bulk of rations were handed out in 1865, but more than 20 million rations were distributed before the program was discontinued in 1866.

Medical care was also an immediate need: Many freedmen and refugees were dying of disease (cholera and smallpox) and poor sanitation conditions. Bureau leaders attempted to improve the medical care available to freedmen and refugees by improving existing clinics and establishing new ones. In summer and fall 1865, for instance, the bureau's hospitals treated approximately 50,000 freedmen and refugees. Further, the bureau attempted to stem pandemics by establishing quarantines and relocating freedmen and refugees.

The bureau also provided free transportation to thousands, so those displaced by the war or separated under slavery could return to their homes and families or to places where they could be employed. The bureau attempted to reunite families—many long divided by slavery—through an informal communication system among regions that agents could use to make inquires.

Howard was often not praised for the bureau's efforts. Even in the first few months of the bureau's operation, Howard heard complaints from both Northerners and Southerners that the rations were too generous and that freedmen and refugees would become idle. Howard himself wanted freedmen to become self-sufficient, so he encouraged his assistants to keep the number of rations issued as low as possible, after which Howard faced accusations that he was persecuting freedmen by denying help to those in need. This problem—the perception (among both government leaders and the public) that the bureau was doing too much or, alternately, not enough—would be an ongoing one for Howard.

Manage Abandoned and Confiscated Property

The bill granted the bureau the authority to rent abandoned and confiscated properties in the South to refugees and freedmen (but "not more than forty acres" to "every male citizen"). And, at the conclusion of the war, there was a large amount of abandoned or confiscated Confederate property controlled by the military that could be used to establish freedmen as landowners.

Indeed, the prospect of "forty acres and a mule" was exciting to many freedmen, and the benefits to freedmen of being landowners were simple but important: some measure of protection from their previous owners and a step toward self-sufficiency. Further, Howard could use the income generated from renting lands to fund the bureau and its initiatives. Radical Republicans hoped the Southern plantation system would be broken through land redistribution, and of course, they hoped newly independent freedmen would vote for Republican candidates.

Some freedmen were able to settle lands under the Homestead Act of 1862 and General Sherman's Special Field Orders, No. 15, issued in January 1865. The field order set aside lands on the Sea Islands and lands from SOUTH CAROLINA to FLORIDA for freedmen to settle. Tunis G. Campbell (1812–91), born free in NEW JERSEY, was sent to the St. Catherine and Sapelo Islands by the bureau to help freedmen organize self-government, and soon he was administering land grants to freedmen on the islands; he did so until he was dismissed in 1866 (after which he became active in education and politics in GEORGIA).

Very few freedmen were able to settle or purchase land, however. President Johnson's Amnesty Proclamation on May 29, 1865, pardoned many Confederates and restored their lands, rendering the creation of a large class of freedmen landowners and massive land redistribution impossible. Although Howard, Radical Republicans, and others opposed the restoration of confiscated land and fought with Johnson over it, thousands of freedmen lost land under the Amnesty Proclamation—land that they had settled and improved. Howard and others began looking for other ways to help freedmen become landowners. They were largely unsuccessful, although the Southern Homestead Act of 1866 did help some freedmen gain land before it was repealed in 1876. In the end, as a result of Johnson's land restoration policy, state laws prohibiting freedmen's ownership of land, the disorganization of land offices, dishonest or unmotivated bureau agents, and the attitude of many whites, relatively few freedmen became landowners.

Supervise Labor Relations

Among the more difficult tasks of the bureau was the supervision of labor relations between planters and freedmen. Some Southern planters kept freedmen agricultural laborers in conditions indistinguishable from slavery, while others conspired to keep wages for freedmen low. Violence against freedmen was also common, especially in places where there were few bureau agents. Bureau agents tried to help freedmen through labor contracts: Agents would help freedmen and planters negotiate contracts and mediate disputes. Contracts generally included information about the kind and frequency of the work required from the freedmen and the payment and supplies they would be provided from the planters.

One such bureau agent was MARTIN DELANY (1812–85) who, during his tenure at Hilton Head, South Carolina, from 1865 to 1868, promoted a "triple alliance" of landowners, laborers, and local capital, each of whom would receive one-third of the crop. Delany, born to a free mother and slave father in West Virginia, was the first black field officer for the U.S. Army during the Civil War; he was also a physician, lecturer, author of articles and books, and proponent for black nationalism. On Hilton Head, he upset many with his arguments that freedmen should own land. (After Delany left the bureau in 1868, he continued to be politically active.)

Both Northerners and Southerners worried that freedmen would become idle, especially in winter 1865, when many freedmen broke their contracts and made their way into cities (they anticipated the government would soon give them "forty acres"). The bureau was criticized for not enforcing labor contracts, and many feared labor shortages would lead to the decline of cotton production. Howard and his agents emphasized that freedmen must work and indicated that vagrants (in some cases, broadly defined as any freedmen who had an offer to work but did not) should be arrested. They also withheld or reduced the number of rations distributed.

By 1868, both freedmen and planters were turning away from the bureau's labor contracts. The planters generally no longer needed to rely on the bureau to supply or enforce labor, and freedmen were disillusioned—they were still not receiving a wage at or above subsistence levels.

Additionally, the bureau faced charges of corruption related to its labor contracts. While some of these charges were fair—in some cases, for example, planters paid bureau agents to contract freedmen to work for low wages—many were overstated by white Southerners who despised the bureau as an agency forced upon them, an agency many saw as usurping states' rights.

The success of the bureau's labor relations efforts was mixed. The bureau did help former slaves find jobs, but pressure from the government and the public to make sure freedmen were not idle and Southern plantations were productive meant that fair compensation for the freedmen's work was less important than creating a stable workforce. Without land of their own and with contracts or conditions designed to disempower them, many freedmen were forced into sharecropping arrangements.

Obtaining Justice for Freedmen

Bureau assistant commissioners and agents soon realized freedmen would not receive fair trials in state courts: Slaves had not been allowed to testify against whites before the Civil War, and Southern states passed BLACK CODES, laws that restricted black rights and freedoms and prevented freedmen from giving testimony against whites. Howard quickly ordered that his assistant commissioners adjudicate conflicts between freedmen and whites in states where freedmen were not allowed to give testimony in court.

Assistant commissioners often appointed their agents to perform this function for minor disputes within the agents' areas, and in some states, a system of three-judge courts developed. In a typical bureau court, however, there would be just one local agent settling the dispute; no jury would be involved. The parties generally could not contest the ruling as the agents' decisions were supported by military power. The bureau agent William A. Golding (1809/13–89) held court sessions in Liberty County, Georgia. Golding was born a slave and was a leader within the slave community prior to the Civil War and among freedmen after the Civil War, acting as their spokesperson to complain about labor conditions.

While the main work of the bureau's courts was to arbitrate disputes over labor contracts between freedmen and whites, the courts also settled conflicts among freedmen and helped legalize slave marriages. And, after the second Freedmen's Bureau Act, renewing the bureau for two years, was passed in July 1866, it began operating a claims division that helped black soldiers and sailors obtain their back pay and pensions.

By 1866, Howard's courts were facing criticism. White Southerners argued that the bureau's courts were biased against them, that bureau judges were ill qualified to perform such a function, and that the courts violated states' rights. Some of these criticisms were fair: The bureau's agents received no training in the law or due process, and bureau courts were unregulated and unorganized. However, prejudice often motivated the criticism: Many Southerners objected to an institution that sought to give equal rights to freedmen.

Also in 1866, the executive, judicial, and legislative branches of the federal government all weighed in on the bureau's courts. President Johnson ordered that civilians should be tried by civil courts if they existed and not by military courts; in April 1866, the U.S. Supreme Court agreed, declaring in *Ex parte Milligan* that citizens should be tried by civil courts unless those civil courts were disrupted in time of war. In the 1866 law renewing the bureau, however, Congress provided that the bureau should have jurisdiction over cases involving racial discrimination.

However, as states began to comply with the Military Reconstruction Acts, the bureau's agents stepped away from their role as judges. The new constitutions drafted by Southern states granted freedmen equal rights with whites to due process and provided freedmen the right to testify. These laws, however, were not consistently enforced, and freedmen still faced discrimination under the law.

Support Education

Before the Civil War, individuals could be severely punished for teaching slaves, and as a result, most freedmen lacked the literacy skills needed to function as citizens and to avoid exploitation (freedmen often could not read the labor contracts they were asked to sign). Howard and others believed that the education of freedmen was a crucial step in their achieving the rights of citizens, and freedmen had a strong desire to read and write—opportunities long denied to them.

By the conclusion of the war, many freedmen aid societies and missionaries were already teaching literacy skills to freedmen, including the American Freedmen's Union Commission and the American Missionary Association. In 1865, the bureau could not contribute financially to the education efforts, so Howard initially helped by coordinating them. In 1866, the Congress allowed the bureau to seize former Confederate government lands for educational use, and Howard provided superintendents with land and buildings rent-free to be used for education. Likewise, Howard helped freedmen when they were building their own schools by finishing their work, calling it "repair." He also provided furniture and books to superintendents and free transportation and pay to teachers.

Freedmen and blacks who had been free before the Civil War played a great role in education, often by becoming teachers. Charlotte Forten Grimké, for instance, was born in Pennsylvania to a prominent black abolitionist family and was among the first of the teachers who journeyed to the South to teach freedmen. She taught freedmen for two years on the Union-occupied Sea Islands in South Carolina, and later, she worked for the U.S. Treasury recruiting teachers.

There were also people of color who were free before the Civil War in the South who taught freedmen. Henry L. Shrewsbury (b. 1846) and his sister, Amelia Henry J. Maxwell (ca. 1836), Whitefield J. McKinlay (b. 1835), Thaddeus K. Sasportas (1844–85), and William J. Whipper (1835–1907) were all born free in South Carolina and taught there after the Civil War. James H. Harris (1832–91) taught in North Carolina; Hugh M. Foley (1847–96) taught in Mississippi. Some of these free people of color had been educated in the North or abroad, many in schools in the South, in places such as New Orleans, Louisiana, and Charleston, South Carolina; others were not formally educated.

Some people of color who were free before the Civil War also worked as school superintendents or administrators,

including Benjamin Randolph (1837–68) and Samuel E. Gaillard (1839–79) in South Carolina and George T. Ruby (1841–82) in Texas. In many cases, superintendents were also teachers, including Ruby, who taught in Galveston, and Gaillard, who taught on St. Johns Island. By 1869, more than half of the bureau's teachers were classified as "Negro."

Some superintendents thought that whites or at least those educated in the North would be better choices for teachers, but communities did not always agree. In some communities, whites and blacks preferred that freedmen be taught by other blacks: In such cases, it would be difficult for a white schoolteacher to find lodging, and many teachers faced verbal threats and physical abuse.

As in some of the other bureau endeavors, there were soon charges of corruption, such as builders' charging too much for schools, teachers' taking advantage of the bureau's systems, and Howard's showing favoritism to certain agencies when he granted funding. Further, in 1867, Howard, school superintendents, and others began voicing their concerns about the quality of teachers working in the South, suggesting that some could not read and write themselves. In May 1867, Howard began working with the aid societies on opening colleges for freedmen in the South: They were successful, and there were 11 colleges in the nation supporting freedmen by 1871. Many of these colleges were turning out desperately needed teachers.

Some Southern whites opposed the bureau's support of education; some objected to the teaching of freedmen altogether, but perhaps more did not object to the teaching itself so much as the ideology that they were sure the many teachers from New England and elsewhere in the North were imparting—ideas such as social, civil, and political equality for people of color. Further, some white Southerners charged—often correctly—that the bureau schoolrooms were being used as pulpits for Republicanism.

The bureau's support of education is often considered its greatest success. While the bureau did not begin the push for educating freedmen, its assistance was critical in establishing and supporting more than 3,000 schools.

Controversy and Continuity for the Freedmen's Bureau

By 1866, the Freedmen's Bureau had gained a number of vocal opponents who charged that the bureau was a violation of states' rights and an unconstitutional continuation of wartime powers. President Johnson agreed and was also angered by what he saw as the bureau's attempts to obstruct his Reconstruction plans (specifically his land restoration policies). In 1867, Johnson offered Howard's job to FREDERICK DOUGLASS and JOHN MERCER LANGSTON. Both were prominent free blacks before the Civil War, and both refused the offer. Some might have seen Johnson's move of putting an African American in charge of the bureau as progressive—and it would have been the most prominent government office an African American had held at that point in history—but it is more likely, as the historian George R. Bentley pointed out, that "he fully expected to wreck the bureau by driving out of it many officers and agents who would not have served under a Negro."

The bureau and its supporters, however, recognized that freedmen needed some protection from violence, prejudice, and discrimination. Indeed, the Southern states' black codes were highly discriminatory, often attempting to restore freedmen to a position near slavery. (See also CIVIL RIGHTS LAWS IN THE UNITED STATES AFTER 1865.)

In January 1866, the moderate Republican senator Lyman Trumbull (1813–96) drafted a new bill that, among other things, gave the bureau more responsibilities and extended its life indefinitely. President Johnson vetoed this bill, and a revised bill that dealt with some of Johnson's objections (for instance, the revised bill limited the life of the bureau to two years) was proposed. Congress passed the second Freedmen's Bureau act over Johnson's veto on July 16, 1866. Overriding a veto was an unusual act at that time; it ensured the survival of the bureau but also set the stage for increased antagonism between Johnson and legislators, especially Republicans.

The law extended the bureau's life by two years and increased its authority. The bureau now had jurisdiction over refugees and freedmen anywhere and retained the use of military jurisdiction in cases where discrimination was a factor (albeit it had this jurisdiction only in former rebel states, and the power ended after the states' representatives were returned to Congress). The bureau was also given funding that it could use for food and for repair of school buildings for freedmen. Further, the bureau could use Confederate government property for freedmen's schools. Finally, it received two more assistant commissioners.

In 1867, Southern states began to grant African-American men the right to vote, though the right did not become universal until the passage of the Fifteenth Amendment in 1870. The bureau's agents were charged with ensuring that freedmen knew their political rights and how to exercise the right to vote. Agents generally did not stop at providing information—they often attempted to persuade freedmen that they should vote for Republicans. Bureau leaders and agents also were involved in organizing Union League meetings and distributing its literature.

Congress renewed the bureau again on July 25, 1868, again overriding Johnson's veto, but the new act limited the bureau's work to its support of education, beginning in 1869. Some wanted the bureau to continue with its earlier powers and responsibilities, but conservative Republicans blocked this.

End of the Freedmen's Bureau and Its Legacy
In March 1872, President ULYSSES S. GRANT asked Howard to leave his duties as commissioner of the Freedmen's Bureau temporarily; Grant needed him to act as the peace commissioner with the Apache and other tribes in Arizona and New Mexico. Before this point, Howard had steadily been reducing the number of agents within each state, and the bureau was running out of funds. Within two weeks of his departure to Arizona, the bureau ran out of funds, and the Congress would provide no more—it discontinued the Freedmen's Bureau in June 1872. Howard returned in October to find his bureau had been dismantled.

The bureau was controversial in its own time, and its legacy is a complex one. It faced charges of corruption, angered many white Southerners as an occupying government that was a continual reminder of their defeat, and frustrated many (both Southerners and Northerners) who began to see the bureau as a violation of states' rights.

Generally, until the 1980s, historians condemned the bureau for failing to make significant changes in the postwar South, especially as related to racial hostility and discrimination. They contended that the bureau did not accomplish many of its goals—few freedmen became landowners; a labor contract system was not established; and prejudice and discrimination became widespread in the South for many decades.

DuBois, in his 1901 article, suggested that "the work it [the bureau] did not do [was] because it could not." And beginning in the 1980s, historians have adopted a view closer to that of DuBois, recognizing the complexity of what the bureau was asked to do and the difficult environment it was asked to do it in. While the bureau had many failures, it also succeeded in providing freedmen and refugees with food, clothing, and medical care; with agents, however flawed, to turn to in order to resolve disputes; and with the opportunity to seek education. The bureau, working with the American Missionary Association and other organizations, established more than 20 institutions for higher learning during the bureau's lifetime. Many are still in existence today, including Fisk University, Johnson C. Smith University, Shaw University, Tougaloo College, and Howard University (named for General Howard).

Summer Leibensperger

FURTHER READING

Bentley, George R. *A History of the Freedmen's Bureau*. Philadelphia: University of Pennsylvania Press, 1955.

Butchart, Ronald. *Northern Schools, Southern Blacks, and Reconstruction: Freedmen's Education, 1862–1875*. Westport, Conn.: Greenwood Press, 1980.

Crouch, Barry A. *The Freedmen's Bureau and Black Texans*. Austin: University of Texas Press, 1992.

DuBois, W. E. Burghardt. "The Freedmen's Bureau." *Atlantic Monthly* 87 (1901): 354–365.

Finley, Randy. *From Slavery to Uncertain Freedom: The Freedmen's Bureau in Arkansas, 1865–1869*. Fayetteville: University of Arkansas Press, 1996.

Foner, Eric. *Forever Free: The Story of Emancipation and Reconstruction*. New York: Alfred A. Knopf, 2005.

———. *Freedom's Lawmakers: A Directory of Black Officeholders during Reconstruction*. New York: Oxford University Press, 1993.

———. *Reconstruction: America's Unfinished Revolution, 1863–1877*. New York: Harper & Row, 1998.

Morris, Robert C. *Reading, Riting, and Reconstruction: The Education of Freedmen in the South, 1861–1870*. Chicago: University of Chicago Press, 2010.

Nieman, Donald G. *To Set the Law in Motion: The Freedmen's Bureau and the Legal Rights of Blacks, 1865–1868*. Millwood, N.Y.: KTO Press, 1979.

Oubre, Claude F. *Forty Acres and a Mule: The Freedmen's Bureau and Black Land Ownership*. Baton Rouge: Louisiana State University Press, 1978.

FREEMASONRY

Freemasonry claims a connection with guilds of ARTISANS from the Middle Ages and indeed with artisans of antiquity, but as an organization it dates to the early 18th century. The first Grand Lodge was that of Britain, formed in 1717. The movement spread with the ideas of the Enlightenment, which it advocates, throughout Europe and the Americas. Freemasonry both took an interest in questions related to slavery and racial discrimination and debated the inclusion of people of color from a very early date in its history.

Masonic Beliefs

Freemasonry is a product of the liberal Enlightenment and generally upholds its ideas about human nature, proper social order, and progress. Masons collectively believe in the freedom of individual humans, especially in matters of conscience and religion. Although most Masonic groups require members to believe in a Supreme Being, none accepts any form of coercion in matters of faith, and this characteristic put Masonic groups at odds with countries that wanted to preserve privileges for an established church in the 18th and 19th centuries. Most Masons support secularism as the most appropriate relationship between church and state. The secularist models that Masons could support ranged from the North American, in which many churches can exist, nondenominational religious expression is common in the public sphere, and atheism is tolerated if not exactly accepted, to the Continental European or Spanish American, in which there is an active hostility toward religion in the public arena. Anticlericalism is common among Masons in the Continental tradition, which is the one most often followed in Latin America. Anticlericalism can mean active hostility to the ROMAN CATHOLIC CHURCH and its clergy, as in MEXICO, or a more limited hostility to any public or political role for the church. Masons in the British and North American tradition are often members of Protestant churches, while in the Continental European tradition it is unusual for a Mason to be a regular church attendee of any denomination, and Catholics who belong to Masonic organizations are excommunicated.

Most Masons also support republican institutions, either wholeheartedly, as most Continental European Masons did in the FRENCH REVOLUTION and revolutions of 1848, or at least in part, as when most British Masons supported political reform and democratization of Britain's monarchy during the 19th century. As a result, Masonic groups were a part of Europe's revolutionary coalition during the early 19th century and have supported gradual liberal reforms since. Most Masons, especially in the Americas, believed at least in theory in the abolition of slavery, though in practice these beliefs were often tempered by racist assumptions about the ability of people of color to survive independently or to participate in society as equals. Many prominent American political leaders were Masons, including Benjamin Franklin and Presidents GEORGE WASHINGTON, JAMES MONROE, and ANDREW JACKSON.

Freemasons also generally believe in progress, that is, that natural laws and/or Divine Providence is moving human society forward toward greater prosperity, freedom, and equality. Acceptance of the dominance of science as a way to discover truth is often a part of this. For many white Masons in the 19th century, this was taken as a promise that, even if racial prejudice meant that they were unable to see blacks as fully equal for the time being, in the future they would become so. Masons in Latin America, such as Porfirio Díaz of Mexico and Benjamin Constant Botelho De Magalhães of Brazil, were prominently associated with positivism, a liberal philosophy that justified temporary racial discrimination in the interests of "uplifting" the "lesser" races through government intervention.

Free People of Color and Freemasonry

One important organizational element of freemasonry that was a barrier to many people of color was the requirement in most lodges of the British tradition that members had to be freeborn. In fact, this did not entirely prevent free people of color from joining Masonic lodges, even when they had been born slaves. In North America, the free black man PRINCE HALL formed the first black Masonic lodge in MASSACHUSETTS in 1775. His background is obscure, and he may have been able to demonstrate that he was born free, but it is also possible that he had been freed and that the British Grand Lodge that enrolled him knew this and overlooked it. Prince Hall fought on the American side in the WAR OF AMERICAN INDEPENDENCE, 1775–83, and during and after the war he formed other lodges in other states in the North among the many black veterans of the conflict. The status of these lodges was questionable, both because many members had been born as slaves and because freemasonry in the United States was organized with one Grand Lodge in each state. Prince Hall's lodges could not affiliate with the white lodges because membership and affiliation votes must be unanimous, and any one white member who harbored racial prejudices could disrupt the process. As a result, the Prince Hall lodges remained organizationally distinct from white freemasonry until the 20th century and still are not fully integrated.

In the rest of the Americas, free people of color had a somewhat easier time fitting into institutional freemasonry. The Grand Orient of France had men of color as members in the 18th century. Freemasonry caught on in Haiti even before the HAITIAN REVOLUTION and remains an important part of elite sociability to this day. The revolutionary leader TOUSSAINT LOUVERTURE was a Mason, probably of high degree, and appears to have been a member of the same lodge as some of the most prominent planters in the colony. His former master, Bayon de Libertat, was a Mason and probably his sponsor in the lodge. In France and the colonies after the fall of Napoléon, there was some reluctance to admit new free colored members, but enough lodges remained true to their liberal ideas that no segregated black Masonic organization sprung up in France. In the Spanish and Portuguese Americas, Masonic organizations were also quite popular in the late 18th and 19th centuries, and as were many other institutions in the Iberian Americas, they were open to free men of color who had the right social connections. Belonging to the right Masonic lodge was an important element of social promotion in MEXICO and BRAZIL during their periods of liberal reform in the mid-19th century. Mexico even had dueling Masonic institutions, the York Rite and Scottish Rite, the former more liberal and open to free people of color, the lat-

ter more linked to aristocratic and royalist groups and harder for anybody with African ancestry to enter.

For free men of color, freemasonry represented another way to achieve common ground with prominent whites and assert claims to common humanity and citizenship. At the same time, it offered an opportunity to form networks among free men of color, especially in the United States. The liberal principles of freemasonry affirmed the equality and citizenship of free people of color, at least in principle.

Stewart R. King

FURTHER READING

Bullock, Steven. *Revolutionary Brotherhood: Freemasonry and the Transformation of the American Social Order, 1730–1840.* Chapel Hill: University of North Carolina Press, 1998.

Grey, David. *Inside Prince Hall.* New York: Anchor Communications, 2004.

Roundtree, Alton G., and Paul M. Bessel. *Out of the Shadows: Prince Hall Freemasonry in America, 200 Years of Endurance.* Forestville, Md.: KLR Publishing, 2006.

FRENCH CARIBBEAN

FRANCE ruled a large number of Caribbean territories at different times during the colonial period. The largest French colony was SAINT-DOMINGUE, now Haiti, which became independent as a result of the HAITIAN REVOLUTION in 1804. France also rule TRINIDAD AND TOBAGO, St. Kitts, St. Lucia, what is now the Dominican Republic, and other smaller territories, for some period. This article focuses on the French presence in the three territories that it controlled in the Caribbean region during the entirety (or nearly the entirety) of the colonial period: Guadeloupe, Martinique, and French Guiana.

Guadeloupe is located in the Lesser Antilles between Montserrat and DOMINICA. St. Martin and St. Barthelemy are small island groups that are today administered separately but in colonial times were under the administration of Guadeloupe; they are located in the northern arc of the Lesser Antilles. The smaller islands of Marie-Galante, Grande-Anse, and the Saintes are located close to Guadeloupe. The principal island of Guadeloupe is the second-largest of the Lesser Antilles after Trinidad. Like the other islands of this chain, it is mountainous and volcanic. There are two lobes connected by a narrow land bridge at the largest city, Pointe-a-Pitre. The larger of the two lobes, Basse-Terre to the southwest, is more mountainous and was settled along the coastline during colonial times. The interior was almost deserted, inhabited by MAROONS and peasants, many of whom were free people of color. Grande-Terre, to the northeast, is flatter and was the site of most of the island's SUGAR CULTIVATION in the

18th and early 19th centuries. On both islands, the volcanic soil is extremely fertile.

Martinique is located to the south of Guadeloupe, between Dominica and St. Lucia. It is very mountainous, with a coastal plain centered on the enormous west coast harbor of Fort-de-France. In colonial times, it was more densely inhabited than Guadeloupe and was the most productive plantation colony in the eastern Caribbean in the early 19th century. At the beginning of the 20th century, an enormous eruption of its central volcano, Mount Pelée, killed more than 30,000 people and destroyed both the colonial capital of Saint-Pierre and extensive agricultural works. Since then, Guadeloupe has become the most prosperous of the French Caribbean territories. Both Martinique and Guadeloupe receive regular rainfall sufficient to grow tropical plantation crops through sugar

and COFFEE CULTIVATION. Martinique, somewhat to the south, has a lower risk of hurricanes than Guadeloupe. In addition, the location of Martinique's most fertile regions on the protected west coast means that agriculture there is less affected by hurricanes than on Guadeloupe.

French Guiana is the easternmost of the three Guyanas, located along the north coast of South America to the east of the Antilles chain. French Guiana is bordered on the west by SURINAM and on the east and south by BRAZIL. As do Surinam and GUYANA, it consists of swampy coastal plains and river valleys extending into a heavily forested and mountainous interior not suitable for plantation development. Settlement in colonial times centered around the river valleys of the Maroni to the west and the Comte in the center of the country. Guiana was the least prosperous of the French territories in colonial times.

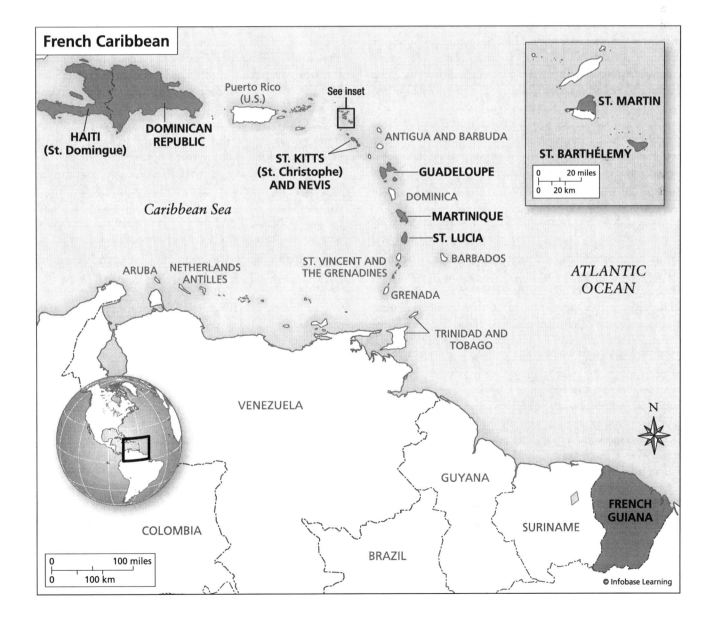

Early Colonial Period: 1635–1788

All three territories were inhabited in precolonial times by Arawak and Carib Indians. These were agricultural peoples, living in villages and governed by chiefs. Their societies were similar to those of the Indians of the eastern woodlands in the United States. The Carib were in the process of conquering the Antilles when Europeans arrived; their societies were warlike and suspicious of newcomers. The first Europeans to visit all three territories were the ships of Columbus's second and third expeditions in 1493 and 1498. For the next century, the Spanish did not make any attempt to settle any of these territories, however. In 1635, the French Company of the American Islands settled Guadeloupe and Martinique from its base on St-Kitts, beginning a campaign that led to the destruction of the indigenous population. French settlers had arrived in Guiana in 1604, as part of the French attempt to settle Brazil, but were driven out by the Portuguese. The French returned in 1643 and were once again driven out, this time by indigenous people. Finally, the colony was definitively established in 1664. The indigenous inhabitants of Guiana retreated from the European presence into the interior and continued to offer resistance to the colonists up to the late 19th century.

The French settlers began producing sugar within a few decades of their arrival. Sugar production in Martinique grew especially rapidly thanks to the favorable geography. Slave imports rose to meet the demand. By the end of the 1600s, Martinique had imported about 66,500 enslaved Africans and Guadeloupe about 12,700. The French priest Jean-Baptiste Du Tertre (1610–87) of the order of DOMINICANS worked in Martinique and Guadeloupe between 1640 and 1658 and produced a detailed history and geography of the islands, published in 1667. It is clear from his account that both colonies, and especially Martinique, were becoming fully evolved plantation societies by that time. According to Du Tertre, the racial lines in this society were very loosely drawn. The rule that the child of a female slave was a slave was not strictly enforced. Slaves and white indentured servants worked side by side and often had mixed-race children, who were often considered free, especially, of course, if the mother were a white servant, but also in some cases if the mother were a black enslaved person. At the same time, free whites and their slaves were having mixed-race children, who were sometimes considered white. Many white CREOLE families, he wrote, had some African ancestry. Color was less important than status and wealth in determining a person's place in that society.

Du Tertre's successor as head of the Dominican mission in Guadeloupe was Fr. Jean-Baptiste Labat (1663–1738), who served in the Antilles from 1696 to 1706. Labat recorded the change in racial climate that was beginning at that time. He bemoaned the fate of the slaves, doomed to eternal exile from society and below the lowest white. His missionary confreres were trying to Christianize the slaves, but the attitude of the white colonists hampered this effort. Even people of mixed race were considered marked by the stain of slavery—no longer were the mixed-race children of influential white men considered white. Labat was not opposed to slavery per se; indeed, he introduced many technical innovations into sugar cultivation and refining that made the Dominicans' plantations much more productive. As new technology was adopted, the sugar plantations on Martinique, Guadeloupe, and Saint-Domingue became the most productive in the region, drawing more slave imports and further deepening the racial divide. But Labat and many other French colonists feared the growing black population and the division between the races. The fear perversely contributed to the further exclusion of blacks in a cyclical process that would only lead to disaster.

The 18th century saw these trends develop. Martinique and Guadeloupe in total imported almost 500,000 slaves between 1700 and the outbreak of the FRENCH REVOLUTION in 1789. Many of the same trends seen in Saint-Domingue were also present in the smaller island colonies, on a smaller scale. The social divisions were perhaps strongest in Martinique, which was home to the most profitable and highly developed sugar plantation sector in the Lesser Antilles in the 18th century. Martiniquan society was divided into wealthy and poor white groups, wealthy mixed-race planters and poor, mostly black urban free people of color, and a vast number of slaves. Society in Guadeloupe was less stratified. There, the wealthy free colored planters still had some ties to their white counterparts, who were often their relatives. Poorer free coloreds often saw the wealthier free colored planters as their patrons. Linkages across lines of class, race, and status had not yet been totally severed by the economic growth of the plantations. In French Guiana, the plantation sector was still establishing itself as the French Revolution began. In a very intriguing but ultimately abortive development, the marquis de Lafayette (1757–1834), GEORGE WASHINGTON's loyal aide during the WAR OF AMERICAN INDEPENDENCE, 1775–83, and an early leader in the French Revolution, bought a plantation in 1785 near Cayenne. The 70 slaves on this plantation were treated almost as free employees. Lafayette paid them salaries, established some forms of self-government in the slave community, and tried to build a self-supporting community. His methods were similar to those of the JESUITS on their plantations on the island colonies in the mid-18th century, although, unlike them, Lafayette was looking toward ultimately granting freedom to his slaves. The Jesuits were expelled from the French colonies in 1762, in part because of the unusual conditions under which their slaves worked. Lay planters were concerned that they were setting a bad example by allowing all slaves to hope to be treated humanely. Lafayette urged his old comrade Washington to follow his example on his plantations, but Washington was not tempted (although years later he did free the slaves in his will). Ultimately, during the French Revolution, Lafayette's plantation was confiscated and sold by the French government, but the slaves gained their freedom thanks to the first abolition of slavery in the French Empire in 1794. French Guiana imported some 37,000 slaves between 1667 and 1789—far fewer than Martinique and Guadeloupe—and had still not fully developed its plantation sector. The loose frontier atmosphere may have allowed Lafayette's experiment to go forward as far as it did; in Martinique, the colonial authorities and neighboring planters would certainly have objected to such an unusual relationship between master and slave.

The French Revolution and Its Aftermath (1789–1848)

As the Revolution broke out, the three colonies were primed for very different experiences thanks to the different courses they had taken during the colonial period. In some ways, the situation in Guadeloupe was like that found in the Southern province of Saint-Domingue, where free colored solidarity ultimately created a revolutionary movement more linked to France than in the more polarized North, where the free black community led the ultimately successful Haitian independence movement. The Northern province of Saint-Domingue, center of the bloodiest slave rebellion of the Atlantic world, was more similar to Martinique. And French Guiana was a frontier region, of little importance economically or militarily, and thus able to work out its revolutionary destiny in relative peace.

In Martinique, there were a number of small uprisings by slaves. No massive rebellion developed there. The small size of the plantation area on Martinique made it easier for the authorities to police the slaves. In addition, the French military commander, Donatien-Marie-Joseph Rochambeau (1750–1813), later to lead Napoléon's expedition to reconquer Saint-Domingue (1802), organized black MILITIA forces in Martinique, promising freedom to those who served. This meant that the most aggressive young men were taken out of the fields and put in uniform, where the authorities could watch them. A number of white and free colored republicans, distrusting Rochambeau's administration and the white planter elite who supported him, went into exile in Dominica and formed a pro-revolutionary government in exile. The white planters of Martinique sent an emissary to the British, and when the French revolutionary government

decided to abolish slavery in the French colonies in 1794, that representative surrendered Martinique to the British. The British kept control of the island until the Peace of Amiens in 1802 returned it to France, then recaptured it in 1806, after hostilities began again. The island remained in British hands until a final peace agreement in 1815. At one point, a Saint-Domingue-born free black man named Jean Kina, who had fought for the British in the Saint-Domingue war and had resettled in Martinique, led a rebellion against British racial policies. He was arrested and imprisoned in Britain. Racial interactions, the roles of free people of color and slaves, and other matters in Martinique were governed according to prerevolutionary French laws, interpreted by British naval officers, during this period. The British tended to apply the rules much more harshly than the prewar French governments had. Many free people of color fled Martinique during this period. Quite a few went to Trinidad, which was under Spanish rule until 1796. The Spanish, French allies by this time, wanted to increase the population and encouraged immigrants regardless of racial status. Other exiles went to Guadeloupe, which remained under French control. Among these migrants was LOUIS DELGRÈS, a free colored officer who was to play an important role in the revolution in Guadeloupe.

Guadeloupe fell into British hands briefly in spring 1794, but an expedition under General VICTOR HUGUES arrived in June. Hugues was a lower-class white man who had lived in Saint-Domingue. While sharing many of the prejudices of other working-class whites against the blacks, both free and enslaved, he nonetheless realized that they were the only group in Guadeloupe who could save the French cause. The white planters were mostly content with British rule, though there were a few who were loyal to the republic. So Hugues appealed to the blacks, proclaiming the French government's decision to abolish slavery and enrolling former slaves in his army. He rapidly defeated the small British occupation force, then turned against British interests throughout the eastern Caribbean. Privateers and raiders operating from Guadeloupe devastated the BRITISH LESSER ANTILLES, seized several islands for a time, and tied up a large British fleet for years (see also PIRACY and NAVY). The black soldiers and sailors of Hugues's forces spread the radical notions of the French Revolution to the rest of the Caribbean and posed a serious threat to white supremacy and colonial rule throughout the region.

Under Hugues's administration, Guadeloupe developed a multiracial society based on free labor. As in the system set up by TOUSSAINT LOUVERTURE in Saint-Domingue, Hugues's government required former slaves to work on the plantations where they had once been enslaved, with regulated wages and working conditions. However, lack of access to global markets meant that the plantations could only operate on a reduced scale, and instead most farmers produced food for the armies. This meant that the former slaves had much more freedom to set working conditions, work for themselves, or negotiate wages than the regulations made it appear. And many former slaves served in the army or found employment supporting the military, thus gaining exemption from field work. Hugues was recalled to France in 1798. The war died down after his departure, as French forces were defeated on several of the islands and the commanders in Guadeloupe contented themselves with holding their ground.

A new government commission and military reinforcements arrived in Guadeloupe in 1800 to strengthen the defenses and rein in radical ideas among the blacks. Among the military escort was Colonel Delgrès, who had served in many of Hugues's campaigns until he was captured on St-Vincent in 1798. Delgrès disagreed with the political agenda of the commission and formed alliances with other prewar free black officers. On October 21, 1801, this group, under the leadership of Delgrès's old commander, another mixed-race officer, MAGLOIRE PÉLAGE, seized control of the island. Delgrès was made commander of the military garrison in Basse-Terre. Pélage tried to show his loyalty to the government in France and called for reforms in the labor system, but Delgrès wanted to go further toward making the former slaves fully free. The new leader of France, Napoléon Bonaparte, sent expeditions to the Caribbean in 1802 to regain control of the French colonies there. The expedition to Guadeloupe was led by General Antoine Richepanse (1770–1802). Pélage bowed to Richepanse's authority, but Delgrès and many of the former slaves of Basse-Terre refused to give in. After a heroic defense, he and his men blew themselves up in their fort rather than surrender to the French.

The French forces reestablished slavery and suppressed resistance harshly. At least 10,000 people were either executed or exiled from the island, often to prison in France—about 10 percent of the colony's population. There were former slaves and whites among their number, but the suffering fell predominantly on the free colored population. Free people of color in the island were especially suspect, since the leaders of the rebellion were almost all prewar free people. Richepanse thought that the colony's security depended on liquidating or driving out any black men who had served in the armed forces. Common soldiers were sometimes overlooked, especially if they had not directly participated in rebellion and were willing to go back to work on their plantations without any fuss. But almost all men who had served as officers or noncommissioned officers had to leave. Even Magloire Pélage was deported to Corsica and made to work on

building roads. A few holdouts fled to the mountains and continued a guerrilla resistance for another two years, finally surrendering and leaving the colony in 1804.

Guiana suffered much less severely during the revolution. There were only about 12,000 people living in the colony in 1789, of whom about 9,000 were slaves and about 1,000 free people of color. The colony was so remote and poor that no foreign invaders arrived until 1809, when the colony was occupied by Brazil. Between 1789 and 1809, the colony served as a dumping ground for people the French Republic wanted to get rid of. In 1792, the first prison colony was established to house Roman Catholic priests who refused to participate in the authorized government church established by the Civil Constitution of the Clergy (1790). They were joined by prisoners of war and political opponents of the regime. Some black soldiers exiled from Guadeloupe were also settled here. Slaves in the colony were freed in 1794, and many left their plantations and moved deeper into the interior to become peasants. When slavery was reestablished in 1802, many of these settlers simply refused to return, becoming MAROONS. The colonial government, under the former Guadeloupe governor Victor Hugues, was not strong enough to deal with them, and perhaps unwilling to force them back into slavery, and most were simply left alone. Under Portuguese rule, from 1809 to 1814, the slave trade resumed, and slave numbers reached 13,000 by the 1820s.

When French rule was restored in Guiana after the abdication of Napoléon, the restoration of the old laws was not a great shock, nor was there repression of free people of color, as had been seen in Guadeloupe. The territory was still very peripheral, and thus racial lines were less sharply drawn than in the islands. The Roman Catholic religious order of the Sisters of St. Joseph of Cluny, under the direction of their formidable abbess Blessed Anne-Marie Javouhey (1779–1851), arrived in the colony in 1823 with the goal of Christianizing and uplifting the black and Indian population. She established an abbey and agricultural settlement at Mana, on a river near the Surinam border. The colonial government assigned 520 slaves to her, and her order purchased hundreds of others. They were educated in trades and prepared for freedom, then the order helped them start businesses or obtain land grants in the interior to settle on as free people. The sisters also visited plantations and heard complaints from slaves about their treatment. The power of the Catholic Church in postrevolutionary France was such that no planter dared refuse when Mother Javouhey asked for some change in the work rules or for the liberation of some slave. As a result of the work of the sisters, and of the frontier conditions that still prevailed in Guiana, there was a large group of free people of color in the colony by the 1830s and 1840s. Guiana was evolving toward free labor well before the second abolition of slavery in the French Empire on April 27, 1848. The population of Guiana in 1848 included about 5,000 free people of color and about 13,100 slaves. These blacks were joined by thousands of RUNAWAY SLAVES from neighboring Brazil, an exodus that sparked border disputes as Brazilian masters sought to reclaim their "property."

The postrevolutionary period in Martinique was similarly peaceful, though there were few steps toward racial justice and progress for free people of color. The British held Martinique from 1806 to 1814. After the abdication of Napoléon, the French government returned, and most of the laws of the old pre-revolutionary days remained in effect. Many of Martinique's free people of color had emigrated during the war. Some returned after the war, but the free colored population remained lower in proportion than in Guadeloupe or Guiana. An 1831 law eliminating taxes and other restrictions on MANUMISSION helped the free colored population grow rapidly. Martinique was still a prosperous sugar-planting region in the 1830s, but increasingly the economy relied on free colored ARTISANS, managers, and small businesspeople. White immigration had never recovered from the breakdown in communications during the Napoleonic Wars. The native-born white population was growing only very slowly. Free people of color became the middle class of the colony by the time the slaves were finally emancipated in 1848.

The harsh repression continued in Guadeloupe for decades after 1802. In 1830, when the blue, white, and red flag of the revolutionary era was once again adopted as the national symbol, blacks on plantations in Guadeloupe came out of their cabins to cheer and weep—and their masters beat them and drove them away. Both sides knew that the republican flag stood for freedom and was a threat to white supremacy. The ultimate abolition of slavery 18 years later found Guadeloupe less well prepared than the other French territories. The free colored middle class was not so vibrant or confident, and the colony suffered riots and disorder and economic decline.

Stewart R. King

FURTHER READING

Dessalles, Pierre. *Sugar and Slavery, Family and Race: The Letters and Diary of Pierre Dessalles, Planter in Martinique, 1808–1856.* Edited and translated by Elborg Forster and Robert Forster. Baltimore: Johns Hopkins University Press, 1996.

Dubois, Laurent. "Citoyens et Amis!' Esclavage, citoyenneté et République dans les Antilles françaises à l'époque révolutionnaire." *Annales* 58, no. 2 (March–April 2003): 281–304.

———. *A Colony of Citizens: Revolution and Slave Emancipation in the French Caribbean, 1787–1804.* Chapel Hill: University of North Carolina Press, 2004.

Labat, Jean-Baptiste. *The Memoirs of Père Labat, 1693–1705.* Edited and translated by John Eaden. London: Routledge, 1970.

Moitt, Bernard. *Women and Slavery in the French Antilles, 1635–1848.* Bloomington: Indiana University Press, 2001.

Stein, Robert Louis. *The French Sugar Business in the Eighteenth Century.* Baton Rouge: Louisiana State University Press, 1988.

FRENCH REVOLUTION

The French Revolution contributed to the crumpling of the slave trade and provided a model, a vocabulary, and justification for slaves' emancipation. More than any previous war or uprising, this conflict changed the face of the Caribbean islands. Lasting from 1789 to 1799, it inspired rebellions in Guadeloupe and Martinque and revolutionized SAINT-DOMINGUE.

While the French Revolution was caused by various and complex factors, the economic crisis in France in the late 18th century certainly set the stage. Massive war debts incurred during the SEVEN YEARS' WAR, 1756–63, and the WAR OF AMERICAN INDEPENDENCE, 1775–83, had depleted King Louis XVI's funds, and to avert bankruptcy, he convened the Estates General (the formal gathering of clergy, nobles, and commoners), a legislative body that had not met in 175 years. Moreover, the calamitous 1788 hailstorm and the severe drought that had destroyed most of the grain crop had driven up the price of bread, which led to spiraling unemployment and helped precipitate a collapse of the economy in 1789. Parisians were starving while only 20 miles away the oblivious royal family and attendants at the court at Versailles feasted lavishly. In this tenuous environment, the Estates General met, and a few missteps by Louis inspired the third estate (the commoners) to empower themselves to make demands and set their own agenda. They declared themselves the "National Assembly," and when denied meeting space by the king, they gathered in an indoor tennis court and vowed not to disperse until they had crafted a constitution for France. They dissolved the other estates and redubbed themselves the "National Constituent Assembly."

When the king fired his financial adviser for suggesting that he and his wife, Marie Antoinette, live within a budget, riots broke out in Paris, and on July 14, 1789, insurgents stormed the Bastille palace, freed some prisoners, and raided its armory; more significantly, they symbolically overthrew an icon of the ancien régime. In a matter of months, France changed from an absolute monarchy that reserved privileges for the clergy and aristocracy to a constitutional monarchy, built on the values of "*liberté, egalité, fraternité,*" as articulated in the Declaration of the Rights of Man and of the Citizen, which

A group surrounds the revolutionary leader Jean-Sylvain Bailly in Paris during the Tennis Court Oath of June 20, 1789. *(Giraudon/The Bridgeman Art Library International)*

French revolutionaries modeled on the recent American Declaration of Independence. Feudalism ended, the ROMAN CATHOLIC CHURCH ceded its powers and property to the state, and, for the first time in French history, the people had a voice and rights. Utopian dreams swelled, and many emerging leaders, such as the Abbé HENRI GRÉGOIRE, believed that the new universal language of the rights of "all men" would permanently transform France and eventually extend globally. Meanwhile, however, radical factions within the assembly gained traction as its forged unity began to splinter. The Legislative Assembly—the body leading France from 1791 until it collapsed in 1792—had to address the unrest in its colonial crown jewel, Saint-Domingue (later Haiti). With so many diverse and mounting challenges to the state vying for attention, the problems in the colonies could not receive sustained focus, but in 1791, Maximilien Robespierre (1758–94) and Grégoire did publicly advocate civil equality of free people of color in the colonies amid tensions surfacing among white colonists who wished to retain hierarchical power. In April 1792, France granted equal rights to free blacks in the colonies. Later that month, the nation declared war on Austria, thus launching the French Revolutionary Wars, which soon would spread across Europe. In June, the king and queen, disguised in servants' clothes, quietly escaped Versailles, headed for the Austrian border, but upon discovery at the border town of Varennes, were paraded back to Paris and placed under watch. The subsequent support Louis's cause attracted from European monarchies—including vows of invasion—further steeled the French people in their rejection of their former king and forced the militarization of the borders. In September, with the assembly dissolved, the National Convention was formed, tasked with writing a new constitution as the basis of the newly declared French Republic. The convention, which ruled from September 20, 1792, to October 26, 1795, assumed executive powers and, as a result of the demands of wartime, suspended the Constitution. This period witnessed the rise of Robespierre and fellow Jacobins, who instituted the Reign of Terror. The guillotine that would symbolize the bloody excesses and whimsical nature of Jacobin rule claimed thousands of lives in this period. The Directory ruled France until 1799, when Napoléon Bonaparte staged the coup that led to the creation of the dictatorial consulate and the end of the republic. With Napoléon's rise, many of the civic gains of the Revolution were lost. He rescinded rights that the republic had at least nominally extended to those in France and the colonies.

Impact on Saint-Domingue

The class conflict that helped spark the Revolution in France existed also in Saint-Domingue. Indeed, the French Revolution threw the colony's delicate system of power into sharp relief. As in Guadeloupe and Martinique, the social and power hierarchy in Saint-Domingue was based on landownership and skin color. In the highest caste were the wealthy white landowners (the *grands blancs*), followed by the poor whites (the *petits blancs*), then the free mulatto population—often descended from a white-slave union and sometimes owning land and slaves—then the free blacks, and finally the large population of slaves. The beleaguered colony could not long sustain peace among the various stakeholders whose balance of power made it so profitable. As news of the Revolution spread, the *grands blancs* sided with the monarch, and the *petits blancs* and mulattoes espoused the revolutionary ideals of liberty and equality, though they did not wish to apply them to the slaves. Through their Club Massiac, the *grands blancs* provided the representatives for the colony in the National Assembly at the beginning of the Revolution; later *petits blancs* and free colored representatives were elected. In addition, the *petits blancs* were not interested in applying ideals of liberty and equality to free people of color, and the areas they controlled were generally hostile to free colored aspirations to civil rights.

The French abolitionist group Société des Amis des Noirs distributed literature in Saint-Domingue that spread the revolutionary ideals of liberty and equality for all people. Rumors that the home government had decreed emancipation sparked slave insurrections throughout the French Caribbean during the first years of the Revolution. Violent uprisings in Saint-Dominigue, Martinique, and Guadeloupe convinced the French government to allow the creation of colonial assemblies in 1790 but after some haranguing decided that only white taxpayers could hold seats. Meanwhile, since the 1780s, Saint-Domingue's most prominent free black planter, JULIEN RAIMOND, had been lobbying legislators in Paris to intervene and legislatively reduce the racial injustices that free people of color faced. In the revolutionary atmosphere of 1789–91, Raimond's arguments resonated, and French leaders identified an opportunity to apply their newfound model to the distant colony. However, when even minor changes were instituted to elevate the status of free blacks in 1791, Saint-Domingue fell into chaos. White planters, who tied their identity to their white purity, fretted as the rights of free blacks increased. The mulatto revolt of 1790 led by VINCENT OGÉ (1755–91), which had sought to secure voting privileges for free men of color, further frightened the wealthy white plantation owners, who staunched the rebellion and then brutally and publicly executed Ogé in February 1791. The National Assembly responded to the execution by offering equality to free people of color in Saint-Domingue in April 1792, but white aristocrats pressured the assembly to reverse the decree, thus sowing the seeds for upheaval. In August 1791, a violent slave insurrection set in motion the series of events that led to the toppling of the colony and the creation of Haiti. Led by a *vodun* priest named Boukman (?–1791), the rebellion drew together nearly 50,000 slaves, who burned plantations and slaughtered white families. Whites retaliated in kind, killing and beheading blacks. The slaves soon found a leader in TOUSSAINT LOUVERTURE, who between 1791 and 1794 trained an army of slaves. The British, who feared a similar slave uprising in its colonies, supported the white planters. When Spain lent support to the rebels, France directed its representative, Léger-Félicité Sonthonax (1763–1813), to abolish slavery in Saint-Domingue in summer 1793; this strategic move prompted the slaves to side with the French in defeating the British and Spanish invaders. In 1797, Toussaint's forces had occupied the Spanish side of the island of Hispaniola, and he had a constitution drafted that claimed autonomy for Saint-Domingue (the French side of Hispaniola) while nominally maintaining loyalty to France. He then appointed himself governor for life. Napoléon, threatened by Toussaint's popularity and power, ordered an invasion of Saint-Domingue and the imprisonment of its governor. Jean-Jacques Dessalines (1758–1806) stepped up and forged a temporary alliance with the French invaders, though once the French forces succumbed to yellow fever, Dessalines renewed the rebellion and in December 1803 declared Saint-Domingue a free republic: the new nation of Haiti. (For a more detailed description of these events, *see also* HAITIAN REVOLUTION.)

Impact on Martinique and Guadeloupe

As in Saint-Domingue, the already tense class dynamic in Guadeloupe and Martinique needed only the catalyst of the French Revolution to erupt into a bloody conflict. The *grands blancs* wanted political representation in the National Assembly, and after new colonial assemblies were established in June 1787, the various colonial stakeholders vied for seats on the assemblies. On March 8, 1790, the French National Assembly decreed the right of free people of color to vote and to be elected, but wealthier mulattoes viewed this decree as a challenge to their own privileged position ahead of free blacks, and they rebelled. The poorer free people of color, therefore, already organized by the colonial government into militias, took up arms and inspired slave rebellions on the plantations. The French National Assembly finally suspended the colonial assemblies and sent a commission to restore peace.

In 1791, when news of the slave rebellion in Saint-Domingue reached Guadeloupe and Martinique, the *grands blancs* who were attempting to become independent of France sided with the British, who were at war with the French Republic. The revolutionary government again sought to intervene in Martinique and sent a naval squadron, which forced the rebellious colonial assembly to recognize the republic. When France sent a new administrator to Martinique in 1793, he tried to dissolve the colonial assembly and to involve the *gens de couleur* in colonial government, but that action inspired a retaliation by the *grands blancs*, who organized and started a civil war in April. Great Britain sided with the monarchical *grands blancs* and, with its overwhelming force, weakened the MILITIA groups and the French troops. On March 20, 1794, Martinique became a British possession, thus gaining autonomy from France and preserving the institution of slavery. Martinique returned to French control with the Treaty of Amiens in 1802, by which time slavery was in the process of being reestablished in what was left of the French colonial empire.

Guadeloupe also fell to the British in 1794. There, the French Revolution had inspired an alliance of the *petits blancs* and *gens de couleur*, but they could not overcome the power of the *grands blancs*. The National Convention voted on February 4, 1794, to abolish slavery in the French colonies, hoping to empower the slaves to rise up and fight the British. France sent two new commissioners to Guadeloupe—Pierre Chrétien and VICTOR HUGUES—whose troops challenged the British occupation. In December, the British accepted defeat, and the French revolutionaries installed a Jacobin regime in Guadeloupe. Under Hugues, slaves were freed, the ports opened to foreign trade, and Guadeloupe remained outside British control. Guadeloupean soldiers and sailors carried the war to British colonies throughout the eastern Caribbean, cooperating with slave rebels there and threatening a regional war for liberty and racial justice. The economy suffered from the fluctuations within the French government and from France's war with Great Britain, and authorities had to confiscate colonial products in order to defray expenses. After Hugues left his position in 1798, Guadeloupe witnessed a revolving door of governments and remained in perpetual turmoil.

Under Napoléon's lead, the French Consulate rescinded the abolition of slavery. White Jacobin leaders in Guadeloupe considered the possibility of declaring independence from France, but Napoléon acted quickly, and, in 1802, after the Peace of Amiens removed the British threat temporarily, dispatched a fleet to close down the Jacobin government and to reinstate slavery in Guadeloupe. A new decree extended French citizenship to landowners and recognized the political rights of *gens de couleur*. Only Saint-Dominique was successful in wresting control from colonial powers and establishing a free, black-led government.

The French Revolution's greatest contribution to free people of color in the Americas lay not in its concrete political achievements, which were limited in the Western Hemisphere, but in the ideas it planted in the minds of people throughout the Americas. The Revolution stood for liberty of all people from arbitrary authority, including from the point of view of the colonies of the Americas, their colonial masters and the institution of slavery. It stood for equality, which for the people of color of the Americas meant an end to racial discrimination as well as aristocratic privileges for wealthy whites. And finally, it stood for brotherhood, especially the brotherhood of a national community of all races and peoples. These ambitious ideals were never quite realized in the societies that grew up in the Americas in the 19th century, but they were powerful motivators for the various rebels and national unifiers who stepped forward in the half-century following 1789. In the Americas, many of these liberators were people of African descent, if not the leaders, then the soldiers in the ranks. The role of the French Revolution as the precursor and enabler of all the liberation movements that followed cannot be denied.

Emily M. Brewer

FURTHER READING

Davis, David Brion. *Inhuman Bondage: The Rise and Fall of Slavery in the New World.* Oxford: Oxford University Press, 2006.

Dubois, Laurent. *A Colony of Citizens: Revolution and Slave Emancipation in the French Caribbean, 1787–1804.* Chapel Hill, N.C.: Published for the Omohundro Institute of Early American History and Culture and Williamsburg, Va., by the University of North Carolina Press, 2004.

Figueredo, D. H., and Frank Argote-Freyre. *A Brief History of the Caribbean.* New York: Facts On File, 2008.

Garrigus, John D. *Before Haiti: Race and Citizenship in French Saint-Domingue.* New York: Palgrave Macmillan, 2006.

Gaspar, David Barry, and David Patrick Geggus, eds. *A Turbulent Time: The French Revolution and the Greater Caribbean.* Bloomington: Indiana University Press, 1997.

Klein, Herbert S. *African Slavery in Latin America and the Caribbean.* Oxford: Oxford University Press, 2007.

FREYRE, GILBERTO (1900-1987) *Brazilian sociologist*

Gilberto de Mello Freyre was born on March 15, 1900, in the northern city of Recife, BRAZIL, into a Catholic family. Freyre was a precocious child, and his family's conversion to Protestantism helped him earn a scholarship at Baylor University in Waco, Texas. After graduation from Baylor in 1918, Freyre went on to earn an M.A. in 1922 at Columbia University, where Franz Boas's teaching on race powerfully influenced his intellectual development.

Freyre spent much of the 1930s in PORTUGAL and the United States, and the racial discrimination he witnessed in the United States had a profound impact on his ideas. Freyre became the leading Brazilian intellectual of the 20th century. His work helped create a new concept of Brazilian national identity at a time of tremendous sociopolitical and economic transformation in that country. Earlier Brazilian intellectuals had viewed race mixture as the cause of the country's underdevelopment. Freyre, on the other hand, argued in his influential 1933 book *Casa grande e senzala (The Masters and the Slaves)* that the socioeconomic and sexual relations between the Portuguese masters and the African slaves during colonial times helped create a modern Brazil that had racial justice and democracy. He argued that Brazil's system constituted a singular form of *racial democracy* in a world awash with racial hatred and inequality. This argument was later encoded in the concept of *lusotropicalism,* which argued that slavery in Brazil was different and more benign than slavery in Anglo-America as a result of the particularities of the Portuguese, who were Catholics and had more consensual relations with their slaves.

Freyre's ideas were revolutionary at the time because most Brazilian intellectuals accepted that Brazil was inferior to Europe and the United States and attributed the inferiority to MISCEGENATION. Moreover, Freyre's ideas fit a new global consensus, as World War II was being waged, partly on the issues of race, ethnicity, and religion. Those ideas remained very popular in Brazil and were embraced by the authoritarian regime of Getúlio Vargas (president 1930–45, 1951–54), which found in these ideas a rallying cry to draw support from poor Afro-Brazilians for his government. Freyre celebrated regional cultures within Brazil, especially in the Northeast, where he was from, and where the culture was strongly influenced by Africans. During this period, the cultural policies of the Vargas regime turned Afro-Brazilian cultural manifestations such as samba, the martial arts–style *capoeira,* and the cuisine *feijoada* into symbols of national pride. In 1936, Freyre published *Sobrados e mucambos (The Mansions and the Shanties)* and in 1959 *Ordem e Progresso (Order and Progress),* both of which expounded on his earlier ideas with a focus on different periods of Brazilian history. *Sobrados e mucambos* focused on the Brazilian Empire in the 19th century, and *Ordem e progresso* on the republic in the first three decades of the 20th century.

Freyre's ideas, which were later criticized by foreign and Brazilian social scientists, had many implications for modern understanding of the role Afro-Brazilians played in their country's history. His analysis of sexual relations between the Portuguese masters and their slaves is the lynchpin of his argument that many slaves tolerated their conditions and sought advancement within the system and that Brazilian slavery was a more benign institution than in other countries. Subsequent observers have presented contrasting examples showing that the brutality inherent in slavery was not absent from Brazil. Freyre's work celebrated miscegenation and racial diversity in a world where racism was rampant. However, Freyre's assertion that Brazil constituted a *racial democracy*, either in the colonial period or when he was writing, in which race was irrelevant to a person's social status and mobility was fundamentally erroneous. Often in Freyre's writing he would try to demonstrate the lack of RACISM AND RACIAL PREJUDICE in Brazil, and yet the evidence he cited often undercut his argument. In *Casa grande e senzala*, he argued that if white families did not let their sons or daughters marry blacks, it was often because of class difference but not race, yet the woman interviewed in the immediately preceding passage said that she would not let her daughter marry a black man because she would fear the way the society would treat their mixed-race offspring. Freyre's sources, whether archival or from oral traditions, often contradict his thesis of Brazilian racial democracy.

Most importantly, many of Freyre's ideas about blackness often restated some of the stereotypes on which white superiority hinged. The idea of the black mammy in American Southern racial lore was reframed as the affectionate Brazilian wet nurse and nanny. Freyre portrayed blacks as libidinous, sensuous, sexual, and often drawn to the arts. Finally, the context within which Freyre was writing is revealing. His concept of miscegenation and his views on the relations between the races in Brazil were written as a contrast to race relations in the United States, where blatant segregation was the norm in the 1930s. In addition, they were an attempt by a Brazilian northeasterner to come to terms with his own nationalist and racial consciousness in a foreign land. In America, his whiteness was questioned in a society that only had two values for race, white and nonwhite. Despite these flaws, Freyre's contribution to the formation of Brazilian national identity remains incontestable. Freyre was founder and director of the Instituto Joaquim Nabuco in Recife, a research institute and foundation dedicated to the study of northeastern Brazilian culture and still an important center for the study of race and ethnicity in Brazil. He died on July 18, 1987, in his native city of Recife.

Martine Jean

FURTHER READING

Butler, Kim D. *Freedoms Given, Freedoms Won: Afro-Brazilians in Post-Abolition São Paulo and Salvador.* New Brunswick, N.J.: Rutgers University Press, 1998.
———. *The Mansions and the Shanties: The Making of Modern Brazil.* New York: Knopf, 1963.
———. *Order and Progress: Brazil from Monarchy to Republic.* Berkeley: University of California Press, 1986.
Freyre, Gilberto. *The Masters and the Slaves: A Study in the Development of Brazilian Civilization.* New York: Knopf, 1946.
Meade, Teresa A. *A Brief History of Brazil.* New York: Facts On File, 2003.
Skidmore, Thomas E. *Black into White: Race and Nationality in Brazilian Thought.* New York: Oxford University Press, 1974.

FUGITIVE SLAVE ACT OF 1850 (Fugitive Slave Law)

Passed by the U.S. Congress, the Fugitive Slave Act of 1850 was one of the most controversial pieces of the Compromise of 1850, a series of laws passed by Congress relating to slavery. The Fugitive Slave Act was intended to mollify slaveholders by strengthening federal enforcement of article IV, section 2, of the Constitution, which provided for the return of persons "held to service or labor in one State . . . escaping into another." An earlier fugitive slave law passed in 1793 was circumvented by the Supreme Court in *Prigg v. Pennsylvania* (1842), in which the Court ruled that the law preempted the rights of the states. The Supreme Court decision gave states the option to refuse to enforce the 1793 act. Slaveholders argued that this ruling undermined their ability to recapture fugitive slaves and was thus an attack on the system of slavery. As part of the Compromise of 1850, the Fugitive Slave Act was a significant concession to slaveholders in an attempt to quiet the sectional crisis over the expansion of slavery. Not surprisingly, the law failed to achieve true compromise. Abolitionists opposed the law on the basis that it weakened the individual states' PERSONAL LIBERTY LAWS, while slaveholders argued that the law placed unnecessary restrictions on their ability to reclaim fugitive slaves.

The Fugitive Slave Act affected not only slaves but free blacks, who were deprived of legal protection. Many who were accused of being fugitives—whether falsely or not—fled to CANADA to escape prosecution. The draconian law strengthened the authority of the federal government to help in recapturing slaves and increased penalties for aiding and harboring fugitives. The law proved extremely unpopular in the North, where abolitionists rallied to block its enforcement. Efforts by slaveholders to recapture escaped slaves led to several notable confrontations in the 1850s and exacerbated sectional tensions in the United States.

Thomas Bahde

FURTHER READING:

Fehrenbacher, Don. *The Slaveholding Republic: An Account of the United States Government's Relations to Slavery.* New York: Oxford University Press, 2002.

Franklin, John, and Loren Schweniger. *Runaway Slaves: Rebels on the Plantation.* Oxford: Oxford University Press, 1999.

FUGITIVE SLAVE ACT OF 1850

The U.S. Congress passed the Fugitive Slave Act of 1850 as part of the Compromise of 1850. The controversial law consisted of 10 sections. The first four sections established the authority of federal commissioners to act as arbiters in fugitive slave cases. Section 5 imposed punishments for marshals or deputies who failed to comply with the law or who allowed fugitive slaves to escape their custody and allowed for specially appointed individuals to act as fugitive slave catchers. Section 6 established the right of slaveholders to recapture fugitive slaves and set forth the procedures by which fugitives could be reclaimed. Section 7 set forth the punishment for anyone caught aiding or harboring fugitive slaves. Section 8 set the fees that were to be charged in fugitive slave cases. Section 9 authorized officers arresting fugitives to employ whatever assistance may be necessary to prevent the escape or liberation of the fugitives. Section 10 allowed slave owners to obtain from a court, commissioner, or judge a certificate of their right to capture specific fugitives. Sections 5, 6, 7, 9, and 10 are reproduced here.

Fugitive Slave Act of 1850

Section 5 . . . That it shall be the duty of all marshals and deputy marshals to obey and execute all warrants and precepts issued under the provisions of this act . . . and should any marshal or deputy marshal refuse to receive such warrant, or other process, when tendered, or to use all proper means diligently to execute the same, he shall, on conviction thereof, be fined in the sum of one thousand dollars, to the use of such claimant, . . . and after arrest of such fugitive, by such marshal or his deputy, or whilst at any time in his custody under the provisions of this act, should such fugitive escape, whether with or without the assent of such marshal or his deputy, such marshal shall be liable, on his official bond, to be prosecuted for the benefit of such claimant, for the full value of the service or labor of said fugitive in the State, Territory, or District whence he escaped: and the better to enable the said commissioners, when thus appointed, to execute their duties faithfully and efficiently, in conformity with the requirements of the Constitution of the United States and of this act, they are hereby authorized and empowered, within their counties respectively, to appoint, . . . any one or more suitable persons, from time to time, to execute all such warrants and other process as may be issued by them in the lawful performance of their respective duties; with authority to such commissioners, or the persons to be appointed by them, to execute process as aforesaid, to summon and call to their aid the bystanders, or *posse comitatus* of the proper county, when necessary to ensure a faithful observance of the clause of the Constitution referred to, in conformity with the provisions of this act; and all good citizens are hereby commanded to aid and assist in the prompt and efficient execution of this law, whenever their services may be required, as aforesaid, for that purpose; and said warrants shall run, and be executed by said officers, any where in the State within which they are issued.

Section 6 . . . That when a person held to service or labor in any State or Territory of the United States, has heretofore or shall hereafter escape into another State or Territory of the United States, the person or persons to whom such service or labor may be due, . . . may pursue and reclaim such fugitive person, either by procuring a warrant from some one of the courts, judges, or commissioners aforesaid, of the proper circuit, district, or county, for the apprehension of such fugitive from service or labor, or by seizing and arresting such fugitive, where the same can be done without process, and by taking, or causing such person to be taken, forthwith before such court, judge, or commissioner, whose duty it shall be to hear and determine the case of such claimant in a summary manner; and upon satisfactory proof being made, by deposition or affidavit, in writing, to be taken and certified by such court, judge, or commissioner, or by other satisfactory testimony, duly taken and certified by some court, magistrate, justice of the peace, or other legal officer authorized to administer an oath and take depositions under the laws of the State or Territory from which such person owing service or labor may have escaped, with a certificate of such magistracy or other authority, as aforesaid, with the seal of the proper court or officer thereto attached, which seal shall be sufficient to establish the competency of the proof, and with proof, also by affidavit, of the identity of the person whose service or labor is claimed to be due as aforesaid, that the person so arrested does in fact owe service or labor to the person or persons claiming him or her, in the State or Territory from which such fugitive may have escaped as aforesaid, and that said person escaped, to make out and deliver to such claimant, his or her agent or attorney, a certificate setting forth the substantial facts as to the service or labor due from such fugitive to the claimant, and of his or her escape from the State or Territory in which he or she was arrested, with authority to such claimant, or his or her agent or attorney, to use such reasonable force and restraint as may be necessary, under the circumstances of the case, to take and remove such fugitive person back to the State or Territory whence he or she may have escaped as aforesaid. In no trial or hearing under this act shall the testimony of such alleged fugitive be admitted in evidence; and the certificates in this and the first [fourth] section mentioned, shall be conclusive of the right of the person or persons in whose favor granted, to remove such fugitive to the State or Territory from which he escaped, and shall prevent all molestation of such person or persons by any process issued by any court, judge, magistrate, or other person whomsoever.

Section 7 . . .   That any persons who shall knowingly and willingly obstruct, hinder, or prevent such claimant, his agent or attorney, or any person or persons lawfully assisting him, her, or them, from arresting such a fugitive from service or labor, either with or without process as aforesaid, or shall rescue, or attempt to rescue, such fugitive from service or labor, from the custody of such claimant, his or her agent or attorney, or other person or persons lawfully assisting as aforesaid, when so arrested, . . . or shall aid, abet, or assist such person so owing service or labor as aforesaid, directly or indirectly, to escape from such claimant, . . . or shall harbor or conceal such fugitive, so as to prevent the discovery and arrest of such person, after notice or knowledge of the fact that such person was a fugitive from service or labor as aforesaid, shall, for either of said offences, be subject to a fine not exceeding one thousand dollars, and imprisonment not exceeding six months . . . ; and shall moreover forfeit and pay, by way of civil damages to the party injured by such illegal conduct, the sum of one thousand dollars for each fugitive so lost as aforesaid . . .

Section 9 . . . That, upon affidavit made by the claimant of such fugitive, . . . that he has reason to apprehend that such fugitive will be rescued by force from his or their possession before he can be taken beyond the limits of the State in which the arrest is made, it shall be the duty of the officer making the arrest to retain such fugitive in his custody, and to remove him to the State whence he fled, and there to deliver him to said claimant, his agent, or attorney. And to this end, the officer aforesaid is hereby authorized and required to employ so many persons as he may deem necessary to overcome such force, and to retain them in his service so long as circumstances may require. The said officer and his assistants, while so employed, to receive the same compensation, and to be allowed the same expenses, as are now allowed by law for transportation of criminals, to be certified by the judge of the district within which the arrest is made, and paid out of the treasury of the United States.

Section 10 . . . That when any person held to service or labor in any State or Territory, or in the District of Columbia, shall escape therefrom, the party to whom such service or labor shall be due, . . . may apply to any court of record therein, . . . and make satisfactory proof to such court, . . . of the escape aforesaid, and that the person escaping owed service or labor to such party. Whereupon the court shall cause a record to be made of the matters so proved, and also a general description of the person so escaping, with such convenient certainty as may be; and a transcript of such record, . . . being produced in any other State, Territory, or district in which the person so escaping may be found, . . . shall be held and taken to be full and conclusive evidence of the fact of escape, and that the service or labor of the person escaping is due to the party in such record mentioned. And upon the production by the said party of other and further evidence if necessary, either oral or by affidavit, in addition to what is contained in the said record of the identity of the person escaping, he or she shall be delivered up to the claimant. And the said court, commissioner, judge, or other person authorized by this act to grant certificates to claimants of fugitives, shall, upon the production of the record and other evidences aforesaid, grant to such claimant a certificate of his right to take any such person identified and proved to be owing service or labor as aforesaid, which certificate shall authorize such claimant to seize or arrest and transport such person to the State or Territory from which he escaped: Provided, That nothing herein contained shall be construed as requiring the production of a transcript of such record as evidence as aforesaid. But in its absence the claim shall be heard and determined upon other satisfactory proofs, competent in law.

Source: The National Center for Public Policy Research. URL: www.nationalcenter.org/FugitiveSlaveAct.html.

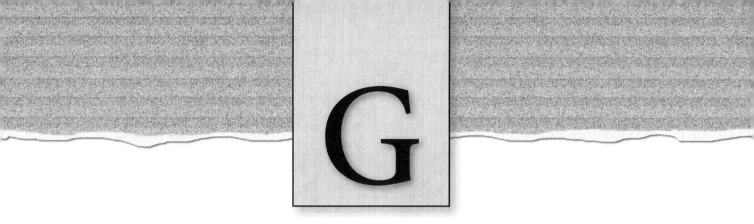

G

GANNIBAL, ABRAM PETROVICH (1696–1781)
Russian engineer and general

Abram Petrovich Gannibal is an example of a very successful free African in European society. Although he never set foot in the Americas, Gannibal's life illustrates how far the influence of Africans spread in the Atlantic world of the 18th century. Born in 1696, Abram was an African slave given by the Ottoman sultan to Czar Peter the Great. Abram was probably from the vicinity of Lake Chad, in the modern nation of Cameroon or Chad, and was sent to the sultan as a hostage at the age of seven. The Ottomans enslaved him because war broke out with his country. He was taken by the Russian ambassador to Moscow in 1704. He was baptized in the Russian Orthodox Church in 1705, with Czar Peter as his godfather. Though there was never any formal act of MANUMISSION for him, nobody ever spoke of him as a slave after this, and probably the baptism was considered the equivalent of manumission.

Abram served as a page in Peter's court until he reached the age of 21, when Peter sent him to Paris to be educated in the arts, sciences, and warfare. While in FRANCE, Abram served with the French army and rose to the rank of captain. It was in France that he adopted the surname of Gannibal, in honor of the Carthaginian general Hannibal, a fellow African. He met or corresponded with such Enlightenment figures as Diderot, Montesquieu, and Voltaire. Voltaire called him the "dark star of the Enlightenment."

Upon his return to Russia in 1722, he put his education to work as an inspector and builder of fortifications for Peter. He also designed canals and other public works. When Peter died in 1725, Gannibal was temporarily exiled to Siberia along with others of Peter's close companions but was pardoned in 1730 and returned to his engineering work. When Peter's daughter Elizabeth staged a coup and became empress in 1741, he rose rapidly in the ranks, becoming a major general and serving as governor of Tallinn in Estonia from 1742 to 1753. He is said to have convinced the father of the future great Russian general Alexander Suvorov (1729–1800) to permit the boy to pursue a military career. Empress Elizabeth gave him an estate near Pskov with several hundred serfs, and he lived there from his retirement in 1762 until his death on May 14, 1781.

Gannibal had 11 children, one of whom, Ivan Gannibal, became general in chief of the Russian armies under Catherine the Great (1729–96); another was the grandmother of the great Russian writer and liberal social critic Alexander Pushkin. His descendants include royalty and nobility throughout Europe, including the current British duchess of Westminster.

Stewart R. King

FURTHER READING

Barnes, Hugh. *The Stolen Prince: Gannibal, Adopted Son of Peter the Great, Great-Grandfather of Alexander Pushkin, and Europe's First Black Intellectual.* New York: Ecco, 2006.
Nabokov, Vladimir. *Notes on Prosody: And Abram Gannibal.* Princeton, N.J.: Princeton University Press, 1964.
Pushkin, Alexander. "The Moor of Peter the Great." In *The Complete Prose Tales of Alexander Pushkin,* translated by Gillon R. Aitken. London: Barrie Books, 1966.

GARNET, HENRY HIGHLAND (1815–1882)
American clergyman, orator, abolitionist, diplomat

Henry Highland Garnet was one of the most militant abolitionists and prominent free blacks in the United States. As a clergyman and orator, he remained an uncompromising opponent of slavery and supporter of equal rights. Son of George Garnet and Henny Garnet, he was born near New Market, MARYLAND, on December 23, 1815. In 1824, the family escaped to freedom and reached New York City in 1825.

Garnet began his education at New York's African Free School (1826–28), where he formed, with other students, the Garrison Literary and Benevolent Association, named for the white abolitionist William Lloyd Garrison (1805–79). He also worked as a cabin boy (1828) and a cook and steward (1829) on ships sailing between New York and CUBA, and New York and Washington, D.C.

An 1882 lithograph of Henry Highland Garnet (1815–82), who was one of the most radical abolitionists in the United States. In 1843, he called for a slave uprising to end slavery and said there was not much hope for the nation's redemption from the sin of slavery without bloodshed. He remained a stalwart opponent of slavery and supporter of full civil rights throughout his life. *(Library of Congress)*

(*see also* MERCHANT SEAMEN). When his family, fearing slave catchers, fled Manhattan in 1829, Garnet relocated to Jericho, Long Island, to work on the farm of Epenetus Smith. In his second year there he suffered a severe knee injury that led to leg amputation 10 years later.

Garnet resumed his formal education in 1831 at the High School for Colored Youth in New York, and in 1835, he enrolled at Noyes Academy, Canaan, New Hampshire. On July 4, 1835, he gave a passionate address at an abolitionist meeting, angering local residents, who, the following month, attacked and burned the Noyes building. Garnet escaped to New York, his health frail, and was bedridden for the next two months. In early 1836, he entered Oneida Institute in Whitestown, New York. There, he developed a reputation for debate and oratory and while still a student delivered an antislavery speech in New York City that established his reputation as one of the nation's most powerful young orators.

Graduating from Oneida in 1840, he moved to Troy, New York; established a school for black youth; and became increasingly involved in abolition (*see also* EDUCATION AND LITERACY and HIGHER EDUCATION). But in December 1840, his badly infected leg had to be ampu-

tated at the hip. Nevertheless, he was ordained an elder in his church, married Julia Ward Williams in 1841, received his license to preach in 1842, and coedited the abolitionist journal *National Watchman*. From 1843 to 1848, he served as the first pastor of Troy's Liberty Street Presbyterian Church and worked on abolition and temperance on behalf of the American Home Missionary Society.

On August 16, 1843, Garnet addressed the National Convention of Colored Citizens in Buffalo, New York (*see also* NEGRO CONVENTION MOVEMENT IN THE UNITED STATES). His "Address to the Slaves of the United States of America" proclaimed, "You had far better all die—*die immediately*, than live slaves. . . . There is not much hope of redemption without the shedding of blood. . . . let your motto be resistance! resistance! resistance!" The address was an important moment as Garnet proved to be a nationally influential figure. The speech highlighted the gulf between his militant approach and that of FREDERICK DOUGLASS, who persuaded the convention against endorsing Garnet's call for an uprising. Garnet was a member of the Anti-Slavery Society in 1838–40, then the rival American and Foreign Anti-Slavery Society after that point. His radical views contrasted sharply with those of the more conservative white abolitionists in the American and Foreign Society, however.

Garnet remained active in abolition and reform over the next two decades. From 1850 to 1852, he toured Britain, France, and Germany, giving antislavery lectures and participating in the World's Peace Conference at Frankfort (1850) and the World's Anti-Slavery Convention in London (1852). He sailed to JAMAICA on missionary work sponsored by the United Presbyterian Church of Scotland in the 1850s, pursuing his interests in colonization.

Upon returning to the United States, he became pastor of New York's Shiloh Presbyterian Church in 1855. In 1859, he founded the African Civilization Society—demonstrating both his support for emigration and colonization, as well as his Euro-American attitudes about Africa. (*See also* EMIGRATION AND COLONIZATION.) "We believe," he said in 1860, "that Africa is to be redeemed by Christian civilization." In 1861, on the eve of the AMERICAN CIVIL WAR, he returned to Britain to generate interest in emigration.

During the Civil War, Garnet pushed the U.S. government to permit black enlistment in the army, recruited black troops, and worked to improve their conditions in the army. On December 31, 1862—the day before President Abraham Lincoln issued the EMANCIPATION PROCLAMATION—he read the proclamation to the crowd gathered at a "Grand Emancipation Jubilee" held at New York's Shiloh Presbyterian Church. In July 1864, he became pastor of the Fifteenth Street Presbyterian Church in

Washington, D.C., and worked on the challenges facing newly freed men. Commemorating congressional passage of the Thirteenth Amendment (which, when ratified in December 1865, officially abolished slavery in the United States), he preached in the House of Representatives on February 12, 1865, the first African American to speak at the Capitol. The address foretold "a model Republic, founded on the principles of justice and humanity and Christianity, in which the burdens of war and the blessings of peace are equally borne and enjoyed by all."

In 1868, he became president of Avery College in Pittsburgh, Pennsylvania, where he also founded Grace Memorial, Pittsburgh's first black Presbyterian church. He returned to Manhattan's Shiloh Presbyterian Church in 1870, the same year his wife, Julia, died. Thereafter, he seemed to decline physically and became depressed and embittered that he had been forgotten while Douglass had gained fame. He lobbied for a diplomatic appointment to Liberia and was appointed U.S. minister to Liberia in 1881. He remarked at a farewell dinner in Washington, D.C., "If I can just reach the land of my forefathers and with my feet press her soil I shall be content to die." Reaching Monrovia on December 28, 1881, he died there a month and a half later, on February 13, 1882.

The radical forerunner of Frederick Douglass, Garnet was one of the foremost leaders of the black nationalist movement. He was a fearsome debater, a powerful orator, and an advocate of black-controlled institutions and black self-improvement. More than any other black leader of his era, he helped to move abolition away from moral suasion and toward more militant tactics.

Kenneth Blume

FURTHER READING

Crummell, Alexander. "Eulogium on Henry Highland Garnet, D.D." In *Africa and America*. Springfield, Mass.: Willey and Co., 1891. Reprint, New York: Negro Universities Press, 1969.

Garnet, Henry Highland. *An Address to the Slaves of the United States of America*. Troy, N.Y.: J. H. Tobbitt, 1843 and 1848. Reprint, Richard Newman et al., eds. *Pamphlets of Protest: An Anthology of Early African-American Protest Literature, 1790–1860*. New York: Routledge, 2001.

———. *A Memorial Discourse Delivered in the Hall of the House of Representatives, Washington, D.C. on Sabbath, February 12, 1865*. Philadelphia: Joseph M. Wilson, 1865.

———. *The Past and Present Condition, and the Destiny, of the Colored Race: A Discourse Delivered at the Fifteenth Anniversary of the Female Benevolent Society of Troy, N.Y., Feb. 14, 1848*. Troy, N.Y.: Steam Press of J. C. Kneeland and Co., 1848. Reprinted in Howard Brotz, ed. *Negro Social*

and Political Thought, 1850–1920. New York: Basic Books, 1966.

Ofari, Earl. *"Let Your Motto Be Resistance": The Life and Thought of Henry Highland Garnet*. Boston: Beacon Press, 1972.

Pasternak, Martin B. *Rise Now and Fly to Arms: The Life of Henry Highland Garnet*. New York: Garland, 1995.

Schor, Joel. *Henry Highland Garnet, a Voice of Black Radicalism in the Nineteenth Century*. Westport, Conn.: Greenwood Press, 1977.

Seraile, William. "The Brief Diplomatic Career of Henry Highland Garnet." *Phylon* 46, no. 1 (First quarter 1985): 71–81.

GARRIDO, JUAN   (active 1501–1538)
Afro-Spanish conquistador

Juan Garrido was probably one of the first people of African descent to arrive in the Americas. He was a child of the Italian-Portuguese community and is reputed to have been born in Africa as a Kongo prince or at least a member of a local royal family in the Kingdom of Kongo sometime in the mid- to late 15th century (*see* Congo and Angola). The Kongo had been evangelized by Portugal in the late 15th century. In 1501, Garrido was living in Seville, Spain, and he traveled to Santo Domingo in the Caribbean as a slave between 1502 and 1503. In 1508, Juan Ponce de León (1474–1521) transported a group of armed Africans to help him in the conquest of Puerto Rico; in a similar action 10 years later, Diego Velázquez de Cuéllar (1465–1524) had black assistants—whether enslaved or free is unclear—in his conquest of Cuba. Later, Juan Garrido asserted that he had participated in both expeditions.

In 1508 and 1509, Garrido, still enslaved but obviously acting with a great deal of independent initiative, settled in Caparras, Puerto Rico, prospecting for gold. In the same period, another free mixed-race man living in the area was killed defending Luisa, a Castilian woman, from the Carib Indians. In 1511, Garrido joined Ponce de León's expedition, purportedly in search of the fountain of eternal youth in Florida. He was probably the first African to set foot in what is now the United States.

Garrido later embarked on the Narváez expedition in 1520 to Mexico, where he was given his freedom and married, apparently with an Indian woman, settled down, and fathered several children. He obtained properties near Hernán Cortés's property in Coyoacán. He also was in charge of guarding the Chapultepec aqueducts, which were constantly attacked by animals and Indians. He also was probably the porter at the cabildo, or municipal administration, headed by Cortés. He seems to have had a troubled relationship with Cortés, especially during an expedition into the northern interior to las Huigueras, where Cortés returned to Mexico City after defeating De Olid. Later, he obtained loans to explore for gold in Michoacán. At the same time, he had a farm growing pigs for market in Mexico City.

In 1538, he wrote a *probanza*, or legal brief, to the king in order to get a pension and *mercedes* (rewards for Indians who had been Christianized thanks to his efforts) to pay for his services during the conquest of Mexico. In the brief, he is said to be living with his wife. The document was witnessed by Juan González, a Spaniard who acted as a Taíno interpreter (and was probably the first Christian to marry in Veracruz). Some of the other witnesses referred to Garrido as the "conqueror" to recognize him as one of the earliest settlers. In the document, and as one of the reasons he merited reward, he claimed to be the first non-Indian to cultivate maize in the Americas.

That same year a conspiracy of slaves was discovered in Mexico City, and many of its leaders were executed; some authors believe Garrido's *probanza* was written to protect him from the repression occasioned by the plot. After this, Garrido disappears from history.

Garrido's life is the best documented of those of a number of black conquistadores who participated, sometimes as servants and sometimes as free members of the company, in the various Spanish *entradas*, or first expeditions of conquest to various areas of the Americas. The role of free people of color in the Spanish conquest of the Americas is a fascinating and little-known story. The role of these black conquistadores in founding Spanish society in the Americas indicates that people of African ancestry were important components of this society from its inception.

Juan Manuel de la Serna

FURTHER READING

Alegría, Ricardo E. *Juan Garrido, el conquistador negro en las Antillas, Florida, México y California c. 1503–1540.* San Juan, P.R.: Centro Estudios Avanzados de Puerto Rico y el Caribe, 1990.

Gerhard, Peter. "A Black Conquistador in Mexico." *Hispanic American Historical Review* 58, no. 3 (August 1978): 451–459.

Restall, Mathew. "Conquistadores negros africanos armados en la temprana Hispanoamérica." In *Pautas de convivencia étnica en América latina colonial (Indios, negros, mulatos, pardos y esclavos),* edited by Juan M. de la Serna, 19–72. México City: UNAM-Gob Edo Guanajuato, 2005.

GENDER ATTITUDES

The employment of women of color as child care workers, HOUSEKEEPERS, and in other, less respectable, but traditionally feminine occupations, along with other

characteristics of the free colored population, led to a set of gender attitudes that whites employed to justify marginalizing and oppressing people of color, both men and women. At the same time, free women of color needed to live and feed their families, and their employment in these roles met real needs in slave societies. This was especially true in places outside the United States where the social attitudes toward gender were different and racial barriers somewhat more permeable.

Free Women of Color, Occupations, and Social Roles
Free women of color pursued a wide variety of different occupations in slave societies. Probably the most common was farmer. Even families living in or near urban areas, in which the male members of the family had urban occupations, kept gardens and small livestock in an effort to supplement their diet and income. The "butter and egg man" is a stock figure of antebellum stereotypes of black roles, but in fact it was as likely or more likely to find a "butter and egg woman" who marketed small amounts of produce to the urban home, often the homes of patrons or wealthier relatives. (*See* PROVISION GROUND FARMING.) The second most common occupation for women, overlapping to some extent with the first, was small retail commerce. A step up from marketing one's own produce to the homes of a few urban purchasers would be to purchase products from small farmers and sell them in a stall in an open-air market or small enclosed store (*see also* COMMERCE AND TRADE). This sort of commerce was and is common in Africa and in Latin America today, and women are prominent as both buyers and sellers throughout the black Atlantic. But somehow these occupations, common though they may have been, did not make the impression on public attitudes that the more stereotypically feminine occupations did.

The occupations most commonly associated with free women of color are those of housekeepers, nannies, maids, cooks, and laundresses, who provided an array of domestic services. These were tasks that were difficult in themselves in the era before labor-saving household machines. They were even more difficult for members of the ruling class to perform for themselves because of unwritten social rules about race and class. However, they often were not the sort of thing that even a wealthy master could justify assigning slaves to do, because they required moving about independently, taking responsibility for valuable property or money, and took people away from the principal productive tasks of the plantation. Some masters did have this sort of work done by slaves, but only the wealthiest and most ostentatious. For less well-off or pretentious people, a hired employee would often prove to be cheaper, more flexible, and more reliable. White female employees were available in some places, especially in the American South after the beginning of

Two engravings dating from the period of the first abolition of slavery in the French colonial empire (1794–1804). The inscriptions *"moi libre"* and *"moi libre aussi"* mean "I am free" and "I also am free." The man is shown as a farmer, while the woman is better dressed and could be a service worker. Many field workers were women, but the pictures illustrate gender stereotypes from before the Haitian Revolution about free people of color. *(Left: Archives Charmet/The Bridgeman Art Library International; Right: After Claude Louis Desrais/Getty Images)*

Irish immigration in the 1840s, but even then unwritten rules of the color line prevented their employment in the more personal kinds of service. These domestic servants sometimes also had or were suspected of having sexual relationships with their masters. The possibility of such relationships was one reason that white women, if any were present in the household, often preferred hiring free women of color—preferably older married ones—to employing slaves in these sorts of roles. A free colored woman at least would be more able to resist unwelcome advances from her employer than a slave woman would. But the free colored housekeeper who was also the sexual companion of the single white master was a common stereotype, especially in the Caribbean, where there was a large gender imbalance in the white population and consequently a lot of single white men. Such relationships were common enough, in fact, that many a free family of mixed race in SAINT-DOMINGUE or JAMAICA could trace its ancestry to one. But there were also many free colored housekeepers who were clearly not the sexual partners of their employers.

Another stereotypical occupation for free women of color, and one that was at once less respectable and more crucial to the physical survival of many people in the society, was as a traditional healer (*see also* MIDWIVES AND TRADITIONAL HEALERS). Formal certification as a medical doctor was only open to men, and in almost all of the slave societies, to men of high racial status. Men of lower racial status could sometimes slip into the field of healing in a formal way by being recognized as members of lower-status healing professions: apothecaries, such as St. MARTIN DE PORRES, or veterinarians, such as TOUSSAINT LOUVERTURE. But for women of color, there were only the informal healing arts. Healers, and especially midwives, were crucial to the community's health. However, the fact that women were exercising the healing arts was somehow disruptive to what was thought of as the proper gender order. The knowledge that traditional healers and midwives used was not gained from the infant medical science of the era but from traditional African, Indian, and European knowledge. All this made practitioners vulnerable to charges of witchcraft and abortion and made them symbols of disordered gender relations.

The third stereotypical occupation for free women of color was as PROSTITUTES AND COURTESANS. While men of the master class could prey upon their slaves, for various reasons they might choose not to or might want to stray further afield. Additionally, there were plenty of single white men who did not own slaves and who might want sexual access to women of color, especially given the gender imbalance of white populations in the Caribbean. Moreover, part of the gender stereotype played back into white sexual desire, as women of color were stereotyped as being especially interested in sexual experience and especially good at giving sexual pleasure. This all represented a potential economic niche for free women of color. There were many who took up the challenge, though perhaps not so many as excited rumor or censorious commentary suggested at the time. Nonetheless, prostitution has always represented a possible source of income for women in grave economic circumstances, as was the case for many free people of color at the time. However, most people would rather establish a long-term relationship with any customer or provider of service, and sexual services are no exception. Many longer-term sexual relationships between free women of color and white men may have been somewhat commercial in origin. It was often assumed by observers at the time, and sometimes by subsequent analysts, that housekeepers were paid sexual companions. They might have been sexual companions in some cases, though housekeeping by itself was a difficult task that required a lot of skill and hard work and was worth a good deal of money. It is hard sometimes to untangle the complex web of motivations in relationships and determine what exactly was being paid for and what the emotional component of the relationship was for both parties. But the assumptions that many people held at the time about the nature of these relationships went a long way toward stereotyping women of color.

Gender Attitudes

These stereotypically feminine occupations, along with some other characteristics of free colored populations, helped skew gender attitudes toward all free people of color. The first point to realize about this gender discourse that the remainder of this article will deconstruct is that it does not need to have much connection to actual behavior of free colored women in order to have power to define them for whites and justify oppression. Indeed, if white public opinion had been able to perceive the reality, they would have realized that free people of color were much like them in their attitudes and values, and this would have made racism and oppression much more difficult to conceive of and execute. But sadly for the people

of color, and happily for white elites who needed racism to unite whites behind their rule, the perception was very different from the reality. So for the remainder of this article we will be speaking of the racial attitudes held by most whites, in Europe and in the colonies, reinforced by the accounts of colonial observers and scientists and reports of travelers. Interestingly, colonial whites, who, one presumes, would have known better from direct observation of their own free colored clients, business contacts, neighbors, and relatives, nonetheless broadly accepted the stereotypes and repeated them to the uninitiated, while viewing those free people of color they actually knew as happy exceptions to the general rule.

The stereotype started with the assumption, often one that slipped into language, that free people of color were "freedmen," that is, former slaves who had gained their freedom. This was in fact untrue of many, a majority in most places by the 18th century, who were born free. But combining this assumption with the observed fact that more adult women than men received MANUMISSION, white society was able to convince itself that most free people of color had gained their freedom in exchange for sexual favors, either by themselves or by their mothers or other female relatives. In truth, a higher percentage of adults receiving manumission were women, in part because they had relationships with white men but also because women in slavery had more access to money through their dominance of small retail, and in addition because families would often choose to ransom a woman in order to gain the freedom of her future children. But the assumption, only partly true even of those who had gained their freedom, naturally compromised the sexual honor of the whole group, in an era that prized female chastity. Free colored men were characterized as dependent on their womenfolk and complaisant in their sexual misconduct.

Women also had more authority within free colored families than white women had in white society for a number of reasons. The occupations that were open to them gave them independent sources of income that would not have been available to most white women. In those cases where there was a long-standing relationship with a white man, in general the couple would not be married. In some countries, including the United States, marriage of members of different racial groups was prohibited by law, and in other places, such as the British Caribbean or the French colonial world, it was lawful but strongly discouraged. If the parents were not married, the children were legally under the authority of their mothers until they were adults. It was very common in the French, Spanish, and Portuguese colonies for fathers of illegitimate children to give the mothers some assets, such as land and slaves, to enable them to support the children. This was a legal requirement in FRANCE. This property would commonly be managed by adult sons but owned by the mother. The subjection of sons to their mother's authority was a further challenge to patriarchal gender roles, especially in Latin countries with a tradition of machismo. So alongside the stereotype that free people of color were sexually promiscuous and owed their advancement to the sexual prowess of their women, a second stereotype, equally loosely grounded in reality, accused their men of being weak and allowing women too much authority over them.

This gendered view of free people of color did not have to be explicit for it to be powerful. That is, ordinary white people did not go around saying to themselves that free colored men were all weak and womanish and free colored women were of loose sexual morals and breakers of traditional gender roles. Sometimes these arguments were made explicitly, in travelers' accounts or popular political discourse. However, the usually unspoken assumption had a real impact on behavior: laws, public opinion, even governmental decisions. So, for example, many places used free colored men as MILITIA or slave catchers, but it was unusual to allow them to be leaders or to make them responsible for guarding prisons. The harshness necessary for a leader or someone responsible for prisoners was incompatible with their presumed effeminate nature. When the Saint-Domingue free men of color said they should be allowed to vote, citing their militia service as proof of their devotion to the common good and usefulness to society, the white public reacted with brutal violence, killing a number of free colored men in pogroms and then inflicting barbaric public torture and execution on the free colored rebels VINCENT OGÉ and JEAN-BAPTISTE CHAVANNES. The spokesmen for the white colonists in the French National Assembly argued that free colored men were unable to exercise the franchise because they lacked the necessary republican manly virtues.

The gendered discourse about free people of color did not end with slavery. Indeed, it has proven to be one of the most enduring elements of racist attitudes, both in the United States and throughout the Americas. Women of color are stereotyped as helpful "mammies" or promiscuous "ghetto girls" in nostalgic novels, hip-hop videos, *corridas*, and other products of popular culture. Men of color are equally stereotyped as sexually promiscuous and preternaturally masculine, but lazy, flighty, devoted to comforts and consumer products, and incapable of truly manly devotion to a family. Attitudes and values are often the last things to change in a society, long after economic relations, laws, and even informal social exclusion have died unlamented deaths.

Stewart R. King

FURTHER READING
Beckles, Hilary McD. *Centering Woman: Gender Discourses in Caribbean Slave Society.* Kingston, Jamaica: I. Randle, 1999.
Gaspar, David Barry, and Darlene Hine, eds. *More than Chattel: Black Women and Slavery in the Americas.* Bloomington: Indiana University Press, 1996.

GEORGIA

Spaniards led by Hernando de Soto in 1540 were the first group of Europeans to visit what is now the U.S. state of Georgia. De Soto described the Mound Builder Indian villages that existed in the area. Other Indian tribes, including the Cherokee and Creek nations, later occupied parts of Georgia. Spain established missionary settlements along the Georgia coast in 1566, but the settlements did not last long after the English colony of SOUTH CAROLINA was established in the 1670s. Named after King George II, the British colony of Georgia was established in 1733 to act as a deterrent to Spanish growth from their bases farther south, in today's FLORIDA. It was the last of the original Thirteen Colonies that would later join to fight against BRITAIN in the WAR OF AMERICAN INDEPENDENCE, 1775–83.

Today, Georgia is bordered on the north by TENNESSEE and NORTH CAROLINA, on the east by the Atlantic Ocean and South Carolina, on the south and southwest by Florida, and on the west by ALABAMA. The northern part of the state is mountainous, and the Blue Ridge Mountains, part of the mountain system known as the Appalachians, are part of the state. Much of Georgia has a subtropical climate with hot and humid summers and mild winters; the northern parts of the state are much cooler and receive snow and ice during winter months. The state is often the victim of tornadoes and, as do other states that border the Atlantic coast, faces hurricanes. The southern coastal regions are fertile agricultural areas, producing many of the crops of the plantation complex including rice, cotton, INDIGO CULTIVATION, tobacco growing, and some SUGAR CULTIVATION. The interior regions were suitable for COTTON CULTIVATION once technologies to process the crop, especially the cotton gin, were created. Georgia was well suited by geography to be a prosperous part of the plantation Americas.

Initial Colonization Efforts in Georgia and British Rule

The first European settlers in what is now Georgia were Spanish missionaries who sailed to Georgia in 1566 and established many missions, primarily along the Atlantic coast of Georgia, in the years that followed. After the Carolinas (which later became the states of North Carolina and South Carolina) were founded and settled by English colonists in the 1670s, the territory between Florida and the Carolinas was the site of many battles as Spanish and English forces contended for control over the area. Carolinians with help from Indians destroyed the Spanish missionary settlements in the early 1700s, but the battles among Spanish, British, and French over boundaries continued for decades. After the War of Jenkins' Ear in 1742 between the British and Spanish, Spain never returned to Georgia, and the controversy was ended decisively in 1763 with the Treaty of Paris, which gave Florida to the British.

The first lasting settlement in Georgia resulted from a charter issued on June 8, 1732. The British government and trustees of the Georgia colony had several goals for the colony: They hoped the colony would help protect South Carolina from encroachment or invasion from Spanish Florida, create another market for British exports, supply manufacturers in Britain with products such as silk and wine, provide a place to settle for European Protestants who were being persecuted, and remove the poor and unemployed from Britain. James Edward Oglethorpe is known as the founder of the colony of Georgia, and his original, albeit unrealized, plan was to use the colony as a haven for people who had been put in debtor's prison.

The first group of settlers arrived in Georgia on February 12, 1733, and settled the land that became the city of Savannah. Oglethorpe led the group of 114 and, as the only trustee present in the colony, functioned as its governor although he never had that title. Under the colony's charter and the laws established soon after settlement, settlers were limited to owning no more than 500 acres, religious freedom was assured to all but Catholics, and slavery and liquor were prohibited in the colony.

Under the restrictions, the colony grew slowly, although settlements (at Augusta and Ebenezer, for instance) and defensive forts (e.g., Fort Frederica on St. Simons Island) were established. Most settlers believed that slaves were needed to develop the colony and that changes were needed in landownership rules. A few slaves did enter the colony at this time. Georgians simply maneuvered around the rules by "renting" blacks for life from South Carolinians.

The colony began to grow more quickly in the early 1750s after two changes. In 1750, settlers in Georgia were allowed to own slaves, and in 1752, Georgia became a royal colony. Settlers in Georgia could now elect an assembly; the British king, however, still appointed the governor. The major products of the colony were rice (grown along the coast), indigo, lumber, and wheat (grown inland). There was also a lucrative fur trade with Indians.

In 1754, the SEVEN YEARS' WAR, known in North America as the French and Indian War, began in PENN-SYLVANIA, and the hostilities between France and Britain soon spread to Europe. While Georgia did not play a large part in the war, it did benefit from it through an increase in its lands, which grew again when the Cherokee and Creek nations ceded land to Georgia.

In 1765, in part to help pay for the expensive Seven Years' War, Britain passed the Stamp Act. Georgia was the only colony to support the act (albeit inconsistently), and later Georgia would be the last colony to support the cause of American independence.

By 1775, Georgia had grown dramatically. It had a population of approximately 50,000, approximately half of whom were slaves. The number of plantations worked by slaves increased throughout the period that Georgia was a royal colony. New settlers began establishing plantations along Georgia's rivers and in time would grow cotton, tobacco, and peaches. Some of these planters spent little time at their plantations.

The slaves who worked these plantations had been imported from rice-growing regions in Africa; the knowledge of these slaves was instrumental in the success of rice production in Georgia: The coast of South Carolina and Georgia became known as the "Rice Coast." These slaves developed a unique culture known as the Gullah or Geechee culture, which has many roots in the culture of SIERRA LEONE; many of its cultural expressions and traditions are still in existence among descendants who live along the coast today.

Revolution, the United States, and Georgia Statehood

In 1776, Georgia joined the rest of the original Thirteen Colonies in signing the Declaration of Independence, but in the revolution that followed, Georgia's participation was not as great as the other colonies' (perhaps because of its relative youth). Savannah itself was captured by British forces in December 1778 and remained under British control until the end of the war, despite a combined French-American assault in 1779 that famously included the participation of many of the leaders of the future HAITIAN REVOLUTION as free colored soldiers in the French army. Georgia's slave population was reduced by at least 5,000 during this time: Many escaped in the disruption of war, and British forces promised freedom to escaped slaves. Many Georgia blacks fought in the Loyalist forces. These freedmen left Georgia for Great Britain, the Caribbean, or CANADA. In 1783, Great Britain recognized the independence of the United States after the American War of Independence.

Five years after the war ended, Georgia ratified the U.S. Constitution on January 2, 1788, the fourth state to do so. The borders of Georgia changed several times both before and after it became an American state. Under an ancient grant from Charles II, Georgia claimed ownership of what are now the states of Alabama and MISSISSIPPI, but Georgia ceded western lands to the federal government. Georgia later received lands from the government that had been ceded by South Carolina. Land-hungry settlers and gold speculators also pushed Indians off their territories, which added to Georgia's land. In 1838, the Cherokee were removed by force in what became known as the Trail of Tears, wherein 4,000 Cherokee died on the march to OKLAHOMA.

In 1793, Eli Whitney invented the cotton gin, transforming cotton growing over the next few decades and increasing its production throughout Georgia and the South.

As cotton production increased, slavery became institutionalized. By 1860, there were more than 450,000 slaves in Georgia; the total population of Georgia was slightly above one million. As settlers became wealthier in the 1840s and 1850s, notions of white supremacy were strengthened and used to defend and rationalize slavery, and those notions (underlined by economic reliance on slavery) help explain the support for secession before the Civil War.

Free People of Color and the Rise of Racial Discrimination

After Georgia became a royal colony, settlers elected an assembly, and one of the first acts of the assembly was to pass a slave or "black" code in January 1755. While the code provided some protection to the slave (it limited the number of hours a slave could work to 16 hours a day and indicated that slaves should be provided with food and clothing), it also included a number of rules that revealed the fear of uprising. Slaves could receive the death penalty for inciting insurrections, setting fire to property, or poisoning a white person; slaves could not have liquor or be taught to read or write, and they could be punished for assembling in groups.

During colonial times, the number of free people of color grew through MANUMISSION by white owners (who sometimes freed mistresses and illegitimate children), through self-purchase by slaves, and through other options available to slaves. Occasionally, slaves might be freed by military service, by their owners' wills, or after a period of service. Slaves also became free in illegal ways—running away and then LIVING "AS FREE." Some slaves escaped to Indian lands or to Spanish Florida.

In general, the status of free people of color and that of slaves did not differ greatly in Georgia. Free people of color were required to have a white guardian and to register with the state. Laws that applied to slaves in Georgia usually applied to free people of color, as well, and free

people of color were threatened with slavery as punishment for some offenses, including harboring RUNAWAY SLAVES.

During the War of Independence, slaves (often escapees) worked as guides, informers, couriers, and spies for the British. They also fought with the British, and a number of runaway slaves who had supported the British chose to remain in Savannah at the conclusion of the war. These slaves did not all reenter slavery peacefully; instead, some formed groups who lived along the Savannah River and raided settlements, sometimes killing whites (see also MAROONS). The Georgia MILITIA finally destroyed these maroon societies in 1786.

In North Georgia, near Cave Spring, the community Chubbtown was founded in the 1860s by free people of color, specifically the Chubb family. The town included farms, mills, and stores, and it had a post office. Chubb Methodist Episcopal Church was built in 1870.

Religion was important to free people of color and slaves at this time. The First African Baptist Church, arguably the first black Baptist congregation in the country, was founded in Savannah in 1777 (see also BAPTISTS AND PIETISTS). The first black missionary in Georgia is generally acknowledged to be George Liele, who was born a slave and later freed. He also became an ordained minister and preached to both slave and white congregations.

By 1790, there were about 400 free people of color in Georgia, and more arrived after the 1792 slave revolt began in SAINT-DOMINGUE. Most free people of color resided in urban areas, especially Washington, Savannah, and Augusta. The trades and professions that free people of color could enter were limited (for example, they could not practice medicine), but some exceptions were made. Generally, men worked in skilled trades (as barbers or tailors, for instance). Women often worked as cooks or seamstresses. A few of these free people of color were landowners and had slaves of their own. Charles Odingsells, for instance, owned three plantations and 73 slaves. The table below charts the evolution of the state's black population after U.S. independence.

As did other Southern states, Georgia attempted to limit the number of free blacks in the state and passed a number of laws to achieve this goal. In 1801, a new law provided that slaves could be manumitted only through an act of the Georgia legislature. This law was later revised to allow manumission in wills, but only if funds for transportation were provided for the newly freed to leave the state. In 1818, a new law prohibited the entry of free blacks from other states (similar laws were passed in the 1830s and 1850s, suggesting that the 1818 law was not enforced consistently). In 1859, manumission by will was prohibited. Further, freedmen were subject to being arrested

AFRICAN-AMERICAN POPULATION OF GEORGIA, 1790–1900

Year	Slaves	Free People of Color	Free People of Color as a Percentage of Total Population	Total Population
1790	29,264	398	0.5%	82,548
1800	59,699	1,919	1.2%	162,686
1810	105,218	1,801	0.7%	252,433
1820	189,656	2,166	0.6%	340,939
1830	217,531	2,486	0.5%	516,823
1840	280,944	2,753	0.4%	691,392
1850	381,682	2,931	0.3%	906,405
1860	462,198	3,500	0.3%	1,057,286
1870		545,142	46.0%	1,184,109
1880		725,133	47.0%	1,542,180
1890		858,815	46.7%	1,837,353
1900		1,034,813	46.7%	2,216,331

and returned to slavery. Also in 1859, free people of color who were judged to be vagrants (defined rather broadly) would be sold into slavery. Local laws were sometimes even worse.

Free people of color could own and inherit property, but they had few civil rights—they could not vote or serve in the militia or on juries. Laws also limited their actions. After 1829, it was illegal to teach free people of color to read or write. For violating the law, whites could be fined, and free people of color could be fined and whipped. This law limiting literacy may have been in response to the several schools that had been created for free black children in Savannah in and after 1818. Some of these schools continued to operate underground after the 1829 law.

In 1831, after the Nat Turner slave revolt in Virginia, legislators enacted several laws, which limited the rights of free blacks. In 1833, Georgia's General Assembly prohibited free people of color to own, use, or carry firearms. In 1840, free people of color were limited in terms of where they could live within cities. The firearm law was reaffirmed in 1848, and the Georgia courts declared in *Cooper and Worsham v. Savannah* that "free persons of color have never been recognized here as citizens."

The laws of Georgia were successful in limiting the growth of the free black population: By the time the Civil War began in 1861, there were only around 3,500 free people of color in Georgia. Ultimately, racial discrimination against free people of color arose from various factors. Some contemporaries believed that free people of color

were a challenge to the Southern way of life: To their way of thinking, the institution of slavery was needed for survival. Many were fearful of slave insurrections and believed that free people of color either were directly responsible for slave revolts or helped encourage slaves to rebel.

The Civil War and Reconstruction
Georgia seceded from the Union in January 1861 and joined the Confederate States of America along with the other Southern states that had seceded from the Union. As in other Southern states, one of the major motives for secession can be traced to economic reliance on the institution of slavery, but both cultural and economic divisions divided the North and South.

Many major battles of the AMERICAN CIVIL WAR, 1861–65, occurred in Georgia, including battles at Atlanta and Chickamauga. The most destructive episode in the Civil War became known as General William T. Sherman's (1820–91) March to the Sea, during which a broad swath of land from Atlanta to Savannah was rendered a wasteland in 1864. Notably, after the Union army gained control of the Florida and Georgia coasts in 1862, General Thomas Sherman (1813–79) gave the barrier islands to freedmen, and four settlements, generally composed of families, were established on Cumberland Island. A unit of black soldiers recruited from among these refugees on St. Simon's Island, the 33rd U.S. Colored Troops, included in its ranks the free colored nurse and laundress SUSIE BAKER KING TAYLOR. The Civil War ended in the Confederacy's defeat in 1865, and Georgia was crippled in the process—tens of thousands died in the fighting or from disease; cities, railroads, and factories were destroyed.

What followed the war was the period known as Reconstruction, wherein Southern states that had seceded worked to regain their status, and slavery was abolished (*see also* RECONSTRUCTION IN THE UNITED STATES). During Reconstruction, Georgia and other Southern states were placed under military rule, and the military government initially thwarted Georgia's attempts at reinstituting a black code in the postwar environment by giving freedmen the right to vote (*see also* BLACK CODES IN THE UNITED STATES and CIVIL RIGHTS LAWS IN THE UNITED STATES AFTER 1865). Black males could vote, and, for a brief time, they made some progress in the state, holding positions of power in government. In 1868, for instance, 29 blacks were elected to the State House of Representatives, and three blacks were elected to the Senate. These blacks were initially expelled by conservatives who claimed that while freedmen had the right to vote, they did not have the right to be elected to office. After federal intervention, the black legislators were admitted to their seats.

Georgia was readmitted to the Union on July 15, 1870, after periods of military rule, but it was soon clear that the state would not willingly create a world where freedmen shared equality with whites or, for that matter, where freedmen had very many rights at all.

Democrats in Georgia began working toward disenfranchising blacks, first using violent intimidation tactics and then institutionalizing disenfranchisement through literacy tests, property requirements, grandfather clauses, and poll taxes. They were successful, and Jim Crow laws that resulted in "separate but equal" transportation, schools, and other public services became common throughout the South. Many blacks moved to towns in the years following the Civil War but found overcrowding and shortages of food. The FREEDMEN'S BUREAU worked to return black labor to the fields, and sharecropping developed as a system that replaced slavery; both blacks and poor whites participated and fell further into debt each year.

Some blacks did work to improve conditions for their fellow Georgians. For example, Henry McNeal Turner (born free in South Carolina), a minister in the AFRICAN METHODIST EPISCOPAL CHURCH, helped found the Republican Party of Georgia and, dissatisfied with the progress of equality, began promoting the Back to Africa movement; Tunis Campbell (1812–91, born free in NEW JERSEY) supervised land claims for the Freedmen's Bureau in Georgia, purchased some land, established an association of black landowners, and made some political gains (he became a Georgia state senator), but he was persecuted for his efforts by whites and jailed; William J. Claghorn (1822–78, born a slave in Georgia but freed before the Civil War) was a businessman who promoted better education for blacks.

Ultimately, however, in the late 1800s and early 1900s, under the weight of repressive laws and severe poverty, most blacks found their condition was little improved. Hundreds of blacks in Georgia were also the victims of lynching, often justified by alleged sexual advances made by black men toward white women or by the alleged murder of a white man by a black man. The KU KLUX KLAN was active in Georgia by the late 1860s, and the Confederate general John B. Gordon, reputed leader of the Georgia Klan, was elected governor in 1886. The deadliest incident of racial violence was the September 1906 Atlanta Race Riot, wherein mobs of white men, inflamed by months of sensationalist newspaper articles, attacked and murdered blacks in the streets and in their homes. The state militia was ordered to search blacks and their homes for weapons and to confiscate those weapons.

Indeed, disenfranchisement and discrimination lasted well into the 20th century and were factors in what became known as the First and Second Great Migrations. In the 1920s and 1930s, and again from 1940 to 1970, hundreds of thousands of African Americans migrated from Georgia to industrial cities, usually in the North, where greater opportunities for education, representation, and advancement could be found.

Beginning in the 1960s, however, Georgia made a number of advances in civil rights, and the state capital, Atlanta, became the headquarters for the Civil Rights movement. Georgia eventually came to stand as a symbol of the New South.

Summer Leibensperger

FURTHER READING
Bellamy, Donnie D. "The Legal Status of Black Georgians during the Colonial and Revolutionary Eras." *Journal for Negro History* 74, no. 1 (Winter–Autumn, 1989): 1–10
Berlin, Ira. *Slaves without Masters: The Free Negro in the Antebellum South.* New York: W. W. Norton, 1974.
Bond, Bradley G. *Political Culture in the Nineteenth-Century South.* Baton Rouge: Louisiana State University Press, 1995.
Coulter, E. Merton. *Georgia: A Short History.* Chapel Hill: University of North Carolina Press, 1960.
Martin, Harold H. *Georgia: A Bicentennial History.* New York: W. W. Norton, 1977.
Mohr, Clarence L. *On the Threshold of Freedom: Masters and Slaves in Civil War Georgia.* Athens: University of Georgia Press, 1986.
Smith, Julia Floyd. *Slavery and Rice Culture in Low Country Georgia: 1750–1860.* Knoxville: University of Tennessee Press, 1985.
Wood, Betty. *Slavery in Colonial Georgia.* Athens: University of Georgia Press, 1984.

GIBBS, MIFFLIN WISTAR   (1823–1915) *American abolitionist, entrepreneur, attorney, and diplomat*

One of the more remarkable figures of the 19th and early 20th centuries, Mifflin Wistar Gibbs lived a rich and varied life that encompassed numerous careers and pursuits. He was an abolitionist, businessman, attorney, judge, diplomat, and banker. Mifflin Gibbs was born on April 17, 1823, in PHILADELPHIA, PENNSYLVANIA, the son of Jonathan C. Gibbs, a minister in the Wesleyan Methodist Church, and Maria Gibbs, both free blacks.

As a young boy, Gibbs became an apprentice carpenter while participating in a Philadelphia literary society for his education. At the age of 12, he visited MARYLAND and saw firsthand the horrors of plantation slavery. This early exposure to slavery awakened his awareness of injustice, and he soon began developing a philosophy of self-help and practical training. In the 1840s, Gibbs met the abolitionist FREDERICK DOUGLASS, who inspired him

Mifflin W. Gibbs (1823–1915) was an early pioneer in California and western Canada. He established California's first black newspaper and led the fight for civil rights there in the 1850s. After the Civil War, he settled in Arkansas and served as an elected state judge. He was a pillar of the Arkansas Republican Party and held many positions in the federal government, including service as U.S. consul in Madagascar. *(The Granger Collection, New York)*

to become an agent for the Underground Railroad and whom he joined on an antislavery lecture tour. In 1850, Gibbs moved to San Francisco, CALIFORNIA, where, in partnership with another free black man, he opened a boot and shoe business. With other black leaders, he published resolutions protesting discriminatory laws in 1851, helped to establish the *Mirror of the Times*, California's first black newspaper in 1856, and fought the California poll tax in 1858. When California ordered black residents to remove their children from public school in 1858, Gibbs and others relocated to Victoria, British Columbia. The governor of British Columbia at the time was Sir JAMES DOUGLAS, a free man of color from Guyana, who encouraged black immigration. In 1867, Gibbs began supplying Fraser River miners with provisions and shipping anthracite from Queen Charlotte's Island to Victoria. In addition, he was twice elected to the Victoria city council.

In 1859, he married Maria Alexander, an Oberlin College (OHIO) student. His wife and children returned to Oberlin in 1867, and in 1870, Gibbs joined them to study law. Afterward, he relocated to Little Rock, ARKANSAS; was admitted to the bar in 1872; and became active in the Arkansas Republican Party. He supported President ULYSSES S. GRANT's reelection in 1872 and, the following year, became the nation's first elected black municipal judge as Little Rock's police judge.

Deeply involved in Republican politics, Gibbs was a delegate to all Republican national conventions from 1876 to 1904, except 1888, and was a presidential elector in 1876. He was appointed registrar of the Little Rock land office by President Hayes in 1877, and after touring KANSAS to assess black immigration in 1879, he became a cautious supporter of the EXODUSTER MOVEMENT. He served as secretary of the Arkansas Republican state committee from 1887 to 1897 and receiver of public monies in 1889.

In October 1897, President McKinley named Gibbs U.S. consul to Tamatave, Madagascar, after the French defeated the Malagasy government and annexed the country. As consul (1898–1901), he reestablished good relations with French authorities and expressed cautious optimism about the benefits of French rule. Nevertheless, he was unimpressed by conditions there.

Returning to the United States, Gibbs immersed himself in economic activities to improve conditions among blacks. In August 1901, he was a delegate of the National Negro Business Men's League. In January 1903, he became president of Little Rock's new black-owned Capital City Savings Bank. Despite distinguished black leadership and substantial deposits, the bank collapsed in June 1908 because of mismanagement and fraud. Gibbs and others were indicted by a grand jury, but he settled out of court and saved most of his personal fortune. Nevertheless, his reputation had been damaged. He lived his last years in Little Rock, where he died on July 11, 1915.

Gibbs's life demonstrated the transition from the 19th-century optimism of Frederick Douglass to the more sober views that developed with Booker T. Washington. Gibbs emphasized the importance of black participation in politics, the need for education and a trade, and hard work and entrepreneurial activity as the road to material success. As an entrepreneur, an apostle of self-help, and a Republican Party loyalist, Gibbs reflected a sense of optimism that drove American developments throughout a turbulent century.

Kenneth Blume

FURTHER READING
Dillard, Tom W. *The Black Moses of the West: A Biography of Mifflin Wistar Gibbs, 1823–1915.* M.A. thesis, University of Arkansas, Fayetteville, 1975.
———."'Golden Prospects and Fraternal Amenities': Mifflin W. Gibbs's Arkansas Years." *Arkansas Historical Quarterly* 35 (Winter 1976): 307–333.
Gibbs, Mifflin Wistar. *Shadow and Light. An Autobiography with Reminiscences of the Last and Present Century.* Washington, D.C., 1902. Reprint, Lincoln: University of Nebraska Press, 1995.
Lapp, Rudolph M. *Blacks in Gold Rush California.* New Haven, Conn.: Yale University Press, 1977.
Woodson, Carter. "The Gibbs Family." *Negro History Bulletin* 11 (October 1947): 3–12, 22.

GILL, ANN   (1781–1865) *Barbadian religious leader*

Ann Gill (née Jordan), free woman of color, was born in BARBADOS in 1781. A stalwart member of the Methodist Church, Gill attracted the attention of the Barbadian civil authorities in 1824 when she assumed leadership of the Bridgetown Methodist congregation in the wake of the Methodist Chapel incident, in which an irate mob of white Barbadians demolished the Bridgetown Methodist Chapel and drove the minister off the island. For two years, Gill acted as the congregation's de facto leader, holding the embattled church together while asserting her right to worship as a Methodist. She was prosecuted by the Barbadian House of Assembly in 1825 and charged with the crime of holding illegal meetings in her home. Gill's case was cited by Thomas Buxton in the British House of Commons as an example of religious intolerance in the British West Indies. Gill's case was eventually dismissed because of the lack of evidence against her.

Ann Gill is one of a handful of free women of color in the British West Indies whose lives have been rescued from historical anonymity. Her father was Edward Jordan, a white man who resided in Barbados. To date, the identity of Gill's mother is unknown, save for the fact that she was a woman of color. Much of the first 18 years of Gill's life remains in obscurity, except that she lived in Bridgetown and was possibly cared for by an enslaved woman owned by her father. In 1799, Gill's father died, leaving her a substantial legacy, which secured her financial circumstances and ensured her position as a member of the propertied free colored community in Barbados. In 1809, she married Alexander George Gill, a free man of color. She was widowed in 1814. Four years later, Gill became associated with the Methodist Church in Bridgetown, where her name appears in the church annals as a financial contributor to the Methodist Chapel building fund. However, it was not until 1820, when the church was under the leadership of the Reverend William Shrewsbury, that Gill became a member and quickly rose to the rank of class leader.

Gill is remembered by the Methodist community in Barbados as a devout member of the church, who "rescued Methodism" in the island. Recently, some historians have portrayed Gill as an antislavery activist who used her platform in the Methodist Church to speak out against slavery. Others have tried to draw connections between Gill's prosecution by the state and the state's persecution of free people of color who at the time were waging a campaign to expand their civil rights. What is clear is that Gill stepped outside the prescribed box allotted to her as a free woman of color and demanded that the white Barbadian patriarchal power structure respect her rights, as a British subject, to freedom of worship. Gill died in 1865. In 1998, the Barbadian government named her a national heroine for her "courage, perseverance, and commitment to religious freedom."

Janette Gayle

FURTHER READING
Beckles, Hilary McD. *Centering Woman: Gender Discourses in Caribbean Slave Society.* Kingston, Jamaica: Ian Randle, 1999.
Handler, Jerome C. *The Unappropriated People: Freedmen in the Slave Society of Barbados.* Baltimore: Johns Hopkins University Press, 1974.

GONÇALVES TEIXEIRA E SOUSA, ANTÔNIO
(1812–1861) *Brazilian writer*

Antônio Gonçalves was an important Brazilian author of the mid-19th century. He is an outstanding example of the important role played by people of color in the artistic and creative community of BRAZIL in the early national period. His work contained explicit criticism of white racism and slavery, and he was probably the most dissident of the imperial period intellectuals. As an explicit critic of Brazilian society, Gonçalves was ahead of his time; most mixed-race intellectuals were loyal supporters of the monarchy.

The son of a Portuguese merchant and his black mistress, Antônio Gonçalves Teixeira e Sousa was born in Cabo Frio, Rio de Janeiro, Brazil, sometime in 1812. When his father fell on hard times in the 1830s, Gonçalves was forced to apprentice as a carpenter and quit school. He managed to continue studying part-time after his father's death in 1835, thanks to the assistance of Inácio Cardoso da Silva, a local surgeon and amateur poet. Later, Gonçalves was to collect and publish his benefactor's poems in tribute to his memory. In 1840, Gonçalves settled in the city of Rio de Janeiro, where he met the publisher Francisco de Paula Brito. He began writing poems for Paula Brito's magazines. Brito, as was most of the free colored literary and intellectual leadership of Brazil, was a monarchist who believed that the system offered the best hope for blacks to advance, even though it maintained slavery and racial discrimination. Gonçalves disagreed with his patron and friend, instead upholding a tradition of black resistance and looking to a future of republican equality and racial justice. He published epic historical poems such as *A independência do Brasil* (*The Independence of Brazil*, 1847–55) and historical novels such as *Gonzaga ou a conjuração de Tiradentes* (*Gonzaga, or Tiradentes's Conspiracy*, 1848–51), based on a 1798 conspiracy in Minas Gerais against colonial rule. His *Três dias de um noivado* (*Three Days of a Marriage*, 1844) includes condemnations of racial discrimination in Brazil and reveals the existence of a dissident black and mulatto voice in early Brazilian literature. He supported himself as a teacher and eventually obtained minor civil service positions, which allowed him to devote more time to writing. He died on December 1, 1861.

Hendrik Kraay

FURTHER READING

Treece, David. *Exiles, Allies, Rebels: Brazil's Indianist Movement, Indigenist Politics, and the Imperial Nation-State.* Westport, Conn.: Greenwood, 2000.

GORDON, GEORGE WILLIAM   (1820–1865)
Jamaican landowner and political leader

George William Gordon was born in 1820 in St. Andrew Parish, JAMAICA, near Kingston. His father was Joseph Gordon, a Scottish plantation manager, who owned a good deal of his own land and many slaves. His mother was one of those slaves, with whom Joseph Gordon had at least four children. Many white fathers in Jamaica neglected their mixed-race slave children, but Joseph Gordon freed his son George and arranged for him to be educated. The boy grew up with his godfather, James Daley, a Baptist missionary. Gordon became a Baptist in the 1830s, when in the wake of the Baptist War (1831–82), this was a dangerous choice. (*See also* BAPTISTS AND PIETISTS.) But he maintained good relations with his father and ultimately inherited one of his plantations, in the St. Andrew Hills just outside Kingston, the capital.

George Gordon built a Baptist church in Kingston and reached out to the poor blacks of the region. The church grew and established branches in other areas of the colony. Gordon ordained a number of deacons, including, most notably, Paul Bogle, of St. Thomas parish at the eastern tip of the island. Gordon also worked to provide more concrete benefits to the poor black population by buying up abandoned land and renting or selling to black squatters at reasonable rates. He also organized a number of small mutual aid societies that had been created by the newly freed through Baptist churches or other community groups into the Mutual Assistance Association, an early life insurance company. In these ways he acquired a following of clients, many of whom were also coreligionists.

Gordon became involved in colonial politics in 1844 when he ran for the Kingston city council. He was elected and served most of the rest of his life in this body. He served several times as mayor of Kingston. In 1862, he was elected to the colonial assembly. In both places, he was a strong supporter of the land rights of poor black peasants. In the aftermath of the abolition of slavery in 1833, many former slaves took up unused land on plantations or public lands that were not being farmed and established peasant farms. When the colonial economy began to revive in the 1850s, the legal owners of these lands often returned to dispossess the black farmers. The farmers' protests unsettled the politics of the colony more than once. Finally, in 1865, a protest movement among black Baptist farmers in Morant Bay led to riots and the death of 15 prominent local whites and dozens of black protesters. The government decided that Gordon's preaching and political agitation had stirred up the unrest and decided to make an example of him. He, Deacon Paul Bogle, and 17 other radical political and religious leaders were executed on October 23, 1865.

Gordon's life illustrates many important characteristics of the lives of Jamaican free people of color. As a wealthy, educated, mixed-race landowner, he, in some colonies in the Americas, would have been divided from poor black farmers by racial and class antagonisms. In Jamaica, however, with its history of harsh enforcement of a binary color line created by the "ONE DROP RULE OF RACIAL IDENTITY," Gordon's solidarity with the black peasantry was not so unusual. Moreover, Gordon was a Baptist. The Baptists

George William Gordon (1820–65) depicted on a Jamaican banknote. Although very light-skinned and the son of a wealthy white planter, Gordon suffered from racial discrimination and was a tireless activist for the rights of poor black Jamaicans. He was executed in 1865 in retaliation for riots and strikes by the poor black workers he championed. *(Georgios Kollidas/Shutterstock)*

particular individual leader much more important to voting behavior than any variables of class or race.

Stewart R. King

FURTHER READING

"Jamaica Declared Gordon a 'National Hero' and Published a Short Biography." Available online. URL: http://www.jis.gov.jm/special–sections/Heroes/Heroes.htm.George. Accessed December 25, 2010.

Johnson, Howard. "From Pariah to Patriot: The Posthumous Career of George William Gordon." Available online. URL: www.kitlv-journals.nl/index.php/nwig/article/viewFile/3594/4353. Accessed December 27, 2010.

Sherlock, Philip, and Hazel Bennett. *The Story of the Jamaican People.* New York: Marcus Weiner, 1998.

GRAND UNITED ORDER OF ODD FELLOWS
African-American fraternal organization, United States

The Odd Fellows are an international fraternal organization, originally organized in Britain in the 18th century. They claim descent from medieval guilds and may have some connection with 17th- and 18th-century tradesmen's organizations. Odd Fellows lodges coexisted with Masons and other secret fraternal lodges in the 18th and early 19th century throughout the Atlantic world. (*See also* FREEMASONRY.) There were more than half a million Odd Fellows members worldwide at the beginning of the 20th century, of whom about 70,000 were African Americans in the United States.

The Odd Fellows in the United States, like other fraternal organizations, were unwilling to accept free people of color into their lodges in the early 19th century. In 1842, Peter Ogden, a free colored sailor, probably from New York, joined the British Victoria lodge of Liverpool, part of the Manchester Unity group of Odd Fellows lodges in the United Kingdom (now officially referred to as the Grand United Order). Ogden drew a number of New York free black men into a new lodge associated with the British organization and not connected in any way with American Odd Fellows lodges, which had separated from the British organization earlier in the century (now known as the Independent Order of Odd Fellows).

Ogden, like many black MERCHANT SEAMEN of the time, was a relatively well-paid and respected member of the black community. However, the Odd Fellows under his leadership stressed the importance of brotherhood among people of all social classes and skin colors. Unlike other elite black fraternal organizations, the Odd Fellows accepted poorer blacks and provided scholarships and other assistance to members to help them rise in society.

and other radical Protestant churches played an important role in uniting poor Jamaicans. The Baptist belief, drawn from Calvinist roots, that anyone could be saved and conversely that anyone could be damned, combined with the often fairly loose morals of the Jamaican white elites, gave black Baptists a sense of moral superiority that empowered them to speak out about racial oppression. The churches were also protected places for oppressed people to meet and plan for a future with less oppression—a role that they have filled in many other places throughout the history of Latin America. Gordon's political career illustrates the role that patron-client relations played in the politics of Latin America in the 19th century. Gordon's supporters certainly saw him as a sympathetic figure because of his black ancestry, and he did work for their interests in protecting land tenure. However, he was also a landowner, and many of his constituents were his tenants. Nonetheless, he gained their support, across lines of class and what we might think of in our modern perspective as economic interest, because they thought of him as a patron who would look out for them in particular. Politics was, and is still to a considerable extent, personal, with the individual voter's relationship with a

The first Odd Fellows lodge, number 646, established in New York City in 1843, was soon joined by a wave of new lodges open to blacks across the North and Midwest. Although the order was officially open to all races, all early members that we know of were blacks. Today, Grand United lodges in the United States are integrated, as are other Odd Fellows groups. After the AMERICAN CIVIL WAR, 1861–65, the Odd Fellows created lodges in the South. By 1900, there were 2,253 Grand United lodges in the United States. True to the Odd Fellows' core value of cross-class brotherhood, Odd Fellows lodges in the South accepted newly freed men as well as former free people of color and worked hard for the social advancement of all blacks. The Odd Fellows were particularly known for establishment of homes for black widows and orphans, providing social services that were very important, especially for Southern blacks who were excluded from government-provided facilities after the end of RECONSTRUCTION IN THE UNITED STATES. Between 1876 and 1936, the Odd Fellows distributed an estimated $247 million in social benefits.

Black fraternal organizations in general were essential institutions for creating black solidarity, organizing black communities, and recognizing community leaders. In the absence of formal participation in the institutions of the larger society, both during slavery and under Jim Crow, the lodge was a crucial community institution for the free people of color. The Odd Fellows, though not so well known as the PRINCE HALL Masons, were, because of their greater geographical spread and willingness to recruit among working-class blacks, very important elements of this group.

Stewart R. King

FURTHER READING

Brooks, Charles H. *The Official History and Manual of the Grand United Order of Odd Fellows in the United States*. Philadelphia, 1902. Available online. URL: http://books.google.com/books?id=Sj-jv2g7utcC&source=gbs_navlinks_s. Accessed December 29, 2010.

Skocpol, Theda, Ariane Liazos, and Marshall Ganz. *What a Mighty Power We Can Be: African American Fraternal Groups and the Struggle for Racial Equality*. Princeton, N.J.: Princeton University Press, 2006.

Tabbert, Mark A. "The Odd Fellows." Available online. URL: http://www.freemasons-freemasonry.com/tabbert5.html. Accessed December 23, 2010.

GRANT, ULYSSES S.   (1822–1885) *U.S. general and eighteenth president of the United States (1869–1877)*

Ulysses S. Grant was born on April 27, 1822, in Point Pleasant, OHIO, the son of a shopkeeper. His father was active in local politics as a Democrat, and the local congressman, Thomas Hamer, appointed Grant to the United States Military Academy at the age of 17. Grant graduated 21st of 39 in the class of 1843 and was posted to an infantry regiment. He opposed the MEXICAN-AMERICAN WAR, fearing that it would allow the opportunity for further expansion of slavery, but when war was declared, he went to MEXICO. He served with distinction, being present at all the major battles of the war and being twice promoted as a reward for his bravery. At the end of the war, he married Julia Dent, the daughter of a planter and slave owner from MISSOURI, and a relative of an important political family there.

Grant left the army in 1852 and tried several civilian occupations, without much success. He was working as a clerk in his father's store in Ohio when the AMERICAN CIVIL WAR, 1861–65, began. American military officers at the time were supposed to remain completely nonpartisan, but Grant's sympathies were with the Northern Democrats. Nevertheless, when war began, he immediately volunteered for service, becoming the recruiting and training officer for the state of ILLINOIS. He took command of troops in the field in fall 1861 and fought with distinction in KENTUCKY, TENNESSEE, and MISSISSIPPI. His victory in the campaign and siege of Vicksburg in 1863 was one of the turning points of the war. After victory in the Battle of Chattanooga in 1863, President ABRAHAM LINCOLN made him supreme commander of Union forces, with the rank of lieutenant general.

After the battle of Shiloh in April 1862, Grant became convinced that the war would be long and that no political solution was possible. He previously had opposed the inclusion of blacks as soldiers in the Union army because he knew the practice would enrage white Southerners. (*See also* REGULAR ARMY.) However, in summer 1862, he changed his policy and directed his officers to gather up all the black men in the regions they passed through who were willing to work against the Confederacy and enroll them in the army. At first, they were employed as labor units or to guard rear areas, but ultimately they made up as much as one-quarter of the Union army. When the Confederate army threatened to sell any captured black soldiers into slavery in 1863, Grant wrote to the Confederate general Robert E. Lee that the United States was bound to protect any soldiers wearing its uniform and that if any black U.S. soldiers were sold into slavery, an equal number of Southern prisoners would be put to hard labor in Northern prison camps. On the other hand, in the preparations for the Battle of the Crater in 1864, he sided with General George Meade, the commander of the Army of the Potomac, who had vetoed the use of black troops to make the breakthrough in what might have been the decisive blow against the Confederate army. The attack went forward with untrained white troops leading the charge. They blundered into the wrong area, were wrapped up by the Confederate defenders, and were slaughtered. The black soldiers who had originally trained for the mission were then sent in to rescue the survivors; they suffered heavy losses as well. Grant later admitted that he had made the wrong decision and said he had refused to send the black troops at first for fear that if they took heavy casualties he would have been accused of putting them in a hot spot because he did not care about black soldiers' lives.

After the war ended in 1865, Grant continued as commander of the U.S. Army and oversaw the occupation and pacification of the South. As white soldiers left the army, his troops became increasingly black. His relations with his black troops were always good, and he insisted that they be treated fairly.

In 1868, at the age of 46, Grant was elected president, serving until 1877. He was the youngest man up to that time to be elected. He pressed for an aggressive policy of RECONSTRUCTION IN THE UNITED STATES in the South, using federal troops to suppress the KU KLUX KLAN and guarantee blacks the right to vote. Under the Grant administration, black Republicans were elected for the first time to the U.S. Senate, House of Representatives, and state governorships in the South. His administration was marred by financial scandals and economic crisis, however, and by 1876, the Northern electorate was in the mood for a change. The election of 1876 resulted in a compromise in which federal troops were withdrawn from the South and Southern white elites were permitted to rescind the rights that the Reconstruction laws and constitutional amendments had granted to blacks. Within another decade, the Jim Crow system in the South would deprive the black population of its civil rights and much of the economic gains it had made up to that point.

Along with Lincoln, Grant was probably the most sympathetic president to black Americans before the 1940s. As was Truman, who desegregated the U.S. Army (again) in 1948 and took other important steps to support the Civil Rights movement, and Lincoln before him, Grant was from a border region and grew up with some unenlightened ideas about race. It is a tribute to his character and intelligence that he was so successful in overcoming those prejudices. The free black abolitionist FREDERICK DOUGLASS said of him that he "was right towards us" and called him a "benefactor" of African Americans. He died on July 23, 1885.

Stewart R. King

FURTHER READING

Grant, Ulysses S. *Personal Memoirs.* New York: C. L. Webster, 1885–86. Available online. URL: http://www.bartleby.com/1011/. Accessed December 27, 2010.

Simpson, Brooks D. "Quandaries of Command: Ulysses S. Grant and Black Soldiers." In *Union and Emancipation: Essays on Politics and Race in the Civil War Era,* edited by David Blight and Brooks Simpson, 123–152. Kent, Ohio: Kent State University Press, 1997.

GRÉGOIRE, HENRI (ABBÉ GRÉGOIRE)
(1750–1831) *French clergyman and abolitionist*

A fervent republican, the French Roman Catholic priest Abbé Henri-Baptiste Grégoire served as an outspoken leader of the FRENCH REVOLUTION and of the abolitionist cause in FRANCE, its colonies, and America.

The only child of modest artisan parents in Lorraine, France, Grégoire was born on December 4, 1750. Gregarious and precocious, Grégoire became a scholarship student and studied under both Jansenists and JESUITS. As a seminarian, Grégoire read voraciously, and through his social circles he was exposed to Enlightenment and Protestant values that would help shape his views on the enlightened religion movement he helped develop. After serving as a local clergyman, Grégoire entered public life and the national stage in 1789, with his appointment to the Estates General. He helped to prod the union of the three estates and to launch the French Revolution, a role immortalized by Jacques-Louis David in his famous painting *The Tennis Court Oath,* which prominently features Grégoire in his priestly robes. Within the Revolutionary coalition, Grégoire served as a Christianizing force, and in addition to eliminating regional dialects and enforcing standard French, extending citizenship to men regardless of wealth, and combating the counter-Revolution, he worked toward abolishing slavery. He held liberal positions, even by Revolutionary standards, championing rights for blacks, Jews, and women. He also supported reform of the ROMAN CATHOLIC CHURCH under the Civil Constitution of the Clergy (1790). When Napoléon signed a concordat with the Vatican in 1801 and repealed the Civil Constitution, Grégoire resigned his post as bishop, though he remained a devout member of the Catholic Church for the rest of his life.

Within the National Assembly, Grégoire advocated rights of free blacks in the colonies and encouraged his colleagues to apply the universal language of the rights of man to the entire French Empire. He adopted their cause after a series of eye-opening encounters with British and French abolitionists and mixed-race property holders from SAINT-DOMINGUE had alerted him to the human cost of the French colonial system in the West Indies. Grégoire bristled at reports of the 500,000 slaves in Saint-Domingue alone and of that colony's legal and social repression of even free blacks and those of mixed race, perpetrated in the pursuit of the island's SUGAR CULTIVATION, COFFEE CULTIVATION, and INDIGO CULTIVATION interests.

A contemporary engraving of Abbé Henri Grégoire (1750–1831), a prominent French clergyman and abolitionist. During the early stages of the French Revolution, Grégoire took up the cause of the free people of color in the French colonies and became a close friend and collaborator of free colored activists such as Vincent Ogé, Julien Raimond, and Jean-Baptiste Belley. Grégoire was a prominent advocate of the law granting equal rights to free people of color in the colonies, and after the Haitian Revolution, he worked with the newly independent Haitian government to seek diplomatic recognition and establish a just and stable government. *(Library of Congress)*

Grégoire therefore joined the newly created Société des Amis des Noirs. It was Grégoire who made the motion that the National Assembly adopted in May 1791, granting equal rights to free people of color in the colonies. A delegate to the National Convention from Blois, he supported the decision to abolish slavery in 1794, though he felt that a period of time would be required to "regenerate" former slaves before they could take their place as citizens.

Having traveled extensively through Europe from 1797 to 1805 and finding the prospects for republicanism bleak, he shifted his focus to the Americas. The unrest in Saint-Domingue that he had cataloged in 1789 bubbled to the surface in 1790, when first an unsuccessful uprising by free people of color, including Grégoire's ally VINCENT OGÉ, and then a successful slave rebellion led by TOUSSAINT LOUVERTURE sparked a struggle for power that eventually led to the colony's emancipation and independence in 1804 (see also HAITIAN REVOLUTION). Grégoire

was a supporter of the Saint-Domingue rebels throughout this period. After Napoleonic France rescinded the abolition of slavery in 1802, Haiti was the first country in the Western Hemisphere to enjoy a lasting end to slavery. During the course of the Napoleonic period, Grégoire continued to follow Haiti's cause peripherally. Before his engagement with Haitian affairs intensified after the restoration of royal rule in 1814, Grégoire established a following among emerging Haitian leaders by the progressive positions toward blacks that he articulated in early-19th-century pamphlets, essays, and books.

Grégoire contributed to the abolitionist cause in France and in the French colonies, but he also challenged accommodation of slavery in the United States by confronting its leaders. Scandalized by the young republic's protection of slavery by the three-fifths compromise in the U.S. Constitution, Grégoire corresponded with various abolitionist groups and, most significantly, with THOMAS JEFFERSON. Jefferson, whose *Notes on the State of Virginia* (1781; published in Paris in 1784) had insinuated that blacks were innately incapable of the intellectual capacity of whites, stung particularly because of his own efforts against the slave trade. In response, Grégoire countered these claims and fingered Jefferson in his important 1808 *De la literature des nègres*: "Who would dare . . . deny that all humans are variations on a single type, and who would claim that some of them are incapable of attaining civilization?" Only historic injustices and the brutality of slavery had hampered blacks, Grégoire responded: "What can become of individuals degraded below the level of brutes, overloaded with word, covered with rags, devoured with hunger, and torn by the bloody whip of their overseer for the slightest fault?" This book systematically refuted contemporary arguments about the inferiority of blacks, highlighting examples of achievement to illustrate parallel elements of intellect and civilization to those found in European societies. Grégoire highlighted the first settlements of self-governing freed slaves in JAMAICA and SIERRA LEONE, as well as the new nation of Haiti, to support his attack on the institution of slavery, the slave trade, and indeed the entire colonial system. Blacks, he insisted, could rule themselves. Because of the book's methodical documentation of the achievements of writers such as OLAUDAH EQUIANO, Phillis Wheatley, and IGNATIUS SÁNCHO, it is a pioneering text of African-American literary criticism. When the English edition appeared in 1810, it became a rallying point for the nascent abolitionist cause in America and inspired abolitionist writings throughout the 19th century.

By 1819, Grégoire, bitterly disappointed by the failure of the French Revolution, the coronation of Napoléon, and the return of the Bourbon monarchy to France, discovered that he no longer had a role in the French government;

therefore, he redirected his focus. He earlier had identified the Haitian Republic as an auspicious site for nurturing the legacy of the Revolution, and he now applied himself wholly to its cause. Because Haiti's republic was so new, Grégoire viewed it paternalistically, as a blank slate onto which he could help write his ideals about "regeneration," or societal improvement and renewal. If successful, Grégoire believed, Haiti could offer an exportable template for republicanism, exuding only the best qualities of European civilization. Although he never visited the West Indies, Grégoire corresponded with wealthy members of Haiti's intellectual and political elite. Since the assassination of Emperor Jacques Dessalines in 1806, Haiti had been divided into two regimes: a black-led kingdom in the North and a *métis*-led republic in the South. Ever the revolutionary, Grégoire was eager to see the monarchy collapse and the republic succeed. After 1820, when the republic absorbed the North after its king committed suicide, General JEAN-PIERRE BOYER and his fellow mixed-race leaders sought Grégoire's advice. In his correspondence with them, and in a series of targeted essays, Grégoire sought to shape the emerging culture in Haiti by projecting on to it lessons gained by the republican experiment in France. The aftershocks of European colonialism had splintered Haiti, which suffered from racial tension, class division, broken families, and a suspicion of outsiders. Grégoire applied his own moral and religious solutions to these societal problems. He encouraged the wealthy, well-educated, and primarily mixed-race leadership to be good role models to the (now all free) black majority, to sanctify the institution of marriage and ban extramarital relationships, to view all men as members of a greater family, to practice morality and religious tolerance, and to encourage intermarriage (which he believed would alleviate tensions and create a stronger race of people). With the passage of time, however, Haitian leaders distanced themselves from Grégoire, who in 1827 removed himself from their affairs.

Grégoire died on May 20, 1831, but he later became an icon of some Haitian leaders and intellectuals. Recent scholarship has questioned the nature of Grégoire's involvement, pointing to ways in which his views on religious universalism inadvertently supported colonial expansion, but his was a progressive voice in his era, and he risked his own political standing in order to further the cause of postcolonial free blacks.

Emily M. Brewer

FURTHER READING

Brière, Jean-François. "Abbé Grégoire and Haitian Independence." *Research in African Literatures* 35, no. 2 (2004): 34–43.

Fick, Carolyn E. *The Making of Haiti: The Saint-Domingue Revolution from Below.* Knoxville: University of Tennessee Press, 1990.

Grégoire, Henri. *De la littérature des nègres, ou Recherches sur leurs facultés intellectuelles, leurs qualités morales et leur littérature.*) (*An Enquiry Concerning the Intellectual and Moral Faculties, and Literature of Negroes.* Translated by D. B. Warden. Brooklyn: Thomas Kirk, 1810.) Paris: 1808. English translation digitized by the University of South Carolina Library's Digital Collections. Available online.URL: http://www.sc.edu/library/digital/collections/gregoire.html. Original French document digitized by Project Gutenberg. Available online. URL: http://www.gutenberg.org/etext/15907. Accessed December 28, 2010.

——. *Mémoire en faveur des gens de couleur ou sang-mêlés de St Domingue & des autres isles françoises de l'Amérique, adressé à l'Assemblée Nationale.* (Report to the National Assembly in favor of people of color or mixed blood from St.-Domingue and the other French islands in America.) Paris: Chez Belin, 1789.

Necheles, Ruth F. *The Abbé Grégoire, 1787–1831: The Odyssey of an Egalitarian.* Westport, Conn.: Greenwood, 1971.

Popkin, Jeremy D., and Richard H. Popkin, eds. *The Abbé Grégoire and His World.* Dordrecht: Kluwer Academic Publishers, 2001.

Sepinwall, Alyssa Goldstein. *The Abbé Grégoire and the French Revolution: The Making of Modern Universalism.* Berkeley: University of California Press, 2005.

GUATEMALA

The modern nation of Guatemala is located south and east of MEXICO on the Central American peninsula. It extends across the peninsula from the Caribbean to the Pacific and is bordered on the southeast by HONDURAS and EL SALVADOR and on the northeast by BELIZE. The government of Guatemala has intermittently claimed the territory that now comprises Belize. The southern part of the country is highlands, and the Pacific coastal strip is fertile and well watered. The capital and largest cities are located in the highlands. There was a dense population of Native Americans in the highlands when Europeans arrived. The northern part of the country is low-lying and heavily forested. In precolonial times, this area was densely settled by Mayan Indians, but their civilization declined after about 800 C.E. When Europeans arrived, this area was impenetrable jungle. The only Spanish settlement in the North was a fort near the modern Caribbean port of Puerto Barrios, which had a village of a few hundred Indians and Afro-Indians outside its walls. In general, the Spanish did not settle the Caribbean coast of Central America.

Spanish conquistadores, accompanied by black and Indian auxiliaries, arrived in Guatemala in 1523, under the command of Pedro de Alvarado (1485–1541). The names of Sebastian Toral and Pedro Fulupo are recorded

Guatemala

N

0   50 miles
0   50 km

MEXICO

Río Usumacinta

Paxban

Lago Petén Itzá

Flores

BELIZE

Barillas

Cobán

Huehuetenango

Río Chixoy

Río Motagua

Lago de Atitlán

Mazatenango

Guatemala

Nueva Concepción

San José

PACIFIC OCEAN

© Infobase Learning

Bay of Honduras

Puerto Barrios

Lago de Izabal

Zacapa

HONDURAS

Jutiapa

EL SALVADOR

among the companions of Alvarado, with the notation "negro," and Toral gained MANUMISSION and an exemption from tribute obligations for his services on the expedition. The somewhat better-documented Juan Bardales (?–1551) was also a companion of Alvarado, though the exploits for which he gained his freedom and a pension took place in Honduras, where he became an important early settler, and it is unclear whether he was in Guatemala. Juan Valiente (1505?–53), a free black man and later one of the leading settlers of CHILE, participated in the conquest of Guatemala as a young man before going to Chile with Diego de Almagro's (1475–1538) expedition.

During the Spanish colonial period, Guatemala's economy did not develop a significant plantation sector. Guatemala City was the seat of the captaincy general, which ruled all the territory down to Panama. But the region remained an economic backwater. Relative poverty and the lack of a plantation sector meant that few slaves were imported. Those slaves who did enter worked as personal servants, skilled workmen, or overseers of Indian laborers on haciendas or in urban workshops. Their relative autonomy often gave them access to the resources necessary to buy their freedom. This, along with the generally looser racial lines and legal encouragement for manumission, meant that most Afro-Guatemalans were free before the end of the colonial period. Because of the large Indian population and the role that many Afro-Guatemalans played in super-

vising Indian workers, many people of African descent had intermarried with the Indian population, creating a relatively large class of mixed-race *ladinos* or CASTAS. The Spanish legal system has a spurious precision in naming the various shades of racial mixture: In fact, record keeping was poor and people often were classified in terms of their wealth and social standing rather than their ancestry. Many mixed-race people of partly African ancestry were counted as mestizos. By the turn of the 17th century, around 1,100 people of African ancestry were counted by the 1594 census in Guatemala City and a similar number lived in smaller towns and rural areas throughout the colony. Most of these were free. Several independent black towns were established in the highlands or along the Pacific Coast, including one at San Diego de la Gomera that had several hundred black or mulatto inhabitants in the mid-1600s. Integration with indigenous populations, however, meant official population declines. A census in 1801 found that the reported number of Afro-Guatemalans had fallen to fewer than 2,000.

During this period, the African-descended population of the Caribbean coast was growing. The British began importing slaves into the region that now makes up the nation of Belize starting in the 1740s. As was common in the Spanish Empire, Guatemalan officials offered freedom to any RUNAWAY SLAVES who converted to Catholicism. A town of several hundred Africans and their Afro-mestizo families gathered around the Spanish fort on the Bay of Honduras at the modern site of Puerto Barrios. Another settlement of MAROONS grew up near the modern Livingston, across the bay from Puerto Barrios. Additional colonies of runaway British slaves settled in the forests of the northern Petén region. After 1793, these settlers were reinforced by BLACK CARIB who ran away from the British colony on Roatan Island in the Bay of Honduras. They had been expelled from St. Vincent in the Lesser Antilles. They still practiced a form of the Catholicism they had been taught by the French, who ruled St. Vincent until 1763. This was enough for the Spanish to see them as potential allies, and Black Carib who reached Spanish-controlled areas were employed as guards for the Spanish towns and forts there. The coast of Guatemala was an almost entirely lawless region. The authorities from Guatemala City could only deal with the runaways and Black Carib as allies and equals. The runaways, their Indian relatives, the Antillean immigrants, and the few Spaniards in the region together created what has become known as the Garifuna culture, which now extends all the way from Belize to Costa Rica along the Caribbean coast of Central America.

The end of Spanish colonial rule occured in 1821. The WAR OF MEXICAN INDEPENDENCE, 1810–21, had little impact in Guatemala. The newly independent nation abolished slavery in a multistep process. With the fall of Mexico's first "emperor" Agustin I in 1823, the former Captaincy-General of Guatemala broke away to become the Federal Republic of Central America. The government of the republic, like that of Mexico to the north, was strongly influenced by liberal ideas, including opposition to slavery. The Central American constitution of 1824 abolished slavery. As in Mexico and elsewhere in the Spanish Americas, this formal abolition did not end the practice of slavery throughout the national territory. Large landowners and the ROMAN CATHOLIC CHURCH never accepted the republic and ultimately rebelled against its authority, dissolving the federation by 1841 and creating the five modern nations of Guatemala, El Salvador, Nicaragua, Costa Rica, and Honduras. Conservatives in Guatemala, led by Rafael Carrera (1814–65), wanted to reestablish slavery formally after 1841, and an American adventurer, William Walker, invaded Honduras, Nicaragua, and Costa Rica in an attempt to introduce slavery and American political domination to the region in the 1850s. Cooler heads prevailed, as liberal leaders turned back the American invaders and, after Carrera's death, introduced liberal rule to Guatemala. The end of slavery in the United States in 1865 also spelled the end of any hope for reestablishment in Guatemala.

The debate over the freeing of slaves had repercussions for the social status of free blacks. RACISM AND RACIAL PREJUDICE have marked Guatemala's independent history. However, this discrimination has been directed principally at Native Americans, especially those of the northern Mayan group. A vicious civil war in the late 20th century resulted in the deaths of tens of thousands of indigenous peoples. The small black population has remained mostly on the sidelines of these struggles. However, the dominance of white conservatives, especially during the middle years of the 19th century, meant that blacks were held back. They remained mostly poor rural villagers and migrant farmworkers throughout most of Guatemala's history. Even the liberal regimes of the late 19th century were strongly affected by positivist ideas. Positivism held that liberal forms of government, with free speech, political democracy, equal rights, and the rule of law, were only appropriate for people who had reached a certain level of social development. Older forms of government were more appropriate for more "backward" people. Positivism was very popular in Latin America because it allowed ruling classes to preserve white supremacy and liberal ideals at the same time by arguing that whites were the most advanced, "scientific" group and deserved to lead. Some limited numbers of people of

color could be defined as "scientific" or "developed" and included in the club, if they spoke good Spanish, were well educated, and conformed to other norms of behavior. The advancement of small numbers of people of color to the ranks of the elite did not disrupt white supremacy but instead allowed it to think of itself as benevolent, as "improving" the "lower" races.

By the 1850s, growing numbers of African-descended people were entering Guatemala as free immigrants from the Caribbean islands. Guatemala finally began to establish plantations under Carrera's rule, for COFFEE CULITVATION for the North American market. This process accelerated under the succeeding liberal governments, especially after the turn of the 20th century, as technical innovations permitted the shipment of fresh bananas. Guatemala was not so strongly affected by this immigration as its fellow Central American countries, however, since it has a shorter Caribbean coastline and less land suitable for banana production. The region around Puerto Barrios, however, still has a significant population of Afro-Guatemalans, some descended from the Garifuna and some from 19th-century Caribbean immigrants. The descendants of the early African immigrants to the highland region have almost entirely disappeared as a distinct population, intermarrying with native people to create an undifferentiated mestizo group.

Stewart R. King

FURTHER READING
Gonzalez, Nancie L. *Sojourners of the Caribbean: Ethnogenesis and Ethnohistory of the Garifuna.* Urbana: University of Illinois Press, 1988.
Handy, Jim. *Gift of the Devil: A History of Guatemala.* Cambridge, Mass.: South End Press, 1998.
Lokken, Paul. "Génesis de una comunidad afro-indígena en Guatemala: La villa de San Diego de la Gomera en el siglo XVII." *Mesoamérica, Mesoamérica/Antigua* 29, no. 50, (2008): 37–65.
Montoya, Salvador. "Milicias negras y mulatas en el reino de Guatemala, siglo XVIII." *Caravelle: Cahiers du monde hispanique et luso-brésilien* 49 (1987): 93–104.
Opie, Frederick. *Black Labor Migration in Caribbean Guatemala, 1882–1923.* Gainesville: University of Florida Press, 2009.
Restall, Matthew. *Beyond Black and Red: African-Native Relations in Colonial Latin America.* Albuquerque: University of New Mexico Press, 2005.

GUERRERO slave ship

The *Guerrero* was a Spanish slave ship that ran aground in FLORIDA in 1827. At that time, the slave trade was illegal under international law, although SPAIN and BRAZIL continued to import slaves from Africa into the 1850s. The fate of the *Guerrero's* slaves was the subject of an important trial in the United States that preceded the more famous AMISTAD CASE of 1839–41.

On December 19, 1827, the British warship *Nimble*, commanded by Lieutenant Edward Holland, pursued the Havana slave ship *Guerrero*, which had a crew of 90 and 561 Africans imprisoned in its hold. The chase of the suspicious-looking brig began at noon near Orange Cay, Bahamas, and continued for hours. As night fell and after a gun battle, the slave ship struck the coral reef six miles off Key Largo, Florida, at 7:30 P.M. Five minutes later, the British warship ran aground on the reef two miles away. Both ships suffered significant damage from their contact with the reef, and the *Guerrero*—a total wreck—rolled over on its side with more than 40 killed.

The next morning, two American ships that specialized in salvaging wrecks, the *Thorn* and the *Surprise*, and an American fishing vessel, the *Florida*, rescued the Spanish and African survivors (41 Africans had perished in the wreck). The *Surprise* freed the warship from the reef, but it could not sail as the rudder had broken off. That day, the Spaniards hijacked the *Florida* and then the *Thorn* with a total of 398 male and female Africans on board to CUBA, where they were illegally re-enslaved.

The *Surprise* with 122 male Africans and only 20 Spaniards on board had been protected by another salvage vessel that arrived on the scene, the *General Geddes*. Those Africans, one of whom died en route, were taken to Key West, 100 miles away.

When the British lieutenant Holland arrived at the island after the American salvage ships helped fit the *Nimble* with the rudder from the slaver, he wanted custody of the Africans, but the American collector of customs, the senior U.S. government official present, William Pinkney, declared that they had landed in American territory so were under the protection of the U.S. government. When the crew of the American salvage ships demanded that Lieutenant Holland submit to the island's unofficial "court of arbitrators," which in collusion with the wreckers would no doubt award a huge salvage fee, the *Nimble* sailed away, without the Africans. Salvaging wrecked ships and extracting huge fees from their owners was the principal business of Key West in the 19th century, and the hundreds of slaves on the *Guerrero* and the British warship represented a potential huge windfall for the Floridians.

The Africans at Key West were well cared for but were in danger, as there was a rumor that the Spanish slave traders were fitting out an armed vessel to sail there, only 90 miles from Havana, and seize them. On learning of the situation, U.S. Marshal of the Eastern District of Florida Waters Smith chartered a vessel from St. Augus-

tine and took the Africans there, for their protection. They had been at Key West for two and a half months, and the evening before Smith arrived, an American coastal slave ship captain tried to bribe Smith's deputy to re-enslave them.

With no funds to care for the Africans, Smith hired the men who could work out to area plantations as slaves. He was later ordered to do just that by Secretary of the Navy Samuel Southard. The Africans were legally free people but in limbo, for the anti–slave trade laws, determined President JOHN QUINCY ADAMS, did not apply to them, as the laws addressed only illegal importation of enslaved Africans and the people in the *Guerrero* had landed by accident from a vessel bound to Cuba. Adams addressed Congress on April 30, 1828, on the situation, proposing a supplemental act to cover their circumstances and to return them to Africa. It was bottled up in committee for almost a year.

Marshal Smith hired out 36 of the Africans to Zephaniah Kingsley, and 20 to Joseph M. Hernandez. The Kingsley Plantation is now a National Park Service site, and part of Hernandez's plantation is now Washington Oaks State Gardens. Three men escaped Hernandez's plantation to live in the woods or with the Indians. Eleven months later, the Indians took them to Smith for a reward.

Boys too young to work were placed with St. Augustine families, while men blind or too ill to work were in the care of Justice of the Peace Francis James Ross of Jacksonville.

After continual efforts by Smith and inadequate response by Secretaries of the Navy Southard and his successor, John Branch, Congress finally authorized an appropriation on March 29, 1829, for transportation of the Africans to LIBERIA. One hundred surviving Africans boarded the chartered *Washington's Barge* at Amelia Island, Florida, on September 30, 1829. Two others were held back because of illness. Another had been released, as he was an African interpreter and a crewman and not part of the slave cargo. One boy was taken aboard the U.S. Revenue Cutter *Marion* at Key West and remains unaccounted for. Of the original group of 121 men and boys to arrive at Key West, six had died on the island and one in the care of Justice Ross, and 10 apparently died on the plantations of northeastern Florida.

The captain of the *Washington's Barge* did not know how to sail to Liberia, and after 89 days at sea put into BARBADOS in distress. At the request of A. Hamilton Mechlin, the appointed superintendent of the Africans, Governor James Lyon of Barbados guaranteed with his own funds payment by the United States for Mechlin to charter the Barbados brig *Heroine* to complete the voyage to Liberia. Five more men died before reaching Barbados, and four more before the *Heroine* arrived at Liberia on March 4, 1830. One of the boys left behind later died. The other was sent from Norfolk for Liberia in July 1831, having been a resident in U.S. territory since his arrival at Key West from the wreck in December 1827.

Upon arrival, the Africans' American-given names were recorded. All had surnames. Many of those names are in the 1843 census of Liberia. The census included their occupations and the names of their wives and children. Most settled in New Georgia with the recaptured Africans from the slave ship *Antelope,* who were already there. They were later joined by recaptured Africans from the slave ship *FENIX.*

Thus, after four years, most of the Africans recaptured from the *Guerrero* returned to Africa. Many no doubt remained far from their homes—we do not know what port the *Guerrero* was originally loaded at but many of the ships in the illegal slave trade to Cuba loaded in Central Africa, at the Portuguese ports in CONGO AND ANGOLA many hundreds of miles from Liberia. Thus, Liberia would have been almost as different from their homes as Cuba or Florida. They worked on plantations in the Americas, even though they were technically free, and they suffered the diseases that most newly arrived Africans experienced. The aggressive Spanish defense of their "property"—armed hijackings of the ships that arrived to rescue them from the reef, threats of invasion of Key West, bribes and double dealings—prefigure the better known *Amistad* case a decade later, when Spanish government officials supported their nationals who took a legal case all the way to the Supreme Court of the United States in an attempt to regain control over escaped slaves.

Gail Swanson

FURTHER READING
Murray, David R. *Odious Commerce: Britain, Spain, and the Abolition of the Cuban Slave Trade.* Cambridge: Cambridge University Press, 1980.

Swanson, Gail. *Slave Ship Guerrero.* West Conshohocken, Pa.: Infinity, 2005.

Thomas, Hugh. *The Slave Trade: The Story of the Atlantic Slave Trade, 1440–1870.* New York: Simon & Schuster, 1999.

GUERRERO SALDAÑA, VICENTE (1782—1831)
independence leader and general, president of México (1829–1830)
Vicente Guerrero was the chief military leader of the pro-independence forces in the WAR OF MEXICAN INDEPENDENCE, 1810–21, and an important politician in the 1820s. He was briefly president and is best known for definitively abolishing slavery in the country.

Born in 1782 in a family of free mulatto *"arrierías"* (muleteers) in the town of Tixtla, located near the Mexico-Acapulco road, Vicente Guerrero Saldaña was a simple man with no education. From his early years, he traveled with his father throughout the country. Through his travels, he learned the physical and human geography of MEXICO's southern territories, the most striking characteristics of which were racial mixing and cultural fusion. He also witnessed violence, social inequality, and exploitation. He identified strongly with the 1810 independence movement principles of freedom and justice, and he soon joined the movement after the outbreak of the armed struggle against Spain.

He soon was recognized for his bravery and military aptitude as well as his leadership skills, and he was rewarded by promotion and military commands. JOSÉ MARÍA MORELOS, an early leader of the rebel movement and also an Afro-Mexican, ordered him to raise armed movements in the coastal region and extend the revolution to the modern state of Oaxaca. This was an area with many Afro-Mexican inhabitants, both free and enslaved. Morelos was unable to commit any men or weapons, so Guerrero initiated his struggle with only one assistant, a mulatto, José del Carmen. Recruiting independence supporters from the towns and settlements and training them, collecting weapons from supporters, he launched a successful campaign in the modern states of Puebla, Veracruz, Oaxaca, and Guerrero, the latter state created in 1849 to recognize his labors.

After Morelos was captured and executed by pro-Spanish forces in 1815, the insurgent movement declined and just a few chiefs remained in the field. Guerrero was the most efficient of these; he reorganized his troops to face the royalist armies. In 1818, he participated in the creation of the Junta de Gobierno (governmental board) and accepted the title of General en Jefe del Sur (general in chief of the South). Brave, a good soldier, and a skilled strategist, he divided the army into three regiments to control the region. Its success in military campaigns compelled the authorities to use other tactics than weapons. Viceroy Apodaca sent his father, Don Pedro, to convince Guerrero to surrender to the authorities, but even while recognizing Don Pedro's authority, Guerrero kept loyal to freedom ideals for Mexico in the celebrated phrase *la patria es primero* (the fatherland comes first), today printed in gold words at the National Congressional Palace.

Undefeated, Guerrero sustained the ideals of freedom and social equality but was unable to extend his operations outside the southern region. This was one of the reasons why he accepted the royalist plan to consummate independence through political compromise. On February 24, 1821, he signed the Plan de Iguala, a program for devolution of power from Madrid to Mexico City in a more federal empire, and placed his troops under the command of the new general in chief of the Ejército de las Tres Garantías (the army of the three guarantees), Agustín de Iturbide.

Iturbide abandoned the plan for political devolution after it was rejected by the king of Spain and proclaimed the independence of Mexico on September 27, 1821. The new government recognized Guerrero's services to the fatherland, named him general, and made him the captain-general of the South. He received the Gran Cruz de Guadalupe, the highest honor awarded by the Mexican government. When the empire was proclaimed, with Iturbide crowned emperor of Mexico on July 21, 1822, Guerrero once again began his efforts to establish a republic, reorganizing his army in his well-known southern territories. In this new military campaign, he was wounded in the chest, a wound that troubled him for the rest of his life. Ultimately, Guerrero and the other liberal chieftains, along with the mercurial Antonio López de Santa Anna (1794–1876), overthrew Iturbide and established the Mexican Republic.

A firm believer in republican institutions and federalism, in 1828, he became a candidate for the presidency against Manuel Gómez Pedraza, a former officer in the colonial military. Gómez was proclaimed the winner, but Guerrero disputed the results and the indirect voting process. His opposition created discontent in the army and among the public. Military uprisings, perhaps manipulated by Guerrero, and massive popular discontent forced a new election, which Guerrero won, assuming power on April 1, 1829. Simón Bolívar and other Spanish-American liberals criticized him for his actions in overthrowing Gómez, but he maintained that he was actually defending the democratic process.

Guerrero began his administration during a severe economic crisis and faced financial problems, but he had wide political and popular support. He was granted extraordinary powers by the Congress to resist foreign aggression feared from SPAIN and FRANCE. He ratified the law that expelled Spaniards and defeated the invasion of Spanish troops under General Isidro Barradas to regain Mexico for the Spanish Crown.

Using the special powers granted him, on September 15, 1829, Guerrero decreed absolute and uncompensated abolition of slavery in all national territory. This important decision had implications in TEXAS, where slavery was growing because of immigration and importation of slaves from the United States. The law did not enter into effect immediately in Texas, but caused discontent among white Texans, both American immigrants and Mexicans, that ultimately led to the independence movement in that state in the 1830s.

Guerrero also abolished the state tobacco monopoly and authorized freedom of cultivation to the benefit of all peasants, abolishing feudal restrictions. To alleviate the situation of mine workers and independent prospectors, he decreed a mining law. His economic policy was basically liberal as the term was then used, focusing on free trade, free labor, and an end to inherited privilege or special protections for economic activities.

Guerrero's foreign policy fit into this liberal mold, as he sought commercial treaties with different nations with the clear purpose to gain international recognition of Mexico as an independent country and open up trade links. He sought to help CUBA obtain its independence by paying for an army organizing in Haiti composed of Cuban exiles and Haitian soldiers who were to disembark in the island and initiate a general insurrection of colored people against Spain.

An uprising by Vice President Anastasio Bustamante (1789–1853) in 1829 obliged him to abandon the capital. He took refugee in his native city of Tixtla, where he resigned the presidency of the republic in the early days of January 1830. This decision provoked a civil war. The fear of Guerrero's popularity and his decision to take up arms again to restore republican order made the established government decide to arrest him. Captured in Acapulco, he was moved to Oaxaca, where a military tribunal judged him and condemned him to death. He was executed in Cuilapa on February 14, 1831.

Today, Vicente Guerrero is remembered principally as an independence fighter and secondarily as the liberator of Mexico's slaves. As an Afro-Mexican, he illustrates the important role that people of African descent played in Mexico's national history. His unwavering defense of republican principles, liberalism, and the national sovereignty of Mexico defined the ideology of an important faction in Mexican political dialogue that has persisted to this very day. In many ways, he is the father of modern Mexico.

Araceli Reynoso Medina

FURTHER READING

Bocanegra, José María. *Memorias para la historia de México independiente.* 2 vols. México City: Instituto Cultural Helénico-INERM, 1986–87.

Costeloe, Michael P. *La primera república federal de México (1824–1835): Un estudio de los partidos políticos en el México independiente.* México City: Fondo de Cultura Económica, 1975.

Lafragua, José María. *Vicente Guerrero el mártir de Cuilapan.* Biblioteca Popular, 124. México City: Secretaria de Educación Pública, 1946.

Mancisidor, José. *Hidalgo Morelos, Guerrero.* México City: Grijalbo, 1970.

Rodríguez O, Jaime E., ed. *The Independence of Mexico City and the Creation of the New Nation.* UCLA Latin American Studies. Los Angeles: UCLA Latin American Center Publications, 1989.

GUYANA

Guyana is located along the northern coast of South America on the Atlantic Ocean. It borders Dutch Guyana, the modern SURINAM, to the east; VENEZUELA to the west; and, beyond a range of hills and a heavily forested region that was not settled by Europeans until modern times, BRAZIL to the south. The coastal plain was swampy and heavily forested when European settlement began. There are two major river valleys, the Essequibo and Demerara, that are the center of settlement. The indigenous inhabitants of the coastal strip and river valleys were Arawak, related to the indigenous peoples of the Greater Antilles. European explorers passed along the coast of Guyana as early as Columbus's second voyage in 1493, but settlement did not begin until Dutch settlers arrived in 1616.

Dutch Colonial Period (1616–1814)

The first European settlers of Guyana were Dutch. They first settled along the river valleys upstream from the coastal plain, establishing trading posts to deal with the native people. When Dutch invaders were driven from northeastern Brazil in the 1650s, however, they took with them the idea for the plantation system, which they had seen in Brazil. SUGAR CULTIVATION required flat, well-watered land, and the Dutch planters thought the coastal plains would serve well for sugar plantations once the swamps were drained. The Dutch had plenty of experience in hydraulic engineering from their swampy, low-lying homeland, and they put this expertise to work to develop extensive plantations around the mouth of the Essequibo, Demerara, and Berbice rivers. The three areas were treated as separate colonies by the Dutch. The Dutch imported very large numbers of slaves into their South American colonies; the best estimate is that around half a million people were taken from Africa, about two-thirds of them to Essequibo, Demerara, and Berbice (and the rest to Surinam and, for a short time, Dutch Brazil). The Dutch slave regime was very harsh, and working conditions were difficult. Many of the newly arrived slaves died before they could even have children, and populations of Afro-Guyanans did not grow rapidly until the late 18th century.

Dutch law permitted MANUMISSION of slaves, and for a long period in the 17th and early 18th centuries, unlike in other European colonies in the Americas, at least some children of enslaved women and free white men were treated as free from birth. Thus, a comparatively large free population of color, many of whom were of mixed race, grew in the colonies, becoming the majority of the free population of Guyana by the 1770s. Slaves were still the vast majority of the population. A number of slave rebellions took place in the colony, including one of the most famous rebellions in the Atlantic world, the Berbice Rebellion of 1763. A slave named Cuffy, an artisan, probably from West Africa, led slaves in a rebellion that threatened Dutch rule in the colony. After the initial uprising, the Dutch governor evacuated more than 3,000 surviving whites and free coloreds from the colony to a nearby fort and was preparing to evacuate entirely when reinforcements arrived from neighboring British and French colonies. With this assistance, and thanks to divisions among the rebels, the Dutch were able to recapture the colony within a few months. One of the important factors in the ultimate Dutch victory in the Berbice Rebellion was that most of the free people of color remained loyal to the white colonial government. In this period,

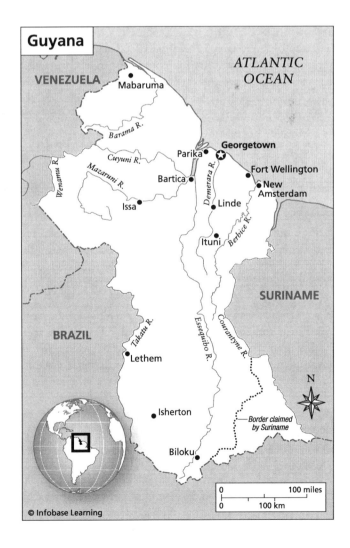

many free people of color lived in the countryside, either with white relatives or on their own slave-worked farms. There were few large free colored planters, but many free people of color identified with the slave-owning white ruling class because of family ties or their own status as slave owners (*see also* SLAVE OWNERS).

The Dutch colonies also had many RUNAWAY SLAVES who founded communities of MAROONS. The extensive and heavily forested interior of Guyana, with its unconquered indigenous inhabitants, was a perfect environment for maroons. The Dutch colonial governments were poorly funded and had few soldiers to spare for attacks outside their area of settlement. The "Bush Negroes" of Surinam are descendants of maroons who managed to preserve their independence from the colonial government there after several wars. The maroons of Guyana were less fortunate, as large settlements were crushed by Dutch attacks in the 1740s and 1760s. Still, many smaller communities of maroons managed to escape the attention of local officials, and there are still many people in the interior of Guyana who refer to themselves as maroons.

British Rule and Abolition of Slavery

The Dutch colonies were attacked by other European powers several times during the 18th century, with periods of British rule in the 1760s, 1780s and 1790s and intermittent French rule during the time of the FRENCH REVOLUTION and the wars of Napoléon. British military occupation turned into a formal change in sovereignty with the surrender of Napoléon in 1814. Britain made many changes to the Guyana colonies. First, the British had abolished the slave trade in 1807, so the flow of new Africans to work in the plantations stopped. Some new slaves were imported into the colonies from other British colonies, but this practice, too, was stopped by the formal transfer of authority in 1814. With the end of slave imports, masters realized that the extremely harsh treatment of the Dutch era had resulted in low birthrates, which threatened their businesses. Treatment, especially the quantity and quality of food supplied to slaves, improved somewhat under British rule. Slave birth and child survival rates increased, and the Afro-Guyanese population rapidly became mostly CREOLE as the slave population decreased overall. Throughout the Americas, creole slaves were more likely to be able to gain their freedom and work effectively against the slave system because of their cultural similarity to the white ruling class, and this was also true in Guyana. In the realm of culture, the Dutch had made little effort to Christianize their slaves, but the British occupation and the rise of Baptist groups in Britain led to the conversion of most Afro-Guyanese to Baptist Christianity (*see also* BAPTISTS AND PIETISTS).

The colonies were more closely connected with the world economy, and the name *Demerara* came to signify a high-quality brand of sugar throughout the English-speaking world. The contrast of increasing profitability from sugar exports and a declining slave workforce meant that planters had to look for alternative sources of labor. Employment of immigrants from South Asia was the ultimate solution, and today people of South Asian descent make up more than 40 percent of the population of Guyana. However, the first Indian indentured servants did not arrive in Guyana until 1838, after the abolition of slavery. During the early years of British rule, planters sought to import free laborers from neighboring colonies and to employ Native Americans and the descendants of the maroons.

The British were less generous to the free colored population than the Dutch had been. They discouraged manumission with an 1815 regulation that required government approval and imposed a tax. Still, by 1820, free people of color constituted about 8 percent of the population of the colony, as opposed to about 6 percent for whites. Many free blacks owned at least some land, though there were few large planters. The "hucksters," or small retail merchants, of the colony were almost all free coloreds, along with many ARTISANS and some larger businessmen. After 1823, regulations on manumission were loosened, in part in response to the Demerara slave uprising of that year. The free colored population grew rapidly from that point until the abolition of slavery. There were still some free colored farmers, but British regulations limiting the right of free people of color to own land and slaves meant that larger farms were hard to operate. Free Afro-Guyanese, as did free people of color elsewhere in the tropical British Americas, tended to concentrate in the towns and cities, with the maroons on the outskirts of the settled areas forming a distinct group.

Guyana experienced one more important slave uprising during the period of British rule, the Demerara slave uprising of 1823. This uprising, unlike the Berbice Rebellion, was not an attempt to seize control of the colony but instead a work stoppage intended to force the colonial government to implement laws that the slaves thought had been ordered by the British government to change working conditions of slaves. They were reacting to debates in the British Parliament on abolition and the regulation of slavery. The slaves mainly refrained from killing or destroying property, instead locking up masters and white supervisors in their homes. The colonial government reacted with great harshness, killing dozens of slaves out of hand and trying and executing more. A white missionary was among those punished with imprisonment, although his conviction was ultimately overturned on appeal. In another difference, this rebellion, or strike, was supported by at least some of the free people of color of the colony, especially those involved with the Baptist Church. The Baptist teachings on racial equality were an important part of the motivation for the uprising, and the harsh treatment meted out to the rebels sparked outrage among Baptists and other religious dissenters in Britain. This outrage led to further modifications of the slave law, and ultimately to the abolition of slavery in the British Empire as a whole in 1834.

Post-Abolition Aftermath

The Guyanese free colored population lost many of its leaders and was cowed by the harsh reprisals after the Demerara uprising of 1823. As a result, there was little overt abolitionist sentiment in the colony leading up to the 1834 declaration. The 1834 act created a transitional regime of "apprenticeship," under which slaves over six years old were to continue to serve their former masters, although they were to be ultimately freed. As did slave populations elsewhere in the British Americas, Guyanese slaves generally simply refused to accept the continuing authority of their former masters, and they fled the plantations in large numbers. Thousands crowded into the towns, while others began farming as squatters on plantation or public land in remote regions. Planters hired free labor as they could, but many of the newly freed refused to work in plantation agriculture for any price. Planters accelerated their search for alternative sources of labor, ultimately bringing in the Indian indentured laborers. The role of Guyana's pre-abolition free colored population during this period was to welcome the newly freed either in the towns or in the remote rural areas. The former free people of color were not the only Afro-Guyanese to enter the middle class at this time, but they had an inside track due to their education and resources. The presence of growing numbers of Indian workers and the racial tension that sprang up between Indo-Guyanese and Afro-Guyanese, however, worked against the creation of an internal distinction between "blacks" and "browns" as is found in many other British former plantation colonies in the Caribbean. Instead, Afro-Guyanese tended to be thought of as a single coherent group from the earliest post-abolition days.

Stewart R. King

FURTHER READING

da Costa, Emilia Viotti. *Crowns of Glory, Tears of Blood: The Demerara Slave Rebellion of 1823*. New York: Oxford University Press, 1994.

Daly, Vere. *The Making of Guyana*. New York: Macmillan, 1974.

H

HAITI *See* SAINT-DOMINGUE.

HAITIAN REVOLUTION

The Haitian Revolution of the 1790s and early 1800s remains the world's only successful slave revolution, in the sense that it overthrew a society in which almost all productive labor was done by slaves and replaced it with one without any slaves. The French island colony of SAINT-DOMINGUE was the richest colony in the Americas before the outbreak of the revolution. It had enormous SUGAR CULITIVATION and COFFEE CULITIVATION on plantations worked by half a million slaves. Overseeing these slaves were about 50,000 free people, about half of whom were free people of color and the rest whites. The free people of color played an important role in the unfolding drama, fighting for their own interests and allying in turn with the French government, invaders from other colonies, and the rebel slaves.

The Haitian Revolution took place at the same time as the FRENCH REVOLUTION, and the two events are connected. The French political discourse on liberty and equality naturally made the slaves and free people of color hope for improvement in their situation. The political chaos in France and the wars that France fought during this period, especially with Britain, the greatest naval power of the age and an important colonial power in the Americas, had an important impact on the unfolding Haitian Revolution.

The colony of Saint-Domingue occupied the western third of the island of Hispaniola in the Caribbean. It had a number of fine ports including CAP-FRANÇAIS/CAP-HAÏTIEN in the north and PORT-AU-PRINCE in the west. The colony was divided into three provinces: the North, the West, and the South. Each province was subdivided into a number of parishes. Geographically, the colony was cut up by a number of mountain ranges, with narrow plains that were the areas most suitable for agriculture. The valley of the Artibonite River, in the center of the colony extending east from Gonaïves, was very fertile but had difficult access to the sea. The Cul de Sac plain in the south-center was very dry, with salt lakes, but broad and flat. The northern plain, around Cap-Français, was broad and had plenty of water and was the first to be exploited for intensive agriculture. The mountains provided refuge to people in danger, including RUNAWAY SLAVES, poor free people of color, and rebel armies, during the revolution.

Colonial Background

Saint-Domingue was the richest colony in the Americas in 1789. There were almost 500,000 slaves, most of whom worked on plantations producing sugar, coffee, indigo, and other crops. Saint-Domingue's production costs were lower than in other large plantation colonies such as JAMAICA or BRAZIL, so as a result much of the sugar and coffee consumed on the European mainland was produced there. Profits were enormous, and the colony was fantastically wealthy—the Saudi Arabia of its time.

The half-million slaves were overseen by a free population of somewhat more than 50,000. Of these, about half were people of color. Free colored people in the island were about half of mixed race and half of entirely African ancestry. There was an increasing social distance among the three groups of free people—the whites, the mixed-race, and the blacks—in the last decades before the revolution, especially in the wealthiest and most densely populated regions of the colony. Discriminatory laws against all people of color played a role in this, as did increasing social class distinctions between wealthy free colored planters and poorer, and often darker, free town dwellers and peasants.

The free colored planter class had once felt itself a part of the planter elite, along with the white planters, who were often their relatives. But humiliating laws passed in the 1760s and 1770s made it harder to preserve that unity. Free colored planters continued to argue for their inclusion in a limited aristocratic ruling class, however, right up to and into the early stages of the revolution.

Free blacks of the cities and smaller free colored farmers, were suspicious of the wealthier planters and formed their own social networks, especially in the North Province. In the North and West Provinces, many of the more

350

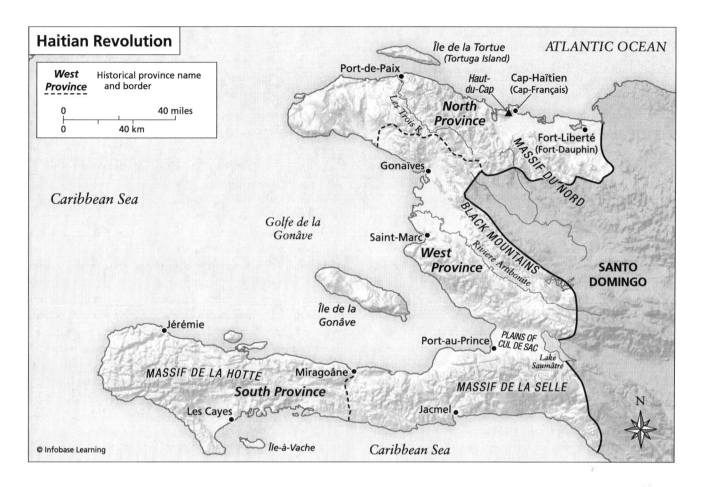

prominent free blacks were MILITIA sergeants or rural policemen, and the military training and networks they established were very helpful in the revolution. Many of the future leaders of the revolution were from this group, TOUSSAINT LOUVERTURE most notably.

Outbreak of the Revolution
The French Revolution broke out in Paris in the summer of 1789. The spark was the meeting of the Estates General, an ancient legislature that had not met in more than a century, which King Louis XVI had called together to help him resolve a financial crisis. The calling of the Estates General in 1788 resulted in a multistage election process and broad debate across France and, although they had no formal representation, in the colonies as well. The white population of Saint-Domingue was represented in the Estates General by a number of absentee planters who had been elected from their home districts in France. These planters worked together as a group called the Club Massiac, which acted as the West India Interest did in the British Parliament at the same time: fighting any move to change the established system in the colonies. Poorer whites felt disenfranchised and began to work for representative institutions in the colony, ones that would, naturally from their point of view, exclude people of color. The wealthy free colored

planters already had representatives in France, JULIEN RAIMOND and VINCENT OGÉ, who had been urging the royal government to enact civil rights laws. After appealing fruitlessly to the Club Massiac, they took their case to the National Assembly, as the Estates General called itself after the fall of the Bastille in July 1789 in the early days of the French Revolution. They got an ambiguously worded resolution, passed in March 1790, that could be interpreted as permitting free colored property owners to be included in the elections to choose local assemblies. This was enough for Ogé, who returned to the colony in October and tried to register to vote. When he was refused by the colonial governor, and when similar requests by other free coloreds met with violence and even lynching in other parts of the colony, Ogé raised the standard of revolt along with the planter activist JEAN-BAPTISTE CHAVANNES. They gathered a small force of free coloreds, refusing to enroll RUNAWAY SLAVES in their army because they did not want to weaken the slave system that had made them wealthy. They put up a fight but were overwhelmed by large professional armed forces sent from the provincial capital of Cap-Français, the colony's largest city, and fled to the Spanish side of the island. Captured and returned by the Spanish, both Ogé and Chavannes were executed in Cap-Français in February 1791.

Whites were also fighting among themselves at this time. Supporters of a poor white–dominated colonial assembly temporarily occupied the colonial capital in Port-au-Prince. Their rule was harsh both for wealthy whites and for their free colored relatives. The colonial governor, supported this time by free colored troops from the countryside surrounding Port-au-Prince, drove the assembly's forces from the city. These free colored activists were not as strong in their support for the slave system as Ogé and Chavannes; they equipped a force of slaves to fight alongside them, called the "Swiss" after the famous mercenaries serving King Louis XVI in France. Like the king's Swiss soldiers, the black "Swiss" of Port-au-Prince were eventually betrayed and slaughtered, but they were the first of many Haitian slaves to fight for their own freedom and the political goals of free colored leaders. The western free colored activists were from a lower social class than Ogé and Chavannes for the most part. Many of them were small farmers who owned few or no slaves, and some were urban free blacks like the rebel leaders of the North.

The 1791 Uprising

In August 1791, the slaves of the North Province rose up in a devastating rebellion. The rebellion was preceded by a *vodun* ceremony at Bois Cayman, presumably celebrated by a *houngan*, or *vodun* priest, named Boukman. (*See also* AFRICAN AND SYNCRETIC RELIGIONS.) Some authorities have said that Boukman was a maroon, and thus a free person of color, though evidence is lacking to be sure what his status was or even to know definitely that he existed. Most of the sugar plantations of the province were destroyed by groups of rampaging slaves. The slaves tried to attack Cap-Français but were driven back by the regular army regiment stationed there. The slaves retreated to regroup and began a classic guerrilla campaign. A new leader rose to prominence among them, a free colored man named Toussaint Bréda. Living at Haut du Cap, on a mountain overlooking Cap-Français, Toussaint later adopted the surname Louverture, and it is under this name that he is known today. Toussaint trained his forces, and they became veterans during more than a year of vicious warfare.

As the colonial government forces stepped up the pressure, Toussaint followed in Ogé's wake and led his troops across to the Spanish side of the island. By this point, in 1792, SPAIN and France were ready to go to war, and the Spanish were happy to have Toussaint's troops on their side. He and the other rebel leaders took commissions in the Spanish army. They said they were fighting for the king of France, who they felt supported the cause of the blacks, while the revolutionary forces, represented in the colony by the poor white–dominated colonial assem-

bly forces, were very hostile to racial equality. Toussaint's forces fought alongside Spanish troops through 1793. In February 1794, the French National Assembly in Paris granted freedom to all slaves in French colonies, and once he heard of this development, Toussaint made his peace with France and switched sides, slaughtering hundreds of his unsuspecting Spanish allies. He became an active, and presumably sincere, republican for the remainder of his career and fought against the kings of Spain and Britain and the royalist French forces.

The Revolution Achieved

With Toussaint as military commander and the French republican commissioner Léger-Félicité Sonthonax as political manager, the French turned to the task of resisting foreign troops and suppressing a variety of internal threats to their rule. The Spanish were routed in 1794, but meanwhile the British invaded the island, committing what would ultimately become their largest expeditionary force of the Napoleonic Wars, eclipsing even the army led by Wellington in Spain. The British used mostly metropolitan British and Irish troops, who suffered horribly from disease. They also recruited local people into their army, including a battalion of soldiers of color led by Jean Kina. Some sources say that Kina was a prerevolutionary maroon or free person, though his principal biographer is convinced that he was a slave until the outbreak of the rebellion, albeit a skilled and apparently well-treated one. Toussaint also had internal enemies: Royalist whites and some of their wealthy free colored allies intrigued against the black general and his loyal white political boss Sonthonax. ANDRÉ RIGAUD and Pierre Pinchinat, both prerevolutionary free coloreds, controlled the southern peninsula and the area of Port-au-Prince. Rigaud and Pinchinat conspired against Étienne Laveaux, a white general and one of Toussaint's supporters. Sonthonax was driven from the colony twice, thanks to his having picked the wrong side in the internal struggles of the French Revolutionaries.

A New Society

Between fighting external and internal enemies, Toussaint tried to restructure society to keep plantation agriculture while ending slavery. This was the crisis that all post-abolition societies were to face; Toussaint's Haiti was just the first, and like the others, he did not have much success. Plantations abandoned by white proprietors who had fled into exile became state property and were generally turned over to military officers to operate. If the owners were still in residence—frequently the case with the wealthy free colored planters—they kept title to the land and buildings while losing their slaves without compensation. The former slaves of each plantation were supposedly required to live and work there unless they had joined the military, under contracts negotiated by a governmental agency. This system was essentially doomed from the beginning. The war required lots of soldiers, and Toussaint was enlisting as many young men as he could. The soldiers expected that they would be rewarded with land at the end of their service, and indeed Toussaint and his generals often gave farms to wounded veterans. They also expected that their extended families would be exempted from the plantation system along with them. Most plantation workers had no interest in continuing work, even for wages. This was especially when the wages were minimal or rarely paid, as was too often the case when powerful military officers exerted their influence over the judges who administered the system. Finally, because of the war with Britain, whose NAVY controlled the seas, export crops such as sugar had difficulty finding a market. Plantations could not stay in business without income.

The cities were in the hands of the revolutionaries' enemy for significant periods of time: The capital, Port-au-Prince, was controlled by the British for most of the 1790s, then by French invaders from 1802 to 1803. The largest city in the colony at the beginning of the war, Cap-Français, was besieged by the rebel slaves from 1791 to 1794, then was assaulted and burned twice, in 1795 and 1802. Urban life declined considerably during the course of the war. Many urban free blacks had rural lands, like Toussaint's farm at Haut du Cap on the mountain overlooking Cap-Français, and they retreated there.

The revolution killed uncounted thousands of people. The population of the colony fell by at least 100,000, and Haiti did not regain its prewar population for half a century. Death, devastation, and loss of markets all led to a profound economic depression. For all these reasons, most Haitians became peasant farmers during the years of the revolution, never to return to large-scale agriculture in any significant numbers.

The colony's political life was in ferment throughout the conflict. Eight different governments set up shop in Port-au-Prince from 1791 to 1804, with styles ranging from legitimist monarchy (the royalist governors) to racially based limited democracy (the colonial assembly), to military dictatorship (Toussaint), to new empire (the revolution's ultimate victor, Emperor Jean-Jacques Dessalines). Every change in government meant a possibility of being killed or driven into exile. Toussaint could drive his white enemies out of the colony—many Saint-Domingue whites settled in the United States, where they waged a lively propaganda struggle against Toussaint's rule. Getting rid of the free coloreds was harder. Ultimately, he and his successors in power conciliated most of their free colored enemies, though in some cases after hard-fought military campaigns accompanied with much slaughter of innocents.

The colony's cultural life changed during the revolution. Prerevolutionary free coloreds had been self-consciously French in their culture, educating their children in France if they could afford it, ostentatiously supporting the ROMAN CATHOLIC CHURCH, and carefully speaking good French if they wished to be taken seriously by their white relatives and business associates. Plantation regulations and colonial laws repressed expressions of Afro-Caribbean culture: Gathering for dances and *vodun* ceremonies was forbidden or harassed. Most whites were fashionably anticlerical and freethinking. The biggest social group in white society were the Masons—even some free coloreds were Masons, including apparently Toussaint Louverture. There was a little high culture: theater, musical societies, libraries encouraged by white reformers and patronized, albeit in bad seats in the upper balcony, by the wealthy free coloreds. The Catholic Church did very little for the slaves, but the free coloreds were serious about their religion. Then the revolution began. The theater impresarios, priests, Masonic leaders, and artists were mostly white, so they left the colony as the fighting spread. The revolutionary government was attacking the church in France and did not have much time for other cultural activities. The revolutionary leaders in Haiti saw no need to encourage European culture. By the end of the revolution, Afro-Caribbean culture was dominant, even among the highest-class former free coloreds.

The Final Victory
Toussaint preserved his power and protected the revolution up until 1802. He finally defeated Rigaud and Pinchinat in 1799–1800, with the help of outside intervention by the United States, which was fighting France and wanted to encourage Haitian independence. With this victory, Toussaint took control of the entire island. Toussaint did not want independence so much as autonomy within the French Empire, but this was too much for Napoléon Bonaparte, who had just taken power in France. After Napoléon signed a peace treaty with the British in 1802, he sent a large force to the island under his brother-in-law, General Charles Leclerc (1772–1802). Leclerc's army contained free colored troops led by Rigaud and ALEXANDRE SABÈS PÉTION, another free colored leader from the West Province. Most of Toussaint's generals bowed to Napoléon's authority, and Toussaint himself was finally defeated, then arrested and imprisoned in France, where he died in 1803.

At first, all was quiet under Leclerc's administration, but the ultimate goal of the expedition was to restore slavery and reestablish the system that had existed before the revolution. As this increasingly became apparent to the Haitian soldiers, one by one, they abandoned their loyalty to Napoléon and France. The rebel armies grew as Leclerc's forces were shrinking from the effects of disease. As the British had, they found that troops from Europe were not able to stay healthy in the colonies for very long, particularly during active service. Leclerc himself died in November 1802 and was replaced at the head of the French forces by Donatien-Marie Joseph de Vimeur, vicomte de Rochambeau (whose father, also a general, had fought the British in the United States during the War of American Independences, 1775–83). The new rebel forces were led by Jean-Jacques Dessalines, who had been a slave at the outbreak of the revolution. Many of his top commanders were former free coloreds, however, including his assistant Louis Boisrond Tonnerre, author of the Haitian Declaration of Independence (issued on January 1, 1804), Pétion, and at least five of the other signatories of the declaration.

Both Dessalines and Rochambeau were believers in a "hard war" and would not accept peace under any conditions other than complete victory. Rochambeau slaughtered prisoners indiscriminately, including the families of Haitian soldiers. Dessalines retaliated by killing most of the whites in the colony, though he famously passed his intended victims in review before sending them to the firing squad, indicating those who were to be spared by saying of each *"li neg,"* "that one is black." Dessalines's forces finally defeated the French at the Battle of Vertières, November 18, 1803, then declared Haitian independence on January 1, 1804. The two heroes of Vertières, François Capois (nicknamed "La Mort") and Alexandre Pétion were both prerevolutionary free coloreds.

The Aftermath

After a brief interlude as "governor-general for life," Dessalines took power under a new constitution as Emperor Jacques I in September 1804. His reign lasted a little more than two years, as he was assassinated by a group of his officers on October 17, 1806. The coup started a period of instability in Haitian politics that ended with the country divided in half. In the North, King Henry Christophe reigned over the Kingdom of Northern Haiti. Christophe himself may have had some claim to free status before the revolution, and his officer corps was full of former free blacks. In the West and South Provinces (now redesignated departments in keeping with Republican reforms in France), Alexandre Pétion was designated President for Life of the Republic of Haiti. Pétion was of mixed race, and his officers included many prewar planters and businessmen. The division between the leaders, their entourages, and their policies reflected the division between the two regions and their prerevolutionary free colored populations. In the West and South, the free coloreds had always been generally homogeneous, with blacks and people of mixed race intermarrying, suffering under the same discrimination, and generally sharing the same politics. In the North, the prewar free coloreds were divided between wealthy mixed-race planters and poorer, usually darker-skinned, city people and small farmers. The free colored planters of the North had mostly disappeared during the revolution—many moved to North America or France. The northern former free blacks dominated a country devoted, as Toussaint had hoped, to continuing plantation agriculture with free labor. As with Toussaint, the outcome was not what the leadership hoped: People did not want to work on plantations if they could avoid it, even for wages. There were regular rebellions, and northern society became a police state. In the end, the military overthrew Christophe. The southern leaders were more concerned with harmony among the racial groups and distributed land widely to former soldiers. Pétion was called *Papa bon-kè* (Father Goodheart) by his subjects.

Christophe and Pétion were succeeded in power by another former free colored, Jean-Pierre Boyer. Boyer was of mixed race, from Port-au-Prince, and had supported Pétion throughout his career. Boyer managed to reunite the entire island for a short time, though his successors lost most of the Spanish side of the island, which became the Dominican Republic, after he was overthrown in 1843. During Boyer's administration from 1818 to 1843, the modern pattern of Haitian society began to emerge. Boyer wanted to encourage cash crop agriculture through a system called *fermage*, a sort of sharecropping on state lands, but poor Haitians rejected this alternative as they had rejected all the previous attempts to make them work on sugar and coffee plantations. Instead, most Haitians persisted in living as peasant farmers. The wealthiest Haitians still owned land in the countryside, in some cases very large amounts, but could not find enough labor to make it profitable, and those who survived economically turned to urban entrepreneurship. The destruction of Cap-Français (called Cap-Haïtien after the revolution) in the war and the concentration of power in the hands of Port-au-Prince natives accelerated the shift of the urban center of the colony to the new capital. By the 1840s, Port-au-Prince was by far the largest city in the country and the home of most of its wealth. Not coincidentally, most of the prominent former free colored families had homes there (though there were, and are, still plenty of members of these families living in smaller cities like Cap-Haïtien, Jérémie, Jacmel, or St-Marc).

After Boyer, Haitian politics became a game of shifting alliances between "black" military and "mulatto" commercial classes. As the years went by, it became harder and harder to predict where any particular individual would place his loyalties, though the prominent prerevolutionary free colored families tended to support the "mulatto" factions. The last actual prerevolutionary free colored to rule Haiti was Jean-Baptiste Riché, in power from 1846 to 1847. Riché was originally put in power by the "mulatto" faction of former president Boyer, but he turned against them and tried to push for racial inclusion and political reform. He was probably assassinated, to be succeeded by Emperor Faustin Solouque, a former slave.

Stewart R. King

FURTHER READING

Bell, Madison Smartt. *Toussaint Louverture: A Biography*. New York: Pantheon, 2007.

Dubois, Laurent. *Avengers of the New World: The Story of the Haitian Revolution*. Cambridge, Mass.: Belknap, 2005.

Garrigus, John. *Before Haiti: Race and Citizenship In French Saint-Domingue*. New York: Palgrave McMillan, 2006.

Geggus, David P. *The Impact of the Haitian Revolution in the Atlantic World*. Columbia: University of South Carolina Press, 2002.

Nicholls, David. *From Dessalines to Duvalier: Race, Color, and National Independence in Haiti*. New Brunswick, N.J.: Rutgers University Press, 1995.

Popkin, Jeremy. *Facing Racial Revolution: Eyewitness Accounts of the Haitian Revolution*. Chicago: University of Chicago Press, 2007.

HALL, PRINCE (ca. 1735–1807) *Continental army soldier, American fraternal organization leader, abolitionist*

Prince Hall was a free man of color who lived in BOSTON in the 1770s. He founded the American black Masonic organization, now known as Prince Hall Freemasonry, in 1775, and organized lodges in several states after the WAR OF AMERICAN INDEPEDENCE, 1775–83. (*See* FREEMASONRY.)

Masonic organizations at the time required that all members be born free, and so an attempt was made at the time and in the official history of Prince Hall freemasonry, published in 1903, to claim that he had been free from birth. Internal inconsistencies make these claims dubious at best, and the broad lines of Prince Hall's early life remain unclear. He may have been born in BARBADOS or Massachusetts, or even in BRITAIN, according to one source, some time around 1735.

Despite the uncertainty of his early life, we do know that Hall was no longer a slave, if he had ever been one, and was living in Boston in 1763, when he married Sarah Ritchie or Richery. He was a member of the Congregational Church, the official church of the colony, a sign that he was accepted by upper-class whites. He owned a house in the city in the 1770s and was a leatherworker and shopkeeper. As a landowner in the city, he was a member of the MILITIA, and as such he joined a military Masonic lodge, associated with a British regular regiment, in 1775 along with several of his black militia comrades. When the American Revolution began in 1775, he may have been involved in plotting against British rule; in any case, when the British left the city in 1776, he did not go with them. His group of black Freemasons continued to meet and were provisionally accepted by the other lodges in the city. In 1777, Hall and eight other Boston free blacks petitioned the Massachusetts government to end slavery, though his petition was referred to the national Congress and never acted upon. In that year, he also enlisted in the Continental army. He met other blacks who were interested in freemasonry while in the military, and after the war many groups asked him to help them organize as Masonic lodges.

Although freemasonry generally supports the principles of the Enlightenment, for a Masonic organization to accept a membership application or affiliate itself with another Masonic group requires the unanimous agreement of all members in a secret ballot. Also, in principle, there is only one Masonic Grand Lodge for each state, and all Masons and Masonic lodges in that state must be associated with the Grand Lodge. Any single member acting out of racial prejudice could keep blacks out, and in most places in the United States, Masonic lodges did not admit black members or accept the existence of the Prince Hall–affiliated lodges. Nevertheless, Prince Hall freemasonry grew rapidly. Many prominent African Americans have been members, including RICHARD ALLEN, MARTIN DELANEY, W. E. B. DuBois, ABSALOM JONES, Booker T. Washington, and Thurgood Marshall.

Prince Hall led the organization during its formative years and achieved recognition by the British Grand Lodge, receiving a formal charter in 1787. He used his position as master of the black Masons of Boston to continue speaking out against slavery and the mistreatment of black workers. The Massachusetts courts had found in 1783 in the QUOCK WALKER CASE that slavery was prohibited under the 1780 state constitution, but for several years thereafter people continued to hold slaves, and the issue was not settled. Prince Hall and the Freemasons played an important role in educating blacks about their newfound rights and in supporting people who sought their freedom. Hall served as Grand Master of the Boston black lodge until his death on December 4, 1807.

Freemasonry was important in the United States as a way for free blacks to build networks and claim equal citizenship with whites under the principles of the Enlightenment. The craft did not, as in other countries in the Americas, offer free men of color a way to make contacts among the white elite but did put the leaders of free black society in contact with each other and with promising young men. Freemasons had to be born free, in principle, although the lodges that descended from the one Hall founded often accepted people who had gained their freedom. Nonetheless, freemasonry in the antebellum period did not accept slave members, and there was a certain amount of social class discrimination. For this reason, other fraternal groups grew up, which nonetheless maintained close relations with the Masons and also worked for racial equality and black community development. The whole universe of black fraternal organizations in the United States ultimately owes its origin to the work of Prince Hall.

Stewart R. King

FURTHER READING

Grey, David. *Inside Prince Hall.* New York: Anchor Communications, 2004.
Roundtree, Alton G., and Paul M. Bessel. *Out of the Shadows: Prince Hall Freemasonry in America, 200 Years of Endurance.* Forestville, Md.: KLR, 2006.

HARRISON, WILLIAM HENRY   (1773–1841)
diplomat, military leader, ninth president of the United States (1841)

William Henry Harrison died in 1841 of complications of a cold he caught at his presidential inauguration, serving only 31 days in office, the shortest tenure of any U.S. president. Nonetheless, he had an eventful career before assuming the presidency and took many steps that affected the lives of free people of color.

Harrison was born on February 9, 1773, in Virginia. He was the last president to be born before American independence. The area he was born in was one of the most heavily developed plantation areas in North America, and his father was a major planter and a member of Virginia's political elite. He grew up surrounded by people of color, both enslaved and free. He went to INDIANA in 1791 as an army officer, part of the army of General Anthony Wayne (1745–96) fighting the powerful Western Confederacy of Ohio Valley and Great Lakes Indian tribes and French Canadian settlers. Wayne's victory at the Battle of Fallen Timbers (August 20, 1794), in which Harrison fought as a junior officer, allowed American settlers to move north of the Ohio River. Indians remained dominant in the Great Lakes region, and the British maintained a fort near today's Detroit.

Harrison left the army after the war and settled in what is now southern Indiana. He served as an assistant to the territorial governor and was acting governor on several occasions. He became governor in 1801. It was during this time that the provisions of the Northwest Ordinance, originally passed in 1787, actually went into force. Among other provisions, slavery was officially prohibited. Many settlers were from KENTUCKY or other slave states and wished to take their slaves with them. Other settlers, from Northern states that were in the process of abandoning slavery, did not like the idea of having to compete for jobs and land against planters with large slave labor forces. Both sides resented free blacks and thought they disturbed some ideal social order—for the Southerners, white supremacy and plantations and for the Northerners an ideal of a white agrarian republic. The territorial government at first resolved all of these conflicting forces by effectively barring blacks, either free or slave, from the territory. This did not entirely stop free blacks from moving to the Ohio valley, but it did both reflect and reinforce a prejudice against them among the white public.

The most important issue for Harrison was encouraging the growth of agriculture, which he hoped to do by reducing the cost of new land for settlers. But he also played to popular prejudices, against Indians mostly, but also against blacks. He tried on several occasions to have the provision of the Northwest Ordinance that outlawed slavery either abolished outright or suspended for a time. Foiled in this endeavor by the slave-owning president THOMAS JEFFERSON, who believed strongly in the dream of a white agrarian republic, he supported attempts to pass laws in the territory barring free black migration. He also called for an aggressive policy against the region's Indians. This policy ultimately resulted in Tecumseh's War (1810–11), which culminated in the victory by troops under Harrison's command at the Battle of Tippecanoe (November 7, 1811) and his subsequent capture of the British forts along the Great Lakes during the War of 1812.

After the War of 1812, he settled in the newly admitted state of OHIO, served in Congress, and was appointed U.S. ambassador to Gran COLOMBIA in 1828–29. In Colombia, he actually was an ally of free people of color, criticizing President Simón Bolívar for, among other things, taking action against prominent free colored leaders from CARTAGENA and the Caribbean coast. His lectures to Bolívar on democracy merely angered the volatile leader, giving rise to the first of many annoyed responses by Latin American leaders when Bolivar said, "The United States . . . seem destined by Providence to plague America with torments in the name of freedom."

Harrison was an early leader of what became known as the Whig Party, opponents of the Democrats under ANDREW JACKSON and MARTIN VAN BUREN in the 1830s. The Whigs supported a strong national government to promote economic development. Whigs tried to compromise on the issue of slavery, and many, such as Harrison's ally Henry Clay of Kentucky, hoped that with economic advancement and modernization, slavery would disappear. Harrison supported laws passed in Ohio prohibiting black settlement there and offered rhetorical support to Clay's AMERICAN COLONIZATION SOCIETY, though Harrison never became a member of the organization. Harrison ran for president in 1836 and lost. He ran again and won in 1840 but held office only a few weeks before his death on April 4, 1841. He was succeeded by Vice President JOHN TYLER.

Stewart R. King

FURTHER READING
Middleton, Steven. *The Black Laws: Race and the Legal Process in Early Ohio.* Athens: Ohio University Press, 2005.
Owens, Robert M. *Mr. Jefferson's Hammer: William Henry Harrison and the Origins of American Indian Policy.* Norman: University of Oklahoma Press, 2007.
Peterson, Norma Lois. *The Presidencies of William Henry Harrison and John Tyler.* Lawrence: University Press of Kansas, 1989.

HAYNES, LEMUEL   (1753–1833) *American Congregational minister and theologian*
Lemuel Haynes, an early African-American religious leader, is believed to be the first African American ordained by a mainstream Protestant Church in the United States (*see* PROTESTANT MAINLINE CHURCHES). In 1783, he became the first African American to serve as pastor of a white congregation, in Rutland, VERMONT. Haynes also produced extensive writings criticizing slavery and the slave trade.

Born in West Hartford, CONNECTICUT, in 1753, Haynes was the son of a white mother and an African American named Haynes. At five months, he was made an indentured servant until the age of 21 to David Rose of Granville, MASSACHUSETTS. Part of the agreement required Rose to educate him. Haynes augmented his education by reading numerous books on theology, including the Bible.

When Haynes's indenture expired in 1774 and he was freed, he joined the Minutemen of the Granville MILITIA and fought in the WAR OF AMERICAN INDEPENDENCE, 1775–83. The militia company marched to Roxbury, Massachusetts, in 1775, following the Battles of Lexington and Concord. Haynes produced one of his first written efforts, a lengthy ballad-sermon about the April 1775 Battle of Lexington. The poem emphasized the conflict between freedom and slavery. After the capture of Fort Ticonderoga in 1776, the Granville militia participated in

the occupation of the fort. Haynes returned to Granville after the end of the northern campaign of the American Revolution.

Haynes became a prolific writer, criticizing the slave trade and slavery. He argued that slavery denied African Americans their natural rights to "Life, Liberty and the pursuit of happyness." (His spelling of Jefferson's phrase inspired the title of the 2006 book and film *The Pursuit of Happyness.*) Comparing the American Revolution with slavery, Haynes wrote, "Liberty is equally as precious to a black man, as it is to a white one, and bondage as equally as intolerable to the one as it is to the other." He also wrote about theological matters and prepared sermons for family prayers.

Haynes turned down the opportunity to study at Dartmouth College after the war, opting instead to study Latin and Greek with clergymen in Connecticut. In 1780, he was licensed to preach, and he accepted a position with a congregation in Middle Granville. Later, Haynes obtained the first of three pastorships, an all-white congregation in Torrington, Connecticut. He left that post after two years, tiring of the prejudice of several members. One member who did not share the prejudice was a young woman, Elizabeth Babbitt. She proposed to Haynes, and they were married in 1783. The couple had 10 children.

In 1783, Haynes began his second pastorship at a primarily white church in Rutland, Vermont. Two years later, in 1785, Haynes was officially ordained a Congregational minister. He spent 30 years ministering to Rutland's West Parish. During this time, he was recognized as a leading Calvinist minister in Vermont. Haynes argued along Calvinist lines that God's providential plan would defeat slavery and lead to the harmonious integration of the races as equals. His position was in contrast to contemporary white republican and abolitionist thinkers who viewed slavery as a liability to America but argued for eventual slave expatriation to Africa. (*See also* AMERICAN COLONIZATION SOCIETY and EMIGRATION AND COLONIZATION.)

In 1804, Haynes's achievements and writings were recognized by Middlebury College in Vermont when they awarded Haynes an honorary degree at the college's second commencement.

Haynes left his church in Rutland, Vermont, in 1818, after conflicts with his congregation over style and politics. There was some speculation, however, that the church's displeasure with him stemmed from racism.

His next appointment was in Manchester, Vermont. There, he counseled two men convicted of murder. They escaped hanging when the alleged victim reappeared. Haynes's writings about the case became a best seller.

For the last 11 years of his life, Haynes ministered to a congregation in Granville, New York. He died on September 28, 1833, at the age of 80.

Lemuel Haynes's writings continued to inspire and teach in the past century. Nearly 150 years after his death, a manuscript written by Haynes around 1776 was discovered. In it, he wrote, "That an African . . . has an undeniable right to his Liberty." The piece condemned slavery and noted the irony of SLAVE OWNERS' fighting for their own liberty while denying it to others.

John McLane

FURTHER READING

"Africans in America/Part 2/Lemuel Haynes." Available online. URL: http://www.pbs.org/wgbh/aia/part2/2p29. html. Accessed December 29, 2010.

Kaplan, Sidney, and Emma Nogrady Kaplan. *The Black Presence in the Era of the American Revolution.* Amherst: University of Massachusetts Press, 1989.

Saillant, John. *Black Puritan, Black Republican: The Life and Thought of Lemuel Haynes, 1753–1833.* New York: Oxford University Press, 2003.

"Virtual Vermont: Vermont History: Lemuel Haynes." Available online. URL: http://www.virtualvermont.com/history/ haynes.html. Accessed December 29, 2010.

HEALERS   *See* MIDWIVES AND HEALERS.

HEALY FAMILY   *American religious leaders and military officers*

The Healy family is a prominent example of a group of mixed-race people with very high proportions of white ancestry who were able to achieve considerable success in the North in the 19th century, not by "passing," but by exploiting the very small amount of flexibility in the racial lines in the United States. Members of the family became senior officials in the ROMAN CATHOLIC CHURCH, while another served as a senior commissioned officer in the precursor to the U.S. Coast Guard.

Michael Morris Healy (1796–1850) was born in Athlone, Ireland, and immigrated to the United States in 1818. He obtained a large plantation in Jones County, GEORGIA, through a lottery and successful purchases. Among his 49 slaves was one named Mary Eliza (ca. 1813–50), who was a mixed-race woman. Almost nothing is known of her ancestry. He began a relationship with her in 1829, which lasted for the remainder of their lives. They had 10 children, of whom nine survived to adulthood, six boys and three girls.

As their children grew up, the parents realized that they had little future in Georgia. Since their mother was never formally manumitted, the children were probably legally slaves, and in this case if their father had financial difficulties they might be sold to pay his debts. It was unlawful to give them any education whatsoever, even basic literacy. Therefore, the Healys decided to send their children to the North. The oldest boys first attended Quaker schools in Flushing, New York, but Michael Healy preferred a Catholic education for his children. He befriended John Bernard Fitzpatrick (1812–66), Catholic bishop of BOSTON, who agreed to help the children get their educations. Therefore, the boys were all sent to College of the Holy Cross, at that time a secondary school, in Worcester, MASSACHUSETTS, when it opened in 1843. The girls attended the convent school of the Congregation of Notre Dame in Montréal, CANADA. Bishop Fitzpatrick became an important patron for the children in their future careers. When both parents died unexpectedly in 1850, Hugh, 12 at the time, went back to Georgia at some risk of RE-ENSLAVEMENT and took his three sisters and his youngest brother to safety. The executors appear to have passed on at least some of the family property to the children as they later had enough money to pay for their educations and start them in their careers.

The children generally followed social paths appropriate to Irish Catholics of means. Three of the sons—James Augustine, Patrick Francis, and Alexander Sherwood—became Catholic priests, and all three daughters—Martha, Josephine, and Eliza—became nuns. One brother, Hugh, went into business and died in his early 20s. Another brother, Michael Augustine, joined the Revenue Cutter Service, the ancestor of today's U.S. Coast Guard, rising to the rank of captain. They appear in most cases to have been treated by society as white Irish, not mixed-race. Their ancestry was known in at least some cases and physically obvious at least in the case of the fourth son, Alexander Sherwood. It is possible that the Irish component to their ethnic background successfully masked their blackness in the eyes of society where another white ethnicity would not have. Irish were also the targets of discrimination during this period, though nothing as harsh as what blacks experienced. But perhaps it was easier to "whiten" to the status of Irish (*see also* "WHITENING" AND RACIAL PROMOTION). Their religion might also have protected them, especially since two of the brothers went on to become very famous churchmen. The Roman Catholic Church had a mixed record in opposing slavery, but a much better record of insisting consistently on at least minimal inclusion of people of all races. Catholics formed a distinct class in American society at the time, as a minority suspected by the Protestant majority of strange religious practices and superstition. Mixed-race people who looked at least a little white could perhaps fit more easily into another separated and oppressed community.

James Augustine Healy (1830–1900), Roman Catholic bishop

James Augustine Healy discovered a vocation to the priesthood quite early in life. He referred to it as his goal in grammar school. Indeed, it was common for the eldest son in pious Irish families to enter the priesthood. After graduating as the valedictorian of the first graduating class at College of the Holy Cross in 1849, James entered a Sulpician seminary in Canada. He had to go to Canada because his first choice, the JESUITS' seminary in MARYLAND, would not accept a student of African ancestry, and neither would any other seminary in the United States. In 1852, he went to Saint-Sulpice seminary in Paris, FRANCE, originally with the intention of earning a Ph.D. and becoming a seminary professor. However, he changed his mind and decided to become a pastor, and in 1854, he was ordained for the Diocese of Boston in Notre Dame Cathedral in Paris. He was the first American of African ancestry to be ordained a Catholic priest. He became an assistant pastor in Boston, then in 1866 pastor of the largest congregation in the city. He was Bishop Fitzpatrick's right-hand man in the diocesan administration as well. As a leading cleric, he spoke out against proposed taxes on churches and Massachusetts laws that discriminated against Catholics. In part as a reward for his outspoken defense of the church, Pope Pius IX (1792–1878, reigned 1846–78) elevated him to bishop of Portland, Maine, in 1875. He thus became the first American of African ancestry to be made a Catholic bishop. He oversaw Catholic activities in Maine for 25 years until his death in 1900, founding many churches and witnessing a rapid expansion in the numbers and respect accorded his denomination. His African ancestry was known, and he was regularly invited to speak to groups of black Catholics or to other groups on topics related to race relations. He always refused these invitations, expressing support for racial inclusion but not representing himself as a black cleric or someone especially interested in racial matters. When Fr. AUGUSTINE TOLTON, often referred to as America's "first black priest," passed through Boston in the 1880s, Bishop Healy met with him but could not be induced to "come out" and address issues of racial equality from an African-American point of view.

Hugh Healy (1832–1854), businessman

The second son, Hugh Healy, also attended College of the Holy Cross. After his parents' death in 1850, he returned to Georgia to escort his sisters and younger brother to safety in Massachusetts. After secondary school, Hugh went into business in Worcester as a hardware retailer and died in an accident at the age of 21.

Patrick Francis Healy (1834–1910), Roman Catholic priest and educator

The third child, Patrick Francis Healy, was a brilliant student at College of the Holy Cross. He graduated in 1850 and entered the Jesuit religious order. The headquarters and seminary of the American Jesuits was in Maryland, a slave state, and Patrick's African ancestry caused controversy. Finally, faced with resistance from donors and some fellow members of the Society, his superiors sent Patrick to study at the University of Louvain, in Belgium. He was ordained to the priesthood

A photograph of Patrick Francis Healy (1834–1910), a Roman Catholic priest of the Jesuit order and president of Georgetown University. Father Healy was the first U.S. person of color to become a member of the Jesuits and the first to be president of a majority-white university. Healy and his numerous siblings were born enslaved in Georgia of a mixed-race mother and an Irish immigrant father and were taken to freedom in Massachusetts by their parents. They were quite light-skinned, and although their racial identity was not unknown to their superiors and colleagues, they did not suffer from as much racial discrimination as other African Americans at the time. One of Patrick Healy's brothers became a bishop, and another became a captain in the precursor to the U.S. Coast Guard. *(Library of Congress)*

in 1864 and received a Ph.D. in 1866, the first American of African ancestry to receive that degree. In that year, he returned to the United States, becoming a professor of philosophy at the Society's Georgetown University, in Washington, D.C. In 1874, he became the 29th president of the university. He was so effective in taking the institution into the modern age that he is often referred to as the "second founder" of Georgetown. He retired from the presidency in 1882 but remained on the faculty and lived on campus until his death in 1910. The office of the president of the university is today located in Healy Hall, an imposing building built with money raised by Father Healy and named after him.

Alexander Sherwood Healy (1836–1873), Roman Catholic priest, musician, and educator

As did his brothers James and Patrick, Alexander Sherwood Healy also felt a vocation to the priesthood. Sherwood, as he was called, had the most distinctively African appearance of the siblings, and there was no question of his studying in the United States. He followed his oldest brother, James, into the Sulpicians, studying for the priesthood at Saint-Sulpice in France. He, too, was ordained at Notre Dame Cathedral in 1858. He was very interested in church music and participated in the revival of Gregorian chant that was occurring at the time. The Abbey of Solesmes, in France, was one of the centers of this movement, and he stayed there for several months. Sherwood remained in Europe for several more years, failing to obtain an appointment as director of the Catholic American College in Rome because leading church figures thought that his race would make him unacceptable to white American students. Finally, he returned to Boston in the 1860s, introducing and popularizing chant music in the liturgy. He was probably also bound for promotion to bishop when he fell ill and died in 1873.

Martha Healy Cashman (1837–1892), teacher

Martha Healy Cashman, like her two younger sisters, was sent to the convent school of the Congregation of Notre Dame, a Catholic women's religious order, in Montréal. She graduated in 1851 and became a novice of the order. She was sent as a teacher to St John's, Quebec, where she served for several years. She did not take her final vows in the order, instead resigning, moving to Boston, and marrying an Irish immigrant named John Cashman in 1859. She lived the rest of her life in suburban respectability in the increasingly well-off Irish community of Boston.

Michael Augustine Healy (1838–1904), Coast Guard officer

Michael Augustine Healy followed much the same path as his older siblings until the age of 15. He was unhappy at the College of the Holy Cross and acquired an extensive disciplinary record. His older brothers gained his admission to a seminary in France, but after a year there he quit, provoking an almost decade-long estrangement from his family. In 1854, he signed on as a crewman on the American merchant ship *Jumna*, rising from cabin boy to officer in the merchant service over the next 10 years. In 1864, he returned to the United States, reconciled with his famous brother James, and married an Irish immigrant woman the following year. He applied for a commission in the Revenue Cutter Service, the predecessor of today's Coast Guard, and was appointed a third lieutenant. This was the same period when a few blacks were permitted to rise to the rank of officer in the U.S. Army and Navy, and a few black cadets were admitted to the U.S. Military Academy at West Point. Michael rose through the ranks of the service and became a captain in 1880. The United States purchased Alaska from Russia in 1867, and the Revenue Cutter Service was responsible for mapping the coastline and exploring the resources of this enormous new territory. Michael Healy made several voyages to the area starting in 1868, and in 1882, he took command of the cutter *Thomas Corwin*, permanently stationed in Alaska. In 1886, he became commander of the *Bear*, the newest and most powerful cutter in the service. He commanded it for 10 years, becoming the leading authority on sailing conditions in the Bering Sea and Gulf of Alaska. He was also almost the only representative of the U.S. government in the area, serving as policeman, social service department, and hospital for a wide range of Alaskans. Native people, prospectors, and seal and whale hunters all knew and respected him. The naturalist John Muir (1838–1914) made several voyages with Healy as part of a mission to catalog the life-forms of Alaska. Healy was known as "Hell Roaring Mike," in part because of a volcanic temper that occasionally got him in trouble with his superiors. He was also occasionally called "Black Mike," which may have been a reference to his racial background or a further, more restrained, description of his temper. His great seamanship and the respect Alaskans had for him protected him from any negative consequences springing from either trait. He retired in 1904 and died later that year. In 1999, the Coast Guard named one of its research icebreakers after Healy.

Josephine Healy (1841–1864), Roman Catholic nun and nurse

Josephine Healy was educated at the Congregation of Notre Dame, as were her two sisters. Instead of joining the congregation, she became a novice in the Hospitallers of St. Joseph, a nursing order, upon graduation in 1856. She died in Ontario in 1864 after working with the order for a few years.

Eliza Healy (1846–1918), Roman Catholic nun and educator

Eliza Healy completed her schooling with the Congregation of Notre Dame in 1861, but instead of joining the order she continued her education at Villa Maria, a Catholic girls secondary school in Montréal, then returned to the Boston area and lived with her younger brother, Eugene. She taught in a school for black children there. After Eugene left home in 1873, Eliza returned to the Congregation and became a novice at, for that time, the advanced age of 28. She was assigned as a teacher at several schools in Quebec and Massachusetts, and then in 1903, she became the headmistress and superior of Villa Barlow, in St. Albans, Vermont. This was a very prestigious school that attracted socially prominent young women, both Catholic and Protestant, from New England. The school was in some disorder, with financial difficulties and a poorly trained and motivated staff. Healy served there for 14 years, resolving all the controversies and becoming one of the most revered educators in the order. In 1918, the order transferred her to the College of Notre Dame in Staten Island, according her the honorary title of Mother Superior. She died in Staten Island later that year.

Eugene Healy (1848–?)

The youngest son, Eugene Healy, experienced a lot of dislocation in his early life. He appears to have had difficulty at school and did not graduate from the College of the Holy Cross. He had problems with alcohol and gambling in later life and was under the care of his next-oldest sister, Eliza, for a while. He left home in 1873, and there is no further record of him after that time.

Conclusion

The Healy family illustrates some of the conditions associated with whitening, or what was called "passing" in the United States. Unlike many light-skinned people who passed for white, the Healy children did not have to cut their ties to their family or deny their heritage entirely. The Healys and their own descendants remained aware of their African ancestry, as did at least some of the people they associated with during their lives. To a considerable extent, they benefited from a looser set of ideas about race than were usually applied in the United States; they were treated more like what might have been the case in Latin America or Catholic Europe. The Dumas family in France, for example, was considered white in the same way as the Healys. Nobody was unaware that the famous General THOMAS-ALEXANDRE DUMAS was a mulatto, but his son and grandson, famous writers, were still generally considered whites. There are a number of reasons for this relative tolerance extended to the Healys. First, although they lived in a variety of places in the northeastern United States and Canada, their life as a family centered on Massachusetts, the most liberal state from the point of view of race relations. Second, they had a powerful patron, deeply entrenched in the power structure of Boston even though he was from a subordinate religious tradition. Third, as Catholics, they benefited from generally positive teachings about race relations from the highest authority in the church. Individual Catholics might harbor racial prejudice, but the church itself was opposed to it and, even in the 19th century, was willing to force members to accept racial minorities. And finally, since they were Catholics and Irish, groups that already experienced discrimination, it was not so much of a stretch for society to overlook their African ancestry than if they had tried to assimilate to white Anglo-Protestantism.

Stewart R. King

FURTHER READING

O'Toole, James. "Passing Free." *Boston College Magazine* (Summer 2003). Available online. URL: http://bcm.bc.edu/issues/summer_2003/ft_passing.html. Accessed December 25, 2010.

———. *Passing for White: Race, Religion, and the Healy Family, 1820–1920.* Amherst: University of Massachusetts Press, 2003.

HEMINGS, SALLY, CHILDREN OF

Sarah "Sally" Hemings (1773–1835), a slave of THOMAS JEFFERSON (1743–1826), gave birth to at least four children and possibly as many as seven. Most scholars now believe Hemings and Jefferson had a sexual relationship, probably long term, and many think Jefferson fathered at least one and perhaps all of her children. A DNA study published in 1998 indicated that Thomas Jefferson or a male-line relative was the father of Hemings's youngest son, Eston.

In fact, the paternity of Sally Hemings's children has been debated since the early 1800s, when Jefferson's political enemies in an attempt to discredit him and prevent him from winning a second term as president charged that he had fathered interracial children. Jefferson was reelected in 1804 despite the controversy, but at the time, the allegation of MISCEGENATION was an embarrassment, an offense based on racial or moral rather than sexual transgression.

As was their mother, Hemings's children were born slaves. Two of her children—Beverley (1798–unknown) and Harriet (1801–unknown)—gained their freedom by "running away" from Monticello and passing as white (see "WHITENING" AND RACIAL PROMOTION). Her two youngest children—Madison (1805–77) and Eston (1808–56)—were freed by Jefferson's will. Hemings herself remained a slave in the possession of Jefferson's acknowledged daughter, Martha Randolph (1772–36), but Sally was allowed "her time" and was informally freed (see LIVING "AS FREE").

Sally Hemings and Thomas Jefferson

Sally Hemings was born to Elizabeth "Betty" Hemings (1735–1807), a slave of John Wayles (1715–73), in Charles City County in 1773. Wayles died within a few months of Sally's birth, after which Betty and her descendants became the property of Thomas Jefferson. Jefferson had married Wayles's daughter, Martha Skelton, in 1772. Most sources suggest that John Wayles was Sally's father; if true, that would make Martha Jefferson (1748–82) and Sally Hemings half sisters.

Her paternity would also explain why she was often described as a "bright mulatto" (meaning light-skinned): If Wayles was her father, then Sally was three-fourths white, known as a quadroon, as her grandfather was also reputed to be white. The lightness of her skin would later allow some of her children to pass for white.

Sally was raised by her mother at Monticello and was nine years old when Martha Jefferson died on September 6, 1782. After Mrs. Jefferson's death, Jefferson went to Paris as the U.S. minister to FRANCE with his eldest daughter, Martha. Later, he asked that his younger daughter, Mary "Polly" Jefferson (1778–1804), then staying with her aunt, Elizabeth Epps, be sent to Paris to join them. And, in 1787, Sally, but 14 at the time, was sent to Paris as a companion to Polly.

Sally remained in Paris for about two years, receiving wages for part of her time there and receiving training in needlework and the care of clothing. She, along with her brother James, could have petitioned for freedom under French law. But she did not and returned to Monticello with Thomas Jefferson in 1789. Her son Madison's memoir claims that Sally was pregnant with her first child before she left Paris. Madison believed that Jefferson was the father and related that Sally refused to leave Paris unless Jefferson promised to free her children.

At Monticello, Sally lived out her life as a lady's maid, chambermaid, and seamstress, giving birth to as many as seven children. She and her four surviving children were house slaves and at the top of the slave hierarchy at Monticello.

The Children of Sally Hemings

Sally gave birth to at least four children and perhaps as many as six or seven. At least two children did not survive to adulthood, including a daughter (by the name of Harriet) who was born on October 5, 1795, and died on December 7, 1797, and a daughter who was born in 1799 and died in infancy.

Madison's memoir also speaks of a third child who died in infancy born after Sally's return from Paris in 1790; Madison indicates that the child lived only a short time. The oral tradition of the Woodson family claims that Thomas C. Woodson (1790–1879), father of the educator LEWIS WOODSON, was that child—the first child of Sally and Jefferson. However, the 1998 DNA study indicated the descendants of Woodson were not a DNA match with the Jefferson line.

Four of Sally's children survived to adulthood: Beverley, Harriet, Madison, and Eston.

Beverley Hemings

Beverley Hemings was born on April 1, 1798, and much of what is known about him (and the rest of the Hemings siblings) is known from Madison's 1873 memoirs or Jefferson's Farm Book.

Little is known about how any of the Hemings children grew up, but generally they seem to have been apprenticed or have had some kind of training beginning at age of 14. As did his brothers, Beverley learned carpentry, and he was also a musician. In 1822, Beverley left Monticello, probably with the tacit approval of Jefferson since Beverley was never pursued.

Madison indicated that Beverley relocated to Washington, D.C., and changed his racial identity to white, passing for white and marrying a white woman from MARYLAND. Beverley and his wife had a daughter, but no living descendants are known.

Harriet Hemings

Harriet Hemings was born on May 22, 1801. She was trained as a spinner and weaver and worked as a spinner in Jefferson's textile shop.

In 1822, Harriet also left Monticello, possibly with her brother Beverley, for Washington, D.C. She also probably had the tacit approval of Jefferson; she was never pursued, and Jefferson made provision for her to be given some funds before she left.

Madison's memoirs indicate that Harriet also changed her racial identity, married a white man, and raised a family of children. Her descendants, if living, are unknown.

Madison Hemings

Madison Hemings was born on January 19, 1805, and was named after Jefferson's great friend JAMES MADISON. At 14, Madison entered into an apprenticeship with his uncle John Hemings (Sally's brother) to learn carpentry. He also learned to play the violin.

Madison was freed by the conditions of Thomas Jefferson's will, after which he rented a house in Charlottesville with Eston, and though Sally was never formally freed, she went to live with her sons there.

Madison married Mary McCoy (a free woman of color) in 1834, and they had 10 children. Two were born in Virginia before 1836, including a son who died as an infant and a daughter named Sarah (1835–84) after Madison's mother. In 1836, Madison and his family moved to Pike County, OHIO, south of Chillicothe. Eston also lived there, and Chillicothe had a thriving free black community. Three sons were born in Ohio, including Thomas Eston (1838–63), William Beverly (1847–1910), and James Madison (1849–unknown), along with five daughters, including Harriet (1839–1925), Mary Ann (1843–1921), Catherine Jane (1844–80), Julia Ann (1851–67), and Ellen Wayles (1856–1940).

Two of his sons served on the Union side in the AMERICAN CIVIL WAR, 1861–65, in the United States Colored Troops. Madison's children and grandchildren were storekeepers, farmers, domestic servants, and laborers.

Madison was a landowner and made his living as a farmer and carpenter. In 1873, when he was 68, Madison shared his family's story and details of his life at Monticello with the journalist Samuel F. Wetmore, who published a series of articles in the *Pike County Republican*.

Madison died of tuberculosis on November 28, 1877. Madison was the only child of Sally's who appears to have remained in the black community.

Eston Hemings
Eston Hemings was born on May 21, 1808. Like Madison, Eston was apprenticed to John Hemings and trained in carpentry. He was a talented musician, playing the piano and violin.

Eston was manumitted at age 21 by the conditions of Jefferson's will, and both brothers were allowed to remain in Virginia through Jefferson's appeal to the state legislature. (At this time, Virginia law required that manumitted slaves leave the state.)

After being freed, Eston worked as a carpenter and woodworker in Charlottesville. And, in 1830, he and Madison purchased a house—Sally lived with him there until she died in 1835. In 1832, Eston married Julia Ann Issacs (a free woman of mixed-raced ancestry), and they had three children. Two were born in Charlottesville, John Wayles (1835–1892) and Anne Wayles (1832–66), taking the last name of Sally's mother's master and Sally's purported father. In 1837, Eston and his family moved to Chillicothe, Ohio. There, Beverley Frederick (1838–1908) was born. Hemings worked as a professional musician in Chillicothe.

In 1852, Eston and his family moved north to Madison, WISCONSIN, perhaps because of the political environment in the Chillicothe community after the passage of the FUGITIVE SLAVE ACT OF 1850. Eston and his family adopted the surname Jefferson and took the opportunity offered by their move into a community of strangers to change their race to white.

Both of Eston's sons served on the Union side in the American Civil War as white men. His eldest son, John, led the Wisconsin 8th Infantry and was promoted to colonel before he was mustered out of service in 1864. Later, John became a prosperous cotton broker, and Beverley a respected hotel owner. Eston's grandsons became businessmen, lawyers, and physicians.

Eston died on January 3, 1856.

The 1998 DNA study revolved, in part, around descendants of Eston. The study showed that John Weeks Jefferson was a descendant of the Thomas Jefferson male line.

Conclusion
The 1998 issue of *Nature* and the case of Sally Hemings and her children and their relationship to Thomas Jefferson cast light on some of the complexities of the time.

Jefferson was certainly not the only slaveholder to have a sexual relationship with a slave, whether through the slave's consent (insofar as consent is possible in such a relationship) or through rape. The children of these encounters existed as shadow families throughout the South, living with and serving the acknowledged white family. Many slaveholders, including Jefferson, never acknowledged their children born to slave mothers. To do so would have violated the social mores of the time.

Matters are never so simple, though, and in some cases these slaveholders did help their children informally. It is telling that so many of Hemings children could play musical instruments when Jefferson himself played the violin and cello. More important, Jefferson ensured that each of the Hemings children learned a trade, perhaps preparing them to support themselves as freedmen.

Likewise, it is significant that three of Hemings's four children changed their racial identity to white. Many light-skinned freed slaves chose to pass for white in order to improve their opportunities in life. But the disavowal of their black ancestry had a cost—usually the freed slaves had to move to a new community and break all ties with their family. They denied their past, sometimes living in fear that they would be discovered. At the time of Madison's interviews, he had not spoken with his older brother and sister for more than 10 years.

The case also highlights some of the limitations of our time. It is worth noting that through the 19th and 20th centuries most of Jefferson's biographers did not believe that he had fathered children by a slave. In that sense this case also serves to reinforce the value and illustrate the reliability of the oral tradition among slaves—the Hemings family oral traditions are more accurate than Jefferson's acknowledged written and legal documents.

Jefferson's acknowledged family, of course, had its own motivations to promote a certain kind of legacy, but the issue is a larger one: The denial of the oral traditions of slaves (especially the treatment of Madison Hemings and Israel Jefferson as liars or glory seekers) both by

Jefferson's contemporaries and later writers reveals that whites were only too happy to sacrifice the honor and identity of slaves and free people of color to maintain the interests of whites. And, in doing so, those writers denied slaves and free people of color the power to define reality and history—to find themselves and their ancestors in the national story.

Summer Leibensperger

FURTHER READING

Brodie, Fawn M. *Thomas Jefferson: An Intimate History.* New York: W. W. Norton, 1974.

Foster, Eugene, et al. "Jefferson Fathered Slave's Last Child." *Nature* 196 (November 1998): 27–28.

Gordon-Reed, Annette. *The Hemingses of Monticello: An American Family.* New York: W. W. Norton, 2008.

Horton, James Oliver, and Lois E. Horton, eds. *Slavery and Public History: The Tough Stuff of American Memory.* New York: New Press, 2006.

Lewis, Jan Ellen, and Peter S. Onuf, eds. *Sally Hemings and Thomas Jefferson: History, Memory, and Civic Culture.* Charlottesville: University Press of Virginia, 1999.

Neiman, Fraser D. "Coincidence or Causal Connection? The Relationship between Thomas Jefferson's Visits to Monticello and Sally Hemings's Conceptions." *William and Mary Quarterly* 57, no. 1 (January 2000): 198–210.

HIGHER EDUCATION

It was very uncommon for anybody to attend college or university before the 20th century. No more than a few percent of the population in any country would have graduated from college. Therefore, it is not surprising to discover that only a very small number of free people of color attended university in all the countries of the Americas. Black university graduates did exist, however, and became more common as racial attitudes began to improve in some places in the early 19th century.

The original purpose for universities when they were first established in Europe in the Middle Ages was to train men for the Roman Catholic priesthood. These medieval universities became important players in the religious debates of the period, with prominent thinkers such as Thomas Aquinas (1225–74), Desiderius Erasmus (1466–1536), and Martin Luther (1483–1546) all serving as members of university faculties. Even before the Renaissance, though, universities had begun to teach other subjects, especially law and "natural philosophy," or science. By the beginning of European colonial expansion in the Americas in the 1500s, European universities were turning out numerous nonclerical graduates who held positions in government or were artists and philosophers. Hernán Cortés (1485–1547), Spanish leader of the conquest of MEXICO, studied law at a university in Spain before traveling to the Americas, and he was one of many university-trained lawyers who governed the Spanish Empire.

Higher education was not open to most people of color in the Americas until the 19th century. Most places in the Americas did not have colleges or universities, since governments of their home countries were suspicious and wanted to keep universities close to home where they could keep an eye on them. Those colleges that did exist in the Americas were small and mostly restricted to training religious leaders.

Franciscan missionaries in Mexico established the Colegio de Santa Cruz de Tlatelolco in 1533 with the intention of training an indigenous priesthood. Some indigenous people were trained as priests, and some people of mixed African and Indian ancestry were also students, according to some sources, but the whole program was closed down when the Spanish authorities decided in 1605 that they would no longer allow nonwhites to become priests. People of color were once again allowed to be ordained priests in the late 1700s, and among others JOSÉ MARÍA MORELOS, a man of mixed race, and one of the heroes of the liberation of Mexico, trained for the priesthood at the Colegio San Nicolás in Valladolid, where the liberal priest and future revolutionary Miguel Hidalgo was rector. The DOMINICANS established universities in Santo Domingo and Lima in the 1550s. Some people of mixed race who were children of powerful white men may have been able to study at these institutions. It is possible that the Peruvian monk MARTIN DE PORRES studied medicine at Lima's university in the early 1600s; he cared for the sick in his convent's infirmary and is sometimes referred to in contemporary documents as a physician, indicating that he had had formal medical training.

BRAZIL and the French and British Caribbean had no universities before the 1800s. Brazilian universities admitted students of color in the 19th century, and some of the most famous black leaders of Brazil, including the journalist José Cavlos do Patrocínio, were university graduates. Some free people of color from the Caribbean studied at universities in Europe, where the racial climate was less harsh and the educational system stronger. ALEXANDRE SABÈS PÉTION, the first president of independent Haiti, was sent by his wealthy white father to the French national military academy.

The Northern states of the United States had a more vibrant higher education system than Latin America, with the first colleges and universities, Harvard, William and Mary, and Yale, founded there in the 17th and very early 18th centuries and a wide range of institutions open by the mid-18th. These North American institutions were originally established for religious training of Protestant ministers but quickly began educating students in a wide range of disciplines. American blacks found it very difficult to gain access to higher education in the United States, despite the relatively large number of schools, however. The first black graduate of a college in the United States was Alexander Twilight (1795–1857), who graduated from Middlebury College in Middlebury, VERMONT, in 1823. The first institution regularly to admit students of color, however, was Oberlin College in OHIO, beginning in 1835. Harvard had allowed a few free men of color to attend classes in the 1700s, but the first black graduate of Harvard did not receive his degree until 1870—and he had spent the first three years of his college career at Oberlin. Yale gave its first degree to a black student in 1857, an M.D.

A number of higher education institutions in the United States were originally intended solely for the education of black students, though today they admit students of all races. The first of these historically black colleges and universities was Cheyney University in PHILADELPHIA, PENNSYLVANIA, originally called the Institute for Colored Youth and founded in 1837 by Quakers to train black schoolteachers. Many of today's black colleges were formed after the AMERICAN CIVIL WAR, 1861–65 in the South in an initiative linked to the work of the U.S. Army's FREEDMEN'S BUREAU.

For anybody, higher education was and is an important door to social mobility. For free people of color in the 18th and 19th centuries, it was an especially important entryway since so many other routes of social advancement were closed to them by racial prejudice. Paradoxically, the segregation of people of color in the British colonies and in the United States created a niche within the society for an educated free black middle class. Segregated schools needed black teachers and administrators; if health care was to be segregated, then there needed to be black physicians and nurses; black churches needed black pastors; and other positions needed professionals with higher education. The creation of this black middle class was one goal of the post–Civil War American civil rights campaigner and educator W. E. B. DuBois (1868–1973), descended from a MASSACHUSETTS free black family. DuBois continually stressed the importance of higher education for blacks and worked to break down segregation and discrimination in universities. In other countries in the Americas, the less virulent racial climate permitted more people of color to attain higher education at an earlier date. Once again, the experience permitted those individuals to rise in society and allowed people of color collectively to raise their profile and break down walls of segregation. Throughout the period and across the Americas, blacks were and remain today less likely to earn college degrees than whites, but the fact that any were successful was important to the struggle of the whole group.

Stewart R. King

FURTHER READING

Baumann, Roland. *Constructing Black Education at Oberlin College: A Documentary History.* Athens: Ohio University Press, 2010.

Bullock, H. A. *A History of Negro Education in the South From 1619 to the Present.* New York: Praeger, 1970.

DuBois, W. E. B. "The Talented Tenth." In *The Negro Problem: A Series of Articles by Representative American Negroes of Today*, edited by Booker T. Washington. New York: James Pott, 1903. Available online. URL: http://teachingamericanhistory.org/library/index.asp?document=174. Accessed March 8, 2010.

Hardin, John A. *Fifty Years of Segregation: Black Higher Education in Kentucky, 1904–1954.* Lexington: University Press of Kentucky, 1997.

Kennedy, Thomas. *A History of Southland College: The Society of Friends and Black Education in Arkansas.* Fort Smith: University of Arkansas Press, 2009.

HONDURAS

Honduras is located in the Central American isthmus. It is bordered on the west by GUATEMALA, on the south by EL SALVADOR, and on the southeast by NICARAGUA. It has a long coastline on the Caribbean Sea and includes in its national territory several islands in the Caribbean (the Bay Islands group). It has a short southern coastline on the Gulf of Fonseca, which opens onto the Pacific Ocean. Most of the country is mountainous, and the Caribbean coastal strip is swampy and heavily forested. The Sula River valley in the Northwest is flat and well watered. The mountainous interior is relatively well watered and supports traditional agriculture of corn, beans, and squash.

The indigenous population of Honduras included an important Mayan cultural center at the city of Copán in the Northwest. Other Honduran indigenous groups were related to the people of central MEXICO. Spanish explorers, beginning with Columbus in 1504, visited the coast and the islands, and the first expedition to penetrate the interior of the country was in 1524. Pedro de Alvarado (1485–1541) suppressed indigenous resistance by 1538, establishing the capital of the Spanish province at Tegucigalpa. The names of Sebastian Toral and Pedro Fulupo are recorded among the companions of Alvarado, with the notation "negro," and Toral gained manumission and an exemption from tribute obligations for his services on the expedition. This makes Toral one of the first free people of color in Honduras, along with the somewhat better-documented Juan Bardales (?–1551), who was also a companion of Alvarado, and for his bravery in combat he was awarded his freedom and a pension. He later became an important early

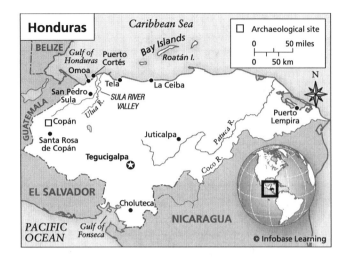

of 15,351. The total population of the colony at the time, including Indians and rural dwellers, was about 95,000.

Aside from the area around Omoa, the rest of the Caribbean coast of Honduras was essentially unexplored and almost unpopulated through most of the colonial period. In the mid-18th century, British and Afro-Caribbean settlers began to move into this region. A number of people of mixed Indian and African ancestry, known as the Garifuna, relatives of the group found in BELIZE, were moved into the area by the British government, who saw them as a disruptive influence in Saint Vincent in the BRITISH LESSER ANTILLES, where they had been living. The Garifuna and related Afro-native groups, such as the Miskito of Nicaragua, developed a distinctive Afro-Caribbean culture that extends all the way from the southeastern coast of Mexico to Costa Rica.

In the late colonial period, after 1770, Spain began to extend its influence over the Caribbean coastal region, in part because of the presence of British settlers there and in part because of the possibility of developing plantation agriculture. COFFEE CULTIVATION increased after the turn of the 19th century, ultimately becoming one of the major exports of the country today. Coffee is grown in Central America mainly by very small producers, but there was a limited demand for African slaves, and Honduras imported several thousand slaves for agricultural labor during the last decades of the colonial period. The survivors of this people, having spent less time under Spanish rule before independence, are the people in Honduran society most likely to self-identify as Afro-Hondurans today.

Honduras gained its independence from Spain along with the rest of the Viceroyalty of New Spain in 1821. The WAR OF MEXICAN INDEPENDENCE, 1810–21, did not have a very strong impact on the territory that became Honduras, though there was some fighting along the Pacific coast and in El Salvador. When Agustín Iturbide's first Mexican Empire fell apart, Honduras and the rest of Central America declared independence in 1823 as the Federal Republic of Central America. The federation was strongly influenced by liberal ideas, one of which was the abolition of slavery, so, as did Mexico to the north, Central America abolished slavery in its constitution in 1824. As in Mexico and elsewhere in the Spanish Americas, this formal abolition did not end the practice of slavery throughout the national territory. Large landowners and the Roman Catholic Church never accepted the republic and ultimately rebelled against its authority, dissolving the federation by 1841 and creating the five modern nations of Guatemala, El Salvador, Nicaragua, Costa Rica, and Honduras. The liberal hero, Francisco Morazán (1792–1842), a Honduran, ensured that the newly independent Honduras would have legal equality of the races

settler. Highland Honduras was a very peripheral part of the Spanish Empire, ruled as a part of the Viceroyalty of New Spain from Mexico City throughout the colonial period. It was part of the Captaincy General of Guatemala and was primarily useful to Spain as a mining center. Elite Spaniards took some black slaves with them as servants, foremen, or technical specialists, but most of the labor was performed by native people. Honduras was never a slave society in the same sense as the coastal regions of Mexico or the Spanish Caribbean islands.

The port of Omoa, located in northwestern Honduras, was a principal port for the entire region. A number of African slaves passed through this port from the 16th century onward, and several hundred royal slaves were imported to work on the fortifications of the city. The royal slaves remained in the area, working on other public works. Since they were slaves of the king and not of any local master, their situation was somewhat easier than that of other slaves. They found it fairly easy ultimately to gain their freedom, joining other free Afro-Hondurans to make the city the largest concentration of PARDOS—people of mixed race—in the colony.

Many of the Afro-Honduran descendants of slaves taken to the highlands also gained freedom during the colonial period. Spanish laws made MANUMISSION fairly simple. The living and working conditions of the first slaves imported to Honduras—as craft workers, domestic servants, and supervisors of Indian work gangs in mines and farms—permitted them some access to money and made them important assets for their masters. These sorts of conditions permitted the growth of a substantial population of free people of color. By the late colonial period, *pardos* dominated the free population of the cities: In a 1770 ROMAN CATHOLIC CHURCH survey of Honduran cities and towns (apparently excluding the rural and predominantly Indian population), there were 10,209 free Afro-Hondurans in a total adult population and no slavery. The American filibusterer William Walker (1824–60), briefly president of Nicaragua in 1857, tried to invade Honduras in 1860. In all his expeditions to Central America, Walker was acting on behalf of groups from the Southern United States who wished to annex territory in Latin America so as to reintroduce slavery there. Walker was defeated by Honduran forces in 1860 and shot after his capture.

As in many parts of Spanish America, many Afro-Hondurans blended into a larger mixed-race community and progressively lost their distinct group identity. From constituting about 18 percent of the population of the colony in the 1770s, people who identify themselves as Afro-Hondurans today make up only about 2 percent of the population. Many other Hondurans have some African ancestry but do not consider themselves Afro-Honduran. The Garifuna still have a distinct identity, and these Afro-Hondurans have contributed a distinctive theatrical form, the Louvavagu, to the country's culture.

Stewart R. King

FURTHER READING
Cáceres Gómez, Rina. "The African Origins of San Fernando de Omoa." In *Trans-Atlantic Dimensions of Ethnicity in the African Diaspora*, edited by Paul Lovejoy and David Trotman, 115–138 London: Continuum, 2003.
England, Sara. *Afro-Central Americans in New York City: Garifuna Tales of Transnational Movements in Racialized Space*. Gainesville: University Press of Florida, 2006.
Gonzalez, Nancie L. "The Garifuna of Central America." In *The Indigenous People of the Caribbean*, edited by Samuel M. Wilson, 197–205. Gainesville: University Press of Florida, 1997.

HOUSE, CALLIE (1861–1928) *American civil rights campaigner*
Callie House was born in 1861 in Rutherford County, central TENNESSEE, during the first year of the AMERICAN CIVIL WAR, 1861–65. House supported the philosophy of restitution for former slaves, and her ideas and words continue to be cited in the modern slave reparations movement.

Callie married William House in 1883. William was probably a relative of Charlie House, who was married to Callie's sister. Callie House had five children, and she helped support her family by going into the laundry business. Both white and African-American families used her services.

After moving to Nashville, House cofounded the National Ex-Slave Mutual Relief, Bounty and Pension Association with Isaiah Dickerson in 1894. The orga-

nization's first convention, held four years later, established the goal of organizing a federal pension for former slaves. The organization formed several local chapters throughout the country and continued to grow rapidly, probably because unlike other relief organizations at the time, the one House and Dickerson founded did not discriminate on the basis of color, religion, or social standing. On the local level, the organization helped fill the void left by the demise of the FREEDMEN'S BUREAU. Locally, the organization provided support for orphans and covered burial expenses. Nationally, it campaigned for the passage of laws that would establish a pension for former slaves.

As the organization grew, the U.S. Pensions Bureau became increasingly suspicious of their activities and began a simultaneous campaign of both covert surveillance and aggressively challenging the legitimacy of the organization. In 1902, House secured the help of the attorney Cornelius Jones to sue the U.S. Treasury Department for $68,073,388.99 in county taxes traced to slave labor in TEXAS. Ultimately, the Pension Bureau used the broad powers of the U.S. Post Office to bring fraud charges in 1899. The legal theory was that, since there was no possibility that Congress would pass reparations laws, any attempt to organize toward such a goal was a form of fraud. The Nashville district attorney Lee Douglas filed indictments against House and other officers of the National Ex-Slave Mutual Relief, Bounty, and Pension Association on May 10, 1916. In 1917, an all-white male jury convicted House of fraud and sentenced her to one year in prison. House served her sentence in a penitentiary in Jefferson City, MISSOURI, from November 1917 to August 1, 1918. She earned early release from prison based on good behavior.

Upon release, she resumed her laundry business in Nashville. The continued hostility caused House to step down as the organization's assistant secretary, although she remained extremely active, organizing more local chapters throughout the South. On June 6, 1928, Callie House died of uterine cancer, and she was buried in an unmarked grave in Nashville at the old Mt. Ararat Cemetery. Although the organization that she helped create disintegrated under the weight of the criminal fraud charges, she is still admired today for her ideas and her organizational efforts. The courage House displayed during a moment in history dominated by discrimination by white male culture continues to inspire the modern-day slave reparations movement.

Holly Heinsohn

FURTHER READING
Berry, Mary Francis. *My Face Is Black Is True: Callie House and the Struggle for Ex-Slave Reparations*. New York: Alfred A. Knopf, 2005.

Tennessee Historical Society. *Callie House: 1861–1928.* 1998. Available online. URL: http://tennesseeencyclopedia.net/image-gallery.php?entryID=C005a. Accessed December 9, 2008.

Vorenberg, Michael. "Slave Reparations: The Untold Story." *Concord Monitor,* 29 September 2005.

"Writing, Reading and Reflections: Famous Women You've Never Heard—#2." Available online. URL: http://writing readingandreflections.wordpress.com/2008/06. Accessed December 14, 2008.

HOUSEKEEPERS

Many free women of color in the Caribbean worked as housekeepers for wealthy white or free colored men. The demographic conditions in some of these colonies, especially in the rapidly growing colonies of the Greater Antilles, JAMAICA, SAINT-DOMINGUE, and CUBA, after 1800, opened a profitable economic niche for them. There were few white women, and many white men were single. Moreover, the work of a housekeeper required individual initiative and independent thinking and so was a job that people were unwilling to entrust to a slave. Although in most European countries, the duties normally performed by a colonial housekeeper might well be done by a male butler or manager, it was quite unusual for men to be employed in this role in the tropical Americas. Perhaps this is because there were stereotypes about men of color and because most white men were employed managing and supervising slaves in productive labor. Housekeepers made good professional salaries and had some job security. Despite, or perhaps because of, the good conditions of this line of work, among the most rewarding for women of color in these societies, women housekeepers were often suspected of being merely courtesans. (*See also* GENDER ATTITUDES and PROSTITUTES AND COURTESANS.)

Housekeepers were more than domestic servants. While they might well perform some domestic tasks, especially in smaller households, they were also responsible for the management of the domestic side of a town home or, more commonly, a plantation. This meant buying a wide variety of goods, such as food, fuel, furniture, tools and utensils, fabric for clothing and linens, and building supplies. In larger households, it meant supervising a staff of domestic servants, who might be either free people of color or slaves. It also meant hiring contractors for household repairs or making and repairing furniture and tools. It required responsibity for health care, either providing it directly or hiring professionals, not only for the domestic staff, but also for the owner, professional staff, and slaves. There was a budget to be overseen. If the owner lived on his plantation, then he would be responsible for the management of the farm. But very often, owners were either absent entirely or lived only part-time on their plantation and traveled to the colonial port city for regular long business trips. Very large plantations would have professional management staff, often young white men who hoped to earn enough money to become planters themselves. But if these managers were not present, the housekeeper might often be a part-time plantation manager herself. Even if there were professional managers, owners often trusted their housekeepers with powers of attorney to exercise some sort of control over management decisions, especially in cases when there was a personal relationship between the two. However, even when such a relationship was clearly not present, housekeepers might well be trusted as a check on the actions of unreliable or inexperienced plantation management staff. A free colored housekeeper who grew up in the colony might well know more about farming and plantation management than a young European man who recently immigrated. Housekeepers could also be entrusted with plots of land, along with slave labor to work them, and livestock for growing food for the domestic staff and owner. All these duties meant that the housekeeper was a professional who needed a wide variety of skills and a good deal of independent initiative in order to be successful at her job.

Pay was quite reasonable, generally comparable to that received by plantation managers. The SAINT-DOMINGUE free mixed-race political leader and merchant VINCENT OGÉ's housekeeper earned 1,500 French colonial pounds a year in 1787, which would be enough to buy a slave off a slave ship or the starting stock for a small retail business. It would also have been a good salary for a manager on a small plantation or a junior official in the colonial government. Unlike for colonial government officials and white professional managers, however, the housekeepers' salary might well be paid in kind and years late. Legal cases in French and British courts show that housekeepers sued their former employers for the payment of wages going back years. Several wills in Saint-Domingue specify that this or that asset of the plantation is actually the property of the housekeeper, who had taken title through her years of work but had kept the slave or field or herd of livestock integrated with the assets of the plantation. This sort of arrangement appears to have been quite common and not remarkable. The ambiguous nature of the relationship between employer and housekeeper appears to have been the cause of this phenomenon.

Housekeepers were often seen as members of the employer's family in a way that no other employee would be, especially when they had a personal as well as business relationship. That is, the housekeeper would have shared in the successes and failures of the plantation in a much more fundamental way than the plantation manager or accountant would. The male professional employees might have a few slaves of their own, and perhaps they would work a little in the fields at harvesttime and earn a rental fee for their masters or harvest some product for their masters' accounts, but there was no sense that the plantation manager was a partner in the whole operation. However, for the housekeeper, this was much more often the case. The housekeeper's slaves would have worked alongside the rest of the plantation's workforce, and if the harvest was profitable, there would be a reward: another slave, maybe a small cash payment or a barrel of the product, but rarely much cash and certainly nothing close to the large annual salary. Instead, the balance owed would build up over the years, and when the housekeeper was ready to retire, there would be enough for a respectable small farm, half a dozen slaves to work it, and a decent house and furnishings.

Of course, the relationship between housekeeper and employer was often personal and intimate as well as merely professional. Colonial society seemed to have assumed that it was in almost all cases. The categories of housekeeper and courtesan were almost completely conflated by colonial society, and indeed by later observers. There were plenty of examples of housekeepers who had numerous children with their employers. Nonetheless, from the employer's point of view, the salaries paid to housekeepers were exorbitant if what was being purchased was merely regular and exclusive sexual access to a woman of color. In any case, these relationships were frequently long-lasting, and after several children one presumes that a man who was merely interested in sex would have traded a courtesan for a younger and less encumbered candidate. This did sometimes happen and led to the lawsuits noted. Some housekeeper-employer relationships ended without lawsuits, presumably because the housekeeper believed that she had been fairly treated in the division of assets. But many others persisted until the death of one of the partners.

Since white men had very low life expectancies in the colonies as a result of tropical diseases, this generally meant that the housekeeper, often with young mixed-race children, had to take care of herself. And this is where the genius of the system reveals itself. If a man's mixed-race companion was a mere mistress, and he had left her something in his will, the heirs back in Europe could contest the will and often break it. Having a mistress was immoral. A man's children born out of wedlock had the right under French law and British common law practice to a small inheritance, sufficient to train them for a skilled trade or provide dowries for respectable marriages. But if the mother were an employee whose wages were severely in arrears, that was a different matter. Her claims on the estate were equal to those of any other creditor, for example, a mer-

chant who had sold slaves to the plantation on credit. So employer-housekeeper relationships often served to provide legal cover for a normal, noncommercial, longterm relationship with a woman of color that could not, for whatever reason, be made legally binding by marriage. Perhaps the man had a wife in Europe, or perhaps he had some government job that he would have to give up if he were married to a black woman, or perhaps he feared social exclusion for marrying "beneath himself." In some British colonies, marriages between whites and blacks were forbidden by law. But this was the next best arrangement for a planter who wanted to ensure that his companion and children would receive part of his property after his death.

Not all employer-housekeeper relationships involved sex. Free men of color who owned plantations also needed housekeepers if they were single or if they and their wives were absent from the plantation for significant lengths of time. Vincent Ogé, for example, hired a housekeeper to take care of his coffee plantation while he was living in Cap-Français/Cap-Haïtien and then in Paris in the 1780s. He was single, but there is no evidence that he was having a sexual relationship with this woman, whom he probably would not have seen more than three or four times a year. Free colored men in both Saint-Domingue and Jamaica were much less likely in general to have sexual relations outside marriage or at least to leave traces of those relationships where subsequent historians or contemporary observers could find them. The assumption at the time was that they were too much under the control of their women to dare to exercise the sexual liberty that white men in these Caribbean colonies took for granted. Today, cultural historians of the black Atlantic argue that more restrictive 19th-century moral codes took root earlier in free colored society, at least in the Caribbean, than among whites, thanks to a more balanced gender ratio and more active participation in the religious movements of the day. White men who were married—and there were some in the Caribbean—would certainly have found it harder to maintain an outside relationship so publicly, and yet we have numerous examples both in Saint-Domingue and in Jamaica of white families who employed free colored housekeepers. Presumably they were paying for professional services only.

The phenomenon of professional housekeepers was less pronounced in the mainland colonies of North and South America and in the Lesser Antilles. In North America, this was a result of the much stronger color line. Assumptions about the abilities and reliability of people of color there would make most white men unwilling to entrust such a wide range of duties to any woman of color. However, the black "mammy," responsible for child care, cooking, and a good deal of household management under the supervision of the planter's wife, is still a stock figure in nostalgic portrayals of Southern plantation life. This stereotype is loosely based in reality—some women of color did perform many of these tasks in mainland North America as well, while not enjoying the high degree of autonomy and responsibility that their sisters in the rapidly growing colonies of the western Caribbean did. In both North and South America, however, it was much more likely that there would be a wife on the plantation. Gender ratios in the white populations of the mainland colonies were much more even. In those places where gender ratios were unbalanced, especially in BRA-ZIL, it was not considered unusual for a planter to marry a woman of African or Indian ancestry. A wife was in a much better position both to manage plantation assets on behalf of her husband and to ensure inheritance of assets for herself and her children. In the Lesser Antilles, which had been settled longer and had fewer recent white immigrants, the more balanced gender ratios in the white population made for more marriages, and the lower productivity of plantations there made for more resident proprietors (and their wives). There were free black housekeepers in all of these places, but they would not have been able to aspire to the same ambiguous position as almost family members that they might have been able to attain in the Greater Antilles, where free women were much fewer in number than free men.

Stewart R. King

FURTHER READING

Bush, Barbara. "White 'Ladies,' Coloured 'Favourites' and Black 'Wenches': Some Considerations on Sex, Race, and Class Factors in Social Relations in White Creole Society in the British Caribbean." *Slavery and Abolition* 2 (1981): 245–262.

Mathurin, Lucille. "A Historical Study of Women in Jamaica, 1655–1844." Ph.D. dissertation, University of the West Indies, 1974.

Rogers, Dominique. "Réussir dans un monde d'hommes: les stratégies des femmes de couleur libres du Cap-Français." *Journal of Haitian Studies* 9, no. 1 (Spring 2003): 40–51.

Rogers, Dominque, and Stewart King. "Housekeepers, Merchants, *Rentières*: Free Women of Color in the Port Cities of Colonial Saint-Domingue, 1750–1790." In *Women in Port: Gendering Communities, Economies, and Social Networks in Atlantic Port Cities, 1500–1800*, edited by Jodi Campbell and Doug Catterall. Leiden, Netherlands: Brill, forthcoming.

HUGUES, VICTOR (1764–1826) *French military leader and colonial governor*

Victor Hugues was the central figure in the French Revolutionary Wars in the eastern Caribbean (*see also* FRENCH CARIBBEAN and FRENCH REVOLUTION). A former white colonist in SAINT-DOMINGUE, he understood the fundamental reality of the colonial Caribbean: that the colonies could only defend themselves with the support of the black majority. He enthusiastically implemented the French assembly's decrees abolishing slavery and giving equal civil rights to free people of color. With his black-majority armed forces, he spread the revolution to the British and Spanish islands of the Lesser Antilles. Ironically, after his recall from the Caribbean, Napoléon reestablished slavery, and Hugues was tasked with implementing this decision in French GUYANA. He performed this task with his usual efficiency and ruthlessness.

Hugues was born in Marseille, FRANCE, sometime in 1764, to a family of small businesspeople. In 1776, at age 12, he moved to Saint-Domingue at the height of its colonial prosperity. He worked as a merchant throughout the Caribbean, sailing to the Americas and eventually establishing a shop in PORT-AU-PRINCE and owning slaves. The HAITIAN REVOLUTION began in 1791, and the insurrectionary climate developing in Saint-Domingue led Hugues to become disillusioned with the dream of colonial prosperity in 1791 or 1792, when rebels burned his shop and killed his brother. He returned to Paris in 1792 to represent the interests of fellow poor whites in the colonies. He absorbed the Jacobin ideology of the French Revolution and attracted the attention of Maximilien Robespierre (1752–94), who groomed him for later work by installing him as a judge of the revolutionary tribunal in the French port town of Rochefort, near the monarchist rebel stronghold of the Vendée. In the subsequent two years, Hugues demonstrated his commitment to the French Revolution in these tribunals, and in spring 1794, the Comité du Salut Public, ordered by the French National Convention to end slavery in the colonies, dispatched him as one of three civil commissioners to Guadeloupe. In June 1794, Hugues led republican troops to the island and, emancipating the slaves upon landing, armed a new black citizen army to join his small detachment of French troops to rout the French royalists and the British who had been occupying the island. By October, he had reconquered the entire island. He trained his new army and paid black and white soldiers equally. Between 1794 and 1798, he turned Guadeloupe into a republican stronghold. (*See also* REGULAR ARMY.) Under Hugues's leadership, Guadeloupe exported armies of former slaves to fight the British on behalf of France in the Lesser Antilles—in Granada, Saint Vincent, and Saint Lucia. By March 1795, the three islands were embroiled in internal war as French forces assisted insurgents. Additionally, Hugues recruited former slaves to sail around the eastern Caribbean as corsairs to capture incoming British merchant vessels as well as neutral ships destined for enemy islands. (*See also* PIRACY.) The freedmen-turned-sailors received loot from their captures and in their travels disseminated the message of emancipation throughout the greater Caribbean.

In the initial months of emancipation, many former slaves moved from plantations to the towns, where the new economy accommodated many at the docks, on fishing boats, and in banks. However, as the plantation labor force became depleted and unharvested crops went bad, Hugues had to rescind some of the measures granted to the newly freed blacks. In presiding over a newly emancipated people, Hugues faced two questions that troubled contemporary advocates of abolition: how to prepare slaves for the adjustments they would inevitably undergo when emancipated, having been denied political and social rights for so long; and how to provide for the economy of France, given its dependence on the colonial plantations fueled by an enslaved workforce. In response, he published an islandwide labor directive commanding all previous plantation workers to return to the fields and justified this move by pointing both to the plantations' need for workers and to the idleness and looting of the former slaves who had fled to the cities. Failure to comply would be considered a treasonous act. On the basis of his observations, Hugues argued that the climate of the island encouraged indolence and that few people would willingly agree to participate in the backbreaking labor of field cultivation, even for wages. He proposed that a policy that forced former slaves to work would teach them how to be free and how to practice citizenship. The system implemented in Guadeloupe and the other French colonies of the eastern Caribbean was not unlike that ordered by the liberator-hero Toussaint Louverture in Saint-Domingue, faced with similar conditions during the Haitian Revolution. Despite the Jacobin philosophy he had been nurturing in the previous half-decade, Hugues started to think that it would be impossible to incorporate former slaves into the republic as full citizens. A letter to former Guadeloupean planters who had relocated to the United States promised them the labor force to which they had been accustomed.

As the black citizen field laborers struggled to create their new identities as nominally free people in familiar roles as plantation laborers, they found that emancipation did not look all that different from slavery. Hugues essentially nationalized the plantations and assumed the duties once the purview of plantation owners: managing, disciplining, and inventorying laborers. Hugues instituted harsh legislation that equated stealing produce from plantations with treason against France. Indeed, as he established Guadeloupe as an outpost of the republic, he imported the Jacobin terror, ruthlessly executing more than 700 traitors to the Revolution with the guillotine. To address these problems, Hugues set limits to former slaves' rights

and justified this action by arguing that they lacked the capacity and readiness to merit full citizenship. Former slaves, therefore, were made to understand that their duty as citizens compelled them to work the fields to assist the colonial economy by SUGAR CULTIVATION, COFFEE CULTIVATION, and COTTON CULTIVATION. The "new citizens" often evaded or resisted Hugues's labor policies as they sought to define and fulfill a vision of liberty in this new post-emancipation society. He used the armed forces and police to compel the "cultivators" to return to their employers.

In 1798, the French Directory called for Hugues's replacement and sent over General Edme Desfourneaux to oust him. When Hugues returned to Paris, he found the political climate much changed since he had left in 1794. The rise of Napoléon had shifted the government's policy for its troubled colonies. In 1802, Napoléon decreed a separation of the laws of the metropole and those of the colonies and later that year sent Hugues to Guiana as the new governor, tasked with overseeing the reestablishment of slavery. He employed a virtual police state, ensuring that French Guiana would maintain slavery until final abolition in 1848. Guiana was invaded in 1809 by Portuguese forces from BRAZIL, and Hugues was forced to surrender. Upon his return to France in a prisoner exchange in 1810, he was accused of failing to put up enough of a fight against the invaders. He was held without trial until 1814, when he was finally granted a court-martial and his name was cleared. He served the restored monarchy after the fall of Napoléon and in 1817 returned to Guiana as a special commissioner. He reorganized the colony's government and reestablished effective French rule after Portuguese forces withdrew. He also became a large-scale planter, employing both enslaved people and the increasing number of free colored laborers in the colony. He remained in Guiana until he fell ill in 1826. Returning to Bordeaux, he died later that year.

Hugues's legacy, therefore, is complex: He implemented the immediate abolition of slavery in 1794, then backtracked and employed a gradualist approach to abolition, and later, in 1802, was deployed back to the colonies to reestablish the institution. He used free black soldiers very effectively in the 1790s, then limited the rights of free blacks (as well as slaves) in Guiana. He was a poor white and a Jacobin who ended his life as a civil servant of an absolute monarchy and a large planter who owned many slaves.

Emily M. Brewer

FURTHER READING
Cormack, William S. "Victor Hugues and the Reign of Terror on Guadeloupe, 1794–1798." In *Essays in French Colonial History*, edited by A. J. B. Johnson. East Lansing: Michigan State University Press, 1997.

Dubois, Laurent. "'The Price of Liberty': Victor Hugues and the Administration of Freedom in Guadeloupe, 1794–1798." *William and Mary Quarterly*, 3rd series, 56, no. 2 (1999): 363–392.

Jenkins, H. J. K. "'The Colonial Robespierre': Victor Hugues on Guadeloupe, 1794–98." *History Today* 27, no. 11 (1977): 734–740.

HULL, AGRIPPA   (1759–1848) *American soldier and farmer*

Agrippa Hull was born free in Northampton, MASSACHUSETTS, in 1759 (the exact date is unknown). He later claimed that he was the son of an African king. His parents were members of a Puritan church where Jonathan Edwards (1703–58) had been the pastor until shortly before Agrippa's birth. Hull's family were an example of the highly assimilated free blacks of Massachusetts, with some comfort in life and some social acceptance from their white neighbors.

Hull joined the Continental army in 1777, at the height of the WAR OF AMERICAN INDEPENDENCE, 1775–83, in the North. He was assigned as an orderly, or messenger, for General John Patterson of Massachusetts (1744–1808), on whose staff he served during the Battle of Saratoga (September–October 1777), the winter at Valley Forge (1777–78), and the Battle of Monmouth (June 28, 1778). In May 1779, Hull was reassigned to the staff of General Tadeusz Kościuszko (1746–1817), a Polish military engineer who joined the Continental army in 1776 and had become its chief engineer by 1779. When Kościuszko was building a powerful fort at West Point on the Hudson River above New York City in spring 1779, Hull gave him important help by organizing laborers, preventing suppliers from cheating Kościuszko, and serving as an essential cultural bridge between the Polish engineer and the rural NEW YORK STATE and Massachusetts workers on the project.

The contact between Hull and Kościuszko helped the Polish aristocrat understand the real meaning of the freedom he was fighting for both in America and in Poland. In one incident, Hull organized a party for the other black workers at the site while Kościuszko was away on an inspection trip. Hull dressed in the general's uniform, sat in his chair, imitated his style of drinking tea, and issued humorous orders. Kościuszko arrived in the midst of this scene, and all the participants were horrified. Dropping to his knees at the general's feet, Hull begged forgiveness, and Kościuszko lifted him up, saying that "the son of a King should not prostrate himself before anyone." Kościuszko then joined in the fun and invited his officers in as well.

Hull and Kościuszko worked together throughout the remainder of the war. From 1780 to 1783, they fought in the South, participating in almost all the battles of the southern campaign from Camden (August 16, 1780) to the "bushwhacking campaign" in SOUTH CAROLINA in 1783. Observing plantation slavery was a moving experience for both of them, especially when they saw the devotion of the black soldiers who fought for the British. Kościuszko became convinced that slavery was inconsistent with republican values and determined that Poland would have to abolish serfdom.

At the end of the war, Kościuszko invited Hull to return to Poland with him, but Hull refused, preferring to return to the area of Stockbridge, Massachusetts, where his aging mother was living. Hull kept the certificates that Continental soldiers were given in lieu of back pay, later using them to buy land. He worked as a servant for the family of Theodore Sedgwick, a lawyer who had won the legal case that overturned slavery in Massachusetts. He worked for Sedgwick until about 1800, by which time Sedgwick had become more conservative, and they parted ways. Hull was a Jeffersonian Democrat, while the white elite of the area remained devoutly Federalist. By 1790, Hull was a substantial landowner. He married in 1785, fathered four children, and married a second time in 1821 after his first wife died. He lived with his children, his first wife's mother, and other kin at the center of a substantial free black community in Stockbridge. He was widely respected and by the 1830s was the best-known Revolutionary War veteran in western Massachusetts.

Kościuszko went back to Poland and ultimately became the leader of resistance to Russian rule. He proclaimed the freedom of the serfs in 1794. His resistance was ultimately crushed, and he was imprisoned in the Peter and Paul Fortress in St. Petersburg, Russia, for two years. Released in 1796, he returned to the United States. In summer 1797, he and Hull met again. After their meeting, Kościuszko wrote a will, with THOMAS JEFFERSON's assistance, offering his substantial fortune in U.S. government securities to Jefferson to purchase the freedom of the Monticello slaves, provide them with land, and educate them. After Kościuszko's death in 1817, Jefferson refused to carry out the provisions of the will, and the money was eventually returned to Kościuszko's distant relatives in Russia.

Hull's story ends more happily. In 1831, he helped dedicate a memorial to Kościuszko at West Point, the first monument erected on the grounds of the United States Military Academy there. He lived on until May 21, 1848, a respected member of his rural Massachusetts community, a patriarch of a large family.

Stewart R. King

FURTHER READING

Nash, Gary B., and Graham Russell Gao Hodges. *Friends of Liberty: Thomas Jefferson, Tadeuz Kosciuszko, and Agrippa Hull: A Tale of Three Patriots, Two Revolutions, and a Tragic Betrayal of Freedom in the New Nation*. New York: Basic Books, 2008.

I

IBN SORI, ABDUL-RAHMAN IBRAHIM (ca. 1762–1829) *African Islamic scholar and judge*
Born around 1762, Abdul-Rahman Ibrahim ibn Sori was from Timbo, the capital of the Fulani state in the Fouta Djallon, in Guinea. He studied at the Islamic university in Timbuktu, Mali, and was an Islamic teacher and judge (*see also* ISLAM). He may have been related to the family of the *almamy*, or king of Fouta Djallon; at any rate, he represented himself as a member of the royal house while in the United States. He was captured in battle in 1788, perhaps by Sosos from the coast of what is now Guinea or Bissau, or perhaps by internal rivals, as Fouta Djallon was experiencing an internal power struggle. He was sold to British slave traders on the Gambia River and carried to Spanish FLORIDA (*see also* SENEGAMBIA). From there, he was sold to an American planter, Thomas Foster of Natchez, MISSISSIPPI.

Foster was a cotton planter, participating in the rapid expansion of COTTON CULTIVATION in the Deep South that was to revolutionize the area's economy and the lives of African Americans and white Americans alike. Ibrahim was from a cotton-growing region in Africa and had good leadership skills. He told Foster that he was from a royal family in Africa and Foster named him Prince. Even though most of Foster's slaves, including Ibrahim's wife, were CREOLE and at least nominal Christians, Ibrahim's leadership, literacy, technical skills, and Islamic legal training allowed him to rise to foreman of the plantation. Some sources suggest that Foster was illiterate or nearly so, and that thus Ibrahim was the only literate and numerate person on the plantation. Foster became very successful, with Ibrahim's help. At a market, Ibrahim met an old acquaintance, Dr. John Cox, an Irish ship's surgeon who was the first white man to visit Timbo many years before. Ibrahim's father had taken care of Cox during an illness, and he owed a debt to Ibrahim. He tried to discharge his debt by buying the freedom of Ibrahim and his family, but Foster would not sell. Cox took a letter written in Arabic from Ibrahim addressed to his family. He gave a copy of the letter to an American politician, Senator Thomas Reed, who, thinking the writer was Moroccan since the letter was in Arabic, forwarded it to the U.S. Consulate in

Morocco, which passed it on to the Moroccan government. The sultan of Morocco then formally appealed for the liberation of Ibrahim. In 1826, Cox and Ibrahim appealed to the president of the United States, JOHN QUINCY ADAMS. Because of the intervention by the Moroccan government, Adams misunderstood that Ibrahim was a Moroccan and arranged with the sultan of Morocco that he should be released. Foster reluctantly agreed, on condition that Ibrahim leave the United States at once, and without his family. Ibrahim instead traveled the United States telling his story and trying to raise money to purchase his family's freedom. Foster objected strenuously to the publicity and threatened Ibrahim with RE-ENSLAVEMENT. He was able to get enough money buy his wife and two of his children, but his other three children remained enslaved. Finally, very ill and afraid that he was about to be returned to Foster's custody, Ibrahim and his wife traveled to Monrovia, LIBERIA, the closest port on the West African coast to his native Fouta Djallon. He died in 1829, four months after arriving in Liberia. He never saw his home or his children again.

Ibrahim is one example of a relatively small number of Africans who regained their freedom and returned to Africa during the era of the slave trade. AYUBA SULEIMAN DIALLO of Bondu and MARYLAND is another well-known case of an African who lived as a slave in North America and then returned to his home in Africa, and there were also some survivors of slave ships such as the *AMISTAD* and the *GUERRERO* who spent some time in the United States before being repatriated. Alongside those who regained their freedom, there were a few voluntary migrants such as the merchant ANNE ROSSIGNOL of SAINT-DOMINGUE and Gorée, Sénégal, and the missionary Phillip Quaque of Cape Coast, Ghana. Their presence indicates how tightly tied Africa was to the complex Atlantic world economy during the era of the slave trade.

The importance of ISLAM to Ibrahim and the role that his Muslim legal training and general education played in his life as a slave demonstrate the real cultural achievements of Islam in the period. Muslim universities were highly respected, and the education students received there was sufficient to make them educated men in the Americas. Ibrahim's technical skills and literacy made him an essential part of the plantation's staff, an indication of the degree to which planters relied on technically skilled slaves to make the plantation system function. Technical and leadership skills could also be a route to freedom for slaves, since in order to motivate such highly skilled employees masters often had to allow them access to money. Moreover, even though apparently none of the other slaves on Foster's plantation was African-born, and, in any case, the Muslim regions of Africa had been yielding fewer and fewer slaves since the middle of the 18th century, Ibrahim's Islamic faith and position as a recognized religious teacher gave him authority over the other slaves. They might not have understood Islam, but they understood that Ibrahim's position in the religion meant that he was a man to be respected.

Stewart R. King

FURTHER READING

Alford, Terry. *Prince among Slaves: The True Story of an African Prince Sold into Slavery in the American South.* New York: Harcourt Brace Jovanovich, 1977.

Austin, Allen. *African Muslims in Antebellum America: Transatlantic Stories and Spiritual Struggles.* London: Routledge, 1997.

ILLINOIS

Illinois is a state of the United States located north of the Ohio River, east of the Mississippi River, and south of the Great Lakes. It borders WISCONSIN, IOWA, MISSOURI, KENTUCKY, INDIANA, and MICHIGAN. It is well watered and fertile, but the climate is unsuitable for the crops of the plantation complex. The indigenous inhabitants were agriculturalists who lived in towns and villages before the arrival of European settlers. They were organized into large tribal federations, the best known of which were the Chippewa. The Illinois Indians had been very numerous up to the 13th century and built the largest single urban complex in the territory of the modern United States at Cahokia. About 40,000 people lived in the city of Cahokia in the 1250s, making it larger than London at the time and larger than any city in the United States until after 1800. The population of the region declined as a result of environmental challenges and the effects of diseases introduced to the Americas by Europeans and Africans from the 16th century. By the time Europeans and Africans began settling in what is now Illinois, much of the land was only very lightly inhabited.

Free blacks may have entered the Illinois territory as early as the mid-18th century, but the early black population of the area was primarily enslaved. The French took the first black slaves into the Illinois country during the 1720s, when the region was part of the French-controlled LOUISIANA territory. A French census of 1732 listed 330 black slaves living in the Illinois territory, and when the British took over the territory in 1763, there were supposedly 900 black slaves. By 1770, the number of slaves had fallen to about 600, but we do not know how many free blacks lived in the territory. The Haitian-born explorer and entrepreneur JEAN-BAPTISTE POINTE DU SABLE is typically acknowledged as the first free black settler in the Illinois territory, who established a trading post in 1779 near what would become the city of CHICAGO, ILLINOIS.

After the Illinois territory was under the control of the United States, as a result of the WAR OF AMERICAN INDEPENDENCE, 1775–83, article VI of the Northwest Ordinance, adopted in 1787, prohibited slavery and involuntary servitude. However, it also stipulated that RUNAWAY SLAVES found in the territory must be returned to their masters. It soon became clear that territorial governor, Arthur Saint Clair (1737–1818), was sympathetic to slaveholders, and he interpreted the ordinance so that residents who already owned slaves could continue to do so. When it became evident that the territory was friendly to slaveholders, more of them migrated from the upland South, especially Virginia, TENNESSEE, and Kentucky.

In 1800, Congress created the Indiana Territory, which encompassed the present-day states of INDIANA and Illinois. In the Illinois portion of the territory, the census of 1800 recorded 298 African-American residents: 163 free people of color and 135 slaves.

Although free people of color slightly outnumbered slaves, a series of territorial laws were passed under the assumption that all blacks in the territory were slaves or servants. In 1803, the Indiana Territory adopted "A Law Concerning Servants," which was based on a Virginia slave statute. The law required that all "negroes and mulattos" under servitude must have voluntarily entered into indenture, thus avoiding any obvious contradiction of article VI of the Northwest Ordinance. However, it is likely that few slaves or servants understood this distinction. Further weakening the rights of both enslaved and free blacks in the territory, the Indiana Territory in 1803 also adopted a law preventing all blacks from testifying against whites, ensuring that abuses of the "voluntary" system of servitude could not legally be reported. Between 1803 and 1809, Indiana enacted more racist territorial statutes, which further limited the rights of blacks, both slave and free. Together, these legislative measures continued to presume that all blacks in the territory were slaves or servants, regardless of their actual legal status.

In 1809, the Illinois Territory was separated from the Indiana Territory, partially as a result of the lobbying of proslavery advocates who wanted Illinois admitted

AFRICAN-AMERICAN POPULATION OF ILLINOIS, 1800–1900

Year	Slaves	Free People of Color	Free People of Color as a Percentage of Total Population	Total Population
1800	135	163	1.3%	12,282
1810*	128	500	6.8%	7,275
1820	916	506	0.9%	55,211
1830	747	1,637	1.0%	157,445
1840	331	3,598	0.8%	476,183
1850		5,436	0.6%	851,470
1860		7,628	0.4%	1,711,931
1870		28,762	1.1%	2,539,891
1880		46,368	1.5%	3,077,871
1890		57,028	1.5%	3,826,351
1900		85,078	1.8%	4,821,550

*Note: The figures for 1810 are fragmentary.

to the United States as a slave state. While the Indiana Territory subsequently dismantled its laws supporting slavery, the Illinois Territory strengthened its own. Most significantly, in 1813, free blacks were prohibited from migrating into the territory and faced whipping and expulsion if discovered. Free blacks already living within the territory were subject to mandatory registration with county officials or faced expulsion from the territory. Illinois was the only free territory to enact such a complete ban on the immigration of free blacks prior to statehood. The territorial governor, Ninian Edwards, also continued to interpret the Northwest Ordinance to allow the supposedly voluntary indenture of blacks for limited periods of service.

When Illinois applied for statehood in 1818, the constitutional convention wrote the prohibition of slavery into the state's constitution, virtually copying the phrasing of the Northwest Ordinance, but left open significant loopholes. This was not a contradiction of their previous policy but instead a reaffirmation—the framers of the state's constitution did not want Illinois to be a slave state, but they wanted to make sure that free blacks were subordinate to their employers, few in number, and unlikely to compete with free white laborers. About 1,000 slaves and indentured blacks lived in Illinois at the time of statehood, and the wording of the constitution provided that all slaves held in 1818 would remain in bondage for the duration of their terms of service. The most significant exception to the antislavery constitution applied to the salt mines of southern Illinois, where outright slavery was still permitted. Slave masters who traveled or settled in the state were also allowed to retain their human property.

After statehood had been achieved, Illinois law mandated strict codes for the legal residence of free blacks, while expanding the ability of slaveholders to take black slaves into the state. In 1819, the new state legislature reinforced the existing laws with "An Act respecting Free Negroes, Mulattoes, Servants, and Slaves," which mandated that any black person or mulatto entering the state had to provide an official certificate of freedom to the local court or face arrest and expulsion. The act also made it illegal to take slaves into Illinois for the sole purpose of freeing them but continued to allow slaveholders to retain their slaves within the state's borders.

Even with these restrictive laws, greater numbers of free blacks settled, lived, and worked in Illinois by the 1830s. Indeed, there were many whites and free blacks who worked to counteract or subvert the state's restrictive and prejudiced laws. In 1819, Illinois became the site of the first MANUMISSION settlement, known as the Edwardsville colony. Established by Edward Coles as part of the Organized Negro Communities Movement, the Edwardsville colony was a white-run experiment in "freedom training" for manumitted blacks, who were urged to farm and become self-sufficient. Edwardsville, as did similar communities through the country, failed through the lack of planning by its organizers.

Of the early black pioneers of Illinois, William Florville is among the best known. In 1833, Florville, a Haitian-born barber, established a shop in Springfield, where he befriended ABRAHAM LINCOLN. As well as being a barber, Florville was a musician and humorist, contributing whimsical verses to the local newspapers. The first Catholic Mass in Springfield is also said to have been performed in Florville's own house. During the

1840s and 1850s, Florville became the largest black property holder in Springfield, investing heavily in numerous real estate ventures. When Lincoln was elected president in 1860, he entrusted Florville with the care of his Springfield house, and when Lincoln's funeral procession arrived in Springfield five years later, Florville was asked to walk near the front, but declined in order to walk at the rear with the rest of the town's black residents.

Frank "Free Frank" McWorter was another of Illinois's early free black pioneers. He was born a slave in SOUTH CAROLINA in 1777 and was taken to Kentucky sometime before 1800. During the War of 1812, while still enslaved, Free Frank established a saltpeter factory and with the profits purchased freedom for his wife, Lucy, in 1817 and his own in 1819. In 1830, Free Frank, Lucy, and their three children moved to Pike County, Illinois, where Frank entered the land-speculation market and raised cattle. In 1836, Free Frank founded the town of New Philadelphia, the only documented antebellum town founded by a black pioneer.

Between 1820 and 1860, the number of free blacks in Illinois increased, while the number of slaves decreased. In 1820, there were still nearly 1,000 slaves in Illinois, especially in the counties of Gallatin, Randolph, Madison, and St. Clair. By 1830, there were 1,637 free blacks in Illinois and only 747 slaves, and by 1840, there were more than 3,000 free blacks and only about 300 slaves. The census of 1850 did not record slaves in Illinois, and the free colored population had grown to more than 5,000. In 1860, just before the AMERICAN CIVIL WAR, 1861–65, there were 7,628 free blacks living in Illinois, with concentrations in the counties of Cook, Madison, St. Clair, Randolph, and Gallatin. The majority of Illinois's free blacks lived in the southern half of the state, an area known as "Egypt," with large numbers in the Mississippi River city of Cairo, but there were also residential concentrations in central Illinois and Cook County, especially in the city of Chicago.

Slavery did not decline in Illinois as a result of abolitionist activism but because of white RACISM AND RACIAL PREJUDICE and concerns about the economic viability of slavery and its competition with free labor. These two factors contributed to the strengthening of Illinois's so-called Black Laws in 1853. (See BLACK CODES IN THE UNITED STATES.) The new laws included "An Act to prevent the Immigration of Free Negroes," which made it a misdemeanor offense for blacks to enter the state and stay longer than 10 days. If a black person convicted of this crime could not pay the fine imposed, he or she could be sold at public auction to whoever could pay the fine. The new "Black Laws" also reiterated laws already in effect, imposing harsh fines and penalties on anyone caught harboring a free black immigrant or fugitive slave, requiring free blacks already in the state to prove their status and to register with local officials, and preventing blacks from testifying in court against whites.

Despite the race prejudice that prompted the majority of the state's laws concerning blacks, the abolition movement in Illinois represented a vocal minority. The most famous black abolitionist from Illinois was John Jones of Chicago. Jones gave frequent public speeches on the abolition of Southern slavery and advocated the repeal of Illinois's own Black Laws. Jones was born free in NORTH CAROLINA in 1816, but his mother apprenticed him to a tailor, fearing that his father might attempt to sell him into slavery. Jones traveled with his employer to Tennessee, where he met and married his wife, the daughter of a free black blacksmith. In 1845, John and Mary Jane Jones moved to Chicago, where they established a tailoring shop. As a free black businessman, Jones based his opposition to the Black Laws on his belief that they prevented all blacks in the state from becoming productive members of society. In 1848, Jones was selected as a delegate to the Colored National Convention in Cleveland, OHIO, where he was chosen vice president. (See NEGRO CONVENTION MOVEMENT IN THE UNITED STATES.) After returning from the convention, Jones began a letter-writing and petition drive to have the Black Laws repealed. He also vigorously opposed the FUGITIVE SLAVE ACT OF 1850, which ensured federal cooperation in returning fugitive slaves to their masters. In 1853, Jones was elected president of the Illinois State Colored Convention, which denounced the Black Laws as well as African colonization schemes. At the 1856 statewide Convention of Colored Citizens, Jones spoke out in favor of public education for blacks, the right to vote, and legal equality. In 1864, Jones published a pamphlet, *The Black Laws of Illinois and a Few Reasons Why They Should Be Repealed*, which, along with more petition drives, led to repeal of the laws in 1865.

In addition to the more formal activities of abolitionists like John Jones, antislavery advocates in Illinois participated in the Underground Railroad, working to provide safe routes and havens for blacks escaping slavery. Despite laws that made it illegal to aid fugitive slaves, the Illinois Anti-Slavery Society and other similar county-level organizations passed resolutions asking their members to help fugitives escape from slave catchers. Although their efforts were never officially organized, and no records kept, the activities of Illinois abolitionists probably helped a number of slaves escape into CANADA.

The DRED SCOTT case was another rallying point for opponents of slavery in Illinois. During the 1830s, Scott traveled and lived with his white master, an army surgeon, in several free states and territories, including Illinois. The case that would become *Dred Scott v.*

Sandford before the U.S. Supreme Court originated in 1846, when Scott and his wife, Harriet, filed petitions in Missouri that the heirs of their previous owner were illegally holding them in slavery. The Scotts argued that since they had lived in free states, they thereby became free. The Missouri courts, however, ruled against the Scotts on a technicality, and the case was submitted to the U.S. Supreme Court in 1854. It was two years before a hearing was granted, and the final decision was handed down in early 1857. Chief Justice Roger Taney delivered the majority opinion of the Court, including the phrase that blacks "had no rights which the white man was bound to respect." Although the phrase was later used out of context by both pro- and antislavery advocates, Taney's decision did affirm the subordinate status of both free and enslaved blacks throughout the country. With the *Dred Scott* decision as precedent, the federal commissioner in Illinois ordered the return of alleged fugitive slaves to their white claimants in 1857, 1860, and 1861.

With the outbreak of the AMERICAN CIVIL WAR in 1861, blacks in Illinois faced new challenges. About 1,811 Illinois blacks served in the ranks of the Union army during the war, representing roughly 24 percent of the black population of the state, an enormous percentage. Many Southern blacks moved to the state during and immediately after the war. Their status was problematic during the war years, especially if they were RUNAWAY SLAVES from Kentucky, which had remained loyal to the United States and where slavery continued to have legal force until the adoption of the Thirteenth Amendment to the U.S. Constitution in December 1865 (*see also* CIVIL RIGHTS LAWS IN THE UNITED STATES AFTER 1865). Illinois's discriminatory laws remained in force, at least until the adoption of the Fourteenth Amendment in 1868. However, the cultural climate changed much more rapidly than the laws. Blacks in Illinois during the war and the subsequent era of RECONSTRUCTION IN THE UNITED STATES enjoyed unprecedented freedom. This freedom was not gained without effort—blacks had to wage political battles for the right to attend public schools, for desegregated access to other public services, and for social equality. The era of formal discrimination—the Black Laws—ended with the passage of the Fourteenth Amendment and parallel legislation at the state level. Discrimination by individuals and businesses and by local officials outside the large cities remained the norm. There were race riots where white mobs, effectively unrestrained by governments, used violence to impose inferior social status on blacks, most notably in the state capital of Springfield in 1908 and in Chicago in 1919. But formal freedom and legal equality allowed blacks to construct social institutions and gain access to at least some public services. In the 20th century, blacks in Illinois became numerous and influential. Illinois remained a place of refuge for Southern blacks fleeing the much harsher discrimination there, and the Great Migrations of the 1920s and 1940s/1950s boosted the black population to around 15 percent of the total population of the state by the end of the 20th century. The first black president of the United States, Barack Obama, though not a descendant of these 19th-century black Illinoisans, was a resident of Chicago at the time of his election and represented Illinois in the U.S. Senate from 2005 to 2008.

Thomas Bahde

FURTHER READING
Cha-Jua, Sundiata Keita. *America's First Black Town: Brooklyn, Illinois, 1830–1915*. Urbana: University of Illinois Press, 2000.
Finkelman, Paul. "Evading the Ordinance: The Persistence of Bondage in Indiana and Illinois." *Journal of the Early Republic* 9 (Spring 1989): 21–51.
———. "Slavery, the 'More Perfect Union,' and the Prairie State." *Illinois Historical Journal* 80 (Winter 1987): 248–269.
Gliozzo, Charles A. "John Jones: A Study of a Black Chicagoan." *Illinois Historical Journal* (Autumn 1987): 177–188.
Grivno, Max L. "'Black Frenchmen' and 'White Settlers': Race, Slavery, and the Creation of African-American Identities along the Northwest Frontier, 1790–1840." *Slavery and Abolition* 21, no. 3 (December 2000): 75–93.
Hart, Richard E. "Springfield's African Americans as a Part of the Lincoln Community." *Journal of the Abraham Lincoln Association* 20, no. 1 (1999): 35–54.
Hodges, Carl G., and Helene H. Levene. *Illinois Negro Historymakers*. Springfield: Illinois Emancipation Centennial Commission, 1964.
Middleton, Stephen. *The Black Laws in the Old Northwest: A Documentary History*. Westport, Conn.: Greenwood Press, 1993.
Walker, Juliet E. K. *Free Frank: A Black Pioneer on the Antebellum Frontier*. Lexington: University Press of Kentucky, 1983.

INDIANA

As in the other states of the Midwest, the first free blacks in Indiana were probably trappers and traders during the period of French control in the 18th century. There were also French slaves in the territory, in the Vincennes area on the Wabash River, dating from at least the mid-1740s. As in ILLINOIS and WISCONSIN, French residents of the territory were allowed to retain their slave property even after the British and subsequent American control of the area.

Despite the Northwest Ordinance of 1787, which prohibited slavery in the Northwest Territory, of which Indiana was a part, many of the first white settlers took their slaves with them from the South. When the Indiana Territory was formed in 1800, proslavery leaders, including Governor WILLIAM HENRY HARRISON, enacted laws evading the slavery prohibition in the Northwest Ordinance and restricting the rights of all blacks in the territory.

In 1803, the Indiana Territory adopted "A Law concerning Servants," which was based on a Virginia slave statute. The law required that all "negroes and mulattos" under servitude must have voluntarily entered into indenture, thus avoiding any obvious contradiction of the Northwest Ordinance. However, it is likely that few slaves or servants understood this distinction. Further weakening the rights of both enslaved and free blacks in the territory, the Indiana Territory in 1803 also adopted a law preventing all blacks from testifying against whites, ensuring that abuses of the "voluntary" system of servitude could not legally be reported. Between 1803 and 1809, more territorial statutes were enacted, further limiting the rights of blacks, both slave and free. Together, these legislative measures continued to presume that all blacks in the territory were slaves or servants, regardless of their actual legal status.

When Illinois was separated from the Indiana Territory in 1809, at the lobbying of proslavery advocates in ILLINOIS, Indiana subsequently dismantled its laws tacitly supporting slavery. When Indiana became a state in 1816, the antislavery faction dominated state politics, and the state's first constitution clearly prohibited slavery and involuntary servitude.

Over the next decade, state supreme court rulings gradually eliminated the few cases of slavery and indentured servitude in Indiana, but nothing was done to affirm the rights of black residents. Suffrage was restricted to white residents, as were MILITIA service and the right to testify in court cases involving whites. As in other states of the Midwest, black children were not allowed to attend public schools, and beginning in 1831, black emigrants to the state were required to register with county authorities and post bond against becoming a burden on local government. In 1851, article XIII of the new state constitution stated that "No negro or mulatto shall come into, or settle in the State, after the adoption of this Constitution" and even provided for sending offenders to LIBERIA. It seems, however, that this provision, like the laws requiring registration and posting of bonds, was not frequently applied.

Despite a general suspicion and hostility toward free black emigration during the antebellum period, legislation was also enacted to provide some small measure of protection to free black residents against the threat of being kidnapped and sold into slavery. Two personal liberty laws were passed in 1824 and 1831. The 1824 law,

however, actually reduced the rights already granted to black victims of kidnapping and made it easier for SLAVE OWNERS to reclaim fugitive slaves, and both laws were rendered essentially meaningless by the reluctance of the state courts to rule against the claimants of alleged fugitive slaves.

In the antebellum era, black emigrants to Indiana typically either were free-born in the Midwest or South or were manumitted slaves from the South, although as the 1850s progressed, more and more black Indianans were probably fugitives from slavery. According to the federal census, there were 11,262 free blacks living in Indiana in 1850 of a total population of 188,000. The majority were from NORTH CAROLINA, VIRGINIA AND WEST VIRGINIA, KENTUCKY, and TENNESSEE. The Quaker population of Indiana was especially active in encouraging former slaves to settle in the state, and Quaker societies provided the bonds required for free blacks to settle in the state before 1851 (see also BAPTISTS AND PIETISTS).

The Underground Railroad was also active in Indiana during the 1840s and 1850s, and the best-known of its black participants was a free-born Virginian named Chapman Harris of Jefferson County, near the town of Madison. Harris along with his four sons and his neighbors Elijah Anderson, Henry Thornton, Griffith Booth, and George Baptiste all helped escaped Kentucky slaves cross into Indiana and in some cases even crossed into Kentucky to assist them.

Although many white Indianans were afraid that these migrants would become a burden on local government, most of the migrants sought only a better life and a good living. Most of the migrants turned to farming, and at least 30 black farm communities were established before 1850, primarily in the central and southern portions of the state. Blacks were also present in skilled trades, including barbers, blacksmiths, masons, shoemakers, and coopers. The Ohio River boat industry attracted many black migrants, as well, although proximity to Kentucky and its enslaved black population probably was a deterrent for many as the epidemic of slave-catching expanded during the 1850s.

In urban areas, antebellum black residents were concentrated in the communities of New Albany, Indianapolis, Richmond, Madison, Terre Haute, Jeffersonville, Charleston, and Vincennes. In New Albany, black residents totaled 627, or more than 7 percent of the total population of 8,181. Indianapolis, with the next largest community of black residents, had only 498, or about 2.5 percent of the total population of 18,611.

Because blacks were excluded from white society, including publicly funded schools, black settlers in Indiana established their own schools, churches, and social organizations. As in other antebellum free black com-

AFRICAN-AMERICAN POPULATION OF INDIANA, 1820–1900

Year	Slaves	Free People of Color	Free People of Color as a Percentage of Total Population	Total Population
1820	190	1,340	0.9%	147,175
1830	3	3,629	1.1%	343,031
1840	3	7,165	1.0%	685,866
1850		11,262	1.1%	988,416
1860		11,428	0.8%	1,350,428
1870		24,560	1.5%	1,680,637
1880		39,228	2.0%	1,987,301
1890		45,215	2.1%	2,192,404
1900		57,505	2.3%	2,516,462

munities, churches provided the focal point for many social activities and organizations. The AFRICAN METHODIST EPISCOPAL CHURCH and Baptist Church were most common, and many of the church leaders also proved instrumental in organizing the black convention movement in the state. State "colored" conventions took place in 1847 and 1851, and there were probably others (*see also* NEGRO CONVENTION MOVEMENT IN THE UNITED STATES). In 1851, delegates specifically addressed the proposed exclusionary language in the proposed 1851 state constitution and passed resolutions opposing the further exclusion of black migration and curtailment of black rights.

Despite the articulation of rights by black leaders, and perhaps because of it, racial violence also occurred during the antebellum period. In 1845, an Indianapolis black pioneer named John Tucker was lynched by a white mob. In Jeffersonville in 1850, two black men who were accused of improper relationship with white women were reportedly dragged before a large crowd, tied to posts, and whipped. In the worst case of antebellum racial violence, armed groups of blacks and whites near Evansville traded shots over the case of a black man accused of beating a white family in 1857. When the man was released on bond, a white mob decided to take justice into its own hands but was confronted by a group of the man's friends, who returned their fire, killing one of the white attackers.

Although the outbreak of the AMERICAN CIVIL WAR in 1861 did redirect some of the racial antipathy of the antebellum decade, there were instances of racial violence during the war as well. In 1862, after reports that two white men had been shot by a group of blacks, New Albany whites indiscriminately attacked the city's black residents. This was the worst of the wartime violence, but across the state, white suspicions of illegal black migration

and fears of economic competition and social degradation accompanied the announcement of the EMANCIPATION PROCLAMATION in 1863.

These fears echoed the reactionary concerns of other states in the Midwest and were largely the product of Democratic tactics to regain the political ground they had lost through Republican Party accusations of treason and Copperhead, or prosurrender, sympathies. As in Illinois, Democrats triumphed in the state congressional elections of 1862 and introduced measures denouncing emancipation and black migration. By 1864, Democrats were less successful at the polls but nevertheless continued to include black exclusion from the state as a significant part of their party platform.

Black Indianans did not have the opportunity to serve in the Union army until 1864. The War Department credited Indiana with 1,597 black soldiers, though some of these may have been men from Kentucky or other slave states who were recruited and armed by the state government. The majority served in the 28th Regiment United States Colored Troops (USCT), organized in Indianapolis. Others served in the 8th, 13th, 14th, 17th, 23rd, and 65th Regiments USCT, as well as the 4th U.S. Heavy Artillery Regiment.

In early 1865, despite the active role Indiana blacks were playing in the Union army, attempts to repeal the exclusionary language of the state constitution and school laws were defeated in spite of a Republican-controlled state assembly. In matters of racial exclusion, this placed Indiana behind even Illinois, where the Black Laws were repealed wholesale by a Republican state legislature at exactly the same time.

The continuing racial hostility was encouraged, in part, by the rapid growth of the state's black population during the 1860s and 1870s. Between the federal census of 1860 and that of 1870, the black population increased by more than 13,000. By 1880, Indiana's black population stood at nearly 40,000. Southern Indiana saw a large percentage of this increase, as freedmen from Kentucky and other parts of the Upper South migrated northward.

In April 1879, in a smaller migration that coincided with the relocation of 20,000 Exoduster migrants to KANSAS, at least 1,000 migrants from the South, many of them from NORTH CAROLINA, entered Indiana (*see also* EXODUSTER MOVEMENT). Although many continued to move farther west, this migration nevertheless contributed to the overall growth of Indiana's black population, as well as the fears of the state's Democratic racial exclusionists, who feared a Republican plot to depopulate the South and artificially swell the black population of the Midwest before the census of 1880.

The most dramatic result of the migrations of the late 1860s and 1870s was the movement of Indiana's black residents from rural areas to cities. While white settlement in rural counties continued to increase, the relative numbers of black residents decreased. By 1900, the percentage of Indiana's black residents in rural areas was just 26 percent, compared with nearly 75 percent in urban areas. Indianapolis experienced the largest growth, gaining almost 2,500 black residents between 1860 and 1870, and another 3,600 by 1880. By the turn of the century, Indianapolis had nearly 16,000 black residents, or nearly 28 percent of the entire black population of the state.

Along with this rural-to-urban movement was a shift in the kinds of work black Indianans performed. No longer primarily farmers or agricultural laborers, blacks now worked in the railroad industry, manufacturing, mining and quarrying, and construction in greater numbers. The number of unskilled workers also rose, in part because of racial discrimination amongst skilled white employees. Efforts by the Knights of Labor and then the American Federal of Labor to include black members were short-lived and generally unsuccessful in overcoming the prejudice of white members, although segregated black unions were formed.

Although discrimination in the economic sector remained pervasive, with a larger share of the population and larger communities, black Indianans also continued and expanded their activism from the antebellum era. Statewide conventions of black citizens became more frequent, with equal access to suffrage and education the primary focal points of the movement. In 1866, the Indiana Supreme Court declared the article on black exclusion from the 1851 constitution invalid but did not address the question of suffrage. The issue was not resolved until Republicans forced ratification of the Fifteenth Amendment to the U.S. Constitution in 1870, rendering the state's constitutional restriction on black suffrage void. Even then, it was several years before the inoperative racial language was removed from the state's constitution.

The cause of equal access to public education also proceeded slowly in Indiana after the Civil War. Most black communities continued to support their own private schools, which enrolled hundreds of black students across the state. In 1869, the legislature approved a law that required school trustees to organize separate black schools within their districts when there was a large enough population to support them.

Indianapolis and Evansville were the first to open separate public facilities for black students, and by 1873, the state superintendent claimed that every county had provided separate facilities. In 1877, the legislature amended the law to provide for integrated schools where there was not a sufficient black population to support a separate school. For the remainder of the century, both integrated and segregated districts remained throughout the state.

In addition to political and educational activism, black Indianans engaged in a greater variety of social and cultural activities in the late 19th century. In addition to the growth of black churches as social centers, all-black fraternal orders elaborated new kinds of black sociability. The United Brothers of Friendship and the Sisters of the Mysterious Ten had 51 chapters in Indiana in 1892. The Knights and Daughters of Tabor and the Independent Sons of Honor and Daughters of Honor were also among the orders that catered to black citizens. In addition to providing a social outlet for blacks, these orders operated assistance funds, supported orphans' and old folks' homes, and offered independent insurance.

Although racial violence and intimidation continued to threaten many of Indiana's black communities by the turn of the 20th century, those communities were also larger, stronger, and more diverse than at any point in the previous century.

Thomas Bahde

FURTHER READING

Bigham, Darrel E. *On Jordan's Banks: Emancipation and Its Aftermath in the Ohio River Valley.* Lexington: University Press of Kentucky, 2006.

———. *We Ask Only a Fair Trial: A History of the Black Community of Evansville, Indiana.* Bloomington: Indiana University Press, 1987.

Blocker, Jack S. *A Little More Freedom: African Americans Enter the Urban Midwest, 1860–1930.* Columbus: Ohio State University Press, 2008.

Butler, Brian. *An Undergrowth of Folly: Public Order, Race Anxiety, and the 1903 Evansville, Indiana Riot.* New York: Garland, 2000.

Thornbrough, Emma Lou. *The Negro in Indiana before 1900: A Study of a Minority.* 1957. Reprint, Bloomington: Indiana University Press, 1993.

Vincent, Stephen. *Southern Seed, Northern Soil: African-American Farm Communities in the Midwest, 1765–1900.* Bloomington: Indiana University Press, 1999.

INDIAN WARS, UNITED STATES

Free people of color played an important role in many of America's wars against Indian tribes, as Afro-Indian supporters of the native people, as settlers of frontier regions affected by the wars, and as soldiers of the U.S. armed forces. African-descended people played a role from the earliest days in confrontations between explorers and settlers and native people. The expedition to FLORIDA headed by Pánfilo de Narváez (1478–1528) included about a dozen enslaved Africans from CUBA and a number of Africans or African-descended people from SPAIN, including ESTÉBAN DE DORANTES, who ultimately was one of the three survivors of the expedition who crossed the entire North American continent from Florida to Sonora, MEXICO. Although most of Dorantes's voyage was peaceful, the expedition had several hostile encounters with Indians in what is now the American South. Dorantes gained his freedom and was killed by Indians in what is now New Mexico while doing advance scouting for the Coronado expedition. The later, and much more violent, expedition of Hernando de Soto (1496–1542) included more than 20 Africans from Cuba, probably all enslaved, and apparently, five free men of color from Spain.

Throughout the Americas, Spanish colonial governments encouraged blacks to flee neighboring colonies and offered them refuge. Florida received many RUNAWAY SLAVES from neighboring GEORGIA; the runaways from the failed Stono Rebellion in SOUTH CAROLINA (1739) were heading for Florida when captured. Some runaways lived with local Indians and became the ancestors of the BLACK SEMINOLE, while others settled among the Spanish. Farther north, native people were also welcoming runaway blacks under some circumstances, while turning others back over to their "owners" in the British colonies and even purchasing slaves of their own. Since Indian tribes were not the harshly regimented slave societies found among whites in the American South, even the descendants of slaves owned by the Indians could often become tribal members. By the 1820s, a significant number of Southern Indians were of partly African ancestry. This deepened racial antipathy to them among Southern whites and helped lead to the expulsion of large numbers of Indians from the Lower South in the infamous "Trail of Tears" (1831–38). Some Indians violently resisted being moved, and most notable among these were the Afro-Indians. They feared RE-ENSLAVEMENT—realistically, as many former owners sought their runaway slaves among the columns of Indians heading west, and even those falsely identified as runaways had little recourse. The Seminole fought three wars against the United States between 1817 and 1858. Black Seminoles were the most unbending of opponents, and after the Second Seminole War, a number of them stole a ship and settled in the Bahamas rather than submit to American rule. Other black Seminole, who had been forcibly relocated to OKLAHOMA, fled to Mexico and, welcomed by the Mexican government as useful allies against the Indians of the Northern states, established a village there that still exists.

The Indians relocated from the South at this time settled in Oklahoma, where many acquired new slaves and welcomed new runaways. By 1861, there were thousands of Afro-Indians in Oklahoma, many of whom fought in the AMERICAN CIVIL WAR, 1861–65. The Civil War in the West was one of America's largest Indian wars, with Indians fighting on both sides while seeking advantage for their own faction. The tribes' capacity for resistance was ultimately broken, as they were driven from their homes and farms into a more nomadic existence. There was wide variation in allegiances, with tribal bonds, family, and patron-client relationships playing important roles, but as a general rule, Afro-Indians and poorer, full-blooded Indians tended to support the U.S. cause while the more wealthy mixed-race Euro-Indians tended to support the Confederate States. U.S. Army troops finally regained control of the region after the Battle of Honey Springs on July 17, 1863. One important component of the American victory was the 1st Kansas Infantry (Colored), a unit of free men of color raised in KANSAS but including people from MISSOURI and ARKANSAS and Afro-Indians from Oklahoma.

After the war, the army decided to control the Indians in the West with a mixture of regular black troops and Indian scouts. Black troops, it was thought, were more capable of bearing up under the hardships of long marches in desolate areas and were also less likely to make trouble about harsh living conditions in isolated posts than white soldiers. The most famous of the Indian scout units were the Seminole Indian Scouts, many of whom were Afro-Indians who had served in the Seminole Wars, the Mexican War of the Reform (1858–61), Mexican Indian Wars, or the Civil War. The regular black troops were the "Buffalo Soldiers" of the 9th and 10th Cavalry and 24th and 25th Infantry regiments. These units made up 10 percent of the total strength of the U.S. Army during the period 1866–1914, but in the inland West and Southwest, they were more than half of the total.

Black units had some of the most difficult and unpleasant assignments in the Indian Wars. Black cavalry troopers from the 9th Cavalry tracked the Apache leader Geronimo (1829–1909) in an 80-day campaign through northern Mexico in 1883 and forced him to return to the Apache reservation in the United States. Geronimo left the reservation again in 1886 and was tracked down by Indian scouts and an officer from the white 4th Cavalry. On May 13, 1880, First Sergeant George Jordan (1847–1904), born a slave in TENNESSEE, led 25 troopers from the 9th Cavalry, to defend Fort Tularosa, New Mexico. He and his men found the fortifications poorly sited and almost completely eroded by the weather. With the help of local civilians, several of whom were black and Latino miners, Jordan's men built a new fortification under Apache fire and held it for several days until relief could arrive. None of Jordan's men or the civilians he was sent to protect was killed. On August 12, 1881, a squad of 19 troopers from the 9th Cavalry under Sergeant Jordan was ambushed by dozens of Apache at Carrizo Canyon in New Mexico. Jordan led his men in a spirited counterattack, which drove the Indians away. For his leadership in these two engagements, Jordan became one of 13 black enlisted men from the Buffalo Soldiers awarded the Medal of Honor.

The army made some effort to train black leaders at the commissioned ranks during the late 19th century. Several black men were admitted to the army's officer training school at West Point. Among these was John Hanks Alexander (1864–94), the child of free black Arkansans. Alexander served as a lieutenant in the 9th Cavalry starting in 1887. He served for seven years, starting an officer training program at Wilberforce College in OHIO, a black college, before dying of heart disease in 1894. Perhaps because he was light-skinned and from a free family, Alexander did not experience the sort of vicious racial harassment faced by other 19th-century black officers. The first West Point graduate, Henry Ossian Flipper (1856–1940), was born a slave in GEORGIA. He was apparently brilliant, further irritating his racist fellow officers. He was persecuted and harassed—no classmates spoke to him for four years during his West Point education. Commissioned in 1877, he persevered for several years, serving with the 10th Cavalry in the Indian Wars. Flipper was finally court-martialed on trumped-up charges and cashiered in 1882. He was posthumously pardoned by President Bill Clinton in 1999.

Black soldiers often encountered racial hostility from white settlers, especially when the threat from Indians seemed to be receding. Sent to suppress violent confrontations between large cattle barons and small ranchers in the Johnson County War in Wyoming in April 1892, the soldiers became targets for the frustrated small operators. Racial prejudice combined with a sense that the army was defending the interests of the wealthy led to violence, and three members of the 9th Cavalry were shot by white civilians. The 9th Cavalry's Troop D, stationed at Rio Grande City, TEXAS, faced hostility from local law enforcement officials. Finally the black soldiers, law enforcement personnel, and Latino civilians had a series of violent confrontations in October and November 1899 that left several people severely wounded. The white officers commanding the black troops tried to protect their men, but the army's high command did not back them up, and several troopers were fined or imprisoned.

In the face of racial hostility and very difficult conditions, black soldiers made an important contribution to the American occupation of Indian lands in the West. At the same time, Afro-Indians resisted American pressure and tried to preserve the traditional Indian way of life and sometimes were among the most irreconcilable of Indians. The black role in the story of the American frontier was overlooked in the creation of the myths that would dominate popular understanding of the West. In reality, blacks were essential parts of the story.

Stewart R. King

FURTHER READING

Bielakowski, Arthur. *Buffalo Soldiers: African American Troops in the US Forces, 1866–1945.* London: Osprey UK, 2008.

Glasrud, Bruce A., and Michael Searles, eds. *Buffalo Soldiers in the West: A Black Soldier's Anthology.* College Station: Texas A&M University Press, 2007.

Porter, Kenneth Wiggins. *The Black Seminoles: History of a Freedom-Seeking People.* Edited by Thomas Senter and Alcione Amos. Gainesville: University Press of Florida, 1996.

INDIGO CULTIVATION

Indigo is a dark blue dye, the color of blue jeans, extracted from a variety of plants including the well-known English species woad. The most common commercial indigo plants are two species of the genus *Indigofera* first domesticated in South Asia but grown throughout the world in the Tropics. Indigo was introduced into the tropical Americas in the 16th century and rapidly became an important plantation crop. The dye is extracted from the plant's leaves, which are fermented, soaked in a strong base such as lye, and then dried and pressed into cakes. The process requires some chemical knowledge and some expensive equipment but is not so expensive or difficult as sugar milling and refining. The chemicals used are dangerous, and many workers were poisoned or burned, but the mortality rate associated with indigo cultivation was much lower than that in SUGAR CULTIVA-

TION. The process concentrates the dye a great deal, and a small amount of dye will serve for a large amount of cloth: The product of an entire farm for a year could be carried by a couple of packhorses. Indigo processing also requires a supply of clean water for the fermenting and washing of the leaves, though the plants themselves are relatively drought-tolerant and do not need irrigation. In the 18th and early 19th centuries, before the development of artificial dyes, indigo was the most common dye used in the world. It worked especially well with cotton, and indigo was in great demand in Asia as well as in Europe.

Therefore, indigo was an important crop for people who lived on the margins of the plantation colonies of the Americas. It could be grown in mountainous or remote regions because the product could be transported easily across mountain trails. Clean mountain springs and streams were actually better for the product than lowland rivers, which were more likely to be polluted or at least muddy. It required some capital investment, but nothing compared to the huge outlays necessary to be a sugar planter. An indigo planter could make a good profit with a dozen slaves, a processing facility that cost about as much as a couple of good horses or a small house, and some land that was not very good for anything else. Many free people of color could manage this level of investment, and many indigo cultivators in the Caribbean and South America were free people of color.

Indigo was widely cultivated in West Africa. The men of the Touareg people of Mali and Niger famously wear indigo face coverings that dye their faces dark blue. Women in the Fouta Djallon and Niger headwaters region make complex tie-dyed fabric using indigo. West Africans entered the Americas with these skills, and some farmers in the Americas sought out skilled African craftspeople to teach them the technology.

The Portuguese first introduced indigo cultivation into the Americas in the 1500s. They were looking for a crop that would give them something to sell in India and China. The Spanish also cultivated indigo in Central America at about the same time, exporting to Asia through their new colony in the Philippines. The Portuguese began by collecting another dyestuff in BRAZIL, Brazilwood, which produces a red dye that was prized in Europe. However, this dye could also be manufactured in Asia, and the Brazilian producers were not very competitive in such a faraway market. But when they introduced indigo, they discovered that, as a nonnative species, it grew remarkably well in the Americas, and soon they were able to undersell Asian producers and capture the market. Indians, RUNAWAY SLAVES, and other marginalized people had dominated Brazil wood production, and they had an important role in the indigo market as well. The Dutch conquered northern Brazil in the early 1600s and learned about indigo cultivation, transferring these

This 17th-century illustration shows the manufacturing of indigo in the Caribbean. *(Library of Congress)*

skills to Dutch and English colonies after their brief rule in Brazil ended. JAMAICA was an important producer in the late 1600s and early 1700s. Curaçao was the center of the trade in the Caribbean, even though little indigo was actually produced there, because Dutch merchants were able to offer better prices to producers than English or Portuguese merchants. The French resisted entering indigo cultivation for some time, because the government wanted to protect French farmers who produced indigo from woad. But protectionist rules were relaxed in the French system in the mid-1700s, and indigo rapidly became an important crop there as well, especially in the southern part of SAINT-DOMINGUE (present-day Haiti). Much of the indigo produced in southern Saint-Domingue was sold to the Dutch, and important Dutch merchant houses maintained agents in Les Cayes and Jacmel. This was despite the fact that export of indigo was strictly forbidden—the Dutch were master smugglers. Indigo is an ideal crop for smugglers because, as drugs do today, it combines high value and low bulk. A small ship could moor in a remote cove along the long coast of southern Saint-Domingue and take on enough cargo in a couple of hours to keep a Curaçao merchant house solvent for a year. Many of these Dutch merchants' agents were free people of color from Curaçao. Some of them were relatives of the planters with whom they dealt. JULIEN RAIMOND, a free colored political activist who went on to become a deputy to the National Assembly and revolutionary political commissioner on the island in the late 18th century, was an indigo planter in Aquin in southern Saint-Domingue with relatives who worked for a Curaçao merchant house.

Indigo was also grown in mainland North America. It was a particularly important crop in SOUTH CAROLINA. There, the business was mostly in the hands of large white farmers in the low country and islands near the coast: No records survive of free black indigo farmers in the Carolinas.

About the time of the AMERICAN CIVIL WAR, 1861–65, German chemists discovered ways to make indigo synthetically, and by the end of the 19th century, a wide range of artificial dyes in eye-popping colors had replaced natural dyestuffs for most uses. The African-American scientist George Washington Carver experimented with a simple way to synthesize dyes from a variety of plants, including soybeans and peanuts, hoping to offer poor black farmers in the post-Reconstruction period a share of the wealth that the chemical dye industry was creating in the early 20th century. Few of these products ever became commercially successful, however.

Stewart R. King

FURTHER READING

Balfour-Paul, Jenny. *Indigo.* London: British Museum, 1998.

Garrigus, John D. "Blue and Brown: Contraband Indigo and the Rise of a Free Colored Planter Class in French Saint-Domingue." *Americas* 50 (October 1993): 233–263.

West, Jean M. "The Devil's Blue Dye: Indigo and Slavery." *Slavery in America.* Available online. URL: http://www.slaveryinamerica.org/history/hs_es_indigo.htm. Accessed December 27, 2010.

INLAND WEST OF THE UNITED STATES

The future states of Arizona, Colorado, Idaho, Montana, Nevada, New Mexico, North Dakota, South Dakota, Utah, and Wyoming were only lightly settled by European and African-descended Americans before the 19th century. The northern portion of this area became part of the United States with the LOUISIANA Purchase (1803), while the southern portion was conquered by the United States from MEXICO after the MEXICAN-AMERICAN WAR, 1846–48 (*see also* CENTRAL AND NORTHERN MEXICO for the history of free Afro-Mexicans in this region before 1848). The United States administered these areas in a variety of ways, but most passed through the status of territories and then were admitted to statehood in the late 19th or early 20th century (Nevada in 1864, Colorado in 1867, North and South Dakota and Montana in 1889, Idaho and Wyoming in 1890, Utah in 1896, and Arizona and New Mexico in 1912).

The geography and climate of these areas make them unsuitable for plantation agriculture. Arid high plains to the east give way to high mountains, then desert or semi-desert scrublands going west to the western mountain ranges—the Sierras and Cascades—that form the climatic division with the Mediterranean and oceanic climates of the Pacific coast. During the 19th century, economic exploitation of the inland west saw an initial wave of fur trading and trapping, then a number of mining booms, the growth of RANCHING, and occasional attempts at rain-fed agriculture. Black Americans participated in small numbers in all of these activities.

The initial African-descended explorers and settlers of this region entered from the Spanish possessions to the south. The Afro-Spanish explorer ESTÉBAN DE DORANTES traversed this region from 1527 to 1540 in the company of Álvar Núñez Cabeza de Vaca (1490–1559) and returned as the chief scout for Francisco Vázquez de Coronado (1510–54). He died somewhere in Arizona in 1540 during Coronado's expedition. Coronado was followed by a succession of conquistadores and missionaries, with their Afro-Mexican servants. By the end of the 18th century, a series of small Mexican towns stood along the Rio Grande, with populations composed mostly of Indians and mestizos, but with small numbers of Afro-Mexicans and whites.

The northern half of this territory was theoretically under Spanish administration from 1763 to 1803, but in fact no Spanish settlements existed there. The first non-Indian visitors to the northern plains arrived from CANADA in the late 1700s, as fur traders working for the Northwest Company and the Hudson's Bay Company. These companies employed many nonwhites, mostly Indians but a small number of people of color. Details of their lives, and even their names, have often been lost to history, with only references to a black cook or *coureur de bois*—woodsman—surviving to mark their presence. The first black explorer in the northern plains we know of is York (ca. 1770–1834?), a slave who accompanied his master, William Clark (1774–1838), on the Lewis and Clark Expedition from St. Louis, MISSOURI, to the Pacific Coast near modern Astoria and back between 1804 and 1806. In the 1820s and 1830s, the northern plains and mountains saw many black fur trappers. Noteworthy among them is JAMES BECKWOURTH, who worked with the Rocky Mountain Fur Company in the 1820s, explored the northern Rockies, lived with the Crow Indians, led wagon trains to CALIFORNIA during the gold rush, and ultimately retired to live with the Crow. Before becoming one of the first settlers of the WASHINGTON TERRITORY, GEORGE WASHINGTON BUSH worked for the Hudson's Bay Company and as an independent trapper in the northern Rockies.

The southern portions of this region remained part of SPAIN until 1821, when they joined newly independent Mexico. Slavery was abolished in Mexico in 1829. A process common throughout Spanish America permitted the integration of Afro-Mexicans into a larger mestizo population, and numbers of people describing themselves as black or mulatto fell throughout Mexico during the 19th century. This process was accelerated in the territories conquered by the United States, as the especially harsh racial climate in antebellum America became obvious to the new citizens. Most Afro-Mexicans were able to escape classification as African Americans and were instead lumped together with Spanish-speaking Indians, mestizos, and whites of Spanish ancestry as Mexican Americans. The New Mexico territory, including what are now the states of New Mexico and Arizona, reported a free colored population of only 22 in 1850. During the 1850s and 1860s, the period surrounding the AMERICAN CIVIL WAR, 1861–65, this territory saw a significant increase in the black population from the American South. In particular, the development of cattle ranching offered opportunities to free blacks as cattle hands and small cattle owners. As many as one-third of the hands working on TEXAS and New Mexico ranches in the late 1860s were African American, and many of the remainder were Mexicans, some of whom were no

doubt of African ancestry. A notable example of the black cowboys was Bill Pickett (1870–1932), born after the end of slavery in Texas. He was a showman, leading a trick riding show that in its time was almost as famous as Buffalo Bill's Wild West Show. Pickett invented the modern rodeo sport of bulldogging. Another famous black cowboy was Nat Love (1854–1921), also known as Deadwood Dick, a rancher in Texas who then ran his own Wild West show, published his memoirs, and worked as a railroad porter. More whites arrived to work in the cattle business later in the 19th century, but nonwhites were in the majority throughout the century. The conventional image of the western cowboy as an English-speaking white man is a product of early 20th-century revisionism and a gross distortion of the real situation in the mid-19th century.

The Homestead Act (1862) offered government land at very low prices to people who wished to become farmers in the West. This law was passed during the American Civil War, and for the first several decades of its existence, there was little discrimination in the allocation of plots. In addition, railroad companies were encouraged to sell their land grants to farmers at reasonable prices and saw these sales as encouraging use of their services. They also were reluctant to turn away potential customers on the basis of race. Many potential black farmers took advantage of these provisions to begin farming in the inland west. The EXODUSTER MOVEMENT of the 1870s and 1880s led to the establishment of black communities in the high plains, most notably in KANSAS but also in Colorado and Wyoming; Dearfield, Colorado, founded in the 1910s by O. T. Jackson (1862–1948), an OHIO man from a free black family, is an example. Dearfield was established as a model agricultural community for blacks following the principles of Booker T. Washington. Most of these communities were later abandoned, both because of long-term droughts that struck the West after the turn of the 20th century and because of increasing discrimination against blacks in the western states.

The future state of Utah was an unusual case. The geography of the Salt Lake Basin favors large-scale agriculture using irrigation from streams descending the Wasatch Range, which receives large amounts of winter snow. The flat land along the lakeshore was permeated with salt and needed to be protected by dikes and washed by freshwater to be useful for agriculture. The large-scale irrigation works and land clearance were managed by the collective labor of the members of the Church of Jesus Christ of Latter-day Saints (the Mormons), who migrated to Utah starting in 1847. The Mormons were opposed to slavery and had liberal attitudes toward blacks similar to those held by northern evangelical Christians (*see also* BAPTISTS AND PIETISTS). Although blacks were not permitted to hold any but the lowest positions in the Mormon Church hierarchy, they were welcome to live in Utah, and small numbers of free blacks joined the Mormon migration. Green Flake, a free black man from MISSOURI, apparently drove Brigham Young's wagon on the great migration to Utah. Three black pioneer families, the Flakes, the Crosbys, and the Lays, are listed among the original Mormon settlers on the pioneer memorial in Salt Lake City. The 1850 census recorded the presence of 25 free and 22 enslaved blacks in Utah; in 1860, these numbers were essentially unchanged, at 30 and 29. Utah's small black population remained relatively well integrated into their community throughout the late 19th and early 20th centuries, escaping the otherwise-pervasive discrimination elsewhere in the region, probably because of the religious ties that bound Mormon Utahans together.

The principal theater of operations of the U.S. Army during the 19th century, with the exception of the four years of the Civil War, was the western frontier (*see* INDIAN WARS, UNITED STATES). Blacks played an important role in the military in the inland west throughout this period. At the end of the Civil War, the black role became especially pronounced with the deployment of the Buffalo Soldiers of the 9th and 10th Cavalry and 24th and 25th Infantry Regiments. These units were a legacy of the black United States Colored Troops (USCT) enlisted in the army during the Civil War. At the end of the war, many Northern states withdrew their state regiments from the army and demobilized them. The postwar occupation of the South was mostly carried out by USCT regiments and the few REGULAR ARMY units that existed before the war. As the military occupation of the South ended, the army decided to keep some of the black soldiers in regular units and deployed them to the West. In addition, blacks served in various units of Indian Scouts, paramilitary units maintained by the army to gather intelligence about hostile Indians and guide regular units. Western Indians often allowed non-Indians to live among them, as James Beckwourth lived among the Crow. They did not discriminate between whites and blacks, at least not in the 19th century. One group of mostly black Indian scouts were the Seminole Indian Scouts, descended from BLACK SEMINOLE who had migrated to Mexico in the 1830s and returned after the Civil War. The black regulars and the scouts were the most professional and hardest-working units in the postwar U.S. Army. They were assigned the most difficult tasks of policing hostile Indian tribes, hunting down escapees from reservations, and enforcing order in lawless frontier regions.

The frontier period almost everywhere in the Atlantic world saw a relaxation of racial and social lines, with opportunities for excluded people—minorities, women, social outcasts, and outlaws—to achieve success. The remarkable progress enjoyed by the quite small black populations of the inland west before the 1880s was in many ways a product of this frontier mentality. As the frontier closed, however, more conventional racial attitudes began to restrict black westerners' lives. The states along the Mississippi from Minnesota to Missouri had placed restrictions on free blacks as soon as they joined the Union, including denying them the vote, restricting the right to bear arms, and requiring registration and special taxes. These black laws were among the cultural baggage of white settlers moving west. A strong consensus existed among western whites that a truly civilized west would have few or no nonwhite residents. As soon as white residents gained political control of these territories, through gaining statehood or electing territorial legislatures, they generally implemented some form of restrictive legislation. The territorial legislature of OREGON passed restrictive black laws as early as 1857, obtaining approval from the Democratic administration of President James Buchanan. As the national government became friendlier toward black interests during the period of RECONSTRUCTION IN THE UNITED STATES, whites in the West gained greater autonomy and were able to continue the process of exclusion of nonwhites. State-level legal restrictions were difficult to implement after the Civil War because of the Fourteenth Amendment to the U.S. Constitution (*see also* CIVIL RIGHTS LAWS IN THE UNITED STATES AFTER 1865), ratified in 1868, but local laws and popular prejudice backed up by informal discrimination by law enforcement, government bureaucracies, and the courts increasingly limited the black role in western society after 1865. One significant opponent of legalized discrimination against blacks in the West was the railroad industry. The rail companies employed many blacks, as sleeping-car porters, firemen, and brakemen and in other menial or low-status occupations. The black employees needed to live close to rail stations and needed some social services. Rail companies prevented towns in many areas from imposing formal "sundown" laws forbidding blacks to reside in city limits and in other ways moderated the effect of the pervasive RACISM AND RACIAL PREJUDICE on their employees.

The labor movement was very strong in the West in the late 19th century. The Knights of Labor, an early attempt at broad-based industrial unionism, accepted black members, but the organization declined after the Haymarket bombing in CHICAGO, ILLINOIS, in 1886. Most craft unions, those representing workers in just one job category, tried to limit black membership and define certain jobs as white-only. The railroad unions of the 1880s and 1890s followed this model, and blacks tended to work in the nonunionized job categories in the railroads. Broad-based labor organizing began again with the formation of the Industrial Workers of the World (IWW) in 1905 and again included blacks as well as other nonwhite and immigrant workers. The IWW was especially strong in mining, in forestry work, and on the docks in the western port cities. Blacks were an important presence in mining in the West. A black woman, Lucy Parsons (1853–1942), born a slave in Texas, helped found the International Working People's Association and the IWW. A mixed-race immigrant from Curaçao, Netherlands Antilles, Daniel DeLeon (1852–1914), was a founding member of the U.S. Socialist Labor Party and the IWW.

The inland western region never had a large black population. For a while, in the frontier days, blacks and other nonwhite residents enjoyed opportunities not available to them in more settled areas of the United States. These opportunities generally disappeared in the late 19th century and many blacks abandoned the region. Today's urban black populations in the inland west are mainly the descendants of immigrants who immigrated during or after World War II, though small numbers of people still trace their ancestry back to those intrepid pioneers of the 19th century.

Stewart R. King

FURTHER READING

Beckwourth, James Pierson. *The Life and Adventures of James P. Beckwourth as Told to Thomas D. Bonner.* 1856. Reprint, Lincoln: University of Nebraska Press, 1972.

Billington, Monroe Lee, and Roger D. Hardaway, eds. *African Americans on the Western Frontier.* Boulder: University Press of Colorado, 1998.

Brooks, James F., ed. *Confounding the Color Line: The Indian-Black Experience in North America.* Lincoln: University of Nebraska Press, 2002.

De León, Arnoldo. *Racial Frontiers: Africans, Chinese, and Mexicans in Western America, 1848–1890.* Albuquerque: University of New Mexico Press, 2002.

Katz, William. *The Black West: A Documentary and Pictorial History.* Seattle: Open Hand, 1987.

Love, Nat. *The Life and Adventures of Nat Love, Better Known in the Cattle Country as "Deadwood Dick," by Himself.* 1907. Reprint, Lincoln: University of Nebraska Press, 1995.

Ravage, John W. *Black Pioneers: Images of the Black Experience on the North American Frontier.* Salt Lake City: University of Utah Press, 1997.

Taylor, Quintard. *In Search of the Racial Frontier: African Americans in the American West, 1528–1990.* New York: Norton, 1998.

Taylor, Quintard, and Shirley Ann Wilson Moore, eds. *African American Women Confront the West, 1600–2000.* Norman: University of Oklahoma Press, 2003.

INTERRACIAL MARRIAGE

Interracial marriage is still the strongest racial taboo. During the time of slavery, public attitudes toward marriage of whites and blacks in the Americas ranged from disdainful bare toleration down to outright prohibition on pain of imprisonment and enslavement. After the end of slavery, these legal prohibitions and social taboos grew stronger, and they still persist even after most other elements of social exclusion and formal discrimination have been abolished.

In the 16th century and earlier, most European countries had no formal restrictions and little informal prejudice against interracial marriage. The few non-Europeans who lived in northwestern Europe had no restrictions on choosing European marriage partners. In SPAIN, there were legal handicaps attached to marriage between Old and New Christians, that is, between people of old Spanish and Jewish or Moroccan ethnic heritage. These restrictions were justified not on racial but on religious grounds. Non-Christian ancestry made one suspect for unorthodox religious practices—and indeed many families who pretended to convert to Christianity continued for centuries to practice Judaism or Islam secretly—and so people with those backgrounds were not permitted to advance to high ranks in the church or state. When Spaniards tried to reproduce their society in the Americas after 1492, however, legal restrictions on interracial marriage grew out of these religious restrictions. At first, the justification was still religious—descendants of Indians were suspected of clinging to Indian religious values—but the perception of differences between Indians and Spaniards quickly aquired have a racial component. Soon, a racial caste system grew up and was reproduced by newer European colonizers when they arrived.

Most colonial powers, especially those where Catholicism was the state religion (*see also* ROMAN CATHOLIC CHURCH), continued to permit interracial marriage, with some limitations, during the period of slavery. Indeed, the CODE NOIR IN FRENCH LAW encouraged it as preferable to informal interracial unions. Single white men who fathered children with their slave mistresses were theoretically required to marry them, though the law was rarely enforced. White men in the Spanish and Portuguese colonies could have their mixed-race legitimate children declared officially white, escaping the principal handicap that interracial marriage imposed on a family (*see also* "WHITENING" AND RACIAL PROMOTION and *CEDULAS DE GRACIAS AL SACAR*).

The Protestant colonial powers, principally BRITAIN and the Netherlands, started with an accepting attitude toward interracial marriage. Famously, the early Virginia settler and tobacco planter John Rolfe married Pocahontas in 1614 (*see also* PROTESTANT MAINLINE CHURCHES). But their religious values and cultural experience with colonialism led them to a more restrictive attitude fairly rapidly. The Protestant nations of northern Europe equated membership in the national church with citizenship. Noncitizens were not encouraged to join the national church, and without being a member of the church, one could not marry legally. So the marriages of blacks and Indians in Protestant colonies were often unofficial or unrecorded. Whites who had relationships with nonwhites were handicapped in society, being excluded from institutions and suffering other sanctions. The state would often take away mixed-race children of white women and bind them as indentured servants, especially if their fathers were African slaves. White women who married Indians could be legally kidnapped and returned to white society. White men who had relationships with African-American women were tolerated, though there was a social price to be paid if one's relationship became public knowledge. It would be especially difficult for a white man who tried to have his African-American companion accepted as his wife, regardless of the religious status of their relationship. Most English colonies passed laws against mixed marriages by the end of the 17th century.

Everywhere, even in the Spanish colonies, restrictions on interracial marriage became stronger as the black enslaved population grew, and as the plantation sector of the economy became more profitable. Interracial marriage was a serious blow to the color line, much more so than an informal interracial sexual relationship. After 1820 in CUBA and PUERTO RICO, the Spanish placed sharp restrictions on interracial marriage. Marriages still took place, particularly between light-skinned women of color and white men, but they were more difficult and caused more social and legal problems for the white partner. This development was in part a result of growing "scientific racism" in the 19th century and in part of an increasing fear of the growing number of black slaves in Cuban society. In addition, Cuba was strongly influenced by North American racial attitudes, through economic contacts and immigration links with the United States.

Despite their efforts to end slavery, most abolitionists did not support overturning the taboo on interracial marriage, even outside the United States. Public attitudes were so strongly opposed to interracial marriage that some countries enshrined prohibitions in law even as they were liberating their slaves. This tendency was especially strong in the United States, where most states had MISCEGENATION laws before 1865, but most of the remainder passed them or strengthened them after the end of RECONSTRUCTION IN THE UNITED STATES. People of color generally supported racial endogamy and did not want to work to overturn laws against miscegenation. FREDERICK DOUGLASS married a white woman in 1884 and was roundly criticized by blacks (including his own children by his first marriage) and whites. In Latin America, a pro-miscegenationist discourse did develop around the concept of "improving the race" through interracial marriage. This discourse, which was somewhat misogynistic, suggested that if newly arrived white immigrant men could be induced to marry women of color, the outcome for the nation would be the disappearance of blackness. This idea was especially strong in BRAZIL, where by the late 19th century, as slavery was ending there, the country began to think of itself as a "racial democracy," following the historical and sociological ideas of GILBERTO FREYRE. Color prejudice remained, especially against Afro-Brazilians, but light-skinned people began to be assimilated as in Spanish America, particularly through interracial marriages.

Into the 20th century, however, interracial marriage remained difficult throughout the Americas. In a 1992 study by the U.S. Justice Department, mixed-race couples reported the highest rate of housing discrimination in the United States, more than single-race couples of any race. Matchmakers' ads in Latin America and Internet Web sites in Spanish and English still promise a mate of the right color. Even members of groups traditionally discriminated against still resist intermarriage. Prominent African-American men married to white women have been the focus of public anger by blacks and whites. This continuing resistance to marriage outside one's own racial group, as other forms of racial exclusion decline and are seen as abhorrent by most people, seems to suggest that there is some deeper explanation for the phenomenon than mere historical accident.

The traditional explanation for prohibitions on exogamy was that people naturally fear the unfamiliar and find it distasteful. This begs the question of why many men from dominant groups in racially mixed societies seek out women of other races for informal sex. Of course, in some cases, as in 16th-century MEXICO, there were very few white women available, but even when there are many white women, white men often seek out women of color at least for informal relationships and often for marriage. Sociobiologists, such as Jared Diamond, have argued that men seek to control sexual access to women they control—members of their own group—while undermining such attempts by males of other groups, thus providing a neat explanation for both restrictions on interracial sex and white male attempts to undermine those restrictions. The problem with socio-biological explanations is that human genetics changes very slowly while popular resistance to racial exogamy in Western civilization has waxed and waned during the last 500 years, a blink of the eye in evolutionary terms.

Much of the explanation for popular opposition to racial exogamy must lie in the realms of socioeconomic, cultural, and ideological changes—historical processes still, but ones that change more slowly than political relationships. In the area of ideology, Christian religious teaching in the 1400s was that human beings had a single origin—as children of Adam and Eve. All people were human and fully eligible for all the sacraments, including marriage. In the 18th century, the Enlightenment reduced the influence that Christian teaching had over Europeans and raised the possibility that the various races had separate origins. Eighteenth- and 19th-century racial ideologies tended to dehumanize the racial other and encouraged whites to preserve racial distinctions in all matters, particularly marriage. The high point of this ideological current was the early 20th century, when the eugenics movement spurred the adoption or strengthening of miscegenation laws in the United States, South Africa, and Germany. The failure of these laws—in Germany at the end of World War II, in the United States in the 1960s, and in South Africa after the end of apartheid—is a signpost of the generalized decline in the power of racist ideologies in the late 20th century. But at the same time, the previously subjugated races were seeking equal rights through organized political movements and building consciousness through cultural movements. Preserving racial identity was important to these cultural movements, and intermarrying with the former oppressor might well seem an act of disloyalty.

Stewart R. King

FURTHER READING

Diamond, Jared. *The Third Chimpanzee: The Biological Roots of Human Behavior.* New York: Harper Perennial, 2006.

Pascoe, Peggy. *What Comes Naturally: Miscegenation Law and the Making of Race in America.* Oxford: Oxford University Press, 2009.

Sollors, Werner, ed. *Interracialism: Black-White Intermarriage in American History, Literature, and Law.* Oxford: Oxford University Press, 2000.

IOWA

The first free black settlers in the territory that would become the state of Iowa probably arrived during the period of French control in the 18th century. Free black trappers and traders would have roamed the Iowa territory as freely as they did the neighboring regions that would become ILLINOIS, INDIANA, and MISSOURI. Enslaved blacks also entered the territory with white masters, many of whom were army officers stationed on frontier posts, including DRED SCOTT's owner, John Emerson, who purchased land on the site of Davenport while stationed across the river at Illinois's Fort Armstrong in the early 1830s.

In 1838, Iowa achieved territorial status with a provision that explicitly prohibited slavery. With a growing popular dislike of slavery, backed by the antislavery provision, the few slaveholding residents of the Iowa Territory gradually moved across the border to Missouri, although many still traveled to Iowa and transacted business there, accompanied by their slaves.

As in most states of the Upper Midwest, Iowa's black population remained small until the AMERICAN CIVIL WAR, 1861–65. The territorial census of 1840 listed 188 black residents, more than 90 percent of whom were recorded as free. Although it is likely that some underreporting took place, there were only a few slaves left in the territory by the time of statehood in 1846. The free black population remained small as well, although the decade of the 1850s witnessed exponential growth. The first post-statehood federal census in 1850 counted only 333 free blacks in Iowa in a total state population of 192,000, and by 1860, there were more than 1,000.

The largest center of free black population in early Iowa was at Dubuque. As early as 1834, a small group of Dubuque blacks, some of them slaves, helped raise funds to organize and build the city's first Methodist church. By 1840, there were 72 black residents, or about 5 percent of the town's total population. Over the next decade, the decline of the local lead mining industry and persistent racial violence had apparently fragmented this small population. Of the 10 free black heads of household listed in the 1840 census, only two remained by 1850. By this time, more than a quarter of Dubuque's remaining black population lived in white homes, presumably as servants.

By 1850, the center of Iowa's free black population had moved from Dubuque to Muscatine, on the Mississippi River, south of Davenport. Sixty-two free blacks lived in Muscatine in 1850, only one of whom lived in a white household. Among the notable local black residents were Benjamin J. Mathews, a former slave, and his family; Thomas C. Motts, a barber and collier, whose real estate was valued at $6,000; and ALEXANDER CLARK, who in the 1850s and 1860s became the state's most outspoken critic of discriminatory legislation and segregated schools.

In Muscatine, as in other centers of black population throughout the Midwest, the free black community organized events and institutions that provided an explicit

AFRICAN-AMERICAN POPULATION OF IOWA, 1840–1900

Year	Slaves	Free People of Color	Free People of Color as a Percentage of Total Population	Total Population
1840	16	172	0.4%	30,945
1850		333	0.2%	192,214
1860		1,069	0.2%	674,913
1870		5,762	0.5%	1,194,020
1880		9,516	0.6%	1,624,615
1890		10,685	0.6%	1,911,896
1900		12,693	0.6%	2,231,833

critique of slavery. In a symbolic sense, these activities joined the smaller frontier black populations with larger communities and created common bonds of activism and ideology. In 1848, Muscatine's black residents organized the Methodist Episcopal Educational and Church Society and, under its auspices, held a celebration of West Indian Emancipation Day on August 1, 1849. By 1851, the AFRICAN METHODIST EPISCOPAL CHURCH of Muscatine was one of the first such churches in the trans-Mississippi West.

In 1857, the first statewide convention of "colored" citizens met in the Muscatine African Methodist Episcopal Church with at least 33 delegates from black communities across the state (*see also* NEGRO CONVENTION MOVEMENT IN THE UNITED STATES). As in many similar conventions throughout the Midwest in the antebellum decades, the Iowa convention passed resolutions against colonization, in favor of suffrage and full citizenship rights, and in favor of equal access to public education. The members of the black convention drafted and signed a petition to the state's upcoming constitutional convention demanding black suffrage, but the latter took no action to incorporate black suffrage in the state's constitution.

Although the black population of Iowa remained small, this did not diminish the popular spirit of racial exclusion that predominated among whites across the Midwest. Iowa's path to statehood included a lengthy territorial period in which the territorial legislatures passed laws barring black migration modeled after those of Indiana and Illinois. Despite early efforts by Quaker and Presbyterian antislavery organizations as advocates against laws that would allow fugitive slaves to be recaptured in the state, the legislature repeatedly adopted legislation allowing the recapture of fugitive slaves and denying suffrage and education rights to free black residents. Despite the vigorous efforts of the Iowa Anti-Slavery Society, the first constitutional convention in 1844 drafted a document that prohibited black suf-

frage and, thus, full citizenship. The original organic document of Iowa statehood also specified that blacks could not serve in the general assembly, would not be enumerated in the state census, and would not be eligible for MILITIA service.

By the eve of the Civil War, exclusionist laws and constitutional language remained in effect, and although the black population of the state remained relatively small, it already showed signs of growth. During and after the Civil War, although the black population grew rapidly, it did not match the larger black populations of states such as Indiana, Illinois, and OHIO. If the fears of Iowa's racial exclusionists were realized during the Civil War, it was only insofar as the war made it possible for freed slaves and other black migrants to move more freely through the states of the Midwest.

Although the numbers were still quite small, the proportion of black residents in Iowa's rural counties multiplied exponentially during the 1860s. The percentage of rural Iowa counties that claimed no black residents dropped from 45 percent in 1860 to just 16 percent in 1870, and 64 Iowa townships gained black residents over the decade. By 1870, there were 5,762 black citizens in Iowa. Over the next three decades, the state's black population continued to grow rapidly. By the turn of the 20th century, more than 12,693 blacks called Iowa home.

The exclusionary racial language of Iowa's constitution was not changed until 1880, but black Iowans were successful in gaining the right to vote in 1868, joining WISCONSIN, NEBRASKA, MINNESOTA, and KANSAS among the states of the Midwest in granting black suffrage before the ratification of the Fifteenth Amendment in 1870.

Thomas Bahde

FURTHER READING

Dykstra, Robert R. *Bright Radical Star: Black Freedom and White Supremacy on the Hawkeye Frontier.* Cambridge, Mass.: Harvard University Press, 1993.

Schwalm, Leslie A. *Emancipation's Diaspora: Race and Reconstruction in the Upper Midwest.* Chapel Hill: University of North Carolina Press, 2009.

ISABEL OF BRAGANÇA (PRINCESS IMPERIAL)
(1846–1921) *also known as Isabel the Redemptress, regent of Brazil (1871–1872, 1876–1877, and 1888)*

The oldest daughter of Dom Pedro II, Isabel Cristina de Bragança e Bourbon, was the next in line for the throne of Brazil. She was a prominent abolitionist and supporter of liberal causes within the Brazilian government. In 1888, when her father was away in Europe for medical treatment, she declared the abolition of slavery in Brazil.

She was born on July 18, 1846, into a life of privilege as the heir to the throne of Brazil. Isabel received the best education Brazil could afford as the intended future ruler of a constitutional monarchy that gave considerable power to its monarch. Her education stressed liberal principles, which she shared to a considerable extent with her father, but she was willing to go much further than he was in putting those principles into effect in Brazilian society. She was married at the age of 18 to a French prince, Gaston d'Orléans, count of Eu, with whom she had three children, but she preserved her independence both from her husband and from her father.

Princess Isabel was deeply involved in the abolitionist movement, even planning, alongside André Rebouças, strategies for mass slave escapes. She was a loyal Catholic, a supporter of the reforming Pope Leo XIII, and for her action in freeing the slaves, Pope Leo gave her a medal and referred to her as the "redeemer" of Brazil. Brazilian political and economic elites disliked the princess and her husband the prince for her fierce religiosity and his abrasive personality. For this reason some tended to prefer that the crown be passed on to her nephew, Pedro Augusto, a more conservative and conciliatory figure.

In 1871, her father left for Europe. He traveled for long periods on three occasions when very serious political issues were under debate, leaving observers at the time and subsequently to assume that he saw Isabel as the person who was willing to implement the tough measures he wanted but did not want to be blamed for implementing. He had maneuvered for the appointment of the liberal viscount of Rio Branco (1819–80) as prime minister, and this was accomplished before his departure. Rio Branco pushed through a law of free birth, passed September 28, 1871, called the Rio Branco law, which freed all slaves born after the adoption of the law on their 21st birthday, with provision for the reimbursement of the masters. The law had little immediate effect, naturally, but was a first step toward the ultimate abolition of slavery. Princess Isabel presided over the passage of the law with pleasure.

In 1888, Isabel's father left once again for Europe. During his absence in 1888, she went further than she had in 1871, using the "Moderator Power" given the monarch under the Constitution to change the country's government to create what would be called the "Abolitionist cabinet." The princess suggested to the new prime minister, João Alfredo Correia de Oliveira (1835–1915), and the abolitionist leader in the Senate, Rodrigo Augusto Da Silva (1833–89) that they, abolish slavery immediately and without preconditions. On May 4, 1888, she invited 14 runaway slaves to dine with her in the Imperial Palace. On May 23, the law abolishing slavery, called the Lei Aurea, or Golden Law, was passed by Congress and signed by her. The law did not provide any recompense for slave owners who lost their "property"; nor did it provide for any special laws to protect or govern the newly freed. Slave owners were outraged.

Dom Pedro had hoped that the absence of the emperor at the time the Golden Law was adopted would deflect the hostility of Brazilian elites from the royal family, or at least from him. The people generally supported the monarchy, especially people of color grateful for their freedom and improving conditions of civil rights. However, local elites in several provinces revolted, the army leadership refused to move, and within 18 months the imperial system fell. The emperor and Isabel fled into exile November 15, 1889. She became the head of the House of Bragança after her father's death in December 1891. There were several promonarchist revolts between 1889 and 1912. Isabel's role in organizing these attempts is unclear. Finally, in 1921, she reconciled with the republican government, and the sentence of exile against her was revoked. She died on November 14, 1921, before she could travel to Brazil. Her family relocated to Brazil, and her many descendants live in Rio de Janeiro today.

Ana Janaina Nelson

FURTHER READING

Barman, Roderick J. *Princess Isabel of Brazil: Gender and Power in the Nineteenth Century.* Lanhan, Md.: SR Books, 2002.
Longo, James Mcmurtry. *Isabel Orleans-Braganza: The Brazilian Princess Who Freed the Slaves.* Jefferson N.C.: McFarland, 2007.

ISLAM

The Islamic faith emerged in western Arabia in the early seventh century when Muhammad (570–632) began reporting the content of visions that he believed were a message from God. His visions were collected and transcribed into the holy book, the Qur'an, which Muslims believe is the complete word of God. Islam is egalitarian in theory, opposed to discrimination on the basis of race, and values education and encouraged every believer to become literate. Islamic law contained a general commercial code, and the requirement to make pilgrimage to Mecca, a city in present-day Saudi Arabia, meant that the large Muslim world was connected by long-distance caravan routes, giving Muslim merchants a great advantage. Muhammad and his followers quickly converted the people of Arabia, defeated the great empire of Persia and much of Byzantium over the next century, and spread the new faith throughout the Middle East and North Africa. Muslim refugees in the very early days of Muhammad's mission introduced Islam to East Africa, where Muslims were welcomed by the local Christian rulers. By 738, Islamic scholars in North Africa were already aware of the existence of large civilizations south of the Sahara in West Africa, suggesting that merchants were already crossing the desert. The Kingdom of Tekur, in SENEGAMBIA, was the first West African state formally to convert to Islam around 850. The Soninke people built the Empire of Ghana in the Niger River valley in the 10th century, and although Ghana was never completely Islamized, its merchants, civil servants, and judges were mainly Muslims. When Ghana fell and was replaced by Mali in the late 11th century, this region also became largely Islamic. From these bases, Islam spread throughout the savannah region of West Africa, and south in many places into the forest, as at least a minority faith of merchants and the educated. West Africa was a center of Islamic learning in the 15th and 16th centuries, with the University of Timbuktu one of the best-known Muslim universities in the world. When Mansa Musa (ruler of Mali 1312–37) made his pilgrimage to Mecca in 1324, he took professors with him to Cairo. He endowed and enlarged the Islamic university there, once the foremost in the Islamic world, but which had fallen on hard times due to political disruptions in Egypt.

Islam as practiced in West Africa was often syncretic, taking on characteristics of African beliefs and religious practice, much as Christianity did among Africans in the Americas (see also AFRICAN AND SYNCRETIC RELIGIONS). Religious practitioners known as fetisheurs, in order to help petitioners with problems in daily life, wrote appropriate quotes from the Qur'an on slips of paper to put in amulets or on boards from which the ink is then washed to make a potion. Often people continued to venerate spirits or ancestors under the guise of djinn, or angels, or Islamic saints. These diversions from strict orthodoxy sometimes provoked forceful reactions from religious reformers and outside observers from the larger Islamic world in precolonial times. Holy wars and disruptive reform movements attacking these vestiges of pre-Islamic beliefs often led to social unrest and political chaos: In the 11th century, the Empire of Ghana was toppled by religiously motivated Almoravid invaders from Morocco, who criticized official toleration of pre-Islamic beliefs, and the movement resisting French colonial expansion in Senegambia, led by El Hadj Umar Tall (1797–1864), was regularly distracted by an ongoing jihad against unorthodox religious practice among the Bambara people in what is now Mali.

This religiously based turmoil in Islamic West Africa, combined with more secular causes, meant that the region was regularly racked by wars. One product of these wars were slaves. In the early days, slaves were exported across the Sahara—in fact, many of the first Africans to reach the Americas in the 16th century were transported by the Moors as slaves from their wars in West Africa. ESTÉBAN DE DORANTES is an example: He was a black man, probably raised as a Muslim, who was a slave in Morocco. He was sold to the Spanish and then accompanied his master on a long exploratory voyage across North America from FLORIDA to Sonora, MEXICO, between 1528 and 1536. After European slave-trading voyages to the coast of West Africa became common, another export route to the South opened up and significant numbers of Muslim slaves began to arrive in the Americas.

Masters in the Americas were of two minds about their Muslim slaves. On the one hand, they often recognized that Muslims were more connected to global culture and thought of them as more "civilized" than "pagan" Africans. Most Muslims could read at least a little Arabic, since the recitation of the Qur'an was so important in religion. Some Islamic slaves were highly literate: AYUBA SULEIMAN DIALLO lived for a few years as a slave in MARYLAND in the 1730s before being freed and repatriated to the Fouta Djallon in modern Guinea. He owed his freedom in part to help from locally prominent whites who realized from his literacy and "affable and noble bearing" that he must be a high-ranking person. Almost a century later, ABDUL-RAHMAN IBRAHIM IBN SORI was a slave on a cotton plantation in Natchez, MISSISSIPPI, in the 1820s and may have been the only literate person there, including the master and his family. When President JOHN QUINCY ADAMS intervened to seek Ibrahim's freedom, his master was unwilling to give him up since Ibrahim had been keeping all the plantation records—in Arabic. Slaves shared this view that Muslims were more civilized, and religious leaders such as Diallo and Ibrahim often became leaders among the slaves. This made them potentially dangerous to the masters, at least if their loyalty could not be guaranteed. Muslims were suspected in many rebellions and plots in the Americas, especially in the Iberian countries that had a long history of struggle with Muslim internal enemies. The most serious rebellion with Islamic connections was the Malê revolt in Salvador, Bahía, Brazil, in 1835. The rebel slaves were mostly from Yoruba country in what is now Nigeria, from the Kingdom of Benin (*see also* Slave Coast, Benin, and the Bight of Biafra). This people of Benin were predominantly not Muslim in the early 19th century, but Islamic teachers and merchants were a respected upper class in society. People from this class led the uprising, while the majority of rebels were not Muslims. Nonetheless, it has come to be known as the great Muslim revolt.

Free people of color were less likely than slaves to become or remain Muslim. In order to gain the degree of acceptance that freedom represented, most people had to make some effort to accommodate the dominant culture. Various cultural practices had to be adopted, and given the importance of religion to Europeans, especially before the 1800s, religious conversion was generally required. In fact, in many places in the Americas, free people of color were among the most dedicated Christians, flocking to revival and reform movements. It is certainly possible that some covert Muslim practices remained, either more fully preserved as a clandestine religious belief covered by a false Christian practice or, more likely, as syncretic practices such as the wearing of amulets or the use of ill-remembered Arabic expressions in folk religious practices.

After the Malê revolt, the Brazilian authorities made intensive efforts to convert Muslim slaves to Christianity. This was a period in which both Catholic and Protestant groups were aggressively proselytizing among blacks, partly in response to the religious movement sometimes called the Second Great Awakening. Foremost among the missionaries in the English-speaking world were Baptists and Pietists, who shared with Muslims the idea that religion should be simple to join, be easy to understand, and treat everyone equally. With their lack of a religious hierarchy, respect for learning or at least literacy, and straightforward style of prayer,

they appealed to people who had been influenced by Islam. Many Baptist leaders in this mission work were free people of color, in such groups as the African Methodist Episcopal Church or the Moravian Brotherhood. In their abhorrence of syncretic practices and holdovers from the pre-monotheistic beliefs of their ancestors, the Baptists also echoed the attitude of orthodox Muslim leaders in Africa. In Brazil and the Spanish Americas, the Roman Catholic Church had been handicapped by the intellectual assault of Enlightenment rationality and political associations with colonial rule and conservative politics. The 1830s saw a revival of Catholicism, which included a concerted attempt to revive Catholic practice among the common people both in Europe and in the Americas. Between these twin assaults, most African-American Muslims abandoned almost all of their religion. There were still a few syncretic practices hanging on by the beginning of the 20th century, especially in northeastern Brazil. The American religious movement the Nation of Islam claims a heritage from African Americans who never abandoned Islam, but despite some survivals, the faith was very weak everywhere in the Americas before the beginning of revival in the 1910s.

Stewart R. King

FURTHER READING

Alford, Terry. *Prince among Slaves.* New York: Oxford University Press, 2007.

Austin, Allen. *African Muslims in Antebellum America: Transatlantic Stories and Spiritual Struggles.* New York: Routledge, 1997.

Curtis, Edward IV, ed. *Encyclopedia of Muslim-American History.* New York: Facts On File, 2010.

———. *Muslims in America: A Short History.* New York: Oxford University Press, 2009.

Diouf, Sylviane. *Servants of Allah: African Muslims Enslaved in the Americas.* New York: New York University Press, 1998.

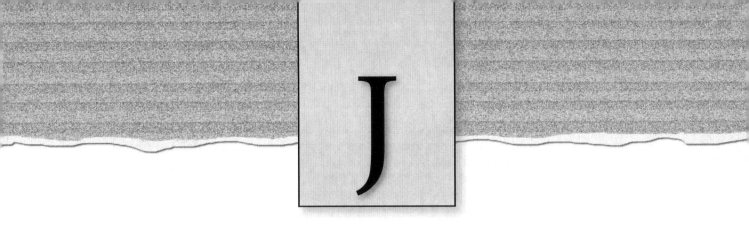

J

JACKSON, ANDREW (1767–1845) *general and seventh president of the United States (1829–1837)* Andrew Jackson was born on March 15, 1767, in NORTH CAROLINA into a poor Northern Ireland Protestant immigrant family. His entire family died during the WAR OF AMERICAN INDEPENDENCE, 1775–83, and he was orphaned at 14. He studied law, moved to TENNESSEE, and went into public service. He was a member of the U.S. House of Representatives, a senator, and justice of the Tennessee state Supreme Court. He was also a merchant and planter, owning as many as 150 slaves on his plantation, Hermitage, near Nashville. During the War of 1812, he commanded U.S. forces in the West, provoking the Indians of the region into war and then crushing them in a series of campaigns between 1812 and 1818. Between 1817 and 1821, he masterminded the conquest of FLORIDA from SPAIN. He also successfully defended NEW ORLEANS, LOUISIANA, against a British expeditionary force. These military victories gave him a national reputation. He ran for president in 1824 but was defeated in a close election, though he had received the most votes, because of a compromise between his two chief competitors, Henry Clay (1777–1852) and JOHN QUINCY ADAMS. Jackson and his supporters saw this outcome as unjust and undemocratic, and the 1828 election saw Jackson ride a wave of democratic outrage into the White House. He served two terms, during which he decentralized government, especially finances; expelled most of the remaining Indians from the Southeast in the infamous "Trail of Tears"; and firmly established the principle of democratic equality among white men in American politics. By eliminating most of the vestiges of aristocratic government that the American system had incorporated in its early days, he became and remains a hero for many Americans. However, he also helped cement racial exclusion as a central element in American politics for more than a century.

His relations with free people of color were mixed. His actions contributed to the opening of the inland South to the expansion of plantation society. These new plantation societies were unwelcoming to free people of color. On the other hand, in LOUISIANA, he cooperated with the large free black community, including free blacks among his soldiers in his 1814–15 campaign against the British and pledging to uphold laws protecting the status of free people of color in west Florida (what is today the Gulf Coast of MISSISSIPPI and ALABAMA) when he captured it from Spain. During the First Seminole War in 1818, Jackson ordered the execution of two British subjects, Alexander Arbuthnot and Robert C. Ambrister, who operated a trading post serving a free colored community in Florida. The two men executed were white, but their crime, in Jackson's eyes, was helping their free black neighbors. These were mostly MAROONS who had run away from slavery in the United States. The Spanish had welcomed them if they were willing to convert to Catholicism, but Jackson saw them as violent RUNAWAY SLAVES and ordered his Creek Indian allies to attack and destroy the settlement.

Many southeastern Indians were of partial African ancestry. This was one reason that Jackson wanted to move them out of the South during his presidency—they provided an alternative paradigm for the inclusion of blacks in Southern society, and some of them, most notably the Seminole, welcomed runaway slaves. On the other hand, federal troops under Jackson's orders protected the exiled Indians during the Trail of Tears from local MILITIA and slave catchers who wanted to enslave or re-enslave Afro-Indians. Those tribes that acceded early to Jackson's demands to relocate to OKLAHOMA met with little harassment.

There is no evidence of any close relationship between Jackson and any free people of color in his private life, but there were many free blacks living in Tennessee during the time he was a planter there. Given what we know about plantation life in the Upper South, he must have had work done by free black craftsmen, rented land or bought produce from free black small farmers, and seen free blacks in the nearby towns.

Andrew Jackson died on June 8, 1845.

Stewart R. King

FURTHER READING

Meacham, Jon. *American Lion: Andrew Jackson in the White House*. New York: Random House, 2008.

Remini, Robert. *The Life of Andrew Jackson*. New York: HarperCollins, 2001.

JACOBS, HARRIET (1813–1897) *American author*

Harriet Jacobs became a prominent figure in African-American life in the United States with the publication in 1861 of her memoir *Incidents in the Life of a Slave Girl*. Her story of a growing horrified understanding of her status, sexual abuse by her master, and plucky and dangerous escape to freedom enthralled audiences in the North and helped to undermine the proslavery arguments of Southerners. Her story was not unusual, of course; only the fact that she told it to a wide audience makes her famous today.

Jacobs was born a slave in Edenton, NORTH CAROLINA, on February 11, 1813. Her parents were enslaved mulattoes. Harriet and her brother, John, had a pretty safe childhood surrounded by her father, Elijah—a carpenter—and her mother, Delilah. With the death of her mother in 1819, Harriet began to realize what her status as a slave meant. In relation to this traumatic moment she would later write, "I was born a slave but I never knew it till six years of happy childhood had passed by." Her first mistress after her mother's death was a Margaret Horniblow, who was kind enough to teach Harriet how to read, write, and sew. However, when Horniblow died, Jacobs was sent to the Norcom family, whom she called the "Flints" in her memoir. Mrs. Norcom was Margaret Horniblow's daughter. In the Norcom household, she would experience firsthand the crude reality of being a slave.

Jacobs was in charge of the Norcoms' three-year-old daughter. Dr. John Norcom was highly respected by the community as a devout Christian and a pious man, but when he was at home he would torture, punish, and whip slaves with no mercy at all. As time went by and Jacobs became an attractive young woman, Norcom repeatedly propositioned her for sex and harassed her verbally. It is unclear from the sources whether Jacobs ever actually had sex with Norcom, as the only source for this period of her life is her autobiography, which was written in the Victorian period when such details were not discussed publicaly. Jacobs always claimed that she resisted Norcom's advances successfully. Norcom's wife was extremely jealous of her husband's affairs with slaves and often took revenge on Jacobs. Jacobs eventually became the lover of Samuel Sawyer, a white lawyer, with whom she had two children.

Norcom threatened to sell her two children, who were his slaves by law, away from her if she did not agree to have sexual relations with him. She finally escaped the Norcom household in 1835 and took refuge in the attic of the house of her grandmother, Molly, in Edenton, where she hid for seven years. As she wrote in her memoir, she lived among mice, with almost no space to move and with almost no light. Sawyer bought their children from Norcom and freed them, and they lived with the grandmother, so Jacobs could see them but for fear of their revealing her location to outsiders she could not show herself to them. After seven years living this way, Jacobs was smuggled onto a boat to PHILADELPHIA, PENNSYLVANIA, perhaps with the assistance of Sawyer. In the North, she became actively involved in the abolitionist movement. Installing herself in New York, she reunited with her children and her brother, John Jacobs, who was living and working there. Both the children and John were legally free. Her brother's employers, the writer Nathaniel Parker Willis and his wife, also employed Harriet Jacobs for some time as a nursemaid to their daughter. They started raising funds to pay for Jacobs's freedom, fearing she might be re-enslaved under the provisions of the FUGITIVE SLAVE ACT OF 1850. They took her to Britain for a while to ensure that she could not be recaptured. Finally, Willis bought the rights to Jacobs from Norcom's son-in-law and heir in 1853, making her legally free. She then moved with her daughter and brother to Rochester, New York.

The abolitionist Lydia Maria Child encouraged and helped Harriet Jacobs to publish her own life story. Jacobs's slave narrative appeared in 1861 with the title *Incidents in the Life of a Slave Girl* and was signed with the pseudonym Linda Brent. With her text, Jacobs gave voice to millions of female slaves who suffered in silence. Hers is a bold text that exposes sexual abuse, the cruelty of slavery, and the hypocrisy of slave masters: "Reader, be assured this narrative is no fiction," she begins. Nonetheless, Southern apologists attacked the narrative as exaggerated, and in the Jim Crow years, as American whites constructed a new narrative of the antebellum South, Jacobs's book went out of print and was nearly forgotten. Scholars in the 1970s republished it, and it has become an important source for understanding the experience of enslaved women.

During the AMERICAN CIVIL WAR, 1861–65, she helped raise money for black refugees and escaped slaves. She lived in Alexandria, Virginia, during the war, working in a hospital and helping local schools and orphanages for children of color. After the war, she worked as a boardinghouse housekeeper and domestic servant in New York and died on March 7, 1897.

Laura Gimeno-Pahissa

FURTHER READING

Fleischner, J. *Mastering Slavery, Memory, Family and Identity in Women's Slave Narratives*. New York: New York University Press, 1996.

Foster, F. Smith. *Written by Herself: Literary Production by African American Women, 1746–1892*. Bloomington: Indiana University Press, 1993

Jacobs, Harriet. *Incidents in the Life of a Slave Girl*. New York: Oxford University Press, 1988

Yellin, J. F. *Harriet Jacobs: A Life*. New York: Basic Books, 2004.

JAMAICA

Jamaica is the third-largest island in the Caribbean, and at 4,200 square miles, it was the fourth-largest colony after CUBA, SAINT-DOMINGUE, and Spanish SANTO DOMINGO (the last two colonies are on the island of Hispaniola). The island is generally mountainous, with a chain of mountains rising to 7,400 feet running east-west the length of the island. There are relatively broad, well-watered coastal plains on the southern side of the island and much smaller river valleys along the northern coast. The island is subject to frequent hurricanes, and the mountains do not protect the primary agricultural zones as they do in Haiti and Cuba. However, the climate is generally favorable to the SUGAR CULTIVATION in the plains and COFFEE CULTIVATION in the mountains. It was a principal producer of both these commodities during the 18th and early 19th centuries. There are several small ports on the north and west coasts of the island, but the main port, and one of the largest in the Caribbean, is the harbor of Port Royal/Kingston.

History

Jamaica was inhabited by around 100,000 Taino Indians when the Spanish explorer Christopher Columbus arrived in 1494. The Spanish settled first on Hispaniola and raided the neighboring islands for slaves, but in 1509, a Spanish expedition arrived with the goal of conquering the island. The Jamaicans had been weakened by persistent raiding and by diseases introduced by the Europeans. They fought for three years, with the remaining survivors mostly committing suicide when resistance proved futile. The Spanish kept some surviving Indians as slaves but fairly rapidly began meeting their labor needs by importing slaves from Africa. It has been suggested that this was done at the urging of the Dominican missionary and defender of the Indians Bartolomé de Las Casas (ca. 1484–1566), but Spain needed no prompting to make use of African workers. African slaves had been working on farms in southern Spain, the Balearic Islands, and the Canaries from the early 15th century. African slaves were at work in Jamaica from at least 1517.

Jamaica's economic development was slowed, however, as in most of the Spanish Caribbean island colonies, by the flow of population, capital, and official attention to the mainland colonies after the conquest of MEXICO

(1521) and PERU (1532). Without new importation of slaves and without the capital needed to sustain sugar cultivation, most of Jamaica became an area of subsistence cultivation. Small amounts of tropical staple crops, primarily tobacco but also some sugar, were exported through Cuba. Most slaves gained their freedom and intermingled with the white population until, by the middle of the 17th century, almost everyone on the island was a free person of African ancestry (though, thanks to the flexible Spanish color line, some were socially defined as white). Then, in 1655, an English expedition arrived to conquer the island, and everything changed with dramatic suddenness.

Establishment of British Rule (1655–1800)

The British generally preserved a very sharp division between the races in their colonial empire. They did not adhere so strongly to the "ONE DROP RULE OF RACIAL IDENTITY," which defined people as black if they had any known African ancestry, as they did in mainland North America. In the British Empire outside mainland North America, lighter-skinned blacks were distinguished from people of entirely African ancestry in some ways, but harsh discrimination was the rule for anybody with any known African ancestry. The British had no recent national history or legal structure for slavery when they began their colonial project in the Americas and adapted their normal property laws that applied to movable property to define slaves as "chattel," almost entirely without legal human personality. The state did not intervene in the master-slave relationship, which was often quite brutal. Free people of color were sharply restricted in what they could do both in BRITAIN and throughout the empire.

When Britain entered Jamaica, there was a brief period before this harsh climate was fully established. The first British inhabitants of the island were buccaneers, living at Port Royal. As with the buccaneers in Tortuga, off the coast of Saint-Domingue, their society was racially mixed

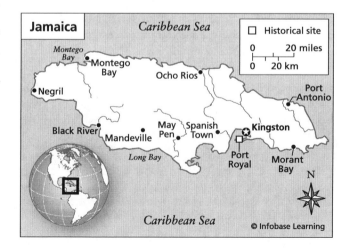

and quite egalitarian (*see also* PIRACY). But the late 17th century was a period when all the European governments were consolidating their power. One of the most important elements of this consolidation was gaining a monopoly on the use of armed force. The buccaneers were important to Britain's naval power in the Americas in the mid-17th century, but by the end of the century, Britain had a regular Royal Navy base in Jamaica and no longer needed informal assistance. Most of the buccaneers who could be socially defined as white were integrated into the larger society, at a higher or lower level, depending on their wealth. Some of them became wealthy planters. The people of color among them were more of a threat because as armed black men they represented a threat to the racial order. Many of them became civilian or Royal Navy seamen, some lived on quietly in the colony, and many were hunted down by the navy. (*See also* MERCHANT SEAMEN and NAVY.)

Once British colonial rule was firmly established in Jamaica, the colony began to grow rapidly in population and wealth. Sugar plantations filled the plains and river valleys. In the highlands, a stubborn population of MAROONS posed a threat to the colony. The colonial authorities launched several military expeditions against them between 1670 and 1738 but were unable to force them to surrender. The maroons were also growing rapidly in numbers and military skill, as their ranks were filled by RUNAWAY SLAVES from the sugar plantations. In many cases, these slaves were already trained soldiers from African armies who had been taken prisoner and sold into the Atlantic slave trade. With the maroons a serious military threat and colonists beginning to be interested in settling the mountains as coffee cultivation was introduced, the government signed a series of treaties with the maroons of the Cockpit Country, beginning in 1738, guaranteeing them their liberty and farmland in return for an agreement to stop raiding the plantations and to return all new runaway slaves. The maroons fought for Britain in defense of the colony and elsewhere in the Atlantic world, including during the Saint-Domingue expedition in the 1790s. Tension between the maroons and the colonial government did not disappear, erupting in fighting in 1795–96 that ended with the entire population of the Trelawney Town maroon community deported to CANADA and ultimately to SIERRA LEONE, where they arrived in time to put down a rebellion by earlier free black settlers there.

After having been a source of slave exports to the British North American colonies for a century, Jamaica received substantial numbers of immigrants from North America after the end of the WAR OF AMERICAN INDEPENDENCE, 1775–83. The immigrants included loyalist whites and their slaves, as well as loyalist free blacks.

North American exiles spread out through the British Empire, with many, both blacks and whites, going to Canada, and others to the smaller Caribbean islands, but Jamaica received the largest contingent from the Southern colonies. This importation of North American ideas, both about race and about individual freedom, proved to be a challenge to the stability of Jamaica.

Colony, War, and Revolution (1800–1900)

Jamaica was the second-largest producer of sugar in the Caribbean in the latter half of the 18th century. It was one of the wealthiest parts of the British Empire, and one of the most strategic. It was during this period that Britain and FRANCE fought three major wars, the SEVEN YEARS' WAR (1756–63), the War of American Independence, and the Wars of the FRENCH REVOLUTION and Napoléon (1791–1815). Jamaica played an important role in each of these wars as a source of wealth for Britain and as a strategic base permitting the projection of British power in the region. Britain and France fought a desperate and very expensive struggle for global naval supremacy during this period. The Caribbean was a major theater for this war, and Jamaica was one of the principal British naval bases in the region. The harbor at Kingston was typically the home port to a squadron of at least a dozen battleships throughout these wars. The British admiral George Rodney, architect of Britain's decisive naval victory at the Saintes (1782), which cemented a new, more aggressive culture and tactics in the Royal Navy and established British naval dominance for the rest of this struggle, was commander of the Jamaica squadron from 1763 to 1774. He built up the dockyards and base facilities to make them the equal of any British naval base in the world. The British attempt to conquer Saint-Domingue during the HAITIAN REVOLUTION was based in Jamaica. After the British invasion was defeated by TOUSSAINT LOUVERTURE's forces in 1799, the British fear that Haitian forces would invade Jamaica led them to sign a treaty with Toussaint, effectively conceding him control of the island of Hispaniola. After this, and after the defeat of Napoléon's navy at Trafalgar in 1805, a navy that included most of the French Caribbean squadron, the strategic importance of Jamaica declined.

However, after the outbreak of the Haitian Revolution in 1791, Saint-Domingue ceased to be an important sugar producer, and Jamaica took over the leading position. BRAZIL and Cuba's production also increased, however, and the fact that British sugar could not be shipped to European markets between 1791 and 1815 because of Napoléon's economic sanctions meant that Jamaican producers did not benefit as much as they expected to from this windfall. In fact, Jamaican sugar producers were always deeply in debt to British creditors and in peril of losing their businesses. The prosperity of the islands was built on a mountain of debt, which the planters always hoped to repay through one big harvest or one big shift in the market. This precarious economic position made Jamaica's planters even more suspicious of change. The enormous wealth that the sugar and coffee trade produced mainly stayed in the hands of the British merchants, who nonetheless formed a political alliance with the planters to create the "West India interest" in the British Parliament. This powerful lobby, supported by King William IV (1765–1837, r. 1830–37), opposed ending the slave trade, fought the abolition of slavery with great ferocity, and, when finally forced to give in, saw their wealth and influence decline sharply.

The British Parliament ended the slave trade in 1807. The effects on Jamaica were enormous. The Jamaican slave population had never maintained an excess of births over deaths, though the situation was improving in the early 1800s as a result of improved medicine and the importation of more women slaves. Jamaican planters realized that the slave trade would soon end and made an effort to promote more births of slaves on their plantations by offering women time off work while pregnant and nursing, providing child care, hiring free women or buying skilled slaves to serve as midwives, and increasing the number of women slaves in their workforces. Prices for newly arrived women slaves were actually higher than for men in the last years of the slave trade. The proportion of Jamaican slaves who were born in the island exceeded 50 percent by 1800, meaning that the black population was nearing the ability to replace itself by natural means. But despite all these efforts, the slave population of Jamaica began to fall after 1807. Planters met the challenge of declining slave population by hiring free laborers and investing in machinery. Increasing demand for free labor meant that more cash was circulating in the black population, providing the means to purchase the freedom of more slaves, further worsening the labor shortage. Ultimately, production was cut, and European consumers grew accustomed to substitutes, principally beet sugar.

At the same time, the slaves became even more restive than they had been up to that point, sensing weakness in the national government's commitment to slavery and their own enhanced bargaining power thanks to the shortage of workers. Jamaica had experienced dozens of rebellions or work actions by slaves before 1807, including a major islandwide struggle in 1760 called Tacky's War that took hundreds of lives. However, there were an increasing number of local work actions after 1807, culminating in a major disturbance in 1831–32 that ultimately helped put an end to the slave system. The Baptist War, as it was called, was organized by black Baptist preachers, the best-known of whom was Samuel Sharpe.

They apparently did not intend to overthrow the entire system or massacre whites, as demonstrated by their restraint in the early hours of the uprising. Their movement was intended to be a colonywide strike by slaves for better conditions. However, the colonial government responded with unrestrained brutality, slaughtering slaves by the hundreds and then rounding up hundreds more for quick "trials" and executions. The savagery stopped the strike, but the effect on British public opinion was such that Parliament abolished slavery in the British Empire in 1834. This was a progressive and compensated emancipation, with masters paid a portion of the market value of their slaves and former slaves above the age of six required to work for their former masters as "apprentices" for a period of up to seven years.

The apprenticeship provisions of the law were largely ignored by the slaves and proved mostly unenforceable. Once the slaves heard they were free, those who could work generally left their plantations and either moved onto unoccupied land, setting up as PEASANT farmers or moved to the towns. Some black farmers continued to work part-time for plantations, though there was a generalized reluctance to return to work for the same plantation where one had been a slave. The apprenticeship provisions of the abolition act were revoked before the seven years ended, and Jamaican blacks were legally entirely free. There was a seasonal migration of black farmers to the plantation regions to work on the harvest. Some planters managed to remain in business by employing free labor. The colonial government also imported indentured servants, or "coolies," from India to work on the sugar plantations, though they only had to work for a limited term of years, and many ran away before their indentures were completed. Sugar and coffee cultivation continued on Jamaica at a limited level, but the colony ceased to be an economically important part of the British Empire after the 1840s.

Free People of Color in Jamaica

The first free people of color to live in Jamaica probably arrived with Columbus, though we can not be sure whether the servant Diego listed as a member of Columbus's crew and described as an African was from Morocco or sub-Saharan Africa. Some sources say that the conquistador Juan Garrido, who was a companion of the conquistador Hernán Cortés and an important landowner in Mexico City, may also have been a participant in the conquest of Jamaica. The generalized poverty and isolation of Spanish Jamaica after the 1520s led to the creation of a racially mixed and relatively egalitarian society by the 17th century. It would not be an exaggeration to say that almost all Jamaicans in 1655 were free people of color.

The early English settlers of the colony after 1655 also included many men of color. Some were runaway slaves from Spanish islands, others were English seafarers, and there were an increasing number of African slaves. The Spanish inhabitants socially defined as white mostly left the colony, but many of the poorer, mixed-race Spanish inhabitants remained. Their descendants, in what was called Spanish Town, became one of the largest urban free colored populations in the colony. As the slave population grew, the lines between black and white and between slaves and free people hardened. Britain did not have national laws about slavery until the time came to abolish the institution in the 19th century. Up to that time, each colony had made its own laws defining slavery and reserving privileges for whites. The various different legal regimes shared some characteristics, however. For the most part, slaves were treated as property rather than as people. They had no legal rights, either to sue or to own property or to exercise any of the rights of a citizen. They could be prosecuted legally for crimes, though most masters opposed this since punishments could deprive them of their property. Masters generally exercised full legal jurisdiction over their slaves, punishing and rewarding as they saw fit, and were civilly responsible for the actions of their slaves.

If a slave were to become free, the master would normally have to request permission from the colonial government. In Jamaica, MANUMISSION was taxed, though not so heavily as in the French colonies. Masters who were not dissuaded could free their slaves, and the newly freed people gained some rights under law. They could be sued and could sue, but their testimony could not be heard in court against a white man. This meant that their property rights, while in theory equal to those of a white, were in fact very insecure. In addition, the colonial government was very concerned about the threat to the idea of white supremacy posed by having a black man in the position of master over slaves. The government, therefore, placed a number of requirements on black property owners, the most onerous of which were the Deficiency Laws, which required that slaves be supervised in their daily work by a certain proportion of white men. At different times in Jamaica, these laws made it either more expensive or nearly impossible for a person of color to be a large-scale planter. There were small farms owned by free Afro-Jamaican families, especially in coffee-growing areas in the mountains, and some free people of color were technical employees on plantations, but for the most part, the free Afro-Jamaican population was concentrated in the towns.

Planters freed their slaves in Jamaica for many of the same reasons that they did in other slave societies. Slaves received their freedom because they were the relatives of white people, often illegitimate children fathered with slave women. Slaves might be rewarded for faithful service by manumission, especially if they were too old to give much more service—though this was frowned upon and governmental permission to free older slaves was often withheld. The government occasionally freed slaves as a reward for some service to the state, usually betraying plots to rebel or run away. The family relationship worked less efficiently in the British colonies than in the French or Iberian ones, however. The conventional social expectation in Atlantic world slave societies that a man would free his illegitimate mixed-race children was not so strong in Jamaica. Many slaves bought their freedom or free people bought the freedom of their enslaved relatives. As the end of the era of slavery approached, in 1829–31, more than half of all recorded manumissions were the result of self-purchase or ransom. The result of this was that the free colored population had a larger proportion of ARTISANS and retail merchants who could raise the money to free themselves and their families. The fact that they were more likely to be trained in urban occupations was another important reason that most Jamaican free coloreds lived in the towns.

One important exception to this rule were the maroons who made their peace with the colonial government in the 1730s and lived as peasants in the countryside. The colonial government used the maroons as shock troops to put down slave insurrections and hunt for runaways. It was not in the government's interest to have the maroons moving to the towns, and in addition, they wanted to avoid having them forge too close an alliance with the urban free coloreds. Therefore, they were generally not permitted to move to the towns, were harassed if they entered plantation areas, and preserved an isolated rural lifestyle in the mountains. The descendants of former maroons are identifiable today, almost two centuries after the end of slavery, by distinctive language and cultural patterns.

Jamaican free people of color were also racially mixed and did not experience the sharp division between free black and free MULATTO in other Caribbean colonies. Part of the explanation for this is the effect of harsh and undifferentiated racial discrimination in the British Empire, even going so far in some places as to define anyone with any known or apparent African ancestry as black. But beyond this, shared legal restrictions and common residence in racially segregated quarters in towns created a sense of community. In fact, free blacks and free people of mixed race intermarried, and within a few generations nearly everyone in the free colored community was "brown."

The free colored population in Jamaica grew rapidly, as was the case throughout the plantation Americas. Significant numbers of manumissions were an important factor, though probably fewer as a percentage of the slave population than in French, Spanish, or Portuguese colonies. Still, for the few years for which there are data, in the 1820s, there were hundreds of manumissions registered each year. At the same time, the free colored population was almost entirely native-born and was gender-balanced. They were also optimistic about their future and strongly influenced by evangelical religion during the late 18th and early 19th centuries, both of which gave them cultural reasons to want large families. Their economic situation was not as prosperous as that of the free people of color in Saint-Domingue, but there was still a lot of wealth in the island, enough so that free coloreds' businesses could count on customers and their farms could count on a market for the crops. Birthrates were high, and death rates were low. By the 1830s, at the end of the period of slavery, free people of color made up more than a third of the island's population.

The Jamaican free colored population experienced intermittent repression. The mixed-race newspaper editor EDWARD JORDON was tried for sedition and imprisoned in 1830 for publishing a pamphlet calling for abolition of slavery. The repression of Jordon sparked resistance by the urban free colored population. Free coloreds gained popular support from Britain, where an active abolitionist movement was making great strides. The colonial government decided to try to reconcile free coloreds by giving them equal legal rights and awarding the vote to free colored men who met the property requirements. The people of Kingston responded by electing Jordon to the House of Assembly, and so after a short time in prison, he was freed and became an important leader of the free colored community.

The Baptist War represented a step backward for free coloreds, especially poor country people. While almost all of the instigators of the Baptist War were slaves, the persecution afterward affected all people of color in the countryside. A number of free people of color from the Baptist Church were accused of collaboration in the plot, though most of them were freed because the evidence against them was from slaves and slaves were not allowed to testify against free people in criminal cases. Some Baptist missionaries, both whites and people of color, were expelled from the colony. However, popular outrage in Britain provoked by the harsh repression of both slaves and free people in the Baptist War was an important factor in Parliament's ultimate decision, in 1833, to abolish slavery.

After Abolition

Former free people of color formed a distinctive group in Jamaican society after the end of slavery. The brown urban middle class to this day have many ancestors who were free before 1834. They are aware of and proud of their connection to their own heritage of freedom. Issues of race and class are tied up in the identity of this group. As among black middle classes throughout the former slave societies of the Americas, the Jamaican middle class recruited some members from the ranks of former slaves, particularly those who had served in the colonial civil service or military. At the same time, they lost some members to poverty or emigration. Free people of color continued to experience discrimination along with the newly freed in access to public institutions, promotion in private employment, and social acceptance. But in each case, this discrimination was more subtle and less handicapping than that experienced by the newly freed. Former free people of color and their descendants continued to exert significant influence in Jamaica's politics and culture for more than a century after abolition. The early civil rights leader GEORGE WILLIAM GORDON, who was executed after the Morant Bay uprising of 1865, was free before 1834. The Jamaican pan-Africanist thinker Marcus Garvey was descended from pre-1834 free black artisans. The Jamaican independence leader Norman Manley was descended from a former free colored family.

Stewart R. King

FURTHER READING

Craton, Michael. *Empire, Enslavement, and Freedom in the Caribbean.* Kingston, Jamaica: Ian Randle, 1997.
Sherlock, Philip, and Hazel Bennett. *The Story of the Jamaican People.* New York: Marcus Weiner, 1998.
Thome, James, and J. Horace Kimball. *Emancipation in the West Indies, a Six Month's Tour in Antigua, Barbados, and Jamaica in the Year 1837.* New York: American Anti-Slavery Society, 1839. Available online. URL: http://www.yale.edu/glc/archive/1158.htm. Accessed December 27, 2010.

JEFFERSON, THOMAS (1743–1826) *author of the Declaration of Independence and the Virginia Statute of Religious Liberty, founder of the University of Virginia, third president of the United States (1801–1809)*

Born in Albemarle, Virginia, on April 13, 1743, Thomas Jefferson was a wealthy planter in western Virginia. He studied law and was a delegate to the Virginia House of Burgesses and was their representative to the Second Continental Congress. He was on the committee selected to draft the Declaration of Independence, and he wrote most of what was finally accepted. He was governor of Virginia during the AMERICAN WAR OF INDEPENDENCE, 1775–83, and U.S. representative to FRANCE after the peace. After the adoption of the Constitution, he returned to the United States, serving as secretary of state to GEORGE WASHINGTON (1789–93), vice president under John Adams (1797–1801), and then president from 1801 to 1809. He generally opposed increasing the power of government and was the chief opponent of Alexander Hamilton and John Adams in the early development of the federal government.

Like any large planter in Virginia, Jefferson had plenty of free people of color who were his employees, dependents, and relatives. He probably had a longtime relationship with his slave Sally Hemings, who lived "as free" after his death in 1826, and apparently fathered most or all of her numerous children. Some biographers have suggested that the father of the children of Sally Hemings was one of Jefferson's cousins, but most historians believe that the evidence of a relationship between the president and Hemings is convincing. Although he owned hundreds of slaves, Jefferson generally opposed slavery. One of the most powerful sections of his draft of the Declaration of Independence condemns slavery and accuses the British government of having imposed the system on America. This passage was deleted by the Congress before passage. Jefferson's book *Notes on the State of Virginia* also condemns slavery, though on the grounds that association with blacks tends to debase whites, who would be more virtuous as independent small farmers. He also wrote in the book that blacks and whites probably could not live together in peace, and Jefferson seemed to support some form of emigration and colonization of blacks to Africa or elsewhere in the Americas as a solution to America's race problem. He supported a plan to resettle American blacks in Haiti after that island gained its independence in 1804, though it came to nothing, and supported the American Colonization Society's work to free slaves and transport them to Africa. In later life, he wrote to the French abolitionist Henri Grégoire in terms that suggest that he might have reconsidered some of his racial prejudices. His draft of the Northwest Ordinance of 1787 contained a provision that would have barred slavery from the territories north of the Ohio River, though he later supported the Missouri Compromise that permitted slavery in some of the territories the United States had purchased from France during his presidency. He died on July 4, 1826.

Stewart R. King

FURTHER READING

Finkelman, Paul. *Slavery and the Founders: Race and Liberty in the Age of Jefferson*. London: M. E. Sharpe, 2001.

Jefferson, Thomas. *Notes on the State of Virginia*. London: 1797. Available online. URL: http://etext.lib.virginia.edu/toc/modeng/public/JefVirg.html. Accessed December 27, 2010.

Wills, Garry. *The Negro President: Jefferson and the Slave Power*. New York: Houghton Mifflin, 2003.

JESUITS

The Society of Jesus, commonly known as Jesuits, was founded in 1534 by St. Ignatius Loyola and other students at the University of Paris with the idea that they would go as missionaries to the Holy Land or wherever else the pope might decide to send them. Many Jesuits worked in various areas in Europe during the Reformation, but missionary work among non-Europeans has always been an important part of the society's work. Jesuit missionaries have often been willing to adopt the lifestyles of the people they live among, and this has become one of the best-known forms of evangelization associated with the society. For example, Matteo Ricci (1552–1610), the Jesuit missionary to China, sought permission from the Vatican to adopt the shaved head and saffron robes of a Buddhist monk. He lived in Beijing and served as a scientific adviser at the Chinese court. Jesuit missionaries in Canada, including St. Isaac Jogues, lived among the Indians and respected many aspects of their society. In another form of evangelization pioneered by the society, Jesuit missionaries in Argentina and Paraguay established *reducciones* (reductions), or mission villages, to house Guaraní Indian converts. The villages were administered by the Jesuits to produce agricultural crops that could be marketed in the colonies, and they proved to be profitable enough to finance all the society's activities in the region. The villages were also easier to defend, and the Guaraní were being attacked by slave raiders moving up from Brazil. Nonetheless, the *reducciones* were a step away from the earlier Jesuit model of missionaries living the life of the people they served.

When the society began evangelizing Africans in the Americas, they followed both of these precedents to some degree. In Saint-Domingue, the Jesuits were assigned as parish priests in rural parishes in the North Province, the area with the largest slave population. They also operated two homes for sick and impoverished people in Cap-Français/Cap-Haïtien. The Haitian revolutionary leader Toussaint Louverture may have worked at one of these centers as a young man. His biographer suggests that he may have learned to read from the Jesuits. They appointed at least two priests per parish, one for the free population who worked at the parish church and the other for the slaves who traveled from plantation to plantation. They also trained lay catechists, many of whom were free people of color. Even years later, some of the former catechists were still working to evangelize and teach the slaves, though without supervision, they often had some odd theological notions. In fact, the *prêt savan*, or bush priest, is a distinctive feature of Haitian *vodun*, and the heir of the Jesuit lay catechist. The Jesuits also owned land in each parish and maintained their own plantations, both for funding their operation and as a sort of refuge for slave converts. But in many cases, the plantations were run by lay professional managers, and the slaves mistreated in some of the same ways as were slaves of secular masters. Nonetheless, their secular neighbors complained that the Jesuits coddled their slaves and made the neighbors' slaves discontented with their lot. The Saint-Domingue Jesuits genuinely tried to evangelize the slaves and to call both slaves and masters to mutual concern and respect, as they believed Christianity demanded. They were so energetic in their demands and so profitable in their plantation operations that the colonial elites finally prevailed on the government to expel the Jesuits and give their parishes to Capuchin friars, who had very little to do with the slaves.

In COLOMBIA, St. Peter Claver (1580–1654) and the Jesuits of CARTAGENA de Colombia established hospitals for people who were sick when they arrived on slave ships that docked there. At the time, Cartagena was a very important port for the slave trade, with thousands of people arriving every year, some in very poor condition. The society eventually owned many of the slaves who recovered, and they established a plantation where they worked and produced food for the hospital and cash crops to fund the Jesuits' activities. Again, the neighbors complained that the Jesuits treated their slaves too kindly and made too much money off the plantation. Claver compounded the offense by visiting those of his converts who had been returned to their masters, criticizing owners who mistreated their slaves. As in Saint-Domingue, the Jesuits trained lay catechists to lead communities in remote areas, and many of these lay ministers were free people of color. There were many complaints from white elites, but the Catholic hierarchy and the society's superiors in Rome backed Claver, and the society's work in Cartagena continued up until the final suppression of the order in the Spanish Empire in 1767.

The society was suppressed in most countries in the late 18th century. Popes tried to defend the order, but the powerful Catholic absolute monarchs of Spain, PORTUGAL, and FRANCE were all opposed, and the popes had to give in. There were many reasons for the hostility of these governments to the Jesuits, but their relationship with blacks and Indians in the Americas was certainly part of the problem, from the governments' point of view.

In MARYLAND, Jesuit priests were theoretically clandestine until the WAR OF AMERICAN INDEPENDENCE, 1775–83, as it was unlawful to hold Roman Catholic services in British territories. In Maryland, many of the wealthiest and most influential people were Catholics, so the Jesuits were tolerated as long as their activities were not obvious. They were known as the "Catholic Gentlemen of Maryland," still the official corporate name of the Jesuit Province of Maryland. As gentlemen farmers,

they owned slaves. As late as 1838, the Jesuit Province of Maryland owned 272 people when they decided to give up slavery on news of Pope Gregory's pending denunciation of slavery and sold their slaves to Catholic planters in LOUISIANA. The Maryland Jesuits shared the predisposition of British Catholics in general, conditioned by harsh repression during the Reformation, to avoid political activity at all costs. Moreover, the ROMAN CATHOLIC CHURCH in general was suspicious of abolitionism, and in the United States it was even more an object of suspicion since it was associated with anti-immigrant political parties. Nonetheless, they preached the Catholic idea of common humanity and called masters to treat their slaves decently, putting them in conflict with the prevailing belief among Southern SLAVE OWNERS that slaves were "chattel," movable property, rather than human beings.

Stewart R. King

FURTHER READING

Lunn, Arnold. *A Saint in the Slave Trade: Peter Claver 1581–1654.* 1937. Reprint, Lanham, Md.: Sheed & Ward, 2008.

Murphy, Thomas J., S.J. *Jesuit Slaveholding in Maryland, 1717–1838.* New York: Routledge, 2001.

JESÚS, URSULA DE   (1604–1666) *Peruvian religious mystic*

Ursula de Jesús was born a slave in Lima in 1604, just as Spanish colonial life in PERU was becoming well established and growing in wealth and power. She either was born in the household of Luisa de Melgarejo Sotomayor, a noted pious white laywoman, or became her slave at a young age. She showed considerable piety, and when her mistress's daughter was sent to the convent, Ursula accompanied her.

The ROMAN CATHOLIC CHURCH had concentrated on converting the Indians and ensuring their religious orthodoxy in the 16th century, but as the 17th century dawned, the church also began to establish more elaborate institutions in the America's. One of these was the order of Poor Clares, a society of religious women founded in medieval Italy by Clare of Assisi (d. 1253), one of the first followers of St. Francis of Assisi, founder of the Franciscans. The order was strictly cloistered and contemplative, and its principal religious duty was to pray for the salvation of its benefactors, society as a whole, and the souls of the faithful dead in purgatory. Its social function in Spanish America was to provide a home away from male influences for women of good family who were not ready to marry, either for a time, in which case they would remain novices under instruction until their families called for them, or permanently, in which case they would become nuns "of the black veil." Although the founding principles of the order were egalitarian and the rule called for all nuns to perform physical labor within the convent as their health permitted, in fact the Convent of Santa Clara in Lima, where Ursula and her young mistress lived, was strictly segregated by class and status. Slaves, newcomers, and poor or free colored nuns, called *donados*, did the labor that kept the institution functioning. Everybody participated in community masses, but the nuns "of the black veil," the socially prominent women who were to live in the convent their whole lives, ruled, studied, and performed most of the daily prayers.

De Jesús lived in this environment as a slave for 29 years, from 1617 to 1646. In her later spiritual writings, she reports that she was willing enough to do the work but suffered from vanity and pride and was easily distracted by things of the world. In 1642, though, she had a transformative experience. While washing a dress and, as she reports, complaining loudly about the person who had borrowed it and left it dirty, she fell into an unused well on the convent grounds. Her fellow nuns were not able to rescue her as she dangled over a drop that would have been fatal. She prayed to the Virgin Mary and, she says, was miraculously preserved from death. After this experience, she realized that vanity and pride were her besetting sins, and she set about heroic works of humility. She treated the sick in the convent infirmary, the more disgusting their illnesses the better. She took on the hardest and most onerous tasks in the daily labor of the monastery. And she began to receive visions of people who had died, asking her to pray on their behalf, and of Jesus, the Virgin Mary, and angels, whom she would ask to have mercy on them. This was not an unusual spiritual gift in her community; several of the senior nuns reported special visions or mysterious urges to pray for some individual. But de Jesús's visions were often of people who had suffered or perpetrated some sort of injustice in colonial society. An early vision was of a man who had cruelly mistreated a slave. She wrote that Jesus told her that the man's punishment could not be reduced because of the gravity of his offense. She also saw a vision of a fellow junior nun who had had a sexual relationship with a senior religious figure, which de Jesús may well have seen as abusive; this person's punishment was reduced because of de Jesús's prayers to Saint Clare. Her visions of purgatory and paradise contained clear messages that in an ideal world ordered according to God's plan, there would be social and racial justice. This was a revolutionary message, but one that, combined with de Jesús's humility and piety, her community was willing to hear. A senior nun, Doña Rafaela de Esquivel, bought her from her owner and freed her. De Jesús became a *donada*, or religiously professed lay sister, of the convent. She lived there for the rest

of her life, dying in 1666. Her reputation for mystical gifts and piety spread around Lima, though she was nowhere near as famous at the time as her near-contemporary Saint MARTIN DE PORRES, a mixed-race lay brother of the DOMINICANS. She kept a spiritual diary in her later years, recording details of her earlier life and spiritual development, as well as her visions. This diary became public after her death and led to continuing fame and local recognition of her sanctity that persists to this day. The diary was recently translated into English, sparking a revival of interest in this visionary figure.

Stewart R. King

FURTHER READING

de Jesús, Ursula. *The Souls of Purgatory: The Spiritual Diary of a Seventeenth-Century Afro-Peruvian Mystic, Ursula de Jesús.* Edited and translated by Nancy van Deusen. Albuquerque: University of New Mexico Press, 2004.
van Deusen, Nancy. "Ursula de Jesús: A Seventeenth-Century Afro-Peruvian Mystic." In *The Human Tradition in Colonial Latin America*, edited by Kenneth J. Andrien, 88–103. Lanham, Md.: SR Books, 2002.

JOHNSON, ANDREW (1808–1875) *Tennessee politician, seventeenth president of the United States (1865–1869)*
Born in Raleigh, NORTH CAROLINA, on December 29, 1808, Andrew Johnson served as president of the United States from 1865 to 1869. Johnson was a white Southerner, who owned slaves before the AMERICAN CIVIL WAR, 1861–65. He served as governor of TENNESSEE from 1853 to 1847 and senator from 1857 until the Civil War in 1861. Johnson was from a pro-Union part of Tennessee, and at the time of the Civil War, he was the only congressman from the seceded states to remain loyal to the U.S. government.

He served as military governor of Tennessee from the time the national forces captured the state until 1865, when he became vice president under President ABRAHAM LINCOLN, having run in 1864 on a "National Union" ticket merging Unionist Democrats and Republicans. While governor of Tennessee in 1864, he proclaimed the abolition of slavery there, and he supported letting freed slaves join the U.S. Army. The Civil War ended on April 9, 1865. Five days later, Lincoln was assassinated, and Johnson became president. During his four years as president, Johnson was generally hostile to expanding the rights of former slaves and free blacks and opposed most of the policies of RECONSTRUCTION IN THIS UNITED STATES enacted by Radical Republicans in Congress. He was impeached by the House of Representatives in 1868 but not convicted by the Senate.

Although personally pretty well-off, Johnson came from and identified himself with the poorer mountain people of the South, who did not own slaves, did not like the white elites who did, and did not like the Confederacy that those white elites had created. As among poor white Northerners, though, there was not a lot of friendship for free blacks in this constituency. In addition, the former abolitionists in the North who were calling for full inclusion of blacks in American society were Republicans, and Johnson's political opponents. So, for political reasons rather than any deep philosophical analysis, Johnson vetoed the civil rights bills and other congressional Reconstruction initiatives in 1866 and 1867. He persevered with Lincoln's relatively benign Reconstruction program, which permitted whites to reestablish state governments in the South if they would swear allegiance to the United States. Lincoln and Johnson hoped that most of the whites who would be willing to swear these oaths would be people like Johnson, poorer Unionists who might be willing to make profound changes in Southern society. But instead, the great majority of white Southerners took the required oaths, including almost all high Confederate officials. The Lincoln plan had excluded the most senior Confederates from the amnesty, but Johnson signed individual pardons for the vast majority of Confederate officials. As a result, the state governments that were created in 1865 after the surrender of the Confederacy were very similar to those that had existed before secession in 1861. Many of the same Southern senators and representatives who traveled to Washington, D.C., for the congressional session of 1866 had represented those states upon secession. Johnson was disappointed, but he supported these Southern state governments, even when they imposed harsh black codes on their newly free black citizens.

Many congressional representatives from the North were not willing to tolerate the presence of their recent enemies, so they ejected them from Congress, dissolved the new state governments, and imposed military law on the South. Congress put its Reconstruction policy into law over the objections of President Johnson, overriding his vetoes by large margins. Congress then implemented these laws through the Department of the Army, still run by Lincoln's secretary of war, Edwin Stanton. Johnson tried to persuade Stanton to be more moderate, and when he failed, he tried to fire him, but Congress argued that it had to be consulted in the firing of cabinet officials. The debate finally led to the impeachment and subsequent acquittal of Johnson, the first American president to be impeached.

Like any Southerner, especially one from the Upper South region, Johnson had plenty of contact with free people of color. There were few slaves in eastern Tennessee where Johnson grew up, but free blacks often found their way to such poor regions of the South to escape prejudice and harsh laws in more settled areas. Paradoxically, the racial climate in these remote areas was not nearly as bad as that found in the plantation regions, or even in the Northern cities. Johnson's politics were less racial than class-based; he and his constituents distrusted wealthy people. They certainly did not believe in black equality, but they were willing to tolerate blacks as neighbors, business partners, and even coreligionists. As were his neighbors', Johnson's attitudes toward blacks were ambiguous. On the one hand, he owned slaves. On the other hand, he freed those of them who stayed with him when the Civil War began, though he was not obliged to do so, and indeed most Southern and border state Unionists were adamant about keeping slavery in their areas. He supported giving the vote to at least some blacks, though under more restrictive rules than for whites. Like many other presidents and politicians, Johnson is not easy to categorize on this issue: neither the racist cartoon of much modern analysis nor the reconciling honest patriot that early 20th-century historians saw.

He died on July 31, 1875.

Stewart R. King

FURTHER READING

Foner, Eric. *Reconstruction: America's Unfinished Revolution, 1863–1877*. New York: HarperCollins, 1988.

Trefousse, Hans. *Andrew Johnson: A Biography*. New York: Norton, 1989.

JONES, ABSALOM (1746–1818) *African-American minister and activist*

Absalom Jones was a prominent activist in PHILADELPHIA, PENNSYLVANIA, and the first African-American priest in the Episcopal Church. Jones was born on November 6, 1746, a slave of the family of the wealthy merchant and planter Abraham Wynkoop of Sussex County, DELAWARE. At a young age, he was taken into the house and bought a reading primer by saving pennies. He later described himself as a singular child. In 1762, his master, Benjamin Wynkoop, decided to move to Philadelphia. After selling Absalom's mother and six siblings, Wynkoop arrived in Philadelphia with only the 15-year-old boy at his side. Jones worked in Wynkoop's Philadelphia dry goods store all day and attended Anthony Benezet's Quaker school in the evenings, further developing his literacy skills.

In 1770, at age 23, Absalom Jones married Mary King, the slave of his master's neighbors, Thomas and Sarah King. They took their vows at St. Peter's Anglican Church. Jones then wrote an appeal for his wife's freedom and took it to prominent Quakers, receiving some donations and loans. By 1778, during the third year of the WAR OF AMERICAN INDEPENDENCE, 1775–83, and as

British troops were occupying the city, they had worked and saved enough to buy her freedom. He then asked Wynkoop to allow him to purchase his own freedom. Wynkoop refused. The Joneses chose not to leave Philadelphia with the British in summer 1778, even though the British were promising freedom to all blacks who would follow them; instead, they purchased a house and lot in early 1779. After five more years, Wynkoop allowed Jones to purchase his freedom in 1784. A free man, Jones continued to work in Wynkoop's store. He continued patiently to save his money, eventually buying a second house to use as a rental property.

In April 1787, Absalom Jones and RICHARD ALLEN cofounded the Free African Society. It was designed for mutual aid and assistance and was a symbol of the growth in institutions within the African-American community. The society had monthly meetings and rapidly grew in membership, but its nondenominational character bothered Allen, a devout Methodist who decried its Quaker and Anglican tendencies. Methodism stressed preaching and an enthusiastic worship style, while Anglican (or Episcopal) worship was more liturgical, or scripted. Both churches shared a history and theological approach, though Methodists tended to have more Protestant beliefs about the nature of divine grace, faith, and redemption. Quakers had a very distinctive style of worship, in which any member was allowed to speak freely on almost any topic during weekly meetings. Quakers stressed the role of the individual and the action of the Holy Spirit in guiding each person to salvation (see also PROTESTANT MAINLINE CHURCHES and BAPTISTS AND PIETISTS). When Allen left the Free African Society in November 1788, Jones assumed sole leadership. He continued to appeal to leading white citizens for funds to build an African church.

After the growth in African-American membership at St. George's Methodist Episcopal Church, where both Jones and Allen worshipped, the church had constructed a balcony. Upon its completion in 1787, the white members assumed that the African Americans would worship in the new space, apart from the whites. When this did not happen, several whites accosted Allen and Jones during church services. Jones requested they wait until after the prayer was finished. The whites then sought physically to remove them. With the prayer finished, Jones stood up and led the African Americans from the church. Though the exact date remains uncertain, in March 1793, they broke ground for an African church on Fifth Street between Walnut Street and Locust Street in Philadelphia. Planning a nondenominational church, Jones and Allen had sought donations and loans to build the church. In late August 1793, they had a roof-raising banquet. A large gathering of white supporters sat at the tables and was served by African Americans. After they were finished, the African Americans sat down and were served by six of the most respectable whites. Despite the early unanimity, Allen had sought to make it a Methodist church, but some African Americans refused to be associated with Methodism because of their treatment at St. George's. Thus, Allen left to start his own church. This first black church affiliated with the Episcopal Church to become the African Episcopal Church of St. Thomas with Absalom Jones as minister. In 1804, Jones became the first African American to be ordained a priest in the Episcopal Church.

Despite their religious differences, Jones and Allen remained friends, seeking to open a nail factory together and coorganizing the African-American response in Philadelphia to the yellow fever epidemic of 1793. Mistakenly believing African Americans to be immune, leading physicians and politicians called for their assistance in fall 1793. Jones and Allen heeded the call and organized the African-American community's response. Allen contracted the fever, so Jones did most of the organizing. In January 1794, Jones and Allen coauthored a pamphlet refuting and rebutting the allegations and accusations about African-American behavior during the epidemic. This was the first copyrighted publication by an African-American author. They not only used facts and figures to make their case, but Jones and Allen also argued for abolition and racial equality, two passions they would both pursue, in their own way, for the rest of their lives.

Jones's patience, evident throughout his life, made him a different and complementary presence to the younger Allen. Unlike Allen's Methodist Church, Jones's Episcopal Church conceded some authority to white bishops in return for peace and recognition. His church grew more slowly than Allen's, but it also had many of the wealthiest African Americans as members, including the sail maker and entrepreneur James Forten (see also FORTEN FAMILY). Jones spoke out against slavery and racism, but in his own way. He petitioned Congress, along with Forten and Allen, but his publications were largely sermons advising thanks, progress, and patience. In 1797, he co-organized the second African Masonic Lodge in the country and was elected its first Lodge Master (see also FREEMASONRY). Throughout his life, he continued to speak, largely from the pulpit, and to publish his sermons, notably on the anniversary of the abolition of the slave trade on January 1, 1808. Though he, along with his friends, had some interest in African EMIGRATION AND COLONIZATION, he ultimately opposed the AMERICAN COLONIZATION SOCIETY. Absalom Jones died on February 13, 1818, leaving his walking cane to his good friend Richard Allen.

Matthew J. Hudock

FURTHER READING

Nash, Gary. *Forging Freedom: The Formation of Philadelphia's Free Black Community, 1720–1840.* Cambridge, Mass.: Harvard University Press, 2003.

Powell, J. H. *Bring Out Your Dead: The Great Plague of Yellow Fever in Philadelphia in 1793.* Philadelphia: University of Pennsylvania Press, 1993.

Winch, Julie. *Philadelphia's Black Elite: Activism, Accommodation, and the Struggle for Autonomy, 1787–1848.* Philadelphia: Temple University Press, 1988.

"A NARRATIVE OF THE PROCEEDINGS OF THE BLACK PEOPLE DURING THE LATE AWFUL CALAMITY IN PHILADELPHIA, IN THE YEAR 1793; AND A REFUTATION OF SOME CENSURES THROWN UPON THEM IN SOME LATE PUBLICATIONS" (1794)

In January 1794, Absalom Jones and Richard Allen wrote and published the first federally copyrighted pamphlet by African Americans. It not only provided a counternarrative to the horrendous yellow fever epidemic, in which more than 4,000 people had died in fall 1793, but also challenged white stereotyping in public and in print. Their pamphlet was a reply to an earlier pamphlet by the Philadelphia publisher and author Mathew Carey. His narrative of events had, in part, attacked African-American behavior during the epidemic.

Mistakenly believing them to be immune, white leaders had called on African Americans for help in fall 1793. Jones and Allen answered and organized the response. Despite this, Carey accused African Americans of negligence and theft by taking advantage of sick whites. Jones and Allen refuted these allegations, but letting no opportunity go to waste, they also added an "Address to Those Who Keep Slaves and Uphold the Practice." Probably authored by Allen alone, this coda attacked slavery and racial prejudice. If the oppression of slavery were removed, African Americans could and would succeed.

The pamphlet was published by William Woodward, a white printer new to Philadelphia. The initial print run was between 250 and 500 copies. It evidently had a fairly wide audience on both sides of the Atlantic, because Carey felt compelled to reply to Jones and Allen in a later pamphlet. Jones and Allen presented copies of their pamphlet to the Pennsylvania Abolition Society and appended a testimonial from the Philadelphia mayor, Thomas Clarkson, attesting to their deeds and words.

Both Jones and Allen were former slaves living in Philadelphia. They founded the Free African Society together in 1787 and would both lead independent black churches. These leaders of the African-American community presented petitions to Congress and founded other groups, such as the local lodge of the African Masons. They would also publish more throughout their lives, consistently attacking slavery and prejudice. This pamphlet was the first in a long line of black efforts to secure abolition and equality in public and in print.

A Narrative of the Proceedings of the Black People during the Late Awful Calamity in Philadelphia, in the Year 1793; and a Refutation of Some Censures Thrown upon Them in Some Late Publications

In consequence of a partial representation of the conduct of the people who were employed to nurse the sick, in the late calamitous state of the city of Philadelphia, we are solicited, by a number of those who feel themselves injured thereby, and by the advice of several respectable citizens, to step forward and declare facts as they really were; seeing that from our situation, on account of the charge we took upon us, we had it more fully and generally in our power, to know and observe the conduct and behavior of those that were so employed. . . .

Our services were the production of real sensibility;—we sought not fee nor reward, until the increase of the disorder rendered our labor so arduous that we were not adequate to the service we had assumed. . . .

Here it ought to be remarked, (although Mr. Carey hath not done it) that two thirds of the persons, who rendered these essential services, were people of colour. . . .

We feel ourselves sensibly aggrieved by the censorious epithets of many, who did not render the least assistance in the time of necessity, yet are liberal of their censure of us, for the prices paid for our services. . . .

We do assure the public that all the money we received, for burying, and for coffins which we ourselves purchased and procured, has not defrayed the expence of wages which we had to pay to those whom we employed to assist us. . . .

We have buried *several hundreds* of poor persons and strangers, for which service we have never received, nor never asked any compensation. . . .

That there were some few black people guilty of plundering the distressed, we acknowledge; but in that they only are pointed out, and made mention of, we esteem partial and injurious; we know as many white who were guilty of it; but this is looked over, while the blacks are held up to censure.—Is it a greater crime for a black to pilfer, than for a white to privateer?

We wish not to offend, but when an unprovoked attempt is made, to make us blacker than we are, it becomes less necessary to be over cautious on that account. . . .

We can with certainty assure the public that we have seen more humanity, more real sensibility from the poor blacks, than from the poor whites. . . .

It is unpleasant for us to make these remarks, but justice to our colour, demands it . . . for we conceive, and experience proves it, that an ill name is easier given than taken away. We have many unprovoked enemies, who begrudge us the liberty we enjoy, and are glad to hear of any complaint against our colour. . . .

When the people of colour had the sickness and died, we were imposed upon and told it was not with the prevailing sickness, until it became too notorious to be denied, then we were told some few died but not many. Thus were our services extorted *at the peril of our lives,* yet you accuse us of extorting a *little money from you.* . . .

We shall now conclude with the following old proverb, which we think applicable to those of our colour who exposed their lives in the late afflicting dispensation:—

God and a soldier, all men do adore,
In time of war, and not before;
When the war is over, and all things righted,
God is forgotten, and the soldier slighted.

An Address to Those Who Keep Slaves and Uphold the Practice

The judicious part of mankind will think it unreasonable, that a superior good conduct is looked for, from our race, by those who stigmatize us as men, whose baseness is incurable, and may therefore be held in a state of servitude, that a merciful man would not deem a beast to; yet you try what you can to prevent our rising from the state of barbarism, you represent us to be in, but we can tell you, from a degree of experience, that a black man . . . can think, reflect, and feel injuries, although it may not be with the same degree of keen resentment and revenge, that you who have been and are our great oppressors, would manifest if reduced to the pitiable condition of a slave. We believe if you would try the experiment of taking a few black children, and cultivate their minds with the same care, and let them have the same prospect in view, as to living in the world, as you would wish for your own children, you would find them upon the trial, they were not inferior in mental endowments.

We do not wish to make you angry, but excite your attention to consider, how hateful slavery is in the sight of that God, who hath destroyed kings and princes, for their oppression of the poor slaves; Pharaoh and his princes with the posterity of King Saul, were destroyed by the protector and avenger of slaves . . . the example of the Israelite shews, who with all that Moses could do to reclaim them from it, still continued in their former habits more or less; and why will you look for better from us? . . .

When you are pleaded with, do not you reply as Pharaoh did. . . . We wish you to consider, that God himself was the first pleader of the cause of slaves.

That God who knows the hearts of all men, and the propensity of a slave to hate his oppressor hath strictly forbidden . . . We feel the obligations, we wish to impress them on the minds of our black brethren. . . .

If you love your children, if you love your country, if you love the God of love, clear your hands from slaves, burden not your children or your country with them. . . .

Will you, because you have reduced us to the unhappy condition our colour is in, plead our incapacity for freedom, and our contented condition under oppression . . . the dreadful insurrections they have made, when opportunity has offered, is enough to convince a reasonable man, that great uneasiness and not contentment, is the inhabitant of their hearts.

God himself hath pleaded their cause, he hath from time to time raised up instruments for that purpose, sometimes mean and contemptible in your sight; at other times he hath used such as it hath pleased him with whom you have not thought it beneath your dignity to contend, many add to your numbers, until the princes shall come forth from Egypt and Ethiopia stretch out her hand unto God.

Source: U.S. National Library of Medicine. National Institutes of Health. Available online. URL: www.ncbi.nlm.nih.gov/books/NBK22124/. Accessed May 6, 2011.

JONES, JEHU, JR.   (1786–1852) *American religious leader*

Jehu Jones, Jr., born a slave, was the first African-American ordained a minister by the American Lutheran Church (*see also* PROTESTANT MAINLINE CHURCHES). He started one of the first African-American Lutheran congregations in the United States, and he also worked to improve the social welfare of African Americans. In the Calendar of Saints of the Lutheran Church, Jones is commemorated on November 24.

He was born in CHARLESTON, SOUTH CAROLINA, on September 4, 1786, the son of a tailor, Jehu Jones, Sr., who obtained his freedom in 1798 and later owned an exclusive hotel in Charleston. Jehu Jones was of mixed-race ancestry, and thus he was able to join the privileged MULATTO elite in Charleston.

A third member of the family to gain fame was Jones's brother, Edward. He was the first African American to receive a baccalaureate degree from Amherst College. In 1827, Edward became an Episcopal priest and missionary to SIERRA LEONE. He was the first principal of Fourah Bay College (now Fourah Bay College, University of Sierra Leone). Edward later died in Britain.

Originally affiliated with the Episcopal Church, Jehu Jones, Jr., joined St. John's Lutheran Church in Charleston in the 1820s. John S. Bachman, the minister of St. John's, recruited Jones to attend the seminary in PHILADELPHIA, PENNSYLVANIA, so he could serve as a missionary to LIBERIA. Jones became an ordained Lutheran minister in 1832 through the New York Synod of the Lutheran Church. When he returned to Charleston after his ordination, he was jailed briefly for violating South Carolina's law prohibiting the immigration of free African Americans. Jones never went to Liberia.

In 1833, Jehu Jones settled in Philadelphia, America's second-largest city at the time. In June 1833, the Pennsylvania Ministry (of the Lutheran Church) appointed Jones to work as a missionary to African Americans in Philadelphia. Jones founded three congregations in Philadelphia. His first congregation, St. Paul's, was composed of free African Americans and was the first African-American Lutheran church in the United States. On February 16, 1834, the congregation decided to build a church and to solicit support from other Lutheran congregations. Jones purchased two lots on Quince Street in Philadelphia for the church.

Jones laid the cornerstone for the building (still standing at 310 South Quince Street) with the assistance of Pastors Philip Mayer of Philadelphia and Benjamin Keller of St. Michael's Church in Germantown. By the time the building was dedicated in 1836, the congregation had paid nearly 40 percent of the costs. The rest of the funding (about $1,300) was not obtained, however, and the building was lost to creditors in 1839.

During his time in Philadelphia, Jones was active in the political and social life of the city. In 1845, he organized a convention at Temperance Hall to unite free African Americans to petition for civil rights (*see also* NEGRO CONVENTION MOVEMENT IN THE UNITED STATES). He and his congregation participated in the Moral Reform and Improvement Society, an association of African-American churches in Philadelphia dedicated to improving the social conditions of the African-American community. Jones served the St. Paul's congregation until 1851.

Jehu Jones, Jr., died on November 24, 1852, in Philadelphia.

John McLane

FURTHER READING
McMickle, Marvin Andrew. *An Encyclopedia of African American Christian Heritage.* Valley Forge, Pa.: Judson Press, 2002.

JORDON, EDWARD (1801–1869) *Jamaican politician*

Edward Jordon was born in Kingston, JAMAICA, on November 13, 1801. He was the child of two free people of color. There does not appear to be an image of him available, but he was apparently quite light-skinned. However, under the British "ONE DROP RULE" OF RACIAL IDENTITY, he was considered nonwhite because he had some African ancestry, and that was enough to make him subject to discrimination and exclusion as a youth. Nevertheless, he managed to get an education and become a journalist. He started a newspaper, the *Watchman*, which criticized the colonial government for corruption, oppression of the free people of color, and mismanagement of Jamaica's economy. In 1830, the newspaper published an article advocating for the abolition of slavery, calling on the colonial authorities to "strike off the fetters" and "bring the system down by the run." For this, Jordon was arrested and tried for sedition, which carried the death penalty. One member of the jury was unable to stomach hanging Jordon for simply speaking out and voted stubbornly against conviction. Finally, the jury was dismissed, and Jordon was sent to prison by executive order.

He was originally given a six-year sentence but was quickly released. Free coloreds gained the vote in 1831, and the people of Kingston elected Jordon to the House of Assembly, so the governor could not keep him in prison. Parliament in BRITAIN abolished slavery, starting in 1833. Former slaves were supposed to go on working as "apprentices" on their plantations, but most of them left and began farming on abandoned land. The apprenticeship system was to end prematurely in 1838. Plantations cut production because they could not get enough laborers. Jordon and many free colored political leaders began to prepare themselves for a post-emancipation society.

During the late 1830s, Jordon became a prominent political leader in the colony. As the economy collapsed, he supported efforts to centralize and strengthen the colonial government, managing the Kingston Savings Bank. He served as a member of the Executive Committee of the assembly in the 1850s and helped introduce a new constitution for the colony. Jordon was a leader of the "city party" in the colonial assembly, supporting the interests of the class of urban brown ARTISANS, many of whom were also former free people of color. His opponents were supporters of rural interests, including those of the plantations and those of the rural black poor. He was appointed a Companion of the Order of the Bath in 1854, the first person of color to hold that ceremonial title. The Morant Bay uprising of 1865 caused him to withdraw from politics for a while. He was no friend of the accused organizers of the rebellion, GEORGE WILLIAM GORDON and Paul Bogle, who represented the "country party," and in fact Gordon had severely criticized Jordon's support for the government. But the rebellion made any black politician suspect, and so Jordon went into retirement for a few years. He was appointed secretary of the colonial government in 1867, however, and was serving in that role when he died on February 8, 1869.

The life of Edward Jordon illustrates several important points about the free people of color of Jamaica. His trial for sedition illustrates the degree to which the colonial governments in the period between the end of the slave trade in 1807 and emancipation 27 years later were willing to go to repress dissent. His "crime" was merely to call the slave system unjust. The context of his editorial was the decision by a prominent white politician, a Mr. Beaumont, who represented a plantation district, to enter the ranks of the abolitionists. Paradoxically, the fact that Jordon and other free colored activists were building cross-racial alliances seemed to enrage the colonial elites further. But the cross-racial nature of his appeal probably saved him: The fact that a white man, as all jury members were in those days, was unwilling to vote to convict even against the strongly expressed wishes of the colonial government was all that saved Jordon. His cross-racial appeal was important to him later on, as he was able to serve in several important roles in colonial government and even be named on the Queen's Honors List during a time when racial tension were high.

Stewart R. King

FURTHER READING

Sherlock, Philip, and Hazel Bennett. *The Story of the Jamaican People*. New York: Marcus Weiner, 1998.

Thome, James, and J. Horace Kimball. *Emancipation in the West Indies, A Six Months' Tour in Antigua, Barbados, and Jamaica in the Year 1837*. New York: American Anti-Slavery Society, 1839. Available online. URL: http://books.google.com/books?id=BlwSAAAAIAAJ&dq=edward+jordon+jamaica&source=gbs_navlinks_s. Accessed March 30, 2010.

JOSEPH, JOHN   (ca. 1831–1858) *Australian gold miner*

Born around 1831, John Joseph was an African-American gold miner who emigrated to the British colony of AUSTRALIA in the mid-19th century. He played a prominent part in the battle for the Eureka Stockade, which occurred on the Ballarat diggings in Victoria, Australia, on December 3, 1854. Joseph's origins are uncertain; various sources suggest he was from BOSTON, New York, or Baltimore. It is unknown whether he was a freeborn man, manumitted, or a fugitive slave.

When in late November 1854 the labor crisis brewing on the Ballarat gold field erupted into armed insurrection, Joseph was one of the diggers who answered the call and took up arms. He never spoke or wrote about his motivations for doing so. When fighting erupted between the miners and the military and police for control of the rough stockade the dissident miners had built at the Eureka Lead, Joseph fought firmly with rifle, shotgun, and musket. He stood his ground when many others fled and was captured in the company of a notably radical

digger near a large tent that had been a central feature of the stockade and around which many diggers had been killed or wounded. Joseph was described as a powerful man of color and had to be forcibly restrained, but even so he attempted to escape and had to be roughly thrown back among the prisoners. Soldiers accused Joseph of firing the shot that had mortally wounded their captain and had to be restrained from shooting him.

Unlike for every other American who had taken part in the uprising and been captured, there was no attempt made by the American consul's representative to secure Joseph's release. Presumably, this was because of his race. As a consequence of this, Joseph found himself among 12 other Eureka "rebels" committed to trial on the capital charge of treason at the supreme court in Melbourne. His defense was conducted pro bono by one of Melbourne's leading lawyers. After some cunning legal maneuvering, Joseph was the first to take the stand. Playing to the racial stereotypes and misconceptions of the day, Joseph's counsel brilliantly used gentle mockery and ridicule of his client's race to convince the jury that such a simple fellow could not possibly have presented a threat to the power and majesty of the British Crown. The ploy worked, and after 30 minutes, the jury returned to acquit Joseph. Uproarious applause erupted in the courtroom and spilled out onto the street, where Joseph was carried through the crowd shoulder high in triumph. Joseph's acquittal created the precedent on which the defense for all the other accused rested and they, like Joseph, were acquitted.

Joseph's stand at the stockade, where the diggers were fighting for their rights and liberties, proved that he was a man not only of courage but also of principle and resolve. His trial and acquittal were notable acts in a train of events that contributed significantly to fundamental political reform and accelerated the shift in colonial Australia from class-bound exclusivist government to a vastly more inclusive democratic model. After his trial and brief flurry of celebrity, Joseph returned to the relative anonymity of the gold fields. He died of heart disease sometime in 1858 and is buried in an unmarked grave at the White Hills cemetery in Bendigo, Victoria.

Gregory Blake

FURTHER READING

Blake, Gregory. *To Pierce the Tyrant's Heart—a Military History of the Battle for the Eureka Stockade 3 December 1854*. Loftus: Australian Military History Publications, 2008.

Carboni, Raffello. *The Eureka Stockade*. Carlton, Australia: Miegunyah Press, 2004.

Potts, E. Daniel, and Annette Potts. *Young America and Australian Gold—Americans and the Gold Rush of the 1850s*. St Lucia: University of Queensland Press, 1974.

State Trials, Queen v. Joseph, 1855, Library of the Supreme Court of Victoria.

JOURNALISM

The barriers to launching a career in journalism were remarkably low in the late 18th and early 19th centuries. The population was increasingly literate, even in the free colored community. Most countries had much poorer literacy rates for free blacks when compared to whites, though few went so far as some states in the United States that legally prohibited literacy training for people of color (*see* GEORGIA, for example). Nonetheless, large numbers of free blacks gained enough education to be able to read a newspaper, and even if some were illiterate, there were sure to be some people in any community who could read a newspaper to others (*see also* EDUCATION AND LITERACY). Sometimes, such arrangements were formalized, for example, Afro-Cuban cigar manufacturers customarily pooled their earnings to hire one of their fellow workers to read to the entire shop.

This newly literate population demanded newspapers. Interest in current events and opinion journalism are a marks of membership in the "public sphere" or "republic of letters" that sprang up throughout the Atlantic world during the Enlightenment of the 18th century. The politics of the Enlightenment were generally liberal, progressive, and antimonarchical, but even more important was the cultural change. People of all shades of opinion and all social classes were increasingly interested in public affairs. People of color, both free and enslaved, participated enthusiastically in this cultural transformation. Older loyalties and cultural patterns were still strong, as when MAROONS from JAMAICA agreed to crush a nationalistic uprising among former RUNAWAY SLAVES in SIERRA LEONE. But a growing sense of national identity and of racial solidarity informed the behavior of people of color in the rebellions and revolutions of the age of revolution (1775–1824). More and more, the African-descended people of the Americas either saw themselves as part of an Afro-descended group that transcended nationality or as part of a nation that included whites and Indians. Either way, with an identity that transcended tribe, plantation, and village, they needed news to connect them. Journalism filled that need.

The economic transformation associated with the Industrial Revolution was slow to come to fruition in the plantation areas. But as it entered, ordinary people gained access to cash employment and acquired a taste for goods from a larger economy. Even people of color, especially in the cities of the Americas, often had paid employment and were able to pay for things they wanted. Printing presses were cheaper and easier to use than ever before. Large corporations did not yet dominate the field.

And, of course, there were no technologies of mass communication such as radio or television to attract people away from newspapers. Because of these favorable circumstances, many people of color were able to work in journalism. However, the supply of paying customers was not bottomless. Many newspapers were launched, published for a few years, and went out of business. The history of early journalism, especially black journalism, is full of bankrupt newspapers. The most successful black journalists were those who had some other activity that could provide a steady income, to which journalism was an important adjunct.

Newspapers were important means of communication in communities of free people of color and important tools for free colored activists to make their views known. Similar developments took place throughout the black Atlantic, at different times and in somewhat different ways, depending on the circumstances in each place.

The United States

Free black activists in the United States began to publish pamphlets around the turn of the 19th century. In PHILADELPHIA, PENNSYLVANIA, the community leaders and ministers ABSALOM JONES and RICHARD ALLEN published "A Narrative of the Proceedings of the Black People, during the Late Awful Calamity in Philadelphia, in the Year 1793, and a Refutation of Some Censures; Thrown upon Them in Some Late Publications" to refute allegations against the black community of theft and profiteering during a deadly yellow fever epidemic. In 1813, James Forten (*see* FORTEN FAMILY) published a series of public "Letters from a Man of Color" protesting antiblack measures being discussed in the state legislature. While not a regularly published newspaper, these letters served a similar purpose by discussing a variety of measures in an episodic manner over an extended period. In 1827, SAMUEL E. CORNISH and JOHN RUSSWURM began to publish the first newspaper owned and operated by blacks, *Freedom's Journal,* in New York City. The paper was a journal of opinion and specialized news reporting, publishing articles on slavery and abolition, on events in the free black community in New York and other Northern cities, and, a special area of interest for the publishers, on the EMIGRATION AND COLONIZATION movement. Like many newspapers of the day, *Freedom's Journal* only lasted a little less than two years, and the editors split up over disagreements on colonization policy. Russwurm ultimately moved to LIBERIA, where he edited the *Liberia Herald.*

The role of *Freedom's Journal* as a forum for editorial opinion was a model that many black newspapers, both in the United States and in Latin America, were to adopt throughout the 19th century. The black abolitionist FRED-

ERICK DOUGLASS published a number of newspapers, the best known of which was the *North Star,* published in Rochester, New York, from 1847 to 1851. He called for immediate abolition of slavery and leveled a harsh critique at American RACISM AND RACIAL PREJUDICE.

Brazil

Free people of color played a key role in the expansion of journalism in BRAZIL from the time of independence (1824) forward. Newspapers were very important tools in the ideological struggle around independence and during the early years of the imperial government. Emperor PEDRO I Bragança gave Brazil a constitution and ruled as a limited monarch, but absolutist and pro-Portuguese forces, supported by the planter class, were continually restive. Finally Pedro I left the country in 1828, returning to play a role in a civil war in PORTUGAL and leaving the throne to his three-year-old son, PEDRO II Bragança. Until Pedro II turned 18, the country continued to be divided between liberal, constitutional forces and conservative absolutists. Most wealthy and influential free people of color were liberals and saw Pedro II as their leader against the aristocratic party.

FRANCISCO DE PAULA BRITO was an outstanding example of a Brazilian free colored journalist. Trained as a printer, starting in 1830, he operated a series of newspapers and literary journals as an adjunct activity to his principal business of printing. He thereby avoided the financial problems that plagued many free black newspapers. For him, the newspapers were useful advertising and a way for him to build connections to other free colored intellectuals and to white society. He was patron to JOAQUIM MARÍA MACHADO DE ASSIS, one of Brazil's greatest writers, who published his first poem in one of Brito's journals.

In the late monarchical period, after the War of the Triple Alliance (1864–70), free people of color became an essential element of popular support for the monarchy. The Afro-Brazilian "prince" CÂNDIDO DA FONSECA GALVÃO (Dom Oba II) published pro-monarchy and antislavery articles in the opposition press. Widely mocked by the white-owned conservative press for his stereotypically (and possibly assumed) "African" behavior and appearance, his articles mobilized support among working-class free coloreds in Rio de Janeiro and linked the abolition struggle to the goals of free black urban workers. Brazil's best-known free colored abolitionist, JOSÉ CARLOS DO PATROCÍNIO, publicized his work against slavery during the 1870s and 1880s in several newspapers with which he was associated, including the *Cidade do Rio.* This paper played an important role in the struggle against the republic, and it was shut down after the Armada Revolt of 1893.

Spanish America

Journalism was in its infancy when many Spanish South American colonies gained their independence between 1808 and 1826. The island colonies of CUBA and PUERTO RICO, however, developed a vibrant press, and free people of color played a notable role. This was especially true during the long struggle for independence and racial equality in Cuba. Juan Gualberto Gómez (1854–1933) is an especially noteworthy example of a Cuban journalist of color. He was born in Cuba and educated in FRANCE, and when he returned to Cuba at the conclusion of the TEN YEARS' WAR in 1878, he established *La Fraternidad* (Brotherhood), a journal of opinion devoted to racial harmony and progress for people of color. Arrested and deported to Spanish Morocco after the Guerra Chica (1880), he traveled to Spain and worked for *El Abolicionista* (The Abolitionist) newspaper in Madrid. His sentence of exile was lifted in 1890, and he returned once more to Cuba. He continued his campaign for racial equality in the pages of *La Igualdad* (Equality), another black newspaper, where he published an article linking national independence to the struggle for equal rights. Arrested once more, he fought stubbornly through the courts for freedom of speech. Finally, after the outbreak of the Cuban War of Independence (1895–1898), he took up arms and joined his fellow journalist José Martí in the field against the Spanish army. After Cuba gained its independence, Gómez continued to write and report, calling for greater autonomy from the United States and racial harmony within Cuban society.

The most famous black journalist from Puerto Rico, Jesús Colón (1901–1974) was active after the end of Spanish rule there, but he was from a free colored family who had been bakers and cigar makers in Cayey for generations. He was first attracted to journalism as a boy when he heard the designated reader in the cigar factory where his family worked reading various radical newspapers to his fellow workers. Colón moved to New York as a young man, started a number of Spanish-language newspapers, and wrote a regular column in the *Daily Worker* for almost 40 years. He is the founder of the "Nuyorican" cultural movement among mainlanders of Puerto Rican ancestry.

It is no accident that many of the foremost black political leaders of the 19th century were journalists, at least part-time. It was an activity that was central to the aspirations and identity of free people of color throughout the Americas. Newspapers allowed them to express their desire for freedom and fair treatment. Newspapers also allowed them to know themselves as a cultural group, to transmit their cultural achievements to a larger audience, and to learn about the ideas of the modern world. The rise of the black press also serves as a sign of the rise of blackness and nationality as identities that transcended tribe, village, or plantation.

See also BLACK PRESS IN THE UNITED STATES.

Stewart R. King

FURTHER READING

Hallewell, L. *Books in Brazil: A History of the Publishing Trade.* Metuchen, N.J.: Scarecrow Press, 1982.

Hutton, Frankie. *The Early Black Press in America, 1827 to 1860.* Santa Barbara, Calif.: Greenwood Press, 1992.

Pride, Armistead S., and Clint C. Wilson II. *A History of the Black Press.* Washington, D.C.: Howard University Press, 1997.

Vogel, Todd, ed. *The Black Press: New Literary and Historical Essays.* New Brunswick, N.J.: Rutgers University Press, 2001.

Wolseley, Roland E. *The Black Press, U.S.A.* Ames: Iowa State University Press, 1990.

Index

Fleetwood, Christian Abraham 289–291
Florida 293–294
Forten family 298
Freedmen's Bureau 303
Garnet, Henry Highland 324
Georgia 332–333
Grant, Ulysses S. 338–339
Hemings, Sally, children of 363
Illinois 377
Indiana 379
Indian Wars, United States 381
Iowa 389, 390
Jacobs, Harriet 395
Johnson, Andrew 403
Kansas 415
Kentucky 418–419
Langston, John Mercer 426
Lincoln, Abraham 444–447
Maine 472
Maryland 491
Massachusetts 494–495
militia 522
Minnesota 524
Mississippi 529
Missouri 531, 533
navy 542
Nebraska 544
New Hampshire 549
New Orleans, Louisiana 557
New York Draft Riots 558–559
New York State 564
North Carolina 568–570
Ohio 576
Oklahoma 578
Pennsylvania 602
Philadelphia, Pennsylvania 616
Pierce, Franklin 619
Pittsburgh, Pennsylvania 624
Polk, James 630, 631
Purvis, Robert 654
Reconstruction in the United States 671
regular army 681
Revels, Hiram 683
runaway slaves 703
segregation 722
sites of African-American participation 26m
Smalls, Robert 733–734

South Carolina 744–745
Tennessee 767–768
Ten Years' War 770
Texas 772–774
Truth, Sojourner 779
Tubman, Harriet 782
Tyler, John 784
United States, abolition movements in 789
U.S. presidents and free blacks 794
Van Buren, Martin 797
Vermont 810
Virginia and West Virginia 813, 817–818
Washington, D.C. 832
American Colonization Society (ACS) xxixc, xxxc, **28–29**
Africa 9
Allen, Richard 22
Connecticut 190
Crummell, Alexander 203
Delany, Martin 217–219
Delaware 221
emigration and colonization 265
Fenix 287
Fleetwood, Christian Abraham 290
Forten family 297
Harrison, William Henry 357
Jefferson, Thomas 401
Jones, Absalom 405
Liberia 443, 444
Negro Convention Movement in the United States 546
New York State 563, 564
Ohio 576
Pennsylvania 602
Philadelphia, Pennsylvania 615
Roberts, Joseph Jenkins 690
Russwurm, John 704
Tyler, John 784
United States, abolition movements in 785–786, 789
American Episcopal Church 203
American Federation of Labor 380
American Freedmen's Union 307
American Indians. *See* Native Americans

American Lutheran Church 407–408
American Missionary Association 307
American Moral Reform Society 298, 546–547, 601, 602, 615, 654
American Negro Academy 203
American Negro Masonic Lodge. *See* Prince Hall Freemasonry
American (Know-Nothing) Party 288, 794
American Revolution. *See* War of American Independence
Amerindians. *See* Native Americans
Ames, Alexander 492
Amherst College 653
Amiens, Treaty of 313, 318
Amis des Noirs. *See* Société des Amis des Noirs (Friends of the Blacks)
Amish 48
Amistad case xxxic, xxxiic, **29–31**, *30*
Adams, John Quincy 8
Connecticut 190–191
Fenix 286, 287
Guerrero 345
Sierra Leone 728–729
Van Buren, Martin 797
Amnesty Proclamation (1865) 305
Anabaptists 48
Ana Muriel 269
Anderson, Elijah 378
Anderson, Jacob 536
Anderson, William 810
Anderson, William T. "Bloody Bill" 533
Andes Mountains 155, 605
Andino, Domingo De 651
Andrew, John A. 24, 89–90
Andros, Edmund 560
Andry, Louise 536
Andry, Simon 534
Andry family 536
Anglican Church. *See* Church of England
Anglican Church Mission Society 202
Anglo-African 77
Angola 105, *187*, 638. *See also* Congo and Angola
Angola, Luis 230
Angola Maconde, Juan 86

animism 11
Anthony, Susan B. 50, 654, 782
anthropology xxivc. *See also* scientific racism
anticlericalism 309
Anti-Slavery Society 324, 431–432
Anti-Slavery Society of Pittsburgh 798
Anti-Slave Trade Squadron 113
Antoine, Caesar Carpentier 558
Antoine, Père 428
Antón 253
Apache Indians 82, 382
Aponte, José Antonio 165, 180, 207, 439
Appeal of Forty Thousand Citizens, Threatened with Disfranchisement, to the People of Pennsylvania xxxiic, 821
Appeal to the Coloured Citizens of the World (Walker) xxxic, 87, 494, 568, 822
Appleton, Jane 618
Appomattox Court House, Virginia xxxvic
apprenticeship system xxxic, 408, 778
Arana, Felipe 36
Arango y Parreno, Francisco de 185
Araucanian people 155
Arawak Indians 52, 72, 312, 347, 755
Arbuthnot, Alexander 394
architecture 246
Arcia, Valentín 142
Ardouin, Beaubrun xxxiiic, xxxivc, **31–32**, 470
Ardouin, Céligny 31
Arévalo, Pedro 804
Argentina xxixc, xxxc, xxxvic, *32*, **32–37**, *33m*
Afro-Argentine population 32–33
aftermath 36–37
Chile 155, 157
economic and social roles 34–35
end of slavery and persistence of racism 35–36
increasing discrimination 33–34